Instructional Development Paradigms

Instructional Development Paradigms

Charles R. Dills
Alexander J. Romiszowski

EDITORS

EDUCATIONAL TECHNOLOGY PUBLICATIONS
ENGLEWOOD CLIFFS, NEW JERSEY 07632

Library of Congress Cataloging-in-Publication Data

Instructional development paradigms / Charles R. Dills, Alexander J.
  Romiszowski, editors.
    p.   cm.
    Includes bibliographical references and index.
    ISBN 0-87778-294-6 (hardcover). — ISBN 0-87778-295-4 (softcover)
    1. Instructional systems—Design.   2. Educational technology.
I. Dills, Charles R.   II. Romiszowski, A. J.
LB1028.38.I576   1997
371.33—dc21   96-52249
                                               CIP

Printed in the United States of America.

Library of Congress Catalog Card Number:
96-52249.

International Standard Book Numbers:
0-87778-294-6 (hardcover).
0-87778-295-4 (softcover).

First Printing: February, 1997.

Dedication
To Thomas F. Gilbert

Thomas F. Gilbert was a major contributor to the theory and practice of instructional development for well over thirty years. His influence on many researchers and practitioners in the field, including the present Editors, has been immense. Tom was working on a chapter for this book when he was stopped by illness, which resulted in his unfortunate and untimely death in late 1995. His chapter has been completed through the efforts of his wife, Marilyn Gilbert, and therefore appears within the body of the book, but Tom's influence on the book affects much more than just this single chapter.

As further explained in the latter sections of the introductory chapter (Chapter One), the overall organizing framework which we have used to assemble the diverse chapters into a meaningful and useful organizing framework has been based on the model of vantage points that Tom introduced in his classic book, *Human Competence*, published in 1978.

As both a tribute to Tom's thinking, writing skills, and contributions to the field, as well as the most appropriate way of giving readers our rationale for adopting the particular organizational structure for this book that can be seen in the contents matrix and the later section introductions, we reprint in this Dedication a small anecdote which Tom used to introduce the vantage points model of analysis to the world. We thank you, Tom, for this and your many other anecdotes, as well as for the many inspirational ideas and practical techniques that we can discover by reading your published work with the attention it deserves.

THE PERFORMANCE MATRIX[1]

O civili, si ergo,
Fortibus es in ero!
O nobili, deis trus.
Vatis enim, causan dus.
—ANONYMOUS

Competence and Vantage Points

Latin students are well advised not to attempt a translation of the bit of verse we owe to Anonymous, unless they wish to waste hours on the futile assumption that the verse is truly Latin. Anyone can translate it in an instant, however, by assuming the correct point of view. And the translation nicely illustrates the impetus for this chapter. I have provided a "translation" below, but the reader may first

---

[1]The Performance Matrix is excerpted from Chapter Four of T. F. Gilbert (1978). *Human competence: Engineering worthy performance.* New York: McGraw-Hill.

want to try. I warn you, however, that it is a simple matter only if you assume a simple-minded vantage point.

The translation illustrates that a language cannot be understood from its syntax, vocabulary, and orthography alone, but is conditioned as well by the way we look at things. Similarly, much of our disagreement and confusion about human competence results from conflicting or unclear vantage points, more than from the details of what we are viewing and talking about. And many subjects that appear to be abstruse can soon be reduced to utter simplicity by a slight shift in our viewpoint, just as the imposing pretentiousness of the "Latin" verse becomes reduced to banal doggerel.

> O see, Willie! See 'er go!
> Forty buses in a row.
> Oh no, Billie, they is trucks.
> What is in 'em? Cows and ducks.

Human performance often seems imposing in its complexity, and disagreements over it unresolvable. But mystery, like beauty, is in the eye of the beholder, and has no objective existence. If we are to make sense of human performance, it will be because we develop simple and useful vantage points when we discuss it. But first a communications network is required. Since both the pillage of New York City and the preservation of Central Park can be valuable accomplishments, depending on one's point of view, we must have a way to sort out our viewpoints and weigh our values if we are going to communicate.

I believe that most of the disagreements people have about values and competence are not a result of applying different standards of value, but of observing the same things from different (or not clearly stated) points of view. As an example, suppose that we have agreed to discuss the competence of the rebellious Virginian, Robert E. Lee. Where would we begin, and what would be the rules guiding us to agreement?

Summer nights in the South encourage talk, especially when mixed with bourbon and good friends on a porch. A child can lie on the steps and listen to the quiet, drawling voices just rise above the whir of the cicadas and the chatter of crickets. And sometimes there is a sorcery in the sounds and sensations, and the conversation becomes as indelibly imprinted as the unforgettable odor of the yellow jessamine and the creak of the old swing.

It is such a moment of magic that I recall long ago on some now-forgotten veranda. The retired Colonel Broadview, as I shall call him, orated rather pompously about General Robert E. Lee and about how the General was the most competent warrior in all of history, recorded or otherwise. The Colonel seemed most to admire the way Lee had outsmarted all the Yankee generals time after time, as he kept a war alive that he should have lost long before.

"He wasn't too smart at Gettysburg," objected old Xavier Cooting. He had been in the army, too, and was gassed in France, which gave him credentials enough (though it was not as if a Southerner needed credentials to engage in debate). "Lee should have been cashiered," Xavier went on. "He trusted men like Longstreet too much, and he should have sacked Jeb Stuart. And Pickett's Charge—what a damn fool Lee was."

"Oh, come on, Xavier," the Colonel replied, rocking a bit more vigorously. "Lee was brilliant, and he really didn't lose at Gettysburg, you know. He fought a bigger enemy to a standstill on its own ground. The whole idea of coming up through Pennsylvania and getting above Washington was the damnedest bit of daring, and marvelous strategy. He drew the Yankees out of Virginia and came close to making them wash their hands of the whole affair."

"But the point is, he didn't succeed. Any damn fool can be daring. I'm not saying he wasn't brave and clever—just that he was an incompetent general," Xavier granted. "How about another drink, Polly?"

Polly Saey, the veteran Southern belle on whose veranda we were assembled, was nothing if not soft-spoken.

"Old Bob Lee only made one mistake, Xavier. He fought on the wrong side," Polly said to everyone's amazement. At least her daughter, Ethel Good, was amazed.

"How can you say that, Mama?" Ethel said. "You of all people! Lee had his home and people back in Virginia, so he had to fight on their side even if he didn't agree with them about slavery and secession. I'd call him a noble man."

"Noble; my ass; he was a damn chauvinist—just another militant bastard," Abby Stracht interrupted. Abby was Polly's cousin, and a feminist of local notoriety.

"Killing people was his hobby. If he had been really noble, he wouldn't have gone to war at all. If he had been a decent man, he would have stayed home and helped his wife wash the dishes. People who fight wars are incompetent by any definition," sneered Abby.

And so the argument went, through the night, with no minds changed until Tony Logisti, the visitor from the North, finally tried to switch subjects.

"What's the big argument all about? Maybe he didn't wash dishes, Abby, but he did take good care of his men. That's what I always admired about Lee; he worried all the time about feeding and clothing his troops. I thought that's why he came up through Pennsylvania in the first place—to supply his army. You can't be a competent general if you don't tend to the details. Besides, that war is over," reasoned Tony.

Although I have long forgotten exactly who those people were on that magic Carolina evening, the arguments have never faded; partly, no doubt, because it was the first time I had heard anyone question the competence of General Robert E. Lee, paragon of Southern virtue and skills. But there was a deeper reason—one that obsessed me in my youth: curiosity about why seemingly intelligent adults, having much the same information, disagree on anything. It seemed to me then that logic must be so simple and commanding that no one could escape its conclusions. And when I asked, I was always told, "It all depends on your point of view."

Years later, I heard two great generals of World War II revive the Lee argument, one attesting to Lee's competence at Gettysburg, the other sharing Xavier Cooting's opinion that Lee should have been cashiered. Surely these men, equally expert in military science, and both scholars of Lee's war, had no room for dispute.

Slowly, I began to see that each of the six friends of that warm Carolina night was correct in assessing Lee's performance, as were the two generals. And we can reconcile the differences. Because they did not really dispute each other—they only seemed to. It wasn't as if they were viewing the same thing and arriving at different conclusions. Rather, they were viewing different things—different aspects of a person's performance—and arriving at quite reasonable though different conclusions. It can be very instructive to sort out their viewpoints and make some sense of them.

Problems of philosophy and analysis are problems of the vantage point. And the problem of vantage points is getting them organized so that we can assess what it means to stand in one place or another. Three of our six friends thought Lee's performance worthy, and three others thought him a fool. So our first sorting of these viewpoints looks like the following table:

LEVELS OF JUDGMENTS OF LEE

Viewer	Level of View	Judgment of Lee
I. Abby Stracht	Philosophical (philosophy of life)	Negative
II. Ethel Good	Cultural (cultural values)	Positive
III. Polly Seay	Policy (institutional goals)	Negative
IV. Colonel Broadview	Strategic (planning)	Positive
V. Xavier Cooting	Practical (execution)	Negative
VI. Tony Logisti	Logistic (supply)	Positive

A vantage point is like a scientist's microscope or telescope—an instrument that sets the range of our observations, and separates and highlights events in which we are particularly interested. To view performance from no vantage point, or from an evershifting vantage point, is really to see nothing of import, and leads only to a collection of confused impressions, no matter how clear and articulate our descriptions may sound.

Once we have chosen our vantage point—set its context and stated its purpose—we shall be looking through the same scope as anyone else who assumes the same outlook. We may disagree about what we see once we look through that scope (is this event a fact or an illusion?) or about our taste for what we see (I hate it; I love it). But at least our disagreements will now be intelligible, and not a result of using different lenses to look through.

The disparities of view about General Lee that we found among our six friends are universal, I believe. They represent ranges of scope, or breadth of generalization of viewpoint, from the most abstract to the most specific.

Preface and Overview

When the present Editors undertook the task of preparing a book with the title of *Instructional Development Paradigms*, we invited representatives of just about every reasonable and prominent tendency and school of thought that we could identify to write chapters. These introductory comments are a mixture of the viewpoints of the Editors, together with frequent reference to those of this large group of invited contributors.

We have structured our comments here and the format of the book in similar ways. First, we discuss instructional design and development from a philosophical vantage point as an area of activity in general: To what extent is it in fact a valid and thriving area? To what extent and in what quarters is it considered to be a dying or irrelevant area? Second, we discuss the instructional development field from a "cultural" vantage point, contrasting the views of authors from specific end-user cultures (e.g., the K through 12 public school environment or the business training environment) or professional specialization (e.g., Needs Assessment or Evaluation). Next we review the theoretical underpinnings of instructional design and development, emphasizing some of the more recent additions to the arsenal of learning and instructional theories that are influencing at least some instructional designers. We follow with a more detailed look at the macro-strategies used for design and development of overall courses and programs. The chapters in this fourth section reflect the practical implementation of the philosophical, cultural, and theoretical viewpoints highlighted in the three earlier sections. We proceed in the fifth part of the book with an analysis of the tactics or micro-strategies used in instructional design, as practiced in the planning of specific lessons and sequences of instructional materials. Once more, the selected micro-level models in most areas reflect one (or a combination) of the theoretical and strategic viewpoints expressed in earlier chapters. We conclude in Part 6 with some comments specifically related to the current trends for the use of technology-based delivery systems, whether by computers or telecommunications or a combination of various such technologies. In this final section, we have also sought to trace some links between the "logistical vantage points" expressed by the authors in the sixth section and the philosophical, cultural, theoretical, strategic, and tactical views presented in the earlier sections.

Before continuing, we would like to emphasize that the book uses the term "paradigm" in its title, as do many of the chapters within the book. Therefore, we would like to define a little more clearly what we mean by this term and discuss what it implies. We feel the need to explain why we believe that it is valid and useful to take a paradigmatic focus on the analysis of trends and issues in the field of instructional design and development at this time.

According to Kuhn (1962, 1970), a paradigm in a scientific field (in this case, a social science field as well as a psychological and cognitive science) is a coherent set of concepts, principles, assumptions, and basic axioms that have come to be accepted by a sufficiently significant number of researchers or practitioners in the field. These axioms are used by those who hold them to create their own unique identifiable knowledge base of research data, case studies, explanations, and methodologies. For these axioms and beliefs to function as a paradigm, they must attract a group of adherents, and this group, acting through the paradigm, comes to be a significant factor within the life and development of that particular domain of scientific endeavor. It has been suggested that the domination and purpose of the paradigm is to give these people the power and authority to develop the field, both socially and in terms of research and theory. But this is not quite true, though it almost is. In fact, paradigms are somewhat like evolution and genetic inheritance. These things don't exist to serve a purpose; it is more accurate to say that since they do in fact exist (in the case of paradigms, since they have been and are being invented), they therefore can and do serve a purpose.

Perhaps the most often heard discussion within the field of instructional technology in recent years that has typically been couched in paradigmatic form is the debate on "behaviorism versus cognitivism," and which of these should be used as the theoretical underpinning for the ISD process. Almost every single issue of almost any of the instructional and educational technology journals contains articles that in some way or another make the claim that ISD grew up from the 1960s onwards based on a behaviorist paradigm, but that now (in the 1990s) a more appropriate paradigm can be extracted from cognitive psychology. Some of these articles proceed to denigrate ISD on the grounds that it has not moved with the times and that it is becoming rapidly irrelevant because it persists within a behaviorist paradigm, rather than evolving towards a cognitivist-based set of procedures and principles. Other articles devote themselves to proposing and illustrating ways in which the ISD process has adapted and evolved so that it is already based more on cognitivist principles.

However, as the comments which follow will show, this dichotomy of behaviorism versus cognitivism is only one of many currently debated paradigmatic issues. It is fair to say that the number of paradigms that one can identify as underlying the ISD process in one or another context may run into dozens and maybe even hundreds. This book touches on a selection of these paradigms; using them, we will try to illustrate a general evolution of ISD that has accompanied the social, philosophical, and theoretical developments that have occurred over the last few decades since ISD has become accepted and widely applied. Indeed, the Editors feel that understanding the complex paradigmatic structure of the ID field is sufficiently important to warrant a complete chapter devoted to it. This is the first chapter of Part 1: The Moving Target.

The comments which follow are organized into six parts or sections, each relating respectively to the six sections of the book. Readers may wish to read the relevant introductory part of this preface before reading the corresponding section of the book. Alternatively, readers may wish to read the whole of this overview first, as a basis for the later selective reading of specific chapters across the various sections as they relate to a particular interest.

Part 1. The Moving Target: Instructional Development from a Philosophical Vantage Point

When instructional design and development were first applied systematically in educational and training situations, the research fraternity was very much concerned with the latest scientific developments in behaviorism. The focus of laboratory experiments, whether with human beings or animals, was on achieving certain behaviors with a given level of probability through the manipulation of schedules of reinforcement and environmental conditions. This just happened to fit well with the educational philosophy and societal customs of the times. The proper job to be performed by schools and training departments was to put people through courses; then they were to be tested whether or not they had mastered pre-specified abilities as a result of those courses. The name of the game was "instruction."

Over the years, this viewpoint has often been challenged, and these challenges have resulted in the creation of alternative paradigms. On the one hand, over the past decade or so, a growing number of practitioners and theoreticians in the general education field has been won over to a conception of education as being less a process of instruction and more a process of creating environments. Within these environments, the learner may choose to participate or not to participate in certain activities. The shared participation in the process has often been the focus, rather than any specific pre-defined learning outcomes. Meanwhile, practitioners and researchers in the field of human resource development began to realize that the mere mastery of a specific technique or behavior did not necessarily lead to improved productivity or job competence, and this led to the development of the "performance" paradigm as a replacement for the behaviorist paradigm as the cornerstone of the HRD process.

We will leave the educational trends toward the creation of collaborative learning environments alone for the time being and concentrate on the trend to a performance-based human resource development technology and away from a behavior-based one. This trend started in the late 1960s, largely as a result of work by Thomas Gilbert (see the chapter by Marilyn Gilbert, Tom's spouse). Already, in the 1970s, in furthering this trend, the U. S. based organization, the "National Society for Programmed Instruction," transformed itself into the "National Society for Performance and Instruction." This was more than a clever change of names; it aided greatly in adapting the image of the society to the emerging paradigms of the time, while preserving the NSPI initials, and so maintaining organization continuity. The chief *guru* of this movement towards a performance paradigm was Thomas Gilbert of the Praxis Corporation, who had previously been devoted to behaviorism; he had conducted experiments on the principles of behavior at the University of Georgia, and then had worked under Professor B. F. Skinner in his laboratory at Harvard University adapting these principles to humans.

It is particularly interesting to note how Gilbert's viewpoints evolved over the years. When he was still involved with laboratory work on the establishment of a technology for the shaping of behavior, he developed a set of procedures for the practical application of this technology to training. He named this particular technology "Mathetics." His writings on Mathetics are among the most clear and precise of all of the presentations to date of how behaviorist theory can be applied in practice to the systematic design of training exercises and materials. Gilbert's Mathetics was quite influential within a limited sector of the ID profession during the 1960s and shaped the approach to the design of training materials followed by many of the key professionals in the field.

In the January, 1962 issue of the *The Journal of Mathetics*, Gilbert said that the shaping of behavior in order to achieve pre-planned learning outcomes with a high level of probability is a very effective process provided that the trainees are motivated to learn the outcomes. Gilbert noted (already in 1962) that nothing within behaviorism deals with the question of how to motivate the learner to learn. As he pointed out, the laboratory pigeon is starved in order to ensure that food will be the reinforcer. What is the analogy for the human learner? How do we ensure that human learners are equally starved, in the sense of being ready to devour the learning experience presented to them? Already, therefore, in the early 1960s, Gilbert was quite clear about the limitations of approaches based exclusively on operant reinforcement analyses to the achievement of effective learning.

In his book *Human Competence* (1978), Gilbert described the methodology he had developed, which established a basis for a paradigm. This paradigm was based on clear distinctions between performance and behavior. It also established a clear understanding that the achievement of the ability to behave in particular ways is no guarantee that the person will perform effectively in a real situation. In Gilbert's pioneering work, the performance-oriented viewpoint has without a doubt become one of the most powerful paradigms for ISD that is currently in place, particularly within the human resource development area. The National Society for Performance and Instruction grew from an association of a few hundred members through the 60s and 70s to many thousands of members in the mid-1980s onwards. Indeed, it has probably become the predominant association of professionals in the training and development field in both the U.S. and internationally (it has since changed its name to reflect this situation, calling itself the International Society for Performance Improvement). The chapter by Ivor Davies provides further details and elaboration on this trend towards a performance view of ISD.

In this second chapter of the book, Davies outlines the focus, both theoretical and practical, that are driving trainers (and now increasingly educators, too) to embrace the performance engineering paradigm, some 20 or more years after its principles and procedures were developed and proven in practice. In the following third chapter, Marilyn Gilbert draws our attention to the impact of the growth in popularity of this paradigm on other aspects of Tom Gilbert's work. She argues that the success of Tom's contribution to developing the performance engineering approach helped to relegate to relative oblivion his equally important contributions to instructional design. There were no doubt several other influencing factors; for example, the swing of general ID philosophy from a behaviorist-oriented basis to one based on cognitive psychology principles or other fashionable paradigms.

Marilyn's chapter is important to this book in several ways. First, it presents a review of the contributions to our field made by her late husband. Second, it illustrates how the "giant" of our field was able to contribute in parallel to two disciplines, and based on their own paradigms, without experiencing any clash or inconsistency in, on the one hand, developing approaches to eliminate unnecessary instruction and, on the other hand, developing one of the most sophisticated and detailed approaches to the design of instruction. Third, it illustrates how the rank and file of our field seem to have difficulty with such a "multi-paradigmatic" basis for their approach.

The power of the performance engineering approach in identifying how frequently the instruction we design, develop, and implement is, in fact, quite unnecessary, should not blind us to the obvious need for precise and powerful techniques for the design of instruction when indeed it is necessary. But, as Marilyn Gilbert's chapter illustrates, we are often thus blinded. Hence the importance of the message presented in the Editors' opening chapter: *Instructional design is, and always will be, a practice based on multiple paradigms*. Work such as Gilbert's can teach us how to integrate apparently conflicting paradigms and orchestrate our thus more flexible approach to instructional design.

Another strong paradigmatic change that is influencing the ISD field is the move from (so-called) "objectivism" to "constructivism." In the constructivist philosophical perspective, both the behaviorist and the cognitivist routes of ISD are seen as being objectivist in that they are both (as normally practiced) driven by system-derived objectives identified and imposed upon groups of students or trainees. The alternative viewpoint, as expressed in the constructivist paradigm, is that education is a process of constructing meaning out of reality rather than of achieving specific outcomes. This paradigmatic shift therefore implies quite substantial changes in the process of education and training, which also places the control of the process very much more in the hands of the learner. The constructivist viewpoint emphasizes that learning is the activity of the learner in interacting with alternative viewpoints and explanations, and with the surrounding reality. This process should be largely learner-driven and largely a process of collaboration and communication among learners. The role of the teacher, as teacher, is played down; the teacher's function is no longer the dissemination of information and the evaluation of students.

This somewhat radically different viewpoint on what learning is all about is leading to quite radical changes in the process of education, particularly in elementary schools. In elementary mathematics teaching, for example, the constructivist viewpoint has become particularly well-rooted and has led to vast curricular and methodological changes in those schools where it has been adopted. The implications for the ISD field of such a move are quite interesting and are elaborated upon by Brent Wilson in the chapter on constructivism as a philosophical basis for instructional design.

Although constructivism is perhaps most strongly rooted in the context of the education of young children, it has become such a popular banner under which to fight one's battles that we hear it used as an underlying paradigm at all levels of education and even within the human resource development and in the corporate and industrial training fields. Very often, all that happens is that the term is used; but the training processes continue much as before and have little to do with implementing the constructivist paradigm in a serious manner. However, it is still worth considering to what extent the constructivist paradigm has relevance in the adult education and industrial training contexts.

These are probably the most pronounced paradigmatic changes at the moment, but some new candidates for change are appearing on the horizon. Among these are a growing group of researchers and practitioners who call themselves postmodernists and who see education and training as embedded within the process of continual change and revolution (or evolution) occurring within any given society. These people often see instructional design and development as somewhat irrelevant to that society and that continuing change process. This is because ID leads to relatively stable and long-lasting curricula and materials. The postmodernists, in contrast, argue from the fact that society is in constant change to the conclusion that the educational processes and materials should also be in constant change. The implications of this trend are explored by P. K. Jamison in her chapter. She explores how to conceive of instructional development as a social practice.

The constructivist and postmodernist philosphical positions would appear to present serious challenges to the established principles and procedures of ID, especially with respect to the methods and the extent of systematic pre-planning of instruction. How do these new perspectives on the educational process match up to the realities of current educational and training systems? What are the benefits to the students of a radical change in teaching/learning methods and content if the criteria by which success is judged (school and national examinations, industry standards, selection and promotion criteria, etc.) remain unchanged? If we accept that I.D. is part of a technology of instruction, we should accept the essential requirements that spring from the basic definition of "technology" (the application of science to the solution of real-world practical problems); that is, ID ultimately stands or falls on the basis of the extent to which real-world problems of teaching and learning are solved. Some action research on the real-world effects of adopting specific ID approaches should be done in order to determine their real-world effects, and so their real-world values. This has been tried in the past, but only in a few cases, because of the cost required to carry out such studies and the number of people, both students and designers, that are required to fill all the required experimental and control blocks involved.

The chapter by Joseph Kessels and Tjeerd Plomp that closes this section of the book presents the results of such a program of research, performed in the context of corporate training and development. The research study was complex and long-term.

In the first phase, evaluations were performed on a large number of real-world training programs in order to identify the extent to which the "success" of the programs (as measured by currently accepted criteria) was related to the methods used for planning, developing and implementing the programs. This phase demonstrated very convincingly that the adoption of a systematic approach to instructional development was an important factor in a project's success.

However, the use of this systematic approach was not a sufficient condition for success. In addition to the adoption of an appropriate "systematic approach" to planning, it was necessary to adopt an appropriate "relational approach" to the implementation of the project. As in so many other spheres of activity, it is not only *what* you do, but even more *how* you do it.

One important outcome of this first phase was to identify and list the principles and procedures, both of the "systematic (ID) approach" and the "relational (implementation) approach" that were found to "get results" in particular contexts. This extended ID model was then used as the basis for the second phase of the research, in which a large number of real-world HRD programs were designed, developed, implemented, and operated for a period of years. These programs rigorously followed the principles and procedures that had earlier been identified as "appropriate." This second phase provided very strong evidence of the appropriateness of both the "systematic" and the "relational" approaches that were prescribed and adopted.

The Kessels and Plomp study is significant in having put alternative philosophies to the test in real-world contexts. Unfortunately, all the contexts are drawn from HRD in business. Similar studies are required in the contexts of primary and secondary education. This is the prime focus of the criticism and challenges that recently-emerging philosophical positions aim at the ID field. But the evidence that the real world of education would be better as a result of these changes in philosophy is also mostly lacking. A series of experiments examining the effects of these new approaches to ID along the lines of the Kessels and Plomp research would go a long way to settle the arguments arising from philosophical differences in a practical sense, possibly showing that if you have the methodologies right, how you visualize the process doesn't matter.

Part 2. Context, Needs, Results, and Acceptable Process: Instructional Development from a Cultural Vantage Point

Such changes in the underlying philosophies of what education and training are all about, and also in the practice that responds to the underlying realities of organizations that are in constant flux, inevitably also have an impact on those aspects of the instructional development process which are not specifically concerned with instructional design. If we conceive of instructional design as the planning and conceptualization of the teaching/learning environment and of the activities that may occur within that environment, we have a number of other components of the total ISD process that also have to be appropriately implemented in order for any design to reach the light of day and to make a difference in the real world. Among these are the processes of diffusion and implementation (see the chapter by Donald Ely) and the processes of evaluation (see the chapter by Thomas Reeves). These are essential processes within the overall ISD effort. Once more, as the realities of workplace, society, and school change, and as the instructional design approaches change in response to these cultural and social changes, the dissemination, implementation, and evaluation stages of a project may have to follow somewhat different procedures than in the past.

One small example is provided by a comparison of the processes of implementation and evaluation as they are practiced within conventional ISD with the way they would have to be practiced in some of the emerging approaches to ISD. In the past, great emphasis has been placed within ISD models on carefully pre-testing and evaluating every module and element of materials produced before they are all put together, and then they must be further evaluated in field tests before being disseminated to a wider public. Today, if we take the position that there is no one "wider public," but rather a myriad of small publics, each of which might wish to learn about a particular topic area for a different purpose and to a different extent, the issue of evaluation must be treated differently. If we also conceive of a fast-changing environment in which today's needs are no longer tomorrow's needs and any response to a training need must be made almost immediately, it is also more difficult to conceive of a systematic step-by-step product validation and evaluation process that precedes the release of the product for use by a wider audience. An analogy could be drawn with the testing of new drugs and medicines. In the past, this has been regulated carefully by national bodies. These bodies typically insist upon careful testing, first in laboratories using animals. Then they test progressively in more and more real lifelike conditions until every doubt about the drug's actions and side effects has been answered. Only then is the marketing of the drug to the population at large permitted. In the case of AIDS research, however, this tradition has been broken. There is a great need for speed in reaching the public with effective drugs if there is to be any hope of dealing with the fast-evolving problem. This requires that any potentially promising drug be put into field-test situations with real patients almost immediately. Some of the laboratory test situations that were mandatory before are now skipped out of necessity. This, of course, is a special case, but the analogy, we think, is valid, in that in the HRD field we have a "moving target" (and not one, but many moving targets). Therefore, our diffusion, implementation, and evaluation processes must evolve so that they can work in a cost-effective manner within this fast-evolving needs situation. This implies that much more of the evaluation effort might have to take place in the real-life context through developers maintaining contact with large-scale users of a product after its release, constantly monitoring and improving the product after release, rather than following the current practice of eliminating all bugs and improving the product in all respects before its release on the market.

Doughty and Romiszowski recognize the need for the integration of all aspects of instructional development with its customers and users, but go further. They argue for a hierarchy of processes, systems, or viewpoints. For a company or a school to optimize itself, to get as great a benefit as is possible from its efforts, it must be multi-paradigmatic. This embracing of paradigms must not be merely horizontal, as in choosing among several different paradigms to do the same job, but also vertical. They argue that instructional development paradigms are components of performance engineering paradigms, and that performance engineering paradigms are parts of organizational re-engineering paradigms. They are all parts of management and management paradigms, and they all fit together into a unified whole, with each individual paradigm contributing where appropriate.

As suggested in the chapter by Davies in the first section, the driving force is the business. Business needs will determine when and how much re-engineering needs to be done, and the organizational development and performance engineering paradigms will decide how this is to be accomplished. Then instructional development and other change engineering paradigms will accomplish these changes.

Abedor and Sachs (1978) proposed a similar hierarchical relationship to that of Doughty and Romiszowski. They proposed a spiral interaction among instructional development, organizational development, and faculty development, acting within the change process in higher education and in the public schools.

Why have so many years elapsed since the need for such a multi-paradigmatic approach to business and education has been recognized, without its being implemented? Why hasn't the full use of performance engineering and instructional development been realized long ago, since such people as Gilbert developed the theory and methodology for these functions as long as 20 years ago? As Davies argues in his chapter, everything hangs on the bottom line. Business has not recognized the need for the multi-paradigmatic, spiral, or hierarchical view, because the decision-makers in business have not been forced by their data to see it. They see not what they want to see, but what the data, the facts of their business lives, *make* them see.

Doughty and Romiszowski argue that only recently have economic and business conditions become such as to require optimum performance from the typical company, and so only recently has the need for the full use of these technologies been required. Further, until outside forces acted upon the company's group mind, that mind did not think in terms of the human engineering and change paradigms. Until the equivalent of Kuhn's scientific revolution had occurred in industry, no new paradigms would enter the minds of the decision-makers. And without these new paradigms, the technologies and processes, and even the guiding questions needed to bring the power of the new paradigm hierarchy (of instructional development, performance management, and corporate re-engineering) into play could not exist, at least not as all-encompassing, integrated tools focussed on a single goal. All that could be done with these types of development technologies was to use them piecemeal, each operating by itself, and each being blown in the winds of fashion.

Doughty and Romiszowski have presented a view that should act as a warning signal to the field. If practitioners don't think in integrated ways about these different paradigms, and communicate this way of thinking to decision-makers, the wind may well continue to decide our futures, as the changing corporate climate continues to tighten our belts and makes more necessary those things we can do to help the bottom line, but which nobody *knows* we can do, except us.

In the area of public education and general education, the trends have been less towards this performance view and more towards the view that education should serve the individual needs of individual participants much more than the predetermined needs established by the system itself. This aspect is elaborated by Mauldin and Gustafson in their chapter of the book. There are several implications here for the ISD process. If we adopt the position that the role of an educational system is to be responsive to individual needs and interests rather than to prepare the individuals to take specific final exams that have been formulated in advance by a small elite, then the ISD process itself must change. Instead of a process that starts by identifying specific objectives extracted from a predetermined curricula, it must become a process that presents materials and exercises relevant to a broad range of users who may have a broad range of different objectives.

This turnabout implies a change in some aspects of the ISD process, and particularly in how the initial analyses (in order to establish content, sequence, etc.) should be carried out. Although the viewpoints implied by this paradigmatic shift are most strongly expressed in the public education sector, in many areas of HRD we are seeing a growing allegiance to the viewpoint that the content and the process of training should be very much more controlled by the learner than by the system (as is currently the case). The reasons for this may be less philosophical and more pragmatic; namely, that in some areas of modern business, particularly at the level of management and also at the level of application of the new technologies, the reality of the organization is evolving so quickly and so continuously that it becomes practically impossible for a system-controlled process of analysis and planning to keep up with the reality of the change. The members of an organization require a continuous upgrading of their education, and the content of this education that is appropriate for one member of the organization may be quite different from the content appropriate for another, even though they appear to have similar job descriptions. It is therefore essential to involve the individuals in the planning of their own training and development. The process of instructional systems design and development should be geared more towards the provision of resources that the learner can exploit to achieve personally defined objectives rather than the development and presentation of fixed modules or courses that many members of the organization would take.

Of course, this trend is not an absolute change from one paradigmatic situation to another, but is just a shift in emphasis. Whereas a few decades ago it could be argued that most training in an organization that was worth doing would involve large groups of trainees having common objectives and with relatively uniform entry-level knowledge and skills, today, we can see a growing number of situations in which this is not true. Rather, there is a fragmentation of needs, with most members of the organization having at least some specific learning requirements that are different from those of most other members of the organization. Therefore, these students all require much more individualized provisions in order for them to maintain themselves at a currently adequate level of skills and knowledge, and therefore be of value to the organization itself. This aspect of the changing role of HRD and the implied changing emphases and procedures of the ISD process is further explored in the chapter by Lent and Van Patten, who present a model of the ISD process as being "customer driven" as opposed to being "systems driven."

Part 3. The Theory/Policy Vantage Point: Theoretical Underpinnings of Instructional Development

In this section, the chapters review some of the predominant theoretical bases upon which the ISD process can be seen to rest. Different ISD approaches and models are commonly based on one or maybe on a combination of these theoretical underpinnings. The Editors would like to stress that one does not necessarily have to view these theoretical viewpoints as alternative and competing camps, but rather can see them as components to be used in combination; together, as well as individually, they can be used to create a firm foundation for the ISD process. Some of these component viewpoints, such as cybernetics and general systems theory, are more concerned with the overall learning process and aspects of its control, while others, such as behaviorism, cognitivism, or humanism, are concerned with aspects of the learning process itself. Not only is it quite clearly possible to have an ID model that is firmly based on a particular view of systems theory and at the same time embody aspects of behaviorism or cognitivism, it is possible at the instructional/learning level to find that some aspects of behaviorism are quite compatible with some aspects of cognitivism and other aspects of humanism. Rather than reading the chapters in this section as representing opposed and mutually exclusive paradigms for the ISD process, the reader is encouraged to look for links and interrelationships.

The science of cybernetics, or general systems theory, is probably the most global and basic theoretical underpinning for the ISD process. It is from this scientific background that the concepts and procedures of the so-called "systems approach" were generated and applied in many contexts, including education and training systems design, during the 1960s and onwards. Through the 1980s, there was a reaction in the instructional design field against the systems approach. Some felt that the systems approach was overly *systematic* and step-by-step, bound by flowcharts which did not represent the practice of the field as experienced by some practitioners. There was also a reaction to the *systemic* aspect of the systems approach on the grounds that the whole field of education and training was too fuzzy and loosely structured to be viewed in systemic terms.

However, the last few years have seen an about-turn in both of these respects. There is now a growing feeling that some level of systematicity is essential in order to get a job done, and that being systematic does not necessarily mean being rigid in terms of blindly following a given list of steps in a particular way. We will analyze in a later section the trend towards the "rapid prototyping" approaches to ISD; these are based on intelligent and creative "breaking" of the systematic rules of the lockstep ISD model in order to increase productivity. This is to some extent a reaction to the rapid "moving target" aspect of ISD as practiced within modern, rapidly changing society and work contexts. However, the rapid prototyping approach, to be manageable and effective, must itself be systematic in its own way.

The other aspect of a systems approach, the systemic view, is going through a rebirth, especially in areas such as the restructuring of schools in the United States. After many decades of trying to repair existing school systems, the vast bulk of innovators have concluded that existing school systems cannot be improved without a total "systemic" redesign of all components and their relationships to each other. Indeed, "systemic design" is currently a catch-phrase among administrators and innovators in the area of school restructuring in the United States, and it is also coming back into fashion among ISD professionals within the business community.

Further aspects of the cybernetic view of educational systems and how this continues to be relevant in the current age of ISD are covered by William Hug in the first chapter of this section. This chapter presents the principal ideas of general systems theory as applied to the analysis and understanding of educational systems. The chapter is short and concise, as it is intended to be a review of the general principles. These principles are then exemplified by the structure and content of many of the other chapters as they provide more precise descriptions of specific theoretical and practical approaches to the design and development of instruction. Norbert Weiner (1948), in his classic treatise on cybernetics, describes in the very readable preface how the science as it developed came to interest so many different groups of researchers in many different areas of both the exact sciences and the social sciences. The "glue" that brought together the theoreticians and researchers from so many disciplines was the realization that the general meta-principles of cybernetics, as they relate to the study of complex systems and their control, were of relevance across many of the traditional disciplinary boundaries. In his chapter, William Hug emphasizes exactly this aspect, by presenting cybernetics and general systems theory as a form of meta-theory that can bring together and interrelate at a higher level of generality many of the ideas that are expressed in the specific, theoretical positions presented in the later chapters. We place Hug's chapter at the beginning of this section in order to allow readers to view the contents of the remaining chapters throughout the book through the "lens" of general systems principles. They can then search for this higher order of generality, through which many of the apparent differences between theoretical positions and the practical models of implementing them can be seen as merely special cases.

We mentioned earlier (in discussing our introductory first chapter) that much has recently been written about the move from behaviorism to cognitive views of the learning process and the resulting paradigmatic change in the preferred models and practices of ISD. However, such changes are never total. Donald Cook in his chapter emphasizes that without detracting from the need for the application of new lessons that have been learned from cognitive science and cognitive psychology, many of the principles and procedures that were based on the behaviorist paradigm continue to be relevant. Indeed, in specific cases they may be the most appropriate and most effective and efficient ways to proceed in the design of instructional systems and materials. Cook presents a historical overview of the application of behavioral psychology principles to the process of instruction, commencing from the early teaching machines and programmed instruction of the 1960s through more sophisticated approaches to the sequencing and planning of instruction. He analyzes the reasons for the rise, followed by the decline and fall, of programmed instruction as a major paradigm among ID practitioners. He then discusses the impact of programmed instruction on both early and later developments in the field of computer-based instruction, pointing out that many of the more valuable principles of behavioral psychology are still being applied, and for very good reasons. He finishes with an analysis of the importance of the appropriate application of behavioral psychology principles to the development of instructional materials in the future and the prospects for co-habitation of principles drawn from behaviorism and from other areas of psychology in one and the same model for instructional design and development. (The Editors note, most sadly, that this chapter was completed by Dr. Cook only days prior to his sudden death in the summer of 1996. He will be sorely missed by the scholarly community.)

How do we, the Editors, therefore see the contribution of cognitive psychology to the ISD process? Our position is well illustrated by the book *Instructional Design: Implications from Cognitive Science* (West, Farmer, & Woolf, 1991). In this book, the authors illustrate the practical ISD techniques that have arisen from the application of cognitive psychology principles. These include, for example, the use of advance organizers, the use of concept mapping, and the use of frames and other techniques for organizing content in a structured manner. The case is made that these new techniques can be used in two very distinct ways. One way is by the instructional designer in the elaboration of materials and presentations that use more structured diagrammatic presentations than is the typical practice. The other way is by the learner constructing his or her own concept maps or frames or organizers as the study process proceeds. West, Farmer, and Woolf consider both methods of applying the lessons learned from cognitive psychology as valid; though they tend to favor the "tools for the learner to learn with" approach as being the more significant and important contribution of cognitivism to the teaching/learning process.

One particularly interesting aspect of the chapters in this book is that the authors address the issue of teaching students to use these new tools for organizing the content of learning. In the process of outlining an ideal methodology for the development of the skills of constructing concept maps or organizational frames for the content being studied, West, Farmer, and Woolf propose a model that is a classic application of behaviorist principles. Indeed, the way in which they present their ideal strategy for the development of skills to enable students to use the new cognitive learning tools could well have been borrowed from Thomas Gilbert's treatise on Mathetics (Gilbert, 1962a, b). Is there any inconsistency in this mixture of paradigms and procedures? We do not think so. We think it is particularly admirable that a group of cognitive psychologists, in the process of explaining the specific ways in which their work has improved upon and extended the power of ISD procedures (that in the past were based primarily on behaviorist principles), have the honesty and humility to adopt procedures based on behaviorist principles for those objectives for which these continue to be of relevance.

We should consider the contributions from various theoretical viewpoints as being additive and cumulative rather than in competition and seeking to replace past practices that, however limited in some respects, have nevertheless proved to be effective in others. This is the general way in which many of the other chapters in the book have approached not only cognitive psychology, but also other theoretical viewpoints such as humanism and constructivism. Brockett, Grabowski, and Coleman, Perry, and Schwen, in their respective chapters in this section, address these three topics. They also stress how it is possible to borrow and integrate ideas from these various theoretical viewpoints in order to strengthen current ISD practices. They prefer this approach to adopting the somewhat destructive approach of throwing current practices out of the window and starting all over again from a completely different paradigmatic viewpoint.

We are reminded here of the admonition that John Dewey made in the 1920s, when he accused the educational systems of the time of suffering from what he called the "baby-and-bath-water syndrome." He argued that every generation of teachers and innovators see some fault with current systems and react by throwing all of these current systems away and starting afresh with a new set of ideas. Thus, maybe they cure one or two old problems but create one or two dozen new ones. It seems that to some extent both in education and the human resource development areas, the baby-and-bath-water syndrome is still with us. It is hoped that these comments, plus the further detail in the following chapters, may help to create an antidote or serum that may in some way control this syndrome in the future.

However, some specific paradigmatic positions have developed over the last few years that quite clearly adopt the baby-and-bath-water position. Among these, constructivism (at least in its more extreme or radical forms) may be included as a prime example. There are, however, a growing number of practitioners and theorists who suggest ways in which constructivist ideas can be creatively and usefully integrated with some of the older procedures and viewpoints without necessarily implying a total change of methodology and approach.

Other paradigmatic positions that may seem to be revolutionary in their intent include the "situated cognition" movement and the "postmodernist" movement. These are described in this section in the chapters by Orey and Nelson, and by Wilson. While both of these chapters try to adopt a balanced view, analyzing the pros and cons, it is nevertheless true that many of the proponents of these two paradigms see themselves as evangelists and revolutionaries rather than as correctors of existing viewpoints.

Situated cognition grew out of research at Xerox, which discovered that in real-life practice, most people learn to use a piece of equipment such as a photocopy machine or a piece of software (such as a word processor or a spreadsheet package) by a trial and error process that is not really plan-based. From this finding the view has grown that this is the way that most learning occurs and is indeed the way that most learning ought to occur. In this respect, the situated cognition movement shares some of the principles of extreme constructivism in that it proposes that learning should occur within a reality situation. Further, both posit that the learners should be given the opportunity to form their own viewpoints on what that reality really is, and how it should be interpreted.

This viewpoint flies in the face of much evidence derived from practical experience, particularly in many industrial training situations, in which escape from the existence of a strong external reality is impossible. Such a reality might even take the shape of an accident or a death if particular procedures are not followed in particular ways. In the chapters mentioned above, the analysis focuses on how such viewpoints can be toned down and tailored so as to form part of a richer and more powerful ISD process, rather than forming an alternative approach requiring the complete dismantling of all previous approaches. The above comments are probably just as relevant and valid when applied to the postmodernist movement as described by Brent Wilson in this section. However, the postmodernist viewpoints expressed by P. K. Jamison in her chapter (included in Part 1) seem somewhat more radical, and might be difficult to implement in small doses along with doses from other, competing approaches. There are many other theoretical viewpoints that might also be considered as candidates for inclusion within a more powerful and diverse theory-base for ISD. In this section, we include just one of these, the science of semiotics. This subject is interesting in that it starts the process of the design of learning sequences and materials from an analysis of the media to be used and the various "coding characteristics" that different media may possess. The use of this starting point is diametrically opposite to the time-honored approach of the mainstream ISD fraternity, who analyze the problem first, trying to keep as open a mind as possible concerning the selection of the solutions that are to be used. Only later in the process do they determine what methods, and finally what media, are appropriate. In the semiotics approach, one starts with the media and from that develops certain principles for how the learning process can be organized. Driscoll and Rowley, in their chapter, analyze this theoretical viewpoint in terms of its relevance to modern instructional systems design methodologies. They find that there are ways in which the semiotics theory-base can contribute to and enrich ISD, and argue that it should not necessarily be viewed as a diametrically opposite viewpoint.

An example of how multiple theoretical viewpoints can be integrated into a more powerful and more versatile practical approach is illustrated in the final chapter of this section. In that chapter, Kerry Johnson and Joan Bragar present the Forum Adult Learning Model and discuss its multiple theoretical roots. The Forum model, in summary, boils down to several general principles for the planning and implementation of adult learning systems. The theoretical roots of the model are derived from and attempt to integrate the work of major theoreticians who have long been recognized as the *gurus* of educational and training systems development and a number of other, more recent contributors to the growing range of theories of adult learning. The Johnson and Bragar chapter is a significant and appropriate closure to this section of the book, as it illustrates through practical example the multi-paradigmatic nature of the ID field that was described from a theoretical perspective by the present volume's Editors in the first chapter.

In summary, therefore, the different viewpoints that are collected together here reflect the Editors' own viewpoint that ISD is indeed multi-paradigmatic and that the theoretical underpinnings for ISD are developing and diversifying. Because of this, we are evolving to higher levels of potential, rather than regressing to lower levels of relevance and applicability, as some other writers would have us believe.

Part 4. The Strategic Vantage Point:
Instructional Systems Development Macro-Strategies

In this section, we review some of the past, present, and potential future approaches to ISD "in the large"; that is, the design and development of whole courses or course units. We start with a reference to one approach that was extremely popular through the 1970s, but then in the late 1980s and early 1990s seems to have suffered almost total rejection. We refer, of course, to the Personalized System of Instruction (PSI), or, as it is often called, the "Keller Plan" (after the name of Professor Fred Keller, who pioneered this approach).

The principal characteristics of the Keller Plan are the study of pre-prepared modules of learning materials designed to promote the achievement of pre-specified standards of competence; the mastery of the contents of the modules is ensured through a process of evaluation and personal tuition from peer tutors (that is, students who have already mastered the module being studied). This combination of well-designed materials plus individual tutoring from one's peers proved to be highly effective in many different applications in the 1970s.

It should be asked, then, why this particular approach is now used so infrequently. In his chapter on PSI, George Semb analyzes this phenomenon and gives a number of probable reasons why an effective, widely accepted, and proven methodology for the design and implementation of courses may in time be rejected. Interestingly, his analysis shows that in some respects the principles and the procedures have not necessarily been rejected, but have been adapted and incorporated into other schemes, and that this is not immediately evident to the causal observer because these other schemes have been given new names.

We have here a combination of two evolutionary factors that are quite common in much of ISD (as indeed, in much of social innovation in general). One factor is that new "plans" labeled by new names have a limited "shelf-life," in that new generations of researchers and practitioners feel they need to improve and modify the plans; having done so, they tend to also change their names. In some cases, they may also create negative propaganda about the original techniques upon which they have based their somewhat evolved and elaborated modifications (the baby-bathwater syndrome). The second factor is that valid principles of learning and instruction will survive even if the specific "plan" or methodology, and the name by which it was originally known, for some reason does not. There are many current instructional plans/models in many training and educational systems in which peer tutoring and/or the mastery model of achievement are still preserved and serving a good purpose.

It is probably true that some of the reaction to the Keller Plan and to its overall structure is characteristic of the swing in education towards the learner-centered philosophies. The constructivist view, for instance, would be completely in opposition to the use of the Keller Plan. This also would be true in the case of the situated cognition movement. It is interesting, however, that the humanist position would not necessarily be against this type of course structure, provided that it was used for those aspects of the total course content and curriculum which were appropriate for mastery to predetermined levels of competence. In his chapter on the Individualizing Instruction Model, Burton Sisco elaborates on the humanist approach and transforms it into the basis for a practical ISD model. In some respects, this model has much in common with the Personalized System of Instruction, while in other respects, it is substantially different. Although the theoretical origins of the approach outlined by Sisco are different from those that led Keller to develop the PSI model, the practical suggestions for implementation are very similar (see also the chapter by Hiemstra in Section 5). We see here an example of how some of the principles of earlier models continue to live on in ID through their incorporation within new models.

Further examples of currently practiced ISD models that owe their pedigree to much earlier work are described by Engelmann in his chapter on Direct Instruction and by Novak in his chapter on Assimilation Theory and Metacognitive Tools as a Foundation for Instructional Design. Engelmann describes the current practice of Direct Instruction, outlining the roots of this approach in the behaviorist movements of the 1960s, but illustrating how the details of the approach have been updated, modernized, and integrated into more current philosophical viewpoints of what education and training are all about. Similarly, Novak describes modern and up-to-date instructional design processes that are nevertheless based on theoretical work that was developed by Ausubel and his students in the 1960s and earlier. We have here examples of two currently thriving instructional design and development macro models that owe their pedigrees to work of 30 or more years ago. In one case, it was from the behaviorists, and in the other case from the cognitive psychology camp. The reader should trace the links between these chapters and the theory-based chapters by Cook and Grabowski included in Part 3.

The chapters by Stahl and by Dorsey, Goodrum, and Schwen are further attempts at integration of various paradigmatic positions applied to ISD. Stahl outlines a model as yet perhaps infrequently implemented, but one that is an attempt to integrate those information processing/cognitive science principles and constructivist principles that have been widely discussed in the literature as ways to integrate them into the practice in ISD and curriculum planning. The reader should trace the links between the suggestions proposed in this chapter and the theoretical viewpoints presented earlier in the chapters of Wilson, Grabowski, and Coleman, Perry, and Schwen.

Dorsey, Goodrum, and Schwen describe the movement towards rapid collaborative prototyping in their chapter by the same name. This is an attempt to adapt to the ISD context the ability of the computer programmer to develop software much more quickly and get it into use much faster by starting with a prototype before attempting to build the final product. The same needs for flexibility and speed are also important in the education and training field. The essential aspect of rapid prototyping is to eliminate or compress many of the conventionally expected steps and procedures of the ISD process, and to go back to perform these only if experience shows that eliminating them results in producing an ineffective and unacceptable final product. The chapter describes how rapid collaborative prototyping is performed in practice, what benefits may be realized, and just how different it is from the conventional ISD processes that we have used in the past.

There also exist many rather less well-known and not always well accepted approaches to ISD. Notable among these are the Accelerated Learning or Suggestopaedia approaches that were pioneered in Eastern Europe in the 1960s and 70s, and which have over the last decade or two slowly been accepted in the education and training fields worldwide. A number of recent adaptations of the initial Suggestopaedia ideas have been made incorporating concepts drawn from a variety of research areas, such as, for example, Howard Gardner's pioneering work on multiple intelligences, and work on mental imagery. One such multidisciplinary approach that is now common in the United States has come to be called Integrative Learning. It is "integrative" because it focuses on integrating learning through many of the seven human intelligences that Gardner has described, and also because it integrates principles derived from a range of psychological, psychiatric, and other theoretical positions.

A thriving and growing interest group now concerns itself with "Human Possibilities." It is actively investigating the practical application within the instructional process of ideas that have been taken from the Accelerated Learning and Suggestopaedia work, from mental imagery research, from psychocybernetics, and from many other areas of study. Some of these approaches are considered to be suspect and not thoroughly "scientifically-based" by the mainstream scientific community. A thriving professional association called the Society for Accelerative Learning Technology (SALT) focuses on these novel and somewhat marginal ISD approaches (see the chapter by Schuster for further details). These new developments, however "novel" and "marginal," have on many occasions shown quite significant positive results in their practical application; and there is a growing feeling that there is much more to be learned than we currently are aware of about the processes of learning and instruction and the organization of environments for effective learning, and instruction.

Some of these more extreme (when compared to currently widely-accepted models) and not necessarily yet fully accepted theoretical positions are also incorporated into the Existential Design and Delivery of Instruction model presented by Terry Flynn in her chapter, "Existentialistic Design and Delivery of Instruction." Flynn considers the specific context of workplace instruction, and she analyzes both the well-established "conventional" approaches (e.g., the Conditions-of-Learning Model of Gagné) and some of the "innovatory" approaches (e.g., the SALT model) as regards their applicability and relevance to this specific context. She finds both the conventional and the innovatory approaches to be lacking in certain repects. This leads her to propose an alternative ID model for use in the workplace training context.

The Flynn model incorporates elements from several already-existing models, but combines them within an overall structure and approach derived from existential philosophy and psychology. Her arguments concerning the drawbacks of earlier models are convincing. Her new model, however, differs not so much in its technical aspects (objectives are still defined, strategies planned, etc.) but rather in the way that the ID process is operationalized and carried out.

Flynn emphasizes that the workers trained in a business organization are adults. Therefore, the adult learning principles proposed by such writers as Brockett, Sisco, and Hiemstra in their respective chapters, and organized into the "Forum Adult Learning Model" in the chapter by Johnson and Brager, hold good and should be applied.

But Flynn argues that the real-world context of workplace training imposes a set of constraints and requirements that are quite different from those assumed by adult education writers, or those that might exist in an educational institution or in an off-the-job setting. Flynn's proposed model takes these differences into consideration by laying particular emplasis on how the ID process is planned and implemented. Flynn's chapter should be read as a specific example of the general findings reported by Kessels and Plomp in their chapter, namely that real-world success always depends on an appropriate combination of systematics and tailored implementation processes.

We round off this section of the book with the chapter by Roberts Braden. His chapter efffectively critiques the whole range of philosophies, innovatory theoretical positions, and alternative "new" ID models so far presented and discussed in the earlier chapters of the book. Braden takes the position that most of the elements of the "conventional" ID models continue to be relevant in real-world contexts. He defends many of the specific steps and characteristics of established ID procedures that have been under attack by recent theorists and model builders. However, he also sees fit to present (or rather to re-present) his arguments in the form of yet one more alternative model. The interesting aspect of his model is that basically it espouses the "linear" sequence of steps so often criticized of late, but then shows by reference to published research that the overly linear appearance of such a model does not necessarily (indeed does rarely) result in unwavering lockstep practice. The apparently lockstep conventional ID models that are encountered in the literature are reactions more to appearance of the process than to its practice in the real world. He also implies that many of the more useful and successful modifications of earlier ID models, although invariably launched in the literature on the basis of some "new philosophical or theoretical paradigms," have been useful and successful because they reflected the real-world requirements of a particular educational problem or context. For example, Braden adds an emphasis in his own model on the systematic design of motivation, in parallel with the systematic design of instruction, justifying this as a very real-world pragmatic consideration. This is one aspect on which the Braden model and Flynn's Existentialist model are in full agreement. Flynn derives the practical need for motivational design at least in part from a philosophical/theoretical background based on Existentialism. Braden comes to similar practical conclusions without a shift in philosophical or theoretical paradigms.

If this book were to conclude at this section, the Braden chapter could be considered a useful and worthy final chapter, or more precisely, a reaction to the multiple paradigmatic viewpoints presented separately by the other authors. Braden questions the validity and usefulness of nearly every one of the innovatory viewpoints presented so far. It remains with the reader to reflect on the validity and usefulness of Braden's critique. In his own words, "a serious analysis of the relative merits of linear ID vs. these contenders would require at least another five chapters. Proponents of these approaches are invited to engage the debate in a future forum."

But the book does not end here. The two remaining sections (which deal with the Tactical and Logistical implementation of specific philosophical or theoretical viewpoints on the teaching/learning process, by means of the selection of specific strategies of instruction) give us the opportunity to engage the debate right here and now.

Part 5. The Tactical Vantage Point:
Instructional Design Micro-Strategies

At the "micro" level, just as at the "macro" level previously analyzed, a multitude of strategies and tactics are actually in use, both in the classroom and in training workshops as well as in the design of various types of instructional materials. This is well illustrated by the classic work by Joyce and Weil on Models of Instruction, which provides detailed descriptions of over 20 approaches to classroom instruction. Timothy Anderson, in his chapter on Using Models of Instruction, updates us on a number of these models.

Some of these models have not been developed within the ISD discipline as we know it, but rather have been developed "at the grass roots" by practitioners through their experience of what works and doesn't work. These models have slowly become accepted by a large enough group of practitioners to be considered as paradigms for practice. Other models are very precisely and clearly derived from specific theoretical paradigms that are part of the basis for the ISD process. Among those that can be so traced is the Precision Teaching model and the Precise Instructional Design underlying it, described by Ogden Lindsley in his chapter. Lindsley traces the behaviorist roots of this methodology and illustrates how it is today being used by a large, and growing, body of teachers—providing practical support for the claims made by Cook in his chapter in Part 3.

Among the newer models that were not listed in Joyce and Weil's book are those that have come from the humanist movement, and from research on Andragogy; for example, the model described by Hiemstra in his chapter on Applying the Individualizing Instruction Model with Adult Learners. Another example is the Strategic Teaching Framework for Learning Complex Interactive Skills (described by Thomas Duffy). Duffy's work has its roots at least partly within the constructivist paradigm, but also makes use of modern technologies and hypermedia as a means for implementing the principles espoused by the model.

More precisely related to computer-based instruction are the models that have been derived under the name of Instructional Transaction Theory, pioneered by M. David Merrill over the last few years. Instructional Transaction Theory is described in the chapter by Cline,

Pratt, and Merrill. One application is further described in the following chapter by Zhang, Gibbons, and Merrill. "Automating the Design of Adaptive Instructional Materials" discusses the application of instructional transaction theory to the production of "templates" that can be filled with relevant content and applied in a variety of different instructional situations. This is an attempt to overcome a major weakness of ISD, particularly in the design of computer-based instruction materials: the high cost in terms of development time of the instructional materials. It is the hope of Merrill and his associates that the application of instructional transaction theory will achieve two main goals: (a) extend detailed systematic instructional materials design from the level of discrete exercises for single objectives (as was the focus of Merrill's earlier work on Component Display Theory) to the development of skills in dealing with multiple objectives and complex domains of subject matter; and (b) reduce the time and cost of developing computer-based instructional materials, thus rendering the ISD process at this micro level more viable in practical contexts, where both the cost of the product and the time from conception to use have now become critical factors. The reader may note the links implied here to the Doughty and Romiszowski chapter on front-end analysis and the Dorsey/Goodrum/Schwen chapter on rapid prototyping.

Merrill and his associates are focusing on an important aspect here in that one limiting factor on the application of computer-based instruction and new technologies in the modern education and training environment is the time and cost of materials development. However, they may be committing the error of trying to over-simplify the theoretical underpinnings and structure of the design/development process, so that the approach, although efficient in terms of production time, may be limited in effectiveness to only certain categories of content or objectives (as was the case with Component Display Theory). There is also the issue of product quality, which many instructional design specialists would consider to be a function not only of a logical design but also of the creative personality that a particular designer brings to a project.

Although the automated design tools advocated by Merrill and his associates could be considered to be useful aids to the design process that would help to cut down the overall time of an ID project, there is a danger that the instructional designer may come to rely too heavily on the tools and even delegate responsibility for final product quality almost entirely to them. But it is questionable whether the tools can replicate those aspects of the design of outstanding educational materials that depend on intuitive and nonlogical aspects of the designer's and subject expert's decision-making processes. It is too early to make final judgments on these issues, though, since the tools to which Merrill and his associates refer are not fully operational and have not been used on a sufficient number of projects to enable their effectiveness and contribution to the instructional design process to be fully evaluated.

At this point, we would like to comment on an interesting methodology which had its birth in the 1960s as a cognitive psychology/humanist philosophy reaction to behaviorist principles applied in programmed instruction; it is called the Structural Communication methodology. Structural Communication was invented in the United Kingdom in the late 1960s as a way of constructing text-based (or computer-based) conversations between a set of study materials and the user that in some ways replicated a Socratic Dialogue model. Structural Communication enables self-study materials to achieve success in the development of complex problem-solving strategies, and also in the mastery of complex domains of information (including the interrelationships between different components of the domain). The principles of Structural Communication are further described in the chapter by Slee and Pusch. This methodology was used to develop materials in various subject areas, particularly such areas as history, social sciences, and philosophy. In areas such as these, it is difficult to say that there are right and wrong answers to certain questions, but rather, there is a range of positions that people can take on a problem. Structural Communication enables students to compare and contrast these positions in the simulated discussion.

After the initial flurry of interest in Structural Communication through the late 60s and early 70s, the technique seems to have remained relatively dormant. In the last few years, however, in the context of new philosophical viewpoints on the process of learning, on learner control, and also on the importance of critical thinking as an essential life skill for employable people, Structural Communication has gained new relevance as a methodology for implementing appropriate teaching/learning experiences, particularly within a computer-based learning environment. A number of recent projects, many of them emanating from the IDD&E Department at Syracuse University, have examined the applicability of Structural Communication as a methodology for presenting the case study methodology on computer networks to groups of people distributed geographically. The research in these recent projects has demonstrated that the use of Structural Communication and other derivative method-ologies for the design of group discussions can significantly extend the applicability of com-puter-based training to areas that would normally be considered the preserve of small-group discussions led by a skilled and competent subject-matter expert/facilitator.

This research is particularly important in the context of the "corporation of the future," because one result of the trend towards so-called "knowledge work" (where the worker uses knowledge in order to create new knowledge) is that critical thinking and creative problem-solving skills will grow in importance as the basis for employability of the work force. In that case, either at school or later after school within their job context, most employees will need to improve their critical-thinking skills. At present, we are aware that small-group discussion techniques led by skilled facilitators appear to be the most effective conventional ways of achieving such objectives. But we may be able to offer technology-based alternatives that could replicate the effectiveness of the rather expensive conventional approach. At the pre-sent time, the use of case-study methodology and other small-group discussion activities is severely limited because of the need to gather people in one place at one time with a skilled facilitator. If these restrictions can be overcome by technology-based replications of such dis-cussions on world-wide networks (such as the Internet and its World Wide Web), we may greatly extend the availability and use of these techniques within the human resource de-velopment area. This is probably one of the more important areas in which new technologies may help us to do a better job as human resource development specialists.

As with macro ID, we have a few "marginal" and not fully "respectable" candidates at the micro-level that are seeking inclusion in our tool box of design techniques. One of these is described by King in his chapter on "Subliminal Perception Studies and Their Implications for Instructional Design." The specific technique of including subliminal messages has ap-parently not proved instructionally effective; and, as King concludes, the promise of the pro-ponents of subliminal perception within the training and educational product development fields have not yet been realized. This is one particular design technique that we may safely say should be left out of our tool box for the future; an example of a candidate paradigm that has not stood the test of time and research-based scrutiny.

The fifth section of the book closes with a detailed account of the Algo-Heuristic ap-proch to ID, pioneered by Lev Landa, originally in the USSR, but for the last two decades in the United States. This chapter is significant in that it presents an ID "micro" model that has withstood the test of time. Based on research work completed in the 1950s, Landa has de-veloped a very detailed approach to the analysis of cognitive processes and the design of ap-propriate tactics for instruction. Historically, the model was developed in parallel with the popularity of behaviorist psychology and the resultant procedures for the systematic analysis of behavior (see the chapter by Cook). Perhaps as a result of this historical factor, or perhaps because the original Russian reseach became available in the USA in English language trans-lation only from the mid-1970s onwards, the apparent impact of this work on the practice of ID seems to be somewhat limited, but Landa quotes evidence to support the claim that, on a worldwide scale, the impact of the Algo-Heuristic paradigm has been significant.

What Landa does not state explicitly is the indirect impact that his pioneering work has had on several current "hot issues" in the ID field. Even when not specifically acknowledged, Landa's work was the basis of much of the work on the design and use of job-performance aids, through the 1970s and 1980s. It is therefore one of the cornerstones of Performance Technology as we know it today (see the chapters, in different sections, by Davies, Horn, and Doughty and Romiszowski).

But the "algorithms" aspect of Landa's work (applied in job-performance contexts) is complemented by the "heuristics" aspect, which is of relevance to the development of general problem-solving and critical-thinking skills. These categories of skills are fast becoming "top priority" issues in both formal education and corporate training (see the last chapter in the book by Romiszowski). Therefore, the relevance of the Algo-Heuristic Approach is on the rise as we enter the 21st century.

The reader may wish to contrast Landa's approach to the development of critical-thinking skills with the approaches proposed or implied by other authors who have addressed the issue of changing needs, curricula, and teaching/learning methods. The proponents of constructivism and constructivistic ID seem to argue for the delegaion of much of the task of knowledge structuring to the learners themselves. In contrast, Landa argues that this is the most important task of the instructional designer.

It is up to the reader to critically examine these opposing viewpoints, not so much to decide which is "right" and which is "wrong" (in our opinion, that's the wrong question), but to identify the real-world relevance and utility of such apparently contrasting viewpoints and seek the "common ground" that may identify (as we believe) how each paradign offers its own unique contribution to an integrated multi-paradigmatic approach to instructional design.

Romiszowski's chapter presents a fairly "rosy" picture of the ID profession in the 21st century: more work to do; more varied work; more challenging work. It also presents a strong practical argument for developing and maintaining a multi-paradigmatic approach to ID in the years to come, thus closing, through practical examples, the arguments that were opened, through theoretical analysis, in the book's opening chapter.

Other somewhat unusual and even strange design techniques may emerge that will prove themselves to be valid candidates for inclusion in our tool box. As we move into the multimedia/hypermedia environments of the future, several such candidates will emerge or are indeed already emerging. A potential paradigmatic foundation for the use of hypermedia and multimedia that many writers of recent times have proposed is that the external storage of information in media would benefit from being modeled after the way in which human beings appear to store and access information in their minds. They appear to do this in a very non-linear, random-access way. It has been suggested by the inventor of the name "hypertext," Theodore Nelson (1967), as well as many of his later followers, that hypertext imitates human behavior in this respect, and so is more effective for information searching and for allowing the learner to study in a more effective and satisfying a manner. These claims are yet to be put to the test in practice. Some of the chapters in the last section of the book attempt to evaluate to what extent such claims and many other aspects of the application of new technologies to training are leading to new and valid paradigms for the planning of the instruction process.

Part 6. The Logistics Vantage Point: Technology-Based Paradigms

In this section, we present some of the techniques and procedures that have been developed over recent times because of the availability of a new technology that was previously not available to the trainer. We start by looking at a technique that, like Structural Communication (see Slee and Pusch in Part 5), is not recent and was not initially developed specifically from a technology basis, but is proving to be especially important for application within a technology-based training context. We refer to the structured writing methodology which was developed in the 1960s and early 1970s by Robert Horn and his collaborators as a more effective way of authoring technical documentation and training materials that could be used for both initial learning and also for later reference on the job. The details of this technique and some of its research support are outlined in the chapter on structural writing by Robert Horn.

Structured writing now has a pedigree of some 25 or 30 years of use and has proven itself to be an effective way of producing print-based materials for both technical documentation and also for training and education purposes. However, like Structural Communication, the structured writing technique is even more relevant in today's technology-based society as more and more information is distributed and made available through hypertext and hypermedia networks. Although much has been written about hypertext and hypermedia and their potential benefits, very few attempts have been made to present or develop methodologies by which hypertext and hypermedia may be designed and organized. There are many tools for creating the final product (ToolBook, HyperCard, etc.), but very few "tools to think with" as to what structure and organization the content should be given to ensure the effectiveness of the product. This is perhaps not surprising, as much of the driving force behind the hypertext/hypermedia movement has come from the computer science field rather than from the educational and training professions. However, without a doubt, there are some potential benefits to the education and training area of the use of well-designed hypertext and hypermedia.

The key term is "well designed." What does this mean and how does one achieve it? Structured-writing procedures and techniques appear at this time to be the most complete and (at least for some types of applications) the most powerful way of approaching the problem of structure and organization. For this reason, it will be particularly important for current workers within the instructional design and development field to become conversant with the techniques and also the history of development and the underlying principles of this methodology. Among other things, this is a lesson in eclectic integration of principles and procedures from many theoretical fields into one integrated and powerful set of tools for "getting the job well done." Materials design techniques such as structural writing are essential factors in getting benefit from the investment that many organizations are making in the computer storage and delivery of their technical information and training materials.

At this point, it is interesting to refer to the chapter by Dreyfus and Dreyfus, which suggests that maybe some of the new technology-in-training proponents are exaggerating their case. Dreyfus and Dreyfus take the position that both theoretical analysis and practical experience suggest that the role of the computer as a tool in the education and training process is in fact limited to basic information presentation and drill-and-practice levels of the teaching/learning process. The authors of this chapter are rather skeptical about the benefits of computers and computer-based educational software at the higher-order learning levels.

This position is in stark contrast to the rather optimistic views expressed by Terry Borsook (in his chapter on Hypermedia) and Gibbons, Fairweather, Anderson, and Merrill (in their chapter on Simulation and Computer-Based Instruction). These authors all see the main value of computers in rather sophisticated applications aimed at enhancing the power of the teaching/learning process at the level of problem solving and other higher-order types of objectives. It is interesting to contrast the viewpoints of these theoreticians. Dreyfus and Dreyfus feel that we have already extended the computer beyond its rightful place and role within the instructional-delivery process. Other writers, who are working actively to extend the applicability of the computer to well beyond its current areas of effective application, see technology as the savior of educational and training systems of the future.

As a complement to these positions, the chapter on Computer-Mediated Communication (CMC) by Romiszowski and Ravitz illustrates yet another potentially far-reaching impact of new technologies in the education and training field. In Computer-Mediated Communication, the computer is used primarily as a communication device; that is, networked computers enable people to contact other people as well as contacting databases of information that may be stored somewhere at a distance. CMC is a new dimension for distance education that is more rapid and more interactive than many of the previously available distance education/communication methodologies. It is also a development that is integrative in the sense that it integrates access to information and access to people in a relatively seamless manner. In many ways it replicates (more closely than any other distance education/communication methodology) the strong points of bringing people together in one place where there is available a rich variety of information resources (e.g., a library or media center). It is worth recalling that the original medieval concept of a university was just that: a place that furnished access to information and opportunities for interaction between interested and knowledgeable individuals (scholars).

The fact that we can now replicate such rich learning environments over distances and indeed unite people who are separated by both distance and time zones to work together as if they were in one place at one time offers many potential advantages to the designers of education and training systems. For these reasons alone, Computer-Mediated Communication might be considered to be a new and developing paradigm for education and training. However, there are other aspects to CMC which are of importance and interest. Among these are the results of some recent research suggesting that in some situations and with some groups of students, communication via computer at a distance in an asynchronous mode may in fact be superior in some respects to the time-honored and sacrosanct paradigm of face-to-face meetings, discussions, and instruction.

Before we are burned at the stake as heretics, we would hasten to add that we are not advocating elimination of human contact, but the extension of opportunities for human contact in a way which, if properly designed and orchestrated, would appear to be in some respects even more effective than the time-honored methodologies of place-based, real-time instruction that are so familiar to us. We still require experts and teachers with whom to interact and communicate, but these experts and teachers may be used in a more effective and efficient manner. Some of the advantages that may accrue from asynchronous distance communication of this nature are that before responding to a statement or question, respondents may analyze it a little more closely, make reference to other sources, make sure that they have thought out their response, and then present it in as clear and precise a manner as they are capable of doing. Another emerging potential benefit is that some people (and indeed, in some cases, whole societies or nations) appear to be relatively inhibited when group discussion and argument are used as a method of education. In some of these cases, it has been shown that people who have exhibited such inhibition in the live classroom situation lose that inhibition and become quite argumentative and assertive when placed in an asynchronous CMC environment.

We could quote other potential benefits that seem to be achievable through the use of CMC. No doubt there are also certain potential dangers or disadvantages. Maybe the lack of live contact detracts through the elimination of much of the non-verbal communication that may occur in personal discussions. Also, some aspects of the socialization process essential to the development of character and interpersonal skills may be lost if CMC is over-used and is incorporated too early in the educational process. However, it is very early yet to be certain. We will learn a lot more over the next few years, since CMC appears now to be the most rapidly growing area of application of computers in education and training, and it is being subjected to the most intensive and extensive programs of research.

We should not leave this section without some comments on Intelligent Tutoring Systems (ITS) or Intelligent Computer-Assisted Instruction (ICAI). This area of research and development has been with us for some 20 years. Today, however, there seem to be more skeptics than there were at the beginning of our interest in this approach. Some of this skepticism is due to slower than expected progress in the implementation of effective intelligent tutoring systems. Other skepticism has arisen from new theoretical viewpoints that now consider that those factors differentiating exceptionally good teaching from average teaching are not capable of being reproduced within computer-based software. The state of Intelligent Tutoring Systems and research in this area is analyzed by Farquhar and Orey in their chapter. They are perhaps more optimistic than we are about the ultimate impact of intelligent tutoring systems on a large scale in everyday education and training. On the other hand, they are quite right that in certain specific areas the results of research in this field will eventually be very significant indeed.

One particular area in which progress has been made and will continue to be made is in the development of intelligent support systems for the use of software such as spreadsheets or word-processing packages. It is now quite predictable that the next generation of software products, as they become available with the benefit of CD-ROM storage, will include in the CD-ROM (in addition to the software package) a full "performance support system." This performance support package will include basic instruction and on-line help systems that are much more helpful than those currently available because they are much more "intelligent" in diagnosing what are the causes of problems that a person may be having with the operation of the package. Procedural tasks that are involved in the use of typical computer-based software applications are relatively easy to analyze and to use in categorizing the causes of possible difficulty. The current state of development of artificial intelligence and expert systems technologies is actually sufficient to enable one to design and develop applications that would replicate the effectiveness of a knowledgeable tutor "peering over the operator's shoulder."

However, as we move (for example) to the use of spreadsheets, then, in addition to being able to use a particular spreadsheet package (for example, Excel) effectively and efficiently, we must also have some basic understanding of what a spreadsheet is and how it may help in a particular job situation. In other words, the design of a particular spreadsheet application is a creative problem-solving exercise that depends on the application of general concepts and principles in a flexible way to the particular task that is being addressed. It is in such areas that intelligent tutoring systems have not yet demonstrated their capability of delivering cost-effective training. The Editors do see some clear situations in which "intelligent" performance-support systems would be used on the job for particular procedures; but these would be preceded by some more conventional instructional designs that may often rely on interaction with human tutors (directly or at a distance through CMC systems) in order to verify that basic concepts and principles have been thoroughly mastered and successfully applied in a creative manner in real-life problem-solving situations.

The themes of the last two chapters of the book examine how new developments such as ITS, CMC, and simulation may be integrated with each other and with other more conventional methodologies in order to satisfy all the needs of human resource development in the 21st century. "The Learning Systems Repository: A Conceptual Framework," developed by Charles Atkinson, is an attempt to integrate many of the ideas that we have been discussing into a conceptual model of ISD as it may appear in the future. The final chapter, by Romiszowski, explores ISD in the context of the future "Networked Society" from the viewpoint of an assessment of future human resource development needs and the creation of a model of what the key action areas for the HRD professional will be in that future. This model is then extrapolated to identify the key areas that ISD should strengthen in order to continue to serve as an effective and efficient tool of the human resource development professional.

Charles R. Dills
Alexander J. Romiszowski
October, 1996

References

Abedor, A. J., & Sachs, S. G. (1978). The relationship between faculty development, organizational development, and instructional development: Readiness for instructional innovation in higher education. In R. K. Bass, B. Lumsden, & C. R. Dills (Eds.), *Instructional development: The state of the art*. Columbus, OH: Collegiate Publishing.

Gilbert, T. F. (1962a). Mathetics: The technology of education. *Journal of Mathetics, 1*(1).

Gilbert, T. F. (1962b). Techniques of exercise design. *Journal of Mathetics, 1*(2).

Gilbert, T. F. (1967). A scientific approach to identifying training needs. *Management of Personnel Quarterly, 6*(3).

Gilbert, T. F. (1978, 1996). *Human competence: Engineering worthy performance*. Washington, DC: ISPI (originally McGraw-Hill).

Kuhn, T. S. (1962, 1970). *The structure of scientific revolutions*. Chicago: University of Chicago Press.

Nelson, T. H. (1967). Getting it out of our system. In G. Schechter (Ed.), *Retrieval: A critical review*. Washington, DC: Thompson Books.

Weiner, N. (1948). *Cybernetics*. Cambridge, MA: MIT Press.

West, C. K., Farmer, J. A., & Wolff, P. M. (1991). *Instructional design: Implications from cognitive science*. Englewood Cliffs, NJ: Prentice-Hall.

Contents

PART 1.
The Moving Target: Instructional Development from a Philosophical Vantage Point

PART 2.
Context, Needs, Results, and Acceptable Process:
Instructional Development from a Cultural Vantage Point

PART 3.
The Theory/Policy Vantage Point:
Theoretical Underpinnings of Instructional Development

PART 4.
The Strategic Vantage Point:
Instructional Systems Development Macro-Strategies

PART 5.
The Tactical Vantage Point:
Instructional Design Micro-Strategies

PART 6.
The Logistics Vantage Point:
Technology-Based Paradigms

Instructional
Development
Paradigms

PART 1

The Moving Target: Instructional Development from a Philosophical Vantage Point

1

The Instructional Development Paradigm: An Introduction

Charles R. Dills
IntelliSys, Inc.
Syracuse, New York

Alexander J. Romiszowski
Syracuse University
Syracuse, New York

Technology and Instructional Development[1]

Instructional development (and the related concepts of instructional design and educational technology) have been defined in many different ways by many different authors (Gentry, 1995). Some of these different ways can be seen in the different paradigms displayed in this book. A typical definition is given by Shrock (1995, p. 12):

> **A self-correcting, systems approach that seeks to apply scientifically derived principles to the planning, design, creation, implementation, and evaluation of effective and efficient instruction.**

Most other definitions share the emphasis upon systems, scientifically-derived principles, and feedback. Many define instructional development as a kind of technology; others define it as an application of a technology. Many emphasize its close ties to learning theory, media technology, curriculum development, and evaluation theories.

Others identify instructional development with education in general, and consider it to be more of a social science than a branch of cognitive science or behaviorism. Still others consider education in general and instructional development in particular to be a hybrid of the social and hard sciences.[2] Bass and Dills (1984) placed a strong emphasis on the artistic, creative, and intuitive dimensions of instructional design, as apparently do the "Scruffies" (discussed later in this chapter). Each of these conceptualizations of instructional development results in a slightly different picture of what instructional development is like. But the resulting descriptions and prescriptions have in common that they can be characterized as technologies (or clusters of technologies). Even the social science and intuitive views of instructional development result in what are generally called "soft technologies." They are so called because they are not normally reducible to algorithmic procedures and rules, but only to heuristic "rules of thumb," and instructional development is seen as a technology.

Technology, in turn, has been defined in many different ways (Finn, 1960; Gentry, 1995; Saettler, 1968, 1990). These definitions may be roughly divided into two groups, those based on machines (product definitions) and those more general ones that talk about systematic ways of doing things (process definitions). These latter include such processes as evaluation, programmed instruction, surgery, writing, and instructional development.

Another approach is to define instructional development not in terms of what it is, but in terms of either its function or its purpose. This is the approach of the editors of this book. As they see instructional development, it exists to provide the world with improved instruction. And it functions as a community of practitioners and researchers who attempt to fulfill this purpose. That is, instructional developers are supposed to be able to produce instructional materials and instructional events, activities, and courses that teach (instruct, meet goals, achieve objectives) more efficiently and more effectively than would otherwise be possible. Sometimes these materials and events are also used (delivered) by the instructional developer, sometimes by someone else who is a specialist in delivery (and therefore, supposedly, can deliver the message, content, instruction, and materials more efficiently and effectively than can anyone else).

Before there were instructional developers, others had already invented this role, and were the experts in efficient and effective education. There were educational technologists in the 1950s and 1960s, and there have been curriculum development specialists and subject-matter specialists, and educational psychologists for far longer than there have been computers and computer-based instruction (CBI).

In Europe, for example, particularly in Central and Eastern European countries such as Germany, Hungary, and Poland, universities have for over a century tended to support departments and even schools of "didactics." The definition of didactics differs little from many of the currently-quoted definitions of instructional development, although its practice was more of an analytic discipline, a description of the teaching and learning process, rather than the current ID emphasis on the systems approach, prescriptive models, and measurable improvements in the process. We, to a large degree, inherit their roles in society and education, even as do those who still use these titles.

Before there were any of these roles or the people who filled them, there were educators. The great cathedral schools of the Middle Ages, the early European universities, all filled the same roles that we do. So did those who taught the traditions to the shamans among the native tribes, or those who currently teach the children of the Amazon to grow up as hunters and medicine men. The roles haven't changed. What has changed?

What is significantly different between the shamans, the great teachers in the Medieval universities, and ourselves as instructional developers is the psychological nature of the world within which we practice our professions. We live in a world in which instruction can be objectively evaluated, and those instructional objects that are evaluated as "good" can be studied to see what makes them good, or what has kept other such objects from being "good." Further, we assume that the human organism is to one extent or another subject to the laws of psychology; learning is at least somewhat orderly, and this order can be discovered; and once discovered it can be used as a basis for the discovery of those factors that make instructional objects either "good" or "bad." This view of the world that we all live in (a part of our "world view") is created within us, by us, and is in the final analysis unique to each of us. But we all share aspects of a common world view, and it is this shared world view that makes us different from those who have gone before us or who now develop instruction outside of the instructional development camp. It is also what makes our instruction different from that developed by these other educators. It is this core set of beliefs and perceptions, those parts of our world views that we as instructional developers hold in common and that are not held in common by those people who create instruction but are not called instructional developers, that we call the "instructional development paradigm."

Hall, Extensions, Cyborgs, and ID: You Become ID

The authors believe that one fruitful approach to the understanding of the instructional development world view, or paradigm, is through the anthropological theories of Edward Hall. Hall (1966, p. 188; 1992, p. 266; 1992, footnote 7 of his Chapter 16) defines technology in terms of its function; the function of technology is to provide the normal human capacities with an expanded repertoire of abilities and functions. Thus, instructional development, thought of as a process technology, is a psychological and cultural extension of the normal human abilities to teach and learn. The world view or paradigm of instructional development, then, is the psychological and cultural extension that we build into or around the student as that student becomes a practicing professional instructional developer. To understand the ID paradigm, then, it is appropriate to attempt to understand how cultural and psychological structures can modify the world people perceive themselves living within in such a way that some of these concepts and processes come to be extensions of naturally occurring human abilities.

Hall talks about human evolution in terms of extensions. Human cultural evolution can be described in large measure as the development of extensions to our physical attributes. Once these extensions begin to evolve, further development consists of honing them to their purpose. Their purpose is always as an interface between the individual and the surrounding environment, whether that environment be another person, some other aspect of the physical and/or biological world, or another interface. Honing them has two aspects: making them perform their function better (improving their interface with the world), and making them easier or more convenient for us to use (improving their interface with us). Examples of such extensions are writing, which is an extension of language (verbal, talking, vocal chords); talking (an extension of our facial gestures and hand motions); government (an extension of our tribal structure); tribal structure (an extension of family structure); and family structure (an extension of individual power).

Such extensions become unconscious functions of our ego, as Freud would describe them, or of our operant repertoire, as Skinner might characterize them; the anthropologist would say that they become bodily functions and serve to define us as a species and as individuals. They become a part of our body as much as would an artificial arm.

We go through life inventing such extensions and making them a natural part of ourselves (a process called "reification," "to reify"). Many of these inventions are second and third order additions to ourselves. That is, we invent an extension to a naturally-existing limb or function; then we invent an extension to that extension. Then we invent a third extension to the second extension, and so on. Eventually some of these extensions can become pretty abstract, specialized, and peculiar to one or a few individuals. But to these individuals, the higher-order extensions seem just as natural, just as much a part of themselves, as do the original limbs, and their use becomes just as subconscious and automatic. In a sense, we become the extension. Technology (in its product sense) can be defined as being the sum total of our extensions, both as individuals and as a society. In its process sense, technology is the invention (design), evolution (development), and honing (formative evaluation) of these extensions.

It is appropriate to consider ourselves as cyborgs, since we now are a blend of our biological self with our technological self, such that our mental or psychological self is partly natural human, partly technological extension, in our thinking, our reacting, our goals, and our needs. We do not have technology, we do not use technology, we *are* technology. As instructional developers, one of the extensions of our Ego and Superego, in Freudian terms, is instructional development as we understand and practice it. In a very real sense, even though we say we are instructional developers, in reality we are instructional development.

This is not to say that all aspects of instructional development technology have been so internalized by us that we are the complete compendium of this technology. But we have internalized the core of ID to the extent that, for many of us, we solve ID problems unconsciously, intuitively, automatically. We have reached the fifth stage of expertise as described in the chapter in this volume by Dreyfus and Dreyfus, or maybe we have even gone beyond that.

Dreyfus and Dreyfus describe the stages a professional goes through in the transition from beginner, or novice, to expert. This process has to do with how the professional views him or her self and his or her tasks, what he or she studies, how he or she organizes cognitive structure, and what kinds of mental objects are used in conceptualizing tasks. At the highest level of expertise, when confronted with a project or problem, the professional operates intuitively and in two steps. First, the professional performs a rapid search-and-retrieval operation on his or her memory of projects and situations, and matches the current one with similar ones in the past. Once identified, a second search is done to retrieve the results of these projects and a list of problems posed and of solutions tried, and the professional intuitively identifies the approach most appropriate for the current project. All this is done intuitively, as if the mind were a holographic film. What characteristics of the current situation are important, and are to be used as the basis of the search, and which ones are unimportant? It varies from situation to situation, and the expert both doesn't know, if he or she is asked, what these characteristics are, or how to derive them in a given situation. Experts just "know," and just perform the search and match. They operate intuitively, but almost infallibly—which is what makes them experts in the first place. They have made the field a part of their cognitive system, their intuitive self. They have internalized the world of ID to such an extent that they do not even understand ID anymore—not explicitly, not deductively. They can, of course, lecture for hours on ID theory, on models and algorithms, and on explicitly-defined procedures. But they do not use these themselves, and can no longer tell you what they really do. ID has become a part of them, just like an arm, a leg, or a stomach. They use these things without knowing how, and without error. Just as an arm is an extension of their mind, so is ID. And just as a person is his or her body, he or she can be ID.

The part of instructional development that has been internalized into the practitioner's intuitions is the basic core of the subject, but this is not in this case the same as the fundamentals. In one sense, the part of sub-atomic physics that is taught to high school physics and chemistry students is the basic core of the subject, the fundamentals. In another sense, even the content taught to post-graduate students in physics is not the real basis of what makes sub-atomic structures and equations work. Perhaps no physicist truly knows the fundamentals in this sense, but physicists eventually gain an insight into these things, a feeling for them, so that if they hear a new theory propounded they can tell, intuitively, whether or not it has much chance of holding up. Or if they hear an experiment proposed, they can guess what the outcome is likely to be. But if they had to write down what they thought this core, these fundamentals, consisted of, they couldn't do it. This is the sense in which instructional developers internalize into their intuitions the fundamentals or core of the subject. This core is what becomes an extension of them, what partitions their phenomenologies into different experiences and populates their experiential world with intellectual objects and what provides these objects and experiences with meanings. They no longer live in the real world, the objective world (nor does anyone else); they now live in a world in which they consist of an awareness/volition with two arms, two legs, language, instructional development concepts, and other body parts and extensions.

The part of ID technology that has been the most deeply internalized in us, that is most properly thought of as an extension of our selves, is the ID paradigm. Each of the elements making up this has been acquired individually, and at various times in the acquisition process the element may have existed consciously within the individual as a belief, or may have existed outside the individual as an offering from another individual, or may have been absorbed subliminally from the environment, or may have been invented by the individual. Much of a college and university education consists of instilling paradigm elements into the individual's subconscious and integrating them there.

A field of study may be defined by the paradigm elements its practitioners hold in common (although unless it is a mature field, there may be no common set of elements all of the practitioners accept), and in turn a field of study may be defined by the activities commonly performed by the community of people who hold a paradigm in common. Thus, the members of that community will all subconsciously possess specified extensions of their minds that serve as interfaces with each other and the world, and will in turn define that world for them. What to ask about that world, how to attempt to answer this question, and how to understand and evaluate the answer, are all determined by the extensions, the interfaces, that the person uses to interact with and filter the world. Everyone experiences the world in this way, in a distorted way, and those who perceive the world through the same extensions experience similar distortions, and are said to have similar world-views. Those parts of the world-view dealing with their field of study are collectively called their paradigm, and those with similar paradigms make up a community of scholars, a field of science. Science is possible because all the scientists studying a given phenomenon in a given period of history build on each other's work, and this is possible because each shares the other's starting point, distorts the world in the same way, through the same extensions, and lives in the same paradigm.

This book is about instructional development paradigms. This chapter is also about instructional development paradigms, and also about the book itself. But more than that, it is about you, and me, and the past and future of our profession. It is about how we can function in that future, how we can control what it becomes, and how we can change it from what it might otherwise be. It is about how we can, to a large extent, ensure that there is such a profession in the future. It is about building or modifying our paradigms.

What is a paradigm, and what makes it so central to our field? How are our research and theory dependent upon the paradigms we follow? How does the routine of our daily lives as practicing instructional developers in industry, education, business, and medicine vary according to the paradigm or paradigms we internalize in our cognitive structure?

Paradigms: Small and Large

According to our dictionary (Urdang & Flexner, 1969), a paradigm is an example or a pattern. Literally, it means, in its original French form, to show side by side. We are all familiar with this kind of paradigm, whether or not we call it by its proper name. This is the kind of paradigm we all use in teaching and in our articles. We have small, self-contained, simplified examples that we use to illustrate procedures, processes, and theoretical points.

These paradigms both mold students into competent developers (as we define competent developers), and at the same time they mold our ideas of what a competent developer is. Our theoretical concepts can mean many different things when brought to the concrete level. What they in fact do mean to us is largely determined by how we express them in these small exemplars, or paradigms. As the exemplars change over the years, so do the meanings of our concepts, and the bounds and definitions of ourselves as professionals. This, of course, is not peculiar to instructional development; all academic subjects, perhaps all things that are explicitly defined and taught, follow this pattern.

A different meaning than that given by Webster and quoted above was introduced into the language of philosophy and scientific method by Thomas Kuhn (1962, 1970) through his book, *The Nature of Scientific Revolutions*. Kuhn's use of the term paradigm also refers to examples and models, but not of the same kind as defined by Webster. Kuhn uses paradigm to mean the underlying assumptions and intellectual structure upon which research and development in a field of inquiry is based. These assumptions and structures are of the most fundamental kind, and are not normally subject to argument. In fact, they are not normally discussed at all. They are the assumptions everyone in the field accepts; those who do not accept them, and do not use them to govern their behavior, are seldom argued with. They are just ignored; they are considered to be outside the field, and possibly they are considered to be cranks or crackpots.

Paradigms and Scientific Method

In the case of a science or technology, and perhaps in any field that can be termed a research field that is still alive and active, there are two kinds of knowledge that form the foundation of the science and that dictate how research is conceived and executed. Only one of these is the paradigm of the field; the other is the scientific method as adapted to the subject matter of that field. But scientific method is widely discussed in the literature; if not the literature of the field, then the literature about the field, especially that published in philosophy of science journals and elementary textbooks and laboratory manuals. Students are explicitly taught scientific method. In fact, one of the chief uses of the paradigm-examples discussed earlier is to teach through examples the scientific method as practiced in the field.

Paradigms are different from the scientific method in several ways, but primarily in two. First, paradigms are pre-logical, while scientific method is itself a kind of logic. Paradigms are pre-logical in that paradigms consist of the collective beliefs of a community of practitioners concerning aspects of their field that verge upon the metaphysical, ethical, epistemological, and the axiomatic. The paradigm also determines the semantic expression of the field's data and the types of constructs used in building the field's theories and models. All of these aspects of the paradigm are embedded deep within the student's cognitive (and often emotive) structure by the time the professional training has been completed. In Freudian terms, the paradigm forms a part of both the student's Superego and Ego, and so becomes an inseparable aspect of the student's personality, his or her world view. Scientific method also becomes deeply embedded within the student's psychological structures, but not as deeply, and it produces no comparable changes in personality. Scientific method functions psychologically at a much shallower level than does the paradigm in the student who is learning a research profession.

Second, a functioning scientific field can be represented as a conceptual hierarchy. At the foundation of this hierarchy is the paradigm. Resting upon the paradigm are the field's particular version of the scientific method and the field's axioms. Upon these rest the fundamental theories of the field, those that form the broad fabric upon which all else rests, and which probably cannot be subjected to experiment. Next come the models, specific theories for special topics, and testable hypotheses. Finally come the experimental literature and research data. The phenomena investigated by the field are outside this structure, but interact with it at all points, in different ways, at each level of the structure. For our purposes, it is important to recognize that the research literature, models, and testable hypotheses can only recognize and work with those phenomena that the paradigm recognizes and gives meaning to, and for which the scientific method and axioms allow experimental manipulations to be formulated. Thus, the paradigm and scientific method differ in their level of fundamentalness within the hierarchical structure of the field. Paradigms establish the world of research-able phenomena and provide the conceptual understanding for interpreting that world, including the understanding needed to interpret any research data from that world. Once this has been established, scientific method then describes the way in which that research data can be obtained.

Paradigms define how the world works, how knowledge is extracted from this world, and how one is to think, write, and talk about this knowledge. Paradigms define the types of questions to be asked and the methodologies to be used in answering them. Paradigms decide what is published and what is not published. Paradigms structure the world of the academic worker, provide its meaning and its significance. It is a largely unarticulated world that is shared by and creates the academic community, and is mostly unaffected by the research findings and controversies within the field. These controversies are eventually resolved, or discarded, in terms established by the paradigms. And the research findings are interpreted in terms of the intellectual constructs defined by the paradigm.

How Do Paradigms Differ— and How Can We See the Differences?

Paradigms can be distinguished from one another along several dimensions, among which are Intellectual Antecedents, Pre-theoretical Ideas, Subject Matter, Analogies, Concepts and Language, and Research Methods (Lachman, Lachman, & Butterfield, 1979). Different paradigms have different histories, so the intellectual backgrounds and foundations differ. Also, the intellectual content currently in use differs from paradigm to paradigm. This seems obvious when the paradigms lie a great distance apart, such as when comparing the Bohr Atom with the Leakey theory of the structure of the Hominid family tree (Morell, 1995). But it sometimes comes as a surprise when one finds such differences among paradigms that lie very close to each other. For example, the model of cognitive styles developed by Keppler, Dills, Selfridge, and Ishwaren (called DISK) has as a pre-theoretical idea the Einsteinian Universe, whereas that of Joseph Hill (1981) has the universe of Descartes and Newton as pre-theoretical ideas. Because of this, distances between the cognitive style scores of Hill's students are represented by the Euclidean distance formula between points in a Cartesian Plane, as we all learned in elementary analytic geometry. But distances between these same points in the DISK paradigm are measured using the Mahalanobis Squared Distance (Mahalanobis, 1936), as this is used in discriminant analysis. Because the intellectual antecedents are slightly different between the two paradigms, distances are measured differently. Therefore, even though both paradigms use the Educational Cognitive Style Inventory of Joseph Hill (as modified by Bass, 1978) to provide the scores, and the scores are interpreted in terms of concepts developed by Hill, two scores may be very similar (close) in one paradigm and extremely different (far apart) in the other.

Further, intellectual antecedents of the DISK paradigm include the mathematics of projective geometry, multi-dimensional statistical distributions, and topology. These appear to play no role in Joseph Hill's paradigm. As a result, the language, analogies, research methods, and even the formulation of the central question under examination all differ between the two paradigms. This is true even though both deal with the cognitive styles of students, assume these to be multi-factored, and ask how these interact within instructional development. And it is especially surprising when one considers that the DISK paradigm developed historically as a new way of looking at the data obtained using cognitive style inventories based on Hill's methodology.

In the chapters of this book, several more examples of paradigms that lie close together can be found. These will be seen to differ along these same dimensions, or maybe only along some of them. The reader can gain a greater understanding of these paradigms by attempting to determine along which dimensions the paradigms differ and in what ways, what significance these differences make to the practitioner living within the paradigms. Also, what differences do these dimensions make in the instructional designs produced by these practitioners? Further, are there other significant dimensions along which these paradigms differ? And suppose the differences were made greater, or just different than they now are, how would the basic paradigms be changed? (This was the exercise played by those who first studied non-Euclidean Geometries. Since they had no understanding of the nature of paradigms, however, they rejected what they found and delayed the development of modern geometry, and possibly modern physics as well, for a century or more.) This will be a better approach to the study of this book than one might at first appreciate, since a majority of the paradigms are not spelled out in explicit presentations. Instead, most of them are presented implicitly within the context of a theory, a model, or some other type of application. The readers must determine for themselves what the paradigm is, although a good many hints and clues are given, and a brief glimpse of the world as it exists within the paradigm is provided. But for the reader who wishes to explicitly examine the paradigm, a good beginning is to tease out the dimensions that define the differences between a given pair of paradigms, and determine the values espoused by each along these dimensions. Incidentally, such a study could lead to several dissertations designed to test the importance of these differences within the instructional development process.

Sociological Aspects of Paradigms

Paradigms are sociological phenomena as well as psychological. Paradigms can be distinguished from one another by identifying the community of scholars who accept them. Those who accept a particular paradigm are likely to publish in the same journals, read each other's books and articles, visit each other, and cite each other as references. Look at learning theory, for example. Those who are experimental behavior analysts cite each other, and the traditional behavioral scientists cite each other. But neither group typically cites anyone from the other group, although both groups supposedly are writing about how humans acquire new behaviors (learn). Again, those who consider there to be similarities between the human psychological processes and the programming processes of computers may be divided into two groups, each of which adheres to different paradigms. There are those who consider the computer processes to be analogies for suggesting experiments and explanations for human processes, and there are those who consider the human and the computer processes to both be special cases of the same general kind of device.

Some overlap among paradigmatic groups in terms of where they publish does occur. In instructional development, for example, those who have their roots in ID as a social science or in education (either K–12 or university-level) often publish in places that differ from those used by those with roots in cognitive science or behavioral science. But both groups share enough in common that they recognize each other as belonging to the instructional development confederation, and both publish in the journals of AECT and ISPI (although members of both groups complain from time to time about the discrimination shown by various journals when the editors belong to a subgroup of the confederation).

One criterion defining a paradigm, as given by Kuhn, is that the candidate paradigm must have attracted a large enough group of adherents to form a self-perpetuating research community. In fact, what may on the surface appear to be one community may be found on deeper inspection to be composed of several relatively independent communities adhering to alternative, sometimes mutually conflicting, paradigms.

All scholarly communities are held together by paradigms. Most of the time, it is likely that some single paradigm controls the community. But at different times, different paradigms dominate the community, and sometimes no paradigm does so. And, sometimes, in some types of communities, several paradigms share control. Special circumstances come into existence which result in the loss of control by the community's dominant paradigm, resulting in a time of turmoil and lively competition between candidate paradigms to gain control. Such a set of special circumstances and resulting events is called a scientific revolution, and the associated change from one dominant paradigm to another is called a paradigm shift. The cause of such a shift is usually the recognition that the existing paradigm is inadequate in some significant way, and also that an alternative or alternatives exist. The result of such a recognition is that the community is thrown into turmoil, and breaks into competing camps. Each camp espouses some new paradigm or defends the existing one, and often scientific precision and method are less important in who gets community support than is the particular camp to which the scientist belongs. Camp membership during such times is especially important when grants are being awarded, when professional societies are honoring individuals at their annual meetings, and when books are being reviewed in journals. Only when one of these camps becomes strong enough to overpower the others does a new paradigm become firmly entrenched and can normal science practices and standards be resumed. This overpowering comes about when a new paradigm attracts enough followers that those who cling to the old paradigm have either died of old age or have been pushed aside as gatekeepers or other arbiters of power, and those supporting other new paradigms have either left the field to start a new one or have been seduced away from their original camp. Until this happens, the field is disorganized and is the constant scene of bloody battles between the camps. No one can objectively evaluate the work of anyone else because standards for evaluation must be grounded in a paradigm, and there isn't one that is generally accepted.

The professional community in normal times, then, can be seen as a community of people operating within commonly agreed-upon parameters, the paradigm. This allows them to perform much like knights at a jousting tournament. But when they disavow the paradigm and begin the search for a new one, the community loses its cohesion and the members begin to operate as knights in a battle. This allows them to fight each other and the community as a whole, and not to be restricted in doing so by commonly-held community standards and previously-made alliances. Evolution occurs, and the fittest paradigm and its supporters will survive; those who refuse to adopt the new paradigm once it has emerged will not survive. Much as knights had to swear allegiance to the victor of the battle, or be beheaded or burned at the stake, the scientists must adopt the new paradigm and practice their science as it dictates, or they will be eliminated from the community—either by retiring, dying of old age, changing to a new field, starting a new field of their own, or by being branded by other, conformist, professionals as out of date or crackpots. Most will join, and the new community will function as the old community functioned, at least until the new paradigm is itself rejected by the community (which, sooner or later, is guaranteed to happen).

How Do Paradigms Develop/Take Control?

To understand paradigms, we must understand ourselves. What are we, where did we come from, and why do we exist? Only by answering these questions can we decide where we should go in the future, or even if we should continue to exist as a profession. The answers to these questions are subjective, of course, and the chapters to follow could be conceived of as the stimulus materials for use in a constructivist-based course in which we interact with others to produce our own answers to these questions. In the editors' view, however, an answer to some of these questions can be arrived at by thinking about how we were trained as instructional developers to begin with.

We, as instructional developers, were and are trained in professional training programs, mostly in universities, or through the apprenticeship system in industry. In either case, we are taught how to analyze tasks, investigate needs, develop objectives and test items, and write instructional scripts. We are taught standard ways of doing this, and if someone from, say, Syracuse University were to go to, say, the University of Twente (in The Netherlands) and watch a student there developing instruction, the Syracuse student would recognize the activities and understand the underlying model and associated theory behind these activities. This is because we are all members of a scientific community which shares these models, theories, and procedures, as well as other things, such as values, standards of behavior, terminology, goals, history, and thought patterns. We all agree (in general) on what good instruction is like, how it is produced, how to use it, why it works, and what is gained by its production and use.

How were we taught these things? We were shown exemplars. We were shown the Shannon-Weaver model of the communication process, for example, or the nine-step model of instructional development produced by the University Consortium for Instructional Development and Technology (Gustafson & Schuller, 1984). These were some of the basic exemplars of the concepts we learned. We were taught standardized procedures for writing objectives, and we were taught standard research designs. We then used these exemplars in practice situations (sometimes called internships, sometimes called class projects) until we had internalized them and shown a degree of proficiency in their use. The final lesson, if we went for a doctorate, was to apply these exemplars in a dissertation. And what is a dissertation? It is a pure exemplar of the fundamental nature of research and thought in our field. And what is the fundamental nature of research and thought in our field? It is our paradigm. A dissertation is a paradigm, in the first meaning of this term that we used. It is a small paradigm, or, if you prefer, a paradigm spelled with a small "p." And what does it exemplify? It exemplifies the large paradigm that the person who prepares a dissertation has internalized by this point in life (and who may live in and with it for the rest of his or her life). We are taught our (large) paradigm through the learning of many (small) paradigms, or exemplars. And the final (formal) test of how well we have learned, internalized, or made into an extension of ourselves, the large paradigm, is to require us to construct our own exemplar of this large paradigm, which we do by creating a small paradigm, called a dissertation (although some students create small paradigms before their dissertation, as, for example, in the research apprenticeships of Syracuse University's Department of Instructional Design, Development, and Evaluation).

The dissertation can be conceptualized in at least three different ways. It is a test of the student to determine whether or not the paradigm has been adequately internalized to permit the student to receive recognition from the paradigmatic community as a full-fledged member, one who is trusted with the teaching of new students and the carrying out of acceptable research. It is the supervised production of a new exemplar for use in the future education of students. And it is the filling in of a small gap in the web of knowledge, theory, and methodology that is the scientific product of the paradigmatic community. It is usually the student's first full-fledged attempt to conduct "normal" science on a more-or-less large scale.

Normal science is the type of science that is "normally" practiced. Under normal (= expected, usual, typical, default) conditions, a snapshot of a science at any point in time, if that science is reasonably mature, has a governing paradigm. This paradigm allows the researchers to determine what are the legitimate phenomena of the field, what are the allowable questions that can be asked about these phenomena, and what research methods can be used to study these questions. The paradigm also tells the researcher what possible interpretations the resulting data can be given and what types of new theories are allowed.

What, then, is the researcher allowed to do? Dissertations. The researcher is allowed to create dissertations, just as does the doctoral student, and also dissertation-type studies that are beyond the capabilities and resources of the doctoral student. The researcher is allowed to select a question from among those allowed by the paradigm, and conduct exploratory studies attempting to tease out aspects of the question and its associated phenomena. He or she is then allowed to carry out more detailed, better controlled, more rigorous studies based upon the exploratory findings. Or the degree of rigor can be reduced in exchange for increasing the degree of perceptiveness in the way the question is asked, using methods specially designed for this purpose, such as surveys, non-intrusive observations, single-case studies, etc. What he or she is doing is creating a series of paradigms (in the small paradigm sense), just as the doctoral student did.

This may not be obvious to the researcher or others in the field, since in the case of the professional researcher, the profundity of the question asked, the rigorousness of the study, and the importance within the paradigm of the findings may be enormous compared to that attempted by the doctoral student. But in fact what the researcher is doing is filling in a hole in the mosaic picture of the subject matter presented by the field within the context of the paradigm.

Normal science can be described as those activities of scientists, conducted within the confines of an existing paradigm, that are defined by the paradigm. These activities are designed to fill in the holes in the picture presented in outline by the paradigm. Recent examples of normal science in educational technology include research on the effectiveness of multi-modal audio-visual presentations as opposed to single-mode presentations, early film research, and the studies of the frame size or frequency and mode of feedback from responses made in the use of programmed instructional materials. Recent examples of anomalous work in educational technology include the various forms of accelerated learning, the use of subliminal perception, the Summerhill School movement, and the teaching methods of Herbert Kohl (King, 1997; Kohl, 1967; Neill, 1960; Rose, 1986; Schuster, 1997).

Why and How Paradigms Change

The paradigm is a finite model, and the world it is trying to control and shape and filter is infinite. Therefore, it ultimately fails. The mechanism for failure is the same as the mechanism for its success: normal science. As researchers perform normal science, their experiments collect results which must be interpreted and understood within the framework of existing theory and the existing paradigm; or, if new theory is needed, it at least must be developed in ways consistent with the paradigm and following lines dictated by the paradigm.

But the world sometimes provides phenomena and data describing these phenomena that do not meet these requirements. These phenomena simply cannot be understood within the normal framework. Sometimes, the normal framework even prohibits the phenomena themselves from existing, or else defines them to be out of the bounds of the science. The scientist practicing normal science says that such phenomena might be legitimate, but don't belong to his or her science. Or, maybe they are said not to be legitimate—they are folklore, or superstitions, or quackery. Or, if it is the data and not the phenomena that are illegitimate, they throw the data away—it is a bad sample, or a bad data point, or the data are the result of the fact that every so often, a data sample is taken that comes predominantly from either the upper or lower tail of a distribution, or the data are strangely distributed when in fact they were analyzed as if they had a normal distribution. In any case, the researcher comes across phenomena from time to time that do not and cannot be made to fit into the bounds of normal science. He has a choice. If he accepts the phenomena, if he insists the data are valid, he runs the danger of being thrown out of the scientific community. If he rejects the phenomena, he stays within the community but runs the danger of throwing away reality. The phenomena (or data sets) that produce such a situation are called anomalies.

Anomalies are all over the place. They exist in the back closets of every science. They are typically ignored, rejected, their existence denied. This situation, again, describes normal science, and every snapshot of every science, at whatever point in time, will show some of these. However, every once in a while one of these assumes an overriding importance. Everybody in the field, or at least those who are trying to establish their reputations, takes notice, and focuses attention on the anomaly. This often happens when a new methodology has been developed, or when somebody presents an alternative set of assumptions for the paradigm. Often the problem is solved by the new methodology, or the interest dies away. But, sometimes, the anomaly is taken to be so important that the field ceases to exist. That is, the paradigmatic community loses its cohesiveness, the paradigm is no longer accepted as an article of faith, and great confusion results. In psychology, it might be called an identity crisis.

The field becomes overpowered by floating anxiety, it becomes schizophrenic, then the old paradigm becomes catatonic. It no longer speaks to the people in the field who used to believe in it. Primarily, the young students and those professionals who have not yet made their place in the field are most deeply affected. The top people are going to try to remain the top people; they are going to cling to the old paradigm as long as possible. But those who have less of a stake in the old are more likely to reject it, or to look favorably on those others who reject it.

The old paradigmatic community collapses, while its members look for a new paradigm within which they can establish a new community. And the new paradigm must be able to deal with the same phenomena and the same questions about them that the old paradigm covered, and in addition it must be able to handle the anomalies, or at least several of the more important ones, that led to the breakdown to begin with. This desertion of the old paradigm and search for a new one is called a scientific revolution.

Those searching for a new paradigm are likely to find several candidates. This is not because paradigms are always available. They are not, although usually the seeds of a new paradigm are lying around, waiting to be developed. But usually the anomalies aren't taken seriously, and don't produce a scientific revolution, until one or more new paradigms have become visible to those in the field. The first followers of the new paradigm show that it can deal with both traditional problems and the new anomalies, and demonstrate the new and improved results they can obtain. When others see these results, the scientific revolution occurs. So the search usually produces several candidate paradigms because the search would never have begun unless it was already known that these candidates existed. This may sound like circularity in a cause-and-effect argument, but it is how the system works.

So, several candidates are found, and these must compete with each other for the allegiance of those who are in the field. Once one or another of these has established itself as more powerful than the others, at least in the sense of its ability to attract followers and establish a coherent community based upon itself, the revolution has in effect come to a halt. Normal science is again practiced, but now the normal science is defined by the new paradigm, not by the old. Standards are now used that would have been rejected in the old paradigm. New questions are asked, and old ones are re-phrased so as to have different meanings. New theories are used to explain experimental results that would have been called heresy or crackpot before.

And the world goes on, constructing itself as it goes. Scientists in the field have cut off their old extensions and have sewed on new ones. The old extensions are gone; it is like their arm was cut off and a new and better arm was sewn on in its place. But the person was unaware of his or her old arm, except when it hurt or when he or she dropped something, and the same is true of the new. The world of the scientist has evolved into a new and different world, but one related to the old world in such a way that the scientist is unaware of the change, and continues to live life the way he or she always has.

The Multiple Paradigms of Educational Technology

The authors wish to put forth the position that the field of educational technology is, and always has been, multi-paradigmatic. That is, there has never been a time when only a single paradigm has been operating in the field, or even a time when a single paradigm so completely dominated the field that those who held rival paradigms were completely excluded from participation in the field as a social and communal activity. That is not to say that no single paradigm has ever held the major part of the field's attention, or dictated most of the research questions being asked. But there were always rival paradigms waiting in the wings, and these were always generating some research, always contributing their language and their pre-theoretical ideas to the stew-pot called educational technology.

The reason for this multi-paradigmatic state may be due to the multiple sources of theoretical foundations supporting the field at any given time. Also, the particular sources of employment in the field at different periods in our history, the influence of the particular sex dominating the membership of the field at any given time, the relative influence of various schools of philosophy and psychology dominating our times, the types of equipment and the way that equipment was conceptualized and utilized, all contributed to the paradigm structure of the people in the field at any given period in history. And at any given period in our history, each of these factors had multiple sources.

For example, when Skinnerian psychology dominated the field, non-Skinnerian behavioral psychology held a close second in influence, and the two fields were locked in combat. At the same time, the previously-strong influence of Freudian psychology was fast disappearing, but was still detectable, and the future strength of cognitive information-processing psychology was visible already. Meantime, the communication theorists were still publishing in *AVCR*, and the audio-visual movement, with overhead projectors, slide projectors, and 16mm film, was developing its own philosophy, eventually leading to the pre-computer form of multimedia, independent of any theoretical school of psychology.

Another example may be seen in the educational developments occurring during the later part of the nineteenth century. During that time, within the folds of the technology of teaching, there were the kindergarten, nature study, object study, the Herbartian movement, the museum education movement, and the Chautauqua adult education movement—all existing through the same time period, all entwined within the then current developments in educational technology and curriculum development, and yet each dominating a different group of people from those of the others, and none completely dominating the whole educational community of the times.

Later, the visual instruction movement, the film study movement, educational radio, Dewey's curriculum reform movement, and the military use of films in training all co-existed, but didn't truly compete, or even involve inter-communication, for the most part, among those involved. All these examples add to the evidence that the field of educational technology (and didactics before it) has always been based on a combination of more-or-less coexisting paradigms.

Similar positions are taken by Saettler (1990, p. 7) when he identifies four paradigms within the field of educational technology during the twentieth century:

(1) **The physical science or media view;**
(2) **the communications and systems concept;**
(3) **the behavior science-based view, comprising the behaviorist and neo-behaviorist concepts;**
(4) **the cognitive science perspective.**

Ivor Davies describes a similar situation when he identifies technology with "know-how" and methodology. He recognizes the association of the word with machines, but points out that this association is quite recent, whereas the use of the word to mean methodology goes back to the Greeks and encompasses the machine usage as a special case (Davies, 1984). He then shows that viewed in this manner, three archetypes (root metaphors, primordial images) have at various times guided educational technology, and that this has led to several different paradigms. He argues that those paradigms that derive from the same archetype can be grouped together because they share so many features. He then discusses these paradigms under the headings of the audio-visual, the engineering, and the problem-solving archetypes.

The paradigmatic structures of other fields within the technology of education have been variously described. The structure of the fields of research and evaluation methodologies has recently been described by several writers. Driscoll (1995) has described at least eight different research paradigms operating within instructional technology research. Clark and Sugrue (1995) describe a paradigm shift between behavioral and cognitive approaches to research design and the formulation of research questions for media research. And Robinson (1995) describes a kind of war between paradigm positions on research in educational technology.

Others have described the paradigm structure, or a part of it, as parts of efforts to achieve some other purpose. For example, Schwier (1995) distinguishes between objectivist and constructivist orientations in discussing various stances concerning how multimedia should be designed. And Reigeluth has recently argued for a paradigm shift from Instructional Systems Development to a new position he describes as Educational Systems Development (Reigeluth, 1995).

Reigeluth (1995) points out, as do many outside the bounds of educational technology, that paradigm shifts are occurring or are about to occur throughout society, and that such shifts are happening at a faster and faster rate as our knowledge base increases and our technological power grows. And as cultures collide, many paradigms that have existed for centuries are disappearing, while others are melding with newer ones to form exotic and inconsistent hybrids within the newly structured cultures resulting from the intertwining of European and non-European peoples.

Saettler (1990, p. 15) has described educational technology as a field in a pre-paradigmatic stage of development, since it obviously has not settled on a single dominating paradigm. The boundaries of the field have not even been well-defined, let alone the appropriate way to think within these boundaries.

The current authors disagree with the conclusions of these descriptions of the paradigmatic structure of educational technology. If a field is defined as a community of people practicing a set of related activities tied together and given meaning and direction through a single paradigm held in common, all sharing commonly held pre-theoretical concepts, speaking a common technical/scientific language, restraining themselves within common research designs and methodologies, and examining the same subject matters, then educational technology is not a field. It is, rather, a loose confederation of fields that are not quite independent of each other and yet that are not merely different aspects of the same field.

The membership of this confederation of fields making up educational technology changes from time to time. Furthermore, even though a field remains within the confederation over a period of time, its position relative to the other fields changes, sometimes abruptly, sometimes gradually, over the life of its membership.

Dynamics of the Educational
Technology Confederation

What makes a field a member of this confederation at any given time? The same things that create a paradigm; they are based upon the same or similar sets of pre-theoretical ideas, languages, methodologies, subject matters, histories, communities of practitioners, and centers for receiving training and initiation into the field. However, unlike the case of the paradigm, individual members of the confederation differ from other members in one or more of these dimensions, sometimes by only a little bit, sometimes by a great deal. As a result, these fields are not different facets of the same subject bound together into the same field and held tightly to the same fate by the values of these dimensions, but are semi-independent areas lightly attached to each other, lightly or strongly interacting for periods of time because of shared values across these dimensions, but eventually torn apart by conflicting values across these same dimensions.

Each of these individual fields is itself held together by its own paradigm. This paradigm holds the field much tighter within itself than the field is held within the confederation of fields. While there are detectable differences among the pre-theoretic ideas, methodologies, etc., of the various fields within the confederation, there are no such differences within the underlying conceptions of the community of people composing a single field.

Thus, for a field to gain or lose its centrality or strength of influence within the confederation, all that is needed is a change in the technologies binding the fields together or a change in the surrounding social fabric within which the confederation is embedded and from which the reinforcement structure of the confederation is derived. No serious and unexplainable anomalies are required, and no scientific revolution must occur. A revolution may, of course, occur, but much more likely is a gradual slipping and sliding of the composite fields among themselves, with occasionally a field going completely extinct or coming into existence.

A scientific revolution, based upon the recognition of unexplainable and significant anomalies, while not needed to modify the structure of the confederation, must occur to significantly change the structure of the particular paradigm governing one of the specific fields of study making up the confederation. In fact, our belief in the cohesion and endurance of the individual subjects in the confederation stems from the fact that during our lifetimes we have seen the confederation change membership and/or configuration many times through non-revolutionary events, but we have never seen an individual subject within this confederation come into or go out of existence, or gain or lose a large segment of its community of adherents, without such a revolutionary event or the appearance of significant and obvious anomalies.

Why is instructional or educational technology (and instructional design/development) structured this way? The authors, of course, don't know. They believe, however, that three propositions can be stated which probably account in large measure for this structure and the accompanying behavior of the member fields. We believe historians and others interested in the nature and development of educational technology would profit considerably by investigating these propositions.

First, many of the components of the confederation are actually composed of specific interest groups belonging to some other field of research and/or development, with their interest in some facet of educational technology exerting only a secondary influence on the group. They participate in the paradigmatic structure of the confederation only to the extent that, at some particular point in time, the characteristics of this structure overlap with those of the field of their major interest. If a change occurs within either the paradigm of their major field of interest or in the technological or social expression of current educational technology, their interest in that technology dissolves and the community moves out of the confederation. Likewise, when such changes occur, the result might be the opposite; that is, a community from some field previously having no connection to educational technology might develop such an interest and so move into the confederation, probably while still maintaining its own self-definition in terms of the paradigm of its field of origin and not in terms of that of its neighbors in the confederation. This confederation draws from the engineering sciences, the social sciences, the psychological, behavioral, and cognitive sciences, and philosophy, just to name a few of the major sources of specialized interest groups.

An example of such a field was holographic imagery, which for a while interested many educational technologists as a teaching tool for the future. A small group of workers from physics, optics, and electrical engineering began exploring the potential of the holograph for education, but soon left the field and returned to their work in physics when nothing exciting, to them, resulted. Although holographs are still used in educational settings, it is no longer a "hot" topic for articles and studies as it once was.

The second proposition is that much of our conceptual structure, many of our pre-theoretical ideas, much of our methodology, and much of our language is borrowed from other fields, thereby creating a temporary community of educational technologists governed by a hybrid paradigm. This paradigm is that governing the field from which the material is borrowed, but modified through the incorporation of the pre-theoretical ideas that are unique to educational technology, applied to the subject matter of educational technology, and asking research questions motivated by this subject matter, but formulated in terms of the language and concepts of the original discipline. Examples include the communications research published in *Audio-Visual Communications Review* in the 1950s and 1960s, which derived from the mathematical measurement of noise in telephone and radio design (Shannon & Weaver, 1949), and mass communications research carried out by the journalism/broadcasting community and various pioneering political scientists and social psychologists beginning primarily in the late 1940s (see Saettler, 1990, for a summary of this work). A more recent example is the change from a behavioristic to an information-processing to a cognitive science outlook for educational technology theorists. All three outlooks, and the change from one to the other, derives from parallel changes in the mainstream outlook of psychologists. If the new questions, concepts, and approaches do not prove fruitful, or the concepts and methods are discredited or discarded by the original discipline, the community formed within educational technology may also dissolve. In the above examples from psychology, this is what happened, and explains in part why behavioral and information-processing paradigms are less popular in educational technology than they used to be. This reaction is sometimes called the "bandwagon effect" in the educational technology literature.

Third, many of our communities have as a central element of their paradigm a wedding to a particular type of hardware, and when that hardware no longer is used, the community dissolves. This happened to the multi-image slide projector community, and it happened to the classroom movie community. These people may or may not leave educational technology, but their community dissolves and they re-distribute themselves. It appears that it is a significant weakness in a paradigm to have as a significant element the attachment to a particular kind of hardware.

Earlier Structure of the Instructional Development Community

Instructional development over the last twenty or so years has exhibited some interesting phenomena regarding its communal composition. First, instructional development has attempted to absorb other fields. For example, the instructional development community during the sixties and seventies considered the study of diffusion of innovations, the use of action research and active interventions within the individual college classroom, and the use of "cut and paste" technology (e.g., overhead transparencies, clay lifts, hot and cold mounts for pictures) to be properly within its domain. Yet, in the first two cases, independent communities existed for the study and development of these areas within the educational technology confederation, and in the third case, almost every community within and without the confederation could lay a claim to the "cut and paste" technology, and within the confederation the audio-visual community had a stronger and a prior claim to it that instructional designers could never equal.

Second, a phenomenon Kuhn discusses is the splitting off from pre-paradigmatic communities of specialized groups that mature faster than does the whole. For example, physics split from astronomy, and biochemistry split from chemistry. Instructional development has produced specialized areas within itself, some of which have, if they have not formed hybrids with outside fields, have at the least been strongly fertilized by these outside areas. One such area is the design of computer-based instruction (CBI). This area started out as an independent area of computer scientists, psychologists, and educators. Then it developed into its own community, and by the time of PLATO and TICCIT, this community had largely been absorbed into the instructional development community (although significant members still remained outside of this community). Then along came the Apple, the Mac, and the PC. Many people started developing software that taught, although they were not instructional developers, or in many cases even educational technologists. They often were members of other educational communities, or just "hackers" who wanted programs to entertain and teach their own children.

Within the educational technology/instructional development confederation, the CBI community has splintered off from instructional development, has taken some of the instructional design community with it, picked up a group of artists from outside the confederation, and become a semi-independent paradigmatic community. It is only semi-independent at this point, because in many of the more involved projects, the CBI designer must rely upon instructional development techniques to acquire the knowledge and develop the knowledge structure that is to be incorporated into the final product. But for many projects, the CBI producer relies upon common knowledge or uses non-ID approaches to knowledge acquisition and design, and remains independent of the instructional development community.

A second example of a significant area that appears to be breaking away from instructional development is instructional design. Instructional design from its beginnings has resided within the instructional development community, and for the most part still does. Most of the people who originated and pioneered instructional design were themselves instructional developers, and still consider themselves so. Their research and development work usually fell within instructional development projects and was funded through instructional development departments and contracts. Instructional design is usually included as an integrated activity within most, if not all, instructional development models, either explicitly or under some other name.

However, there now exist several instructional design models that are independent of any formal front-end analysis procedures other than those explicitly incorporated within the model's structure (e.g., Landa or Scandura, both in Reigeluth, 1983, 1987). Further, many instructional designers base their work on pre-theoretical ideas that are not a part of the set defining the more general instructional development community. And the instructional design community is beginning to publish books and journals that do not include material from the more general instructional development community. Students are also being trained in the design of instruction without being offered or required to take training in other aspects of instructional development, especially when the instructional design is intended for application to computers or is offered as a part of a behavioral training program for special education students. These are all signs that instructional design may eventually break away into a separate field within the confederation. When it does, it may remain as one of the components of the confederation, or it may completely leave the confederation and cease to think of itself as educational technology, much as the testing and curriculum communities do not.

Another example of a community that came into existence within instructional development and that is in the process of breaking out (although it has not completely done so as yet) is the human performance technology community. It evolved originally within the instructional development paradigm, then modified it, and finally embraced many people within the educational, management, and human relations communities that had never been a part of the instructional development community. Many people live in both worlds at the present time, and this seems to be all that is holding the two sets of people within a single community. It seems possible that as the new performance improvement paradigm evolves, a complete split will occur, although the new community will likely maintain the techniques, models, and processes of instructional development within its armamentarium, even though it will use them and conceptualize them in new ways. If such a separation occurs, the needs analysis community may similarly split between the performance improvement and the instructional development communities; or it may conceivably form its own separate community (the latter possibility, however, seems unlikely).

Two examples present themselves of communities that should logically find themselves, if not totally within the instructional development community, then at least closely tied to it, and that yet seem almost unaware that instructional development exists. One is the educational and instructional television community, and the other is the curriculum and instruction community of public and higher education. Both contain small groups of instructional developers, of course, but these are few enough to be the exception rather than the rule.

A related situation exists that calls into question the boundaries of instructional development, or even its right to exist as a field. At an international conference of instructional developers in Caracas, Venezuela in 1988, a great debate was held that pitted the "Neats" against the "Scruffies." The Neats are those instructional developers and designers that follow models, executing each box of the model in sequence, possibly following M. David Merrill's or someone else's design prescriptions (Reigeluth, 1983), and generally behaving during all phases of the instructional development process as the voices of their paradigm says they should. The "Scruffies" are designers who dismiss all of this as nonsense.

Have the Scruffies become aware of the many gaps in our design knowledge, of the anomalies in our theory and prescriptions that we cover over with heuristic and intuitively executed rules of thumb, and therefore ignore as we sweep them under the rug? Or are they merely rebels who shouldn't be trusted with a flowchart, and who probably are rejecting the systematic approach because deep down they don't really understand it to begin with? The authors have difficulty in fully believing the latter, since there are many bright and conscientious Scruffies. And we ourselves sometimes (maybe more often than not) behave as Scruffies. You could argue, theoretically, that we are always acting as Scruffies, whether we follow the rules or not, since clearly the rules and models are not algorithms but are merely rules of procedure which at the level of execution are seen to be rules for the application and guidance of intuition in the application of art within the bubble created by our paradigms and philosophies. The real question is whether we are acting on blind intuition without regard to any underlying axioms, theories or principles, or whether we are acting on enlightened intuition, having reached that highest level of expertise as described by Dreyfus and Dreyfus.

Future Structure of the
Instructional Development Community

What then are we left with? At first we are tempted to claim that a scientific revolution is at hand for the instructional development community. When instructional development was first devised, and the first elements of a community of practitioners and theorists began to form, they had a specific set of pre-theoretical ideas in mind, crafted a common language and knowledge representation scheme, applied their work to a common subject matter, and developed common approaches. For the most part, the people had a common educational background, coming either from the audio-visual or the military training communities. Programs were provided in several universities to train people in this new paradigm, and these programs were for the most part very similar.

When the commonly-accepted psychological paradigms changed, some splitting of the community occurred and some left, while others remained within the community but remained within the older psychological parameters. For the most part, however, these changes in psychological outlook resulted in a molding of the ID paradigm in a slightly different direction rather than in fundamental changes. This was at least partly because the psychological theories were never a deeply embedded part of the ID structure; they were superstructure, and affected how ID was practiced only in its surface structure. So instructional development survived as a unified, strong, united community of practitioners and researchers who accepted the same paradigm expressed in the same dimensions and taught through the same or very similar example-paradigms.

Only gradually did some conceive of the paradigm in slightly different ways, because they introduced some novel pre-theoretic ideas from the outside, and these gradually evolved into the separation of the groups mentioned above. In spite of these events, the community remained coherent for most of its history. Now, however, this situation seems to be changing.

Now, new pre-theoretic ideas, language, methodology, subject matter, and philosophical outlooks are being introduced into the community, some from the outside and some originating from within (resulting from the fresh recognition and analysis of various previously-unrecognized or ignored anomalies). These changes are widespread, and are burrowing deeply into the fundamental substance of the paradigm, and are being introduced into the training programs for new entrants into the community, providing new and novel example-paradigms and changing or modifying previously-used example-paradigms in the traditional curriculum. These events are widespread not only in the instructional development community, but are even stronger within the instructional design part of that community, and are also equally strong in areas outside instructional development, such as testing and evaluation, program evaluation, media production, and educational psychology. Not everyone in the community accepts these new paradigm elements as compelling, but the journals are filled with lively debate about them, they are generating much of the more recent empirical studies, and they seem not to be going away.

The authors recognize these as cues that a paradigm shift or a scientific revolution is about to occur. However, because of the nature of educational technology in general, as described earlier, and of instructional design and development in particular, we hesitate to proclaim or predict such an event. When we began this book, we were convinced that such a paradigm shift or revolution was occurring. Now, however, we believe that instructional development and instructional design, like the educational technology community as a whole, and like many other fields within the educational technology confederation, is in the process of rapidly becoming multi-paradigmatic.

Right now a great many new and older but revised paradigms are being introduced into the field. In the case of the older paradigms, they are either ones that were introduced a long time ago and didn't catch on but held the attention of a small group until now, or they appeared, were tried and published, then were completely ignored and ceased to exist in practice at all, but have recently been revived. These paradigms are both of the larger, encompassing kind and of the smaller example-paradigm kind. Most of the literature being currently published on these topics tends not to make a distinction, or even to recognize them as paradigms; these paradigms are typically described as new approaches, as new models, or as new techniques. However, a discussion attacking those elements that formed the underpinnings of the historically-dominant paradigm and substituting new elements usually accompanies such presentations and articles, leaving no doubt of a paradigm offering.

We believe this is a healthy situation, because it provides the instructional developer with new tools not previously possessed, and new ways of understanding instructional problems not previously available. We believe that with the new paradigms, current anomalies will fall to scientific advances, better theories will be developed, and practice will jump ahead in quantum leaps. If the Scruffies are currently correct in their assessment of our current technology of design and development, maybe they will not be so correct in the future.

There are difficulties, however, with the process as it is currently occurring. Many of the paradigms are incompatible, especially philosophically. But they are being accepted as technological alternatives. Perhaps they can be practiced together, or alternately by the same person, but only by treating them differently than their internal structures would dictate. This results in less favorable outcomes than would probably be obtained were they adopted in toto.

Further, some of them are unsuitable for some uses, and they are as likely to be tried in these applications as in those for which they are suitable. Thus, mixed reviews of results will appear in the literature concerning their value, and much time will pass, and many projects will suffer, before we have obtained a proper understanding of each new paradigm.

In the end, if the field does become multi-paradigmatic, many of these paradigms will survive into the final mixture, some as general-purpose approaches to instructional development, some surviving only in specialized niches and for specialized applications. Others will disappear altogether. Many years may be required for this puzzle to sort itself out fully. Much of this sorting will appear confusing to the practitioner, will lead the theoreticians into many dead-end arguments, and will consume much paper needlessly.

The authors have attempted to speed up this shake-out process and make it more systematic and less painful and wasteful. They have attempted this through the present book. This book is an attempt to present as many as possible of the currently available paradigms and paradigm offerings to the instructional development community. These paradigms, presented in the words of their inventors and advocates, as seen through their own eyes, are made explicit to the community. In addition, the community is given the reasons for and against these paradigms, as mustered by their best advocates, their inventors and their critics. Hopefully, by presenting a kind of catalog of such paradigms, people in the field will more quickly become aware of them, study them explicitly, and evaluate them for use in their own work. They will be able to compare and contrast them, to determine for what purposes and in what niches they seem appropriate and inappropriate, and whether they are based on pretheoretic ideas, philosophical concepts, and methodologies that the worker finds acceptable or is able to adopt.

By doing this, we hope to artificially speed up the process through which instructional development is becoming multi-paradigmatic, and hopefully that much sooner introduce to the ID community a new generation of technology and achievement. The chapters that follow are the selection of paradigms that we have gathered for this purpose. Some of these are major paradigms, some are example-paradigms that merely imply and illustrate the major paradigm they support. We have not explicitly distinguished between these in the book, since how you see it determines its classification, and if allowed to examine a paradigm without our bias, you may reach different conclusions than you would were we to tell you how to think of it in advance. We do wish to provide you with an overview of the chapters, however, and to suggest some trends among the chapters and to suggest several different approaches for you to follow in your study of them. Also, with a book of this scope and size, we are obliged to use some overall organizing principles and structure. This structure and these organizing principles are described in the following sections, as well as in the Preface.

The Client or End-User

So far in this chapter, we have focused on instructional development from the viewpoints of the theoretician, researcher, and professional instructional developer. However, other valid viewpoints that ought to be considered are those of the clients or end-users of the products of the instructional development process, that is, school teachers, instructors, training departments, specific educational institutions, or whole educational systems. The viewpoints of the consumers or customers and their paradigmatic assumptions are just as important in the analysis of what future trends and changes may occur as are the viewpoints of theoreticians, researchers, and professionals in the field. Two contrasting examples taken from other fields may illustrate that the paradigmatic assumptions of the professionals and of their clients are not always the same, and any differences may significantly influence the tendencies for change and acceptance of an innovation.

The first example is now a classic, often quoted to illustrate how the professionals in the field may overlook important new trends because these do not fit into their existing paradigms. However, the resistance of the theoreticians and professionals may not necessarily result in the rejection of the innovation. In 1968, Switzerland held 65% of the world's watch market. Ten years later, by 1978, the market share had dropped to below 20%. In contrast, in 1968, Japan had virtually no share of the world market for watches, but by 1978 it held the major share of the market. What was it that led to this incredible transformation of market share in the short period of one decade? The answer to this question, as we all know, is the impact of the quartz electronic watch movement which, in addition to being much cheaper to manufacture, is much more accurate than its spring predecessors and much simpler, involving no bearings or springs and few moving parts, and not needing regular winding or automatic winding mechanisms. It would seem obvious that such progress in the science of timekeeping should lead to improvements in the technology of watches and transform the industry. However, the Swiss watchmakers did not see it that way. Even though the quartz electronic watch technology was a Swiss invention, it was rejected by all major Swiss manufacturers in the 60s and was considered so irrelevant to the future of watchmaking that the companies who employed the scientists that developed the new technology did not even bother to take out patents to protect the invention. The result of this was that other companies, notably Seiko in Japan and Texas Instruments in the United States, took up the new technology and within a very few years more or less demolished the Swiss watch industry's dominance in the world market.

However, the existence of the superior new technology was not a sufficient condition for the demolition of the older technology. What was also required was an acceptance of the new quartz watches by the public at large. In this particular case, cheaper and more accurate watches filled the requirements of the majority of customers and the trend towards quartz watches was rapid and is still continuing even today. Of course, there is still an ever more limited demand for high quality mechanical watches such as the Rolex, but this now amounts to a very small proportion of the total market. Even in Switzerland now, the major sales of watches are the later developed "Swatch" series of quartz watches, which has done a little toward regaining Swiss market share in this field through applying superior aesthetic design to the technology which the Japanese, the Americans, and others put on the market so effectively. What we may learn from this story is the importance of re-examining our paradigms in relation to new ideas as they come along and recognizing that the old ways of doing things may well have to change in order to satisfy changing market needs.

The second story relates to the short history of the capital city of Brazil. Brasilia was an artificially created federal capital that was founded in the 1950s, strategically placed within the geographical area of Brazil but in fact not conveniently placed in relation to existing centers of population, networks of transport, and so on. The placing of a capital in this way is not unusual. Other examples include Canberra in Australia and Ottawa in Canada. The focus of our case, however, is not on the geographical position of Brasilia but on its architectural and town planning aspects. As this was a new city, the town planners and the architects who were employed had a free hand in implementing their viewpoints and ideas in the design. As regards town planning, a popular paradigm at the time was the "Garden City" concept: a large, urban area so organized as to appear to the inhabitants to be composed of small, semi-rural, village-like communities. Welwyn Garden City in the United Kingdom was one exemplar of this paradigm that had worked reasonably well since its founding in the

1930s, and this model was replicated in many other locations in the United States and elsewhere. The town planners of Brasilia adopted and elaborated on this paradigm, creating a town plan that combined modern architecture, freeways, and other transport innovations with the Garden City concept.

The overall plan of Brasilia resembles the shape of a bird or an airplane. The body running on one axis is devoted to public buildings, sports arenas, and military and governmental complexes, whereas the broad wings running on another axis at 90 degrees are made up of a symmetrically organized set of mini-villages located on each side of a main superhighway. Each mini-village or "super square" as it is called is composed of from 10 to 20 apartment blocks set in a parkland context and divided from each other by transversal roads that feed into the superhighway. Each super square was initially self-contained in that it had all the locally required grocery and food shops, a daycare center, and laundry and other facilities. These were located in buildings along the dividing roads. In this way, the residents would walk through the parkland to the local shops, leaving their children at the local daycare center or elementary school and walking back to their home. The shops and business buildings on the transversal roads were therefore built with imposing marble-faced frontages facing into the super squares' parkland, and their rear doors were on the transversal roads with space for trucks to pull in for loading and unloading of goods.

What actually happened over a very short period of time was that the residents did not in fact walk to the local shops but decided to drive and take up the spaces originally designed for delivery trucks, and the local shopkeepers therefore *turned around* their stores, utilizing the back doors as the front entrance and stacking their trash up against the marble facades within the park. Furthermore, in a relatively short period of time, the village-like organization of local shops supplying the every-day needs of each of the super squares broke down as some of the transversal roads became dominated by one or other trade, such as auto car spare parts or electrical equipment or furniture. By the 1970s, twenty years after the city's founding, the urban structure of Brasilia from a physical viewpoint still reflected the planner's model of futuristic architecture and super square layout, but from a sociological and organizational perspective, the way the commerce was organized had more in common with medieval London than with the paradigms and models used by the town planners. This second example therefore illustrates how professionals working from a particular new paradigmatic position may in fact make errors in estimating to what extent the paradigms of the end-users and consumers have changed or are likely to change so as to accept the innovations that are being designed for them. Both of the examples illustrate the importance of balancing theory and philosophy against practical reality and assuring that there is a match between the paradigmatic axioms of the theoreticians and designers on the one hand and of the end-users and consumers on the other.

Many examples of lack of understanding of possible gaps between the assumptions of the providers and of the consumers abound. For instance, in 1943, Thomas Watson, chairman at that time of the company that would soon be renamed IBM, is quoted as saying, "I think there is a world market for about five computers." More recently, in 1977, Ken Olson, then president of Digital Equipment Corporation, is quoted as saying, "There is no reason for any individual to have a computer in their home." We need to look only at the changes that occurred within the decade that followed this pronouncement and the even larger and faster changes which are now occurring to see how much professional viewpoints may be out of touch with consumer realities.

In our own field of instructional development, we may find similar examples. In the 1950s, as color television became the norm, the British Broadcasting Corporation in Great Britain carried out extensive research on the impact of color on learning and on the relative effectiveness of color and black and white versions of similar instructional programs. On the basis of the results of this research, which showed that color has no effect on learning in controlled experimental situations unless color is part of the message that is being communicated, the BBC decided that although entertainment broadcasting was going to color, educational broadcasting would stay in black and white for the next ten years or so. Only one year later, the BBC reversed this policy decision because, as color TV became common in households, the actual usage of educational television dropped so significantly that despite whatever the research says, it became absolutely essential to go to color in order to motivate the consumers to actually partake in the programs that were being provided. This example is analogous to the quartz watch.

An example that may well be analogous to the urban realities of Brasilia is one of the chief discussion points within the last few years in the literature of instructional development. We are referring to the often voiced "complaint" that although instructional development theory has for years now espoused cognitive psychology, information processing theory, and more recently constructivist and situational approaches to the planning of teaching and learning processes, the bulk of the practice of instructional development continues to be largely embedded within a "behaviorist paradigm." If for the sake of argument we take this position as being true, we may nevertheless ask whether this is poor instructional design practice on the part of the practitioners charged with the development of teaching materials for different groups of clients and consumers, or whether, as in the case of the super squares of Brasilia, there is in fact a large gulf separating the paradigmatic assumptions of the theoreticians in the field and the end-users and consumers of the field's products. Maybe we should ask ourselves whether many of the new paradigms that are further analyzed in the following chapters are being driven mainly by innovative philosophical and theoretical thinking, or are they a response to changing needs of the market place?

In the following sections of the book, the editors have attempted to represent a variety of viewpoints from a variety of sources. For example, in this volume, we are exploring from a philosophical viewpoint the basic paradigm of instructional development as a field of activity. Some chapters look at the field from specific end user viewpoints. For example, the chapter by Lent and Van Patten examines instructional development from the viewpoint of the business environment as the ultimate client. The chapter by Mauldin and Gustafson examines the formal education context as a client for instructional development. Wilson, on the other hand, examines new philosophical positions such as constructivism as a starting point for reconsidering whether instructional development paradigms are in the process of change and whether indeed they should be in such a process of change. Yet other chapters, for example, Ivor Davies's analysis of the ID field, try to keep a balance between the philosophical and theoretical paradigms of the researchers and professionals and the practical real-world paradigms of the end users and clients. In the later sections of the book, we have also tried to select chapters which mix the theoretical/professional approach with the practical/end-user approach, in order to create as good a balance as we could between these two essential components that should be integrated within the multi-paradigmatic structure of a field such as instructional development.

The preceding paragraphs have illustrated one aspect of the need for coherence between different but related viewpoints of a field such as instructional development. These could be referred to as the "theoretical practitioner" vantage point and the "practical client or end user" vantage point. Another somewhat different concept of different "vantage points" will also be useful in making links between the various chapters the authors have assembled in this book. This is the concept of vantage points so well explained by Thomas Gilbert in his book on *Human Competence* (Gilbert, 1978). The authors have dedicated this present book to the memory of Tom Gilbert, who unfortunately died during its final editorial stages. In the dedication to this book, we are reprinting a small story taken from *Human Competence* which illustrates Tom Gilbert's suggestion that what is often an unclear process of argument between people with different viewpoints on a topic, on closer analysis are revealed to be viewpoints expressed from different systems levels or vantage points. Gilbert in that story identifies six levels of view, that he refers to as the philosophical, the cultural, global/policy, strategic, tactical, and logistic levels. This model of vantage points has been found by the editors to be of great value in many different contexts, including the creation of an organizing structure for complex books on complex topics such as instructional design and development. One of the current editors has indeed authored a series of three books covering the instructional design and development field in an overview manner using an adaptation of Gilbert's vantage points model as the organizing structure for the books (Romiszowski, 1984, 1986, 1987). In the present book, the authors propose to use Gilbert's model of vantage points as one organizing dimension for the chapters.

Organization of the Book and How to Use It

The six sections into which the book is divided reflect, as closely as we have been able to manage, the six vantage points or levels of view illustrated by the anecdote from Gilbert's *Human Competence* (reproduced in the preface/dedication). In the present section, we have assembled some chapters which take philosophical stances on instructional development and its potential roles and appropriateness in a general sense to current and future educational practices. In the second section, the chapters take what may more appropriately be seen as a cultural vantage point, examining instructional development from particular cultural contexts such as the formal K–12 context or the business training context. In the third section, the chapters look at general educational/training policy which in our context has included also theory of learning and instruction. Chapters in this section include viewpoints from the more classical positions expressed within the educational and educational psychology literature (behaviorism, humanism, cognitive theory, etc.) and also chapters presenting new viewpoints on the goals, the role and the underlying theories that are the basis for a "new wave" of policy for the education systems of the 21st century (constructivism, situated cognition, post-modernism, etc). In the fourth section, the editors have included chapters that can best be characterized as expounding a strategic planning level of viewpoint. The authors of chapters in this section are looking at how to apply specific philosophical or theoretical paradigmatic positions as an overall underlying basis for the planning of education, educational systems, whole courses, and curricula. In the fifth section, the chapters take a more tactical vantage point, dealing with specific procedures suggested for particular forms of lesson or instructional exercise. However each of the procedures reflect certain paradigmatic positions expressed within the philosophies and theories underlying the instructional development field. We therefore find that through the strategic and tactical sections, there are cross-sectional links to the philosophical, cultural and policy/theoretical viewpoints expressed in sections one through three.

Finally, in the sixth section, we have assembled a series of chapters that deal with particular hardware or delivery-system-based innovations such as hypertext, hypermedia, computer-based simulations, etc. These are seen as analogous to Gilbert's logistic vantage point. As mentioned earlier in this chapter, it may be somewhat dangerous and not always fruitful to base one's paradigms for instructional design and development on a particular hardware or software innovation. However, practice shows that this is often done, and some authors even suggest that it is the rule. For example, some suggest that the reigning delivery technologies of a period are one of the prime factors that influence which philosophical and theoretical viewpoints on the nature of education are proposed and accepted. Whether or not we agree with this view, as regards the importance of the delivery technologies or the logistics of a particular period on the philosophies and theories espoused by practitioners, we cannot deny the links between theory and practice. Once more we often may see in the chapters included in the sixth section clear links to all five of the earlier sections. In most cases, therefore, there are quite clear threads that can be traced through the six sections indicating how philosophical, cultural, and theoretical paradigmatic elements play a role in determining the strategic, tactical, and logistical decisions within the practice of the field.

We may therefore see a matrix-like structure developing for the book. Not only do we have six vantage points or levels of view as defined by Gilbert and reflected in the six sections of the book, but we also have threads of strong interrelationship running through the levels. These interrelationships are illustrated in the matrix diagram presented with the contents pages and are further elaborated in the introductions to each of the later sections. We hope that this elaboration on the finer detail of the structure that the editors perceive within the book as a whole will be of help to the readers in making their own links and interrelationships between the various diverse philosophies, theories, cultural factors and practical aspects of the strategies, tactics, and logistics of instructional development.

Notes

1. The authors wish to thank Dr. Donald P. Ely for his comments and suggestions following a review of this chapter's early manuscript.
2. Donald P. Ely (1996). Personal note, bringing to the authors' attention the nature of instructional development as a social science. There is a subset of paradigmatic values that are held by the members of the instructional development confederation having roots in the general education and social science community that are not always shared with those entering instructional development from other traditions. This subset of values are in addition to or slightly different from those held by those groups having their roots in the behavioral engineering tradition.

References

Bass, R. K. (1978). Educational cognitive style inventory (unpublished measuring instrument).

Bass, R. K., & Dills, C. R. (1984). *Instructional development: The state of the art* (Vol. 2). Dubuque, IA: Kendall/Hunt Publishing Co.

Clark, R. E., & Sugrue, B. M. (1995). Research on instructional media, 1978–1988. In G. J. Anglin (Ed.), *Instructional technology: Past, present, and future* (2nd ed.). Englewood, CO: Libraries Unlimited.

Davies, I. (1984). Instructional development: Themata, archetypes, paradigms, and models. In R. K. Bass & C. R. Dills (Eds.), *Instructional development: The state of the art* (Vol. 2). Dubuque, IA: Kendall/Hunt Publishing Co.

Dills, C. R., & Bass, R. K. (1978). *Cognitive style mapping and the personalization of instruction: A problem in profile interpretation and matching solvable problems using DISK.* Paper given at Seventeenth National Conference on Media and Instruction, Saskatoon, Saskatchewan, Canada.

Driscoll, M. P. (1995). Paradigms for research in instructional systems. In G. J. Anglin (Ed.), *Instructional technology: Past, present, and future* (2nd ed.). Englewood, CO: Libraries Unlimited.

Finn, J. D. (1960). Technology and the instructional process. *Audio-Visual Communication Review, 8*(1), 9–10.

Gentry, C. G. (1995). Educational technology: A question of meaning. In G. J. Anglin (Ed.), *Instructional technology: Past, present, and future* (2nd ed.). Englewood, CO: Libraries Unlimited.

Gilbert, T. F. (1978). *Human competence: Engineering worthy performance.* New York: McGraw-Hill Book Company.

Gustafson, K. L., & Schuller, C. F. (1984). Professional education in instructional development at Michigan State University. In R. K. Bass & C. R. Dills (Eds.), *Instructional development: The state of the art* (Vol. 2). Dubuque, IA: Kendall/Hunt Publishing Co.

Hall, E. T. (1966). *The hidden dimension.* New York: Doubleday.

Hall, E. T. (1992). *An anthropology of everyday life: An autobiography.* New York: Doubleday.

Hill, J. E. (1981). *The educational sciences: A conceptual framework.* West Bloomfield, MI: Hill Educational Sciences Research Foundation.

Keppler, K., Dills, C., Selfridge, G., & Ishwaren, C. (1982). *DISK: A computer program for classification using multi-dimensional distributions.*

King, J. M. (1997). Subliminal perception studies and their implications for incorporating embedded communications into instructional design products. In C. R. Dills & A. J. Romiszowski (Eds.), *Instructional development paradigms.* Englewood Cliffs, NJ: Educational Technology Publications.

Kohl, H. (1967). *36 children.* New York: New American Library.

Kuhn, T. S. (1962). *The structure of scientific revolutions.* Chicago: University of Chicago Press.

Kuhn, T. S. (1970). *The structure of scientific revolutions* (2nd ed.). Chicago: University of Chicago Press.

Lachman, R., Lachman, J. L., & Butterfield, E. C. (1979). *Cognitive psychology and information processing: An introduction.* Hillsdale, NJ: Lawrence Erlbaum Associates.

Mahalanobis, P. C. (1936). On the generalized distance in statistics. *Proceedings of the National Institute of Science in India,* Vol. 12, 49–53.

Morell, V. (1995). *Ancestral passions: The Leakey family and the quest for humankind's beginnings.* New York: Simon and Schuster.

Neill, A. S. (1960). *Summerhill: A radical approach to child rearing.* New York: Hart Publishing Company.

Reigeluth, C. M. (Ed.). (1983). *Instructional design theories and models: An overview of their current status.* Hillsdale, NJ: Lawrence Erlbaum Associates.

Reigeluth, C. M. (Ed.). (1987). *Instructional theories in action: Lessons illustrating selected theories and models.* Hillsdale, NJ: Lawrence Erlbaum Associates.

Reigeluth, C. M. (1995). Educational systems development and its relationship to ISD. In G. J. Anglin (Ed.), *Instructional technology: Past, present, and future* (2nd ed.). Englewood, CO: Libraries Unlimited.

Robinson, R. S. (1995). Qualitative research: A case for case studies. In G. J. Anglin (Ed.), *Instructional technology: Past, present, and future* (2nd ed.). Englewood, CO: Libraries Unlimited.

Romiszowski, A. J. (1984). *Developing instructional systems: Decision making in course planning and curriculum design.* London: Kagan Page.

Romiszowski, A. J. (1986). *Producing instructional systems.* London: Kogan Page.

Romiszowski, A. J. (1987). *Developing auto-instructional materials.* London: Kogan Page.

Rose, C. (1986). *Accelerated learning.* Cambridge, England: Topaz Publishing Limited.

Saettler, P. L. (1968). *A history of instructional technology.* New York: McGraw-Hill.

Saettler, P. L. (1990). *The evolution of American educational technology.* Englewood, CO: Libraries Unlimited.

Scandura, J. (1983). Instructional strategies based on the structural learning theory. In C. M. Reigeluth (Ed.), *Instructional design theories and models: An overview of their current status.* Hillsdale, NJ: Lawrence Erlbaum Associates.

Schuster, D. H. (1997). SALT and accelerated learning. In C. R. Dills & A. J. Romiszowski (Eds.), *Instructional development paradigms.* Englewood Cliffs, NJ: Educational Technology Publications.

Schwier, R. A. (1995). Issues in emerging interactive technologies. In G. J. Anglin (Ed.) *Instructional technology: Past, present, and future* (2nd ed.). Englewood, CO: Libraries Unlimited.

Shannon, C., & Weaver, W. (1949). *The mathematical theory of communication.* Urbana: University of Illinois Press.

Shrock, S. A. (1995). A brief history of instructional development. In G. J. Anglin (Ed.), *Instructional technology: Past, present, and future* (2nd ed.). Englewood, CO: Libraries Unlimited.

Urdang, L., & Flexner, S. B. (1969). *The Random House dictionary of the English language, college edition.* New York: Random House.

2

Paradigms and Conceptual ISD Systems

Ivor K. Davies
Indiana University, Bloomington

*What determines your destiny is not the hand you're dealt, it's how you
play your hand. And the best way to play your hand is to face reality . . .
see the world the way it is . . . and act accordingly.*

J. F. Welch

Instructional Systems Design (ISD) is at a crossroad. It is time to re-examine the role
we continue to play, ought to play, and must play in contemporary education, training, and
business. As Jack Welch reminds us, it is necessary "to face reality . . . see the world the way
it is . . . and act accordingly." As with programmed instruction, many of whose concepts we
absorbed, many ISD principles have now in turn become part of the mainstream of best practice in education and training. It is a measure of our success that they have become commonplace. The question is, what hand have we been dealt today, and how should we play
that hand—how can we continue to add significant value?

ISPI, the most sensitive of our professional bodies to shifts in the field, changed its
name in 1995 from the "National Society for Performance & Instruction" to the "International
Society for Performance Improvement." Some thirty years ago it was known as the "National
Society for Programmed Instruction." In the debate over a name change at that time, it fortunately resisted a suggestion that they call themselves the "Nebulous Society for Piecemeal
Instruction" (Mager & Davies, 1964). Piecemeal seemed rather apt in 1964 because of their
previous devotion to small or medium chunks of information called frames.

In this time of re-invention (Davies, 1995), we need to ask ourselves two basic
questions:

Why do we do *what* we do?
Why do we do it the *way* that we do?

In other words, what are the tacit rules and basic assumptions (the theory) that underlie the practice of our profession? Only in this way will it be possible to determine the worth of our present day contribution. (Worth,[1] it is important to remind ourselves, is the *margin* that remains when cost is deducted from value.) Our own paradigm is changing, but the reality of the paradigm of the world we face on a day-to-day basis has already changed. We are laggard in our audit, and one paradigm is out of step with the other.

As we enter the late 1990s, the descriptor *Human Performance Technology* (HPT) better captures the direction the profession is taking. There is a growing realization that a preoccupation with instruction artificially cuts short the full value of our effectiveness. Instructional and non-instructional interventions are *both* important in the acquisition and maintenance of performance. *Human Reliability and Performance Technology* (HR&PT) is an even more apt descriptor of our competence. The concept of "reliability" brings into play current concerns with authentic tasks and consistency, quality, and durability. This is a particularly important consideration, for a period of great change and constant innovation invariably implies opportunities for significant variance in human performance.

HR&PT also meshes well with current concerns in business. Renewed customer and client demands for system reliability have highlighted the importance of systematically reducing variance in performance—particularly at the person-process interface. The traditional focus of instructional development, instructional systems design, and even performance technology on tasks, roles, jobs, structures, and people has become myopic. It reduces our general effectiveness. In business, there is an important movement away from an excessive concentration on inputs and outputs, towards a process orientation (Davies, 1994).

Process-based thinking is replacing task-based thinking. It is in processes that work is done. Process re-design is now a central strategy in business productivity enhancements. Human reliability and performance technology has a central role to play in this effort, if only because of our historic concern with design and systems thinking. HR&PT, like ISD, inherited both of these concepts from the earliest formulations of our field.

Adam Smith's late eighteenth century interest in breaking down work into its simplest tasks and sub-tasks, and then assigning them to specialist functions, has greatly influenced us. Businesses today, however, are less concerned with this approach, and more concerned with systems thinking. Their focus is less on the individual *steps* of obtaining an order from a customer, and more on the whole *process* of customer fulfillment. Such a process includes sales, pricing, production, shipping, installation, and after-sales support. This more accurately describes the way that work is or should be carried out. Furthermore, seeing production as part of the process of customer fulfillment casts a new light on the manufacturing function. A process perspective, furthermore, better ensures that processes are managed—instead of the individual tasks, functions, or people. This has important consequences for the theory, role and formatting of task analysis.

A World in Transition

Change is in the wind, not necessarily for the sake of change, but because of a dramatic shift in the character of the problems we face. In a 1993 study, a task force of the American Society for Training & Development (ASTD, 1993) recognized five major forces at work in society. They were: changing organizations, a technology explosion, changing employee roles and responsibilities, changing workforce demographics, and a changing external environment (see Figure 1). These same forces, to which might be added the specific reality of "global competitiveness," also affect the theory, practice, and perceived contributed value of ISD and even more of HR&PT. Such forces lie at the very roots of the change that is affecting not

---

[1]Worth = value − cost.

- Changing organizations—reassessment of what is needed
- Technology explosion—new opportunities & challenges
- Changing employee roles & responsibilities—different expectations
- Changing workforce demographics—no longer a homogeneous constant
- Changing external environment—sophisticated global competition on- and off-shore

SOURCE: Based upon ASTD Professional Concerns Committee Report, *"News & Notes,"* August 1993.

Figure 1. Forces changing current ISD theory and practice.

only business but society at large. However, the word "change" is misleading. Its singular case fails to acknowledge the multiple challenges that we face. It presents change as a single event rather than a continual and dynamic process.

When change of the magnitude currently facing society occurs, three things happen. An ending takes place as a period of transition gets underway, and steps are taken to prepare for a new beginning. However, during the transition, remnants of the ending remain, tending to block or slow the transition while stopping the new beginning from occurring. Similarly, remnants of the transition remain, and they in turn get in the way of realizing the future (see Figure 2, after Bridges, 1991). All of this holds back the process. It becomes more painful, particularly as the history of the past lives on in both the present and the future.

Each stage of the process (ending, transitioning, and beginning) brings its own particular problems and opportunities. Each stage imposes its own demands. Many things have to be done simultaneously. Time is not on the side of western business, and there is no great constituency lobbying for change to occur—particularly with the massive job losses that are still occurring. For these reasons, there is little or no point in waiting.

At the moment, western business has entered the stage of transition, where many of its fundamental beliefs and behaviors are outmoded or suspect. It is a tempestuous time, a moment of "white water," when change is constant, and no end is in sight. Persistence is the name of the game. Competitiveness, cost reduction and productivity are the issues, and reliable human performance the means. Business and industry are being forced to let go of practices that made for success in the past, while searching for different ways of dealing with the turbulence of the present. The compass is being replaced, while the maps are re-drawn. Survival has become a major concern even for large and previously successful companies. Some famous companies are already dinosaurs (Loomis, 1993), relics of a past golden age.

Some 40% of the companies on the *Fortune Five Hundred* list in 1985 *no longer exist!* Since 1990 (the recession technically ended in March of 1990) over 11.9 million white collar workers have lost their jobs. In 1972, eighteen of the twenty most valuable companies on earth were American. These days (Loomis, 1993), only seven are still on this select list, and two of those are new to the category (Microsoft and Intel). The remainder have failed, merged with others, or are simply significantly smaller. They have been replaced by companies from southeast and north-east Asia, most of them in the service rather than the manufacturing sector.

To compete in this new global market place, radical change is essential. Re-structuring is seen as the solution (see Champy, 1995; Tichy & Sherman, 1993), even for Korean companies that no longer have the advantage of inexpensive labor and cheap Korean currency. In the western world, "Foreign competitors are becoming tougher. Workers, many aging and

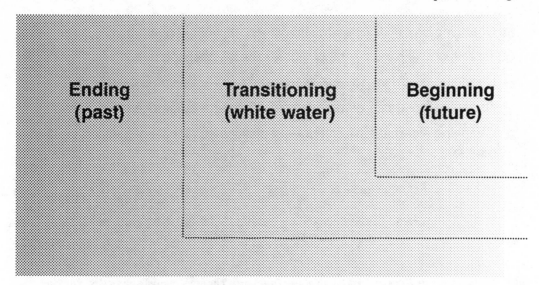

Figure 2.   Change as a three-stage process.

underskilled, are clamoring to be empowered. And customers are demanding the highest quality, latest technology, and speediest delivery—all at the lowest cost. . . . This may be a time of immense uncertainty, but it is a certainty that Western companies are in for ten years of competitive hell" (Henkoff, 1990). That prophecy has been fully realized in the years since 1990, and things are likely to get tougher still. Jack Welch, Chairman & CEO of GE, believes that "the value decade has begun, with it global price competition like you've never seen. It's going to be brutal" (Welch, 1995). It is not just that the world of business has changed. Rather, we are in transition toward a radically new way of doing things. The paradigm is shifting toward a *global* reality, and the world of business, like the world of education, will never be the same again.

The new business environment of a customer oriented global market is creating a "demand pull" for new products, services, and ways of delivering them. Simultaneously, a "technology push" is forcing business to radically re-think how work is done. These forces, coupled with the promise of information technology (see Tapscott & Caston, 1993), offer us a means of more effectively tapping new ideas of *design* that can *transform* instructional systems technology. It is only through re-thinking our field that we will be better able to contribute meaningfully to the incessant demand of business for productivity, growth and competitiveness.

The Role of Paradigms

The succession or series of changes that society has undergone in the last ten years has led to the realization that change has been more radical, patterned, and cumulative than was anticipated. The pain of a long recession has sharpened this perception. Companies have to deal with the challenge of changing from domestic businesses selling offshore into global companies competing in the global market place. This is the sign that a global shift of some magnitude has taken place in the way that business thinks and behaves.

The lens through which people view opportunities has altered. They have a new "pre-scription" for looking; they even "frame" things differently. Some things are seen more clearly; much is seen differently. If learning is indexed by experience (see Honebein, Duffy, & Fish-man, 1993), then the paradigm shift may have made much of that experience outdated. This places people at a disadvantage, unless they are willing and able to change. Sadly, some are unable to make the accommodation, or refuse to believe that it is necessary. Their thought style is out of phase with the paradigm shift that has taken place around them. They too, like some businesses, have become dinosaurs.

Fleck's original term "thought styles," to express ideas that are common to everyday thinking in a community of scholars, was the latent root from which Kuhn derived his idea of a "paradigm" (see Harré, 1993). A paradigm represents a set of shared values, which bind people together into a common community. Such shared values help establish common boundaries. They provide rules and regulations for what is to be taken for granted (Kuhn, 1970). Such rules and regulations, explicit or tacit, increase the probability of success if they are followed (Barker, 1993, p. 32). Paradigms, which are by their very nature highly restrictive, filter information. If data does not fit the paradigm, we are resistant to it. Such data is ignored or bent, so that it is made to fit the paradigm. Data that contradicts the paradigm may not even be seen. Paradigms control not only the way that people see things, but the way people think.

Kodak refused the rights to Xerography, since the process did not use a photo negative. Sensitive to the need to keep close to their core competencies, Kodak defined photography too narrowly. It missed a major business opportunity. When the paradigm shifts, the game changes. In fact, "everyone goes back to zero" (Barker, 1993, p. 140). A company which has been number one in its traditional markets goes back to zero, along with its competitors. A new race to be number one in the *global* market place begins, in which everyone starts from a new starting line. It is a new game, and the past counts for very little.

What is impossible under the rules of the old paradigm may be possible under the rules of the new. A business, however, must be willing to become a "learning organization" (Senge, 1992), ready to acknowledge mistakes and learn from them. Francis Bacon's[2] acute observation that "truth emerges more readily from error than from confusion" is a rationale for such a prescription. There is no place for the "not invented here" syndrome. Values have changed and every company must begin a new learning curve.

As is common with all paradigm shifts, the cultural change that businesses like GE, AT&T, Allied Signal, Ford, and Whirlpool have undergone has cast them in the role of mentors. They have become mentors to those who have not yet dared make the changes, or are still attempting to make the passage. To use the words that Thomas Kuhn (1970) employs to describe two key properties of paradigm shifts: "Their achievement was sufficiently unprecedented to attract an enduring group of students away from competing modes of scientific activity. Simultaneously, it (their experience) was sufficiently open-ended to leave all sorts of problems for the refined group (i.e., followers) to resolve." Mentor companies provide ideals from which the new paradigm ultimately emerges. They are not early adopters; they originate the new reality that the new paradigm finally comes to represent.

ISD and the New Paradigm

In its relatively short history since the 1940s, the ISD field has moved through three paradigms of its own. They were the audio-visual paradigm, the engineering paradigm, and the systems paradigm (Davies, 1984). Each of these paradigms represented a different set of values; each had its own rules and regulations; each tended to ignore the literature of its predecessor. All three paradigms reacted to key forces in their environments, and in the end came to represent these environments.

---

[2]Bacon, F. (1597). *Novum Organum*, Vol. VIII. J. Spedding, R. L. Ellis, & D. D. Heath (Eds.). *The Works of Francis Bacon.* New York: D. D. Heath, p. 210.

The audio-visual paradigm viewed instructional development as fulfilling the dream of a *technology of education.* It explains why media departments in many universities have been so closely associated with the development of our field. Under this paradigm, the principles of instructional development were seen as offering four broad advantages. They helped in the design of classroom presentations, seemed to solve the problems of distance education, enhanced the efficiency of teaching and learning, and offered novel instrumentation for assessment and testing procedures.

The engineering paradigm viewed instructional development as fulfilling the dream of a *science of teaching and learning.* It was heavily influenced by the work of Professor B. F. Skinner in the 1960s. Operant conditioning and the shaping (engineering) of human behavior became part of a radically new technology, which generated much emotion among educators and trainers. A great deal of initial effort was expended in comparing the efficiency of one methodology with another. The efficiency of teachers was compared with that of programmed texts, behaviorally stated objectives, aims, and goals stated in a more generalized form, and goal-centered evaluation with goal-free evaluation.

In order to find the "one best way," the whole process of instructional development was flowcharted, complete with boxes, arrows, and feedback loops, in an attempt to lay down a systematic step-by-step process. It was prescribed that the ends must always be defined before the means. The systematic approach was emphasized as the only way to go. Small steps were valued over large ones, lean steps over more content-generous ones. The orientation of the paradigm emphasized the priority of learning over teaching.

The systems paradigm was viewed as fulfilling the dream of a *systems view of human performance.* Instructional development began to be called instructional systems design after 1970, or performance technology after 1975. Design was seen as central to the function of ISD, and design came to be recognized as a key competency required for success in the field. Effectiveness[3] rather than efficiency became the name of the game. The importance of looking at things holistically or systemically was repeatedly emphasized.

A clear distinction was made (see Davies 1971) between fitting the person to the task, and fitting the task to the person. Fitting the person to the task (FPT) was achieved through selection, guidance, and instruction to overcome performance problems due to knowledge, skill, or attitudinal deficiencies. Fitting the task to the person (FTP) was achieved through task and tool redesign; the availability of essential information and feedback; motivation, recognition, and incentives; and the optimal arrangement of working conditions to overcome skill discrepancies. The discriminator *"Can they do it if their life depends upon it"* (Mager, 1970) distinguishes discrepancies from deficiencies. It replaced the old ID bias toward identifying the "one best way." The orientation of this paradigm emphasized the priority of performance over learning. Problem solving and action learning became important design strategies.

The renunciation of the "one best way" is especially important in this paradigm shift. Scientists have drawn a clear distinction between tidy, regular phenomena, and messy, random phenomena. The former was beloved of physics (e.g., the trajectory of a missile), and the latter by statistics (e.g., the toss of a coin). Standardized tests, like the General Management Aptitude Test (GMAT), with their true-false and multiple-choice questions, are founded upon such a paradigmatic view of reality. GMAT is still a useful predictor of performance in most MBA programs, but it is now a less useful predictor of an MBA graduate's performance during his or her first three years in business—the world of business has changed and is in a constant state of flux.

---

[3]Effectiveness is concerned with doing the right things, efficiency with doing things right (Davies, 1973).

Today, we understand much better that the world is also full of things that are neither regular nor random. We are living through an age of paradox (see Handy, 1994), perhaps of the absurd (Farson, 1996); some things we experience are both regular and random at the same time (e.g., the weather and human behavior). Chaos theory and fractal geometry have taught us that order and disorder co-exist in the hard sciences, in the affairs of business, and most certainly in human performance (see Goerner, 1993; Peters, 1994). Educators and many instructional systems designers and performance technologists still have to come to terms with this finding, obvious though it is to keen observers of the human condition.

Effective human performance became the goal of the systems paradigm. During the 1970s and the 1980s, this orientation well served the needs of business and industry. However, during the current period of transition, while business prepares for a new beginning, something more is needed. The business paradigm has shifted with the change to global markets, with their sophisticated global customers, global competitors, and global brands. Instructional systems design and the performance technology field must also change and become more business-sensitive. Education is one of the most resistant of professions. However, educators are already busily engaged in restructuring school systems in North America and Europe, but most of the major players are not members of our field. AECT's Systemic Change Division, which is concerned with educational restructuring, was only formed in 1994.

ISD and PT Competencies and Training: Meeting Business Needs in the Mid-1990s

In an ad hoc study of educational technologists[4] in two large American corporations (Davies, 1989), their strengths and weaknesses were assessed by managers outside the educational technology function. They were perceived as highly able, technically competent in their professional activities, possessing valuable analytical skills, and having good people skills.

However, they were also perceived as lacking a business orientation, management skills, and experience, and lacking an issue or problem orientation. Their vocabulary was criticized for being predominately that of education, and not that of the business that employed them. They were also criticized for being reactive, rather than proactive, and for being individual entrepreneurs rather than team players. While they had a well-developed "educational technology" network, their education and business networks were perceived as poorly developed.

Managers believed that promotion to other roles outside the function of educational technology was unlikely, despite their undoubted ability, unless they became more business and issues oriented. Interviewees sensed that something else was lacking, but they had difficulty verbalizing it. The missing ingredient is best captured by the expression "impact orientation." In other words, the paradigm under which educational technologists worked lacked the impact component of the business paradigm. Learning is important, performance is essential, but impact is the ultimate aim. Impact affects the key measures by which businesses judge themselves.

Such measures deal with productivity, cost reduction, growth, and competitiveness. In business, things that are measured get done. Performance is continually tracked. Three new global paradigm values help to drive these measures. They are speed, simplicity, and self-confidence (Welch, 1989). Stretch targets and customer service that include the essential variable of quality, should be added (Welch, 1994). Under the international standard of ISO 9000, quality is a prerequisite for selling goods and services in the European Union (EU) market.

---

[4]Although their job title was "educational technologist," they were operating under the instructional systems design/performance technology paradigm.

Simplicity is tied to speed, for it involves getting rid of the mind-numbing bureaucracy that increases costs and lengthens cycle times. But simplicity also implies working smarter, questioning every task, job, and function that does not add value to the enterprise. "Just as surely as speed flows from simplicity, simplicity is grounded in self-confidence" (Welch, 1989). Self-confidence is essential. Nothing will change the way things are done, if people don't have the confidence to stand up and be counted. Without self-confidence, ideas will not be shared, opportunities will not be exploited, and people will follow rather than lead.

The problem facing business today is too much management, and too little leadership. Speed, simplicity, and self-confidence are keys to effectiveness in the current global business environment, but speed is especially important. Welch (1989) points out that "we have to get faster (getting there first) if we are to win in a world where nothing is predictable except the increasing pace of change." All of this calls for another stage to be added to the total training and education process. Figure 3 shows a continuum along which three types of training, education and development are arrayed as three stages in one ISD migration process. Stage one in the migration involves education for knowledge, stage two involves knowledge for performance, and stage three involves performance for impact. Programs can begin with stage one, laying down a firm knowledge platform for further stages. Programs could begin with stage two, and migrate as necessary to stage one, gaining essential knowledge on a "just in time" basis, and then forward, as necessary, to stage three. Alternately, some programs could begin with stage three, with students and trainees migrating back to stage one and stage two to gain additional competencies along the way.

Education for knowledge, associated with the improvements initiated by the science of teaching and learning paradigm, properly values the acquisition of knowledge, skills, and attitudes. The output of such training is knowledge, and the outcome, hopefully, is visionary ideas. Unfortunately, some education and training programs are content to end there, rather than continue on to the next stage.

■ **Education for Knowledge**	■ **Knowledge for Performance**	■ **Performance for Impact**
▶ Creates a framework for critical thinking	▶ Translates vision into actionable outcomes	▶ Adjusts tools & skills for the variables of individual contexts
▶ Illustrates various models for understanding inter-connectedness of things	▶ Builds competencies for achieving outcomes	▶ Innovates unique solutions to unique situations and solves problems via market driven perspective
▶ Concept & rule-based learning environment	▶ Activity-based learning environment	▶ Impact oriented environment
Outcome: Visionary ideas	**Outcome:** Implementable skills and tools	**Outcome:** Measurable business results
Conceptualization ⟷	**Conversion** ⟷	**Execution**

Figure 3. ISD migration strategy.

The acquisition of knowledge, skills, and attitudes is an essential prerequisite of knowledge for performance activity. This stage is associated with the human performance systems paradigm. It seeks to *transform* knowledge, skills, and attitudes into the active forms of knowing, doing, and valuing. The output is performance, i.e., implementable skills and tools. Most education, training, and development programs tend to end at this point. Indeed, some educators place such value on knowledge that they see little need to migrate to this stage—they view performance as the "vocational" domain.

As the critics of educational technologists noted, performance today is not enough. Knowledge and performance training passes on an enormous problem to the operating departments in business and industry that receive its graduates. Operating departments must engage in assimilation training to ensure, if time and resources are available, that people use at work what they have learned in training. If such a result does not occur within some three months of graduating, there seems to be little likelihood that it will ever happen. In effect, trainers make operating departments responsible for ensuring that transfer to the work environment takes place. If the effects of training are not discernible in the work place, the investment in training will not have been fully realized.

If speed, simplicity, and self-confidence mean anything, the message is clear for instructional systems designers and performance technologists. They, too, must share these three values, and enter into an active partnership with the operating departments. Training needs to be carried a stage further. Instructional designers and performance technologists must themselves assume responsibility, along with the operating departments, for ensuring that education and training have impact on the way that work is done (see Figure 4). Speed, as a prime value, also implies that training must occur at exactly the right moment, when knowledge and skills need to be put to use at the right moment in the pursuit of meeting business productivity goals. Such timely or "just-in-time" training needs to replace expensive "just-in-case" training, for which there may be no immediate business need.

Designing for impact and authentic activities adds an additional process or module to the ISD process. This is shown by the area of darker shading in Figure 4. The diagram indi-

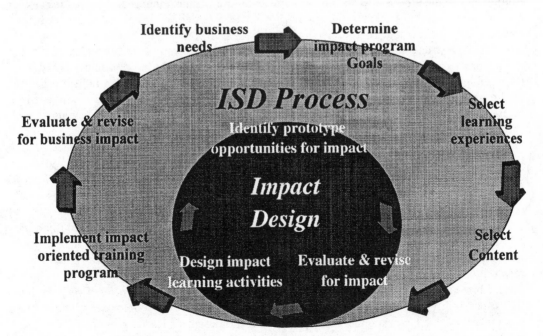

Figure 4. Instructional systems design for impact.

cates that the design entry point can be at any location in the multi-phase process. Instructional systems designers can begin with identification of business needs, followed by deciding the needs of the impact program itself. Alternatively, designers can begin with the impact design module, or perhaps with the selection of the content—which is where many designers begin anyway. Different opportunities call for different sequencing, as well as differences in what to include and what to exclude. Scope and sequence are challenging theoretical and practical problems in instructional systems design, especially when designing for impact.

In these circumstances, training and operating must be boundaryless, with both functions working in partnership as one process team to enhance productivity and reduce costs. This implies that while learning and most performance acquisition mainly take place in educational or training facilities, achieving impact must largely take place in the operating environment. This setting challenges ISD and HPT to rethink the matter of learning environment design. A green fields approach, in which education and training take place almost exclusively in a world apart from the world of work, is no longer tenable. An ISD paradigm, with an emphasis on boundarylessness, has three consequences important for ISD practice.

First, if training is to accept the additional responsibility of training for impact, instructional system designers and performance technologists must design experiences that train not just individual contributors for particular functions, but also intact work teams. Many of these teams will be multi-functional at times, if not multi-level. Some intact work teams will be permanent and some temporary in nature. Some team members will be direct employees (i.e., making product), and some indirect. An increasing number will be temporary or contingency employees (Fierman, 1994), who form a just-in-time work force made up of part-timers, free-lancers, and independent professional people. In most of American business today, over 60% of the work is carried out by high performance work groups or teams. In some businesses, the contingency work force comprises anything up to 25% of the total work force. It will perhaps be numbering 60 million people by the year 2000.

Second, while most of the training for learning and performance involves preparation for specific tasks and roles, training for impact implies training in how work is done. This involves training in the process environment. Subject matter experts (SMEs) will be the hourly people who actually do the work—not supervisors and not their managers. For this reason, a process orientation, as well as a process improvement orientation, are essential pre-requisite competencies for ISD and HPT professionals.

Third, instructional systems designers and human performance technologists must rethink their seemingly inbuilt preference for hierarchies. Under the new business paradigm, the traditional organizational structure is increasingly flat. There has been a radical pruning of the many levels that perpetuated the hierarchical principle of control and command inherited from the military at the end of the Second World War. The pyramid has also been turned upside down, with customers and vendors at the top interfacing with sales and service people at the source of the cash flow. General managers, vice-presidents, and CEOs lead from behind. Today, direction in business is upwards and outwards to customers and vendors, while execution is downwards and inwards to the processes. This is a design principle that ISD and HPT professionals need to adopt if they are to leverage their own professional contribution and that of other stakeholders.

In companies that have been re-engineered (see Champy, 1995; Hammer & Champy, 1993), people communicate with whomever they need. Control is vested in the people who work the process under conditions of great autonomy. Supervisors, who typically had some seven direct reports, have been replaced with coaches who work with thirty or more people. Leadership, coaching, facilitating, and influencing are essential competencies. Everyone has the responsibility of being a change agent, and total quality or zero defects are more than slogans. All of this has profound consequences on the design of learning, performance, and impact experiences.

ISD Model and Cycle Time Reduction

Since speed and productivity are important business issues in the global market place, it is essential that instructional systems designers give greater thought to how they can reduce the time it takes to design and continuously improve programs and courses. In business, the first two products or services brought to market tend to gain some 60% of market share. Speed is a two-edged weapon. Speed in program and course design is one benefit, speed in implementation is another. The first reduces cycle time, so that ISD productivity is enhanced and costs reduced. The latter speeds up market entry, so that a program or course is more competitively positioned. It also ensures faster program or course implementation, so that training impacts business processes more quickly than would be the case under the old paradigm.

Figure 5 illustrates a different way of organizing ISD design and development work. A comparison of Figures 4 and 5 graphically illustrates the advantages of concurrent (or parallel) design over serial design. Serial instructional systems design has many of the characteristics of a relay race. First one thing is completed, followed by the next, and so on. Such a process can be continuously improved, but only a radical re-design of the design and development process will result in a significant reduction in the time it takes to do the work.

To gain significant cycle time reductions of the order of perhaps 30 to 45%, concurrent strategies are essential. By using a parallel strategy, in which many ISD functions are carried out simultaneously, significant productivity gains can be achieved. The creative scrum and scramble of concurrent instructional systems design, however, is not for the faint hearted. Some designers will feel that determining goals while designing impact prototypes and simultaneously identifying appropriate subject matter content is logically absurd (see Davies, 1992, 1994; Lee, 1993).

Nevertheless, Japanese product designers and developers in the manufacturing and service industries are employing concurrent engineering, as it is called in industry, with con-

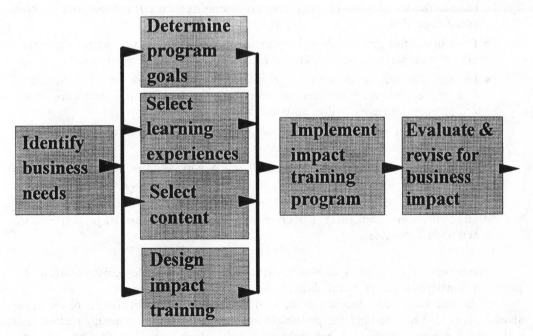

Figure 5. ISD process improvement: speed through concurrence.

siderable success. They have achieved significant speed and productivity enhancements. Creative forces, previously hemmed in by working in the boxes of serial design, have been unleashed. Chaos, as it were, works as natural feedback loops in the on-going process of continuous improvement. Most importantly, instructional systems designers who employ concurrent strategies will be seen as taking a leadership role in the global business revolution.

ISD and HPT Best Practices

All instructional systems design and human performance technology activities represent so many "case studies." Case studies (e.g., Keller & Taguchi, 1996) specific to a particular time and place, to a specific process and people needs, to specific problems and emerging opportunities. Such cases are inter-woven around two common strands of thought. Both strands must be taken seriously, since they reflect upon our art, craft and science. They involve, first, certain basic themes or "themata," and second, particular paradigms (Davies, 1984).

The term "themata" identifies certain themes that run through and across the literature of our field. They provide insights into the activities of professionals, and a bridge over areas of ignorance. They are believable propositions, which are difficult to corroborate or refute (Holton, 1973). Themata have a strong hold over the minds and hearts of instructional system designers and human performance technologists, showing great persistence over situations and over time.

An ongoing study by the author of practices in the instructional systems design and human performance technology community, consistent with the new business paradigm, has tentatively identified major themata that permeate best global practice. The themata, or global best practices in training and development, offer this advice to the field:

- Ensure that training directly impacts the realization of the strategic objectives of the business.

- Design primarily around processes, not just tasks. Recognize that order and disorder coexist. The world is full of things that are neither regular nor random, but are both at the same time.

- Enter into a full partnership with operating departments. Ensure the total effectiveness of both partners, and flatten the hierarchy in training departments.

- Leverage instructional systems design and human performance capability through a strategy that impacts individual contributors, intact high performance work teams, and business processes. Utilize authentic activities.

- Use concurrent rather than serial strategies in the design and development of instructional systems programs and courses.

- Emphasize system speed, cost reduction, and quality as three themes in *one* total meta-strategy. (By themselves, quality programs work to increase costs, slow product and service delivery times to customers, and increase bureaucracy.)

- Make clients and participants players, not spectators, in the knowledge, performance and impact strategies.

These best practices, acting as benchmarks, can be used to guide activities during this period of transition, when paths are difficult, if not impossible, to discern.

Associated with these themata, as with all paradigms, is a particular set of emerging shared values that help to bind the profession together in a time of seemingly endless radical changes. A tentative listing of these values and beliefs is given in Figure 6. They are com-

Traditional Values	New Values
■ Rewarded for work done	■ Rewarded for value created
■ Functional environment	■ Boundaryless environment
■ Focus on outputs	■ Focus on processes
■ Doing what it takes	■ Speed (cycle time reduction)
■ Relay race model	■ Concurrent model
■ Individual contributor	■ High-performance teams
■ Project is well-managed	■ Project team is well-led
■ Emphasis on meeting project goals	■ Emphasis on meeting client needs & expectations

Figure 6. ISD and HPT values and beliefs.

pared with values and beliefs that helped hold us together as a community of scholars in the past. It will be seen that significant changes are indicated, particularly the change from a reward structure for work done to a reward structure for value or wealth created. Attention is also drawn to the importance of working in a boundaryless environment, of exercising leadership, and of using concurrent design. The days when designers and technologists worked alone as individual contributors seem to be lost for ever. Design and development under the new paradigm has become a multi-functional, multi-level, high performance team activity.

Conclusion

Every theory of Instructional Systems Design involves a re-interpretation of the essential inter-relationships implicit in the components of its conceptual system. Each theory interprets data in an idiosyncratic way. Each conceptual system has its own reality. That reality is the paradigm, for paradigms control not only the way that we see things but, what is more important, what we take for granted.

The paradigm of instructional design and performance technology has changed radically in response to global business changes. It has not changed enough. It is out of phase with the way that many instructional systems designers, and even some human performance technologists, see opportunities through the eyes of an educator, rather than the eyes of a professional working in the global world of business.

Even when designers and technologists understand the new paradigmatic realities of business, and see the value of them for the operating departments, they fail to apply the values to their own professional activities. They "talk the talk," but fail to "walk the talk." Change mandates a new set of priorities, a new set of values: change mandates congruence between the global business paradigm and the ISD and HPT paradigm.

Speed, simplicity, and self-confidence are key. So are stretch targets and customer or client service. Traditional training that emphasized learning and performance have been found wanting. Western businesses demand that ISD and HPT professionals leverage training to achieve worthwhile impacts in client systems, and so help them create wealth. What determines the destiny of our field is not the hand we have been dealt, but how we play that hand. We must face the many new realities, and act accordingly.

References

ASTD. (1993). Professional Concerns Committee Report. *News & Notes, 6*(7), p. 1.

Barker, J. A. (1993). *Paradigms: The business of discovering the future.* New York: HarperCollins.

Bridges, W. (1991). *Managing transitions: Making the most of change.* Reading, MA: Addison-Wesley.

Champy, J. (1995). *Reengineering management: The mandate for new leadership.* New York: Harper Business.

Davies, I. K. (1971). *Competency based learning: Technology, management, and design.* New York & London: McGraw-Hill.

Davies, I. K. (1973). *The organization of training.* New York & London: McGraw-Hill.

Davies, I. K. (1984). Instructional development: Themata, archetypes, paradigms, and models. In R. K. Bass & C. R. Dills (Eds.), *Instructional development: The state of the art* (Vol. 2) (pp. 13–15). Dubuque, IA: Kendall/Hunt Publishing Co.

Davies, I. K. (1989). Total educational technology (TET): Challenging current limits. *Canadian Journal of Educational Technology, 18*(2), 132–137.

Davies, I. K. (1992). *Process mapping: A path to a vision.* Unpublished presentation to joint DID & ITED Session of the National Convention of the Association for Educational Communications and Technology, Washington, DC.

Davies, I. K. (1994). Process re-design for enhanced human performance. *Performance Improvement Quarterly, 7*(3), 103–113.

Davies, I. K. (1995). Re-inventing ISD. In B. Seels (Ed.), *Instructional design fundamentals: A reconsideration* (pp. 31–44). Englewood Cliffs, NJ: Educational Technology Publications.

Farson, R. (1996). *Management of the absurd.* New York: Simon & Schuster.

Fierman, J. (1994, January 24). The contingency work force. *Fortune,* 30–36.

Gaines-Robinson, D., & Robinson, J. C. (1989). *Training for impact.* San Francisco: Jossey-Bass.

Goerner, S. J. (1993). What is chaos? Or can science's sense of the world really change? *The General Psychologist, 29*(3), 87–93.

Hammer, M., & Champy, J. (1993). *Reengineering the corporation: A manifesto for business revolution.* New York: HarperBusiness.

Handy, C. (1994). *The age of paradox.* Boston: Harvard Business School Press.

Harré, R. (1993). Paradigms, experiments, and the discursive turn. *The Psychologist, 6*(6), p. 263.

Henkoff, R. (1990, December 31). How to plan for 1995. *Fortune,* p. 70.

Holton, G. (1973). *Thematic origins of scientific thought.* Cambridge, MA: Harvard University Press.

Honebein, P. C., Duffy, T. M., & Fishman, B. J. (1993). Constructivism and the design of learning environments: Context and authentic activities of learning. In T. M. Duffy, J. Lowyck, & D. H. Jonassen (Eds.), *Designing environments for constructive learning* (p. 88). New York: Springer-Verlag.

Keller, J. M., & Taguchi, M. (1996). Use of the systems approach to training design and delivery in Japanese corporations. *Performance Improvement Quarterly, 9*(1), 62–76.

Kuhn, T. S. (1970). *The structure of scientific revolutions.* Chicago: University of Chicago Press.

Lee, W. (1993). The parable of concurrent development. *Performance & Instruction, 32*(8), 12–13.

Loomis, C. J. (1993, May 3). Dinosaurs? *Fortune,* p. 37.

Mager, R. F. (1970). *Analyzing performance problems or 'you really oughta wanna.'* Belmont, CA: Fearon Publishers.

Mager, R. F., & Davies, I. K. (Verra Ewe & O. Sopedantic). (1964). Phrames are out: Phootnotes are in. *Journal of the National Society for Programmed Instruction, 5*(4), 4–7.

Peters, E. (1994). *Fractal market analysis.* New York: John Wiley & Sons.

Senge, P. M. (1992). *The fifth discipline: The art and practice of the learning organization.* New York: Doubleday.

Tapscott, D., & Caston, A. (1993). *Paradigm shift: The new promise of information technology.* New York: McGraw-Hill.

Tichy, N. M., & Sherman, S. (1993). Walking the talk at GE. *Training & Development, 47*(6), 26–35.

Welch, J. F. (1989). *Speed, simplicity, self-confidence: Keys to leading in the '90's.* Executive Reprints, GE Corporate Publications Center, General Electric Company.

Welch, J. F. (1994). *General Electric Company Annual Report.* Fairfield, CT: GE Corporate Publications Center.

Welch, J. F. (1995, May). Upfront. *Director, 48*(10), p. 19.

3

Tom Gilbert and the Educational Revolution

Marilyn B. Gilbert

Introduction

This chapter is my own impression of Tom's work and his contributions to instructional design. My fear is that these contributions might be overlooked because of his more exciting development of performance technology. And while I certainly don't mean to diminish that achievement, I want to be sure his work in instructional design is acknowledged and used. I am equally sure he would have wanted that, too.

Maybe the current perception of Tom's dedication to instructional design was inevitable, since performance technology emphasizes interventions other than training. Tom's message, in fact, was to warn that training is costly and not always the solution to a performance problem. Workers may know how to do their jobs, but they may not perform for other reasons—poor data, no feedback, a punishing environment, and so on. The job of the performance technologist is to uncover the real causes of poor performance, and, as Tom always pointed out, 95 percent of all jobs can be improved. Clumsy procedures that insiders never challenge are readily discernible to outside observers. Where training *is* required, I believe that the mission of the instruction is often changed when the principles of performance technology are employed; but performance technology hasn't changed the nature of the instruction itself.

In his later years, Tom was swept up by the fame of performance technology. Incentives and information are "sexier," as Tom would say. Nowadays, only old-timers know of Tom's pioneering work on learning (Gilbert, 1962). And not even the old-timers know much about his later work on instructional design—work that he actively pursued for thirty plus years longer.

In writing this chapter, I could see a completed life's work: how it started, how it developed, and how it ended. Unlike most other authors in this book, who can refine their theories or even change them entirely, Tom's work is done. I didn't need to suspend my conclusions while waiting for new revelations. Although a full description of Tom's system of instructional design is beyond the scope of this chapter, I can supply here an historical record and what I consider to be some highlights. Of course, if I have fractured some science, please remember my usual disclaimer: I am not a psychologist. If I have omitted some important principles that others have contributed, please remember my other disclaimer: I read novels. And if I want you to believe that Tom was a genius, please remember my final disclaimer: I loved the guy.

Because of my experience as an editor, however, I think I can separate my relationship with Tom as his partner in work from my relationship with him as his partner in life. Tom was the "father of performance technology"; he developed a whole system, which he shared generously with everyone. But he was also a master of a system of instructional design, and that system mostly lies hidden in his files and in obscure writings. I believe that his work promotes instructional design to a new level that others should know about, should use, and should extend. I'm writing in the hope that those of us who want an educational revolution can stand on Tom's shoulders and produce one.

In the Beginning

In the early 1950s, B. F. Skinner's chief assistant and collaborator at Harvard University was my then husband Charles B. Ferster. At that time, Skinner and Ferster did the considerable ground work on schedules of reinforcement, which they described later in a primitive-looking book of remarkable content called *Schedules of Reinforcement* (Ferster & Skinner, 1957). Their subjects in those days were likely to be pigeons, but Charlie often talked with Fred about applying the principles of reinforcement to human animals. In 1954 or thereabouts, he began to write the first programmed instruction textbook, attempting to teach German 101 to Americans. Charlie was a student of the German language, although not fluent enough, as it turned out. A German colleague reviewing Charlie's homemade programmed text pointed out that the German word for "arm," which Charlie had taught meant one of a pair of upper appendages on a human body, actually meant a single member midway down. After that enlightenment, Charlie preferred to deal with the hardware of programmed instruction, designing one of the first practical teaching machines; and he limited his research with human beings to what we now call behavior modification.

Meanwhile, Tom was teaching psychology at the University of Georgia. Unlike Charlie, who had studied at Columbia under Professors Keller and Schoenfeld and was an early Skinnerian disciple, Tom had been a student of psychometrics and clinical psychology. In graduate school, his knowledge of Skinner, he told me later, was limited to a few biographical paragraphs. I don't know who turned him on to operant conditioning, but his conversion was thorough and immediate. Soon he began to run Skinnerian-type experiments with animal subjects. He also practiced a few behavior modification experiments on himself and his students, with varying degrees of success. At the same time, he began to dabble in programmed instruction and wrote a programmed textbook on algebra. He even built his own clumsy teaching machine, which had some surprising consequences. Years later, his friend and colleague Joe Hammock found this early device and sent it to New Jersey, thinking Tom might want to have it. As this clumsy package sat unattended on our porch, Tom characteristically tripped over it and broke his big toe. He appreciated my comment: "At least it taught you something."

In 1958, at Skinner's invitation, Tom left Georgia and went to Harvard as a postdoctoral fellow. Along the road to Cambridge, Tom stopped at Bell Labs in Murray Hill, New Jersey, where he developed an ingenious system for remembering the color code for resistors. Resistors—in case you've forgotten—are devices that introduce different degrees of resistance, measured in ohms, into electrical circuits. But since these devices are very small, their resistance value, in ohms, would be difficult to read if stamped directly on them. For this reason, a resistor wears four or five color bands, each color representing a different number. The first two bands are read as digits; the third band is read as a number of zeroes following the two digits; the fourth band is interpreted as the heat tolerance of the resistor.

Previous instruction on reading resistors had been through a poem, requiring students to remember a sequence of color associations. The poem worked, but it was clumsy, because students had to review the entire sequence in order to reach the associations they might encounter on the job. Only with continuous application could they reach immediate recall. Tom reasoned that the pattern of behavior required for applying the color code for resistors was not a sequence of steps—that is, a chain—as the poem had assumed, but was actually a multiple discrimination. In working with resistors, technicians would see one of several bands (stimuli) at random, each requiring a different response or reading. That meant they would experience considerable competition for responding correctly. So, Tom abandoned the usual poem and set up instruction for students to learn the associations directly. This was his first important departure from the usual way to teach the resistor code: He designed the instruction so it would follow the pattern of the behavior, not conflict with it. Then, recognizing how difficult it would be to remember these responses, he provided a second departure: He supplied memory aids relating each color to a number. This departure was courageous, since many educators at that time thought that using a memory aid was cheating.

Tom chose his mediators very carefully. In his search for a mediator for the association of brown and No. 1, for example, he could have selected any number of brown objects—hair, say, or a leaf. The difficulty with hair is that it can be any one of several colors and it has no pre-existing association with the number 1. The problem with using a leaf is similar: Leaves are red, gold, green, and brown. And nothing about them connotes singularity. The mediator Tom picked was "1 brown penny," and it was perfect. What made a penny so strong as a mediator, of course, was that it related the stimulus to the required response: A penny is brown and it has a value of 1 cent. Similarly, Tom used "a red heart has two sides" as a mediator for a red band, which has a value of 2. A heart is usually red, and it always has two sides. With just a little practice, the mediators drop out, and the students remember the associations directly.

Tom has always adapted the training to the pattern of the behavior required—something very few course developers know how to do or even know that they *should* do.

By the time he reached Harvard, Tom had pretty much left hardware and animal research behind forever, devoting himself exclusively to instructional design. Here, he was pretty much a maverick, although extremely productive. He was in Cambridge for only a year, but in that brief time, he developed the basic principles of the system he called *mathetics*. He also conceived the dream of a gigantic research laboratory in Tuscaloosa, Alabama, which would be devoted to education and learning research. After leaving Harvard for a teaching position at the University of Alabama, he wrote what has to be the most remarkable proposal ever for funding of a research laboratory, attracting some of the most distinguished behavioral scientists of that time (Gilbert, 1960). Tom's proposal was turned down, and Tom went on to other educational pursuits.

The Birth of Performance Technology

In 1963, Tom set up a mathetical instructional design and development unit at the Centers for Disease Control (CDC) in Atlanta. One of his first projects there was to develop a course for lab technicians, teaching them how to identify the bacteria causing amoebiasis. This course was a great success. Tom had a problem with it, however, when he learned that amoebiasis was extremely rare in the United States. He realized he had developed very effective training where training wasn't really needed.

He thought about this CDC experience later, as he developed training products for such forward-looking companies as AT&T and Xerox and for agencies of the Department of Agriculture. He also recalled an earlier consulting assignment for the military during the Korean War. His charge was to develop a training program for soldiers on preventing trench foot and frostbite. While doing his research, however, he learned that the only training the soldiers actually needed was a warning to keep their socks dry. What they really needed was some timely information, not training. Yet, again, training seemed to be the only solution anyone ever recommended to fix a problem.

Another of Tom's fundamental observations was that although organizations paid homage to the need for measurement, they usually measured the wrong things. They actually measured activities—behaviors—rather than accomplishments. They measured how fast typists typed, for example, when all that mattered were the typed pages themselves: Were they typed accurately and completely and produced in a timely manner? This observation led him to emphasize the importance of distinguishing between behavior and accomplishment. And, later, when he found that people had real difficulties doing this, he devised a simple test:

> *Behavior you take with you; accomplishments you leave behind.*

These early observations were the seeds of performance engineering, or performance technology.

Tom also recognized that training animals was fairly simple compared with training people. Despite an ancient Columbia University cartoon showing the rats controlling the experimenters, in point of fact the experimenters controlled the rats' complete environment. But this was not true in training or in the education of human animals. Tom pointed out that we need to address the larger context of performance before deciding that the solution to a problem is training. In an early explanation, he formulated the question: Is the deficiency one of knowledge or of execution? He also defined forever the measure we can use to identify a deficiency of knowledge:

> *If the student can not perform, not even if his life depends on it,*
> *the deficiency must be one of knowledge.*

But if the student would be able to perform the task or the job if absolutely necessary to save his own skin, then we should look for other reasons for his poor performance. These reasons might have any number of sources. Maybe no one ever told him how well he was performing, or how poorly. Maybe no one seemed to give a damn what he did. Maybe the job had such punishing aspects that he simply avoided doing it. Maybe the student experienced so many interruptions that he just didn't have enough time to perform the required task. And a host of other reasons.

For the next few years, Tom investigated all the possible sources of these deficiencies of execution. He then sorted and classified them into a matrix, based on the symbolic representation for the components of behavior. He called it the Behavior Engineering Model (Gilbert, 1978, 1996). A discriminating stimulus is the information needed before performance can occur. The response is the instrumentation required. The reinforcing stimulus represents the motivation. In other words, before performance can occur, some information is needed, some instrumentation, and some motivation. Furthermore, these components may exist in two areas: as environmental supports and within the person's repertory of behavior. The environmental support for information is data; the behavioral repertory needed is knowledge. The environmental support for the response is the instrument—the tools; the behavioral repertory needed is the capacity—mental, physical, and emotional. The environmental support for motivation is the incentive; the behavioral repertory required is the intrinsic motive—an inner motive or strength.

Next to the distinction between an accomplishment and behavior, this matrix is probably the most useful of all the performance tools that Tom developed. What it does so successfully is to act as a litmus test for analyzing any accomplishment: What data do you need, what knowledge, and so on. Later, Tom made the model even more useful with the diagnostic tool Probe, which is a set of questions to ask about any aspect of any accomplishment being investigated.

While others were selling training, Tom was selling the reality that training was not always the solution to a problem—that performance problems needed to be viewed in a larger context. When instruction is viewed in that larger context, its mission might need to be changed. Furthermore, when training *is* required, it can't take place in a vacuum, without any supports, or never mind doing it at all. In addition to the actual instruction to do a job, trainees may need a lot of direction, adequate tools, efficient procedures, good incentives, and immediate feedback that training is successful.

In essence, what Tom said was that we live by a set of beliefs that he called the "topsy-turvy truths." Every popular tenet we hold about behavior is 180 degrees off.

And a funny thing happened. Slowly, the logic of Tom's message about performance began to win supporters, probably as a result of the publication of *Human Competence: Engineering Worthy Performance* (Gilbert, 1978, 1996). Consultants eager to include performance technology in their repertories renamed themselves "Performance" something or other. Tom also made several converts among the staffs of his clients in the mega-companies. A surprising number of them left their jobs as training directors to become performance technologists and to compete directly with their former consultant.

Perhaps the organization ISPI best illustrates the evolution. It was born NSPI, representing the National Society for Programmed Instruction. After a time, it renamed itself as the National Society for Performance and Instruction. This organization now calls itself ISPI, for the International Society for Performance Improvement. *Instruction* has completely vanished from the name—not because no one's doing any instruction any more, but because instruction is no longer the emphasis of the Society.

During his life, Tom was acknowledged and honored as the founder of performance technology. But performance technology was an outgrowth of his work in instructional design, which, as I said, is largely ignored. And his work in instructional design is just an outgrowth of his training as a psychologist. (He wouldn't have liked me to say this, though; when confronted, he always said he was a Baptist.)

The Educational Revolution

In the early days, Tom approached education in much the same way as other psychologists: intoxicated with a desire to do it better and convinced he could. He and others proclaimed the *Great Educational Revolution.* Like Tom, many who normally would have clung to academic posts and would have begun the steady (sometimes wiggly) climb up the academic ladder, shed academia and set up training shops instead. I say "training shops" rather than "education shops" because, interestingly enough, their clients came mostly from industry and government. Even Wall Street listened; only the schools hung back. But reasoning that you had to start somewhere, most practitioners compromised and started with some government agencies and the forward-looking companies.

Those early times were exciting to me, but many of my illusions were punctured when I saw some would-be revolutionaries more lured by the promise of riches than by the prospects of educational reform. I remember saying, "So this is what happens when psychologists discover money."

At first, the emphasis was on the hardware. I can recall going to an American Psychological Association Conference in Cleveland many years back and witnessing a teaching machine that was so large it filled a 9- by 12-foot room. I should say "glass-enclosed refrigerator," because this teaching machine had to be maintained at very low temperatures before it could work. Two psychologists I knew back then were in attendance to its needs. It was so big and complex that even Rube Goldberg would have been impressed. Of course, no one really knew whether the big machine would work or not, since it had no software to accompany it. That was a common problem of even the more approachable teaching machines: although ready page-turners, they had no pages to turn. This situation led to Tom's speech before another APA convention, this time in Cincinnati in 1959, when he urged everyone to throw away their teaching machines; if they still had a yen for a machine that they couldn't resist, he advised them to get a toaster instead.

Whether as a result of Tom's words or their own good sense, the early timers forgot about the hardware and focused their efforts on the software, most of it in the format of programmed textbooks. In attempting to apply the principles of animal behavior to human beings, the psychologists who ventured into business as instructional designers developed their own version of what became known as programmed instruction. Mainly, these designers broke the content down into short bits of information followed by questions—all encased in small boxes, which they called *frames*. They reasoned that the students would then always know whether they were learning or not, because the right answers to these questions were placed close by to reinforce the learning. Instruction was individualized, and students proceeded at their own pace.

The designers argued about some traditional learning principles, such as whether the rule should precede the example, or vice versa. They also argued a lot about where to place the answers, since immediate reinforcement of the behavior was an important principle. They also embedded at least one or two of their adaptations of Skinner's beliefs about verbal behavior into early frames. They avoided the use of the words *quite* and *very*, for example. And they used the "prompt," a hint to the right answer, which would prompt the student to respond correctly. For example, if the right answer to a frame was "physics," other text in that frame might contain the word "physical," or even something less related but starting with the letter "p."

Tom used the prompt in a similar way in early instructional lessons when he advised a three-step course of instruction: demonstrate, prompt, and release. The first step demonstrated to the student the stimulus and the behavior required to make the appropriate response. The second step, the prompt, featured some hint prompting the student to make the appropriate response. Finally, the release presented the bare stimulus and required the student to actually make the appropriate response unaided. In later work, the other programmers dropped their version of the prompt feature. Tom was likely to use some form of mediator as a prompt, but otherwise, in his later work, he too dropped the prompt step of his model.

Many early examples of programmed instruction advised the student to "Go to the Next Page" on every page—as if the reader coming to the end of a page would otherwise halt, not knowing where to go next. Jim Evans, psychologist and early developer of programmed instruction, claimed that the origin of this advice was a note from an editor to the typist that somehow became an integral part of every page of programmed text (Evans, 1966).

Then, as now, every training course started with a set of behavioral objectives (Mager, 1962, 1970). It was said that these objectives needed to be measurable, but in practice this often meant avoiding such phrases as "knowing how to" do certain things. Although measurement was implied, the measures by which the objective was evaluated were rarely defined.

But even with objectives measurable and measures defined, Tom still questioned the usual assumptions about learning objectives. To him, the problem was larger than the simple wording of the objective; it was the lack of an accomplishment-based training design. Either the learning objectives were behaviors, not accomplishments, or they encouraged the inclusion of material that wasn't significant and didn't need to be learned.

One feature that an early faction of the Educational Revolution used was called *branching,* in which students pursued different parts, or branches, of a book depending on their learning needs. They took a test at the end of a section of instruction to determine whether it would be advisable for them to take some extra instruction, located in a special part of the book, or to continue. Though cumbersome, branching followed the concept of individualized instruction by allowing students to learn at their own pace and in accordance with their own individual needs. In this respect, it was a cut above the usual linear flow of frames.

Tom also recommended a form of branching. Theorizing that the only way to discover what people needed to learn from a mathetical lesson was to assume that they needed as little instruction as possible, Tom was the first proponent of "lean" programming. He also realized that some target students might need more than this minimum, and he advised designing a remedial course of instruction for them (Gilbert, 1962). In practice, however, Tom did not actually prepare two sets of mathetical designs. And probably for the same reasons others had not pursued branching; it was too tough and too tedious to do. Instead, he relied on the pilot test to determine what the lean programming might have failed to cover.

Overall, all the developers of instructional materials in those days at least gave lip service to the Skinnerian tradition, "the animal is always right." If the animal failed to respond to a stimulus as might be expected, the experimenter was at fault and not the animal. The experimenter had overlooked something in the setup. If the human student failed to learn after taking a course of instruction, the fault was the designer's, not the student's. The designer needed to find out what was wrong, not blame the student. And I suppose course developers follow this practice in general. In any case, the warning always makes great fodder for speeches on training at meetings and conventions.

The Legacy of Programmed Instruction

Programmed instruction without the branching option was pretty easy to develop. Fairly soon, the field was inundated with the work for hire of non-psychologists who were able to write equally good frames, despite lacking the foundation of the learning principles borrowed from the training of rats and pigeons in the laboratory. It didn't matter much, since, as I have pointed out, most of the psychologists were not really applying these principles in a sophisticated manner themselves. They simply broke a subject matter down into small steps, and then they tested everything they said. Most people would agree that the results didn't provide much beyond the offerings of an ordinary textbook—which also covered the subject matter and often tested important points at the end of each chapter. Besides, unlike an ordinary book, a programmed textbook generally lacked any table of contents or even an index, so that students might never know where they were going or how to get back to what they had already read. For these reasons, many questioned the value of programmed texts.

In point of fact, most of the psychologists were too busy—either supervising the work of the non-psychologists or marketing and searching for funding—to engage in the pursuit of better instructional design. Probably the main innovation in those years was the ban on copy frames, which everyone realized were a waste of time. For those who have forgotten that copy frames were ever used, I'll briefly explain. At the start of every instruction, the beginning frame presented a definition and then asked students to "write"—"copy"—the definition as their response. I think the origin of this copy-frame-writing practice was the decree that every frame must contain a question for the student to answer. Otherwise, how would the developer know that the student was really attending to the instruction? Copying an answer was at least proof that the student had read the instruction. Besides, what other question could the developer possibly ask the student to answer in that first frame?

But keep in mind that as soon as they could, the writers of early programmed instruction left the writing to others. That was not surprising news. If you've ever tried to write a frame, you know what a boring task this is. Eventually, as we all know, programmed frames of instruction collapsed under their own weight. Only a few concepts survived. One was that each course would start with a set of learning objectives for the students. Another was the principle of individualized learning, based on individual needs, and a course of procedure at one's own pace. The offspring of these concepts is self-instruction, which bears only some minor resemblance to early programmed texts.

Still another concept of programmed instruction that survived is the branching approach. Although it represented a degree of innovation, branching was dropped in a book format because of its cumbersome publishing requirements. But the branching concept has been adapted in many computerized applications, where it can be accomplished by the click of a mouse. Students can study a principle and practice it for as long as necessary.

By the early 1980s, training companies had sprung up everywhere, although many of them faded just as quickly. Training consultants hired themselves out to mega companies that wanted to train their people better. And, actually, training overall did improve as a result of all the attention. School materials changed somewhat too, in that many publishers began to insist on a statement of objectives for every chapter of their textbooks. Also, most teachers learned what behavior modification was all about, and a few even practiced it to some extent. But all of these were small gains compared with the problems at hand. Except with some practitioners of Precision Teaching (see the chapter by Lindsley in this book) and Fluency (Binder, 1993)—and maybe some others I don't know about—the spirit of revolutionary reform seemed to be mostly gone. Around that same time, Tom, with characteristic audacity, proclaimed, "I call the Educational Revolution off."

Tom's Way with Instruction

From the beginning, Tom had set himself apart from the other psychologists. He had dropped frames almost from the outset, refusing to limit instruction to a set physical space. He then began to develop what I believe is now, about forty years later, our most comprehensive system for designing instructional materials. The name he gave it, *mathetics*, was from the Greek root *mathein*, meaning "to learn." Mathetics was his transposition of the learning principles used in training rats and pigeons in the behavioral laboratory to the education and training of human beings in the classroom. However, mathetics as a system did not spring forward, fully formed. It evolved over the years, based mostly on Tom's experiential evidence rather than on any research he had conducted in a laboratory. I like to say that Tom didn't create data himself, but he used the data of others extremely well.

Clearly, early mathetics had some serious shortcomings that inhibited any widespread adoptions. The most obvious of these was its name. In 1960, when Tom was invited to Indianapolis to make a presentation on mathetics to experimenters at the Psychiatric Research Institute of the Indiana University Medical Center, someone misspelled *Mathetics as Mathematics* on the poster announcing his lecture. It was a hot August afternoon in Indianapolis. Hardly anyone wanted to hear a dry presentation on mathematical formulae, so, of course, only a few diehards showed up. But to those who listened—and I was one of these—Tom's presentation was compelling.

But I also saw then that Tom was not infallible, and that his system was not without its faults. One of Tom's early mathetical lessons was to teach young children how to tie their own shoelaces. And since my then five-year-old child needed to learn this skill, I offered Billy as a willing subject. Not realizing it would matter, I neglected to mention that Billy was left-handed. Tom, completely right-handed himself, had developed the lesson always assuming right-handed five-year-olds as subjects, and forgetting about the other 10 percent. The combination was perfect: a very bright teacher and a very bright student, yet the student failed to learn. Tom acknowledged his defeat, renaming his lesson "Teaching Right-Handed Children How to Tie Their Shoelaces." Billy's kindergarten teacher taught him how to tie his shoelaces.

Mathematics was a common substitution for *Mathetics*—with the obvious consequences. Recently, when I edited a paper sprinkled with mentions of *mathetics* while I traveled on the bus to New York City, the man sitting behind me tapped my shoulder and whispered, "Pardon me, ma'am, but *mathematics* is spelled incorrectly on your paper. I thought you'd like to know."

Why Didn't Mathetics Catch On?

In 1962, Tom published his work on mathetics in a journal called *The Journal of Mathetics* (Gilbert, 1962). There were only two issues, the first in January and the last in April of the same year. Tom wrote every article except two: "The Control of Eating," by Charles B. Ferster, John I. Nurnberger, and Eugene B. Levitt, in the January issue; and "The Maintenance of Ongoing Fluent Verbal Behavior and Stuttering," by Israel Goldiamond, in the April issue. Probably so he could convince his readers that mathetics was a widespread movement, and not simply a Gilbertian creation, Tom attributed some of his own articles to other authors, real and invented. Or maybe this was just Tom's joke. We did have some laughs about the famed scientist Dr. Ljungberg Fox.

The Journal of Mathetics was a critical triumph, but the system of mathetics was never a public success. Aside from the confusion between the words *Mathetics* and *Mathematics*, the name *Mathetics* itself connoted academic dryness—exactly what proponents of educational reform always try to avoid. As Tom taught us, the word *mathetics* was not his invention. The word was in fact listed in Webster's *Unabridged Dictionary*, Third Edition, where it was also called archaic. Tom was always very particular about the words he chose to define the concepts he used. But even though he was precise and could cite the dictionary to confirm his choices, often his words had different popular connotations—connotations that interfered with the understanding of the concepts themselves.

I should point out here that those early days produced several real "matheticists"—some of them still at work today. I had the honor of being crowned "M-I" by Tom, meaning the First Matheticist. And we early converts were very enthusiastic—so enthusiastic that early hyperbole was probably another drawback of the mathetics movement. I myself recall faltering, temporarily, when one of Tom's overexcited revolutionaries informed everyone that "we" would drop a mathetical reading bomb over India to wipe out illiteracy in that country forever. Such was the fervor of the people around the charismatic Tom Gilbert.

But there were more serious gaps in the mathetical system and one glaring technical error, which I will discuss shortly. All of these, coupled with its own strangeness, retired mathetics prematurely to a back seat in the public eye of education and training. Even those who admired mathetics viewed it only as an example of Tom's genius, but not as a practical system that others could apply. And there was considerable truth in this view. Tom's students, slogging through cumbersome S→R prescriptions and domain theories, never found the unique solutions to the training problems that Tom was able to discover. He appeared to extract solutions from the ether, rather than from his system. Students of mathetics had to wonder whether the holes were in the system, or were actually in their heads.

Nor did Tom's words assure them of their own worth and restore their self-esteem. He would say that the advantage of applying mathetics was that every matheticist would come up with the same solution. How dismaying to find that it wasn't true. Nor, of course, could it be true even now, when mathetics is a much more complete system. I probably should say *especially* now. That's because Tom's insistence that every matheticist would produce the same results violated another of his beliefs: that the way to generate the most differences would be to teach everyone the same skills. He thought that in education, individual differences are confused with the value we place on human individuality. We fear that individuality will be destroyed if we teach all people the same skills. This fear arises, Tom said, from the common view that the ability to perform and the decision to perform are at equal strength in people. Tom pointed out that art schools have traditionally avoided teaching traditional skills, presumably to protect the student's creativity, which Tom assumed meant the student's decision to use these skills in unusual combinations (Gilbert, 1962).

Typically, though, Tom's students never challenged him; they accepted nearly everything he said—even when he seemed to contradict himself. Mathetics is a system that depends on the art of human beings to apply. But people can apply the same skills in different ways. An individual may even apply the same skills in different ways at different times. And we have only to recognize and appreciate the differences in pieces of pottery handcrafted by the same potter to know that we human beings have a way of incorporating our own uniqueness into our work. We never can reproduce either ourselves or our products in exactly the same way twice. *Sameness* is for computers and other machines. What makes mathetics so intriguing to me is that it provides the principles and the tools that even a novice can apply to a subject matter—and then enjoy the possibility of creating something new and wonderful.

Besides these points, my own private view of what really set mathetics back was the serious error I alluded to earlier. In his attempt to transpose principles of learning from animals to people, Tom tried to apply the principle of chaining to human beings in the same way experimenters work with animals. Experimenters proceed backwards, step by step in the chain, always showing the animal what it would accomplish by performing the next step. Likewise, Tom advised early matheticists to start the development of a mathetical lesson by teaching the last step first, and then to work backwards step by step to the beginning. In a linear process, the last mathetical step would actually be the first step. In learning long division, for example, students were to start with the result and work backwards to the last step, which was to set up the problem by identifying the dividend and the divisor and positioning them properly. Long division had been a nemesis for Tom in grammar school, he told me. I had been a math major in college, but trying to develop a long division lesson according to Tom's mathetical design was my nemesis as a matheticist. I remember protesting, "My mind doesn't work that way."

But Tom was stubborn. I recall his returning home after one early convention of developers with an enormous gash on his head. Colleagues teasing him about his use of the principle of chaining had challenged him to explain how he would teach diving. Tom insisted he would do this mathetically, last step first. After inviting everyone to the hotel pool, he demonstrated. (I suspect a few trips to the hotel bar had preceded the poolside lesson.) This bravado certainly confirmed his confidence in the principle of chaining. And since he knew the headlong plunge would be the first step, he was aware that a mathetical diving lesson could have some serious consequences. What he didn't know, though, was that the pool didn't have enough water for a proper demonstration.

Eventually, of course, Tom did yield the point of chaining a procedure in a backwards sequence. (Some instructional designers cling to chaining as a teaching device, calling it "backwards chaining," and I can't comment about this because perhaps there are some occasions when this methodology is appropriate.) Tom conceded that the tactic we must employ in teaching a procedure to people must be different from the tactic we would employ with animals. Human beings have a common language, which we share. If animals have a common language—and many say they do—it isn't one they share with us. We have to show animals what comes next; we can't simply tell them.

The principle of first pointing out what the learning should accomplish became the cornerstone of all of Tom's later work. He started every project, whether training was involved or not, by first defining the mission and the major accomplishments; and he started every instructional lesson by first telling the students what they were expected to accomplish.

In the leap from animals to human beings, Tom didn't have to give up the principles of learning that had already been confirmed by animal research. These principles held, whether for human beings or for animals. What had to be different were the tactics that could be employed. Just as experimenters had to vary their tactics somewhat when they switched to different animal subjects, they would need to arrange a whole set of different accommodations when they worked with human beings.

The Search for the Reinforcer
and the Myths It Produced

What makes human beings learn? Or, better, what will motivate the human animal to learn? As Charlie Slack, an early *Revolutionary Extraordinaire*, put it, our students are not knocking at the doors of knowledge thirsting for education (Slack, 1962). Hardly.

Probably the most significant difference between the design of an animal experiment and one with human beings is that with animals, the reinforcer is never in doubt. Before any experimentation ever begins, animals are starved to 80 percent of their total body weight. (Animal rights enthusiasts can be assured that the animals are kept healthy while on this rigid diet.) The animals are put into the experimental room or cage only when they are hungry, and they work at learning only until they are sated. When they succeed at performing a simple task, they are reinforced with food. They eat when they're hungry; they quit when they're full. It's as simple as that. Animals don't work for the love of the learning they receive; they work for food. So, what should we do with human beings? Starve them down to 80 percent of body weight? If it's not the love of learning itself that drives them, what can we give to people that will motivate them to learn and will reinforce them when they do?

Money is the obvious answer, yet not even money is a foolproof reinforcer for human behavior. And even if money is sufficiently rewarding, the provider of the reinforcement must be sure that the behavior being rewarded is the behavior he or she wants to reoccur. Parents who try to reward their children's "A's" and "B's" with dollars, thinking they are teaching a love of learning, can only count on the possibility of creating richer children. They are not reinforcing the learning in itself—only the value they and their school place on that learning. In my own experience, I recall my ex-husband, Charlie Ferster—a distinguished behavioral scientist—silently and repeatedly pulling our errant two-year-old son away from a piece of furniture. What the toddler didn't know was that Charlie's intent here was to extinguish the climbing behavior. Charlie, of course, was attempting to apply the principle that behavior ceases if it is not reinforced. But people surrounded by a multiplicity of stimuli in the free environment are not so easy to control. They will respond to the stimulus of highest strength to them, and too bad what the experimenter had in mind. Instead of extinguishing or even diminishing, Sam's climbing behavior became more frequent and was accompanied by great whoops of laughter. What really happened was that Charlie was providing the child with a span of his attention, which actually reinforced the behavior he thought he was extinguishing.

We would suppose that no one would dispute the fact that people do pretty much what it pays off for them to do. But if you ever voice this to a group of people, someone will object, since the "paying" seems to imply money, and we all acknowledge Shakespeare's "filthy lucre." Who knows for sure what a good reinforcer would be for you: Is it money, power, attention, compliments? Or is it simply a love for learning new things? Besides, what reinforces you may not be what reinforces me.

So, we can't be surprised that the early developers of programmed instruction worried about the reinforcer they could use with people to induce them to learn. They reasoned that even though they couldn't use food as the reinforcer for human beings, they could still apply the principles of reinforcement. For example, the results in animal laboratories proved that the reinforcement—whatever it was—needed to follow the desired behavior immediately. Otherwise, the animal wouldn't be able to associate the reward with the behavior that produced it. They also knew that any behavior they didn't want would extinguish if it were not reinforced. Their assumption for human learners of programmed instruction, then, was that a right answer immediately following every question not only confirmed the learning, but also reinforced it. In other words, right answers would be motivating enough to maintain the learning provided they checked their answers soon after the learning. This implied, of course, the students' insatiable appetite for right answers and their need for the immediacy of the confirmation, since, otherwise, they might not know why they were being reinforced. Some researchers thought that "dirty" pictures might be reinforcing enough to keep people learning. Again, this implied the student's insatiable appetite for such pictures and their need to know they were right, lest they become confused.

Furthermore, the developers warned that students must not see incorrect answers for fear that these inappropriate responses would become fixed in their heads. They would then learn the incorrect responses rather than the desired ones. And, certainly, animals would become confused if we reinforced their mistakes. Again, human beings are considerably more complex, and they are hardly in a controlled environment. I believe these developers also forgot how much they themselves have learned just because they did make mistakes. I also wonder whether they underestimated the desire that some people can have to learn some things and their persistence, no matter how many times they may have failed earlier.

I believe this prohibition on mistakes contradicts another learning principle that the behavioral scientists have always espoused: "To learn, one has to emit lots of behavior." I don't know how many times I have heard psychologists say that. Logically, we would expect fear of making mistakes to inhibit the emission of lots of behavior. Yet fear of making mistakes doesn't prevent children from emitting all the behavior needed to learn how to ride a two-wheeler. They try and fail, try and fail, try and fall, until—suddenly—they're aloft. Obviously, the ultimate goal of riding the bike is reinforcing enough to sustain all that failure. And, as anyone will tell you, once we learn to ride a bike, we have with us a skill we never forget.

Tom's definition of a creative person was someone who made a lot of mistakes. (His actual words were much saltier.) Creative people emit lots of behavior: Some of it is great, some of it is not so great, and some of it is nonsense. He cited baseball's great home run kings, who also struck out considerably more often than average hitters. Lots of behavior and an acceptance of some inevitable failure characterize the creative person.

Although Tom's mathetical lessons demanded right answers, he obviously didn't have the same fear of mistakes the other developers exhibited. Because of his emphasis on lean programming, not all students would be able to achieve 100 percent success initially on a mathetical lesson. Perhaps the student lacked a prerequisite skill, or perhaps the matheticist had overlooked a critical step. No matter. The student would make a mistake and the proper correction would be made. On the other hand, if the matheticist had anticipated and provided for all possible contingencies, the training might have been unnecessarily long, because there would be no way of knowing if the student would have learned despite the omission.

I should interject a disclaimer here about the principle of making mistakes. Obviously, Tom did not extend this freedom to make mistakes to the learning of all skills. Flying an airplane is one skill that must be learned perfectly, with no permission for mistakes. Basic skills, too, must be learned so thoroughly as to be fluent. Otherwise, they will inhibit the learning of more advanced skills that depend on them (Binder, 1993). I suppose that in our pursuit of how people learn, we should avoid the impression of a handy generalization. The safest assumption is that nothing works all the time.

Tom addressed the issue of motivation and reinforcement of behavior in a different way. As a start, he defined "motivation" as having two aspects: "intrinsic" motivation and "extrinsic" motivation. And what we really should consider is the transaction between the two. Intrinsic motivation, or the inner desire to learn, resides deep within the person. Although Tom agreed that some people simply had a deep built-in thirst for knowledge and other people didn't have this same thirst, he didn't pretend to know how to change anyone's thirst or lack of it. Nor did he think that anyone else knew any more than he about how to accomplish this change.

Extrinsic motivation, on the other hand, consists of the incentives that can be applied to reinforce learning so that it will continue. In industry, keeping a job is the main incentive; people either need to learn how to do their jobs—or risk losing them. Other common incentives for maintaining performance are well-known: money, power, attention, and—of course—success. Furthermore, these incentives can be applied in accordance with the various schedules of reinforcement defined by the Skinnerian researchers. Tom addressed the issue of extrinsic motivation at length, producing some remarkable incentive systems for salespeople and others. Not one of these incentive systems, however, is guaranteed to increase the love of learning.

In his instructional materials, however, Tom didn't incorporate any incentives besides right answers. Like others, he believed that young children have a natural love for learning, and their reinforcement is their ability to navigate their environment. Once they accomplish this, however, many kids get turned off to learning in school, and Tom would theorize as well as anyone else about why this happens. But he believed in the power of good instructional design to overcome any resistance to learning. He would say that unless students are in some way incapacitated, they will learn if presented with instructional materials of excellent design, and then the learning in itself would be reinforcing. Of course, we really don't know whether this is true or not; but in seeking cures for our educational system, providing good instructional design as extrinsic motivation should be a potential solution worthy of our consideration.

This search for a reinforcer—usually known as a motivator—is a pervasive legacy of the early educational revolutionists. In training departments today, although we see some efforts at simulation, particularly with online operations, as well as some games in which the learning is applied, we still continue to see mostly the same traditional teaching methods, such as straight lecture and leader-led instruction. Some training directors, having read somewhere that "learning should be fun," try to lighten up the dullness of the training materials by employing a theme—a trip to foreign lands, for example, when a tour of a system is required. These themes are harmless in themselves, except for the extra time the course developers must take to design them, but in the main, they do nothing to promote learning.

So many simplistic solutions are offered—the endless tapes of pep talks presented to new salespeople, for example. Still, the search continues, and mostly it produces more talk than deeds. Many training directors repeat the truism that everyone learns differently—some by seeing, some by hearing, and so on. But I have never seen a course designer, in preparation for developing a training project, pretest every target student's learning style first, then, having done so, offer different sets of the training to accommodate the different styles of learning. Nor do I imagine that learning will improve appreciably if we rely on new delivery systems like computers without making a substantial investment in excellent design.

But not everything is bleak. In classrooms where Precision Teaching and the techniques of fluency are employed, everyone there is engaged. Instructors are the directors, orchestrating the students' responses as a group learning basic math or English. The students I observed at Malcolm X College, for example, were extremely motivated to learn (Laynge, 1994). After having received diplomas from a Chicago high school, they still didn't qualify to enter even a two-year college—never mind the University of Chicago. They also knew that failure to acquire basic skills would doom them to an underclass life forever.

The instruction in the remedial classroom was extremely stylized. Instructors couldn't simply pick up the special instructor guides and expect to use them to conduct a class without any preparation. They had to study these guides and practice their delivery before facing a group of students. As I watched the interactive performance between teachers and students at Malcolm X College, I was fascinated. To critics who complain that students are learning by rote, I can only say that students did actually appear to be learning to perform quickly by repetition and practice. Undoubtedly, the system was a major improvement over any existing classroom instruction of adult students that I had seen before.

What the course developers in search of a fun theme or a solution to the different styles of learning should do first is to master all of the recognized principles of instructional design. Then they can try to incorporate the applicable principles into some novel method that will take a potentially dull subject matter and transform it into something that becomes fun, or at least interesting to learn. Tom was able to do this. To me, that seemed to be happening at Malcolm X College as well.

Tom's Instructional Design

Tom developed the best system of instructional design that exists anywhere today. Why doesn't everyone already know about it? Why don't they teach his methods in schools for instructional design?

A natural preference for performance technology can't claim all the blame for the lackluster interest in what Tom knew about instructional design. Let's give some of that blame to Tom himself. I can also share some secrets that might explain Tom's share of this blame. First, *The Journal of Mathetics* is hard to follow, and it certainly is not intended for those who must engage in just-in-time training. Some of the material is out of date, and it's also incomplete. Tom himself didn't follow all the procedures he prescribed in *The Journal of Mathetics*, or in his other writings on design, when he developed instruction.

I suppose Tom was like the other experts he warned us about. As he advised, we must *observe* what the experts do when they work; we cannot rely on what they say about what they do. This is not because they are trying to confuse us or they don't want to share their secrets with us, but because they may not know precisely what they really do. Even though Tom never wrote down, step by step, exactly what he even thought he did, he has written enough and I have observed him at work enough to be able to deduce and describe his methodology—not perfectly, perhaps, but reasonably well. Tom, I hope, would forgive me for ignoring his work on the performance audit here, since he has already described this system at length elsewhere. I will limit my descriptions to just his approach to the instructional design itself.

What I have learned especially from watching Tom, and with or without his verbal prompting, was that he always tackled a problem in the same way. He started by defining what he called the mastery model for the performance. What should this instruction accomplish? What do we want students of this instruction to be able to do once they leave the training room? Here, Tom did not rely on what clients said they wanted. He snooped around, he asked many questions, and he noticed what people were doing. When he was asked to develop a training course for pre-divestiture AT&T repair clerks, for example, the client had in mind the usual kind of scenario: answering the phone, handling the irate customer, and so on. But this emphasis on irate customers got Tom wondering why people were so angry. He found that the customer was mad because, after calling to report the problem, there was a wait for a tester to come out to the house to assess the problem. If it was one requiring a repair inside the home, there was another wait until a repairman could be dispatched there. The repair clerk was simply making the appointments, and the customer was hard to reach because the phone—remember—was out of order. Tom found that all the tester did was to determine whether the problem could be solved in the central office, or whether the repair had to be made in the house—a decision that actually could be made by asking a few key questions. Tom reasoned that if the repair clerk could be trained to ask these questions, the central office could make the repair immediately, or else the clerk could make the appointment for the home repair. A tester wasn't needed, and the customer didn't have either an opportunity to be irate, or the need: The customer was too busy answering key questions to vent rage at the repair clerk.

The tool that Tom used to define the mastery model of the repair clerk training we recognize as the Behavior Engineering Model, even though he hadn't yet formulated it. By using the method of the Behavior Engineering Model, he completely changed the mission and the mastery model of the training he later developed.

The mastery model is not always clearcut in education, either. What do we want our students to be able to do after studying history, for example? Tom suggested four possible mastery models:

- History can be defined as a written record of past events. In that case, we would want our students to be able to maintain such a written record. Our students could then become library scholars and teachers.

- History can be defined as what storytellers do: relate and interpret the events of the past. Students could become journalists, propagandists, essayists, or historical novelists.

- History could be defined as what history makers do. In that case, we could train our kids to be politicians, philosophers, or even revolutionaries.

- History could be defined as a model to learn from. In that case, we could teach our children to be explainers of the past and predictors of the future.

Tom asked about a hundred people which mastery model they might choose for their own children. Just about all of them chose the last model: They wanted their children to be able to deduce the variables that help account for events; then forecast the direction present events might take, and, finally, perhaps even visualize how to alter them. This is not what happens in the schools, as we all know. Too often, history teachers take the easy course, requiring their students to match a series of events with a series of dates; a very forgettable exercise.

I have applied this S→R paradigm to many problems myself. In education, particularly, I have applied it to teaching people how to edit their writing. I often say that Tom taught me the difference between a stimulus and a response, but I don't mean this literally. What I really mean is that he taught me to notice what the stimulus is, and then let this stimulus drive the response I want the student to make. For editing, I wanted students to be able to recognize situations in their own writing that would confuse or bore their readers. This led me to discover something significant about how we typically teach writing and English grammar in particular. Instead of teaching students how to recognize the troublespots in their own writing, educators concentrate on teaching students to make responses. This describes precisely what the schools do in teaching punctuation: "Here's how to use the comma . . ." "Here's how to use the semicolon. . . ." And so on. All are responses, which students then forget to use in their own writing, because they never learned to recognize their own troublespots and to then select out and apply the appropriate responses to them.

So, Tom's Part One on the road to excellent instructional design was to select the mastery model, using the tools of the Behavior Engineering Model and the Probe Diagnostic Questions. Once he had selected the mastery model, he then defined it—rigorously. Part Two is deciding which behaviors must be performed in order to produce the mastery model, and Tom had a method here as well. Either in his head or on paper, he drew an S→R paradigm to represent the accomplishment he wanted to produce, given the stimulus that presented itself. This paradigm is a powerhouse in that it permits the designer to define the problem exactly. If you want a repair clerk to ask key questions rather than make an appointment for a tester, your procedures will be quite different. If you want your students to be able to explain and predict, your procedure will be much different from the procedure you would design so that students could match a set of dates with historical events. Once the scope is limited, the next step is to find a solution—and not just *any* solution, but the *best* solution. And Tom always reasoned that the best solution was also the shortest solution.

To pick the best solution, Tom tested all the possible paths that he could follow to produce that accomplishment, and then he picked the one that would produce the results most effectively and efficiently under the other constrictions that usually exist—like money and time. The question is, how do you find all the possible paths you might use? Here, again, Tom called on the Probe Diagnostic Questions—ideal for helping designers find solutions to a performance problem once we know exactly what we want to cure. That's because instruction cannot exist effectively and efficiently in a vacuum. In deciding on the type of instruction, we must consider the kinds of direction that might be needed, the kind of feedback that might be required, the procedures that would be most efficient, and so on.

Now for Tom's Part Three, the instruction itself. As I've said, probably Tom's main contribution to instructional design was to apply to human beings so many of the learning principles that emerged from routine basic experiments with animal subjects in the animal laboratories. In doing so, of course, he made extrapolations required for working with human beings. He has described this basic course of instruction for human beings as a *Progression*, relating each step to the action the experimenter takes with an animal subject.

What experimenters do first is introduce the animal to the experimental environment. Tom called Step 1 in a progression for human subjects the *inductive*, in which we familiarize the students with the subject matter to be learned. This is usually accomplished in an overview, now typically called the "big picture," or perhaps an analogy. Another hope for the inductive is that it could possibly also motivate the person to learn. This might happen, for example, if we said why it was important to learn this skill—or, sometimes, what might happen if students *failed* to learn that skill.

Next, Step 2, is to teach any preliminary skills. For a rat, this step is to teach the animal how to reach its food—its reinforcement. This is necessary because experimenters use naive animals so their results will be pure. Naive animals, of course, need to be trained how to perform this elementary skill, but Step 2 for human beings is not always necessary. In many jobs, employees are selected because they already have the preliminary skills. Nowadays, though, since so much of even entry-level work is done on computers, this is less likely to be true. New hires may have never used a computer before. These people would require some preliminary training—or, as Tom first called it, a *Propaedeutic*. After subjecting him to a lot of harassment, I was able to persuade him to change this word to *Tools*. I'm not sure this is an accurate-enough term, but it's an improvement.

Step 3 is to teach the rat the essentials of the task—that bar pressing produces food, but that the food is present only when a light is on. The teaching is accomplished through rewards of food. But since the animal will not perform correctly at first, the experimenter will reward successive approximations to the performance so that it won't become discouraged and quit. Behavior is then "shaped" by the gradual increase in the level of performance demanded of it, until it reaches the desired standard. Unfortunately, Step 3 is probably the most ignored of all steps in a teaching progression for human subjects. Yet students learn the steps of a skill better if they are given the essential elements of the system first—a generalization or concept explaining the behavior. If we were teaching a student how to troubleshoot and repair a turbine engine, for example, a necessary concept would be how a turbine works. Students should know that heat from burning gas fuel makes a fan turn. This first fan is connected to a second fan, which draws in oxygen and compresses it—that is, it keeps up the pressure. The result is a non-reciprocating engine that runs without exploding fuel.

Tom called Step 3 the *Theory*, so it was always confused with the traditional notion of the many theories and background information about a subject that only dedicated scholars needed or cared to know. Later, he changed the name of this step to *Concept*.

Step 4 is to teach the skills of mastery, which Tom called the *Praxis*. Here, the animal is taught how to make the required discriminations. In many organizations today, course developers for the training of human subjects are likely to attend to only the skill training, but they do this in the absence of any knowledge about how to teach these discriminations. Finally, Step 5, the *Application*, is to apply this training in a real setting. Tom distinguished this step from Step 4. But I think his example of letting the rat perform before an audience as the application of the skill is contrived. With animals, application is not even a step. With human beings, it is *the* major step, which is why a simulation for teaching the skill (Step 4) is ideal. Step 5 is appropriate in only those rare situations in which students cannot learn the skill directly.

The progression is basic to any instruction. But, depending on the subject matter, other tactics of learning methodology can be applied to great advantage, depending on the pattern of the behavior. Tom was the first to note that full-scale instruction was not always required for providing knowledge that people needed in order to do their jobs. In fact, he documented the criteria for determining when to use training and when to use guidance. He also designed and used three different kinds of guidance, again depending on the pattern of the behavior required. The simplest of these is what he called the *Directory*, which he would prescribe for a step-by-step procedure or a checklist. He called a second type of guidance an *Ensampler*, which he used to teach a skill that is never performed in exactly the same way twice. How about an ensampler for the teaching of instructional design? for the preparation of taxes? and a million other skills. Probably the most interesting of the lot was the *Query*, which he used to teach people a skill for which the student is the authority and best able to make the ultimate decisions.

When full-scale instruction was actually required, Tom was able to employ behavioral science, and with unusual results. One scientific principle that Tom applied with particular success was shaping—letting the subjects make successive approximations to a solution. To do this, he worked from the general context in which the behavior occurs, down to the specific behavior to be taught. What happens is that the student is led gradually to make the specific response desired.

Often, in using shaping, Tom also applied the common-sense principle that a picture is worth a thousand words. Of course, the picture has this value only if it can be used instead of the words. For the Centers for Disease Control project to teach lab technicians how to detect the presence of amoebiasis in lab specimen, which I mentioned earlier, Tom's design was a brief booklet of pictures. In the first set, he showed the gross difference between perfect and imperfect cells. Next, he gradually narrowed the imperfections until students were actually discriminating between healthy cells and diseased cells. What Tom did—what Tom *always* did—was to peel the onion.

In another training project—this time, for an airline manufacturer—I recall we were asked to develop materials that would train technicians to assemble parts in the wing of an airplane. Most course developers would have approached this task in the usual tedious way, explaining the details on the blueprints step by step. What Tom did instead was to design a series of drawings and then hire a graphic artist to produce them. First, the artist created drawings of the whole wing, showing exactly where the major parts belonged. Next, he drew pictures of the interconnections, so the students could see how everything fit. Then the students looked at pictures of the small parts they would be working with; they saw the parts and the connections that they would make. (Nowadays, of course, computerized drawings could produce that design in half the time.)

In 1992, Tom and I wrote up a method we have used to teach children multiplication (Gilbert & Gilbert, 1992). This example illustrates several other scientific principles that Tom used routinely. Whereas most teachers start with the 1s, we dismiss the 1s—the children already know them. We advise heading out with the 6s, 7s, and 8s, instead. Our rationale is to teach the hard discriminations first, when they are easier to learn without the competition of the easier discriminations. With our sequence, the discriminations gets easier as the children go. The traditionalists usually teach the 2s next. But we say to teach the 6s, 7s, and 8s together simultaneously. The principle here is to group the most confusing stimuli together. This tactic forces the children to notice what is different about them so they can make the discriminations and remember them easily. We then say to teach the 9s and 5s last, because these are supported by excellent memory aids. Overall, we advise requiring high speed from the very beginning, since fluency is mastery, and letting students know their progress instantly, since they need to know how well they do at all times.

Conclusion

The variety of Tom's instructional solutions was so vast that I cannot record them all here. Overall, though, if I dare to generalize about what Tom did that made him great, I would say that he always adapted his methods to the pattern of the behavior required to accomplish mastery. No easy roads or handy bandwagons for him.

When I agreed to write this chapter, I didn't realize what a bold and difficult undertaking this would be. It is my small contribution to ensuring that while Tom inevitably had to take his behaviors with him, enough of his real accomplishments would be left behind.

References

Binder, C. (1966). Personal communication.

Binder, C. (1993). Behavioral fluency: A new paradigm. *Educational Technology, 33*(10).

Evans, J. (1996). Personal communication.

Ferster, C. B., Nurnberger, J. I., & Levitt, E. B. (1962). The control of eating. *The Journal of Mathetics,* Vol. 1.

Ferster, C. B., & Skinner, B. F. (1957). *Schedules of reinforcement.* New York: Appleton-Century-Crofts.

Gilbert, T. F. (1960). Unpublished manuscript.

Gilbert, T. F. (1962). *The Journal of Mathetics,* Vol. 1.

Gilbert, T. F. (1978, 1996). *Human competence: Engineering worthy performance.* New York: McGraw-Hill; Washington, DC: ISPI.

Gilbert, T. F., & Gilbert, M. B. (1992). Potential contributions of performance science in education. *Journal of Applied Behavior Analysis, 24.*

Goldiamond, I. (1962). The maintenance of on-going fluent verbal behavior and stuttering. *The Journal of Mathetics,* Vol. 1.

Laynge, J. (1994). Personal communication.

Mager, R. W. (1962, 1970). *Preparing instructional objectives.* Palo Alto, CA: Fearon.

Slack, C. (1962). Personal communication.

[Handwritten annotations at top of page: "constructivist → building blocks to move to next step of learning"]

4

Reflections on Constructivism and Instructional Design

[Handwritten annotations: "no pre-conceived notion of the content to be discussed" / "objectivism - set objectives + content to be discussed"]

Brent G. Wilson
University of Colorado at Denver

The field of instructional design (ID) is in a state of rapid change. Recent expressions of constructivist theorists (Bednar, Cunningham, Duffy, & Perry, 1991; Duffy & Jonassen, 1992) have engendered a lively debate. If our Instructional Technology (IT) department is any indication, graduate students across the nation are engaging their professors in heated discussions concerning the fundamental models in our field, and how these models hold up to the constructivist onslaught.

This is good. I feel better about the future of ID than I have since I was a graduate student myself. For years, M. David Merrill has pled that more serious attention be given to the development of ID theory. He finally seems to be getting his wish, but perhaps not the result he anticipated. For a long time, thoughts about the nature of ID theory and its practice have been fermenting in my mind. This chapter is a forum for developing some of those thoughts and sharing them with a wider audience. The tone is personal because it deals with underlying assumptions I have made in doing ID. In a way, the paper is a sort of confessional—my tone and stance are much less temperate than in any of my previous writings. Narrative forms of research have recently been gaining esteem among educators and social scientists (Connelly & Clandinin, 1990; Polkinghorne, 1988; Witherell & Noddings, 1991); I ask you to consider this chapter a sort of narrative documentation of my professional beliefs about ID.

A Short Personal History—Why I Care About This

In the nearly two decades that I have been associated with instructional design, I have seen a gradual but painful transition from behavioristic roots toward a broader theory base. As a graduate student, I was privileged to have worked closely with M. David Merrill and Charles M. Reigeluth at Brigham Young University, particularly in the development of elaboration theory (Reigeluth, Merrill, Wilson, & Spiller, 1978, 1980). I bought into the field—its theories, models, and aims—yet I always felt an ambivalence toward what I perceived as cut-and-dried design prescriptions in areas that I felt so personally "mushy" about. My respect for the complexity and difficulty of design decisions always made me hesitant about explicit, canned procedures and models that were meant to answer all questions. I felt that ID lacked a sense of perspective or a sense of modesty toward the awesome task of meeting people's learning needs. Recently I came across some old notes I had made, dated 15 March 1978, titled "Issues that still haven't been resolved in SSDP" (Structural Strategy Diagnostic Profile—the old name for elaboration theory). Excerpts of those notes are reproduced in Table 1. Re-reading those notes reminded me that many of the issues are still pertinent to today's discussion, including the nature of knowledge and content, the role of context, parts versus wholes, and accommodation of alternative structures. The task of adapting ID theories to address these issues still remains.

In the ID articles I have written since then, I have tried to steer a delicate balance between being too accepting of the "received view" about ID and being too radical. I did not want to lose my audience. My moderate tone sometimes belied the urge within to shout, "Wait—don't you see? We've got it wrong!" That urge was heightened by the recent comments of an anonymous IT/SIG reviewer on a paper critiquing elaboration theory (Wilson & Cole, 1992):

> You have put your finger on a fundamental difference in approaches taken by those who believe that instruction can be designed to teach knowledge and those who believe that knowledge is constructed by learners . . . I would go so far to say that the two positions are irreconcilable. If you accept what the "humanistic theorists" say, then you cannot simply revise [elaboration theory] in the ways you propose to make it fit in with these views. You have to throw it out entirely!

I'm not as pessimistic about the possibility of reconciliation. *In fact, that is a major theme of this chapter, that there can be a constructivist theory of instructional design.* But I am coming to believe that the best way to handle theoretical differences is not to be coy, not to down-

---

Table 1.   Excerpts from my elaboration theory, circa 1978.

How do our ideas of structure relate to learning/ memory theorists' ideas about how memory is organized? Mayer, Greeno, Ausubel, Kintsch, Craik & Tulving, Norman & Lindsey, Quillian & Collins, McConkie, etc. . . .

The problem of "segmentation": Are we sure the contents of a discipline can be broken down into individual concepts, principles, etc.? What about what theorists call "verbal information," "meaningful verbal materials"—facts that are important to know but don't connect to any principles directly . . . Are we rather talking about a mere skeleton in our work, which, to be complete, needs to be fleshed out by facts, details, context, etc.? . . .

It seems to me that there are certain kinds of content whose purposes do not admit to use of synthesizers/epitomes or an elaborative approach. Narratives, for example, often have a dramatic component, as if the teacher/author were telling a story. It would be senseless to let the cat out of the bag prematurely simply to "stabilize" the content for the learner. An effective alternative (in certain situations) is having the student on the edge of his seat waiting in suspense for what happens next. . . .

Bruner (1966) distinguishes between passive and active learning, between what we know and what we do with what we know. How do these seemingly separable kinds of knowledge relate to our scheme? Is true active learning on the rule-finding or rule-using level? Are procedures and principles real problem-solving behaviors? Would Ausubel object that we devalue facts and verbal information unnecessarily? . . .

Is 'content' defined as "What is," "What is presented to the student," or "What is expected to be learned?"

play problems, but to be honest and straightforward in criticism, and aggressive in offering alternative design concepts. My experience has now started me to wondering how many other professionals who, rather than confront their problems with the models, have simply walked away from the problem by disengaging themselves from the models or from the field.

On the Objectivist/Constructivist Debate

Rather than comprehensively examining the issue, I want to raise a few selected points. Still, the central claims of constructivism should become apparent after reading this section.

1. *Constructivism is more a philosophy, not a strategy.* In general, I reject the idea that a particular instructional strategy is inherently constructivistic or objectivistic. Constructivism is not an instructional strategy to be deployed under appropriate conditions. Rather, constructivism is an underlying philosophy or way of seeing the world. This way of seeing the world includes notions about:

- the nature of *reality* (mental representations have "real" ontological status just as the "world out there" does);
- the nature of *knowledge* (it's individually constructed; it is inside people's minds, not "out there");
- the nature of *human interaction* (we rely on shared or "negotiated" meanings, better thought of as cooperative than authoritative or manipulative in nature); and
- the nature of *science* (it is a meaning-making activity with the biases and filters accompanying any human activity).

When we see the world in constructivist terms, we go about our jobs in a different way, but the difference cannot be reduced to a discrete set of rules or techniques. Let me give an example.

My son Joel recently turned eight, and for his birthday we presented him with a computer-based math-drill game. He is a good math problem-solver—he likes to play with numbers and invent routines—but because of a schooling mixup, he is behind in mastering his math facts. I essentially said, "Joel, this is a fun game you will enjoy; it will also help you learn the addition and subtraction skills that you're a little behind in. It's no big deal. You will be glad, because learning that stuff is something you want, too."

Does my gift of a drill-and-practice program make me an objectivist? I deny that it does. I also deny that I am violating my deeply held constructivist principles about people and the way we learn. People do construct meaning from their experiences; learning should be meaningful and derive from an authentic context; people should be allowed to pursue individual learning goals. I believe that Joel has a pretty good idea of what the game is doing for him, and the kind of fun he is deriving from it. As he chooses to make use of the game, he *is* actively constructing meaning and new knowledge. Joel has plenty of other opportunities to exercise his more creative talents; his use of the game is filling a needed learning gap to meet the expectations and pace set by his school. He was much happier in school two weeks later, when he aced the timed math test and came home to tell us about it.

My point is that a given instructional strategy takes on meaning as it is used, in a particular context. If I had tricked my son, "Joel, look at this computer game. It's better than Nintendo!" and pretended that he was already great at his math facts, and that the game had no bearing on his schooling, then I would have felt in violation of my philosophy. So the same instructional technique can have vastly different meaning (and effects) depending on its context of use.

Another example—a journal entry from Scott, a teacher in my *Reflective Educator* class in a recent semester:

> Third hour composition I went to a seating chart, the first time I've done that here. I caught them as they came in and told them where to sit. Great improvement. Everyone working hard on their papers. . . . I sense the students are relieved that I've imposed more structure.

Scott teaches at an alternative high school. His philosophy, as expressed in journal entries, class contributions, and teaching methods, is definitely constructivistic and anti-authoritarian. Yet imposing a seating chart on a class is a clear act of asserting authoritative control and imposing structure. Is Scott betraying his principles, or can an ostensibly "objectivist" instructional technique actually serve his constructivist learning and teaching goals? The students' answer to that is clear: they welcome the new arrangement and view it as supporting their own learning goals.

Too often, constructivism is equated with low structure and permissiveness—imposing predefined learning goals or a learning method is somehow interfering with students' construction of meaning. In extreme cases, that may be true. Yet to help students become creative, some kind of discipline and structure must be provided. Laurel (1991) cites Rollo May (1975), who makes this point very well:

> Creativity arises out of the tension between spontaneity and limitations, the latter (like river banks) forcing the spontaneity into the various forms which are essential to the work of art. . . . The significance of limits in art is seen most clearly when we consider the question of form. Form provides the essential boundaries and structure for the creative act. (quoted in Laurel, 1991, p. 101)

In other words, an instructional strategy that imposes structure may actually help learners make constructions needed for learning. Joel's computer game or Scott's seating chart may be hindering or serving constructivist learning goals. You can't tell by looking only at the strategy; you have to look at the entire situation and make a judgment. That is the role of the teacher or instructional designer—to make professional judgments about such things.

2. *You don't have to be a philosopher to take a position.* Among the contributors to Duffy & Jonassen (1992), originally appearing in the May and September 1991 issues of *Educational Technology*, Perkins and Cunningham have considerable training in philosophy, but to my knowledge the remaining writers are, like you and me, relative novices in that domain. Our interest in these issues derives from a desire to do the right thing, and to be knowledgeable about sources of bias and damaging assumptions we can make in our work. I hope that practitioners and researchers do not defer to the "experts" on issues so central to defining the field. At the same time, I am busy trying to expand my breadth and knowledge base about philosophy. As I read more Schön, more Bruner, and more postmodern philosophy, my perspective toward ID is necessarily influenced. That change in perception is for the good; I like the feeling that I am growing in my understanding of the meaning of my field. (And I confess I tend to grow impatient with fellow researchers who show no inclination to broaden their understanding of the issues squarely facing the field.)

3. *Nobody I know admits to being an objectivist.*[1] Objectivism, in the context of the debate within instructional design, is not a true philosophy; rather, as Molenda (1991) points out, it is primarily a pejorative label given by constructivists to the offending others (Bruner,

---

[1] That was true at the time of writing; since that time, I have met a couple of colleagues who claim to be objectivists. However, I have blocked their names out of my consciousness!

1986; Johnson, 1984; Lakoff, 1987). That fact alone is enough cause to worry. It's hard to talk seriously about a philosophical position that no one admits to. This goes for caricatures made by both ideological sides of the dialogue. Very few people hold radical positions of either persuasion.

Please note that my complaint has to do with labels and descriptions; there are many people who may not call themselves objectivists, but whose way of seeing may be very different from a constructivist perspective. Philosophers holding this more traditional view of the world call themselves *realists* (House, 1991; H. Putnam, 1990). To my understanding, realists do believe that there is a "reality" out there, and that the quality of mental representations can be judged by their correspondence to that reality. This "correspondence theory of truth" is one of the many issues hotly debated by philosophers. If they can disagree about it, I imagine the rest of us can as well.

The cross-talking going back and forth about constructivism reminds me of an anecdote from *Readers Digest* (Safire, 1991) about a Florida politician, asked to take a position on a county option to permit the sale of liquor:

> If by *whiskey,* you mean the water of life that cheers men's souls, that smooths out the tensions of the day, that gives gentle perspective to one's view of life, then put my name on the list of the fervent wets. But if by *whiskey,* you mean the devil's brew that rends families, destroys careers and ruins one's ability to work, then count me in the ranks of the dries. (p. 14)

Similarly, if by constructivism you mean the solipsism and subjectivism portrayed by Merrill or Molenda, then I am a strident opponent. But if by constructivism you refer to the moderate philosophy of a Cunningham or a Perkins, then count me in as a constructivist.

4. *Neither side is right.* I am suspicious of simple dichotomies like the idea that reality is either inside or outside of the mind. The analogy implicit in such claims is that the mind is like a box (Faulconer & Williams, 1990; Heidegger, 1984). Inside the box are reflections of what lies outside. Martin Heidegger's ontology rejects the box metaphor of mind, and the inner/outer dualism that goes with it (see Dreyfus, 1991; Faulconer & Williams, 1990; Winograd & Flores, 1986).

> Rather than accepting the metaphor of the box, with the human subject walled off from the nonhuman, objective world, Heidegger's analysis leads to the conclusion that human being is already being-in-the-world. There is no inside walled off from the outside. (Faulconer & Williams, p. 46)

According to Heidegger, the starting point is recognizing that we simply are in the world, working, acting, doing things. Turning Descartes' famous maxim on its head, the motto becomes "*I am* [in the world]; *therefore I think.*"

In this view, individual cognition is dethroned as the center of the universe and placed back into the context of being part of the world. This philosophy is reminiscent of the socially oriented, connected ways of knowing found among women by Belencky and colleagues (Belenky, Clinchy, Goldberger, & Tarule, 1986). I am attracted to such holistic conceptions of the world, even if my understanding of the philosophy is still incomplete (see Polkinghorne, 1990 for a good, short introduction to many of the issues). My reading is enough to make me suspect that much of the objective/constructive debate is based on the wrong questions.

Implications for Design Theories

In this section, I turn to the more difficult issue of articulating implications of a constructivist philosophy for doing instructional design. But first I discuss the notion of an ID theory, and how it relates to professional practice.

What Is Instructional-Design Theory?[2]

Traditionally, ID theories are seen as *prescriptive* in the the sense that:

- they provide recipes or heuristics for doing designs, and
- they also specify how end-product instruction should look.

Thus, in both a product and a process sense, ID theories serve as guides to professional practice. Conceptually, ID theories are much closer to engineering than to science. They are about how to get something done, how to design a solution, not about how the world is. In that sense, they are really less theories and more models for action, for problem solving.

Such design theories may be based on a lot of hot air, or they may have some validity. On what kind of knowledge base are these theories built? Several forms of knowledge may contribute to an ID model, including:

- scientific knowledge about learning and related sciences;
- craft knowledge about effective design, based more on teaching practices than on formal scientific research;
- idiosyncratic knowledge about instruction unique to the ID profession, untested by formal research, yet functionally important to ID practice.

Reigeluth (1983a) has outlined a prescriptive framework for embodying this knowledge. A series of rules is developed connecting existing conditions, desired outcomes, and recommended methods to instrumentally obtain those outcomes. For example, if your learners are new to a concept and you want them to learn it at an application level, then you might present a statement of the definition followed by examples and practice opportunities to classify new cases. An ID theory builds a collection of similar IF-THEN rules; designers are then supposed to apply these rules to their various situations.

This is a fairly technical view of design activity. Schön (1983, 1987), in fact, refers to exactly this type of thinking as *technical rationality*.

> From the perspective of technical rationality . . . a competent practitioner is always concerned with instrumental problems. She searches for the means best suited to the achievement of fixed, unambiguous ends . . . and her effectiveness is measured by her success in finding . . . the actions that produce the intended effects consistent with her objectives. In this view, professional competence consists in the application of theories and techniques derived from systematic, preferably scientific research to the solution of the instrumental problems of practice. (Schön, 1987, p. 33)

Schön's technical rationality looks a lot like Reigeluth's conditions/outcomes/methods framework. Schön does not deny that some problems encountered are routine ones that relate to the rules and concepts of the discipline. However, professionals go far beyond technical rationality when they encounter novel problems:

---

[2]Some colleagues object to the use of the term 'theory' when applied to instructional design. They suggest that these alleged theories are really nothing more than technological models. I retain 'theory' for two reasons: (1) to distinguish between ID theories and instructional development models that prescribe an entire methodology for managing ID projects (cf. Andrews & Goodson, 1980), and (2) because philosophers of science liberally apply the terms 'theory' and 'model' to a variety of frameworks of varying complexity, formality, and power (Suppe, 1977).

There are also unfamiliar situations where the problem is not initially clear and there is no obvious fit between the characteristics of the situation and the available body of theories and techniques. It is common, in these types of situations, to speak of "thinking like a doctor"—or lawyer or manager [or instructional designer!]. . . . We would recognize as a limiting case the situations in which it is possible to make a routine application of existing rules and procedures. . . . Beyond these situations, familiar rules, theories, and techniques are put to work in concrete instances through the intermediary of an art that consists in a limited form of reflection-in-action. And beyond these, we would recognize cases of problematic diagnosis in which practitioners not only follow rules of inquiry but also sometimes respond to surprising findings by inventing new rules, on the spot. (Schön, 1987, p. 35)

Technical rationality suggests a clear demarcation between theory and practice, with categories of basic knowledge, applied knowledge, and practice. Theory is what gets written in textbooks and professional journals, while practice tends to be mistrusted, since practitioners never have the good sense to apply theory correctly. On the other hand, Schön's reflective practitioner model blurs the line between theory and research, suggesting that practitioners embody personal theories of practice, and often assume a kind of research stance toward their work (see also Winn, 1990). Schön makes clear the philosophical basis of his view of practice:

[T]he practitioner [is] *constructing*[3] situations of his practice, not only in the exercise of professional artistry but also in all other modes of professional competence. . . . [O]ur perceptions, appreciations, and beliefs are rooted in worlds of our own making that we come to *accept* as reality. (Schön, 1987, p. 36; italics added)

In contrast,

technical rationality rests on an *objectivist* view of the relation of the knowing practitioner to the reality he knows. In this view, facts are what they are, and the truth of beliefs is strictly testable by reference to them. All meaningful disagreements are resolvable, at least in principle, by reference to the facts. And professional knowledge rests on a foundation of facts. (p. 36)

Thus, Schön is setting certain conditions for a constructivist model of instructional design. If you buy into a constructivist idea of the world, learners become active creators of meaning (and teachers of this meaning to others), and teachers are continual learners.

Communities of practitioners are continually engaged in what Nelson Goodman (1978) calls "worldmaking." Through countless acts of attention and inattention, naming, sense-making, boundary setting, and control, they make and maintain the worlds matched to their professional knowledge and know-how. . . . When practitioners respond to the indeterminate zones of practice by holding a reflective conversation with the materials of their situations, they remake a part of their practice world and thereby reveal the usually tacit processes of worldmaking that underlie all of their practice. (Schön, 1987, p. 36)

I have cited Schön heavily because I am convinced that we need to rethink the roles of formal ID theory and of the ID practitioner. Schön's model is not complete—for example, he does not pursue the ethical/moral dimensions of professional decision-making in an institutional context. But his views serve as a valuable starting point for discussion.

The expert/novice literature within cognitive psychology reaches similar conclusions about the nature of expertise. Researchers have found that expertise is:

---

[3]Schön uses the term 'constructionism' to refer to this philosophy of practitioners building their own worlds and perceiving things within those worlds. Because this term has been appropriated by Papert to denote a somewhat different idea, we are retaining our use of the term 'constructivism.'

- largely intuitive and inaccessible to direct reflection (e.g., Bloom, 1986);
- more pattern-matching than rule-following (Bereiter, 1991; Suchman, 1987);
- more qualitative than quantitative (White & Frederiksen, 1986); and
- highly context- and domain-dependent (Brandt, 1988–89).

Such a view of expertise seems also to fit the field of ID. We know that professional designers are highly flexible and adaptive in applying their knowledge to working problems (Nelson, Magliaro, & Sherman, 1988; Nelson & Orey, 1991; Thiagarajan, 1976); moreover, instead of applying formal theories in a rote, straightforward way, many practitioners regularly cut corners, combine models and ideas, and develop their own idiosyncratic approaches (Tessmer & Wedman, 1992; Wedman & Tessmer, 1990). With this view of ID expertise, the precise role of traditional ID theory is left in question. If ID theories are not descriptive science, and not a set of rules to be unambiguously applied to problems, then what are they and what value do they have?

One possibility is that the recipes contained in ID theories may have some value to novice designers. Putnam (1991) found that when learning a complex subject, novices tended to grasp onto formulas and recipes to support initial performance, then changed their use of the recipes as they gained expertise. The main problem with this rationale, though, is that ID theories are not formulated as simple recipes; they are *not* easy-to-use "hooks" into a subject. Rather, ID theories are typically represented as formal, technical-sounding systems with extensive jargon, big words, and acronyms. The ID theory papers I have read are anything but a support to novices. ID theories are written as though they were serious science; novices would require another type of representation altogether to support their initial learning needs.

Another possibility is that ID theories are not really meant to be used by human designers in normal situations, but rather are best suited to computer-based training and automated instructional design. This possibility is much more promising, even though both Gagné and Merrill have denied the need for separate formulations of ID theory for computers and traditional media (Gagné, 1988; Merrill, 1988). Of course, there is still the question of whether theorists can successfully represent design knowledge with computers. It may turn out that the IF-THEN rule approach to design may be unable to capture true design expertise. This is, however, an empirical question worthy of continued investigation.

In summary, ID theory, with its prescriptive orientation toward both procedure and product, lies in conceptual limbo. Its role and status remain unclear in light of cognitive/constructivist views on expertise and professional problem-solving. In spite of these difficulties, I believe at this time that there can be such a thing as a constructivist theory of instruction. At the paper's conclusion, I will recommend several changes to revitalize ID theory and its place within practice and within the discipline.

The Cooperative Metaphor

P. Kenneth Komoski, director of the EPIE Institute—a "consumers' union" for educators—raised an issue a few years ago that has continued to affect my views. Citing Buchanan's (1963) study of ancient Greek and medieval thought, Komoski suggested that technologies can be divided into two distinct groups, the first being called "exploitative" technologies:

> In the first group are the arts practiced on matter and on the many things and forces found in nature. These arts, such as sculpture, agriculture, hydrology, painting, carpentry, cooking, etc., are arts in which "the form in the artist's mind . . . could be impressed on the matter . . . which could be fashioned and formed [Buchanan, 1963]." [O]ur uses of all technologies have been—and continue to be—influenced by this view of "technology as a system of exploitation." (Komoski, 1987, p. 9; italics removed)

The second group constitutes the "cooperative" technologies because they require the cooperation of the "object" being worked with. Cooperative technologies are:

> those arts "practiced on human beings, who also have artistic capacities." In humans there are "natural processes which if left to themselves might accomplish their ends, but if aided by the professional would accomplish their ends more easily and more fully. Medicine and teaching were the frequently discussed examples of such arts. They were called coopera-tive arts because they were understood to be cooperating with rational natures." The physi-cian who gains the cooperation and confidence of patients, and the teacher who gains the willing cooperation of students, are much more apt to end up with healthy patients and competent learners than those doctors and educators who fail to gain such cooperation. (Komoski, 1987, p. 9)

Komoski notes that "it is the *exploitative technologies*, with their undeniable and demon-strable efficiency and effectiveness, that have shaped our thinking about, and our practices of, all technologies—including those such as medicine and teaching that, presumably, func-tion more effectively when practiced as *cooperative technologies*" (Komoski, 1987, pp. 9–10; see also Mumford's [1967] distinction between authoritarian and democratic technologies).

It would be an interesting exercise to classify various known educational technologies on the exploitative/cooperative continuum. Where would ID theories fall? From the standard conceptualization, I am afraid it falls too neatly into the exploitative category, with attendant consequences. The despised factory model of schools has a close cousin in the machine model of ID. The content of current ID theories also belies this orientation. In Reigeluth's "green" book (Reigeluth, 1983b), only the Gagné chapter and Keller's ARCS chapter treat student attitudes in any lengthy way. ID's manipulative bent is ironic, given the recent emphasis on working with schools and teachers in restructuring initiatives (e.g., Banathy, 1991) and on cognitive apprenticeships (e.g., Wilson & Cole, 1991). We clearly need more cooperative metaphors and rhetoric in our ID literature. I raise this point because an exploitative view of learning technology bears a strong similarity to objectivist views. A cooperative view of tech-nology leaves open the possibility for a constructivist orientation.

Task/Content Analysis and the Nature of Knowledge

Does all learned (or taught) knowledge have to be pre-analyzed? Of course not. There is much learned within any instructional environment that goes far beyond the instructional objectives. Curriculum theorists and media critics have been making that point for years (Hidden curriculum reference; Hlynka & Belland, 1991). Yet ID theorists and practitioners give every indication that their method of slicing up the world is *the* method, and that the content resulting from their analysis is *the* content to be taught to students. More than any-thing else, this aspect of ID theories has troubled me (see Wilson & Cole, 1992 for a similar discussion).

Eisner (1988) puts the counter argument succinctly in an abstract to a paper:

> Knowledge is rooted in experience and requires a form for its representation. Since all forms of representation constrain what can be represented, they can only partially repre-sent what we know. Forms of representation not only constrain representation, they limit what we seek. As a result, socialization in method is a process that shapes what we can know and influences what we value. At base, it is a political undertaking. (p. 15)

In other words, the conceptual schemes we apply to the world constrain that world. Similarly, the schemes instructional designers apply to content constrain and shape that con-tent, necessarily distorting it to fit our preconceived notions. If by some chance the educa-tional community were to agree on knowledge categories, then we might have some basis for using those consensual categories in content and task analyses. But educators do not agree.

Alexander, Schallert, and Hare (1991), in a recent review, found 25 distinct knowledge types cited in the educational literature on language and cognition. And that article was an attempt to simplify the problem!

If our knowledge categories are faulty (which they are), then how can we design adequate instruction? A short answer is, don't make the quality of your instruction rise or fall on the quality of your analysis. There is more to instructional design than analysis. Bunderson made essentially the same point years ago in his discussion of the "lexical loop" (Bunderson, Gibbons, Olsen, & Kearsley, 1981). The lexical loop refers to the parade of print-to-print translations we put content through as part of a traditional design process, beginning with needs and content analyses and ending in paper-based tests (see Table 2). As an alternative, Bunderson proposed a series of qualitative "work models" progressing in difficulty and fidelity to the target setting. These work models or learning environments are highly reminiscent of White and Frederiksen's (1986) progression of practice environments based on careful cognitive task analysis of mental models; I believe that such analyses remain highly relevant to the design of instruction, particularly multimedia products.

The role I am advocating for analysis is fairly modest. Analysis provides an overall framework for instruction, and provides extra help on some tricky parts, such as identifying likely misconceptions or previous knowledge that may undercut students' efforts to under-

Table 2.   Two paths from mastery to mastery
(derived from Bunderson *et al.,* 1981, p. 206).

Knowledge of the Master

The Lexical Loop

Translation to goal statements through goal/job analysis.

Translation to objectives list through task analysis.

Translation to print-based tests through test item technologies.

Translation to print-based media using text-design principles.

Students expected to transfer text material into skills ot the master.

(Actually, negligible transfer occurs to everyday life.)

Work Models

Master performance is documented through multiple media.

Work models are designed of progressively increasing difficulty.
  —Learning environments simulate real-life environments.
  —Students practice holistic as well as parts skills.
  —Authentic tools are available.
  —Info can be accessed through job aids, help systems, and other resources.
  —Coaching, mentoring, and peer consultation is available as needed.

Students complete work models *1 . . . n.*

Student demonstrates master's knowledge/skill in real-life performance environment.

Knowledge of the Master

stand the content. The role of the designer is then to design a series of experiences—interactions or environments or products—intended to help students learn effectively. Neither the instruction nor the assessment of learning can be as confidently dictated as has been thought to be possible in the past. But the important point to keep in mind is that the design role is not lost in such a revised system; the design still happens, only it's less analytical, more holistic, more reliant on the cooperation of teachers and materials and learners to generously fill in the gaps left gaping by the limitations of our analytical tools. Instruction thus construed becomes much more integrally connected to the context and the surrounding culture. ID thus becomes more truly *systemic* in the the sense that it is highly sensitive to the conditions of use.

In summary, no matter whose 2 x 3 scheme you use, the world doesn't always fit such neat epistemological categories. Force-fitting people's expertise into ID taxonomies sometimes can do more harm than good. My recommended alternative is not to throw away the taxonomies entirely, but simply to:

1. admit the tentativeness of any conceptual scheme applied to content;
2. realize that no matter how thorough the task-analysis net, it doesn't come close to capturing true expertise;
3. realize that since content representation is so tentative, designed instruction should offer holistic, information-rich experiences, allowing opportunities for mastery of un-analyzed content;
4. always allow for a lack of fit between the conceptual scheme and any given content;
5. realize that the very points of lack of fit can be the most critical to understanding that content area; and
6. always be on the lookout for those critical points of idiosyncratic content demands.

Viewed in such a way, content analysis is less a leveling exercise and more an exploration of the terrain, noting and even exploiting rough spots. Rules, verbal information, and other such categories cease to have such literal epistemological status, and become mere tools in the design process. The change is largely one of attitude and stance. I personally do not write behavioral, typed objectives anymore unless required by the sponsoring agency. I try not to teach each content type separately (i.e., verbage apart from skills). Rather, I do what Gagné and Merrill (1990) have advocated: I try to combine all the learning outcomes into problem-solving instruction. There is a variety of possible strategies to address this problem, ranging from conservative to radical. All, however, should be able to fit within a constructivistic ID framework.

The Mystery of Expertise

A constructivist view of knowledge leads to another dilemma central to the ID process:

> *Subject matter experts know the content best but often*
> *have least access to it.*

Because expert knowledge gets automatized, conscious representation typically drops out of the picture. The corollary is just as disturbing:

> *To go beyond routine mediocre rule-based ID,*
> *a designer needs to know content deeply.*

Shulman (1987) talks about the many kinds of sophisticated knowledge required of teachers. In addition to knowing the content, they must know how to teach it. This typically does not come automatically, but only after years of teaching the same subject (Berliner,

1986). Designers who script instruction from a newly acquired, superficial content knowledge cannot be expected to find just the right analogy, just the right way of approaching a topic. They do have an advantage over the non-teaching expert in that their understanding of the subject is freshly acquired; that means they have greater access to strategies that worked for them. But this advantage applies only to initial learning levels: Once instruction moves to non-elementary tasks, the designer is on more wobbly ground and lacks the insight needed to create the *best* teaching methods (if such a thing indeed exists). Falling back on known design concepts is not the optimal design solution, but becomes a means of only resort in such situations.

Together, these two problems pose a formidable paradox for ID: The people who know the subject best often can't relate to the learner, while the designer, with a good general schema for teaching and a closer feel for the learner's needs, doesn't have a feel for the subtleties of the content and is thus left to deal in superficiality.

The role of the knowledge engineer—the designer's counterpart in AI—is a subject of continuing debate (e.g., Dreyfus & Dreyfus, 1986; Winograd & Flores, 1986); thus, I am surprised that the designer/SME relationship is not more controversial than it is. We should be asking the same tough questions of designers that we ask of AI knowledge engineers: Where does the expertise really come from? What is lost in the translation? Are IF-THEN rules sufficient to characterize expertise, or do we need a neural network? Can expertise be digitally represented? How can we make use of a greater variety of representation forms in our designs? (See the chapter by Dreyfus and Dreyfus, this book.)

The standard metaphor for the designer/SME relationship is *extraction:* The designer has good people skills, asks the right questions, pushes the right buttons, and presto!—out comes the expertise, on paper no less. But of course things cannot be so simple. The level of communication between SME and designer needs to move beyond superficialities; somewhere between the two of them there must occur a synthesis of meaning; the design process must be deeply collaborative for good design to occur. I personally don't know how this happens. It remains a mystery.

Instructional Strategies

ID needs a richer language, a deeper conceptual framework for classifying instructional strategies. While this is not the place for such an effort, I have sketched out in Table 3 a number of instructional strategies that seem to facilitate more active construction of meaning (see also Wilson & Cole, 1991).

Table 3.   A sampling of alternative instructional strategies.

Simulations
Strategy and role-playing games
Toolkits and phenomenaria
Multimedia learning environments
Intentional learning environments
Storytelling structures
Case studies
Socratic dialogues
Coaching and scaffolding
Learning by design
Learning by teaching
Group, cooperative, collaborative learning
Holistic psychotechnologies

A defender of traditional ID could suggest that our present theory base already contains prescriptions for designing all of the above. I would only counter that each of the above strategies deserves its own mini-design model, and that many traditional design concepts seem only to get in the way. It seems ludicrous, for example, to discuss simulation design using terms such as "expository," "inquisitory," "synthesizer," and "summarizer." A new framework and accompanying language is needed.

Student Assessment

Shepard (1991) recently reported some interesting findings about psychometricians' beliefs. About half of those surveyed believe in close alignment of tests and instruction and careful, focused teaching of tested content. Shepard argues, however, that such beliefs correspond to a "behaviorist learning theory, which requires sequential mastery of constituent skills and explicit testing of each learning step" (p. 2). She argues for a constructivist alternative that emphasizes more authentic methods of assessment such as interviewing, observations, and holistic task performances (see Linn, Baker, & Dunbar, 1991; Perrone, 1991).

Jonassen (1991a) takes what I consider to be a more radical stance towards assessment, extending Scriven's (1973) notion of goal-free program evaluation to the goal-free assessment of student outcomes.

> Constructivistic outcomes may be better judged by goal-free evaluation methodologies. If specific goals are known before the learning process begins, the learning process as well as the evaluation would be biased . . . Criterion-referenced instruction and evaluation are prototypic objectivist constructs and therefore not [sufficient] for constructivistic environments. (p. 29; change based on Jonassen, 1991b)

I take exception to Jonassen's position for reasons I discuss below, but I am ambivalent about the general issue of assessment. Surely ID theory makes assumptions that make some people feel uncomfortable; for example, that instruction is purposive and goal-directed, and that attainment of those goals can be assessed. I believe these assumptions can be wholly compatible with a constructivist philosophy; here I differ with Jonassen. And certainly, assessment need not go to the extreme of being goal-free. It seems that a key question to ask is, "Does the test performance require all of the contextualized reasoning and performing that the target performance would require?" (Frederiksen & Collins, 1989). The question is one of fidelity and validity, not of goal-directedness.

I do not have a problem with the idea of goal-directedness and measurement, but I do have a problem with how it is often done. A true mastery model with micro levels of assessment would only be appropriate with highly defined technical content; I believe that such methods would rarely be appropriate in public schools, though somewhat more often in training settings. Instructional designers in both school and corporate settings feel the need for better assessment methods that can be more fully integrated into their performance and instructional systems. I have not sorted out all the issues; I raise the question because of its clear importance to the field and to society at large. I continue to believe that improved assessment methods can be developed that are more consistent with a constructivist framework.

Concluding Thoughts

The central issue of this chapter is this: Is a constructivist theory of instructional design possible? And, if so, what might it be like? In typical backwards fashion, let me return to the question of the nature of ID theory by defining terms.

Instruction—teacher(s) and student(s) in interaction trying to learn something. Together they form an instructional subsystem within a larger system and community.[4]

Design—"the process by which things are made . . . designers make representations of things to be built" (Schön, 1990, p. 110). Design is always done within constraints.

Constraints inherent in the design of instruction include:

a. Some situations don't even have teachers *per se*. Thus, the teacher may be broadly thought of as the guiding agent, directing the learner toward accomplishing the goals of instruction. Learners themselves often function in the teacher role, as do instructional materials and programs.

b. Designers can usually exert more direct influence on the teacher side than on the learner side of the instructional system. At the same time, designers ignore considerations of the learner at their peril.

c. Designers can usually exert more direct influence over materials and tools than over the interaction between learners and teachers. At the same time, the nature of the precise interaction between learners and teachers is at the heart of understanding instruction.

These constraints pose dilemmas for constructivist designers. As much as we may like to focus on individual learners' cognitions, often our access is extremely indirect and limited. This also helps to explain why ID is often a goal-based, stimulus-design oriented endeavor, working within a noisy system that is near chaos. It is no wonder that we get no respect; my response to critics who think we should get entirely out of such a messy business is, "If we didn't do it, somebody else would. Practitioners of ID need somewhere they can turn to, and our theories are as good as the next guy's." (I am actually serious about this.)

I have become convinced that a field is largely shaped by the central questions it puts to itself. In the case of ID, the questions are tough; there are no good answers, the best we can do is put forth some best guesses. We pay attention to stimulus design (a "dirty word" among cognitivists) because we have no choice. We prescribe general principles of message and interface design because those are aspects of the instructional system that lie somewhat within our power to influence. For good reasons we tend to get beat up by cognitivists, constructivists, and humanists; yes, it's a dirty job, but somebody's got to do it!

The next generation of ID theory needs to better fit the needs of the practitioner:

-   ID theories need to be thoroughly grounded in a broad understanding of learning and instructional processes. That foundation needs to be continually evaluated and revised.

-   We need more modest principles that designers can flexibly apply. These principles should be generic and principle-based in order to to be relevant to the wide variety of situations encountered in everyday practice.

-   In addition to generic principles, we need specific heuristics for dealing with recurring problems and situations in ID practice. In particular, heuristics should be developed that are sensitive to:

---

[4]Note that this systemic definition differs from definitions that emphasize teacher behaviors. Instruction is not strictly what the teacher designs, intends, or does; it is that *plus* what students design, intend, and do.

—*setting* (schools, business, museums, etc.),
—*media* (computer, instructor-led, workbook, etc.),
—*product type* (stand-alone product, program, system, etc.),
—*resources* (time, money, constraints).

- ID theories need to reflect a view of ID as a profession. Designers need sophisticated schemas of design that go beyond the "technically rational" models presently available. Students should be encouraged to develop personal models of action through extensive practice in authentic settings with coaching and opportunities for reflection. (Note the theme of reflection running through students, teachers, and designers.)

Let me conclude by drawing a parallel with a couple of other disciplines, lest we think that we're alone in this chaotic science of design. Artificial intelligence right now is facing some of the same crises we are confronting. So is the field of human/computer interface design. Both of these fields have a strong tie to learning and cognitive psychology. Both rely heavily (at least in theory) on user testing and field validation. Old-time AI theorists presently are being challenged by connectionists, who believe that parallel processing via neural networks is a more promising way to go than symbolic manipulation of IF-THEN rules. The controversy goes beyond symbolic versus networked processing. A growing number of AI researchers have lost faith in traditional views of the representability of knowledge; the "situated" movement within AI goes so far as to deny that knowledge is a structure, and that memory is anything more than process (Brooks, 1991; Clancey, 1991). The field of interface design is going through similar growing pains, moving from a screen-design view of the field to a global, holistic view of the entire human experience with computers (Laurel, 1990, 1991). This revised view of interface design has more to do with human activity than with icons, buttons, and windows, more with dramatic metaphors, agents, and virtual worlds.

I don't doubt that AI will be around in twenty years. Nor do I doubt that people will still be studying how computers and humans work together. The theories and concepts may change, but the basic questions are still there; they cannot be ignored. Likewise, ID will not go away; this is because the questions behind the field are genuine questions. The challenge for ID theorists is to continue to adjust our theories, or to replace them with better ones. The goal is to make our theories worthy of the questions.

Author's Note

This paper is based on a talk I gave to the Instructional Science Department, Brigham Young University, 4 December 1991. I wish to thank Peggy Cole, David Jonassen, and Lyn Taylor for comments on an early draft. Thanks also to students and faculty of Brigham Young University—in particular, Jane Birch and Rob Boody—for their stimulating comments on the issues addressed. An earlier version of this chapter is published in the 1993 *AECT Research Proceedings*, edited by Michael Simonson.

References

Alexander, P. A., Schallert, D. L., & Hare, V. C. (1991). Coming to terms: How researchers in learning and literacy talk about knowledge. *Review of Educational Research, 61*(3), 315–343.

Andrews, D. H., & Goodson, L. A. (1980). A comparative analysis of models of instructional design. *Journal of Instructional Development, 3*(4), 2–16.

Banathy, B. H. (1991). *Systems design of education.* Englewood Cliffs, NJ: Educational Technology Publications.

Bednar, A. K., Cunningham, D., Duffy, T. M., & Perry, J. D. (1991). Theory into practice: How do we link? In G. Anglin (Ed.), *Instructional technology* (pp. 88–101). Englewood, CO: Libraries Unlimited.

Belenky, M. F., Clinchy, B. M., Goldberger, N. R., & Tarule, J. M. (1986). *Women's ways of knowing: The development of self, voice, and mind.* New York: Basic Books.

Bereiter, C. (1991, April). Implications of connectionism for thinking about rules. *Educational Researcher,* 10–16.

Berliner, D. C. (1986, August/September). In pursuit of the expert pedagogue. *Educational Researcher,* 5–13.

Bloom, B. S. (1986, February). Automaticity: The hands and feet of genius. *Educational Leadership,* 70–77.

Brandt, R. (1988–89, December/January). On learning research: A conversation with Lauren Resnick. *Educational Leadership,* 12–16.

Brooks, R. A. (1991). Intelligence without representation. *Artificial Intelligence, 47,* 139–159.

Bruner, J. S. (1964). Some theorems on instruction illustrated with reference to mathematics. In E. R. Hilgard (Ed.), *Theories of learning and instruction* (pp. 306–335). Chicago: National Society for the Study of Education (63rd yearbook).

Bruner, J. S. (1966). *Toward a theory of instruction.* Cambridge, MA: Harvard University Press.

Bruner, J. S. (1986). *Actual minds, possible worlds.* Cambridge, MA: Harvard University Press.

Buchanan, S. (1963). Technology as a system of exploitation. In C. F. Stover (Ed.), *The technological order: Proceedings of the Encyclopaedia Britannica conference* (pp. 151–159). Detroit, MI: Wayne State University Press.

Burton, R. R., & Brown, J. S. (1979). An investigation of computer coaching for informal learning activities. *International Journal of Man-Machine Studies, 11,* 5–24.

Bunderson, C. V., Gibbons, A. S., Olsen, J. B., & Kearsley, G. P. (1981). Work models: Beyond instructional objectives. *Instructional Science, 10,* 205-215.

Clancey, W. J. (1991). The frame of reference problem in AI. In K. vanLehn & A. Newell (Eds.), *Architectures for intelligence: The twenty-second Carnegie Symposium on Cognition.* Hillsdale, NJ: Lawrence Erlbaum Associates.

Connelly, F. M., & Clandinin, D. J. (1990). Stories of experience and narrative inquiry. *Educational Researcher, 19*(4), 2–14.

Dreyfus, H. L. (1991). *Being-in-the-world.* Cambridge, MA: MIT Press.

Dreyfus, H. L., & Dreyfus, S. E. (1986). *Mind over machine: The power of human intuition and expertise in the era of the computer.* New York: The Free Press.

Duffy, T. M., & Jonassen, D. H. (Eds.). (1992). *Constructivism and the technology of instruction: A conversation.* Hillsdale, NJ: Lawrence Erlbaum Associates.

Eisner, E. W. (1988). The primary of experience and the politics of method. *Educational Researcher, 17*(5), 15–20.

Faulconer, J. E., & Williams, R. N. (1990). Reconsidering psychology. In J. E. Faulconer & R. N. Williams (Eds.), *Reconsidering psychology: Perspectives from continental philosophy* (pp. 9–60). Pittsburgh, PA: Duquesne University Press.

Frederiksen, J. R., & Collins, A. (1989, December). A systems approach to educational testing. *Educational Researcher,* 27–32.

Gagné, R. M. (1988, February). *Presidential session: A conversation on instructional design.* Paper presented at the meeting of the Association for Educational Communications and Technology, New Orleans. [Response to question from the audience.]

Gagné, R. M., & Merrill, M. D. (1990). Integrative goals for instructional design. *Educational Technology Research and Development, 38*(1), 23–30.

Goodman, N. (1978). *Ways of worldmaking.* Minneapolis, MN: Hackett.

Goodman, N. (1984). *Of mind and other matters.* Cambridge, MA: Harvard University Press.

Hannafin, M., Rieber, L., Merrill, D., Tobin, K., Streibel, M., & Hooper, S. (1991, February). *Alternative perspectives on the design of learning and instrumental environments.* Symposium of the Association for Educational Communications and Technology, Orlando, FL.

Harel, I. (1991, April). *When mathematical ideas, programming knowledge, instructional design, and playful learning are intertwined: The Instructional Software Design Project.* Paper presented at the meeting of the American Educational Research Association, Chicago.

Harel, I., & Papert, S. (1990). Software design as a learning environment. *Interactive Learning Environments, 1*(1), 1–32.

Heidegger, M. (1984). *The metaphysical foundations of logic* (M. Heim, translator). Bloomington, IN: Indiana University Press.

Hidi, S. (1990). Interest and its contribution as a mental resource for learning. *Review of Educational Research, 60*(4), 549–571.

Hlynka, D., & Belland, J. C. (Eds.). (1991). *Paradigms regained: The uses of illuminative, semiotic, and postmodern criticism as modes of inquiry in educational technology.* Englewood Cliffs, NJ: Educational Technology Publications.

House, E. R. (1991). Realism in research. *Educational Researcher, 20*(6), 2–9.

Johnson, M. (1984). *The body in the mind: The bodily basis of meaning, imagination, and reason:* Chicago: The University of Chicago Press.

Jonassen, D. H. (1991a, September). Evaluating constructivistic learning. *Educational Technology, 31*(9), 28–33.

Jonassen, D. H. (1991b). Personal communication.

Komoski, P. K. (1987). *Educational technology: The closing-in or the opening-out of curriculum and instruction.* Syracuse, NY: ERIC Clearinghouse on Information Resources.

Komoski, P. K. (1989, March). *The future of educational technology.* Invited paper presented to the Special Interest Group on Instructional Technology, American Educational Research Association, San Francisco.

Lakoff, G. (1987). *Women, fire, and dangerous things.* Chicago: University of Chicago Press.

Lakoff, G., & Johnson, M. (1981). *Metaphors we live by.* Chicago: University of Chicago Press.

Laurel, B. (Ed.). (1990). *The art of human-computer interface design.* Reading, MA: Addison-Wesley.

Laurel, B. (1991). *Computers as theatre.* Reading, MA: Addison-Wesley.

Linn, R. L., Baker, E. L., & Dunbar, S. B. (1991, November). Complex, performance-based assessment: Expectations and validation criteria. *Educational Researcher,* 15–23.

Lumsdaine, A. A. (1961). Some conclusions concerning student responses and a science of instruction. In A. A. Lumsdaine (Ed.), *Student response in programmed instruction.* Publication 943, National Academy of Sciences. Washington, DC: National Research Council.

May, R. (1975). *The courage to create.* New York: W. W. Norton.

McDaniel, M. A., & Schlager, M. S. (1990). Discovery learning and transfer of problem-solving skills. *Cognition and Instruction, 7*(2), 129–159.

Merrill, M. D. (1988, February). *Presidential session: A conversation on instructional design.* Paper presented at the meeting of the Association for Educational Communications and Technology, New Orleans. [Response to question from the audience.]

Molenda, M. (1991, September). A philosophical critique of the claims of "constructivism." *Educational Technology, 31*(9), 44–48.

Mumford, L. (1967). *The myth of the machine: Technics and human development.* New York: Harcourt, Brace, & World.

Nelson, W. A., Magliaro, S., & Sherman, T. M. (1988). The intellectual content of instructional design. *Journal of Instructional Development, 11*(1), 29–35.

Nelson, W., A., & Orey, M. A. (1991, April). *Reconceptualizing the instructional design process: Lessons learned from cognitive science.* Paper presented at the annual meeting of the American Educational Research Association, Chicago.

Perrone, V. (Ed.). (1991). *Expanding student assessment.* Alexandria, VA: Association for Supervision and Curriculum Development.

Polkinghorne, D. E. (1988). *Narrative knowing and the human sciences.* Albany, NY: State University of New York Press.

Polkinghorne, D. E. (1990). Psychology after philosophy. In J. E. Faulconer & R. N. Williams (Eds.), *Reconsidering psychology: Perspectives from continental philosophy* (pp. 92–115). Pittsburgh, PA: Duquesne University Press.

Putnam, H. (1990). *Realism with a human face.* Cambridge, MA: Harvard University Press.

Putnam, R. W. (1991). Recipes and reflective learning: "What would prevent you from saying it that way?" In D. A. Schön (Ed.), *The reflective turn: Case studies in and on educational practice* (pp. 145–163). New York: Teachers College Press.

Reigeluth, C. M. (1983a). Instructional design: What is it and why is it? In C. M. Reigeluth (Ed.), *Instructional design theories and models: An overview of their current status* (pp. 3–36). Hillsdale, NJ: Lawrence Erlbaum Associates.

Reigeluth, C. M. (Ed.). (1983b). *Instructional design theories and models: An overview of their current status.* Hillsdale, NJ: Lawrence Erlbaum Associates.

Reigeluth, C. M., Merrill, M. D., Wilson, B. G., & Spiller, R. T. (1978, July). *Final report on the structural strategy diagnostic profile project.* A final report submitted to the Navy Personnel Research and Development Center, San Diego.

Reigeluth, C. M., Merrill, M. D., Wilson, B. G., & Spiller, R. T. (1980). The elaboration theory of instruction: A model for structuring instruction. *Instructional Science, 9,* 195–219.

Resnick, L. B., & Klopfer, L. E. (Eds.). (1989). *Toward the thinking curriculum: Current cognitive research.* Alexandria, VA: Association for Supervision and Curriculum Development.

Rosch, E., Mervis, C., Gray, W., Johnson, D., & Boyes-Braem, P. (1976). Basic objects in natural categories. *Cognitive Psychology, 8,* 382–349.

Rossett (1991). *Coaching successful performance.* Paper presented at the meeting of the Association for Educational Communications and Technology, Orlando.

Safire, W. (1991, November). If by whiskey . . . *Readers Digest,* p. 14.

Schön, D. A. (1983). *The reflective practitioner.* New York: Basic Books.

Schön, D. A. (1987). *Educating the reflective practitioner.* San Francisco: Jossey-Bass.

Schön, D. A. (1990). The design process. In V. A. Howard (Ed.), *Varieties of thinking: Essays from Harvard's Philosophy of Education Research Center* (pp. 110–141). New York: Routledge.

Scriven, M. (1973). Goal free evaluation. In E. R. House (Ed.), *School evaluation.* Berkeley, CA: McCutchan.

Shepard, L. A. (1991, October). Psychometricians' beliefs about learning. *Educational Researcher,* 2–16.

Shulman, L. S. (1987). Knowledge and teaching: Foundations of the new reform. *Harvard Educational Review, 57*(1), 1–22.

Spiro, R. J., Feltovich, P. J., Coulson, R. L., & Anderson, D. K. (1989). Multiple analogies for complex concepts: Antidotes for analogy-induced misconception in advanced knowledge acquisition. In S. Vosniadou & A. Ortony (Eds.), *Similarity and analogical reasoning.* Cambridge, UK: Cambridge University Press.

Spiro, R. J., & Jehng, J-C. (1990). Cognitive flexibility and hypertext: Theory and technology for the nonlinear and multidimensional traversal of complex subject matter. In D. Nix & R. J. Spiro (Eds.), *Cognition, education, and multimedia: Exploring ideas in high technology* (pp. 163-205). Hillsdale, NJ: Lawrence Erlbaum Associates.

Suchman, L. A. (1987). *Plans and situated actions.* Cambridge, UK: Cambridge University Press.

Suppe, F. (Ed.). (1977). *The structure of scientific theories* (2nd ed.). Urbana, IL: University of Illinois Press.

Tessmer, M., & Wedman, J. (1992). *A survey of instructional-design practitioners.* Paper presented at the meeting of the Association for Educational Communications and Technology, Washington DC.

Thiagarajan, S. (1976). Help, I am trapped inside an ID model! Alternatives to the systems approach. *NSPI Journal,* 10–11, p. 22.

Wedman, J., & Tessmer, M. (1990, July). Adapting instructional design to project circumstance: The layers of necessity model. *Educational Technology, 31*(7), 48–52.

White, B. Y., & Frederiksen, J. R. (1986). *Progressions of quantitative models as a foundation for intelligent learning environments.* Technical Report #6277, BBN.

Wilson, B. G., & Cole, P. (1991). A review of cognitive teaching models. *Educational Technology Research & Development, 39*(4), 47–63.

Wilson, B. G., & Cole, P. (1992). A critical review of elaboration theory. *Educational Technology Research & Development, 40*(3), 63–79.

Winn, W. (1990). Some implications of cognitive theory for instructional design. *Instructional Science, 19,* 53–69.

Winograd, T., & Flores, F. (1986). *Understanding computers and cognition: A new foundation for design.* Norwood, NJ: Ablex.

Witherell, C., & Noddings, N. (Eds.). (1991). *Stories lives tell: Narrative and dialogue in education.* New York: Teachers College Press.

5

How Is Instructional Development a Social Practice? Instructional Development in a Postmodern World

P. K. Jamison
Indiana University School of Medicine, Indianapolis

Reflect for a moment and seriously question the philosophical assumptions of the field known as educational technology, and the associated areas of instructional technology, instructional development, and instructional design. What would occur in education if individuals were to confront the typical view that education, instruction, teaching, and learning are neutral "events" that can be standardized and scientifically monitored? What would happen to instructional development if it were to move away from a strict reliance on quasi-scientific belief systems that mask the underlying social practices impacting people and settings?

Enter the postmodern world of instructional development. Several individuals in the field of educational technology have explored the relationship between people and social settings more deeply, as well as the influence of sociopolitics, technosciences, and philosophy of education. The postmodern world of instructional development does not rely on the typical language, theories, practices, or texts of the field that encourage individuals to focus on the analysis, design, and evaluation of efficient systems of instruction (Banathy, 1991; Briggs *et al.*, 1991; Dick & Carey, 1990; Gagné & Wager, 1992). Instead, this work makes use of a variety of critical perspectives and approaches to instructional development written by individuals who are disenchanted with the typical theory and practice of the field of educational technology (Damarin, 1994; Hlynka, 1991; Koetting, 1994; Yeaman, 1994). These individuals draw their ideas from critical theory, postmodern studies, feminism, and the broad area of cultural studies, including anthropology, sociology, literary theory, and aesthetics. (See Berger, 1972; Bush, 1983; Haraway, 1989; Harding, 1987; Jameson, 1991; Pacey, 1983; Trinh, 1989.)

More recently, a few of these authors have begun to develop alternative conceptual frameworks based on these writings and their professional/personal experience as developers and educators (Jamison, 1992, 1994a, 1994b; Yeaman, 1994).

Postmodernism presents many new possibilities for instructional development. But new beginnings are not always clear, and certainly not simple. To understand this approach to instructional development, one must be willing to embrace multiplicity, conflict, contradiction, uncertainty, ambiguity, and chaos as constituents that inform instructional development.

> . . . we are constantly confronted with multiple understandings of the "seemingly same reality" (the world, schooling, "educational technology," etc.). The challenges we pose to each other through our differing understandings, as well as the challenges posed by our study, present us with certain contradictions. These contradictions have to do with our individual experiencing of the world, and the public representation of that world. When the public and the private are in conflict, an unquietness can result. (Koetting, 1994, p. 55)

The Postmodern Problem of Instructional Development

This essay acknowledges the unquietness of one area within the field of educational technology, instructional development. It presents postmodernism as both a critique of instructional development and as an actual framework for instructional development. While postmodernism may be criticized and characterized as too abstract, intellectually exclusionary, or elitist, it is one approach that is highly reflective of the unquietness of late industrial society, and directly challenges the theoretical and practical traditions of instructional development. Furthermore, postmodernism provides broader aesthetic, conceptual, and research experiences in instructional development activity; depicts instructional development as an activity that should expand, not limit, the multiplicity of experiences available to students, teachers, and clients; and finally, encourages individuals to view instructional development as a *social practice:* a socially manufactured change process that challenges social and organizational conditions.

Instructional development has provided society and education with a variety of philosophical and political exercises. Recently, postmodern educational technologists have taken greater interest in the interpretation of instructional development and a recurring problem that has been identified in the literature on the philosophy of instructional development. *The problem assumes a form of inquiry, "How is instructional development a social practice?"* Such a question has led postmodernists to explore the many ways in which instructional development is embedded in and reflective of social ideology (theory) and activity (practice).

Clearly, the exploration of instructional development as a social practice is complex. Struggling with an inherited philosophical distinction between theory and practice, yet working in a field that requires the bridging of both, many instructional developers are bewildered by the criticism of educators situated in critical and postmodernist positions. Both theoretically and practically, instructional developers are trained to focus their activity on the development of plans, goals, and systems using a set of organizational theories that draw heavily upon rationalism and empiricism (Yeaman, 1994). Consequently, rather than embrace the quality of meaning constructed in lived settings, including the richness of ambiguity and confusion, instructional developers often attempt to develop what Clark (1985) refers to as the "bureaucratic organization" in every instructional situation. Substituting the supposed real for the more illusory real, the typical instructional development model began as an imitation or simulation of instructional processes, people, events, and settings intended to facilitate instruction, but now it "has taken over and become its own reality" (Hlynka, 1991, p. 518). More and more, educators are persuaded that instructional and organizational models are constructed to match their ideal "social reality."

No longer is there any imperative to submit to the model, or to the gaze. "YOU are the model!" "YOU are the majority." Such is the slope of a hyperrealist society, where the real is confused with the model, as in the statistic operation . . . (Baudrillard, 1991, p. 467).

Britzman, writing on the significance of the "renovation of theory as social practice" and its impact on research directions for teachers, indicates the importance of moving away from imposed models of "reality":

> First, images of theory as reflective practice can dissipate a view of theory as imposed from above and situate it as constructed rather than received. Both theory and practice can thus be viewed as a problem of interpretation. Second, in positioning theory as dialogic to lived experience, the traditional dualism of theory and practice can be reconceptualized as a *problem of praxis.* When this occurs, practice can be understood theoretically. Third, an emphasis on personal practical knowledge values the activity of theorizing as a tenuous yet transformative activity. Teachers can experience themselves as authors and interpreters of their lived experience. To see teachers as interpreters of theory dismantles the view of theory as monological. Finally, these research directions re-establish a qualitative understanding of the complexity of the teacher's work. Through the use of qualitative research methods, research grounded in voices and in the contradictory realities of teachers implicitly opposes technocratic research directions that seek to "improve" education without teachers' knowledge. (Britzman, 1991, p. 54, *italics* added)

Similarly, postmodernists who have worked as instructional developers have begun to frame instructional development as a problem for inquiry and to deconstruct the language, philosophy, and activity of the social practice known as instructional development.

> Deconstruction is the sign of postmodern thinking. It is not a step-by-step formula. Nor is it ideal for uncovering the absolute truth. It is a mode of criticism, and it uncovers why someone thinks there is truth in a certain situation. Texts chosen for deconstruction are ones with which deconstructors identify or feel a positive relationship. Deconstruction seeks the deconstructive moment or place where texts contradict themselves and fall away from their official meaning. . . Each text can be deconstructed not once but in many different ways. (Yeaman, 1994, p. 16)

Mechanisms and Meaning

Generally, instructional development has been considered a link between educational research and practice that "seeks to apply scientifically derived principles to the planning, design, creation, implementation, and evaluation of effective and efficient instruction" (Shrock, 1995, p. 12). Shrock regards the history of instructional development as the "story of a gradual confluence of ideas, which took place over several decades" (p. 11). Consequently, instructional development *has been constructed* by the field of educational technology to focus on mechanisms (analysis, design, and evaluation) that emphasize the "development of standardized language and, formal or 'expert' values, observable and concrete outcomes, and objectivity" (Jamison, 1994a, p. 1). The practice of instructional development, then, can be likened to Koetting's view of the practice of social reform known as "school reform." It is a conceptualization of reform and change (i.e., development) that purposefully characterizes social settings as environments that are "supposed to be predictable, that are supposed to be controlled," and instructional development is seen as "fine tuning the social system" (Koetting, 1994, p. 55).

To seriously challenge the typical practices of instructional development, one must inquire into the mechanistic philosophy of instructional development, and to deconstruct its functionalist/structuralist position.

> Moving beyond the quasi-scientific analysis of tasks, behaviors, and needs, (associated with most models and systems in educational technology), what "other ways of knowing" do individuals experience beyond the mechanical and technical, such as aesthetic, emotional, kinesthetic, and social? (Jamison, 1994b, p. 67)

Furthermore, if instructional development is to be viewed as a bridge between research and practice, then it must become the problem of praxis that Britzman (1991) speaks of. In this way, instructional developers begin to explore and develop postmodern approaches to instructional development *in a search for meanings,* rather than mechanisms. As Britzman illustrates, theorizing is either a search for mechanisms or a search for meaning:

> A search for *mechanisms* entails a functionalist account of how things work, or do not work. It is a concrete search that attempts to posit explanations for specific problems and to prescribe solutions. A search for *meaning,* a style of theorizing. . .begins with a different set of assumptions. Such a search is interpretive, constructivist, and critical, moving back and forth between the story, its telling, and the contingencies of perspectival borders. This style of theorizing, rooted in narration, is reflexive and not reducible to discrete variables. (Britzman, 1991, p. 14)

There are many ways of framing instructional development as postmodern and as praxis. More importantly, different persons and settings would frame instructional development as social inquiry and as social activity (and their echoing of each other) differently.

> Method and substance are joined in the common recognition that everyone shares in the same world and responds to it somehow. (Vidich & Lyman, 1994, p. 42)

One approach encourages instructional developers to adopt positions that reflect their participation in their social practice. This approach challenges developers to resist objectivity and to inquire into the variety of assumptions, meanings and interpretations embedded in social practices. Therefore, this approach recognizes that:

> Given the inseparability of ourselves as researchers and as persons, the questions we must ask are no longer on the order of epistemological ones like, Are my results correct in the sense of accurate? but rather on the order of moral ones like, What kind of person am I or do I become? or What kind of society do we have or are we constructing . . . we are at the end of a history of describing ourselves and our work in methodological terms and at the beginning of describing ourselves and our work in ethical (and therefore participatory) terms. (Heshusius, 1994, p. 20)

There is some discussion among postmodern theorists as to whether there can actually be a discourse of "ethics" (see Caputo, 1993, for example). The adoption of "ethical behavior" as an approach can be framed in such a way that it, paradoxically, assumes that a "general idea" of thinking and acting "ethically" can be identified that is acceptable to all individuals. However, the concept of taking responsibility for participating in the construction of social practice raises important questions that are integral to postmodern development. Questions such as, "Who decides what in the instructional development process?" and "Who benefits from instructional development?" are characteristic of postmodern inquiry.

A second, and related, postmodern instructional development approach is drawn from literary theory and suggests that developers need to become comfortable with, and indeed embrace, the ambiguity, uncertainty, and unanticipated meanings constructed in social settings; their "unquietness."

> If modernism is certainty, then postmodernism is uncertainty. If modernism provides metanarratives, then postmodernism provides disbelief of these. If modernism is singular, then postmodernism is plural . . . breakups are not by outside interference, but by internal inconsistencies. . . . (Hlynka, 1991, p. 517)

This approach is best conceptualized by folklorist Susan Stewart (1978), but is also mirrored in the writings of educational technologists such as Yeaman (1994) and Hlynka (1991). It is a position that suggests that "unquietness" is the tension between common sense and nonsense. Both inform social settings, each shaping the other, together informing/bridging theory and practice. Common sense is that which is best described as "an organization of the world, as a model of order, integrity, and coherence accomplished in social life," and non-sense is "considered as an activity in which the world is disorganized and reorganized" (Stewart, 1978, p. vii). As Stewart suggests, this approach asks different kinds of questions; different questions than are commonly asked by instructional developers. Questions such as, What is the problem? and What is wrong with the system? are replaced with:

> How is it possible for us to talk about something while, at the same time, we are caught up in or implicated in that something? And, second, how do we use what we've got? (p. vii)

Stewart's questions address the paradox of commonsense and nonsense; the conflict of meaning, interpretation, and activity lived by persons in social settings. Furthermore, this approach strives to conceive of settings as cultural, rather than as natural systems.

> Cultural systems invoke a 'humanistic coefficient.' While natural systems may be objecti-fied, may be seen to operate independently of the desires, purposes, and interpretations of men, cultural systems are ontologically defined by such desires, purposes, and interpreta-tions and cannot be taken into account outside of their human universe. (p. 7)

Rather than merely identifying problems and providing solutions, both of these ap-proaches suggest that instructional development is a process of socialization for the *developer* and the clients or participants, and the setting. Furthermore, as Britzman (1991) suggests in her interpretive study of teacher practice, this process of "becoming" for both the developer and the setting participants "is not limited to what happens to persons" but includes "un-derstanding what they make happen because of what happens to them and what it is that structures their practices" (p. 56). Again, instructional development moves away from con-trol, compliance and resolution and towards "a form of inquiry, but also a process of dis-covery. It is an event beckoned by a setting and people who live within it" (Jamison, 1994a, p. 2).

Postmodern Instructional Development as Social Inquiry: The Bridge to Activity

The contrast between the typical and, often, technical paradigm of instructional devel-opment and the postmodern approach of instructional development as social inquiry resem-bles the artist David Hockney's frustration with traditional still photography and his love of polaroid imaging. The difference is between a single photograph (traditional instructional de-velopment) and Hockney's development of multiple polaroid images constructed as collages (postmodern instructional development); overlapping images of time, people, settings, and life that helped Hockney learn to convey and to see his lifeworld.

> My main argument was that a photograph could not be looked at for a long time . . . Life is precisely what they don't have—or rather, time, lived time. All you can do with most ordinary photographs is stare at them . . . photography is all right if you don't mind looking at the world from the point of view of a paralyzed cyclops—*for a split second*. But that's not what it's like to live in the world, or to convey the experience of living in the world. (p. 9)

For Hockney, traditional still photography lacked the movement and expression of the lifeworlds we actually construct and embed ourselves in. In contrast, his collages brought new meaning and interpretation to his own lifeworld for himself and his viewers.

> It takes time to see these pictures—you can look at them for a long time, they invite that sort of looking. But, more importantly, I realized that this sort of picture came closer to how we actually see, which is to say, not all-at-once but rather in discrete, separate glimpses which we then build up into our continuous experience of the world. Looking at you now,

my eye doesn't capture you entirely, but instead quickly, in nervous little glances. I look at your shoulder, and then your ear, your eyes (maybe, for a moment, if I know you well and have come to trust you, but then only for a moment), your cheek, your shirt button, your shoes, your hair, your eyes again, your nose and mouth. There are a hundred separate looks across time from which I synthesize my living impression of you. And this is wonderful. If, instead, I caught all of you in a frozen look, the experience would be dead—it would be like looking at an ordinary photograph. (p. 11)

Hockney's ideas can assist the deconstruction of the formal paradigm of instructional development. It suggests that a developer is situated in a social setting as an observer and interpreter. It is a highly "personal and metaphorical," rather than "example based," approach. Metaphors may "constrain thinking" as well as "provide a way of seeing" (Hlynka, 1991, p. 516); but, more importantly, metaphors suggest interpretation. In contrast, examples often are constructed to operate as overly mechanistic and functional models of reality. Examples lack deeper meaning because they are constructed simply to persuade an individual to accept a model, system, activity, or experience without personal or critical examination. Examples are designed towards simplicity and objectivity, and away from complexity and subjectivity.

> To say that personal meanings are contradictory—they simultaneously express the said and the unsaid, pose myths and construct realities, and can be seen as belonging to individuals and cultures—is not to assert a dreary relativism that all meanings are equal, accurate, just, or empowering, or that communication is either impossible or a mere matter of individual thought and determination. Just the opposite: This capacity for contradiction, or the situation of multiple and conflicting meanings that constitute the heteroglossic in language, can serve as a departure for a dialogic understanding that theorizes about how one understands the given realities of teaching as well as the realities that teaching makes possible. Central to this study, then, is the problem of how subjects produce and reproduce meanings and myths about education through their theories, practices, routines, discourses, contexts, and reflections on educational life, and how such meanings produce identities. (Britzman, 1991, p. 15)

Therefore, instructional development is social, personal, constructed, metaphorical and often partial. And, if instructional development is a social practice, then it must be self-reflexive and deconstructionist. Even some of the language and concepts of the traditional instructional development texts, paradoxically, deconstruct: analysis, feedback, evaluation; postmodernism encourages instructional developers to further interrupt the linearity of technical models and to imagine other possibilities:

> It is generally assumed that texts "construct" or "reconstruct" meaning . . . in fact the opposite is the case . . . careful analysis of a text shows its contradictions, its instability, its uncertainty . . . careful analysis of a text will result in its "deconstruction." (Hlynka, 1991, p. 514)

Postmodern Instructional Development as Social Activity: The Bridge to Inquiry

Technical instructional development practice conceives of people and settings as "real objects" that not only can be, but must be, analyzed, designed, and evaluated. Hence, this activity frames people, settings, and reality in a particular way.

As it is typically portrayed, instructional development formalizes settings and people along a systematic path. It tends in its resolution of educational problems towards a preconceived hierarchical, top-down characterization. The technical model of instructional development is oriented towards identifying a problem (or problems), and often presents a model as reflective of the problem and its associated resolution. A technical model of instructional development and some of its associated concepts are shown in Figure 1. This model masks the complexity of the activities of people and settings, as well as instructional problems and events. The model focuses on a simple, linear process that either hides social activity or situates it on the periphery of the development process.

However, models, systems, and hierarchies provide only temporary, and temporal, descriptions of social activity as reality.

> It is no longer a question of a false representation of reality (ideology), but of concealing the fact that the real is no longer real and thus of saving the reality principle. (Baudrillard, 1991, p. 453)

Postmodern instructional development recognizes that "real" is itself an illusion, a "simulacrum," often created for political or social purposes to restore an organization or setting to a preferred state, and sometimes to obscure transformation or change.

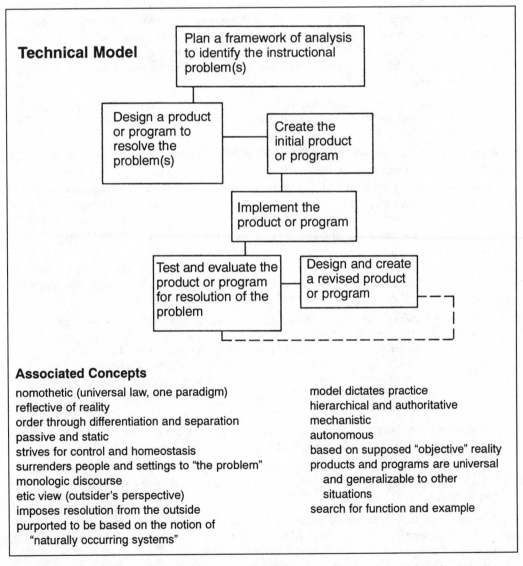

Figure 1.   Technical model of instructional development and associated concepts.

It is characteristic of postmodern society, that the simulacrum, the image, no longer follows reality, but in fact displaces it . . . First the simulacrum reflects reality, then it masks
reality, then it masks the absence of reality, and finally it deconstructs reality such that
there is no relation between reality and its simulacrum. (Hlynka, 1991, p. 518)

The continued search for supposed "scientific" theories, "effective" education programs,
and "verifiable" research activity by many instructional developers represents a desire to identify and designate instructional mechanisms that control people and settings. In turn, these
mechanisms promote theories and practices that portray the illusion that "order" is a first requirement towards development (learning, instruction, social change).

It is impossible to critique instructional development without breaking (deconstructing)
its representation of "real" posed through particular language, models, and discourse. As
Baudrillard (1991) points out, different language and conversations are necessary because
"the established order" (the traditional field theories and practices) "can do nothing against
it (p. 491)." In response to criticism, traditionalists will often fall back on the use of language,
models, and discourse that represent their particular conceptualization of social activity and
"order." While late twentieth century societies continue to experience widespread social and
political unrest, many instructional developers refuse to embrace this uncertainty, and are
adamant about defining the real "order" of events as necessary for educational activity. In
fact, one might say that "real" and "order" are synonymous in technical models of instructional development.

Hence, *failing the real*, it is here that we must aim at order . . . This is why order always
opts for the real. In a state of uncertainty, it always prefers this assumption. . . .
(Baudrillard, 1991, p. 461)

Postmodern instructional developers asks different questions in an effort to help educational settings and participants "breathe"; to explore new outlets for looking at social environments. Such an approach provides developers an opportunity to challenge neutrality and
the language of authority common to the traditional view of educational technology, and
seeks to encourage others to embrace uncertainty and ambiguity, accept resistance, recognize
chaos and freely experience the changes that continuously occur in a setting. Postmodern instructional development activity is located in a gray area and conceives of itself as a practice
that is dedicated not to resolutions, but to the responsible interpretation of educational lifeworlds through exploration. Exploration is the path to broadening one's understanding of the
social, as well as technical, meaning of educational activity.

The core of postmodernism is the doubt that any method or theory, discourse or genre,
tradition or novelty, has a universal and general claim as the "right" or privileged form of
authoritative knowledge. Postmodernism *suspects* all truth claims of masking and serving
particular interests in local, cultural, and political struggles. But postmodernism does not
automatically reject conventional methods of knowing and telling as false or archaic.
Rather, it opens those standard methods to inquiry and introduces new methods, which are
also, then subject to critique. (Richardson, 1994, p. 517)

For some postmodern instructional developers the objective, technical view can be situated next to postmodern development without any problem since:

. . . positivist methods are but one way of telling a story about society or the social world.
They may be no better or no worse than any other method; they just tell a different kind
of story. (Denzin & Lincoln, 1994, p. 5)

Hlynka (1991), for example, suggests that "in educational technology, a postmodern
view would challenge monolithic, technical and systematic models of instruction" (p. 517),
but this would not mean that the postmodern view is exclusive. From Hlynka's point of view,
"postmodern educational technology would see technical, practical, and critical models

existing side by side, sometimes contradicting, but often complementing each other." (p. 517)

For others, there can be no bridge between the technical view and the postmodern view. Yet, whether one embraces in part the traditional methods and criteria of instructional development, or rejects them altogether, postmodern developers recognize "alternative methods" for exploring people and social settings "including verisimilitude, emotionality, personal responsibility, an ethic of caring, political praxis, multivoiced texts, and dialogues with subjects" (Denzin & Lincoln, 1994, p. 5).

As the developer inquires and participates in the setting, begins to know the people, learns about their interpretations and search for meaning, and suggests some of his or her own interpretations, instructional development is woven into the inquiry. Therefore, instructional development is not focused on the development of an "outcome," but is a process constructed *by* the interaction of people and social settings. And so, instructional development is an actual social practice. The developer struggles with negotiating entry (does not command it) and becoming part of the setting . . . observes and learns about the people and setting over time (does not simply analyze them), explores the variety of overlapping activities and practices in the setting . . . including individuals' current construction of instructional development (does not engineer reality), and actively participates in the interpretation and meaning making of that setting as it is constructed by the participants and, *now,* the developer (does not impose a model upon them). This view of instructional development envisions power relationships as constructed and negotiated:

> Understanding the *context* of power, in concert with the *relationships* it articulates and effectuates, allows us to move beyond the abstract notion of individual autonomy to construct a cultural theory of meaning grounded in social circumstances and material practices. Moreover, any theory of power must also be sensitive to the capacity of persons to interpret and intervene in their world. (Britzman, 1991, p. 19)

A postmodern inquiry into instructional development suggests that settings and people are undifferentiated from social activity, and are constantly engaged in inquiry.

> The dichotomy between theory and practice, which represents, in actuality, the fragmentation of knowledge from lived experience, is challenged when the context of theory is practice, not other theories. (Britzman, 1991, p. 54)

Instructional developers who learn to inquire into their social practice through creative questioning, who can facilitate a variety of discourses, and who are able to look at that which is taken for granted in the traditional components of the development process, are more likely to participate in educational activity that is socially responsible and meaningful, and at its best, partial:

> . . . a postmodernist position does allow us to know something without claiming to know everything. Having a partial, local, historical knowledge is still knowing. (Richardson, 1994, p. 518)

Furthermore, an instructional developer who can deconstruct the theory and practice of instructional development, and conceive of it as a social practice, will be capable of crossing borders, thinking about different meanings, creating new meanings, and transgressing the static identity associated with the stereotype of an "educational technologist." Once again, enter the postmodern world of instructional development:

> You go in at one point, you rocket around until you think it's time to come out, and there you are. Where is 'there'? Why, that's the surprise that's in store for you, because you never know until you get there. And sometimes not even then.
>
> When you took the Jump . . . how sure were you *where* you would emerge? The timing and the quantity of the energy input might be as tightly controlled as you liked

. . . but the uncertainty principle reigned supreme and there was always the chance, even the inevitability of a random miss . . . a paper-thin miss might be a thousand light-years. *(Paul Nahin, 1993, p. 81: quoting science fiction writers Pohl and Asimov on the trouble with hyperspace travel.)*

Instructional development in late industrial society is reflective of, and has much more in common with, the ambiguous and uncertain experience of hyperspace travel than supposed "orderly" systems. Postmodern systems are entropic: in a continuous state of breaking down. Likewise, instructional development in the postmodern world suggests negotiation, collaboration, and criticism. A critical approach to instructional development and some of its associated concepts are shown in Figure 2.

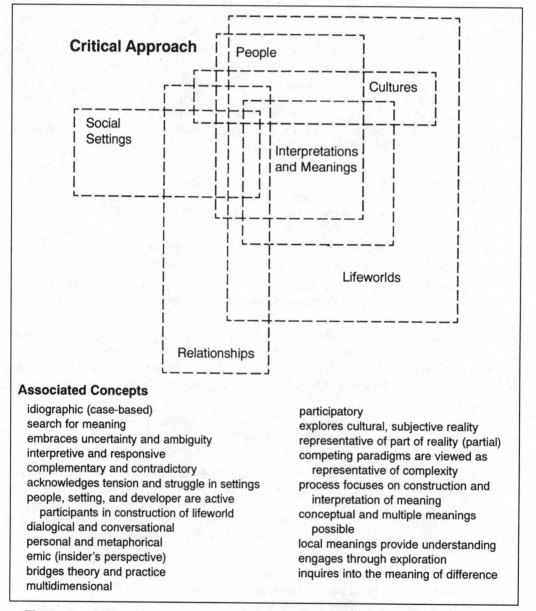

Critical Approach

People

Cultures

Social Settings

Interpretations and Meanings

Lifeworlds

Relationships

Associated Concepts

idiographic (case-based)
search for meaning
embraces uncertainty and ambiguity
interpretive and responsive
complementary and contradictory
acknowledges tension and struggle in settings
people, setting, and developer are active
   participants in construction of lifeworld
dialogical and conversational
personal and metaphorical
emic (insider's perspective)
bridges theory and practice
multidimensional

participatory
explores cultural, subjective reality
representative of part of reality (partial)
competing paradigms are viewed as
   representative of complexity
process focuses on construction and
   interpretation of meaning
conceptual and multiple meanings
   possible
local meanings provide understanding
engages through exploration
inquires into the meaning of difference

Figure 2.   Critical approach to instructional development and associated concepts.

Implications of Instructional Development as Praxis: Bridging Theory and Practice

At this point in the discussion, a developer with a good sense of postmodern humor might suggest that the implications for instructional development practice are not much so about ensuring that one knows what is meant by "postmodern instructional development," only that one is sure "what it is not." It is not focused on the development of outcomes or models. It is not viewed as a practice through which an individual or expert defines a setting and people. It is not about defining a "problem," and then outlining solutions. Instead, it suggests that developers must "explore how individuals' lived experiences often differ from those defined within current educational technology systems" (Jamison, 1994b, p. 67). As a social practice, it must acknowledge its own culture, but also the culture of other practitioners.

> Culture is where identities, desires, and investments are mobilized, constructed, and re-worked. It is the site where antagonistic meanings push and pull at our sensibilities, deep investments, and relationships with others. And consequently there is not one monolithic culture that communicates unitary meanings. Circulating within and persuading any culture are an array of contesting and contradictory discourses that vie for our attention. (Britzman, 1991, p. 57)

Postmodern instructional developers search for meaning. They are interpretive and recognize that "the individuals who make up different societies are held in relation to one another not by natural or scientific laws, but through a variety of overlapping and often contradictory social processes" (Jamison, 1994b, p. 66). As a practice, development is playful and personal, but also responsible.

> Postmodern thinking does not dispute the value of trying to improve both the world and human relations, but it does question the possibility of doing so with only science and technology. Belief in industrial, urban solutions accomplished the development of the modern world. The utopian dream of navigating cyberspace and controlling all things by pressing a few keys underlies this type of thinking. (Yeaman, 1994, p. 16)

Postmodern instructional development is an interpretive practice that provides the opportunity to participate, responsibly, in the process of different educational inquiry and activity. It moves away from the commonly held view that its activities should focus on the provision of outcomes, answers, or solutions to supposed "real problems" in instructional settings. Instead, postmodern instructional development is like looking into a swimming pool on a hot and windy day:

> *Unlike a stationary glass of water, the heat, water, and air transform the shape and bottom of the pool, and the bottom becomes something other than flat, static, motionless. Nothing is clear, it is all moving and blurry. You cannot tell the depth of the water, because the bottom no longer provides any meaning. The water is and isn't clear. Still, it is hot and you plunge into the water. You feel your way around and now you have to reinterpret the water, pool, air, environment. The instructional process, like the heat surrounding you on this hot day, begins to melt away and you begin to welcome the pool as comforting. You begin to deny the heat, respect the water, and take ownership of your presence in the pool. You become integrated into all that surrounds you, but aware that you are able to create your own transformations and impact the water. And, then, you look amongst the two hundred and fifty other people in the pool to find a place where you might begin . . . to swim.*

References

Banathy, B. (1991). *Systems design of education: A journey to create the future.* Englewood Cliffs, NJ: Educational Technology Publications.

Baudrillard, J. (1991). The precession of simulacra. In D. Hlynka & J. C. Belland (Eds.), *Paradigms regained: The uses of illuminative, semiotic, and postmodern criticism as modes of inquiry in educational technology* (pp. 441–480). Englewood Cliffs, NJ: Educational Technology Publications.

Berger, J. (1972). *Ways of seeing.* London: BBC and Penguin Books.

Briggs, L. *et al.* (1991). *Instructional design: Principles and applications* (2nd ed.). Englewood Cliffs, NJ: Educational Technology Publications.

Britzman, D. P. (1991). *Practice makes practice: A critical study of learning to teach.* Albany, NY: SUNY Press.

Bush, C. G. (1983). Women and the assessment of technology: To think, to be, to unthink, to be free. In J. Rothschild (Ed.), *Machina ex dea: Feminist perspectives on technology.* New York: Pergamon Press.

Caputo, J. D. (1993). *Against ethics.* Bloomington, IN: Indiana University Press.

Clark, D. (1985). Emerging paradigms in organizational theory and research. In Y. Lincoln (Ed)., *Organizational theory and inquiry* (pp. 43–78). Newbury Park, CA: Sage.

Damarin, S. K. (1994). *Would you rather be a cyborg or a goddess? On being a teacher in a postmodern century.* Paper presented at the annual American Educational Research Association Conference, New Orleans, LA.

Denzin, N. K., & Lincoln, Y. S. (1994). *Handbook of qualitative research.* Thousand Oaks, CA: Sage.

Dick, W., & Carey, L. (1990). *The systematic design of instruction* (3rd ed.). Glenview, IL: Scott, Foresman.

Gagné, R., & Wager, W. (1992). *Principles of instructional design* (4th ed.). Fort Worth, TX: Harcourt Brace Jovanovich.

Haraway, D. (1989). A cyborg manifesto: Science, technology, and socialist feminism in the late twentieth century. In L. Nicholson (Ed.), *Feminism/postmodernism.* New York: Routledge.

Harding, S. (1987). *Feminism and methodology.* Bloomington, IN: Indiana University Press.

Heshusius, L. (1994). Freeing ourselves from objectivity: Managing subjectivity or turning toward a participatory mode of consciousness. Unpublished paper.

Hlynka, D. (1991). Glossary. In D. Hlynka & J. C. Belland (Eds.), *Paradigms regained: The uses of illuminative, semiotic, and postmodern criticism as modes of inquiry in educational technology* (pp. 513–520). Englewood Cliffs, NJ: Educational Technology Publications.

Hockney, D. (1984). *Cameraworks.* New York: Alfred Knopf.

Jameson, F. (1991). *Postmodernism, or, the cultural logic of late capitalism.* Durham, NC: Duke University Press.

Jamison, P. K. (1992). No Eden under glass: A discussion with Donna Haraway. *Feminist Teacher, 6*(2), 10–15.

Jamison, P. K. (1994a). Providing alternative views of context, instruction, and learning in graduate and continuing professional education courses in instructional development. Paper presented at the Center for Urban Ethnography Conference (CUE), Philadelphia, PA.

Jamison, P. K. (1994b). The struggle for critical discourse: Reflections on the possibilities of critical theory for educational technology. *Educational Technology, 34*(2), 66–69.

Koetting, J. R. (1994). Postmodern thinking in a modernist cultural climate: The need for an unquiet pedagogy. *Educational Technology, 34*(2), 55–56.

Nahin, P. (1993). *Time machines: Time travel in physics, metaphysics, and science fiction.* New York: American Institute of Physics.

Pacey, A. (1983). *The culture of technology.* Cambridge, MA: MIT Press.

Richardson, L. (1994). Writing: A method of inquiry. In N. K. Denzin & Y. S. Lincoln (Eds.), *Handbook of qualitative research.* Thousand Oaks, CA: Sage.

Shrock, S. A. (1995). A brief history of instructional development. In G. J. Anglin (Ed.), *Instructional technology: Past, present, and future* (2nd ed.). Englewood, CO: Libraries Unlimited.

Stewart, S. (1978). *Nonsense: Aspects of intertextuality in folklore and literature.* Baltimore: Johns Hopkins University Press.

Trinh, T. Minh-ha (1989). *Woman, native, other.* Bloomington, IN: Indiana University Press.

Vidich, A. J., & Lyman, S. M. (1994). Qualitative methods: Their history in sociology and anthropology. In N. K. Denzin & Y. S. Lincoln (Eds.), *Handbook of qualitative research.* Thousand Oaks, CA: Sage.

Yeaman, A. (1994). Deconstructing modern educational technology. *Educational Technology, 34*(2), 15–24.

6

The Importance of Relational Aspects in the Systems Approach

Joseph Kessels
Leiden University, The Netherlands

Tjeerd Plomp
University of Twente, The Netherlands

Introduction

The aim of the study reported in this chapter was to identify a set of practical instructional design standards, validated by empirical research, that can be used in the context of corporate education. Although the importance of learning rarely has been questioned, there is increasing doubt as to the effects of the actual activities geared towards the facilitation of learning processes. Training and development activities absorb a costly part of an organization's manpower capacity, budget, and opportunities, but the resources needed become scarce in periods of economic decline (Harrison, 1992). In organizations, the need for successful adaptation to an ever-changing environment, and thus also for learning, is most urgent in such periods of economic instability. At present, learning is widely recognized as a major vehicle for organizational survival and change, and great interest is shown in emerging and re-emerging concepts such as 'learning to learn,' 'organizational learning,' and the 'learning company' (Pedler, Burgoyne, & Boydell, 1991; Senge, 1990).

Curriculum Design. Curriculum design plays an important role in creating an educational environment that fulfils the needs for learning. Descriptive theories on how learning is organized are available, but prescriptive theories and their related design instructions are scarce (Reigeluth, 1983).

The study reported here partially fills this need, and offers a theoretical and an empirically tested basis for curriculum design standards that should lead towards goal-oriented and cost-effective learning situations. These learning situations are not restricted to the typical classroom environment. In principle, an organization offers a wide variety of learning opportunities. Specifically, the environment outside the classroom seems to play a dominant role in achieving the desired effects of intentionally organized learning situations (Broad & Newstom, 1992; Kirkpatrick, 1975; Robinson & Robinson, 1989).

Design standards for corporate education focus primarily on the acquisition of skills that are sustained by the work environment; skills that should bring about intended changes in employee performance and subsequently have an impact on the organization. The body of knowledge on public education provides the broad theoretical foundation for such design standards. Moreover, the complex mechanisms in corporate education, where cognitive operations of individual learning intertwine with social processes of an organizational context, demand not just an adapted theory, but an extended theory that seeks to explain the existing successes and failures of training systems and predicts the results of new actions. However, such a study should avoid the immodesty of presenting a grand theory that pretends to solve all problems in the field. Nor can it inquire in depth into trainer behavior and such trainee background variables as age, gender, intelligence, culture, and previous education.

Corporate education provides intentionally designed learning situations aiming at the mutual effects of individual and organizational behavior. Therefore, the curriculum design theory needed should not only incorporate indicators for the development of curriculum materials, but also prescribe approaches that relate to the strategic issues of an organization and to structural feedback mechanisms, as well as to the design of a work environment that inherently holds constructive educational values.

Research Questions. Thus, the aim of this study was to develop a prescriptive theory and validated design standards for corporate education, and as such addresses the following research questions:

1. Which factors in curriculum design influence quality in corporate education?
2. How do these factors operate?
3. Can curriculum design standards control these factors?

Curriculum Typology

Building onto Taba's definition of the term curriculum (Taba, 1962, p. 76), curriculum in the context of corporate education is defined as:

— the course of action open to an organization
— for influencing the necessary skills of employees
— that contribute to goal-oriented changes in their performance and in their work environment
— thus striving for a desired impact on the organization
— by applying planned learning activities and the resulting learning processes.

Goodlad's curriculum typology (Goodlad, Klein, & Tye, 1979) provides a springboard for the development of a curriculum typology for use in corporate education. However, for the application of these concepts in this context, other labels have been used. Furthermore, much emphasis has been placed on the contingencies among the subsequent curricula. Moreover, the consistency among the curricula will be considered as an expression of their quality. It is this concept of consistency that leads to the major hypotheses of this research. The modified version of Goodlad's curriculum typology is depicted in Figure 1. The arrows indicate the mutual influences of the related elements that are described in the following sections. The typology distinguishes between two principal curricula:

— the ideal curriculum: what should be strived for, and
— the attained curriculum: what has been achieved.

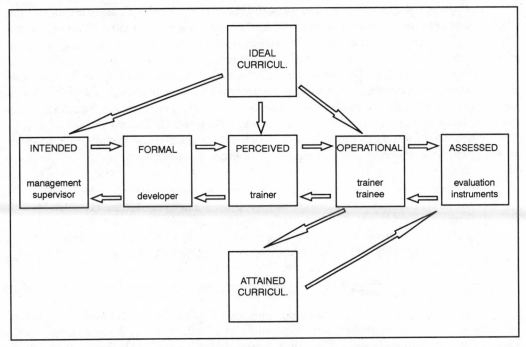

Figure 1. A curriculum typology for corporate education.

The following intermediate curricula bridge the ideal and attained curriculum:

— the intended curriculum: the assignment from management to develop and conduct training;
— the formal curriculum: the documented design of the interventions needed;
— the perceived curriculum: The trainer's perception of what kind of education is needed;
— the operational curriculum: the real learning environment;
— the assessed curriculum: the evaluation of results.

External Consistency. External consistency refers to the congruence in the perceptions of the above mentioned curricula by the actors: (top) management, developer, supervisor, trainer and trainee. Establishing such a coherence does not only depend on activities of the developer but is also favored by a positive learning climate and an active corporate education policy.

Internal Consistency. Next to the need for consistency among the actors' perceptions, a curriculum should be consistent in itself. This concept of internal consistency applies to the logical contingencies between:

— the changes that are needed in the work environment,
— the necessary skills of managers and employees to bring about these changes, and
— the learning situations that facilitate the acquisition of these skills.

By the same token, internal consistency also implies for the curriculum that learning processes should enable employees to acquire skills that influence their performance, so that the affected work environment has an impact on the organization.

The concept of curriculum consistency—the contingencies between its elements and the congruences between its appearances—is inspired by Stake's model for curriculum evaluation (Stake, 1973). Throughout this study, curriculum consistency, both internal and external, is used as a descriptive framework for quality in corporate education.

Design Approaches. The main purpose of developing and applying design standards is to improve the internal consistency of a curriculum and to gear towards a strong external consistency between the curriculum perceptions of the actors in corporate education, thus resulting in an attained curriculum that is consistent with the ideal curriculum.

When design standards are to influence curriculum consistency, the question arises as to which mechanisms bring about internal and external consistency.

> The theory developed here advocates both a systematic and a relational approach that trigger a powerful combination of systems thinking and social integration. The integration of a systematic and a relational approach in design standards is held responsible for curriculum consistency and subsequently for corporate education of a high standard.

Systematic Approach. The systematic approach implies the logical design sequence of orientation, design, development, implementation, and evaluation. (Branson & Grow, 1987; Plomp, 1982, 1992; Romiszowski, 1981, 1984; Rothwell & Kazanas, 1992; Tracey, 1971, 1984). Specific instruments and methods used are needs assessment and job/task analysis techniques, instructional objectives, learning strategies, training materials, guidelines for trainers and evaluation instruments. The systematic approach, when skillfully applied, leads to a well structured and logically ordered curriculum design with a strong internal consistency. This design on paper is referred to as the formal curriculum.

Relational Approach. The relational approach provides activities that challenge actors to become involved in the design and implementation process and that reveal their perceptions of the ideal curriculum. When the mutual perceptions of the actors involved are explicit, they can be influenced and gradually become compatible. The relational approach facilitates actors' involvement in the design and implementation process and has an impact on management commitment to corporate education. When skillfully applied, the relational approach leads to a strong external consistency among actors' curriculum perceptions, which is considered to be a necessary condition for a successful implementation of the new curriculum and its presupposed effects.

The Research Design

Exisiting theory served as an important source for design standards that result in internally and externally consistent curricula. Identification and validation of the standards were based on empirical research encompassing four main stages: analysis of 17 contrasting cases, development of design instructions, the training of 30 developers, and finally the development, implementation, and evaluation of 28 new curriculum projects.

Seventeen Case Studies. The cases, comprising existing training programs in 8 different organizations, were divided into two contrasting groups—9 successful and 8 unsuccessful (the criterion 'success' initially to be determined by the training manager). The cases were analyzed on the degree of internal and external consistency, and to see whether the systematic and relational design approaches had been applied. The characteristics found were related to the attained effects (as evaluated by independent assessors). Most successful cases showed strong internal and external consistency. They also revealed a strong systematic and relational design approach. The unsuccessful cases showed weak curriculum consistency, both internal as well as external. Both the systematic and relational design approaches were poor in the unsuccessful cases.

Development of Design Standards. In addition to theoretical justification, the case studies provided an empirical basis for a set of curriculum design procedures, which were to be tested in the second empirical study.

Training of 30 Developers. At the outset of the second empirical study, 30 developers were trained in mastering the design instructions. The training course took place over a period of eight months during which the participants worked simultaneously (but not full time) on projects to be implemented in their organizations.

Twenty-Eight Curriculum Projects. The design instructions used in this second study incorporated the systematic approach and the relational approach. The main hypothesis of the second study was as follows: the skillful application of design standards, based on a relational and systematic approach, will generate educational programs that accomplish better results than programs that are not supported by such approaches. A total of 28 projects were submitted for further research. Three judges per project assessed the curriculum documents. Up to nine months later, data on the attained curriculum were collected by means of a questionnaire from (top) management, supervisor, trainer, trainees and developer.

The Systematic Approach

A Theory of Instructional Design

This study aims at *prescriptive* models for designing corporate education, as it seeks to create optimal instructional environments directed towards desired outcomes within the framework of the specific conditions of an organization.

Plomp's generic model for educational problem solving (Plomp, 1982) provides a systems approach by:

- analyzing conditions and desired outcomes;
- designing and developing an educational environment in which methods and strategies are selected and applied;
- testing and revising the system;
- evaluating the outcomes.

This generic model involves a process of iterative problem solving and solution finding. Each following phase in the process may require further analysis of components from previous steps. This cyclic nature is required not only because of the lack of prescriptive theory, but due to the fact that activities and products in the succeeding stages often require specific information that can not be collected in the initial phase. When applying Plomp's problem solving model to the design of the formal curriculum, the systematic approach comprises activities, as schematized in Figure 2 (see also Figure 3).

1. Analysis of problems or goals on the organizational level requires needs assessment for defining the aims of the design process and for determining the educational and non educational implications of the projected solution (analysis of outcomes and conditions). This type of analysis, often called needs assessment, produces the overall goals of the project and the criteria for evaluating its future impact on the organization (Kaufman, 1982, 1990; Kessels & Smit, 1994; Rossett, 1992).

2. Analysis of the desired changes in the work environment requires job and task analysis for determining the educational and non-educational components and interventions. Analysis may include traditional hierarchical task analysis (breaking up tasks into sub tasks) and psychological analysis (revealing cognitive and metacognitive operations and knowledge

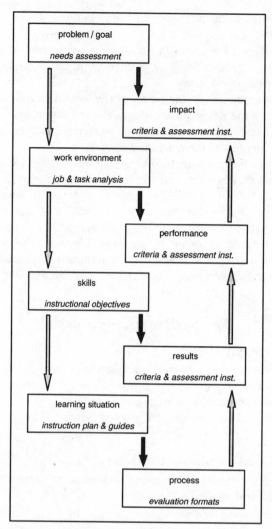

Figure 2. Design of the formal curriculum.

representation) (Carlisle, 1986; Kessels & Smit, 1994; Merrill, 1987; Patrick, 1991, 1992; Rossett, 1987). Analysis of the desired work environment also includes determination of the various target groups and data collection on their specific characteristics. This type of analysis produces specific goals of the project, types of interventions, and the basis for stating instructional objectives and criteria for evaluation on the performance level (analysis of outcomes and conditions).

3. Analysis of the required skills and the transformation of these requirements into instructional objectives, demands for in-depth examination of data collected in the previous stages. These desired educational outcomes, in terms of cognitive skills, interactive skills, reactive skills, and psycho-motor skills (Romiszowski, 1981), provide the criteria for evaluation on the level of training results and for selecting instructional methods and strategies (analysis of outcomes).

4. The design of learning situations and the development of supporting materials require careful consideration with regard to generally, training strategies and specific methods. The selection is based on instructional theory and on learning theory, but also on what is feasible in the work environment, or more generally, the corporate organization. Theories that

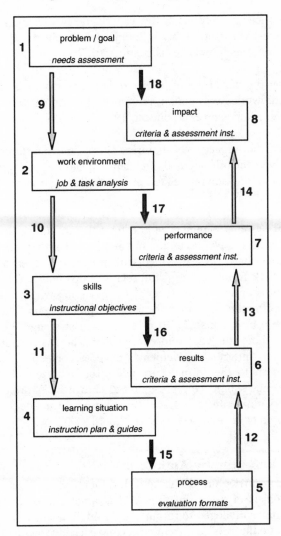

Figure 3.   Adequacy and consistency of the formal curriculum.

provide information on the effectiveness and efficiency of instructional strategies, methods, and delivery systems also provide information on adequate learning processes and ways in which learning may be enhanced, induced, or controlled (Fleming & Levie, 1992; Lowijck, 1991; Reigeluth, 1983; Reigeluth & Curtis, 1987; Romiszowski, 1981, 1984). The development of materials requires subject matter expertise, content analysis, and organizing principles of instructional sequencing. These design and development activities produce instructional plans, materials, and guides for creating learning situations both in work environment settings and in dedicated training settings.

5. Evaluation on the process level requires procedures, instructions, and formats for collecting data on reactions of trainees, trainers, and other actors in the learning situations to be created. These are procedures for formative purposes, pilot testing and revising, and for more permanent control of learning processes during the project (Kirkpatrick, 1975; Stake, 1973; Stufflebeam, 1971).

6. Evaluation on the results level requires criteria and assessment instruments for collecting data on the progression in skills acquisition. These are instruments that provide a

demonstration of proficiency referenced by criteria derived from instructional objectives (evaluation of outcomes) (Kirkpatrick 1975; Robinson & Robinson, 1989). Furthermore, cost-effective analysis on training approaches is conducted (Kearsley, 1982; Nijhof, Mulder, & Van Wijk, 1992).

7. Evaluation on the performance level requires assessment instruments for collecting data on changes in the work environment, referenced by criteria derived from project objectives (Kirkpatrick, 1975; Robinson & Robinson, 1989; Seashore, Lawler, Mirvis & Cammann, 1983).

8. Evaluation on the impact level requires criteria and instruments for assessing organizational change. These include methods for data collection on progression of the projects in achieving project goals and solving related problems (Kirkpatrick, 1975; Robinson & Robinson, 1989; Seashore *et al.* 1983).

The constituent systems elements of the formal curriculum have been described by their function and products as well as by the manner in which they are interrelated. For practical use, these elements have been provided with procedures, methods and techniques described in Kessels (1993). Examination of the relationships between the various elements of the formal curriculum is an important strategy for assessing whether a systematic approach has been accomplished by the developer or the development team. The Instructional Quality Profile (Merrill, Reigeluth, & Faust, 1979) offers such a strategy. The curriculum elements should be judged for their adequacy and consistency. The Instructional Quality Profile focuses on the following interrelated elements: purpose, objectives, tests and instruction. Applying their approach to the formal curriculum, as analyzed above, the evaluation of adequacy and consistency should be represented as shown in Figure 3.

The formal curriculum can be assessed by examining the adequacy of the products in 1 to 8 and the consistency of their relations in 9 to 18.

Competencies for a Systematic Approach

The profession of curriculum design and development requires specific competencies. They have been the object of study since the 1930s, ranging from adult learning as a sort of charity given to the underprivileged to formulating guidelines for developing a graduate program for training adult educators, and from criticizing excessive reductionism and behaviorist foundations to recent statements on ethical standards. Henschke's review (1991) reports on 30 of these studies.

ASTD (McLagan, 1983, 1989) and The International Board of Standards for Training, Performance, and Instruction, IBSTPI (Foshay, Silber, & Westgaard, 1986) conducted large-scale research projects on design and development competencies. ASTD reports on 11 roles, their outputs, the required competencies and related ethical issues. The IBSTPI Standards describe sixteen instructional design competencies, each embedded in a rationale, and performance indicators and assumptions. Rothwell and Kazanas (1992) based their book *Mastering the Instructional Design Process: A Systematic Approach* entirely on the sixteen IBSTPI instructional design competencies, and claim to offer the first volume grounded on an underlying foundation of solid research (Rothwell & Kazanas, 1992). Tracey (1981) developed a 600-page self-evaluation manual for HRD managers and specialists. Part Five of this giant checklist is devoted to the development, implementation, and evaluation of HRD delivery systems.

To accomplish a systematic approach in curriculum design, as advocated in the previous sections, a selection of competencies from the above mentioned sources has been made. This selection is justified by the requirements of an adequate performance of the elements in Figure 2. The numbers refer to the specific components and their contingencies:

Conduct needs assessment (Figure 3: 1).

Identify ideal and actual performance and performance conditions and determine causes of discrepancies. Employ strategies for analyzing individual and organization behavior.

Perform job and task analysis (Figure 3: 2 and 9).

Employ analysis strategies and reporting procedures.

State instructional objectives (Figure 3: 3 and 10).

Transform job requirements into objectives, so that performance measurement and selection of instructional strategies is facilitated.

Develop performance measurements (Figure 3: 6 and 16, 7 and 17, 8 and 18).

Transform needs, performance requirements, and objectives into evaluation criteria and appropriate assessment instruments.

Sequence the performance objectives (Figure 3: 4 and 11).

Draw a blueprint for the desired learning environment, appropriate for achieving the desired changes of performance.

Specify the instructional strategies (Figure 3: 4 and 11).

Devise instructional interventions to put the blue-print learning environment into action.

Design instructional material (Figure 3: 4 and 11).

Develop print, audio-visual, or electronic-based learner materials, job aids, trainer guides, and plans to facilitate the instructional interventions.

Evaluate the educational interventions.

Appraise the instructional methods, sequences, and materials, and improve (Figure 3: 5, 15, and 12).

Assess results, performance improvement, and the related impact on the organization (Figure 3: 6, 7, 8, 13, and 14).

The Relational Approach

In the preceding sections it is argued that external curriculum consistency can be influenced if the developer applies a relational approach. As curriculum affairs are mainly activities involving human beings communicating with each other, the relational approach consists of all the contacts between the developers and relevant actors. Besides the actors referred to in the curriculum typology ([top]managers, supervisors, trainers, trainees, developers), other parties may be involved, in particular clients, customers, coordinators, sponsors, and opinion leaders. Unlike the systematic approach with its clear and rigorous logic, the relational approach may often seem fuzzy, using informal networks, balancing power and influence, and striving for consensus within the limits of culturally determined feasibility (Duncan & Powers, 1992). Political awareness, cultivating support, developing relationships and gaining visibility seem to be ingredients of this aspect of curriculum design (Warshauer, 1988). In Plomp's generic model for educational problem solving (Plomp, 1982), 'implementation' starts from the very beginning of a project by involving all stakeholders. This model implicitly suggests a relational approach, however, without elaborating it. Activities that belong to the relational approach are sometimes characterized as "walk and talk the job" (Harrison, 1992). Banathy (1987) states that the process of arriving at better decisions is not a process of optimization; it is rather a process of negotiation among those with different points of view and value systems in order to find a satisfying solution. Subsequently, he advocates a participative design approach, comprising several spiralic and iterative phases that pay attention to context and environment of the system (Banathy, 1987, p. 93).

Although chaotic design processes may produce apparently high quality programs, for reasons of efficiency, planning, and control, a more orderly application of the relational approach is to be recommended (Lippitt & Lippitt, 1986; Phillips & Shaw, 1989).

The relational approach refers to the developer's activities in the domain of interpersonal dynamics of decision making about educational planning. It aims at developing homogeneous notions among actors on what the problem is and how it should be solved, and at gaining their commitment, involvement and support for implementation. In the next sections, several tactics to help achieve these goals are discussed, such as project management, rapport-building activities during needs assessment and task analysis, involvement of line management, creating similarity between learning situation and work environment, and recruiting trainers with practical experience in the subject matter field.

Project Management

Project management is a widely accepted form of planning and control. Sometimes it is seen as an administrative process of planning activities, allocating resources, monitoring costs, and ensuring conformity to time lines and specifications. Sometimes it is seen as an interpersonal process that manages relationships through such actions as making sure the right people are involved in the right way, and adopting a style that conforms to the need or preferences of the people involved (Jackson & Addison, 1992).

Project management facilitates the various phases of educational program design (AECT, 1977; Plomp 1982). Project management is important not only for planning and control reasons, but also for disseminating innovative ideas on corporate education in general and program features, in particular among important stakeholders. In many organizations project management is an accepted strategy, if not a *conditio sine qua non*, for research, development, and marketing activities. Therefore, it is recommended for educational program design that a strategy similar to the one the organization is acquainted with is adopted.

Common project functions comprise planning, scheduling, and control (Rothwell & Kazanas, 1992), and will recur during the different phases of a project. Although labels may differ, phases referred to here comprise: Preliminary inquiry, design, construction, test & revision, and implementation and are derived from the generic problem-solving model (Plomp, 1982):

- Preliminary inquiry involves recruitment of a project leader, assigning the role of principal to one or more executives constituting a project team, needs assessment, stating goals, and planning of activities and resources.

- Design involves task analysis, stating objectives and evaluation criteria, and blueprinting the learning environment.

- Construction involves selection of trainers and coaches, devising instructional strategies, and development of supporting materials and delivery system.

- Test & Revision involve pilot testing, formative evaluation, and revision.

- Implementation involves delivery and assessing effects, evaluation of evolving needs, and adaptation of the instructional and delivery system.

In perspective of the relational approach, project management and the processes it evokes can be regarded as a most important learning process for the organization. Particularly, organizations that consider training an isolated activity to be delegated to the training department or contracted out to a commercial agency may benefit from the intrinsically educational values of project management. The developer, in the project leader's role, is offered many chances to inform participants on contingencies across needs, interventions, and outcomes. Essential conditions for successful program implementation and their implications need to be discussed extensively. Apart from the education policy-making process on the corporate level, project management is a foremost opportunity to convey that, though an organization may farm out the training process, the learning process ultimately has to take place in the work environment.

The Relational Approach to the Formal Curriculum

Some elements in the formal curriculum do not depend exclusively on a systematic approach and require a relational approach as well. *Needs assessment* and *task analysis* need to be mentioned specifically. Mostly, where management has commissioned a training program, the initial problem has already been perceived as a training problem. Subsequently, the developer introduces needs assessment in order to revalidate these assumptions. Whether management is prepared to support the upheaval of time consuming needs assessment depends largely on the image of the training function in general and on the credibility of the developer in particular. Turning needs assessment and task analysis into a model of action research requires consulting skills from the developer, so that he or she may adequately play the role of change agent. Activities of such nature require other competencies from the developer over and above mere skillful application of data collection techniques and logical reasoning.

Moreover, task analysis is not just a meticulous process of determining how things are done and should be done. It is also establishing a rapport, thus evoking critical, though often unconscious, know-how. A positive and non-threatening climate during the data collection process is of great value for the quality of the information sought (Kessels & Smit, 1994). The nature of the established relationships with management, employees and clients during needs assessment and task analysis are of preeminent importance for successful implementation, which starts here, right from the initial phase of the development process (Plomp, 1982).

Compensatory Quality of the Relational Approach

As mentioned previously, many educational programs have been conducted without any formal assignment. Others have been developed because the training staff anticipated a demand for such programs, without having first clearly analyzed any perceived problem. Education departments and commercial training agencies may offer training programs of a certain kind because these are fashionable at the time. Numerous training programs are not based on an elaborate formal curriculum. Except for the few lines in a flyer or program catalogue and some transparencies, documentation is often sparse. The program is in the trainer's head. However, these training activities can still be perceived as high quality programs, even when formal evaluation did not take place. Missing or poorly stated formal curricula will by their nature cause internal curriculum discrepancies. However, it is not inevitable that these discrepancies will cause a decrease in quality. Under certain conditions, specific factors might compensate for these discrepancies. We are hypothesizing that the relational approach bears such correcting qualities. Factors that are assumed to influence quality in corporate education comprise: the role of line management, similarity between learning environment and work environment, practical experience of the trainer, and the selection of trainees. Although we contend that weaknesses in the formal curriculum might be compensated for, the relational approach does not substitute for the formal curriculum. Nonetheless, the factors described here are of critical importance for attaining positive program results.

Competencies for a Relational Approach

The quality of the relational approach is heavily related to the personal effectiveness of the developer. However, the image of the training function and its position in the structure of an organization are the foremost conditions that determine the opportunities for a relational approach within a single project (Buckley & Caple, 1990). Management's acceptance of the developer and the extent to which management legitimizes the developer's role are essential for the problem-solving effort (Lippitt & Lippitt, 1986). Interpersonal and consulting skills seem to be indispensable for an effective relational approach.

Many sources offer analyses of competencies professionals should dispose of when they enter into the relational approach. Often the performance oriented corporate educationalist is portrayed as a 'change agent' (Clark, 1991; Phillips & Shaw, 1989; Pont, 1991). When comparing curriculum design with the planned change tradition, the profiles of the change agent may be of great value for the developer (Argyris, 1982; Bennis, Benne, & Chin, 1969; Lippitt, Watson, & Westley, 1958).

The ASTD research projects (McLagan, 1983, 1989), as well the IBSTPI Standards (Foshay *et al.*, 1986), define several competencies for developers that may apply to the relational approach. Furthermore, recent publications on consulting and coaching offer a variety of requirements and competencies for developers to adopt in their relational approach (Block, 1981; Gilley & Eggland, 1989; Lippitt & Lippitt, 1986; Phillips & Shaw, 1989; Rothwell & Kazanas, 1992; Sink, 1992; Tosti & Jackson, 1992).

The most salient competencies are listed below:

1. Communication skills: listening, observing, interviewing, relating to others, self-expression, and exchanging constructive feedback.
2. Project management skills: leadership and chairperson skills, planning, monitoring and negotiating skills.
3. Consulting skills: building open collaborative relationships, clarifying mutual expectations and responsibilities, ability to influence others and gain commitment, facilitating change, encouraging widespread participation in the design and implementation of a project, and dealing with friction and resistance.
4. Experimental flexibility, self-insight, and self-esteem.
   Ability to create an atmosphere of tact, trust, politeness, friendliness, and stability.

Hypotheses

The previous sections presented a theory of curriculum consistency in corporate education. The curriculum typology forms the basis for describing external consistency between the various appearances of a curriculum. External consistency is influenced by a relational approach of the developer. The formal curriculum is analyzed in terms of internal consistency. Internal consistency is effected by a systematic approach of the developer. This conceptual framework and its constituent factors lead to the following chain of reasoning, which will result in a set of hypotheses.

A Chain of Reasoning

The chain of reasoning developed for this study consists of a number of components which are related to each other on the basis of assumptions in the curriculum consistency theory and the supporting systematic and relational approaches (Figure 4).

1. Design standards, comprising a systematic and relational approach, should generate educational programs that bring about positive effects (acquired skills, improved performance and impact).

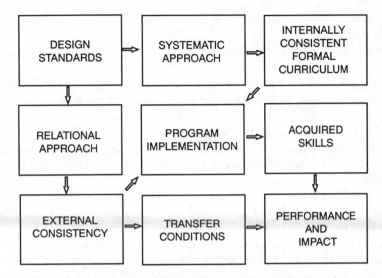

Figure 4. A chain of reasoning in corporate education.

2. Design standards are used to prepare educational programs (formal curriculum). These preparations result in tools such as plans, materials, and guides. The desired effects are assumed to be attained following proper implementation of the program according to plan. The trainer enacts the plan.
3. Effective design standards require skillful application by the developer. The developer needs to be trained to apply the design standards appropriately; that is, mastering both a systematic and relational approach.
4. The effects of a program find expression in the newly acquired skills of the participants. Ultimately, however, improved performance and a contribution to solving the initial problem (impact) are to be seen as positive effects.
5. Transfer of newly acquired skills into improved performance is facilitated or impeded by conditions in the participants' work environment.
6. Design standards should stimulate the developer to apply both a systematic and a relational approach (Figure 4).
   a. The systematic approach effects an internally consistent formal curriculum. Therefore, logic contingencies are to be found among purpose, objectives, evaluation criteria and instruments, and instruction presentation. The internal consistency of the formal curriculum enables powerful educational interventions and, subsequently, positive results.
   b. The relational approach generates homogeneous notions among parties involved as to what the problem is and how it could be solved: external consistency. If managers, supervisors, trainers, trainees and the developer share coherent opinions about the purpose and about the means to that end, their efforts will lead to successful program implementation, favorable transfer conditions and positive effects.

Hypotheses to Be Tested

The concept of curriculum consistency and the ensuing chain of reasoning lead to the following hypotheses to be tested:

1. Skillful application of design standards, based on both systematic and relational approaches, will generate educational programs that accomplish better results than programs that are not supported by such approaches.

2. Design standards advocating a systematic approach lead to internally consistent formal curricula.
3. Internal consistency of the formal curriculum and program effects are related positively.
4. Design standards advocating a relational approach lead to external consistency (homogeneous notions among concerned parties as to the nature of the problem and its possible solution).
5. External consistency and program effects are related positively.
6. The relational approach compensates for weaknesses in the systematic approach.
7. The systematic approach does not compensate for weaknesses in the relational approach.

Educational provisions should be cost effective. A cost-effective program design generates the best effects at the lowest costs. As the largest cost factor in corporate education are trainees' salaries and their opportunity costs (the loss of potential contribution to the organization), the program with the shortest training time per employee is the least costly. But the shortest program is not necessarily the most effective. Therefore, though conducting cost-benefit analysis is an important aspect of curriculum design, this activity itself does not generate better program effects. This observation leads to an additional hypothesis:

8. Though cost-benefit analyses are important for selecting efficient solutions to educational problems, they are not related to program effectiveness.

These hypotheses will be tested against the empirical findings of the two research projects described in the following sections. The results of the analyses obtained from these projects will contribute to the validity of the curriculum consistency theory. If evidence can be inferred regarding the systematic and relational approaches, design standards can be improved on the basis of the empirical findings. Skillful application of such design standards will lead towards high quality educational provisions in labor organizations.

Empirical Study #1: Seventeen Case Studies

The major research questions addressed in the first study are:

1. What factors in curriculum design affect the quality of corporate education?
2. How do these factors operate?

Study #1 was designed to find an empirical basis for the existence of the predicted relationships between the systematic approach, internal consistency, and program effects, and the relationships between the relational approach, external consistency, and program effects.

Variables

From the conceptual framework and its constructs described above, the following six variables have been derived:

Variable: Systematic Approach

A systematic approach implies adequate application of design procedures including the following items:

— adequate assessment of training needs
— adequate description of goals
— adequate task analysis
— adequate instructional objectives
— adequate establishment of evaluation criteria
— adequate construction of evaluation instruments
— adequate design of learning situations
— adequate development of course materials

Variable: Internal Consistency

In an internally consistent formal curriculum, a logical relationship exists between assignment, objectives, evaluation criteria, evaluation instruments, instructional strategies, and training materials. The formal curriculum comprises the following items:

— consistency between goals and needs assessment
— consistency between task analysis and preceding elements
— consistency between instructional objectives and preceding elements
— consistency between evaluation criteria and preceding elements
— consistency between evaluation instruments and preceding elements
— consistency between learning situations and preceding elements
— consistency between course materials and preceding elements

Variable: Relational Approach

A relational approach comprises activities that favour the involvement of managers and supervisors during design and implementation, the selection of trainers who have recent, practical experience in the subject matter field, and the creation of a learning situation that closely resembles the work environment. The relational approach comprises the following items:

— adequate assessment of training needs
— adequate task analysis
— creation of favorable conditions for implementation
— adequate selection of trainers and coaches
— adequate selection of trainees
— involvement of line managers
— design of learning situations that resemble the work environment
— selection of trainers that have experience with the work of trainees

Variable: External Consistency

External consistency refers to the homogeneity of ideas and perceptions among managers, supervisors, developers, trainers and trainees on the nature of the problem and its possible solution through an educational provision. External consistency comprises the consistency between views of:

— (top) manager and developer
— (top) manager and trainer
— (top) manager and supervisor
— (top) manager and employee (= trainee)
— developer and trainer
— developer and supervisor
— developer and trainee
— trainer and supervisor
— trainer and trainee
— supervisor and employee (= trainee)

Variable: Cost-benefit Analysis

The cost-benefit analysis variable comprises the following item:

— direct costs, salaries of trainees, overhead costs, lost opportunity costs, and estimation of benefits

Variable: Effects

Program effects comprise the acquired skills, changes in performance and the impact on the organization as perceived by:

— (top) managers
— supervisors
— developers
— trainers
— trainees

Research Design

Study #1 may be characterized as a multiple case study with multiple units of analysis, focusing on theoretical replication and not at statistical generalization, described by Yin as a Type 4 study (Yin, 1989). The within-site and cross-site data analyses were carried out by means of display techniques as described by Miles and Huberman (1984).

As these case studies aimed to detect factors in curriculum design that affect the quality of the outcomes, the research design comprises the analysis of two sets of contrasting cases: successful and unsuccessful. Unlike Empirical Study #2 (where curricula have been designed deliberately as part of the research project), Study #1 concentrates on existing, implemented curricula. In that respect, the design may also be considered as a *post-facto* design (Sprinthall, Schmutte, & Sirois, 1991, p. 71). The cases have been selected by the local training managers on the basis of their subjective measure of the Effects variable (successful/unsuccessful). During the study, a reliability test was run on the correct use of the labels 'successful' and 'unsuccessful'. The results of this test are reported later in this chapter.

Selection of the Cases

Selection of the cases raised the following questions:

— What type of organizations should be addressed?
— Which kinds of programs should be reviewed?
— Who determines whether programs are successful or unsuccessful?

Theoretically, there was no reason for the exclusion or inclusion of specific types of organizations, nor did the kind of program matter. The only criterion was that the program had to have been developed at the request of the organization. Off-the-shelf courses and packages were to be excluded. The course design could have been carried out by either the in-house training staff or by an outside agency.

At the outset of the project, the definition of success or failure was left to the training manager. The researcher was mainly interested in the contrast between programs that were considered to be successful and those considered to be unsuccessful in the context of the organization itself.

Discussing the research project with training managers soon revealed that the main problem was to obtain access to cases, especially the unsuccessful ones. In general, managers are reluctant to offer failures for outside inspection. Furthermore, the research design called for the cooperation of developers, trainers, managers, supervisors and trainees. Publicly designating their program as unsuccessful would make them reluctant to participate and inhibit a collaborative attitude. These concerns could be met by promising the participating organizations that the cases would be studied anonymously. These considerations led to the following selection process:

Fifty training managers were invited to offer two contrasting training programs: one successful and one unsuccessful. To avoid insulting anyone, the label 'less successful' was used.

Fourteen training managers responded that they were willing to participate in the project (28 cases).

When the time came to submit the cases for analysis, only nine training managers succeeded in finding (top) managers, supervisors, developers, trainers and trainees—who had been involved in the program—willing to participate in the data collection.

Nine successful and nine unsuccessful cases were examined. Yet, during the data collection, one of the unsuccessful cases was withdrawn (Case 17) because top management objected to further analysis.

The remaining 17 cases were all tailor made or adapted to the organization's specific need. They included the following types of programs:

Case:

1, 2, 11, 12	technical skills
3, 4, 7, 8	interpersonal skills
5, 9, 10, 13, 14	computer skills
6, 15, 16	servicing skills
18	management skills

The participating organizations come from the fields of banking, insurance, public service, industry, transportation, and consulting.

Data Collection

Data collection was conducted by eight trained investigators according to a data collection protocol. The protocol contained 28 pages of detailed guidelines for the investigator. The guidelines were derived from the variables and their constituting items. The protocol covered the following sections:

A. General information on the case
B. Guidelines for the study of documents
C. Guidelines for interviews with the actors
D. A framework for writing a case report

Data reduction was accomplished by applying coding and display techniques as described by Miles and Huberman (1984). The qualitative analysis was completed by quantitative analysis. The researcher and analysts rated the items of the main variables on a 5-point scale, so that Likert scales could be constructed for the variables Systematic Approach, Internal Consistency, Relational Approach, External Consistency, Cost-Benefit Analysis, and Effect. Values <3.00 were defined as low. For the quantitative analysis, data were rejected when jury $\alpha < .60$, scale $\alpha < .70$, and sub scale $\alpha < .60$. The probability level $p < .10$ is justified by the small number of cases.

The Effect variable was quantified by means of two series of rating sessions. In series #1, two judges (expert training consultants) each assessed the actors' statements on the perceived effects by rating the statements on a five-point scale (1 = no effect; 5 = highly effective). The rating took place according to prescribed instructions from the researcher. Once all cases had been rated, the two judges compared their ratings and discussed differences. This discussion was considered necessary because the quality of the statements in the displays varied considerably. Statements referred to reactions of trainees, test results, changes in performance, and effects on the department or organization. In series #2, the same rating process was repeated in a different setting with different judges. Comparison of the two rating series showed a correlation of $r = .85$. The results of these ratings and the statistical checks allow relabelling of the cases: Unsuccessful is an Effect score <3.00, successful is an Effect score >3.00. On the basis of the two ratings, a Likert scale for the Effect variable was constructed. This scale was used to calculate the correlations of the variables Systematic Approach, Internal Consistency, Relational Approach, External Consistency, Cost-Benefit Analysis, and Effect. The ratings of the perceived effects of the 17 cases made it possible to rank the cases according to their new total scores ($\overline{X}$ of the two rating series). Tied case scores were broken by using the combined ratings of managers and supervisors as a second ranking key.

Discussion of Study #1

This section formulates answers to the research questions to the extent that it would be possible to generalize on the basis of the theory developed in the conceptual framework. To that end, the main variables and their constituting elements will be discussed, and the hypotheses will be compared with the findings.

Conclusions

To visualize the differences between the two sets of contrasting cases, data are depicted in graphic form. The cases are ranked according to their Effect value. The numeric values are represented by the graphic sign (#). Thus, Table 1 shows a graphic pattern of the results for the variables.

The observations that follow are made on the basis of the values of the main variables and the statistical comparison of successful and unsuccessful cases, combined with additional qualitative information.

Systematic Approach. In unsuccessful cases (Effect < 3.00) a significantly poorer systematic approach is applied than in the successful cases (Effect > 3.00), t (12.14) = −3.18, $p = .008$. However, in most cases, whether successful or unsuccessful, documentation on the design and development process is poor. Some conclusions from the data are:

— Reports on training needs assessment and task analysis are mostly absent in both types of cases.
— Instructional objectives of unsuccessful programs tend to be stated in terms of reproductive knowledge aspects.
— Instructional objectives of successful programs tend to be stated in terms of reproductive as well as productive skills.
— In both types of cases, evaluation criteria are neither stated nor documented.
— In both types of cases, evaluation instruments are restricted to the lowest levels of evaluation: reaction to learning processes and tests of training results. Virtually none of the cases used instruments to assess performance or organizational impact.
— In the successful cases, the designed learning situations show a greater variety of activities than in those that are unsuccessful.
— Almost all cases used elaborate training materials. Successful cases devoted more attention to guidelines for trainers.

Table 1. Display of case scores in a graphic pattern, ranked according to the Effect value.

Case	Systematic Approach	Internal Consist.	Relational Approach	External Consist.	Cost-Benefit Analysis	Effect
12	###	####	####	###	###	####
11	###	####	####	####	#	####
18*	####	###	###	####	###	####
2	####	###	####	###	###	####
8*	##	#	###	##	#	###
10*	##	##	####	####	#	###
16	####	###	####	###	####	###
14*	##	###	####	###	##	###
6*	##	#	###	####	#	###
15	##	##	##	##	##	##
7*	#	#	#	##	#	##
13*	#	#	#	###	#	##
4*	##	#	#	#	#	##
3*	#	#	#	##	#	##
9*	##	##	#	###	#	##
1*	##	##	#	#	###	#
5	##	##	#	##	#	#

Odd numbers denote the cases that were originally labeled unsuccessful. Even numbers denote the cases that were originally labeled successful.

(*) denotes that developer and trainer are one and the same person.
(#) denotes value $1 \leq \# < 2$
(##) denotes value $2 \leq \#\# < 3$
(###) denotes value $3 \leq \#\#\# < 4$
(####) denotes value $4 \leq \#\#\#\# \leq 5$

Internal Consistency. Unsuccessful cases had significantly poorer internal consistency between the assignment, objectives, evaluation, learning situations, and training materials than the successful cases, t (11.39) = −3.64, p = .004.

Relational Approach. Unsuccessful cases applied a significantly poorer relational approach than the successful cases, t (15) = −9.38, p = < .001.

From the qualitative data the following conclusions can be drawn:

— Actors' involvement during development and implementation is strong in successful programs. The successful cases show strong involvement by line managers in particular. The unsuccessful cases do not.

— The similarity between learning situations and work environment is extremely strong for the successful cases and is weak for the unsuccessful cases.
— Practical experience in the subject matter field of the trainer is extensive in the successful cases and limited in the unsuccessful cases.
— In six of the nine successful cases, special emphasis was put on creating favorable circumstances for implementation. None of the unsuccessful cases emphasized this aspect.

External Consistency. In the unsuccessful cases, consistency between actors' perceptions of the initial problem at hand is significantly weaker than in the successful cases, t (15) = −3.56, p = .003.

Cost-Benefit Analysis. In general, cost-benefit analysis is given little attention. Still, unsuccessful and successful cases differ significantly, t (11.57) = −1.91, p = .081. Some of the successful cases included records of the salary costs of developers and trainers. Records of salary costs of trainees were available in four cases. One case mentioned overhead costs of training staff. One case provided an estimation of lost opportunity costs. Only one case contained an estimation of benefits.

Findings Related to the Hypotheses

To relate the findings to the hypotheses, relevant correlations between variables have been computed. On the basis of these findings, the hypotheses are examined and discussed in relation to the conceptual framework (Figure 3). The probability level p < .10 is justified by the small number of cases.

Hypothesis 1: A systematic approach leads to internally consistent curricula. Significant correlation was found, r = .87, p = < .001. None of the cases reveal a high value for systematic approach together with low internal consistency (see Table 1). This hypothesis should not be rejected.

Hypothesis 2: The internal consistency of the formal curriculum and program effects are related positively. Significant correlation was found, r = .77, p = < .001. This hypothesis should not be rejected. Deviations appear in Cases 8, 10, and 6 (see Table 1). They reflect low values for internal consistency, <3.00, but are nevertheless ranked among the successful cases. Apparently, low internal consistency does not affect program effects in these cases.

Hypothesis 3: A relational approach leads to external consistency. Significant correlation was found, r = .54, p = .013. This hypothesis should not be rejected. Only Case 8 shows a high value for relational approach (3.50) in conjunction with low external consistency (2.95), although this value is close to 3.00. Cases 13 and 9 (Table 1) reveal that the relational approach is not conditional for external consistency.

Hypothesis 4: External consistency and program effects are related positively. Significant correlation was found, r = .61, p = .005. This hypothesis should not be rejected. Of all successful cases, only Case 8 has a value for external consistency <3.00 (2.95). Cases 13 and 9 contradict the hypothesis. They have high values for external consistency but are ranked among the unsuccessful cases (Table 1). Further examination of the qualitative data on these cases revealed that both cases concern computer training. In Case 9, the developer/trainer was a management trainee, who was inexperienced in both the subject matter field and in the training profession. In Case 13, the external developer/trainer was unfamiliar with the organization, the equipment, and the computer application to be instructed.

These observations stress the importance of hiring a trainer who is both a training professional and a subject matter expert. Apparently, external consistency can not compensate for poor qualifications in trainer performance nor in subject matter expertise. Selection of the trainers and their practical experience in the subject matter fields are critical elements in the relational approach. This conclusion implies that training of trainers should emphasise subject matter expertise as well as intensive coaching and mentoring of novices.

Hypothesis 5: The relational approach compensates for weaknesses in the systematic approach. Successful cases with a weak systematic approach, defined as <3.00, (Cases 8, 10, 14 and 6; see Table 1) all exhibited a relational approach ≥ 3.00. The high value for the relational approach seems to compensate for the low value of the systematic approach, as these cases are considered successful. On the basis of this reasoning, this hypothesis should not be rejected. As the relational approach and external consistency are closely related, as are the systematic approach and internal consistency, a similar method of reasoning applies to the compensating quality of external consistency in case of weak internal consistency. Cases 8, 10 and 6 show low internal consistency. Their external consistency, which is ≥ 3.00 (#8: 2.95), might compensate for that weakness.

Hypothesis 6: The systematic approach does not compensate for weaknesses in the relational approach. In the group of successful cases, none shows a relational approach ≤ 3.00. In other words, there are no low values to be compensated. In the unsuccessful group, Cases 4, 9, 1, and 5 show stronger systematic than relational approaches, although <3.00. As these cases are ranked lowest, a presumed compensating quality is not effective. Furthermore, the unsuccessful cases show a negative correlation between systematic approach and effects, $r = -.51$, $p = .096$. This figure indicates that investments in systematic design of the formal curriculum may become counterproductive when the development process does not satisfy the relational approach. The research design does not permit conclusions whether the relational approach is satisfactory alone for program effectiveness. On the basis of this reasoning, this hypothesis should not be rejected.

The combination of Hypotheses 5 and 6 might indicate that, although the systematic approach is indispensable for internally consistent curricula, it can be effective only when combined with a relational approach resulting in external consistency. This assumption would explain why successful programs have benefitted from the systematic approach (internal—effect: $r = .62$, $p = .037$), whereas unsuccessful programs have not (systematic—effect: $r = -.51$, $p = .096$).

Hypothesis 7: Although cost-benefit analyses are important for selecting efficient solutions to educational problems, they are not related to effectiveness. No significant direct or reverse correlation was found concerning a relationship between cost-benefit analysis and effect. This hypothesis should not be rejected.

One might argue that performing a cost-benefit analysis for an educational program is part of a systematic approach. Analysis of numbers of participants, of trainee salary costs and their (lost) opportunity costs direct the making of decisions about instructional strategies, course length, selection of media, group size and number of trainers, in view of the expected benefits. Here, cost-benefit analysis is treated as an independent variable, separate from the systematic approach, that apparently does not contribute to program effectiveness.

In an additional analysis, we compared the values of the main variables of the group of cases in which one individual is both trainer and developer (Cases 1, 3, 4, 6, 7, 8, 9, 10, 13, 14, 18) with the other group (Cases 2, 5, 11, 12, 15, 16), in which the roles of developer and trainer are served by two (or more) different staff members. Statistical comparison was established by performing *t* tests. The two groups do not significantly differ on the variable effect, t (15) = −1.01, p = .328. This finding indicates that it is unlikely that a curriculum will be effective only when the trainer is also the developer. The two groups neither differ significantly on the variable relational approach, t (15) = −1.74, p = .103, nor on external consistency, t (15) = −.48, p = .641.

However, splitting the tasks of trainer and developer appears to affect the systematic approach, t (15) = −2.32, p = .035, and internal consistency, t (15) = −3.25, p = .005. The mean values of these variables are significantly higher when the trainer and the developer are not one and the same person. It is plausible that, when an organization specifically employs the function of instructional developer, the quality of the formal curriculum is likely to be high (internal consistency) because the design procedures (systematic approach) have been applied more skillfully. When the trainer designs the program, it is likely that more attention is devoted to the operational curriculum than to the formal.

Development of Design Standards and Training Developers

The aim of this study was to develop a coherent set of design standards, validated by empirical research. The theoretical underpinnings have been explored in the context of the conceptual framework and tested in the case study research. Now, the relational and systematic approaches need to be presented in a practical format so that they can be applied by developers.

A Blueprint for Design Standards

In principle, it is irrelevant whatever practical form design standards take and in what model they are casted. One could even argue that developers should be encouraged to adapt and customise their own design model, as this is the only one that they will put into action. However, the results of Study #1 suggest that developers can increase the effectiveness of their designs and the efficiency of the development process by phrasing their models following the framework of the generic problem-solving model and by applying the elements of the relational and systematic approaches. In the blueprint for the design standards, the elements of the relational and systematic approaches are compiled and presented in the matrix of Figure 5. On the basis of this blueprint, two planning models have been drawn up, both making part of the design standards: *The Curriculum Design Model* (Figure 5: central column) and *The Project Management Model* (Figure 5: right column). A curriculum development project needs to be coordinated and controled. This management function is provided by the project management model, and assists in planning the development team and controlling the necessary resources. The presented model for curriculum design is the researchers' customized design model and reflects the logical structure of the systematic approach. *The activities supporting the relational approach in the design model are marked with * in the Figure.*

The complete set of procedures for the project management model and the design model is described fully in Kessels (1993). The formats for the two models and their operating procedures are inspired by the texts of authors on curriculum design and development that were discussed in the preceding sections. Many references are made to Tracey (1971, 1984, 2nd edition), Romiszowski (1981, 1984) and to Rothwell & Kazanas (1992). Romiszowski's analytical treatment of the heuristics in curriculum design supported the systematic approach. Rothwell & Kazanas' procedures for '*Mastering the instructional design process*' (1992), which are based on '*Instructional design competencies. The Standards*' (Foshay et al., 1986), provide valuable suggestions for both systematic and relational approaches.

Notwithstanding our recommendation of spiralic, iterative, and cyclic procedures (Banathy, 1987), the graphical representation of the models reflects a linear format, as the multitude of possible iterations and simultaneity would otherwise blur the desired clarity of the presentation.

Generic Model	Curriculum Design Model	Project Management Model
Preliminary Inquiry	1. Training Needs Assessment*	Appoint a project manager Designate a top manager in the role of principal State the assignment Plan the project (including activities, capacity, schedule, and budget) Recruit project team Discuss operating procedure Assess the training need Determine the major goals of the curriculum
	2. Goals	

Design	3. Task Analysis*
	
	4. Instructional Objectives
	5. Evaluation Criteria
	6. Evaluation Instruments
	7. Design Learning Situations
		Execution of task analyses
		Instructional objectives
		Evaluation criteria
		Evaluation instruments
		Design learning situations
		  — educational format
		  — instructional strategies

Construction	8. Select and Instruct Trainers* 9. Develop Training Materials 10. Favorable Condition for Implementation* 11. Select Trainees*	Choose the project team members, such as trainers, coaches, and mentors Compile the course material Plan the execution Instruct trainers and other members of the project team Select trainees
Test & Revision	12. Conduct Training Program 13. Evaluate Process & Results	Run a pilot program Evaluate the learning process Evaluate the learning results Adjust the learning situations
Implementation	14. Evaluate Performance and Impact	Deliver the program Evaluate changes in the work environment Assess the impact on the original problem Adjust the design Take procedural measures Conclude the project

*Activities supporting the relational approach.

Figure 5. A blueprint for design standards.

Training of Developers

Availability of design standards does not ensure skillful application. The developer must put these procedures into action. Simply knowing about the standards is insufficient for verifying their value. It is a prerequisite that developers master the design standards, and above all, that they be motivated for applying these procedures in their own organizations. To that end, 30 developers registered for a course on instructional development of which the objectives are geared towards the skillful application of the design standards. The course was taught to two groups of 15 participants. The training course took place over a period of eight months while participants devoted part of their time to training development projects to be implemented in their organizations. As the main features of the program combined working on a project with being coached by two experienced developers and by individual mentors (supported by guest lecturers on specific topics), it turned into a reflective practicum (Schön, 1987).

The participants were training officers, human resource managers and training consultants. The criteria for enrolling in the program were:

— the candidate's current position permits professional curriculum design;
— the candidate has been assigned to develop an educational program;
— the candidate has a degree from higher education.

The two program directors (the first author is one of them) interviewed eligible candidates, and discussed the implications of the selection criteria, the objectives, as well as the facilities required for practical assignments. Out of the 30 developers who started with the program, two participants could not finish their projects due to illness.

The program consisted of ten modules of two successive days each, distributed over eight months. Course materials comprised the design standards (first version), selected readings, and assignments for practical work. The program directors arranged separate meetings with the participants' mentors. They discussed the objectives and the characteristics of the course, as well as the mentor's supportive role in helping to perform the activities of the relational and systematic approaches. The mentors were provided with documents on the design standards.

Empirical Study #2: Twenty-Eight Curriculum Projects

Study #2 can also be characterized as a multiple case study with multiple units of analysis. This second empirical study is both a replication of the preceding case study and an evaluation study of the design standards. To that end, the hypotheses developed above apply also to this part of the research. As the specific use of design standards is emphasized, Hypothesis 1 above has been restated as follows: Skillful application of design standards, based on both a systematic and a relational approach, will generate educational programs that accomplish significantly better results than those of unsuccessful cases.

Variables: Study #2 is based on the same variables and their constituting elements as Study #1, with one exception: in the variable relational approach, the item of *adequate project management* has been added.

Procedures

Data Collection. Data collection was conducted by professional assessors using an assessment manual for curriculum design and by means of questionnaires for (top) managers, supervisors, developers, trainers, and trainees to obtain data on perceptions of the initial problem and program effects. The assessment manual was applied to pilot analyses by three assessors. The pilots tested whether the guidelines offered sufficient help in rating the adequacy and consistency of the various curriculum elements. These pilots led to revisions of the assessment manual, mainly rearrangements of the coding system for adequacy and consistency.

Data collection took place in three stages. The following procedures have generated values for the main variables and their constituting items.

- **Stage 1: Assessment of Curriculum Design: Systematic and Relational Approach, and Internal Consistency**
    - a. In late May, 1992, the researcher received three copies of the files containing the curriculum documents for the 28 projects. Three independent assessors studied the documents and carried out a preliminary analysis guided by the assessment manual.
    - b. In June, 1992, for each of the 28 projects, the three assessors and the developer of the project met to discuss specific features and aspects that raised questions during the preliminary analysis. After the interview the assessors completed their manuals and submitted these to the researcher.

- **Stage 2: Assessment of Effects**
    - a. In October, 1992, for each program developed, the researcher sent out the questionnaires on effects to the top manager, the supervisor, the developer, the trainer and to the trainees.
    - b. In May, 1993, the last set of questionnaires was returned to the researcher. Sets arriving after that date could not be included in the analysis.

    Effect was based on the actors' answers to the questionnaire referring to:
    = satisfaction
    = acquisition of skills
    = improved performance
    = impact on work environment and department
    = impact on the organization.

- **Stage 3: Assessment of External Consistency**

    The data on the external consistency were collected as follows:
    - a. The researcher collected the answers to two specific questions of the questionnaires and entered them on a separate display for each project.
        Question 1: What instigated the development of this educational program?
        Question 2: Which new skills should participants acquire in this program?
    - b. For each project, three judges assessed the consistency between perceptions of managers, developers, trainers, supervisors and trainees. The judges assigned scores for the consistency between ten pairs of actors.

In Stage 1, the assessors analyzed the curriculum documents of 28 projects. However, in Stage 2 the questionnaires could be retrieved for only 17 projects. The developers reported on various circumstances responsible for this disappointing response. Due to internal restructuring of the organization and mergers, three projects had to be postponed because responsibilities and target groups had to be redefined. Two projects were not implemented because all training activities had to be cancelled or postponed due to the economical recession. Two projects were still in progress. No data on effects could be reported at that time. The activities for needs assessment, task analysis and creation of favorable conditions for implementation finally convinced top management in two projects that major changes in the organization were necessary for successful implementation. The projects were postponed. One project was postponed because the system for which the program was developed had not yet been implemented. Another project was postponed because the trainer went on maternity leave.

Results of Study #2

This chapter presents the results of the second empirical study. The reliability of the criterion variable effect is discussed, as well as the values for the predictor variables. The chapter concludes with the comparison of implemented and postponed projects.

Reliability of Effects Measures

Questionnaires were returned for 17 projects. The number of respondents per project varied from 1 to 12. The reliability of the effect measures was secured by applying the following criterion for accepting a project: at least 75% of the actors, for whom the scores of at least four (out of five) effect items are available, should show a jury a $\geq$ .60. Three projects did not meet that criterion and had to be rejected. The correlations between variables are therefore based on the 14 remaining projects.

The value of the effect variable is based on the following items: satisfaction, skills, performance, impact on work environment and department, and impact on the organization. The logic of the five effect items is that (in time) satisfaction facilitates the acquisition of skills, performance benefits from skills, performance has an impact on work environment and department, and work environment and department have an impact on the organization as a whole. The correlations between the five effect variables showed the following pattern:

	satisfaction	skills	performance	department (*) denotes: sign. $p < .001$
satisfaction				
skills	.04			
performance	.20	.79*		
department	.06	.38	.56	
organization	−.05	.36	.51	.77*

Apart from the pair *satisfaction–skills*, the pairs of adjacent effect variables show the highest correlations. This pattern may be interpreted as an indication that the measure of an effect variable over time is mainly influenced by the variable directly preceding it. Moreover, this empirical evidence supports the conceptual relationships between the effect items as described above.

Values of the Main Variables in Projects

On the basis of the values from the assessment manuals, the questionnaires, and the external consistency judgements, Likert scales have been constructed, in a way similar to Study #1. Table 2 shows a summary of the scales. The scales for the variables systematic approach, internal consistency, and relational approach are based on the data from 28 projects. The scale for the variable external consistency is based on the data from the 17 implemented projects. The scale for the variable effect is based on the 14 implemented projects where at least 75% of the actors, for whom the scores of at least four effect items were available, showed a jury $\alpha \geq .62$.

Table 2.　Scale analysis in projects.

Scale	k	min.	$\bar{X}$	s	scale α
Systematic Approach	5	3.33	4.00	.46	.87
Internal Consistency	5	3.07	3.74	.52	.88
Relational Approach	5	3.58	3.85	.36	.89
External Consistency	5	2.33	3.25	.63	.75
Cost-Benefit Analysis	5	3.33	4.26	.46	jury α = .62*
Effect	5	3.10	3.59	.26	.73

As the Cost-Benefit variable is based on one item, its reliability is expressed by the jury α of the three assessors.

k = number of scale points

Scale point:　1 = not at all adequate/consistent/effective
　　　　　　　2 = slightly adequate/consistent/effective
　　　　　　　3 = somewhat adequate/consistent/effective
　　　　　　　4 = very adequate/consistent/effective
　　　　　　　5 = highly adequate/consistent/effective

Comparison of Implemented and Postponed Projects

As implementation has been postponed for 11 projects, experimental mortality might affect the findings. Therefore, we were interested in whether the values for the variables systematic approach, internal consistency, and relational approach of 17 implemented projects differed significantly from those in the group of 11 postponed projects. For both groups, the values of these three variables were available. For this comparison, t tests were run for the two groups. Comparing the three variables showed that the 17 implemented projects did not deviate significantly from the 11 postponed at p < .10. Therefore, experimental mortality is not likely to affect the validity of the effect values at hand.

Discussion of Study #2

A general conclusion is that the projects show homogeneous values for the six variables (Table 2). Only the variable external consistency is weak (that is, <3.00) for three projects (projects 5, 10, 18). The variable cost-benefit analysis is very strong (>4.00) for all but three projects. Regarding the effects variables, all the 14 projects have succeeded when the same criterion for success was applied as in Study #1 (>3.00). This homogeneous achievement is rewarding to the group of developers and their organizations, but the limited variance in the data caused psychometric problems. Between relational approach and external consistency, no substantial correlation could be established due to small variances, s = .36 and s = .63, respectively. This was also the case with the correlation between relational approach and effects, s = .36 and s = .26, respectively.

Findings Related to the Hypotheses

To relate the findings to the hypotheses, the relevant correlations between variables have been computed. On the basis of these findings, the hypotheses are examined and discussed.

Hypothesis 1: Design standards advocating a systematic approach lead to internally consistent formal curricula. The correlation between systematic approach and internal consistency is $r = .88$, $p = <.001$. This hypothesis should not be rejected. Study #1 showed similar high correlations: $r = .87$, $p = <.001$.

Hypothesis 2: Internal consistency of the formal curriculum and program effects are related positively. The correlation between internal consistency and program effects is $r = .47$, $p = .043$. This hypothesis should not be rejected. It is remarkable that the five projects with the lowest effect values (<3.50) show a negative correlation $r = -.72$, $p = .086$.

These figures indicate that internal consistency and the related systematic approach probably have to be embedded in a prerequisite condition to be effective. These findings form a basis for a plausible explanation that further efforts to obtain internal consistency of the formal curriculum might become counterproductive when the design process does not satisfy the prerequisite elements of the relational approach and external consistency.

Hypothesis 3: Design standards advocating a relational approach lead to external consistency (homogeneous ideas and perceptions among parties involved on the nature of the problem and possible solutions). No significant correlations were found for this hypothesis. All the correlations found were close to 0. This might indicate that, from a statistical perspective, the hypothesis should be rejected. Compared to Study #1, this shift is dramatic (Study #1: relational approach → external consistency $r = .54$, $p = .013$; relational approach → effects $r = .86$, $p = <.001$).

A plausible explanation for this deviant pattern is as follows: In view of the strong correlations found in Study #1, it is unlikely that there is no empirical evidence for the theoretical construct of the relational approach and its presumed impact on external consistency and effects in the projects of Study #2. The deviant pattern may be of psychometric origin. The variance of the relational approach is too small ($s = .36$) to obtain substantial correlations.

In view of the findings in Study #1 and the small variance of the variables, it is justified not to reject the hypothesis.

Hypothesis 4: External consistency and program effects are related positively. The correlation between external consistency and effects is $r = .40$, $p = .077$. This hypothesis should not be rejected.

Hypothesis 5: The relational approach compensates for weaknesses in the systematic approach. When weakness of the systematic approach is defined as <3.00, this hypothesis does not apply to any of the projects. No empirical data are available for testing this hypothesis.

Hypothesis 6: The systematic approach does not compensate for weaknesses in the relational approach. When weakness of the relational approach is defined as <3.00, this hypothesis does not apply to any of the projects. No empirical data are available for testing this hypothesis.

Hypothesis 7: Though cost-benefit analyses are important for selecting efficient solutions to educational problems, they are not related to program effectiveness. As no significant correlations between cost-benefit analysis and effect could be found, this hypothesis should not be rejected.

Hypothesis 8: Skillful application of design standards, based on a systematic as well as on a relational approach, will generate educational programs that accomplish significantly better results than those of unsuccessful programs in Study #1. The minimum value found for the systematic approach is 3.33. The minimum value for the relational approach is 3.58. These values justify the conclusion that in all projects of Study #2, the systematic approach as well as the relational approach have been skillfully applied. The programs in Study #1 were not developed on the bases of the design standards that the developers in Study #2 applied. In the Study #1, the criterion for success is effect >3.00. All projects in the second study present effect values >3.00. Provided that it is permissible to compare the effect values of the two studies, the conclusion that skillful application of the design standards generates educational programs that accomplish results that are significantly better than those of unsuccessful programs in Study #1 is justified. This hypothesis should not be rejected.

Conclusions

Answers to the General Research Questions

The aim of this study was to develop a prescriptive theory and validated design standards for corporate education. It addresses the following research questions:

1. Which factors in curriculum design influence quality in corporate education?
2. How do these factors operate?
3. Can design standards control these factors?

The questions will be answered here, to the extent permitted by the limitations of the study:

Question 1: *Which factors in curriculum design influence quality in corporate education?*
A theory has been developed in which the systematic and relational approaches of the developer are related to the internal and external consistency of a curriculum. Curriculum consistency is used as a descriptive framework for quality in corporate education. The paradigms of the theory are:
A. Systematic Approach. A systematic approach generates logical contingencies between purpose, objectives, evaluation criteria and instruments, and the instructional presentation. The systematic approach results in an internally consistent formal curriculum and enables powerful educational interventions. Consequently, an internally consistent curriculum enables the acquisition of new skills, improvement of performance and a positive impact on the work environment.
B. Relational Approach. A relational approach stimulates management involvement and team work during the design and implementation process. It engages trainers with practical experience in the subject matter field and facilitates learning situations that resemble the work environment. The relational approach generates external consistency, defined as homogeneous notions of the parties involved, on the nature of the problem and possible solutions through educational provisions. When managers, supervisors, developer, trainers, and trainees share coherent opinions about the purpose of a program and the strategy to follow, their efforts will lead to successful program implementation, favorable transfer conditions and positive effects.

> The research findings have inferred empirical evidence for the application of the systematic and the relational approaches. External consistency appears to be conditional for internally consistent curricula to become effective. Moreover, without these prerequisites, an internally consistent curriculum can become counterproductive.

Question 2: *How do these factors operate?*

The systematic approach involves a logical and intellectual endeavor. The developer collects and analyzes data on the desired outcome and the target group, draws up a plan, selects instructional strategies and constructs course materials. Intellectual versatility and skillful application of instructional theory are major ingredients.

> The study shows that efforts to take a systematic approach increase the internal consistency of the curriculum. Internal consistency of the formal curriculum and program effects are related positively.

The relational approach involves social intervention and skilled communicative interaction. The developer organizes meetings and interviews managers, supervisors, employees, potential trainees and trainers. These procedures entail consulting with concerned parties, problem solving, negotiating, reaching a consensus, gaining support, and strategically applying gentle pushes and decisive pulls. The goal of these efforts is to achieve a consensus among parties involved on methods of solving the problem, implementing the program, and creating favorable transfer conditions in the work environment.

> The study shows that the relational approach, external consistency, and program effects are positively related. The creation of favorable conditions for implementation, adequate selection of trainers, coaches, and trainees, project management, and involvement of line management are essential elements in the relational approach.

Question 3: *Can design standards control these factors?*

The developers who participated in the second study were trained in the application of design standards, that emphasise both the systematic and the relational approach. Experienced specialists with excellent reputations in the training profession assessed the curricula they developed. The average values for the systematic and relational approaches and for internal consistency, as well as those of their constituting elements were all satisfactory (>3.00). When we investigated the effects of the programs, all projects passed the criterion for success (>3.00). All but three projects satisfied the criterion for external consistency (>3.00).

Cost-benefit analysis is the easiest factor to influence by design standards. The values for the adequacy of this variable were among the highest. This result was in contrast with the preceding study, which showed very poor performance on this item. However, the cost-benefit analysis does not have a significant impact on program effects.

> The procedures for systematic curriculum design were learned and adopted successfully and generated programs with high internal consistency. This quality has a distinct impact on effects, provided the program is embedded in an externally consistent environment.

The procedures that encouraged the developer to apply a relational approach were implemented properly. Unfortunately, their intended impact on external curriculum consistency could not be measured, because the variance in the data was too small. Nevertheless, comparable achievements in Study #1 clearly show effects on external consistency and program outcome.

In the framework of a single program, the developer is unlikely to achieve high external consistency when the organizational system fails to respond. Management involvement and close links with the work environment are essential for establishing external consistency. If the training function is isolated or has a negative image, the first attempts at a relational approach will not automatically result in strong external consistency and consequently in effective programs. It is obvious that, apart from the inductive activities of a single program developer, an organization will benefit most from the relational approach when the educational policy at the managerial level advocates curriculum design that integrates the systematic and relational approaches. Thus, quality in corporate education is not solely dependent on skillful application of relational and systematic approaches of the developer, but also on the organizational climate in which an integrated educational strategy can flourish.

> External consistency is a prerequisite for optimal benefits from the formal curriculum. It appears, however, that external consistency does not increase in proportion to the amount of energy the developer puts into the relational approach. The organization must also react positively to the developer's efforts. It really does take two to tango.

In view of the preceding findings, the answer to the third research question is affirmative. The design standards with which the developers were provided could be mastered within a period of eight months and successfully applied to their projects.

> The curriculum projects in Study #2 performed significantly better than the unsuccessful cases in Study #1 as to effect, systematic approach, internal consistency, relational approach and cost-benefit analysis.

In addition to these observations, it should be stated that this study only investigated the program effects when design standards were being applied deliberately. For most developers, this project was the first they ever developed according to prescribed operating procedures. The findings do not predict whether the developers of this study will continue applying these design standards in future projects.

Suggestions for Further Research

This study has not questioned the foundations of internal consistency (the logic contingencies among purpose, objectives, evaluation criteria and instruments, and instructional strategies). Whereas external consistency is viewed as conditional, internal consistency is considered the driving force behind a curriculum. It might, however, be interesting to investigate curriculum design procedures that neither are rigorously rational nor strive for logical contingencies in the formal curriculum. If curriculum design were also perceived as professional artistry, additional categories of design principles could be explored, for example:

— the learning situation mirrors the work environment
— the manager is the prime educator
— the trainer is an experienced colleague
— trainer and trainee agree on the importance of their educational encounter.

The research design did not permit separate statements on each of these postulates detached from the framework of the systematic approach. Of course, the application of these relational design principles should be applied in a systematic way, but emphasis would primarily be put on the dynamics of the interactional context of curriculum design. The findings of the present study justify the conclusion that in striving for quality in corporate education, gaining external curriculum consistency should be a high priority. As a consequence, design standards that strive only for an internal, rigid logic, but meanwhile hinder the integration of the actors' interests, values, believes and priorities (external consistency), should be abolished and replaced by intervention strategies mainly focusing on the interpersonal dynamics of educational decision-making: procedures that aim at reaching a consensus on the practical implications of the above mentioned alternative design principles. In particular, professional curriculum designers (not being the trainer) should be alerted not to focus unilaterally on the structured and internally consistent formal curriculum. Curriculum development should be regarded, more than up till now, as a social enterprise. Therefore, developers should also elaborate on their management role within that social enterprise of the educational decision-making process.

Thus, the end of this study states some 'daring and fresh hypotheses that do not take for granted as true what has merely become habitual' (Bruner, 1966, p. 171):

- Curriculum development that unilaterally focuses on internal consistency and neglects external consistency may create a major source of design inefficiency.

- Effective educational provisions are not constructed, but negotiated (as part of the relational approach).

- To become effective, curriculum development should be embedded in a positive educational environment. Such a climate is supported by a formal and sophisticated education policy, as well as by informal and personal commitment of top managers.

- Successful curriculum designers are above all competent social engineers, who skillfully manage the social enterprise of educational decision-making.

References

AECT (Association for Educational Communications and Technology). (1977). *The definition of educational technology.* Washington, DC: AECT.

Argyris, C. (1982). *Reasoning, learning, and action.* San Francisco: Jossey-Bass.

Banathy, B. H. (1987). Instructional systems design. In R. M. Gagné (Ed.), *Educational technology: Foundations* (pp. 85–112). Hillsdale, NJ: Lawrence Erlbaum Associates.

Bennis, W. G., Benne, K. D., & Chin, R. (Eds.). (1969). *The planning of change.* New York: Holt, Rinehart, and Winston.

Block, P. (1981). *Flawless consulting: A guide to getting your expertise used.* San Diego, CA: University Associates.

Branson, R. K., & Grow, G. (1987). Instructional systems development. In R. M. Gagné (Ed.), *Instructional technology: Foundations* (pp. 397–428). Hillsdale, NJ: Lawrence Erlbaum Associates.

Broad, M. L., & Newstom, J. W. (1992). *Transfer of training: Action-packed strategies to ensure high payoff from training investments.* Reading, MA: Addison-Wesley.

Bruner, J. S. (1966). *Toward a theory of instruction.* Cambridge: Harvard University Press.

Buckley, R., & Caple, J. (1990). *The theory and practice of training.* London: Kogan Page.

Carlisle, K. E. (1986). *Analyzing jobs and tasks.* Englewood Cliffs, NJ: Educational Technology Publications.

Clark, N. (1991). *Managing personal learning and change. A trainer's guide.* London: McGraw-Hill.

Duncan, J. B., & Powers, E. S. (1992). The politics of intervening in organizations. In H. D. Stolovitch & E. J. Keeps (Eds.), *Handbook of human performance technology* (pp. 77–93). San Francisco: Jossey-Bass.

Fleming, M., & Levie, W. H. (Eds.). (1992). *Instructional message design: Principles from the behavioral and cognitive sciences.* Englewood Cliffs, NJ: Educational Technology Publications.

Foshay, W., Silber, K., & Westgaard, O. (1986). *Instructional design competencies: The standards.* University of Iowa and The International Board of Standards for Training, Performance, and Instruction.

Gilley, J. W., & Eggland, S. A. (1989). *Principles of human resource development.* Reading, MA: Addison-Wesley.

Goodlad, J. I., Klein, M. F., & Tye, K. A. (1979). The domains of curriculum and their study. In J. L. Goodlad *et al., Curriculum inquiry: The study of curriculum practice* (pp. 43–76). New York: McGraw-Hill.

Harrison, R. (1992). *Employee development.* London: Institute of Personnel Management.

Henschke, J. A. (1991). History of human resource developer competencies. In N. M. Dixon & J. Henkelman (Eds.), *The academic guide: Models for HRD practice* (pp. 9–30). Alexandria, VA: ASTD.

Jackson, S. F., & Addison, R. M. (1992). Planning and managing projects. In H. D. Stolovitch & E. J. Keeps (Eds.), *Handbook of human performance technology* (pp. 66–76). San Francisco: Jossey-Bass.

Kaufman, R. (1982). *Identifying and solving problems: A system approach.* San Diego: University Associates.

Kaufman, R. (1990). A needs assessment primer. In E. L. Allen (Ed.), *Needs assessment instruments. ASTD trainer's toolkit* (pp. 224–228). Alexandria, VA: ASTD & Pfeiffer & Company.

Kearsley, G. (1982). *Cost, benefits, & productivity in training systems.* Reading, MA: Addison-Wesley.

Kessels, J. W. M. (1993). *Towards design standards for curriculum consistency in corporate education.* Doctoral dissertation. Enschede: Twente University.

Kessels, J. W. M., & Smit, C. A. (1994). Job analysis in corporate education. In T. Husén & T. N. Postlethwaite (Eds.), *International encyclopedia of education* (2nd ed.). Oxford: Pergamon Press.

Kirkpatrick, D. L. (1975). *Evaluating training programs.* A collection of articles from the Journal of the American Society for Training and Development. Madison, WI: ASTD.

Lippitt, G., & Lippitt, R. (1986). *The consulting process in action.* San Diego: University Associates.

Lippitt, R., Watson. J., & Westley, B. (1958). *The dynamics of planned change.* New York: Holt, Rinehart, and Winston.

Lowijck, J. (1991). The field of instructional design. In J. Lowyck, P. De Potter & J. Elen (Eds.), *Instructional design: Implementation issues* (pp. 1–30). Procedings of the I.B.M./K.U. Leuven Conference, La Hulpe, December 17–19, 1991.

McLagan, P. A. (1983). *Models for Excellence.* Alexandria, VA: ASTD.

McLagan, P. A. (1989). *The models: Models for HRD practice.* Alexandria, VA: ASTD.

Merrill, M. D., Reigeluth, C. M., & Faust, G. F. (1979). The instructional quality profile: A curriculum evaluation and design tool. In H. F. O'Neil (Ed.), *Procedures for instructional systems development* (pp. 165-204). New York: Academic Press.

Merrill, P. F. (1987). Job and task analysis. In R. M. Gagné (Ed.), *Instructional technology: Foundations* (pp. 141-174). Hillsdale, NJ: Lawrence Erlbaum Associates.

Miles, M., & Huberman, M. (1984). *Qualitative data analysis.* London: Sage.

Nijhof, W. J., Mulder, M., & Van Wijk, M. (1992). *Cost indicators for developing corporate training.* St. Paul, MN: University of Minnesota Training and Development Center.

Patrick, J. (1991). Types of analysis for training. In J. E. Morrison (Ed.), *Training for performance* (pp. 127–166). Chichester: John Wiley & Sons.

Patrick, J. (1992). *Training: Research and practice.* London: Academic Press.

Pedler, M., Burgoyne, J., & Boydell, T. (1991). *The learning company: A strategy for sustainable development.* London: McGraw-Hill.

Phillips, K., & Shaw, P. (1989). *A consultancy approach for trainers.* Aldershot Hants: Gower Publishing Company.

Plomp, Tj. (1982). *Onderwijskundige technologie: Enige verkenningen* [Exploring educational technology]. Inaugural lecture, Enschede: Universiteit Twente.

Plomp, Tj. (1992). Onderwijskundig ontwerpen: Een inleiding [Introduction to educational design]. In Tj. Plomp, A. Feteris, J. M. Pieters, & W. Tomic (Eds.), *Ontwerpen van onderwijs en trainingen* (pp. 19-38). Utrecht: Lemma.

Pont, T. (1991). *Developing effective training skills.* London: McGraw-Hill.

Reigeluth, C. M. (1983). Instructional design: What is it and why is it? In C. M. Reigeluth (Ed.), *Instructional design theories and models: An overview of their current status* (pp. 4–31). Hillsdale, NJ: Lawrence Erlbaum Associates.

Reigeluth, C. M., & Curtis, R. V. (1987). Learning situations and instructional models. In R. M. Gagné (Ed.), *Instructional technology: Foundations* (pp. 175–206). Hillsdale, NJ: Lawrence Erlbaum Associates.

Robinson, D. G., & Robinson, J. (1989). *Training for impact.* San Francisco: Jossey-Bass.

Romiszowski, A. J. (1981). *Designing instructional systems.* London: Kogan Page.

Romiszowski, A. J. (1984). *Producing instructional systems.* London: Kogan Page.

Rossett, A. (1987). *Training needs assessment.* Englewood Cliffs, NJ: Educational Technology Publications.

Rossett, A. (1992). Analysis of human performance problems. In H. D. Stolovitch & E. J. Keeps (Eds.), *Handbook of human performance technology* (pp. 97–113). San Francisco: Jossey-Bass.

Rothwell, W. J., & Kazanas, H. C. (1992). *Mastering the instructional design process. A systematic approach.* San Francisco: Jossey-Bass.

Schön, D. A. (1987). *Educating the reflective practitioner.* San Francisco: Jossey-Bass.

Seashore, S. E., Lawler III, E. E., Mirvis, Ph. H., & Cammann, C. (1983). *Assessing organizational change. A guide to methods, measures, and practices.* New York: John Wiley & Sons.

Senge, P. (1990). *The fifth discipline: The art and practice of the learning organization.* New York: Doubleday.

Sink, D. L. (1992). Success strategies for the human performance technologist. In H. D. Stolovitch & E. J. Keeps (Eds.), *Handbook of human performance technology* (pp. 564–575). San Francisco: Jossey-Bass.

Sprinthall, R. C., Schmutte, G. T., & Sirois, L. (1991). *Understanding educational research.* Englewood Cliffs, NJ: Prentice-Hall.

Stake, R. E. (1973). The countenance of educational evaluation. In B. R. Worthen & J. R. Sanders (Eds.), *Educational evaluation: Theory and practice. Frameworks for planning evaluation studies* (pp. 106–124). Belmont, CA: Wadsworth Publishing Co.

Stufflebeam, D. L. (1971). *Educational evaluation and decision making.* Itasca, IL: Peacock.

Taba, H. (1962). *Curriculum development: Theory and practice.* New York: Harcourt, Brace, & World.

Tosti, D., & Jackson, S. F. (1992). Influencing others to act. In H. D. Stolovitch & E. J. Keeps (Eds.), *Handbook of human performance technology* (pp. 551–563). San Francisco: Jossey-Bass.

Tracey, W. R. (1971). *Designing training and development systems.* New York: American Management Association.

Tracey, W. R. (1981). *Human resource development standards.* New York: American Management Association.

Tracey, W. R. (1984). *Designing training and development systems* (rev. ed.). New York: American Management Association.

Warshauer, S. (1988). *Inside training and development. Creating effective programs.* San Diego: University Associates.

Yin, R. K. (1989). *Case study research: Design and methods.* London: Sage.

PART 2

Context, Needs, Results,
and Acceptable Process:
Instructional Development
from a Cultural Vantage Point

7

Is Instructional Development a Paradigm for Public Education?

Mary P. Mauldin
Medical University of South Carolina, Charleston

Kent L. Gustafson
University of Georgia, Athens

Current Status of Instructional Development in Schools

Analysis, design, evaluation, and dissemination constitute the four basic elements addressed in the majority of instructional development models associated with the instructional development paradigm (Briggs, Gustafson, & Tillman, 1991; Gustafson, 1991). These four elements, some would call them activities, are included in one form or another in virtually all variations of the ID paradigm that have appeared over the last 30 years (Andrews & Goodson, 1980; Branson, 1975; Gerlach & Ely, 1980; Gustafson, 1991; Hamreus, 1968; Stamas, 1973). The ID paradigm has been demonstrated to improve the effectiveness of instruction and the efficiency of the development process in a wide array of settings from individual classrooms (Gerlach & Ely, 1980) to remaking the entire educational system of a country (Morgan, 1989). When taken separately, each one also (except perhaps dissemination) appears to be crucial to effective classroom instruction. Yet, if that is the case, why do school administrators, instructional supervisors, and classroom teachers respond to inquiries regarding their use of instructional development procedures with statements such as:

- "I'm already doing that."
- "That's OK in theory but it's not relevant to what I do."
- "I already know those theories."
- "If I use that theory, I'll have to change my teaching methods."
- "That can't be useful for me. It was developed in another context."
- "I can't afford the time to plan/design instruction."
- "Instructional development is okay if you're using AV or computers, but it's not really relevant to other means for providing instruction." (Snelbecker, 1987)

How did the instructional development paradigm receive such a negative connotation in the field of public education? There are probably as many answers to this question as there are public educators, and perhaps that is not the critical question anyway. More pertinent questions are: Does instructional development have a place in public education? If so, is there an effective way to incorporate the process into a teacher's repertoire of skills? Would public educators and their students benefit from a shift in thinking regarding the instructional development paradigm? We think the answer is "yes," as described later in this chapter.

At the present time, educators are being bombarded with information regarding how the entire current school system is ineffective (Bagley & Hunter, 1992; Earle, 1990; Kemp, 1991; Mecklenburger, 1992; Shrock, 1990). George Bush, when President, encouraged business leaders and educators to make a shift in their paradigms regarding public education by designing totally new models for schools (Mecklenburger, 1992). As the entire educational system of the U.S. is being challenged to make systemic changes, individual classroom teachers also are being encouraged to make changes in their individual classroom instruction as well (Bagley & Hunter, 1992; Kemp, 1991; Kerr, 1981; Knirk, 1988; Reiser & Radford, 1990). In order to design these new effective schools (from the classroom to the entire system), the four areas of instructional development (analysis, design, evaluation and dissemination) may provide guidance in the movement toward effective classroom instruction, product and system development, and systemic restructuring.

However, instructional developers need to be aware that even if a person is armed with all of the positive research findings related to instructional development's effectiveness (Shrock, 1990), there are hurdles to get across regarding public education's strong traditions, its apparent negative attitude toward instructional development, and the general lack of knowledge of the ways that instructional development might contribute to schools (Rossett & Garbosky, 1987). Gaining widespread acceptance of instructional development in schools is a difficult and complex task (Burkman, 1987), and an area in which educators and instructional developers should conduct research, collaborate, and plan as a team. One of the most critical issues relative to the non-acceptance of the instructional development paradigm is addressed in this chapter: Is there a way that educators can select instructional development models that are matched to their specific purposes and that will truly meet their instructional needs? A complicating factor for anyone incorporating the instructional development process is the evaluation and selection of an appropriate model(s), since they vary widely in their purposes, the amount of detail provided, and the technical jargon they contain. Educators would also benefit from the knowledge that no single instructional development model is useful in all settings and for all purposes (Gustafson, 1991).

Instructional Development Needs at Different Levels of "School"

The instructional development paradigm can be applied at different levels within schools (see Figure 1) to meet a number of needs. These levels range from the individual classroom to the board room of the school district as answers are sought to some of the many problems currently being faced by schools.

While entire educational systems are being challenged to make systemic changes, individual classroom teachers are also being encouraged to make changes in their classroom instruction as well (Bagley & Hunter, 1992). In order to design these new effective schools (from the classroom to the entire system), examination of various approaches to ID, known as models, rather than a totally new ID paradigm, is required. The numerous models contained within the ID paradigm provide the developer with the opportunity to select an appropriate model based upon identified needs. Therefore, the degree of emphasis placed on each element of the ID model may look quite different from one setting to another. For example, a classroom teacher may select an ID model which emphasizes the design/development of content, while an instructional designer of computer-based instruction programs may select an ID model that places a much heavier emphasis on design/development and evaluation. A group of educators designing a reading program for grades one through three may decide that an ID model that focuses equally on analysis, design/development, evaluation, and dissemination is necessary for their purpose, while school administrators considering systemic restructuring may decide to select an ID model especially focusing on analysis and evaluation. Although these models may appear to be different, each resides within the ID paradigm. No matter where the emphasis lies, with analysis, design/development, evaluation, and/or dissemination, the conscious use of an ID model may provide guidance in the movement toward effective classroom, product and system development, as well as total systemic restructuring.

Figure 1 displays one way in which to think about the activities of a school as they would relate to the instructional development process. At the most global level, referred to as systemic restructuring, a school district may be interested in restructuring itself to better respond to the demands being placed on it by society. Reigeluth (1992) and others have written to this need. At the instructional system development level, comprehensive new curriculum might be developed in areas such as robotics or computer technology, with the entire system being carefully designed, developed, evaluated, and implemented across multiple sites. At the instructional product development level, a team of teachers might be asked to systematically develop a unit on AIDS or sex education to meet the needs and desires of a local community. At the individual classroom level, teachers are seeking more and better ways of teaching with and without the many technological devices now becoming more common in schools. Each of these levels is described in greater detail below, starting with individual teachers, whom we believe are the foundation for any improvement we can hope to see in schools.

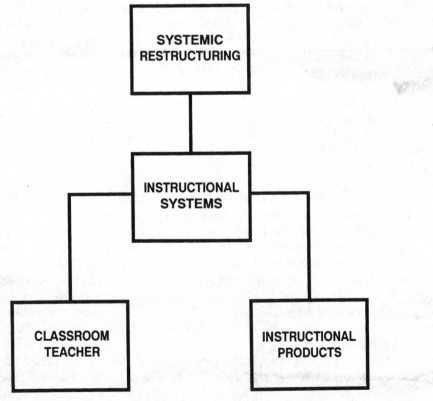

Figure 1. Possible foci of instructional development efforts in public schools.

The classroom teacher uses a systematic design process when s/he consciously considers student needs and/or levels, selects appropriate objectives to meet these needs, and then designs instruction and evaluation to match the objectives. Not only does the teacher receive critical information from formal evaluation of the students, but s/he is also provided with information from a mental review of the instruction (a formative evaluation) such as examination of effective and ineffective techniques. Some of this information can then be immediately applied to other instructional situations with the same students, regardless of subject matter, while other content-specific evaluation data may not be used for an entire year until that topic is again taught to a new group of students.

If a designer of an educational product conducts an analysis of needs and objectives prior to development, the actual development time may be shorter than if these analyses were not conducted in a systematic fashion. Evaluation throughout the entire process of analysis and design/development will ensure a product which is more effective than one haphazardly designed without analysis of needs and objectives. Thus, the product developer will chose to emphasize different elements of the ID process than the classroom teacher.

When designing an instructional system, such as an alternative math curriculum, an analysis of needs will assist the developers in determining goals, from which objectives can be derived. The analysis of these objectives will lead to evaluation items, as well as specific content to be included in the design/development. Formative evaluations of this instructional system will further refine the objectives and design, and results of summative evaluations will assist in the acceptance of this instructional system when dissemination is desired. Obviously, the process of designing integrated instructional systems to meet specific needs must emphasize the ID elements of analysis and dissemination so that the system will match to, and be accepted by, people in the target organization

Development of goals and objectives based on the results from a needs analysis, and determination of evaluation methods are components of instructional design critical to the process of systemic restructuring. A State Department of Education committee challenged to restructure its school districts must first determine the needs from which goals and objectives can be developed. The determination of systematic evaluation methods is crucial in order to justify whether or not the structuring should be expanded, modified, or returned to the drawing board. Also, they must be alert to changing conditions and modify the plan as it evolves.

From these examples, it is apparent that ID does not look the same in every situation, yet all of these models can be considered part of the same ID paradigm. It is these models' relationship to the ID paradigm and the ID paradigm's relationship to public education that is the focus of the remainder of this chapter.

A Taxonomy of Instructional Development Models

Figure 2 is designed to assist educators in examining the relevant attributes of various instructional development models and to guide their selection on one that is appropriate for their specific needs. Educators may want to use the matrix for conducting a comparison of various development models relative to their immediate purpose, thereby assisting them in evaluating which one (or combination of several) is most appropriate. Hopefully, use of the matrix will also encourage the development of educators' confidence in their ability to select and apply only those parts of various models that would be appropriate for their purpose, whether designing instruction for an individual classroom, planning a product or system, or seeking a systemic change.

There are four distinct foci in the model classification scheme presented in Figure 2: (1) the individual classroom teacher; (2) instructional product(s); (3) instructional systems; and (4) systemic restructuring. The four foci are represented in a hierarchy, with systemic restructuring being composed of the areas listed below it in the hierarchy as well others unique

Focus of ID Effort	Typical Output	Resources Committed	Team/Ind. Dev. Effort	Dev./Select Mtls.	Amt. Analysis	Amt. Tryout & Revision	Amt. Distribution	Scope of Impact	Amt. Staff Dev.	Amt. Theory/Res. Base
Classroom	Hr. of Inst.	Very Low	Ind.	Select	Low	Low	Low	Small	Low	Low
Inst. Product	Pkgs. & Kits	Med/High	Team	Dev.	Low/Med.	High	Very High	Low/Med.	Low/Med.	Low/High
Inst. System	Curriculum	High	Team	Select & Dev.	Low/High	Low/High	Low/Med.	Variable	Variable	Low/Med.
Systemic Restruc.	New Struct.	High	Team	Select & Dev.	High	High	Low	High	High	Variable

Figure 2. A matrix of instructional development model foci and selected variables.

to itself such as community concerns and state requirements and mandates. Similarly, instructional systems represent design efforts of individual teachers and instructional products, as well as such concerns as district level curriculum design and continuing staff development activities.

At the individual classroom level, teachers operate in a dynamic and evolving environment that must be responsive to minute-by-minute changes. Teachers generally work within a given curricular structure and have very limited amounts of time available for planning. Thus, any ID model that they can apply will involve selection from existing resources, with minimal amounts of front-end analysis, and will permit little structured formative evaluation. There is scant evidence that instructional developers are actively engaged in working with teachers at this level at the present time.

Instructional product development usually is characterized by at least some front-end analysis, careful selection of instructional strategies, and formative evaluation. Instructional product development occurs only to a limited degree in schools. Occasionally, groups of teachers, media specialists, curriculum specialists, and perhaps others will systematically design and develop instructional units for distribution within a school or district. However, most instructional products are developed outside of schools and marketed to them by commercial vendors.

An instructional system is a comprehensive package of substantial size covering an extended amount of time. It may be on a single topic (e.g., a year-long math program) or may include several areas (e.g., whole language programs that promote many objectives including especially reading and writing). Development of instructional systems is characterized by a major investment in front-end analysis, rigorous design and development, extensive formative evaluation, usually in a variety of settings, and carefully planned marketing or implementation.

Systemic restructuring involves making fundamental changes in the very structure of schools. Everything from the way schools are governed to the way students are organized into classes is reexamined during school restructuring. State requirements such as time per subject and even the conceptualizing of how the curriculum is organized also may be examined. And, obviously, the very nature of the learning experience of the student is redesigned. While there have many calls for such major systemic restructuring (Bowsher, 1992; Morgan, 1992; Reigeluth, 1992), to date the most notable efforts are being mounted by the New American Schools Development Corporation (Rundell, 1992) and the various state efforts, such as Florida Schoolyear 2000 (Salisbury, 1992, 1996) designed to aid schools in their states in making major changes.

A number of attributes can be examined for each one of the four categories (see Figure 2) of instructional improvement efforts and related instructional development models. These attributes include: typical outputs of the design effort; amount of resources typically committed to the effort; whether development is typically a team or an individual effort; whether the emphasis is on selecting from existing materials or creating new ones; the amount of analysis done (and why) before actual design begins; how much, if any, formal tryout and revision occurs; whether distribution and/or adoption/dissemination to a specific target audience is expected to occur; the nature of the impact expected; the degree of the design effort; the amount and type of staff development required during development and at the time of implementation; and the amount of research and theory upon which the instruction is based.

To clarify how this matrix might be used, examples of a variety of ID models are provided for each area of four levels of the hierarchy as they relate to each of the attributes listed in the matrix. In a later section we describe how the matrix might be used to select an appropriate model.

Individual Classroom Teacher

There appears to be disagreement in the field regarding how teachers plan and whether or not they actually do think like instructional developers (Kerr, 1981). Kerr states that teachers may start the instructional development process by thinking through situations, activities, or other elements of the teaching environment, while Higgins (1980) reports that teachers actually plan just around activities. Martin (1990) reports a study of teachers trained in instructional development versus those not trained in instructional development and found that both groups used some instructional development skills and processes in planning. However, no teachers reported use of specific *research and theories* in their development process, leading one to deduce that the amount of research and theory would probably be rated low in this area.

Suppose a teacher plans to develop a social studies lesson around the topic of the three branches of government in the United States and their associated system of checks and balances. The teacher could examine the matrix to assist in developing a set of criteria to apply and then select an appropriate model (or components of various models) to incorporate. Depending on the learners, the *output* of this lesson could range from one to several hours of instruction spread across several days. An *individual* teacher rather than a team would probably design this instruction with very few *resources* allocated to its design. Since teachers have only small amounts of planning time and frequently are limited to county and/or state adopted materials, the *materials* for use would probably be selected rather than produced (although teachers sometimes develop supplemental materials). The teachers would more likely than not feel they were aware of the students' existing knowledge on this subject and the needed prerequisite skills; therefore, only a small amount of *front end analysis* would be required. *Staff development* training required for the teacher to develop and deliver this lesson would be of limited importance when compared to the training that would be required, for example, if a school district decided that teachers would team teach in social studies with an emphasis on discovery learning. The *impact* of this lesson might be great on the 20 to 30 students in that classroom, but small when compared with the impact of a systemic change. Generally, the teacher would not provide other teachers with this plan, therefore, *distribution* of the instruction would probably be non-existent. This development effort probably would be only modestly *revised* for the following year with any changes being based on results of the initial implementation rather than upon implementation following a tryout revision cycle as is depicted by most instructional development models.

Instructional Product

An instructional product could be either commercially produced or teacher prepared. Examples are provided of a teacher-prepared, as well as a commercial product.

Teacher-Prepared Product: A group of teachers, all in the same school, realized that, although their students could name the three branches of government, they could not list the duties of each nor identify any checks and balances that each branch possessed. The teachers discussed their project in relation to the matrix and made the development decisions described below. Also, after determining the areas of emphasis from the model, various components of several models were combined for use in developing the product. Since commercially developed supplemental materials were not provided to accompany their textbook, the teachers chose to produce their own supplemental materials. They decided that an effective way to provide instruction was to have the students participate in an activity in which they assumed the roles of the three branches of government, including activities that demonstrated how each branch provides checks and balances for the others. However, they also knew that there would need to be explicit instruction before, during, and after these activities. Therefore, the *output* of this effort was to be both a teacher and student manual with *low resources* committed to the development project. Although this was a *team* effort, a similar project could have involved only a single teacher.

The teachers *developed* the materials, since they were not aware of appropriate materials already developed and available. There was a moderate amount of *front end analysis* conducted (i.e., teacher interviews and examination of student work samples, etc.) and the entire development process was based on a very low amount of *research and theory*. A small amount of *staff development* was required to train the participating teachers in use of the materials and the *impact* was low (although numerous students and teachers participated, the project was confined to one school). The *distribution* of this program would be considered low if it remained only in the one school but could become higher if designers (or others) promoted its use outside of the one school.

Commercially Prepared Instructional Product: A commercially produced and marketed computer program designed to teach the three branches of government and the system of checks and balances is another example of an instructional product. The *output* of this design effort would be the computer program along with a teacher's guide and student books, if appropriate. There would probably be a high degree of *resources* committed to the development project and the product often, but not always, would be designed by a team, with emphasis placed on *development* rather than selection of the materials. A moderate amount of *front end analysis* likely would be conducted (e.g., surveys, task analysis) to justify the selected goals and objectives, as well as influence consumers. The amount of *tryout and revision* might be based on the allocated resources, but typically would be fairly high, again with the idea that documentation of this information would positively influence potential consumers. This producer of the commercial material would more than likely report extensive use of *research and theory* in making instructional decisions. *Staff development* would probably receive a low rating for this program (depending upon detail of documentation and the contents of the teacher and student guides) but some commercially prepared materials may require a great deal of staff development (e.g., implementing an extremely structured and extensive commercially prepared reading program in a K–5 school). The *distribution and impact* of the computer program may be high based upon its popularity and effectiveness. The developers of commercial instructional products could examine the matrix to determine which attributes to emphasize and which model to chose to guide their development efforts.

Instructional Systems

Examples of instructional systems include school districts that incorporate cooperative learning across all grade levels, a specific reading or math program mandated for a particular school or district, the curriculum designed for an entire school district, etc. Figure 1 also illustrates the fact that instructional systems include individual classroom teachers and instructional products in addition to other areas, such as the provision of specific training in the areas listed above (i.e., training in cooperative learning, specific math or reading programs, etc.). For example, a school realized that students were experiencing significant problems not only in the area of social studies (e.g., discussing checks and balances of the three branches of government) but in other areas as well, such as language arts, math, and behavior. Therefore, the school decided to address the learning and behavioral problems of *all* students, and not just those previously identified as having difficulty with a social studies topic. To do this, the matrix was examined to determine areas of emphasis; various portions of development models were selected and the result was a graduate level course taught to the faculty. The goal of this course was for the faculty to develop a school-wide plan designed to address learning and behavior problems specific to their school.

For this project, the *output* was a written school-wide plan, including goals, objectives, justifications, timelines, methods of evaluation, etc. *Resources* committed to the development process would vary, sometimes depending on the impact, as well as other financial and personnel considerations. In this case, *resources* were moderate with only school and district level support. Instructional systems will usually be designed by a *team* and they will either *develop and/or select materials* depending on needs. This project was developed by a team composed of school and district level personnel, as well as college professors. There will usually be a high amount of *front end analysis,* due in part to its potential impact and *distribution.* The project in this case was based on needs assessments and discussions with the entire faculty and school administration. The amount of *tryout and revision* will be related to the resources committed to the development process, as well as the impact, and theory/research upon which the instructional system is based. This project was not subject to a great deal of *tryout and revision* due to budgetary constraints and timelines. However, for each replication of the project, revisions were made based upon previous experiences and information. The actual amount of *research and theory* upon which the instructional system is based will vary due to school district requirements, team members' own beliefs/philosophies, etc. This project was based on a substantial amount of research but no actual theory. The amount of *staff development* for this particular project was extensive and intense, but this variable could change based upon the actual instructional system. The *impact* of this system was high for the one school, as any instructional system will typically have a high impact (whether it is for one school, a school district, or state-wide). The *distribution and dissemination* for this system was moderate since other schools in the same district modeled similar programs after this one. Instructional systems will usually have a moderate to high level of distribution/ dissemination.

Keep in mind, however, that individual teachers and instructional products are part of any instructional system. Individual classroom teachers were involved in designing lessons for their own classes based on goals/objectives and staff development from the training sessions. Teachers (individuals and groups) also designed instructional products to meet the needs of some of the identified students, as well as selected additional commercially prepared materials to meet their needs.

Development of instructional systems, though, consists of more than the design of lessons by individual teachers and product development. In this case, developing the instructional system also included conducting extensive training, developing a school-wide plan, implementing and monitoring the plan, and designing and conducting the evaluation of the plan.

Systemic Restructuring

Systemic restructuring focuses on the complete restructuring of a school district, (e.g., the "break-the-mold" idea of the New American Schools Development Corporation; Mecklenburger, 1992). As an example, a school district decided that one school's effort to address student learning and behavior problems was not sufficient and wanted to implement system-wide changes, including dissolving existing grade levels. Instead, students would progress based upon the mastery of objectives. Work/study programs would be involved at the middle and high school levels, as well as opportunities for participation in advanced courses of academic study, and replacement of academic credits toward a diploma with the number of hours of instruction based upon individual student need. The *output* for this example would be "new" schools with extensive *resources* committed to its development (both financial and personnel). This plan would have to be developed by a *team* not only due to its magnitude but also due to the need to gain support from the educational system, parents, and the community. Materials for systemic restructuring may be either developed (e.g., forms for timelines, goals, objectives) or selected (e.g., forms, information, etc., from districts that have undertaken restructuring). There would be a high degree of *front end analysis* required, as well as a solid base in *research and/or theory*. A high degree of *tryout and revision* would be crucial, with one school being selected as the pilot study prior to district wide implementation. The amount of *staff development* would be high, since teachers and administrators would need to be trained in their new roles. Parents and the community would also need opportunities to receive information and ask questions regarding the new system. The *impact* would be high due to the large number of people affected by this system change (students, teachers, parents, community, etc.). *Distribution/dissemination* would probably vary based upon tryout and revision from the pilot school, but if success was shown, this attribute on the matrix would be rated as high.

Systemic restructuring affects all the levels depicted in the matrix. It affects classroom teachers; requires that new products be developed or selected; and instructional systems also must be incorporated. However, systemic restructuring is more than this. For example, it also includes examining teacher retraining related to the systemic change, the impact on schools and the community, and the theory and research employed. The matrix can be used to guide selection of one or more instructional development models or combination of models.

When Figures 1 and 2 are studied, it appears that the variables grow in size as you progress up the chart. For example, systemic restructuring produces a greater impact than instructional systems and so requires more tryout and revision, more resources allocated, more front end analysis, etc. Notice, again, that each level incorporates those below it in the hierarchy, but is more than simply the sum of those parts.

As teachers and other individuals design instruction, develop products, introduce instructional systems, or work to bring about systemic change, perhaps the matrix presented in this chapter would be useful for two purposes:

(1) Figure 1 allows designers and other educators to determine areas that need to be considered in the design process. For example, if an instructional system were being designed, participants could see that teachers and products would also be affected and, therefore, would need to be included in the design plans.

(2) Figure 2 provides guidance for designers and other educators to determine areas of emphasis in specific design models. By considering these attributes, instructional development projects can be more systematically planned and executed.

Using the Matrix to Select an ID Model

As should now be clear, one cannot expect to apply a single model to the diverse conditions found in schools or to the array of instructional improvements educators might decide to undertake. This fact has implications for both instructional designers and the educators with whom they might work. We believe the matrix can be of value to educators desiring to select ID models to match specific situations.

In the case of instructional developers, they must become much more flexible in their thinking about how to apply the paradigm via the variety of types of models described earlier. Rather than being tied to a single somewhat rigid ID model, as is so often the case today, designers will need to become competent in applying a variety of models in a flexible manner as the contexts dictate. Instructional developers also will need to employ new instructional theories and technology-based design and delivery tools as they assist public schools to restructure and change *at all levels*, from the classroom to the central office to the state department of education. However, instructional developers cannot and should not simply wait for educators to come to them for assistance. It is quite clear that educators will need to be convinced of the efficacy of the ID process, not through exhortations, but through the proactive efforts of developers who are willing and able to go into the schools and stay there long enough to make a difference.

For their part, educators must become more willing to seriously consider applying the systematic development process rather than simply responding to the latest fad or purchasing the newest of the ever-emerging technological hardware in the hope that significant improvements will result (see Hackbarth, 1996). Instructional development has already demonstrated the power to make a difference in selected situations (e.g., Morgan, 1989). What is now needed is for educators to create an open environment in which it can be more fully tested in a variety of forms in a variety of settings.

It is also essential that both developers and educators keep in mind that systemic change has little hope of resulting in significant educational improvement without concomitant change in individual classrooms, and classroom teachers have little hope of bringing about major changes without concomitant systemic change. Clearly, public education is a system with multiple and interacting elements that only can be best understood by applying our knowledge of general systems theory. The need is for developers to work with educators at all levels to promote application of the ID process; in the individual classroom, in the product development lab, in the instructional system project, and in the administrative office to demonstrate the power of the process. To do less is to guarantee either failure or at best rather marginal successes that are not convincing and that will have minimal impact.

As evidence of the inadequacy of present one-sided approaches, one need only look at the efforts of the New American Schools Development Corporation to bring about dramatic improvement of schools. Sherry (1992) reports that there were few true examples of "break-the-mold" proposals submitted to the New American Schools Development Corporation during its national competition. While one could argue that perhaps this was due in part to the vague challenge for designers to ". . . design an educational environment to bring every child in this community up to world class standards . . ." (Olds & Pearlman, 1992, p. 296), the fact remains that there was scant evidence that instructional designers were involved in preparing any of the proposals. Developers of the proposals often emphasized their processes for planning the design, rather than providing any real substance for the design (Sherry, 1992). This observation points to the fact that the skills of instructional developers in the area of task analysis, instructional design, evaluation, and feedback will be crucial to planning any systemic restructuring efforts.

In summary, there are two keys to successfully applying ID to improving public education. First, both educators and developers must be more willing to reach out to each other and become proactive in exploring how, when, and where the ID process might be applied.

Second, any exploration or opportunities must recognize that ID must occur across the spectrum, from the classroom to the boardroom, if we are to expect the quantum gains in performance of children so grandly announced as goals by Former President Bush and the governors but more earnestly felt by every parent of a school-age child.

Can Instructional Development Really Happen in Schools?

Now, to return to the questions posed at the beginning of this chapter:

Does instructional development have a place in public education? We strongly believe that instructional development does have a place in the public schools. Although the development process may not appear to match their traditional models, educators need to develop the confidence to select the appropriate features from various ID models in order to meet their development needs.

If so, is there an effective way to incorporate the process into a teacher's repertoire of skills? Yes, we believe that an effective way to incorporate the instructional development process into teachers' repertoire of skills is to encourage the use of tools such as the matrix presented in this chapter, with emphasis on *selection* of various components of models appropriate to the goals and contexts of the planned improvement effort.

Would public educators and their students benefit from a shift in their thinking regarding the instructional development paradigm? The current emphasis on school restructuring will affect everyone involved in the public educational process. Educators must be prepared to make a shift from traditional to "break-the-mold" paradigms. Be aware that although public educators' models may not look the same as the "traditional" instructional development models, their selection and use of various components of models would facilitate effective systemic change (Shrock, 1990).

References

Andrews, D., & Goodson, L. (1980). A comparative analysis of models of instructional design. *Journal of Instructional Development, 3*(4), 2–16.

Bagley, C., & Hunter, B. (1992). Restructuring, constructivism, and technology: Forging a new relationship. *Educational Technology, 32*(7), 22–27.

Bowsher, J. E. (1992). What can we learn from corporate education about systemic change? *Educational Technology, 32*(11), 51–54.

Branson, R. (1975). *Interservice procedures for instructional systems development* (4 volumes plus executive summary). Tallahassee, FL: Florida State University, Center for Educational Technology. (National Technical Information Service, 5285 Port Royal Rd., Springfield, VA 22161. Document Nos. AD-A019, 486 to AD-A019 490.)

Briggs, L. J., Gustafson, K. L., & Tillman, M. H. (Eds.). (1991). *Instructional design: Principles and applications* (2nd ed.). Englewood Cliffs, NJ: Educational Technology Publications.

Burkman, E. (1987). Prospects for instructional systems design in the public schools. *Journal of Instructional Development, 10*(4), 27–32.

Earle, R. S. (1990). Performance technology: A new perspective for the public schools. *Performance Improvement Quarterly, 3*(4), 3–11.

Gerlach, V., & Ely, D. (1980). *Teaching and media: A systematic approach.* Englewood Cliffs, NJ: Prentice-Hall.

Gustafson, K. L. (1991). *Survey of instructional development models.* Syracuse, NY: ERIC Clearinghouse.

Hackbarth, S. (1996). *The educational technology handbook: A comprehensive guide.* Englewood Cliffs, NJ: Educational Technology Publications.

Hamreus, D. (1968). The systems approach to instructional development. In *The contribution of behavioral science to instructional technology.* Monmouth, OR: Oregon State System of Higher Education, Teaching Research Division (EDRS: ED 041 448. Microfiche only).

Higgins, N. C. (1980). Formative evaluation of teacher managed instructional programs. *Educational Technology, 20*(12), 22–25.

Kemp, J. E. (1991). A perspective on the changing role of the educational technologist. *Educational Technology, 31*(6), 13–18.

Kerr, S. T. (1981). How teachers design their materials: Implications for instructional design. *Instructional Science, 10*, 363–377.

Knirk, F. G. (1988). Implications of instructional technologies for the future of education. *Journal of Instructional Development, 11*(3), 10–15.

Martin, B. L. (1990). Teachers' planning processes: Does ISD make a difference? *Performance Improvement Quarterly, 3*(4), 53–73.

Mecklenburger, J. A. (1992). The braking of the "break-the-mold" express. *Phi Delta Kappan, 74*(4), 218–289.

Morgan, R. M. (1989). Instructional systems development in third world countries. *Educational Technology Research and Development, 37*(1), 47–56.

Morgan, R. M. (1992). Educational reform: Top-down or bottom-up? *Educational Technology, 32*(11), 47–51.

Olds, Jr., H. F., & Pearlman, R. (1992). Designing a new American school. *Phi Delta Kappan, 74*(4), 296–298.

Reigeluth, C. M. (1992). The imperative for systemic change. *Educational Technology, 32*(11), 9–13.

Reiser, R. A., & Radford, J. M. (1990). Preparing preservice teachers to use the systems approach. *Performance Improvement Quarterly, 3*(4), 40–51.

Rossett, A., & Garbosky, J. (1987). The use, misuse, and non-use of educational technologists in public education. *Educational Technology, 27*(9), 37–42.

Rundell, R. (1992). To start a school: NASDC as a catalyst for systemic change. *Educational Technology, 32*(11), 13–16.

Salisbury, D. F. (1992). A special report: Toward a new generation of schools: The Florida Schoolyear 2000 initiative. *Educational Technology, 32*(7), 7–12.

Salisbury, D. F. (1996). *Five technologies for educational change: Systems thinking, systems design, quality science, change management, instructional technology.* Englewood Cliffs, NJ: Educational Technology Publications.

Shrock, S. A. (1990). School reform and restructuring: Does performance technology have a role? *Performance Improvement Quarterly, 3*(4), 12–33.

Sherry, M. (1992). Searching for new American schools. *Phi Delta Kappan, 74*(4), 299–302.

Snelbecker, G. E. (1987). Instructional design skills for classroom teachers. *Journal of Instructional Development, 10*(4), 33–39.

Stamas, S. (1973). A descriptive study of a synthesized model, reporting its effectiveness, efficiency, and cognitive and affective influence of the development process on a client. (Doctoral dissertation, Michigan State University, 1972). *Dissertation Abstracts International, 34* (University Microfilms No. 74–6139.)

8

Exploring the Paradigm of Instructional Design: Implications in Business Settings

Richard Lent
Brownfield & Lent
Acton, Massachusetts

James Van Patten
Trinity Performance Systems
Manchester, New Hampshire

Prologue

This chapter concerns paradigms—those ". . . beliefs, values, techniques, and so on shared by members of a given community" as described by Thomas Kuhn in *The Structure of Scientific Revolutions* (1970). Given this definition, the question isn't whether or not the field of instructional design has a paradigm, it is how the paradigm affects the "beliefs, values, techniques, and so on" of those who provide and consume instructional design services.

Nowhere are assumptions, beliefs, and values more in play than in the give-and-take between customers and providers as they attempt to define the scope, goal, and activities of an instructional design project. The following is a brief hypothetical example of one client's assumptions as they look for help with a supervisory performance challenge:

Dear Instructional Designer:

We have identified an opportunity to improve the performance of our first-level managers, some of whom are less successful than others in implementing our corporate strategy to move towards work teams. We understand your company has experience in solving similar performance problems, and would like to hear from you on your approach to our situation. Would you please specify:

(1) Analysis: What procedures would you use to clarify the cause of the performance gap between our successful and unsuccessful supervisors?
(2) Design: What are the likely components of the performance system you might develop to close this gap: training? re-organization? compensation? job design?
(3) Implementation: What are the appropriate roles for you and our personnel? How can we work together to improve efficiency?
(4) Evaluation: How will you assess the success of the performance system?

In addition to the nature of your approach to performance systems solutions, would you please identify your approach to project management, including:

- typical project phases and their deliverables
- a "ballpark" cost range
- the management, subject-matter expertise and other personnel supports you would require from us

Of course, no quoted prices and project specifics will be considered final until contract signing. Thank you for your assistance in improving our supervisors' performance.

Sincerely,
The Client

Our designer offers his or her response and, a few weeks later, receives a Request for Proposal . . .

Dear Instructional Designer:

Thank you for your response to our request for information. The Supervisory Steering Committee would like to invite you to submit a proposal concerning our supervisory performance system. We found your experience to be quite impressive and your approach to be very creative, though a bit different from our expectations. Therefore, in your proposal, we would like you to pay special attention when describing the milestones and deliverables of your project. Specifically, please identify:

- the data gathering, analysis, and reporting processes used in your needs assessment
- the typical contents and level of detail of your design document
- the number of pilot tests allowed for the budget specified
- how you intend to conduct "train-the-trainer" sessions for any classroom training components we would be responsible for implementing
- the number and duration of review meetings and the recommended audience of each

We look forward to meeting you at your proposal presentation.

Sincerely,
The Client

Our designer gathers additional information from the client and prepares and presents the proposal. Though the presentation was spirited, the results, it seems, were disappointing.

Dear Instructional Designer:

Thank you for presenting your proposal last week. We continue to find your approach to our project very creative, and hope you found the resulting conversation as stimulating as we did. As they say in diplomatic circles, "We had a frank and honest exchange of ideas."

However, it is the decision of the committee to not proceed with your company at this time. We have selected another vendor for our request. If we find ourselves in need of your services in the future, please be assured we will contact you. Please accept our sincere thanks in responding to our request. If we find ourselves in need of your services in the future, please be assured that we will contact you.

Sincerely,
The Client

Though it is possible that this designer "missed the mark" for any number of reasons, it also very possible that the reason this designer and customer didn't "fit" is because the paradigm used by the designer is different from the one used by the customer. More and more, members of the instructional design community—customers and designers—find they no longer share their ". . . beliefs, values, techniques, and so on" with others. Could it be that there is a change brewing in the instructional design paradigm? Perhaps. But what is that paradigm, and how can we be sure that the change is for the better?

Introduction

About thirty years ago, there were no common assumptions about instructional design because there was no profession called instructional design. Decisions involving instructional design were made by the instructor, who was usually the content expert as well. Because of their expertise, instructors were expected to give the most accurate presentations, ask the hardest questions, and provide the most detailed answers. As long as students paid attention to the expert instructors, they were bound to learn.

As our understanding of the process of teaching and learning grew in the 1960s, we found that providing accurate presentations, hard questions, and detailed answers was not all that there was to learning. Variables were found which greatly affected learning but had very little to do with the content. They had to do with the way the content was organized and designed. Banathy (1968) and others began to define a new perspective on the task of instructional decision making, one which conceived of instructional "systems." Thus was born the concept of "instructional systems design" (ISD) and the beginning of a whole new orientation to research and practice in this area.

Today, we believe that ISD represents the basic "paradigm" which guides instructional designers' activities, focuses our attention, and affects the way future designers learn our practice. The ISD paradigm is useful in that it creates some norms of thinking, belief, and action that are assumed to be held in common by its practitioners.

As Kuhn (1970) pointed out, there is something special about the nature of a paradigm as long as its appropriateness is accepted and unquestioned. Little consideration is given to the possibility of an alternative conceptualization of the field. Researchers, practitioners, clients, and students will have their activities affected by their paradigm but rarely question its appropriateness. In this chapter, we intend to raise an awareness of the existing ISD paradigm. We believe that becoming more aware of how perceptions are shaped by this paradigm will enable us to respond more successfully to the challenges of improving learning in business and other settings.

But beyond simply becoming more aware of the effects of the ISD paradigm, we also intend to question whether or not the "ISD process" models are still the best way of educating and training adults. Over the last three decades there have been many developments which impact the effective use of instructional design in business and industry. Specifically, much has changed: our understanding of adult learning, the technologies available for instruction and learning, our understanding of management practices, the workplace and "work," and the role and expectations of students and other customers of instructional services. If the basic ISD concept was formed from the available theories, models and technologies present thirty years ago, one has to wonder, "What would the instructional designers' paradigm look like if it were created today for the first time?"

In response to this last question, the latter half of this chapter poses observations and questions relevant to the creation of a new paradigm that's focused on serving the multiple customers of instructional design; a paradigm that incorporates today's thinking about learning, managing, and working, and the change of focus from improving the individual's performance to improving organizational performance.

The Benefits and Liabilities of Paradigms

In *The Structure of Scientific Revolutions*, Thomas Kuhn (1970) explains that paradigms provide models and examples which function like explicit rules in defining how to solve typical problems. Furthermore, a paradigm provides a particular community of practitioners with a whole approach to reasoning, working, communicating, and problem solving. It defines a universe of appropriate goals as well as means for achieving them. It isn't questioned—it defines "the way things are done."

Paradigms serve a very useful purpose. Bohm and Peat (1987) explain that paradigms help to support productive interaction and communication among a group of professionals working in a common area. Writers such as Peter Senge have stressed the importance of paradigms as "mental models" that determine the way individuals and organizations behave. As Senge notes, "Our 'mental models' determine not only what sense we make of the world, but how we take action" (1990, p. 175).

But paradigms also limit creativity and flexibility. As Bohm and Peat note, paradigms exact "a price in that the mind is kept within certain fixed channels that deepen with time until an individual . . . is no longer aware of his or her limited position" (1987, p. 53). And Senge clarifies that "the problems with mental models lie not in whether they are right or wrong—by definition, all models are simplifications. The problems with mental models arise when the models are tacit—when they exist below the level of awareness" (1990, p. 176). When this occurs, goals, processes, and activities are unquestioned and guided by the assumptions which define the model. The difficulty occurs when past assumptions (which are now unquestioned) become out of step with current realities. In a descriptive science—such as the physics paradigms described by Kuhn—the paradigm is so strong that *descriptions* of phenomena are sometimes unconsciously "bent" to fit the assumptions, thereby slowing the progress of the field. In a prescriptive science—such as instructional design—it is the *prescriptions* that get bent to fit the assumptions, also slowing the field's progress.

The Instructional Systems Design Paradigm

Over the last three decades, instructional designers have worked to create and clarify an alternative to the traditional instructor-centered or subject-matter expert (SME) approach to course design (e.g., Hannum & Briggs, 1982). The explicit basis of the new approach is the body of procedural and conceptual models that has become known as instructional design, and more specifically as instructional *systems* design to highlight its reliance on general systems theory as a primary conceptual foundation (Richey, 1986, p. 22).

In 1986, Richey defined the field of instructional design as *"the science of creating detailed specifications for the development, evaluation, and maintenance of situations which facilitate the learning of both large and small units of subject matter "*(p. 9). Borrowing ideas about the design process from architecture and engineering (Reigeluth, Bunderson, & Merrill, 1978), the ISD approach was created around a core set of steps or phases beginning with analysis and concluding with evaluation and implementation. Where the core of the older instructor-centered or SME approach was the content itself, the core of the ISD approach became a phased process for guiding the designer's activities. As Richey explains:

> The most prolific amount of activity relates to the construction of procedural models. Andrews and Goodson (1980) have identified and analyzed forty instructional design models in the literature. To a great extent, these models provide the structure for the bulk of design projects completed today, and these models are all procedural in nature. Essentially, they provide a list of steps to follow, and in most cases, provide a rationale for the steps. (Richey, 1986, p. 29)

Prior to the mid-60s, instructional design was barely recognized as a field. In Saettler's (1968) history of the larger field of instructional technology, instructional design is barely mentioned. Over the next few years, as the properties of the ISD approach became clear, a number of efforts were made to communicate and promote its use, including the development of the Interservice Procedure for Instructional Systems Design (Branson, Rayner, Cox, Furman, King, & Hannum, 1975) for technical skills training, and, for classroom instruction, the U.S. Office of Education's Instructional Development Institute (circa 1970–74). These efforts all emphasized the procedural nature of instructional design.

Over time, the development and widespread adoption of the ISD approach provided many of the benefits common to a paradigm. By standardizing a common process with a common vocabulary, researchers and practitioners have been able to exchange ideas and experiment with improvements. Journals, professional societies, and graduate programs have evolved to focus on building professional practice in each phase of the process. As a paradigm, however, the ISD approach also seems to suffer from certain weaknesses as well. Recent research by Wedman and Tessmer (1993) indicates that, at least today, there is a considerable difference between what is espoused and what is practiced in the name of ISD. Perhaps the ISD paradigm is suffering from certain inherent weaknesses that limit its utility and benefits in "the real world."

Weaknesses of the ISD Paradigm

It is the nature of a true paradigm that its principles seem so obvious and fundamentally logical that they often go unquestioned. This seems to be true in the case of the ISD paradigm:

> One thing that most, if not all, persons involved in the design and development of instructional materials or training systems can agree upon is that the basic [instructional systems design] model and its underlying systems approach to instructional development is sound. (McCombs, 1986, p. 68)

Little has changed since the McCombs comment in 1986. Consider the 1993 criteria used by the National Society of Performance and Instruction (NSPI) for determining its award for "Outstanding Human Performance System":

> All steps in the systematic approach applied to the submission will be evaluated for, but not limited to, the:
>
> - Analysis procedure that results in the selection of this intervention.
> - Design, development, testing, and revision procedures.
> - Evaluation system design
> - Usability and reliability. (NSPI, 1993, p. 5)

One can assume that if a process was followed that did not include analysis, design, development, testing, revision and evaluation, then the resulting human performance system would be rejected automatically. It appears that to the NSPI, following the prescriptions of the ISD model was fundamentally logical, an unquestioned nessessity: *a paradigm.*

Over time, however, the world in which the paradigm exists changes, and eventually practitioners of a paradigm begin to experience some tension between the way they believe their discipline is to be practiced and the expectations and constraints of the environment in which they work. Since paradigms are difficult to change (as pointed out by consultant Joel Barker in his books and videotapes), the world may change around the practitioners and their paradigm, creating a gap between theory and practice. We believe this has happened to the ISD paradigm.

Reflect for a moment on just some of the developments that have changed the environment in which instructional designers practice their craft over the last quarter century:

- Originally, "programmed instruction" was a print-based medium, and computer-based instruction was just being conceived. (And personal computers, electronic performance support systems, and interactive video were the stuff of science fiction.)

- Most training assumed the traditional, pedagogical classroom model. While attention had begun to be given to adult "students," the importance of continuous learning throughout one's career was yet to be given any attention. The distinction between androgogy and pedagogy was first being made and there was no conception of "organizational learning."

- The practice of educational evaluation had yet to be defined as distinct from research or measurement.

- Project management was based on earlier product development and engineering technology that emphasized linear steps with decision "gates" between each step. The processes of concurrent engineering, continuous improvement, and rapid application development were yet to be defined (particularly in the western world).

- B.F. Skinner and Carl Rogers were among the most visible and influential advocates of theories of learning. Cognitive learning theories, constructivism, and theories of multiple intelligences and learning style differences were yet to appear.

Given such changes, it is hardly surprising that the paradigm of ISD has begun to show difficulties in its practice. Various writers began noting problems, questioning key aspects of the ISD paradigm even before the paradigm had reached its twentieth birthday (e.g., Braden, 1984; Heinich, 1984; Winn, 1987, 1990). Some of these criticisms began to raise fundamental questions about the paradigm. For example, Carroll (1990) questioned the utility of instructional objectives, one of the most distinctive features of the ISD paradigm:

> A major theme in the standard systems approach (e.g., Gagné & Briggs, 1979) is the hierarchical decomposition of learning objectives. There is no reason in principle that an analysis of learning objectives cannot be coupled with a synthesis of those objectives into a variety of realistic tasks for learners, but in fact we found that this did not occur. The learning objectives were treated as ends in themselves, addressed by structured curricula for building skills from the bottom-up, by step-by-step drill and practice. We found that learners often tenaciously tried to accomplish real tasks, confounding the step-by-step guidance of their training materials. (p. 7)

As early as 1982, Leslie Briggs began to question how well the prescriptions of the ISD approach fit adult learners. He noted that the acceptance of learning objectives by adult learners is not guaranteed. That is, even if the systematic analysis produces performance gaps which are translated into learning objectives, adult learners might refuse to cooperate during the training. Briggs goes on to suggest that the entire treatment of learners—and adult learners in particular—by systems models is not very successful. It is interesting to note that the field of adult development and learning evolved in parallel to but was largely ignored by the field of instructional design throughout the 70s and 80s. Today, issues of learner differences, motivation, job-relevance, and group processes are still not well-handled by current models. Efforts are being made to integrate constructivism with instructional design's prevailing theoretical foundations in behaviorism and cognitivism (Ertmer & Newby, 1993).

Recently, writers such as McAlpine (1992) have suggested that the problems with design models have grown acute. She provides a good picture of the gap between theory and practice of ISD:

> There are many instructional design models presented in the literature, and when I have tried to use them as heuristic or job aids, I have increasingly come to see their lack of fit, the mismatch or dissonance between concept and reality when brought to bear on my real life situations. . . . It is apparent to me from my practice and from discussion with other practitioners that the instructional design process seems rarely to match the linear progression of steps (goals, objectives, etc.) that is so often described. Rather the process can start in a variety of places, doesn't always involve all the elements or stages, and is recursive. (p. 16)

The existence of a gap between theory and practice could mean that practitioners should do a better job of following the prescriptions. However, just considering the changes in the environment in which ISD is practiced, such gaps are hardly surprising. We think it is time to break out of ISD's constaints and consider alternative models for training, development, and performance in the workplace.

A New Paradigm Focused on the Customer(s)

There are many perspectives from which to consider revisions to the existing paradigm. For example, new communication technologies or concepts like just-in-time training offer a variety of insights into alternative paradigms for instructional design. We have chosen to use the perspective of the Total Quality Management (TQM) movement, defining training and development as one of a number of TQM management strategies. As with all TQM strategies, we have chosen to focus our considerations on how instructional design serves its various customer's. Specifically, we propose the development of a new paradigm that would address key interests of *all* the customers of the instructional design effort. Such a "customers" paradigm for instructional design would focus less on a consistent, step-wise development process and more on addressing varying customers' definitions of quality: quality of results as well as quality of the process delivering the result. This paradigm for instructional design would balance a focus on the student with a focus on the other clients and stakeholders of the effort.

In the remainder of this paper, we will examine what some of the properties of this new paradigm may be. How could the paradigm of instructional design be designed to address the requirements of the various different customers of its activities? We will look at four different customers in the typical business setting—learner, worker, manager, and client—and suggest how their requirements might shape the future paradigm.

Learners as Customers. Though most instructional designers feel they are already focused on the learner, the ISD paradigm tends to emphasize the "client" or person making the decisions about the project and funding. Though the learner is an important stakeholder of the training, learners have different and considerably less influence than clients on most process decisions: clients determine the quality of the result and of the interim deliverables supplied by designers, while learners only provide feedback on whether some predetermined outcomes were achieved (and even those outcomes were not the learner's to specify). Quite possibly, this lack of involvement of the learner in design decisions is due to the ISD paradigm's historical roots in pedagogy. But, today, with design activities increasingly focused on serving adult learners, the lack of recognition of the adult learner's role in design decisions is short-sighted. What would a paradigm for instructional design look like if it emphasized making the adult learner an active participant in design decisions?

If we were to design a paradigm that reflected the requirements of adult learners, we believe that instructional decision-making would proceed along a different path. Adults have a very rich and evolving context for their learning. Decisions about instructional events would emphasize the integration of new learning with existing understandings, all within an environment in which the learner is constantly testing the utility of the new skills and information. Furthermore, adults may pass through distinctive developmental stages in their acquisition of some skills and its application to their work. Writers such as Chris Argyris, Joan Bragar and Kerry Johnson, and Donald Schön are providing some distinctive insights into the unique challenges of designing instruction to serve adult learners. For example, in his article on "Teaching Smart People How to Learn," Chris Argyris (1991) presents a thoughtful picture of the challenge of designing workplace learning when the learner is highly skilled at avoiding any embarrassing failures and hence avoids many opportunities to learn. In a new paradigm, how might instructional activities be designed to avoid defensive reactions and "closed-loop" reasoning?

Joan Bragar and Kerry Johnson (1993) present an analysis of adult learning research and suggest new principles for designing instruction. They present a view of the adult learner as moving through three stages of competence: preparation, apprenticeship, and mastery. They then suggest that the learning requirements of individuals in each stage are unique to that stage, but are composed of the same three elements: building awareness, providing practice, and ensuring meaningful application. Under a new paradigm, how might instructional designers develop and evaluate their efforts to support these stages and requirements of individual development? And how might instructional designers help learners in the knowledge-era workplace to go beyond these stages to knowledge generation and exchange?

Finally, Donald Schön offers further insight into the concept that training must support the learner's "meaningful application" of the subject of instruction. Schön (1988) differentiates between "knowing-in-action"—the type of fluent, effortless performance usually associated with training—and "reflection-in-action"—the iterative process used by designers, artists and other problem solvers where actions are conscious (and halting) and their results direct future actions. The current ISD paradigm defines learning outcomes by identifying lists of cognitive, affective, and psychomotor objectives which define "knowing-in-action" performance. What type of learning objectives might instructional designers create to define "reflection-in-action" outcomes for workers in tomorrow's organizations?

Workers as Customers.   The customers of instructional design efforts are also workers with a job to do. Training must help them do their jobs better and more efficiently in order to contribute to their success (and ultimately the success of the business).

If we define human capacity—knowledge, skill and attitude—as resources which can be stored, our current paradigm assumes that workers can effectively "warehouse" an incredible inventory of behavior capacity. That is, the ISD paradigm assumes that a training product or event is developed, produced, and then delivered in a place different from where it will be used—at the workplace. Presumably, this "just in case" design and delivery of training ensures that each person will have the information and skill necessary whenever he or she subsequently requires it. It also assumes there is little or no "spoilage" to the warehoused knowledge, skill and attitude.

By designing "just in time" performance management and support systems, which function together to build skill and knowledge at the workplace, we could *ensure* a more effective and efficient delivery of skills and knowledge. Our workers would have the ability to act, reflect on their work, learn from it and then to improve their future actions accordingly. Gloria Gery (1991) and others have identified the advantages and technologies for such an integration of work and learning. What is lacking, however, is an instructional design model that supports the development of more timely training products. Borrowing from relatively recent developments in hardware and software engineering, we could use a process of rapid application development. How could a new paradigm help us identify new ways of building training and information systems more efficiently so that learning and performance support are "just in time," not "just in case?"

Taking this concern for the worker as a customer a step further, we wonder about how the existing paradigm identifies the opportunities for training. The current ISD paradigm has its roots in the traditional "top-down" management style (of businesses or schools), in which required knowledge and skill are pre-determined for each learner and then instruction is developed and "pushed" out accordingly. Instead of prescribing training to address predicted needs, how might a new instructional design paradigm support a learning process which uses a "pull" strategy initiated by learners consistently improving themselves or their work processes? For example, what would happen if we replaced traditional needs analysis and its emphasis on gap identification with a version of the total quality management technique known as Quality Function Deployment (Akao, 1990; King, 1987), in which customer requirements are used directly to define the desired properties and performance of the finished product which, in turn, are used to define work processes, which define jobs. The worker sees how his or her job has changed and "pulls" in the training required to succeed.

Customers as Managers of "Learning Organizations." The Total Quality perspective changes management from a results-only perspective (e.g., "If it ain't broke, don't fix it!") to a process and results perspective (e.g., "Nothing's perfect, so how do we make this better?"). The organization that results from such a change is one that continues to *learn* from its environment, processes, employees, and customers. The manager is concerned with the learning of the organization as a whole system, rather than with the learning of each individual worker.

This "learning organization" perspective raises a number of important implications for the existing and potential future paradigms of ISD. First of all, it redefines the *potential* value of ISD services from tactical and reactive (e.g., "Train these sales people by next Friday so I can roll this product out this quarter!") to strategic and proactive (e.g., "I need a process for continually sending out product information to the field and bringing in customer information from the field."). For example, Arie deGeus of Royal Dutch Shell has been widely quoted (e.g., Beckhard & Pritchard, 1992, p. 15) for stating that in today's competitive environment, a learning organization "may be the only sustainable competitive advantage," since it means that the organization can keep up with, or ahead of, the constant change in the marketplace. Meanwhile, the existing paradigm of ISD is based on identifying and closing identified gaps in current performance. How might ISD be conceived if it was also intended as means of building the core competence and future capabilities of an organization? That is, what is the role and goal of "instructional design" in a learning organization?

Closely related to the concept of the learning organization are the concepts of total quality and continuous improvement mentioned throughout this chapter. Collectively known as *Total Quality Management* (TQM)—despite Dr. Deming's reluctance to use this term—this movement shatters the traditional view of management's role in planning and promoting learning by espousing such principles as:

- All workers "own" their work process, and follow it.

- All work processes are continuously improved by the workers.

- Process improvements either add value to the customer, reduce waste to the company, or both.

- Customers decide the quality of the result.

- Most of the organization exists to support workers.

Walter Dick recently offered his analysis of the ramifications of a total quality approach to training:

> When one considers typical procedures used in training and education organizations, it is clear that a number of things likely would change if a quality training system were put in place. These changes would impact the following:
>
> - systems and performance thinking
> - customer identification and focus
> - use of a variety of solutions to organizational problems
> - reconsideration of design and development processes
> - a new spirit of process improvement
> - emphasis on data collection and review
> - emphasis on reduction of cycle time for both learners and training staff. (Dick, 1993, p. 42)

Clients as Customers of the Designer.   Finally, we turn to the relationship of the instructional design process to the decision-maker or client who requests the project. The existing paradigm contains an implicit role for the designer as a consultant to the client as an expert on instructional design. (This role is generally the same whether or not the designer is internal to the client's organization.) The designer is expected to provide the "answers" to the client's training requirements and control the predictability of the process through carefully planned "deliverables" and review points.

Recent efforts to improve the quality and productivity of consultant/client relationships have noted weaknesses in the approach of consultant as expert (e.g., Weisbord, 1987). More effective, efficient, and sustainable improvements result from projects in which a collaborative consulting model is used. What are the implications for the client-instructional designer relationship and the paradigm of ISD?

Alexander J. Romiszowski (1990) provided one forecast of the changing relationship between clients and designers. He looked at trends in corporate training and predicted that the training department as a centralized training implementation agency would disappear, replaced by multidisciplinary teams that work with and report to their clients to address changes in all aspects of organizational performance.

This leads to a further question: What would happen to the existing paradigm if being responsible for producing or delivering effective training were not enough—instead, if the designer became responsible for collaborating *with* the client to produce change? Brinkerhoff and Gill (1994) provide one picture of such a paradigm:

> We believe that in most organizations today the capacity of the training function to provide high-quality training interventions has greatly increased. Many training departments have the instructional technology to deliver solid learning interventions. It is the capacity of the total organization to manage the learning process for maximum value that is in need of attention. . . . The new training paradigm is a set of beliefs about the way training is perceived and structured within the organization. These are beliefs about the following:

- The way training goals are established and related to strategic needs
- How training plans and strategy are formulated.
- How the nontraining stakeholders in the process are involved.
- How learning interventions are designed and delivered.
- How learning results are managed so that learning increases and is transformed into added value products and services. (pp. 9–11)

Conclusion

In this chapter, we have tried to provide a starting point for considering the nature and the strengths and weaknesses of the existing ISD paradigm, and to suggest directions for changing this paradigm towards one more customer-focused. We have only begun to describe some of the changes and trends that may shape the future paradigm. To paraphrase a common statement in management strategy sessions, we believe it is time "to get outside the nine dots" and re-think some of our most basic assumptions about the practice of instructional design.

Epilogue

Let's revisit the communication between the client and the instructional designer we saw in the Prologue, but this time, let's see how our designer responded to our client using a different, more customer-focused paradigm of instructional design. . . .

Dear Client:

Thank you for your interest in me and my firm. We have had success in helping many organizations improve their management systems. Though our approach doesn't easily fit into the four categories you've identified in your letter, I will use those categories to describe our value to customers and the activities we use to deliver that value.

We assume that you are currently dissatisfied with the way your supervisory system is aligned with your other management systems—especially your team management system. Given this, our general approach would include:

(1) Analysis: Rather than focus our analysis on the level of the individual supervisor (i.e., by locating performance gaps between successful and unsuccessful supervisors), we suggest exploring your set of management systems (i.e., by locating discrepancies among the results of your current set of management systems, the results desired by your external customers, and the results required by your core work process).

Specifically, we would be interested in four management systems and how they are aligned:

- Self-management by individuals: What work instructions exist and are they being followed? This includes worker as well as supervisor work instructions.
- Self-management by teams: How are teams deployed by your managers? Specifically, what is the relationship between natural and cross-functional work teams?
- The coordination and alignment of individuals: How do your systems of employee selection, job description, performance review, training, and compensation interact?
- The coordination and alignment of teams: How do your systems of team assignment, charter, support, and rewards interact?

We would conduct a series of focused meetings with as many individuals as possible from across the your organization. These meetings of 8–12 employees each would seek to build organizational consensus concerning management practices by:

- articulating current customer requirements
- identifying organizational core and support processes
- identifying current management practices (from the four systems described above) which serve those processes
- finding ways to improve the management practices

(2) Design: Historically, our "analysis" activities have resulted in significant organizational improvement in and of themselves. We've found that by including as many people from across an organization as possible in the analysis of an issue, the solution and resolution of that issue appear simultaneously. But when additional intervention is required, we suggest the creation of a "design team" to develop that intervention across functions. In this way, we act as a facilitator and monitor of the process, ensuring that the committee achieves its mission.

(3) Implementation. After the design team identifies the appropriate interventions, we offer any support required—from desk-top publishing, to delivery, to coaching facilitators. Our intent is to help build a complete solution by partnering with your internal resources.

(4) Evaluation. Our philosophy of evaluation is to gather the information required to facilitate the decision at hand. Given your supervisory challenge, we believe the decisions at hand might include:

- Who is the supervisors' customer in your environment of self-directed work teams?
- When and how do supervisors add value to work teams? How is that value measured?
- How should supervisors work as a team to improve their own work?

As you can imagine, our intended project will not fit the traditional phase and cost model you describe in your RFP. For example, we cannot describe specific deliverables until they are developed by the focus groups. We can offer a "typical" project composed of the following events. We call them the three "As":

(1) Alignment. All parties directly involved in the supervisory system are brought together to build a common perspective on the challenge of supervision in an environment of self-directed work teams.

Deliverable: a mission statement for supervisors and clarification of their role in the customer supply chain.

(2) Agreement. All stakeholders come to consensus on how to proceed to implement the supervisory mission.

Deliverable: functioning supervisory improvement teams and a support system.

(3) Action. Stakeholders agree to changes in supervisory work standards and request specific support.

Deliverable: training, organization, compensation, job focus, etc.

I'm sorry, but we cannot provide a typical "ballpark" cost for these events but will work with you to define and manage the costs relative to the value of specific activities. We look forward to working with you to achieve this important learning opportunity for your company.

Sincerely,
Instructional Designer

The client decides to hear more about this designer's approach and requests a more formal proposal. After a few calls with the client and the steering committee, the designer responds . . .

Dear Client:

Thank you for your request for a proposal. It is heartening to know you support our basic approach to performance improvement. We understand your Steering Committee's need for specificity concerning process, deliverables, and price, but we are currently unable to offer much more detail. I have enclosed a copy of our standard contract terms and conditions and will be happy to discuss our experience and approach at the proposal presentations later in the week.

Please remember, our intent is to partner with your organization to accomplish three tasks:

- *Alignment* of stakeholders
- *Agreement* on appropriate improvements
- *Action* by individuals to change the four management systems

We do not believe a traditional needs analysis, design document, development, evaluation, implementation approach is successful in developing long-lasting, successful organizational learning. I look forward to meeting with you later this week and discussing your challenge further.

Sincerely,
Instructional Designer

Unfortunately, as we saw in the prologue, the client chose to work with another bidder. Maybe the safest route is to stay with the old paradigm? In one reported effort to apply quality concepts to instructional design, Debby King and Ann Dille (1993) described the influence that the existing paradigm had on their project:

> In retrospect, we now realize that the familiarity that the [customers] had with the design teams and the ISD model used by the teams, introduced a bias in their identification of customer requirements. . . . Their requirements were stated in terms of the existing instructional design system to which they had been educated. They shaped the requirements into statements that complied with and upheld that ISD model. (p. 59)

But while it may be easier in the short term to stay within the existing paradigm, beware getting caught when the paradigm does change, as the history of other fields suggests it surely will.

References

Akao, Y. (Ed.). (1990). *Quality function deployment: Integrating customer requirements into product design.* Cambridge, MA: Productivity Press.

Andrews, D. H., & Goodson, L. A. (1980). A comparative analysis of models of instructional design. *Journal of Instructional Development, 3*(4), 2–16.

Argyris, C. (1991). Teaching smart people how to learn. *Harvard Business Review, 69*(3), 99–109.

Banathy, B. (1968). *Instructional systems.* Palo Alto, CA: Fearon.

Barker, J. A. (1990). *The business of paradigms.* Burnsville, MN: Charthouse International.

Beckhard, R., & Pritchard, W. (1992). *Changing the essence: The art of creating and leading fundamental change in organizations.* San Francisco: Jossey-Bass.

Bohm, D., & Peat, F. D. (1987). *Science, order and creativity.* New York: Bantam.

Braden, R. A. (1984). Instructional design: A discrepancy analysis. *Educational Technology, 24*(2), 33–34.

Bragar, J. L., & Johnson, K. A. (1993). *Principles of learning.* Paper presented at the annual meeting of the American Society for Training and Development, Atlanta, GA.

Branson, R. K., Rayner, G. I., Cox, J. L., Furman, J. P., King, F. J., & Hannum, W. H. (1975). *Interservice procedures for instructional systems development* (5 vols.). Ft. Monroe, VA: US Army Training and Doctrine Command.

Briggs, L. J. (1982). Instructional design: Present strengths and limitations, and a view of the future. *Educational Technology, 22*(10), 18–23.

Brinkerhoff, R. O., & Gill, S. J. (1994). *The learning alliance: Systems thinking in human resource development.* San Francisco, CA: Jossey-Bass.

Carroll, J. M. (1990). *The Nurnberg funnel: Designing minimalist instruction for practical computer skill.* Cambridge, MA: The MIT Press.

deGeus, A. (1988). Planning as learning. *Harvard Business Review,* March/April.

Dick, W. (1993). Quality in training organizations. *Performance Improvement Quarterly, 6*(3), 35–47.

Ertmer, P. A., & Newby, T. J. (1993). Behaviorism, cognitivism, constructivism: Comparing critical features from an instructional design perspective. *Performance and Instruction, 6*(4).

Gagné, R. M., & Briggs, L. J. (1979). *Principles of instructional design* (2nd ed.). New York: Holt, Rinehart, and Winston.

Gery, G. (1991). *Electronic performance support systems.* Boston: Weingarten.

Gustafson, K. (1981). *Survey of instructional development models.* (ERIC Clearinghouse on Information Resources, ED 211 097.)

Hannum, W. H., & Briggs, L. J. (1982). How does instructional systems design differ from traditional instruction? *Educational Technology, 22*(1), 9–14.

Heinich, R. (1984). The proper study of instructional technology. *ECTJ, 32*(2), 67–87.

King, D., & Dille, A. (1993). An early endeavor to apply quality concepts to the systematic design of instruction: Successes and lessons learned. *Perfomance Improvement Quarterly, 6*(3), 48–63.

King, R. (1987). *Better designs in half the time: Implementing quality function deployment in America.* Methuen, MA: Goal/QPC.

Kuhn, T. S. (1970). *The structure of scientific revolutions.* Chicago: University of Chicago Press.

Masterson, P. M. (1981). *Development and evaluation of a participatory planning/learning model for introducing study of the future to state education agency staff.* Tallahassee: Unpublished doctoral disseration, Florida State University.

Markle, D. G. (1977). First aid training. In L. J. Briggs (Ed.), *Instructional design: Principles and applications.* Englewood Cliffs, NJ: Educational Technology Publications.

McAlpine, L. (1992). Highlighting formative evaluation: An instructional design model derived from practice. *Performance & Instruction, 31*(10), 16–18.

McCombs, B. L. (1986). The instructional systems development [ISD] model: A review of those factors critical to its successful implementation. *ECTJ, 34*(2), 67–81.

Mezirow, J. (1991). *Transformative dimensions of adult learning.* San Francisco: Jossey-Bass.

NSPI (1993). *1993/1994 awards of excellence: Call for nominations.* Washington, DC: National Society for Performance and Instruction.

Reigeluth, C. M., Bunderson, C. V., & Merrill, M. D. (1978). What is the design science of instruction? *Journal of Instructional Development, 1*(2), 11–16.

Richey, R. C. (1986). *The theoretical and conceptual bases of instructional design.* New York: Nichols.

Romiszowski, A. J. (1990). Trends in corporate training and development. In M. Mulder, A. J. Romiszowski, & P. C. van der Sijde (Eds.), *Strategic human resource development.* Amsterdam: Swets & Zeitlinger.

Saettler, P. (1968). *A history of instructional technology.* New York: McGraw-Hill.

Schön, D. A. (1988). *Educating the reflective practitioner.* San Francisco: Jossey-Bass.

Senge, P. M. (1990). *The fifth discipline.* New York: Doubleday.

Wedman, J., & Tessmer, M. (1993). Instructional designers' decisions and priorities: A survey of design practice. *Performance Improvement Quarterly, 6*(2), 43–57.

Weisbord, M. R. (1987). *Productive workplaces.* San Francisco: Jossey-Bass.

Winn, W. (1987). Instructional design and intelligent systems: Shifts in the designer's decision-making role. *Instructional Science, 16*, 59–77.

Winn, W. (1990). Some implications of cognitive theory for instructional design. *Instructional Science, 19*, 53–69.

9

Emerging Paradigms in Diffusion and Implementation

Donald P. Ely
Syracuse University
Syracuse, New York

The popular current use of Thomas Kuhn's original concept of changing paradigms (Kuhn, 1962, 1970) probably has more to do with the ways in which change can be described than with the paradigms themselves. Kuhn's description of the change process as a deviation from the accepted scientific norms has become a handy vehicle for use in interpreting any alteration of the status quo in almost any field. As a field matures with new research findings and applications of knowledge, new approaches to solving current problems are introduced. These new approaches sometimes alter or link with traditional processes and sometimes replace them. In either case, the focus is on change—of the individual, of management, of the institution, or of the society.

Diffusion (or dissemination) has always been with us. Since the mid-20th century, it has branched out under new labels, such as *diffusion* (Rogers, 1983), *marketing* (Kanter, 1983), *organization development* (Miles & Eckholm, 1985), and *transfer of technology* (Creighton, Jolly, & Laner, 1985). The goals of dissemination, however, have not changed substantially. Most efforts are focused on *informing, promoting,* and *changing.*

Early Paradigms

At the most elemental level, diffusion (or dissemination) can be described as the sending of purposive messages. Dissemination is rarely done without purpose. Much of the early thinking and writing used a basic communication model (Rogers, 1962) as a graphic representation of the diffusion process. The dominant paradigm from that point through the work of Rogers and Shoemaker (1971) was the classic communication model (Shannon & Weaver, 1949) in a modified form. The thrust was toward "getting the message out"; hence *diffusion,* as in the spreading of seeds. The emphasis was on reaching people, often as many as possible, through the mass media. The purpose was largely to *inform* and to *persuade*. Receivers of information were considered to be passive and rational. They were identified as "the audience," as if there was a group waiting to receive "the word." By and large, the audience was considered to be open to persuasion (Hovland, Janis, & Kelley, 1953).

As educators began to embrace the basic diffusion paradigm of the 1960s and early 1970s, a context emerged in which *change* was dominant. Thus, the United States Office of Education began to use the R D D and E "model"—Research, Development, Dissemination, and Evaluation (Clark & Guba, 1972). The linearity of the communication process continued to dominate the R D D and E approach, since one phase was intended to be "complete" before the next phase began. For example, research and development had to occur before dissemination could take place, and evaluation could not begin until after dissemination had occurred.

The Move Toward Implementation

As studies of the diffusion process were completed, new approaches (or "models") were introduced that moved toward the *use* of an innovation. These studies focused on *implementation*—the actual use of an innovation in context. The earlier models emphasized adoption. Once an innovation was adopted, it was assumed that use would follow naturally. In the 1970s and early 1980s, Hall and his colleagues at the Research and Development Center for Teacher Education at the University of Texas at Austin conducted a series of major studies of the change process in education. These studies were based on various dimensions of the Concerns-Based Adoption Model (CBAM), which explained the change process from the user's point of view (Hall & Hord, 1987), using a problem-solving approach. Havelock (1973) likewise advocated a problem-solving approach in his model. About the same time, Fullan and Pomfret (1977) reported on implementation research. Fullan's own research continued through the 1980s and is still in process (Fullan, 1991).

Institutionalization: Completing the Paradigm

Even though implementation seemed to be the ultimate goal of the diffusion process, an additional step appeared in the late 1980s—*institutionalization*. Some of the early work from outside the field of education was done by Yin and Quick (1978). Later, with some influence from European researchers, a more formal and comprehensive analysis was developed and reported (Miles, Eckholm, & Vandenburghe, 1987). Institutionalization (or "routinization") has created a circle rather than an extension of the R D D & E line. A successful innovation, according to this paradigm, is one that is routinely used in settings for which it was designed. It has become integral to the organization and is no longer considered an innovation.

All of these extensions and modifications of the original diffusion model have caused some reflection among the social scientists who follow this literature and participate in field applications. One such set of reflections is contained in Lehming and Kane (1981). They attempt to consider approaches to school improvement through the research knowledge that has already been produced. It is in this volume that Berman discusses the original diffusion paradigm (which he calls the "technological-experimental paradigm"). Basically, this paradigm holds that ". . . developers could produce replicable products . . ." and assumes that ". . . new technologies were fixed and constant treatments, as required by experimental design" (p. 257). Berman (1981) continues to analyze this paradigm and proposes a series of "meta-propositions" that seem to bridge the dominant paradigm with potentially new paradigms. For example, Meta-Proposition 1: "Educational change typically involves an implementation-dominant process." Meta-Proposition 2 holds that "The educational change process consists of three complex organizational sub-processes—mobilization, implementation and institutionalization—that are loosely, not linearly, coupled." Thus, the stage is set for newly emerging paradigms that incorporate the concepts of *implementation* and *institutionalization.*

Much of the attention paid to the diffusion of innovations has been directed toward education, and that is the focus of this chapter. However, it should be noted that there are other models that grew out of marketing, anthropology, organizational development, and transfer of technology. When these models are compared, many conceptual similarities can be found. The *process* of change can be described in many sectors of society and in many different contexts, but the fundamental elements are strikingly similar. For example, there is a shift away from the linear, step-by-step approach to innovation to a systemic, all-at-once approach. Other changes mark the new paradigms, almost regardless of the context. We will consider several of the most important changes. Each change will use the "from-to" pattern, e.g., *from* institution *to* individual.

From Institution to Individual

The *unit of analysis* is often ambiguous when developing strategies for dissemination and implementation. In the beginning, change agents attempted to influence large bodies in education—the school system, the university, or even an entire state. Much of the early research focused on the institution as the unit of change. Much of this effort was "top-down," with school superintendents, principals, and deans being the key gatekeepers and most of the effort directed towards them. Individuals were not neglected, but they were considered to be just one element among many that had to adopt an innovative practice. Collective action was required to be "successful."

Further research indicated the central role of the individual and special designations were assigned to *opinion leaders, early adopters, late adopters,* and *laggards* (Rogers, 1962). Decisions were made by individuals, usually classroom teachers, who inverted the process to "bottom-up." They became more critical in their decisions to adopt and moved from adoption by replication to "mutual adaptation" (Fullan & Pomfret, 1977). Initially, adoption required a specified use of materials and procedures. The premise was that an innovation, such as team teaching, would not work or could not be guaranteed to be "successful" if the basic procedures were violated. However, some educators felt that there were local social and cultural factors that were inconsistent with the assumptions made by the proponents of the innovations. For example, the social science curriculum "Man: A Course of Study" was altered to meet local conditions rather than blindly following its specified procedures. Adoption therefore became adaptation. New teaching resources and procedures needed to be customized for *their* students, who they felt were not "typical" of the students for whom the innovation was designed. Serious debate occurred between those who held out for *replication* and those who practiced *mutual adaptation.* There is still a division of opinion.

From a Behaviorist to a Constructivist Approach

Early paradigms emphasized diffusion strategies that were aimed at specific persons. These individuals were the *object* of change, often considered to be a significant challenge in the process. The task was to *persuade* people to do something differently—to *adopt* a new program, procedure, or product. In effect, the individual was expected to adopt new ideas that would bring about change. The desired changes, as perceived by the change *agent,* were brought about by following certain principles that usually influenced an individual to *accept* the innovation. In family planning, it was the acceptance of procedures that would assist in the process. In education, it was the adoption of team teaching or programmed instruction. In many settings, the objective was specific (or behavioral) and could be observed and measured.

In the early days of the diffusion/adoption paradigm, professionals in the field of educational technology saw immediate applications for the use of diffusion principles in "selling" their programs to colleagues who, in turn, would use these innovations to improve instruction. During this period, the introduction of programmed instruction with its emphasis on behavioral objectives was compatible with the goals of the diffusion process. It seems obvious now, in hindsight, that diffusion/adoption had a behavioral orientation.

From Replication to Mutual Adaptation

As implementation became more dominant, the behavioral approach that championed *replication* according to specifications gradually gave way to adaptation or "mutual adaptation." This approach called for modifications of an innovation that reflected local conditions, the unique characteristics of local learners, and the addition of elements that local educators thought would make more sense than to follow the instructions that usually came with the new product or practice. After all, the argument went, the local professional could make a better assessment of the needs and potential reception of the innovation than the original researcher or developer.

Once professional educators realized that they could modify programs, products and practices, it was a short step to constructivism. A California-based curriculum initiative in mathematics (Cohen & Ball, 1990) that used "constructivist" approaches, pointed out that ". . . any teacher, in any system of schooling, interprets and enacts new instructional policies in light of his or her own experience, beliefs, and knowledge . . . Teachers view themselves as independent, autonomous professionals . . . Even the most obedient and traditional teachers [that were] observed, enacted policies in their own ways and were proud of their contributions" (p. 253).

Huberman (1973) documented the shift from "stimulus-response" psychology to constructivist teaching and learning." If people can interact with those who produce new knowledge, articulate how they might modify it, suggest how the originator of the program or project producer can revise it to make it more applicable, potential adopters might feel a greater sense of propriety over the knowledge base" (Hutchison & Huberman, 1993, pp. 11–12). Constructivism in diffusion and implementation is tangentially related to the concept in teaching and learning. If an attempt is made to connect current knowledge with new knowledge and adapt that new knowledge in the existing context, it can be used for local applications and will not be a "top-down" directive.

From Innovation to Reform

Current discussions and efforts aimed at "restructuring education," "systemic change in teaching and learning," and "school redesign and reform" cry out for all types of innovations in the organization and management of education as well as in classrooms and laboratories. Emerging paradigms of diffusion and implementation offer models for bringing about change. The major difference in the present models compared with earlier models is the comprehensive nature of the process. From *diffusion*, through implementation, to *institutionalization*, the new paradigm is systemic. Lessons from earlier studies (Berman & McLaughlin, 1978) show that change of key personnel and termination of federal funds caused school-based innovations to cease. The case studies of these innovations describe a "top-down" procedure that eventually shifted to a "bottom-up" process, whereby teachers themselves were active in assessing local needs, gaining personal and professional rewards, and using new products and practices that seemed to "fit" in their settings.

From "Top-Down" to "Bottom-Up"

Neither "top-down" nor "bottom-up" approaches by themselves are sufficient to bring about the reforms that are called for today. Both are necessary at one point or another and should be linked to "middle-out" strategies that Hutchison and Huberman (1993) describe as "indirect." The "middle-out" strategies involve *linking agents* who serve as bridges between knowledge producers and knowledge users. These linking agents use person-to-person approaches to diffuse and facilitate adoption of innovative ideas. One good example is the National Diffusion Network (NDN) that uses State Facilitators to disseminate validated programs. These linking agents provide information about programs that work, and help local users to connect with substantive experts who are called Developer-Demonstrators. Hutchison and Huberman (1993) see this "middle-out" strategy as a promising paradigm.

> The combination of elements such as choice, ample in-person assistance from a variety of people, and high-quality services, information, and use of craft (and oftentimes more scientific) validation of its programs appears to contribute to this relatively successful dissemination system. These ingredients were already in the formula for "what works," at least in middle-out dissemination strategies. In particular, the combination of 'bottom-up' features (attention to local needs, connection to personal and professional incentives, focus on 'usable' characteristics of the knowledge base) and the 'middle-out' characteristics just reviewed, appears to predict fairly well the extent of implementation in a set of given school districts. (p. 17)

The New Emphasis on Institutionalization

The current paradigm is not complete unless it encompasses *institutionalization*. It is this step, beyond implementation, that offers the true test of adopted innovations. "Institutionalization . . . is an assimilation of change elements into a structured organization, modifying the organization in a stable manner. Institutionalization is thereby a process through which an organization assimilates an innovation into its structure" (Miles, Eckholm, & Vandenburghe, 1987). There are a number of characteristics that help to identify the stabilization of an innovation:

1. Implementation success: the innovation . . . is effectively carried out, achieving positive results, as seen by users and others (a pre-condition, but not sufficient).
2. Extension of use: spreading the use of the innovation more widely through the school/district; growth of program in organization. Also diffusion across organizations. Both internal and external diffusion tend to increase legitimacy, 'taken-for-grantedness.'
3. Removal of old (replaced) practice.
4. Embedding: fitting the change explicitly into curriculum, schedule, organizational structure, and procedures. Essentially organizational change to accommodate the innovation; includes idea of 'interconnecting' or 'integrating' program and organization. Redesign of the organization's routines to incorporate the innovation. Can also be seen as transferring responsibility from the temporary project system to the permanent system.
5. Resource allocation: Time, expertise and money needed for routine operation are put in place for current and future years (Miles, Eckholm, & Vandenburghe, 1987, p. 40). Initiation (that is, the diffusion and adoption of an innovation), implementation and institutionalization, taken together, in a systemic fashion, provide the basis for the current paradigm. No one element is sufficient to bring about change which is the ultimate goal of the process. Each component has sufficient research support to create guidelines that facilitate the process. Whether or not these principles are visible parts of the paradigm or not, they *do* exist and can be used at each step along the way.

The purpose of the dissemination process, according to the current paradigm, is to bring about change in education. Instructional development, by definition, is a process that brings about change (Diamond, 1989). Diffusion/implementation is most frequently an *external* process; instructional development is most frequently an *internal* process. If, after testing, the products and practices created by the instructional development process meet acceptable criteria for use in a classroom, school, or institution, the next step is to *inform* others about the new approach; then, to *persuade* others to adopt and use it, thus bringing about *changes* in teaching and learning. The process of change is launched within the scope of instructional development.

The diffusion paradigm as it currently exists is an integral part of the instructional development process. It is *not* an event that occurs once the development process ends. In the same manner in which evaluation is considered to be integral to the systematic development of instruction, so is diffusion—diffusion that includes implementation and institutionalization. A diffusion plan which begins when instructional development begins is much more likely to succeed because the ultimate users have been identified and the likely adjustments that will have to be made are projected or known. Change is not a surprise but a visible expectation.

The importance of dissemination in the instructional development process is spelled out by Michael Scriven (1993) in his Foreword to a special issue of *Evaluation and Program Planning*. He suggests that there is a ". . . need to treat dissemination as having the same importance as creation and development." Further, he "suggest(s) an explanation of our reluctance to recognize the roles of dissemination . . . (is) our bewitchment by an inappropriate paradigm" (p. 209). He concludes that ". . . those of us concerned with changing the world need to get the evaluation and dissemination phases of our projects planned, and planned well, and well linked to each other, not only before we fund them but also at each stage where we consider increasing our investment in them" (p. 211). To follow this advice, we must consider the new paradigm for diffusion that includes implementation and institutionalization within specific contexts.

References

Berman, P. (1981). Educational change: An implementation paradigm. In R. Lehming & M. Kane (Eds.), *Improving schools* (pp. 253–288). Beverly Hills, CA: Sage Publications.

Berman, P., & McLaughlin, M. W. (1978). *Federal programs supporting educational change.* Santa Monica, CA: Rand Corporation.

Clark, D. L., & Guba, E. G. (1972). A reexamination of a test of the research and development model of change. *Ed. Admin., 2*(8), 93–103.

Cohen, D. K., & Ball, D. L. (1990). Relations between policy and practice: A commentary. *Educational Evaluation and Policy Analysis, 12*(3), 249–256.

Creighton, J. W., Jolly, J. A., & Laner, S. (1985). *Technology transfer: A think tank approach to managing innovation in the public sector.* Monterey, CA: Naval Postgraduate School.

Diamond, R. (1989). *Designing and improving courses and curricula in higher education.* San Francisco: Jossey-Bass.

Fullan, M., & Pomfret, A. (1977). Research on curriculum and instruction implementation. *Review of Educational Research, 47*(1), 335–397.

Fullan, M., with Steigelbauer, S. (1991). *The new meaning of educational change.* New York: Teachers College Press.

Hall, G., & Hord, S. (1987). *Change in schools: Facilitating the process.* Albany, NY: SUNY Press.

Havelock, R. G. (1973). *Planning for innovation through dissemination and utilization of knowledge.* Ann Arbor, MI: Institute for Social Research.

Hovland, C. S., Janis, I. L., & Kelley, H. H. (1953). *Communication and persuasion.* New Haven, CT: Yale University Press.

Huberman, M. (1973). *Understanding change in education: An introduction.* Paris: UNESCO.

Hutchison, J., & Huberman, M. (1993). *Knowledge dissemination and use in science and mathematics education: A literature review.* Washington, DC: National Science Foundation.

Kanter, R. M. (1983). *The changemakers.* New York: Simon and Schuster.

Kuhn, T. S. (1962, 1970). *The structure of scientific revolutions.* Chicago: University of Chicago Press.

Lehming, R., & Kane, S. (1981). *Improving schools.* Beverly Hills, CA: Sage Publications.

Miles, M. B., & Eckholm, M. (1985). What is school improvement? In W. van Velzen, M. B. Miles, M. Eckholm, N. Hameyer, & D. Robin (Eds.), *Making school improvement work* (pp. 33–67). Leuven, Belgium: ACCO.

Miles, M. B., Eckholm, M., & Vandenburghe, R. (Eds.). (1987). *School improvement: Exploring the process of institutionalization.* Leuven, Belgium: ACCO.

Rogers, E. (1962). *Diffusion of innovations.* New York: Macmillan.

Rogers, E. (1983). *Diffusion of innovations* (3rd ed.). New York: Free Press.

Rogers, E., & Schoemaker, F. F. (1971). *Communication of innovation.* New York: Free Press.

Scriven, M. (1993). Foreword. *Evaluation and program planning, 16*(3), 209–211.

Shannon, C. E., & Weaver, W. (1949). *The mathematical theory of communication.* Urbana: University of Illinois Press.

Yin, R. K., & Quick, S. K. (1978). *Changing urban bureaucracies: How new practices become routinized.* Lexington, MA: D. C. Heath.

10

Established and Emerging Evaluation Paradigms for Instructional Design

Thomas C. Reeves
University of Georgia, Athens

Introduction

Including the word "paradigms" in a chapter about evaluation within the context of instructional design and development may seem a bit premature. Although popularly used in recent years to describe everything from a change of philosophy to a change of clothes, "paradigm," in the scientific sense, represents a well-established, clearly-delineated approach to conducting inquiry in a field. The status of evaluation within instructional design or development is hardly "well-established" or "clearly-delineated." (The fact that there is only one chapter focused on evaluation in this book of more than forty chapters could be one indication of the limited application of evaluation within instructional design.)

According to the *International Encyclopedia of Educational Evaluation* (Walberg & Haertel, 1990), the predominant usage of "paradigm" refers to the explicit and tacit assumptions that guide inquiry within a field. In his much-discussed book, *The Structure of Scientific Revolutions*, Thomas Kuhn (1962) described how paradigms change within fields, e.g., how the shift from Newtonian to quantum physics required fundamental changes in the philosophy, assumptions, theories, and methodology of research in this "purest" of sciences. According to Kuhn, the dominant mode of inquiry within a field at any given time depends upon complex interrelationships of theories, measurement assumptions, research methods, and analytical procedures. Kuhn's "revolution" thesis holds that, as a mode of inquiry is practiced over time, anomalies accumulate concerning the assumptions within a field and thus reconceptualization is required. Eventually, a new paradigm emerges.

The prospect of a new paradigm for inquiry emerging from time to time in a field is a very powerful one. However, within the context of instructional design (and indeed, within the field of education as a whole), there is a problem. Evaluation is so infrequently and inconsistently applied that anomalies have few opportunities to be revealed and reconceptualization is rarely required. Much more effort is put into creating new methods of evaluation (usually called models) than applying them, and thus no clearly dominant paradigms have emerged. As a result, the field of evaluation is replete with competing paradigms and models (Shadish, Cook, & Leviton, 1991).

On the other hand, some scholars maintain that the lack of a dominant paradigm may be appropriate within instructional design and related fields (Hlynka & Belland, 1991; Yeaman, 1990). Kuhn (1962) suggests that the social sciences (including sociology and psychology explicitly, and education by implication) are "pre-paradigmatic" because researchers in these fields have not been able to reach consensus concerning the fundamental theories, methods, and assumptions for conducting inquiry. On the other hand, widespread acceptance of an established paradigm is no guarantee of successful inquiry. Bohm and Peat (1987) maintain that over-emphasis on paradigmatic purity is to blame for much of the fragmentation in physics and other "hard" sciences. They maintain that a paradigm can be, and often is, detrimental to the creativity that underlies authentic inquiry.

The situation described above presents instructional designers with a dilemma. On the one hand, the lack of a dominant evaluation paradigm leaves instructional designers with insufficient guidance for conducting evaluation within the context of instructional design. On the other hand, having competing evaluation paradigms from which to choose provides them with insufficient direction for applying one or more specific evaluation models to support instructional design activities. What are instructional designers to do?

Purpose

The remainder of this chapter is a description and analysis of four existing and emerging paradigms of evaluation and eight discrete evaluation models that exemplify these paradigms. Further, the chapter reveals ways that these paradigms and models might be applied to support various instructional design activities. The result is not intended to be a recipe for evaluation within the context of instructional design, but rather a presentation of the strengths, weaknesses, and applicability of each of these paradigms and their related models so that practitioners can make more informed choices among them.

Evaluation Paradigms

According to Soltis (1992), there are currently "three major paradigms, or three different ways of investigating important aspects of education" (p. 620) in use:

- the positivist or quantitative paradigm,
- the interpretivist or qualitative paradigm, and
- the critical theory or neomarxist paradigm.

In the *International Encyclopedia of Educational Evaluation* (Walberg & Haertel, 1990), Schubert and Schubert (1990) use different terms to describe basically the same three paradigms:

- the empirical-analytic paradigm,
- the hermeneutic paradigm, and
- the critical theory or praxis paradigm.

Soltis (1992) concludes that these paradigms currently coexist within the educational community "in a state of tolerance and struggle" (p. 621). Schubert and Schubert (1990) point out that there is considerable variation within each paradigm and that many educators resist being categorized according to one paradigm or another. Some view the three paradigms as necessary to yield a full and complete picture of educational phenomena (cf., Salomon, 1991) whereas others regard them as incompatible (cf., Cziko, 1989, 1992).

In light of the controversies surrounding paradigmatic assignments and the interrelationships among the paradigms, a fourth "paradigm" is recommended by the author as an alternative to the three listed above. This fourth set of assumptions that can guide evaluative inquiry is an "eclectic" or "mixed-methods" paradigm (Mark & Shotland, 1987; Reeves, 1992). Grounded in the pragmatic philosophy espoused by John Dewey (1938), this paradigm seeks to integrate selected aspects of the other three inquiry paradigms into a practical, problem-focused approach to evaluation.

The remaining sections of this chapter describe the four paradigms listed above in more detail. The assumptions and methods of the four paradigms have been purposefully overstated to distinguish among them more sharply. Their actual implementation in evaluations conducted within the context of instructional design would rarely approach the "paradigmatic purity" described below.

Two discrete evaluation models are categorized under each paradigm. The models have been categorized on the basis of the strength with which they adhere to the basic tenets of the paradigm under which they are subsumed. At the same time, it must be recognized that any given model may include aspects of one or more of the other paradigms. Also, there are scores of other evaluation models that could be assigned to one or another paradigm; the models discussed below have been chosen because of their usefulness in characterizing the various paradigms.

The rationale for including evaluation models in this analysis is that instructional designers and evaluators usually concern themselves with discrete models rather than paradigms. Further, Alkin and Ellett (1990) maintain that "Evaluation models either describe what evaluators do or prescribe what they should do" (p. 15). Prescriptive evaluation models are more specific than descriptive models with respect to procedures for planning, conducting, analyzing, and reporting evaluations. According to Alkin and Ellett, descriptive models are more general in that they describe the theories that undergird prescriptive models. In this regard, descriptive, theory-based models are akin to inquiry paradigms. There are dozens of prescriptive evaluation models, but descriptive models are still relatively rare.

Analytic-Empirical-Positivist-Quantitative Paradigm

The "Analytic-Empirical-Positivist-Quantitative Paradigm" represents the most established of the paradigms that guide evaluation in education and the social sciences. The "analytic" aspect of this paradigm reflects a belief in a mechanistic, deterministic reality whereby parts can be separated from wholes and cause and effect relationships among parts can be revealed. The "empirical" aspect refers to the goals of inquiry as being the definition, prediction, control, and explanation of physical phenomena as revealed through experience (induction) and experiments (deduction). The "positivist" aspect represents a faith in scientific progress and the perfectibility of mankind. Finally, the "quantitative" aspect stems from a reliance on measuring variables and analyzing the relationships among them with descriptive and inferential statistics.

Subscribers to the "Analytic-Empirical-Positivist-Quantitative Paradigm" believe in a separate, material reality that exists apart from the beliefs of individuals, groups, or societies. Following E. L. Thorndike and other early measurement theorists, they believe that if anything exists, it can be measured. They seek to explain changes in aspects of reality through controlled experimentation. Detachment from the phenomena under study is preferred to maintain objectivity. Mathematical analysis and statistical significance are held in the highest regard.

Although evaluation is generally underutilized, the "Analytic-Empirical-Positivist-Quantitative Paradigm" is the most widely-used evaluation paradigm within the field of education as a whole. The reliance upon this paradigm stems partly from the desire to determine the comparative effectiveness or worth of one program or product over another. Often, the first question asked about an innovative instructional program or product under development or a newly implemented instructional innovation is: "Is the innovation better than the competing programs or products, e.g., another innovation or the existing program or product?" Classical experimental or quasi-experimental methods are frequently the preferred method of determining the comparative superiority of one program over another (Campbell & Stanley, 1966).

The dominance of this paradigm also derives strength from the degree to which it is entrenched in the universities where many novice evaluators learn their craft. Many members of the tenured generation of educational psychology and instructional technology faculty who dominate the teaching of evaluation as well as instructional design methods were schooled in positivist, quantitative methods and may be unfamiliar with or uncomfortable with alternative paradigms. This may be changing as more graduate students enroll in courses concerning alternative paradigms, e. g., qualitative methodologies.

Describing the evaluation models that can be categorized under the quantitative paradigm would entail writing a veritable history of evaluation. Therefore, the following summaries of two positivist evaluation models represent only the highlights of a parade of largely analytic, empirical, positivist, quantitative models that exist and are widely used.

Tylerian Objectives-Based Evaluation Model.   No description of positivist, analytical evaluation models would be complete without including the seminal contributions of Ralph W. Tyler and his many followers (Smith & Tyler, 1942; Tyler, 1949). According to Alkin and Ellett (1990), the essence of the Tylerian model is that "evaluation should judge that a program is good if, and only if, its objectives are achieved" (p. 16). Tyler changed the focus of evaluation from assessment of the inputs into educational programs to a comparison between its objectives as stated and as achieved.

Tyler's emphasis upon the importance of objectives has influenced many aspects of education, including instructional design. The specification of objectives is a major factor in virtually all instructional design models (Gustafson, 1991). A major benefit touted for specifying objectives during instructional development is that they provide the basis for the development of measurement procedures and instruments that can be used to evaluate the effectiveness of instruction. Indeed, it is difficult to imagine how instructional design might proceed very far without some attempt to delineate the objectives of the development effort.

Tyler's approach is deceptively simple. Establish goals, derive specific behavioral objectives from the goals, tailor instruction and performance measures to the objectives, collect performance data on the objectives, and finally judge the effectiveness of a program based upon the learners' achievement of the objectives. If only it were that simple, there would be no need for this book, much less this chapter!

First, there is the problem that many goals cannot be specified in terms of easily measured behavioral objectives, e.g., the goal of preparing children to be good citizens. Second, measurement of even the most behavioral of objectives is often a difficult process involving complex issues of feasibility, reliability, and validity. Third, programs often have unintended outcomes that are more important than the stated goals of a program, either positively or negatively. Focusing on the specific objectives of a program under evaluation may obscure what critical theorists call the "hidden curriculum." Fourth, focusing on whether or not the

	Time			
	1 **(pre)**			**2** **(post)**
Experimental Group	R	O	X	O
Control Group	R	O		O

R = Random Assignment. O = Observation. X = Treatment

Figure 1. The True Control Group, Pretest-Posttest Design (Fitz-Gibbon & Morris, 1987).

objectives have been attained does not address the worth of the objectives themselves. For these and other reasons, the Tylerian evaluation model has been succeeded by numerous other models.

Experimental Evaluation Model. The experimental (or more often, quasi-experimental) model is a widely accepted and frequently employed approach to evaluation and research within education. Not surprisingly, it has had many proponents, both in the past and in the present (cf. Campbell & Stanley, 1966; Rossi and Freeman, 1989; Tate, 1990). The most familiar version of this approach is represented in Figure 1.

House (1991) identifies Suchman (1967) as one of the originators and strongest advocates of the experimental approach to evaluation:

> The logic of this design is foolproof. Ideally, there is no element of fallibility. Whatever differences are observed between the experimental and control groups, once the above conditions are satisfied, must be attributed to the program being evaluated. (Suchman, 1967, pp. 95-96; cited in House, 1991, p. 7)

It is difficult to argue with authorities who speak in terms of their approach being foolproof or infallible. It is also difficult to oppose an approach that is so entrenched in the minds and actions of so many educators. However, there is a distinct contrast between the advocacy of experimental methods by many evaluators and academics (cf., Fitz-Gibbon & Morris, 1987; Gage, 1989; Schrag, 1992) and the rejection of these methods by contemporary philosophers of science (cf., Casti, 1989; House, 1991; Phillips, 1987). Phillips (1987) remarks on this irony, "New approaches to the design of evaluations of educational and social programs are being formulated that make the "true experiment" seem like a lumbering dinosaur, yet some folk persist in thinking that dinosaurs are wonderful creatures" (p. viii).

What are some of the problems with experimental and quasi-experimental approaches to evaluation? First, the concern for controlling the treatment variables as required by experimental methodologies is impractical in most instructional settings. The hard-earned lessons from decades of implementation studies clearly indicate that there are substantive differences between the designs of innovative programs and products and their actual implementation (Berman & McLaughlin, 1978; Cuban, 1986). Second, the emphasis on measuring educational outcomes via tests in this approach is rarely matched by a concomitant effort to establish the reliability and validity of those measures. In addition, the tests themselves are often poor indicators of the important outcomes of instructional programs (Stake, 1990). Third, the experimental approach can only support or fail to support pre-stated hypotheses; it cannot discover unexpected effects of a program or product within an instructional context. Fourth, randomized experiments are extremely difficult to conduct and can be unethical in some situations. Hence, the vast majority of evaluations conducted within this paradigm are "quasi-experimental," a compromise that introduces many difficulties with respect to the analysis and interpretation of findings. As a result, evaluators operating within this paradigm frequently concentrate on using designs that can be most easily managed, focus on variables that are easiest to measure, apply statistical methods without meeting the assumptions underlying their use, and draw conclusions that have little or no practical applications (Schwab, 1970). Readers interested in a more extensive critique of experimental and quasi-experimental approaches to evaluation are referred to Cronbach (1980), Guba and Lincoln (1989), and House (1991).

The application of experimental methods within the context of instructional design is limited by several factors, especially by the time and resources usually required by this approach. Carey and Dick (1991) sum up its limited utility as follows:

> Such experimental studies are rarely employed in summative evaluation field trials for lengthy instruction because it is almost impossible to hold constant all factors in the design, much less those in the instruction. The list of study limitations often exceeds the list of study questions. (p. 300)

Carey and Dick recommend alternatives to the experimental evaluation approach, including expert judgments and detailed analyses of the relationships among implementation and outcome variables.

Constructivist-Hermeneutic-Interpretivist-Qualitative Paradigm

If the "Analytic-Empirical-Positivist-Quantitative Paradigm" represents the most established of the paradigms that can guide evaluation, the "Constructivist-Hermeneutic-Interpretivist-Qualitative Paradigm" can be described as first among the up-and-coming alternatives. Interest in qualitative evaluation methodologies in education has grown steadily during the past fifteen years. One small but telling indicator is that the president of the American Educational Research Association in 1993 was Elliot W. Eisner, a long-time proponent of qualitative evaluation and educational criticism (Eisner, 1977, 1985).

The "constructivist" aspect of the "Constructivist-Hermeneutic-Interpretivist-Qualitative Paradigm" reflects the belief that humans individually and collectively construct reality. The "hermeneutic" aspect of this paradigm has its original meaning in the analysis of religious texts, especially in reference to different scholarly interpretations of the Bible. More recently, hermeneutics has come to mean the analysis of curriculum in the broadest sense and instructional programs and products in a more focused sense, including attempts to expose the values underlying these phenomena (Schubert & Schubert, 1990). The "interpretivist" aspect stresses the need to put analyses in context, presenting the interpretations of many, sometimes competing, groups interested in an evaluation's outcomes. The "qualitative" aspect represents the emphasis on the human being as the primary evaluation instrument, rejecting the mathematical modeling of phenomena upon which the quantitative paradigm depends so heavily.

Proponents of the "Constructivist-Hermeneutic-Interpretivist-Qualitative Paradigm" have sharply divergent views about the nature of reality from those of proponents of the quantitative paradigm. They believe that "Truth is a matter of consensus among informed and sophisticated constructors, not correspondence with an objective reality" (Guba & Lincoln, 1989, p. 44). Further, they are concerned with understanding the nature of this constructed reality from multiple perspectives, emphasizing the roles of culture, sex, context, and other factors in the construction of "reality." With regard to evaluation methodology, they have adopted many anthropological methods of inquiry, especially human observation. Not surprisingly, immersion in the context of an evaluation is highly preferred over the detachment of the classical laboratory scientist.

The emphasis on observation as an evaluation strategy is especially relevant to evaluation within the context of instructional design. Observational methods are among the most effective strategies for collecting formative evaluation information during the development of an instructional program or product. Formative evaluation is focused on finding ways of improving a program or product under development. According to Flagg (1990), "Formative evaluators employ a wide range of data collection measures, drawn mainly from four categories of methods: self-report, observation, tests, and records or documents" (p. 149). Masters of observational methods for evaluating instructional programs include the creators of "Sesame Street" at the Children's Television Workshop (Schauble, 1990) and operators of software usability testing labs at companies such as Bell Laboratories and the IBM Corporation (Hix & Hartson, 1993; Nielsen, 1993).

Several evaluation models developed during the last fifteen years can be categorized according to the "Constructivist-Hermeneutic-Interpretivist-Qualitative Paradigm." Although the popularity of qualitative methods is growing in some circles, they are by no means accepted everywhere (cf., Cizek, 1995). Early interest in qualitative methods grew out of a frustration with the lack of practical implications for education resulting from quantitative, comparative research, and a strong desire to have more impact on educational practice (Cronbach, 1980). Recent qualitative approaches are much more radical than earlier alternatives to the dominant quantitative paradigm, sometimes despairing of the prediction and control long promised but little realized by the quantitative perspective (Guba & Lincoln, 1989).

Patton's Qualitative Evaluation Model.   Although the earliest efforts to define qualitative methods for educational evaluation originated in Great Britain (cf., Hamilton, 1976), a major contributor to this movement has been Michael Quinn Patton (1980) and his colleagues at the Center for the Study of Evaluation at the University of California at Los Angeles. Patton (1987) stresses that qualitative methods are "particularly useful for studying variations in program implementation" (p. 13). He also stresses the value of qualitative methods, especially observations, if the intent of an evaluation is formative, i.e., focused on improving a program or product.

Patton (1980, 1987) describes several different methods of qualitative evaluation, including observations, case studies, interviews, and document analysis. He also stresses rigorous training for qualitative evaluators. Quantitative evaluators and researchers are often subjected to a regimen of statistics and research methodology courses before they can undertake inquiry. Patton and others (cf., Preissle, 1991) maintain that disciplined training and careful preparation are required for qualitative evaluators as well.

Critics of the qualitative approaches advocated by Patton (1987) and others claim that it is too subjective and that the results of qualitative inquiry lack generalizability (Cizek, 1995). Opponents also maintain that qualitative evaluators have a bias against the precision and accuracy of numerical data. Patton, however, claims that the numbers derived from quantitative methods are seductive because they "convey a sense of precision and accuracy even if the measurements which yielded the numbers are relatively unreliable, invalid, and meaningless" (pp. 165–66). Patton says that he is not anti-numbers, but pro-meaning.

Instructional designers conversant with the formative evaluation methods described by Flagg (1990) will find support and guidance in the writings of Patton (1980, 1987, 1990). Dick and Carey (1991) also promote the value of early one-on-one observations and later field trial observations within ID projects. Reeves (1992) suggests that qualitative methods are particularly appropriate in instructional design projects within school settings where more formal, controlled methods are unfeasible.

Fourth Generation Evaluation Model.   The constructivist aspect of the "Constructivist-Hermeneutic-Interpretivist-Qualitative Paradigm" is perhaps best characterized by the model that Guba and Lincoln (1989) call "Fourth Generation Evaluation." Guba and Lincoln (1989) state: "It [constructivist evaluation] takes the position that evaluation outcomes are not descriptions of the 'way things really are' or 'really work,' or some 'true state of affairs,' but instead represent meaningful constructions that individual actors or groups of actors form to 'make sense' of the situations in which they find themselves" (p. 8). Constructivists generally view measurement as a futile act because the act of measuring always affects what is being measured.

Guba and Lincoln (1989) present seven principles that underlie their model:

1. evaluation is a sociopolitical process;
2. evaluation is a joint, collaborative process;
3. evaluation is a teaching/learning process;
4. evaluation is a continuous, recursive, and highly divergent process;
5. evaluation is an emergent process;
6. evaluation is a process with unpredictable outcomes; and
7. evaluation is a process that creates reality.

A primary outcome of "Fourth Generation Evaluation" is "rich, thick" description based upon extended observation and careful reflection. Constructivists seek more effective ways of sharing understandings of the world, but ultimately despair of the prediction and control so integral to the quantitative measurement perspective. Guba and Lincoln (1989) go so far as to maintain that "To accept the basic premises undergirding responsive constructivist evaluation is virtually to abandon hope that solutions to social problems can ever be found" (p. 47).

This latter statement plays right into the hands of the critics of Fourth Generation Evaluation as described by Guba and Lincoln (1989). Advocates of the quantitative, positivist paradigm who believe in the ultimate perfectibility of mankind criticize the lack of emphasis on generalizability within this model. On the other hand, critical theorists (see below) who believe in social action and commitment criticize the hopelessness of Guba and Lincoln's perspective. Constructivists would respond to their critics that the burden of generalizability and action should be placed on the consumers of an evaluation rather than the evaluators themselves.

A common element in both Fourth Generation Evaluation as an evaluation model and instructional design as a process is the importance of negotiation. Guba and Lincoln (1989) recommend negotiation strategies for reaching consensus about the purposes, methods, and outcomes of evaluation. Similar negotiation strategies can also be used by instructional designers attempting to develop instructional innovations within the constraints of limited time, money, and personnel. Although hard-core positivists will almost certainly find the relativism espoused by Guba and Lincoln disconcerting, their approach has the potential to help instructional designers deal realistically with the complexities they will inevitably face in everyday education and training contexts.

Critical Theory-Neomarxist-Postmodern-Praxis Paradigm

Whereas proponents of the quantitative paradigm proclaim their objectivity, and believers in the qualitative paradigm revel in their subjectivity, advocates of the "Critical Theory-Neomarxist-Postmodern-Praxis Paradigm" wear the label "social activists" with pride. Critical theorists condemn the "Analytic-Empirical-Positivist-Quantitative Paradigm" as reactionary and the "Constructivist-Hermeneutic-Interpretivist-Qualitative Paradigm" as unengaged. In fact, members of the neomarxist faction of this paradigm view themselves as the forces of liberation engaged in mortal conflict with the powers of oppression.

The "Critical Theory" aspect of the "Critical Theory-Neomarxist-Postmodern-Praxis Paradigm" relates to a concern "with questions of power, control, and epistemology as social constructions with benefits to some and not to others" (Muffoletto, 1993, p. 4). The "neomarxist" aspect of this paradigm is derived from the liberation education movement led by Paulo Freire (1970) and Ivan Illich (1970). Neomarxist evaluators seek to expose the "hidden curriculum" underlying instructional technology and other educational reforms. The "Postmodern" perspective questions the conception of instructional technology "as neutral or as leading inevitably to progress" (Hlynka & Yeaman, 1992, p. 2). Postmodernists deconstruct the "texts" inherent in the products and programs developed by instructional designers, seeking to reveal contradictions and the exclusion of minority interests. Deconstruction, which has its roots in literary analysis, is a process of revealing the hidden meanings of texts. The "praxis" aspect represents a desire to abandon the search for truth as sought by empiricists or understanding as desired by interpretivists in favor of seeking "little truths which are situationally appropriate" (Anderson, 1993, p. 1).

From the perspective of evaluation within the context of instructional design, the "Critical Theory-Neomarxist-Postmodern-Praxis Paradigm" may be difficult to conceive, much less apply. After all, why would proponents of this anti-authoritarian paradigm seek to serve a process that has its roots in systems models developed for large-scale weapons production by the military-industrial complex? Nonetheless, the "critical theory" perspective should be taken seriously because it encourages evaluators and instructional designers to question again and again the cultural, political, and gender assumptions underlying an instructional product or program. Skepticism and questioning are the basic tenets of this paradigm. For example, Michel Foucault, a major figure in this movement, demands "that we question everything, including law, science, religion, and Western philosophy" (Anderson, 1993, p. 1).

The primary modes of inquiry for followers of this paradigm are criticism and deconstruction. For postmodernists, the basic notion of evaluation is superseded by the practice of criticism. Hlynka & Yeaman (1992) regard evaluation as a strategy for improving the effectiveness and efficiency of instructional design and the innovations it develops, whereas they promote criticism as having the more important role of "constantly rethinking and deconstructing our beliefs, tools, and technology" (p. 2).

Eisner's Art Criticism Evaluation Model. Elliot W. Eisner, a former art teacher, coined the term educational connoisseurship to describe the first of two primary facets of his art-based evaluation model (1977, 1985). Just as there are connoisseurs in the worlds of literature, drama, and art, Eisner argues that education should have its own connoisseurs, individuals with refined tastes and sensitivity to educational phenomena. The second primary facet of Eisner's approach is educational criticism, i.e., the public expression of the connoisseur's observations and appraisals of education.

Educational criticism has three major dimensions: description, interpretation, and assessment. It is the last dimension, assessment, that distinguishes Eisner's approach from traditional qualitative inquiry. As Barone (1990) describes, ". . . it is also the task of the educational critic to *explicitly* appraise features of the critical object according to personally held educational criteria" (p. 198, author's italics). The critic has the responsibility to convey his/her values to the public so that they may judge the worth of the critic's assessment.

Traditional empirical methods are concerned with internal and external validity. Eisner (1985) has described two related processes that he calls "structural collaboration" and "referential adequacy." The former is concerned with the coherence, cohesiveness, and persuasiveness of the criticism. The latter is related to the insights or "psychological generalizability" of the critique. These two processes have the goals of assuring that the reader finds the critical piece credible and that it moves the reader to some decision or action.

Educational connoisseurship and criticism, as proposed by Eisner (1977, 1985), has not been widely implemented. Opponents of educational criticism claim that it is too subjective. Proponents of this model respond that positivists are also subjective when they formulate research questions, choose instruments, and interpret data, but that their subjectivity is hidden. Educational critics, on the other hand, have an explicit responsibility to disclose the values underlying their subjectivity; they do not suffer from the illusion of objectivity (Barone, 1990).

Another reason for the limited application of Eisner's ideas may be the difficulty in training people to be connoisseurs and a lack of venues for expression of educational criticism, especially in established research journals. Eisner (1985) suggests that anyone involved in education (teacher, student, parent, or administrator) has the right and responsibility to be a critic, but that certain people can be trained in the approach and eventually establish a reputation for the refined tastes and appreciation that are indications of authentic connoisseurship.

Can instructional designers apply Eisner's ideas to the challenges they face? Certainly, the frequent use of expert reviewers as an evaluation strategy within instructional design has something in common with educational connoisseurship and criticism. When employing expert reviewers during formative or summative evaluation, instructional designers should seek to clarify the underlying values that influence the expert's assessment. In addition, those interested in the creative aspects of instructional design will find the art-based concepts and ideas that Eisner (1985) adopts of considerable interest.

Postmodern Evaluation Model.   According to Jencks (1989), postmodernism advocates multiple, often contradictory ways of knowing in contemporary society. The "post" in postmodernism reflects a belief that we are existing in a time beyond the failed modernity of the industrial age. "Modern" is meant in a pejorative sense to refer to the misplaced faith in science, technology, and progress that have left the world with the threat of nuclear holocaust, the destruction of the environment, and global racism and intolerance (Hlynka & Yeaman, 1992).

Hlynka and Belland (1991) present multiple perspectives on postmodernism and related evaluative perspectives such as critical theory. They criticize the field of educational technology for overemphasizing modern technologies and positivist modes of inquiry. They point out that educational technology can be viewed as a series of failed innovations ranging from motion pictures, television, programmed instruction, instructional systems design, computer-based instruction, and intelligent tutoring systems. They recommend the postmodern perspective as an approach to revealing the political agendas hidden in each of these "innovations."

Hlynka and Yeaman (1992) describe how to be a postmodernist:

1. Consider concepts, ideas and objects as texts. Textual meanings are open to interpretation.
2. Look for binary oppositions in those texts. Some usual oppositions are good/bad, progress/tradition, science/myth, love/hate, man/woman, and truth/fiction.
3. "Deconstruct" the text by showing how the oppositions are not necessarily true.
4. Identify texts which are absent, groups which are not represented, and omissions which may or may not be deliberate but are important. (pp. 1–2)

What are the lessons of the postmodernist perspective for the instructional designer? Basically, instructional designers should not automatically assume that their systems models and instructional technologies are the best methods for establishing conditions for teaching and learning. Further, they should constantly examine and re-examine their motives and methods to assure that minority perspectives are included. In addition, they should invite alternative views that can be used to rethink and deconstruct the programs and products they develop (Yeaman, 1994).

Not surprisingly, critics of the postmodernist model see it as anti-technology, anti-progress, and anti-science. Postmodernists respond that positivism and science have had their chance to perfect the world and have failed miserably. Postmodernists seek to empower the disenfranchised in contemporary society, especially female, third world, and non-white interests (Anderson, 1994). The difficulty with postmodernism within the context of instructional design and evaluation is that postmodernism largely rejects these as modes of development and inquiry. ID is criticized as a tool of those positivists who hold onto the false hope of linear progress. Further, criticism is valued over evaluation because of its emphasis on identifying "dysfunctions as well as functions" (Hlynka & Yeaman, 1992, p. 2). Although the incongruency between instructional design and postmodernism is problematic, there is certainly some value in the postmodernist perspective as a method of checking instructional programs and products for aspects that may be racist, sexist, and/or culturally insensitive.

Eclectic-Mixed Methods-Pragmatic Paradigm

This last "paradigm" for evaluation within the context of instructional design cannot be found in any traditional analysis of paradigms for inquiry in education (cf., Schubert & Schubert, 1990; Soltis, 1992). Nonetheless, it is perhaps the most important of the four paradigmatic orientations described in this chapter because it is the one approach most capable of handling the complexity that is the hallmark of contemporary society and technology (Casti, 1994; Sedgwick, 1993).

The concept of complexity is exceedingly relevant to evaluation within the context of instructional design. Sedgwick (1993), in an article titled "The Complexity Problem," maintains that "It is becoming increasingly clear that the comfort of a good fit between man and machine is largely absent from the technology of the information age" (p. 96). A similarly pessimistic observation can be made about the fit among teachers, learners, and the instructional programs and products resulting from systematic instructional design. According to Leshin, Pollock, and Reigeluth (1992), the major problem with existing ID models is that "they have totally ignored guidance as to what makes good instruction" (p. 1). Leshin *et al.* (1992) also maintain that traditional ID models can be followed rigorously and still yield poor instruction.

At least part of the poor success record of systematic instructional design results from the inadequate, simplistic evaluation methods incorporated within most ID models (Reeves, 1989). In other words, the failure of instructional innovations that result from ID to transform practice in education and training can be partially attributed to a failure to evaluate in ways that adequately account for the complexity involved in instruction and learning.

The "eclectic" aspect of the "Eclectic-Mixed Methods-Pragmatic Paradigm" refers to its openness to borrowing the methods of the other three paradigms to collect information and solve a problem. The "mixed methods" aspect relates to the recognition that multiple perspectives are necessary to "triangulate" or "bracket" information and conclusions regarding complex phenomena. The "pragmatic" aspect reflects the practical orientation that, although ultimate prediction and control may never be achieved in education and training, things can get better.

Adherents to the "Eclectic-Mixed Methods-Pragmatic Paradigm" rarely concern themselves with ultimate conceptions of reality, preferring to deal with the practical problems that confront them as educators and trainers. They view modes of inquiry as tools to better understanding and more effective problem-solving, and they do not value one tool over another any more than a carpenter would value a hammer over a saw. They recognize that a tool is only meaningful within the context in which it is to be used. Pragmatists accept their interconnectivity with the phenomena they seek to understand and change (Bruce & Rubin, 1992). They also recognize the weaknesses of their tools, and struggle against the odds to ensure that evaluation will affect decision-making more than will politics, ignorance, intuition, habit and prejudice. Finally, they are honest with themselves and their audiences about the tentative and probabilistic nature of the recommendations they make.

There are few indications that instructional design theorists or evaluators in general recognize the importance of an eclectic approach to evaluation within instructional design (Mark & Shotland, 1987). An exception to this trend is Johnson (1989) who describes the complex problems that instructional designers face amid a world of "chaos, connectivity, and computers" (p. 182), and argues for applying the science of chaos within instructional design. The more common approach in the instructional design literature is to fall back on traditional notions of formative and summative evaluation (cf., Briggs, Gustafson, & Tillman, 1991; Leshin, Pollock, & Reigeluth, 1992).

Nonetheless, contemporary instructional design theorists recognize the need for enhanced approaches to instructional design (cf., Seels, 1993). Some seek to build new tools that can support instructional designers (cf., Merrill, Li, & Jones, 1990). Others call for a major examination and renewal of the fundamentals of instructional design (cf., Gustafson, 1993). Perhaps these and other theorists will find some grounds for improving the effectiveness and efficiency of instructional design in the eclectic models of evaluation described below.

Stake's Responsive Evaluation Model.   One of the earliest attempts to prescribe an evaluation model that falls within an Eclectic-Mixed Methods-Pragmatic Paradigm is the Responsive Evaluation Model advocated by Robert E. Stake (1980). Upon first consideration, Stake's responsive model might appear to fit within the qualitative paradigm, but this is not so according to Stake (1990). "There is a common misunderstanding that responsive evaluation requires naturalistic inquiry or qualitative research" (p. 76). Stake claims that the methods for responsive evaluation are negotiated by the "stakeholders" in the evaluation. Sometimes they will be naturalistic or phenomenological; other times they will be quantitative or goal-oriented. More often, responsive evaluators will attempt to "triangulate" issues and findings using multiple methods.

According to Stake (1990), the key distinction of this model is "that of emphasizing the issues, language, contexts, and standards of stakeholders" (p. 77). Stakeholders are defined as the diverse people who are affected by a program, including administrators, teachers, students, parents, community members, program developers, and representatives of funding sources. The evaluators themselves are also viewed as critical stakeholders, and their judgments are given equal weight as the perspectives of others in evaluation reports. However, the evaluators must endeavor to expose the subjectivity of their own judgments as rigorously as they do those of other stakeholders.

Another essential element of responsive evaluation is the continuous nature of observations and reporting. Responsive evaluators begin to provide feedback to stakeholders as early as possible within an evaluation, fully expecting to please some people and displease others. The questions and methods of evaluation are modified throughout the evaluation period in response to the evolving concerns of the stakeholders.

Critics of the Responsive Evaluation Model argue that "too much attention is given to subjective data, for example, the testimony of participants" (Stake, 1990, p. 76). Stake defends the approach by maintaining that subjectivity is inherent in any type of observation or measurement. He claims that responsive evaluators endeavor to expose the origins of their subjectivity whereas other types of evaluators may disguise their subjectivity by using so-called objective tests and experimental designs. Responsive evaluation can also be criticized because it requires a level of trust and cooperation within an evaluation context that may be unrealistic, especially when the financial or political stakes are high.

The utility of responsive evaluation within the context of instructional design may rest more in the values espoused by Stake (1980, 1990) than in specific methodological aspects of the model. Being responsive to the multiple audiences likely to be affected by an instructional program or product under development should be a key ingredient of the analysis phase of any ID model. This responsiveness, of course, is an ideal rarely attained in many ID projects, and attention to the ideas and values inherent in Stake's Responsive Evaluation Model may improve the degree to which minority issues are considered by instructional designers.

Multiple Methods Evaluation Model. In 1987, the American Evaluation Association published an important volume in the New Directions for Program Evaluation Series called *Multiple Methods in Program Evaluation* (Mark & Shotland, 1987). What Mark and Shotland and their co-authors present is not so much a unitary model for evaluation as a set of guidelines for applying an eclectic approach to evaluating instructional inputs, processes, and outcomes. They maintain that the primary benefits of "multiple methods" are addressing different but complementary questions in an evaluation and reducing the inappropriate certainty associated with traditional experimental methods.

Using multiple methods is not just a simple matter of two or more methods being better than one. Two poorly designed and sloppily conducted evaluation strategies will yield no better picture of the findings than one poor study. Mark and Shotland (1987) maintain that multiple methods are only appropriate when they are chosen for a particular purpose, such as investigating a particularly complex program that cannot be adequately assessed with a single method.

Key issues in Mark and Shotland's (1987) approach are "triangulation," a term popularized by the methodologist Donald Campbell, and "bracketing." Triangulation usually involves using multiple measures to converge on a more accurate estimate of the "true" value of a variable. For example, if an instructional designer needs to determine the motivation of students, s/he might use a questionnaire, an interview protocol, and a personality scale in an effort to gain a more precise assessment of student motivation. The triangulation approach assumes that errors in one type of measure are canceled out by errors in another type. According to Mark and Shotland, this is an optimistic view, especially in education and other social sciences.

Bracketing, on the other hand, involves using multiple measures to provide a range of estimates of the value of a variable. This is a subtle but important difference. The instructional designer interested in student motivation might use the same three measures (questionnaire, interview, and personality scale), but s/he would look at the results differently. Whereas from the triangulation perspective s/he would assume convergence of the measures on a more accurate assessment of motivation, the instructional designer employing a bracketing perspective would interpret differences among the measures as reflecting a range of motivation. Mark and Shotland maintain that the bracketing approach is more practical in evaluation because of the complexity and uncertainly involved in education and other social science contexts.

Probably the most valid criticism of the multiple measures approach is that it is so complex in terms of design, implementation, analysis, and interpretation that few evaluators and instructional designers will be able to apply the approach without the assistance of a team of methodologists and statisticians. However, the benefits of considering the approach and employing aspects of it are considerable. Evaluations focused on the effectiveness of instructional innovations in comparison to other programs have often led to findings of no significant differences (Clark, 1992). Although methodological issues may have invalidated many of these studies, there is also a strong possibility that a single weak outcome measure was used. Bracketing the outcomes of instructional innovations with multiple methods may yield a more realistic portrayal of the outcomes of systematic instructional design efforts.

Conclusions

Four paradigms that have the potential to guide evaluation activities within the process of instructional design have been described, along with eight evaluation models exemplifying them. Instructional designers are advised to investigate these and other evaluation approaches more carefully in order to enhance their repertoire of evaluation options (cf., Bruce & Rubin, 1992; McLellan, 1993).

Some in the field of instructional design may feel uncomfortable with evaluation options. A colleague recently remarked that he is a "quantitative evaluator," and that as such, qualitative methods hold little interest for him. This kind of statement seems ludicrous, akin to a workman claiming to be a "hammer carpenter," stating that the saw and the screwdriver hold little interest. Paradigms and models are only tools, and as such, should be selected only after the purpose or question of the evaluation is understood. Some questions are certainly more susceptible to quantitative, positivist methods, others to a qualitative methodology, and still others may cry out for the skeptical analysis that only a critical theory approach can provide. More likely, multiple methods will be appropriate to "triangulate" or "bracket" the phenomena and provide a more balanced perspective.

The bottom line is that the purpose of evaluation within instructional design is not crunching numbers, telling stories, or deconstructing meaning, but supporting the overall goals of the ID effort, improving human learning and ultimately the human condition. Eisner (1985) makes an eloquent case for viewing evaluation as an art rather than as a science. An essential element underlying the growth and development of the arts is the freedom that artists have to express themselves in many different media. For example, Michelangelo, perhaps the greatest of artists, created paintings, sketches, murals, sculptures, and other art forms. Before we lock ourselves into one or the other evaluation paradigm or model, we might do well to remember Michelangelo's motto, *"Ancora imparo"* (I am still learning). For who could deny that when it comes to evaluation within instructional design, we are still learning?

References

Alkin, M. C., & Ellett, F. S. (1990). Development of evaluation models (pp. 15–21). In H. J. Walberg & G. D. Haertel (Eds.), *The international encyclopedia of educational evaluation.* New York: Pergamon Press.

Anderson, J. (1993, January). *Foucault and disciplinary technology.* Paper presented at the Annual Conference of the Association for Educational Communications and Technology, New Orleans, LA.

Anderson, J. (1994). The rite of right or the right of rite: Moving toward an ethics of technological empowerment. *Educational Technology, 34*(2), 29–34.

Barone, T. E. (1990). Curricular implications of educational connoisseurship and criticism. In H. J. Walberg & G. D. Haertel (Eds.), *The international encyclopedia of educational evaluation* (pp. 197–200). New York: Pergamon Press.

Berman, P., & McLaughlin, M. (1978). *Federal programs supporting education change. A model of education change, Vol. VIII: Implementing and sustaining innovations.* Santa Monica, CA: Rand.

Bohm, D., & Peat, F. D. (1987). *Science, order, and creativity.* New York: Bantam Books.

Briggs, L. J., Gustafson, K. L., & Tillman, M. H. (Eds.). (1991). *Instructional design: Principles and applications* (2nd ed.). Englewood Cliffs, NJ: Educational Technology Publications.

Bruce, B., & Rubin, A. (1992). *Electronic quills: A situated evaluation of using computers for writing in classrooms.* Hillsdale, NJ: Lawrence Erlbaum Associates.

Campbell, D. T., & Stanley, J. C. (1966). *Experimental and quasi-experimental designs for research.* Chicago, IL: Rand-McNally.

Carey, L. M., & Dick, W. (1991). Summative evaluation. In L. J. Briggs, K. L. Gustafson, & M. H. Tillman (Eds.), *Instructional design: Principles and applications* (pp. 269–311). Englewood Cliffs, NJ: Educational Technology Publications.

Casti, J. L. (1989). *Paradigms lost: Images of man in the mirror of science.* New York: William Morrow.

Casti, J. L. (1994). *Complexification: Explaining a paradoxical world through the science of surprise.* New York: HarperCollins.

Cizek, G. J. (1995). Crunchy granola and the hegemony of the narrative. *Educational Researcher, 24*(2), 26–28.

Clark, R. E. (1992). Media use in education. In M. C. Alkin (Ed.), *Encyclopedia of educational research* (pp. 805–814). New York: Macmillan.

Cronbach, L. J. (1980). *Toward reform of program evaluation.* San Francisco: Jossey-Bass.

Cuban, L. (1986). *Teachers and machines: The classroom use of technology since 1920.* New York: Teachers College Press.

Cziko, G. A. (1989). Unpredictability and indeterminism in human behavior: Arguments and implications for educational research. *Educational Researcher, 18*(3), 17–25.

Cziko, G. A. (1992). Purposeful behavior as the control of perception: Implications for educational research. *Educational Researcher, 21*(9), 10–18, 27.

Dewey, J. (1938). *Logic, the theory of inquiry.* New York: Henry Holt.

Dick, W., & Carey, L. M. (1991). Formative evaluation. In L. J. Briggs, K. L. Gustafson, & M. H. Tillman (Eds.), *Instructional design: Principles and applications* (pp. 227–267). Englewood Cliffs, NJ: Educational Technology Publications.

Eisner, E. W. (1977). On the uses of educational connoisseurship and criticism for evaluating classroom life. *Teachers College Record, 78,* 345–58.

Eisner, E. W. (1985). *The art of educational evaluation: A personal view.* London: Falmer.

Fitz-Gibbon, C. T., & Morris, L. L. (1987). *How to design a program evaluation.* Newbury Park, CA: Sage.

Flagg, B. N. (1990). *Formative evaluation for educational technologies.* Hillsdale, NJ: Lawrence Erlbaum Associates.

Freire, P. (1970). *Pedagogy of the oppressed.* New York: Herder & Herder.

Gage, N. L. (1989). The paradigm wars and their aftermath: A "historical" sketch of research on teaching since 1899. *Teachers College Record, 91,* 135–150.

Guba, E. G., & Lincoln, Y. S. (1989). *Fourth generation evaluation.* Newbury Park, CA: Sage Publications.

Gustafson, K. L. (1991). *Survey of instructional development models* (2nd ed.). Syracuse, NY: Syracuse University, ERIC Clearinghouse on Information Resources.

Gustafson, K. L. (1993). Instructional design fundamentals: Clouds on the horizon. *Educational Technology, 33*(2), 27–32.

Hamilton, D. (1976). *Curriculum evaluation.* London: Open Books.

Hix, D., & Hartson, H. R. (1993). *Developing user interfaces: Ensuring usability through product and process.* New York: John Wiley & Sons.

Hlynka, D., & Belland, J. C. (1991). *Paradigms regained: The uses of illuminative, semiotic, and post-modern criticism as modes of inquiry in educational technology: A book of readings.* Englewood Cliffs, NJ: Educational Technology Publications.

Hlynka, D., & Yeaman, A. R. J. (1992, September). Postmodern educational technology. *ERIC Digest.*

House, E. R. (1991). Realism in research. *Educational Researcher, 20*(6), 2–9, 25.

Illich, I. (1970). *Deschooling society.* New York: Harper & Row.

Jencks, C. (1989). *What is post-modernism?* New York: St. Martin's Press.

Johnson, K. A. (1989). Chaos, connectivity, and computers. In K. A. Johnson & L. J. Foa (Eds.), *Instructional design: New strategies for education and training* (pp. 182–191). New York: Macmillan.

Kuhn, T. S. (1962). *The structure of scientific revolutions.* Chicago: The University of Chicago Press.

Leshin, C. B., Pollock, J., & Reigeluth, C. M. (1992). *Instructional design strategies and tactics.* Englewood Cliffs, NJ: Educational Technology Publications.

Mark, M. M., & Shotland, R. L. (Ed.). (1987). *Multiple methods in program evaluation.* San Francisco, CA: Jossey-Bass.

McLellan, H. (1993). Evaluation in a situated learning environment. *Educational Technology, 33*(3), 39–45.

Merrill, M. D., Li, Z., & Jones, M. K. (1990). Second generation instructional design (ID$_2$). *Educational Technology, 30*(2), 7–14.

Muffoletto, R. (1993, January). *Schools and technology in a democratic society: Equity and social justice.* Paper presented at the Annual Conference of the Association for Educational Communications and Technology, New Orleans, LA.

Nielsen, J. (1993). *Usability engineering.* Boston: Academic Press.

Patton, M. Q. (1980). *Qualitative evaluation methods.* Newbury Park, CA: Sage.

Patton, M. Q. (1987). *How to use qualitative methods in evaluation.* Newbury Park, CA: Sage.

Patton, M. Q. (1990). *Qualitative evaluation and research methods* (2nd ed.). Newbury Park, CA: Sage.

Phillips, D. C. (1987). *Philosophy, science, and social inquiry.* New York: Pergamon Press.

Preissle, J. (1991). The choreography of design: A personal view of what design means in qualitative research. In M. J. McGee-Brown (Ed.), *Fourth Annual Qualitative Research in Education Conference,* (pp. 55–66). Athens, GA: The University of Georgia.

Reeves, T. C. (1989). The role, methods, and worth of evaluation in instructional design. In K. A. Johnson & L. J. Foa (Eds.), *Instructional design: New strategies for education and training* (pp. 157–181). New York: Macmillan.

Reeves, T. C. (1992). Evaluating schools infused with technology. *Education and Urban Society Journal, 24*(4), 519–534.

Rossi, P. H., & Freeman, H. E. (1989). *Evaluation: A systematic approach* (4th ed.). Newbury Park: Sage.

Salomon, G. (1991). Transcending the qualitative-quantitative debate: The analytic and systemic approaches to educational research. *Educational Researcher, 20*(6), 10–18.

Schauble, L. (1990). Formative evaluation in the design of educational software at the Children's Television Workshop. In B. N. Flagg (Ed.), *Formative evaluation for educational technologies* (pp. 51–66). Hillsdale, NJ: Lawrence Erlbaum Associates.

Schrag, F. (1992). In defense of positivist research paradigms. *Educational Researcher, 21*(5), 5–8.

Schwab, J. J. (1970). *The practical: A language for curriculum.* Washington, DC: National Education Association.

Schubert, W. H., & Schubert, A. L. (1990). Alternative paradigms in curriculum inquiry (pp. 157–162). In H. J. Walberg & G. D. Haertel (Eds.), *The international encyclopedia of educational evaluation.* New York: Pergamon Press.

Sedgwick, J. (1993, March). The complexity problem. *The Atlantic,* pp. 96–104.

Seels, B. (1993). Instructional design fundamentals: A review and reconsideration: Introduction to a special issue. *Educational Technology, 33*(2), 7–8.

Shadish, W. R., Cook, T. D., & Leviton, L. C. (1991). *Foundations of program evaluation: Theories of practice.* Newbury Park, CA: Sage Publications.

Smith, E. R., & Tyler, R. W. (1942). *Appraising and evaluating student progress.* New York: Harper.

Soltis, J. F. (1992). Inquiry paradigms. In M. C. Alkin (Ed.), *Encyclopedia of educational research* (pp. 620–622). New York: Macmillan.

Stake, R. E. (1980). Program evaluation, particularly responsive evaluation. In W. B. Dockrell & D. Hamilton (Eds.), *Rethinking educational research.* London: Hodder and Stoughton.

Stake, R. E. (1990). Responsive evaluation. In H. J. Walberg & G. D. Haertel (Eds.), *The international encyclopedia of educational evaluation* (pp. 75–77). New York: Pergamon Press.

Suchman, E. A. (1967). *Evaluative research.* New York: Russell Sage.

Tate, R. (1990). Experimental design. In H. J. Walberg & G. D. Haertel (Eds.), *The international encyclopedia of educational evaluation* (pp. 553–561). New York: Pergamon Press.

Tyler, R. W. (1949). *Basic principles of curriculum and instruction.* Chicago, IL: University of Chicago Press.

Walberg, H. J., & Haertel, G. D. (Eds.). (1990). *The international encyclopedia of educational evaluation.* New York: Pergamon Press.

Yeaman, A. R. J. (1990). An anthropological view of educational communications and technology: Beliefs and behaviors in research and theory. *Canadian Journal of Educational Communications, 19*(3), 237–246.

Yeaman, A. R. J. (1994). Deconstructing modern educational technology. *Educational Technology, 34*(2), 15–24.

11

Organizational and Performance Engineering Paradigms and Their Relationship to Instructional Systems Development

Philip L. Doughty
Alexander J. Romiszowski
Syracuse University
Syracuse, New York

The Changing HRD Paradigms in Business and Industry

From Behavioral to Performance Engineering

In this chapter, we address the business and industry context and analyze the transformations and changes occurring in this context and their impact on how instruction and therefore instructional design and development are viewed and practiced. In his chapter earlier in this book, Ivor Davies identifies five forces that are influencing current instructional development theory and practice: changing organizations; the technology explosion impacting organizations in terms of opportunities and challenges; changing employee roles, responsibilities, and expectations; changing workforce demographics; and the changing external environment due to globalization of the majority of activities undertaken by today's business organizations. An alternative way of saying much the same thing would be through the employment of systems terminology: The modern organization, as a system, is experiencing constant change in terms of expected outputs, in terms of the available inputs, in terms of the structures and the processes employed to achieve those outputs with the available inputs; and all of this occurs in an ever more rapidly changing environmental context. Change is the name of the game in business and industry today.

According to Peter Dean (1994): "Organizations that are going to survive and thrive in the 21st century must possess the attitudes, practices, and technology that will enable them to constantly monitor and anticipate the needs of their customers and quickly change their products to meet these needs and maintain customer satisfaction. To achieve these goals, there must be change and often dramatic change in the way that organizations are run. In fact, it is widely recognized that business and industry are undergoing paradigm shifts in attitudes and practices. Attitude changes include a re-orientation towards total quality and towards customer satisfaction. Some of the practices include process redesign and re-engineering, outsourcing, utilizing product work teams, and cooperating with the competition." Changing paradigms and practices in the business environment inevitably lead to changes down the line that impact the training and development profession and, ultimately, instructional design and development. Lent, Brownfield, and Patten, in their chapter in this book, pick up on this general business trend in describing how customer orientation may be perceived as a new paradigm in the instructional design and development field. In the present chapter, we analyze the changing practices in the business and industry environment and their impact on the paradigms and practices of instructional developers who work in both contexts.

Marilyn Gilbert, in her chapter in this book, presents a historical review of the contribution to the instructional design and development field of her late husband, Tom Gilbert. She emphasizes the instructional design contributions of his early pioneering work in the rational application of behavioral science principles to the development of a "Technology of Education," which Gilbert named "Mathetics," and his more recent work on the systematic planning of education and training systems. She also refers to his better known work on performance engineering and technology as being partly responsible for the fact that his work on instructional design is less well known in the field. It is this work that formed the foundation for the behavior-to-performance (engineering) paradigm shift.

Both Marilyn Gilbert and Ivor Davies refer to the NSPI (now renamed ISPI) in their chapters, analyzing how this organization's name has evolved from a focus on instruction to one on performance improvement. They fail to mention that the growth in membership of this organization over the years, if taken as an indicator of the presence or absence of a new paradigm (applying Kuhn's criterion of attraction of a significant group of professionals away from other paradigmatic viewpoints) is in itself sufficient to place performance technology and the performance engineering movement within the area of interest of this book. Membership of the NSPI, which was counted in the hundreds through the 1960s and 1970s (when it was the National Society for Programmed Instruction) has in the last decade grown exponentially to include thousands of new members as it changed its name to reflect the shift from "Programmed Instruction" to "Performance Improvement." The name change from "National" (as in NSPI) to "International" (as in ISPI) also indicates that the shift in focus has led to the attraction of growing numbers of researchers and practitioners.

The main concepts, principles, and procedures of performance technology, or performance engineering, were laid out by Gilbert in his ground-breaking book entitled *Human Competence: Engineering Worthy Performance.* Originally published in 1978, the book was allowed by the publishers to go out of print at one time, but now, in the 1990s, it has been republished due to the growing interest of the training and development profession in the ideas it presents. One of the key ideas presented is the clear distinction between behavior and performance, that is, between what it takes to do something and what the results are of that doing. Performance is seen as the accomplishments that result from the behaviors in which people engage. A focus on performance as opposed to behavior is the first underlying principle of a revolutionary change in perspective on both the role and methodologies of instruction within the business context.

The second underlying concept which Gilbert introduced into the conceptual structure of the training and development professional was the "PIP," or "Potential for Improving Performance." This essentially is a novel approach to the analysis and quantification of the return on investment in the development of human resources of the organization. The revolutionary change of perspective is associated with another key concept, that of the "exemplary" or "master" performer. Gilbert suggests that instead of comparing actual performance achieved with a typical performance (or norm referencing), one would do better to compare the performance actually achieved with world class or best known performance, thus establishing the size of theoretically achievable improvement. This avoids the development of the mental set of being "satisfied with the average" as well as serving as the basis for calculation of the "PIP" and other performance improvement indicators.

The third important shift in thinking about instruction and its role was contributed by Gilbert in his emphasis on the underlying causes of performance problems, first exemplified in his treatise entitled "Praxeonomy" (Gilbert, 1967), and which is the basis for what is now commonly referred to as performance problem analysis or, more broadly, front-end analysis. This innovation, introduced by Gilbert and then popularized by a number of authors and training consultants (e.g., Harless, 1971; Mager & Pipe, 1970; Romiszowski, 1981; Rossett, 1987; Rummler, 1976), is perhaps the best known "trademark," or identifying characteristic, of the performance technology movement as it exists today. It involves the realization that training and instruction are but two of the many interventions that may be considered in order to "turn around" and improve inadequate human performance. Other major categories of intervention include the management of the incentives, the consequences, and the managerial systems that surround the performer, and also improvement of the tools used or the environmental conditions that influence the performer's chances of achieving and maintaining the desired performance criteria.

These three conceptual shifts underly the three principal phases of analysis that, together, are referred to as the performance engineering approach. These three phases are: first, determining the desired performance results or accomplishments; second, measuring and tracking the opportunities for improvement in these results or accomplishments; and, third, analyzing in a systematic and systemic manner the underlying causes of any performance deficiency and then selecting combinations of techniques for performance improvement that match the causes. This approach enables the desired accomplishments to be achieved with greater probability, and therefore positively impacts the performance indicators defined by the PIP.

A further contribution of Gilbert's philosophical approach to training and development, also initially launched on the world in his 1978 book, was the concept of vantage points and their use as an analytical tool. Gilbert suggests six systemic levels or "vantage points" within an organization, from which almost any problem or event may be observed. These represent different perspectives from which a manager can analyze what happens within the organization and how the organization operates. The six vantage points are:

1. Philosopical Level—the overall vision and ideals which govern the organization's business and operational principles.
2. Cultural Level—the overall environment within which the organization exists and operates.
3. Policy Level—which defines the missions and purposes of the organization.
4. Strategic Level—at which business plans are formulated and overall future change is designed.
5. Tactical Level—which concerns the specific tasks and duties that have to be accomplished in order to achieve the strategic objectives.
6. Logistics Level—which encompasses the various technical and support systems that must be in place to enable the tasks and duties to be performed.

This multi-level vantage points model has indeed been adopted as an organizing framework for the present book in order to be able to better perceive the systemic structure and interrelatedness that exists among the various paradigms presented by the many authors of the different chapters. However, the model is even more useful as a powerful analytical tool for understanding how an organization operates and works and why certain actions at certain levels of decision-making may be likely to succeed or fail in the achievement of their goals. As Gilbert (1978) states, "at whatever level we ultimately wish to draw conclusions about performance, we must begin by identifying the context at a higher level. And even to identify that high context appropriately we need at least to understand its context" (p. 120). In other words, in order to expect a successful resolution of a problem identified within a particular organizational level, it is important to design the solution taking into consideration all relevant factors operating within the broader environment within which the problem under investigation is embedded. And that requires further understanding of that environment's environment, and so on.

It is appropriate, therefore, to analyze the conceptual environment within which the performance engineering methodology may be applied in today's modern organizations. Change in organizational thinking has come from many sources, Gilbert's performance engineering paradigm being but one of them. The congruence in focus and impact of several such paradigmatic changes can be perceived by analysis of the higher-level contexts within which training and indeed performance technology occur. The analysis of these higher-level contexts and the design, development, implementation, and evaluation of improvements and innovations at these higher levels and contexts may be defined as organizational engineering or, as more commonly referred to in today's literature, Organizational Re-engineering. In the next section, we shall examine this trend and its principal component disciplines.

Organizational Re-engineering and Its Components

The perspective that one adopts when viewing change in an organization, change in a project, or change related to instruction influences how one thinks about strategy, processes and outcomes. Figure 1 suggests organizational re-engineering or organizational redesign as

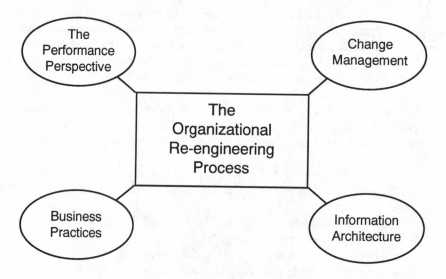

Figure 1.   The organizational re-engineering perspective.

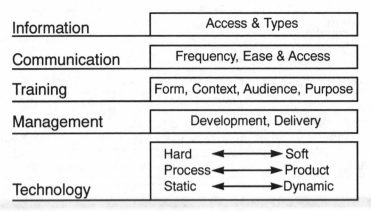

Figure 2. Integration of fields, functions, and technologies.

a perspective to adopt. One subcomponent of this particular organizational re-engineering perspective is performance, both large-scale organizational performance and work-group or individual performance. This is the primary target area for performance engineering or technology.

A second component is change management. Is the organization like a leaf, tossed about by the winds of changing technology, or is technology change and transfer a planned, mission-oriented, and well-managed process? Other people's views of technology transfer also are relevant in this situation. For example, a recent study comparing multiple high-tech company approaches to the design and implementation of a technology transfer process studied the integration of human resource development, human resources, and human performance technology within a technology transfer process (Jassawalla, 1996).

A third component relates to all aspects of information: information architecture, information technology, and networking, perhaps combining communications within information or information as a part of communication. Many view this as the starting point for a large-scale organizational change in which the import of new technology, particularly information and communication technologies, drive that change.

A fourth component of organizational re-engineering relates to the notion of business practices, or organizational practices. How does or should an organization do its work? The answer to this question could include strategic plans for integrating training and development, strategic plans for integrating human performance technology within a larger scale organizational structure, and practices that reflect a concern for return on investment, for example, Kirkpatrick's (1976) "Level 3 and Level 4 evaluation" notion of training as an investment.

Figure 2 portrays this integration of fields, functions and technologies in a somewhat different way. Here the primary thrusts related to information, communication, training, management, and technology (both as a process and as a product) are viewed as forces influencing organizational performance. The types of available information and access to information have direct impact on how an organization functions in both process and product terms. The notions of access (ready, quick, just in time) and types of information (customizable, generic, job-specific) are factors of great relevance here. The concept of communication is difficult in many ways to separate from information in that information, when well-designed and well-formatted, can lead to appropriate kinds of communication between work groups and teams. Thus the opportunities for communication, in terms of frequency, ease, and access for all concerned, are important factors to consider as part of the organizational re-engineering process.

Teaching	Process Focus
Learning	Outcome Focus
Training–Education	Purpose & Function Differences
Delivery	Via Technology
Methods	Interactive • Distance • Instructor Based
Strategies	Video • Computers • Interactive Video • Print
Tactics	Feedback • Individualized • Independent

Figure 3.   The meaning of instruction in an HPT context.

Development and training, whether it involves formal training, group or individual training, "just-in-time," "embedded," or "integrated" (all relatively new concepts related to training) fit well in the overall concept of an integrated performance support system that should be present within any organization. Of course, the management of all this (the organization itself and the change process it is experiencing) includes information, communication, staff development and training, management development, and the like. Thus, management may be viewed as the "glue" or integrating force that directs and controls the interaction of the other forces influencing the change process.

Finally, technology in some contexts is viewed merely as the delivery mechanism for change: the systems, software, and equipment to implement an innovation. In other contexts, technology may be perceived as the causal factor that is driving the requirement for change. It is seen as both hardware and software. It is understood in both process and product terms. Consequently, the impact of technology on an organization varies widely from something that is quite dynamic, open, and flexible to something that is not at all flexible, quite rigid and restrictive. Of course, the goal is that technology will support the process of organizational re-engineering and be a prime driver for the integration of the other four forces of information, communication, instruction and overall change process management..

Figure 3 addresses the next more detailed level of concern related to the human performance technology (HPT) component of the re-engineering process and the role of instruction within that component. The figure suggests a variety of ways of looking at instruction and thinking about instruction. Within today's HPT contexts, all of these have relevance. Figure 3 suggests how these issues should be addressed once one figures out whether the overall intended organizational change requires interventions designed to change human performance through instruction. Given these seven (not so randomly selected) issues, one should examine how their treatment is different when viewed within a human performance technology context than when viewing the same issues in any other approach to planned change. The key difference is that many of these teaching, learning, training, and delivery issues now are viewed as parts of a larger scale organizational intervention and are selected and employed when the front-end analysis data suggest that it makes sense to train or teach, rather than as an initial almost reflex-like selection of training as the solution to any organizational problem.

The ultimate purpose of the exercise from the organization's standpoint is not performance and is not technology but productivity. In this context the concept of productivity includes quality, efficiency, cost, and some kind of balance between them: a kind of three-legged stool. The colloquially expressed notion of "good, fast, and cheap" sometimes used to emphasize these three criteria sounds simplistic but in some ways makes excellent sense. The concept of "good" includes quality, "fast" includes notions of efficiency, just-in-time, and just-in-case, and the "cheap" notion really means affordability or working within realistic budgets. Thus, how to improve productivity translates into how to improve the quality and efficiency of work and how to manage resource requirements for that work. The tools used to achieve this include: change management strategy, improved or expanded technology transfer plans, human performance technology interventions (that may include human resource development, training or staff development) changes in information architecture and in business practices.

Most ISD models or approaches employ the general notions of analysis, design, development (perhaps with production separated from development), and evaluation as major components. In the broader HPT context the same overall scheme can guide the ISD process. However, the new models have stronger "front-end analysis," "needs assessment," or "curriculum analysis" components. No longer do we jump immediately into instructional design and development with little attention paid to the initial, broader-context, analysis phases. In almost any human performance technology or organizational performance technology context, the "front-end analysis" phase is a pre-eminent component such that only when that's finished or well along, does the consideration of training or instruction as an intervention or ISD to define the details of that intervention come into play.

The HPT-Based Paradigm for Instructional Development

Changing Views of Analysis and Its Role in ISD

Within a human performance technology (HPT) context, a "macro" or "total systems" orientation often drives how one then conducts analysis. Figure 4 suggests at least four different ways to think about analysis in this way. The approach called discrepancy or gap analysis concentrates on the performer's job context and suggests some kind of needs assessment. The identified needs may include many other component factors in addition to instruction, and occasionally may not incude instruction at all. A second approach is that of marketing, in which the goal is not to analyze the performance problem but to identify sales, productivity, and other kinds of problems and opportunities. Marketing is both the point of view and the justification for a planned-change intervention. Yet another analytical approach is based on the decision-informing and decision-making paradigm in which problem-identification, problem-clarification, and problem-solving is the purpose of the exercise. A fourth approach identifies the training requirements aspect of large scale strategic planning exercises or at least the systematic definition of tactical planning requirements. The planning and eval-

Activity	Rationale
Discrepancy Analysis	Needs Assessment
Marketing	Justification
Decision Informing and Making	Problem Solving
Planning and Evaluation	Consistency of Intent and Action

Figure 4. Analysis perspectives.

Context Activity	Rationale
Strategic Planning	Decision Informing & Making
Restructuring	Applied Planning
Planned Change	Advocacy
Human Resource Development	Cost vs. Investment
Evaluation	Judgment
Problem Analysis	Discrepancy or Deficiency Analysis
Organizational Audit	Documentation

Figure 5.   Contexts for front-end analysis.

uation paradigm underlying such approaches requires a kind of consistency of purpose and intent, or "ends and means" linkage.

Figure 5 suggests a variety of contexts within which the front-end analysis process may occur. This incudes at the macro level strategic planning, organizational restructuring, and a variety of planned change models that are applied in a variety of settings. This also includes the more traditional contexts of: human resource development (and perhaps human resource management), evaluation, assessment and performance appraisal, the problem analysis approach addressed earlier, and the notion of an organizational audit or comprehensive assessment of an organization. The justification or rationale for these, as shown in Figure 5, suggests that frequently there are different explanations and different reasons for engaging in these kinds of front-end analysis and planning ventures.

The concept of gap or deficiency analysis flows through many of these front-end analysis schemes. Whether one follows the general models of Harless (1971), Gilbert (1967), Mager & Pipe (1970), or the more specific suggestions of Romiszowski (1981), Rossett (1987), Kaufman, Rojas, and Mayer (1993), the notion of a "need," that is, the identification of some kind of gap or deficiency, is seen as the underlying goal of the initial analysis phase of almost any HPT-based ISD approach. Figure 6 suggests that needs can be defined in a variety of ways. The first and foremost one is as a discrepancy, deficiency or gap between a desired and an actual state of the system under analysis. This makes the most sense most of the time. At times, however, opportunities, possible solutions, or various innovations made possible by new technologies suggest or imply a future need which may well trigger performance technology interventions. Yet another source of need is existing requirements and mandates, whether they be state or federal (i.e., external) or managerial (i.e., internal). The notion of need as a want or a desire (more like a solution rather than a gap) arises from a client-oriented approach to needs analysis. The bottom line is that the concept of need and the process of gap analysis are components in most systemic approaches to problem solving and therefore appear within most HPT models as well as in recent ISD models.

Why one would engage in any kind of front-end analysis or needs analysis may vary depending on the environment. Figure 7 suggests there are several possible reasons for conducting these kinds of analyses, including problem solving (in general), strategic and tactical

- As Discrepancies, Deficiencies, and Gaps

- As Opportunities and Solutions

- As Requirements and Mandates

- As Wants and Desires

- As a Component in Problem Solving

Figure 6. Needs in context.

planning, description and documentation, evaluation, and resource allocation, where the primary focus is on planning and budgeting. However, when the solution of choice, or the implementation of a particular innovation is the focus, the process becomes a marketing analysis to support, advocate, or justify the planned change. Finally, the last item is that of planned change, which analyzes how to build involvement and develop a sense of ownership and cooperation in all concerned with the innovation.

Figure 8 reflects the fundamental model of front-end analysis in which the notion of human performance deficiencies or discrepancies is the focus. Embedded within this model is a three-part schema of skill and knowledge/deficiency, lack of incentives or motivation, and environmental barriers. This figure is based on the suggestions of Gilbert (1967, 1978) and Harless (1971). An expansion of this model is presented by Allison Rossett (1987) in her *Training Needs Assessment* text, in which she breaks out the incentive and motivation components into separate elements, thereby suggesting a more refined analysis and a more refined identification of potential solutions and combinations of solutions to address a given performance deficiency.

Romiszowski's (1981) concentric circles model presented in his *Designing Instructional Systems* text further breaks out the kinds of primary and secondary questions to ask when analyzing a performance deficiency and explicitly suggests a broader range of potential solutions to the problems being analyzed. The concentric-circles presentation of this model is de-

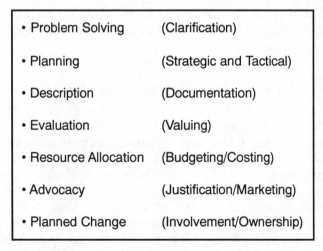

• Problem Solving	(Clarification)
• Planning	(Strategic and Tactical)
• Description	(Documentation)
• Evaluation	(Valuing)
• Resource Allocation	(Budgeting/Costing)
• Advocacy	(Justification/Marketing)
• Planned Change	(Involvement/Ownership)

Figure 7. Needs analysis purposes.

- ■ Skill Knowledge Deficiencies
  - Don't Know How To   (Training)
  - Don't Know What Is Expected   (Standards)
  - Don't Know Present Performance   (Feedback)

- ■ Motivation/Incentive Barriers
  - Not Rewarded for Appropriate Behavior
  - Punished for Appropriate Behavior
  - Rewarded for Inappropriate Behavior

- ■ Environmental Barriers
  - Insufficient Resources
  - Deficient Equipment
  - Conflicting Demands/Standards

Figure 8.   Causes of deficient performance.

signed to represent the integration and "one-ness" of a complex system of ideas, communicating the non-linear and "systemic" aspects of the front-end analysis process. Another "systemic" aspect is the notion of the various organizational levels at which one performs front-end analysis, as ilustrated by Kaufman, Rojas, and Mayer (1993) in their "mega/macro/micro" model of needs assessment. Without consideration for community, societal, and/or larger organizational concerns, small-scale interventions based on localized problem or gap analysis, though well intended, may lead one down a garden path which does not lead to a full solution of the problem.

Of course, viewing front-end analysis as needs assessment alone also severely limits the notion of front-end analysis. Jonassen & Hannum (1991), in their book chapter on analysis of task analysis procedures, describe a large variety of front-end analysis methods and tools in addition to needs assessment, including content analysis, conceptual analysis, job and task analysis, and the like. This begins to present the wide array of potential tactics, tools, and methods that can be employed in the process of front-end analysis, all of them geared towards first identifying "the right thing to do" before proceeding to the question of "doing it right."

Interventions with HPT Implications

Although the "flavor of the month" or "flavor of the year" training and development intervention often is embedded within an HPT argument, there are also others that are presented almost as if they are independent of human performance technology and indeed independent of any kind of instructional system design/development paradigm. For example, the currently popular notion of the "Learning Organization" (Senge, 1990) has implications for organizational redesign and for systems planning and also has considerable implication for training, instruction, career pathing, and job performance aids. Most of the quality movements, whether it be Total Quality, Quality Improvement, Process Improvement, the ISO 9000 strategies, or the like, also have considerable implications for information, communication, and instructional intervention. Svenson and Rinderer's (1992) *Training and Development*

Strategic Plan Workbook suggests a comprehensive approach to strategic planning within a large scale company or corporation which has broad implications for training and development. Their approach includes organizing, staffing, managing, positioning, and planning functions. Although not strong in the ISD components, this workbook has major implications for the front-end analysis and planning for training and development that then leads to planning for ISD. All these approaches to organizational re-engineering share many concerns and some strategies with the HPT-based approaches. Yet none of them were born within the HPT movement and few of their "early adopter" practitioners have seen themselves as members of this fraternity. Nevertheless, as these various separate planned-change movements become accepted and institutionalized, one may see them as complementary components of an integrated approach to organizational re-engineering.

Examples of the integration of strategic planning, or at least strategic thinking, organizational change (development), and training are becoming more frequent in the literature. The Spuches and Evensky (1991) study reported recently in the *Journal of Staff, Program, and Organizational Development* suggests just such an integrated venture. It includes a blending of strategic planning, ISD and organizational development in a higher education context. Such multi-faceted and integrated model ventures now drive many contract R&D firms and in-house organizational change agencies for whom strategic planning, training, information technology and organizational communication are all integrated or partially integrated to address a comprehensive problem. Several of the chapters presented in this book (for example, Davies, Kessels & Plomp, Lent *et al.*) illustrate or advocate this trend. There is evidence of ever-greater integration of the underlying paradigms of the various disciplines that study and attempt to influence the productivity of organizations.

Problem Solving as a Foundation for Action

One way to think about instructional systems development and human performance technology approaches to planning is to address the range of models that can be and have been employed in this context. Figure 9 suggests that there are at least six ways to think about such an integrated instructional systems and human performance technology. They include problem solving, strategic planning, goals and objectives or requirements models,

---

- Problem Solving Models

- Strategic Planning Models

- Goals and Objectives Models

- Theory-Based Models

- Philosophical Approaches

- Vocational-Technical Perspectives

Figure 9. Where to start ISD/HPT planning?

learning theory based models (addressed elsewhere in this book), as well as philosophical approaches (also addressed in other chapters) and the basic "push vs. pull" model for curriculum design in which the vocational/technical requirements of the field drive goals, which drive objectives, which drive strategies, which drive assessment, which drive practice, and the like.

A variety of creative problem-solving strategies are of relevance here. They include various problem-solving strategies that are almost independent of the ISD approach: using analogies and metaphors as ways of thinking; changing representation or presentation or point of view and perspective; spending considerable time defining and clarifying the questions prior to design and development; in essence, being quite clear on the ends before addressing the means. Techniques such as constraint analysis and risk analysis also apply in this kind of environment, where one is looking for either stable or not so stable structures that would guide both analysis and development. Kaufman's notions of inductive and deductive planning also merit consideration. Sometimes, when in the development stage, one could work from the requirements or the competencies backwards to strategies and techniques and goals and objectives, ultimately inferring gaps.

A fundamental and basic approach to addressing this means-and-ends planning scheme for both ISD and human performance technology development is presented in Figure 10a, b, c, and d. This simple "Why, What, How, and How Well" diagram portrays basic elements inherent in human performance technology as well as on ISD planning. The initial notion of "why" can be driven by either organizational or personal philosophy, perspectives of the organization, the agency or individuals within the agency, as well as the kind of ethical issues related to political, social, and/or economic concerns (see Figure 10a). Related to this, of course, is the notion of values, whether they are societal, organizational, group, or individual. The explanation or rationale may be driven by one of these previous notions or may be driven by the important concepts of gap, performance deficiency, productivity, and the like. In theory, all of these lead to priorities, either priorities in terms of sequence or criticality, which then lead to further conversations about purpose.

The second component of this scheme (Figure 10b), addresses "what to do" when engaging in the design and development component. The "front end analysis" list addresses many of the issues identified in previous sections in this chapter. But there are some additional elements. The notion of constraint analysis hasn't been addressed in depth before, but merits inclusion here. The notions of standards, benchmarks, or benchmarking and all the requirements issues, including competencies and organizational or professional standards, fit in here as well. The notion of content analysis as well as job and task analysis also fits within our broadly-based concept of front-end analysis. Finally, we include the futures invention issue, since the goal of the front-end analysis may be to in some way engage in planned change or technology transfer for building a better future for the organization, the society, or for specific work groups.

In the "how to do it" phase of our model, the four items listed in Figure 10c represent at least some of the levels of action and some of the procedures to be employed at these levels, once one figures out why some intervention is necessary and what form of intervention that should be. This multi-level notion of course, curriculum, lesson and materials development also applies within the instructional analysis phase of our ISD scheme.

Finally, Figure 10d presents the evaluation, or "how well was it done" phase. This component of our basic model suggests evaluation and validation both of a formative and a summative nature, as well as both process and product evaluation. Careful consideration should be given to all kinds of criteria here, to ensure that the structure, processes and outcomes reflect the initial analysis of the problem, its causes and its organizational or human "costs". One could add to this list of criteria some considerations of "Level 3" and "Level 4" evaluation (Kirkpatrick, 1976) or some aspects of return on investment. Investment in training often

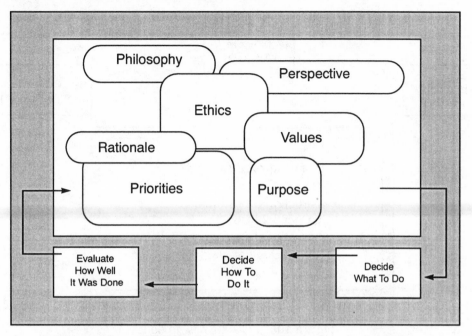

Figure 10a. ISD/HPT development: Determine why to do it.

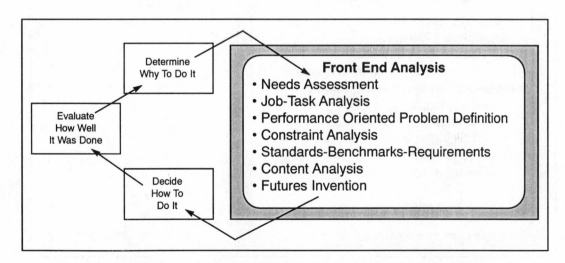

Figure 10b. ISD/HPT development: Determine what to do.

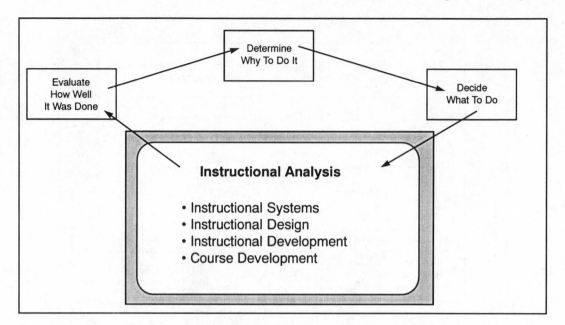

Figure 10c.   Decide how to do it.

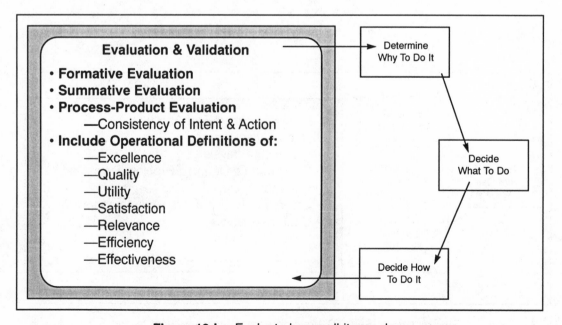

Figure 10d.   Evaluate how well it was done.

cannot be easily assessed, but in cases where it can be, and especially when there are organizational-level reasons for assessing the return on investment, such further criteria should be operationally defined so as to make it possible to track and measure them over time.

An interesting example of an instructional systems design/development model is that created by Molenda, Pershing, and Reigeluth (1996) at Indiana University. Their model follows the typical analysis, design, development, implementation, and evaluation stages, but adds a significant component for the front end. In this case, front-end analysis serves not only instructional systems design, but also human performance technology intervention design. Their model, called a Business Impact ISD Model, considers both non-training and training or instructional interventions. A general overview of this model, or at least its underlying philosophy, is presented by Ivor Davies (also from Indiana University) in his chapter of the present book. This model for systems analysis and human performance technology planning, though not new in theoretical terms, is perhaps one of the first to present practical procedures for implementing a fully integrated ISD and HPT model. Although it is the case that a number of performance technology contract R&D firms have been employing these paradigms in an integrated manner for some time, little has been presented in the literature reflecting why they do what they do and how they do what they do.

Focus on the Bottom Line:
A Change-Based Rationale for Instructional Development

Figure 11 suggests that there are many influences on workers, on work groups, and on organizations. Although the standard approach to interpreting this diagram would be to suggest that ISD should address training and job aids and perhaps management and supervision, leaving the others for some other kinds of intervention, the new integrated ISD/HPT approaches suggest otherwise. If one looks at methods, whether they are work methods, communication methods, information transfer methods, or the like, then potential human performance technology interventions, which may perhaps include training and instructional interventions, usually also come into play. Once one completes a policy analysis, as an example, what does one do to promote, practice, implement and evaluate new policy? This implies training, staff development, and management development.

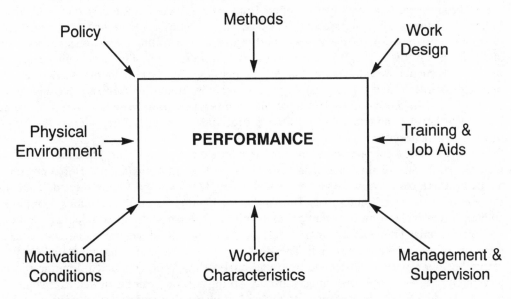

Figure 11.   Influences on worker performance.

• Process vs. Product

• Practical vs. Conceptual

• Depreciation vs. Obsolescence

• Investment vs. Operation

• Sizzle vs. Steak

Figure 12.   Implications of change for ISD/HPT decisions.

It is also likely that training, instruction, perhaps job aids and job performance tools could also be considered as components of work design and improving and maintaining an appropriate physical environment. John Keller's (1983) ARCS model speaks eloquently to the motivational conditions, at least as far as instruction and training is concerned. Improving the quality of the workers who are selected and promoted can be at least partially impacted by training and instruction. Although not exhaustive, this view of comprehensive analysis with implicatons for instructional interventions hopefully serves to illustrate the range of influences.

Figure 12 suggests that there are a number of components embedded within the concept of planned change that have implications for instructional systems developers. Whether one focuses on improving the process, such as total quality, ISO 9000 and the like, or on the product with emphasis on competence, or "Level 3" and "Level 4" evaluation, the ISD models within HPT in some way ought to reflect these kinds of concerns. Larger scale strategic and conceptual planning as well as practical and tactical planning make sense here as well. The notion of instruction or training or job aids as an investment that can be depreciated much like other kinds of capital investments rather than considered a cost or overhead has implications for how training proposals are presented and how to conduct the analysis that precedes the proposal. The notion of a sound front-end, well-designed instruction, and nicely integrated delivery using multimedia should be viewed much like one views any other kind of capital investment, particularly where both initial and operating costs are significant. The last point in this figure suggests moving away from a focus on design, development and delivery of instruction overall (i.e., the "sizzle") to focusing more heavily on the "steak" (i.e., the benefits, the results and the impact). Front-end analysis, human performance technology interventions, and impact-driven ISD must all be integrated in a systemic process of events leading to "Level 3" and "Level 4" evaluation procedures that effectively address the notion of return on investment.

More practical considerations about all this are portrayed in Figure 13a under the headings "Scope or Size of the Enterprise" and "Approach to Implementation." How one thinks about instructional systems development within an HTP context in some ways depends on the size or scope of the enterprise. Thinking of one course as an intervention, or multiple courses or curricula as an intervention, and ultimately, large scale interdisciplinary training and instructional interventions across multiple departments all suggest a "micro-to-macro" focus on improving the organization. This does not necessarily imply that more and larger is better, but often once a substantive front-end analysis has been conducted, limiting the intervention to a few people or a small subset of an organization can be viewed as myopic. Of course, the detailed implementation of any kind of instruction or training venture may vary quite widely, depending on a number of theoretical and practical considerations. Subsequent

> • **Scope or Size of the Enterprise**
>   —One Course
>   —Multiple Courses
>   —Interdisciplinary Across Multiple Departments
> • **Approach to Implementation**
>   —Individualized
>   —Modularized
>   —Mediated
>   —Self Instructional
>   —Mastery Based
>   —Non-Time Based
>   —Criterion Referenced

Figure 13a. Practical considerations in ISD/HPT planning—Part I.

chapters in this book address many approaches to the design, development, and delivery of instruction, illustrating the wide variety of possible approaches. The list presented in Figure 13b identifies just some of the elements that ought to be considered whenever the practical considerations of ISD come into play after the large scale front-end analysis has been conducted. Although not exhaustive, these approaches to implementation, along with integration provided by multimedia delivery systems, all fit within the proposed ISD/HPT planning schema.

The newly evolving software to support group development suggests many of the components listed under the "Development Process" heading in Figure 13b. A team focused on a specific project, but not necessarily all working in the same context or using the same approach to development may integrate and cross over many disciplines, may be content based or process based, or some combination of content and process. A non-linear, non-sequential kind of approach to design and development also is possible, through the use of "rapid prototyping" models (see the chapter by Dorsey, Goodrum, & Schwen in this book), facilitated by information and communication technology software and tools (see the chapter by Zhang, Gibbons, & Merrill in this book).

> • **Development Process**
>   —Team Focused
>   —Multi-disciplinary
>   —Content Based
>   —Process Based
>   —Systems Approach
>   —Incremental Decision Making
> • **Planning and Evaluation**
>   —Internal and External Support
>   —Purposes
>   —Audiences
>   —Issues
>   —Methods
>   —Reporting

Figure 13b. Practical considerations in ISD/HPT planning—Part II.

While still not supported wholeheartedly by many clients, evaluation, testing, measurement, and assessment all play a role in any substantive ISD planning venture (see the chapter in this book by Reeves). The question of how the market for ISD views the notion of evaluation as related to planning could merit extensive conversation. It is often the case that clients suggest that if planning is well done, evaluation is unnecessary. This suggests that planning, if well-conceived, well-executed, and well-validated, may in fact make evaluation easier or less costly. However, theoretical considerations, such as the laws of cybernetics and general systems theory, teach us that when dealing with complex and probabilistic systems (which is the case of any human activity system such as a training program), it is almost impossible to predict all aspects of system operation with accuracy. Therefore, superior quality planning may indeed reduce the cost and complexity of the evaluation process, but it never totally eliminates the requirement to perform one or several cycles of formative evaluation. The currently popular push for more systematic "Level 3" and "Level 4" evaluation within organizations sits well with the human performance technology model, in which the focus is less on training satisfaction and immediate post-training performance and more on the impact on the bottom line. All these theoretical and practical considerations combine to make the evaluation-to-planning link all that much more important. This is where the human performance technology and ISD models support one another in very powerful ways.

The Bottom Line: Converging Paradigms

This chapter started by outlining how the instructional design/development paradigms held by a large proportion of the business training and development community have been subsumed into a broader performance engineering paradigm, which itself is now part of an even broader organizational re-engineering paradigm. It also indicated that this organizational re-engineering paradigm really has a number of sources, each of which could be considered as a paradigm for human resource management or even for the general management of organizations. Today, in the fast changing society that we are entering, the different areas of study and practice referred to as total quality management, organizational development, organization and methods, human resource management, and many others are converging to work as integrated components in a broader approach to the systemic planning of change in organization.

At this broader level of the organization, a multi-paradigmatic approach seems to be developing, similar to the one that is suggested by the editors of this book in the introductory chapter when discussing the field of instructional systems design and development. Furthermore, we have argued in the later sections of the present chapter that instructional systems development can best be seen as a component within a broader organizational re-engineering or organizational development approach. In reflection over this chapter and its place and role within the book as a whole, we may state that not only is the field of instructional systems design and development (ISD) multi-paradigmatic but that ISD fits into a multi-paradigmatic context of organizational design and development. In effect, the multiple vantage points model which Gilbert proposed for organizational analysis and problem solving may well be a model which has value beyond the structuring of the present book to the structuring of one's views regarding how alternative paradigms in our field may not necessarily be alternatives at all, but may best be viewed as contributing components which often are relevant at different levels of systemic analysis of the problems we try to solve.

A second final observation is to question why, given that the bulk of fundamental theory building and research which led to the performance technology or performance engineering movement was completed through the 1960s and 1970s, is it only in the 1980s and 1990s that we see a significant adherence to this new paradigm. Why has it taken 20 or more years for the paradigm shift to occur? One possible answer is that paradigm shifts often do occur over a considerable period of time and that 20 years is fairly typical. It reflects the typical period of time between a given generation of students completing their graduate and post-graduate studies in a field, and reaching the level of organizational authority to be able to influence the adoption of what they learned as a model for action. The human resource department directors and human resource development managers of today are those who had the opportunity to study the principles of the performance technology movement in the 1960s and 1970s, but only now have the power to implement them in a systematic and organized manner.

However, an alternative line of argument is that the basic research and theory building which led to the performance technology movement originated a little before its time in a period when, at the higher levels of organization, the pressures for productivity, competitiveness, and customer orientation were not felt as strongly as they are today. We may compare the time it took for the performance technology paradigm to take root with the much shorter time that the total quality movement, the organizational re-engineering movements, and other movements such as "right-sizing," etc., have taken to become almost household words within the business sphere. This can be ascribed to a very much more rapidly changing environmental context within which modern businesses operate, the globalization of markets, and strong international competition, and thus to the general need to improve productivity as an essential requirement for organizational survival.

Given this change in its macro environment, the organization (as does any system) rapidly moves towards internal change in order to adapt itself to its new environmental conditions. In so doing, the macro organizational policy and strategic planning levels (in Gilbert's model) create the environmental conditions for the subsystem of human resource development to be required to rapidly adapt itself to its new environmental conditions. Thus, in turn, by the laws of general systems theory, the ISD fraternity now finds itself within a working environment in which human performance technology principles are the ruling environmental pressures for change.

If there is one major "bottom line" lesson to be drawn from the analysis of the growth of the human performance technology paradigm, its absorption of ISD as a sub-component, and its own absorption into broader total quality and organizational re-engineering paradigms, it is that the paradigms of today are the results of the environmental requirements, pressures, and conditions of today. This being an observation based on general systems theory, it may be considered equally relevant for the analysis of what is happening, or probably will happen, in formal education. Maybe what has been happening over the last decade or so at a very rapid rate within the business training context could be considered a model for what is likely to happen, perhaps a little more slowly and a little later, within the general educational field.

References

Dean, P. J. (Ed.). (1994). *Performance engineering at work*. Batavia, IL: International Board of Standards for Training, Performance, and Instruction.

Gilbert, T. F. (1967). Praxeonomy: A systematic approach to identifying training needs. *Management of Personnel Quarterly, 6*(3).

Gilbert T. F. (1978). *Human competence: Engineering worthy performance*. New York: McGraw-Hill.

Harless, J. (1971, 1975). *An ounce of analysis (is worth a pound of programming)*. Washington, DC: Harless Performance Guild, Inc.

Jassawalla, A. (1996). Unpublished doctoral dissertation, Syracuse University School of Education.

Jonassen, D. H., & Hannum, W. H. (1991). Analysis of task analysis procedures. In G. J. Anglin (Ed.), *Instructional technology: Past, present, and future*. Englewood, CO: Libraries Unlimited.

Kaufman, R., Rojas, A. M., & Mayer, H. (1993). *Needs assessment: A user's guide.* Englewood Cliffs, NJ: Educational Technology Publications.

Keller, J. M. (1983). Motivational design of instruction. In C. M. Reigeluth (Ed.), *Instructional design theories and models: An overview of their current status.* Hillsdale, NJ: Lawrence Erlbaum Associates.

Kirkpatrick, D. L. (Ed.). (1976). *Evaluating training programs.* New York: McGraw-Hill.

Mager, R. F., & Pipe, P. (1970). *Analyzing performance problems.* Belmont, CA: Fearon Publishers.

Molenda, M., Pershing, J., & Reigeluth, C. (1996). Designing instructional systems. In *Training and development handbook* (4th ed.). Alexandria, VA: American Society for Training and Development.

Romiszowski, A. J. (1981). *Designing instructional systems.* London: Kogan Page.

Rossett, A. (1987). *Training needs assessment.* Englewood Cliffs, NJ: Educational Technology Publications.

Rummler, G. A. (1976). The performance audit. In R. L. Craig (Ed.), *Training and development handbook* (2nd ed.). Alexandria, VA: American Society for Training and Development.

Rummler, G. A., & Brache, A. P. (1990). *Improving performance: How to manage the white space on the organization chart.* San Francisco: Jossey-Bass.

Senge, P. M. (1990). *The fifth discipline: The art and practice of the learning organization.* New York: Doubleday.

Spuches, C. M., & Evensky, J. (1991, Winter). Instructional improvement revisited: Lessons in strategic design. *The Journal of Staff, Program, & Organization Development, 9*(4).

Svenson, R. A., & Rinderer, M. J. (1992). *The training and development strategic plan workbook.* Englewood Cliffs, NJ: Prentice-Hall.

PART 3

The Theory/Policy
Vantage Point:
Theoretical Underpinnings of
Instructional Development

12

The Cybernetic View of Educational Systems

William E. Hug
University of Georgia, Athens

Introduction

Meta-theories such as cybernetics and general system theory attempt to look for patterns and phenomena in the natural world. They provide a view from outside the educational system and look for similarities and differences that affect all systems. Meta-theories can help avoid the problem of looking at and talking to self. How educational institutions view themselves can be quite different from the way communities see an institution. This tends to be true on all levels. Librarians believe that school libraries are essential to a quality education. Yet, some teachers never use the school library and fail to see the librarian or the school library as a critical part of the instructional program. Do school librarians have an exaggerated view of their value? Are teachers who fail to make use of the library inferior? Arguments generated by questions such as these tend to lead nowhere. On the other hand, cybernetic theory would point out that an instructional system, like other man-made systems, acquire, evaluate, modify, translate, use, generate, transmit, and export information to achieve their purposes. This characteristic of systems and institutions can provide insight into the roles of school librarians, instructional program developers, teachers, administrators, and other educational professionals and how they might collaborate to improve the educational system.

The use of meta-theories can also help professional educators escape from forceful factors that repeatedly exercise their influence in shaping an educational institution and its instructional programs. Educational systems are distorted by economic, ethnic, religious, and political pressures. They are also plagued by simplistic answers to complex problems—experience based, core, broad fields, competency based, and other educational fashions, past and present. Thinking about educational systems using principles from meta-theories elevates thinking and thus helps avoid jumping on bandwagons, focuses on purposes, and looks critically at the information, structures, and relationships needed to produce results.

Traditional View
of Curriculum and Instruction

"That's not what I said at all!" exclaimed the teacher. "That is too what you said," replied the student. What was the content of the message? Was it what the teacher thought she said, or was it what the student thought he heard? This little dialogue represents the dilemma in trying to define instruction. Nonetheless, most teachers think of instruction as the implementation of a planned lesson which is part of the curriculum. The more theoretically minded take a more comprehensive view of curriculum and instruction.

TRADITIONAL VIEW OF CURRICULUM

What is said and what is understood are too frequently different. In a theoretical sense, what students learn from an instructional sequence is different for every child. How could it be otherwise? Each child has different experiences, different capacities, and may or may not be attending to the lesson. Does the real curriculum include everything that teaches a child at school—the words on the bathroom walls and the rumbles in the halls? How does the instructional program contribute to the attitude of the principal, the ethos of the school, the way teachers and students use educational resources, abuse facilities, and contribute to class discussions?

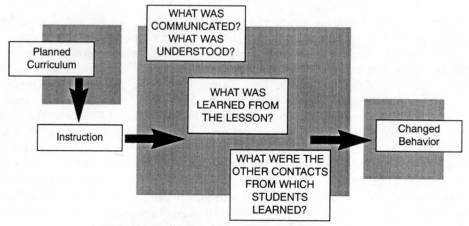

CURRICULUM AS ALL SCHOOL EXPERIENCE

To develop this notion further, if information exchange is viewed as the basic element of any instructional program and the process of exchanging information described as an interface, shown by crossing lines of communication, then the instructional program could be defined as a mesh of interfacings.

The pattern and number of contacts illustrated by the mesh would differ for each child. Each day produces an imprint, "fingerprint," which distinguishes individuals. Consequently, to know what the instructional program is for each child, a map of the interfacings, lines of communication, or contacts would have to be made and analyzed. Awesome, but is anything else accurate?

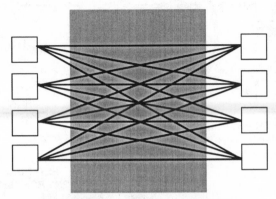

**THE INSTRUCTIONAL PROGRAM
AS A MESH OF INTERFACINGS**

The implications of this view of the instructional program as a mesh of interfacings among components (boxes in the above diagram) are more complicated. The diagram of the traditional view of instruction supports the common, less complicated, and probably less accurate view of the curriculum. The diagram above illustrates the concepts of the "real" experiences as students interact with instructional program components.

> The term *interface* is increasingly being employed to describe the relationships between entities in the educational program. Any time a man or machine is exchanging information an interface is established. An interface also applies to tasks: it refers to the actions that are organized to achieve objectives. Interfacing suggests the dynamic aspect of relating tasks; this point of view creates a concern for what is happening in the program. Most task descriptions suggest numerous interfaces which are easily categorized. Consequently, task analyses and competency lists imply a virtual catalog of interfacings. (Hug, 1975, p. 69)

Cybernetic View of an Educational System

The definition of cybernetics has many implications for education. In the simplest terms, the definition of cybernetics includes a study of (1) the information needs of a system, (2) the ways a system utilizes information, (3) the information generated by the system, (4) what information is communicated to its suprasystem, and (5) how information is communicated within the system as well as with its environment. Cybernetics tends to define information as any stimuli that have the capability of producing a man or machine reaction. Consequently, cybernetics may also be defined as a study of actions and reactions.

Note that the boundaries of each system—schools, administration, and external environment—show various degrees of permeability by the shading (see below). The diagram suggests that schools are the most closed. This also means that what is going on within schools is better known, more predictable, and constant over time. Policy formation, on the other hand, is a task that takes place over an extended period of time. When policies will be changed, how they will be changed, and why the changes are necessary may vary and be less predictable.

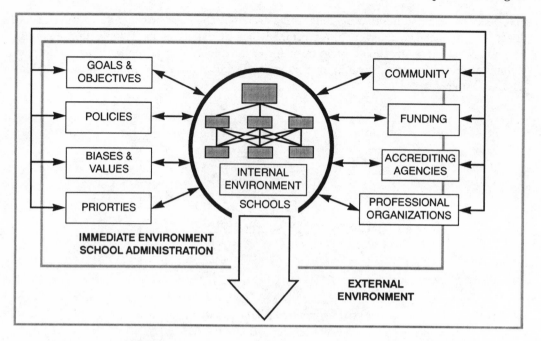

CYBERNETIC VIEW OF AN EDUCATIONAL SYSTEM

Feedback. The feedback loops are essentially closed according to cybernetic theory. The observed state of the system is determined by the characteristics of the feedback—sporadic, delayed, distorted, relevant, etc. Feedback can present many problems. It can be incomplete, not available at the time needed for action, changed to fit the personal biases of individuals, and so forth. Consequently, the quality of feedback determines the effectiveness and efficiency of the educational system. In a sense, feedback is an action that promotes a reaction, as shown below.

	TYPE OF INFORMATION COMMUNICATED TO SCHOOLS	ACTION	REACTION
GOALS & OBJECTIVES	Directive—informs schools what should be taught	Curriculum development	Implement curriculum
POLICIES	Administrative—informs schools of operational procedures	Implement policies	Improved operations
BIASES & VALUES	Hidden, obscure—vague indicators that influence decision making and rewards	Unpredictable reaction to perceived implications	Confusion trust distrust loyalty, etc.
PRIORITIES	Directive—informs schools of change of emphasis	Reallocation of resources	Changed programs

EXAMPLES OF ACTIONS AND REACTIONS
TO ADMINISTRATIVE COMMUNICATIONS

Characteristics of Information

Information is a source of energy that enables a culture to perpetuate itself and to transcend that which is. The availability of information, the degree to which new information is generated, and the way it is used define the creative parameters of a culture. In this sense, education consists of developing a population that can find, generate, evaluate, and utilize information.

Sources of Information. The way information is obtained, identified, and utilized to bring about learning and understanding is called an instructional strategy. Some strategies stress social interaction, such as role playing, case studies, and sensitivity training, while others use more traditional forms of media such as textbooks. The environment provides basic information in developing competencies such as surveying a piece of land, observing and recording ecological changes, and developing the ability to utilize information resources of a given community. Action, experimental, and other research may also be considered instructional strategies.

A carefully selected, artfully articulated, and readily accessible collection of information resources is essential if an instructional strategy is to realize its full potential. What is important is that the informational support be suitable to the mode of inquiry. For example, school library media specialists need a media center, not an archive, for their apprenticeships. Environmental structures are their primary information resource. In another instance, strategies stressing social process would defeat their purposes if students were programmed individually through materials without the opportunity for interpersonal relationships.

Forms of Information. Information comes in a variety of forms. A cold mass of air, the echo from a canyon wall, the fragrance of a flower, the blast of a fog horn, falling leaves, a paragraph in a book, and the magnetic strip on a charge card all provide information. In fact, there does not seem to be any natural way to identify what provides information and what does not without being both artificial and arbitrary. Consequently, information may be in the form of body language: a red face may indicate embarrassment, trembling may mean fear, applause may express approval, and a frown may show disapproval. Aural symbols such as fire and ambulance sirens and visual symbols such as highway signs and mathematical equations provide still other forms of information.

Oral and recorded languages are traditionally the most valuable forms of information and have supported the great accomplishments of the past and will continue to do so in the future. Language unlocks the power of the human mind and enables one to remember, discriminate, analyze, and evaluate. The word *sphere* assists in remembering the shape of balls and planets. The words *verb* and *noun* assist in discriminating among parts of speech. Recognizing a non-sequitor or syllogism assists in the analysis of a philosophical work. Having the vocabulary to express and defend an opinion assists in evaluation. To make sense, however, verbal communications use both a subject and predicate to convey thought.

Another kind of information exists in the way entities are arranged—the relationship of one thing to another. For example, four parallel lines of equal length are recognized as parallel because of their placement. They could have different relationships, forming a square, box, or the letters "TV." In this case, understanding how the lines or components of a system are "communicating" with one another provides the necessary information for conceptualizing the whole.

Value of Information. Still another aspect of information is the usefulness of a particular piece of information. For example, the word *cherries* can be communicated by both print and sound. The first time a learner encounters cherries, information may be provided by pictures, words, sound, and/or the cherries themselves. In subsequent encounters, redundant information may equal no information. Consider a person who asks the advice of another. If the advice received is already known, the person received no information.

The concept of redundant information equaling no useful information has implications for all educational programs, the most important one involving the tying of programs to the needs of the population. Providing things without careful consideration of whether or not they supply needed information is obviously poor practice. Closely associated with this concept is the notion of information as something that reduces anxiety. For example, if a person is not sure how to mix gas and oil for his outboard motor, finding the formula reduces his anxiety. In this example, the formula represents the needed information. If, in a search for a new automobile route from Chicago to St. Louis, one finds the only routes are those traveled before, no useful information has been received (except, perhaps, that there is no other route). A message, then, may or may not contain needed information. Thinking in these terms is important to educators because such reasoning encourages a consideration of the interrelationships among what a message could contain, what a message does contain, and what the user needs. The kind and the quantity of information in a message must be linked to an understanding of the kind and amount of information needed to fill a specific information request. The ability to perceive this comes from a principle of cybernetics: an educational system must take in a great deal of information if it is to have the capacity to select the most appropriate for a specific need. In other words, the choice made by the sender of a message is controlled by the number of possibilities at the sender's disposal. *The critical linkages are between that which can be transmitted and that which is transmitted, between that which is transmitted and that which is needed.*

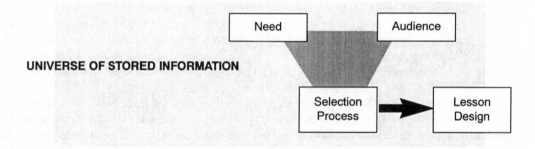

FACTORS INFLUENCING LESSON DESIGN

In a cybernetic sense, the power of any educational program depends upon the system's ability to choose, generate, and use the most appropriate information for the task at hand.

Encoding Forms

Each form of media provides a unique experience and as such stands as a metaphor suggesting a likeness or analogy between objects and ideas. Since media are metaphors, they inevitably stress and suppress what they represent. Hence, each has its particular purposes, strengths, and weaknesses. Translating information from one form or package to another involves adding, summarizing, reducing, clarifying, and sometimes even obscuring the original content. Translations also require an understanding of encoding forms—*language, symbols, pictures*—utilized by a specific media or media-mix. The way information is coded in an encoding form is different from a media format (book, microfilm, filmstrip, computer program, etc.). The format is the package; the way the information is presented is the encoding form (environmental structures, realia, models, still and moving images, graphics and cartoons, oral and written language, and abstract symbol systems).

For the purpose of understanding the kind of information utilized in typical instructional settings, a concept of encoding forms is useful. The English language is an encoding form. Encoding structures are the forms information take, the way information is presented in formats such as films, books, etc. Note the difference between encoding form and the media or format. Media usually use more than one encoding form.

ENCODING FORM	CONSIDERATIONS FOR COMMUNICATIONS	SAMPLE MESSAGE
Environments	Can communicate through all senses; is the most real and concrete; persistent	Convey how it smells and feels to walk through a flowering cherry orchard
Realia	Can communicate through all senses; is real and concrete; persistent	Show different types of minerals
Models	Can communicate through all senses; is real and concrete; persistent	Make visible small objects or reduce large objects to make them easier to study
Still Images	Communicates visually; is real to abstract; persistent	Show different breeds of dogs
Moving Images	Communicates visually; is real to abstract; transient	Illustrate movement of amoebas
Audio Communication	Communicates aurally; is abstract to very abstract	Spoken words; music
Printed Words	Communicates visually; is abstract to very abstract	Read a poem
Symbols	Communicates visually and aurally; is abstract to very abstract	Blast of a fire warning horn; music notation; mathematical symbols; Braille

Typical formats for information resources include:

Artifacts—contain actual objects such as Babylonian clay tablets, original manuscripts, and museum items

Audiotapes—contain music, recorded speech, oral history

Bibliographies—list of related items

Catalogs—index to information resources

Computer printout—presents results of a computer database search

Fiction and nonfiction books—contain factual or creative content

Filmstrips—present a series of still images generally accompanied by written captions or a sound tape.

Microforms—include microfilms, microfiche, and microcards

Newspapers and magazines—contain up-to-date information

Periodical indexes—lead to magazine or newspaper articles

Phonograph records—contain music, plays, poetry, and the like

Reference works—non-fiction materials such as dictionaries, atlases, encyclopedias, handbooks, and directories

35mm slides—contain a variety of material such as pictures of paintings and real subjects, e.g., butterflies

35mm motion pictures—combines many encoding forms in various genres

Vertical files—organize clippings, pictures, pamphlets, and the like

Video tapes—combine many encoding forms in various genres

Media formats employ a mixture of encoding forms such as language, symbols, and pictures. Consequently, most formats are considered *multimedia.* Books contain pictures, moving pictures make use of captions, and so on. The principal value in considering media in terms of the types of *encoding forms* employed in a particular format is that once the encoders are known, identifying strengths and weaknesses in the communication is facilitated. The consideration here is the way encoders form *metaphors.* Effect depends on how media condense or expand reality, eliminate distractions, speed up or slow down information output, and reduce the cost of information transmission.

The point is that educators need to determine the message before selecting the media. Too frequently educators decide to use a film, filmstrip, or other material before the message to be communicated is analyzed in terms of the encoding forms needed. A better procedure is to design the message carefully with a particular audience in mind and then select the media that are appropriate for both the message and the audience.

Creative communication demands both freedom and constraint. Freedom must be exercised in order to investigate, experiment with, and combine materials and communication (presentation) forms in new and original ways. Constraint must be practiced in order to recognize and evaluate strengths and limitations (capacities) of materials and presentation forms. Learning to utilize the unique characteristics of all encoding forms requires continuous practice. The potential for creatively responding increases as the components—time, personnel, facilities, materials, and equipment—are expanded.

Degrees and Hierarchies

Cybernetics, as a study of actions and reactions, is concerned with the consequences of having or not having information. The discrepancies between the intents of the goals and objectives of a school and the implemented curriculum as well as the effects of priorities on current programs are all important to the evaluation of the system. Discrepancies are expressed in terms of degrees: the degree the goals and objectives are met, the degree that bias and values determine how decisions are made, and the degree that biases and values block objectivity.

The notion of degree from cybernetics is closely associated with the concern over identifying hierarchical structures found in general system theory. Hierarchies are found when entities are arranged in a graded series—simple to complex, large to small, important to unimportant, etc. Hierarchies are present in any system and are important since they provide a view of the structure of a system—human made organizations (president, supervisor, worker), biological organisms (cell, tissue, organ, organism), and even subject matter (add, multiply, divide). How do the hierarchies explain how a system behaves as it does? To what degree do the hierarchical structures facilitate or block the mission of the system? Can the hierarchies be changed to improve the system? The answers to these types of questions constitute one way cybernetic theory can be applied to instructional as well as other systems.

More broadly, cybernetic theory is concerned about how information shows the degree of dependence, complexity, analytical depth, overlap, independence, credibility, and the like.

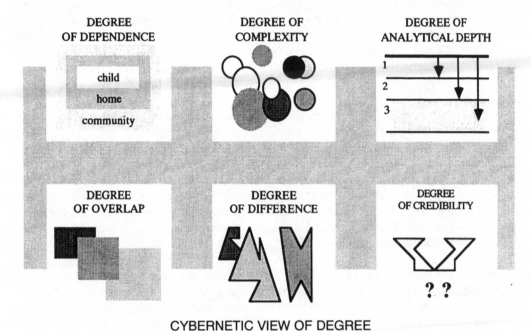

CYBERNETIC VIEW OF DEGREE

Structure of Knowledge

Giving structure to the universe of information is necessary for understanding a discipline as well as for teaching and learning the subject. Knowledge is organized in many different ways. The structure of a discipline may be a natural or an obvious hierarchy or a contrived structure. In biology, the simple to complex organizational structure is a natural hierarchy—cell, tissue, organ, system, organism. In history, a thematic approach is contrived—causes of war, influence of Darwin, the eras of human achievement. In cybernetic theory, the concern is for the degree a hierarchy is natural or contrived, since natural hierarchies are better in the sense that people tend to agree with the basic structure. Agreement about contrived hierarchies is rarely found. Think of a short title for the organization of knowledge presented in the following diagrams. Is the hierarchy natural or contrived?

Knowledge can be structured in many ways—socio-economic status, size, and purpose. Socio-economic status and the classification of human habitats are more natural than the purposes for communications.

Implications from Cybernetics

An educational system must have the ability to take in and process a great deal of information in order to select the best, most appropriate information to convey to students. In education, this tends to be an awesome task. First, keeping up in their disciplines poses a difficult problem to teachers who have little time left after planning, teaching, and evaluating lessons. Likewise, mastering the principles of teaching concepts, problem solving, decision making, critical thinking, scientific inquiry, and the like seems endless. Nevertheless, a current, in-depth knowledge of subject matter increases the choices teachers *can* make in designing lessons. Also, when teachers know that what they are teaching—large bodies of knowledge, concepts, problem solving, critical thinking, etc.—they can apply principles that can greatly improve the instructional strategies employed.

Operating on incomplete, distorted, and/or fallacious information will ultimately destroy an educational system. Every attempt must be made to make value judgments about instructional systems on facts, consequences, sound principles, and available alternatives. Obstacles to ad-vancement in education frequently involve lack of agreement, personality conflicts, politics, and funding. Lack of agreement appears in many forms. For example, defenses of educational programs that include the use of glittering terms, oversimplification, and vagueness are de-structive. Personality conflicts as well as political conflicts usually grow from the beliefs, values, and personal aspirations of individuals.

Manmade systems can be described by the information they value and subsequently use in the decision-making process. Leadership styles illustrate this point.

Defeat and Exploit (Spoils of War). The principal administrator uses information to sell his educational program. Propaganda and distorted information may be used to eliminate competitors, exploit people and resources, and gain power. The organizational structure is arranged so that top administrators receive the information they want to hear. Opposing views are suppressed. Success is judged mainly in terms of the administrator gaining com-plete control. Failure is due to flawed information fed by subadministrators.

Surrender and Endure (Top-Down). Purposes and goals are established from infor-mation provided from some authority. Information gained from subordinates establishes the effectiveness of each level to reach predetermined goals and objectives and to establish re-wards and punishments for personal performance. Competence is assessed by an individual's ability to use and produce information that expresses a positive contribution to the system (surrender and endure).

Collaborate and Relinquish (Political Model). Leadership is the ability to gather and use information to negotiate and to relinquish as few resources as possible to the opposition. System purposes and goals shift as information is made available to secure additional re-sources; hence, educational program development tends to follow the path where monetary resources become available. The tendency is to use information to make deals with personnel within the district and agencies outside the district. Success is judged in terms of the system's ability to find information which will increase power and bureaucratic structures.

Unite and Agree (Empowerment Model). Leadership is any action that encourages using information to arrive at consensus. Every effort is made to gain objective information that can assist the group in making unbiased decisions. Success is judged by the degree the organization can collectively set and achieve purposes. Administrative structures assist the group in finding information needed to arrive at consensus and strive to relinquish power as the organization becomes more efficient.

Instructional systems need to teach the organization of knowledge as well as the content of disciplines. The most important point here is that if students know the type of knowledge they seek, then designing a search strategy becomes easier and more precise. Also, knowing how a discipline is structured is frequently necessary to find information and gain knowledge. For example, "A map is not like a musical score, which is not like the equation for a function, which in turn differs from an evolutionary tree" (Leinhardt, 1992, p. 3).

A greater understanding of the way knowledge is coded will increase the power to communicate. The most important encoding form is language. Campbell (1985) writes:

> Essential to the learning process in man is language; some form has likely been with us from the beginning. The development of language introduced a drastic revision in the function of the hemispheres of the new brain. One complete side of the neocortex is generally devoted to techniques of performance associated with language—science of all kinds, applied mathematics, analytical abilities, all learned techniques of explicit performance. The other half is devoted to intuitive perceptions, esthetic appreciation, visual-spatial assessments, and the formation of related concepts. It can understand language but it has no capacity for explicit expression. (p. 64)

Programs Sharing Principles
Congruent with Cybernetic Theory

Cybernetics as a meta-theory can be translated into many different kinds of systematic processes. Such diverse efforts as building educational programs, developing distribution systems for goods and services, evaluating the informational needs of an operation, and building robots, are examples. These processes emphasize determining the information needs of a system, establishing the ways a system uses information, recognizing the information generated by the system, and identifying what information is communicated within the system and to its environment. All information processing strategies for teaching and learning show most of these attributes in one way or another. However, coping with the information age has been more instrumental in bringing cybernetic theory into educational thought and action than a conscious attempt to apply cybernetic principles directly. In other words, current initiatives struggling to use information technologies to meet the multitude of problems facing education have inadvertently incorporated many of the same notions developed in cybernetics. The following examples illustrate these relationships.

Interdisciplinary approaches connecting the subject areas are becoming a practical reality with the development of information superhighways. Perhaps the best example of the need for interdisciplinary approaches relates to using and contributing to the Internet. Armbruster (1994) explains that:

> Like a superhighway system formed from many converging highways, the Internet is a worldwide computer network made up of thousands of autonomous and separately administered networks of many sizes and types. However, the Internet is a "network of networks" with a phenomenal annual growth rate: one new network joins the Internet approximately every 10 minutes. (p. 1)

Using the Internet as well as other information resources requires the development of conceptual frameworks to access, process, and utilize the mass of information available. Perkins' education "for insight" mandates developing and teaching new ways to gain intellectual access to information. He believes that people learn from "acting on information and making up their own information more than just soaking up information" (Perkins, 1991). The current interest in synergistic pedagogy is putting these notions into practice. Units are developed using related subjects and teaching in a manner that makes them inseparable (Bonds, 1993). *Dimensions of Thinking* (Marzano *et al.,* 1988, v–vi) lists the thinking skills that need developed to help students use the glut of information surrounding them. These include

Focusing Skills	Analyzing Skills
Information-Gathering Skills	Evaluating Skills
Remembering Skills	Generating Skills
Organizing Skills	Integrating Skills

The Association for Supervision and Curriculum Development (ASCD) is promoting the use of instructional strategies to develop these core thinking skills. These include structured lessons which emphasize decision making, composition, and synectics. The breakthrough is that educational programs now have the technology to identify more precisely the materials that are needed to support and implement an interdisciplinary, integrated curriculum. Expanding the information base of schools puts the use of traditional textbooks into proper focus. Textbooks should help students find, evaluate, and generate information rather than attempting to provide comprehensive coverage of a given subject. Schools that use information superhighways are the smart schools.

Smart schools are computer networked and make comprehensive use of city, regional, state, and world databases. Students and teachers not only use databases but they also share information which contributes to the development of information resources (Stallard, 1991). The concept of smart schools is not new. Over fifteen years ago, a list of the advantages of interactive computer systems included the ability to:

1. design and administer performance tests developed by students, teachers, and subject matter experts,
2. pool performance tasks and units of instruction,
3. correct deficiencies of individuals or groups *immediately* following a completed task,
4. equalize the difficulty of subjects and tasks in many languages,
5. place more responsibility on students to manage their own learning,
6. provide an opportunity to individualize and personalize the curriculum,
7. keep lessons, databases, tests, and the like current,
8. streamline writing and editing,
9. eliminate or sharply reduce printing and distributing costs,
10. establish profiles of individuals or groups,
11. estimate the investment needed to move an individual or group to the next higher level of performance, and
12. locate individuals or groups with specific expertise. (Hug, 1978a)

The current interest in resource-based education is another example of an attempt by educational planners to develop smart schools.

Resource-based education makes extensive use of information retrieval systems and avoids the limitations of texts. Textbooks have many disadvantages caused by economic, political, ethnic, and other social problems. Publishers limit the number of pages in order to be profitable and control the content to avoid offending anyone.

> . . . textbooks tend to be bland and uninteresting and to use a controlled vocabulary that curbs the development of language facility. Resource-based education can solve many of these problems and make learning more individualized. Through resource-based education, students can approach assignments and problems by using diverse resources giving them equal access to information and ideas. Equal access, regardless of the socioeconomic inequities among schools, makes school less biased because many points of view are represented in non-textbook approaches. (Hug, 1992, p. 7)

Perhaps the most important advantage to resource-based learning is that it responds to the needs of a more diverse population of students. Establishing equity has become a monumental problem in American schools. Teachers play a critical role in helping students access, evaluate, and generate information necessary for the implementation of an integrated curriculum and also in providing equal access to information for all students regardless of their socioeconomic status. The discrepancies between schools serving the poor and affluent and among schools serving Hispanic, African, and Asian American communities are staggering.

The literature-based, integrated language arts program and whole language approaches are strategies that utilize a broader base of information. Basal readers tend to be dull, use limited vocabularies, and respond to the same social and economic pressures as textbooks. A literature approach integrates reading, thinking, and writing. The teacher writes down the stories of children who will eventually write for themselves using word processors. This technology provides children with access to the use of data bases, spelling and grammar checkers, and thesauruses. The computer redistributes textual control by empowering students who use these technologies (Johnson-Eilola, 1992, p. 381). In other words, the computer works with the student by providing tools as well as rules and accessing information that is needed rather than being provided by the teacher or textbook whether needed or not.

Whole language approaches place meaning-making at the center of teaching and learning (Ruddell, 1992). Active involvement is designed to enlighten. This is an individual process typically pursued under these conditions:

1. Students and teachers can expect predictable as well as unpredictable outcomes within a planned activity.
2. Learner outcomes are unique to each individual.
3. Activities are based on student's ideas, interests, and experiences.
4. Socioeconomic differences are accommodated due to the individualized nature of the activities.
5. A wide variety of information resources are used in additional to traditional textbooks (Veatch, 1988, p. 9).

Whole language approaches also provide an opportunity to individualize and personalize the curriculum, as well as keeping lessons, databases, tests, and the like current.

Information literacy will become the vehicle for lifelong learning. Practically any technology that schools have is available in the home workplace. The first, and perhaps the most difficult, task is to teach people to recognize their need for information. Next, they must have the skills to identify, locate, obtain, and evaluate the information in relation to their need. Being information literate allows people to be interactive and self-directed in a resource-based environment. When this is achieved, the notion of "going back to school" to keep current will be only one of several options for obtaining information and training (Hancock, 1993).

References

Armbruster, L. (1994). *Internet essentials.* Indianapolis: Que.

Berlo, D. K. (1960). *The process of communication* (p. 32). New York: Holt, Rinehart, and Winston.

von Bertalanffy, L. (1968). *General system theory.* New York: George Braziller.

Bonds, C. W. (1993, Summer). Curriculum wholeness through synergistic teaching. *Clearing House,* 252–254.

Brewer, J. H., Ainsworth, J. M., & Wynne, G. E. (1989). *Power management: A three-step program for successful leadership.* Jackson, MS: Associated Consultants in Education.

Caine, R. N., & Caine, G. (1991). *Making connections: Teaching and the human brain.* Alexandria, VA: Association for Supervision and Curriculum Development.

Campbell, R. (1985). *Fisherman's guide: A systems approach to creativity and organization.* Boston: New Science Library, Shambhala.

Churchman, C. W. (1971). *The design of inquiring systems: Basic concepts of systems and organization.* New York: Basic Books.

Dupuy, J.-P. (1989, May–July). The autonomy of social reality: On the contribution of the theory of systems to the theory of society. *World Futures,* 153–176.

Etzioni, A. (1991, May–June). The good policy: Can we design it? *American Behavioral Scientist,* 549–563.

Hancock, V. E. (1993, May). Information literacy for lifelong learning. *ERIC Digest.* Syracuse University; ERIC.

Hug, W. E. (1975). *Instructional design and the media program.* Chicago: American Library Association.

Hug, W. E. (1978a). *Instructional technology: Factors influencing the field.* Occasional Paper Number 1. Syracuse University, ERIC.

Hug, W. E. (1978b). Review of products, procedures, and personnel used in developing soldiers' manuals, commanders' manuals, job books, and skill qualification tests. Unpublished report.

Hug, W. E. (1992). Trends and issues in school library media programs, In J. B. Smith & J. G. Coleman, Jr. (Eds.), *School library media annual.* Englewood, CO: Libraries Unlimited.

Hug, W. E., & King, J. M. (1984). Educational interpretations of general system theory. In R. K. Bass & C. R. Dills (Eds.), *Instructional development: The state of the art, II.* Dubuque, IA: Kendall/Hunt.

Johnson-Eilola, J. (1992, Fall). Control and the cyborg: Writing and being written in hypertext. *Journal of Advanced Composition.* 381–399.

Leinhardt, G. (1992, April). What research on learning tells us about teaching. *Educational Leadership,* 20–25.

Leinhardt, G., Putnam, R., & Hattrup, R. A. (Eds.). (1992). *Analysis of arithmetic for mathematics teaching.* Hillsdale, NJ: Lawrence Erlbaum Associates.

Lochhead, J. (1991, November). Guest comment: Why is good teaching so clearly confusing? A tale of two theories. *American Journal of Physics,* 969–971.

Marzano, R. J. et al. (1988). *Dimensions of thinking: A famework for curriculum and instruction.* Alexandria, VA: Association for Supervision and Curriculum Development.

Meindl, J. D. (1989). *Brief lessons in high technology.* Stanford, CA: Stanford Alumni Association.

Miller, J. G. (1970). *The living systems involved in the educational process.* Washington, DC: Academy for Educational Development.

Perkins, D. N. (1991, October). Educating for insight. *Educational Leadership,* 4–8.

Porush, D. (1989, Winter). Cybernetic fiction and postmodern science. *New Literary History,* 373–397.

Resnick, L. B., & Klopfer, L. E. (1989). *Toward the thinking curriculum: Current cognitive research: 1989 ASCD Yearbook.* Washington, DC: ASCD.

Ruddell, R. B. (1992, December). A whole language and literature perspective: Creating a meaning-making instructional environment. *Language Arts,* 612–620.

Schlechty, P. C. (1990). *Schools for the 21st century: Leadership imperatives for educational reform.* San Francisco: Jossey-Bass.

Smith, J. B. (1984). Library orientation. Duplicated class syllabus.

Stallard, C. K. (1991). Implementing smart school technology at the secondary level.

Stonum, G. L. (1989, Winter). Cybernetic explanation as a theory of reading. *New Literary History,* 397–413.

Veatch, J. (1988). En garde, whole language. In J. B. Smith (Ed.), *School library media annual.* Englewood, CO: Libraries Unlimited.

Veneris, Y. (1990, March). Modelling the transition from the industrial to the informational revolution. *Environmental and Planning,* 399–417.

Weil, M., & Joyce, B. (1978). *Information processing models of teaching.* Englewood Cliffs, NJ: Prentice-Hall.

Wiener, N. (1948). *Cybernetics.* New York: John Wiley & Sons.

13

Behavioral Analysis as a Basis for Instructional Design

Donald A. Cook
Cambridge Center for Behavioral Studies
Cambridge, Massachusetts

Introduction

The point of view of this chapter can be characterized in two ways. First, the theoretical stance has its sources in the experimental analysis of behavior, which stresses the primacy of operant behavior in human life and extends the principles of operant behavior to the field of instructional design. Second, the chapter reflects the experiences and convictions of a participant in this attempt. That participant—myself—was schooled in analysis of operant behavior (at Columbia) and has devoted most of his adult life to the design of instruction from that point of view. It seems only fair to say that this background might engender certain biases, but it is equally fair to say that is it also the source of kinds of knowledge not otherwise easy to find.

Operant Behavior

The study of operant behavior as characterized by that term owes most to the formulations of B. F. Skinner (1904–1990). Skinner is usually classified as an experimental psychologist, although at various points in his career—and among some of his followers—there is to be seen a sharp disaffection with the rest of psychology, amounting in certain ways to a "declaration of independence" from that field as normally understood.

What is characteristic and essential about Skinner's approach can readily be seen in his first major integrated collection of papers, *The Behavior of Organisms* (Skinner, 1938). This book is based entirely on an extensive series of investigations carried out with the white rat as subject. The rat, however, is regarded as a "representative organism," and the reader is told, "Let him extrapolate who will." It seems clear that Skinner believes extrapolation of the main functional relations treated in this work to be possible and sound as long as provision is made for differences characteristic of species and all required adjustments of quantity. The principle of reinforcement as herein stated is meant to apply possibly to all mammalian life. The question of "what all the reinforcers are" for various species—or even one species—is carefully left open in this statement.

More important than the choice of species is the fact that all of the experiments described in Skinner's book yield reproducible results when carried out with a single organism at a time. In most of the experiments, replications on several animals are reported—and the regularities are duly observable—but only once or twice in the book are averages resorted to. Many others in psychology were using rats as subjects—Clark Hull and Edward Tolman and their students are notable examples—but almost never will results derived from a single organism be found in their research.

It is of more than passing note that to find examples of single-animal experimental results would have required looking back to the work of Lynn Thorndike (1898) or, significantly, to numerous critics of "behaviorism."

Along with the emphasis upon the single case is to be found a parallel willingness to see significant behavioral change arising from a single event in the organism's experience. What is usually regarded as "trial and error" may require repeated instances to produce its effects; but the properly arranged "trial and success" can yield major effects in a single instance. These facts are worth noting as they point to dimensions in which Skinner differed, most significantly, from others classed as "behaviorists." This ambiguity has persisted until the present time; we see Skinner even now being attacked as "a behaviorist" with properties ascribed to that position which, although to be found in other behaviorists, are distinctively absent in Skinner.

This point is not trivial. In the year 1950, in a graduate course with one of the best-known behaviorists of the Hullian school—Kenneth W. Spence—Murray Sidman and I pointed out an implication of Hull's theory (as Spence was expounding it) which was contradicted by Skinner's findings on schedules of reinforcement. "Who can take those results seriously?" said Spence. "They are reported on just a couple of animals!" Our reply was this: "How many cases would you like to see? Tell us the number, come downstairs to the lab with us, and we will give you verification in the desired number." The course was at Columbia, and the class was in a building whose lower floors contained an extensive operant laboratory system. Our challenge was never taken.

More important than doctrinaire encounters is the experience of reliable replication. As a laboratory assistant and a course instructor, I have seen the basic functions adumbrated in *The Behavior of Organisms* recaptured in hundreds of animals serving as subjects for an equal number of students in the basic lab course. The experiments always worked, with results obtained from the individual animal. The individual organism was demonstrably orderly. This observation applies to the students as well. Graduates of such a lab course share some typical attitudes: that individual behavior is lawful; that a technology can be mastered which can put this fact to useful service; that showing, telling, and explaining are often weak sources of behavior change in the absence of more powerful interactive engagements; and that punishments—including its milder forms of threats, exasperation, intimidation, disapproval—are not reliable tools of the educative process, despite what might appear to be short-run effectiveness.

Such a set of views is not widely understood to be a consequence of a "behavioristic" position. Yet it would seem, on the face of it, to comport well with educational applications, in which the individual is taken seriously, and data based upon averages is never regarded as telling the entire story.

Until his development of the first teaching machines, Skinner's own experimental work was primarily limited to non-human species. For many years, the pigeon became his preferred subject, for reasons which include their excellent eyesight and their long life span. A few studies with humans and extensive notes taken over a period of ten years form the basis of the book *Verbal Behavior* (Skinner, 1957). But these studies cannot be said to have altered the fundamental formulations of the operant behavior process, which remained stated at a level of generality which permits application to a wide range of species.

The Contingency in Operant Behavior

Many names exist which refer to roughly the same thing: voluntary behavior, trial-and-error learning, instrumental behavior, and operant behavior. The reasons for such behavior also have several names, which have roughly the same meaning: rewards, reinforcements, positive consequences, the Law of Effect—and perhaps others.

Modern psychology has been plagued by a serious problem in accepting the notion that we do things because of their consequences. It cannot be the consequences which will follow the act, because you never know what's really going to happen this time. All right, you say, it is the consequences which have happened in the past. But how, comes the answer, can the effects of an act "work backward in time" to have an impact on the response? Well, you say, the consequences do not work backward on the act which has just happened; they work forward on future actions like the one that just happened. There is even more to this argument, which is seemingly endless.

It is my belief that we are ready to accept this principle and put it to work. I know that some scientists are still worried about being unscientific if they speak of "purposive" behavior, and that they yearn for a specific stimulus which must precede every response. This way of thinking has a long history, going back at least to the Cartesian notion of a "reflex." At the same time, the very idea that "stimulus-response" thinking lies at the heart of Skinner's principles is the basis on which he is most often attacked ("We must go beyond mere mechanistic stimulus-response thinking"), and it is important to understand that Skinner is not a stimulus-response theorist. This disclaimer can be found repeatedly in his writings—it is not a matter of my (or anybody's) interpretation of what Skinner "really" meant.

The term "contingency" is used in the experimental analysis of behavior to refer to the "if-then" relation which connects behavior with its consequences. If you press the light switch, the bulb will light up; there is a contingency between the response of pressing the light switch and the consequent illumination. If the production of light (in the room, for example) has been reinforcing, then under the right circumstances, you will press the switch.

In a contingency, then, the response is an operant, and its effect is upon the environment. The connection between them is the contingency:

$$R: \text{(press light switch)} \rightarrow S: \text{(light goes on)}$$

This is the simplest possible operant contingency, and it contains two terms—the response and the stimulus produced by that response. Note that the important stimulus, which acts to reinforce that response, appears after the response in time. The order of R and S is the reverse of that seen in traditional "reflex" S-R accounts.

The two-term contingency quickly becomes more complex in the lives of most organisms. We usually do not throw switches if we know they are broken, or if the light is already on in the room. Walking along the street, we usually do not cry out the name of an old friend unless we see that friend in the crowd. We click the mouse cursor on an icon, but not on an empty screen. In most contingencies, then, there are three terms:

$$S: \text{icon} * R: \text{click} \rightarrow S: \text{program opens}$$

The two-term contingency has become a three-term contingency. A stimulus (such as the icon on the screen) sets the occasion for the response (clicking on the icon) to produce the reinforcing result (program opens).

"Mistakes" may occur: We forget that the switch is broken, and press it anyway. Lonely for a friend, we may "see" him or her in the crowd and cry out the name, only to apologize to a stranger. In a hurry to communicate, we may activate the e-mail when we have not yet written the letter. But that is the stuff of the study of operant behavior.

Contingencies may become more complex than three-term. But the basic three-term notion—discriminative stimulus, response, and consequence to that response—will carry us deep into the design of instructional exchanges from the operant point of view.

Transition to Human Behavior

The transition to human applications was in my case strongly supported by earlier experience. My thesis advisor at Columbia, Fred S. Keller, had already brought dramatic improvements to the teaching of copying skills in International Morse Code to human learners during World War II by the application of reinforcement methods (Keller, 1943). A friend and colleague of Skinner's from Harvard days, he had developed the "Code-Voice" method, in which learners responded to each code signal with a written guess as to the corresponding character, then received a voiced confirmation over the same phones through which the signal had been sent. The ensemble of some 40 signals (26 letters, 10 numerals, and 4 punctuation signs), would be sent and resent in random order, treated in this manner as a series of discriminated operants. If the response was correct, the learner would get that confirmation immediately; if incorrect, the correct character (as voiced) would be written in a space right under the incorrect guess. This procedure may nowadays sound sensible enough to suggest itself "without benefit of theory," but if so, that fact suggests that basic reinforcement ideas have entered the general climate in the last 50 years. It was not obvious to the Signal Corps, if current practice be taken to reflect ideas, and the dramatic gains resulting from the method were acknowledged only after some struggle.

In my own dissertation (Cook, 1972) on learning to copy Morse Code, carried out under contract with the U. S. Air Force, the method was employed in a further extension to messages of varying degrees of complexity and "meaningfulness" in the English language. Details aside, the results made two things clear to me: (a) the application of relatively simple aspects of operant reinforcement theory could bring striking improvement to practical training problems, as compared with traditional practices; and (b) in the seventeen human subjects in my study, though the specific numerical values on their skill improvement graphs varied from one to the other, the trends were the same and the order of difficulty for the various kinds of material was identical from one subject to the next.

It remains true for me today that most instructional applications of an operant-based theory of learning consist primarily in establishing an environment in which three-term contingencies maintain a high degree of interaction. In addition, the contingencies must be arranged in a sequence so that the behavior of the learner "goes somewhere," in the direction of the final objectives which are the aim of the instructional design. To understand contingencies and how to sequence them is to understand instructional design from the viewpoints of the operant laboratory. To me, this is not the stuff of profound philosophic wonderment, unless it is wonderment arising because the world still so little puts these principles to work.

The Teaching Machine

First Formulations

The general idea of a "teaching machine" can be found as early as the 19th century, if not before. The records of the U. S. Patent Office show an "Improvement in Apparatus for Teaching Spelling" obtaining patent No. 52,758 in 1886, granted to one H. Skinner. "H" is for Halcyon—no relation, apparently, to B. F. Skinner. For a "Machine for Intelligence Tests," Patent No. 1,749,226 was granted to S. L. Pressey in 1930. The Pressey machine, acknowledged by Skinner, implemented a contingency—knowledge that an answer was correct or incorrect—but did not govern a sequence of events.

Some 19 machines after H. Skinner's, and 15 machines after Pressey's, a "Teaching Machine" registered by B. F. Skinner was granted Patent No. 2,846,779, in 1958.

The Strict Contingency

As we undertake a review of the concept of teaching machine as an export from the operant behavior lab, we quickly encounter a basic problem: What teaching machine concepts should we study? In my opinion, there occurred very early in the teaching machine movement a shift in the nature of the contingency mediated by the machine. The early form of the contingency I shall call "strict," and the later form I shall call "loose."

In a strict contingency, the correct response and only the correct response will advance the program:

S: frame display * R: correct response → S: advance of program

The advance of the program to the next frame might or might not be accompanied by ancillary reinforcers: the statement "correct," a statement of the total number correct so far, a token in some current token economy. Whatever these details, the contingency is strict in that the correct response and only that event will produce the advance.

Skinner's first two teaching machines are strict contingency machines, and are described in the 1954 article, "The Science of Learning and the Art of Teaching" (Skinner, 1954). "On the top surface is a window through which a question or problem printed on a paper tape may be seen. The child answers the question by moving one or more sliders upon which the digits 0 through 9 are printed. The answer appears in square holes punched in the paper upon which the question is printed" (the word "answer" here refers to that constructed by the student through use of the sliders). "When the answer has been set, the child turns a knob. . . . If the answer is right, the knob turns freely and can be made to ring a bell or provide some other conditioned reinforcement. If the answer is wrong, the knob will not turn. . . . The knob must then be reversed slightly and a second attempt at a right answer made. (Unlike the flash card, the device reports a wrong answer without giving the right answer.) When the answer is right, a further turn of the knob engages a clutch which moves the next problem into place in the window" (Skinner, 1954, pp. 22–24). A parallel description in the figure caption states that "The machine senses the composed answer . . ." thanks, of course, to the positioning of the sliders. Two features of this description are distinctive: First, the production of consequences is strictly contingent upon the composition of the correct response; and second, among the consequences mentioned—conditioned reinforcers and advance to the next problem—a statement of the correct answer is not to be found among them. This last fact is highlighted through the comparison with flash-cards.

This same article describes a second machine for teaching both spelling and arithmetic, and the description is similar, except that the sliders can manipulate both letters and numerals: "When the sliders have been moved to complete the material, the pupil turns a crank. If the setting is correct, a new frame of material moves into place and the sliders return to their home position. If the material is wrong, the sliders return but the frame remains and another setting must be made" (Skinner, 1954, p. 25).

From Strict to Loose Contingency

In a loose contingency, a response is called for, but advance and feedback are not truly contingent upon the properties of the response. The shift from strict to loose contingencies took place within the specifications and descriptions of the three main teaching machines described by Skinner himself. The first two machines—for teaching spelling and arithmetic—implemented strict contingencies; the third machine, for programming verbal knowledge, employed loose contingencies. Thus, in two key early papers—the first appearing in 1954 and the second in 1958—a shift occurred which compromised the nature of the contingency, before even machines themselves were abandoned for "programmed instruction." It is reminiscent of the very fraction of a second following upon the big bang which created the universe; the disposition of matter and energy taking place in the blinding glare prefigured for long eternities the shape of problems, issues, and disputes to come.

By 1958, as the range of applications for teaching machines enlarged, a shift could be detected. The influential 1958 paper, published in *Science* (Skinner, 1958), begins by briefly describing the same machines, but then goes on to say, "For more advanced students—from junior high school, say, through college—such a machine is unnecessarily rigid in specifying form of response" (p. 35). It is odd to see Skinner applying the pejorative term "rigid" to his own key procedure for controlling behavior. Could it be because he is preparing us to give it up? He continues: "Fortunately, such students may be asked to compare their responses with printed material revealed by the machine" (p. 35). What follows is the description of the disk machine, in which printed frames appear to the student in windows, answers are written on paper strips and moved to inaccessible positions so they cannot be erased, and the correct answer comes to view. The contrast with the strict contingency is twofold: First, the program proceeds when the student asks it to (by moving a lever), regardless of whether the response made is correct or not—and indeed, regardless of whether any response at all has been made; second, what is produced by the advance is the correct answer to the frame, followed in turn by advance to the next frame. The two contrasts both spring from the critical fact that the written response cannot be "sensed" or "read" or "parsed" by the machine, as in the case of the strict contingency.

In the light of the technology available today, I believe that we must entertain the idea that the development of the disk teaching machine with its loose contingency simply reflects the fact that written responses could not easily be sensed and thereby employed in a strict contingency. In the sentence "Fortunately, such students may be asked to compare their responses with printed material revealed by the machine," we may be seeing a virtue made of necessity. The statement contains a note of caution in stating merely that students may be asked to behave in a specific way, without asserting that they indeed will do so, nor stating with what effect. Many issues are raised by the shift from the strict to the loose contingency: If the learner's response was correct, does seeing the correct answer act as a reinforcer? If the response was wrong, is the reason for that error now corrected? Such issues, which could be discussed at length, remained unresolved as the "educational revolution" gained momentum and hurtled on. I now believe that some of the force of Skinner's own technology of behavior was lost in the move from strict to loose contingencies. I will later argue that we can today realistically and practically consider, thanks to computers and their programs, the restoration of the strict contingency to a central position in automated instruction.

Errors and Repetition

Skinner's strategy in this compromise is not an isolated phenomenon. We can, in fact, formulate two principles of the behavior of instructional psychologists when faced with a complex learning task:

1. When the learning task becomes complex, give up the strict contingency, accept any response, then give the right answer, then move on to the next step. Assume that presentation of the "correct answer" acts to reinforce a correct answer from the learner, and to correct an incorrect answer from that learner.

The second principle arises out of a recognition that this first principle may leave something to be desired, and is an attempt to compensate for that fact. It is:

2. If you retreat to a loose contingency and present correct answers in uncontingent fashion, then institute repeated trials covering the same material, until a criterion is reached.

In his use of the disk teaching machine Skinner exemplified the second principle as well as the first, as can be seen in the following:

[If the student's response corresponds to the right answer] he moves a lever horizontally. This movement punches a hole in the paper opposite his response, recording the fact that he called it correct, and alters the machine so that the frame will not appear again when the student works around the disk a second time. . . . The student proceeds in this way until he has responded to all frames. He then works around the disk a second time, but only those frames appear to which he has not correctly responded. When the disk revolves without stopping, the assignment is finished. (The student is asked to repeat each frame until a correct response is made to allow for the fact that, in telling him that a response is wrong, such a machine tells him what is right.) (Skinner, 1958, pp. 35–36)

Notice that the criterion of correctness has shifted in part from the single response, with program advance contingent upon its correctness, to a group of responses, selectively repeated until each has been made correctly once. Skinner says of this scheme: "Like a good tutor, the machine insists that a given point be thoroughly understood, either frame by frame or set by set, before the student moves on" (Skinner, 1958, p. 39). The tutor has relaxed. It's a very good compromise, but there is a compromise in the insistence that the learner answer each frame correctly, no matter how many trials are required: In the limiting case, with but one frame still unanswered, the learner can hold the correct response echoically for a moment while the disk spins to a repetition of the same stubborn frame.

Evidence of difficulty with this procedure is provided in a report on the Teaching Machine project written by Skinner and James G. Holland (1958) and submitted to the Fund for the Advancement of Education. They write: "There was a strong tendency to put down a quick, careless response in order to uncover the correct response in the machine. The more highly motivated the student, the stronger the tendency appeared to be. Many students were content to get the response right the second time around. It seems to be necessary to make correct first-cycle responses more important. This can be done by adding a slight punishment for a wrong response . . ." (Skinner, 1958).

This is a sad moment, and brings us to the third "realistic" principle to be discerned in the life of the instructional psychologist:

3. When strict contingencies must be abandoned and loose ones enter the scene, it may be necessary to add a bit of punishment to discourage the shortcuts that can develop.

Although the initial enthusiasm for the teaching machine was to lose much of its force, there is much creative variety in the thinking of that time. Skinner was aware of the compromises being undertaken, and gives evidence of wishes to improve upon the situation. Specifically, the design of an improved machine is described, in which more space and larger windows are available, so that the material exposed after the student has entered an answer "may tell him that his response is wrong without telling him what is right. For example, it may list a few of the commonest errors, one of which may be his response. He makes a second response if necessary on a newly uncovered portion of the paper strip. This is covered by a further operation of the machine, which uncovers the correct response" (Skinner

& Holland, 1958, p. 37). Thus, the correct answer is withheld, corrective feedback given, and a second try allowed at the same frame. Two are better than one, but the limit is clearly set by the technology and not by a view of the learning process.

But these improvements never saw commercial realization. The only "teaching machine" which attained widespread distribution was the Min-Max of Teaching Machines, Inc., which had one small window to write in, no feedback other than the right answer no matter what you wrote, and not even a disk to repeat missed items. We remind the reader that the technology for achieving the subtler effects hinted at in these pages is becoming commonplace.

Code-Voice Reconsidered

In Fred S. Keller's "code-voice" method of teaching the reception of Morse Code, as noted above, the student listens to a code signal transmitted through earphones, then writes a best guess at the corresponding character on specially ruled paper, then, after a brief pause, hears a voiced statement of the character through the same phones that transmitted the signal. If the guess was correct, the student merely awaits the next signal; if it was wrong, the correct character must be written in a correction space underneath the guess. The three-term contingency of the discriminated operant is clearly present, but it is a loose contingency. The procedure moves on no matter what you wrote, and your own correction is made after you've been told what it should be. Of course, ordinary writing paper cannot parse your response, and large numbers of trainees were receiving instruction at once.

Here again, then, is the theme of the weaker contingency, with the correct answer, backed up by repetitions of that kind of trial until a criterion is reached. Despite these limitations, the method resulted in code training superior to any hitherto achieved in the U. S. military forces. The method in stricter form would now be easy to implement with a computer program which, unlike the ruled paper on which Keller's subjects wrote, could parse the response made—presuming the response is typed—and hold to a strict contingency when desired.

In discussing these examples, I am suggesting that the specific management of the contingencies of learning in some typical and important applications of our technology is a result of a complex blend of ideal theoretical notions—most well-supported in the laboratory—and the practical exigencies of the situation in which the application takes place. The two-model mixture, whatever its roots may be in animal vs. human research, and whatever its theoretical dressing may be in "behaviorist" vs. "cognitive" controversies, is in fact, to a large extent, a product of non-theoretical actualities. Were these actualities to change, our models and patterns for the arrangement of instruction might change also, and we might surprise ourselves by discovering that we knew better all along.

Programmed Instruction

Those of us who worked in the field remember that rather quickly, the machine itself was set aside and supplanted by the paper-and-pencil booklet called "programmed instruction." This step was even defended by some as a true advance: "It's the program that counts," they would say; "the machine is merely a page-turner." This statement, wrapped as it was in the lingo of anti-mechanical humanism, perpetuated a fundamental mistake. The machine as a controller of contingencies was lost, and we had to worry about masks and sliders to cover the answers in programmed books, or the arrangement of programmed texts so that answers to frames were only to be found by turning pages. We had to worry as well about the honesty of students, peeking, and the rest of it. We became skilled at writing initial exhortations to students not to "cheat," as they would learn more in the long run by composing their answers before looking at the printed one, etc.

"Revisions" of Operant Theory

The loss of the strict contingency brought in its wake not merely the unsatisfactory compromises of the programmed textbook format, but also subjected us to pressures to represent as "operant conditioning theory" statements which had little if any laboratory backup. Perhaps the central tenet of this kind was the notion that seeing the correct answer would reinforce the student who had obtained the correct answer, and would also correct the misunderstanding which had led to any incorrect answer.

On the first point, Donald H. Bullock (personal communication) carried out a study in Sweden in which obtaining a look at the correct answer to a frame was given a slight cost—five button-pushes were required to see it. The student had the option of continuing, without this slighly "costly" feedback, to the next frame. At the same time, each student was asked to rate his or her confidence in his or her constructed response. The finding was that the effort to see the correct response took place most often when confidence in one's own response was low. Not a surprising result, perhaps, but what does this do to the notion that "good programmed instruction should generate a low rate of error"?

The view that the correct answer constitutes adequate or appropriate feedback remains quite general in the world of educational practice. I believe it to be not only wrong but also injurious. It is widely held because any alternative requires a more serious level of individualization, a stop to the unrushing pace of mass-level instruction. The group instructor must stop a class and probe and prompt when a student cannot answer, and must also pay attention to the individual differences in that class. Even a private tutor, or a teaching machine, must have recourse to some minimal theory of "trouble-shooting" an incorrect answer, which calls upon a method of identifying what is missing and then remediates to the point at which the correct answer emerges.

The practitioners of programmed instruction also had to defend the lack of "branching"—instructional moves dependent upon the response made at any given step.

All of these problems were addressed in one breathless formulation: Branching was absent, and steps were small, so that the error rate would be low, and the correct response served sufficiently well as a reinforcer, and as a correcter also of any rare mistakes that did happen, since the step was sufficiently small so that the correct answer would suffice without further elaboration!

If the consequence of these practices was programs with steps *so* small as to be wasteful or boring, that was the inevitable cost of a highy reliable instructional technique.

A Five-Point "Credo"

The reasoning above soon formalized itself into a five-point "credo" for programmed instruction:

1. **Small Steps.** The program advanced knowledge of the subject in a series of small and well-ordered steps.

2. **Active Response.** Each step ended with a requirement for an active response from the learner, in which the new material was integrated with that previouly learned and put to use.

3. **Immediate Feedback.** The response to each step was followed by immediate feedback to the learner. As we have seen, the only form of feedback that was considered seriously (and therefore defended theoretically) was the correct response.

4. **Self-pacing.** Each learner progressed at "his own best pace," free from the constraints of instruction in a group. A possible subtlety here, namely, whether the flexibility of timing pertained to the time required to complete a response to a frame, or alternatively to the time interval between successive frames, was rarely discussed.

5. **Low Error Rate from Learners Due to Cycles of Test-and-Revision.** The commitment to empiricism appears here. Primarily salutary, it nonetheless deserves some immediate sobering comment. The slogan was often repeated with an enthusiasm that might have aroused suspicion in some. "Programs are tested on actual students," it was said. What might be the alternative to "actual" students? It was said, "The test-revise cycle may take place from two to nine times." Nine times? I would guess that by nine cycles of testing and revision, something was drifting badly—the objectives of the program, the management team, the type of students being tested—something! Most testing and revision was carried out on a small number of subjects, and in parallel with editing. The wide range of possibilities that might result from testing and editing was never fully formalized: One might improve the instructional frames, one might remove certain difficult objectives, one might raise higher the level of prerequisites required to begin the program—these options all deserve a look in clear and steady light. One of the few treatments to take a broad view worthy of consultation today is the work of Susan M. Markle (1967).

1. **Small Steps.** It would be possible to mock this "credo" in several ways. For example: What is the measure of "small" in small steps? Might it not be that "small" steps are achieved by incorporating such prompting of the correct answer, that this correct answer can be obtained without learning what new material there might be on the frame? We soon came to call such frames "overprompted" or "overcued." Markle called them "idiot frames."

The vision of "steps so small as to generate no errors" was haunting. The distinction between steps which were small but truly taught something, and steps which were so overprompted as to make for no steps at all—this distinction could never be clarified in a satisfactory manner. In both cases, it might be that no errors were generated, but for strikingly different reasons. The possibility that learners might "get frames right but for the wrong reasons" became like the fear of the Evil One—hard to detect but always ready to bring destruction to the instructional process.

Measures were finally developed to address these problems, which will be discussed below. These measures remain important today, and their critical nature remains insufficiently appreciated.

2. **Active Response.** The active response requirement served both a pedagogical and an accounting function. The latter lay in the fact that an empirical record was generated in which errors (or subtle variations in response format) could be identified for the sake of program evaluation and repair. The case for the pedagogical function was more complex: was it really true that an overt form of each resonse was required? Well, perhaps that depended upon step size, and we are thus returned to another issue. Some research of James Holland (1967), and also of Eigen and Margulies (1963) shed some light upon the conditions under which active responses can make a difference.

Educational applications of psychological principles often take on an unconditional "all-or-none" quality: If the principle is worth attending to, then it must never be violated. As a result, some subtleties of the original theory may be swept aside. A major aspect of research with operant behavior has been to show that rather infrequent deliveries of reinforcement may serve to keep responses at high strength—at least as measured by the rate of emission. The variety of "ratio" and "interval" schedules—with "fixed" and "variable" versions of each, was first hinted at in Skinner's *Behavior of Organisms* (Skinner, 1938), amplified in great detail in the Ferster and Skinner (1957) *Schedules of Reinforcement,* and has remained a staple of fascinating and important research in the operant laboratory. But practices derived from the consideration of schedules of reinforcement have been given little play in the more open educational setting.

As early as 1962, Cook suggested that useful effects might be obtained if responses could be "brought to strength" but not always demanded. The learner would indicate, via a given "ready" response, that he/she was prepared to emit the response on demand, and would then be informed, depending upon the schedule in operation, whether the response would be requested in the given instance. The use of such a schedule of "intermittent demand for overt responses" might be expected to have two effects: (a) time would be saved to the extent that responses were skipped without emission; and (b) possibly the practice in bringing responses to the point of emission which yet remain covert might strengthen the definition and precision of the kind of covert behavior required for effective thinking.

Speculations such as these, despite their plausible basis in well-known elements of a theory of behavior, have been allowed to drift untested as broader hypotheses have moved into the spotlight and then out again. It seems clear that one reason for the neglect is that studies of this type would require the instrumentation afforded by prototypic laboratory teaching machines. The required ongoing link between laboratory investigations and instructional applications was not forged.

3. Immediate Feedback. Criticism has already been made of the claim that "knowing the correct answer" acts as a reinforcer if the response was correct, and as a corrective if it was not. In programmed instruction, the effect of self-paced progress to the next step is preserved, regardless of the informational feedback given. This feature of self-paced instruction— even if the contingencies are otherwise loose—seems to have become widely appreciated, and could be said to have been absorbed by many approaches to instruction which are not otherwise very rigorously defined.

4. Self-pacing. The possibility of self-pacing, then, could be seen as an important kind of "feedback," with reinforcing and motivating effects. A possible subtlety here—whether the flexibility of timing implied by the term "self-pacing" pertained to the time required to complete responding to a frame, or alternatively to the time interval between successive frames was rarely discussed. Even studies employing teaching machines of some kind almost never recorded data on response latency to successive frames (most machines had no such provision), and none, in my recollection, employed latency measures as part of the criterion for the "correctness" of the response.

This restricted attention to time intervals, typical of most of the early work with programmed instruction, stands in contrast to the current emphasis seen in a more recent crystallization of work from the operant laboratory, "Precision Teaching." This topic is explored in a separate chapter in this book, written by its founder and chief exponent, Ogden R. Lindsley, one of the early workers in Skinner's labs, who sought practical applications based directly upon the central measures studied in operant behavior. The measure seen as central by Lindsley is rate of response—expressed as number of instances per unit of time. The field of Precision Teaching takes as its main instructional objective the generation of high rates of the kinds of behavior that are defined as desirable. In so doing, it sets itself off from educational concerns which emphasize the accuracy of desired behavior, measured as "percent correct," and even from a concern with avoiding high rates of inaccurate behavior—at least at first.

The emphasis is: Get relevant behavior going vigorously, and it can be shaped and sharpened and tuned later. Techniques which stress the attainment of high rates of desired behavior have begun to be labeled as "fluency" measures, and a considerable literature is now developing in this area. Discussion of the fine points of this emphasis might be most valuable, but here we will merely note that the interest in rate is indeed traceable to a basic measurement technique of the operant laboratory, and that it was not to be found in most work with teaching machines or programmed instruction.

There is still some feeling that the measurement of rate and the attainment of high rates are impeded by the mechanics of teaching machines, even in their modern dress as computers, because of the use of "frames." These take up much of the screen, each requests a response to one defined step, and each entails varied mechanics in the transition from one screen to the next. It is worth stressing that this restriction can be eliminated if desired. Ian Spence (Spence & Hively, 1993) has developed a computer-based teaching system which implements Precision Teaching methods, including the use of problem sets in which high rates of student response can be generated, accommodated, and measured. Each "screen" contains a number of problems of the desired type—performing a subtraction in arithmetic, for example—and the student responds to the array as rapidly as he or she can. Using this specially adapted screen, there is little impact from inter-screen transition time upon the flow of behavior, or its appropriate measurements.

A nice feature of this instrumentation is that the same screen can be used to present, to the same student, graphs showing the progression of the very rates of behavior—correct and incorrect plotted separately—which he or she has been generating.

Before leaving the topic of Precision Teaching, it may be worth noting that the method has been most intensely applied to learning tasks in which children must speak aloud—as in early reading—and in which the parsing of the required behavior has depended upon the skills of teachers who can listen to the spoken utterances and in some way reinforce or correct the behavior. This kind of teaching exchange has not been instrumented at all until very recently, and the technology for doing so is still relatively crude and very expensive. Thus, it might be possible that conflicting evaluations about the relative merits of one application of operant learning methods over another have at least some of their origins in the state of the art of technological automation, rather than differences in "theory" or in "schools of thought."

We have mentioned two distinct time-intervals of possible importance in self-paced learning: (a) the latency between presentation of an instructional step and the commencement or completion of the behavior appropriate to that step; and (b) the interval between the completion of a given step and the inception of the next one. Rather than ask to which of these intervals does the term "self-pacing" apply, it might be more productive to attend henceforth to the distinction, and possibly give these two measures distinguishing names, such as "latency" for the first, and "ISI" ("interstep interval") for the second, respectively. Typical programmed instruction studies conflated latencies and ISIs. But with contemporary computer-based teaching instrumentation, it is possible to become much more refined, and on a routine basis.

We not only note that "behavioral" methods are not identical, but that at times they seem to be in conflict with each other. To some, the philosophy of "self-pacing" is seen as antithetical to the aim of producing rapid behavior. Close analysis will reveal that this need not be so, despite the momentum of tradition. We need to recognize both intervals in instruction: an intra-trial latency or reaction time, and the ISI. The magnitude of the intra-trial latency may enter into the specification of objectives as a fluency criterion; if many similar problems are presented seriatim, then latencies blur into a rate; if it is presumed that no stimulus is playing a role, then the rate seems even more natural.

In contrast, the ISI is a pause within which the events may be unspecified. This does not mean that there are no events! Important cases arise in any examination of yet another method deriving from the operant tradition: the Personalized System of Instruction (PSI) of Fred S. Keller and J. G. Sherman (Keller, 1968; Sherman & Ruskin, 1978). That method, as with Precision Teaching, is treated in a separate chapter [Semb], and will not be extensively examined here. But we must note the varieties of ISI which can take place in PSI. In such a course, for example, the interval between attempts at unit mastery quizzes may be filled with restudy of a failed unit, new study of the next unit, or a trip to Venezuela. If one plots graphs only of units successfully passed (as is typical in the recording of PSI data), it is not possible to tell whether any given ISI is made up of study behavior, failed attempts at the same unit, behavior outside of the domain of the course, or any mixture of these ingredients. Experience with PSI will render familiar all of these alternatives. In theory, also, PSI could incorporate fluency into its toolkit: I have worked with the Columbia University School of Oral and Dental Surgery on the PSI version of a course in prosthodontics, in which one of the unit quizzes consisted in the task of making a cast of the mouth before the material hardened. The speed of making the cast was critical, while the interval between attempts was not part of the criterion.

5. Low Error Rate. Despite the frequent invocation of the "low error rates" as a desirable quality of effective programs, attained as a result of the testing and revision of several versions, few studies were published which either examined the meaning of the term, or offered guidelines on the use of error data to correct or improve programs.

In attempting to define "low" in some satisfactory manner, it becomes evident that a zero error-rate may be difficult to obtain, especially if learners emit some errors for reasons other than faults in the program. My own rough experience with a number of programs began to suggest to me that error rates might vary between nearly zero and as high as 10 or 15%, and that if these levels of error were fairly random in their distribution, variations in error rate might remain uncorrelated with achievement on final examination.

Thus, it seemed worthwhile to consider an alternative approach wherein errors may occur, but are not ascribed to the program if they are random—if they are not systematically positioned in the program frames. However, if a large number of subjects provide data during testing, and if their error data are combined, some piling up of errors would take place by chance, and should not impugn the program itself. The problem is to determine that level.

The problem is one in which errors have a low probability (an error on any given frame is unlikely), but a large number of opportunities to occur (because there are many frames in the program). The limiting case of this type—in which p approaches zero and n approaches infinity, but their product n*p has a real value—is the Poisson distribution. That distribution can be put to use in assessing error patterns in programmed instruction.

Cook (1992) studied three programs, each about 800 frames in length, tested on learner populations ranging from 12 to 40 in size. "Set Theory" was tested with 6th, 7th, and 8th graders. "Chemistry" was tested with high-school students. "Wide Area Telephone Service" was tested with phone company employees. Testing was carried out in supervised settings, over several days within a week's time. Materials were printed and responses handwritten, answers to each frame were provided under a mask which could be moved after responding. Progress was self-paced. No help was given by supervising staff, and written work was collected immediately upon completion.

Comprehensive final exams were administered to each student upon completion of the teaching program. For each frame, the total number of errors made by the test population was determined. For each program, these numbers served as the basis of a distribution of the relative frequency of each value for "number of errors." The average number of errors for each distribution was taken as n*p, which is the single determining parameter of the Poisson distribution. Theoretical Poisson values were calculated and superimposed upon the empirical distributions (Parsons, 1974).

All programs taught well, yielding over 90% of each learner group scoring over 90% on the exams. Overall error rates, on a subject-by-subject basis, ranged between a few percent to about 15 percent.

The Poisson functions matched the empirical curves well in all three cases. The pattern of discrepancy, however, was the same for all three distributions: (a) There were more cases of no errors than expected in the Poisson calculation; (b) there were fewer cases of 3–5 errors than expected by Poisson; (c) there were more cases of 6 or 7 errors than expected by Poisson. These last frames identified under (c), then, seem to be the ones to focus upon in making corrections.

It might seem obvious in revising a program to first address the most frequent errors. The Poisson method refines the obvious by suggesting a cutoff value dependent upon different average error rates and number of subjects employed. One can draw a line at error-rates which can be regarded as random.

Two warnings are in order: (1) The frame collecting the errors need not be the locus of the problem; (2) In locating the problem, the nature of the errors, as well as the degree of uniformity among the errors, should also be consulted.

Procedures of this type illustrate the use of mathematical or statistical methods, which should not be dogmatically banished from a science of behavior. I say this in an attempt to counter a bias, whose source is also the operant laboratory, that with sufficiently powerful experimental "control" of the subject matter—the behavior of organisms—results are so "overwhelming" that recourse to statistical methods is never of use.

A more sophisticated conception of "low error rate" may become useful in the testing of computer-based learning material, especially as multi-tasking environments simplify the collection of data while programs are being tested.

The other aspect of this problem—how to use error data to correct or improve instructional programs—has also been given little attention. One exception is the study by Stolurow and Frinche (1966).

Some Lessons from PI for Today's ID

Stimuli and the Instructional Contingency

We have said that the contributions to instructional design from the operant laboratory could be grouped under the two rubrics of (a) contingency and (b) sequence. Considerable discussion has been devoted to the ways in which the strict contingencies embodied in the very first teaching machines were compromised in the third machine, and even further in programmed instruction.

But despite its compromises, programmed instruction worked well under certain conditions. In part, this may be due to the fact that even weak or "loose" contingencies made themselves felt in contrast to the relative passivity of most instructional activities. But another part was no doubt due to the attention given to the sequencing of instruction, even in the face of loose contingencies. As methods of writing programmed instruction developed, a great deal was learned about the development of teaching sequences. Though we couldn't control our contingencies tightly, we could—and did—work on the stimulus control side of the process. Much was learned that is little used by today's practitioners of "instructional technology."

A set of memoranda written by Francis Mechner for use in the programming department of Basic Systems Incorporated remains, in my opinion, the best codification of knowledge about the problem of writing instructional "frames" which "give the answer away" by some form of prompting (Mechner, 1961a, 1961b, 1963, 1967). Overprompted frames (also called overcued, giveaway, copy, or "idiot" frames) allow the learner to emit the correct response for the wrong reasons. The result may be a low error rate—but only until a criterion or exam question comes along, for the required transfer of stimulus control has probably failed to take place. Mechner's memoranda described in detail many types of defective prompting, and showed how such frames could be repaired. Unfortunately, the Mechner material was never fully published.

As we learned how to avoid giveaway frames, we came to see that the trend-setting *Analysis of Behavior* by James Holland and B. F. Skinner (1961)—an influential model if there ever was one—contained many examples of the frames we saw as problematical. An example is presented in Figure 1.

In this sequence, Frame 2 tells the student to replace the term reward with its "technical" equivalent, "reinforcement." The third frame shifts the example from food to water, and asks for the "technical" term. For this frame to "work," several assumptions must hold: that the learner can generalize from the food to the water example of acts that reinforce behavior, that the shift from the active verb to the passive form will take place (just as the shift from noun form to verb is assumed in Frame 2), and that the term "technically" has gained

Frame	Correct Answer
1. Performing animals are sometimes trained with "rewards." The behavior of a hungry animal can be "rewarded" with _____.	food
2. A technical term for "reward" is reinforcement. To "reward" an organism with food is to _____ it with food.	reinforce
3. Technically speaking, a thirsty organism can be _____	reinforced with water

Figure 1. Three frames from an early teaching program (Holland & Skinner, 1961).

control as a prompt. However, the frame might still be answered correctly for another reason—the answer desired was the correct answer for the last frame (barring the shift in tense)! The temptation is strong in writing programs to compensate for possible problems in the teaching sequence by presenting cues which permit correct answers without mastery. In this case the prompt, as described by Mechner, is sequential.

A ruthless determination to answer Frames 2 and 3 correctly without learning much about operant behavior could employ this advice:

For Frame 2:

If a new term is introduced and defined, it will be the correct answer to the frame that introduces it.

(Some frame-writers provide the extra prompt of putting the new term in italics!)

For Frame 3:

The same new term is likely to be the correct answer for several frames in a row.

Early programmed instruction was rich in overprompting. But so is much that transpires in the attempt to teach. The fine-grained records provided by this new endeavor make that truth quite visible for the first time. Many interactive sequences on today's computers reveal the very same defect.

The principles at stake in frame design were further clarified by Stuart Margulies' work, *Some General Rules of Frame Construction* (Margulies, 1963). He begins by contrasting two frames which are superficially similar (Figure 2). Both are "easy" to answer correctly, and

Frame with Critical Information	Correct Answer
* is the equivalent of plus 4 * 3 = _____	7
Frame with Non-Critical Information	
* is the equivalent of plus 4 + 3 = _____	7

Figure 2. Frames illustrating critical and non-critical use of the same information. From Margulies (1963).

Criterion Frame	Correct Answer
7 * 11 = _____	18

Figure 3. A criterion frame. The likelihood of a correct answer is higher if preceded by a frame in which the information is critical (see Figure 2).

yield the desirable low error rate. But when the learner confronts a criterion frame (Figure 3), only one of the earlier teaching frames will reliably be followed by a correct answer here.

Thus, it is not sufficient, in producing "transfer of stimulus control," for the old and new stimulus to be merely contiguous in space and time. If we hold with a two-factor model of learning, we would say that the mere pairing of stimuli in a Pavlovian procedure can't be counted upon to "transfer" control. Adherents of operant conditioning might say "Of course; learning from programmed instruction is an operant process." Yet, paradoxically, we can detect the ghost of Pavlovian thinking in the very phrasing of some of the concepts that emerged in the early days of programmed instruction. Terms such as "fading" or "vanishing" of stimuli suggest—not definitively, to be sure—that it is the intensive properties of the original stimulus which is critical, and that can be "faded" as the new stimulus takes control. To speak this way is almost to invoke the laws of reflexes.

I offer as an example of "reflex-like" thinking the analysis of how control gets transferred from one stimulus to another. Is this a Pavlovian process of pairing, or is there a discriminative aspect? If the latter, then "fading" is not a function of the intensity of the stimulus.

Israel (1960) had suggested, and had experimented with, a technique of fading or vanishing of stimuli (letters which spell a word) in which the physical intensity or clarity of outline is gradually diminished (by derangement of a focusing mechanism which leads to blurring of the pattern). I questioned (Cook, 1960) the analysis underlying the method: "Are we to assume that presenting a stimulus nearer and nearer threshold value acts to strengthen the response it controls? An alternative explanation appears equally plausible. For some subjects, this procedure may act, or come to act, as a warning that this position of the stimulus will disappear 'soon.' In the presence of such a warning, rehearsal to strengthen that fragment will be reinforced. If this is correct, it would be simpler to teach directly in the program a warning signal which would signalize the impending disappearance."

We have learned to say that a critical feature of the study of operant behavior lies in the role of the three-term contingency relating stimulus, response, and reinforcement. Yet we still have difficulty in applying this paradigm to a complex stimulus field, and fall back upon a model based primarily upon pairing. Here lies the path to the experimental analysis of cognitive phenomena—a path still awaiting our exploration.

Stimulus Control and the Editing of Instruction

The principles formulated by Mechner and Margulies were restated by Donald H. Bullock in an editing language, used by course developers in the description, evaluation, and improvement of instructional sequences. The system is described in Editing System for Self-Instructional Material (Bullock *et al.*, 1973). This editing language contains terms which name significant features of interactive instruction.

An example: the term "non-crit" identifies the material in a frame which is apparently of importance but which can be skipped in getting to the correct answer. The usual reason that important material "can be skipped" is that the frame is overcued. Strictly, the editor does not judge whether the material is important or not—but merely identifies the presence of material which can be ignored in responding correctly to this specific frame. (Whether it is "safe" to ignore this material in the light of future frames is another question.) Often the material which the editor finds to be "non-crit" is in fact important, but has not been critical to obtaining a correct answer, thanks to the presence of other material which overprompts that answer. An editor using this system simply circles all "non-crit" material, labels it "nc," and returns it to the author. The author must then decide whether the material labeled "nc" is in fact important. Specifically, will later frames build upon it? Will a criterion frame ask for it? If the answer is no, the "nc" material can be eliminated. But if it is yes—and this is more usual—then the author rewrites in such a way as to render the "nc" material critical to obtaining the correct response. This is often done by removing the over-prompting material.

A second important edit is "no-pri," short for "no prior strength." If a question is asked on a frame which cannot be answered on the basis of responding to the previous frames, this question or request will be labeled "no-pri. Typically, "non-crits" in a teaching sequence are followed by subsequent frames which lead editors to use the code "no-pri." In more everyday terms: material which needn't have been attended to when originally encountered will probably not be remembered when later asked for directly. The iron law of ineffective instruction can thus be given this terse statement: Non-crits are followed by no-pri's. When repairing this situation as a result of instructional editing, no-pri's need not be re-written, if the non-crit's are re-written so that the important material is rendered critical.

Does It Matter? Some Evidence

During the period when the above principles were formulated, two studies examined the impact of good interactive writing upon the resulting learning. In the first study, by Eigen and Margulies (1963), students were asked to learn three three-letter words through exposure to four successive frames. The words to be learned were of three kinds: (a) unfamiliar, unpronounceable groups of consonants; (b) pronounceable but meaningless groups of consonant-vowel-consonant; and (c) familiar meaningful words. (The familiar words were called "low-information" and the unfamiliar, unpronounceable words were called "high information." The meaningful words are low in information because they are familiar, their appearance is not a surprise, they are somewhat predictable; the strange words are high in information their appearance most surprises us.) In all cases, the request for a response was followed by the correct answer. The three words were always embedded in a seven-word sequence, and constituted the middle three of the seven. The purpose of the four "extra" words was to serve as "incidental" material to ask for on the posttest.

The posttest asked for all seven of the words. It was thus like a final exam which asks for the material you have studied intensively but also asks about information in footnotes in the text which was never even mentioned in class. In terms of the edit-code vocabulary, it asked for material which was critical in each of the previous frames but also for the non-critical material. In Bullock's language, part of the posttest could be labeled "no-pri."

Results demonstrated that the low-information words were the most fully learned of the three types of words. The next highest percentage correct was for the intermediate information words, and the least best learned words were those strange words of highest information level. Next, for all information levels, the best learning took place when the responses were overt and relevant. This is the critical case of the well-written frame, which asks for a response and makes the important information relevant to getting that response right. The ideal conditions are those in which the response is both overt and relevant. The request for active responding is helpful if it pertains to relevant material, and most of all if that material is novel or has high-information-value. Where covert responding is used, it is not surprising that better learning takes place under conditions of relevance than with incidental material. But the final contrast is interesting: When overt responses are employed and incidental material is asked for, learning seems inferior to when covert responding is used. It's as if the emphasis on the response drew attention away from the other material—which, it turns out, was what you were supposed to know. The authors applied statistical tests of significance to this data and concluded conservatively: "It may be concluded that overt responses are superior to covert responses only if a relevant response is called for and the information value is not low" (Eigen & Margulies, 1963, p. 52).

The practical implications of this study seem to be that the value of interactive responding in CAI or CBT will be realized only if the instructional design is good, i.e., if the response is relevant to the material, or to put it the other way around, that the material is critical to the response. Otherwise, the response adds little and may even detract. This impact is greatest when the material has high or intermediate information, i.e., is unfamiliar. There the response requirement can multiply the amount learned by five- or six-fold. This gain is much smaller with low-information or familiar material, where the material is so easy to learn that it is inefficient to invest in the technology of CBT.

A second study, by James Holland, is less well-controlled, but uses lengthy instructional programs from the real world (Holland, 1967). Twelve such programs were used, each several hundred frames long, covering such topics as statistics, electricity, set theory, functional wiring of IBM office machines, and diagnosis of myocardial infarction by electro-encephalograph. Since these were existing products, Holland could not create or change the nature of the frames they presented. Instead, he measured them, choosing for his study those programs that were high and low in his measure. Holland's measure, the "blackout ratio," is defined as the percent of the material in the program which could be "blacked out"—literally covered up or omitted, while still permitting the learner to answer the frame correctly. Thus, material blacked out in a frame is the same as the material labeled "non-crit" in a Bullock edit. The blackout ratio is high if much of the material is non-critical to obtaining the correct response on a frame-by-frame basis. Blacked-out material may be important in the final sense that it will be asked for on criterion frames. Holland's subjects studied these programs, not being told anything about their blackout ratios. Each program was encountered by two groups of learners. In one group, learners made the requested written responses; in the control group, the answers were supplied, written into the appropriate spaces beforehand, and learners were asked to "read these programs and learn the material." As each learner completed his or her program, a post-test was given. Holland's question was: Did overt responding make a difference as contrasted to reading, and if so, was this difference related to the program's blackout ratio?

The answer was: For the four programs with lowest blackout ratios, overt responding produced superior learning, when contrasted with the results for the versions which were merely "read and studied." For the remaining eight programs—all with higher blackout ratios—the difference between responding and reading had no significant impact on the amount learned. The changeover point came at a blackout ratio between 30 and 35%—programs with lower blackout ratios profited from learner response; with higher blackout ratios it did not matter.

Holland says: "When the answer given by the subject has little or no relationship to the critical content of the item it does not matter whether the subject writes an answer, thinks an answer, or answers not at all. It is only when the critical content serves as a contingency for correct answers that the overt response is important" (p. 220).

These studies suggest that any interactive instructional material can be critically reviewed by moving quickly through samples of it, asking yourself, "How much of this am I able to get right without really understanding what's going on?" This is the blackout test, or the edit for non-crits. The results can be devastating.

As a one-time employee of Basic Systems Incorporated, I cannot resist the temptation to state that the four "winning" programs in the Holland study were all products of that company. The eight "losers" were all products of other organizations. Not for nothing was Basic

Systems the company of Francis Mechner, Stuart Margulies, and Donald Bullock (all, incidentally, products of Columbia's Psychology Department).

Both the Eigen-Margulies and the Holland experiments show that effective programmed instruction does not owe its power to "blind responding" of the sort that critics like to ascribe to operant theorists, but rather to the relationship between the response which is required and the material which that requirement makes critical. This is the three-term contingency of the discriminated operant, and it is the basis of the link to cognitive processes. As this awareness became salient, while at the same time the torrent of poorly written programs continued unabated, it became fashionable to deny the term "program" to those products which exhibited no behavioral design—or at least to use the term "program" in quotes, or to call them by a derogatory term, such as "Swiss-cheese programs."

Today's teaching programs, presented by computer-assisted instruction, present the same challenges to applied learning theory, and the incidence of well-designed materials is no more common or frequent than it was in the heyday of programmed instruction. In my own workshops on instructional design, I teach aspiring CBT writers the same principles. Often I dramatize them as the "perverse student edit." The perverse student, who wants to get out of a course with as little effort as possible, attacks a frame this way: She looks first at the blank to be filled in or question to be answered, then scans back for the minimal material absolutely needed to fill that in. With an abundance of overprompted material, response blanks can be filled in with little effort and less behavior change of the sort called learning. A preponderance of material is "non-crit" and can be "blacked out." If there is much such material, the programming is poor. Exposure to the perverse student edit—and revisions based thereon—can make a valuable contribution to the education of an instructional designer and writer.

Behavioral Analysis as a Paradigm for ID

The "Instructional Package": Some Examples

One's biases are nowhere better revealed than in the choices one makes in selecting "first events" which begin a new epoch. This caveat stated, I proceed to list B. F. Skinner's 1954 article, "The Science of Learning and the Art of Teaching," as the key germinal paper in the field of modern behavioral analysis. Between 1954 and 1958, Skinner published three papers which established the concepts of teaching machines and the application of laws of learning to the development of instructional programs which should teach a wide range of subjects via such machines.

In 1960, the first signal success was reported: the Hollins College experiment, in which algebra had been taught by teaching machine in a nearby school in Roanoke, Virginia. The chief result of this study was that an eighth grade class completed ninth-grade algebra in half a school year, without exception, and entirely thanks to the programs on the machines (Rushton, 1963). A non-profit clearinghouse—the Center for Programmed Instruction—was set up with Carnegie Corporation funds; in short order, newletters, workshops, and a journal helped spread the word of the new technology and its promise.

By 1960 also, the first companies had appeared whose business was to produce teaching machines and the associated teaching programs for use in such machines. At the same time, "programmed instruction" made its appearance; here one saw the organization of lessons into sequences of printed small steps in book-like bound format, which could be distributed and used without a machine. In such programmed texts, spaces were provided for student responses at each step, and feedback in the form of "the correct answer" was also given. About 60 programmed steps could be completed in an hour, and a book-sized teaching program might contain 800 such steps. To prevent the student from spying the correct answer before responding—or while responding—elaborate sliders, masks, page-turning printing formats, and even invisible inks have been used along with programmed texts. A number of publishers, hesitant at making the full leap into the world of teaching machines, published these programmed texts. They felt they had grasped the essentials.

However, it cannot be said that a unified and purposeful group of researchers and practitoners came into existence. Rival groups disputed with a viciousness worthy of the most acid scorn of a Swift pamphlet. Differences in emphasis and interest were represented to be profound differences in concept, model, or perhaps both concept and model. New and grandiose expressions for old if inexact notions were accorded the status of revolutionary paradigm shifts.

Today, in the face of dissatisfaction with the achievements of the current educational system in the United States, a ferment has developed in which alternative approaches compete for a chance to show what they can do. Sorting out the competing claims is not easy for several reasons. The competing claims often concern different levels of the educational system: In the battles of private sector vs. public sector schools, we hear little of what is to be taught; battles of diversity vs. American value curricula do not tell us how anything, once chosen, will be taught or learned. Battles among advocates of whole word learning, whole language learning, and phonic-linguistic approaches to reading do not tell us whether students will employ books, filmstrips, teaching machines, or shouting in unison. These confusions of level of analysis are worse than "mixing apples and oranges"—these can at least be counted, and also, they can be eaten with some expectation of nourishment.

Among the alternatives scrambling for a hearing in this messy confusion are those approaches calling themselves "behavioral." This has become a term somewhat cut loose from a clear definition, but it is employed with conviction bordering on the passionate, at least by its advocates. Despite claims to a unified position, we find not one behavioral approach, but a number of them. Well-known examples are: programmed instruction, the Personalized System of Instruction (PSI or Keller Plan), Precision Teaching, Direct Instruction, CABAS (comprehensive application of behavior analysis to instruction), and (to some degree) computer-based instruction.

This list might not be complete, but it is pretty representative. Some behavior analysts would question the legitimacy of some entries in this list: The developers of Direct Instruction do not speak the behaviorist language (the term I keep hearing among some of my colleagues is "they do not speak and write carefully"), but since their methods have racked up strong results and a good track record, Direct Instruction is allowed into the club. To me, the great strength of Direct Instruction is that it contains positive principles of the design of instructional sequences. This is a feature of instruction in which behavior analysis is not notably strong, rarely going beyond the injunction that instructional sequences should be developed "carefully." Note that inhibiting term again; sometimes it is said that the steps in instructional sequences should be "small"—also not too well defined. (And one notable figure in the educational revolution, Thomas F. Gilbert, claimed that, on the contrary, steps should be "as large as possible." A meliorist theorist could argue that there is really no contradiction here, and that, for the organisms for whom we usually develop instructional programs, the largest steps possible are—small).

Another item whose place on the list is often questioned is computer-based instruction. The statement is made that this term refers to an interactive delivery technique, independent of the quality of the instructional material so delivered. This is correct, and so the concept of good CBT vs. bad CBT has a legitimate place in any discussion. But let us extend this notion: Is there such a thing as bad programmed instruction in addition to good programmed instruction? This is not a small matter in the history of programmed instruction and in the analysis of its fate. You will hear that the mere fact of interaction, active responding, and feedback in programmed instruction (as in computer-based instruction) is no guarantor of effective learning. The hint emerges, then, that there are underlying principles which should guide the use of these methods.

Is there, then, such a thing as bad Direct Instruction as well as good? Is bad Precision Teaching a possibility as well as good? *Aficionados* of these schools of thought may feel that bad instances are impossible almost by definition. It is as if one believed the Anselm proof of God, which states that the very definition of His perfection implies existence, and that no further evidence is necessary.

It is my sense that each of us has his or her strongest historical attachments, depending upon the corner of the educational revolution in which each has encountered the most thrilling visions, the greatest chapters of growth, or even moments of disillusion. For those behavioral packages from which we are most distant, we readily admit of the distinction between better instances of that method and less well-done cases. But for those packages on which we were ourselves fed and weaned, we tend to be convinced that the method of persisting interest to us embodies the underlying principle, so that the method we champion is by definition good, since if the important underlying principles are not incorporated, the "example" is not really an example of the package under discussion.

I have been speaking of packages on the one hand, and underlying principles on the other. Let me crystallize one of my main points now by saying that the terms listed above—programmed instruction, PSI, Precision Teaching, Direct Instruction, CABAS, and CBT—are the names of packages. The name on the outside of a package is often an uncertain guide to the contents to be found inside the package. Continuing the analogy, the contents inside the package are the underlying principles which make any instance of an educational method good or not good.

The Recurring Issue of Strict vs. Loose Contingencies

The shift from a strong to a weak contingency with the correct answer as feedback and the consequent emergence of trials to criterion of few errors are not unique to the work of B. F. Skinner. In fact, it plagues the history of psychology. Usually, though, matters are the other way around. The weak contingency existed long before the strong, and has long characterized the field of human verbal learning. The standard serial learning list from Ebbinghaus on—and its cousin the paired associate, are typically presented—as in the case of the memory drum—with a pause for a response to each stimulus, followed by the correct answer, no matter what, and on a strict timetable to boot. For long, that has been the *paradigm* of learning. Variations might be introduced, such as holding the feedback until some response is made, or repeating only those items missed (as with Skinner's disk teaching machine); but these were icing on the cake of uncontingent confirmation and trials to a criterion.

The alternative view—the use of a strict contingency—entered psychology with research on animals. With animals one could neither show nor tell, and so the game changed to wait and reinforce. The change can be detected in the work of Thorndike, who waited, and who therefore measured time instead of trials to criterion. Even Thorndike did not wait forever, as can be seen in the following: "In many cases the animal failed in some trial to perform the act in ten or fifteen minutes and was then taken out by me. Such failures are denoted by a break in the curve either at its start or along its course" (Thorndike, 1898).

The competing models of strong contingencies and weak contingencies with repetition and a criterion, can be seen in the work of reinforcement psychologists other than Skinner. I refer once again to Fred S. Keller's "code-voice" method of teaching the reception of Morse Code: The student listens to a code signal transmitted through earphones, then writes a best guess of the corresponding character on specially ruled paper, then, after a brief pause, hears a voiced statement of the character through the same phones that transmitted the signal. If the guess was correct, the student merely awaits the next signal; if it was wrong, the correct character must be written in a correction space underneath the guess. The three-term contingency of the discriminated operant is clearly present, but it is a weak contingency. The procedure moves on no matter what you wrote, and your own correction is made *after* you've been told what it should be. Of course, the paper cannot parse your response, and scores of trainees were receiving instruction at once. What is less well-known about Keller's procedure as it was employed in practice is this: As trainees progressed on in the system, they moved from one table to another in the training quarters. At each table, messages were being sent at differing speeds, ranging from low to high for the distribution of trainees at that time. All the earphones at any one table carried messages at the same speed. Any given trainee remained copying code at the same table—at a given speed—until a criterion of 90% accuracy was achieved at that speed; only then could he move on to the next table, where messages were sent at a higher speed.

Here again, then, is the theme of the weaker contingency, with the correct answer, backed up by repetitions of that kind of trial until a criterion is reached. The short-run loose contingency is backed up by a stricter long-run contingency. The method resulted in code training superior to any hitherto achieved in the U. S. military forces. The method would now be easy to implement with a computer program which, unlike the ruled paper on which Keller's subjects wrote, *could* parse the response made—presuming the response is typed—and hold to a strict contingency when desired.

The two-fold model is pervasive. When Keller (1968) later developed the PSI method for college course instruction, the same dual process again made its apperance: the short-run contingencies involved in studying, quiz-taking, and tutoring are hardly specified except for the binary aspect of passing or failing attached to each unit quiz; the number of attempts allowed is unlimited; and the long-run contingency—advance only after passing—is strictly enforced. The rule prohibiting movement to a new unit until the prior one has been passed at a high level may be strictly enforced, but the system is less clear about what should happen during the proctorial or tutorial interaction with a student who has failed a given attempt. This fine-grained process is left to the wits, devices, materials, and procedures of the local user of the system. The statement of guidelines offered me informally by J. Gilmour Sherman, co-developer with Fred Keller of PSI, is illuminating: "I give my proctors three rules. One, don't tell them the right answers to questions they have missed. Two, observing the first rule, try everything in your power to get *them* to come up with the right answers themselves. Three, chew a minted chewing gum."

Analysis of Verbal Behavior in a CAI/CBT Environment

I hope that I have convinced the reader that the specific managment of the contingencies of learning in some typical and important applications of instructional technology is a result of a complex blend of ideal theoretical notions—most well-supported in the laboratory—and the practical exigencies of the situation in which the application takes place. The two-model mixture, whatever its roots may be in animal vs. human research, and whatever its theoretical dressing may be in "behaviorist" vs. "cognitive" controversies, is in fact to a large extent a product of non-theoretical actualities. Were these actualities to change, our models and patterns for the arrangement of instruction might change also, and we might surprise ourselves by discovering that we knew better all along.

I shall now try to show that developments in computer programming technology offer a number of actualities which make just such changes possible. To characterize an instructional situation comprised of computer, program, and student, we should have to know perhaps four main groups of functional specifications:

(1) The stimuli which the system can present.
(2) The responses which the system will accept as inputs.
(3) The program's capacities to parse, interpret, or judge those responses.

(4) The consequences which can be produced and made to result from—be contingent upon—the processing of responses carried out in (3).

I am assuming in the above list that we take for granted the capabilities of a modern programming language. That is, we have little trouble in generating control logic to a sufficient degree of complexity.

The question of stimuli appears in both (1) and (4). Beyond assuming that the system can present the usual range of visual stimuli on a screen, I will defer this question until we come to point (4), where it appears as a matter of consequences.

Regarding point (2)—response input—I will today stay with alphanumerics as entered by the keyboard. But I want to point out that the rapidly developing use of touch-sensitive screens and "mouse" pointers greatly widen the range of acceptable reponses to include pointing and touching, which can be parsed with respect to position relative to a display and to temporal properties as well. Thus differential reinforcement of positional responses, response latencies, and other non-alphanumeric behavior becomes possible.

But it is point (3)—the program's capacities to parse or interpret a learner's behavior—especially keyboard behavior—that I see as critical to my theme. I shall sketch out a few examples of what can now be accomplished by some currently available *authoring languages*—computer languages expressly written for the purpose of developing instruction via computer. In the last 20 years, several hundred authoring languages have been developed. Some of these are capable of subtle support for those developing instruction via computer. This support includes the capacity to generate complex stimuli, whether alphanumeric, graphic, animated, or colored, and with sound effects too; but it is the response-judging or parsing capability I want to consider here.

In frame-based instruction, every frame—whether or not it is encountered by any given student—is specifically written by the author in advance of program implementation, and as such, is stored in the program files. (These restrictions may sound obvious, but they do *not* hold in some of the more imaginative "generative" authoring languages now available, nor do they hold in some of the more "artificially intelligent" instructional development systems now coming off the drawing boards.)

The focus on frame-based authoring languages carries the implication that the programming language employed can perform the following functions:

1. Present a screen which "presents information" but will not accept a student response.
2. Present a screen which can present information *and also* accepts student responses on that same screen. (As a default case, the screen can present a "question" alone with no preceding "information.") This type of frame is the key element in interactive instruction.
3. Accept student responses of reasonable complexity, including those called free-form, or open-ended, or constructed responses—as well as multiple-choice and other indicated selections. Ideally, these responses should be storable for both administrative and evaluative purposes. If long-run storage is not possible, short-run storage is necessary for the sake of counting trials.

In addition to the three basic functions just listed, frame-based languages can all—to a greater or lesser degree—check such student responses against stored correct answers, or formats or generators of correct answers, to assess whether the response offered as the correct answer shall be judged correct, partially correct, inappropriate in format (but not counted as "wrong"), wrong in some way which the author has anticipated (each of those ways being spelled out in the judging system), or wrong in any way *not* spelled out (and therefore called "unanticipated"). This functionality of an authoring language has many different names: ex-

DISPLAY PRESENTATION

QUESTION PRESENTATION

ANSWER ENTRY: Multiple-choice, true-false, checkoff, matching, open-ended.

SPECIFICATION OF CORRECT ANSWERS
    FEEDBACK FOR CORRECT ANSWERS

SPECIFICATION OF ANTICIPATED INCORRECT ANSWERS
    FEEDBACK FOR ANTICIPATED INCORRECT ANSWERS
    FEEDBACK FOR UNANTICIPATED ANSWERS

SPECIFICATION OF UNGRADED RESPONSES

SPECIFICATION OF HINT, HELP, OR GLOSSARY REQUESTS

SPECIFICATION OF ADMINISTRATIVE REQUESTS

SPECIFICATION OF TRIAL COUNT AND SUBSET OF APPLICABLE FRAMES
    FEEDBACK WHEN TRIAL LIMIT IS REACHED

BRANCHES FOR
    RIGHT ANSWER
    ANTICIPATED INCORRECT ANSWER
    TRIAL LIMIT EXCEEDED
    ADMINISTRATIVE REQUESTS

Figure 4.   Typical capabilities of CAI/CBT authoring languages.

amples are "answer judging," "parsing," "response evaluation," etc., and the authoring systems available today exhibit a corresponding variety in how they work and how subtle they are.

The frame-based languages typically provide for the categories of student response shown in Figure 4.

A number of these current authoring languages operate interactively with the author—that is, they present prompts from the above list of categories to guide the author as to the nature of the entry expected; they then file the entry given in an appropriate file, and handle the program logic of relating these categories as the student encounters the lesson. The prompts can be ignored and bypassed where not applicable. Often the author can easily toggle back and forth between the authoring mode and the student mode, experiencing as he composes how it will appear to the student for whom he is writing.

As we turn to the specification of anticipated answers—whether correct or incorrect—we come upon the existence of delimiters in these languages which allow us to specify class properties of our answer specifications. Figure 5 shows a number of typical delimiters.

The capability of answer-judging methods in an authoring language, and also the degree of skill with which the user can put answer-judging to work, say much about the quality and flexibility of instruction which will be produced in one's CBT effort. Currently available authoring systems differ significantly from each other in their answer-judging capabilities; further, instructional developers with *any* system seem frequently not to appreciate what can and can't be done with their particular product, and to oscillate between writing impoverished material which hardly stretches their system, and drafting ambitious interactions which their system can't handle.

Here is a test case which will tell you much about how any given authoring system works. The question is "Say whether the number 20 is a prime number, and if it is not, list those divisors which show that it is not prime." The clearcut wrong answer is "yes," but if you're sophisticated you might also want to accept "is prime" or "is a prime" or even "prime" are wrong answers if the word "not" is not also there. If you are willing to accept these as

Delimiter	Meaning
CASE (Principle)	Ignore caps vs. lower case letters
?	Accept any letter in this position
#n(believeable)	Accept n omissions or substitutions
#P(Dr. Strangelove)	Ignore punctuation
+not+	String embedded in any context
ot.	String exact match only
Alice ! +sister+	or (at least one)
gunpowder & flame	and (all items listed)
:(2 & 4 & 5 & 10):	elements in any order
:n:(a, b, c, d):	any n of the elements in any order
::(Mars, Venus...)::	elements in exact order
::n(argon, neon...)::	any n elements but in order
(+prime+) − (n?t)	but not if

Figure 5. Typical delimiters in a frame-based authoring language.

elements of a larger answer, then you want to search for them embedded in any arbitrary string, and you want an answer judger which will do that. Turning to the correct answer, we at first want to accept "no" and its variants—"it's not" and "it isn't," so we would like a wild card "?" which lets us write "n?t" to cover all these cases, again embedded in any arbitrary string. We also need an "or" operator, so we can write "'no?'" or "'n?t'" as the specifier for the first part of the correct answer. The first term covers "no" and "not," and the second term covers "isn't" and—redundantly—"not" again. We also need to say that these fragments can be embedded in anything and still be OK—that is, that we are not looking for an exact match.

Most languages offer a way of making this distinction. Now we need to look at the list of divisors. So we need an "and" operator to indicate that the answer has two parts, and that both must be stated by the student. The second part must specify that the divisors 2, 4, 5, and 10 are *all* to be stated, so we need the "and" again. If the authoring system is good, it will have a "delimiter" which will specify whether a number of elements needed for an answer must be given in a specific order. In this case, the order within the answer is obviously not important, since the point is merely to list the divisors. If the language does not offer this order-delimiting feature, there are three ways out: (a) don't ask questions like this; (b) go ahead and ask the question, but be prepared to specify the correct answer class by listing every possible permutation of the numbers 2, 4, 5, and 10 (there are 24 of them!), all connected by the operator "or"; (c) ask a question which restricts the free range of answers by taking on the clause, "and list those divisors in order from smallest to largest," so that your student must carry out bookkeeping work which makes up for the limitations of the program, and which is not intrinsic to the purposes of either instruction or assessment. Such is the kingdom of restricted authoring languages.

The "Is 20 prime?" test case will allow one to explore much of the answer-judging capability of any authoring language. But it will also reveal the linked problems which arise when planning instruction with open-ended responses. For example, there's more to be said about programming anticipated answers to this question. We've spoken as though the only way to indicate that the number in question is not prime is to use some variant of negation—"no? or n?t". But there's another way: Suppose that our learner is a bit more sophisticated than many—perhaps more so than the author is!—and enters, "The number in question is composite." The judgement routines specifications described above will not know what to do with this, and will in fact reply with whatever has been entered for the category "unanticipated answer." A common (and cautious) example of such feedback is: "That's not what I was looking for. Please try again." But the answer is correct! The classic delight of enemies of the testing process is the correct answer which the system has not provided for. Authoring languages have no such category as "unanticipated correct answer." This case could have been handled if the author had used the "or" operator and added "composite" to the specification for the correct answer. That specification would then read something like:

[("no?" or "n?t"; embedded anyhow) or ("composite";embedded anyhow)] and [2 and 4 and 5 and 10; only; any order]

No existing authoring language would put it exactly this way, but this statement is very close to what an actual example would look like. It is saying that the student would have to either make a negation or use the term "composite," and that in either case, she would also have to list the four critical divisors.

You may have been wondering about those divisors. Why are 1 and 20 not on the list? They are, after all, divisors of 20. But the question asked for "those divisors which show that it is not prime," and every number has 1 and itself as divisors. The critical instructional point is that we have encountered a *near miss* (almost no instructional theorists deal with this important concept; one who does calls it the "close-in non-example"). How a teacher-author deals with it might well depend on the stage of learning. Early in the sequence, one might want to call an answer correct if it included 1 and/or 20 (either? both?)—though you surely wouldn't want to insist on their inclusion; so there's another big "or" again; later one might attach special feedback to 1 and 20 if together, pointing out that they are divisors but not decision-making divisors. The answer-judgments which I have presented—in which the inclusion of either of these numbers invalidates the answer (notice the "only" in the judgement specification) would be typical of a late stage in teaching the concept.

The isolation of near misses for varied treatment as learning progresses lies at the heart of the process of shaping new behavior. Instructional psychologists have several names for this process: "the progressive refinement of a discrimination," "the elaboration of a concept," or, more simply, "shaping." Most authoring languages permit you to engage in such shaping through the combined use of "this answer along with anything else" versus "this answer only." Some languages have an additional command which is especially useful in this process: It says "but not if."

If a purist who insisted that there were only five vowels asked the question: "What are the vowels?" she might specify her answer as follows:

("a" and "e" and "i" and "o" and "u"; any order) − ("y")

where the minus sign carries the "but not if" message.

Before leaving this lengthy example, I want to stress the subtleties of "covering all bases" in constructed response programming. The example above, though now in fairly good form, is not invulnerable. Suppose a learner answers the question "Is 20 prime. . . ?" by entering "It is, isn't it?" This answer will be scored as correct by the specification described above! A rereading of the discussion above will make clear why this is so. Perhaps it's no surprise that so much time is required to write a small amount of CAI or CBT.

One reaction to the problem of seemingly endless ambiguities in the answer-judgment area is to retreat to multiple-choice questions. Though this tactic is quite understandable, I would urge that it be resisted, that multiple-choice and other "indicator" questions, such as true-false and matching items, not be awarded an exclusive role in CBT. Many authoring systems offer established formats for organizing frames of all these types, and for filing specifications for answers. My own tendency is to use constructed response frames and multiple-choice frames for both teaching and assessment with criterion frames, and to reserve matching and checkoff frames for assessment alone. Also, I find constructed response and multiple choice frames attractive to use in giving feedback for wrong answers and for permitting multiple tries. But matching and checkoff frames less readily lend themselves to feedback other than "right" or "wrong."

I believe that capabilities of the kind here illustrated carry us far towards the ability to ask for and parse classes of responses broad enough to be worthy of a complex organism with a complex verbal history, who will not legitimately claim that we are being trivial or picky when we reject "a is smaller than b" because the correct answer is "b is larger than a," or ignorant because we left out "composite" as a way of saying "not prime." Of course, the latter case reflects more than the capability of an authoring language; it reflects the subject-matter sophistication of the author. No matter how good the authoring system, classic problems will remain. There may always be a tendency to avoid the need to parse classes of utterances beyond our control by restricting the properties of the acceptable response somewhat artificially. To considerately prompt the learner of this fact may still not eliminate her feeling of being cramped and fussy. We may compromise by blending multiple-choice formats, formats in which model right answers are shown, and truly open response formats. We may even retain in our course designs the two-model mixture, in which some weak contingencies with right answers—and even repetitions to criterion—are mixed with true open responses which are parsed by the delimiters. But the balance is dramatically changed from what could be accomplished by mechanical means alone. The delimiters of an authoring language represent a genuine advance of the human verbal community into computer software, and as such can contribute to the automated shaping of human verbal behavior of considerable complexity.

The importance of the ability to parse constructed responses is twofold. So far we have stressed the importance to the teaching system of its ability to ask for and then discriminate whether a learner's response falls into the class defined by delimiters as correct, anticipated incorrect, or unanticipated. With this ability, replying with the correct answer becomes a less appealing procedure, and other consequences can be allowed their force. But we have not mentioned those consequences. This is point (4) at the top of page 237.

The Future Role of Behavioral Analysis in ID

Skinner says somewhere that when you ask for the salt in good French, if you are in a French class you will get an A, but in France you will get the salt. He means to stress the artificiality of reinforcers typically used in education. However, the choice of a primary reinforcer renders the contrast in some respects atypical. One might get neither an A nor the salt, but a charming reply, "Mais oui." Would that be better? In much of our verbal knowledge, the reinforcers need not be primary, and we needn't wait for computers with pantries attached to produce consequences of some power. The display capabilities of the current computer can be used to *simulate* many properties of the world, the control of which constitute the aims of education: graphical displays, probability distributions, colors, sounds, alterations in text, Boolean searches in databases, three dimensional views and revolutions, simulations of plane crashes. In a teaching environment, the student can be asked, what will happen to the bridge if you change the load upon it? To the harmonies if you change the chord progressions? To the course of the courtroom trial if you object at this point in the testimony? The simulation allows you to see the consequences of your own behavior in a manner that resembles reality in important respects, but is unreal enough to avoid danger, expense, and the time costs of repetition with variation. Simulation explorations can be as tightly programmed or as loose as the pedagogy suggests at any point. They constitute a class of consequences for the behavior being shaped in an instructional program whose instructive and discriminative and reinforcing values extend far beyond *either* being informed that you are right or wrong, or having the correct answer supplied. But to set the parameters of any specific simulation, the learner must enter those parameters into the program. To do this, constructed responses which the program can parse are necessary. Depending on the values you enter into the equation, the tennis ball will go one way or the other, the recessive gene will make itself felt or not, the atomic pile will reach critical mass or not, the music will sound like Bach or Mozart. The representations are not reality, but they mimic its properties in the forms used to govern our technical, professional, formal, mathematical, and verbal lives, even when our official education is done. Thanks to this development, the response of a student can lead to consequences which depend upon the properties of that reponse in a manner extremely close to those prevailing in the extended world and community. With a strict contingency, the responses can control detailed properties of the consequences. I have completed my case for the serious attention to computer-assisted instruction on the part of a science of behavior. But I have a concluding historical note to share.

Among the statements made which may have impeded the fertile union of the behavioral analysis of learning and instruction via computer is this one, made in a paper read in Washington in 1963 and published in an influential volume in 1965: "Nothing we now know about the learning process calls for instrumentation as complex as computer technology." The statement appears on the second page of a paper entitled "Reflections on a Decade of Teaching Machines," and its author is B. F. Skinner. This paper is the first in a collection entitled *Teaching Machines and Programmed Learning, II: Data and Directions*, edited by Robert Glaser and published by the Divison of Audio-Visual Instruction of the National Education Association of the United States. Though many of us may have no difficulty in construing "senses" of this remark with which it would be hard to disagree, I think it more honest of me, and I hope it to be more to the point today, to say that it is the only statement known to me made by this remarkable man that I believe to be wrong. At least today.

Skinner's first two teaching machines—for arithmetic and spelling—maintained a strict contingency because the mechanical topography of the response could be put into one-to-one, or isomorphic, correspondence, with its status as correct or incorrect. Therefore, mechanical "parsing" was isomorphic with verbal parsing. In a spelling course, to insist upon exact spelling is not to substitute easily-tested objectives for the true and important ones; in an arithmetic course, it is the numbers which count. But in the "disk" machine, where verbal knowledge is at stake, the machine utilized was quite different: It retreated to a weak contingency, gave feedback regardless of the nature of the response (which it could not parse), and, since the feedback was uncontingent, it could only offer as feedback an announcement of the correct answer. (And, to compensate for the shift in the contingency from strong to weak, the additional procedure of repetition to a criterion appeared: The learner must repeat attempts with this circular wheel until the errors are cleaned up.) Thus, the moment the step is taken to verbal knowledge of the type which admits of "semantic equivalents"—in which it makes sense to speak of the same thing being said in a number of ways—then the problem arises of specifying the class of events whose elements consist of all the ways of saying the same thing. Without this step, the strict contingency must be given up. The needed specification can be done by enumeration—risky because lists may always be incomplete (as in the case of "composite" as an equivalent for "not prime"); or it can be done by stating the rule which defines all instances of the answer. In the first case, you need at least a mechanism for coupling Boolean "or's" with all the enumerated cases; in the second case, you need more than that. We have seen a few steps in this direction with the delimiters illustrated above. It is here that I expect to see advances in our understanding of verbal behavior. In carrying out the task of teaching machines what meaning is, so that machines will respond correctly to all instances of the same class of verbal events as would a competent teacher listening or reading, we will discover the operational stipulations necessary, including the syntactical formalisms and the referential contexts needed, to know what humans do when they do it. As this task is accomplished, it will become possible to embark upon the automated teaching of complex knowledge—call it verbal, conceptual, cognitive, or what you will—with the strict contingency operating as a powerful tool in the shaping of operant behavior. The field of "parsing theory" in computer sciences is already moving in this area.

Students of behavior have much to learn from this work, and, potentially, much to contribute. The formal structure of computer programs able to respond to human verbal inputs represents the embodiment of the verbal community in an interactive sense, with no human present at the moment, in just the same way that the book is the non-interactive record of the same human verbal community. Therefore, in my opinion, the field of complex verbal learning and the field of computer technology do indeed stand in need of each other, and it can be said that their intimate collaboration would be a marriage of true minds, and that their offspring might soon transform our verbal environments. To this enterprise, let us admit no impediment.

References

Bullock, D. N. *et al.* (1973). *Editing system for self-instructional material.* Report for U.S. Air Force.

Cook, D. A. (1960). On vanishing stimuli in instructional material. *Journal of the Experimental Analysis of Behavior, 3,* p. 292.

Cook, D. A. (1962). *Industrial training problems.* American Management Bulletin #22. New York: American Management Association.

Cook, D. A. (1972). *Message type as a parameter of learning to receive International Morse Code.* Columbia University. Unpublished Doctoral Dissertation.

Cook, D. A. (1992). Unpublished study of three programs, one on chemistry, one on set theory, and one on wide-area telephone systems.

Eigen, L. D., & Margulies, S. (1963, Spring). Response characteristics as a function of information level. *Journal of Programmed Instruction, 2,* 45–54.

Ferster, C. B., & Skinner, B. F. (1957). *Schedules of reinforcement.* New York: Appleton-Century Crofts.

Glaser, R. (Ed.). (1965). *Teaching machines and programmed learning, II: Data and directions.* Washington, DC: DAVI.

Holland, J. G. (1967). A quantitative measure for programming instruction. *American Educational Research Journal, 4*(2), 87–101.

Holland, J. G., & Skinner, B. F. (1961). *The analysis of behavior.* New York. McGraw-Hill.

Israel, M. L. (1960, July). Variably blurred prompting: I. Methodology and application of the analysis of paired-associate learning. *Journal of Psychology, 50,* 43–52.

Keller, F. S. (1943). Studies in International Morse Code: 1. A new method of teaching code reception. *Journal of Applied Psychology, 27,* 407–415.

Keller, F. S. (1968). Good-bye, teacher . . . *Journal of Applied Behavioral Analysis, 1,* 79–89.

Margulies, S. (1963). *Some general rules of frame construction.* New York: Basic Systems.

Markle, S. M. (1967). Behavior analysis and instructional sequencing. In P. Lange (Ed.), *Programed instruction: The sixty-sixth yearbook of the National Society for the Study of Education, part II.* Chicago: University of Chicago Press.

Mechner, F. (1961a). *Programming for automated instruction.* Available from Behavioral Science Applications, Inc., 200 Central Park South, New York, NY 10019.

Mechner, F. (1961b). Behavioral contingencies. In J. G. Holland, C. Solomon, J. Doran, & D. A. Frezza (Eds.), *The analysis of behavior in planning instruction* (pp. 50–62). New York. Addison-Wesley.

Mechner, F. (1963). *A new approach to programmed instruction.* Available from Behavioral Science Applications, Inc., 200 Central Park South, New York, NY 10019.

Mechner, F. (1967). Behavioral analysis and instructional sequencing. In P. C. Lange (Ed.), *Programed instruction: The sixty-sixth yearbook of the National Society for the Study of Education, part II.* Chicago: University of Chicago Press.

Parsons, R. (1974). *Statistical analysis: A decision-making approach.* New York: Harper & Row.

Rushton, E. (1963). *The Roanoke story.* Chicago: Encyclopaedia Britannica Press.

Sherman, J. G., & Ruskin, R. S. (1978). *The Personalized System of Instruction.* Englewood Cliffs, NJ: Educational Technology Publications.

Skinner, B. F. (1938). *The behavior of organisms.* New York: Appleton-Century-Crofts.

Skinner, B. F. (1954). The science of learning and the art of teaching. *Harvard Educational Review, 24,* 86–97.

Skinner, B. F. (1957). *Verbal behavior.* New York. Appleton-Century-Crofts.

Skinner, B. F. (1958). Teaching machines. *Science, 128,* 969-977.

Skinner, B. F., & Holland, J. G. (1958). *The use of teaching machines in college instruction: Final report.* New York: Fund for the Advancement of Education.

Spence, I., & Hively, W. (1993, Oct.). What makes Chris practice? *Educational Technology, 33*(10), 15–20.

Stolurow, L. M., & Frinche, G. (1966). A study of sample size in making decisions about instructional materials. *Educational and Psychological Measurement, 26,* 643–657.

Thorndike, E. L. (1898). Animal intelligence: An experimental study of the associative processes in animals. *Psychology Review. Monograph Supplement #8.*

14

Humanism as an Instructional Paradigm

Ralph G. Brockett
University of Tennessee, Knoxville

Introduction

Effective instructional design begins with an understanding of the basic assumptions that underlie the design and development process. This is, essentially, the philosophy that an educator brings to the instructional situation. One's educational philosophy can be articulated by responding to such questions as: (1) What do I believe about human nature? (2) What is the basic purpose of learning and instruction? and (3) What do I believe about the abilities and potential of the learners with whom I work?

Humanism provides a way of looking at the instructional design process that emphasizes the strengths the learner brings to the instructional setting. It is an optimistic perspective that celebrates the potential of learners to successfully engage in the instructional process. Although humanism is sometimes subject to criticism regarding its basic tenets, and is perceived by some as an irrelevant way to deal with instructional needs of the present and future, most of these criticisms are based on misunderstandings of beliefs underlying the paradigm and how these beliefs are played out in practice. Ultimately, humanism can and should have an important role to play in the future of instructional development.

The purpose of this chapter is to offer an examination of humanism and its potential within the state of the art of instructional design theory and practice. The chapter will begin with a look at the philosophical and psychological underpinnings of humanism. Emphasis will then shift to an examination of how principles of humanism can be applied to the instructional development process. Next, some potential limitations of the paradigm will be mentioned. Finally, several conclusions will be gleaned from the discussion relative to the value of humanism as an instructional design model.

The Nature of Humanism

Humanism has variously been described as a philosophy, a theory of psychology, and an approach to educational practice. Each of these is accurate. Philosophy and psychology provide a foundation for understanding humanism, while education serves as a "playing field" upon which these principles are implemented in practice. This section will examine the philosophical and psychological backgrounds, while the following section focuses upon the application of these principles to instructional practice.

Humanism as a Philosophy

Humanism is a paradigm that emphasizes the freedom, dignity, and potential of humans. According to Lamont (1965), humanism can be defined as "a philosophy of joyous service for the greater good of all humanity in this natural world and advocating the methods of reason, science, and democracy" (p. 12). Elias and Merriam (1980) state that humanism is "as old as human civilization and as modern as the twentieth century" (p. 109). Early threads of humanist thought can be found in the works of Confucius, Greek philosophers such as Protagoras and Aristotle, Renaissance philosophers Erasmus and Montaigne, Spinoza in the 17th century, and Rousseau in the 18th century. In the 20th century, Bertrand Russell, George Santayana, Albert Schweitzer, and Reinhold Niebuhr have all made contributions to contemporary humanism. Similarly, Nietzche, Tillich, Buber, and Sartre have contributed to the development of existentialism, a contemporary form of humanism (Elias & Merriam, 1980; Lamont, 1965).

Rooted in the idea that "human beings are capable of making significant personal choices within the constraints imposed by heredity, personal history, and environment" (Elias & Merriam, 1980, p. 118), principles of humanist philosophy stress the importance of the individual and specific human needs. Lamont (1965) has outlined 10 central propositions of humanist philosophy. These can be summarized as follows:

1. Humanism is based on a naturalistic metaphysics that views all forms of the supernatural as myth.
2. Humanism believes that humans are an evolutionary product of nature and, since body and personality are inseparably united, one "can have no conscious survival after death" (p. 13).
3. Humanism holds that "human beings possess the power or potentiality of solving their own problems, through reliance primarily upon reason and scientific method applied with courage and vision" (p. 13).
4. Humanism holds that because individuals "possess freedom of creative choice and action," they are, within limits, "masters of their own destiny"; in this way, humanism is in contrast with views of universal determinism, as well as fatalism and predestination (p. 13).
5. Humanism stresses a view of ethics or morality based in present-life experiences and relationships and emphasizes "this-worldly happiness, freedom, and progress" of *all* humans (p. 13).
6. Humanism believes that individuals attain the good life by combining personal growth and satisfaction with commitment to the welfare of the entire community.
7. Humanism places great value in aesthetics, and thus, emphasizes the value of art and the awareness of beauty.
8. Humanism values actions that will promote the establishment of "democracy, peace, and a high standard of living" throughout the world (p. 14).
9. Humanism advocates the use of reason and scientific method and, as such, supports democratic procedures such as freedom of expression and civil liberties in all realms of life.
10. Humanism supports "the unending questioning of basic assumptions and convictions, including its own" (p. 14).

In summarizing the essence of these points, Lamont (1965) offers the following observation:

> Humanism is the viewpoint that men [sic] have but one life to lead and should make the most of it in terms of creative work and happiness; that human happiness is its own justification and requires no sanction or support from supernatural sources; that in any case the supernatural, usually conceived of in the form of heavenly gods or immortal heavens, does not exist; and that human beings, using their own intelligence and cooperating liberally with one another, can build an enduring citadel of peace and beauty upon this earth. (p. 14)

In a discussion of humanistic philosophy directed toward application to the field of adult education, Elias and Merriam (1980) summarize the major beliefs of humanism as: (1) human nature is inherently good; (2) individuals are essentially free and autonomous within the constraints of heredity, personal history, and environment; (3) each person is unique with unlimited potential for growth; (4) self-concept plays a key role in influencing development; (5) individuals possess an urge toward self-actualization; (6) reality is a personally defined construct; and (7) individuals are responsible to themselves and to others. While it is clear that the ideas presented by Elias and Merriam are compatible with those of Lamont, by emphasizing notions such as self-concept and self-actualization, the Elias and Merriam description serves as a natural link between humanism as a philosophy and as a theory of psychology.

Humanistic Psychology

For the first half of the 20th century, psychology was influenced primarily by two schools of thought. One of these was psychoanalytic theory, perhaps best represented by Freudian psychoanalysis. The other was behaviorism, reflected in the research and theories of Watson, Hull, and Skinner. However, throughout the 1930s, 1940s, and 1950s, psychologists such as Gordon Allport, Henry Murray, Gardner Murphy, and George Kelly began to present views "which rejected both the mechanistic premises of behaviorism and the biological reductionism of classical psychoanalysis" (Smith, 1990, p. 8). Thus, it was out of response to both the determinism inherent in psychoanalysis and the limited importance placed on affect, dignity, and freedom found in behaviorism that gave rise to what is sometimes called the "third force" of psychology: humanism.

In describing the development of humanistic psychology, Smith (1990) has noted that the approach began to be recognized as a "movement" during the mid-1960s. It is important to note, however, that there is no single conception of humanistic psychology; rather, many individuals contributed different elements to the movement. For instance, Charlotte Buhler emphasized the notion of life-span development. Rollo May emphasized European existentialism and phenomenology. The encounter group movement was a vital aspect of humanistic psychology in the 1960s and 1970s, particularly through the work of J. L. Moreno and his development of psychodrama, Kurt Lewin and field theory, and Fritz Perls and his work with Gestalt therapy. And Viktor Frankl, in part through his personal experiences during the Holocaust, developed Logotherapy as "an account of the human predicament that emphasizes the human need to place death and suffering in a context of human meaning that can be lived with" (Smith, 1990, p. 14).

Probably the two individuals who have had the greatest influence on humanistic psychology, however, were Carl Rogers and Abraham Maslow. Rogers' approach to therapy was originally described as "nondirective counseling" (1942), but was later recast as "client-centered therapy" (1951, 1961). The essence of Rogers' thinking was that human beings have a tendency toward self-actualization; however, the way in which individuals are socialized often blocks that urge. According to Rogers, a therapeutic relationship based on the values of unconditional positive regard, accurate empathic understanding, and honesty and integrity can help individuals fulfill their greatest potential (Smith, 1990). Through this process, Rogers demonstrated his belief in the potential of his clients and his trust in their ability to take responsibility for their lives.

A major goal of Rogerian therapy is to help individuals foster a greater level of self-direction. According to Rogers, self-direction "means that one chooses—and then learns from the consequences" (Rogers, 1961, p. 171). Self-direction is where a person can see a situation clearly and take responsibility for that situation (Rogers, 1983). This notion of self-direction has important implications for educational practice, which will be discussed later in this chapter as well as in subsequent chapters in this volume by Sisco and Hiemstra.

Maslow developed a theory of human motivation originally presented in his 1954 book *Motivation and Personality*, which was revised in 1970. This theory holds that needs are arranged in ascending order: physiological needs, safety, love and belonging, esteem, and self-actualization. Maslow described the first four levels as "deficiency" needs, in that one must be able to meet needs at a lower level prior to working toward the needs at the next level.

Like Rogers, Maslow designated "self-actualization" as an ideal to work toward achieving. Self-actualization, according to Maslow, is the highest level of human growth, where one's potential has been most fully realized. Maslow held that self-actualizers tend to "possess a more efficient view of reality and a corresponding tolerance of ambiguity; be accepting of themselves and others; demonstrate spontaneous behavior that is in tune with their own values and not necessarily tied to the common beliefs and practices of the culture; focus on problems that lie outside of themselves, thus demonstrating a highly ethical concern; maintain a few extremely close interpersonal relationships rather than seek out a large number of less intense friendships; and possess high levels of creativity" (Brockett & Hiemstra, 1991, p. 126).

An important element of Maslow's theory is the notion of the "mystic or peak experience" (Maslow, 1970). These are highly intense periods during which a person is transformed through new insights. A more recent exploration of this notion can be found in the work of Csikszentmihalyi (1990) and his concept of "flow." Maslow's theory has been widely embraced in many areas, such as business and education. Unfortunately, however, it is often treated in an oversimplified manner. This misuse may lead some to dismiss the theory. While an extensive debate of the merits of Maslow's theory is beyond the scope of this chapter, it is important to note that the importance of the theory to this discussion is the value Maslow placed on the potential of human beings to strive for and achieve greater levels of growth.

Humanism and Instruction

Humanistic education is a natural outgrowth of principles derived from humanistic philosophy and psychology. Patterson (1973) has stated that *"the purpose of education is to develop self-actualizing persons"* (p. 22). He goes on to suggest that there are two aspects of humanistic education: facilitating instruction in a "more humane way" (p. x) and developing affective aspects of the learner, which is designed to lead to greater understanding of self and others. Valett (1977) suggests that humanistic education is a lifelong process designed "to develop individuals who will be able to live joyous, humane, and meaningful lives" and that the priorities of this approach should be "the development of emotive abilities, the shaping of affective desires, the fullest expression of aesthetic qualities, and the enhancement of powers of self-direction and control" (p. 12). Similarly, Simpson (1976) has offered the following comment:

> Affect and cognition, feelings and intellect, emotions and behavior blend in an affirmative framework of values derived from the humanities and from positive conceptions of mental health. These are the hallmarks of humanistic education. (p. 16)

Elements of Humanistic Instructional Development

How do the goals and principles of the humanist paradigm translate into instructional development practice? Elias and Merriam (1980) have provided a synthesis of principles relative to humanistic instruction. While their discussion is directed specifically to adult educators, the authors note that these basic elements are relevant to a humanistic approach to education in general. First, humanistic education is student-centered. This means that the learner is a unique individual who brings a unique set of experiences and needs to the instructional situation. Second, the role of the teacher is "that of facilitator, helper, and partner in the learning process" (p. 125). The effective facilitator is one who is able to set a climate that values and emphasizes the unique experiences and needs of each learner. Third, the act of learning is highly personal. The most valuable learning takes place when what is learned is perceived to be "necessary, important, or meaningful" to the person (p. 126). This is analogous to the idea of "experiential" learning and is based on such elements as self-concept, self-evaluation, intrinsic motivation, perception, and discovery. Fourth, since the goal of humanistic education is to help learners become self-actualizing persons, curriculum (or content) is not an end, but rather, a means of promoting the goals of humanistic education. Fifth, since individual growth and development do not take place in isolation, growth is "best fostered in a cooperative, supportive environment" (p. 129). Competition is typically viewed as detrimental to the process of humanistic instruction.

Shapiro (1986) surveyed 40 well-known writers in the field of humanistic education to determine what these individuals perceived to be the "basic principles" of humanistic education. He later conducted a similar follow-up study with 49 additional authors (Shapiro, 1987). From these 89 experts, Shapiro derived the following 16 instructional principles associated with humanistic education:

1. Emphasis on the process of learning.
2. Self-determination, as reflected in learner autonomy, self-direction, and self-evaluation.
3. Mutual caring and understanding among teachers, learners, and others (connectedness).
4. Relevance of material, including readiness of the student to learn.
5. Integration of affect and cognition in the teaching-learning process.
6. An "awareness of the environment, culture, history, and the political and economic conditions in which learning takes place" (Shapiro, 1987, p. 160).
7. Preference for affective and experiential learning approaches.
8. An approach to social change that is anti-authoritarian with the intent to "serve society by improving its education institutions" (p. 160).
9. Equity, consensus, and collaboration through democratic participation in the learning process.
10. A personal growth orientation that stresses self-actualization via self-awareness.
11. A people orientation based on trust and a positive view of humanity, such as is reflected in McGregor's (1960) "Theory Y."
12. Emphasis on individualism.
13. A concrete, pragmatic view of reality.
14. Self-evaluation that emphasizes formative over summative evaluation.
15. Variety and creativity, as reflected in spontaneity, originality, and diversity in learning.
16. A transpersonal orientation that stresses holistic development of the person, including potential for spirituality.

It can be seen that the principles identified through Shapiro's research corresponds closely with the elements identified by Elias and Merriam (1980).

Humanistic Instruction in School Settings: Two Examples

A powerful illustration of this approach can be found in the book *36 Children* (Kohl, 1967). In this book, Herbert Kohl describes his first year as a teacher, in a sixth grade class at an inner city school in New York City. Kohl found that most of these young students had already given up on school. He goes on to describe in detail the strategies he used to reach the "36 children" and to help them discover their previously untapped potential as learners. By the end of the year, the vast majority of the group were actively engaged in learning with an enthusiasm that they had never experienced. Unfortunately, as the students moved on to the next grade and back into a more traditional classroom setting, most of the group reverted to their previous approach to school and learning.

Another illustration of humanistic instruction with children is the work of Gibbons and Phillips (1979, 1982, 1984), who have described their efforts to help elementary and secondary students move from an authority-directed approach toward greater self-direction in learning. They describe a four-stage program that includes the following elements: at the preschool level, parents model self-directed learning and provide an environment conducive to self-direction; students in the elementary grades are encouraged to undertake individual and group projects of personal interest; secondary students are challenged to engage in a process of developing learning contracts and negotiating learning outcomes; finally, as students make the transition to adulthood, they are given information and skills that will allow them to engage in continuous learning beyond the classroom.

Educational Technology and the Humanist Paradigm

Melton (1990) argues that the field of educational technology was very much dominated during the 1950s and 1960s by a behaviorist-oriented "mechanistic" approach to the design and development of instruction. Citing authors such as Tyler (1949), Skinner (1957), Mager (1962), and Gagné (1965), Melton states that this view stresses objectivity and "the development of techniques to reduce—or even eliminate—the vagaries of human judgment" (p. 27). Over the next two decades, Melton notes a change in orientation, as reflected in the following observation:

> By the 1980s the complexity of the situations to which educational technologists needed to respond was emerging much more clearly, and it was generally recognized that learning was likely to be affected by a variety of complex interactions between the personal characteristics of student and teacher, the style of learning and teaching preferred by each, the demands of the subject being studied and the learning-teaching style adopted for this purpose. (Melton, 1990, p. 27)

To illustrate this emphasis on a more humanistic orientation to educational technology, Melton describes three examples from the British Open University. The first example focuses on the development of instructional materials, where course team members have not communicated adequately with one another prior to engaging in materials development. The result can be the development of "inappropriate" materials, which in turn can lead to criticism and conflict among team members. From this, Melton suggests that the success of a course development team can be hampered by negative judgments stemming from inadequate communication, and that such concerns can often be avoided if group members pay attention to the nature of interpersonal relationships.

In the second example, difficulties in conventional approaches to the evaluation of teaching and teaching systems was discussed. Melton pointed out that such "evaluator-centered" approaches, where the evaluator is expected to pass judgment, can be quite threatening, and can lead to rejection of the findings and recommendations. An alternative approach to evaluation is a "non-judgmental" approach where the role of the educational technologist is "to help others to gather information and to think about the issues in a supportive, non-threatening environment" (p. 29).

Is it appropriate to foster qualities such as creativity and self-motivation among staff members, when such activities may not be directly linked to meeting specific goals of the institution? This is the theme of Melton's third example. He suggests that when the institutional environment is supportive and non-judgmental, with individuals exchanging views and concerns with each other, then it is possible for both the individual *and* the institution to benefit from such efforts.

The basic conclusion offered by Melton is "that interpersonal skills are an important part of the human dimension within the field of educational technology, and that they should be developed as an important part of the repertoire of every educational technologist" (p. 30). This conclusion clearly links to several of the basic principles of humanistic instructional design addressed earlier in this chapter.

Humanistic Practices in Adult Education and Training

Humanism has long been a major influence on the fields of adult education and training. As early as 1926, Eduard Lindeman, an adult educator and social philosopher who was greatly influenced by Deweyian progressivism, discussed the compatibility of individual growth and social change as desirable goals by making the following observation: "Adult education will become an agency of progress if its short-time goal of self-improvement can be made compatible with a long-time, experimental but resolute policy of changing the social order" (Lindeman, 1989, p. 103).

Perhaps the most enduring contribution to the humanist influence on adult education and training is found in the work of Malcolm Knowles. In the 1950s, Knowles played an important role in the movement to promote group dynamics, sensitivity training, and experiential learning with adults. His writings over four decades show the evolution of an approach that, even in its earliest versions, placed great trust in adult learners and their potential for growth. Knowles popularized the term "andragogy" in North America and presented it as a model for understanding and facilitating adult learning. Initially, andragogy was viewed as an approach to adult learning, diametrically opposed to pedagogy, the teacher-directed approach most often used with children (Knowles, 1968). After various writers challenged Knowles to rethink his position (Davenport & Davenport, 1985), Knowles (1980) concluded that pedagogy and andragogy should be viewed along a continuum, where andragogy plays an increasingly important role as the learner matures.

The essence of Knowles' approach to andragogy can be found in several assumptions about learners as they mature (Knowles, 1989). These include the following:

1. Learners need to know *why* they need to know something before engaging in learning.
2. Self-concept moves from dependence toward a need for self-direction.
3. Experience plays an increasingly important role in the learning process.
4. Readiness to learn is determined increasingly by what is needed to deal with real-life situations.
5. Orientation to learning moves from subject-centered to problem-centered, or life-centered.
6. Motivation to learn shifts from extrinsic motivators to intrinsic ones.

These six assumptions form the basis for Knowles's approach to instruction. The principles of andragogy have been applied successfully in a wide range of settings, including business, government, colleges and universities, continuing professional education, religious education, adult basic education, and elementary/secondary settings. Knowles (1989) provides a personal account of andragogy's development and current status, and Brockett and Hiemstra (1991) offer an annotated bibliography of sources related to andragogy.

A second application of the humanist approach in the context of adult education and training can be found in the area of self-direction in adult learning. As was mentioned above, the importance of self-direction was central to Knowles's idea of andragogy. Since the early 1970s, self-direction has emerged as one of the most prominent areas of theory, research, and practice in the area of adult learning. While there are many definitions of self-direction, most emphasize one or both of two dimensions: (1) learner control of the planning, implementation, and evaluation of the learning process and (2) an internal desire or preference for taking responsibility for one's learning. In the present discussion, "self direction in learning refers to both the characteristics of an instructional process and the internal characteristics of the learner, where the individual assumes primary responsibility for a learning experience" (Brockett & Hiemstra, 1991, p. 24).

Self-direction in learning is an often misunderstood idea. Some of the myths associated with self-direction that have particular relevance to instructional development include the following:

1. Self-direction is an all-or-nothing, either/or concept.
2. Self-direction takes place in isolation.
3. Self-direction is little more than a current educational fad.
4. The time and energy required to implement self-directed learning far outweighs the benefits of the approach.
5. Self-direction is only relevant in learning situations emphasizing reading and writing skills.
6. Facilitating self-direction is an easy way out for educators who may be unprepared or uninterested (Brockett & Hiemstra, 1991).

Research on the phenomenon of self-direction in adult learning has mushroomed since 1970 and has included descriptive surveys of participation in self-directed learning, quantitative studies involving the measurement of self-direction in relation to a host of personological variables, and qualitative investigations designed to provide rich descriptions and/or theoretical foundations relative to self-direction. Together, these investigations have contributed to an understanding of self-direction from several theoretical and methodological perspectives.

The humanist influence on current work in self-direction might be understood more fully through the concept of "personal responsibility." Personal responsibility, according to Brockett and Hiemstra, means that individuals assume ownership for their thoughts and actions. It does not necessarily mean that individuals always have control over their environment or personal circumstances; however, it does mean that such persons have control over how they respond to these elements. It is similar to the Rogers conception of self-direction, which states that one is free to make choices, but then is responsible for the consequences of these choices. The Personal Responsibility Orientation (PRO) model was developed as a way to link the internal and external elements in self-direction to a common thread. That thread is personal responsibility (Brockett & Hiemstra, 1991).

Not all adult educators have embraced the humanistic orientation to self-direction. For instance, Flannery (1993) has argued that this humanistic view affords inadequate attention to elements of sociology, such as "the socialization process to roles and one's place in the social strata" (p. 110). Candy (1991) has proposed a different model of self-direction, which is derived from principles of constructivist sociology. The points to be emphasized here are, first, that humanism offers only one lens with which to view the concept of self-direction and, second, that humanism does not necessarily emphasize the individual at the expense of ignoring social context. This latter point was addressed earlier in the quote by Lindeman (1989) and is discussed more fully in the following section.

In terms of application to instructional design, the humanist foundation of self-direction is perhaps best reflected in the "Individualizing Instruction" model, developed by Hiemstra and Sisco (1990) and addressed elsewhere in this volume in chapters by Sisco and by Hiemstra. This model emphasizes the "teaching-learning" dimension of self-direction. As for the "internal" elements, these can be found in ideas derived from writings in humanistic psychology, such as those mentioned earlier in this chapter. Three applications of approaches designed to foster learner self-direction include facilitating critical reflection (Brookfield, 1987; Mezirow, 1985), promoting self-direction (Ellis & Harper, 1975), and use of "helping skills" in the teaching-learning process (Egan, 1986).

Some Challenges to the Humanist Paradigm

Humanism is a celebration of human goodness and the virtually unlimited boundaries of human potential. As such, it serves as a foundation for an approach to instruction that builds on the natural strengths of learners. Yet, as with any instructional paradigm, the approach is likely to raise a number of questions from those who may challenge humanism's basic tenets and/or the way these tenets are translated to practice. Three such challenges are addressed below.

Views on the Supernatural and Immortality

One of the most immediate criticisms of humanism is the underlying view of the supernatural and immortality. Essentially, humanism stresses the view that because human nature is basically good, the notions of supreme being and afterlife are rejected. As Lamont states: "Humanism is the viewpoint that men [sic] have but one life to lead and should make the most of it in terms of creative work and happiness" and that "the supernatural, usually conceived of in the form of heavenly gods or immortal heavens, does not exist" (Lamont, 1965, p. 14). For this view, humanism is frequently the target of attack, especially from fundamentalists on the religious right.

To be sure, it is not hard to understand how individuals with a strong religious conviction could have difficulty accepting humanism in its most basic form. Yet, it is important to remember that humanism need not be construed as an "all or nothing" viewpoint. Elias and Merriam (1980), for example, have pointed out that not all humanists see incompatibility between the affirmation of autonomy and the existence of a god. In addressing this issue in the context of educational practice, Hiemstra and Brockett (in press) offer the following comment:

> While this assumption may dissuade some individuals from fully embracing humanism, we believe that teachers, trainers, or administrators do not have to abandon traditional theologies in order to celebrate the good of humanity and to engage in practices designed to facilitate self-direction.

The position advocated here is not that one should feel free to "pick and choose" the elements of a paradigm that one wishes to espouse while uncritically dismissing those parts that are difficult or impossible to embrace. Rather, it is suggested that, just as a non-Christian can share in some or even many of the basic values of Christianity, one need not abandon one's personal theology in order to apply the basic practices of the humanist paradigm.

Emphasis on Individual Vs. Societal Concerns

A second criticism of humanism is that it is sometimes erroneously viewed as a self-centered, or selfish approach. As was noted earlier, the humanist paradigm seems to have blossomed during the decades of the 1960s and 1970s. Smith (1990) has discussed how the development of humanistic psychology coincided with the counterculture of the 1960s. Several features of the counterculture seemed to share common ground with humanistic psychology, such as individualism, human perfectibility, self-disclosure, emphasis on the "here and now," hedonism, and irrationalism (e.g., dispute with the scientific method).

Here, a related concern is the view held by many of those who believe that the primary purpose of education should be social change. The argument is made that humanism stresses development of the individual to the exclusion of concern about the larger society. Actually, however, such is not the case. Most humanist writers stress the centrality of serving the common good. For instance, Lamont (1965) has noted that the highest good can be achieved by "working for the good of all" (p. 15). In addition, one of the characteristics of Maslow's (1970) self-actualizers is the tendency for individuals to focus upon concerns that lie outside of themselves.

One of the clearest illustrations of how humanism and social change can go hand in hand is presented by O'Hara (1989), who offered a comparison of the ideas of Carl Rogers and the Brazilian educator Paulo Freire. While the contexts in which Rogers and Freire have made their contributions are vastly different, O'Hara provides evidence that the basic values held by these two men are very much in concert. She points out that both Rogers and Freire "unabashedly celebrate human existence and our evolutionary potential" and that neither man "gives up on people" (p. 13). Indeed, while most of Rogers' career was spent focusing on the development of individuals, some of his later writings emphasized how the basic principles of the client-centered approach can be used to address broader social issues (e.g., Rogers, 1977).

Conflicts with Behaviorist Thought

A third set of challenges to humanism emanate from those who adhere to a strong behaviorist or competency-based approach to instruction. Indeed, it is quite likely that the strong systems orientation, with its emphasis on measuring observable performance outcomes, which has characterized instructional development, has minimized the impact of the humanist paradigm within the field to date. While there are clearly some fundamental differences between behaviorism and humanism, particularly with regard to views about human nature, and different emphases on outcomes and process, there is also much common ground between the two views. Hiemstra and Brockett (in press) have identified the following shared elements between the two paradigms:

1. Learning should focus on practical problem solving.
2. Learners enter a teaching-learning setting with a wide range of skills, abilities, and attitudes, and these need to be considered in the instructional planning process.
3. The learning environment should allow each learner to proceed at a pace best suited to the individual.
4. It is important to help learners continually assess their progress and make feedback a part of the learning process.
5. The learner's previous experience is an invaluable resource for future learning and thus enhancing the value of advanced organizers or making clear the role for mastery of necessary prerequisites.

Other examples that lend support to the idea that humanism and behaviorism can share common ground include a discussion by Miller and Hotes (1982) on ways to humanize the systems approach to individual instruction. While these authors advocated the use of measurable behavioral objectives, practice, and task analysis, they made the point that it is possible to make the system responsive to the needs of individual students through such activities as modeling, learning by doing, and providing positive reinforcement. Still another more recent example can be found in Stoneall's (1992) discussion of how flexible objectives are more valuable than performance-based ones in situations involving learning for personal growth, development of leaders, and providing information.

The point here is that despite some key differences, it is possible to blend elements of both paradigms in a way that will truly strengthen the instructional development process. Again, it important to warn against uncritical "picking and choosing"; however, this is very different from a thoughtful comparison of common ground shared by different paradigms.

Conclusion

Humanism has had an important influence on education, including the area of instructional development, over the past three decades. This influence has made a clear contribution to educational practice on several fronts. As a way of bringing closure to this chapter, let us examine several major contributions of the humanist paradigm to instructional development.

First, by emphasizing the importance of human potential, the humanist paradigm provides an alternative to deterministic theories. In instructional development, this means that it is important to create a climate of equity, where *all* learners are treated with respect and dignity, since each learner is viewed as having the potential to succeed.

Second, by stressing the importance of affect, the humanist paradigm contributes to a holistic view of the instructional process. While the basic tenets of humanism may differ sharply from behaviorist and cognitive approaches to instruction, the *practice* of humanistic instructional design can compliment other paradigms and, thus, contribute to a comprehensive theory of instruction.

Third, as can be seen from illustrations throughout this chapter, humanism emphasizes the development of the person across the entire lifespan. The clear implication for instructional development is that learning is a lifelong process and it is crucial to understand the needs of learners at different points of the lifespan.

In closing, humanism holds much promise for the future of instructional design. While its basic assumptions differ somewhat from the systems view that has been so influential in the field, humanism addresses some areas that have sometimes been less fully explored by other paradigms of instructional development.

References

Brockett, R. G., & Hiemstra, R. (1991). *Self-direction in adult learning: Perspectives on theory, research, and practice.* London and New York: Routledge.

Brookfield, S. D. (1987). *Developing critical thinkers.* San Francisco: Jossey-Bass.

Candy, P. C. (1991). *Self-direction for lifelong learning.* San Francisco: Jossey-Bass.

Csikszentmihalyi, M. (1990). *Flow: The psychology of optimal experience.* New York: Harper & Row.

Davenport, J., & Davenport, J. A. (1985). A chronology and analysis of the andragogy debate. *Adult Education Quarterly, 35*(3), 152–159.

Egan, G. (1986). *The skilled helper* (3rd ed.). Monterey, CA: Brooks/Cole.

Elias, J. L., & Merriam, S. (1980). *Philosophical foundations of adult education.* Malabar, FL: Robert E. Krieger.

Ellis, A., & Harper, R. A. (1975). *A new guide to rational living.* Englewood Cliffs, NJ: Prentice-Hall.

Flannery, D. D. (1993). Review of *Self-direction in adult leaning: Perspectives on theory, research, and practice. Adult Education Quarterly, 43*(2), 110–112.

Gagné, R. M. (1965). *The conditions of learning.* New York: Holt, Rinehart, and Winston.

Gibbons, M., & Phillips, G. (1979). Teaching for self-education: Promising new professional role. *Journal of Teacher Education, 30*(5), 26–28.

Gibbons, M., & Phillips, G. (1982). Self-education: The process of life-long learning. *Canadian Journal of Education, 7*(4), 67–86.

Gibbons, M., & Phillips, G. (1984). Applications in elementary and secondary education. In M. S. Knowles & Associates, *Andragogy in action* (pp. 365–378). San Francisco: Jossey-Bass.

Hiemstra, R., & Brockett, R. G. (in press). From behaviorism to humanism: Incorporating self-direction in learning concepts into the instructional design process. In H. B. Long (Ed.), Untitled manuscript. Norman, OK: Oklahoma Research Center for Continuing Professional and Higher Education of the University of Oklahoma.

Hiemstra, R., & Sisco, B. (1990). *Improving instruction: Making learning personal, powerful, and successful.* San Francisco: Jossey-Bass.

Knowles, M. S. (1968). Andragogy, not pedagogy! *Adult Leadership, 16,* 350–352.

Knowles, M. S. (1980). *The modern practice of adult education* (revised and updated). Chicago: Association Press (original edition published in 1970).

Knowles, M. S. (1989). *On becoming an adult educator.* San Francisco: Jossey-Bass.

Knowles, M. S., & Associates. (1984). *Andragogy in action.* San Francisco: Jossey-Bass.

Kohl, H. (1967). *36 children.* New York: New American Library.

Lamont, C. (1965). *The philosophy of humanism* (5th ed.). New York: Frederick Unger Publishing Co.

Lindeman, E. C. (1989). The meaning of adult education. Norman, OK: Oklahoma Research Center for Continuing Professional and Higher Education (originally published in 1926).

Mager, R. F. (1962). *Preparing instructional objectives.* Palo Alto: Fearon.

Maslow, A. H. (1970). *Motivation and personality* (2nd ed.). New York: Harper and Row.

McGregor, D. M. (1960). *The human side of enterprise.* New York: McGraw-Hill.

Melton, R. F. (1990). The changing face of educational technology. *Educational Technology, 30*(9), 26–31.

Mezirow, J. (1985). A critical theory of self-directed learning. In S. Brookfield (Ed.), *Self-directed learning: From theory to practice.* (New Directions for Continuing Education No. 25, pp. 17–30.) San Francisco: Jossey-Bass.

Miller, B. W., & Hotes, R. W. (1982). Almost everything you always wanted to know about individualized instruction. *Lifelong Learning: The Adult Years, 5*(9), 20–23.

O'Hara, M. (1989). Person-centered approach as conscientizacao: The works of Carl Rogers and Paulo Freire. *Journal of Humanistic Psychology, 29*(1), 11–36.

Patterson, C. H. (1973). *Humanistic education.* Englewood Cliffs, NJ: Prentice-Hall.

Rogers, C. R. (1942). *Counseling and psychotherapy.* Boston: Houghton Mifflin.

Rogers, C. R. (1951). *Client-centered therapy: Its current practice, implications, and theory.* Boston: Houghton Mifflin.

Rogers, C. R. (1961). *On becoming a person.* Boston: Houghton Mifflin.

Rogers, C. R. (1977). *Carl Rogers on personal power.* New York: Delacorte.

Rogers, C. R. (1983). *Freedom to learn for the eighties.* Columbus, OH: Charles E. Merrill.

Shapiro, S. B. (1986). Survey of basic instructional value in humanistic education. *Journal of Humanistic Education and Development, 24*(4), 144–158.

Shapiro, S. B. (1987). The instructional values of humanistic educators: An expanded, empirical analysis. *Journal of Humanistic Education and Development, 25*(3), 155–170.

Simpson, E. L. (1976). *Humanistic education: An interpretation.* Cambridge, MA: Ballinger Publishing Co.

Skinner, B. F. (1957). *Verbal behavior.* New York: Appleton-Century-Crofts.

Smith, M. B. (1990). Humanistic psychology. *Journal of Humanistic Psychology, 30*(4), 6–21.

Stoneall, L. (1992). The case for more flexible objectives. *Training and Development, 46*(8), 67–69.

Tyler, R. W. (1949). *Basic principles of curriculum and instruction.* Chicago: University of Chicago Press

Valett, R. E. (1977). *Humanistic education: Developing the total person.* St. Louis: C. V. Mosby.

15

Mathemagenic and Generative Learning Theory: A Comparison and Implications for Designers

Barbara L. Grabowski
The Pennsylvania State University, University Park

A Shift in Paradigms

The field of instructional technology is experiencing a major shift in thinking from a behaviorist to a cognitive approach (Clark, 1989; Clark & Salomon, 1987; DiVesta, 1989; DiVesta & Rieber, 1987; Hooper & Hannafin, 1991; Jonassen, 1988; and Winn, 1989). Researchers and designers are now recognizing the mind as an important mediating variable between instruction and outcome. Research and theory from cognitive psychology are, therefore, being given serious attention over the previous influence of behavioral psychology that guided our designs for so many years. Instruction from a behaviorist viewpoint would be "carefully sequenced, successively approximated, with discriminatively reinforced contingencies" (Wittrock, 1974a, p. 88). A cognitive approach considers the learner as an "independent, autonomous learner using his previously acquired information processing strategies to construct adaptive, even creative responses to solve personally important problems" (Wittrock, 1974a, p. 88) with the resulting instruction adapted and adaptable to the learner.

Along with this shift in paradigms, the terms mathemagenic or generative learning have appeared in numerous scholarly articles, often implying a variety of definitions (see, for example, Blanchard, Chang, Logan, & Smith, 1985; Burton, Niles, Lalik, & Reed, 1986; Peper & Mayer, 1986; Sutliff, 1986). Both terms reflect the rise in emphasis on the learner as an active participant in creating personalized meaning from instruction. In the field of instructional technology, these terms appear to have gained increased popularity, especially for developing instructional strategies for the newer technologies (see, for example, Allen, 1987; Jonassen, 1988).

Rothkopf's (1966, 1970) concept of mathemagenic effects was one of the first conceptions which focused on the learner's internal transformation of the stimuli, moving away from the black box of stimulus-response behaviorism. Wittrock (1974a), in his Generative Learning Model, carried the idea of an active learner one step further in proposing that learners generate their own meaning by generating relationships between their existing knowledge and new information.

What Are Mathemagenic Effects?

Rothkopf (1966, 1970) observed that learners often learn something different than is expected from the instruction. He hypothesized that this discrepancy results from the learners actively observing and transforming the stimulus object presented in the instruction to generate their own interpretations. To describe the effects he observed, Rothkopf selected two Greek roots, *mathemain* which means "that which is learned," and *gignesthai*, which means "to be born." The combined term, mathemagenic, refers to behaviors that "give birth to learning" (1966, p. 241).

Rothkopf (1970) divided mathemagenic activities into three classes of learner behaviors that give birth to learning. The first class involves the learner's *overt*, observable behaviors of physically acquiring the materials, and the second pertains to attending to these materials. Although these two classes are important—students cannot learn from materials they do not have or do not attend to—his most significant contribution to instructional design comes from the third class, translation and processing of the new information. This third class refers to those *covert* thought processes which recast learning into an individual experience. Sutliff (1986) cleverly describes this as "learn[ing] by doing inside their heads" (p. 45).

When a learner is put into an environment involving informational or instructional stimuli, learning, whether defined internally by the individual or externally by the instructor, is not guaranteed. These stimuli can have one of four mathemagenic effects: positive, negative, neutral, or unknown. Mathemagenic positive and negative effects are most important to instructional design in that they describe the effect of stimuli which are conducive to (positive) or interfere with (negative) the mental activity required to learn specified objectives or acquire personally defined objectives. The goal of instructional design is to create learning experiences that will maximize the probability that positive effects will occur and minimize the negative ones.

Rothkopf (1970) describes the study of mathemagenic behaviors as a "study of the students' actions that are relevant to the achievement of specified instructional objectives in specified situations or places [where situations are defined as] instructional settings or specific characterizations of instruction materials" (p. 328). In other words, understanding the conscious and unconscious mental and behavioral activities of each learner confronted with instructional materials is paramount to understanding the effects produced by various stimuli which, in turn will help to better predict positive vs. negative mathemagenic effects. Rothkopf found that mathemagenic activities "are relevant to a restricted set of performance objectives or to *classes* of such objectives" (1970, p. 327).

Rothkopf (1970) feels that the study of mathemagenic activities should suggest methods of design for instruction that place emphasis on "promoting those activities in the student that will allow him to achieve instructional goals with available materials" (p. 334). This suggests that he is promoting the study of internal events such that external events can be designed to cultivate these internal activities. In other words, the desired result is what Frase (1969) calls cybernetic control, which puts learner response and selected stimuli in a cycle each based one on the other.

Internal Events: Mental Activities

The mental activities specified by Rothkopf (1970) that give birth to learning encompass set, attention, orienting reflex, information processing, cognition, rehearsal, translation, segmenting, and processing. Sutliff (1986) adds inducing, conceptualizing, organizing, integrating, reinforcing, and reviewing to that list. Barry (1974) classified mental activities by levels of information processing and included rehearsal, coding and imaging, invoking decision rules, organizing schemes, retrieval strategies, and problem solving techniques as mathemagenic activities. These mental activities appear to be the same as the thought processes in the information processing, cognition and metacognition literature (see, for example, Hooper & Hannafin, 1991; Nisbet & Shucksmith, 1986).

Barry's (1974) contribution to this construct was matching specific (mental) mathemagenic activities with differing types of information processing required by the task. By knowing the type of information processing required by the task, learning activities which facilitate these processing strategies could be designed. For example, in a situation in which the learner only needs information for a short period of time, the learning activities should include only rehearsal and imaging. For those requiring recognition in unfamiliar settings, the activity should emphasize organizational schemes or retrieval strategies. Stein and Bransford's work (1979) on transfer also supports Barry's notion of this match between information processing and task demands. Hooper and Hannafin (1991) and DiVesta and Rieber (1987) do not use the same terms but have developed frameworks for matching phases of information processing with specific instructional strategies as well. Table 1 summarizes the interrelationship of these terms. These activities affect the nature of the learner's internal representation of the external instructional materials, which consequently determines what is learned.

Table 1. Mathemagenic activities by types of information processing.

Rothkopf (1970)	Sutliff (1986)	Barry (1974)	Hooper & Hannafin (1991)
Set/Attention			Presenting
			Sequencing
Orienting Reflex	Inducing		Orienting
	Conceptualizing	Imaging	
Segmenting		Coding	Encoding
	Organizing	Invoking decision rules	
		Organizing schemes	
Translation	Integrating		
	Reviewing	Retrieval strategies	Retrieval
Rehearsal	Reinforcing	Rehearsal	
Information Processing/Cognition		Problem solving	

External Events: Instructional Stimuli

Two methods of controlling mathemagenic activities have been specified: directive control and inductive control (Rothkopf, 1976). Directive or deductive control is gained through carefully crafted directions to the students to learn certain materials. Inductive control involves instruction which sparks mental activities. An example of directive control would be the use of behavioral objectives, whereas inductive control would be inserted questions. This dichotomy is similar to Rigney's (1980) categories of embedded vs. detached instructional strategies—detached being related to directive control, and embedded related to inductive control. Rigney's detached strategies are described independent of the content and can be bypassed if the learner considers them irrelevant. These can either be self-assigned or externally assigned (e.g., by the materials or by the instructor). In a detached, self-assigned strategy, the learner may decide to mentally rehearse a procedure. In a detached, externally assigned strategy, the teacher may instruct the learner to compose a mental image of a concept. Embedded strategies are explicitly assigned, generally by the instructional materials, and induce the learner to use a strategy unknowingly. For example, an embedded, externally assigned strategy could be conveyed by the arrangement of the concept structure (Rigney, 1980).

Uses of the Term

Not all authors agree on this inclusive definition of mathemagenic activities. Carver (1972), in a rather critical analysis of mathemagenic behavior, calls the term "barbaric" and contends that it is an empty concept because its broad nature mixes overt observable behaviors with covert unobservable thought. Rickards (1979) claims that the term defies detailed analysis because of its "amorphous" nature (p. 182). Rothkopf (1974), in response to Carver's criticisms, points out that Carver focuses mainly on the first two classes of behavior, which concentrate on largely observable aspects of mathemagenic activities, while avoiding discussion of the translating and processing behaviors. He claims Carver is ready to hypothesize about learners' internal activities, which cannot presently be observed or measured (1974). Although these critics raise some very important points, the concept has served an important function by elevating the significance of learner *activity* as an integral part of the learning process. Rothkopf was one of the first to take the black box from behaviorism and open it for inspection.

Jonassen (1988) rejects the control by the instructional materials he sees implied in mathemagenic activities and dismisses the importance of mathemagenic effects, since he interprets their effect as reductive. He states that learners under mathemagenic control are regarded as "active performers whose mental behavior should be strictly controlled by the activities imposed by the lesson" (p. 152). While Rothkopf (1976) contends that shaping of mathemagenic behaviors is a practical possibility, ". . . not . . . all mathemagenic activities are under instrumental control" (p. 333). In fact, in another article, he describes the learner as having "complete veto power over the success of the written instruction" (Rothkopf, 1976, p. 94). What is very important in mathemagenic activities is not that the mental behavior is strictly controlled but rather that an environment can be created which cultivates active mental engagement in learning. Jonassen interprets mathemagenic too narrowly, only addressing Rothkopf's first two classes of learning and ignoring the third and most significant contribution of Rothkopf's work—that of covert thought processes.

To examine the appropriateness of the use of the term in the instructional technology field, two very important attributes from the above description must be emphasized. The first is that mathemagenic effect is a theoretical construct which affects learning. At least for translating and processing behaviors, mathemagenic effects are mental processes. The second is that mathemagenic activities must be performed by the learner to create learning for him/herself, internally. In other words, they are conscious and unconscious active mental processes caused by some overt or covert action on the part of the learner. Instructor-provided embedded questions, outlines, or analogies certainly could cause (through inductive control) mathemagenic behavior (translation, segmenting, or processing, for example), but they are not in and of themselves mathemagenic activities. The instructor-provided question, outline, or analogy is part of the instruction; the actual mental response of the learner (or non-response), such as responding to the question, or reading the outline, is the mathemagenic activity.

What Is Generative Learning?

Wittrock (1974a, 1974b) developed a model of generative learning which integrated several areas of cognitive psychology, including cognitive development, human learning, human abilities, information processing, and aptitude treatment interactions. A basic assumption behind his model, like mathemagenic activities, is that the learner is not a passive recipient of information, but rather is an active participant in the learning process, working to gain meaningful understanding of the information.

Defining meaningful understanding first will help in the development of the attributes of the model. Meaningful understanding extends way beyond simple regurgitation of information. It would lie on the qualitative end of Schmeck's (1988) "understanding" continuum which is characterized by "the interpretation and reinterpretation of experience to produce self-actualization or personal growth and development" (p. 318). Meaningful understanding, therefore, has a constructive element in which the learner creates meaning by drawing relationships from the information presented in the environment, and then relating those to existing information in cognitive structures (Wittrock, 1985). DiVesta (1989) identified several observable manifestations of meaningful understanding, including better retention of information, better retrieval, meaningful structures created by the learner, and better explanations of the information.

In the generative model of learning, Wittrock (1985) characterizes the learner to be:

1. active at generating . . . relationships;
2. motivated or responsible, in part at least, for exerting the effort to construct them;
3. attentive to the underlying structure of the information to be learned;
4. aware of and making use of learning strategies and metacognitive processes that will facilitate generating these relationships. (p. 123)

The importance of asking the learner to generate his/her own meaning is clearly summarized by Wittrock's statement that "although a student may not understand sentences spoken to him by his teacher, it is highly likely that a student understands sentences that he generates himself" (Wittrock, 1974b, p. 182). It is, as Harlen and Osborne (1985) call it, "learning through the person" (p. 137).

In terms of information processing theory, the brain selectively attends to or ignores information in the environment and then constructs meaning from prior experience, which it stores by connecting it to existing schema in long term memory. The conscious construction of meaning occurs in short-term or working memory where information is being drawn both from long term memory and the environment (Osborne & Wittrock, 1983). According to this model, the learners bring with them prior experiences and understandings which will affect how they learn various materials. What is unique to this model is that meaning is not simply related to existing cognitive structures; rather, new meaning is constructed from interactions between the learner and the environment. Examples of strategies which learners can use to generate meaning include the creation of paraphrases, analogies, explanations, inferences, outlines, summaries, creative interpretations, images, cognitive maps, diagrams, drawings, relevant examples, titles and headings, and questions (Goetz, 1983; Jonassen, 1986). DiVesta (1989) adds identifying scripts within narratives, creating mnemonics, using recursive rules in multiplication, questioning, clarifying, predicting, identifying important information in a passage, and establishing relationships between what is known and prior experience. Only those activities which involve the actual creation of meaning would be classified as examples of generative learning strategies. Activities such as highlighting, tracing, or underlining, therefore, would not be.

According to Wittrock (1974a), "cognitive theory implies that learning can be predicted and understood in terms of what the learners bring to the learning situation, how they relate the stimuli to their memories, and what they generate from their previous experiences" (p. 93). With this as a main assumption underlying instructional technology, the goal of instructional design is to determine the effects of instruction based on what it causes the learner to do. "Effective instruction [in the generative model of learning] causes the learner to generate a relationship between new information and previous experience" (Wittrock, 1974b, p. 182). DiVesta (1989) states that the importance of instruction is its influence on the learner's achievement and understanding.

How Are the Two Terms Related?

Generative learning does not appear to be as fuzzy or as amorphous, using Rickards' terms (1979), as mathemagenic effects, primarily because it deals with mental activities rather than abstract mental processes. Whereas mathemagenic behavior includes all conscious and unconscious covert mental processes and overt physical processes which cause learning to occur, generative learning is limited to those overt and covert manifestations of covert mental activities. Whereas translating and processing mathemagenic activities include all mental processes that give birth to learning, generative learning refers only to those specific mental activities in which the learner engages to generate meaning from instructional materials or from the environment. See Table 2 for a comparison of the concepts and examples of each. In the table, the activities and effects are arranged by level of processing. As can be seen from the table, the overt, physical activities of *getting material* and *underlining phrases* in a text cause the mental processes of orienting and coding, respectively. Likewise, the covert activities of *attending* and *mental repetition* cause the mental processes of attention and rehearsal. In either case, however, the activities are not meant for the learner to generate new or individual meaning from the learning of instructional material, whereas all of the activities in column two are.

Based on this analysis, it appears that mathemagenic activities subsume generative activities. Since generative learning involves the construction of meaning, a mental activity which the learner performs to give birth to learning, it seems reasonable to classify generative learning as a subset of mathemagenic activity. All generative learning produces a mathemagenic effect, but not all mathemagenic activities can be classified as generative.

Whether we are dealing with mathemagenic or generative learning, an argument for designing instruction based on these theories is compelling. Research investigating the effects of mathmagenic and generative activities is also extensive, the results of which add more reason to attend to the message of Rothkopf and Wittrock. The following section provides a very brief summary of several subcategories of generative and mathemagenic research.

Table 2. Match of mathemagenic and generative activities and effects.

MATHEMAGENIC ACTIVITIES Covert/Overt Conscious	GENERATIVE (and Mathemagenic) ACTIVITIES Covert/Overt Conscious	MATHEMAGENIC EFFECTS Covert Conscious/Unconscious
Getting Materials		Orienting Reflex
Attending to Materials		Attention
Repetition		Rehearsal
Underlining Highlighting Tracing Answering Questions		Coding
	Creating Titles and headings Creating Mnemonics	
	Outlining Summarizing Diagramming	Organization
	Paraphrasing Explaining/Clarifying Creating semantic networks Creating concept maps Identifying important information Creating images or creative interpretations	Conceptualization
	Creating relevant examples Relating to prior knowledge	Integration
	Creating analogies Creating metaphors Synthesizing	
	Evaluating Questioning Analyzing Predicting Inferring	Translation

Research Summary

While much of the research on mathemagenic effects focused on the use of adjunct or inserted questions, two other types of activities, imaging and underlining, are included in this brief overview. Studies which investigate the viability of the generative model of learning have researched the effects of imaging, underlining, notetaking, and other meaning generation strategies (familiar stories, summaries, and hierarchies).

Inserted Questions

In the past twenty years, mathemagenic effects of inserted or adjunct questions have been studied extensively. In numerous studies, post-questions have been shown to be most effective for increasing both intentional and incidental learning; superordinate questions have been more effective than subordinate detail questions; and overt responses have been more effective than allowing covert responses (Anderson & Biddle, 1975; Brody & Legenza, 1980; Burton, Niles, Lalik, & Reed, 1986; Rickards, 1979; Sutliff, 1986; Woods & Bernard, 1987).

Underlining

Rickards and August (1975) tested the concept of subject generated versus experimenter-provided underlining strategies under six treatment conditions. Results indicated that when learners had an opportunity to underline text that they considered most relevant, they performed much better on the post-tests on both objective specific and incidental learning (total recall). In fact, a very interesting result was that in the learner generated condition, in which the subjects were asked to underline the least important items, they did poorest of all.

Rickards (1979) considered underlining a generative activity. Since learners are not generating their own meaning from the instructional materials, this strategy might be more appropriately described as a mathemagenic activity.

Imaging

Mathemagenic effects of imaging have also been investigated extensively. Studies have shown that overt imaging is more effective than covert; learner-generated imaging is more effective than instruction-provided imaging; and visual images may be more effective than verbal ones, unless integrated strategies were combined with verbal imaging (Anderson & Kulhavy, 1972; Bull & Wittrock, 1973; Carnine & Kinder, 1985; Laney, 1990; Linden & Wittrock, 1981).

Notetaking

Notetaking may be a highly generative activity; however, quality of notes, type of elaborations, and opportunity for review can affect what, how much, and for how long information is learned. Peper and Mayer (1986), Shrager and Mayer (1989), and Barnett, DiVesta, and Rogozenski (1981) classified notetaking as a generative activity. Barnett, DiVesta, and Rogozenski (1981) also classified it as mathemagenic. These findings were similar to the research findings on questioning, underlining, and imaging, in that notetaking has shown positive effects, but there were mixed findings when compared with type of learning.

Meaning-Generation

The last topic deals with a variety of meaning generation activities. These studies address three key questions regarding the generative model of learning: the effect of learner-generated vs. the effect of learner-reproductive learning; learner-generated vs. instructor-provided constructions of meaning—including organization as a variable; and the general effects of generated elaborations. These studies on generative learning have shown learner generated activities have resulted in significant gains in learning, although issues of organization of lesson content and quality of response may affect the degree of the effect (DiVesta & Peverly, 1984; Doctorow, Wittrock, & Marks, 1978; Stein & Bransford, 1979; Wittrock & Carter, 1975).

In general, results have shown increased gains in learning when the learner is an active vs. a passive participant in the learning process. Research on these topics is currently attempting to tease out the circumstances in which generative learning will have the greatest effect—where there are mathemagenic positive rather than mathemagenic negative results.

Conclusion

While much research has been conducted on many of these questions, their results, except for adjunct question and imaging research, have either not been synthesized to produce a prescriptive model or theory, or have been mixed. Because of their solid theoretical bases, I believe these concepts are not just part of a passing phase or promised panacea. Because they have the substance to form the basis for instructional design prescriptions, an effort to sort out this research would make a major contribution to the field of instructional technology.

The principles behind both concepts, mathemagenic and generative learning, offer the instructional designer much guidance for developing effective instruction. Both emphasize the learner as an active partner in the instructional process. The challenge to the designer is to create a learning environment which promotes this active mental processing at all stages and levels of learning. Various new media have the capability to engage the learner covertly by including questions, complex stimuli, etc. However, what emerging technologies have to offer is a capability for the learner to actually respond by active and *overt manipulation* of information. The key to applying the principles behind these concepts to design of instruction will be to break out of and go beyond the old stimulus-response modes to create a learning environment which taps into the true capabilities of both the learner and the medium.

References

Allen, B. S. (1987). A theoretical framework for interactivating linear video. *Journal of Computer Based Instruction, 13*(4), 107–112.

Anderson, R. C., & Biddle, W. B. (1975). On asking people questions about what they are reading. In G. Bower (Ed.), *Psychology of learning and motivation.* Vol. 9. New York: Academic Press.

Anderson, R. C., & Kulhavy, R. W. (1972). Imagery and prose learning. *Journal of Educational Psychology, 63*(3), 242–243.

Barnett, J. E., DiVesta, F. J., & Rogozenski, J. T. (1981). What is learned in note taking. *Journal of Educational Psychology, 73*(2), p. 18.

Barry, R. J. (1974). The concept of mathemagenic behaviors: An analysis of its heuristic value. *Perceptual and Motor Skills, 38,* 311–321.

Blanchard, J., Chang, F., Logan, I., & Smith, K. (1985). An investigation of computer based mathemagenic activities. *Texas Tech Journal of Education, 12*(3), 159–174.

Brody, P., & Legenza, A. (1980). Can pictoral attributes serve mathemagenic functions? *Educational Communication and Technology Journal, 28*(1), 25–29.

Bull, B. L., & Wittrock, M. C. (1973). Imagery in the learning of verbal definitions. *British Journal of Educational Psychology, 43*(3), 289–293.

Burton, J. K., Niles, J. A., Lalik, R. M., & Reed, M. W. (1986). Cognitive capacity engagement during and following interspersed mathemagenic questions. *Journal of Educational Psychology, 78*(2), 147–152.

Carnine, D., & Kinder, C. (1985). Teaching low-performing students to apply generative and schema strategies to narrative in expository materials. *Remedial and Special Education, 6*(1), 20–30.

Carver, R. P. (1972). A critical review of mathemagenic behavior and the effect of questions upon retention of prose material. *Journal of Reading Behavior, 4*(2), 93–119.

Chen, C. C. (1989). As we think: Thriving in the hyperweb environment. *Microcomputers for Information Management, 6*(2), 77–97.

Clark, R. E. (1989). The future of technology in educational psychology. In M. C. Wittrock & F. Farley (Eds.), *The future of educational psychology.* Hillsdale, NJ: Lawrence Erlbaum Associates.

Clark, R. E., & Salomon, G. (1987). Media in teaching. In M. C. Wittrock (Ed.), *Third handbook of research on teaching.* New York: Macmillan.

Cofer, C. N. (1973). Constructive processes in memory. *American Scientist, 61*(5), 537–543.

DiVesta, F. J. (1989). Applications of cognitive psychology to education. In M. C. Wittrock & F. Farley (Eds.), *The future of educational psychology.* Hillsdale, NJ: Lawrence Erlbaum Associates.

DiVesta, F. J., & Peverly, S. (1984). The effects of encoding variability, processing activity, and rule-examples sequence on transfer of conceptual rules. *Journal of Educational Psychology, 76*(1), 108–119.

DiVesta, F. J., & Rieber, L. (1987). Characteristics of cognitive engineering: The next generation of instructional systems. *Educational Communication and Technology Journal, 35*(4), 213–230.

Doctorow, M., Wittrock, M. C., & Marks, C. B. (1978). Generative processes in reading comprehension. *Journal of Educational Psychology, 70*(2), 109–118.

Foss, C. L. (1989). Tools for reading and browsing hypertext. *Information Processing and Management, 25*(4), 407–418.

Frase, L. T. (1969). Cybernetic control of memory while reading connected discourse. *Journal of Educational Psychology, 60*(1), 49–55.

Goetz, E. (1983). *Elaborative strategies: Promises and dilemmas for instruction in large classes.* ERIC Document: ED 243073.

Harlen, W., & Osborne, R. (1985). A model for learning and teaching applied to primary science. *Journal of Curriculum Studies, 17*(2), 133–146.

Hooper, S., & Hannafin, M. J. (1991). Psychological perspectives on emerging instructional technologies: A critical analysis. *Educational Psychologist, 26*(1), 69–95.

Johnsey, A., Morrison, G. R., & Ross, S. M. (1992). Using elaboration strategies training in computer-based instruction to promote generative learning. *Contemporary Educational Psychology, 17,* 125–135.

Jonassen, D. H. (Ed.). (1986). *Technology of text.* Vol. 2. Englewood Cliffs, NJ: Educational Technology Publications.

Jonassen, D. H. (1988). Integrating learning strategies into courseware to facilitate deeper processing. In D. H. Jonassen (Ed.), *Instructional designs for microcomputer courseware.* Hillsdale, NJ: Lawrence Erlbaum Associates.

Kourilsky, M., & Wittrock, M. C. (1992). Generative teaching: An enhancement strategy for the learning of economics in cooperative groups. *American Educational Research Journal, 29*(4), 861–876.

Laney, J. D. (1990). Generative teaching and learning of cost-benefit analysis: An empirical investigation. *Journal of Research and Development in Education, 23*(3), 136–144.

Linden, M., & Wittrock, M. C. (1981). The teaching of reading comprehension according to the model of generative learning. *Reading Research Quarterly, 17*(1), 44–57.

Lewis, V., & Boucher, J. (1991). Skill, content, and generative strategies in autistic children's drawings. *British Journal of Developmental Psychology, 9,* 393–416.

McAleese, R. (1990). Concepts as hypertext nodes: The ability to learn while navigating through hypertext nets. In D. H. Jonassen & H. Mandl (Eds.), *Designing hypermedia for learning* (pp. 97–115). Berlin: Springer-Verlag.

Nisbet, J., & Shucksmith, J. (1986). *Learning strategies.* London: Routledge and Kegan Paul.

Osborne, R. J., & Wittrock, M. C. (1983). Learning science: A generative process. *Science Education, 67*(4), 489–508.

Peled, Z., & Wittrock, M. C. (1990). Generated meanings in the comprehension of words problems in mathematics. *Instructional Science, 19,* 171–205.

Peper, R. J., & Mayer, R. E. (1986). Generative effects of notetaking during science lectures. *Journal of Educational Psychology, 78*(1), 34–38.

Rickards, J. P. (1979). Adjunct post-questions in text: A critical review of methods and processes. *Review of Educational Research, 49*(2), 181–196.

Rickards, J. P., & August, G. J. (1975). Generative underlining strategies in prose recall. *Journal of Educational Psychology, 67*(6), 860–865.

Rigney, J. W. (1980). Cognitive learning strategies and dualities in information processing. In R. E. Snow, P. Frederico, & W. E. Montague (Eds.), *Aptitude, learning, and instruction.* Vol. 1. Hillsdale, NJ: Lawrence Erlbaum Associates.

Rothkopf, E. Z. (1966). Learning from written instructive material: An exploration of the control of inspection behavior by test-like events. *American Educational Research Journal, 3*(4), 241–249.

Rothkopf, E. Z. (1970). The concept of mathemagenic activities. *Review of Educational Research, 40*(3), 325–326.

Rothkopf, E. Z. (1974). Barbarism and mathemagenic activities: Comments on criticisms by Carver. *Journal of Reading Behavior, 6*(11), 3–8.

Rothkopf, E. Z. (1976). Writing to teach and reading to learn: A perspective on the psychology of written instruction. In N. L. Gage (Ed.), *The psychology of teaching methods.* Chicago: The University of Chicago Press.

Sayeki, Y., Ueno, N., & Nagasaka, T. (1991). Mediation as a generative model for obtaining an area. *Learning and Instruction, 1,* 229–242.

Schmeck, R. R. (1988). Strategies and styles of learning: An integration of varied perspectives. In R. R. Schmeck (Ed.), *Learning strategies and learning styles.* New York: Plenum Press.

Shrager, L., & Mayer, R. E. (1989). Note-taking fosters generative learning strategies in novices. *Journal of Educational Psychology, 81*(2), 263–264.

Stahl, N. A., Brozo, W. G., Smith, B. D., Henk, W. A., & Commander, N. (1991). Effects of teaching generative vocabulary strategies in the college developmental reading program. *Journal of Research and Development in Education, 24*(4), 24–32.

Stein, B. S., & Bransford, J. D. (1979). Constraints on effective elaboration: Effects of precision and subject generation. *Journal of Verbal Learning and Verbal Behavior, 18*(6), 769–777.

Sutliff, R. (1986). Effect of adjunct postquestions on achievement. *Journal of Industrial Teacher Education, 23*(3), 45–54.

Wilson, K. S. (1987). *The Palenque optical disc prototype: Design of multimedia experiences for education and entertainment in a nontraditional learning context* (Technical Report No. 44). (Paper presented at annual meeting of AERA, Washington, DC, April 20–24, 1987.) ERIC number ED 319 377.

Winn, W. (1989). Toward a rationale and theoretical basis for educational technology. *ETR&D, 37*(1), 35–46.

Wittrock, M. C. (1974a). Learning as a generative process. *Educational Psychologist, 11*(2), 87–95.

Wittrock, M. C. (1974b). A generative model of mathematics education. *Journal for Research in Mathematics Education, 5*(4), 181–196.

Wittrock, M. C. (1985). Teaching learners generative strategies for enhancing reading comprehension. *Theory into Practice, 24*(2), 123–126.

Wittrock, M. C. (1990). Generative processes of comprehension. *Educational Psychologist, 24,* 345–376.

Wittrock, M. C. (1991). Generative teaching of comprehension. *Elementary School Journal, 92,* 167–182.

Wittrock, M. C. (1992). Generative learning processes of the brain. *Educational Psychologist, 27,* 531–541.

Wittrock, M. C., & Alesandrini, K. (1990). Generation of summaries and analogies and analytic and holistic abilities. *American Educational Research Journal, 27,* 489–502.

Wittrock, M. C., & Carter, J. (1975). Generative processing of hierarchically organized words. *American Journal of Psychology, 88*(3), 489–501.

Woods, J. H., & Bernard, R. M. (1987). Improving older adults' retention of text: A test of an instructional activity. *Educational Gerontology, 13*(2), 107–120.

Yankelovich, N. (1986). *Intermedia: A system for linking multimedia documents* (IRIS Technical Report 86-2). Providence, RI: Brown University, Institute for Research in Information and Scholarship.

Recognition and appreciation are extended to Eileen Schroeder and to Christopher P. Rynd for their insightful comments and editorial assistance.

16

Constructivist Instructional Development: Reflecting on Practice from an Alternative Paradigm

Scott D. Coleman
J. David Perry
Thomas M. Schwen
Indiana University, Bloomington

Introduction

During the past few years, a number of authors have written about the implications of the *constructivist paradigm* for learning and, by consequence, for the design of instruction (e.g., Bednar, Cunningham, Duffy, & Perry, 1991; Duffy & Jonassen, 1992). However, little has been written about the constructivist paradigm and the practice of *instructional development*, a term which we take to be broader than instructional design. This chapter will focus on the implications of constructivism for the entire development process, rather than on the narrower design of learning activities.

The general plan for the chapter is this:

- Explain what we mean by instructional development.
- Describe the constructivist paradigm and contrast it with the conventional paradigm.
- Examine some implications of the constructivist paradigm for instructional development.
- Offer some concluding comments.

Our Working Definition of Instructional Development

There is no clear consensus in the field about the term "instructional development." Instructional development is sometimes considered to be broader than the term "instructional design," sometimes narrower, and sometimes used interchangeably with it. For the purposes of this chapter, here is our working definition, which closely resembles that suggested by Heinich, Molenda, and Russell (1985, p. 398):

Instructional development is a set of activities carried out in order to:

- *determine needs*, problems, or purposes for instruction;
- *analyze* instructional goals, learners, and settings;
- *design* instructional plans, activities, and materials;
- *evaluate* processes and outcomes.

It may be helpful to note three particular features of this definition:

1. It includes the process of determining needs. This is sometimes assumed to take place prior to the initiation of the development process.
2. It encompasses the activities of instructional design.
3. Although the phases are placed in a logical sequence, there is no mandate to conduct the activities in this order, nor is there any requirement that all instructional development efforts include activities from all four phases.

A related assumption that we make about instructional development is that it can be characterized as a form of inquiry; that is, an attempt to resolve some problematic or uncertain state of affairs.

Paradigms: Conventional and Constructivist

A paradigm is a set of foundational beliefs and assumptions. Though often unconscious, these fundamental understandings greatly influence our thinking. They are the basis for deciding, among other things, what is good, what is fair, and what is rigorous. The concept "paradigm" is a useful tool in explaining differences in the way people look at the world. In the field of instructional development, as well as in many other fields of endeavor, there is a predominant set of beliefs or assumptions that has been labeled by various authors as the "conventional" or "scientific" paradigm. This conventional paradigm includes such beliefs as:

1. The possibility and importance of value-free inquiry.
2. The feasibility and importance of stripping away context to get at the essential variables that will allow prediction and control.
3. The aim of inquiry to discover a single, objective reality that exists independently of any inquirer's interest in it.

A "non-conventional" paradigm has been proposed in recent years and has been labeled by various authors as the "alternative," "naturalistic" or "constructivist"[1] paradigm. The constructivist paradigm includes these beliefs:

---

[1]Most authors seem to use the term "constructivist" when referring to learning, and "naturalistic" when referring to inquiry. However, Guba and Lincoln (1989) have adopted the term constructivist in the belief that it communicates more clearly and avoids confusion with positivist inquiry that takes place in a natural setting. For consistency, we have chosen to use their terminology.

1. Values are of central importance in inquiry and always, whether recognized or not, deeply affect the outcome of any inquiry.
2. The context in which an inquiry takes place is unique to that situation; to view an event separate from its context is to miss the essence of the event.
3. The goal of inquiry is to understand and share different viewpoints about the situation being studied for the purpose of building a joint, sophisticated "construction."

Does the Constructivist Paradigm Really Make Sense?

The constructivist paradigm, when looked at superficially, is quite odd. In particular, the paradigm is frequently characterized using its strange assertion that there are multiple realities, all of which are equally "real." However, whether there "actually" is or is not one true reality is not an essential issue. One does not have to abandon his or her fundamental philosophical and theological beliefs to accept the idea that in our day-to-day interaction with other people it is useful to assume that each individual has a unique perspective that is just as "real" as anyone else's perspective.

Neither does the constructivist paradigm ask us to believe that there are no important differences in the utility of different persons' realities. Accepting that each person's beliefs are as important and worthy of understanding as the next does not mean that all realities are equally useful or relevant in a particular context. The paradigm recognizes that some realities are much more "sophisticated" than others. In fact, the goal of inquiry in the constructivist paradigm is to increase the sophistication of every participant's construction.

To summarize, the constructivist paradigm rejects the idea that the focus of inquiry is to find the one "real" way of looking at world; rather, this paradigm holds that it is more useful to accept and explore everyone's "reality" in the search for an informed and sophisticated construction.

Another strange constructivist assumption has to do with the impossibility of having an "unbiased" inquirer. Does this mean that the inquirer can be corrupt and careless? No, definitely not. Standards for fair and rigorous inquiry do exist (Lincoln & Guba, 1985), though they are somewhat different than conventional standards. The inquirer's values and assumptions deeply influence any study and its outcomes. Since there is no way that a person can ignore his or her values, the best course of action is for the investigator to make these values conscious and to openly acknowledge them. This does not mean that the investigator's values should be the predominant factor in the inquiry, but only that these values should be recognized as an influence. From the constructivist perspective, a claim of "objectivity" is very suspect, as it can serve as a screen under which inquirer or client values and assumptions are given special, incontestable sway (Reason & Rowan, 1981).

A third peculiar idea associated with the constructivist paradigm is its apparent rejection of the "scientific method." Such traditional procedures as isolating independent and dependent variables, setting up controlled experiments, and making statistically-based inferences are no longer accorded their status as premier "truth-finding" tools. However, constructivist inquiry is not a rejection of science, but only a questioning of the traditional way of operationalizing the "scientific method." The reason for this stance is simple: a recognition that in simplifying situations to make them fit the traditional "scientific" model, the essence of those situations can be lost. The alternative proposed by the constructivist paradigm is loyal to the essence of scientific inquiry. In the openness of the constructivist investigator, in the requirement to share ideas openly among all stakeholders, in the tentativeness of its conclusions, always open to additional data, the constructivist paradigm is true to the ideals of science. See Table 1 for a view of the conventional and the constructivist paradigms.

TABLE 1.   The "theorems" of inquiry.

Readers who are interested in a deeper understanding of the two paradigms may find the following table useful. It is adapted from Guba and Lincoln's (1989) contrasting theorems of conventional and constructivist inquiry.

Conventional view:	Constructivist view:
The truth of any proposition can be determined by testing it empirically in the natural world.	The "truth" of any proposition is determined by submitting it to the judgment of a group of informed and sophisticated holders of what may be different constructions.
Whatever exists exists in some measurable amount. If it cannot be measured it does not exist.	Constructions typically cannot be measured. If something can be measured, the measurement plays, at best, a supportive role in the construction.
Facts are aspects of the natural world that do not depend on the theories that guide an inquiry. They are independent of the values that may later be used to interpret them.	"Facts" are always theory-laden and value-laden. They have no meaning except within some theory framework and some value framework.
Every observed action (effect) has a cause, and every cause has an effect.	Any observed action is the instantaneous resolution of a large number of mutual, simultaneous shapers; however, one or several of these may be singled out arbitrarily for some specific purpose.
The success of a science can be judged on whether it displays ever-increasing ability to predict and control its phenomena.	The success of constructivist inquiry can be judged on whether it displays ever-increasing understanding of its phenomena.
Scientifically devised problem solutions have widespread applicability.	Problem solutions devised through recon-struction have local, temporary, applicability only.
Change is a process that must be stimulated by outside forces; it must be managed.	Change is a continuously ongoing process that requires neither outside stimulation nor direction, even though such intervention may be useful.

A Distinction Between Paradigms and Methods

Oddly enough, it is not altogether clear which paradigm instructional developers are op-erating from. Instructional developers often speak in a language associated with the scientific paradigm. We use terms and concepts drawn from scientific or applied science disciplines, such as psychology (e.g., stimulus materials), communication (feedback), and engineering (flowchart, design). On the other hand, the practice of instructional development is often con-sistent with the basic beliefs of the constructivist paradigm. For example, many developers have come to recognize the importance of deeply understanding the learner and client con-texts. Unfortunately, it may not be possible to determine a developer's "guiding paradigm" simply by looking at his or her activities. This is because paradigms and the methods used in practice are very different things.

When we talk about paradigms, we mean a fundamental set of beliefs and assumptions. In our view, a paradigm may suggest certain methods, but it does not necessarily determine or constrain those methods. Thus, a developer who ascribes to one paradigm may legitimately use tools and methods more commonly associated with another paradigm. Guba and Lincoln (1989) have illustrated this nicely:

> To take a homely example, it may not be possible to tell whether an individual holding a hammer is a carpenter, an electrician, or a plumber, but the person holding the hammer knows, and that intention will lead to the hammer being used in very different ways. Similarly, while it may not be possible to label an individual a positivist simply because he or she is using a survey instrument, or a constructivist simply because he or she is conducting an interview, those persons know (or should know) from which paradigm they operate, and that knowledge has significant consequences for the ways in which those tools are used. (p. 158)

To follow on Guba and Lincoln's example, both "conventional" and constructivist developers might use a survey instrument, perhaps even the same instrument. However, the instruments would likely be created in different ways, used at different times, and serve different purposes. A positivist developer might create a survey based on a predetermined set of requirements or assumptions, administer it at the start of data collection, and use it as a primary source of data for a needs analysis. On the other hand, a constructivist developer might create a survey based on open-ended interviews and observations, administer it late in the data collection process, and use it to confirm or extend findings from naturalistic methods.

This distinction between paradigms and methods is important, because it explains why some developers use methods that seem consistent with constructivism, although their beliefs may be more consistent with the conventional or scientific paradigm. In this chapter, while we do discuss some methods, our primary concern is with broader implications, such as the ways we think about instructional development (ID), the purposes it serves, and its impact on client relationships.

Implications of Constructivism for Instructional Development[2]

The constructivist paradigm, when contrasted with the conventional paradigm, is a source of some interesting implications for the practice of instructional development. In this section we discuss five such implications, derived in part from Guba and Lincoln's theorems

---

[2]The phases of instructional development, though they are useful concepts in many ways, may be difficult to distinguish in practice. This is particularly true when practice is guided by the constructivist paradigm. For example, during the negotiation of needs, information about learners and instructional designs may emerge as the developer interacts with the client system. Also, the groundwork and essence of evaluation occurs throughout the development process as the evaluator/developer becomes aware of and builds individual and joint constructions. This notion that the phases of ID are indistinct is certainly not a novel one, but we are further suggesting it may be useful to think of these phases as being orchestrated simultaneously by the developer. Viewed in this way, an instructional development effort is holographic—the phases are so interwoven that it should be possible to understand the whole of the process from the perspective of any one of the four phases.

Such a conception requires a clear understanding of the purpose of each phase, since these phases are not at all distinguished by the developer's activities, nor by when they occur in the process. The reader should understand that, while we find it convenient to discuss the implications of constructivism for each of the four phases, we recognize that such distinctions are somewhat artificial and arbitrary.

for constructivist inquiry. The first four implications correspond to the four phases of instructional development; the fifth applies to ID as a whole.

Implication 1: The search for needs is best characterized as a process of negotiation, not assessment.

From the perspective of the constructivist paradigm, the search for needs, traditionally the starting point for instructional development, requires an exploration of the beliefs and values of the clients, learners, and others who have a stake in the situation being considered. The search for needs is dependent on finding the most informed and sophisticated construction possible, given the available resources. Following from the basic tenets of the constructivist paradigm, the instructional developer must consider his or her own values and assumptions as part of the search for needs. Also, the methodology used in identifying needs must be the establishment of a dialectic between the instructional developer and other stakeholders.

The relative nature of needs.   The idea of exploring needs while operating from within the constructivist paradigm has been termed "needs negotiation" (Coleman, 1989). Rather than viewing needs as objective constructs that can be measured and categorized, the needs negotiator recognizes that needs are a creation of the process used to find them, in the same way that the determination of the nature of light (wave or particle) is dependent upon the experiment used in the investigation. Any set of needs that has been "found" by a developer is dependent on who was involved in the process, how they were involved, how their words were interpreted by others, and many other non-objective factors.

The process of needs negotiation.   Needs negotiation begins with the developer's reflection on his or her own constructions about the situation and about how a fair search for needs should be conducted in that situation. For example, a developer exploring needs before developing a mathematics textbook might write introspectively about how he or she believes children learn, which educational goals are most important, which math content is most appropriate to reaching important goals, which methods of instruction are most valuable, what the clients expect, how important it is to involve teachers in the process of exploring needs, and which needs appear to be most important. The needs negotiator views his or her construction as necessarily tentative and incomplete—the starting point for the more informed and sophisticated construction that will be developed as the negotiation continues.

In many ways, the beginning and all phases of needs negotiation are introspection or self-study. The needs negotiator must be conscious of his or her own beliefs about such matters as how people learn and what is important to know.

Once this initial introspection has been completed, the needs negotiator "purposefully samples" the constructions of other stakeholders, perhaps mathematicians, administrators, teachers, parents, and students. Those persons selected are those the needs negotiator believes may have differing perspectives, values, and understandings that are related to needs. The needs negotiator is interested in understanding each construction and learning how it is similar to and different from other constructions, including his or her own. In selecting and interviewing respondents, the needs negotiator makes an effort to involve respondents from all stakeholding groups and carries out interviews in such a way that the underlying values and assumptions of each respondent come to light.

As the needs negotiation continues, the needs negotiator shares his or her understanding about the differences and similarities between constructions. Ideally, each respondent is asked to consider the differences between his or her own construction and the constructions of the other respondents, including the needs negotiator, who should also share his or her own ideas. One way to facilitate this sharing process is to represent constructions in writing, directly authored by each respondent or paraphrased by the needs negotiator from interview notes and checked for accuracy and completeness by the respondent.

After constructions have been shared among respondents, and each respondent has read and reacted to each construction, the needs negotiator drafts a sophisticated joint construction that encompasses the perspectives of all the respondents. This draft is shared with the respondents who then respond to it. A revised joint construction is then written by the needs negotiator describing what "needs to be done" based on this joint construction.

An important part of needs negotiation is documenting that the exploration of needs was conducted ethically and rigorously—providing evidence that the needs negotiation was conducted in a fair and reasonable way—and showing that the needs were truly negotiated, not dictated by the client or invented by the needs negotiator.

Comparing needs negotiation and needs assessment. Some of the features of needs negotiation are not unlike those prescribed for needs assessment. For example, Rossett (1987, p. 67) has said that needs assessment:

- relies upon opinions and feelings gathered through interviews, surveys and group meetings;

- seeks information on all five purposes; optimals, actuals, feelings, causes, and solutions;

- involves as many concerned sources as you can afford;

- is conducted in stages, with what you learn in the first stage influencing the questions you ask and data you examine in later stages.

In particular, the importance of understanding the client and stakeholders is emphasized in both models. However, the constructivist paradigm provides a powerful rationale for the intimate involvement of the needs negotiator in the process. Following from the conventional paradigm, the investigator must maintain a value-free stance and not let his or her beliefs influence the determination of needs. From the constructivist view, the investigator cannot help but influence the determination of needs, and should do so in an open and fair way.

Implication 2: Analysis and design are processes for reducing the number of competing constructions so that closure can be achieved.

In constructivist analysis and design, competing arguments, methods, and values are arrayed in opposition to each other as a framework for choosing an intervention.

Although the goal of needs negotiation is the creation of a joint construction, some of the competing constructions that surfaced in needs negotiation may be carried into analysis and design. To further complicate matters, the process of job or task analysis also entails value decisions. It is probably obvious, but worth restating, that analytic tools operate from a number of explicit and tacit assumptions about learning. For example, a procedural analysis of a complex task, conducted with the aid of an expert performer, is often linked to the use of mentoring as an instructional technique. Mentoring relationships are typically accompanied by a high degree of tolerance for individual learning paths. On the other hand, a hierarchical learning analysis probably suggests convergence on a single learning path and may move rather quickly to the development of self-instructional materials. These techniques, like others, carry their own social and value implications for the organization. The developer must communicate these implications so that the client can make informed choices.

Similarly, values are also embodied in instructional designs. A particular design or framework for instruction could accommodate, ameliorate, or accentuate a value position. For example, a mastery learning model assumes certain prerequisites, time available to learn, availability of materials, and certain groupings of learners. The prescriptions from this model are not value-free. They have social meaning for the students and the managers of the learning environment. These values may or may not be consistent with the values of the client system. Often clients are not aware of the values embodied in a design until they see the instruction in practice. At that point it is often impractical to make major changes in the instructional protocol. This may be particularly true of naive clients. The authors of this chapter have a wide set of experiences with clients. We have often been confronted with failures or partial successes that are hard to explain. As we have matured in our professional practice, we have come to believe that a silent value conflict between us and our clients, or within a client group, may have led to many of the unexplained problems in practice. Thus, value-based decisions become an explicit part of the constructivist design process, in contrast to conventional instructional design, whose practitioners often take the position that designs are value-free.

In constructivist design, different intellectual positions, methods of solving problems, and value positions, are placed in opposition to one another. The point of the design is to array the reasonable options that are available to address the performance issue. When thoughtful and rigorous arguments surface in our development projects, we seek consensus because it is practical to have one solution. When that is not possible, we seek the least number of feasible solutions (constructions) to an analysis/design problem because that is the next most practical thing to do. Eventually, the client and the designer are forced to closure, and must find a balance between efficient action and accommodation of differing viewpoints.

What is new in the constructivist perspective of instructional analysis and design is that we no longer have the convenience of believing we can identify the one best approach, or the "truth" of a situation. Rather than pursuing the truth, we pursue a situation-specific rigor and discipline that integrates our values with our technical analyses, makes tacit assumptions explicit, exposes the weaknesses as well as the strengths in our arguments, and leads to purposeful action.

Implication 3: Design is characterized as a set of macro-level decisions made in advance of instruction, and micro-level decisions made during instruction.

A constructivist instructional design typically consists of frameworks, structures, and processes, rather than carefully delimited content, specific sequencing, and predetermined practice and testing.

Constructivist designers are predisposed to create active, individual processes, in which the learner builds on prior learning. Designers often empower learners to make—or at least negotiate—decisions about sequence, efficiency, etc.

Constructivist designers typically create environments that allow for a social learning process. Because the fundamental notion is that knowledge is a social construction, collaboration is essential. Interdependent structures or frameworks are created that demand active dialogue to complete learning tasks. A related assumption is that complex skills are learned best in mentoring relationships. Such relationships are characterized by trust and empowerment of the learner. Thus, the designer's challenge is to provide frameworks within which mentors are available, but not responsible for completion of the learning tasks.

Constructivist designers are often concerned with capturing, simplifying, and portraying "authentic" situations and behavior. The constructivist operates on the assumption that the learner is best motivated by "real" problems. Further, the constructivist takes the view that artificial or contrived representations of knowledge and skills inhibit transfer (Resnick, 1987).

So the constructivist will often create "microworlds" within which real behavior can be simulated without distorting the richness and diversity of real-life problem solving. In a certain sense, the constructivist takes the view that knowledge should not be learned out of context. The expectation is that the school experience can be a series of microworlds within which learners are empowered to solve real problems in a reasonably idiosyncratic fashion. Mentoring processes would be available to ensure quality, provide guidance, and make necessary judgments about the efficiency of the designs.

As a result of these characteristics, instructional design is a set of processes that must occur during instruction as much as before instruction. As Streibel (1989) suggests, there is not necessarily a distinction between constructivist design and the instructional process itself. Much of the design process consists of real-time decisions made by teachers as mentors interacting with empowered students, and often negotiated between teacher and student.

Implication 4: Evaluation can best be characterized as a process of creating a joint construction of the worth of the ID effort.

When examined from a constructivist perspective, the evaluation aspects of an instructional development effort rest on three major principles:

1. Evaluation is, inherently, a values-based process.
2. The perspectives of multiple stakeholders need to be taken into account.
3. Evaluation entails looking beyond the stated goals of the ID effort.

Thus, evaluation, like needs determination, can be thought of as a process whereby the views of relevant stakeholders are shared to create a joint construction of the worth or merit of the development effort.[3]

Evaluation as a values-based process. No matter how we choose to conduct an evaluation, the fact is that we have made choices, for example, to look at some parts of an entity and not others; to apply certain processes and procedures and not others. Since there is often no empirical basis for making these choices, they must reflect values to some degree. For example, a common model for the evaluation of training (Kirkpatrick, cited in Smith & Geis, 1992) proposes four levels to be considered: (1) trainee attitude, (2) trainee learning, (3) change in job performance, and (4) change in organizational performance. These would each entail very different kinds of evaluation processes. How would one choose which to address?

We could also pose similar questions for the evaluation of school learning, where the choice is often between "testing" for subject-matter mastery and "assessment" of transferable skills. These correspond to levels 2 and 3 of Kirkpatrick's scheme.

The point of this is not to suggest that there is no role for logic or reason in choosing instruments and objects of evaluation. Rather, the point is that, ultimately, such choices are a reflection of the values of the individual or organization making the choices.

Evaluation to serve multiple stakeholders. In a corporate training effort, the relevant stakeholders might include the students, their "home" managers, instructors, instruc-

---

[3]There are a related set of issues, which we will not address in this chapter, concerning the assessment of outcomes of constructivist *learning*. Jonassen (1992) has noted that constructivist learning raises some thorny problems for evaluation. For example, if the outcomes of constructivist learning are individualized knowledge constructions, then what standards does one apply to test learning? While we acknowledge this set of concerns, ours are somewhat broader. We are interested in the implications of constructivist *inquiry* for the evaluation of instructional development efforts.

tional designers, and both the stockholders and customers of the corporation. In a school learning effort, the stakeholders might include the students, their parents, teachers, principals, and citizens of the community. It seems very likely that such different stakeholders—in either setting—would be interested in different things.

For example, in the corporate setting, students might be interested in whether the instruction was enjoyable, and whether they could apply it on the job, but might care little about how they scored on a posttest (unless the test entailed some reward or punishment). The instructors might be interested in student attitudes toward the instruction, and also in how they scored on a posttest. Instructional designers might want to know whether students learned, and whether they actually perform differently on the job following the instruction. Managers might be most concerned with job performance, while stockholders and customers would be most concerned with organizational performance.

In the school setting, students might be concerned with enjoyment and test scores, teachers and principals with test scores, parents with test scores and transferability to occupational or higher educational settings, and citizens with occupational skills.

The point of these examples is to show that there are, legitimately, multiple stakeholders in any instructional development effort, and that their concerns about the effort are likely to differ.

Beyond goal-based evaluation. As we noted earlier, evaluation in ID cannot simply be a matter of asking whether the instruction met its stated goals or objectives, for several reasons:

1. Stated objectives are often not a good basis for determining the purpose of the instruction. Objectives often evolve during the development process, and written documents may not reflect these changes.
2. Since objectives are usually written with an eye toward measurability, they tend not to address things that we know will be difficult to measure, such as higher-order skills of analysis and synthesis.
3. Even if the stated objectives are well constructed, they may entail the concerns of only one stakeholder group (e.g., the client or the instructional designer).
4. Even when it can be determined whether the instruction met its stated objectives, this says nothing about other consequences, good or bad, of the intervention.

Goals are so problematic for evaluation that some theorists (e.g., Scriven, 1973) contend that the evaluator should not know the goals of the entity or intervention, for fear that he or she will be unduly biased by them. Without going to such an extreme position, we think we have demonstrated that goals would not be a sufficient basis for organizing an evaluation. Rather, we propose that the organizing principle for constructivist evaluation of ID should be the consequences of the intervention for the individuals and organizational system(s) of interest, as expressed through the perspectives of various stakeholders.

The methods of constructivist evaluation. Since evaluation methodology has been thoroughly addressed by numerous authors, we will not discuss this in detail. In brief, Guba and Lincoln (1989) suggest that constructivist evaluation is a process of identifying the concerns of relevant stakeholders and creating a mechanism whereby those concerns can be shared and negotiated, leading to a consensus about the entity being evaluated. The specific techniques are largely those of qualitative inquiry: interview, observation, and document analysis. However, quantitative methods may be used as well, provided they are employed within the overall framework of constructivist evaluation. As we pointed out earlier, we are not proposing that constructivist methods must always be used in ID evaluation, but that constructivism is a useful framework for thinking about evaluation.

Evidence for the utility of constructivist evaluation. The utility of the constructivist approach to instructional evaluation is suggested by the experiences of two groups of professionals: evaluators and instructional developers.

In its brief history, the evaluation field has gone through a considerable evolution. Initially, the field was characterized by a focus on objective measurement designed to support the needs of decision makers—usually managers or funders. Today, the field is characterized by multiple methods, a concern with multiple stakeholders, and aims that are as broad as enlightenment and social justice (Shadish, Cook, & Leviton, 1991). The reasons for this evolution are complex, but one of the most significant factors has been the realization that the quantitatively-oriented evaluation data of the past were seldom ever used to make decisions. As Geis and Smith (1992) have noted, "Decisions rest as much on beliefs, attitudes, and political realities as on the outcomes of evaluations." Thus, this evolution in evaluation can be explained in part by the very pragmatic desire for evaluation data to be useful. If "beliefs, attitudes, and political realities" are the basis for decisions, then evaluations need to take these into account.

Instructional developers should also have reason to favor a form of evaluation that takes into account the the values and concerns of multiple stakeholders. We (the authors) have had numerous experiences in which the success or failure of an ID intervention depended less on its instructional quality than on unplanned effects for some stakeholder group who may or may not have been considered in the development process. We assume that other developers have had similar experiences. The purpose of a broader framework for evaluation, then, is not merely epistemological correctness. Rather, our purposes are very practical ones: to account for how interventions affect the individuals and organizations in which they are set, and to reveal and resolve conflicts that can undermine such interventions.

The feasibility of constructivist evaluation in ID. It is reasonable to ask whether it is feasible to conduct a constructivist evaluation within the framework of instructional development. Our first answer to this question is that there are certainly issues of scale and cost-benefit ratio to be raised here. A two-hour training session designed to improve employees' performance with a software tool already in use probably does not call for a complex, far-reaching evaluation plan. On the other hand, a forty-hour curriculum designed to introduce total quality management to a department would seem to call for an evaluation that goes well beyond trainee attitude or short-term retention. In between the extremes, of course, lie countless gray areas where good judgment is needed. As we mentioned earlier, what we suggest is not that developers always adopt the *methods* of constructivist evaluation, but that they consider constructivism as a *framework* for thinking about evaluation. Using constructivist evaluation as a framework means being aware of what one chooses *not* to do, as well as what one chooses *to* do. As developers, we can choose to focus on particular aspects of an intervention, particular outcomes, or particular stakeholders. But we should make such choices with an awareness of the tradeoffs and risks involved. At the least, the paradigm helps us be aware of our *own* construction of the entity we are evaluating; that ours is one of many possible constructions; and that others are likely to hold very different constructions.

Another way of looking at the feasibility question is within the larger context of constructivist ID. If one has conducted the processes of needs determination, analysis, and design in accordance with the constructivist paradigm, then the evaluation is just a continuation of that process. In other words, if the need for the intervention was determined through a negotiation among the relevant stakeholders, then the evaluation simply continues that process of communication and negotiation. Ultimately, this points in the direction of the "cybernetic," or learning organization in which evaluation is conducted not just to judge the worth of a particular intervention, but as part of a continual process of monitoring and feedback that leads to organizational evolution (Geis & Smith, 1992).

Product evaluation, and formative vs. summative evaluation.   In this discussion of evaluation, we have not touched on the sort of evaluation that most instructional designers and developers are familiar with: that of product evaluation, or evaluation of instructional materials. This kind of evaluation, which uses concepts such as expert reviews, learner validation, small group evaluation, and field trials (e.g., Smith & Ragan, 1993), is still useful in the scheme we have described. However, it is only a small part of the evaluation of an ID *intervention*. The focus of product evaluation is on the clarity and design of the instruction itself, rather than on its impact for the larger system or organization.

Another notion familiar to developers is that of formative and summative evaluation. Formative evaluation is conducted in order to develop the product or intervention. Summative evaluation is conducted in order to certify that the intervention is effective. This distinction seems much less useful within the framework of the constructivist paradigm. Summative evaluation seems to suggest some final and perhaps cross-context judgement about the worth of the intervention. However, one of the tenets of constructivism is that generalizations across contexts are highly problematic. Even if an intervention could be determined, in some summative way, to be appropriate for a particular setting and time, a constructivist would be reluctant to assume anything about its appropriateness in a different setting, or even in the same setting at a different time.

Implication 5: Increasingly sophisticated constructions are the cornerstone of improved practice.

Is there ultimately one right way to practice instructional development? Will research converge on a law-based system that will infallibly guide the production of effective instruction once a given context has been described? Can the effective practice of instructional development be reduced to the careful application of generalizable, scientifically-verified principles regarding needs, objectives, learners, methods and evaluation? The two paradigms suggest different answers to these questions.

The logic of the conventional paradigm allows one to answer "yes" to these questions: one day it may be possible to guide all instructional development using generalizable principles, although the full discovery and implementation of such a law-based system may not be easy or practical.

A constructivist way of organizing the understanding of ID.   The basic beliefs of the constructivist paradigm lead to the conclusion that effective instruction will never follow from the application of generalized "principles." Quite simply, the world is too complex and value-laden to be reducible to generalizable cause-effect relationships. Instead, effective instruction will always be the result of the application of a sophisticated construction in a specific context. This sophisticated construction will necessarily be a joint construction built by the instructional developer and the stakeholders—each contributing their unique understandings and values.

The construction of an individual instructional developer might be put into writing in the form of "rules" and "principles." It is also true that any written or spoken ideas about how to carry on instructional development (including the entire body of ID literature) can be accommodated by the constructivist paradigm as long as these ideas are considered to be individual constructions, not generalizable rules.

Is there then any essential difference between rules that may some day be proven to be laws and rules that are used to organize the thinking of an individual developer? Is the distinction that follows from the two paradigms really worth making? We think so, because we recognize important differences between a field of ID that values the discovery of generalizable principles and procedures, and a field of ID that rejects generalized principles but values the ever-increasing sophistication of its practitioners' individual constructions. In the former case, the field of ID and the practitioners who read and apply research findings improve through the conventional model of research. In the latter case, individual developers, and other developers who consider how those constructions increase their own understanding, improve by building ever more sophisticated constructions.

The importance of the ID community to the constructivist developer. From the constructivist perspective each developer holds unique, perhaps very different views that are equally "real" about how to develop instruction. Each developer has a construction that is based on values and experience. As one gains and reflects on experience and the experience of others, this construction grows more sophisticated. The direction being moved towards is not the discovery of immutable laws applicable by all developers in all situations, but towards the sophisticated individual construction that will lead to good instruction being developed in the sphere within which the developer operates.

From the constructivist perspective, there is still much value in considering the viewpoints of other developers, as they are expressed in writing or in conversation. This is one important way of making our own constructions more sophisticated. But it is essential that each developer consciously continue to build his or her own unique construction about the development of instruction and its foundational values and assumptions. Reflection about one's own ideas and practice is the primary, most essential factor in professional growth.

Consider two instructional developers. One has a strong interest in computer-based instruction and primarily develops military training. The other has an interest in the social aspects of ID and works with corporate clients, helping large businesses maximize performance through training and environmental design. How should these developers, with different experiences, different responsibilities, and different skills increase their effectiveness? Though the constructions of these two individuals would be quite different, due to their different orientations and spheres of activities, both would grow in effectiveness by alternating between experience (which can include reading about and listening to ideas about ID) and the inward-looking process of construction building.

Concluding Thoughts

We believe that there is considerable experiential evidence that the scientific paradigm is an inadequate basis for understanding the practice of instructional development. Like other fields, ID has perpetuated the myth that Schön (1987) calls "technical rationality":

> Technical rationality is an epistemology of practice derived from positivist philosophy, built into the very foundations of the modern research university . . . Technical rationality holds that practitioners are instrumental problem solvers who select technical means best suited to particular purposes. Rigorous professional practitioners solve well-formed instrumental problems by applying theory and technique derived from systematic, preferably scientific knowledge . . . But, as we have come to see with increasing clarity over the last twenty or so years, the problems of real-world practice do not present themselves to practitioners as well-formed structures. Indeed, they tend not to present themselves as problems at all, but as messy, indeterminate situations. (pp. 3–4)

While science may be well-suited for resolving clearly-defined problems, it is not well-suited for resolving "messy, indeterminate situations." Schön's analysis suggests that the most critical aspects of ID are those we can be least certain about: the processes by which we frame or make sense of problems and opportunities before we set about resolving them. These processes draw heavily on our judgment and intuition, shaped by our prior experiences. They take the form of a kind of conversation with the situation at hand. Schön refers to this conversation as reflection-in-action.

One reason the constructivist paradigm holds such appeal for ID and other professions is that it explicitly accommodates this notion of multiple frameworks or ways of seeing a situation. In this chapter, we have suggested some implications of constructivism for the practice of ID, and we have acknowledged that we find it to be a powerful alternative to the scientific paradigm. However, we would stop short of advocating constructivism as the ultimate, "true" guiding paradigm for the field. Like any other human construction, constructivism itself is subject to debate, negotiation, reflection, refinement, and, ultimately, replacement.

What we *do* want to advocate is Schön's notion of reflection-in-action, not only as a process that individual developers engage in, but also as a public conversation that we as practitioners carry on about our field. If we are committed to this kind of conversation, then it is more likely that, whatever paradigms guide our practice, they will be frameworks that expand our opportunities to influence the people and organizations with which we work, rather than boxes that confine us.

References

Bednar, A. K., Cunningham, D., Duffy, T. M., & Perry, J. D. (1991). Theory into practice: How do we link? In G. J. Anglin (Ed.), *Instructional technology: Past, present, and future* (pp. 88–101). Englewood, CO: Libraries Unlimited.

Coleman, S. D. (1989). *Needs negotiation.* Unpublished doctoral dissertation, Indiana University, Bloomington.

Duffy, T. M., & Jonassen, D. H. (Eds.). (1992). *Constructivism and the technology of instruction.* Hillsdale, NJ: Lawrence Erlbaum Associates.

Geis, G. L., & Smith, M. E. (1992). The function of evaluation. In H. D. Stolovitch & E. J. Keeps (Eds.), *Handbook of human performance technology* (pp. 130–150). San Francisco: Jossey-Bass.

Guba, E. G., & Lincoln, Y. S. (1989). *Fourth generation evaluation.* Newbury Park, CA: Sage.

Heinich, R., Molenda, M., & Russell, J. D. (1985). *Instructional media and the new technologies of instruction* (2nd ed.). New York: John Wiley & Sons.

Jonassen, D. H. (1992). Evaluating constructivistic learning. In T. M. Duffy & D. H. Jonassen (Eds.), *Constructivism and the technology of instruction: A conversation* (pp. 137–148). Hillsdale, NJ: Lawrence Erlbaum Associates.

Lincoln, Y. S., & Guba, E. G. (1985). *Naturalistic inquiry.* Beverly Hills, CA: Sage.

Reason, P., & Rowan, J. (Eds.). (1981). *Human inquiry: A sourcebook of new paradigm research.* New York: John Wiley & Sons.

Resnick, L. (1987). Learning in school and out. *Educational Researcher, 16,* 13–20.

Rossett, A. (1987). *Training needs assessment.* Englewood Cliffs, NJ: Educational Technology Publications.

Schön, D. A. (1987). *Educating the reflective practitioner.* San Francisco: Jossey-Bass.

Scriven, M. (1973). Goal-free evaluation. In E. R. House (Ed.), *School evaluation: The politics and process* (pp. 319–328). Berkeley, CA: McCutchan.

Shadish, W. R., Cook, T. D., & Leviton, L. C. (1991). *Foundations of program evaluation.* Newbury Park, CA: Sage.

Smith, M. E., & Geis, G. L. (1992). Planning an evaluation study. In H. D. Stolovitch & E. J. Keeps (Eds.), *Handbook of human performance technology* (pp. 151–166). San Francisco: Jossey-Bass.

Smith, P. L., & Ragan, T. J. (1993). *Instructional design.* New York: Merrill.

Streibel, M. J. (1989, February). *Instructional plans and situated learning: The challenge of Suchman's theory of situated action for instructional designers and instructional systems.* Paper presented at the meeting of the Association for Educational Communications and Technology, Dallas.

17

The Impact of Situated Cognition: Instructional Design Paradigms in Transition

Michael A. Orey
University of Georgia, Athens

Wayne A. Nelson
Southern Illinois University at Edwardsville

At a time when instructional design models have been undergoing revision in order to incorporate advancements in cognitive theories of learning (Hannafin & Rieber, 1989a, 1989b; Merrill, Li, & Jones, 1990a, 1990b; Orey & Nelson, 1993; West, Farmer, & Wolff, 1991), along comes another perspective that threatens to shake the foundations of our field. Debate regarding theories of situated cognition and related philosophies of constructivism has dominated the instructional design field (see, e.g., the May and September 1991 issues of *Educational Technology* and McLellan, 1996), as well as the larger field of education (Brown, Collins, & Duguid, 1989), for the past several years. Some have suggested that situated cognition and the idea of cognitive apprenticeships are merely a modern version of Dewey's (1938) experiential notions of education (Wineburg, 1989). Others have welcomed these new ideas as the foundation upon which to build educational reform (Greeno, 1989; Lave & Wenger, 1991; Pape & McIntyre, 1992; Silver, 1990; Streibel, 1989).

These new conceptions of learning propose alternatives to current cognitive theories of learning that will require new approaches and procedures for the design and development of instruction. Instructional design has traditionally focused on the variables and conditions necessary to improve learning in settings featuring intentional learning and direct instruction (see the chapter on Direct Instruction in this book). Systematic procedures for specifying outcomes, structuring content, selecting media, and assessing learning have been developed to facilitate the design and development processes (Briggs, Gustafson, & Tillman, 1991; Dick & Carey, 1990; Gagné, Briggs, & Wager, 1992). The problem is that a systematic approach such as that typified by the work of Gagné and Briggs (Gagné, Briggs, & Wager, 1992) is not particularly applicable to situations in which incidental learning, discovery-based learning, or other forms of instruction are desired. Furthermore, our current models of instructional design, and the direct instruction that results from utilizing such models, do not readily facilitate transfer of learning to other problem-solving settings. In fact, it has been suggested that few models of teaching used in today's schools are successful in this regard (Resnick, 1987). Current models of instructional design assume that content can be sufficiently structured and that enough activities can be provided for the learners to acquire the desired knowledge and skills (e.g., Gagné, Briggs, & Wager, 1992; Reigeluth, 1983; Scandura, 1983). As has been noted elsewhere, the instruction designed using these models also reflects the beliefs and assumptions about learning held by the designer (Duffy & Jonassen, 1991; Nelson & Orey, 1991; Rowland, 1992). Many leaders in the field of instructional design are calling for a reexamination of our basic assumptions in order to better reflect the alternative views on learning currently being proposed in the literature (Bednar, Cunningham, Duffy, & Perry, 1991; Hannafin, 1992). It may indeed be time to expand the horizons of instructional design to embrace new assumptions about learning.

Howard Gardner (1985) provides a clear history and perspective of the field of cognitive science. Within his book, he describes cognitive science as an interdisciplinary approach that encompasses the fields of psychology, artificial intelligence, philosophy, neuroscience, linguistics, and anthropology. The majority of work in cognitive science has been dominated by those interested in the interaction between psychology and artificial intelligence, with applications to education in the form of intelligent tutoring systems (see Farquhar & Orey in this volume). Cognitive theories assume that information is stored in complex network structures in memory, and that thought and actions are largely the result of symbolic computations occurring in the mind that utilize this information or "data" (Atkinson & Schiffrin, 1968; Collins & Quillian, 1969). Learning is a result of the cognitive processing undertaken by an individual, and this processing is highly dependent upon the ways knowledge is represented and stored in the mind of the individual. Traditional instructional design is concerned with structuring content and designing learning activities so that information can be efficiently acquired by learners. It assumes that knowledge is stored in the mind of the individual, and that learning basically involves the acquisition of information and subsequent modification of the learner's cognitive structures so as to incorporate the information and use it to complete various tasks (Norman, Gentner, & Stevens, 1976).

Within Gardner's framework, situated cognition tends to focus to a large extent upon the interaction between anthropology and psychology. The alternative view suggested by situated cognition is that learning as a result of individual cognitive processing is not the primary phenomenon. Rather, social practice is the primary phenomenon, and learning is one of the characteristics of social situations (Lave & Wenger, 1991). The essential idea of situated cognition is that knowledge cannot be known or understood independent of its context. This view is radically different from current conceptions of learning, and requires that we take a different view of knowledge and its role in learning. Furthermore, situated cognition contends that learning occurs as a component of authentic activities that are common to the community of practice in which the learner is involved. So, rather than designing ways for learners to acquire and represent knowledge in their minds, instructional designers should be considering ways that social interactions can be structured to maximize learning. The need for this is even more acute since major theorists in situated cognition make no attempts to propose how their ideas can impact schooling or instruction, only suggesting that the theory could "inform educational endeavors by shedding new light on learning processes, and by drawing attention to key aspects of learning experience that may be overlooked" (Lave & Wenger, 1991, p. 41).

It is likely that instruction designed from the perspective of situated cognition will be radically different from the kinds of direct instruction common to current models of instructional design. The remainder of this chapter examines situated cognition as an alternative to current cognitive theories of learning. The various philosophical assumptions and descriptions of learning that characterize situated cognition will be contrasted with current cognitive theories, and several instructional models based upon situated cognition will be presented. Finally, implications for the practice of instructional design will be suggested in the hope that designers can begin to develop procedures and strategies that can be utilized to design instruction that better reflects the assumptions and characteristics of situated cognition.

Learning and Instruction: The Cognitive View

The most widely accepted current explanation for human cognition is the computational metaphor, which explains aspects of human behavior by the existence of a computational system in the human mind that utilizes symbolic knowledge structures and cognitive processes that operate on those symbols to recognize, understand and act in the world. A major focus of research on learning from this perspective has centered on the structural characteristics of knowledge in the mind, such as propositional networks (Anderson & Bower, 1973), productions (Newell & Simon, 1972), and schemata (Norman, Gentner, & Stevens, 1976). This focus on knowledge structures and the cognitive processes necessary to receive information from the world and internalize it within existing structures depicts learning as an individual, internal activity through which the learner acquires information and modifies knowledge structures in order to accommodate new information. In fact, theories suggest that if enough practice is completed, the knowledge structures eventually "compile" into more efficient structures that control automatic responses in various situations in which expertise has been achieved (Anderson, 1989; Norman, 1978).

Instruction designed from this perspective takes into account the varieties of learned capabilities humans can exhibit, including attitudes, intellectual skills, cognitive strategies, motor skills and verbal information (Gagné, Briggs, & Wager, 1992). Each type of skill requires different conditions to facilitate learning (Gagné, 1985). For example, verbal information is thought to exist in the mind of the learner as networks of propositions, and may best be learned through the provision of verbal or other cues, with the possible addition of imagery and elaboration. According to this theoretical perspective, there are different levels of intellectual skill, each requiring different learning conditions (e.g., discrimination tasks, retrieval of concepts, and application of rules). External conditions that may facilitate the acquisition of intellectual skills include repetition and reinforcement, presentation of examples and nonexamples, demonstration, and verbal communication. It may also be necessary for intellectual skills to be acquired in a hierarchical sequence from simple to more complex. Attitudes, motor skills, and cognitive strategies are also represented in a variety of formats in the mind of learner, and require varying external conditions for learning to occur (see Gagné, Briggs, & Wager, 1992).

One problem with this view of learning and instruction is that it often results in knowledge structures that are isolated and disconnected from other pieces of knowledge in the mind. Bransford et al. (1990) refer to this form of knowledge as "inert knowledge." It has been acquired in the traditional sense, but serves no useful purpose outside of the context in which it was learned. Recent suggestions to expand conceptions of instruction to include knowledge structures that are organized "based more on employment needs than on attribute or hierarchical associations" (Tennyson, Elmore, & Snyder, 1992, p. 10) reflect alternative knowledge organizations and representation theories that have been proposed recently, such as stories (Schank & Jona, 1991) or mental models (Gentner & Stevens, 1983).

Alternatively, Orey and Burton (1992) use a three-dimensional matrix to depict the many types of knowledge that might make up a person's "understanding" of the world, including declarative and procedural knowledge, syntactic and semantic knowledge, and formal and informal knowledge. They argue that knowledge is learned in both formal and informal ways and that most knowledge acquired in a school setting, especially in mathematics, tends to be knowledge that has been carefully extracted from the world and represented in a symbol system that makes semantic manipulation more efficient.

Informal knowledge is very similar to formal knowledge. However, rather than the knowledge being provided by someone or something else (a teacher or a textbook), the individual has extracted meanings (and facts and procedures) from his or her own experiences in the world. To assess what the individual knows about the world requires the determination of all these types of knowledge; therefore, to educate learners would require both formal and informal methods. But even these theoretical extensions do not fully address the problem of how people acquire and employ situation-specific knowledge, largely because the theories are still based on a computational metaphor for human cognition that views knowledge as internal to the individual.

Situated Cognition: Alternative Conceptions of Learning

Situated cognition proposes a radically different explanation of learning, conceiving it as a largely social phenomenon. Rather than occurring within the mind of the individual, learning is instead described as a characteristic of many social interactions that take place within a framework of participation (Hanks, 1992). Increasing participation in "communities of practice" has the effect of engaging the whole person, focusing on "ways in which it [learning] is an evolving, continuously renewed set of relations" (Lave & Wenger, 1991, p. 50). Indeed, from the perspective of situated cognition, learning requires a rich repertoire of essential actors and participatory relationships beyond those common to education and training as now practiced. Situated cognition also proposes a different location for knowledge, and a different role for knowledge in the learning process, along with an emphasis on legitimate peripheral participation in social groups that is characteristic of learners in a variety of settings and cultures.

Situated Action

Theories of situated cognition take the view that human activity is complex, involving social, physical, and cognitive factors. Proponents of these theories believe that rather than acting on symbolic representations of the world that are located in the mind, we are in direct contact with the environment. Cognitive representations only become necessary when normal, situated activity fails (Dreyfus & Dreyfus, 1986; Greeno, 1989; Winograd & Flores, 1986). Suchman (1987) describes two types of activity in which humans engage: ad hoc improvisation during action and representations of action as plans or retrospective accounts. Situated action is not driven by plans, or in other words, humans "do not anticipate alternative courses of action, or their consequences, until *some* course of action is already underway" (Suchman, 1987, p. 52).

For example, suppose we wanted to build a robot to navigate the rocks, boulders, and craters of Mars. We have two basic approaches. In the first approach, we can build a robot with an "intelligence" based on the computational metaphor of the mind. The robot would utilize video input devices to view the terrain, convert the input into symbols used by the on-board computer to recognize patterns in the terrain, then carefully compute plans about where to move next (e. g., which leg, how far, what angle, etc.). In the second approach, we could build a robot that had "mini-intelligent" legs and arms that could automatically sense the changes in terrain and adjust to the undulations each leg might encounter. Its actions would be situated in the context of walking on Mars, and it would only need to stop and "plan" if it encountered a vertical wall, a canyon or some other obstacle that caused its "mind-less" functioning to stop. The outcome of purposeful, goal-directed behavior has seemingly been achieved by each robot, the former using symbolic computation methods, the latter by situated action.

As a more realistic example, consider Lave's (1988) systematic examination of the nature of situated mathematics as a part of the Adult Mathematics Project. One of the most commonly reported anecdotes from her work is the description of a man who is implementing a diet program and trying to cut his intake of food by three-fourths. One of the items he needs to use in a recipe is two-thirds of a cup of cottage cheese. Instead of selecting the appropriate school-based algorithm and performing the necessary calculation to determine the appropriate measurement, the man uses a somewhat "unorthodox" approach. He measures two-thirds cup of cottage cheese, empties the contents of the measuring cup on the counter, shapes the substance into a pie-shaped pile, cuts it into quarters, and removes a quarter section. The man's actions are situated, in the sense that he employs a procedure that is largely based on the context of the situation, even though it reflects some school-based knowledge (e. g., a circle represents the whole, divide the circle into equal fractional portions, etc.). If there were many of these calculations, the man's problem-solving strategies might change to a more efficient approach that incorporates some form of planning—perhaps he might even choose to use an algorithm. But this change in strategies would only occur after the man stopped his situated action in order to reflect on the situation so as to develop a more efficient plan of action.

Schön (1983) has extended the notion of situated action to include an important additional characteristic; that practitioners often reflect on their situated action in order to deal with some troublesome phenomenon of the situation. For Schön, knowledge is "ordinarily tacit, implicit in our patterns of action and in our feel for the stuff with which we are dealing. It seems right to say that our knowing is *in* our actions" (p. 49). As practitioners become more experienced, this tacit knowledge increases in its complexity and usefulness, but all practitioners still experience problems in which it is necessary to cope with divergent situations in which their situated actions are not effective in solving the problem. In these cases practitioners employ reflection-in-action to construct new ways of framing the problem so that situated action can resume. Studies of practitioners in a variety of domains, from design to psychotherapy to town planning, reveal practices that alternate between situated action and reflection-in-action. If such behavior is characteristic of practitioners, it may be advantageous to encourage learners to adopt similar behavior when learning to solve problems.

Assumptions About Knowledge

The nature and role of knowledge in the learning process is challenged by situated cognition. Rather than viewing knowledge as internal to the mind, situated cognition suggests that knowledge is a relation between an individual and a social or physical situation. Greeno (1989) explains that such a conceptualization is ". . . analogous to the concept of motion in physics. The velocity and acceleration of an object in motion are not properties of the object itself, but are properties of a relation between the object and a frame of reference" (p. 286). In fact, the objective nature of knowledge has been questioned by many in the social sciences with some suggesting that there may be no "right" way to represent knowledge or structure content (Wilson & Cole, 1992). The view offered by Suchman (1987) is that the common practices of participants in social situations are the source of an individual's knowledge structures and rules governing her or his behavior. Objectivity is accomplished through "systematic practices, or members' methods for rendering our unique experience and relative circumstances mutually intelligible. The source of mutual intelligibility is not a received conceptual scheme or a set of coercive rules or norms, but those common practices that produce the typifications of which schemes and rules are made" (pp. 57–58).

There is a growing body of evidence, much from the study of the learning of mathematics, suggesting that knowledge acquired in specific situations is more powerful and useful than so-called general knowledge that is often decontextualized and represented in abstract structures that cannot be applied in specific situations. This idea manifests itself in the phenomenon that many people's mathematical constructions are independent and quite different from the mathematics that people learn in schools. One of the most often cited studies in this regard is the Carraher, Carraher, and Schliemann (1985) study of children's mathematical abilities in the streets of Brazil. These children were able to perform complex mental arithmetic in the context of street vending in their parents' stands. However, given pencil and paper in the classroom, these same children were unable to perform even the most simple calculations. Further, when the arithmetic problems were stated in terms familiar to the children, they were still unable to perform the calculations. Even though the study may be somewhat flawed due to the mixing of ethnographic methods with quantitative analyses, the results remain compelling.

Saxe (1988) suggested that these children had certain limits in their ability to perform the school-based tasks, specifically that the children in the Carraher *et al.*, study had little or no school-based mathematical knowledge (orthographic mathematics). Saxe argued that the differences would disappear if the children had more prior knowledge of school-based learning. Working with the Carrahers in Brazil, Saxe carried out a similar study using children who were street sellers, urban children from the same community who were not involved in street selling, and a group of rural children with limited exposure to currency and transactions with currency. The latter two groups were matched with the sellers on age and school background. Performance on the orthographic problems was clearly related to educational background. Those students with less than a third grade level of education correctly solved 40% of the problems, while children with more than a fourth grade level solved close to 90% of the problems correctly. In analyzing strategies, the children with more schooling tended to make use of school-based algorithms in the context of the street calculations. Apparently, it is not that cognition is situated, but that the greater the knowledge of school-based mathematics, the more likely a person will use school-based knowledge in other contexts.

Does the knowledge gained in the street transfer to the school? In the Saxe (1988) study, second and third grade sellers' and non-sellers' performance on school-like computations and word problems revealed that second-grade sellers performed better than the second-grade non-sellers. This result was attributed to the fact that the second-grade sellers used strategies that were very much like those used in selling candy in the street. By the third grade, the non-sellers caught up to the sellers; however, the sellers still used many of the strategies they learned in the street, while the non-sellers continued to use their school-based knowledge. The results suggest that the extent to which mathematical knowledge is situated is much less than that suggested by the Carraher *et al.* study. Apparently the better a child can use school-based knowledge, the more it can be used in other situations, and knowledge that children acquire outside of school can be used in school to some extent. The degree to which this knowledge is ultimately useful, however, will certainly be dependent upon the contexts for learning provided in the schools.

Shirley Brice Heath (1983) conducted an extensive ethnography in Appalachia that focused upon three different communities; its purpose was to better understand how learning was valued in the institutions within these communities. After determining the kind of knowledge and abilities that were valued within the three communities, school-based programs were designed to take advantage of cognitive abilities and remediate cognitive weaknesses. The instructional interventions were quite successful, focusing on the knowledge utilized in the community domain and how the knowledge within the school domain could be made to correspond to the community knowledge. In order to help learners to find these correspondences, a variety of translation processes were used. For example, community verbal knowledge largely consisted of opinions, sayings, proverbs, and the like. The corresponding verbal knowledge in school was predominantly written, consisting of facts, scientific principles, scientific methods and the like. Translations would require the specification of gaps between knowledge types and identification of common elements. This explicit activity helped learners see the utility of both forms of knowledge. Furthermore, many of these activities brought the community into the classroom, meaning that many family and community members participated more fully in the education of the children.

Clearly, this method has broader social aspects. The increased involvement of significant others in the schooling process increases the motivation of the learners, helping them to see the importance of schooling. If it is important for a parent to come to class, then the information that is being learned there perhaps has some merit. Given the above evidence, it becomes apparent that knowledge is acquired in both formal and informal ways, and that these types of knowledge can interact through purposeful activities that are designed to take advantage of the strengths of one or the other knowledge types. It may also be concluded that *all* knowledge is not necessarily situated, as advocated in the radical view of situated cognition. Formal knowledge can be used in an informal context if the formal knowledge is understood well enough.

Characteristics of Situated Learning

Learning requires more than just thought and action, or a particular physical or social situation, or just receiving a body of factual knowledge; it also requires participation in the actual practices of the culture. Adopting a relational view of knowledge and situated activity changes the focus of the analysis of learning to characteristics of social participation in communities of practice. Lave and Wenger (1991) suggest that participation is a key element, requiring negotiation of meanings in various situations, with the result that "understanding and experience are in constant interaction" (pp. 51–52).

Cognitive Apprenticeship or Legitimate Peripheral Participation?

One of the most widely discussed features of situated cognition as it was originally proposed is the notion of cognitive apprenticeships as a means for learners to become participants in communities of practice. As described by Brown and his colleagues (Brown, Collins, & Duguid, 1989; Collins, Brown, & Newman, 1989), cognitive apprenticeships provide a general framework with four components—content, methods, sequence, and sociology—for designing learning environments. Content includes domain knowledge, heuristic strategies, control strategies, and learning strategies, all of which are well explicated in the literature on cognitive learning theories and instructional design. Methods refer to teaching methods, including modeling, coaching, scaffolding, fading, articulation, reflection, and exploration. Instructional sequence includes notions such as increasing complexity, increasing diversity, and global-before-local skills. Sociology, the only category that seems to have emerged directly from theories of situated cognition, includes five aspects: situated learning, culture of expert practice, intrinsic motivation, exploiting cooperation, and exploiting competition. Motivation, cooperative learning and competition have each played a role in the design and development of instructional systems for some time. That leaves only the first two as something to be incorporated into our design models. The second, the culture of expert practice, is actually something that should always be examined in instructional design. Part of the analysis phase of design is to determine the tasks to be performed and how they are performed, including the devices that are employed and the skills required to use such devices. The only difference is that Collins *et al.* argue for a fairly "rich" analysis that incorporates many subtle aspects of the culture, including all of the various nuances of communication that occur in expert practice. Rather than taking the final aspect, situated learning, to mean that the knowledge ought to be situated within the context in which it exists, Collins *et al.* imply that knowledge can be situated if it is acquired in the process of learning-by-doing. If learning involves some activity encompassing the to-be-learned knowledge that requires the active participation of the learner, then according to Collins *et al.*, this knowledge is situated.

It is curious that the only element of the Collins *et al.* model that directly relates to situated cognition is a distinct component. Rather than trying to integrate situated cognition into a model, it is left as a separate component. The use of the term apprenticeship has also been criticized because the characteristics of master-apprentice relationships in many cultures may represent too narrow a view of situated learning. Lave and Wenger (1991) prefer to describe the central concept of situated learning as legitimate peripheral participation, in order to promote a decentered view of learning that shifts analysis away from the notion of "master as locus of authority" to an analysis of "the intricate structuring of a community's learning resources" (p. 94). The notion of legitimate peripheral participation differs from cognitive apprenticeships in several ways, not the least of which is that the terminology does not include the social connotations commonly associated with the word apprenticeship. For Lave and Wenger, learners must be "legitimate" members of the community, not passive observers, and their activities must be performed in the context of the work of the community. "Peripheral" participation refers to the fact that by their nature as novices, learners cannot be full participants in all community activities, but at the same time they must be recognized as participants in some aspects of the work of the community. There should be time to learn and to discuss ideas with peers and old-timers. The old-timers should not be threatened by the potential of the newcomer, but should be in a position to offer the best of their knowledge and skill. "Participation" means apprentices (newcomers) should be doing the thing that they are learning to do, not just observing.

Lave and Wenger suggest that legitimate peripheral participation is the mechanism of enculturation for a learner that includes relationships between apprentices and masters, but also includes all of the other participants, skills, artifacts, symbols, and ideas that are part of the culture of practice. As a result, their study of legitimate peripheral participation focuses on that form of social participation which includes learning as a necessary component. Learning as a characteristic of social interaction cannot be extricated from its legitimate context. Finally, legitimate peripheral participation is not an instructional method. Rather, it is a lens for viewing and understanding learning in new ways.

Patterns of Situated Learning

Legitimate peripheral participation serves to help learners develop a holistic view of what the community of practice is about, and what there is to learn within that community. Opportunities for learning are structured by the requirements of work, rather than teacher-student relations. In fact, Lave and Wenger (1991) note that in many situations apprentices learn mostly from other apprentices. For example, among Liberian tailors learning their trade (Lave, in preparation, as cited in Lave & Wenger, 1991), much of the communication of technique comes from more experienced peers. The old-timer (master) mainly serves as a model for the ideal professional in the field performing the daily duties, and only to a lesser degree does the master provide formal instruction. What they also learn is how to talk within the community. The shared practice within a community includes both "talking within" to share information about ongoing activities, and "talking about" through stories that support "communal forms of memory and reflection" (p. 109). The case of the "nondrinking" alcoholics (Cain, in preparation, as cited in Lave & Wenger, 1991) demonstrates that the role of language in situated learning does not just contribute to the development of complex skills. Predominantly, the learning activities employed in the Alcoholics Anonymous organization are based upon language, in the form of public speaking to groups and writing in newsletters. Older members adapt their personal story telling to the experiences of newcomers, while newcomers learn to construct personal stories from the models that are provided.

Lave and Wenger (1991) also suggest that learning in communities of practice is not highly structured and sequenced, but rather "unfolds in opportunities for engagement in practice" (p. 93). There are no rules dictating what should be learned, or when it should be learned. Opportunities to learn are mainly improvised from the situation at hand, following a curriculum that includes the resources of everyday practice. Mayan midwives (Jordan, 1989, as cited in Lave & Wenger, 1991) do not provide any explicit instruction at all. In fact, the midwives report that much of their knowledge comes to them in dreams. The data indicates that they actually learn their profession by observing the practices and participating in increasingly complex practices from a very young age. U.S. Navy quartermasters (Hutchins, in press, as cited in Lave & Wenger, 1991) stated that they preferred apprentices (newcomers) who had not received the traditional classroom instruction prior to coming on-board, because it took more time to correct this erroneous learning than it did to work with someone who knew little or nothing. Also, while there were some "traditional" instructional materials (workbooks) on-board, most of the learning occurred in the context of the actual operation of the ship. Newcomers were to perform increasingly more complex tasks in a spiral curriculum that included previously learned tasks. These tasks were performed under the constant guidance of the old-timer, who would correct errors or take over the task if needed. The case of the Liberian tailors (Lave, in preparation, as cited in Lave & Wenger, 1991) again confirms that curriculum can emerge from the practice of formal apprenticeships. The situations involving the Mayan midwives and the Navy quartermasters were not strictly defined as apprenticeships, but the Liberian tailors entered into a formal contract with the old-timer. An interesting attribute of the tailors' learning is that the curriculum is reversed. Rather than beginning with the initial steps in the procedure of making clothes, the apprentices begin at the end, working on finishing touches first in order to observe the quality of workmanship and models for the finished product. In all of the cases cited here, curriculum is situated in practice, and cannot be "considered in isolation, manipulated in arbitrary didactic terms, or analyzed apart from the social relations that shape legitimate peripheral participation" (p. 98).

Implications for Instructional Design

As mentioned above, the descriptions of learning provided by theories of situated cognition are based upon assumptions about learning and instruction that are vastly different from those embodied in current instructional design models. Several general principles have been suggested that can guide instructional designers in the development of strategies to facilitate situated learning. For example, the Cognition & Technology Group at Vanderbilt (1992) suggests that "students need to engage in argumentation and reflection as they try to use and then refine their existing knowledge and attempt to make sense of alternate points of view" (p. 67). They emphasize that instruction should be "anchored" in meaningful contexts that allow situated learning to be simulated in classrooms (Cognition & Technology Group at Vanderbilt, 1991). In this way, environments can be designed that allow "sustained exploration" of the various aspects of a problem, helping students to "understand the kinds of problems and opportunities that experts in various areas encounter and the knowledge that these experts use as tools" (Cognition & Technology Group at Vanderbilt, 1992, p. 67). This sustained exploration can also be facilitated by technology, as in the approach to developing cognitive flexibility suggested by Spiro and his colleagues (Spiro, Feltovich, Jacobson, & Coulson, 1991; Spiro & Jehng, 1991). In this application, learners examine various cases or scenarios from many perspectives, assisted by the rapid and efficient access to information provided by hypermedia technology. Rieber (1992) echoes these suggestions in discussing guidelines for designing computer-based microworlds. He advocates the design of meaningful contexts that support self-regulated learning, establishing a spiral curriculum, and nurturing incidental learning.

As noted above, one area that will require extensive consideration in designing instruction based upon the principles of situated learning is the amount of control that is provided to the learners. Current models of instructional design tend to assume a great degree of control for the teacher (or the "system") with respect to sequencing, strategies, questioning, etc. Tobin and Dawson (1992) note that this problem leads to a "dysfunctional learning environment" in which learners have "little autonomy, and hence lose interest in the curriculum" (p. 81). Several alternative approaches to teaching have been cited as examples that better support situated learning. One example is Schoenfeld's (1985) approach to mathematics instruction, in which the teacher explicitly models problem-solving strategies to the students, and students are given chances to generate their own problems. Reciprocal teaching (Palincsar & Brown, 1984) is another approach in which control of the learning activities is given to the learners. In this method, small groups of learners assume roles including "teacher," "critic," and "producer" in the process of comprehending written passages. Control of learning activities and communication among learners also can be encouraged with technology, as in the Computer-Supported Intentional Learning Environment (CSILE project described by Scardamalia & Bereiter, 1991). At a school where CSILE has been tested, children of varying grade levels share ideas, criticisms and explanations over a computer network, reflecting characteristics of the legitimate peripheral participation discussed earlier. In these and many other similar cases, the role of the teacher seems to be more like "Yoda" from the "Star Wars" trilogy, rather than "Professor Kingsfield" as depicted in the television series "Paper Chase." Learners are in control, while the teacher serves as a model and facilitator rather than directly controlling the instructional process.

Deciding what needs to be learned is a major step in the instructional design process, often requiring many hours of analysis and reams of paper containing flowcharts and hierarchical diagrams. Situated learning may not require such extensive analysis because "the instructional materials and interactions provide a setting wherein students can develop the subtle and often unidentified knowledge needed to succeed in the given task" (Wilson & Cole, 1991, p. 60). While it may not be necessary to employ great precision in identifying outcomes or analyzing or structuring content, situated learning may require more attention to analyzing the learning environment in order to design authentic learning activities. Tessmer (1990) has suggested procedures to more thoroughly analyze the instructional environment that also may be employed to design situated learning activities. Other instructional design theorists are also beginning to suggest ways that traditional instructional design can evolve to better reflect the alternative conceptions of learning proposed by situated cognition and other current theories, including integrative goals (Gagné & Merrill, 1990), contextual analysis (Tennyson, Elmore, & Snyder, 1992), and the design of learning environments (Hannafin, 1992; Rieber, 1992).

Criticisms and Future Directions

We have sketched the descriptions of learning that are associated with situated cognition in the hope that designers interested in improving instruction can incorporate the alternative assumptions that are contained within the theory. Some critics of situated cognition note that it is similar to the views of learning espoused by Dewey (1938). However, a major difference between the experiential view of learning advocated by Dewey and the current explanations of situated cognition is the interpretation of the effects of experience. Dewey's view could not incorporate current theories of cognition. Situated cognition affords a framework for coming to understand the role of experience in the cognition of learners. This may seem trivial, but we do not think that it is. It is certainly accepted that cognitive interpretations of old ideas can be powerful. Farquhar and Orey (this volume) describe the theoretical perspective of Anderson (1989). It can be argued that Anderson's framework does not differ greatly from the idea of shaping developed by behavioral psychologists. However, the specificity of Anderson's cognitive theory actually changes the instructional program considerably, from a reinforcement schedule to an intelligent tutoring system. Therefore, although situated cognition may sound like Dewey's ideas of experiential learning, its acceptance actually may change the ways we interpret experience and understand the impact of experience upon learning.

Others have criticized situated cognition because its predictions about the role of knowledge in learning may not be scientifically verifiable and because its characteristics already can be accommodated in current models (Kornberg, 1992). Part of the problem with these criticisms is that they do not accept the ethnographic methodologies employed in research on situated cognition. The criticism that situated cognition offers nothing beyond current practice (Merrill, 1991) may be the result of misinterpretations of the theory. Furthermore, situated cognition is associated with constructivism (Duffy & Jonassen, 1991; Jonassen, 1991), but there are subtle differences that are not always recognized (Kornberg, 1992). Because situated cognition emerges from an anthropological area of inquiry, it differs from other theories of learning. Constructivism suggests that humans construct meaning in the mind based upon experiences in the world. For constructivists, the mind is centered in the brain. Situated cognition, however, claims that the mind is more than just constructing meaning from experience, it is the things of experience as well. Situated cognition takes mind to be something that is not only in the brain, but includes artifacts from the environment. Because of this fundamental difference, situated cognition stands alone from other paradigms in this volume.

The ultimate role for situated cognition in the advancement of learning theory may already have been achieved, however, given the response it has generated in the larger field of cognitive science. Researchers are already proposing models that reconcile the seeming dichotomy that exists between the conception of mind offered in the computational metaphor (the artificial intelligence explanation) and the "radical" position offered by situated cognition (the anthropological explanation). For example, Greeno (1989) has proposed a compromise between the two positions that accepts the notion of situated knowledge, and explains cognition as a mapping of the world objects and actions to mental models. What is important for the current discussion is that this model admits the possibility for the occurrence of both situated and non-situated cognition. Situated cognition can be described in this model as the processing of information that is both brain-based and world-based. This implies that the mind is larger than brain. To understand the human mind requires an analysis of the individual within the context of activity, because thinking can include both mental and physical manipulations. Similar work has been done by Larkin (1989), who uses the computational theory of problem solving developed by Newell and Simon (1972) to show that much problem solving activity can occur without cognitive representations in the mind, because the representations are already available in the environment. These models suggest a compromise between the two positions (situated and non-situated cognition) because, again, it is assumed that knowledge can exist outside of the mind, situated in the context of the current problem solving environment.

Theories of situated cognition and the instructional principles that have been proposed may not be appropriate for all types of learning. It may not be advisable to use cognitive apprenticeship methods for initial learning, since the learners never discover what they need to know. But for learning at advanced levels and consolidating knowledge so that it can be utilized in increasingly divergent situations, the methods based on situated cognition provide an exciting alternative to current instructional approaches. We will all need to participate in the development of new design procedures that employ principles of situated cognition and in testing the resulting instructional solutions in a variety of settings, if we are to continue as a field situated at the crossroads of learning theory and instructional application. If we do not, we will be left behind as newer conceptions of learning advance while we cling to our older notions of instructional design.

References

Anderson, J. R. (1989). The analogical origins of errors in problem solving. In D. Klahr & K. Kotovsky (Eds.), *Complex information processing: The impact of Herbert A. Simon* (pp. 343–372). Hillsdale, NJ: Lawrence Erlbaum Associates.

Anderson, J. R., & Bower, G. H. (1973). Human associative memory. Washington, DC: Winston & Sons.

Atkinson, R. C., & Schiffrin, R. M. (1968). Human memory: A proposed system and its control processes. In K. W. Spence & J. T. Spence (Eds.), *The psychology of learning and motivation: Advances in research and theory.* Vol. 2. New York: Academic Press.

Bednar, A. K., Cunningham, D., Duffy, T. M., & Perry, J. D. (1991). Theory into practice: How do we link? In G. J. Anglin (Ed.), *Instructional technology: Past, present, and future.* Englewood, CO: Libraries Unlimited.

Bransford, J., Sherwood, R., Hasselbring, T., Kinzer, C., & Williams, S. (1990). Anchored instruction: Why we need it and how technology can help. In D. Nix & R. Spiro (Eds.), *Cognition, education, and multimedia* (pp. 115–141). Hillsdale, NJ: Lawrence Erlbaum Associates.

Briggs, L. J., Gustafson, K. L., & Tillman, M. H. (Eds.). (1991). *Instructional design: Principles and applications* (2nd ed.). Englewood Cliffs, NJ: Educational Technology Publications.

Brown, J. S., Collins, A., & Duguid, P. (1989). Situated cognition and the culture of learning. *Educational Researcher, 18*(1), 32–42.

Cain, C. (in preparation). *Becoming a non-drinking alcoholic: A case study in identity acquisition.* Anthropology Department, University of North Carolina, Chapel Hill.

Carraher, T. N., Carraher, D. W., & Schliemann, A. D. (1985). Mathematics in the streets and schools. *British Journal of Developmental Psychology, 3,* 21–29.

Cognition & Technology Group at Vanderbilt. (1991). Technology and the design of generative learning environments. *Educational Technology, 31*(5), 34–40.

Cognition & Technology Group at Vanderbilt. (1992). The Jasper experiment: The exploration of issues in learning and instructional design. *Educational Technology Research and Development, 40*(1), 65–80.

Collins, A., Brown, J. S., & Newman, S. E. (1989). Cognitive apprenticeship: Teaching the crafts of reading, writing, and arithmetic. In L. B. Resnick (Ed.), *Knowing, learning, and instruction: Essays in honor of Robert Glaser* (pp. 453–49). Hillsdale, NJ: Lawrence Erlbaum Associates.

Collins, A. M., & Quillian, M. R. (1969). Retrieval time from semantic memory. *Journal of Verbal Learning and Verbal Behavior, 8,* 240–247.

Dewey, J. (1938). *Experience and education.* New York: Macmillan.

Dick, W., & Carey, L. (1990). *The systematic design of instruction* (3rd ed.). Glenview, IL: Scott, Foresman and Co.

Dreyfus, H. L., & Dreyfus, S. E. (1986). *Mind over machine.* New York: Free Press.

Duffy, T. M., & Jonassen, D. H. (1991). Constructivism: New implications for instructional technology. *Educational Technology, 31*(5), 7–12.

Gagné, R. M. (1985). *The conditions of learning* (4th ed.). New York: Holt, Rinehart, and Winston.

Gagné, R. M., Briggs, L. J., & Wager, W. W. (1992). *Principles of instructional design* (4th ed.). New York: Harcourt, Brace, Jovanovich.

Gagné, R. M., & Merrill, M. D. (1990). Integrative goals for instructional design. *Educational Technology Research and Development, 38*(1), 23–30.

Gardner, H. (1985). *The mind's new science.* New York: Basic Books.

Gentner, D., & Stevens, A. (1983). (Eds.) *Mental models.* Hillsdale, NJ: Lawrence Erlbaum Associates.

Greeno, J. G. (1989). Situations, mental models, and generative knowledge. In D. Klahr & K. Kotovsky (Eds.), *Complex information processing: The impact of Herbert A. Simon* (pp. 285+318). Hillsdale, NJ: Lawrence Erlbaum Associates.

Hanks, W. F. (1992). Foreword. In J. Lave & E. Wenger, *Situated learning: Legitimate peripheral participation.* New York: Cambridge University Press.

Hannafin, M. J. (1992). Emerging technologies, ISD, and learning environments: Critical perspectives. *Educational Technology Research and Development, 40*(1), p. 64.

Hannafin, M. J., & Rieber, L. P. (1989a). Psychological foundations of instructional design for emerging computer-based instructional technologies: Part I. *Educational Technology Research and Development, 37*(2), 91–101.

Hannafin, M. J., & Rieber, L. P. (1989b). Psychological foundations of instructional design for emerging computer-based instructional technologies: Part II. *Educational Technology Research and Development, 37*(2), 102–114.

Heath, S. B. (1983). *Ways with words: Language, life, and work in communities and classrooms.* New York: Cambridge University Press.

Hutchins, E. (in press). Learning to navigate. In S. Chaiklin & J. Lave (Eds.), *Understanding practice.* New York: Cambridge University Press.

Jonassen, D. H. (1991). Objectivism versus Constructivism: Do we need a new philosophical paradigm? *Educational Technology Research and Development, 39*(3), p. 14.

Jordan, B. (1989). Cosmopolitical obstetrics: Some insights from the training of traditional midwives. *Social Science and Medicine, 28*(9), 925–944.

Kornberg, W. (1992). The science of learning math and science. *MOSAIC, 23*(2), p. 44.

Larkin, J. H. (1989). Display-based problem solving. In D. Klahr & K. Kotovsky (Eds.), *Complex information processing: The impact of Herbert A. Simon* (pp. 319–342). Hillsdale, NJ: Lawrence Erlbaum Associates.

Lave, J. (1988). *Cognition in practice: Mind, mathematics, and culture in everyday life.* New York: Cambridge University Press.

Lave, J. (in preparation). *Tailored learning: Apprenticeship and everyday practice among craftsmen in West Africa.*

Lave, J., & Wenger, E. (1991). *Situated learning: Legitimate peripheral participation.* New York: Cambridge University Press.

McLellan, H. (Ed.). (1996). *Situated learning perspectives.* Englewood Cliffs, NJ: Educational Technology Publications.

Merrill, M. D. (1991). Constructivism and instructional design. *Educational Technology, 31*(5), 45–53.

Merrill, M. D., Li, Z., & Jones, M. K. (1990a). Limitations of first generation instructional design. *Educational Technology, 30*(1), 7–11.

Merrill, M. D., Li, Z., & Jones, M. K. (1990b). Second generation instructional design. *Educational Technology, 30*(2), 7–14.

Nelson, W. A., & Orey, M. A. (1991, April) *Reconceptualizing the instructional design process: Lessons learned from cognitive science.* Paper presented at the annual meeting of the American Educational Research Association, Chicago, IL.

Newell, A., & Simon, H. A. (1972). *Human problem solving.* Englewood Cliffs, NJ: Prentice-Hall.

Norman, D. A. (1978). Notes toward a theory of complex learning. In A. M. Lesgold, J. W. Pellegrino, S. D. Fokema, & R. Glaser (Eds.), *Cognitive psychology and instruction.* New York: Plenum Press.

Norman, D. A., Gentner, S., & Stevens, A. L. (1976). Comments on learning school and memory representation. In D. Klahr (Ed.), *Cognition and instruction.* Hillsdale, NJ: Lawrence Erlbaum Associates.

Orey, M. A., & Burton, J. K. (1992). The trouble with error patterns. *Journal of Research on Computing in Education, 25*(1), 1–17.

Orey, M. A., & Nelson, W. A. (1993). Development principles for intelligent tutoring systems: Integrating cognitive theory into the development of computer-based instruction. *Educational Technology Research and Development, 41*(1), 59–72.

Palincsar, A. S., & Brown, A. L. (1984). Reciprocal teaching of comprehension-fostering and compre-hension-monitoring activities. *Cognition and Instruction, 11*, 17–175.

Pape, S., & McIntyre, D. J. (1992). *Utilizing protocols to enhance teacher reflective thinking.* Paper pre-sented at the annual meeting of the Association of Teacher Educators, Orlando, FL.

Reigeluth, C. M. (1983). *Instructional design theories and models: An overview of their current status.* Hills-dale, NJ: Lawrence Erlbaum Associates.

Resnick, L. B. (1987). Learning in school and out. *Educational Researcher, 16*(9), 13–20.

Rieber, L. P. (1992). Computer-based microworlds: A bridge between construction and direct instruc-tion. *Educational Technology Research and Development, 40*(1), 106.

Rowland, G. (1992). What do instructional designers actually do? An initial investigation of expert prac-tice. *Performance Improvement Quarterly, 5*(2), p. 65.

Saxe, G. B. (1988). The mathematics of child street vendors. *Child Development, 59*, 1415–1425.

Scandura, J. M. (1983). Instructional strategies based on Structural Learning Theory. In C. M. Reigeluth (Ed.), *Instructional design theories and models: An overview of their current status* (pp. 213–246). Hillsdale, NJ: Lawrence Erlbaum Associates.

Scardamalia, M., & Bereiter, C. (1991). Higher levels of agency for children in knowledge building: A challenge for the design of new knowledge media. *Journal of the Learning Sciences, 1*(1), 37–68.

Schank, R. C., & Jona, M. Y. (1991). Empowering the student: New perspectives on the design of teaching systems. *Journal of the Learning Sciences, 1*(1), 7–35.

Schoenfeld, A. (1985). *Mathematical problem solving.* Orlando, FL: Academic Press.

Schön, D. A. (1983). *The reflective practitioner.* New York: Basic Books.

Silver, E. A. (1990). *Treating estimation and mental computation as situated mathematical processes.* (ERIC Document Reproduction Service No. ED 342 645.)

Spiro, R. J., Feltovich, P. J., Jacobson, M. J., & Coulson, R. L. (1991). Cognitve flexibility, constructivism, and hypertext: Random access instruction for advanced knowledge acquisition in ill-structured domains. *Educational Technology, 31*(5), p. 33.

Spiro, R. J., & Jehng, J. C. (1991). Cognitive flexibility and hypertext: Theory and technology for the nonlinear and multidimensional traversal of complex subject matter. In D. Nix & R. Spiro (Eds.), *Cognition, education, and multimedia.* Hillsdale, NJ: Lawrence Erlbaum Associates.

Streibel, M. J. (1989). *Instructional plans and situated learning: The challenge of Suchman's theory of situ-ated action for instructional designers and instructional systems.* Paper presented at the annual meeting of the Association for Educational Communications and Technology, Dallas, TX.

Suchman, L. (1987). *Plans and situated actions.* New York: Cambridge University Press.

Tennyson, R. D., Elmore, R. L., & Snyder, L. (1992). Advancements in instructional design theory: Con-textual module analysis and integrated instructional strategies. *Educational Technology Research and Development, 40*(2), 9–22.

Tessmer, M. (1990). Environmental analysis: A neglected stage of instructional design. *Educational Tech-nology Research and Development, 38*(1), 55–64.

Tobin, K., & Dawson, G. (1992). Constraints to curriculum reform: Teachers and myths of schooling. *Ed-ucational Technology Research and Development, 40*(1), p. 81.

West, C. K., Farmer, J. A., & Wolff, P. M. (1991). *Instructional design: Implications from cognitive science.* Englewood Cliffs, NJ: Prentice-Hall.

Wilson, B., & Cole, P. (1991). A review of cognitive teaching models. *Educational Technology Research and Development, 39*(4), 47–64.

Wilson, B., & Cole, P. (1992). A critical review of Elaboration Theory. *Educational Technology Research and Development, 40*(3), 63–79.

Wineburg, S. S. (1989). Remembrance of theories past. *Educational Researcher, 18*(4), 7–9.

Winograd, T., & Flores, F. (1986). *Understanding computers and cognition.* Norwood, NJ: Ablex.

18

The Postmodern Paradigm

Brent G. Wilson
University of Colorado at Denver

For more than ten years, a small group of postmodern researchers and theorists has existed within the Association for Educational Communications and Technology (AECT). For years, they behaved like a persecuted minority—a "cult" of sorts. They complained that journal editors were biased, even ignorant, and unwilling to publish their radical writings. They struggled to have papers and symposia accepted on the AECT program.

The main forum for the postmodern group was an annual "foundations symposium," which year by year found its way onto AECT's program. I have attended these symposia for the last several years, and have noticed two things. First, the crowds are getting bigger and seemingly better informed. Second, I have noticed a change in the presenters. I see less defensiveness and fewer signs of being persecuted. Instead, I see a growing maturity of perspective and a growing confidence that a postmodern perspective has something hopeful and positive to say to our field. It is in that same spirit of hopefulness and honesty that I approach this chapter. I am not a member of the postmodern clique. I am an instructional designer—a moniker unpopular in many postmodern circles. But I approach the task of articulating postmodernism with a belief that there are some worthwhile ideas here, and that the field of ID can be improved by listening closely to "alternate voices" currently abounding in our field.

Three recent publications symbolize the growing acceptance of postmodern thinking within educational technology:

- Dennis Hlynka and Andrew Yeaman prepared a carefully written two-page digest of postmodern thinking for publication as an ERIC Digest (Hlynka & Yeaman, 1992). This is the first source I would recommend for instructional designers interested in a brief and clear introduction to postmodern thinking.

- In 1991, Educational Technology Publications published a collection of postmodern writing edited by Dennis Hlynka and John Belland, titled *Paradigms regained: The uses of illuminative, semiotic, and post-modern criticism as modes of inquiry in educa-*

tional technology: A book of readings. This book serves as a valuable resource for educational technologists in search of alternative perspectives for interpreting their field.

- The February 1994 issue of *Educational Technology* was devoted to postmodern topics. The issue made postmodernism more visible within the educational technology community, but also included some real dialogue, spurred by Barbara Martin's (1994) call for better communications between postmodern critics and the educational technology community.

The purpose of this chapter is to provide a short, guided tour of postmodern thinking for practicing instructional designers raised in the "old school" of Gagné, Briggs, and Merrill. I will assume that you have been exposed to some measure of constructivist thinking, yet postmodern philosophy remains a mystery. To help make a transition to postmodern ways of thinking, the second half of the chapter offers a set of recommendations for doing traditional ID steps in ways more sensitive to postmodern perspectives.

Also at the outset, please remember that labels such as "constructivist" or "postmodern" embrace a whole range of ideas and methods. This chapter is my best shot at elucidating postmodern philosophy for an ID audience, yet I approach the task as an admiring outsider, not really an expert. What I can bring to the discussion is my understanding of instructional designers and their preconceptions. The next step for any reader would be to consult original sources—either the educational technologists referred to above, or the postmodern philosophers and critics they rely upon in their writing.

An Introduction to Postmodern Thinking

I have decided that the best way to provide a conceptual overview is to tell a simple story. This story is not true, but it has some truth in it. It is meant to serve as a scaffold for making sense out of the word 'postmodern.'

A Story About Worldviews

The ancient worldview. In many ways, the ancients of Greece and Rome were a lot like us. They faced some of the same questions we face now—namely—How is it that we know things? How can we get at the truth? How is the world made up? The ancients recognized that appearances can be deceiving—that what looks reliable and stable on the surface may actually be in flux and changing. How can we get at the way things *really* are? To address this problem, the ancients differentiated between the world that we see with our eyes and the "real" world, which was perfect, whole, and divine. The divine, in fact, was what made it possible for us to catch glimpses of the "real," idealized world. Left to our own inclinations, we see imperfection, weakness, and lots of jagged edges. With the help of divine logic and mathematics, the jagged edges become smooth, and the perfect thing-behind-the-thing is made manifest to us. Concepts are divine revelations of the way the world really is—our everyday usage of "ideas" stems from the ideal forms sought by the ancients.

The modern worldview. The ancient view of things dominated our thinking for many years, in fact through the Medieval Era. Beginning with the Renaissance, however, we gradually shifted our focus. Taught to look to God for truth—and for God in the Church and in received texts—many bright thinkers instead started to believe their own eyes and faculties. Rather than God assuming the central role in the universe, man himself[1] became the stan-

---

[1] I am retaining the gender-exclusive 'man' because it best reflects the historical mindset of the time.

dard for judging the truth of things. Man's intellect was capable of discerning truth from error. Certain defined methods for discovering truth and evaluating evidence came to be considered reliable and sufficient for gaining access to the "truth." Superstition and tradition were replaced by rationality and the scientific method. Technology and the progress of science would signal a corresponding progress in society, until man perfected himself and controlled nature through his knowledge and tools.

Still, philosophers troubled themselves over the same questions of how do we know the truth? Kant realized that we will never really get at the way things *really* are, but that we can get pretty close—we create schemas in our mind that roughly match up with how things are. The word 'phenomenon' comes from Kant, and means essentially "close to the real thing."

Over the years, however, it became clear to philosophers that there remained an insurmountable gulf between ourselves and the truth. We live in a specific time and place, conditioned by a particular culture and set of experiences. Without God to connect us to the truth, how can we get there? How can we *transcend* our limitations and reach beyond ourselves to the way things really are? These are tough questions that have not gone away through the ages.

The postmodern worldview. 'Postmodernism,' as the term implies, is largely a response to modernity. Whereas modernity trusted science to lead us down the road of progress, postmodernism questioned whether science alone could really get us there. Whereas modernity happily created inventions and technologies to improve our lives, postmodernism took a second look and wondered whether our lives were really better for all the gadgets and toys. Postmodernism looked at the culmination of modernity in the 20th century—the results of forces such as nationalism, totalitarianism, technocracy, consumerism, and modern warfare—and said, we can see the efficiency and the improvements, but we can also see the dehumanizing, mechanizing effects in our lives. The Holocaust was efficient, technical, coldly rational. There must be a better way to think about things.

So what about the age-old questions about truth and knowledge? A postmodernist might say, "Truth is what people agree on," or "Truth is what works," or "Hey, there is no Truth, only lots of little 'truths' running around out there!" Postmodernists tend to reject the idealized view of Truth inherited from the ancients and replace it with a dynamic, changing truth bounded by time, space, and perspective. Rather than seeking for the unchanging ideal, postmodernists tend to celebrate the dynamic diversity of life.

In their *ERIC Digest,* Hlynka and Yeaman (1992) outline some key features of postmodern thinking (liberally paraphrased for simplicity):

1. A commitment to plurality of perspectives, meanings, methods, values—everything!
2. A search for and appreciation of double meanings and alternative interpretations, many of them ironic and unintended.
3. A critique or distrust of Big Stories meant to explain everything. This includes grand theories of science, and myths in our religions, nations, cultures, and professions that serve to explain why things are the way they are.
4. An acknowledgment that—because there is a plurality of perspectives and ways of knowing—there are also multiple truths.

In a lovely section, Hlynka and Yeaman (1992) suggest (ironically!) four easy steps to becoming a postmodernist:

1. Consider concepts, ideas and objects as texts. Textual meanings are open to interpretation.
2. Look for binary oppositions in those texts. Some usual oppositions are good/bad, progress/tradition, science/myth, love/hate, man/woman, and truth/fiction.

3. "Deconstruct" the text by showing how the oppositions are not necessarily true.
4. Identify texts which are absent, groups that are not represented, and omissions, which may or may not be deliberate, but are important (pp. 1–2).

Postmodern thinking grew out of the humanities tradition—philosophy, literary criticism, the arts. This helps to account for some of the misunderstandings that can occur between instructional designers and postmodern critics. As C. P. Snow argued in *The Two Cultures and the Scientific Revolution* (1969), people in science see things very differently than people in the humanities. The field of instructional design, evolving from behavioral psychology, systems technology, and management theory, sees the world through the "scientific" lens, whereas postmodernists tend to see things through a critical, humanities type of lens. The goal of an artist or critic is not so much to explain, predict, and control, but to *create*, *appreciate*, and *interpret* meanings. Over the years, postmodern approaches have expanded to encompass science, feminism, education, and the social sciences, but the orientation remains that of *interpretation* rather than *prediction* and *control*.

An Example of "Deconstruction": Conditions-of-Learning Models

As an illustrative exercise, I have attempted a postmodern deconstruction of traditional ID models. Conditions-of-learning or "CoL" models are the type of models we find in Reigeluth (1983). Gagné, Briggs, Merrill, and Reigeluth are the classic "CoL" theorists. Wilson and Cole (1991) described the basic conditions-of-learning paradigm:

> [CoL] models are based on Robert Gagné's *conditions-of-learning* paradigm (Gagné, 1966), which in its time was a significant departure from the Skinnerian operant conditioning paradigm dominant among American psychologists. The conditions-of-learning paradigm posits that a graded hierarchy of learning outcomes exists, and for each desired outcome, a set of conditions exists that leads to learning. Instructional design is a matter of clarifying intended learning outcomes, then matching up appropriate instructional strategies. The designer writes behaviorally specific learning objectives, classifies those objectives according to a taxonomy of learning types, then arranges the instructional conditions to fit the current instructional prescriptions. In this way, designers can design instruction to successfully teach a rule, a psychomotor skill, an attitude, or piece of verbal information.
>
> A related idea within the conditions-of-learning paradigm claims that sequencing of instruction should be based on a hierarchical progression from simple to complex learning outcomes. Gagné developed a technique of constructing learning hierarchies for analyzing skills: A skill is rationally decomposed into parts and sub-parts; then instruction is ordered from simple subskills to the complete skill. Elaboration theory uses content structure (concept, procedure, or principle) as the basis for organizing and sequencing instruction (Reigeluth, Merrill, Wilson, & Spiller, 1980). Both methods depend on task analysis to break down the goals of instruction, then on a method of sequencing proceeding from simple to gradually more complex and complete tasks. (p. 49)

The critique that follows is an edited revision of an e-mail post I sent to some author-friends who are writing a chapter on "conditions-of-learning" models:

Conditions-of-learning (CoL) models rely on a number of assumptions and distinctions, including:

Description versus prescription. The precise stance of CoL models is somewhat ambiguous—are they "scientific" models or are they "engineering" procedures? In some ways CoL models are descriptive—"There are these kinds of learning outcomes, these kinds of strategies"—but descriptive only of highly artificial activities and structures (cf. Simon, 1983). CoL models rest on a loosely defined knowledge base—a little psychology, a little instructional research, a little systems theory, a little information theory. CoL models also serve a prescriptive function for ID, but in a strange sense. Because of their difficulty, they are more than simple "recipes" or "hooks" for the novice to use and then grow out of. They are kind of saying: "Instruction *should* be like this, so do it this way." To complement instructional systems development (ISD) models—which focus more on procedures and processes—CoL models focus more on the product, saying "Good instruction should *look* this way; go and do likewise."

Another way of looking at this question is to consider what defines good instruction:

1. *Craft/process definition.* Instruction made by jumping certain hoops. Instruction made in a certain way—following ISD steps—is good.
2. *Empirical definition.* Instruction that demonstrably results in targeted learning. This is an assessment-based definition. This is a pragmatic, commonsense approach to it— if it works, it's good.
3. *Analytic/scientific definition.* Instruction that has all the desired attributes. This is the product definition of goodness. The product incorporates effective principles, contains certain features, looks a certain way. You can tell by examining the product, rather than the process used to create it or its effect on learners. This approach is most characteristic of CoL models, defining good instruction in terms of its use of certain instructional strategies and components. If the lesson has an advance organizer, clear writing, lots of examples, lots of practice, etc.—then it is good instruction.

Orthogonal independence of content and method. This is analogous to Richard Clark's claims about media and strategy—that they're independent and crossable. I may learn a concept via examples or via a definition or via a bunch of practice. In each case, however, I've learned the same thing—the target concept. An alternative view (that would need some defense) would be that different strategies necessarily lead to qualitatively different outcomes, even if some of the behaviors exhibitable by the person may be the same.

CoL models assume that there is a *class* of methods that fits a *class* of learning goals, and that I can reliably draw upon one in service of the other. But let's say your goal is to make a "Yale man" out of me. Can I accomplish those learning goals by attending Front Range Community College? Can I generalize the strategy used in one setting and replicate it in another setting? How transferable/generalizable are different "contents" and "methods"?

The "real" status of content and method. Trying to find "content" in the experiences of experts can be as hard as finding "method" in the experiences of teachers and designers. Where precisely is the content? Does it "exist" in the objectives list? In people's heads? Where is the "method"? Do I look it up in Reigeluth's books (Reigeluth, 1983, 1987)? Both content and method are rooted in the actual experience and practice of people engaged in instructional activities. Yet CoL models tend to treat textbook objectives and strategies as if they had a clear, unproblematic, unambiguous ontological status. I think that the challenge for designers is not so much in following the models properly, but in determining how a model relates to a practical situation. How can you make sense out of a CoL model when you encounter a messy real learning situation?

Instructional theory versus the practice of design. CoL approaches are all built on the conditions-goals-method framework that Reigeluth articulates in the "Green Book" (Reigeluth, 1983): Depending on the conditions and your instructional goals, you "select" the appropriate instructional strategy to accomplish those goals. Such a view defines ID as adherence to a set of rules, and places the expertise or knowledge into the textbook—or the rule-based expert system. The advantages of this approach are that the knowledge can be codified, owned, controlled, and communicated unambiguously to others. Technician-level people can even do it, even if they don't really understand what they're doing, just following numbers. What an advance! The down side is that it doesn't work beyond a poor level of "output."

Schön (1987) calls this aspect of practice "technical rationality." He doesn't deny its place; all disciplines have a technical component. But he says that's only a starting point for design or for professional practice. Technical rationality is the formal, abstract statement of theory that gets all the attention of the researcher but which utterly fails to "capture" the real expertise of the practitioners' culture. When M. David Merrill first attempted to convert his theories into expert systems, he found a whole new layer of problems and decisions he had previously ignored. I am saying that between expert systems and real life, there is yet again a whole huge layer of expertise, and that expert systems are inherently incapable of capturing it. Hence the chasm between theory and practice, between researcher and practitioner. The theorist takes seriously this formalism, this set of algorithmic rules for practice; the practitioner depends on a huge "bank" of additional knowledge and values—including how to use the technical rules—that accounts for successful practice.

The situation is similar to research on cognitive strategies. Researchers (Butterfield & Belmont, 1975) found that retarded learners were perfectly capable of mastering the specific strategies—it was in knowing when and where to use those strategies, and how to adapt them to situations, that they failed. Our theories are like the strategy repertoires of retarded learners—of themselves they do not add up to true expertise because they are missing the intangible, unanalyzable ingredients that go into everyday cognition and decision-making.

Of course, the same criticism can be leveled at attempts to define content via standard objectives and task analyses. It can't be done. Over-reliance on objectives and analyses can easily lead to failed instruction for the same reason that dogmatic adherence to CoL models will lead to failed instruction: There's more to it than what's written down in the books. People need to have experiences that place them in positions where they'll learn important things. Who knows exactly what they'll learn, but one thing for certain: If you sterilize and control the learning environment and teach *only* your targeted objectives, learners will *fail* to learn how to be the thing you want them to be. They may learn some *things* you want them to learn, but they will fail at the role you're asking them to play in a real world of practice.

Design versus implementation. CoL models assume that decisions about intended learning outcomes and instructional strategies can be made in a context removed in time and setting from practice. Winn (1990) developed this argument fairly well. Following traditional ID procedures, designers and subject experts sit together in a room around a table and make decisions about how teachers and students are going to spend their lives. We can make these decisions out of context. Sometimes we may not know that much about the context of use. Tessmer's (Tessmer & Harris, 1992) work on environmental analysis is an attempt to reintroduce some "systems" thinking back into instructional design, realizing that contexts of use are inexorably related to the design.

In an interesing self-analysis, Clancey (1993) noted that after years of work developing GUIDON and other expert systems for medical problem-solving, virtually no product ever achieved day-to-day use by medical practitioners. He faulted the design team's removal from the context of practice. The design team assumed that practitioners would welcome an expert system into their work; they thought the transition to the field would be relatively unproblematic. They failed to include implementation factors in their design, failed to achieve *praxis*—the interaction between theory and practice that keeps both fresh. There is a danger that when ID decisions are removed from the context of real instruction, similar problems will occur.

The role of the instructional designer. According to typical ID models, the instructional designer comes onto a new subject, gets fed the content by the subject-matter expert (SME), and spits it back out in the form of quality instruction. By contrast, Shulman (1987) found a whole array of different kinds of knowledge that an effective teacher must have in order to teach effectively. There is accumulating research to suggest that teachers who don't know the content inside out don't teach it as well. That's the problem with elementary math—too many elementary teachers are math phobic, don't really understand the concepts and underlying structure, and hence don't teach it well. It is amazing to me how we can expect designers who are neophytes to a subject to somehow design good instruction for it.

Instructional strategies (and types of learning outcomes) "selected" from a pool. Beside the problems of technical rationality stated above, having a finite set of strategies (or objectives types) carries a unique danger—that of locking ourselves into set ways of thinking and not being open to innovations or new solutions. Following a CoL model will likely "bias" me toward a certain defined class of strategies or learning outcomes and "blind" me to other possible ways of viewing learning outcomes or strategies. The examples are obvious—CoL models tend to view motivational variables as "add-ons"; they tend to neglect social cognition and cultural variables; they still don't have a good language for metacognitive and problem-solving outcomes. On the strategy side, a variety of constructivist strategies—simulations, games, cognitive tools—were neglected in "classic" CoL models, with updating and revisions currently going on.

The point is that traditional CoL models grew out of a particular time and place and its attending ways of seeing the world. The two Reigeluth books reflect pretty much a 1970s psychology, translated into 1980s instructional theory. Any model or theory reflects a perspective of a defined time and place. In contrast, professional practice is never-ending, always changing, just as our views are always changing. In the real world, change is the norm; unfortunately, we don't yet have a mechanism for continually updating our formal theoretical models in the same continuous way.

Of course, none of the assumptions above need be devastating to the use of CoL models. Each carries a set of risks (which I have emphasized above) but also yields a certain economy or efficiency in practice. The cumulative danger, though, is that use of CoL models will result in lowest-common-denominator, mediocre-at-best instruction rather than creative or genuinely good instruction. Certainly failure to even think about assumptions like these increases the probability that CoL models will be uncritically and inappropriately used.

Postmodern Roots of Constructivism

There may be some confusion as to how postmodernism is different from constructivism—certainly the more common term found in the ID literature. I confess to some confusion myself, and to occasionally mixing up the two terms (see Wilson, Osmon-Jouchoux, & Teslow, 1995). I think it helps to clarify the issue to think of postmodernism as an underlying philosophy about the world, and constructivism as a very general theory of cognition, suggesting how the mind works and how we know things. The roots of many constructivist beliefs about cognition are traceable to postmodern philosophies which depart from the rationalist, objectivist, and technocratic tendencies of "modern" society. Table 1 illustrates this relationship between constructivism and an underlying postmodern philosophy.

In truth, not all constructivists are postmodern in their orientation. In psychology, constructivism originally reflected the thinking of people like Piaget and Vygotsky, who were basically modern in orientation. The current instructional models of Spiro, Jonassen, Bereiter, Resnick, Lesgold, etc.—while definitely constructivist—show varying degrees of postmodern influence (although some may be postmodern without realizing it!). It is possible to have a constructivist view of cognition while still retaining a fairly traditional, modern view of science, method, and technology.

It should also be noted that postmodern thinking can lead to what I consider positive or negative outlooks on life. On the down side, some postmodernist theories can lead to despair, cynicism, moral indifference, wimpishness, and a kind of myopic self-centeredness. At the same time, other theorists are using postmodern ideas to fashion very positive, hopeful—even spiritual—approaches to life (Spretnak, 1991; Tarnas, 1991). My slant on postmodernism in this paper has been positive, as I believe it must be to have an impact on instructional design.

Table 1. A situated-cognition flavor of constructivism and its underlying postmodern philosophy.

Underlying Philosophy	Theory about Cognition
Postmodernism	**Constructivism (Situated-cognition Flavor)**
Postmodern philosophy emphasizes contextual construction of meaning and the validity of multiple perspectives. Key ideas include:	—Mind is real. Mental events are worthy of study.
• Knowledge is constructed by people and groups of people;	—Knowledge is dynamic.
	—Meaning is constructed.
• Reality is multiperspectival;	—Learning is a natural consequence of performance.
• Truth is grounded in everyday life and social relations.	—Reflection/abstraction is critical to expert performance and to becoming an expert.
• Life is a text; thinking is an interpretive act.	—Teaching is negotiating construction of meaning.
• Facts and values are inseparable;	—Thinking and perception are inseparable.
• Science and all other human activities are value-laden.	—Problem solving is central to cognition.
	—Perception and understanding are also central to cognition.

Guidelines for Doing Postmodern ID

In the spirit of subtly changing the meaning of traditional terms, I offer the following laundry list of tips for doing ID with a postmodern twist. The list should provide a clearer idea of how postmodern concepts can infiltrate and change designers' conceptions of their work.[2]

General Methodology

- *Be willing to break the rules.* Theories and models are meant to serve human needs. Wise use of these models implies when and where to use them, and where to change the rules or forget about them altogether.

- *Place principles above procedures, and people above principles.* The skilled designer will find ways to follow the principles underlying the procedures. Procedural models of ID are seen as flexible and changeable. Even key principles should be continually tested against the real needs of the people involved in the project.

- *Include all interested parties in the design and development process.* Incorporate participatory design techniques, with design activity moving out of the "lab" and into the field. Include end users (both teachers and students) as part of the design team. Make sure all interested parties—the "constituencies"—have some kind of voice contributing to the outcome of the project.

- *Don't believe your own metaphors.* Be aware of the pervasive influence that labels and metaphors have on our thinking—e.g., "delivery" of instruction, memory "storage," learning "prerequisites," "systems" design, strategy "selection," instructional "feedback," and learning "environments." While such metaphors are necessary for our thinking, they each carry a certain connotative baggage that may blind us to alternative ways of seeing.

---

[2]Please be forewarned that these recommendations are based upon my interpretation of postmodern concepts. Many radical critics would probably eschew the whole idea of revamping ID; instead, they would advocate *not* doing ID in any recognizable form.

Needs Assessment

- *Make use of consensus needs assessment strategies, in addition to gap-oriented strategies.* Gap models of needs assessment attempt to portray the "ideal" situation, compare it against the present state, leaving a need in the gap. The technical fix suggested by gap models of needs assessment may be appropriate for certain work settings. However, not all instruction is designed to improve performance in a specific work setting. Schools may develop curriculum based on a consensus among very different constituencies; the "ideal" situation may be a political compromise.

- *Do an "environmental impact" analysis.* Gap analyses always need to be supplemented with consideration of the "environmental impact" of proposed fixes. After addressing the targeted needs, what kinds of unintended outcomes may be anticipated?

- *Resist the temptation to be driven by easily measured and manipulated content.* Many important learning outcomes cannot be easily measured. It may or may not be possible to reduce value down to a number. The postmodern designer will be sensitive to subtle yet highly valued outcomes and effects.

- *Ask: Who makes the rules about what constitutes a need? Are there other perspectives to consider? What (and whose) needs are being neglected?* These questions arise out of the postmodern notion that all human activity is ideologically based. The possible political and social consequences of our actions need to inform our decisions.

Goal/Task Analyses

- *Allow for instruction and learning goals to emerge during instruction.* Just as content cannot be fully captured, learning goals cannot be fully pre-specified apart from the actual learning context. See Winn (1990) for a thorough discussion of this issue.

- *Don't sacrifice educational goals for technical training.* Acknowledge that education and training goals arise in every setting. Schools train as well as educate, and workers must be educated—not just trained in skills—to work effectively on the factory floor. The postmodern designer will be especially tuned to the need for educational goals that strengthen conceptual understanding and problem-solving skills in a domain.

- *Use objectives as heuristics to guide design.* There is no special value in operational descriptions of intended learning outcomes; in fact, these may constrain the learners' goals and achievements. Pushing goal statements to behavioral specifications can often be wasted work—or worse, lead to misguided efforts. The "intent" of instruction can be inferred by examining goal statements, learning activities, and assessment methods. Goals and objectives should be specific enough to serve as inputs to the design of assessments and instructional strategies.

- *Don't expect to "capture" the content in your goal- or task analysis.* Content on paper is not the expertise in a practitioner's head (even if you believe expertise resides in someone's head!). The best analysis always falls short of the mark. The only remedy is to design rich learning experiences and interactions in which learners can pick up on their own the content missing between the gaps of analysis.

- *Consider multiple models of expertise.* Expertise is usually thought of as having two levels: Expert or proficient performance and novice or initial performance. Of course, a two-level model is insufficient for accurate modeling of student growth over time. A series of qualitative models of expertise may be needed for modeling students' progression in learning critical tasks (Dreyfus & Dreyfus, this volume; White & Frederiksen, 1986). Postmodern theorists would pose an even more radical thought: that expertise does not follow a linear progression of stages, but takes on different forms in different people. Instruction needs to respond to where a learner "is," and support their growth, regardless of their positioning in the expertise "universe."

- *Give priority to contextualized problem-solving and meaning-constructing learning goals.* Instead of rule-following, emphasize problem solving (which incorporates rule-following but is not limited to it). Rules change according to context. But even problem solving is not all there is to cognition—perception is also central. Instead of simple recall and memory tasks, ask learners to practice seeing—making sense out of material and demonstrating their understanding of it (Prawat, 1993).

- *Define content in multiple ways. Use cases, stories, and patterns in addition to rules, principles, and procedures.* Human memory, according to some theorists, is largely story- or narrative-based (Schank, 1991). Other theories, such as situated cognition (Brown, Collins, & Duguid, 1989; Clancey, 1992, 1993) and connectionism (Marshall, 1991), emphasize pattern development and learning from authentic cases. Rich cases, stories, and patterns of performance can be alternative metaphors for finding and representing content. These multiple modes of representation can then find their way into instruction, providing richer, more meaningful experiences for students.

- *Appreciate the value-ladenness of all analysis.* Defining content and goals for learning is a political, ideological enterprise. Valuing one perspective means that other perspectives will be given less value. One approach is given prominence; another is neglected. Somebody wins, and somebody loses. Be sensitive to the value implications of your decisions.

- *Ask: Who makes the rules about what constitutes a legitimate learning goal? What learning goals are not being analyzed? Whose interests does the project serve? What is the hidden agenda* (Noble, 1989)? Twenty-five years ago, a designer using 'understand' as a verb in a learning objective would have been laughed out of the office. 'Understanding' was fuzzy; it was forbidden. Are there other expressions of learning outcomes that remain taboo? Are there other dimensions of human performance that remain undervalued within ID discourse? The cultural? The spiritual? Good postmodern ID would pursue answers to these questions and be unafraid of reexamining current practice.

Instructional Strategy Development

- *Distinguish between instructional goals and learners' goals; support learners in pursuing their own goals.* Ng and Bereiter (1991) found that students showed signs of having three kinds of goals: (1) student task-completion goals or "hoop jumping," (2) instructional goals set by the system, and (3) personal knowledge-building goals set by the student. The three do not always converge. A student motivated by task-completion goals doesn't even consider learning, yet the behavior of many students in schools is driven by just such performance requirements. Postmodern instruction would nourish and encourage pursuit of personal knowledge-building goals, while still supporting instructional goals. As Mark Twain put it: "I have never let my schooling interfere with my education."

- *Appreciate the interdependency of content and method.* Traditional design theory treats content and the method for teaching that content as orthogonally independent factors. Postmodern ID says you can't entirely separate the two. When you use a Socratic method, you are teaching something quite different than when you use worksheets and a posttest. Teaching concepts via a rule definition results in something different than teaching the same concepts via rich cases and class discussion. Just as McLuhan discerned the confounding of "media" and "message," so designers must see how learning goals are not uniformly met by interchangeable instructional strategies.

- *Allow for the "teaching moment."* Situations occur within instruction at which the student is primed and ready to learn a significant new insight. Good teachers create conditions under which such moments occur regularly, then they seize the moment and teach the lesson. This kind of flexibility requires a level of spontaneity and responsiveness not usually talked about in ID circles.

- *Be open to new ways of thinking about education and instruction.* The postmodern designer will always feel somewhat ill at ease when "applying" a particular model, even the more progressive models such as cognitive apprenticeship, minimalist training, intentional learning environments, or case- or story-based instruction. Designers should always be playing with models, trying new things out, modifying or adapting methods to suit new circumstances.

- *Think in terms of designing learning environments and experiences rather than "selecting" instructional strategies.* Metaphors are important. Does the designer "select" a strategy or "arrange" a learning experience? Postmodern designers would usually think of instruction in interactive, experiential terms rather than as a simple product or presentation.

- *Think of instruction as providing tools that teachers and students can use for learning; make these tools user-friendly.* This frame of mind is virtually the opposite of "teacher-proofing" instructional materials to assure uniform adherence to designers' use expectations. Instead, teachers and students are encouraged to make creative and intelligent use of instructional tools and resources. In some respects the designer is surrendering control over the use of the product, but in so doing participates more meaningfully in the total design of the experience.

- *Consider strategies that provide multiple perspectives that encourage the learner to exercise responsibility.* Resist the temptation to "pre-package" everything. Let learners generate their own questions and goals, then seek out information and experiences to address those questions. Of course, this runs the risk of not giving the learner enough guidance, or of exposing too much confusion and complexity. Certainly there are times to simplify and reduce complexity; the designer needs to exercise best judgment and find methods for support in the midst of complexity.

- *Appreciate the value-ladenness of instructional strategies.* Sitting through a school board meeting is enough to convince anyone of this. Instructional strategies grow out of our philosophies of the world and our value systems. Not only the content, but the strategy can be a threat to particular ideological positions or to learner motivation. Good designers will be sensitive to the "fit" between their designs and the situation.

Media Selection

- *Include media biases as a consideration in media decisions.* Different media send different "messages" to an audience, independently of the instructional content. A TV show means something different to a child than another worksheet. Look for any "hidden curriculum" elements in different media choices. Avoid negative stereotypes and cultural biases. Consider the rhetorical goodness of fit between media choice and overall instructional purposes.

- *Include media literacy as a planning consideration.* Designers should be sensitive to an audience's media sophistication and literacy, paying particular attention to humor, media conventions, and production values.

Student Assessment

- *Incorporate assessment into the learning experience where possible.* Skilled teachers will be assessing students informally all the time. Assessment should be seamlessly integrated into meaningful learning experiences and not tacked on at the end.

- *Critique and discuss products and performances grounded in authentic contexts, including portfolios, projects, compositions, and performances.* Product and performance reviews can complement more traditional measures of knowledge acquisition and understanding (Cates, 1992). Include different perspectives in the critiquing process.

- *Use informal assessments within classrooms and learning environments.* Informal assessments refer primarily to teacher observations of eye contact, body language, facial expressions, and work performance. These observations can complement formal assessments as a basis for instructional adjustments.

Conclusion

If my purpose has been accomplished, you will have gained an appreciation of postmodern ideas and how they can relate to ID practice. As we continue to grow professionally, the same old terms begin to take on different meanings. At the same time, I hope you are cautious and critical in evaluating these ideas. Avoid any bandwagon phenomenon. Test any of the ideas in this chapter or book against the reality of your practice. All theories and ideas need to be put into the service of real-world practice and usability. Remember the postmodern slogan: "Question authority (before they question you!)."

References

Brown, J. S., Collins, A., & Duguid, P. (1989, January–February). Situated cognition and the culture of learning. *Educational Researcher, 18*(1), 32–42.

Butterfield, E. C., & Belmont, J. M. (1975). Assessing and improving the executive cognitive functions of mentally retarded people. In I. Bialer & M. Sternlicht (Eds.), *Psychological issues in mental retardation.* Chicago: Aldine-Atherton.

Cates, W. M. (1992, April). *Considerations in evaluating metacognition in interactive hypermedia/multimedia instruction.* Paper presented at the meeting of the American Educational Research Association, San Francisco.

Clancey, W. J. (1992). Representations of knowing: In defense of cognitive apprenticeship. *Journal of Artificial Intelligence in Education, 3*(2), 139–168.

Clancey, W. J. (1993). Guidon-Manage revisited: A socio-technical systems approach. *Journal of Artificial Intelligence in Education, 4*(1), 5–34.

Clark, R. E. (1983). Reconsidering research on learning from media. *Review of Educational Research, 53,* 445-460.

Dreyfus, H., & Dreyfus, S. Chapter, this volume.

Gagné, R. M. (1965). *The conditions of learning* (1st ed.). New York: Holt, Rinehart, and Winston.

Hlynka, D., & Belland, J. C. (Eds.). (1991). *Paradigms regained: The uses of illuminative, semiotic, and postmodern criticism as modes of inquiry in educational technology: A book of readings.* Englewood Cliffs, NJ: Educational Technology Publications.

Hlynka, D., & Yeaman, R. J. (1992, September). *Postmodern educational technology. ERIC Digest* No. EDO-IR-92-5. Syracuse NY: ERIC Clearinghouse on Information Resources.

Marshall, S. P. (1991, December). *Schemas in problems solving: An integrated model of learning, memory, and instruction.* San Diego: Center for Research in Mathematics and Science Education. Final Report for Office of Naval Research Grant No. ONR N00014-89-J-1143.

Martin, B. L. (1994, March). Commentary on deconstructing modern educational technology. *Educational Technology, 34*(2), 64–65.

Ng, E., & Bereiter, C. (1991). Three levels of goal orientation in learning. *The Journal of the Learning Sciences, 1*(3 & 4), 243–271.

Noble, D. D. (1989). Cockpit cognition: Education, the military and cognitive engineering. *AI & Society, 3*, 271–297.

Prawat, R. S. (1993). The value of ideas: Problems versus possibilities in learning. *Educational Researcher, 22*(6), 5–16.

Reigeluth, C. M. (Ed.). (1983). *Instructional design theories and models: An overview of their current status.* Hillsdale, NJ: Lawrence Erlbaum Associates.

Reigeluth, C. M. (Ed.) (1987). *Instructional theories in action: Lessons illustrating selected theories and models.* Hillsdale, NJ: Lawrence Erlbaum Associates.

Reigeluth, C. M., Merrill, M. D., Wilson, B. G., & Spiller, R. T. (1980). The Elaboration Theory of Instruction: A model for structuring instruction. *Instructional Science, 9*, 195-219.

Schön, D. (1987). *Educating the reflective practitioner.* New York: Basic Books.

Schank, R. (1991). *Tell me a story: A new look at real and artificial memory.* New York: Simon and Schuster.

Shulman, L. S. (1987). Knowledge and teaching: Foundations of the new reform. *Harvard Educational Review, 57*(1), 1–22.

Simon, H. (1983). *The sciences of the artificial* (2nd ed.). Cambridge, MA: MIT Press.

Snow, C. P. (1969). *The two cultures and the scientific revolution.* Cambridge: Cambridge University Press.

Spretnak, C. (1991). *States of grace: The recovery of meaning in the postmodern age.* San Francisco: HarperCollins.

Streibel, M. J. (1986). A critical analysis of the use of computers in education. *Educational Communication and Technology Journal, 34*(3).

Tarnas, R. (1991). *The passion of the western mind.* New York: Harmony Books.

Tessmer, M., & Harris, D. (1992). *Analysing the instructional setting: Environmental analysis.* London: Kogan Page.

White, B. Y., & Frederiksen, J. R. (1986). *Progressions of quantitative models as a foundation for intelligent learning environments.* Technical Report #6277, BBN.

Wilson, B. G. (this volume). Constructivism.

Wilson, B., & Cole, P. (1991). A review of cognitive teaching models. *Educational Technology Research and Development, 39*(4), 47–64.

Wilson, B. G., Osman-Jouchoux, R., & Teslow, J. (1995). The impact of constructivism (and postmodernism) on ID fundamentals. In B. Seels (Ed.), *Instructional design fundamentals.* Englewood Cliffs NJ: Educational Technology Publications.

Winn, W. D. (1990). Some implications of cognitive theory for instructional design. *Instructional Science, 19*, 53–69.

19

Semiotics: Toward Learning-Centered Instructional Design

Marcy P. Driscoll
Kurt Rowley
The Florida State University, Tallahassee

It is always the story related by William James: novelties are first repudiated as nonsense; in a second stage, they are declared to be obvious and trivial; until in the third stage, the former opponents claim to have discovered them themselves.

—von Bertalanffy, 1967, p. 113

With the telling of that story, von Bertalanffy (1967) hoped that the perspectivistic philosophy implied by the general theory of systems he proposed would become commonplace in psychology and education. "The systems concept," he argued, "implies a new epistemology—in short, replacement of absolutistic by perspective philosophy" (1967, p. 93). Moreover, this perspectivistic view is "tolerant of other philosophies and other experiences—in arts, morals, religion—which may mirror other facets of an unfathomable reality" (1967, p. 113).

The importance of general systems theory as a foundation for theory and practice in instructional systems design can hardly be overstated. Certainly, the cybernetic and engineering aspects of systems theory have had a strong influence on instructional design models that are prominent in the field (e.g., Dick & Carey, 1990; Gagné, Briggs, & Wager, 1992). However, the influence of von Bertalanffy's perspectivistic philosophy is less clearly detected in our instructional design models and theories as they currently exist. Can it yet exert a desirable influence on the theory and practice of instructional design? We think the answer is yes, and in our view, semiotics offers the means to realize von Bertalanffy's hope.

In this chapter, we present one possible view of semiotics as a core paradigm for instructional systems design (ISD). Our view hinges on basic principles originally set forth by Charles Sanders Peirce, beginning in 1867[1], and presents ISD as a *learning-centered* process.

We begin our discussion with the argument that the current ISD paradigm is *instruction*-centered, and we describe how the adoption of semiotic principles enables a more *learning*-centered approach. Then, we outline characteristics of a semiotic ISD paradigm and consider both what challenges this paradigm may face and what new methods and tools for instructional design it may require. Next, we contrast the semiotic paradigm with other current trends in the field that seem to share common concepts, and show how semiotics provides a unifying framework for these trends. We also review several approaches taken by other researchers to apply semiotics to various aspects of instructional design. Finally, we conclude with a few thoughts about the possible future of semiotic ISD.

The Current ISD Paradigm as Instruction-Centered

As a first step to describing how semiotics offers a different approach to instructional systems design and actually extends the current paradigm, it is useful to review the processes and procedures of that paradigm. Generally stated, ISD is a process used by a designer to provide instruction to a learner on a topic s/he may or may not want to learn (Dick & Carey, 1990; Gagné, Briggs, & Wager, 1992). Designers attempt to accomplish this process through a series of systematic procedures designed to identify performance objectives, analyze tasks and behaviors, analyze the related knowledge base, determine the learner's entry skills relative to the knowledge base and desired objectives, design and develop appropriate instruction, and finally, validate and revise that instruction. This is primarily a problem-solving process that supports the practitioner in identifying overall goals and related objectives of instruction (Gagné, Briggs, & Wager, 1992; Kaufman, 1988; Mager, 1975), systematically designing and developing instruction around theories of learning (Dick & Carey, 1990; Gagné, 1985), adjusting that instruction until the objectives are met (Cronbach, 1975; Stufflebeam, 1973), and finally solving the original problem. The best possible technologies, in other words, are assembled in order to analyze the problem context and develop appropriate instructional solutions.

We suggest at this point that the ISD paradigm as described above is *instruction-centered*. What we mean by this is perhaps best illustrated by an example.

Belland (1991) described an auto-tutorial course in biology that was developed and implemented at the Ohio State University in the late 1960s. Evaluation studies of this course showed that students who took it performed well on end-of-course objectives-referenced tests, and it cost a fraction of what public education did at the time. So, you ask, what was the problem? Although the course designers developed instruction that successfully met the performance objectives of the Biology Department, they failed to consider what impact the "lived experience" of the students in the class would have on their future actions. Even though general education requirements for undergraduates included several courses in science, students who took the auto-tutorial class rarely enrolled in another biology course!

This example illustrates the distinction that Shank (1992) made between knowledge as objective truth and knowledge as the making of meaning. He argued that researchers and educators alike tend to focus on knowledge as truth to the exclusion of knowledge as meaning. In other words, we claim to "know" something when we can ascertain that it is true, i.e., verify it through some objective means. Shank presented an example of a patient whose symptoms are diagnosed as cancer. Like the researcher conducting tests of hypotheses, the doctor verified the supposition that the patient had cancer by conducting certain laboratory tests. The tests derive their meaning from their association with cancer, and so we say that we know the *truth* that the patient has cancer because the results of these tests were positive.

But can we also say that we know what having cancer *means* to this patient, her attending physician, or her family? Knowing the objective reality—this patient has cancer—is only part of the story, argued Shank, who suggested that we must also inquire as to what any event means to its participants. Effective treatment of the cancer, for instance, involves not just the doctor's prescriptions based on test results, but also the patient's acceptance of and participation in these prescriptions. And how she construes these prescriptions in the context of other meanings in her life will affect what actions she takes regarding them.

To revisit Belland's auto-tutorial biology course, we can see a situation analogous to Shank's cancer patient. Although we know that the instruction was effective, based on the evaluation results, we have no idea what meanings the students derived from their experiences in this course. They learned biology at a reduced cost to the Biology Department, which satisfied the identified problems, but something else also occurred relative to what the course meant to them so that they chose to forego any further study of biology.

By instruction-centered, then, we suggest that the current ISD paradigm has operated under the assumption that the content of instruction and the content of knowledge are essentially isomorphic. In other words, learners are thought to acquire the same information and skills as the instruction was designed to convey. As has been argued elsewhere (see, for example, Cunningham, 1992; Jonassen, 1991), this is consistent with the positivist epistemological view that knowledge is something external to the learner and verifiable in objective reality. Reality is viewed in terms of a physical environment that can be conceived independently of the individual and that serves as a source of stimulation to the individual. When it is determined, then, that learners don't possess some knowledge (truth) that they should, instruction is designed to transmit that knowledge to learners. As a consequence of this view, the ISD process solicits input from learners to judge how much of the desired knowledge these learners already have (entry level), what methods of transmission are likely to be most successful with these learners (learning styles and preferences), and in formative evaluation, what problems of transmission must be corrected for the instruction to be deemed effective. The quality of instruction is typically judged on the basis of how many learners can demonstrate that they have acquired the desired knowledge to some specified degree of proficiency.

We agree with Shank (1992), however, that the present instruction-centered ISD paradigm, with its emphasis on knowledge as truth, would benefit from an exploration of what happens when the paradigm is expanded to include knowledge as meaning. In our view, such a shift promotes a learning-centered approach to instructional design by requiring that we focus on *what is being learned* in any instructional situation. This is best done, we will argue, through a semiotic approach because semiotics allows us to directly address the process of making meaning through experience.[2]

Introduction to Semiotics

To begin with, semiotics is a lot of different things to a lot of different people and areas of study. For some, it is a point of view involving the whole phenomenon of human communication, which includes the phenomena both of culture and of nature (Deely, 1990a). Others have wondered, sometimes whimsically, whether semiotics is a theory, a perspective, or a disease (Sebeok, 1986). According to Shank (1992), semiotics is "the general theory of how things act as signs" and is therefore "naturally concerned with meaning."

Although branches of semiotics are specifically devoted to the grammar of communication (syntactics, pragmatics, and semantics) as well as interpretation of texts (hermeneutics), and literary criticism (including critical theory), researchers in a variety of fields from anthropology to architecture to geography to medicine have adopted the language and principles of C. S. Peirce as a productive framework for investigating and interpreting phenomena within their own fields. Like these researchers, we believe that Peirce's ideas can underpin the field of instructional systems and can transform the field in ways yet to be imagined. We explore a few of these ways in this chapter.

Charles Sanders Peirce was an American philosopher who grew up in the 19th century (b. 1839–d. 1914). Houser (1992) said this of Peirce: "He was regarded as a prodigy in both science and philosophy, and more brilliant in mathematics than even his father . . . As great a thinker as any that America has ever produced. . ." Among Peirce's contemporaries and friends were John Dewey and William James, who, it is said, founded American pragmatism on a "central idea he borrowed from . . . Peirce" (Edie, 1987, p. 66). Unfortunately for Peirce, the academically conservative times in which he lived severely limited his influence; only recently has his importance to American philosophy become recognized. But in "the rapidly growing field of study known as semiotics, Peirce is universally acknowledged as one of the founders, even *the* founder, and his theory of signs is among the most frequently studied and systematically examined of all foundational theories" (Houser, 1992, p. xx).

Peirce was interested in the human world in its broadest sense, both the natural surroundings as well as the mental world within. His thinking and writing is characterized by a lifelong tension between idealism and realism. To begin with, he believed that "the real is of the nature of thought" and that the mind has the power to originate ideas that are true. This is an idealist view. But Peirce also believed that "experience is our only teacher" (quoted in Houser, 1992, p. xxxiv), so that ideas, to be proved true, had to be indexed to experience. This synthesis of views led Houser (1992) to suggest that Peirce's philosophy might best be represented as "*ideal-realism,* which 'combines the principles of idealism and realism' " (p. xxxv; emphasis his).

Another way to understand Peirce's philosophy is to consider the world of imagination or possibilities as an initial purveyor of thought. But thoughts are independent of what actually exists in the physical world. "No cognition . . . has an intellectual significance for what it is in itself, . . . the existence of a cognition is not something actual" (Peirce, quoted in Houser, 1992, p. xxvi). In order to reference thought to actual situations or to the physical world, then, Peirce recognized the need for indices—or signs—to represent meaning. But as signs represent meaning, they do not necessarily correspond to the physical world. That is,

> How can we know that our representations of the world are correct? The only answer seems to involve checking those representations against the world to see if they in fact match, but, by assumption, the only epistemic contact we have with the world is via the representations themselves—any such check, therefore, is circular. (Bickhard, 1992, p. 63)

The world of meaning and experience, then, also called the objective world (Deely, 1990b), includes both thought and aspects of the physical world, with each being mediated

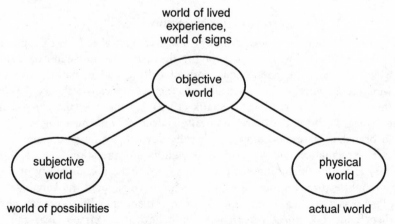

Figure 1.   Peirce's conception of thought and physical reality as indexed to the world of experience.

by signs (see Figure 1). Peirce set out to study this world of signs with the intent of developing an empirically grounded or informed philosophy. This was a very unusual approach for his time, but it is particularly useful in an applied field of symbolic communication such as ours.

Peirce's Sign Theory

Over time, Peirce attempted to analyze fundamental communication across all natural phenomena, and he began a catalog of possible signs, a kind of periodic table that eventually contained over 66 distinct classes of signs and symbols in nature. However, in doing this he discovered that all symbolic conceptions possessed three universal properties: firstness, secondness, and thirdness. "Firstness is that which is as it is independently of anything else. Secondness is that which is as it is relative to something else. Thirdness is that which is as it is mediate between two others" (Houser, 1992, p. xxx). In other words, firstness is a primary object, secondness is a sign or symbol of that object, and thirdness is the interpretation of the sign or symbol.

This triad of object, sign, and interpretant is at the heart of semiotic discourse, and it is a foundational concept that semioticians in all fields have accepted. It essentially establishes interpretation as the primary activity of experience and that which leads to knowledge. To paraphrase an example discussed by Peirce, imagine a pot of liquid on the stove in which a candy thermometer has been placed. As the temperature of the liquid rises, so does the mercury in the thermometer. The observed rise in mercury level is an indexical sign of the rising heat in the candy. The heat is the firstness. There is also a physical cause-and-effect relation here, a secondness, in that the heat causes the mercury to rise. But it's only the cook's experience of the relation between rising mercury and rising heat that gives it particular meaning. The cook's experience establishes the interpretant (or how the sign is to be interpreted), and the original physical relation takes on a thirdness and becomes a semiotic relation.

A similar example can be seen in a person's experience and interpretation of certain bodily sensations, such as a rumbling in the stomach. The firstness is the condition of the absence of food. Again, a cause-and-effect relation (secondness) is present, in that gastric juices are felt when the stomach is devoid of food. When the person interprets the sensation as hunger, then a thirdness is established and the relation, like the cook's experience of rising heat in the previous example, becomes a semiotic one. These two examples, the candy thermometer and hunger, begin to illustrate the broad range of semiotics and its ability to depict the making of meaning from experience with signs.

According to Peirce, signs differ in the types of relations they bear to their objects. *Indexes* bear a direct connection with their objects, as smoke is an index of fire, clouds are a sign of rain, and a windvane is an indication of wind direction. *Icons*, by contrast, are images of their objects in the way that pictures or photographs provide images of their subjects. So, for example, a picture of a dog is not the dog itself, but an image, a likeness. Similarly, icons used in hypermedia programs are meant to represent how specific functions are like the object for which the icon stands. Finally, *symbols* are related to their objects by habit or convention, which describes, for example, the signs of language and mathematics. Specific examples of these three types of signs are shown in Figure 2.

As his theory evolved, Peirce also distinguished, for every sign, two types of objects and three types of interpretants. The immediate object is the "object as the sign represents it," whereas the dynamic object is "the really efficient but not immediately present object" (Houser, 1992). This is essentially the difference between proximal and ultimate causes of signs or associations of signs with their objects (Houser, 1987). As for interpretants, the immediate interpretant is what is signified in the sign, the dynamic interpretant is the effect

INDEXICAL SIGNS	ICONIC SIGNS	SYMBOLIC SIGNS
a flag streaming straight back as a sign of winds greater than 30 mph	sign near an airport:	most advertising logos, such as the 3-pronged emblem of Mercedes-Benz
the glow of an electric burner indicating how hot it is	dairy farm sign:	the word "beauty" for all that it connotes the variable x in algebraic equations
the color that litmus paper turns to indicate PH levels	sign at bike path entrance:	

Figure 2.   Examples of three different types of signs.

produced by the sign at a given time, and the final interpretant is the effect produced by the sign after a history of semiotic interaction with the dynamic object. An example should help to make these distinctions clear.

Suppose that the sign under investigation is an icon that looks like a parachute, used in a hypermedia program. What are its respective objects and interpretants? Assume that it is meant to stand for the function of quitting the program; that would be the sign's immediate object. Its dynamic object is the general concept of quitting that is embodied in the metaphor, "bailing out." The immediate interpretant for the sign, what it visually represents, is the parachute itself. The dynamic interpretant, or the immediate effect produced by the sign, will depend upon whether the program user has experienced this sign relation before. If s/he has, whether or not the dynamic object (i.e., the metaphor of bailing out) is known, s/he will click on the icon to quit the program. However, if s/he has not experienced this sign relation before (i.e., parachute icon stands for QUIT), and if s/he is not familiar with the underlying metaphor of "bailing out," then it is likely that confusion will be the dynamic interpretant. Alternatively, a program user who understands the metaphor will click on the icon to quit the program because s/he correctly interprets the icon as representing the dynamic object (final interpretant; see Figure 3).

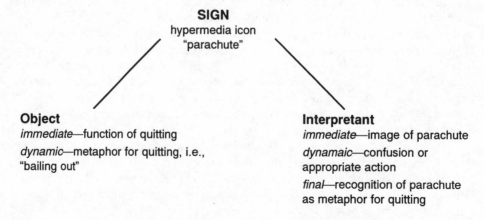

Figure 3.   A semiotic analysis of a hypermedia icon.

In this example, the fact that more than one dynamic interpretant is possible illustrates that, for the most part, signs incompletely represent their objects. Because of this incomplete equivalence, signs are free to have characteristics of their own, which makes possible both misinterpretation and deliberate deception. Of course, some signs must be interpreted for what they actually are in order to assure the survival of the one who is doing the interpreting. For example, an animal must properly interpret food as food and shelter as shelter (Deely, 1990a).

The triad of object, sign, and interpretant offers an analytic framework for investigating an individual's experience, whether it be a student in a classroom, a patient in a doctor's office, or a hunter in search of game. In each case, it is important to determine what signs are perceived by the individual as relevant and what interpretation is made of each sign. As seen in the parachute example above, the future action of the individual may also be identified, because the effect of the sign is inherent in the sign relation as the dynamic interpretant. What makes for miscommunication, or difficulty in analyzing sign relations, is the very arbitrariness of signs—the fact that their interpretation changes with experience, context or new understandings. Signs are also interpreted differently by different people, which can cause confusion when a sign is used in one way but understood in another. A teacher, for example, employs certain signs in the expectation that students will interpret the sign as standing for what the teacher intended. In the case of the hypermedia icon described above, the designer clearly intended for its dynamic object (the metaphor) to be apprehended, so that the student would use the icon to quit the program, even the first time the program is encountered.

The following example illustrates a situation in which a student apprehends a sign in the way it was intended by the teachers. In this unpublished account, the student describes what happened during the first session of a course designed to teach alternative views of teaching and learning in which the instructors wanted students to experience those very views:

> The first activity of our class on the first night session was the rearrangement of the class-room. Our desks had been arranged (undoubtedly by a dualistic-thinking objectivist) in the traditional arrangement whereby the students faced forward toward the all-knowing instructor. We were asked to place the desks in a circle (a symbol which has no obvious beginning or end) whereby learners faced each other. This semiotic suggestion (sign) gave notice that instructors were mere equals to the students, sharing equal positions on the circle, ready to participate. . .ready to collaborate.

The student goes on to describe how this class was markedly different from other classes he had taken and how it altered his personal perspective on teaching and learning. What does this example illustrate? On the face of it, one would have no reason to expect a relation between the arrangement of desks in a classroom and learning. Yet because of his previous experience with desks in rows facing the teacher, this arrangement signified to the student what roles to expect of himself and the teacher. The change in desk arrangement to a circle (the sign) brought a new meaning to the roles of teacher and learner in this class.

Semiosis, or a Process of Sign Interpretation and Construction

Peirce's sign theory not only enables the investigation and interpretation of an individual's experience, it provides a new conception of learning, which also has important implications for a semiotic ISD paradigm. The process of learning, in this framework, is one of interpreting meaning and assembling signs and symbols (Cunningham, 1987, 1992; Houser, 1987). This is often referred to as signification (Saussure, 1959), or what semioticians call semiosis. Put another way, experience must give rise to signs and interpretations, and learning occurs as a consequence of the interaction of signs, objects and interpretants (Houser, 1987). The learner therefore develops a complex network of hierarchical and relational signs and symbols that work together in meaningful systems and structures. These systems and structures then serve to mediate new experiences so that some signs in the environment are perceived whereas others are ignored. Thus, semiosis is a particular definition of learning as an ongoing dialogue, a continuous process of assembling signs and interpretations.

The idea of learning as semiosis is that learning is not what a student sees or hears (perception), it is not whether a student knows the formal definition of what was seen or heard (knowledge), nor whether the student remembers details about what was seen or heard (mastery). Under the semiotic paradigm, learning is how the student perceives a sign as relevant, interprets that sign, and relates that interpretation to the object of what was mediated to the student. Learning as semiosis is also the connection of the student's interpretation with other persons' interpretations to construct meaning. Finally, semiosis involves all actions taken by the student in response to the signs (i.e., the dynamic interpretants), from random responses or active avoidance, to intentional memorization, to understanding, and eventually, to performance.

This concept of learning is transformational, with every element in the environment contributing to that transformation. Important to this transformation is making and testing predictions about what signs mean (Houser, 1987). In other words, the learner perceives a sign and generates a tentative interpretant that provides some notion of what the object related to the sign might be. With repeated experience, the learner either rejects the initial interpretant in favor of others that seem more accurate, or adopts this interpretation as the final interpretant (at least until some later experience calls this interpretation into question). What is important to remember is that the dynamic object might never actually be known, but it is supposed, based on the evidence at hand. Consider the following example.

In a study by Emihovich (1981), who videotaped interactions among kindergarten children, one episode showed the teacher at the blackboard with the children clustered around a table placed near the board. The teacher had drawn overlapping circles on the board, one in blue to represent all animals with four legs and the other in red to represent pets. The teacher asked the children to suggest animals that could be classified in either circle or in their intersection. With each correct classification, the teacher handed her chalk to the student answering correctly, who then came to the board to put a mark in the circle where the animal belonged. At other times, the teacher held the chalk close to her chest. What are the children learning here?

On one hand, they are clearly learning concepts. Suppose, for example, that one of the children suggested "dog" as an instance to classify. The spoken word is the sign and its dynamic object (the intended association to be learned) consists of the two concepts, "pet" and "4-legged animal." The immediate object is the actual animal, dog. As for interpretants, the immediate interpretant is the thought of a dog that comes to the child's mind when the word is spoken. This might be the child's own pet, some dog in the neighborhood with which the child has had contact, or a prototypical representation of dog. The dynamic interpretant is the voiced answer that the child gives as to which circle the dog belongs in. If the child's experience with dogs has been frightening, the dynamic interpretant could also include a feeling of fear. The final interpretant is the anticipated and desired interpretation that a dog is both a four-legged animal and a pet (see Figure 4). For the child who has been frightened by dogs, however, the final interpretant may never come to include the concept of dog as a personal pet.

What other signs are there in this episode to be interpreted (and thus, learned) by students? One is the piece of chalk which is given to any student who provides a correct classification. If the chalk is the sign and its immediate object the chance to go to the board, then what is its dynamic object? In all likelihood the teacher is not aware that the chalk can be interpreted for anything more than she intends. But if she is the only one who has access to the chalk except when she chooses to give it away, the dynamic object becomes one of control or authority, and the children will learn this as readily as their intended lessons.

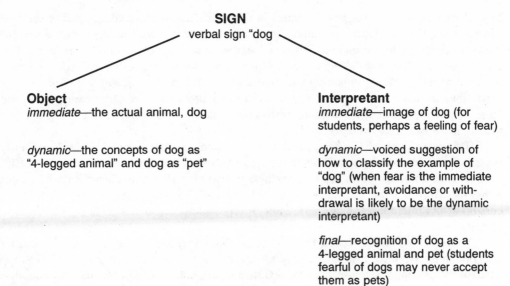

Figure 4. A semiotic analysis of the verbal sign "dog" in a kindergarten lesson on the concepts of "4-legged animals" and "pets."

It is important to recognize that learners construct their own signs as well as interpret the signs of others. These signs may then become available for interpretation by the learners' teachers, peers, and parents. Results of a recent study, for example, showed that students constructed a number of different "codes" for behavior in family, peer, and school cultural settings (Phelan, Davidson, & Cao, 1991; reported in Shank, 1994). Interpreting these codes enabled the researchers to make sense of the students' behaviors in these settings.

The notion of a semiotic paradigm as learning-centered should now be reasonably clear. The theory of signs and the process of semiosis require that attention be focused on the phenomenon of what is being interpreted and learned in any situation. This is the core of semiotic thinking. In order to determine whether this thinking is adequate to develop a paradigm or metaphor for instructional systems design, we present next a hypothetical semiotic model of ISD oriented around the principles of sign, object, and interpretant. With learning defined as semiosis, we believe that a semiotic ISD model offers a fundamentally naturalistic approach to instructional design that enhances the instruction-centered aspects of the current ISD paradigm.

Towards a Semiotic ISD Paradigm

If we accept the semiotic assumption that the learner derives meaning through a process of interpreting and constructing signs and symbols, we can begin to outline a semiotic, or interpretation-oriented, ISD. Instructional designers have traditionally viewed the learner as a recipient and evaluator of instructional materials. Under the semiotic paradigm, however, the learner assumes a more central position as the principal maker of meaning, with all that is available in the learner's environment constituting the materials of instruction. Now the main task in designing instruction is to determine what signs and symbols are being connected to the objects of instruction and how these are interpreted by the learner.

Before we describe how this might be done, it is important to note that under the semiotic paradigm, the environment itself is also viewed differently. Although its components (e.g., instructor, learners, materials, etc.) contribute to its reality, it is assumed to have integrity and meaning in its own right. This is analogous to the different "realities" produced by a single shot versus a sequence of shots in film. Although one is a component of the other, the interpretations that can be realized from each are unique and independent. So to fully understand the kindergarten class discussed earlier, one must consider what is integral and unique to the class beyond what can be accounted for by its individual components of teacher, students, chalk and blackboard. Shank (1994) argued that qualitative researchers, by definition, are open and sensitive to the reality of larger orders of organization and coherence. By the same token, the semiotic instructional designer must be open to the realities of instructional systems at various levels of organization.

This recognition of the dynamic reality of systems is consistent with von Bertalanffy's perspectivistic philosophy, and it strengthens general systems theory as a foundation of ISD. It also seems consistent with the broader perspective of performance technology (Stolovitch & Keeps, 1992), but that is a story for another chapter. For our purposes, we will focus discussion at the micro level—how the learner interprets and constructs signs in the context of instruction.

For semiotic ISD to proceed, then, we must find a way to analyze and reduce a learner's interpretation. We must also find a way to orient the desired interpretation of the learner, perhaps by creating a semiosis agenda. Following the semiotic triad concept, semiotic objectives would logically be derived from an analysis of gaps between actual and desired interpretations of signs and symbols, or a type of semiotic needs assessment.

This is the point at which the divergence between a traditional and a semiotic paradigm becomes clear. Instead of (or perhaps in addition to) performing an analysis of content, an instructional designer working under a semiotic paradigm would inquire extensively into the semiosic process by which the learner interprets materials. Remember, however, that "materials" refers not just to the traditional instructional materials, but to all other possible signs in the learner's environment. Signs are embedded in the instructional content, in the means by which instruction is delivered, in the interactions with other participants (whether other learners or an instructor), and in the overall culture or system within which the learner must operate. Out of this semiosic interpretation inquiry, then, would be created a design for the development of instruction. Moreover, through the ongoing monitoring of interpretation across many learners, revisions of the design would help to maintain a learning-centered orientation. We see this process as being similar to rapid prototyping (e.g., Goodrum, Dorsey, & Schwen, 1994, and their chapter in this volume) and to Pea's (1993) notion of configuring distributed intelligence, because designers are "continually creating new objects and environments, interpreting their meaning, and revising their designs accordingly" (Pea, 1993, p. 55).

What form might this interpretation inquiry take? During the design of an instructional module, for example, we envision the designer selecting a prototypical learner, presenting the learner with a knowledge base or a subject-matter tutor,[3] and questioning the learner during guided learning. When we say "prototypical learner," we mean one from the target population for which the instruction is being designed. In the selection of this learner, there are several important factors to consider. For one thing, the sign systems that learners develop and use over time will differ according to their culture and experience. Culture is meant broadly here to include ethnic differences, religious heritage, and even corporate culture. Experience is important because the more exposure learners have had to the sign systems and means of signification among various cultures, the more likely they are to hold their interpretants as tentative until enough evidence is obtained to assure them that their interpretation is appropriate or correct. Therefore, the designer would be wise to select as the prototypical learner one who has inculcated the sign systems of the target environment. If diversity among participants is expected, then selecting more than one prototypical learner may be considered. This might be true, for example, in the case of a worldwide manufacturing company seeking to train certain employees from each of its many plant locations on a new piece of equipment about to be installed.

As for conducting an interpretation inquiry, the designer could follow the steps of a talk-aloud protocol or use other, naturalistic techniques for determining the learner's interpretations as well as semiosis (development and linkage of new signs and symbols). Possible questions to ask of the learner during guided learning include:

- what are you thinking?
- what is important to you next?
- what are you learning?
- how are you learning (interpreting) this?
- what are you relating these ideas to?
- what metaphors or analogies about this occur to you?
- how does this compare to—?
- how do you feel about this?

The inquiry protocol would also certainly be informed by theories and important issues raised by traditional ISD, and it should probe interpretation of signs in the environment that affect the learner's use of the meanings to be gained through instruction. By using these and other, perhaps more pointed questions, the designer would identify patterns and issues that would then suggest specific instructional strategies, curriculum concepts, implementation strategies, and the like. We expect that this type of applied learning analysis (of semiosis, or interpreting) would produce different instructional approaches than would the traditional paradigm. The identification of metaphors, for instance, is extremely important to a semiotic theory of learning because they call up interpretants that might not otherwise be associated with a dynamic object (Houser, 1987). Cates (1994) has discussed the use of metaphor in designing hypermedia interfaces, and has pointed out the need for examining auxiliary metaphors that are called to mind by the dominant metaphor.

To summarize, then, instructional design performed under a semiotic paradigm would go something like this: Find one or more prototypical learners, expose them to an organized knowledge base, guide their learning, inquire into the symbolic construction or signification of their understanding of specific concepts as they learn, and probe the context of their understandings-in-use.

A General Semiotic ISD Model

The semiotic paradigm by itself does not suggest a singular solution to the design of instruction. What we have presented thus far is only one possible application of semiotic thought to instructional design. Nevertheless, it serves as an example to show how a learning-oriented instructional design model might differ from traditional ISD models, how it might be informed by traditional ISD models, and how it might borrow from naturalistic inquiry paradigms. Ultimately, a semiotic ISD model as we have outlined it would follow these steps, at a minimum:

- Conduct a semiotic learning analysis, including interviews and naturalistic inquiry, into the signification, or symbol and sign interpretation, of prototypical learners during a guided or facilitated process of semiosis, or learning. The facilitation would follow a semiotic agenda and lead to the discovery of missing interpretations, which then become the semiotic objectives.

- Develop from the semiosis analysis a design for instruction in the form of instructional prototypes. Refine and improve these prototypes in iterations with further prototypical learner interviews and naturalistic, semiotic inquiry during guided learning.

- Produce one or more instructional products, environments, or support systems based on the successful prototypes. On an ongoing basis, the instructor or learning facilitator would be expected to evaluate and improve these products. The evaluation would consist of further iterations of naturalistic semiotic inquiry during guided learning.

This is an example of a simple process of instructional design relying on a semiotic paradigm. In a way, this model is a reverse-engineered tutorial or learning-support process. This semiotic ISD is also not isolated from traditional ISD thinking. Elements of the traditional approach to ISD are still present, such as the identification or production of a knowledge base, the generation of objectives, and the systematic approach to product improvement. As Briggs (1978) noted, a minimal utilization of ISD involves congruence among objectives, methods and materials, and evaluation. These traditional elements serve to support the semiotic approach.

It is useful at this point to speculate about the nature of semiotic objectives as specified in the model above. In seeking a semiotic objective, we would start with a learning, or semiosis, agenda. As the agenda is pursued, the objectives would arise as a consequence of interpretations that are incongruous with the desired learning, or missing altogether. Identifying semiotic objectives requires that we depart somewhat from the traditional thinking about objectives. Rather than identifying objectives from an analysis of instructional content, we generate them from the problems and issues a learner encounters in the process of semiosis. This again keeps the focus learning-centered and helps to avoid redundant and unnecessary content-oriented objectives.

Writing semiotic objectives also requires a modification of traditional ISD procedures. Objectives no longer comprise specific conditions and behaviors but rather express standardized learner interpretations. This is rather like a common analogy to how pieces of metal become magnetized: imagine a rowboat carrying four educational theorists, each paddling in a different direction (based on their individual interpretations of where they intend to go). Like magnetism aligning the atoms in the piece of metal, an interpretation agreed upon by all four theorists permits progress to be made in a common direction. Thus, semiotic objectives are defined as standards of interpretation, with standards of performance being a natural derivative of an alignment of interpretations,

Under the semiotic paradigm, most conditions cannot be generalized. This is because interpretations are subjective to the learner and vary depending upon signification. For instance, recall the kindergarten teacher whose goal is for students to acquire the concepts of "pet" and "4-legged animals." In another interaction recorded by Emihovich (1981), one of the children suggests "monkey" as a pet, which the teacher takes to be a wrong answer. Yet for some of the children, monkey is an appropriate sign for pet, because they are familiar with Curious George, a monkey (in a series of children's books) who is treated as a pet. Although it is recognized that interpretations are unique to each learner, nevertheless, the function of semiotic objectives is to bring about some agreement among learners and instructors concerning what something means. In this example, then, the teacher could have discussed the case of Curious George in terms of the unusual circumstances that enabled a monkey to become a pet.

An implication of defining objectives as learner interpretations is that semiotic objectives may describe—individually or collectively—behaviors or actions, cognition or thoughts, and feelings. Peirce's theory of signs, with its distinctions among types of interpretants, essentially integrates into one system thoughts, feelings, and actions. This enables all three to be equally available for identification and specification within a semiotic objective.

Under the semiotic objective, then, the intent of the learning process is that, when a specified object is encountered, the student will interpret its sign according to the desired criteria of semantic meaning, syntactic format, and pragmatic utility. This holds true regardless of whether objects are independent or are components of complex, interrelated systems (Deely, 1990a; Eco, 1976; Peirce, 1955). Ironically, complex systems such as algebraic equations or graphic notation, which allow for efficient interpretation and use of signs, can be very opaque to novice learners in these domains. According to Pea (1993):

> A person has to have been introduced to, and preferably to have participated in, the activities that give meaning to these inscriptions [i.e., sign systems]. After such initiations, one may have the sense of directly perceiving the patterns the inscriptional system was designed to make "obvious," but before such initiation, the conventions and uses of the inscriptions are usually obtuse. Mature users of an inscriptional system know the kinds of tasks it is good for—the questions it enables them to answer, the inferences it enables them to make—as well as its limitations. (p. 62)

What is important to note is that a semiotic agenda and the semiotic ensuing objectives seek harmony of interpretations between the student and external signs and symbols—including those of other members of society.

Challenges to Semiotic ISD

There are several logical challenges to the approach we have outlined thus far. The first issue concerns how authentic the measurement of the learning process will be, given that questioning will interrupt the learning. This issue has been extensively studied by cognitive psychologists, who find that properly constructed talk-aloud protocols do not, in fact, interfere significantly with the underlying processes being measured (Ericsson & Simon, 1993).

Another challenge to this semiotic approach to ISD is the difficulty of performing an analysis of learning in a new or complex domain before a knowledge base has been completely organized into instructional "content." In order to address this challenge, it may be helpful to locate learning support tools that allow the instructional designer to provide guidance and a knowledge base for the learner to use in pursuing learning, or semiosis. These tools should format the knowledge base in a way that will not interfere with the natural and optimal course of learning (we shall have more to say on this point shortly). It will also be cost-effective if support tools do not require extensive traditional instructional design, as the outcomes of the talk-aloud inquiry will act as inputs into how the instruction is ultimately to be organized.

A third issue concerns the degree to which multiple instructional designs are warranted from interpretation inquiries conducted with several prototypical learners. If the learners are quite diverse, it may be difficult to generalize instruction for them following this type of prototypical learner approach. This, of course, would present a difficulty under any paradigm, not just a learning-centered one. A possible solution under the semiotic paradigm is to use the information garnered from the interpretation inquiries to develop a sort of "interpretation guidebook" to the instruction. In other words, when it is expected that learners may misinterpret signs in instruction, various types of help could be provided in order to facilitate their apprehending the intended meanings. This is characteristic of the approach a person might take, for example, who intends to study in another country and language.

Advantages of Semiotic ISD

One of the advantages of a semiotic approach to ISD is the minimal instructional analysis required in many situations. The analysis may be limited to identifying the semiosis agenda and finding or developing a knowledge base for use by the prototypical learner during the learning inquiry process. Some additional analysis may be necessary in order to correctly identify the existing sign systems in use by the learner and to catalog the meaning of relevant signs and symbols in various contexts.

The natural relevance of a semiotic ISD is important here in two ways. First, it helps to clarify the goals of instruction and to establish the context in which these goals should be learned. For example, mathematics instruction has always, it seems, included practice in calculating numbers in the expectation that such practice will enable students to apply these calculations to tasks such as balancing their checkbooks.

Because such problems have stripped away all other signs except strictly mathematical ones, there is no reason to believe that learners will apprehend signs related to the appropriate applications of the skills when they encounter them. Thus, as mathematics educators are coming to discover, these skills may be more meaningfully learned for application purposes when they are accompanied by signs associated with calculation-in-use.

The second point to be made about relevance is that some signs in the learning environment may be ignored by learners in favor of others perceived as more immediately relevant to the task at hand. The example that comes to mind concerns apprentice navigators who, because their lives and livelihoods depend upon it, learn celestial patterns in a hut on the beach from lectures given by an authoritarian-style teacher (Lewis, 1978). These students (navigators) find a high degree of relevance in the lecture approach, ignoring the format (signs) to learn the content. Questions of transfer, then, become redefined in a semiotic paradigm. The issue is not whether a learner can "transfer" a skill learned in one context to another context in which it can be appropriately performed. Rather, the issue is whether the learner has apprehended the signs and symbols that are relevant to the performance of a skill in the desired context. This should be revealed in the learning analysis, so that those signs and the desired semiosis can be the focus of instruction.

Another advantage of a semiotic approach to ISD comes about as a consequence of semiosis as a constant, ongoing process. Instruction designed from a semiotic perspective need not be constrained to discrete pedagogical, systematic presentations. In fact, all that may be necessary for some semiotic instruction would be to provide experiences that foster the signification sought. The signification could even be enhanced by stimulating the student to ask questions that help generate appropriate sign-object interpretations. These experiences, combined with an appropriate knowledge base available as a reference, could be monitored and analyzed by learning facilitators during the student's learning. Tools of the semiotic paradigm could then be used to transform the results of such analysis into designs for the development or replication of the instructional process.

For example, upon interviewing learners and using talk-aloud protocols, the instructional designer might determine that the best way for some learners to develop certain understandings is through a field experience or even through supervised employment activity. The designer would then create materials to guide the facilitator of the student's experience in the field or in supervised employment. The role of the instructor changes from one of teaching to one of monitoring and supporting the ongoing semiosis, or learning and performance, of the student.

New Tools for Semiotic ISD

Reflect for a moment on the types of signs that could and should be revealed through an interpretation analysis of a prototypical learner's semiosis. Imagine, for example, a company poised to install a new computer system for billing. The billing clerks have been notified that they will be expected to participate in training so as to learn how to use this new system. What are some of the signs and interpretations that might be uncovered in a semiotic learning analysis conducted with a single billing clerk? There may be signs of affect (e.g., fear of being replaced by the computer, resistance to learning something new, or pleasure at getting out of work for the duration of training). There will be signs of commitment and interest, or lack thereof. As guided learning proceeds, there will be signs related to the learning process and development of relevant meanings.

There are apparently limitless numbers and types of signs and symbols that can be identified during an interpretation inquiry. These signs and symbols exist along many different dimensions, from affect to cognition to action, and each dimension may involve a different kind of sign system. Evaluating the components of semiosis and signification of the learner is therefore not necessarily a simple task. What types of tools are necessary to identify and organize the signs and symbols and the interpretations of semiosis, or learning? What types of new roles might semiotic instructional designers be called upon to assume?

We suggest first that semiotic ISD calls for tools that are naturalistic and qualitative in nature, such as talk-aloud protocols, observations of learner environments, measurement of attitudes, and interviews conducted with and without specific protocols. Some of these semiotic tools exist already, appearing as needs assessment tools or cognitive psychology research tools. Rossett (1987), for example, describes in detail how to use interviews and observations to acquire information during a training needs assessment. In a manner reminiscent of semioticians, she recommends using all the clues that are available in the setting to build "a multidimensional picture that approaches a truth that plain words may not" (p. 134). Likewise, Ericsson and Simon (1993) discuss methods for both conducting and analyzing talk-aloud protocols. There are certainly other traditional naturalistic tools extant which semiotic ISD designers would find useful.

In order to develop new tools for semiotic ISD, however, we may wish to incorporate, modify, or abridge naturalistic tools used in other fields. We may also wish to invent and develop new tools, but in either case we must ask how we can efficiently and reliably direct and measure the semiosic processes of prototypical learners.

Many other questions and issues surround the development of semiotic tools of ISD as well. For example, once we analytically reduce the process of learning and performance to signs, symbols, and interpretations, how do the tools help us validate and replicate the analysis? How do we ensure that the results of interviews and talk-aloud protocols with a prototypical learner will generate meaningful designs, objectives and methods for other learners? How do we guide the entire semiotic ISD process? How do we design the learning inquiry protocols and agendas? When we take on the perspective that various interpretations of signs and symbols are based on signification—the connecting of prior meanings to new signs and symbols—and that the construction of meaning is not identical across students, how do we identify and measure a common standard of performance? The answers to these questions will inform the identification and development of new tools.

The new tools for semiotic ISD can come only after research and development under the semiotic paradigm and after extensively measured field experience. Because of this, it is not possible at the present time to identify the full nature of the tools necessary for a semiotic ISD. What we can predict, however, is that these tools will be abductive in nature, rather than inductive or deductive. Abduction is the semiotic form of reasoning in which the researcher or practitioner searches for a rule to help in understanding some set of puzzling circumstances (Shank, 1987, 1994; Shank, Ross, Covalt, Terry, & Weiss, 1994). According to Peirce (1955), abductive inferences generally follow this form:

> The surprising fact, C, is observed;
> But if A were true, C would be a matter of course;
> Hence, there is reason to suspect that A is true. (p. 151)

Used systematically, abduction can enable the designer to discover significations, or at least to infer the best interpretation of the information gathered during a semiotic inquiry process (e.g., Shank, 1994). In many fields in which a semiotic paradigm has been adopted or discussed, research and inquiry methods have been explored that take advantage of abductive reasoning. These existing semiotic tools can form a starting point for exploring the nature and function of tools necessary for a semiotic ISD.

Once appropriate tools are available for semiotic ISD, what skills will be required of instructional designers to use them effectively? And what new roles might instructional designers be expected to assume in the ISD process? To begin with, semiotic ISD designers must know how to identify and classify signs and symbols, objects, and interpretations as they occur in the minds of prototypical learners and possibly in the minds of prototypical instructors and tutors as well. Semiotic ISD designers would also have to manage talk-aloud protocols, knowing how to frame the right questions to gather information about applied learning processes.

As for new roles and specializations that might emerge under a semiotic ISD paradigm, the most obvious is the learning, or semiosis, analyst. A second possibility is the facilitation specialist. Because the product of the semiotic learning analysis may or may not be instruction as currently conceived, instructional products could become much broader, perhaps requiring of designers a more general ability to facilitate and coordinate. Finally, when developing instructional materials, designers will follow detailed semiotic maps, perhaps utilizing standard media and script-writing skills.

The job of the semiotic instructional designer is to analyze the process of interpretation and semiosis in an authentic situation and to follow the subsequent steps of the model defined earlier. The job is to facilitate, measure, record, and analyze the learning process in the subject area, and thus identify requirements for the development of necessary products, environments, and support systems for other learners. This is a humanistic process, drawing from naturalistic, qualitative methods.

Juxtaposing Semiotic ISD with Other Current Trends in Education

Reminiscent of Cunningham's (1992) "Isn't semiotics just like—?," we believe that a semiotic ISD paradigm addresses some of the same issues that have recently prompted other movements in education generally and instructional design specifically. Some of these trends include constructivism, multicultural education, situated cognition and authentic activity, and distributed intelligence. In our view, a semiotic paradigm offers a theoretical base that allows a closer alignment of ISD practice with many effective practices discovered by practitioners in education and educational technology.

Most of the movements we wish to discuss are founded, not so much on working theoretical models or extensive empirical research, but rather on rational or critical attempts by educators and educational researchers to improve practice. They acknowledge that the current theoretical base for learning encompasses only a subset of the natural phenomena of learning and performance. What they have in common with the semiotic paradigm is a natural learning-centered focus that recognizes the individual nature of learning and understanding. In this sense, a semiotic paradigm is harmonious with many pragmatic approaches to learning and teaching. What a semiotic paradigm offers, however, is a theoretical foundation that can help to unify these trends and provide a direction for continued research and development of theory.

Semiotics and Constructivism

Constructivism today encompasses an array of teaching approaches largely resting on the epistemological assumption that knowledge is constructed by learners as they attempt to make sense of their environments. Whether constructivism is yet a theory is arguable. Theory or not, however, constructivism "tacitly accepts the very dualism that this approach criticizes in others" (Bredo, 1994, p. 33; see also Shank, 1990). Like objectivists, constructivists fail to distinguish between truth and meaning. Whereas objectivists collapse meaning into truth (i.e., knowledge comes from knowing that something is true), constructivists collapse truth into meaning (i.e., knowledge comes with the learner's construction of meaning). On an epistemological level, then, semiotics offers a means to resolve this dilemma by including both perspectives and provides a consistent theory for understanding and developing constructivist practices.

What *are* some of the implications for instructional design that constructivists have proffered? Lebow (1993) proposed that constructivism embodies an alternative set of values which include: concern for affective outcomes, facilitation of both personal autonomy and collaboration, need for authenticity of learning experiences, support for self-regulation, and enhancement of the learner's strategic exploration of errors. Constructivist learning environments, then, are generally microworlds (e.g., Rieber, 1991) or macrocontexts (e.g., cognitive apprenticeships; Brown, Collins, & Duguid, 1989) that embody instructional strategies designed to support these values.

How does a semiotic perspective handle the concerns expressed by constructivists? To begin with, we suggested previously that some of the signs to be uncovered by an analysis of semiosis are affective in nature. They would naturally arise during the inquiry process and would be as important as any other signs for developing instruction. To our minds, a semiotic paradigm offers a synthesis of affective and cognitive outcomes that is currently not available in traditional ISD. At present, designers must consult models of motivation that are separate from models of instructional design and development in order to assure that affective objectives related to motivation are adequately addressed. This is an instruction-centered approach to affect. Moreover, it is not clear whether all affective concerns that might be identified in a semiotic analysis would be so discovered using current models of motivation.

Authenticity of learning experiences was also discussed previously, in that signs must be identified which relate to the use of meanings in a desired context, so that these same signs can provide an appropriate context for instruction. In addition, however, authenticity in a semiotic paradigm necessarily means more than it is currently taken to mean in most constructivist learning environments. To date, researchers and educators have concentrated on the degree to which the performance required of students in instruction is authentic. They have also examined the fidelity of learning conditions, i.e., how closely the conditions of instruction simulate the conditions of the desired context of use. However, a semiotic approach requires as well that attention be paid to signs that are reflective of the individual's disposition toward learning. For example, if the billing clerks mentioned earlier interpret signs in their environment to suggest that the new computer system will not be in place for a year, then no amount of "authenticity" in instruction will necessarily increase the likelihood of their acquiring the skills to operate the system.

The notions of collaboration and strategic exploration of errors are as important to the semiotic paradigm as to a constructivist one. From a semiotic perspective, both entail the exploration by the learner of other sign systems—either those used by other participants in their environment so that some common interpretations can be reached, or those which can offer alternate interpretations that might be useful in correcting errors. In either case, exploration of multiple sign systems should also support an awareness of perspectives other than the learner's own (pluralism) and a reasoned commitment to one's own individual perspective (personal autonomy).

Semiotics and Multicultural Education

Multicultural educators recognize that learners construct knowledge relative to their existing social schemas and that those social schemas vary in a socially integrated environment (e.g., Scheel & Branch, 1993). The thrust of most multicultural education programs is to make individuals aware that their perspectives of the world are not necessarily shared by others. Often, an additional goal is to expose the oppression practiced by the dominant culture on minority subcultures. As we have already discussed, we believe that the semiotic ISD paradigm readily permits these issues to be addressed. We have argued that representative prototypical learners from the learner pool should be consulted and their semiotic processes extensively studied. This may require particular skill on the part of designers, because they must be alert to the potential influence of their own significations on their interpretation of the signification processes of learners from different cultures.

Other individual differences that can be accommodated through a semiotic approach include learning styles and gender differences, among others. What is important is that the prototypical learners selected for semiosis analysis are representative of the diversity of learner populations represented in the overall learner pool.

Semiotics and Situated Cognition

The concept of situated cognition is perhaps as closely aligned philosophically with a semiotic perspective as any of the ideas thus far discussed. To quote Peirce's pragmatic maxim: "Consider what effects, which conceivably have practical bearings, we conceive the object of our conception to have. Then our conception of these effects is the whole of our conception of the object" (quoted in Houser, 1992, p. xxvi). Likewise, situated learning theories have argued that knowledge and one's use of knowledge are inseparable: "Situations might be said to coproduce knowledge through activity. Learning and cognition . . . are fundamentally situated" (Brown *et al.*, 1989, p. 32). Ironically, Tripp (1993) claimed that nearly everything said by situated cognition theorists was better said by the philosopher Michael Oakeshott more than 30 years ago (Oakeshott, 1962). Yet, the semiotic tradition established by Peirce is more than 100 years old!

As situated learning theorists have emphasized the need for a community of practice, so Peirce emphasized identification with community as fundamental for the advancement of knowledge, or the "end of the highest semiosis" (Houser, 1992). In both traditions, culture is viewed as an important influence on the negotiation and construction of meanings. Thus, in the sense that a semiotic approach to ISD involves the gathering of information from learners during culturally authentic learning and performance situations, it may be considered a situated approach to instructional design. However, a semiotic ISD may also help to surmount some of the problems that Tripp (1993) noted with current applications of situated learning.

One problem, according to Tripp, is an overemphasis on the importance of immersing students in an authentic situational location of learning and an underemphasis on the usefulness of didactic instruction. This, once again, is the problem of what is meant by "authentic," a problem which is solved by examining the hierarchy of sign systems in the context of use. For the apprentice navigators, didactic instruction was effective because it meant their survival, and it was far more efficient to conduct it in a hut than to wait for clear, starry nights.

Tripp (1993) also suggested that two types of problem solving should be distinguished—that which involves acting upon real objects in the real world and that which involves constructing and evaluating propositions (p. 76). He argued that instructional programs such as those developed by the Cognition and Technology Group at Vanderbilt (1991, 1993) facilitate the first type but not the second, which he called critical thinking. He further asserted that critical thinking is best taught in a classroom, where it can be modeled by a teacher.

From a semiotic perspective, both types of problem solving identified by Tripp are aspects of sign interpretation and signification. In the first place, most real-world or practical problem solving comes easily to people because it involves rather automatic interpretation of signs. The South American drug lords mentioned by Tripp have only to apprehend signs related to the transportation of goods to America to generate tentative interpretants for how their cocaine might best be smuggled. On the other hand, critical thinking requires the re-flexive, or metacognitive, use of signs. That is, an individual must become aware of how signs function in the signification process in order to construct and evaluate particular sign-object relations. Because Peirce's theory of signs is itself an algebra of logic, then providing learners with exposure to multiple sign systems and the analysis of semiosis would go a long way toward teaching critical thinking.

Semiotics and Distributed Intelligence

In his recent work, Pea (1993; Pea & Gomez, 1992) has argued for a concept of intelligence that goes beyond its being a property of individuals. Rather, intelligence is claimed to be distributed—"across minds, persons, and the symbolic and physical environments, both natural and artificial" (Pea, 1993, p. 47). Pea describes knowledge as existing in the social and material artifacts (systems) created by humans, so that intelligence is manifested in the activities which are used to exploit these artifacts for achieving particular aims. Moreover, "the environments in which humans live are thick with invented artifacts. . . ," which are ". . . mediating structures that both organize and constrain activity" (Pea, 1993, p. 48).

These notions are consistent with Peirce's view of the experiential world, where "the sign is seen to mediate knowledge over time" and "semiosis is a correspective process structured by and structuring of 'reality'" (Deely, 1986, p. 265). From the point of view of instruction, this means that designers produce instructional materials using particular sign systems, which affect learners' interpretations of and actions with the materials. However, learners can also invent new uses of the materials within alternate sign systems, thus designing, in Pea's words, distributed intelligence for their own purposes.

The trends we have discussed in this section (and there are probably others that we have overlooked) are not only informed or encompassed by the semiotic paradigm, they bring something to the semiotic discussion. In each case, categories of signs emerge as likely candidates for reduction in the semiosis analysis. For example, signs of autonomy and self-regulation can be investigated during a semiotic learning inquiry, as can signs of critical thinking or distributed intelligence. Signs of cultural differences and cultural values are, in fact, the primary interest of critical theorists, as will be seen in the next section. There, we take a brief look at several efforts to apply semiotic thinking within the field of instructional systems design. To some extent, these efforts show how semiotic thinking might be articulated in a specific phase of the ISD process or with respect to particular media.

Other Views of Semiotics in ISD

At least three other approaches to the application of semiotics to ISD deserve mention. They include (1) Susan Tucker and John Dempsey's recently published semiotic model of program evaluation, (2) the application of sign theory to media, and (3) the related application of critical theory and feminist approaches to ISD. We describe each briefly.

Semiotic Program Evaluation

Against a backdrop of educational reform and social change, Tucker & Dempsey (1991) have proposed that program evaluation, as currently practiced, inadequately addresses the human dimension in education and training. Under existing evaluation models, values and judgments of all program participants often go unheard, and data collected do not serve well to facilitate continuous program improvement. Tucker and Dempsey argued that an interpretive perspective would better serve the goals of program evaluation and proposed a semiotic model based on five core "signs." These five were: holism, or representation of multiple perspectives; negotiation; synthesis of inductive, deductive, and abductive investigative methods; vulnerability of evaluator; and futurist orientation.

The *holistic* assumption requires that evaluators consider the total picture of a program and recognize that no one view of it will be entirely accurate. Therefore, multiple views must be sought through the significations of many constituent groups participating in or in some way affected by the program under evaluation. *Negotiation* occurs when these constituent groups determine what questions should be the focus of the evaluation, what sources of evidence should be sought, and what criteria or standards should be used in judging program quality. As the evaluation proceeds, information is gathered through *inductive, deductive,* and *abductive inquiry methods* in the belief that each provides a different dimension of meaning. Evaluator *vulnerability* refers to the subjectivity of the evaluator. That is, the evaluator must be constantly alert to the effects of personal signification on the interpretation of others' points of view. Finally, a *futurist orientation* is adopted to avoid present "realities" becoming an excuse for inaction. This enables "signs of possibilities" to be examined in the light of judgments about program usefulness or effectiveness (Tucker & Dempsey, 1991).

Sign Theory and Media

In the preface to the second edition of *Interaction of Media, Cognition, and Learning,* Salomon (1981) wrote that "although symbols of communication have been dealt [with] extensively by philosophers and semioticians, they have not . . . been integrated into psychological and educational theories" (p. xix). At least one author, however, had attempted to investigate signs in media prior to Salomon's integrated theory. Stevens (1969, 1971) identified what he called "sign behavior" in the perceptual interpretation of visual information. He argued that the viewer interprets symbolic information in visual media as either iconic or dissimilar to the represented object based on prior experiences and enculturation. In other words, the viewer makes inferences about the symbolic information perceived in a picture in order to predict the nature of the represented object and draw conclusions about it.

Salomon, too, has been interested in symbol systems as the essence of media, and he has articulated a comprehensive theory pertaining to the differential role of media's symbol systems in the acquisition of knowledge and the cultivation of mental skills (Salomon, 1994). In essence, his claims are threefold. First, different symbol systems convey contents, and therefore meaning, in different ways, so that "how something is perceived and what we can know about it depend on the symbol systems we can use or choose to use" in a given medium (1994, p. 64). Second, "thinking employs a variety of symbolic forms and . . . these are called upon and evolve in interaction with communicational symbol systems" (1994, p. xxi). Finally, the "environment changes as abilities grow" (1994, p. 239). This means that learners are able to perceive more signs in meaningful ways as they gain experience with more symbol systems.

What are some of the implications of this theory for media design and use in instruction? Salomon (1994) names two that he considers to be particularly important. First of all, media "should be used as unique sources of symbolic forms, which are potential candidates for adoption as mental tools" (1994, p. 243). In other words, it is not necessarily useful to use alternative media for conveying the same information. Rather, learners should be shown how different symbol systems effectively highlight some aspects of the natural or symbolic world, at the same time obscuring other aspects. Finally, in developing the mental skills of learners, we must beware of the fact that learner preferences for less cognitively-demanding symbol systems can lead to failure to develop skills for handling more cognitively-demanding systems.

Critical Theory in ISD

As indicated earlier in the chapter, an entire branch of semiotics has been devoted to the critical analysis and interpretation of literary texts. Many of the principles used in these analyses have been applied to the "deconstruction" of meaning in video or computer presentations, instructional programs, and indeed, the very processes of instructional systems design. The intent of such deconstruction is to expose tacit assumptions and values that underlly our knowledges and practices. Doing this frees us to imagine alternative values and assumptions and to explore the implications of these alternative assumptions for knowledge and practice. Streibel (1991, 1993) has called this approach "critical pedagogy" and "emancipatory evaluation."

Others have used ideas of critical theory to criticize "up-with-technology" assumptions and to examine the ethical position of educational technology in society (e.g., Muffoletto, 1994; Nichols, 1994; Yeaman, 1994). In large part, the aim of this work is to show how technology can exacerbate unequal social relations, removing some groups of people from the communicative processes of democracy (Yeaman, Koetting, & Nichols, 1994).

In a similar vein, Damarin (1991, 1994) has taken a feminist perspective to show how the voices of women and other groups have gone mostly unheard in mainstream educational technology. She proposed that feminist pedagogy can help instructional designers uncover the significations of women in respect to the use of technology in education. Such awareness of and responsiveness to cultural differences and values also provides a more ethical approach to ISD.

Cautionary Note

Because this is a somewhat brash attempt at proposing a semiotic ISD paradigm, the reader is urged to use caution and thoughtfulness in approaching any type of naturalistic, postmodern, or semiotic ISD, such as those we have suggested and reviewed here. Mixing semiotic and naturalistic technologies with traditional ISD could create misunderstandings and cause one to be viewed with suspicion by traditional instructional designers and educators. It is important to point out that a semiotic ISD expands the ability of ISD to achieve its mission.

It is also important to remember that semiotics has been developed in many fields, and we are here talking about developing it fresh for our field starting with the original assumptions. Because of this fresh start, it is important to learn from what other fields have attempted in the application of semiotic theory to practice. There have been many lessons learned (Sebeok, 1991).

The real question about the semiotic paradigm is, will a semiotic paradigm be a superior means of handling instructional design in all cases? Is the semiotic approach sufficiently generalizable? For example, how would the semiotic model proposed here fare in tackling challenging problems of intelligent tutoring systems, or performance support, or integrated learning systems? What about the design of large scale educational systems? It may well be that this semiotic approach will work best under certain conditions, thus becoming a contingency-oriented ISD model. On the other hand, it may be a more universal approach than the traditional ISD model. A semiotic ISD paradigm faces head-on complex issues that the traditional model does not or cannot manage. This may mean that those who develop and use the semiotic paradigm should be prepared to swim in deep waters.

Conclusion

So what does the semiotic ISD paradigm suggest for our field? It expands on and perhaps replaces the traditional paradigm in many contexts. Yet it relies on input from the traditional paradigm. What semiotics seems to do to the ISD paradigm is to link it to a broader, qualitative view of learning and instruction, to help the paradigm more closely match reality and better accomplish its mission. The semiotic ISD paradigm verifies what many practitioners already know—that the development of human learning systems is not a hard science of deliberate engineering but rather a hybrid activity drawing on all of our abilities and contingent upon the details of each new situation.

Does this expansion of the paradigm mean that semiotics is going to make ISD more expensive? That it will take longer? Perhaps in some cases. Yet in many situations, the semiotic paradigm seems to suggest that extant instructional materials may suffice and, in fact, should be sought in order to compose the knowledge base for prototypical learners to use in monitored semiosis. Semiotic ISD encourages us to focus on the process of learning itself and not on the presentation of instruction. This should cause us to develop new instruction only as a last resort and only as need is indicated by inquiry into specific, applied, learning processes.

Even though semiotic ISD is a more naturalistic paradigm than traditional ISD, the systematic processes, and the task, objective, and content analysis of the traditional paradigm are still essential. These characteristics of traditional ISD are critical in the generation of knowledge bases that must be used to facilitate the inquiry into semiosis. In a sense, the semiotic paradigm does not replace the traditional ISD paradigm but rather shifts the role of traditional approaches to ISD to that of developing reference materials and knowledge bases.

The semiotic paradigm brings a new, learning-centered orientation to ISD. It adds an important link to the learner, a missing and needed piece in the puzzle of instructional design and development. The semiotic paradigm allows us to be more responsive to individual differences, and it allows us to include strategies that learners favor and that work, regardless of whether they fit into our theoretical constructs. The semiotic ISD paradigm allows us to be highly sensitive to the needs and wants of learners. There is every reason to be optimistic that semiotics will bring us closer to a learning-centered ISD.

Notes

1. The history of semiotics, as Deely (1990a) pointed out, has roots in the thinking of medieval (e.g., Augustine, c. 397 A.D.) as well as modern philosophers (e.g., John Poinsot, 1632; John Locke, 1690). Moreover, Ferdinand de Saussure is generally credited with giving semiotics its name. But it is Peirce who achieved a "doctrinal convergence" that established semiotics as "a form neither of realism nor of idealism, but beyond both" (Deely, 1990a, p. 116).
2. We are not suggesting that knowledge as meaning supplants knowledge as truth, which would be consistent with idealist, or constructivist, notions. Rather, semiotics suggests that both truth and meaning are essential aspects of knowledge.
3. On the basis of Bloom's (1984) report that tutoring results in an achievement increase of two sigmas, we are inclined to believe that providing subject-matter tutors would be the better means for facilitating learning in the interpretation inquiry.

References

Belland, J. C. (1991) Developing connoisseurship in educational technology. In D. Hlynka & J. Belland (Eds.), *Paradigms regained: The uses of illuminative, semiotic, and post-modern criticism as modes of inquiry in educational technology.* Englewood Cliffs, NJ: Educational Technology Publications.

von Bertalanffy, L. (1967). *Robots, men, and minds.* New York: George Braziller.

Bickhard, M. H. (1992). How does the environment affect the person? In L. T. Winegar & J. Valsiner (Eds.), *Children's development in social context.* Hillsdale, NJ: Lawrence Erlbaum Associates.

Bloom, B. S. (1984). The 2-sigma problem: The search for methods of group instruction as effective as one-to-one tutoring. *Educational Researcher, 13*(6), 4–16.

Bredo, E. (1994). Reconstructing educational psychology: Situated cognition and Deweyian pragmatism. *Educational Psychologist, 29*(1), 23–35.

Briggs, L. J. (1978). Introduction. In L. J. Briggs (Ed.), *Instructional design: Principles and applications*. Englewood Cliffs, NJ: Educational Technology Publications.

Brown, J. S., Collins, A., & Duguid, P. (1989). Situated cognition and the culture of learning. *Educational Researcher, 18*(1), 32–42.

Cates, W. M. (1994, February). *Designing hypermedia is hell: Metaphor's role in instructional design*. Paper presented at Annual Meeting of the Association for Educational Communications and Technology, Nashville.

Cognition & Technology Group at Vanderbilt. (1991). Technology and the design of generative learning environments. *Educational Technology, 31*(5), 34–40.

Cognition & Technology Group at Vanderbilt. (1993). Anchored instruction and situated cognition revisited. *Educational Technology, 33*(3), 52–70.

Cronbach, L. J. (1975). Course improvement through evaluation. In D. A. Payne & R. F. McMorris (Eds.), *Education and psychological measurement*. Morristown, NJ: General Learning Press.

Cunningham, D. J. (1987). Outline of an education semiotic. *American Journal of Semiotics, 5*, 201-216.

Cunningham, D. J. (1992). Beyond educational psychology: Steps toward an educational semiotic. *Educational Psychology Review, 4*, 165–194.

Damarin, S. K. (1991). Feminist unthinking and educational technology. *Educational and Training Technology, 27*(4), 111–119.

Damarin, S. K. (1994). Equity, caring, and beyond: Can feminist ethics inform educational technology? *Educational Technology, 34*(2), 34–39.

Deely, J. (1986). Semiotics as a framework and direction. In J. Deely, B. Williams, & F. E. Kruse (Eds.), *Frontiers in semiotics*. Bloomington, IN: Indiana University Press.

Deely, J. (1990a). *Basics of semiotics*. Bloomington, IN: Indiana University Press.

Deely, J. (1990b). Sign, text, and criticism as elements of anthroposemiosis. *The American Journal of Semiotics, 7*(4), 41–82.

Dick, W., & Carey, L. (1990). *The systematic design of instruction* (3rd ed.). Glenview, IL: Scott Foresman.

Eco, U. (1976). *A theory of semiotics*. Bloomington, IN: Indiana University Press.

Edie, J. M. (1987). *William James and phenomenology*. Bloomington, IN: Indiana University Press.

Emihovich, C. E. (1981). Social interaction in two integrated kindergartens. *Integrated Education, 19*, 72–78.

Ericsson, K. A., & Simon, H. A. (1993). *Protocol analysis*. Cambridge, MA: The MIT Press.

Gagné, R. M. (1985). *The conditions of learning* (4th ed.) New York: Holt, Rinehart, and Winston.

Gagné, R. M., Briggs, L. J., & Wager, W. W. (1992). *Principles of instructional design* (4th ed.). New York: Holt, Rinehart, and Winston.

Goodrum, D. A., Dorsey, L. T. & Schwen, T. M. (1994, February). *A socio-technical perspective of instructional development: A change in paradigms*. Paper presented at the Annual Meeting of the Association for Educational Communications and Technology, Nashville.

Houser, N. (1987). Toward a Peircean semiotic theory of learning. *The American Journal of Semiotics, 5*(2), 251–274.

Houser, N. (1992). Introduction. In N. Houser & C. Kloesel (Eds.), *The essential Peirce: Selected philosophical writings, Vol I*. Bloomington, IN: Indiana University Press.

Jonassen, D. H. (1991). Objectivism versus constructivism: Do we need a new philosophical paradigm? *Educational Technology Research & Development, 39*(3), 5–14.

Kaufman, R. (1988). *Planning educational systems*. Lancaster, PA: Technomic Publ. Co.

Lebow, D. (1993). Constructivist values for instructional systems design: Five principles toward a new mindset. *Educational Technology Research & Development, 41*(3), 4–16.

Lewis, D. (1978). *The voyaging stars. Secrets of the Pacific island navigators*. London: Collins.

Locke, J. (1690). An essay concerning humane understanding. In J. Deely, B. Williams, & F. Kruse (Eds.), *Frontiers in semiotics*. Bloomington, IN: Indiana University Press.

Mager, R. F. (1975). *Preparing instructional objectives*. Belmont, CA: Pitman Management & Training.

Muffoletto, R. (1994). Technology and restructuring education: Constructing a contrast. *Educational Technology, 34*(2), 24–28.

Nichols, R. G. (1994). Searching for moral guidance about educational technology. *Educational Technology, 34*(2), 40–48.

Oakeshott, M. (1962). *Rationalism in politics.* London: Methuen & Co.

Pea, R. D. (1993). Practices of distributed intelligence and designs for education. In G. Salomon (Ed.), *Distributed cognitions: Psychological and educational considerations.* New York: Cambridge University Press.

Pea, R. D., & Gomez, L. (1992). Distributed multimedia learning environments. *Interactive Learning Environments, 2*(2), 73–109.

Peirce, C. S. (1955). *Philosophical writings of Peirce.* J. Buchler (Ed.). New York: Dover.

Phelan, P., Davidson, A. L., & Cao, H. T. (1991). Students' multiple worlds: Negotiating the boundaries of family, peer, and home cultures. *Anthropology & Education Quarterly, 22,* 224–250.

Poinsot, J. (1632). *Tractatus de signis,* subtitled *The semiotic of John Poinsot.* Arranged by J. Deely. Berkeley: University of California Press, 1985.

Rieber, L. P. (1991, February). *Computer-based microworlds: A bridge between constructivism and direct instruction.* Paper presented at the Annual Meeting of the Association for Educational Communications and Technology, Orlando, FL.

Rossett, A. (1987). *Training needs assessment.* Englewood Cliffs, NJ: Educational Technology Publications.

Salomon, G. (1981). *Interaction of media, cognition, and learning.* San Francisco: Jossey-Bass.

Salomon, G. (1994). *Interaction of media, cognition, and learning* (2nd ed.). Hillsdale, NJ: Lawrence Erlbaum Associates.

Saussure, F. (1959). *Course in general linguistics.* New York: Philosophical Library.

Scheel, N., & Branch, R. C. (1993). The role of conversation and culture in the systematic design of instruction. *Educational Technology, 33*(8), 7–18.

Sebeok, T. A. (1986). *I think I am a verb. More contributions to the doctrine of signs.* New York: Plenum Press.

Sebeok, T. A. (1991). *Semiotics in the United States.* Bloomington, IN: Indiana University Press.

Shank, G. (1987). Abductive strategies in educational research. *American Journal of Semiotics, 5*(2), 275–290.

Shank, G. (1990). Qualitative vs. quantitative research: A semiotic non-problem. In T. Prewitt, J. Deely, & K. Haworth (Eds.), *Semiotics: 1989* (pp. 264–270). Washington, DC: University Press of America.

Shank, G. (1992). Educational semiotic: Threat or menace? *Educational Psychology Review, 4*(2), 195–209.

Shank, G. (1994). Shaping qualitative research in educational psychology. *Contemporary Educational Psychology, 19,* 340–359.

Shank, G., Ross, J. M., Covalt, W., Terry, S., & Weiss, E. (1994). Improving creative thinking using instructional technology: Computer-aided abductive reasoning. *Educational Technology, 34*(9), 33–42.

Stevens, W. D. (1969). Sign, transaction, and symbolic interaction in culture mediation. *AV Communications Review, 17*(2), 150–158.

Stevens, W. D. (1971). Pictorially aroused information. *Viewpoints, 47*(4), 66–72.

Stolovitch, H. D., & Keeps, E. J. (Eds.). (1992). *Handbook of human performance technology.* San Francisco: Jossey-Bass.

Streibel, M. J. (1991). A critical analysis of the use of computers in education. In D. Hlynka & J. Belland (Eds.), *Paradigms regained: The uses of illuminative, semiotic, and post-modern criticism as modes of inquiry in educational technology.* Englewood Cliffs, NJ: Educational Technology Publications.

Streibel, M. J. (1993). Queries about computer education and situated critical pedagogy. *Educational Technology, 33*(3), 22–26.

Stufflebeam, D. (1973). Educational evaluation and decision making. In B. Worthen & J. Sanders (Eds.), *Educational evaluation: Theory and practice.* Belmont, CA: Wadsworth Publishing.

Tripp, S. D. (1993). Theories, traditions, and situated learning. *Educational Technology, 33*(3), 71–77.

Tucker, S. A., & Dempsey, J. V. (1991). A semiotic model of program evaluation. *The American Journal of Semiotics, 8*(4), 73–104.

Yeaman, A. R. J. (1994). Deconstructing modern educational technology. *Educational Technology, 34*(2), 15–23.

Yeaman, A. R. J., Koetting, J. R., & Nichols, R. G. (1994). Critical theory, cultural analyses, and the ethics of educational technology as social responsibility. *Educational Technology, 34*(2), 5–13.

20

Principles of Adult Learning: A Multi-Paradigmatic Model

Kerry A. Johnson
Joan L. Bragar
The Forum Corporation
New York

Introduction

Without question, there is an abundance of learning paradigms and theories. Cognitive, behaviorist, and humanist viewpoints compete with cybernetic, semiotic, and postmodern paradigms for a share of the instructional designer's mind. Developmental psychology vies with constructivist theory in guiding the designer's direction. In the long-run, each instructional theory and paradigm offers the designer insight; taken together, however, they offer chaos.

In an effort to guide its design philosophy for product development and custom training projects, and to make some sense of the chaos, The Forum Corporation periodically reexamines its own assumptions about learning and design, and explores the academic research for new insights. New ideas seem to come from the design field and related other fields in a continuous stream. They only offer valuable insights when we examine our own practices against current theory, and seek ways to maximize the impact of what we do and the way we do it.

The application of design theory in the marketplace through the training business increasingly requires clear demonstration of results. Corporations generally want to maximize the return on their training dollar; and more specifically, simply want to understand the impact of that investment. They want to know that they will see the change in performance they require to meet their targeted strategic need.

As a result of these two factors—a need to continuously challenge assumptions, and a need to produce clear results—training companies that want to maintain their competitive edge in an increasingly competitive marketplace must seek their own paradigms for learning and design. They must create a clear image of their assumptions, and clearly and consistently communicate that image to everyone involved in the design process.

Furthermore, these paradigms must enable designers and producers to be both effective and efficient. They need to know that what they produce will have immediate and long-term impact on both the individual's performance and overall capabilities, and the company's business results. They also need to be assured that they can create this training reliably and quickly.

Forum's goal in conducting the research reported here was to create a set of principles to reliably, clearly, and effectively guide our design. We required our own simplified yet robust design paradigm that took what we viewed to be the best synthesis of theory and practical field experience, and organized it in a way that is clear to our customers and our designers alike.

The result is a set of five principles that inform both our design decisions and our macro-design decisions. They reflect our needs and the needs of our customers, and in that sense, take liberties with the pure intent of some of the theories upon which we drew. However, the principles are practical, and they work. They raise the level of our thinking, and the subsequent degree to which we help our customers achieve their goals.

Most of all, these five principles provide us with a language with which to describe both what we want to accomplish and the way in which we try to accomplish it. That language allows us to talk with customers on a common ground. They know why we are making the design decisions we make and giving the advice we give. More importantly, they can challenge those decisions and that advice on a solid conceptual basis if they have alternative viewpoints. It raises the level of dialogue about what can and should be expected from training alone. It also provides a clear rationale for the need to make an investment beyond training in order to achieve results and accomplish the stated goals.

We chose to focus on adult learners in creating these principles for obvious reasons—they are our learners. Adults bring a special set of learning needs to the table. Most significant of these is that they have an extremely strong and active belief system that mediates all of their learning. As adults, we tend to use a backdrop of these existing beliefs to regularly validate what exists in our mental model of the world.

Adults have much more numerous, complex, and intransigent belief systems than small children, so changing any one of these beliefs or systems is not easy. It requires time. It demands awareness. It needs confrontation. It depends upon powerful new experiences, either mental or emotional, to be successful. It must also take place in the broader context of the adult's complex life in which competing demands and powerful consequences for action and inaction are constantly in play.

Adults also demand, even more than children, to feel in control of their own learning and to understand the practical results that they can hope to realize. Adults want to take what they are learning in a training experience and use it the next day (or the next minute, for that matter) on the job. Granted, there are a host of adult learning situations in which learning is "for fun" and such practical application is not an issue. We are not concerned with these situations since, while important, they are less directly related to the results the corporate customer is after.

Our focus in the research was on creating the kind of paradigm that would offer us an opportunity to engage the adult learner sufficiently to change his/her belief system and its corresponding behaviors. This was quite a challenge. It is still a challenge, not only because each situation is unique for the individual, but also because the contingencies in the work environment are unique from corporation to corporation, and are presently in a state of rapid, significant, and, possibly, irreversible change.

The resulting paradigm is designed to reflect the current business world. It is designed to allow us to be fast, flexible, practical, and successful in responding to our customers' training and learning needs. It combines a number of theories without being theoretical. It brings a number of viewpoints together at a macro-design level without limiting the use of other viewpoints at a micro-design level. It is also supported internally within Forum by a rigorous set of processes which allow us to reliably apply it across our full customer-base worldwide.

Background: Theoretical Foundations

Real learning gets to the heart of what it means to be human. Through learning we re-create ourselves. Through learning we become able to do something we never were able to do. Through learning we reperceive the world and our relationship to it. Through learning we extend our capacity to create, to be part of the generative process of life.

Peter M. Senge, *The Fifth Discipline*, 1990

People engage in a continuous process of experience, reflection, and design of effective action (Dewey, 1933). For example, Jean Piaget (1970) observed infants as they conducted repeated experiments to learn how to do such things as putting their fingers together to grasp objects and bring them to their mouths. Based on experiments like these, people create interpretations, or models, in their minds to help make sense of their worlds. They create physical models (like the relation of their hand to their mouth), social models (knowing who feeds them), and linguistic models (make this sound and others smile)—and then compare all new experiences with these existing models.

Over a lifetime, learners create increasingly structured models. Young children develop an intuitive understanding about language and about their physical and social worlds, which enables them to function effectively in these worlds. As they grow older, they begin to formalize their understanding into rules and models that help them to develop further knowledge and skills (Gardner, 1991; Piaget, 1970). Finally, as adults, they develop the ability to apply their knowledge and skills appropriately in many different types of situations (Bruner, 1990; Knowles, 1978; Knox, 1977).

These models govern the way people see the world and are extremely difficult to change once formed (Argyris, 1982). Understandings gained early in life have a powerful effect on all future interpretations. Perhaps the most startling research finding about learning in the past 15 years is that early intuitive understanding about the world becomes fixed in the mind by the time children are six or seven years old. This understanding can even override instruction and schooling. For example, honors students in physics, when asked basic science questions outside the classroom, tended to rely on intuitive models learned in childhood, even though they had learned that the theories supporting these models were wrong (Gardner, 1991).

Adults must transform their models in order to learn new ways of thinking and acting that conflict with their existing, ineffective models. Powerful interventions are required. To overcome inertia, learners must have an opportunity to unfreeze their previous learning (Lewin, 1948), to link the learning to critical personal needs (Knox, 1977; Mezirow, 1991), to engage actively in learning (Argyris, 1982; Dewey, 1933), and to learn with others (Senge, 1990).

As the world and its economic conditions change more and more rapidly, the ability to learn and exchange knowledge becomes a critical competitive advantage of nations, of companies, and of individuals. All will need to commit themselves to continuous learning and the pursuit of mastery (deGeus, 1988; Deming, 1986; Senge, 1990).

The multiple origins of the theoretical ideas that underlie the Forum model, only some of which are referred to in the preceding paragraphs, are summarized in Tables 1 and 2. These tables will illustrate the multi-paradigmatics forms upon which the Forum model is constructed.

Based on these ideas about learning and on its own experience, Forum developed five learning principles that contribute to the design of the most highly effective learning experiences. These principles are intended to guide the design of adult learning programs and processes, and to ensure that they are linked to the needs of both learners and their organizations. They describe what it takes to have significant, sustainable learning occur in the workplace.

Table 1.   The original foundations of Forum's principles of adult learning.

	B. F. Skinner	Albert Bandura & R. H. Walters	Carl Rogers	Abraham Maslow	Kurt Lewin	David McClelland	G. H. Litwin and R.A. Stringer	Jean Piaget	John Dewey
Major Work	*Science and Human Behavior,* 1953	*Social Learning & Personality Development,* 1963	*On Becoming a Person,* 1961	*Motivation & Personality,* 1954	*Resolving Social Conflicts,* 1948	*Human Motivation,* 1973	*Motivation & Organizational Climate,* 1968	*Genetic Epistemology,* 1970	*How We Think,* 1933
Contribution	Showed that the rate of learning increases when the learner receives concrete feedback.	Demonstrated the importance of "modeling," or showing examples of desired behaviors, and the importance of rewarding newly learned behaviors.	Showed that the rate of learning is increased when the learner has a positive self-image and is held in high regard. Described the qualities of a good facilitator (genuine, accepting, etc.).	Reaffirmed the importance or of human qualities—such as freedom, choice, and subjective experience—that make people more than objects for scientific inquiry. Identified the human need for self-esteem and self-actualization.	Developed group-dynamics theory. Emphasized understanding all the social forces acting on the learner. Showed how participative decision-making enhances learning and commitment.	Demonstrated that a strong need for achievement motivates people to set goals and solve problems with greater creativity and energy. Showed that measurable change is more likely when people believe that change is possible and desirable.	Showed that organizational climate (created through managers' actions) can motivate people to be more productive.	Described learners as continually, actively trying to make sense of the world. Learners use their existing rules and categories to understand their experiences and change those rules and categories to accommodate new experiences.	Pioneered the field of experiential learning. Identified reflective thinking as the goal of education.
Effect on Forum's Principles of Adult Learning	1, 2, 4	2, 3, 4	4, 5	3, 5	3, 4	1, 3, 5	2, 4, 5	1, 2, 3	2, 3

Principles of adult learning
1. Learning is a transformation that takes place over time.
2. Learning follows a continuous cycle of action and reflection.
3. Learning is most effective when it addresses issues that are relevant to the learner.
4. Learning is most effective when people learn with others.
5. Learning occurs best in a supportive and challenging environment.

Table 2. New contributions to Forum's principles of adult learning.

	Malcolm Knowles	Alan B. Knox	David Kolb	Jack Mezirow	Jerome Bruner	Howard Gardner	Peter Senge	Chris Argyris	Mary Field Belenky et al.	W. E. Deming
Major Work	*The Adult Learner*, 1978	*Adult Development and Learning*, 1977	*Experiential Learning*, 1984	*Transformative Dimensions of Adult Learning*, 1991	*Acts of Meaning*, 1990	*Frames of Mind*, 1983	*The Fifth Discipline*, 1990	*Reasoning, Learning, and Action*, 1982	*Women's Ways of Knowing*, 1986	*Out of the Crisis*, 1986
Contribution	Popularized "self-directed learning," which emphasizes the learner's needs and goals. Emphasized the creation of a receptive learning climate and the use of the learner's previous experience.	Showed how adults are constantly learning in response to role changes and other new situations, and how they use new information to make sense of their previous experiences.	Stressed the need to understand different learning styles and use a variety of techniques to both accommodate and challenge the learner. Emphasized experiential learning.	Focused on becoming aware of how assumptions constrain the way people perceive the the world, and on learning how to change those assumptions so they can act more effectively.	Showed that humans seek to create systems of meaning and that learning involves changing meaning systems.	Showed that there are different kinds of intelligence: personal, bodily-kinesthetic, linguistic, musical, logical-mathematical, and spatial.	Showed the importance of building "learning organizations" by using five disciplines: personal mastery, mental models, shared vision, team learning, and systems thinking.	Demonstrated how "double-loop" learning, or uncovering one's "operating assumptions" (theories in action), is critical to learning and acting effectively.	Studied how women learn; high-lighted the importance of respecting the learner's viewpoint, collaborating with others to develop ideas, and building on adults' life experiences.	Emphasized the need to drive fear out of the workplace so people are free to learn, cooperate, and be productive. Stressed continuous learning and improvement.
Effect on Forum's Principles of Adult Learning	2, 3, 5	2, 3, 5	2, 5	2, 5	1, 2, 3	2, 5	1, 2, 3, 4, 5	2, 3, 4, 5	1, 2, 3, 4, 5	3, 5

Principles of adult learning

1. Learning is a transformation that takes place over time.
2. Learning follows a continuous cycle of action and reflection.
3. Learning is most effective when it addresses issues that are relevant to the learner.
4. Learning is most effective when people learn with others.
5. Learning occurs best in a supportive and challenging environment.

Principles of Adult Learning: Overview

These five principles summarize Forum's point of view on how learning occurs and on the conditions that facilitate it.

1. *Learning is a transformation that takes place over time.* Learning is the process by which people change the way they interpret, or make sense of, their experiences. Learning creates new frames of reference that guide future ideas and actions. The learning process occurs in phases over time, moving from preparation to apprenticeship to mastery. In order to reach mastery, it is necessary to engage in learning activities that build awareness, provide practice, and encourage application of new ideas and actions.

2. *Learning follows a continuous cycle of action and reflection.* People learn by doing and then thinking consciously about what they did. Actions that have been reflected on— that is, examined and assessed—lead to new understandings, which in turn guide future actions.

3. *Learning is most effective when it addresses issues that are relevant to the learner.* People learn what they need to know in order to respond to conditions in their environment. They are motivated by either a personal desire to acquire new knowledge and skills or by understanding the consequences of not learning. When learning activities are linked to personal or organizational problems, learning is accelerated.

4. *Learning is most effective when people learn with others.* When people learn together, they share and build on one another's perceptions. As a result, they are able to hear other interpretations and test their own. This increases the likelihood of their creating new interpretations that can guide more effective personal and organizational actions.

5. *Learning occurs best in a supportive and challenging environment.* When the environment is not threatening to status or security, people are more willing to take risks, to explore new ideas, and to try new actions. It is essential, however, to balance support with a sufficient level of challenge. Unless people are challenged intellectually and emotionally, they typically will rely on existing habits and will not stretch themselves to find new ways of thinking and acting.

Principle 1: Learning Is a Transformation That Takes Place Over Time

Learning is a process by which each individual creates his or her own understanding of the world and how to interact with it. People form models in their minds that help them make sense of their experiences. For example, in a hierarchical organization, people create models of how employees at different job levels should behave. These models define which behaviors are considered appropriate for each level.

These mental models and belief systems underlie the assumptions that guide thought and action. Learning is the process of identifying and questioning existing models and then testing new assumptions for use as guides to more effective action. For example, a manager may have a mental model that workers are incapable of leadership in the organization. This leads him or her to assume that workers should not be included in decision making. This model must be identified and questioned before a new assumption—that workers are capable of leadership—can take effect. The new assumption opens a realm of action that was previously unavailable.

Changing mental models, beliefs, and assumptions is a very difficult task. Given this difficulty, learning takes time.

This is an important point for understanding how to design and deliver effective learning experiences. Often training designs underestimate the extent to which learners cling to their existing ways of thinking. Training may also fail to provide the high-impact experiences that are necessary to unfreeze existing views. In addition, training curricula often do not accurately assess the time required to learn new ways of thinking and acting.

The Forum Learning Model conveys the learning process as a journey toward mastery; the journey is depicted as an arrow. This model mirrors the one that describes the process of organizational transformation (Forum's Align-Improve-Measure Model). Both models depict the transformation as occurring over a series of three phases. Both also describe the types of activities that take place in these phases.

Each of the learning phases and the types of learning activities will be explained in detail on the following pages.

Learning new ideas, beliefs, or skills generally does not occur as the result of a single experience. Learning evolves. In order to learn, one begins by examining new experiences in light of one's existing knowledge. Then, one creates new models of understanding. Over time and with practice, new knowledge and skills become second nature, and the learner is able to call upon them naturally in all appropriate situations. This "learning by heart" is central to mastery. The process of attaining mastery occurs in three phases, described briefly below and in more detail on the following pages.

Phase 1: Preparation. In the preparation phase, learners become aware of their existing assumptions, encounter new ideas, and practice and apply new behaviors. This is the initial phase of the journey toward mastery. In this phase, the emphasis is on creating awareness of existing assumptions and on introducing new patterns of behavior. For example, a traditional management training program focuses on the preparation phase. It allows participants to examine the gap between what they currently are doing and what they could be doing. It also allows participants to practice and apply new behaviors in a protected setting.

Phase 2: Apprenticeship. To become fluent with new knowledge or skills, learners must use them in a variety of work situations, under different conditions, and under the watchful eye of a master or coach. Apprenticeship provides a protected setting in which to do this. During apprenticeship, the emphasis is on practicing new learning in real work situations. Much of the learning that takes place during apprenticeship results from learners reflecting on their actions and creating improved guides for future actions. For example, a junior partner in a law firm works with a senior partner who provides continual coaching and feedback on how to apply new learning to the practice of law.

Phase 3: Mastery. Mastery is the aim of the learning process. To achieve mastery, learners must pass through the initial phases of preparation and apprenticeship and be willing to take on the responsibilities of leading, teaching, continually improving, and innovating. The emphasis in this phase is on the application of knowledge and skills.

Masters intentionally challenge assumptions about what works and push themselves to new levels of performance. Yet they always return to basics. Think of a master pianist or a professional athlete; to maintain a high level of performance, each requires continuing instruction, daily practice, and surrender to what is "learned by heart." Through teaching, masters further refine their own knowledge.

The Preparation Phase

Mastery requires the creation of a firm foundation on which to build and develop new skills. Traditionally, training courses in business are designed as ends in themselves rather than as preparation for continuous learning. They run the risk of having an effect in the classroom, but not providing long-term benefit. Training programs designed as part of the preparation phase should include activities that are linked with what is to follow in the apprenticeship phase.

All three types of learning activities—awareness, practice, and application—are used in the preparation phase, but the emphasis is on awareness.

- Learners must become acutely *aware* of their current ideas and behaviors in order to accept new ones. For example, immersion exercises can put learners in situations in which they confront their habitual behaviors.

- The use of new ideas and behaviors must be *practiced* in a supportive yet challenging way, so that they can be internalized. For example, role-plays can provide learners an opportunity to practice new behaviors.

- New ideas and behaviors must begin to be *applied*, so that they can be transferred to the job and eventually mastered. For example, action planning can direct learners to apply new concepts and skills to work issues.

All three types of learning activities should engage learners in a continuous cycle of action and reflection. This gives them time to experience the new ideas or behaviors and the opportunity to assimilate them. For example, reading and discussing case studies allows learners to analyze situations and propose solutions. The group debriefing allows learners to reflect on their own solutions as well as the methods they used to arrive at them. (This is what Chris Argyris and Donald Schön (1978) refer to as "single- and double-loop learning.")

In the preparation phase, it is important to prepare both the learner and the learner's work environment. One way this can be done is to include intact work groups in the training; this will foster a better learning environment back on the job. Another way is to engage the learner's manager in the training by having him or her identify expected learning outcomes, provide feedback on performance, or take related training. A third way to link learning to work is to use feedback from customers and colleagues.

At the end of the preparation phase, learners will be aware of key ideas and skills. They will have had an opportunity to practice using these ideas and skills in a protected setting. They also will have had a limited opportunity to apply the new learning, either through action planning or through resolving an actual work issue with other work-group members or by themselves.

The Apprenticeship Phase

In the shops of traditional artisans and craftsmen, "learning at the master's knee" was the norm. Apprenticeship—following the moves of the master—has been widely practiced in some settings for centuries and continues to be practiced today. The current challenge is to bring the effectiveness of the apprentice system into the modern organization; this requires managers to become effective mentors and coaches, capable of giving feedback and guiding improvement.

Most training programs address the introductory needs of new learners, and most consulting interventions focus on the needs of senior people who are working toward mastery. There is a shortage of training programs that address the on-the-job learning needs of the apprenticeship phase.

All three types of learning activities—awareness, practice, and application—are used in the apprenticeship phase, but the emphasis is on practice.

- Learners need to be *aware* of the critical ideas and skills that will help them get their work done. They must be aware of the vision of their organization and their work group. This requires communication with the managers who coach them. Learners should also receive ongoing feedback, guidance, and encouragement from their coaches and work associates so that they can develop shared learning and monitor their own progress.

- *Practice* is the main activity of the apprenticeship phase. Through repetition, the learner assimilates new ideas and behaviors until they become a part of his or her repertoire. For example, basketball star Larry Bird practiced free throws for hours every day since boyhood in his long apprenticeship toward the mastery of his sport.

- Apprenticeship also provides an opportunity to take the fundamental ideas and skills introduced in the preparation phase and *apply* them on the job. Apprentices are capable of resolving real work issues by applying and refining their abilities. Apprentices should be provided opportunities to take on and lead their own projects and be coached when needed.

At the end of the apprenticeship phase, learners will have increased their awareness of key ideas and skills. They will have had an extended period of time practicing the new ideas and skills with coaching and feedback from both mentors and work associates. They will begin the ongoing process of continually applying the new learning on the job and begin to lead their own projects and monitor their own progress.

The Mastery Phase

What do world-class pianists, Wimbledon tennis champions, and Nobel Prize economists have in common? They appreciate that mastery is an endless journey toward perfection. Mastery can lead to a state of harmonious, effortless knowing and doing. It can result in a sense of flow—a natural, pleasant rhythm that accompanies action (Csikszentmihalyi, 1990).

Success in business requires dedication to mastery. Too often in the training field, for instance, "taking a course" is confused with mastering a set of skills. When the desired outcomes are not achieved within the 3- or 5-day program, there is disappointment and, typically, the course or the instructor is blamed. In truth, the fault usually lies in the design's inability to address mastery as the aim of an ongoing process. Training programs need to provide learning activities that will prepare and develop learners to achieve mastery.

George Leonard (1991) said, "Man is a learning animal. . . . In this light, the mastery of skills that are not genetically programmed is the most characteristically human of all activities." Leonard offered five keys to reaching mastery: (1) instruction, (2) continual practice, (3) discipline, (4) creating and sticking to a clear vision, and (5) striving for new insights. Training programs designed to address the needs of learners in the mastery phase must take these into account.

All three types of learning activities—awareness, practice, and application—are used in the mastery phase, but the emphasis is on application.

- In mastery, learners continue to become *aware* of their assumptions and remain open to new learning. They are mindful of what they do and do not know. They receive continual instruction and feedback from mentors and associates. They work with new learners so that their fundamental assumptions are always tested. For example, senior-level professors often teach freshman courses to get new perspectives on their thinking.
- Learners continue to *practice* their basic skills, like concert pianists who practice scales. It is this continual practice, and the surrender to the need for it, that enables the learner to achieve mastery.
- In mastery, learners *apply* their knowledge by sharing it with others through performing, writing, and teaching. They encourage and develop shared learning. They take responsibility for continual improvement and innovation. They exhibit leadership and share their excitement with others.

Unlike the preparation and apprenticeship phases, the mastery phase has no end. Masters remain open to new learning. They surrender to the need for continual practice and dis-

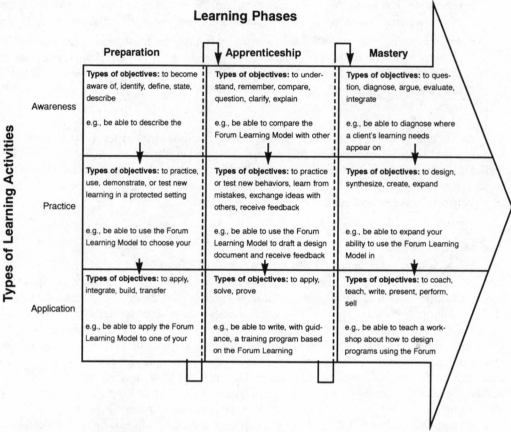

Figure 1.   Instructional Objectives Matrix (for each cell of the Forum Learning Model).

cipline. They seek out teachers and accept their guidance. When temporarily frustrated, masters know what causes the frustration and believe the obstacles can be overcome. In fact, obstacles often become the challenges that keep the flow going. Masters continually create new ways of thinking and acting that advance their fields.

Learning Activities

Learning is an active transformation of existing beliefs and behaviors. As learning evolves, the learner progresses through phases of preparation, apprenticeship, and mastery. In each phase, different types of learning activities are emphasized. In the preparation phase, emphasis is placed on awareness, on gaining an understanding of what is known and what needs to be learned. During the apprenticeship phase, effort is spent on practicing new concepts in protected settings. Finally, in the mastery phase, the emphasis is on applying new beliefs and behaviors to work situations.

To understand how the learning activities progress throughout all three phases of learning, refer to the Instructional Objectives Matrix (see Figure 1). The matrix employs the example of learning the Forum Learning Model. It shows how, in the preparation phase, learners will engage in awareness-building activities that enable them to describe the model. Later, in the mastery phase, when learners have completed many types of activities, they will be able to use their knowledge of the model to create programs and teach others about it.

Awareness. The first fundamental requirement of learning is for learners to understand how they currently make sense of what they observe and how they act in the world. Once they understand the models and assumptions they use to guide their actions, they can examine the usefulness of those models and assumptions and choose to test new ways of thinking and acting. To transform learners' firmly held mental models requires powerful awareness-building activities that can unfreeze existing ways of thinking and acting. The purpose of awareness-building activities is to help learners understand what they currently know and what they need to learn. Building awareness is necessary in all three phases of learning.

Practice. Practice involves using new knowledge and skills in an environment that allows for experimentation, coaching, making mistakes, and a free exchange of ideas. New ideas and behaviors must be practiced to make them part of the learner's repertoire. This involves using the new ideas and behaviors and reflecting on that use, building them into routine ways of thinking and acting. Practice allows learners to take risks and develop new ways of solving problems. Practice is necessary in all three phases of learning.

Application. Learners need to apply the new knowledge and skills in real work situations to accelerate and transfer learning. This speeds learners' comprehension and skill building, and enables them to move toward mastery. Applying new knowledge and skills enables learners to gain confidence using them. Application is necessary in all three phases of learning.

Principle 2: Learning Follows a Continuous Cycle of Action and Reflection

Much of the recent research on learning confirms what Socrates and John Dewey knew and practiced: that learning must consist of action—mental or physical or both—followed by an opportunity to reflect on the action and its outcome. Forum calls this cycle of action and reflection active learning.

Forum holds that active learning can begin with either action or reflection:

- The process can start with action that is then reflected on and summarized as new knowledge. For example, immersion exercises that force managers to act in situations that simulate managerial dilemmas can give the managers an opportunity to reflect on more effective ways of solving problems.

- Active learning can also begin with reflection. Learners can test the validity of new ideas by seeing their effectiveness in practice. Effective ideas are used as guides to further action. For example, reflecting on customer-focused quality ideas can lead to improved management actions.

The purposes of experiential activities are to give learners opportunities to:

- Become powerfully aware of their existing interpretations and habitual ways of behaving.
- Design and practice new, more effective actions.

Course designers must know which of these two purposes they intend to achieve when using experiential learning activities.

The purposes of reflection are to give learners opportunities to:

- Consciously examine their actions and their existing interpretations.
- Create new models and theories that can guide effective future actions.

Action

Learners require dramatic, active experiences to transform long-held ideas and ingrained habits. Without relevant, high-impact experiences, learners are less likely to reconsider existing patterns and to consider new ones.

In short, action must be:

- Direct and personal enough to change firmly held habits and beliefs.
- Concrete enough to allow the practice of specific new behaviors.
- Flexible enough to fit the style, experience, and needs of individual learners.

Learning exercises that start with action place learners in circumstances that force them to stretch—to try on new behaviors and see things from new perspectives. Examples include:

- **Role-plays.** Role-plays provide an opportunity for learners to try on new behaviors in realistic situations and improve them through reflection and practice.
- **Simulations and "real plays."** In a simulation or a "real play," participants play themselves as they try to solve problems in a fictitious environment. They then have an opportunity to debrief and reflect on their actions. In the Leadership program, there is an example of a computerized business simulation; "Site/Central" is an example of a Forum "real play."
- **Survival exercises.** Learners pretend to be stuck in dangerous situations with limited supplies of resources. Similar to role-plays and simulations, survival exercises start with action and then provide time for participants to reflect on behaviors and outcomes.

Reflection

Reflection allows learners to examine experiences and make meaning of them. John Dewey (1933) described reflection as "active, persistent, and careful consideration of any belief or supposed form of knowledge in the light of the grounds that support it and the further conclusions to which it tends." The important point is that reflection ties new experiences to existing frames of reference and prepares the learner to interpret future experiences.

The main principles of reflection are that:

- Reflection is the process of uncovering the underlying assumptions that direct behavior.
- Reflection enables learners to constantly adjust their performance to meet new conditions.
- Reflection must occur soon after an activity in order for learners to gain maximum value.

Reflective thinking can be either divergent or convergent. Often it is both. Divergent thinking about the action allows for a free flow of new ideas. Convergent thinking provides learners an opportunity to summarize their thinking and choose a new course of action.

Examples of learning exercises that start with reflection include:

- **Feedback.** Forum's feedback technology focuses learners on the effectiveness of their job-related behaviors. It gives them an assessment of the importance of those behaviors in the context of the job. Other types of assessment activities that support reflection include talking in small groups, writing journals, conducting interviews or focus groups, and making site visits.

- **Brainstorming.** Brainstorming allows a free flow of ideas about a given topic. It also facilitates the process of divergent thinking. One way that Forum programs facilitate brainstorming is by including diverge/converge exercises and recording participants' responses on flipcharts.

- **"New perspectives" exercises.** These exercises allow participants to view their situations from new vantage points. For example, the participants can imagine that they are living in another time or country in order to create a new perspective on their situation. Or, they can employ certain language techniques (such as the use of metaphors or action verbs) to describe their situations in new ways. This lets learners reframe their existing ideas.

Principle 3: Learning Is Most Effective When It Addresses Relevant Issues

When people are pursuing their own goals, they are motivated to learn. Individuals in organizations also need to align themselves with organizational goals and learn what they need to know in order to implement those goals. For example, if the organization has the goal of having each business unit become self-sufficient, its business managers will need to learn aspects of finance and marketing.

When ideas and behaviors known to lead to high performance are identified and learners are able to practice using them, the learners are more likely to apply the new ways on the job (Litwin, 1978). Training goals typically are related to improving performance in response to either: (1) a change in corporate strategy, or (2) a need to enhance skills.

During all three phases in the Forum Learning Model—preparation, apprenticeship, and mastery—links to work requirements motivate the learner, increase learning effectiveness, and ensure that the learning is transferred and sustained over time.

Preparation. All programs need to specify how they connect to the organization's overall strategy and vision. Program objectives should be described in relation to the organization's business goals. Intact work groups, including managers, should be encouraged to participate together in training programs. Specific, clear action plans must be developed during training to guide transfer of learning to the job and sustain learning over time.

Apprenticeship. Programs in this phase of the Forum Learning Model often combine on-the-job training with classroom work. Learners resolve actual work issues. Where possible, apprenticeships should be conducted on the work site and involve different levels of the organization. They need to include hands-on tasks, coaching, and feedback. Training can also be provided to improve the way teams learn and work together.

Mastery. In the mastery phase, learners are responsible for designing their own learning programs. When working with learners in the mastery phase, it is important to aid them in identifying their learning needs and appropriate strategies for addressing them. Activities such as receiving feedback from associates can help learners identify areas for improvement.

Principle 4: Learning Is Most Effective When People Learn with Others

When learners have an opportunity to exchange ideas and interact with others, they are able to question their own existing interpretations and become open to new ways of thinking and doing. Reading books or instructional materials is one way of learning from others; using interactive media that enable learners to practice and apply new concepts is another. Dialogue, however, provides the most effective means of exchanging and developing new concepts.

It is important to learn with others in all three phases of learning. In the *preparation* phase, learners need to be exposed to other people's ideas. Colleagues and instructors present new ideas and behaviors and provide feedback. Practicing new ideas and behaviors with others improves the learners' understanding of the new material. They then are able to apply the new learning more rapidly.

In the *apprenticeship* phase, learners need coaches and colleagues in order to apply the new learning and get feedback. They also need to be able to work in groups of people who can provide feedback and timely advice. Working with others enables learners to engage in inquiry that can stimulate further thinking, which helps refine and improve practice. This is the way most people learn "on the job."

Mastery requires learners to act as genuine colleagues and fellow travelers with others on the same journey. To improve continually, it is essential that learners receive ongoing instruction, feedback, and coaching from others. Masters must be open to continual reflection on their actions. In the mastery phase, learners take on the role of teacher and continue to develop their ideas as they transfer them to others.

Learning with others is the principle that underlies team and organizational learning. These processes are crucial to building organizations that are responsive and competitive in business today. They are defined briefly below.

Team Learning. When learners have an opportunity to experiment and reflect in teams, they elevate their ability to learn together. Team learning requires an environment in which people feel free to reveal their assumptions. A facilitator can help create this environment by modeling how to accept others' interpretations without immediate rebuttal (Senge, 1990). Team learning helps to initiate organizational learning. But, for organizational learning to continue, learning also must be systematically exchanged across teams.

Organizational Learning. This is the process of continually creating common models of understanding so that organizations can produce their intended results. Organizational learning requires that individuals learn, but it also requires structured organizational processes for developing and transferring shared learning.

Principle 5: Learning Occurs Best in a Supportive and Challenging Environment

In the process of learning, people need to change their existing beliefs and behaviors. This is difficult because the mind has a strong tendency to cling to what it finds familiar and to defend itself against what threatens to disturb its equilibrium (Argyris & Schön, 1978; Bohm & Peat, 1987; Bruner, 1990).

When the need for learning is triggered by major organizational changes, there are additional elements of uncertainty. In high-stress environments, people encounter enormous demands to learn. Under these conditions, they often question their ability to learn.

Research has found that both the efficiency and effectiveness of learning are greatly improved when learners believe they can, will, or should change (McClelland, 1973). This is facilitated by a learning environment that acts as a lab for experimenting with new ideas. People learn by reflecting on the outcomes of their experiments—those that meet their expectations (what they consider "successes") as well as those that don't (what they consider "failures") (Minsky, 1986). A supportive environment provides opportunities for learners to reflect on those outcomes and to receive feedback from coaches (Schön, 1986; Senge, 1990). Course designers, facilitators, managers, and sponsoring organizations are all responsible for creating supportive and challenging environments.

Supportive. The environment must be nonjudgmental. Learners need to be rewarded for examining their thinking and their work (Litwin, 1978). They must be free to take risks, to assume unfamiliar roles, and to take untried positions on issues. A supportive environment enables learners to admit to not knowing and to making mistakes, and encourages them to try what they have not mastered. It is helpful if, in the preparation phase, the learning environment is different from the everyday work environment. This lets learners step back from the routine and see old problems and issues from new perspectives.

Challenging. Learners also need an environment that forces them to reevaluate their current thoughts and actions. Learners are invested in their existing interpretations and tend to refine what they already know, rather than learn new ideas and behaviors. They can become inflexible and resist creating new interpretations (Minsky, 1986). Learners adopt new ideas and behaviors only when they are fully convinced that their old ways are no longer appropriate. Powerful experiences and adequate opportunity to reflect on those experiences enable people to think and act in new ways. Experiences that provide emotional, intellectual, and action components have the greatest effect on challenging existing beliefs and behaviors.

References

Argyris, C. (1982). *Reasoning, learning, and action: Individual and organizational.* San Francisco: Jossey-Bass.

Argyris, C., & Schön, D. (1978). *Organizational learning: A theory of action perspective.* Reading, MA: Addison-Wesley.

Bandura, A., & Walters, R. H. (1963). *Social learning and personality development.* New York: Holt, Rinehart, and Winston.

Belenky, M. F., Clinchy, B., Goldberger, N., & Tarule, J. (1986). *Women's ways of knowing: The development of self, voice, and mind.* New York: Basic Books.

Bohm, D., & Peat, F. D. (1987). *Science, order, and creativity.* New York: Bantam Books.

Bruner, J. (1990). *Acts of meaning.* Cambridge: Harvard University Press.

Csikszentmihalyi, M. (1990). *Flow: The psychology of optimal experience.* New York: Harper & Row.

deGeus, A. P. (1988, March–April). Planning as learning. *Harvard Business Review,* 70–74.

Deming, W. E. (1986). *Out of the crisis.* Cambridge: Massachusetts Institute of Technology, Center for Advanced Engineering Study.

Dewey, J. (1933). *How we think* (2nd rev. ed.). Boston: D. C. Heath.

Gardner, H. (1983). *Frames of mind: The theory of multiple intelligences.* New York: Basic Books.

Gardner, H. (1991). *The unschooled mind: How children think and how schools should teach.* New York: Basic Books.

Knowles, M. S. (1978). *The adult learner: A neglected species* (2nd ed.). Houston: Gulf Publishing.

Knox, A. B. (1977). *Adult development and learning.* San Francisco: Jossey-Bass.

Kolb, D. A. (1984). *Experiential learning.* Englewood Cliffs, NJ: Prentice-Hall.

Leonard, G. (1991). *Mastery: The keys to long-term success and fulfillment.* New York: Dutton.

Lewin, K. (1948). *Resolving social conflicts.* New York: Harper & Row.

Litwin, G. H. (1978). Principles of adult learning. Unpublished manuscript.

Litwin, G. H., & Stringer, Robert A., Jr. (1968). *Motivation and organizational climate.* Boston: Graduate School of Business Administration, Harvard University.

Maslow, A. (1954). *Motivation and personality.* New York: Harper & Row.

McClelland, D. C. (1973). *Human motivation* (2nd ed.). Glenview, IL: Scott, Foresman.

Mezirow, J. (1991). *Transformative dimensions of adult learning.* San Francisco: Jossey-Bass.

Minsky, M. (1986). *The society of mind.* New York: Simon and Schuster.

Piaget, J. (1970). *Genetic epistemology.* New York: Columbia University Press.

Rogers, C. R. (1961). *On becoming a person.* Boston: Houghton Mifflin.

Schön, D. (1986). *Educating the reflective practitioner.* San Francisco: Jossey-Bass.

Schrage, M. (1990). *Shared minds: The new technologies of collaboration.* New York: Random House.

Senge, P. M. (1990). *The fifth discipline: The art & practice of the learning organization.* New York: Doubleday/Currency.

Skinner, B. F. (1953). *Science and human behavior.* New York: Macmillan.

PART 4

The Strategic Vantage Point: Instructional Systems Development Macro-Strategies

21

The Personalized System of Instruction (PSI) and the Three Rs: Revolutions, Revelations, and Reflections*

George B. Semb
University of Kansas, Lawrence

Vignette—Being Taught and Learning: An Important Distinction

I took my first flight in 1951. I was eight. It originated in Philadelphia. I was to spend a month with my aunt and uncle in Alabama. My parents stood near the gate as I boarded the Eastern flight. My father waved good-bye and my mother cried. The flight was exciting, but the long approach and sweeping turns were too much. I threw up. I also lost my wallet.

My uncle, a World War II veteran and pilot, met me at the gate. He realized immediately what had happened. In retrospect, it would have been hard for anyone who could see or smell to miss it. By the next morning, I had forgotten the flight until the doorbell rang and there stood a messenger with nothing less than my wallet. Can you imagine a messenger driving 50 miles to deliver a wallet that contained a Cub Scout card and a $10 bill? That *was* service, the way it used to be!

I flew again eight years later, shortly after my father returned from a business trip. He had just flown on a jet, a Boeing 707, from Denver to Chicago, and he was excited. He offered to give me flying lessons. We lived in a small town in northern Wisconsin. The nearest airport was 13 miles away. There were a few planes and one instructor, a man named Don.

*This chapter is dedicated to Dr. Fred S. Keller (1899–1996). Fred was a great man who touched thousands of lives both personally and professionally, mine included. His Personalized System of Instruction (PSI) is, I believe, one of the most effective instructional delivery systems of this century.

The plane had a tail wheel and two seats, arranged one behind the other. Don gave me a quick overview of the front seat and panel: "the knob on the panel is the throttle—it controls thrust; the pedals on the floor (rudders) control right and left; the thing in the middle is the stick—it controls up and down and right and left." How two things could control right and left was not clear, but before I could ask, Don told me me to climb in. He added that he would show me how this plane could fly. I quickly learned that "showing" and "teaching" are different concepts.

My father waved as we taxied to the runway and took off. Soon Washburn, where I lived, came into view. It was awesome. I would be the first 16-year-old in my class to fly an airplane. Then Don yelled, "I'm going to show you a couple of turns." The plane banked left and I could see the barn below us. A few second later I could see the same barn off the right wing. My stomach wasn't happy, but I guessed that was part of flying. All the time I noticed that my feet were moving and that the stick between my legs was moving from right to left and front to back. My thought pattern was interrupted when Don yelled, "It's yours, give me a left turn." We were drifting up and to the right, so I pushed hard on the left pedal. At the same time, I pushed the stick forward and to the left as far as it could go. The airplane responded with enthusiasm. We were headed down and to the left in what I later learned was called a dive. I could see the ground in front of us, right under the nose. Don yelled: "Let go, let go." I could feel back-pressure on the stick, so I let it go.

Next, we tried climbing. My turn. Pull back on the stick; it didn't go up too much, so I pulled the stick into my gut and held it there. Don screamed, "Let it go," just as we experienced one of the most stunning stalls I've ever encountered. My stomach was not happy. Don was not happy. We landed a few minutes later. I got out of the plane and, in what was now becoming a tradition, threw up. My father handed Don a $10 bill, which Don rejected with the simple epitaph, "George will never be a pilot."

I had failed, but my father did not reinforce that line of reasoning. He told me that someday I might try again. I swore that I wouldn't, but, hedging a bit because I had peers to impress, I vowed that if I ever did, it would be with someone who knew how to teach. That day didn't come until January 1964 when I was working in southern California on a study of visual ranging among, of all people, Navy pilots. They encouraged me to try again. They gave me the name of a civilian instructor named Charlie at the Oxnard airport. Charlie knew how to teach. Within two weeks I had soloed and three months later I earned my Private Pilot Certificate. Today, I co-author a course for private pilots (Semb & Taylor, 1993). Over the years, I have learned a lot about teaching. The University of Kansas even hired me to teach a large introductory course, which I designed using Keller and Sherman's[1] (1974) Personalized System of Instruction (PSI) as a model. The course has been offered in a PSI format for the past 22 years[2] and has produced over 37,000 students, almost all enlightened, almost all happy.

Introduction

Fred S. Keller, J. Gilmour Sherman, and two Brazilian colleagues, Rodolpho Azzi and Carolina Martuscelli Bori, first conceptualized the system in 1963 (Keller & Sherman, 1974). The system was based on principles of learning. As Sherman (1992) notes, "instruction must provide for (a) presentation, (b) performance, and (c) consequences, each constantly adjusted to meet the need of every individual student." Adopting this view of instruction has some implications for how instruction is designed and delivered. Presentation sounds very much like lecturing, and in conventional instruction, lecturing is the primary means of transmitting information. However, in PSI, lectures are seldom given; rather, content is transmitted through written or recorded material to which students have continual access. Performance in academic settings typically refers to *student* behavior such as that emitted on a quiz, exam, or essay. In conventional instruction, occasions for students to behave occur infrequently;

thus, opportunities for consequences to be applied to their behavior occur at a low rate. In PSI, students behave often because they are tested frequently. In such an interactive environment, it is easy to adjust the system to meet the needs of individual students.

I emphasize the word "system" in PSI to distinguish it from what is traditionally called instructional design. Design is an integral part of the process, and without it, the system would fail, but it is only a part of total system. PSI also addresses: (1) instructional delivery—how the material is presented, (2) the interface—how students come in contact with it, (3) evaluation—how they are assessed, and (4) remediation—how deficiencies in learning are fixed.

Systematic approaches to instruction are not new. Nearly 200 years ago, Joseph Lancaster and Andrew Bell designed one of the first educational systems that deviated from the lecture as a method of delivering instruction (Kaestle, 1973). Called the monitorial method, it used student monitors (tutors) who worked with small groups of students over course material that had been carefully programmed by subject matter specialists. It even had a token economy in which students could exchange points earned for academic progress for candy and prizes. The system flourished in the early 1800s. At one point there were as many as 13,000 schools serving primarily lower-class children throughout England and Scotland. The system was even exported to the United States. As with most innovations, however, the schools disappeared when their sponsor, the Church of England, stopped supporting them.

It is at first ironic that Keller and Sherman's (1974) system so closely resembled the monitorial method. Perhaps it is not ironic, however, when one considers that most systematic approaches to instruction put the student, rather than the teacher, at the center of the system. In student-centered systems, things are done to *ensure* that the student succeeds. In her recent essay, "On College Teaching," K. Patricia Cross (1993) asserts that "the ultimate criterion of effective teaching, of course, is effective learning." She continues:

> But we are beginning to see that learning probably depends more on the behavior of students than on the performance of teachers. Thus, research on teaching is shifting from observing how well the teacher is performing to observing how well students are responding. Good teaching is not so much a performing art as an evocative process. The purpose is to involve students actively in their own learning and to elicit from them their best learning performance.

Cross's (1993) remarks are relevant here not because they are new but because they were made in 1993. Keller and Sherman (1974) and others had been making the same point for decades. PSI was an attempt to design a system with the student in the center and the instructor at his or her side as a guide or coach. This is similar to recent attempts to design learner-centered alternatives to conventional instruction such as anchored instruction (Cognition & Technology Group at Vanderbilt, 1990), situated cognition (Brown, Collins, & Duguid, 1989), cognitive apprenticeships (Collins, Brown, & Newman, 1989), and reciprocal teaching (Fantuzzo, Dimeff, & Fox, 1989; Palincsar & Brown, 1984; Palincsar, Brown, & Martin, 1987), all of which actively engage learners in enriched learning environments.

The Basic Components: Theory, Research, and Practice

The differences between conventional lecture instruction and PSI are perhaps best appreciated visually. Figure 1 depicts conventional instruction and Figure 2 illustrates a PSI classroom. What makes PSI such a radical departure from conventional instruction? Keller and Sherman (1974) cite five defining characteristics: (1) a "unit perfection requirement," by which students progress to more advanced material only after having demonstrated mastery of prerequisite material; (2) self-pacing, in which students advance through the material at a rate commensurate with their ability and other demands on their time; (3) stress on carefully prepared written or recorded material to which students can have continued access and

Instructor

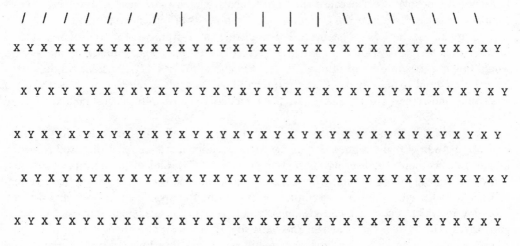

Students

Figure 1.   Conventional instruction (lecture).

which specify in detail (e.g., through objectives, advanced organizers, and study questions) the material to be learned; (4) the use of more-advanced students (what Keller & Sherman call proctors[3]) to tutor or coach less advanced students; and (5) the use of lectures to motivate rather than to transmit essential information. These five features define the *system* that Keller and Sherman came to call PSI. As Sherman (1992) points out, there have been several variations of the basic design, and that has made it difficult to decide when something is PSI and when it is not. The system is so robust, however, that when it is implemented as prescribed, I do not know of a single study in which it has been shown to be inferior to conventional (i.e., lecture) instruction.

It was not until Keller (1968) published the paper titled "Good-bye, teacher . . ." that PSI became popular. Then came the researchers, and there were hordes of them, who compared PSI to everything from the lecture method (Hursh, 1976) to Socratic dialogue (Smith, 1987) and who dissected it like a zealous coroner (Kulik, Jaska, & Kulik, 1978). The research progressed from comparative studies and component analyses to summative reports and meta-analyses. The data were clear: PSI produced high levels of academic performance (Hursh, 1976; Kulik, Kulik, & Bangert-Drowns, 1990; Kulik, Kulik, & Cohen, 1979), particularly among lower ability students (Cross & Semb, 1976). It also engendered high levels of student satisfaction (Kulik *et al.*, 1979) and high levels of knowledge retention (Corey & McMichael, 1974; Semb & Ellis, 1994; Semb, Ellis, & Araujo, 1993). Furthermore, each of the components also proved to be important to the overall success of the system (Kulik *et al.*, 1978).

Keller and Sherman (1974) argued that the system would be incomplete without all of its components. They adopted this position for a simple, but often-overlooked reason—the components are logically interrelated. If you are going to require students to master prerequisite material before they move on to more advanced topics, you *must* let them work at their own rate. Group-pacing simply will not do, because it requires that everyone work at the same rate. What happens if someone falls behind or lurches ahead? Only by allowing students to work at their own rate can you accommodate these individual differences. However, self-pacing imposes further constraints on the system. For example, it would be difficult to

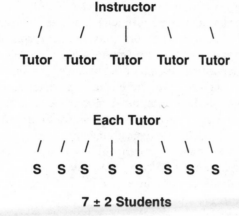

Figure 2. The Personalized System of Instruction (PSI).

prepare a different lecture for each student; thus, lectures are not a good way to disseminate what is to be learned. Rather, the instructor must develop or adopt course materials (e.g., study guides, audio-tapes, and CD-ROMs) to which students have continual access.

Next, if there are prerequisites for advancing from one unit to the next, there must be assessment, and to be most effective, these assessments must occur frequently. Thus, PSI evaluates student progress often and on a regular basis; in most PSI courses, it occurs almost daily. These assessments typically take the form of unit tests[4] that are administered after students have studied the required material. Frequent testing, in turn, requires frequent evaluation. There are only a limited number of hours in a term and most instructors cannot evaluate every student response. PSI's solution to this problem is to employ more advanced students to grade tests and provide one-on-one tutoring. Proctors enable the system to fulfill its goal of maintaining a unit perfection requirement.

In summary, to accommodate individual differences in learning, PSI uses self-pacing. This obviates the lecture as a method of delivering instruction and promotes the development of materials to which students have continual access. Because mastery is required each step of the way, evaluation occurs frequently, a labor-intense job made possible by the use of student proctors.

We begin with the unit-perfection requirement, sometimes called the mastery requirement, because it is arguably the most important component of the system (Buskist, Cush, & DeGrandpre, 1991; Kulik *et al.*, 1978). It is also the least volatile politically—it is hard to argue with a simple, unobtrusive procedure that promotes higher levels of learning.

The unit-perfection requirement. The concept of mastery learning was not new. At about the same time Keller and Sherman were inventing PSI, John B. Carroll (1963) published his theory of mastery learning. Benjamin S. Bloom (1968, 1976) extended this theory and articulated its practical implications in the form of a teaching system called Learning for Mastery (LFM). It is ironic that Keller's classic paper on PSI, "Good-bye, Teacher . . . ," and Bloom's classic paper, "Learning for Mastery," were both published in 1968. The two camps came from different theoretical perspectives—Keller from psychology and, in particular, behavior analysis, and Bloom from education. They occasionally met at the same forum,[5] but for the most part they have led separate, but productive, lives.

The two camps defined mastery in different terms. In Bloom's (1968) LFM, learning outcomes were clearly defined and students were given two attempts to "master" those objectives. According to Bloom, two chances were sufficient for 95 percent of the students. Overall, LFM courses produced academic performance that was about one-half a standard deviation above the mean when compared to more conventional forms of instruction (Kulik *et al.*, 1990). In Keller and Sherman's (1974) PSI, mastery was couched in terms of the "unit-perfection requirement," under which students did not engage in new or more difficult material until previous content had been mastered at a predetermined level, the mastery criterion. This meant that some students attempted an exercise several times before they met the criterion. While PSI theoretically gave students *unlimited* opportunities to demonstrate mastery of an assignment, in practice, this typically meant three to five attempts. Similar to LFM, PSI produced performance that was superior to conventional instruction (Kulik *et al.*, 1990). Recent empirical comparisons of PSI and LFM have indicated that PSI produces significantly higher levels of academic performance than LFM on both course posttests and tests of long-term retention (Semb *et al.*, 1993).

To implement the use of the unit perfection requirement, most PSI instructors first develop a series of unit assignments. A unit assignment can be anything from a chapter in a text to a laboratory exercise or a writing assignment. Calhoun (1976) suggests that relatively short assignments optimize student performance, and research clearly shows that breaking long or complex tasks into smaller parts enhances learning. Semb (1974) demonstrated that short assignments produced higher performance on both unit quizzes and a retention (midterm) exam when compared to long assignments. It should be noted that in one out of perhaps a dozen studies, Born (1975) found no significant differences between long and short assignments. Finally, just as it is important to break long or complex assignments into shorter units, so it is important to include "integration" or "review" units in which students put smaller parts back together (Semb, Spencer, & Phillips, 1976).

The level at which the unit perfection (mastery) criterion is set also influences performance. Parsons and Delaney (1978) found a significant correlation between the unit perfection criterion and exam performance. These results are consistent with Johnston and O'Neil (1973) and Semb (1974)—both of these studies demonstrated that a high criterion produced high levels of academic performance. Furthermore, empirical evidence suggests a high mastery criterion benefits low-aptitude students more than it does high aptitude students (Cross & Semb, 1976; Morris & Kimbrell, 1977).

Lectures. Keller and Sherman (1974) intended for lectures to motivate and reinforce students. Lectures were also used to explain material and to answer questions. In his review of the literature, Hursh (1976) concluded that lectures were poorly attended unless students were required to attend them or earned something for doing so. Edwards (1977) found that attendance at optional lectures was initially high, but that it diminished rapidly over time. Lloyd, Garlington, Lowry, Burgess, Euler, and Knowlton (1972) demonstrated that attendance increased when lectures emphasized course assignments and when students earned course credit for attending them. Finally, Calhoun (1976) found no differences in academic performance or student ratings between PSI courses that included lectures and those that did not. Taken together, these findings have led Kulik *et al.* (1978), Lloyd *et al.* (1972), and Calhoun (1976) to conclude that lectures do not serve to motivate or reinforce students as Keller and Sherman (1974) originally intended. As I will point out later, however, lectures may be an important political component of the system, because they provide the classroom instructor with added visibility.

Emphasis on the written word. Most PSI classes provide material through written or recorded sources such as a textbooks, manuals, workbooks, audiotapes, videos, CD-ROMs, and computer-assisted instruction (CAI) software packages. This is done so that students can have access to the content whenever and wherever they want. Emphasis on the written/recorded word also includes some effective instructional design strategies such as the use of study guides, objectives, pre-questions, and advance organizers, all of which improve student performance. For example, Semb, Hopkins, and Hursh (1973) demonstrated that students who had access to study questions performed about 30 percent better than students who did not.

Designing material for use in a PSI course frequently requires a great deal of advance planning and development, a factor that may be foreign to many educators, particularly those who conceptualize education in terms of lectures and class discussions (Semb, Ellis, Montague, & Wulfeck, 1992). Furthermore, poor and/or outdated material must be revised and new material added on a timely basis. It is also important to distinguish between content and delivery (Semb *et al.*, 1992). Criticisms about course content should always be leveled at the course developer, not at the method of delivery (Reboy & Semb, 1991). Whether PSI or lecture is used to deliver content, the results will reflect the quality of the instructional material, not the method of delivery. Thus, if course content stresses low-level objectives, that will be the educational outcome, regardless of the method used to delivery them.

As an example of how *not* to design PSI materials, consider the Navy's attempt to implement PSI in one of its "front end" courses that had a history of high attrition and numerous complaints (Semb *et al.*, 1992). The course was poorly designed—no task analysis was ever performed and the material was not relevant to executing the job. Many students failed and the course was abandoned. Another Navy course was also discontinued due to problems in course design (Ellis & Wulfeck, 1988). It had been rewritten using Instructional System Development (ISD) methodology, but no one from the classroom was included in the process. An analysis group turned it over to a design team who turned it over to a development team. Semb *et al.* (1992) report:

> These actions caused two serious problems. First, because the school felt left out of the process, the developers received very little cooperation from the subject matter experts who were instructors at the school. These were the same instructors who were to teach the new curriculum when it was developed. Second, because of the separation of responsibilities, a great deal of information and knowledge was lost when products moved from group to group. In the end, the instruction was lengthy, not very effective, and not well received by the school or the fleet. Unfortunately, self-paced instruction took much of the blame for the poorly designed and developed instruction. The moral of the story is that unless there is feedback to the developers from those who are going to implement it, the outcome is likely to be a disaster.

In summary, the demand for developing quality content is no different for a PSI course than it is for a conventional one—quality materials are essential for both. Ironically, one can imagine that PSI would do a better job than conventional instruction in teaching inferior content (Semb *et al.*, 1992). The point here is that one should design and develop course content and objectives first. How that content will be delivered comes next and will be constrained by the types of tasks and objectives of the course.

Self-pacing. The PSI learning environment is student-centered. While the instructor or others prepare the materials to be learned, the student has some control over the rate of learning. Keller and Sherman (1974) used self-pacing to allow students to progress through a course at a rate commensurate with their available time, ability, and motivation. Thus, PSI not only allows students to determine when instruction will occur but also at what pace. This enables students who are more proficient or more highly motivated to work at a faster rate and less proficient or less motivated students to take the extra time needed to meet or surpass the unit perfection requirement. It also allows for unexpected events such as dead batteries, illnesses, and war (Glick, 1978).

The underlying rationale for self-pacing is that individuals learn at different rates. Thus, PSI attempts to adapt instruction to individual differences to gain efficiency as well as to ensure achievement (Semb *et al.*, 1992). Research has clearly demonstrated that in addition to

PSI, a variety of self-paced formats such as computer-based instruction are more effective and more efficient than conventional instruction (Orlansky & String, 1981). Furthermore, studies have shown that PSI is more highly preferred and engenders more positive attitudes about learning than instructor-paced courses (Born, Gledhill, & Davis, 1972; Glick & Semb, 1978; Hoberok, Koen, Roth, & Wagner, 1972; Miller, Weaver, & Semb, 1974).

A common argument leveled against the use of self-pacing is that students may put off many of the to-be-completed tasks until the end of the term. This phenomenon is commonly referred to as the "procrastination" problem. Indeed, research indicates that a problem frequently arises in how students distribute their work in PSI courses (Glick, 1978; Born & Moore, 1978; Hoberok *et al.,* 1972; Miller *et al.,* 1974). A question of practical importance is: How many students will postpone work until a deadline approaches? Glick and Semb (1978) found that in an unrestricted self-pacing environment, 30 percent of the students worked ahead of schedule and finished the course before the end of the term. Another 20 percent distributed their work uniformly across the term and finished before the end of the term. However, 50 percent postponed work and had trouble finishing the course—typically, there was a burst of responding as the final deadline approached.

Several attempts to solve the procrastination problem have been reported (Semb, Conyers, Spencer, & Sanchez-Sosa, 1975). Glick and Semb (1978) taught students time-management skills as a way to reduce procrastination and it worked. Miller *et al.* (1974) used predefined target dates to reduce procrastination. Roberts and Semb (1980) required students to test every day until they had caught up with a pre-defined minimum rate line that listed a series of target dates. In both of these studies, students procrastinated less. Finally, Roberts, Fulton, and Semb (1988) demonstrated that students who set their own deadlines procrastinated much less and finished the course much earlier than students who followed instructor-set deadlines.

In summary, research has shown that setting and enforcing minimum rate requirements does not adversely affect academic performance. However, the best arrangement is to let students define the minimum rate at at which they will work and then have the instructor enforce it (Roberts & Semb, 1989). Semb *et al.* (1992) note:

> Assuming all contingencies can be reasonably anticipated and that a plan of action can be described, there are many advantages to be derived from a self-paced environment. Students benefit because learning is spaced (as opposed to massed), there is the opportunity to do things over if they are not done right the first time (mastery), and they learn to become more responsible for their own actions and their own learning (self-control). Instructors benefit not only because students benefit as just described, but also because the entire system produces superior results. Finally, the institution benefits because resources are put to maximum use and instructional time per student is minimized.

Student proctors (tutors).   This component of PSI provides the "P" in PSI, the "personalization." Sherman (1974) asserted that "one characteristic, the proctors, does set us [PSI] apart." A proctor is a student who has completed the course and who returns to serve as a classroom assistant (Keller, 1968), or a student presently enrolled in a course who has mastered more advanced material and who volunteers to tutor less advanced students (Sherman, 1974). The former are called "external" proctors because they are recruited from outside the course, whereas the latter are referred to as "internal" proctors because they are recruited from currently enrolled students. Proctors lower student-to-teacher ratios and increase opportunities for individualized instruction (Born, 1970). Sherman (1977) states:

> There has been an assumption of long-standing duration in education that students need to be taught by experts, and the more expert the better. This turns out not to be true, but the belief has led us into a wasteful, gross mis-allocation of talent. The mistake is expensive. The proctor has proven in many instances to be a more effective instructor than the professional. The gap between those who know almost everything about a subject and

those who know almost nothing about it is too large to bridge easily, comfortably or effectively for long periods. I am constantly embarrassed to find my proctors doing a better job of explaining something than I can. We do need experts. They have an important teaching function *when their talent is required,* and an important role to monitor the system—but proctors can carry much of the instructional role, and do it better.

Most of the research literature has concentrated on external proctors. Several studies have demonstrated that proctoring affects the behavior of the students they serve. Farmer, Lachter, Blaustein, and Cole (1972) showed that students who were proctored progressed through their course at a faster rate than students who were not proctored. Johnson and Sulzer-Azaroff (1975) and Farmer *et al.* (1972) both reported that students who were proctored took fewer quizzes over again than students who were not proctored. Students also appear to rate the proctoring component of PSI highly (Arp & Semb, 1977; Fernald, Chiseri, Lawson, Scroggs, & Riddell, 1975; Fitch & Semb, 1992; Hoberok *et al.*, 1972; Hursh, Wildgen, Minkin, Minkin, Sherman, & Wolf, 1975).

However, some studies have suggested that proctoring does not affect the subsequent *academic* performance of their students (Arp & Semb, 1977; Barton & Ascione, 1978; Caldwell, Bissonnette, Klishis, Ripley, Farudi, Hochstetter, & Radiker, 1978; Carsrud, 1979, Hursh, 1976; Hursh *et al.*, 1975; Johnson & Sulzer-Azaroff, 1975; Kulik *et al.*, 1978). A problem with all of these studies is that it is not clear if the proctors were trained to be effective peer teachers. Two recent studies (Fitch & Semb, 1992; Kuti, Hinton, Fitch, & Semb, 1992) have reported that students who were exposed to trained proctors performed significantly higher on subsequent exams than students who were exposed to untrained proctors. These results suggest that the training proctors receive affects how well their students perform on subsequent course tasks.

The question of interest here is: What are the skills that contribute to effective tutoring? Fitch and Semb (in press) conceptualize the tutor as a "coach" who guides and shapes students' learning using a three-step process of assessment, intervention, and evaluation. To implement these functions, tutors must possess or learn a variety of skills such as prompting, listening, observing, questioning, clarifying, and providing feedback and reinforcement. Fitch and Semb (in press) analyze the tutor's functions from both behavioral and cognitive perspectives. From a behavioral perspective, the tutor arranges contingencies for students to demonstrate their understanding of the material. Corrective feedback helps to clarify material and to reinforce students' comprehension of the material. From a cognitive perspective, tutors help students organize and elaborate material by building a framework for remembering it and for relating it to other information and concepts. The tutor offers the personal advantages of frequent verbal rehearsal and individual feedback (Schmidt & Bjork, 1992). Furthermore, tutors require students to reconstruct what they have studied, a technique that makes the material more memorable in the future. These are challenging tasks that are not intuitively obvious to most tutors (or teachers, for that matter)—they involve skills that must be trained.

The first step in the process, assessment, is a skill that involves listening and questioning to determine the discrepancy between what the student knows and what defines a competent level of performance. Assessment sets the stage for generating a course of action for the tutor and for shifting the focus of instruction from the tutor to the student. During the second step, intervention, the tutor clarifies material, provides examples, models, and prompts. Prompting and questioning should always set the occasion for the student to respond; however, prompts and questions that require elaborated responses are most effective. The intervention itself is a continuous, iterative process in which the tutor not only prompts, but also evaluates students by providing information about the accuracy or adequacy of their performances. Again, to be most effective, these skills must be trained.

As mentioned previously, tutors who were trained in the use of these skills engendered improvements in the performance of the students they tutored (Fitch & Semb, 1992; Kuti *et al.*, 1992). Is is also the case that proctors benefit from the experience. For one thing, they "see, moment to moment, student progress" (Sherman, 1992). They also benefit academically. Arp and Semb (1977) found that proctors gained seven points more from the pretest to the end of the course than did the students they proctored. Semb *et al.* (1993) conceptualized tutoring as a form of overlearning. They found proctors retained significantly more than the students they proctored. The academic effects may have been due to several factors including increased exposure to course content, continued contact with it, and the experience of tutoring students. PSI is a win/win system—students learn a lot, proctors learn even more.

Finally, our interest in proctor training has implications for the design and analysis of expert systems. The proctor in PSI is the interface between the student and learning, much as the computer may serve as the interface in an expert system. The potential we see is in an analysis of the proctor's behavior. The typical proctor is *not* an "expert," but rather somewhere between the "novice" and the "expert." In PSI, it is the proctor, not the expert, who does most of the one-on-one teaching and from whom we may be able to learn something about how one makes the transition from "novice" to "intermediate" to "expert."

Politics

PSI thrived throughout the late 1960s and 1970s. As Sherman (1992) noted, it produced over 2,000 research studies. It was not, however, the educational panacea its founders thought it might be (Ainsworth, 1979). Despite empirical demonstrations of its effectiveness, it sometimes met harsh resistance (Sherman, 1992). For example, even though data from some 40 studies supported its continued use (Orlansky & String, 1981), the Navy in 1983 decided to phase out self-paced courses and the software systems that managed them (Ellis & Wulfeck, 1988). In another instance, one of the founders of PSI, Sherman (1992) was told by his department chair that 50% of class time had to be devoted to lecturing because "it is the clash of intellects in the classroom that informs the student."

What is it about PSI that leads to such political confrontations? Semb *et al.* (1992) have analyzed several misperceptions, misunderstandings, and criticisms of self-paced instruction. Although they limited their review to self-paced courses, their findings have clear implications for PSI.

PSI is frequently confused with individualized instruction.   The first misunderstanding is that PSI is the same as individualized instruction. Semb *et al.* (1992) note:

> Individualized instruction typically refers to systems in which the material is designed to accommodate different entry levels and/or different branches or routes through the materials. Students' progress through the material is determined initially by their entry level skills and later by their prior performance. Thus, in individualized instruction, students typically begin at a level commensurate with their ability and then progress, sometimes by alternate paths, through the material. For example, in many remedial settings, the instructor administers a pretest and then places the student at the appropriate place in the curriculum.

PSI is a step in the direction of individualization, but it is only a step. Most PSI courses have a set curriculum, but the student controls the presence, absence, and pace of contact with that curriculum. As Sherman (1992) notes, *"There is a difference between providing instruction for individuals and focusing on the learning of individual students."* PSI focuses very much on the latter.

PSI is said to deliver poor quality instruction and to stress low-level objectives. A second accusation is that PSI delivers poor quality instruction and stresses low-level objectives. As discussed previously, these criticisms are often the result of poor instructional design, not the method of delivery (Reboy & Semb, 1991). Perhaps one of the harshest critics of PSI in this arena was Meek (1977), who asserted that "the appropriate goals to be pursued in most courses in the humanities and social sciences are much broader and much more difficult to measure than those selected by the defenders of PSI." The harshness of his comments can best be summarized by the following quote: "I think its [PSI's] contribution to solving the perceived learning problems of the society is all too much like the Nazi choice of genocide as a means of solving the perceived problem on nationality." It is difficult to understand how an educational system could provoke such viciousness, but it did.

Again, it is important to point out that the objectives of instruction, not the method of delivery, determine what is taught. PSI has always had an interest in developing critical thinking skills in its students (Reboy & Semb, 1991). This has its roots in the early days of analyzing a student's ability to apply concepts, to solve novel problems, to generate novel examples of concepts, and to integrate material in ways not explicitly taught (Semb & Spencer, 1976). These are noble goals, but we wondered how well our colleagues were doing meeting these goals in the conventional courses they taught. First, we developed some simple, but reliable, definitions of "low-level" tasks (recognition and recall) and "high-level" tasks (comprehension, generalization, integration, and application). Next, we surveyed 34 professors of major introductory courses. We asked them to estimate the percentage of questions they used on major exams to assess "low-level" objectives and the percentage they used to evaluate "high-level" objectives. Twenty-nine of the 34 professors responded; they estimated that 33 percent of their exams emphasized "high-level" concepts, whereas the other 67 percent emphasized "low-level" objectives.

The problem was that without adequate knowledge of course content, there is no way to know if their estimates were valid. So, we recruited students from those courses to collect notes, exams, and reading assignments. We asked these students to use our definitions and to trace each test item back to its source. The results? There was absolutely no correlation between the percentage of "high-level" tasks estimated by instructors and the actual percentage found by our student observers. Instructors estimated that 33 percent of their questions emphasized "high-level" objectives, but our students found that only eight percent of the questions met that objective. If we eliminate courses in physics and chemistry in which "high-level" items are common, 98 percent of the items in the social sciences and humanities addressed "low-level" objectives. Similar to the research presented earlier on the effects of high and low mastery criteria, if we do not design "high-level" tasks, we are not going to get the kinds of critical thinking skills we all deem important.

PSI is said to eliminate the need for the instructor. A third erroneous perception of PSI is that it eliminates the need for an instructor. Nothing could be further from the truth. Indeed, one of the most radical differences between PSI and conventional instruction is in the role of the classroom instructor, who is transformed from a transmitter of information and authoritarian figure standing in front of the classroom to a facilitator of learning, a tutor, and a problem-solver. In conventional instruction, the instructor is the "sage on the stage"; in PSI, the instructor is the "guide on the side."[6] And therein lies the rub. Many instructors are not willing to adopt such an unconventional role in the classroom. They find the transformation difficult if not impossible to make, not to mention distasteful (Semb *et al.*, 1992). Cross (1993) asserts that "teachers' actions, especially at the college level, are determined more by the predilections, personalities, and perceptions of the teacher than by the needs of the students." Most college teachers teach exactly as they were taught. With such a model, it is not hard to see why most innovations are doomed to fail. More optimistically, Semb *et al.* (1992) pointed out, "It is probably naive to assume that instructors will adopt and accept a new role without training."

To be successful, a PSI course must have the support of the instructors who will implement it. Instructor dissatisfaction was one factor responsible for the Navy's decision to phase out such courses during the 1980s (Ellis & Wulfeck, 1988). Semb *et al.* (1992) stated:

> Asking an instructor to change his or her way of doing things is certainly a potential pitfall. It requires retraining teachers and instructors not only in how to do things differently in the new environment, but also in how to conceptualize that environment. To conceptualize the learning environment as a place where instructors work with students one-on-one or in small groups is a far cry from the authoritarian, sometimes adversarial, role of the conventional instructor. Promoting changes in the instructor's view of the learning environment and his or her role in it involves both selection and training.

Training is important because instructors must learn new behaviors that are appropriate to the PSI environment, such as interacting one-on-one with students (as opposed to lecturing) and prompting students for more information (as opposed to giving it). Much as proctors in PSI need to be trained in the execution of these skills, so do instructors.

As might be imagined, in a system in which the instructor is a facilitator rather than a highly visible authoritarian figure, there is the potential for abuse. One potential abuse is the "disappearing act," in which the instructor disappears from the classroom. In many instances this has happened, and the system loses in the process. It does not take much imagination to see how this "freedom" could be abused. Finally, it may be helpful for instructors to give occasional lectures as a way to maintain visibility in the classroom for both students and colleagues.

It is controversial to pay tutors with course credit to provide instructional services.   A fourth way PSI differs from conventional instruction is in the use of more advanced students to tutor less advanced students. Proctors (tutors) are typically students from a previous term who have mastered the course content and who return to serve as course tutors (frequently called "external" proctors). The immediate problem is how to pay them. For some instructors, they are part of the course budget, but this appears to be rare. Most instructors "pay" tutors with course credit. Typically, this occurs in the form of a course or seminar for tutors (Sherman, 1974). On a theoretical level, it is difficult to justify giving proctors course credit for content they have already mastered, even if they learn it more thoroughly (Semb *et al.*, 1993). Furthermore, it seems contradictory to give students course credit for tutoring, particularly when *they* must, in turn, *pay* for those credits. This argument, too, has merit, especially when tutoring involves a large number of administrative tasks in addition to tutoring. On the other hand, proctoring involves a complex set of tutoring skills (Fitch & Semb, in press). Furthermore, these skills must typically be trained, and such training has academic merit. In our proctor seminar, we not only teach tutoring skills but also the theory behind PSI, as well as several aspects of instructional design and delivery. Still, there are critics who question the academic merits of proctoring.

In fact, as of early 1995, the Committee on Undergraduate Services and Advising (CUSA) at the University of Kansas has banned *all* courses in which course credit is awarded for *any* type of tutoring. CUSA imposed this ban because they view the awarding of course credit for tutoring as a conflict of interest with the mission of the University. That is, students cannot earn credit in a course in which they provide administrative and/or instructional services. While we intend to vigorously fight this ban, there are other avenues to pursue.

Internal proctors. One option is the use of internal proctors. Sherman (1974) was the first to propose this permutation on the system. We have used it in our course at Kansas for several semesters, but we have never been happy with the outcome. For one thing, unless students are trained in tutoring skills, internal proctoring is not of very high quality. We have found that internal proctors do not do much more than grade quizzes and provide right/ wrong knowledge of results. Furthermore, whereas Sherman (1974) stated that students responded enthusiastically to the opportunity to proctor, our students did not, even when offered extra credit to do so. Finally, many of the people who volunteered to proctor were among the least well-prepared academically. I do not mean to discredit internal proctoring, for at some institutions and with some students, it works just fine. For example, in 1976 I used the system with great success at Georgetown University.

Computer-based solutions. Another option is to put a computer at the center of PSI to handle the administrative chores. During the past year, we have developed an integrated, on-line test management system.[7] It is a Windows application that allows instructors to create tests for delivery on-line over a network. Students can take tests on-line in the classroom or in a computer lab, and results from on-line activities are automatically posted to a powerful grade book program, one designed to handle the variety of contingencies found in the typical PSI course. What sets this program apart from many others is that the three separate, but related, functions—test generation, on-line presentation, and record-keeping—are fully integrated.

The Test Generation Program lets instructors create on-line tests, hard copy tests, or both. Instructors can select items individually, over a range of items, randomly, or while viewing items. The program fully supports graphics and multiple item types (e.g., multiple-choice, true-false, fill-in, essay, problems, and more). For some courses, it is also possible to select items on the basis of key concepts, item difficulty, and an item taxonomy (fact, recall, application, problem, etc.). Instructors can view tests on-screen before printing using a built-in word processor, or export the test to other file formats (e.g., Word, WordPerfect, or Rich Text Format).

The Grade Book Program can be used simultaneously with different books and/or courses. It can track up to 2000 students, and supports up to 200 instructor-defined activities per book or course. Designed as a spreadsheet, instructors can direct the on-line testing program to automatically post results to the Grade Book, or they can manually enter (or import) data from other sources (e.g., rosters, a term paper, or a lab activity). The Grade Book has functions to post, store, sort, and calculate common statistics (e.g., mean, standard deviation, and frequency distribution). Furthermore, using one of the many formula functions, instructors can drop the lowest of several test scores, sum scores, and define IF statements (e.g., if the first score on a quiz with repeated attempts is greater than 100, award 10 bonus points). Finally, the instructor can define cut-off points and the program will automatically assign grades and calculate a grade distribution.

The On-Line Presentation Manager promotes greater individualization and flexibility. It also reduces opportunities for cheating. Its primary function, however, is to present tests on-line over a network, or on individual computers. It supports practice exercises (e.g., self-study quizzes), repeated testing, and highly secured exams (e.g., midterms and finals). In conjunction with the Grade Book Program, the instructor controls: (1) the order of tests and exercises, (2) whether feedback occurs after every item or at the end of the exam, (3) whether results are printed out, and in what form, and (4) how much each test or exercise counts. In our computerized PSI class at the University of Kansas, students receive a printed output listing the questions they have missed. They take this output to their proctor for tutoring. After they have remediated incorrect answers, they can either re-take the quiz to improve their score, or move on to the next unit.

The program has worked flawlessly for the past year in several sections of our introductory child psychology course at the University of Kansas.[8] We fully expect it to handle the majority of our 600+ students per semester. We are waiting for budget allocations to determine how many work stations we can afford. In the meantime, this program has allowed us to fully automate the administrative functions of the PSI classroom. This is no trivial accomplishment because proctors in the past spent roughly fifty percent of their time performing these tasks. Furthermore, proctors can now spend almost *all* of their available class time tutoring. Thus, we expect to reduce the number of tutors needed by at least half. Furthermore, as we build more remedial exercises for the computer, the need for tutors will be reduced even further. While it may appear "impersonal" to replace tutors with computers, it also can be argued that human tutors should be saved for the difficult exercises that the computer cannot handle.

Section Summary. Confusion with individualized instruction, accusations of inferior materials and low-level objectives, a major change in the role of the instructor, and paying student proctors with course credits have all raised serious political issues. Some of these have led to instructors abandoning, or being forced to abandon, PSI. Yet, there have been, and continue to be, successful applications of the technology.

One regret I have is that PSI has not taken advantage of recent advances in instructional design technology. PSI researchers and practitioners have assumed that design will take care of itself. However, this is clearly *not* the case—design, like every thing else, must be thoughtfully planned and executed. On the other hand, PSI is a superb delivery system. Contemporary approaches to design technology such as anchored instruction, situated cognition, and cognitive apprenticeships could learn a great deal from PSI about how to deliver instruction.

Conclusion

PSI works. It is a win/win system in which students learn a lot and proctors (tutors) learn even more. The unit-perfection requirement insures that students do not engage in more advanced material until prerequisite material has been mastered. Course materials are carefully designed, making lectures an obsolete way to deliver content. Students work to meet the unit perfection requirement at their own rate. Evaluation occurs frequently and insures that students know where they are going. Proctors make it all happen by providing one-on-one instruction and individual encouragement. Research clearly supports the overall system and the inclusion of most of its components, the use of the lecture being the most questionable. Confusion with individualized instruction, accusations of inferior materials and low-level objectives, a change in the role of the instructor, and paying student proctors with course credit have all raised political issues. These have led some instructors to to abandon PSI. Yet, there have been, and continue to be, successful applications of the technology, especially in the area of computer-based, integrated, on-line test management systems. I, for one, would not do it any differently.

Notes

1. *The PSI Handbook: Essays on Personalized Instruction,* by Fred S. Keller and J. Gilmour Sherman, was first published in 1974. It was reprinted in 1982, and a limited number of copies are still available from Trilogy Systems, Inc., 8020 Monrovia, Lenexa, KS 66215-2727. A related book, *The Personalized System of Instruction: 48 Seminal Papers,* edited by Sherman, Ruskin, and Semb (1982), is also available from the same source. The latter title includes several articles from out-of-print series such as the *Journal of Personalized Instruction* and various PSI conference proceedings. Finally, *The Personalized System of Instruction,* by Sherman and Ruskin, a volume in the Instructional Design Library (1978), is available from Educational Technology Publications, Englewood Cliffs, NJ 07632.
2. During most semesters, there were 12 to 16 PSI sections, and two lecture sections were taught using a Learning-for-Mastery model (Bloom, 1968).
3. I have never liked the term "proctor." It conjures up an image of someone who watches students while they are taking a test. Webster defines a proctor as "one who is employed to manage the af-

fairs of another; a steward; a proxy." With respect to academic institutions, Webster elaborates further by defining a proctor as "an officer in a university or college who enforces order and obedience." The proctor's role in PSI is much more that of a tutor or coach, someone who works one-on-one with the student, and for that reason, we typically call them tutors (Fitch & Semb, in press).

4. Tests are common in most academic courses, but in more skill-based applications, evaluation might be conducted on how well a learner can perform a task such shooting free throws or performing an accelerated stall.

5. In April 1974, some of us shared the stage with Bloom and other mastery proponents at a meeting of the American Educational Research Association in Chicago, IL.

6. This is a great quote. Ogden Lindsey told it to me, but he doesn't know the source.

7. For more details about this integrated, on-line test management system, contact George Semb, Department of Human Development—4056 Dole, University of Kansas, Lawrence, Kansas 66045-2133. Phone: (913) 864-0521 (o), (913) 492-4541 (h), (913) 492-4549 (fax), or e-mail (semb@falcon.cc. ukans.edu).

8. The system has also been field tested with other courses at several other sites.

References

Ainsworth, L. L. (1979). Self-paced instruction: An innovation that failed. *Teaching of Psychology, 6*, 42–46.

Arp, L., & Semb, G. (1977). An analysis of the use of student proctors in a personalized college business course. *Journal of Personalized Instruction, 2*, 92–95.

Barton, E. J., & Ascione, F. R. (1978). The proctoring component of personalized instruction: A help or hindrance? *Journal of Personalized Instruction, 1*, 15–22.

Bloom, B. S. (1968). Learning for mastery. *Evaluation Comment, 1*(2). Los Angeles: University of California at Los Angeles, Center for the Study of Evaluation of Instructional Programs.

Bloom, B. S. (1976). *Human characteristics and school learning.* New York: McGraw-Hill.

Born, D. G. (1970). *Proctor Manual: Initial Draft.* Unpublished manuscript. University of Utah, Center to Improve Learning and Instruction.

Born, D. G. (1975). Exam performance and study behavior as a function of study unit size. In J. M. Johnston (Ed.), *Research and technology in higher education* (pp. 269–282). Springfield, IL: Charles C. Thomas.

Born, D. G., Gledhill, S. M., & Davis, M. L. (1972). Examination performance in lecture-discussion and personalized instruction courses. *Journal of Applied Behavior Analysis, 5*, 33–43.

Born, D. G., & Moore, M. C. (1978). Some belated thoughts on pacing. *Journal of Personalized Instruction, 3*, 155–158.

Brown, J. S., Collins, A., & Duguid, P. (1989). Situated cognition and the culture of learning. *Educational Researcher, 18*(1), 32–42.

Buskist, W., Cush, D., & DeGrandpre, R. L. (1991). The life and times of PSI. *Journal of Behavioral Education, 1*, 215–234.

Caldwell, E. C., Bissonnette, K., Klishis, M. J., Ripley, M., Farudi, P. P., Hochstetter, G. T., & Radiker, J. E. (1978). Mastery: The essential essential in PSI. *Teaching of Psychology, 5*, 59–65.

Calhoun, J. F. (1976). The combination of elements in the personalized system of instruction. *Teaching of Psychology, 2*, 73–76.

Carroll, J. B. (1963). A model of school learning. *Teachers College Record, 64*, 723–733.

Carsrud, A. L. (1979). Undergraduate tutors: Are they useful? *Teaching of Psychology, 6*, 46–48.

Cognition and Technology Group at Vanderbilt (1990). Advanced instruction and its relation to cognition. *Educational Researcher, 19*(6), 2–10.

Collins, A., Brown, J. S., & Newman, S. E. (1989). Cognitive apprenticeship: Teaching the crafts of reading, writing, and mathematics. In L. B. Resnick (Ed.), *Knowing, learning, and instruction: Essays in honor of Robert Glaser* (pp. 453–494). Hillsdale, NJ: Lawrence Erlbaum Associates.

Corey, J. R., & McMichael, J. S. (1974). Retention in a PSI introductory psychology course. In J. G. Sherman (Ed.), *Personalized System of Instruction: 41 germinal papers* (pp. 17–19). Menlo Park, CA: Benjamin.

Cross, K. P. (1993). On college teaching. *Journal of Engineering Education, 82*(1), 9–14.

Cross, M. Z., & Semb, G. (1976). An analysis of the effects of personalized instruction on students at different performance levels in an introductory college nutrition course. *Journal of Personalized Instruction, 1,* 47–51.

Edwards, A. K. (1977). Attendance at lectures and films in a self-paced course. *Journal of Personalized Instruction, 2,* 35–38.

Ellis, J. A., & Wulfeck, W. H. (1988). Computer-managed self-paced instruction in Navy technical training: Problems in implementation. Presented at the American Educational Research Association, New Orleans, LA.

Fantuzzo, J. W., Dimeff, L. A., & Fox, S. L. (1989). Reciprocal peer tutoring: A multimodal assessment of effectiveness with college students. *Teaching of Psychology, 16,* 133–135.

Farmer, J., Lachter, G. D., Blaustein, J. J., & Cole, B. K. (1972). The role of proctoring in personalized instruction. *Journal of Applied Behavior Analysis, 5,* 401–404.

Fernald, P. S., Chiseri, M. J., Lawson, D. W., Scroggs, G. F., & Riddell, J. C. (1975). Systematic manipulation of student pacing, the perfection requirement, and contact with a teaching assistant in an introductory psychology course. *Teaching of Psychology, 2,* 147–151.

Fitch, M. A., & Semb, G. B. (1992, April). Peer teacher training: A comparison of role playing and video evaluation for effects on peer teacher outcomes. Paper presented at the meeting of the American Educational Research Association, San Francisco, CA.

Fitch, M. A., & Semb, G. B. (in press). Peer-tutoring: Theory and research. *Review of Educational Research.*

Glick, D. M. (1978). If there is a pacing problem in PSI, will we recognize it when we see it? *Journal of Personalized Instruction, 3,* 158–161.

Glick, D. M., & Semb, G. (1978). Effects of pacing contingencies in personalized instruction: A review of the evidence. *Journal of Personalized Instruction, 3,* 86–91.

Hoberok, L. L., Koen, B. V., Roth, C. H., & Wagner, G. R. (1972). Theory of PSI evaluated for engineering education. *IEEE Transaction on Education, 15,* 18–24.

Hursh, D. E. (1976). Personalized systems of instruction: What do the data indicate? *Journal of Personalized Instruction, 2,* 91–105.

Hursh, D. E., Wildgen, J., Minkin, B., Minkin, N., Sherman, J. A., & Wolf, M. M. (1975). Proctors' discussions of students' quiz performance with students. In J. M. Johnston & G. W. O'Neil (Eds.), *Behavior Research and Technology in Higher Education* (pp. 159–167). Springfield, IL: Charles C. Thomas.

Johnson, K. R., & Sulzer-Azaroff, B. (1975). The effects of different proctoring systems upon student examination performance and preference. In J. M. Johnston & G. W. O'Neil (Eds.). *Research and Technology in Higher Education* (pp. 159–185). Springfield, IL: Charles C. Thomas.

Johnston, J. M., & O'Neil, G. (1973). The analysis of performance criteria defining course grades as a determinant of college student academic performance. *Journal of Applied Behavior Analysis, 6,* 261–268.

Kaestle, C. F. (1973). *Joseph Lancaster and the Monitorial School Movement: A documentary history.* New York: Teachers College Press.

Keller, F. S. (1968). Good-bye, teacher. *Journal of Applied Behavior Analysis, 1,* 79–89.

Keller, F. S., & Sherman, J. G. (1974). *The PSI handbook: Essays on personalized instruction.* Lenexa, KS: Trilogy Systems, Inc.

Kulik, J. A., Jaska, P., & Kulik, C. C. (1978). Research on component features of Keller's Personalized System of Instruction. *Journal of Personalized Instruction, 3,* 129–141.

Kulik, J. A., Kulik, C. C., & Bangert-Drowns, R. L. (1990). Effectiveness of mastery learning programs: A meta-analysis. *Review of Educational Research, 60,* 265–299.

Kulik, J. A., Kulik, C. C., & Cohen, P. A. (1979). A meta-analysis of outcome studies of Keller's Personalized System of Instruction. *American Psychologist, 4,* 307–318.

Kuti, M. B., Hinton, J. A., Fitch, M. A., & Semb, G. B. (1992, April). Training peer tutors: The effects of video training and live role-playing. Paper presented at the meeting of the American Educational Research Association, San Francisco, CA.

Lloyd, K. E., Garlington, W. K., Lowry, D., Burgess, H., Euler, H. A., & Knowlton, W. R. (1972). A note on some reinforcing properties of university lectures. *Journal of Applied Behavior Analysis, 5,* 151–155.

Meek, R. L. (1977). The traditional in non-traditional learning methods. *Journal of Personalized Instruction, 2,* 114–118.

Miller, L. K., Weaver, F. H., & Semb, G. B. (1974). A procedure for maintaining student progress in a personalized university course. *Journal of Applied Behavior Analysis, 7,* 87–91.

Morris, C. J., & Kimbrell, G. McA. (1977). Individual differences and PSI: A reanalysis. *Journal of Personalized Instruction, 2,* 47–49.

Orlansky, J., & String, J. (1981). Computer-based instruction for military training. *Defense Management Journal,* 1981, 46–54.

Palincsar, A. S., & Brown, A. L. (1984). Reciprocal teaching of comprehension-fostering and comprehension-monitoring activities. *Cognition and Instruction, 1*(2), 117–175.

Palincsar, A. S., Brown, A. L., & Martin, S. M. (1987). Peer interaction in reading comprehension instruction. *Educational Psychologist, 22*(3 & 4), 231–253.

Parsons, J. A., & Delaney, H. D. (1978). Effects of unit-quiz mastery criteria on student performance. *Journal of Personalized Instruction, 3,* 225–228.

Reboy, L. R., & Semb, G. (1991). PSI and critical thinking: Compatibility or irreconcilable differences? *Teaching of Psychology, 18,* 212–215.

Roberts, M. S., Fulton, M., & Semb, G. (1988). Self-pacing in a personalized psychology course: Letting students set the deadlines. *Teaching of Psychology, 15,* 89–92.

Roberts, M. S., & Semb, G. (1980). Daily testing: a consequence for not meeting deadlines in a PSI course. *Journal of Personalized Instruction, 4,* 67–69.

Roberts, M. S., & Semb, G. B. (1989). Student selection of deadline conditions in a personalized psychology course. *Teaching of Psychology, 16,* 128–130.

Schmidt, R. A., & Bjork, R. A. (1992). New conceptualization of practice: Common principles in three paradigms suggest new concepts for training. *Psychological Science, 3*(4), 207–217.

Semb, G. (1974). The effects of mastery criteria and assignment length on college-student test performance. *Journal of Applied Behavior Analysis, 7,* 61–69.

Semb, G., Conyers, D., Spencer, R., & Sanchez-Sosa, J. J. (1975). An experimental comparison of four pacing contingencies. In J. M. Johnston (Ed.), *Behavior research and technology in higher education* (pp. 348–368). Springfield, IL: Charles C. Thomas.

Semb, G. B., & Ellis, J. A. (1994). Knowledge learned in school: What is remembered? *Review of Educational Research, 64,* 253–286.

Semb, G. B., Ellis, J. A. *et al.* (1993). Long-term memory for knowledge learned in school. *Journal of Educational Psychology, 85,* 305–316.

Semb, G. B., Ellis, J. A., Montague, W. E., & Wulfeck, W. H. (1992). Self-paced instruction: Perceptions, pitfalls, and potentials. In T. M. Schlechter (Ed.), *Problems and promises of computer-based training.* Norwood, NJ: Ablex Publishing.

Semb, G., Hopkins, B. L., & Hursh, D. E. (1973). The effects of study questions and grades on student test performance in a college course. *Journal of Applied Behavior Analysis, 6,* 631–642.

Semb, G., & Spencer, R. (1976). Beyond the level of recall: An analysis of complex educational tasks in college and university instruction. In L. E. Fraley & E. A. Vargas (Eds.), *Behavior research and technology in college and university instruction* (pp. 115–126). Gainesville, FL: Department of Psychology, University of Florida.

Semb, G., Spencer, R. E., & Phillips, T. W. (1976). The use of review units in a personalized university course. In B. A. Green (Ed.), *Personalized instruction in higher education* (pp. 140–145). Washington, DC: Center for Personalized Instruction, Georgetown University.

Semb, G. B., & Taylor, D. E. (1993). *Study guide for an invitation to fly* (4th ed.). Belmont, CA: Wadsworth.

Sherman, J. G. (1974). A permutation on an innovation. In J. G. Sherman (Ed.), *Personalized System of Instruction: 41 germinal papers* (pp. 163–166). Menlo Park, CA: W. A. Benjamin.

Sherman, J. G. (1977, September). Individualizing instruction is not enough. *Educational Technology, 17*(9), 326–330.

Sherman, J. G. (1992). Reflections on PSI: Good news and bad. *Journal of Applied Behavior Analysis, 25,* 59–64.

Sherman, J. G., & Ruskin, R. S. (1978). *The Personalized System of Instruction.* Englewood Cliffs, NJ: Educational Technology Publications.

Smith, H. W. (1987). Comparative evaluation of three teaching methods of quantitative techniques: Traditional lecture, Socratic dialogue, and PSI format. *Journal of Experimental Education, 55,* 149–154.

22

Direct Instruction

Siegfried Engelmann
University of Oregon, Eugene

Introduction

The designation *"Direct Instruction"* has different meanings in the educational field. For some it means merely direct teaching, as opposed to facilitating, or setting the stage for learning. A more specific meaning is expressed by behavioral checklists of teacher and student behaviors. Rosenshine (1983) and others (Stallings, 1973) have proposed checklists that refer to time on task, number of tasks per minute, and other measurable features of the presentation. Within this context, interactions would be classified as "direct instruction" if they involved oral responses, possibly scripted presentations, the students engaged in tasks a high percentage of the available time, and similar features.

The notion of Direct Instruction referred to in the present chapter is more specific than either direct teaching or the criteria suggested by Rosenshine. This version of direct instruction was first described as *direct verbal instruction* by Bereiter and Engelmann (1966) and has been subsequently incorporated in demonstrations and instructional programs designed by Engelmann and his colleagues. These applications are characterized by all the details referred to in the various checklists of "Direct Instruction." They also contain several important features that are not implied by these checklists:

1. The sequence of tasks specified for the teaching of a particular skill has been both modified and validated through field tryouts with learners and teachers.
2. The design is based on analytical procedures that permit construction of sequences that predictably will teach learners the targeted skills.
3. Analytical procedures have been used to design teaching sequences that span a wide range of learning—from simple motor responses to advanced math and history, and higher-order thinking skills.
4. The procedures and the design are mobilized to (a) teach all of the content that is required for a particular outcome (including all the generations that are implied) and (b) teach nothing that is not implied by the outcomes or by logically associated outcomes.

371

5. The procedures take into account and are consistent with facts about learning—memory, fatigue, and rate phenomena.
6. The programs that are developed according to this formulation are designed to teach all students who meet the entrance criteria for the program, and to teach them at a relatively accelerated rate.

Bateman (1992) refers to the difference between Engelmann's version of direct instruction as "upper-case DI" and the less specific version as "lower-case di." The main difference between the two designations is that DI accounts for more details that are relevant to the details of the teaching presentations, specifically the curricular details.

A basic assumption of DI is that the teaching must accelerate learning. Acceleration is possible only if the delivery system is able to teach more than the learner would be expected to learn in a particular time span. Since the major details of what is taught are governed by the curricular sequence—what is taught and how it is taught and tested—effective teaching is not uniformly possible without an effective sequence for presenting the content.

The history of this notion of direct instruction began with the teaching of naive children (Engelmann, 1962). The initial demonstrations were designed to show something of the limits that could be achieved through instruction. The skills that were taught to four-year-olds were considered beyond the ken or developmental level of young children. Topics included sophisticated math and logical problems that required formal operations. Later studies extended the work to teaching deaf to "hear" through tactual vibrations, teaching absolute pitch to children in first grade, teaching skills to head-injured subjects, and modifying behaviors of severely antisocial and noncompliant subjects (Engelmann & Colvin, 1983).

In addition to these "limit setting" demonstrations, Becker (1977), Carnine, and others worked with Engelmann on projects involving school-age children. As part of this work, the investigators developed more than 50 instructional programs. The content ranges from beginning reading, math, and language to earth science, and beginning chemistry. Some programs target the corrective reader and the older student who is deficient in math.

Many of the instructional programs have been involved in comparative studies. The largest comparison made between DI and other approaches was Follow Through, which was designed to determine which instructional approaches were effective with disadvantaged children in grades kindergarten through 3 (Abt Associates, 1977). Thirteen major sponsors, representing the full range of "prejudices" about how to combat the effects of poverty on school performance, worked with different cooperating school districts. The sponsor with the most consistent record across different ethnic types, neighborhood types and subjects, was the DI model. This model took first place in teaching basic skills, in higher-order skills, in all academic subjects—language, math, and reading—and in inducing the most positive self-images among the children (Abt Associates, 1977).

The DI approach has been subjected to many other comparisons and analyses. The book *Theory of Instruction*, by Engelmann and Carnine (1982), articulates the theoretical basis and assumptions of direct instruction. It also summarizes some of the studies that Carnine has conducted to verify the efficacy of the different principles and procedures that are incorporated in DI programs. These include studies on the effects of faster pacing, of different patterns of positive and negative examples, and of predicted generalizations following different types of initial teaching. Virtually every assumption and principle of DI has been the focus of empirical investigations, and all have been supported by the outcomes of these studies.

The Need for Logical Analysis

Although a DI classroom may give an observer the impression that the children are engaged in oral, rote recitation, they are actually following a sequence of tasks that unfolds slowly, combining simpler skills into more complex algorithms that arm children with generalized skills for solving problems of increasing sophistication. The analysis that generates this sometimes invisible pathway is the first step in the development of a DI program. This analysis of the content takes a great deal of time, primarily because it does not automatically accept the traditional ways of teaching a particular topic or subject. Rather, it starts with the assumption that only the desired outcomes are "given." The details of how these outcomes are to be achieved are negotiable, and if greater gains are to be achieved with the range of students who enter the program, inventions are needed. The content must be rearranged and packaged in a way that permits faster, more uniform learning. If the content is presented in a traditional manner, the only way greater gains are possible is to use more "muscle" (increased time on task, homework, motivational hype, and extensive remedial work). DI assumes that greater gains imply a reordering of the content.

The approach also makes assumptions about the learner. The learner is assumed to behave lawfully, which means broadly that the learner will learn to respond differently to particular properties or discriminative stimuli. In other words, the learner who received sufficient practice will learn what is taught. If the teaching shows the learner how to respond and shows the conditions that control this particular type of response, the learner will learn. The problem that frequently occurs in a traditional instructional scene is that the learner may learn something quite different from what the teacher intends to teach. Merely because the teacher intends to teach the naive learner a new concept does not mean that the communication the learner receives is sufficiently precise to induce this concept.

The problem is one of ambiguity. The teacher presents information and examples that are consistent with the intended concept. However, the presentation is also consistent with one or more unintended concepts. The learner will learn something that is consistent with the presentation; however, learning the unintended concepts is possible, which means that a percentage of learners will predictably learn unintended interpretations.

Let's say the task is to teach the learner the concept of "triangle shape." During the initial instruction, the learner is to respond one way to triangular shapes and a different way to other shapes. Let's say that all the triangles the teacher presents to teach this discrimination are blue and none of the other shapes are blue. The learner is now in a position of being able to respond correctly to the directions, "Touch the triangles," but has not learned to discriminate between triangles and not-triangles. Furthermore, an observer who sees the learner responding correctly to every task the teacher presents would have no way of knowing what the learner has learned and whether the learner is responding to the blueness of the positive examples or to the triangularity of these examples.

This situation has all the properties of more involved instructional problems:

1. The teacher is unaware of the possibility that the learner could learn something other than what is intended (and interprets the learner's correct responses to mean that the learner has learned the concept of triangle).
2. Not all learners who are put through the flawed sequence learn the same thing because there are different logical possibilities. The major possibilities are: (a) the learner learns to identify triangles regardless of color; (b) the learner learns to respond to blue objects, regardless of their shape; (c) the learner learns to respond to objects that are blue and triangular in shape.

Although this scenario is incredible, it is common. The teacher apparently assumes that the learner will learn what the teacher intends to teach. This implies that the learner is capable of performing feats that are supernatural—somehow reading the teacher's mind and knowing which of the possibilities exhibited by the presentation is the preferred one.

The problem with the instruction may be ascertained logically or experimentally. Identifying the problem logically does not involve working with learners or securing responses of any sort. It involves simply examining the program and noting all the *samenesses* that are shared by all the positive examples but by none of the negative examples. In the instance above, all positive examples (examples that are labeled *triangle*) have two features that are shared by none of the negative examples: the three-sidedness and the blueness. These qualities identify the only possible bases that a learner would have for learning "triangle" from the set of examples the teacher presents.

The advantage of the logical analysis is that it can be conducted without reference to the type or the use of the learners and is therefore a powerful tool for the program developer. It provides the developer with a devil's-advocate test of instructional strategies. After laying out the proposed sequence, the developer can examine the unique samenesses shared by the positive examples and determine whether a learner going through the sequence would be forced to attend to relevant features of the examples, or whether the design has unwittingly created options—examples that share an unintended sameness that could permit a learner to respond correctly to the positive examples without attending to their relevant features.

This analysis does not assume that the learner will learn what is intended, merely that *the presentation offers possibilities*. If a particular feature is present every time the teacher labels an example as "triangle," and is not present when the teacher indicates that the example is not a triangle, the feature is a possibility. The learner may use that possibility as the basis for judging whether an example is a triangle or not. If a possibility is present, learners will learn it. It is, after all, quite as real as any other possibility generated by the presentation of examples. Clearly, a presentation that generates more than one possibility is an inferior presentation and will create mislearning or confusion in at least some learners.

To identify the problem with the triangle sequence experimentally, we would present a test of "generalization" to ascertain the learner's basis for identifying things as triangles. This test would consist of examples that did not appear in the initial teaching set; various geometric forms, including those that are very similar to triangles (triangular shapes with rounded corners, for example, or three-dimensional pyramid shapes). The set could also include triangles in various spatial orientations and in different colors.

The learner's responses to the various items would show relatively precisely what the learner "thinks" is necessary for something to be labeled as a triangle. Note that this "thinking" is not necessarily conscious and certainly not "verbal." It is, however, revealed behaviorally. If the learner responds correctly to all the triangles regardless of color or position, the learner has learned the intended meaning. If the learner correctly identifies triangles that are blue but no other triangles and no other blue objects, the learner has learned that "triangle" means a blue object with a triangular shape.

The assumption of the DI analysis is that *the generalization has already been learned* during the initial teaching and that the learning of the generalization is necessary for the learner to perform on the initial set of teaching examples. This treatment of generalization differs from the classical notion that first something is learned, then it is generalized. Unless the learner identifies (either consciously or unconsciously) a feature that serves as the basis for identifying things as triangles, it is highly unlikely that the learner could correctly perform on the examples presented in the initial-teaching set of examples. Most probably the learner has learned some sort of "rule" about what triangles are. The learner simply applies this rule to new examples in the generalization set.

The prediction is that if the initial teaching set eliminates possible false interpretations or rules, the learner's generalization performance will reflect this difference. For instance, a possible misinterpretation is that something is a triangle only if it is a particular size. This interpretation would be possible in a teaching set that had lots of objects labeled as triangles, all these objects were the same size, and no negative examples were the same size.

The possibility that the label "triangle" involves size is contradicted several different ways. One is a teaching set that varies the size of the objects that are labeled as triangles. If different-sized objects are called "triangles," the label cannot refer to an object of a particular size. The learner who went through a teaching set in which size is varied would generalize to triangles of sizes other than those shown in the teaching set. This generalization is categorically predicted. If all examples in the teaching set were the same size, the set provides the learner with an option. The learner could reasonably assume that it's a triangle only if it's the same size as the triangles shown in the teaching set. Or the learner could assume that triangles are like other objects the learner is familiar with and therefore include size variations other than those shown in the teaching set. Both possibilities are perfectly consistent with the information conveyed by the initial teaching; therefore, both describe a possible pattern of generalization.

Designing tests of generalization implies the same logical analysis that is used to determine the basis for the learner's response to examples of "triangle." The pattern of generalization depends on the teaching set. If all triangles presented to the learner during teaching have a point at the top and a horizontal base, some learners would be expected to identify rotated triangles as not-triangles. If all of the triangles were equilateral, some of the learners would be expected to identify non-equilateral triangles as not-triangles. If the only *negative* examples of triangles presented during the teaching were circles, some learners would be expected to identify squares or rectangles as triangles (given that these learners had no prior knowledge of how to classify these objects). By analyzing the teaching examples, a designer is able to make accurate predictions about the performance of the learner with examples that are not included in the training set (Horner & Albin, 1988).

In summary, the logical analysis of the teaching examples in a sequence simply articulates the possibilities, that is, the different interpretations that are consistent with the examples presented and the information provided about these examples. The assumption is that if there is more than one possibility, different learners will generalize in different ways. All generalizations will be consistent with the set of teaching examples; however, different learners will select different possibilities. If the teaching set generates only one possibility (not more than one), the analytical assumption is that there's only one basis for generalization, and all learners will generalize the same way following successful completion of the teaching set. These analytical assumptions are confirmed by experimental data. The business of designing effective instruction is therefore largely a logical game. If the set of examples used to teach "triangle" contradicts the various undesired generalizations, all learners who meet the entrance criteria for going through the program (basic following-directions skills and language skills) would learn "triangle" and would generalize appropriately.

The first items in this set might teach the basic features of triangles. All the examples presented to the learner—triangle and not-triangle—would be the same color and roughly the same size. This set contradicts the possibility that triangles have a unique color or size. (If both triangles and non-triangles are the same size, size cannot be a basis for discriminating between the triangles and not-triangles.) The negative examples in this set would be rectangles, circles, and possibly triangular shaped objects with slightly curved sides or curved corners. If these are presented, they would be shown dynamically by converting a triangle into a non-triangle by rounding the corners. "Now, it's a triangle. Watch . . . Now, it's not a triangle." Following the demonstration examples in this set would be "test examples," a variety of triangles and non-triangles that vary in spatial orientation, size and color.

A second group of teaching examples would show the difference between three-dimensional and two-dimensional objects. The negative examples would consist of triangular prisms and pyramids. The positive examples would be triangles that are the same size as the three-dimensional objects. A learner would successfully complete the lesson by successfully identifying so many consecutive objects as either triangle or not-triangle. ("Tell me *triangle* or *no* for each thing I point to.")

Specifying so much detail about the teaching of something like triangle may seem to be a pedantic exercise that has little point. After all, naive learners learn to discriminate between triangles without going through such elaborate programs. Why, therefore, would anybody bother with such detail? The answer is: Teaching the concept of triangle through examples is a microcosm of teaching concepts that are much more sophisticated. Although the concept of triangle can be taught more easily by using a verbal rule: *It's flat and it's got three straight sides,* presenting the same information through examples shows the information that is conveyed by the verbal rule—both the number and type of examples that would be needed to convey the details implied by this rule. The triangle example also shows a model of the steps involved in designing sequences that will teach complicated skills.

Instructional Programs

The obvious advantages of a well-designed teaching set would seem to lead to the conclusion that instructional programs used by teachers should first be analyzed for possible mislearning that might be induced by an inappropriate set of examples or ambiguous explanations. If the teacher uses material that is logically capable of inducing inappropriate generalizations or concepts, the material will retard the performance of some learners and it will require the teacher to deviate from the "program" in order to correct student mistakes (modifying the set of examples so that it contradicts the inappropriate aspects of the initial set). If this remedy is not provided on the level of the teacher, it will not occur, and the mistake or misinterpretation may go unnoticed.

A program that has explanations and example sets that are relatively unambiguous provides the teacher with much better information about the lawfulness of the learners who go through the instructional sequence. Some instructional sequences, however, are very complicated and do not lend themselves to a precise analysis of whether the activities are consistent with more than one interpretation. The difficulty of providing a logical analysis of all the details of a well-designed program for teaching third-grade arithmetic, for instance, becomes overwhelming because on a given lesson, material may be reviewed, new concepts may be introduced, and earlier-taught operations may be expanded. Analysis of the communications permits the designer to identify some possible problems, but analysis of other details of the program becomes complicated. An easier way to find out about the adequacy of the program is to subject it to a field tryout, during which data are recorded and *mistake patterns* are identified. A pattern is revealed when more than one or two students make the same sort of mistake. The mistake pattern implies that either the teaching implied more than one possible "interpretation" or the amount of practice provided by the program was inadequate to induce mastery. If a misinterpretation is implied, the remedy is to re-do the teaching so it provides a contradiction to the inappropriate responses.

Although these steps are reasonable, they are rarely followed and are not required in the development of commercial programs. A very small percentage of commercial programs used for the initial teaching of reading, arithmetic, or other skills in the elementary grades has either been analyzed for possible misinterpretations or tried out with a single teacher or learner before publication (Watson *et al.,* 1987). Furthermore, these programs are often replete with faulty sequences. For example, in traditional grade-one arithmetic sequences, fact learning may introduce and repeatedly present the problems in this order:

0 + 1   1 + 1   2 + 1   3 + 1   4 + 1   5 + 1.

Students may respond perfectly; however, their responses do not mean that they know any of these facts. Students may simply be applying a rule that the answers are the counting numbers: *1, 2, 3, 4, 5, 6, . . .* This interpretation is consistent with the presentation. What students learn could be disclosed by presenting the problems in a different order (which is what sometimes happens on the test that follows the unit on addition and completely confuses the teachers because they had assumed that their students were doing well).

The initial work with fractions in many commercial programs induces mislearning. These programs provide three fractions: *1/2, 1/3, 1/4.* Students select the picture for the fraction shown, complete pie diagrams, and write fractions from pie diagrams. The apparent logic behind this sequence is that students should start with simple examples and work up to more difficult ones. The fractions presented have the smallest possible numbers—1 in the numerator and 2, 3, 4 in the denominator. The problem induced by this work is a very serious misleading of the learner. A logical principle is that if we work on a very narrow range of examples, we'll imply that the sameness shown by these examples is a universal sameness. This principle (referred to as *stipulation*) suggests that the more exposure we provide to the narrow set of examples, the more difficult it will be for the learner to generalize to examples that fall outside the range of examples presented. All examples of fractions the learner encounters have a numerator of 1, all translate into a picture that has one part used, all fractions are less than one whole. It would be possible for a learner to perform appropriately on all the tasks presented in the traditional sequence by attending *only to the denominator of the fraction* and following the rule, "If it's 4, look for the group that has four parts, or make four parts." The enduring misinformation that derives from this teaching is observed in the repertoire of many adults (and many teachers) who believe that fractions are less than one. They failed to learn the fundamental notion that the divisions on the number line may be less than one, but the value of the fraction may be less than one or more than 3000. (Teachers may also have strange ideas about the parts being equal-sized. This misunderstanding probably comes about from excessive work with diagrams rather than with other applications involving fractions, such as 3/4 of the people were men. [Are the men the same size as the other people?])

As noted earlier, the procedure for correcting any of these problems is to provide information that contradicts the possible misinterpretation. For the addition facts, we could contradict the inappropriate generalization by presenting the problems in a non-counting order: *2 + 1, 5 + 1, 1 + 1 . . .* This order of problems does not serve as a prompt for the correct answers; therefore, the learner is forced to attend to other features of the problems when responding to them.

The fraction misrules to be contradicted are: (a) fractions are less than 1; (b) the numerator of the fraction does not play a role in determining the picture of the fractions; and, (c) the picture always shows one part. Preempting the stipulation created by repeatedly presenting only three examples (all of which have 1 as the numerator) is achieved by introducing a wide range of fraction variation in the initial teaching sets. All the contradictions could be provided by introducing *a procedure for translating fractions* accompanied by a set of examples that shows a full range of fractions (those that are more than 1 and those that are less than 1).

> Here's a possible translation. Teacher: "The bottom number tells how many parts are in each whole unit; the top number tells how many parts you use (or color)."
> For 3/7: "How many parts are in each whole unit?" *7.*
> "How many parts do you use?" *3.*
> "Find the picture that shows 7 parts in each whole unit and 3 of those parts colored."
> For 6/4: "How many parts are in each whole unit?" *4.*
> "How many parts do you use?" *6.*
> "Make the picture. Show 4 parts in each unit. Color 6 parts."

By applying this translation to various fractions, the program provides a contradiction to all the possible misinterpretations generated by the inappropriate sequence.

Two principles of logical analysis are illustrated by the fraction example:

1. One contradicts a presentation that *stipulates* by presenting examples that *show sameness* across a wide range of variation.
2. To show how things are the *same,* present examples that are greatly *different* from each other and treat them in the *same way.*

To show that fractions encompass a full range of variation, arrange the juxtaposed examples so that the numbers in the fraction follow no pattern and the examples vary in whether the fraction is more than one, one, or less than one. By applying the same "paradigm" to them (first translating the denominator to indicate the number of parts in each unit; then referring to the numerator for the number of parts that are colored), students are required to respond to the sameness of the examples—fractions have two values. All bottom numbers tell about the divisions in the units. All top numbers tell about the parts that are used.

The traditional presentation of fractions (working with 1/2, 1/3 and 1/4) is based on the idea that the learners will proceed in a linear manner, first learning about fractions with a numerator of 1, then much later, possibly learning fractions that have a numerator of 2, then 3, and so forth. Later learning is assumed to require as much work as earlier learning. This is obviously not the case and is lavishly contradicted by the language behavior of children.

Logical Hierarchies

Much has been written about hierarchies and how they are related to learning (Gagné, 1985). The direct-instruction analysis holds simply that there are *logical* hierarchies based on *the component skills and concepts of specific tasks.* After students have learned to read simple directions, they have acquired a component skill that is necessary for tasks in which they follow written directions such as, "Go to the door . . . ," "Stand in front of the window . . . ," "Hold your hand over your head."

Students who are able to *decode the words accurately* have mastered another component skill needed for successful performance of the tasks. Because the following-directions tasks have more than one component, the ability to decode the words accurately does not guarantee successful performance; however, a categorical certainty is that *if* we choose to present written tasks that require following directions, we must teach the learner to decode *before* we present the tasks. The analysis does not suggest that these tasks have special developmental value, that they are salient with respect to some learning tendency, that they must be presented to the learner in a particular order, or that successful performance on these tasks is correlated with developmental tendencies (such as foot growth or counting ability). The identification of component skills suggests only a *possible cause of student failure.* The causes are expressed as a categorical logical necessity. The burden of proof for a counter interpretation would be on the protagonist, who would have to show how it would be logically possible for the learner to follow written directions without understanding the code for deciphering these directions. (Given that the learner can't interpret Morse code without training, why would conventional writing be any different?) We could also state with the categorical certainty that if the learner does not understand the meaning of the word *over* in the sentence, "Hold your hand over your head," the learner will fail the task and fail the set of following-directions tasks that use the word *over* in the positional sense.

The hierarchical analysis of activities is actually what some writers have referred to as task analysis (Markle & Tiemann, 1974). The task represents a possible performance goal for the teaching. The components of the task reveal the possible causes of failure. If the goal is to successfully teach the learner to respond to the targeted task (or set of tasks with the same features), each component represents a discrimination or operation to be taught to the learner before the target task is presented.

Generalizations and Limitations

The analysis of components shows the extent to which the learner would be capable of generalizing to the application and the extent to which additional skills and operations must be taught to ensure a generalization.

For instance, students learn to work equivalent-fraction problems of the form:

$$\frac{3}{4} = \frac{\square}{12}$$

After the students master a set of problems, their instructional program presents this problem:

If 3 out of 4 cars in the lot were clean and if there were 20 cars in the lot, how many of them were clean?

An analysis of the word problem reveals that the solution to the problem could be expressed as:

$$\frac{\textbf{clean cars}}{\textbf{all cars}} \quad \frac{3}{4} = \frac{\square}{20}$$

The traditional notion of generalization suggests that this type of word problem is a reasonable test of generalization. If the student knows how to work the equivalent-fraction problem, the ratio problem represents a generalization. Although some students who learn the mathematical manipulations will perform correctly on the ratio problem, this extension of the equivalent-fraction problem is not a legitimate test of generalization. This sort of generalization test is based on what the learner *might learn*, not what the teaching presentation *has taught*. Analysis of the teaching presentation for equivalent fractions does not reveal either translation procedures or the unique language conventions associated with ratio problems. The presentation does not even suggest that the ratio problem can be expressed as a pair of equivalent fractions, or suggest the conventions for setting up such a problem.

The *difference* between the knowledge that would be needed to work the problem and the knowledge that could be unequivocally assumed by the learner's successful performance on the equivalent-fraction problems shows why generalization would not occur in most cases. More important, it shows why—with references to specific skills and operations. *Each skill that is missing is a skill that should be taught.* The missing skills are: Identifying the names and the ratio numbers in the word problem; writing the ratio numbers as the first fraction; identifying the unknown from the question the word problem asks; writing the fraction after the equal sign with a box for the unknown and a number for the value given in the problem; figuring out the number that goes in the box; and using this number and the unit name to answer the question the word problem asks. These skills should be taught, something that is not systematically or adequately done in traditional math programs. Also, the skills should be sequenced efficiently.

The difference between the equation problem and the ratio word problem reveals the basis for hierarchical sequencing. One of the problems includes *all of the components of the other problem* and has additional components. A sequencing rule in such cases is that the simpler problem form should be taught first. The reason has to do with the amount of learning that is required, or, conversely, the possible causes of student failure. If the teaching starts with the equivalent-fraction problems, the students would have to learn so many more skills, which could be indicated as N skills than otherwise. To learn the word-problem application requires all the skills of the equivalent-fraction problem plus five others.

The causes of mistakes parallel the amount of learning that is required. Learning the equivalent fraction algorithm implies N possible mistakes. Starting with the word problems implies N and S possible mistakes. Successful performance on the word problem implies far more competencies than does the equivalent fractions problem because (a) the learner would have to learn more, and (b) until the learning has mastered all of the components, the learning would continue to fail.

Just as the word problem is more complicated and therefore logically subsequent to the equivalent-fraction application, real-life extensions are logically subsequent to word problems because they involve *all the components* of the word problem but do not give the measurements or summarize the information needed to solve the problem. Such summaries must be derived by examining the application and comparing it to the goals of the activity (the desired solution). Real-life applications should therefore be sequenced after work with word problems.

Some of the more incredible trends in math instruction hold that the way to teach math is to start with real-life applications and to teach the skills as needed (Prawat, Remillard, Putnam, & Heaton, 1992). However, real-life situations (e.g., figuring out the size of a playground based on a scale drawing and then marking the different areas of the playground) place students in a situation that would logically require incredible amounts of learning and practice. The students probably will not receive this practice because of the amount of time required by different aspects of the activity. For many students, mastery would require the same project to be presented possibly 4–6 times. Instead, it is presented one time, and students tend not to learn much from it.

The most manageable learning sequences *keep the causes of failure minimized,* thereby increasing the probability of successful performance on the initial applications, which are relatively simple, and on the later applications, which have additional components but which require only a small amount of new learning—only that learning associated with the new components.

This sequence minimizes the amount of learning required of the learner at each step and increases the possibility that a learner will be able to complete each step successfully; therefore, the design increases the possibility that the learner will master the real-life applications.

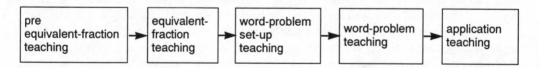

Familiarity vs. Logic

The traditional approaches to curricular development assume that there is undefined magic in real-life situations and that if students are immersed in applications that have familiar elements, they will learn the material more readily. For example, the assumption is that if students work a ratio problem involving bars of soap or units of measurements they are familiar with, they will perform better than they would on a problem that referred to wallabies and earwigs, such as:

If 3 out of 4 wallabies had earwigs on them and if there were 321 wallabies with earwigs on them, how many wallabies would there be in all?

According to the logical analysis, that problem is no more difficult than this one:

If 3 out of 4 bars of soap in a grocery store were on sale and if there were 321 bars of soap on sale, how many bars of soap were in the grocery store?

The learner does not have to know what wallabies are or what earwigs are so long as the learner understands that they are countable things. Knowledge of wallabies, earwigs, or the relative improbability that 3 out of 4 wallabies have earwigs does not alter the difficulty of the problem, compared to the other. Both the soap problem and the wallaby problem name a subclass (bars of soap on sale and wallabies with earwigs on them). Both problems name an entire group (all the soap in the store, all the wallabies under consideration). The ratio numbers are provided for each problem (3 of the subclass for every 4 of the whole group) and an actual number is provided for the subclass (321 bars on sale and 321 wallabies with earwigs). Each problem, therefore, provides information for the same equation:

$$\frac{\textbf{bars of soap on sale}}{\textbf{bars of soap}} \; \frac{3}{4} = \frac{321}{\Box} \quad \Big| \quad \frac{\textbf{wallabies with earwigs}}{\textbf{wallabies}} \; \frac{3}{4} = \frac{321}{\Box}$$

Clearly, the calculations are the same for both problems; therefore, calculation cannot be a variable. Nor can the relationship between the ratio numbers given (3 out of every 4) and the answer to the problem. For both, the learner would check the *reasonableness of the answer* not by reference to whether there could be that many wallabies or that number of bars of soap in a store, but rather by saying something like, "So the answer should be about a third more than 321—about 100 more. Is my answer in that range? . . . So it looks okay."

Efficiency

The goal of the Direct-Instruction sequences is not merely to avoid misconceptions generated by traditional sequences or to break down traditional sequences into more teachable units, but to design sequences that are relatively *efficient*. Efficiency is a function of how much input must be provided to account for a given output in performance. If the required teaching were trivial and if this teaching could analytically account for performance on many different problem types, the sequence would be very efficient. Because it would involve relatively little learning, it could be taught in relatively less time.

The relative "output" that is achieved for the "input" or teaching provides a basis for comparing a sequence to other possible alternatives. Maximizing efficiency in program design requires strategies for sequencing instruction that are different from those used in traditional programs.

Tracks

The traditional "lessons" in a program may consist of units or work on a single topic. The traditional spiral curriculum is a succession of lessons on different topics. This design is not efficient for introducing new material or for reviewing material that had been taught earlier. A more efficient practice divides the class period into time slots, called *tracks. Each track is devoted to a different skill* and is relatively independent of the others that occur in the period; however, the tracks are coordinated so that any skills needed by the student are pretaught. During a single class period, a third-level math student would possibly work on fractions, multiplication facts, review of whole-number operations, measurement, and work on some new word problems. On the following day, most of the same tracks would be repeated, but the activities in each track would be different, as the track moves toward more sophisticated applications and skills.

Tracks are sound from a learning standpoint because they permit inclusion of sufficient numbers of problems to induce high-rate performance. Instead of trying to cram the work on a topic into one or two lessons, the same work may be distributed over a dozen lessons. Working on the material for a short period of time each day reduces the saturation and information overload that occurs when an entire period is devoted to a topic. The format also requires the learner to follow directions more and therefore to become more facile at learning. (In the single-topic lesson, students often spend a lot of time doing the "same thing" with different problems. They are therefore not required to follow directions to the extent that they would in tracked lessons.) The track format also permits timely reviews, which are cumulative—a feature of all Direct-Instruction programs.

Vertical Sequences

Another efficiency device is the *vertical sequence*. A vertical sequence is one that cuts across a wide range of activities or problem types, some of which are traditionally presented years later than they might occur in the vertical sequence. The sequence starts with an algorithm or set of steps for solving a problem. Following this work is a large number of problems that admit to the solution strategy. The vertical sequence is based on the same analysis that suggests that the wallaby problem is no more difficult than the soap problem. If the learner has been taught calculation steps for solving a particular type of problem, the learner is ready to work on the full range of problems that involve these particular steps. The goal is to teach an operation and then use it. The extensions are ordered so that the first are the simplest. Those that require either additional steps or more difficult calculations appear later in the sequence. The vertical series is efficient because it requires a relatively small amount of teaching for the output in student performance. An example is simple fractions. By introducing the routine that the bottom number tells the number of parts in each unit and the top number tells the number of parts that are used, the student is provided with a powerful tool that works for all fractions, including improper ones. Instead of waiting until the fifth or sixth grade to introduce these, the vertical sequence presents improper fractions at the same time that proper fractions are introduced. All are the same because all admit to the same analysis. For example:

$$\frac{5+4}{13} \qquad \frac{28}{4} \qquad \frac{0}{3}$$

None of these fractions require significant additional learning or teaching.

The first example shows that the value in the numerator can be expressed as addition or subtraction over a single-number denominator. This arrangement can be used to show students a method for working problems that have a common denominator:

$$\frac{5}{13} + \frac{4}{13}$$

Test: Can you write the problem as addition with a single denominator? *Yes.*
Write it that way:

$$\frac{5+4}{13}$$

This test provides students with a relatively fail-safe method of determining whether fractions can be added or subtracted without recalculating them. The same test applied to this problem:

$$\frac{5}{13} + \frac{4}{12}$$

reveals that this problem cannot be worked the way it is written.

The second example is important because it sets the stage for expressing the number of wholes that fractions like 28/4 equal.

"The fraction says to make 4 parts in each unit and use 28. Are you using more than there are in each unit?" *Yes.*

"So is the fraction more than 1?" *Yes.*

"You can figure out how many whole units the fraction equals by counting by the number of parts in each unit. How many parts is that?" *4.*

"So every time you count 4 parts, you count 1 whole unit. Figure out how many times you count by 4 to get to 28. That's the number of whole units." The extension requires very little new teaching.

The example 0/3 shows that some fractions equal zero. The learner is instructed to make 3 parts in each unit and use none of them. The result is neither a fractional value nor a whole number.

Inventions

Inventions present another method for reorganizing curricular content. Inventions are used either to make apparently disparate items "the same," or to create a larger difference between items that are otherwise difficult to discriminate. An example of the latter application would be the orthographic conventions used in *Reading Mastery*, Level 1 (Engelmann & Bruner, 1995).

The first level of the program uses a modified alphabet with joined letters: th, er, and so forth, macrons to guide pronunciation of long-vowel sounds ($\bar{e}$, $\bar{a}$, etc.) and small letters that are "silent." With these conventions it is possible to present words that are spelled correctly, but that guide the pronunciation of each "sound."

The word *were* is written as: w er e

The word *where* is written as: wh e r e

The learner is able to process both words by saying the assigned sound for each letter or symbol unit. Note that the learner does not pronounce the final e. This system permits a great expansion of words that are "regularized" by the orthography and at the same time prompts the learner to attend to the spelling of words.

Inventions that create sameness provide prompts that facilitate the development of vertical sequences by collapsing what seem to be different types of problems or applications into a single category. These sameness inventions may consist of an "algorithm," which may be supported by a unique sign or symbol to key the discrimination.

An example is the number family. It is first used to introduce work with facts in *Connecting Math Concepts* (Engelmann & Carnine, 1982). Students work with number families that generate all the addition-subtraction "facts." Here is a group of related families:

$$\frac{2 \quad 2}{} \longrightarrow 4 \qquad \frac{2 \quad 3}{} \longrightarrow 5 \qquad \frac{2 \quad 4}{} \longrightarrow 6$$

$$\frac{3 \quad 3}{} \longrightarrow 6$$

All families have the same property of having a big number (at the end of the arrow) and two smaller numbers (above the arrow).

1. The three numbers that are shown always go together.
2. If two of the numbers are missing, it is possible to figure out the missing number by either addition or subtraction.

If the big number is missing, it is found by adding the two small numbers shown.

If either small number is missing, it is found by starting with the big number and subtracting the small number that is shown.

3. If more than one number is missing in the family, it is not possible to determine the two other numbers (except as possibilities).

The application of the number families to the teaching of addition and subtraction provides a potential savings in learning effort. The reason is that each family processes all the addition facts and the subtraction facts involving the three unique values. For instance:

$$\underrightarrow{2 \quad 3} \quad 5$$

generates:

$$2 + 3 = 5$$
$$3 + 2 = 5$$
$$5 - 3 = 2$$
$$5 - 2 = 3$$

The great savings associated with the number families, however, is not related to facts but to problem solving. Two basic problem types processed through number families are "classification" problems and "comparison" problems. Classification problems mirror the basic logic of the number family. A larger class is divided into two and only two smaller divisions.

Here are two classification problems:

1. There were 76 cars on the lot. 43 of them had full gas tanks. How many cars had gas tanks that were not full?

$$\underset{43}{\text{full}} \quad \underset{}{\overset{\text{not}}{\text{full}}} \quad \underrightarrow{\text{cars}} \quad 76$$

The problem gives a number for all the cars (the big number) and a number for cars with full tanks. The missing small number is computed by working the problem: 76 minus 43.

2. There were 17 boys and 31 girls on the playground. How many children were on the playground?

$$\underset{17}{\text{boys}} \quad \underset{31}{\text{girls}} \quad \underrightarrow{\text{children}}$$

The problem gives values for the two small numbers. The big number is computed by adding 17 and 31.

Comparison problems differ from the classification problems because they don't tell about a whole class and a subclass but make reference to the difference between two groups. The difference is conveyed by information about how many more or how many less. The difference number is the value that is named immediately before the word *more* or *less* (or *greater* or *smaller*, etc.).

The car weighed 345 pounds more than the trailer. The car weighed 2340 pounds. How much did the trailer weigh?

The first sentence tells the difference number, gives the names for the other two values, and implies which is the big number. It's the name that has the larger value: *The car weighed more than the trailer.* Therefore, the car is the big number:

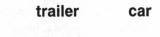

trailer   car

The difference number tells how much more:

dif   trailer   car

345

The rest of the problem gives a number for the car:

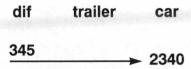

dif   trailer   car

345   2340

The missing number is computed by subtraction: 2340 minus 345.

Number families can be presented vertically as well as horizontally. The combination of vertical and horizontal families permits the presentation of problems that are very difficult without number families. Some of these problems are quite complicated.

Example:

> **Two hospitals have in-patients and out-patients. The hospitals are Bernard Hospital and Hope Hospital. The total number of all patients for both hospitals is 1000. The number of in-patients at Bernard is 250. The total number of patients at Hope is 480. 236 of those are out-patients. How many out-patients are there at Bernard? What's the total number of in-patients for the two hospitals? How many of those patients are in Hope?**

A 3 x 3 table organizes the information into related number families, three horizontally oriented and three vertically oriented. The table makes the problem much easier to solve. Here's the table with the names and the numbers the problem gives:

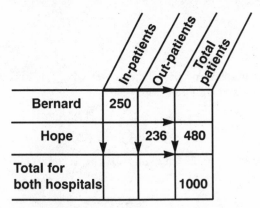

	In-patients	Out-patients	Total patients
Bernard	250		
Hope		236	480
Total for both hospitals			1000

The arrows indicate that each row and each column is a number family. The big numbers are at the end of each row and at the bottom of each column. The same rules that hold for single number families hold for the table. If two numbers are shown for a row or column, the missing number can be computed by addition or subtraction.

The middle row has two numbers. The missing number can be computed by working the problem: 480 minus 236. The last column has two numbers. The missing number can be computed by working the problem: 1000 minus 480.

After these problems have been worked, there are two numbers in the first column and two numbers in the top row. Therefore, the first column and top row can be completed. The remaining value is the big number for the middle column, which can now be computed:

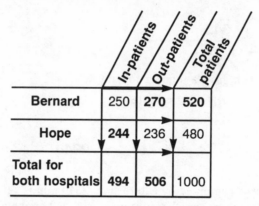

	In-patients	Out-patients	Total patients
Bernard	250	270	520
Hope	244	236	480
Total for both hospitals	494	506	1000

The numbers in the table answer the various questions the problem asks.

Another type of problem involves ratio tables. For these tables, the same "multiplier" is used for all rows. The columns, however, have the features of vertical number families. Any pair of rows can be written as equivalent fractions.

3	
↓	↓54
total 12	

The bottom row of the table shows the totals (the big numbers in the two families). A value is missing in the first column. It can be computed by working the problem, 12 minus 3. After this number is entered into the table, the middle row has the numbers 9 and 54. A pair of equivalent fractions can be created by using that row and either of the other rows. Here's the problem that uses the top row:

$$\frac{3}{9} = \frac{\square}{54}$$

Students work the problem by first figuring out what 9 is multiplied by to get 54, then by multiplying by 1 that same value on top:

$$\frac{3}{9} \left(\frac{6}{6}\right) = \frac{\boxed{18}}{54}$$

When 18 is put into the table, the total for the second column can be computed by adding: 18 plus 54.

3	18
↓9	↓54
total 12	72

Various ratio-table problems can be designed for classification formats.

A pond had perch and bass in it. The ratio of bass to perch was 3 to 5. If there was a total of 400 fish in the pond, how many were perch? How many were bass?

Perch	3	
Bass	5	
Total	8	400

By working either of these problems:

$$\frac{3}{8} = \frac{\square}{400} \quad \text{or} \quad \frac{5}{8} = \frac{\square}{400}$$

students can obtain a second number in the second column. The third is computed by subtracting.

Some problems utilize number families and ratio tables. For instance:

A bag has 12 cards in it. 5 are black cards and the rest are not black. A person took trials at drawing cards from the bag and then returning them to the bag. The person drew 35 black cards. About how many trials did the person take? About how many cards that were not black did the person draw from the bag?

The first part of the problem tells about a *fraction* number family:

$$\underset{\text{black}}{\frac{5}{12}} \quad \underset{\substack{\text{not} \\ \text{black}}}{\frac{7}{12}} \longrightarrow \underset{\text{cards}}{\frac{12}{12}}$$

The fractions show the composition of the bag, expressed in terms of expected trials. If each object in the bag had one opportunity to be drawn, the person would take 12 trials (draw 12 cards). On 5 of those trials, the person would be expected to draw a black card. So the fraction for black cards is 5/12. On 7 trials, the person would draw a card that is not black. So the fraction for not black is 7/12.

The numerators are ratio numbers. They show the expectations if each card had only one opportunity to be drawn:

black	5	35
not black	7	
cards	12	

By working either ratio problem:

$$\frac{5}{7} = \frac{35}{\Box} \quad \text{or} \quad \frac{5}{12} = \frac{35}{\Box}$$

a second number is obtained for the second column (49 or 84).

The number-family logic is used in all these applications. More important, the applications permit a progressive development, which means that the later applications have earlier-taught components, and the difference between the applications is not great. Note also that the approach provides for the articulate teaching of how to process the various word problems and how to discriminate between them.

The number families, the ratio tables, and their applications are inventions. They were generated to make the teaching of applications articulate. Without them, the teacher must often appeal to the students' intuitions. Some students do not have the intuition. The following problem, for instance, involves relationships that are easily shown through number-family logic, but not readily conveyed to the student who hasn't internalized some of the relationships that are assumed by traditional solutions to the problem:

> **The sale price of the couch is 35% less than the regular price. If the sale price is $650, what's the regular price? How much would a person save by buying the couch on sale?**

Finding 35% of 650 and adding the answer to 650 will not yield the correct answer. Explaining why often does not help students to understand. With the number family, however, the difficulty is avoided and the answer to why is obvious.

The percents are fractions. The problem compares the sale price to the regular price. So the regular price is therefore 100%. The percents can be shown as fractions in a number family:

$$\frac{35}{100} \quad \frac{65}{100} \longrightarrow \frac{100}{100}$$

dif   sale   regular

The numerators are ratio numbers that go in the first column of a ratio table. The value 650 goes in the second column.

dif	35	
sale	65	650
regular	100	

It is now easy to compute the missing numbers in the second column. The regular price of the couch is $1000. A person saves $350 by purchasing it at the sale price.

There are certainly other inventions and other solution strategies than those shown for working the problem types outlined above. It may be possible to improve the analysis of the math content and thereby simplify or reduce the problem types and therefore the amount of teaching that is needed to teach solution strategies. However, the inventions shown do serve the purpose of providing a way for students to learn relationships and strategies for problems that are predictably difficult and often not mastered by adults. Because the inventions permit teaching that is progressive and that involves relatively small increments of difficulty, all students who enter the program should be able to learn the content.

Although some studies have been conducted to document the relative efficiency of the DI approach, very little has been done to show the cumulative gains that result from the combination of effective teaching practices and DI programs. A prediction is that the intellectual performance of children would be greatly accelerated over children taught through traditional methods. Hopefully, such demonstrations will be conducted during the next decade and will receive enough publicity to counter current trends and confirm the DI assumption that the children are not the cause of the kind of failure observed in schools today—the teaching practices are.

References

Abt Associates. (1977). *Education as experimentation: A planned variation model (Vol. IV)*. Cambridge, MA: Abt Associates.

Bateman, B. (1992). *The essentials of teaching*. Creswell, OR: Otter Ink.

Becker, W. C. (1977). Teaching reading and language to the disadvantaged—what we have learned from field research. *Harvard Educational Review, 47*, 518–543.

Bereiter, C., & Engelmann, S. (1966). *Teaching disadvantaged children in the preschool*. Englewood Cliffs, NJ: Prentice-Hall, Inc.

Engelmann, S. (1962). Teaching mathematics to four-year-olds. Personal 16mm film.

Engelmann, S., Becker, W. C., Carnine, L., Meyers, L., Becker, J., & Johnson, G. (1975). *Management and skills manual*. Chicago: Science Research Associates.

Engelmann, S., & Bruner, E. (1995). *Reading mastery I*. Chicago: Science Research Associates.

Engelmann, S., & Carnine, D. (1982). *Theory of instruction: Principles and applications*. New York: Irvington Press.

Engelmann, S., & Carnine, D. (1991). *Connecting math concepts, level C*. Chicago: Science Research Associates.

Engelmann, S., & Colvin, G. (1983). *Generalized compliance training: A direct-instruction program for managing severe behavior problems*. Austin, TX: Pro-Ed.

Gagné, R. M. (1985). *The conditions of learning and theory of instruction* (4th ed.). New York: Holt, Rinehart, and Winston.

Horner, R., & Albin, R. (1988). Research on general-case procedures for learners with severe disabilities. *Education and Treatment of Children, 11*, 375–388.

Markle, S., & Tiemann, P. (1974). Some principles of instructional design at higher cognitive levels. In R. Ulrich, R. Stachnick, & J. Mabry (Eds.), *Control of human behavior, Vol. 3*. Glenview, IL: Scott Foresman.

Prawat, R., Remillard, J., Putnam, R., & Heaton, R. (1992). Teaching mathematics for understanding: Case studies of four fifth-grade teachers. *Elementary School Journal, 93*(2), 145-152.

Rosenshine, B. V. (1983). Teaching functions in instructional programs. *The Elementary School Journal, 83*, 335–351.

Stallings, J. A. (1973). Implementation and child effects of teaching practices in Follow Through classrooms. *Monographs of Society for Research in Child Development, 40*(7–8, Serial No. 163).

Watson, D., Goodman, K., Freeman, Y., Murphy, S., & Shannon, D. (1987). *Report card on basal readers: The report of the Commission of Reading*. Washington DC: National Council of Teachers of English.

23

The Individualizing
Instruction Model for
Adult Learners

Burton Sisco
University of Wyoming, Laramie

Introduction

During the past twenty years, a significant number of books, articles, and conference proceedings have appeared focusing on adults as learners. Many organizations, such as colleges and universities, are seeing record numbers of adults returning to the classroom for skill improvement, job advancement, and personal understanding. In business and industry, training programs to help workers keep current and competitive are growing exponentially. As we look to the future, more and more adults from all walks of life will be continuing their learning in a myriad of settings.

Various authors have written about adults as learners. For example, Apps (1981) talks about adults who are returning to college campuses. Smith and Associates (1990) devote an entire book to the concept of learning how to learn across the lifespan. Mezirow (1991) describes the dynamics of how adults learn and how their perceptions are transformed by learning. Merriam and Caffarella (1992) synthesize much of the research on adult learning and offer a typology for organizing this literature. Merriam (1993) reviews a number of promising theories pertaining to learning in adulthood. Authors from other parts of the world, such as Jarvis (1985), Tennant (1988), and Candy (1991), have also focused attention on adults as learners.

Despite this growing literature on adult learning, the actual process of instructing adults has received far less attention until recently. Certainly, a good deal of work has been given to the andragogical process, an instructional approach popularized by Knowles (1980). Over the past twenty years, Knowles has written extensively about andragogy, which he refers to as a system of concepts related to teaching adults.

A parallel area of writing and research that has implications for adult instruction is the growing body of knowledge about self-directed learning. Various researchers, using Tough's (1979) seminal research on adults' learning projects, have demonstrated that mature learners frequently prefer to be in charge of their own learning with only minimal direction from an instructor, trainer, or other resource. Both of these areas of study have prompted a change in the role of the instructor from that of content giver to that of learning manager, facilitator, and resource locator. It is this changing role—and a commitment to individualizing instruction whenever possible for adults—that is a major theme of this chapter. The chapter begins with a look at a number of dominant philosophies that have guided educational practice in the United States since its early history and suggests that many adult educators are now articulating an eclectic view about teaching and learning. This eclectic view is described in some detail under the rubric of effective learning in adulthood. The chapter then introduces a model for instructing adults and highlights some of the advantages of using the model.

Philosophies About Adult Instruction and Learning

Essentialism to Eclecticism

There are a number of dominant philosophies that have guided educational practice in the United States for some time. For example, essentialism has been a pervasive force in American education for much of the country's history. Its goal has been to help shape the individual's knowledge and values through the transmission of cultural essentials. The emphasis has been on content mastery, with instructors serving primarily as transmitters of knowledge. Essentialists believe that schools play a vital role in the development and maintenance of society and their role is to pass current knowledge on to youth in their formative years.

Another significant educational philosophy is that espoused by progressive scholars such as John Dewey (1938, 1956). Dewey believed that education was a continuous process of reconstructing experiences and that learners should play an active role in the learning process. He also maintained that an instructor's role was to guide the learning process and that the school is a social institution that should both reflect and enhance culture. The present emphasis by John Goodlad (1990, 1994) and others on school restructuring and renewal is reminiscent of progressive ideals.

Liberalism is another philosophical approach that has had significant impact on education in the Western world (Elias & Merriam, 1980). Rooted in classical Greek philosophy, liberal education was a foundation for early Christian approaches to education as well as a predominant force in early American schooling. The emphasis on developing the intellectual powers of individuals by exposure to classical thinkers was further developed in American higher education and also formed the basis of early adult education efforts in the United States, such as the Great Books Program.

There has been and continues to be considerable debate between the essentialists and those who believe in a liberal education. Even among adult educators, there are many differences regarding the purposes of education and the role adults play in the learning process. Some feel that the purpose of adult education is to help develop mature individuals who will contribute positively to society. Others believe that the aim is to liberate and empower the individual mind. Still others believe that the education of adults should focus on keeping individuals current in a rapidly changing occupational and technological world. There are also many educators who fall somewhere in between these beliefs and those who have been affected by behavioral, humanistic, or radical beliefs. Elias and Merriam (1980) provide an excellent summary of these various belief systems.

It is clear that many instructors of adults have become eclectic in their philosophical bases. They have selected elements from various philosophies, doctrines, values and belief systems, an approach that best fits their instructional needs and situations. Hiemstra and Sisco (1990), for example, have drawn heavily from various educational philosophies in building their Individualizing Instruction Model. They have been influenced by humanistic beliefs (see especially the Brockett chapter in this book), arguing that instructors should help learners take an active role in the educational process and that instructors themselves should become facilitators. They have also been influenced by behaviorists who emphasize detailed planning with prescribed outcomes by using learning contracts that help learners specify what, when, and how they will learn something. This eclectic view has a number of implications for organizing instruction for adults, beginning with an enlarged role of the learner in the educational process.

Enlarged Learner's Role

The use of facilitator techniques in which learners are encouraged to take an active role in the entire learning process is an eclectic derivation from instructional practices for adults. This role includes participating in various activities, such as assessing individual learning needs, planning content emphases and methodological approaches, and serving as a learning resource in the educational setting. Usually, because of this active role, learners take greater responsibility for their learning efforts.

Many researchers have demonstrated that mature learners prefer to be in charge of their own learning, even in formal classroom settings (Brockett & Hiemstra, 1991; Brookfield, 1985; Knowles, 1975; Long & Associates, 1988). McClusky (1964), in relating psychological theory to the field of adult education, suggested that the adult learner is both autonomous and independent. He concluded that learning activities should be problem centered, facilitate active participation, and be highly meaningful to the adults concerned.

There are many ways in which learners can greatly increase their self-directed learning skills and enhance their personal control of decision making. Hiemstra and Sisco (1990) identify at least nine instructional variables that learners can control in an individualizing process. As Figure 1 illustrates, the level of control between a learner and facilitator varies from situation to situation.

Learners are encouraged to seek a variety of ways to link the learning activities to the practical realities of home, job, and community. They also have the freedom of selecting a range of written or mediated resources to strengthen their command of the subject matter, especially after the learning experience is completed and new needs arise.

Teacher as Facilitator

Another eclectic belief about adults as learners concerns the instructor's role in the learning process. Traditionally, the role of an instructor was to impart knowledge to receptive learners. We see this type of instructional practice in K–12 settings as well as in colleges and universities. However, this type of instruction is far less sensible when mature adult learners are involved, since they bring a variety of experiences to the learning situation and prefer being in control of their learning.

But does this mean that instructors should ignore content or subject matter so that adult learners are more involved? The answer to this question is yes and no, since there are many times when instructors will need to maintain control to varying degrees over the topics studied because of the nature of the subject and the learners' limited background. For example, an instructor in a continuing professional education session for physicians may possess the latest information about the deadly disease AIDS and need to impart that information in as direct, quick, and efficient a manner as possible. A business trainer may be working with a group of executives on a new management technique and must therefore be concerned about time, cost, and efficiency in getting the material across.

In most situations involving adult learners, time is much less a factor than is instructor control and giving up old habits. In fact, an instructor in a facilitator role will need to believe in the overall potential of promoting self-direction in learning, accept input, criticism, and independence, and seek out a variety of learning resources. Changing one's approach or attitudes toward instruction and the potential of mature learners may be the most difficult step to take, but it is a step well worth taking in the long run.

Stimulating the Learners to Learn

An important variable in facilitation lies in providing an environment that stimulates learners to become excited about a subject matter so that they will want to excel. This often entails helping learners to locate a variety of resources and reinforcing the notion that they can use these resources in the discovery of new ideas.

Research evidence supports the contention that the facilitative approach to instruction does in fact promote a positive attitude toward learning. Cole and Glass (1977), Pine (1980), and Verdros and Pankowski (1980) have studied the impact of personally involving adults in assessing needs, determining instructional approaches, and carrying out instructional activities. In general, these researchers found that individualized involvement usually does not affect content mastery. However, they noted a correlation between ownership and learning satisfaction, as well as a greater desire to study the content further after the formal learning experience ended.

Even though considerable research has shown that many adults prefer to be self-directed and in charge of their learning, the moment that some adults enter any formal classroom or training setting they revert to prior teacher-centered expectations. In this case, the instructor's role should become one of encouraging learners to be more self-directing, to help them to be more involved in the instructional process, and to reinforce the importance of being responsible for their own actions. By modeling facilitative behaviors, encouraging personal responsibility, and selecting a wide range of teaching and learning methods, instructors of adults can and will be more effective.

Why Individualizing Instruction Makes a Difference

Clearly, the form and content of teaching has begun to change in the eighties and nineties and there is every reason to believe this trend will continue into the twenty-first century. The importance of keeping up with change, increasing amounts of leisure time, more education at younger ages, and the public's acceptance of lifelong learning as the norm are some of the reasons for this trend. Concomitantly, an increasing recognition that adults often require or at least desire non-traditional instructional styles and uses of instructor's expertise have lead to the development of an individualizing process of instruction (Hiemstra & Sisco, 1990). Before describing this model, a look at three broad approaches to instruction enunciated by Jarvis (1985), "didactic, Socratic, and facilitative," may be useful since they necessitate quite different roles for teachers and learners:

1. Didactic—the instructor controls most of the direction and content through a lecture format. Learners are expected to acquire and retain knowledge primarily through memorization.

2. Socratic—the instructor uses questions to take the learner through a prepared and logical sequence of content acquisition. Learners are expected to respond to the questions.

3. Facilitative—the instructor creates an educational environment in which learning can occur. A variety of instructional techniques can be used. Learners are expected to assume increasing responsibility for specific content determination and acquisition.

Variables	Learner Control Possibilities
Needs Identification	Various techniques are available to assist learners in identifying learning needs associated with a study area's contents. Re-diagnosis of needs throughout a learning endeavor also should be possible.
Content Area and Purpose	The specificity of topics and purpose for the learning process should be controlled by the learner. A learning plan or contract can be a useful tool, and a facilitator can assist with any refinement activities as needed or desired throughout the learning process.
Expected Outcomes	The nature of the desired or expected outcomes should be controlled by the learner. Such outcomes typically relate to needs and purposes. The facilitator provides advice and concrete suggestions as needed.
Evaluation and Validation	Learners should select those evaluation or validation methods that suit personal learning styles and preferences. Facilitators serve as evaluators as needed.
Methods of Documentation	Learners should choose those methods for documenting and demonstrating accomplishments that have long-term uses, such as diaries, logs, journals, scholarly papers, or physical products.
Appropriateness of Learning Experiences	Learners should select those learning experiences best suited to their individual situations or needs. Facilitators can obtain feedback on the appropriateness of various experiences.
Variety of Learning Resources	A variety of potential learning resources permits learners to choose as needs and interests dictate. Facilitators work to locate and make available such resources.
Adequacy of Learning Environment	Learners should select those components of the learning environment that best meet their needs. Facilitators promote an environment that will foster excitement, intellectual curiosity, and involvement.
Pace of Learning	Learners should select a pace best suited to their particular needs or life situations. The facilitator and learner may need to negotiate a pace or completion date for learning activities.

Figure 1. Learner control of instructional variables.
Adapted from Hiemstra (1988) and Hiemstra and Sisco (1990).

The notion that the instructor is an expert who dispenses knowledge to learners is central to the first two models. Learners are viewed as empty vessels into which content is poured, rather than mature people who can assume responsibility for their own learning. This criticism is not meant to denigrate techniques such as lecturing, Socratic questioning, and discussion, or standardized testing, since all can be used effectively in an individualized instructional approach. Yet, the successful instructor of adults is one who uses facilitation techniques and serves as a manager of the various learning transactions rather than simply providing expert information.

There are a number of specific roles that instructors must undertake in any facilitative approach that has individualization as an intended educational goal. Hiemstra and Sisco (1990) identify eight such roles that contribute to more effective teaching and learning of adults.

1. As in more traditional approaches, there will be many instances in which you must serve as a content resource for learners. Instructors usually have considerably more expertise and knowledge about the subject than do learners, and learners will expect this expertise to be shared in various ways. However, using content specialists in areas outside your expertise may be necessary to meet all learning needs.

2. You must take responsibility for managing a process of assessing learner needs rather than presupposing what all those needs might be. The uniqueness of each set of learners necessitates such a role.

3. Once you have uncovered the needs or at least have arrived at some initial understanding of the needs, you will have to arrange and employ the resources necessary for your learners to accomplish their personal goals. In some instances this will require finding or creating new resources, obtaining knowledge or expertise in new areas of relevance to the learning experience, and making outside experts available.

4. We have found it important to use a variety of instructional techniques and devices to maintain learner interest or to present certain types of information. This may seem contrary to our view that each individual must take personal responsibility for learning. But making various techniques and devices available gives learners more control by giving them a wider range of choices and by allowing them to make individual choices.

5. You also need to be aware of techniques for stimulating and motivating learners so that all can reach their potential. Wlodkowski (1985) presents many strategies for motivating adults.

6. Another role is helping your learners develop positive learning attitudes and positive feelings about their ability to be independent. Such attitudes and feelings will vary from learner to learner, with some people having acquired negative feelings about their abilities or past learning experiences. Thus, at times you will need to become a cheerleader or encourager and be willing to spend time helping insecure learners increase their confidence.

7. A very difficult task when learners are using various resources and taking quite different approaches to the achievement of goals is to determine whether or not learners are reflecting on what they have learned. You can help learners accomplish personal reflection through techniques such as small-group discussions, personal interactive journals, theory logs, and statements of personal philosophy.

8. A final role has to do with evaluation of learner progress. You need to evaluate learner achievements in various ways, ranging from more traditional testing to critiquing of written materials to less traditional techniques such as personal interviews with learners. It is also important to stimulate various types of self-evaluation by learners (Hiemstra & Sisco, 1990, pp. 17–18).

Many instructors will find it initially difficult to incorporate all eight of these roles into a personal repertoire of teaching. Some adult learners who are unfamiliar with an individualizing approach may also find these to be difficult roles. Yet, with dedication, hard work, and a commitment to seeing the process though, instructors and learners new to the process will find success. In the next section, the Individualizing Instruction model is introduced, starting with some assumptions about adults as learners.

Assumptions of the Individualizing Instruction Model

As noted earlier, the potential of mature human beings is greatest when instructors systematically provide opportunities for them to make decisions regarding the learning process. The Individualizing Instruction model is rooted in a number of assumptions about the nature of adults, sound principles of learning and instruction, and how to organize instruction effectively. The assumptions are as follows:

1. Adults can and do learn significant things throughout their lives.

2. Educational interventions ought to be organized so that growth and development is the ultimate outcome.

3. The potentiality of humans as learners can only be maximized when there is a deliberate interaction among three elements: the learning process, learning needs and interests, and available instructional resources.

4. When given the opportunity, adults prefer to be in charge of their own learning and actually thrive under such conditions.

5. Adults are capable of self-directed involvement in terms of personal commitment to and responsibility for learning, choice of learning approach, choice of learning resources, and choice of evaluation or validation techniques.

6. An instructor's role is multidimensional, including being a facilitator, manager, resource guide, expert, friend, advocate, authority, coach, and mentor.

7. Empowering learners to take responsibility for their own learning is the ultimate aim of education.

8. Educational interventions ought to promote a match between the needs of each learner and the needs of the instructor.

9. Teaching and learning excellence is the result of subject matter expertise, careful planning, a good deal of patience and flexibility, and a commitment to helping learners reach their potential.

10. The Individualizing Instructional process can be utilized in nearly every educational endeavor with commensurate success. (Sisco & Hiemstra, 1991, pp. 60–61)

The Individualizing Instruction Model

The Individualizing Instruction model consists of six specific steps as illustrated in Figure 2. In each step, an instructor is involved in considerable planning, analyzing, and decision-making as the model is implemented. The model serves as an organizing framework for instructing adults, usually in a group setting such as a course, workshop, or training session, and should be used flexibly as a means of dealing with any individual or institutional constraints. It incorporates many of the instructional design elements presented throughout this book; Hiemstra, in a later chapter, provides a detailed description of how the model is used in a typical adult teaching and learning situation.

Step One—Activities Prior to the First Session

There are many activities to plan and decisions to be made before the initial meeting for the learning event. For example, the instructor often starts by developing a course rationale that describes the purpose of the learning experience, why learners should be interested in it, how it will help them professionally, and what competencies or outcomes they can expect to attain. Usually, some attention is given to the requirements of the learning experience, identifying any support materials such as books, articles, or audio/visual tapes, and locating outside speakers for guest presentations. Other preplanning activities typically involve the preparation of a workbook or study guide that includes information about the syllabus, learning activities, bibliographic references, special readings, and other related materials. Some additional preplanning activities often include scheduling a meeting room where the learning event will take place, reserving any required audiovisual equipment, and making sure that the coordinating administrator has all the pertinent information for advertising the learning event.

Step Two—Creating a Positive Learning Environment

Once the learning experience is underway, there are a number of activities that can help ensure a positive learning environment. Ideas to consider include paying attention to the physical layout of the meeting room, scheduling a break midway through the session for refreshments and a restroom visit if needed, and creating a relaxed and trusting environment in which participants are encouraged to meet each other and express their own opinions without risk of retribution. In addition, some thought should be given to introducing the course content, how the participants will get to know one another, and how the instructor will become acquainted with the participants. Sisco and Hiemstra (1991) call this the "Three Rs": relationship with the subject matter, relationship with each other, and relationship with the instructor.

Step Three—Developing the Instructional Plan

The next step in the Individualizing Instruction model involves spending time on such matters as potential learning topics, activities, and objectives. This is usually accomplished through a needs assessment procedure that is completed individually by participants and which describes their experience, interest level, and competence. Small groups are often formed for sharing and consensus building. The instructor uses these to develop a learning plan that describes the topics to be studied, in what sequence, and through what kinds of instructional methods and techniques. This learning plan is then given to participants for final review and adoption.

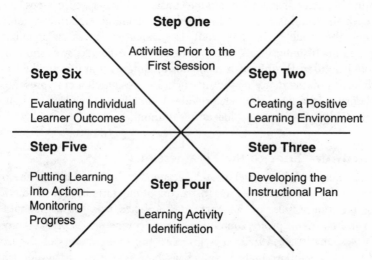

Figure 2.   Individualizing Instruction Model.
Used with permission from Hiemstra & Sisco, 1990, p. 45.

Step Four—Learning Activity Identification

This step is designed to help participants identify what it is they intend to learn, how they are going to learn it, what form the learning will take, when the learning activities are due, and what evaluation strategies will be used to demonstrate mastery of the subject(s) under investigation. A learning contract (Knowles, 1986; O'Donnell & Caffarella, 1990) is typically used here to document the various learning activities, to help participants personalize their learning objectives, and to foster greater control of their learning. Learning activities may take many forms, including the interactive reading log, the theory log, and the personalized journal, so that learners can synthesize, analyze, and reflect on their newly acquired knowledge.

Step Five—Putting Learning into Action and Monitoring Progress

Once the learning plan has been established, the next step in the Individualizing Instruction model is putting it into action and monitoring progress. A number of instructional techniques are typically used, including lectures and mini-lectures, case studies, role playing, small and large group discussions, individual learning projects, field trips, and so forth. As the learning plan is implemented, the instructor monitors group and individual learner progress through formative evaluations, which permit adjustments to be made as needed.

Step Six—Evaluating Individual Learner Outcomes

The sixth and final step in the Individualizing Instruction model involves evaluating individual learner outcomes. Here the emphasis is on helping learners to demonstrate mastery of their learning objectives and activities as outlined in the personal learning contract. Through the use of the learning contract, each learner describes intended learning activities and the criteria associated with each of them. This "criteria referenced evaluation" process allows learners to document their learning outcomes in many ways, while at the same time emphasizing content mastery, personal development, reflective thinking, and critical observation.

A key ingredient of the six-step Individualizing Instruction model is the promotion of effective educational practice through the creation of an instructional system that celebrates individual differences, experiences, and learning needs. By taking advantage of the resident expertise so common in older, more mature learners, the instructor can create optimum conditions for learning to occur. This is one of the guiding principles of instructional design and certainly is a hallmark of the Individualizing Instruction model. Understanding the instructional process, being flexible and supportive when the need arises, helping learners assume greater control of the learning process, and varying the instructional methods and techniques so that active learning is emphasized all add up to instructional success.

Conclusion

The purpose of this chapter was to introduce and describe a comprehensive model for teaching adults—the Individualizing Instruction model. The origins of the model may be traced to a bevy of research studies on self-directed learning, the continuing work on andragogy, and an emerging eclectic philosophy combining humanism, behaviorism, and progressive goals into a coherent system of adult instruction. Human beings are adults much longer than they are children, and our educational systems ought to embrace this reality. It is hoped that the Individualizing Instruction model will help instructors better understand their roles as change-agents charged with facilitating growth and development in adulthood.

References

Apps, J. W. (1981). *The adult learner on campus.* Chicago: Follett.

Brockett, R. G., & Hiemstra, R. (1991). *Self-direction in learning: Perspectives in theory, research, and practice.* New York: Routledge.

Brookfield, S. (Ed.). (1985). *Self-directed learning: From theory to practice* (New Directions for Continuing Education, No. 25). San Francisco: Jossey-Bass.

Candy, P. C. (1991). *Self-direction for lifelong learning: A comprehensive guide to theory and practice.* San Francisco: Jossey-Bass.

Cole, J. W., & Glass, J. C., Jr. (1977). The effects of adult student participation in program planning on achievement, retention, and attitudes. *Adult Education, 27,* 75–88.

Dewey, J. (1938). *Experience and education.* New York: Macmillan.

Dewey, J. (1956). *Philosophy of education.* Totowa, NJ: Littlefield, Adams.

Elias, J. L., & Merriam, S. (1980). *Philosophic foundations of adult education.* Huntington, NY: Krieger.

Goodlad, J. I. (1990). *Teachers for our nation's schools.* San Francisco: Jossey-Bass.

Goodlad, J. I. (1994). *Educational renewal: Better teachers, better schools.* San Francisco: Jossey-Bass.

Hiemstra, R. (1988). Self-directed learning: Individualizing instruction. In H. B. Long & Associates, *Self-directed learning: Application & theory* (pp. 99–124). Athens: University of Georgia, Adult Education Department.

Hiemstra, R., & Sisco, B. (1990). *Individualizing instruction: Making learning personal, empowering, and successful.* San Francisco: Jossey-Bass.

Jarvis, P. (1985). *The sociology of adult and continuing education.* London: Croom-Helm.

Knowles, M. S. (1975). *Self-directed learning.* New York: Association Press.

Knowles, M. S. (1980). *The modern practice of adult education* (rev. ed.). Chicago: Association Press.

Knowles, M. S. (1986). *Using learning contracts: Practical approaches to individualizing and structuring learning.* San Francisco: Jossey-Bass.

Long, H. B., & Associates. (1988). *Self-directed learning: Application & theory.* Athens: University of Georgia, Adult Education Department.

McClusky, H. Y. (1964). The relevance of psychology for adult education. In G. E. Jensen, A. A. Liveright, & W. Hallenbeck (Eds.), *Adult education: Outlines of an emerging field of study* (pp. 155–176). Washington, DC: AEA of the U.S.A.

Merriam, S. B., (Ed.). (1993). *An update on adult learning theory* (New Directions for Adult and Continuing Education, No. 57). San Francisco: Jossey-Bass.

Merriam, S. B., & Caffarella, R. S. (1991). *Learning in adulthood: A comprehensive guide.* San Francisco: Jossey-Bass.

Mezirow, J. (1991). *Transformative dimensions of adult learning.* San Francisco: Jossey-Bass.

O'Donnell, J. M., & Caffarella, R. S. (1990). Learning contracts. In M. W. Galbraith (Ed.), *Adult learning methods.* Malabar, FL: Krieger, 1990.

Pine, W. S. (1980). The effect of foreign adult student participation in program planning on achievement and attitude (Doctoral dissertation. Auburn University, 1980). *Dissertation Abstracts International, 41,* 2405A.

Sisco, B., & Hiemstra, R. (1991). Individualizing the teaching and learning process. In M. W. Galbraith, (Ed.), *Facilitating adult learning: A transactional process.* Malabar, FL: Krieger.

Smith, R. M., & Associates. (1990). *Learning to learn across the lifespan.* San Francisco: Jossey-Bass.

Tennant, M. (1988). *Psychology and adult learning.* New York: Routledge & Kegan Paul.

Tough, A. M. (1979). *The adult's learning projects* (2nd ed.). Austin, TX: Learning Concepts.

Verdros, K., & Pankowski, M. L. (1980). Participatory planning in lifelong learning. In G. C. Whaples & D. M. Ewert (Eds.), *Proceedings of the Lifelong Learning Research Conference.* College Park, University of Maryland, Department of Agriculture and Extension Education.

Wlodkowski, R. J. (1985). *Enhancing adult motivation to learn: A guide to improving instruction and increasing learner achievement.* San Francisco: Jossey-Bass.

24

Ausubel's Assimilation Theory and Metacognitive Tools as a Foundation for Instructional Design

Joseph D. Novak
Cornell University
Ithaca, New York

Introduction

For most of this century, psychology in North America has been dominated by behavioral psychology, which held that the proper study of learning phenomena is through the study of manifest behaviors. While this approach might be defended for lower organisms, and indeed, most of the research was done with animals lower on the phylogenetic scale than human beings, it perhaps was never warranted as a basis for understanding how people acquire knowledge and how instruction should be designed. Nevertheless, most school practices and research on school learning followed closely the behavioral paradigm for learning. For example, there emerged during the 1950s almost universal application of "behavioral objectives" as the foundation for instructional planning and evaluation. The idea was that only criteria that were clearly observable should be used for setting instructional objectives, criteria such as naming specific instances, identifying or classifying information or individuals, or recording instances. Words such as understand, meaning, and comprehension were banned from the vocabulary of the behaviorally driven curriculum planner and instructional evaluator.

Behavioral psychology was the foundation for Bloom's (1956) *Taxonomy of Educational Objectives* and later the hugely popular book by Mager (1962), *Preparing Objectives for Programmed Instruction*. In point of fact, these ideas remain dominant today in most school-based instructional planning, and in many instances the planners fail to recognize both the behavioral psychology that is the foundation for this mode of instructional planning and the positivistic epistemology that undergirds these strategies.

In Europe, there was a less fervent embrace of behavioral psychology and, in fact, the most prodigious researcher and writer concerned with development of knowledge structures in children, Jean Piaget, proceeded to research and theorize on the ways in which children's *cognitive* development proceeded. Of course, little of his writing received attention in North America, and it was not until the 1960s that Piaget was "discovered" (Ripple & Rockcastle, 1964). In Asia, there was also little acceptance of behavioral psychology, but competing, theory-based, instructional design was not developed, to the best of my knowledge.

David Ausubel first put forward his cognitive theory of human learning in 1962, elaborated in 1963 in his *The Psychology of Meaningful Verbal Learning*. Throughout the early 1960s, Ausubel and his students experienced considerable difficulty in identifying publication outlets for their work, since the editorial boards of most psychological journals and corresponding manuscript review panels were overwhelmingly dominated by persons religiously committed to behavioral psychology and to positivistically oriented "experiments" defined by the narrow criteria of positivistically oriented science. Ausubel experienced the resistance commonly found by individuals who advanced a new paradigm, and his work and the work of his students suffered the rejection Kuhn describes as follows:

> At the start a new candidate for paradigm may have few supporters, and on occasions the supporters' motives may be suspect. Nevertheless, if they are competent, they will improve it [the paradigm], explore its possibilities, and show what it would be like to belong to the community guided by it. And as that goes on, if the paradigm is one destined to win its fight, the number and strength of the persuasive arguments in its favor will increase. More scientists will then be converted, and the exploration of the new paradigm will go on. Gradually the number of experiments, instruments, articles, and books based upon the paradigm will multiply. Still more men, convinced of the new views' fruitfulness, will adopt the new mode of practicing normal science, until at last only a few elderly hold-outs remain. And even they, we cannot say, are wrong. Though the historian can always find men—Priestley, for instance—who were unreasonable to resist for as long as they did, he will not find a point at which resistance becomes illogical or unscientific. At most he may wish to say that the man who continues to resist after his whole profession has been converted has ipso facto ceased to be a scientist. (Kuhn, 1962, p. 159)

It is interesting that in the 1990s, it is not the researcher who embraces cognitive psychology who is considered the non-scientist, but rather the researcher who continues to embrace behavioral psychology, although there are now few to be found. Perhaps we have gone into a new period of "disciplinary purification," as Wilshire (1990) describes the game in academia, in which scholars who do not play by the conventional rules are refuted or expelled from the inner circles. It is the modern version of the "purification" described in the Bible when the heretics and non-believers are driven from the temple, only in this case the temple is the journals and publications advisory boards of the field. It might be interesting to speculate on who the new heretics are in educational psychology and how the adherence to the "cognitive revolution" now drives out or curtails any incursion of their emerging ideas into mainstream territories.

In spite of the initial difficulties Ausubel experienced in publishing his ideas, his *The Psychology of Meaningful Verbal Learning* attracted a considerable following, including our research group, then at Purdue University, and his *Educational Psychology: A Cognitive View* (1968) was widely recognized as a significant achievement. Nevertheless, his ideas failed to find their way into the mainstream of psychology, and popular books on theories of learning made no mention of Ausubelian ideas or, indeed, cognitive psychology, until relatively recently.

One of the difficulties for the widespread adoption of Ausubel's assimilation theory of cognitive learning was the fact that Ausubel presented his ideas with great precision in text that many readers found difficult, if not opaque. Rather than working to understand what

I believe was a brilliant theoretical formulation, they simply chose to ignore his work, except for the idea of the "advanced organizer," which is easily the most researched idea in Ausubel's theory. More on this follows below.

In my own work, I never saw the relevance of behavioral psychology to human learning in the sciences and chose instead to base my early research on a cybernetic model of learning (Novak, 1958). My Ph.D. studies and subsequent work by myself and my graduate students produced data that was not consistent with expectations from cybernetic theory. We were beginning to experience great frustration with the cybernetic paradigm when Ausubel's work came to our attention in 1964. Immediately we saw the explanatory power of his ideas for the data we had collected in previous years, and also for the design of new research studies that could focus on the acquisition of meanings necessary to facilitate problem solving. From this point onward, my research program, now embracing over 100 M.S. and Ph.D. studies, was rooted solidly on Ausubel's assimilation theory.

One of the fundamental tenets of Ausubel's theory is his principle cited in the epigraph to his 1968 book:

> If I had to reduce all of educational psychology to just one principle, I would say this: The most important single factor influencing learning is what the learner already knows. Ascertain this and teach him accordingly.

At first glance, this appears to be a simple idea, but in practice it is indeed very difficult to ascertain what a learner knows that is relevant to new instruction in a particular domain of knowledge. It was through our efforts to do this in different domains of science, using primarily modified Piagetian interviews as our data-collection tool, that we developed a new tool we call concept mapping (Novak & Musonda, 1991). Concept maps show in hierarchical structure the concepts and propositions that represent the relevant knowledge of a student in any specific domain. It is also possible to express feelings on concept maps, thus giving affective qualities to the knowledge structure as well as cognitive explicitness. Figure 1 shows a concept map that describes my view on the nature of good concept maps.

Although the tool of concept mapping was first used in our group for research, we soon found it to be effective both for the design of instruction and for helping students understand how to learn *meaningfully.* This has led to a whole program of activities associated with helping students learn how to learn (Novak & Gowin, 1984).

It also became increasingly evident over the years that one of the fundamental problems teachers face in moving learners away from rote-mode learning and toward meaningful-mode learning is the widely pervasive positivistic epistemology. In our studies of student learning in science laboratories, it became clearly evident that there was little understanding of the relationship between the conceptual frameworks that were brought to bear on an inquiry and the methodological and procedural activities associated with knowledge construction. In the struggle to characterize the problem and to identify solutions, my colleague, D. B. Gowin, invented the Vee heuristic. Figure 2 shows the various epistemological elements of the Vee heuristic, which served to define all of those components that interact with one another in the process of knowledge construction. We have found this tool to be enormously helpful in our own research programs but also for wider applicability in the design of instruction and in helping students understand constructivist epistemology, both as spectators to research and as individuals engaged in their own inquiries.

At the present time, there is a growing worldwide recognition of the importance of metacognitive learning tools and the reception to our own work has been increasingly positive. Currently, *Learning How to Learn* (Novak, 1984, 1988) is available in six languages, with an Arabic translation in press. It is my conviction that metacognitive tools will be one of the important components of the methodology of the new constructivist paradigm for instructional planning and the facilitation of learning (Novak, 1988).

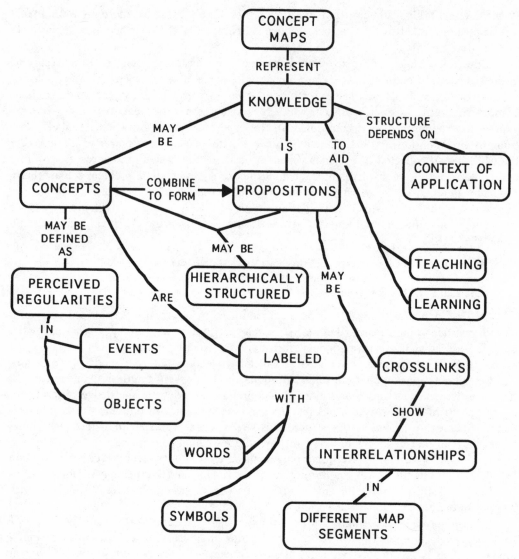

Figure 1. A concept map showing the characteristics of concepts, propositions, and features of a good concept map.

Ausubel's Assimilation Theory

The most fundamental idea in Ausubel's theory is that each learner must construct his or her own conceptual framework based on both observations of events in the world around him or her and on *reception learning,* namely, learning in which concepts and relationships are defined and presented verbally, perhaps with supporting experiences, and the learner does not autonomously construct these concepts or relationships. Indeed, most school learning is reception learning, and efforts over the past two decades to encourage "discovery learning" have largely ignored the distinction between reception learning that is rote in character and reception learning that can be designed to be highly meaningful. It was a plea for the latter kind of instruction that Ausubel expressed in his *The Psychology of Meaningful Verbal Learning* (1963).

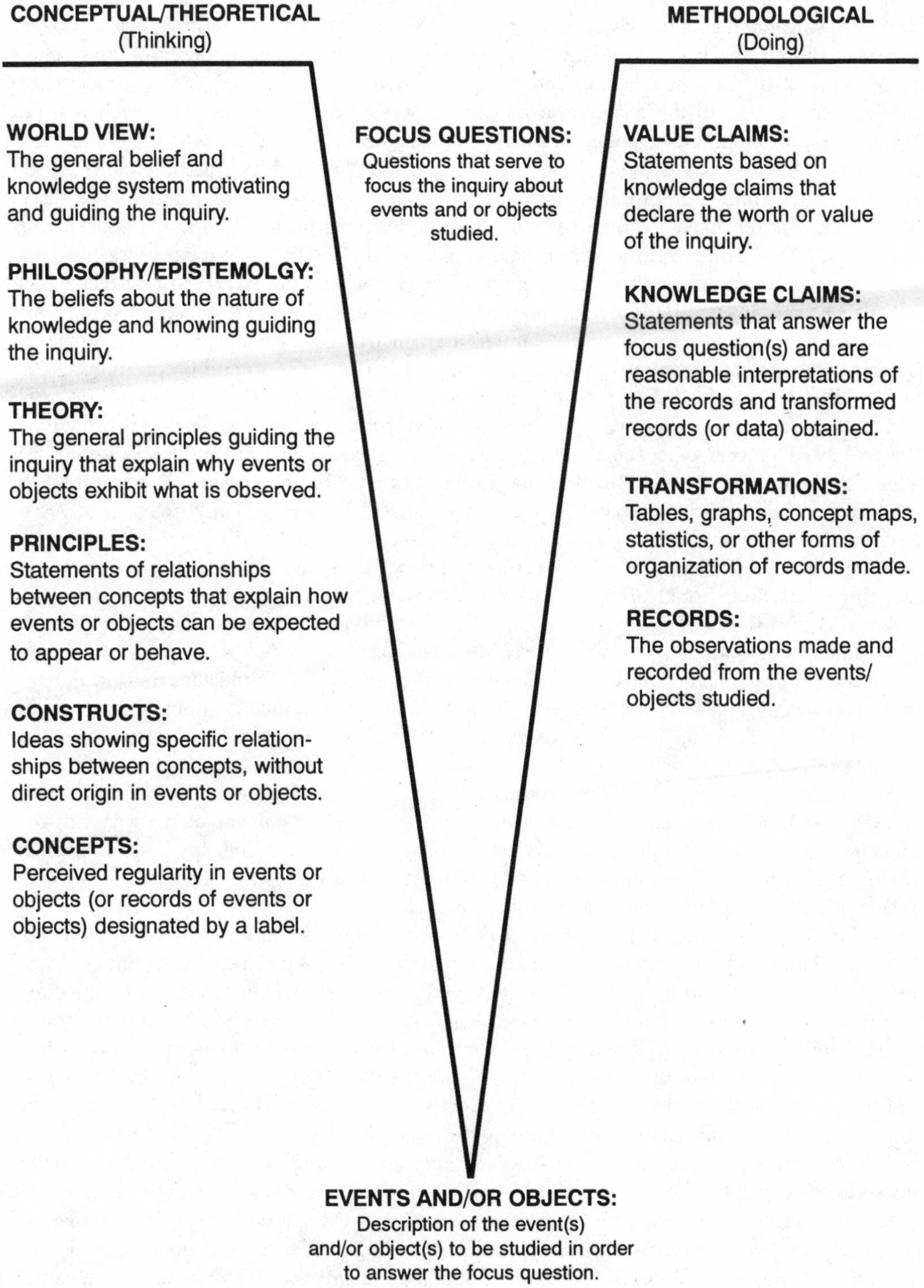

CONCEPTUAL/THEORETICAL
(Thinking)

METHODOLOGICAL
(Doing)

WORLD VIEW:
The general belief and knowledge system motivating and guiding the inquiry.

PHILOSOPHY/EPISTEMOLGY:
The beliefs about the nature of knowledge and knowing guiding the inquiry.

THEORY:
The general principles guiding the inquiry that explain why events or objects exhibit what is observed.

PRINCIPLES:
Statements of relationships between concepts that explain how events or objects can be expected to appear or behave.

CONSTRUCTS:
Ideas showing specific relationships between concepts, without direct origin in events or objects.

CONCEPTS:
Perceived regularity in events or objects (or records of events or objects) designated by a label.

FOCUS QUESTIONS:
Questions that serve to focus the inquiry about events and or objects studied.

VALUE CLAIMS:
Statements based on knowledge claims that declare the worth or value of the inquiry.

KNOWLEDGE CLAIMS:
Statements that answer the focus question(s) and are reasonable interpretations of the records and transformed records (or data) obtained.

TRANSFORMATIONS:
Tables, graphs, concept maps, statistics, or other forms of organization of records made.

RECORDS:
The observations made and recorded from the events/objects studied.

EVENTS AND/OR OBJECTS:
Description of the event(s) and/or object(s) to be studied in order to answer the focus question.

Figure 2. Gowin's Vee heuristic, showing the twelve elements that characterize the structure of knowledge. In production of new knowledge, all twelve elements interact with each other.

If new learning must build on prior concepts and concept relationships to be meaningful, how does the process get started in young children? Ausubel describes the distinction between concept formation and concept assimilation. The former is largely a discovery process, wherein the learner identifies regularities in events or objects observed and begins to recognize that these regularities can be described with verbal labels. Some concept formation occurs prior to the recognition that these perceived regularities can be labeled, but by age one, most children respond to language labels and associate these with certain regularities in their experience. Bedtime, cookies, hugs, and similar things become concepts abstracted by the child from experiences that acquire language labels early in life. By age three, all normal children have acquired several hundred concepts primarily through concept formation and have associated the appropriate language labels with these concepts, at least for the language prevailing in their environment. This is an extraordinary learning feat which will never again be replicated by any learner. In the future, almost all concept learning will be *concept assimilation,* wherein new meanings are constructed for concepts and relationships between concepts (propositions) by using previously learned concepts and propositions. Thus, we begin to explain to children the meaning of new concepts such as green plants, dinosaurs, and hatred, using concepts already in their cognitive frameworks. Most learning throughout life will be a process of concept assimilation wherein new concepts and propositions are added to the developing child's conceptual framework with the process accelerating in early years and perhaps reaching its peak in secondary school or college. Only exceptionally creative people continue concept formation to some extent.

Another fundamental idea in Ausubel's theory is the distinction between rote and meaningful learning. Rote learning occurs when learners choose to incorporate new words or statements into their cognitive framework but fail to integrate these words and statements with already existing concepts and propositions. The result is that these rotely learned concepts and propositions are never assimilated into the conceptual framework and do not become part of the functional knowledge of the individual. In addition, the unintegrated, rotely learned components are rapidly forgotten and after this can actually interfere with the learning of new, similar material.

By contrast, when the learner chooses to learn meaningfully, he or she makes a deliberate effort to seek the integration of new concept and propositional statements with existing concepts and propositions. This process can be represented on a concept map as explicit linking of new concept meanings and propositional meanings into the existing concept map of the individual. Figure 3 shows an example of this.

Material that is meaningfully learned may also undergo some loss of retrieval, but because the knowledge has been assimilated into a larger cognitive framework, interference does not occur when future learning involves either highly similar information, or information that is related but distinct. Therefore, Ausubel has given the phenomenon of loss of retrieval following meaningful learning the name of *obliterative subsumption* to distinguish it from the classical forgetting characteristic of many learning experiments done in the behavioral tradition. These behavioral forgetting experiments established "laws of learning" that apply only when learning is rote rather than meaningful.

The process by which new knowledge is incorporated into cognitive structure usually proceeds most readily when new concepts and propositions bear a subordinate relationship to existing concepts and propositions. Ausubel describes this form of knowledge assimilation as *subsumption.* In the process of subsuming new meanings under more general, more inclusive concept meanings, cognitive structure undergoes *progressive differentiation.* The latter phenomenon involves construction of greater explicitness of meaning, which might lead to distinctions between finer elements of the relevant events or objects. For example, young children often have experience with doggies and may label any four-legged animal a doggie, including cows and horses, especially if seen at a distance. Soon children learn to discriminate between dogs, cats, horses, and dinosaurs, while recognizing all of these as some form of animal. The animal concept may have existed before or may be introduced as a superordinate concept. *Superordinate learning* involves the acquisition of new, more inclusive, more general concepts that subsume existing concepts and propositions in cognitive structure. Thus, superordinate learning would occur when a child sees that all of the animals that nurse their young are grouped under the concept of mammal, whereas those cold-blooded animals that swim in the water may be subsumed under the concept of fish. Of course, the child must later learn to discriminate whales and dolphins from fish and recognize these as another form of mammal. Such cognitive development proceeds with subsumptive learning and occasional superordinate learning, leading to progressive differentiation of a concept-and-propositional framework. We can see this evidenced in Figure 4, showing concept maps drawn from interviews with a young child in Grade 2 and the same child, after instruction in science, interviewed in Grade 12.

While Ausubel distinguishes two forms of subsumption, and another form of concept assimilation that is neither superordinate or subordinate, namely *correlational* learning, it could be sufficient to utilize ideas of subsumption and superordinate learning to characterize most of the development of cognitive structure resulting from meaningful learning. It is important to know, however, that rote learning does not lead to cognitive structure differentiation with the integration and clarification of ideas.

It is now widely recognized that learners acquire not only valid concepts and propositions, valid in terms of how experts currently view phenomenon and events in the universe,

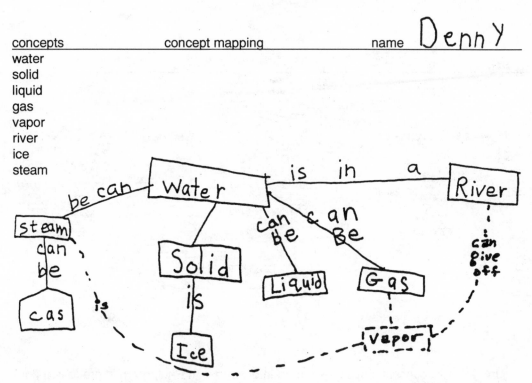

Figure 3. A concept map produced by a 1st grade child. If Denny were to learn the meaning of *vapor* meaningfully, it could be represented as shown with the dash structure added.

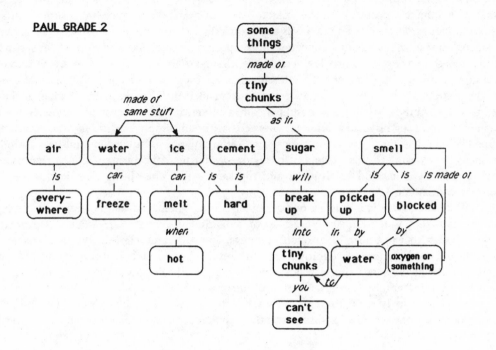

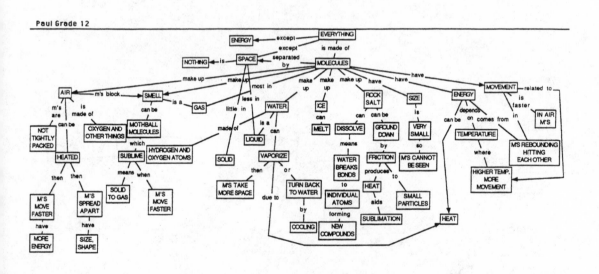

Figure 4. Two concept maps drawn from interviews with Paul, given in grade two (top) and grade twelve (bottom). Note how Paul's knowledge structure has undergone progressive differentiation and integration of concept and propositional meanings over 10 years (from Novak & Musonda, 1991).

but also they acquire invalid concepts and propositions. These *misconceptions or alternative frameworks* are notoriously immune to change by conventional instruction (Helm & Novak, 1983; Novak, 1987, 1993a). The fundamental problem is that most students are learning primarily by rote in most conventional instruction, and thus they do not modify their existing concept and propositional frameworks. The consequence is that the concept and propositional frameworks remain in some respects limited or inappropriate. To recognize the fundamental cognitive difficulties with "misconceptions," I have suggested that we label them instead as LIPHs (Novak, 1993b), an acronym for Limited or Inappropriate Propositional Hierarchies. These limited frameworks can function for passing many ordinary exams, but often fail in novel problem solving or other real-world applications. The consequence is that we sometimes see students performing very well on school examinations, but doing very poorly when they need to apply knowledge in a domain or when their knowledge structures are evaluated critically with effective interviewing strategies.

In summary, we see that the fundamental commitment of instructional design should be the facilitation of meaningful learning, and to the complementary discouragement of rote-mode learning. In my experience, it is not possible to achieve high levels of meaningful learning for all students in most classes unless one also incorporates metacognitive tools. More on this below.

In current cognitive psychology, there is often a distinction made between declarative knowledge and procedural knowledge (Dillon & Sternberg, 1986). Declarative knowledge is defined as the facts and information associated with the content of any discipline. Procedural knowledge, on the other hand, deals with that knowledge necessary to perform particular tasks in a discipline. In my view, this distinction does more to obfuscate than to clarify understanding of cognitive development. For one thing, all knowledge is concept and propositional in nature. Viewed from the perspective of the Vee heuristic, procedural knowledge employed on the right side of the Vee also needs to be inextricably integrated with concept propositional knowledge represented on the left side of the Vee if the inquiry is to proceed intelligently. One of the difficulties that students have in any laboratory or field study is that they employ the procedures on the right side without being guided by the concept propositional frameworks on the left side that give meaning to the entire process. The consequence is the widely recognized experience of most students in science laboratories and in field study that, although they completed the activities, they have little understanding of the phenomena that were involved in the experience; they cannot explain the results in any coherent fashion.

I view the design of instruction rooted on assimilation theory to require a clear understanding on the part of the curriculum planner, as well as by the learners, of the important distinction between rote-mode and meaningful-mode learning. This means that a portion of every instructional syllabus should include instruction on how human brains work to organize knowledge into conceptual frameworks. Every syllabus should also make clear that the most powerful learning derives from deliberate efforts on the part of the teacher and the learner to construct hierarchically organized concept propositional frameworks (Novak, 1991, 1993b).

Instructional Planning

From the perspective of assimilation theory, the fundamental task in the design of effective instruction is the organization of knowledge to be presented into concept maps representing both broad global ideas to be learned and including specific concepts and propositions to be detailed in subsequent lessons. Therefore, the first task is to design a small map presenting the most general, most inclusive ideas. Figure 5 shows a concept map I use in my own instruction to begin to introduce ideas on the constructed nature of knowledge

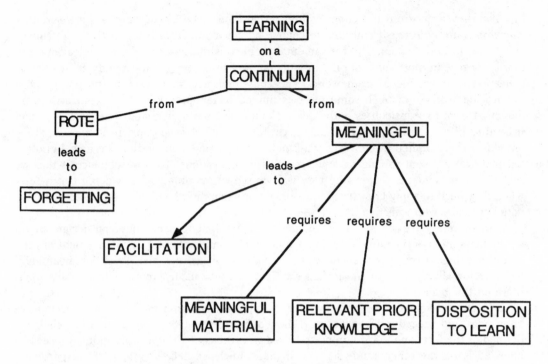

Figure 5.   A simple concept map used to introduce key concepts on learning.

and the fact that each learner must construct his or her own knowledge. Subsequently, I deal with more explicit ideas on the nature of learning presenting the key ideas from assimilation theory. These are represented in Figure 6.

The objective is to begin with ideas that are relatively easily anchored into existing knowledge frameworks of learners and that present the broad general ideas needed to anchor subsequent more explicit concept and propositional ideas. The instruction must be designed to facilitate the process of subsumption, and occasional superordinate learning, with an explicit focus on the progressive differentiation of relevant concept and propositional frameworks.

It is also important to utilize instructional sequences that will help learners understand the constructed nature of knowledge by engaging in activities that center on knowledge construction. The design of these activities is best accomplished by employing the Vee heuristic. An example of a Vee heuristic used in my own courses is shown in Figure 7.

I require all of my students in most of my courses to conduct clinical interviews with a group of subjects on some topic of interest to them. Subsequently, my students prepare a concept map for each subject showing the knowledge structure revealed through their clinical interviews. They also prepare some Vee diagrams to represent how individual subjects view the subject matter under discussion. Figures 8 and 9 show examples of these. This process of designing instruction to focus on the concept and propositional frameworks involved both in the general understanding of the field and in understanding of specific events in the field leads to an integration of knowledge that is far more comprehensive and more relatable to the real-world experiences of learners than would be the case if only concept maps and corresponding reception learning were used. The use of the Vee heuristic and appropriate related activities provide a form of guided discovery learning that can be very powerful both

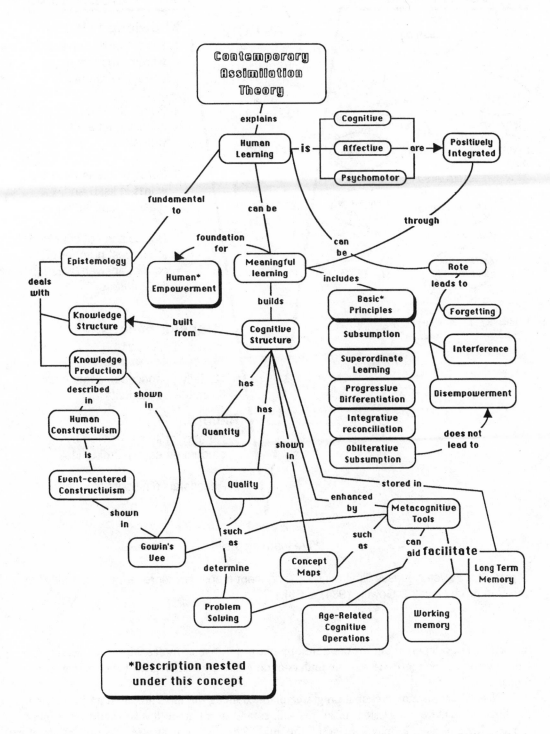

Figure 6. A concept map showing key ideas in Ausubel's assimilation theory of learning.

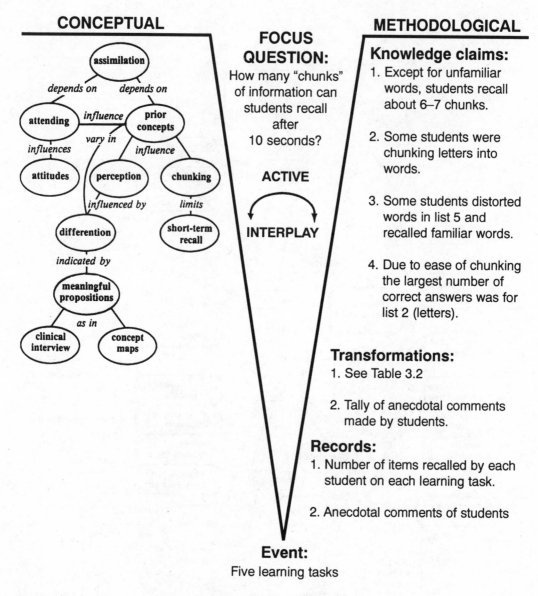

CONCEPTUAL

assimilation

depends on   *depends on*

attending   *influence*   prior concepts

influences   *vary in*   *influence*

attitudes   perception   chunking

influenced by   *limits*

differention   short-term recall

indicated by

meaningful propositions

as in

clinical interview   concept maps

FOCUS QUESTION:
How many "chunks" of information can students recall after 10 seconds?

ACTIVE

INTERPLAY

METHODOLOGICAL

Knowledge claims:
1. Except for unfamiliar words, students recall about 6–7 chunks.

2. Some students were chunking letters into words.

3. Some students distorted words in list 5 and recalled familiar words.

4. Due to ease of chunking the largest number of correct answers was for list 2 (letters).

Transformations:
1. See Table 3.2

2. Tally of anecdotal comments made by students.

Records:
1. Number of items recalled by each student on each learning task.

2. Anecdotal comments of students

Event:
Five learning tasks

Figure 7. A Vee heuristic illustrating how concept maps can represent the "left side" of the Vee (from Novak & Gowin, 1984, p. 68).

in cognitive development and in the development of positive attitudes. Moreover, these provide concrete experience for use in understanding the epistemological ideas of constructivism.

Needless to say, instructional programs planned along the lines proposed and involving the kinds of activities suggested, in all disciplines and at all grade levels, would be revolutionary. Remote as this may appear in the mid-1990s, we already see the utilization of concept maps in most secondary science textbooks, and more recently Vee diagrams have appeared in laboratory guides. While it is far too early to predict the long-term consequences of instruction that is based both on constructivist learning principles and on constructivist

CONCEPTS:	QUESTIONS:	METHODOLOGY:
World View: Working hard makes one more efficient. **Philosophy:** The understanding of the material comes from hard work. **Theory:** The knowledge of different strategies and contents lead to better use of them. Seeing relationships between concepts leads to under-standing. **Principle:** The more you know about your ability to deal with infor-mation, the better your use of the information obtained. Specific strategies are used for quantitative and non-quantitative subjects. **Key concepts:** Study, strategies, efficiency, proficiency, math, (re) read, identify, understand, relate derive, equations, numbers, (non) quantitative	1. Which strategies do you use to study? 2. Which ones are more efficient? Why? (Can you give me examples?) 3. Have you tried other strategies? If not,why? If yes, why you do not use them? 4. Do you think you could improve your strategies? If yes, what do you think would help you learn more? If not, why? **EVENT:** Interview with a business graduate student regarding the use of study strategies.	**Value claim:** Dislike for studying in group. Non-quantitative subjects are more difficult. **Knowledge claim:** Different strategies are used for different subjects and have different efficiency. The strategies used to study are known and chosen. **Transformation:** Transcription of tape, concept mapping and Vee diagram. **Record:** tape of interview

Figure 8. Epistemology map to guide interview study with Japanese business students concerning students' study strategies. This map was typed in these columns for use in production, but retains the Vee heuristic feature.

epistemological principles, and which includes the use of metacognitive learning tools, the evidence to date suggests that we could easily expect an order of magnitude improvement in learning achievements, and realistically, two or three standard deviations of improvement in performance, based on criterion tests that have true validity. We are seeing the beginnings of this kind of instructional development in the sciences and, more slowly, in other disciplines, and also in corporate settings including industrial organizations. It is likely that profit incentive will drive the incorporation of these strategies in business and industry settings more rapidly than in schools. In any case, I feel confident that when we enter the twenty-first century, we will be seeing in a wide variety of settings increased application of assimilation theory ideas and metacognitive learning tools to facilitate both the design of instruction and the enhancement of individual meaning making.

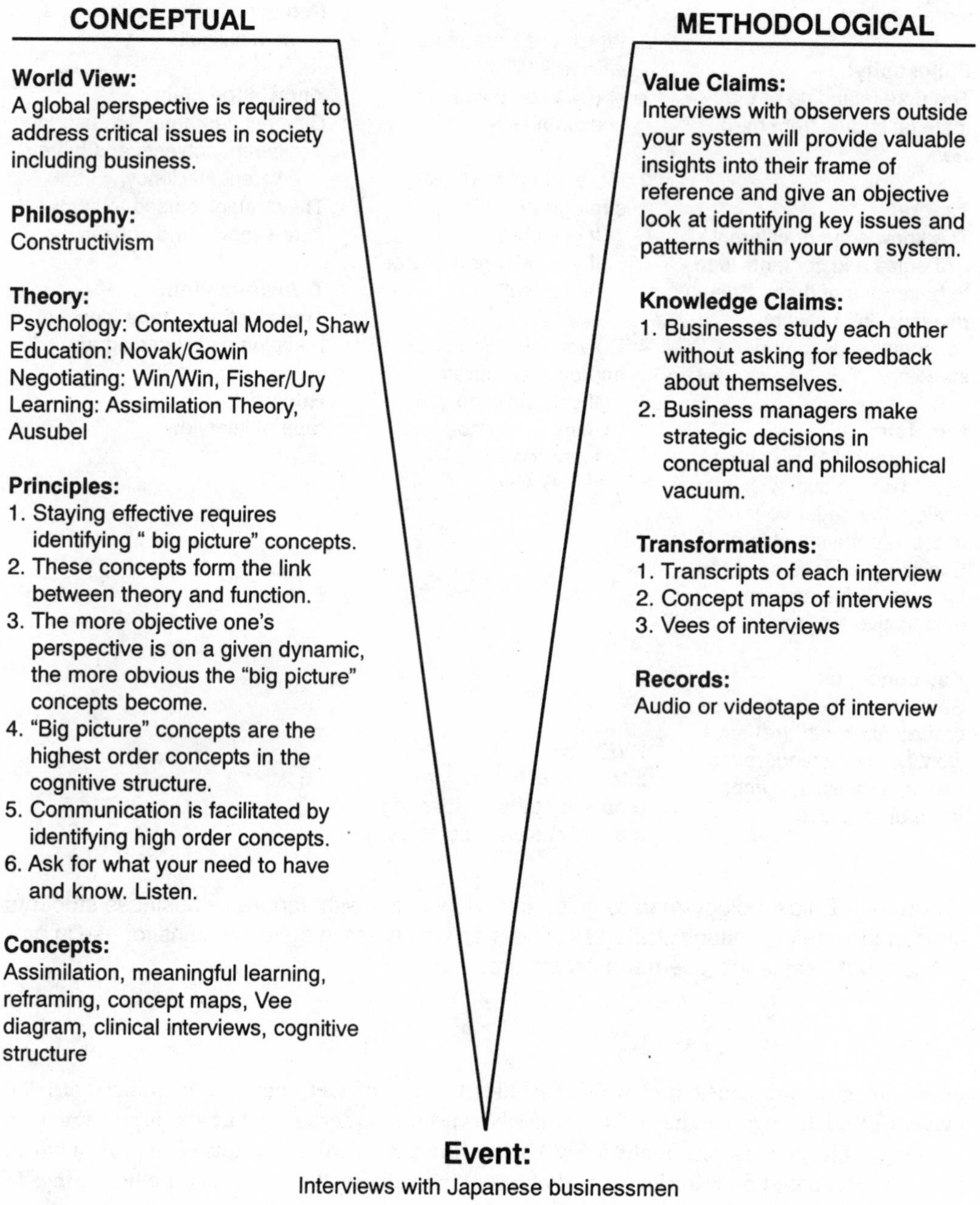

CONCEPTUAL

World View:
A global perspective is required to address critical issues in society including business.

Philosophy:
Constructivism

Theory:
Psychology: Contextual Model, Shaw
Education: Novak/Gowin
Negotiating: Win/Win, Fisher/Ury
Learning: Assimilation Theory, Ausubel

Principles:
1. Staying effective requires identifying " big picture" concepts.
2. These concepts form the link between theory and function.
3. The more objective one's perspective is on a given dynamic, the more obvious the "big picture" concepts become.
4. "Big picture" concepts are the highest order concepts in the cognitive structure.
5. Communication is facilitated by identifying high order concepts.
6. Ask for what your need to have and know. Listen.

Concepts:
Assimilation, meaningful learning, reframing, concept maps, Vee diagram, clinical interviews, cognitive structure

METHODOLOGICAL

Value Claims:
Interviews with observers outside your system will provide valuable insights into their frame of reference and give an objective look at identifying key issues and patterns within your own system.

Knowledge Claims:
1. Businesses study each other without asking for feedback about themselves.
2. Business managers make strategic decisions in conceptual and philosophical vacuum.

Transformations:
1. Transcripts of each interview
2. Concept maps of interviews
3. Vees of interviews

Records:
Audio or videotape of interview

Event:
Interviews with Japanese businessmen

Figure 9. A Vee diagram used to show the plan for an interview study on study strategies with Japanese business students.

References

Ausubel, D. P. (1962). A subsumption theory of meaningful learning and retention. *Journal of General Psychology, 66,* 213–224.

Ausubel, D. P. (1963). *The psychology of meaningful verbal learning.* New York: Grune & Stratton.

Ausubel, D. P. (1968). *Educational psychology: A cognitive view.* New York: Holt, Rinehart, and Winston.

Ausubel, D. P., Novak, J. D., & Hanesian, H. (1986). *Educational psychology: A cognitive view.* New York: Werbel & Peck.

Bloom, B. *et al.* (1956). *Taxonomy of educational objectives.* New York: Longman.

Dillon, R. F., & Sternberg, R. J. (1986). *Cognition and instruction.* New York: Academic Press.

Helm, H., & Novak, J. D. (1983). *Proceedings of the International Seminar on Misconceptions in Science and Mathematics, June 20-22, 1983.* Ithaca, NY: Cornell University, Department of Education.

Kuhn, T. S. (1962). *The structure of scientific revolutions.* Chicago, IL: University of Chicago Press.

Mager, R. F. (1962). *Preparing objectives for programmed instruction.* San Francisco: Fearon Publishers.

Novak, J. D. (1958, March). An experimental comparison of a conventional and a project centered method of teaching a college general botany course. *Journal of Experimental Education 26,* 217–230.

Novak, J. D. (Ed.). (1987). *Proceedings of the Second International Seminar on Misconceptions and Educational Strategies in Science and Mathematics.* Ithaca, NY: Cornell University, Department of Education.

Novak, J. D. (1988). The role of content and process in science teacher education. In P. F. Brandwein & A. H. Passow (Eds.), *Gifted young in science potential through performance* (pp. 307–319). Washington, DC: National Science Teachers Association.

Novak, J. D. (1991). Clarify with concept maps. *The Science Teacher, 58*(7), 45–49.

Novak, J. D. (Ed.). (1993a). *Proceedings of the Third International Seminar on Misconceptions and Educational Strategies in Science and Mathematics.* Ithaca, NY: Cornell University, Department of Education.

Novak, J. D. (1993b). Opening remarks. In J. D. Novak (Ed.), *Proceedings of the Third International Seminar on Misconceptions and Educational Strategies in Science and Mathematics.* Ithaca, NY: Cornell University, Department of Education.

Novak, J. D., & Gowin, D. B. (1984). *Learning how to learn.* New York: Cambridge University Press.

Novak, J. D., & Musonda, D. (1991). A twelve-year longitudinal study of science concept learning. *American Educational Research Journal, 28*(1), 117–153.

Ripple, R. E., & Rockcastle, V. N. (Eds.). (1964). *Piaget rediscovered.* A Report on the Conference on Cognitive Studies and Curriculum Development, March 1964. Ithaca, NY: Cornell University, Department of Education.

Wilshire, B. W. (1990). *The moral collapse of the university: Professionalism, purity, and alienation.* Albany, NY: State University of New York Press.

25

An Information-Constructivist Framework for Instructional Design and Curriculum Planning

Robert J. Stahl

Arizona State University, Tempe

The pre-instructional decision-making phase of instructional design and curriculum planning is often viewed as not facilitative of effective instruction (Wedman, 1989). Curriculum developers, instructional designers, and classroom teachers frequently perceive systematic, pre-instructional decision-making as all of the following: too time consuming; as less important than "live" teaching; as a step which requires them, too far in advance of actual teaching, to decide and describe the specific abilities students are to attain during and maintain after all instruction has ended; as the time to primarily focus on selecting the content that is to be "covered," and the specific activities and resources that are to be used; and as a "necessary evil" to fulfill some external requirement imposed by those not directly involved with in-classroom instruction.[1] Furthermore, when decisions concerning objectives are made, most educators still ignore deciding on and describing the *permanent* abilities and states of being they expect as student outcomes of—rather than merely activities during—their teaching efforts.[2]

Those who hold these notions about planning for instructional events, when required to complete pre-instructional decision-making tasks, tend to focus on variables related to the content and activities that are to be included, completed, or "covered." They view instructional objectives primarily in terms of teacher or student intentions, classroom activities, and/or student production tasks. For instance, when asked to state instructional objectives, the statements they posit take such forms as: "to solve problems 1–15 on page 16 . . . ," "students will be in small groups to . . . ," "to enable students to be critical thinkers . . . ," "to read the short story entitled . . . ," or, "to lecture on . . . ." In addition, many other of their pre-instructional decisions are made with little or no conscious attention paid to *actual* critical learner-learning variables. Even those who do take the pre-instructional time and decision-making process very seriously tend to emphasize a limited number of the internal variables which are most important for successful learning.

The most viable learner-learning outcome-aligned frameworks for making instructional design decisions are those that are directly applicable to a wide range of student outcome abilities, focus on and are aligned with critical inside-the-learner-learning variables, and lead to outcome-aligned decisions and tangible records of those decisions. This chapter describes one instructional design framework, currently used in pre- and in-service curriculum development, methods of teaching, and instructional design courses, that is consistent with these criteria.[3] Before this framework or model is described, background details concerning the Information-Constructivist (IC) perspective of thinking and learning, the foundation for this approach to instructional design, are provided.

The Information-Constructivist (IC) Perspective: A Brief Overview

The Invention of the Information-Constructivist (IC) Perspective

The IC perspective is an outgrowth of the author's work in the classroom with secondary school students, as well as undergraduate and graduate students in teacher-education programs. The impetus to pursue this viewpoint came from (a) personal concerns as to why pre- and in-service teachers had problems with comprehending and using Bloom's Taxonomy (Bloom, 1956) as a model of cognitive outcomes; (b) personal involvement in developing a practical tool to describe, guide, and monitor verbal interaction in the classroom (Casteel & Stahl, 1973); and (c) personal interactions with students at all levels about what seemed to help as well as hinder their success in the classroom. In addition, a number of inconsistencies between and shortcomings of existing models and conceptions of cognition and learning as they might be applied to classroom settings were noted. A perspective emerged that allowed for the human elements of invention, construal, and personal sense making, as well as one that accounted for more of what seemed to occur in all learners across nearly every instance (Stahl, 1992a, b; Stahl & Verdi, 1992).

In generating a viable model of thinking and learning, the notions of social psychologists, such as Bandura (1986), Kelly (1955), and Mead (1934); cognitive psychologists, such as Ausubel (1963, 1968), Neisser (1967, 1976), and Wittrock (1978, 1986); phenomenologists Combs and Snygg (1959; also Combs, Richards, & Richards, 1976); and scholars in the various social and behavioral sciences and the humanities, such as Beard (1934), Becker (1955), Carr (1961), Croce (1941), McGhee (1978), and Murphey (1982), were integrated along with the author's interpretations of research in thinking, learning and human physiology. The result was a theoretical perspective that has generated a number of models relative to human cognition[4] (Stahl, 1982, 1984a, 1987, 1989a, 1992a, b, c, d, 1994). The IC perspective emphasizes the crucial roles information plays in all cognitive activity and structures and includes the word "information" in its name to distinguish this extremely strong information-oriented view from other constructivist views and theories.

While much has been said about processing, constructing, and the kinds of "knowledge" and processes learners could acquire, the essential, common element of all cognition, affect, and psychomotor actions, "information," has been virtually ignored. What exists outside the learner are objects, phenomena, and behaviors as potential sources of information. The learner, and the learner alone, has to attend to, make sense of, assign meaning to, and organize in personally meaningful ways every bit of information *in, from, and about* these different sources of information. During and after the continuous meaning-giving activities are completed *within the learner*, the learner essentially stores only information. As a general rule, the IC does not use the terms "knowledge," "truth," and "reality."[5]

For the IC, information is the fundamental ingredient of all internally-directed, brain-related activity, including cognitive, affective, and psychomotor events, operations, decisions, and processes. The brain, as an active, continuous processing organ, cannot perform its many cognitive operations, activities, and functions without information. Information is not only vital to sense-making, thinking, and learning, *it is the essential ingredient.* Consequently, all cognitive activities, abilities, and products can be described within the context of the specific information that learners may or may not encounter, invent, use, organize, manipulate, transform, store, and forget.

An IC views each person and the multiple internal activities associated with thinking and learning as being dynamic, active, and constantly making decisions, whereby personal versions of the world, self, and experiences are continually being generated, constructed, revised, applied, tested, and assessed (Stahl, 1982, 1987, 1989a, 1992a). Each person alone and internally decides what phenomena, entities, and data are to be attended to and how each phenomenon and *infobit*[6] will be made meaningful and be organized. Furthermore, learners invent or construct meaning and make sense of what they encounter by applying existing sets of information to act upon and manipulate the information encountered through the sense organs, retrieved, and re-presented from permanent storage and via recent inventions within the brain.

The ingredients and results of all inventing, sense-, and meaning-making activities, which are given such labels as constructs, conceptions, world views, perspectives, and info-schemata, are nothing more and nothing less than personally invented and organized clusters of information. All meanings, perceptions, conceptions, and the results of "sense-making" decision-making events *take the form of information* which the learner either stores or allows to be forgotten.

Thinking is defined *as any and all active brain-involved operations, activities, and events that include or make use of information under the conscious or nonconscious direction of the learner.* A person cannot think in the present or about past or future states, behaviors, or phenomena without information.[7] All acquired thinking processes are information-based, -driven, -guided, and -producing internal events which learners can initiate and successfully complete only to the extent that they possess and use the information base that would allow the particular process to occur (Stahl, 1982, 1985, manuscripts in preparation). In addition, the actions a person engages in at a particular moment are determined by the information activated and directed to the muscles milliseconds before the behavior.

Each learner decides, almost always nonconsciously, how just-invented infobits as well as permanently stored infobits, constructed and arranged into infoschemata, will be used to "make sense" of and assign meaning to encountered entities and data and to decide whether something is or is not a problem or worthy of further attention. Details on what constitutes an infoschema and the roles of infoschemata are described in Stahl (1992c) and Stahl and Casteel (1990).

Individuals assign personal meaning to all information and phenomena that are encountered and perceived to exist and to all information and conceptions that are generated internally. This meaning and this meaning alone influences personal judgments about what something is and is not, regardless of whether what is being considered is currently being encountered, was encountered, may be encountered, or has been recovered from permanent storage and is being re-presented and re-encountered.[8]

Much of what one remembers is actually a collection of infobits representing decisions a person made and stored at a previous time and which are, in part, *retrieved and blended with* other infobits the person activates at the moment of recollection and re-presentation. Bartlett (1932) found that humans unconsciously and automatically fabricate a great deal of information in their remembrances of past events and that for them, at the time of the remembrance, the fabricated information is accepted as being correct and as much a part of what they originally experienced as the information stored about the actual experience. In this sense, much of what one remembers as a reconstruction of a prior phenomenon or experience is a nonconscious blend of (a) data from and about a prior experience as the person perceived it at the moment of permanent storage, (b) data just-invented or just-encountered that serve to cue and associate the past incident with the present situation, (c) data "fabricated" at the moment of recall in order to complete an acceptable version of the experience, and (d) present perspectives and expectations that the individual chooses as useful in constructing a "whole" memory to meet the person's contemporary needs.

Within the IC view are a number of complementary models that may be used in instructional settings to describe what is needed for success from an inside-the-learner perspective. One of those models is described below.

For educational settings, the IC perspective defines *learning* as *acquiring new information, one or more infoschemata, or abilities to use information; making permanent changes in one's infoschemata or cognitive-beliefs; or acquiring a new status for an ability such that any one of these is within the person 23 and more hours beyond the period where these were first encountered or done* (Stahl, 1983, 1989a, 1992a; 1994).[9] Learning involves an active series of appropriate internal information processing events that each person completes for him/herself in order that the information appropriate to the construction and use of each ability is placed in permanent storage. In addition, part of one's learning events may, but need not, include the means to gain easy access to the information once stored so that executable abilities and behaviors can occur later. Essentially, learning involves actually making one or more changes in a person's existing infoschemata network, housed in permanent storage, and in his or her abilities to use particular infobits in these infoschemata in future situations.

The ultimate goal of any instructional design model is to enable students to complete the internal processing tasks that are needed to ensure permanent storage and later use of the information that students need so that they can actually complete expected or desired academic tasks.

An Inside-the-Learner Context for Instructional Design:
The IC Model of School Learning

Instructional designers need a model of learning in school settings that provides a comprehensive view of what is needed for learner success from an inside-the-learner perspective and that is functional for making decisions within all phases of instructional design and implementation.

The *IC Model of School Learning* (Stahl, 1987, 1989a, 1992a), an expansion of Carroll's time-based model (1963, 1989), describes what is needed for learner success from an inside-the-learner perspective in a manner that is functional for making decisions within all phases of instructional design, implementation, and evaluation. Briefly, the model states that the degree of learning of any acquirable ability, perspective, or orientation is a function of the quality and quantity of (a) the *appropriate information* one has and can use relative to the information one needs to have and use, (b) the *appropriate internal processing tasks* one has already completed and can complete relative to the processing tasks one needs to complete successfully and is able to complete successfully, and (c) the *productive time* one has spent learning relative to the time one needs to spend learning. At the beginning of instruction, learners will vary in the extent to which they need and can use must-learn outcome-aligned information, can complete appropriate internal processing tasks, and have spent productive time learning the must-learn information and completing must-complete processing tasks.[10]

Having more than what is needed of one or two of these three variables will not compensate for inadequacies in and insufficiencies of the other(s). For instance, enabling learners access to greater quantities of information will not compensate for their failure to complete adequate and correct internal processing events or their failure to spend the necessary time in on-task learning. In addition, increasing one's effort to learn without access to and use of the information, processing, and time needed will not make up for inadequacies in any of these three areas. Yet, in typical instructional settings, teachers operate as though only one or two of these three variables is all that is needed by learners. Acting upon this assumption, they provide learners an overabundance of either information, processing tasks, or time, and limit or prevent access to the other one or two variables.

These three variables are critical for several reasons, the most important of which is that all acquired or being-acquired sets of information, infoschemata,[11] abilities, behaviors, affective orientations, and dispositions require an *information base*, an *ability to use that information base*, and *time to acquire them*. All the various "thinking skills" and "higher order thinking" abilities which have been proposed as processes within classroom tasks and as outcomes of instruction are not possible without these three variables (Stahl, 1989a). No outcome performance ability that an individual may acquire directly or indirectly from instruction is free of all three of these variables.

The IC Model of School Learning is especially relevant to educators and academic learning in classrooms in four ways. First, expected achievement will rarely occur when the learner is limited solely to the information within and making up the particular concept to be acquired and applied. Secondly, the extent of achievement, at any moment, corresponds to and is dependent on the interrelationships among and fulfillment of three distinct variables, not just one or two, and not independent of one another. Thirdly, it points out the need for curriculum planners and teachers to articulate more clearly ahead of time at least the categories of the must-learn information base underlying each targeted ability; to provide learners more frequent opportunities for engaging and successfully completing appropriate processing events; and to allow students to actually spend the on-task time needed. Fourthly, if the targeted ability is to be refined, as well as be maintained, instructional situations must build in appropriate information recycling/rehearsal activities over an extended number of days after the initial success (e.g., Dempster, 1988).

An Instructional Design Model Aligned with the IC Perspective and the Three Critical Variables of Learning

Various models of instructional design enable individuals to proceed systematically to complete required decision-making steps and to generate one or more tangible products which reflect these decisions (e.g., Andrews & Goodson, 1980; Dick & Carey, 1990; Gagné, Briggs, & Wager, 1988; Posner & Rudnitsky, 1994). Appropriate ID models are characterized as requiring decisions and actions that align need-to-have learner variables and instructional variables with desired, permanent learner-exiting abilities. One way to help individuals consciously consider these variables as an integral part of the ID process is to provide clear criteria and procedures both for making relevant decisions and for formulating clear, tangible descriptions of these required decisions. The tangible records of these decisions reflect the extent to which the designer has taken the learner-learning variables into account. These records also serve as the public documentation of the internal decisions that have been made. Furthermore, these descriptors of decisions should never serve as an end in themselves.

The ID model proposed here (see Figure 1) begins with considering the possible permanent abilities that learners could attain, followed by the selection of one or more abilities as target student outcomes. This decision becomes the source for conducting an information-base analysis; i.e., first considering *may-need-to-learn* infobits and then deciding on the *must-learn* infobits from what the learners need rather than on what is convenient to provide. In my work with teachers and instructional designers, I have found that all too often, both select information to have students learn that is nonaligned with the targeted outcome or is insufficient, inadequate, incomplete, or incorrect.

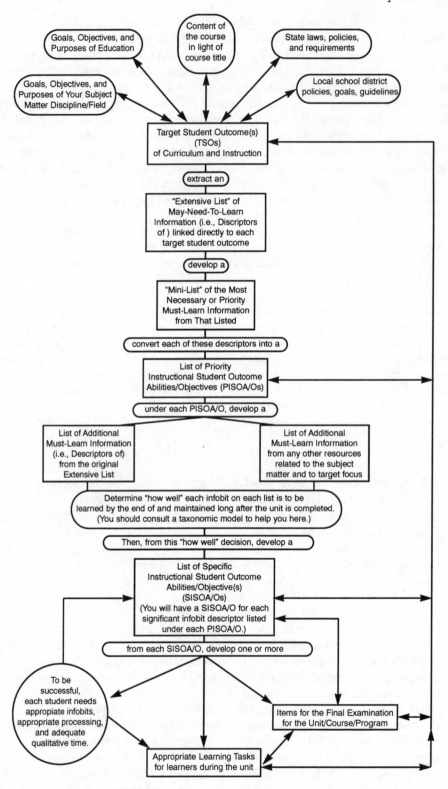

Figure 1. A schematic of a model of curriculum planning and instructional design aligned with the IC perspective (Stahl, 1987).

The Components of This IC ID Model Represent Critical Major Decision Points in the ID Process

Within the IC view, *planning* is defined as all decision making relative to a particular course of action prior to initiating an action. A *plan* is a set of decisions made before action is taken:[12] *To plan* means to make or expect to make a set of decisions prior to initiating action. Designing also involves making decisions, with the requirement that the decision-making process is systematic, follows particular established guidelines, and meets other appropriate criteria. Designing is a subset of planning. Given these definitions, the IDer is compelled to make a number of decisions.

Using these definitions, a written design or curriculum plan is a tangible record of the decisions that have been made in reference to the objectives and goals of a particular unit, course, or program of instruction exclusive of decisions concerning instructional behaviors or events. The instructional designer must view moving through the components of any ID model as making a series of appropriate decisions at particular moments.[13]

A particular type of decision at a particular moment within the design process is referred to as a *decision point*. Decision points constitute the phases, components, and sub-components of a design model. The author often stresses decision points rather than components of instructional design in order to emphasize the nature of the pre-instruction process as consisting of a number of very important and interdependent decisions that should be made. When presented within this context, pre- and in-service teachers report a conception of curriculum planning that emphasizes the dynamics of making appropriate pre-teaching decisions, rather than filling in components of a "curriculum plan."

In the section below, the major decision points in the decision-design process as phases and components of one IC ID model are labeled and defined in the order in which the decisions are made (see Figure 1). A brief description of the content of and guidelines for the decisions for each decision point are included. In many instances, one or more exemplars of each decision are provided. Finally, at least one reason for including particular decision points in the entire system of decision-making steps is provided to clarify the role and value of the phase or component within the sequence of the entire design process.

(A) *Consideration of possible learner outcome abilities.* Decisions here are made within the context of the particular educational setting as well as in regard to other variables that affect or may affect the specific learner outcome(s) selected and the instructional environments that may be possible. IDers are rarely free to decide upon just any learner abilities as *the* permanent outcomes of instruction. Sources such as state- or district-mandated objectives or exit skills and the curriculum guidelines provided by various professional associations may be taken into account.

An appropriate needs assessment is conducted.

There are at least seven *domains of learner outcomes* from which particular target learner outcome abilities may be selected[14] (Stahl, manuscripts in preparation). Three of these are compatible with the domains proposed by Gagné (1985). One example of the domain of *task completion abilities* follows:

"At the end of this course, after all instruction has ended, learners will be competent at designing a course using one model of instructional design."

An example of an *information uniprocessing ability* is also provided:[15]

"At the end of this course, after all instruction has ended, learners will be proficient at comparing any two or more entities."

After existing documents are reviewed; the educational goals, aims, and intents are considered; and concerned individuals are queried; the IDer converts statements of course, teacher, or program intentions, aims, activities, and non-outcome goals into clear statements of precise permanent learner abilities or states. For instance, a statement such as, "To enable learners to use scientific methods of inquiry" would be restated as "Learners will be proficient at using scientific methods of inquiry." The result is a collection of recorded descriptions of expected outcome abilities or states of being that will serve as a *pool of possible target outcomes*. Recording these descriptors provides a public documentation of the decisions made at this time and enables the IDer, at a future time, to review and assess these initial decisions.

(B) *Select and specify one or more Target Learner Outcome (TLO) abilities or states.*[16] From the pool of possibilities generated in step A, the IDer selects the most important mustlearn abilities and must-attain states that learners are to attain during and maintain beyond the end of all instruction for the unit.[17]

These descriptors of Target Learner Outcomes (TLOs) are *not* to be equated with either descriptors of priority (or general) or specific instructional learner outcome objectives; these will be determined and stated in later planning phases. Rather, TLOs are descriptors of the most important to-be-acquired-and-maintained outcome abilities toward which all other planning and instructional decisions and actions are to be aligned. TLOs are *never* to be viewed as "objectives" in the traditional sense of this term.

(C) *Complete an information-base analysis of each Target Learner Outcome.*   This phase requires the conscious consideration of the information that learners *may need* to encounter and acquire in order to attain each TLO ability. This investigation amounts to a content analysis to generate a list of the specific kinds of information that learners may need to learn to be successful in this unit. The categories of information considered may include, but are not limited to, those listed in Table 1.

Each decision takes the form of a descriptor of a piece of *may-need-to-learn information* that is stated in the following form: "definition of ____," "attributes of ___," "reasons for ____," and "procedures for ____." One of the requirements for these decisions is that this list may not include descriptors of information pertaining to any subject matter that was not specifically mentioned by name in the original statement of the TLO. A second is that this list is generated to reveal the largest possible pool of information that students could and may need to acquire. It is not to be limited to information that the instructor at the time of planning wants to teach or "cover." This list never includes descriptors of activities, processing tasks, or action verbs. The list generated at this state is an extensive one.[18,19]

When these descriptors are recorded, this list, labeled the *Extended List of Descriptors of May-Need-to-Learn Information*, allows the IDer to study the range of the information that learners may need to encounter, acquire, and use relevant to each TLO.

(D) *From the Extended List of Descriptors of May-Need-to-Learn Information, select the most important (or priority) must-learn pieces of information.*   Here the designer reviews the large number of descriptors and then selects the one to seven that are most essential if learners are to be successful in acquiring the targeted outcome ability. As a general rule, for a five day unit, based upon approximately one hour of instruction per day, only one major piece of information would be selected from the extensive list.[20]

The information selected should encompass a number of other pieces of important information as it is being learned. For instance, rather than select a descriptor like "definition of a scientific method" or "attributes of scientific methods," the IDer would likely select the one that states "procedures for completing each scientific method," because to comprehend and apply procedures successfully often requires having relevant definitions and attributes. The tangible product of this decision phase is actually a repeat of one or more descriptors from the preceding extensive list. This short list of one to seven descriptors of priority infobits is labeled the Mini-List of Descriptors of Priority Must-Learn Information. Steps C and D, as well as E, F, G, H, and J, represent phases in this set of decisions that are not found in other models.

Table 1. A non-exhaustive list of categories of information learners may include in an infoschema.

GROUP A

[These words serve to describe the information]

advantage(s) of
assumption(s) underlying
attribute(s) of
axioms(s)
belief(s)
belief statement(s)
benefit(s) of
biconditional definition(s) of
canon(s)
characteristic(s) of/for
cause(s)
code(s)
conceptualization(s)
conclusion(s) of or drawn from
connection(s) between/among
consequence(s) of
creed(s) of
criterion(ia) for
cue(s) for
decision(s)
definition(s)
description(s)
disadvantage(s) of/for
doctrine(s) of
effect(s) of
explanation(s) of/for
feature(s) of
formula(s) for
frame(s) of reference of/for
generalization(s)
guideline(s)
hypothesis(es) of/for
idea(s)
ideology(ies)
implication(s)
indicator(s) of
inference(s) about/concerning
interpretation(s) of
justification(s) of/for
law(s)
limit(s) of
linkage(s) between
moral reason(s)
mores
norm(s)
origin(s) of
perception(s)
position held by
position statement(s) on
postulate(s)

premise(s)
principle(s)
property(ies)
purpose(s) of
quality(ies)
rationale(s) of/for
rationalization(s)
reason(s) for/why
recipe(s) for
relationship(s) between/among
relevant attribute(s)
relevancy of
result(s) of
rule(s) for
specification(s)
standard(s)
taboo(s)
tenet(s)
terminal point of
trait(s)
value(s)
world view(s)

GROUP B

[Each of these items are also to be preceded by the descriptors from Group A]

plan(s)
policy(ies)
procedure(s)
scheme(s) (as plan)
theory(ies)

GROUP C

[the word "exact" precedes each of the items below]

amount(s) of
address(es) of
age(s) of
date(s) of/for
distance(s) of
emblem
heading(s) of/for
label(s)
location(s) of
name(s)
symbol
temperature(s) of
title(s)
time of/for
weight(s) of

GROUP D

[Each of these items must always be preceded by at least one descriptor from Group A]

case(s) of/for
category(ies) of/for
cell(s) of/for
class(es) of
compartment(s) of/for
component(s) of
composition of
condition(s) of
degree of
element(s) of
example(s) of
exemplar(s) of
factor(s) of
form(s) of
kind(s) of
method(s)
methodology(ies)
model(s)
part(s) of/for
phase(s) of
process(es)
program(s) to/for
range of
routine(s) for
section(s) of/for
setting(s)
shape(s) of
situation(s)
space(s) of/for
stage(s) of
status of
step(s) of/to
strategy(ies)
style(s)
system(s)
tactic(s) of/for
technique(s) of/for
tool(s) of/for
type(s) of

(E) *Convert each descriptor of priority must-learn information in the mini-list into a descriptor of a Priority Instructional Learner Outcome Ability (PILOA) that is directly aligned with that information.* Each learned internal ability is dependent upon one or more pieces of information and one or more ways the learner can make use of this information at a particular moment. For our purposes, it is useful to view internal learned abilities as falling into four generic classes: recollection, recognition, placement, and application. These four classes of internal abilities represent the only four ways that learners may make use of any learned infobit. When steps C and D are completed correctly, PILOAs always emerge from the pool of critical information which learners must acquire and make use of beyond the end of instruction.

The results of this decision and accompanying conversion step is a descriptive sentence which begins with a phrase like the following: "At the end of this unit, after all instruction has ended, learners will _____," placed immediately prior to each descriptor selected during step D and included in the mini-list. The space following "learners will" is replaced by one of the four labels for permanent abilities (i.e., apply, utilize, recall, recognize[21]). An example of a correctly stated descriptor of a PILOA is: "At the end of this unit, after all instruction has ended, learners will apply the procedures for completing one scientific method." If there are three descriptors selected for the mini-list as critical must-learn information for a particular target outcome, the unit will have three statements of PILOAs.

This procedure guarantees that the PILOAs for a unit or course are directly aligned with the TLO and are not directed too soon to related case- or situation-specific problems, tasks, issues, or subject-matter content such that the original focus of instruction is lost in the planning phase even before instruction actually begins. Using this approach to planning, the descriptors of PILOAs will always be directly related to the critical information that learners must learn. These descriptive statements are *not* referred to as General Instructional Learner Outcome Objectives (GILOOs).[22]

(F) *Decide whether the unit will have one or more Priority Instructional Learner Outcome Objective(s) (PILOO).* When IDers accept a particular PILOA as a descriptor of a permanent ability that they expect learners to acquire during the unit, and then commit themselves to do whatever is needed to enable nearly all learners to attain and maintain this ability at a high level of proficiency, then and only then does the descriptive statement of a PILOA become a descriptor of a *Priority Instructional Learner Outcome Objective (PILOO).*[23]

(G) *Under each PILOA/O, make a list of descriptors of additional must-learn information aligned with that particular ability.* This list, usually consisting of three to eight or more descriptors of must-learn information, represents the information the IDer believes that learners *must also acquire* during the unit if they are to attain the ability described by the TLO and PILOA/O.[24] This set of infobit descriptors takes into account the specific information from one or more subject-matter areas that students also must learn within the context of the information linked to the PISOA. Some of these descriptors may be taken from the extended list generated earlier as step C. The IDer returns to the original extensive list and selects from it descriptors of information "left behind" that he or she now perceives that learners must also learn in order to be successful.

Must-learn infobits may now be selected from one or more specific subject-matter content areas. Note that it is this late in the planning phase that the IDer moves to include subject-matter information that is not mentioned specifically in the original TLO. The decision to delay the IDer from attending to and including other relevant subject-matter information until this late in the process was made to offset the tendency to ignore many critically important outcome-aligned infobits—the very information that would enable learners to attain the target outcome ability. In addition, this delay helps offset a second tendency, which is to focus far too soon on specific and immediate activities, subject-matter content or topics, resources, tasks, situations, or problems at the expense of TLO-aligned must-learn infobits.

Stated in the same form as descriptors in the extensive list and using categories like those found in Table 1, provided earlier, the less-extensive list of descriptors under each PILOO specifies the must-learn information and provides the information base for all end-of-the-unit specific learner outcome abilities and test items.[25] This list includes only must-learn infobits rather than any or all infobits students may study, will "cover," or could learn.

(H) *Determine "how well" learners are to acquire the use of each infobit selected as must-learn information.* This decision point actually consists of three decisions. The first requires the IDer to decide whether learners are to recognize, recall, utilize, or apply the particular infobit selected as the most critical use they need to make of that infobit. As for PILOAs, there is no other choice. The second decision is the selection of one of four types of cue situations within which learners are expected to make use of this information and perform relevant actions. These four cue situations, labeled "direct," "indirect," "embedded," and "imposition," refer to the quality of the clues or directions that are provided to inform learners as to the specific infobit they are to make use of in a particular situation. The third decision requires the selection of the degree of mastery students are to attain relative to the use of the particular infobit in the cue situations selected above. The options here range from "Initial Mastery" to "Skill-Level Mastery." These decisions must be made before the specific learner outcome abilities can be determined.

(I) *Determine and write descriptors of Specific Instructional Learner Outcome Abilities (SILOAs).* These performance descriptors state what each learner will be able to do and publicly exhibit on his or her own on the day after completing all instructional tasks during the unit. These descriptors of exact, expected public performances and products reveal the evidence that learners must provide and that others may witness to verify that the expected exiting conditions and abilities were attained and maintained to the needed level of proficiency. An example of a completed descriptor serving as a SILOA follows:

> When provided a not-previously-studied, written description of a person solving a problem and directed to provide five reasons why the person's actions do or do not fit the procedures for completing one scientific method, learners will write a narrative including five correct reasons why the person's actions are or are not consistent with the procedures of the one method studied and applied during five days in the unit [Extension: Directed Exposition[26]–MM[27]].

In this approach to selecting and describing specific learner outcome abilities,[28] the action verb characteristic of conventional ID performance objectives is dropped in favor of a specific description of the exact public product or performance that the learner must complete. For instance, the IDer would expect students to "write a correct interpretation of . . ." rather than merely to "interpret" a particular poem. In a second case, the IDer would actually expect learners to "write (or mark) correct solutions" rather than "solve" 9 of 10 problems. One cannot see a learner "interpret" or "solve" since these occur internally. However, one can observe, measure, and assess a "written interpretation" and "10 written solutions." The criteria for correctness is described in this descriptor in the form of the information base learners are to use to arrive at correct interpretations, answers, solutions, etc.

(J) *Decide whether the unit will have one or more Specific Instructional Learner Outcome Objectives (SILOOs).* Tangible products of this decision step include a number of clear statements of precise outcome abilities that can be included in course guides, syllabi, and manuals that state learner objectives. As a general rule, there is one descriptor of a SILOA developed for each descriptor of must-learn information generated during step G. Descriptors of SILOAs will serve as the *Specific Instructional Learner Outcome Objectives (SILOOs),* when and only when the teacher commits himself or herself to doing whatever is needed to ensure that nearly every learner actually achieves the abilities described.[29]

This manner of describing these specific abilities also has utility in serving as the basis for test item development for pretests or diagnostic tests as well as formative, summative, and delayed posttests.[30] In addition, because the SILOA/Os usually describe the specific resources or conditions learners will need at least during the final exam (e.g., When given a new sample of each of two previously studied categories of rocks . . . , When shown three Picasso prints not previously examined . . . , When given ten quadratic equations not previously studied . . . .), the specific types of materials and resources needed by learners for both during- and after-instruction tasks are almost always named.

(K) *Develop and construct standard-reference test items aligned directly with the specific must-learn information and must-acquire exit abilities described in the statements of the SILOA/Os.* When constructed in direct alignment with the decisions made in step H, the set of final exam test items will serve to gather public evidence to directly measure the external performance abilities and products described in the set of SILOA/Os. Ideally, the IDer develops and constructs the final exam *prior to* instruction as a way to visualize more clearly just what it is that each learner needs to be able to do on his or her own after all teaching has ended. This descriptor of a SILOA as criterion should also be used as a basis for developing all tests used in connection with this unit of instruction. Certainly attaching a copy of a final exam with the earlier decisions adds to the quality and quantity of the tangible products generated prior to instruction.

Many unit and course designers resist constructing the final exam until instruction has nearly ended (Wedman, 1989). This delay enables them to construct a test which is more consistent with what was "covered" or with what the instructor expected to be learned in light of what was "covered." However, such tests often do not reflect content and abilities that were selected by the instructor prior to the unit as the major outcomes of his or her teaching, or were consistent with the learning tasks that learners spent time completing.[31]

(L) *Determine the sequence in which learners are to acquire, master, and maintain must-learn sub-abilities and information.* There are four general classes of options for how information and sub-abilities may be sequenced during instruction: (a) prerequisite, (b) random, (c) preferred, and (d) model of instruction requirement. Prior to planning specific learning tasks, selecting materials, and finalizing specific instructional strategies, the IDer will want to examine the list of must-learn sub-abilities and information to determine whether certain of these must be learned before others can be learned. Premature concern for resources and instructional strategies often wind up handicapping learners, thus contributing to their becoming remedial learners rather than successful ones.

This approach thus builds the initial set of decisions without reference to any particular teaching method or model. Consequently, it is entirely possible for all teachers in a particular department or district to have the exact same set of "curriculum decisions" and "curriculum guide," but to arrange for and engage learners in different instructional tasks based upon differences in teaching methods, resources, and sequencing of must-learn information and sub-abilities.

(M) *Determine and specify entry abilities, characteristics, and states.* At this time, the IDer describes the specific abilities, characteristics, and states that learners are most likely to need to have attained and maintained to acceptable levels of proficiency prior to the start of instruction. While the learners' prior experiences are to be taken into consideration, these experiences are not to be equated with appropriate learning or achievement. For instance, because a learner has completed fourth-grade math and used a particular book does not, in itself, shed adequate light on the quality and quantity of his or her math proficiency. More importantly, it does not reveal anything about what the learner could have achieved were instructional variables more favorable to what she or he needed in order to learn the math to a high degree of mastery. The meaning and importance of these entry variables are described elsewhere (e.g., Bloom, 1976; Gagné, Briggs, & Wager, 1988; Guskey, 1985). These entry variables enable the IDer to determine what information learners should have acquired and be able to use and what processing events they may have to complete with new or acquired information in order to be ready to start the new unit of instruction.

As these decisions are made, the IDer may choose to record a list of descriptors of the should-have-acquired information base for the prerequisite abilities and of the need-to-successfully-complete internal processing events that learners must complete. Typically, once this task has been completed, descriptors of specific types of instructional tasks that learners will need to complete any specific materials they may (or will) need to use will emerge. In addition, a brief description of the previous experience of learners may be included, along with a description of what may be used to enable them to become motivated, interested in, or ready for the about-to-be-encountered new unit of instruction.

(N) *Select one or more models of instruction.* Note that in this instructional design and curriculum planning model, the above decisions can be completed without reference to the teaching methods or strategies to be used.

(O) *Select appropriate instructional resources and learning tasks.* This set of decisions is identical to that found in other ID models. However, the selection is based upon the learners (a) gaining access to the must-learn infobits, (b) completing must-complete relevant internal processing tasks, and (c) spending sufficient productive time with "a" and "b."

(P) *Design and conduct diagnostic test(s).* This set of decisions is also identical to that found in other ID models. For this reason and for concerns about space, this component is not described here in detail. However, before moving to the next phase, a brief statement concerning the nature of external performance indicators needs to be made. The IC conception of learning helps explain the loss of a great deal of information and a large number of abilities that fade or are forgotten from storage-memory within seconds or minutes after being received or completed. The information and abilities that learners may exhibit may be temporary or permanent, be improved or worsen, or become more or less accessible to the learner over time. Public products, performances, and other "outputs" represent evidence of the current condition of the learner so that the view of the learner as a dynamic, active, developing—as well as a forgetting—individual is maintained throughout the entire ID process. In this perspective, a *test* is any device that is being, has been, may be, or will be used to obtain public information about the condition, performance ability, status, properties, or achievement of an entity at a particular moment in reference to some standard.

(Q) *Engage in instructional activities.* Here the actual actions associated with instruction are completed.

(R) *Design and conduct formative evaluation to collect information to be used in assessing and revising instructional variables to maximize learner success.* When possible, field tests should be completed using small numbers of potential learners to supplement and enhance the quality of the decisions already made and the materials that have been developed. These one-on-one and small group sessions can contribute substantially to the quality and quantity of the unit and its related tangible products. For instance, additional materials or learning tasks may be suggested by participants, and alternative or more powerful examples or analogies may be generated by the IDer or instructor. Areas of inadequacies or inappropriateness concerning any aspect of the unit may be discovered by anyone involved in this activity. This evaluation may bring about many modifications in the ID decisions.

(S) *Conduct and analyze summative test(s) and their results.* This set of decisions is also identical to that found in other ID models. For this reason and for concerns about space, this component is not described here in detail.

(T) *Assess past and future instructional design decisions, actions, and products, including instructional events and tasks and the quality and quantity of student achievement in light of data from summative test(s).* This set of decisions is also identical to that found in other ID models.

The above descriptions provide a brief introduction to the components and sequence of steps toward generating a curriculum plan or initial instructional design decisions for any educational program or course. Note that little mention was made throughout the components (or decision steps) of teaching models or strategies as well as specific resources, learning activities, and student tasks that may be used during the program or course. Notions related to how some of these decisions are to be made are introduced in the next section.

Making the Transition from Initial Instructional Design and Curricular Decisions to Daily Instructional (or Pedagogical) Decisions[32]

Here, as in all other phases of planning, teachers having to proceed from initial instructional design decisions to matters of daily instructional activities, content, etc., are faced with a series of options. For instance, the teacher may start by determining the sequence in which students are to acquire the must-learn information. This decision should start with determining whether certain information is prerequisite to other information. If such prerequisites exist, then the foundational information must be provided earlier in the instructional sequence. All remaining information then may be encountered in an order based upon the teachers' preferences. The selection of sequence of information that is to be encountered by students in a particular order is usually made independently of the teaching model or strategy that may be used. In general, teaching models and strategies focus on the kind and the order of teaching/instructional events rather than on the specific content that is to be taught.

Ways Students May Gain Access to the Must-Learn Information

There are four ways in which students can gain access to the must-learn information:

a. **By direct encounter via external sources.** The resources, such as lectures, textbooks, handouts, a peer in a cooperative learning activity or lab team, filmstrips and/or tutors, actually contain or provide the "exact" infobits learners need to acquire. When these resources are available and used, students must be helped to attend to, consider, and store the must-learn infobits presented to them as direct input.

b. **By invention through internal self-generation.** Here instructional resources do not contain or provide the must-learn infobits. Rather, learners must consider and process infobits about and from resources until they generate or discover the target infobits for themselves. In extreme instances, they personally must invent and construct all of the infobits they need in order to learn. Resources used in conjunction with indirect models of teaching represent instances in which such invention must occur. This invention may be self-initiated or guided via external cues, questions, and instructions. When this means of access is selected, teachers bear the burden of providing what is needed to guide students to generate the appropriate information.

c. **By selective recovery and arrangement of internally-stored information.** Here, a resource may be used to enable learners to search in and recover from their Permanent Storage[33] information concerning thoughts, academic content, feelings, and behaviors that they need to attend to, process, and use. These resources do not provide information that needs to be learned or require learners to invent new infobits. Rather, resources such as questions help learners retrieve infobits they already have learned so that they can reconsider and arrange them in terms of conceptions, abilities, or perspectives they are now considering and learning.

d. **By a combination of any two or all three of the above-mentioned ways.**

None of these four is inherently "better" than the others. They are described here to demonstrate ways that students have available to gain access to critical information (Stahl, 1987; Stahl & Verdi, 1992).

Generic Classes of Models of Instruction (or Teaching)

Each model of teaching was/is originally designed to set up a particular environment for learning. This environment involves resources, learners, and a teacher interacting in particular ways at particular moments. Models vary in the number and types of abilities and outcomes that they can help students to acquire. For instance, a model may be useful in helping students acquire only particular types of concepts. Another model may be intended to help students learn nearly any ability that teachers may want students to attain. Models of instruction vary in the quality and amount of the details that they provide to help teachers plan for, establish, carry out, and assess the particular environment that they advocate for learners and learning.

Decisions regarding instructional implementation may also be viewed as being consistent with one of three generic approaches. One approach requires that students directly encounter the must-learn information from or within one or more external sources. These sources may be but are not limited to teacher lecture, the textbook, or library resource. The second approach requires students to invent and construct the must-learn information for themselves. The third approach requires that some of the must-learn information be encountered directly in external resources with students inventing and constructing the rest. Any student activity chosen will fit one of these approaches and must eventually get students access to the must-learn information they need in order to be highly successful.

If specific models and strategies of "indirect instruction" are to be optimal, then the instructional activity chosen must enable students to invent some to all of the information students must learn in order to achieve the TLO selected. While one way this may be accomplished is by allowing students to engage in inquiry tasks that lead to invention of the must-learn information, there is no guarantee that student involvement with the inquiry will actually lead to their invention of all of this information. For example, if students are to acquire the definition of a short story by inventing it, a text providing a number of short stories *may* be appropriate. Students would need to sort through, make sense of, and assign meaning to information they were reading in these stories in order to construct a viable definition that would hold for all short stories. The teacher's job would be to facilitate this invention, meaning-making, and construction activity to ensure that such a definition actually does result from the students' involvement.

While "processes" and "processing" are critical dimensions of the inquiry approach to instruction, these must lead eventually to the invention and acquisition of targeted information, infoschemata, and conceptions. A well-defined inquiry strategy is not the only model that can be used in indirect instruction situations. Any instructional approach in which the external activity or resources do not contain all the must-learn information for students to encounter in a direct manner is an invention strategy.

In nearly every case, models of instruction concern themselves with initial attainment of the information-base and abilities aligned with a TLO, PILOA, or SILOA (Stahl, 1989b, 1994; Stahl & Verdi, 1992). They rarely provide the additional opportunities for students to gain access to complementary information, to complete necessary and sufficient processing, and to spend the time each needs to spend in attaining and maintaining the abilities to the levels expected. This failure to articulate such extensions and the failure even among proponents of a model to direct teachers to provide for such information, processing, and time are major reasons why students seem to "lose" so rapidly what they appeared to have "learned" inside the classroom.

So, once the instructional events associated with a particular model or strategy have been completed as described, the teacher must deliberately and constantly extend learning tasks directly aligned with the must-learn information and processing in order to increase the likelihood that students will complete their internal tasks and spend the time they need to spend in mastering the content, processing, and ability. In most situations, this requires both in-class and out-of-class on-task rehearsal tasks with descriptive feedback.

Because of this variety and diversity, models could be organized into any number of classes, depending on the criteria one wanted to use (Joyce & Weil, 1972).

An alternative way to organize the various approaches, techniques, strategies, and models is by the extent to which students have direct access to the must-learn information relative to the degree to which they must invent the information they need to be successful. Arranging instructional models in this way generated three generic classes within which all teaching models may be placed.

The Three Generic Classes or Models of Teaching/Instruction

In view of the role and importance of having and using relevant information in order to acquire and maintain any selected cognitive, affective or psychomotor ability or state, we have generated generic classes based upon the quantity and quality of the must-learn information that is to be directly provided to students in the external resources they are to use. Using this criterion, three generic classes emerged: *Supply, Invention,* and *Combination* (Stahl, 1987; Stahl & Verdi, 1992). These have no priority, nor is one automatically "better" or "more effective" than the others.

A. Supply Models. Models, strategies, and approaches are included in this class when they require that students be directly given or be directed to external sources that contain the must-learn information so that they gain access to this information. In other words, students are provided the actual information they need to have in very explicit form in resources they are given, directed to locate and use, or find on their own. For instance, suppose students are to learn to apply a definition for a term. If they obtain access to this definition via a lecture, an overhead, chalkboard or computer screen, a handout, textbook, or dictionary, or by a tutor, movie, cooperative group member, audiocassette, or guest speaker, they have been involved in activities consistent with a supply model of instruction. If they are directed to find the definition in some specific reference book or are instructed to use any resource available to get a definition and they do encounter the definition they are to learn directly from such resources, this is supply model-oriented instruction.

In all these instances, students obtain the must-learn information by directly encountering it in straightforward language within external resources. No inferences, interpretations, or translations are used to get this information except those which come via literal comprehension events. For instance, students who are to learn the attributes of a concept, the procedures for balancing chemical equations, or the rules for punctuation would come face-to-face with this information in at least one external resource they encounter. The teacher should note that processing events—tasks such as comprehension and interpretation—may be needed immediately after this encounter to help assign meaning to the information.

By definition, models fitting this class require that students be provided 100 percent of the must-learn information in explicit form in one or more resources. They are not to "think up" any of it. It is possible to provide learners all of the information they must learn in direct form.

That these models must provide the must-learn information directly to students does not mean that only lecture or textbook materials can be used as resources. These models rarely limit the actual resources that can be used. Even tutors and members of cooperative learning teams, as well as small group problem-solving activities, can serve as "carriers" of the information. Teachers should not limit the resource variety merely because the information must be presented in a direct manner to learners.

Each model in this class instructs teachers as to how to give students direct access to all the must-learn information. However, a type of resource should not be confused with this class of model. A lecture, handout, textbook, or team member, for instance, may or may not include all the information they need to learn. Only when the instructional resources provide it all does the model as used fit this class.

B. Invention Models. Models, strategies, and approaches in this class require students to invent, generate, or discover, and then organize all the must-learn information entirely by internal processing tasks. The must-learn information-products (i.e., attributes, procedures, definitions, and policy options or any other information such as listed earlier in Table 1) are direct results of each student's constructive processing. Students do not obtain this information from any external sources. Rather, they must make it up for themselves as a product of their activated "prior knowledge," infoschemata, and processing events as they interact with available resources, their environment, and others. For instance, students may be shown a number of exemplars of a particular concept and be asked to generate or invent a definition or set of relevant attributes for the concept in light of these exemplars. This may or may not be the exact same definition or set of attributes that the teacher could provide in a handout or lecture. However, in this case, students get this definition in an entirely different way; that is, students are required to invent 100 percent of the need-to-learn information.

The responsibility of the strategies and models that fit this class and of teachers who use these strategies is to guide and facilitate students in processing the information they encounter so that they generate on their own the information they need to learn. In many cases, descriptions of such strategies and the actions of teachers who use them are far too inadequate to guide students to inventing and constructing all of the information needed to achieve the desired outcome. Because teachers are not aware of these responsibilities or inadequacies, these strategies tend to fail in many classrooms. Perhaps these are major reasons why teachers tend to abandon such strategies and resort to activities that they perceive are more appropriate to cover the information targeted.

C. Combination Models. Models, strategies, and approaches in this class represent a blending of ways in which students obtain the must-learn information. Part of this information will come via direct access to resources which explicitly contain it while the rest is invented and constructed internally by the learner. By these two means, the student encounters all of the critical information needed. Nearly all models in actual operation fit this class, because the resources used tend to provide some of the information, and students are left to invent the rest.

Within the environment established, models vary widely in the extent to which they contain the specific information students are to learn and appropriate rehearsal processing that they need to complete. The degree of directness-indirectness models in terms of the amount of the must-learn information students will be directly provided or can locate in an explicit form is depicted below in visual form:

Direct	Combination	Indirect
X		X
100%	Between 1 and 99%	0%
of must-learn	of the must-learn	of must-learn
information	information is provided	information
is directly	directly with the rest	is directly
provided and/	invented internally	provided and/
or encountered		or encountered

The Three Generic Models Illustrated

This section will describe a sample teaching strategy for each generic model, strategies that are used within typical classrooms. Each is described briefly in the context of the IC framework. These descriptions are illustrative overviews of selected applications of the IC perspective to curriculum and instructional decisions.

(a) Supply Model: A Lecture/Text Strategy as an Example. In this strategy, the teacher decides that the students will be directly supplied with all of the must-learn information needed to attain a particular set of abilities. One reason for this decision is to ensure that students do get access to this information in a focused and timely manner. A second reason is to reduce ambiguity among students as to what information they need to pay most attention to, process, and store for later use.

Once this decision is made, the teacher makes an outline of the lecture notes. Pages of the textbook that contain this information may be assigned. Decisions are made about pace, style, and tone of the oral presentation.

During the lecture itself, the teacher needs to allow pauses of silence for students to write relevant information in their notes, as well as to make sense of, assign meaning to, consider, and reflect upon the information provided. Such time enables many to construct their personalized version of the content and context of the information being heard.

After the lecture, the teacher needs to provide opportunities for students to systematically process the just-provided, must-learn information. These opportunities, which may include group interaction or comprehension and application exercises, provide extra time for students to make more sense of, assign greater meaning to, reconsider, and reflect further upon the information just provided. These on-task activities and appropriate feedback/feedforward information enable students to construct relatively adequate versions of the information encountered via the lecture and readings during the period. If the information is expected to be applied by students at the end of the unit/course, then the teacher should arrange for students to complete at least one monitored application exercise before the class period ends.

Once the initial instructional activity has been completed, students need to continue to process the must-learn information over an extended number of days following the completion of this first class. Teachers need to assign homework that will require students to continue working with the information in outcome-ability relevant ways until they have gained the proficiency expected.

(b) Invention Model: A Lecture/Text Strategy as an Example. In this strategy, students will not be directly supplied any of the must-learn information aligned with a targeted set of abilities. One reason for the teacher's decision to use this approach is to ensure that students get involved in working through relevant information in order to make sense of it and to eventually invent the information they need to learn. A second reason is to alter the means by which students gain access to must-learn information.

In this example, the teacher decides to use the familiar lecture and textbook resources. However, these resources will be used differently than in the past. Particular must-learn information is not provided at any time during the presentation. Pages of the textbook that contain relevant but not the must-learn information are assigned to be read ahead of time, or may be read during breaks in the lecture, and/or after the lecture has ended. Decisions are also made about pace, style, and tone of the oral presentation of the lecture.

During the lecture itself, the teacher allows pauses of silence for students to write relevant information in their notes as well as to make sense of, assign meaning to, consider, and reflect upon the information provided. Such time enables many to construct their personalized version of the content and context of the information.

After lecture, the teacher provides opportunities for students to systematically process the just-provided information. This processing typically occurs in three phases.

The first phase is concerned with monitoring students to determine whether they attended to the information presented and comprehended this information. The teacher is aware that if students did not get the information presented and/or failed to comprehend it adequately, then students have a weak data base—and it is this data base that must be processed in order for them to invent the must-learn infobits.

The second phase is processing of relevant non-must-learn information in such a way that students actually invent the must-learn information. This generation and construction activity has as its single focus the production of the information that students must learn. The invention opportunities, which may include group interaction or comprehension and clarification exercises, provide extra time for students to make more sense of, assign greater meaning to, reconsider, and reflect further upon the information just provided in order to invent the information that has not been provided. These on-task activities when appropriate feedback/feedforward information is also provided, enable students to construct relatively adequate versions of the must-learn information not encountered via the lecture and readings.

The third phase involves processing the freshly-invented must-learn information in such a way that students comprehend and assign relevant meanings to what they have just made up. These opportunities, that may include group interaction or comprehension, clarification and application exercises, provide extra time for students to make more sense of, assign greater meaning to, reconsider, and reflect further upon the just-invented must-learn information. These on-task activities, when appropriate feedback/feedforward information is also provided, enable students to construct relatively adequate versions of the must-learn information not encountered via the lecture and readings.

Once the initial instructional activity has been completed, students need to continue to process the must-learn information over an extended number of days following the completion of this first class. Teachers need to assign homework that will require students to continue working with the information in outcome-ability relevant ways until they have gained the proficiency expected.

(c) Combination Model: A Concept Attainment Strategy as an Example. Concept attainment models are widely supported approaches to facilitate instruction. These models typically have three phases to facilitating students' acquisition of concept-aligned content and to help students use valued reasoning patterns or "thinking strategies" to attain other concepts in the future. These models and strategies can be used over a wide range of descriptive and normative concepts in diverse subject-matter fields. Moreover, when used correctly, these models are expected to enable students to attain a portion of the many inquiry and thinking strategy goals of education.

Effective use of the model used in this example requires that before instruction begins, the teacher articulates the to-be-learned information aligned with the concept-linked outcome abilities that students are to acquire. This decision includes selecting the relevant term or concept-label, definition, and set of attributes of the selected concept. The teacher must select and locate descriptions of one or more examples and non-examples of the phenomena associated with the concept that students are to acquire. For instance, if the concept selected is "sexual harassment," then a number of written, video, and/or role play examples and non-examples of sexual harassment need to be obtained prior to instruction. Then, the teacher must review the requirements of each phase of the selected model and be prepared to move students through each of the phases as required. Finally, the teacher must double-check his or her planning so that the primary information base that students will acquire and later apply is aligned with the target goals for that unit. By doing these things, the teacher is prepared to guide students on-task throughout their interactions and inventive tasks.

The initial stage in the sample strategy is the *Opening Set* (or Set Induction). Here the teacher announces the label of the concept students are to construct and acquire and describes the steps students will complete during the acquisition process. The reasons why the concept is important as well as details concerning where and when the concept is used or can be applied may be given now or toward the end of the period.

During phase two, the *Encounter-the-Examples Phase,* the teacher facilitates the students' access to adequate descriptions of one, two, or three examples of the phenomena. Depending upon the concept selected and resources available, these examples may be in the textbook, on handouts, in videos, by role play, or even replicas, realia, or pictures.

In phase three, the *Search for and Invent Common Characteristics Phase,* students freely interact with the data in the description(s) as they seek to answer the question: If these are examples of the concept X, what are the specific characteristics or features that are common to all these examples? Allowing students sufficient time to explore and interact with the descriptive data enables the construction of possible patterns and common attributes concerning the phenomenon at hand. In some instances, teachers have been known to provide one or more nonexamples to help students attend more closely to the common features of the examples. Students emerge from this phase with a list of the most viable descriptions of attributes or common pattern(s) that are supported by the data in the examples and nonexamples encountered.

In phase four, the *Test and Refine the Set of Relevant Attributes Phase,* the focus is the completion of investigative, sense-making, meaning-making, and generative processing tasks wherein students check out the attributes they initially developed by testing them through application to new examples and nonexamples. They add to, revise, drop, or rewrite the attributes as they refine the set toward assembling the list of relevant or critical attributes that serve as the boundary of the concept. They again "test" these attributes via application to already as well as not yet studied examples and nonexamples. When all goes well, students leave this phase with the most viable set of relevant attributes consistent with accepted examples of the concept.

In phase five, the *Attributes Comprehension Phase,* students take the time to rephrase each attribute as they translate each into words and phrases each student personally comprehends. While this comprehension and sense-making has been occurring throughout the earlier phases, this time students attend to comprehending the "final" set of relevant attributes for the particular concept.

During phase six, the *Concept Solidification Phase,* students spend productive time formulating a definition for the concept by combining the relevant attributes into a descriptive sentence; considering infobits concerning the *whens* and *wheres* of the concept's use; and the importance and relevance of the concept to their academic study, everyday situations, and real-world situations that they may never directly experience. For instance, if the concept selected is "civil war," they may study current events in another nation to determine whether those events can be labeled a civil war. During this phase, students are supplied with or invent specific information that may furnish, complement, or replace information generated about the concept besides the attributes they invented. Here students may be provided any variety of resources, including lecture, a handout, textbook, etc., that would include this complementary must-learn information, without which the targeted concept would have little meaning or relevance. Consequently, the teacher must see this information as being of no less importance than the set of relevant attributes for that concept.

The seventh phase is the *Concept Application Phase.* At this time, students apply the newly constructed concept (i.e., its information base in the form of relevant attributes, definition, details on when and where, etc.) to previously unstudied examples and nonexamples. Students are given opportunities to extend their information base by applying what was just constructed to new situations. Moreover, the additional applications of the newly invented information and concept serve as a second source of validation for the concept and its information base. Students are provided the opportunity to assess the extent to which their personal concepts are viable in other situations and to refine and strengthen the concept as needed. During this phase, students are provided with opportunities to actually test and further refine their freshly-invented concept through appropriate rehearsal tasks within the classroom. Ample on-target descriptive feedback is needed in order to ensure that adjustments students make are consistent with acceptable versions of the concept's critical attributes. Students are successful to the extent they retain and apply the information base of the concept to discriminate between exemplars and nonexemplars.

In the final phase of the strategy, the *Closure Phase,* students reflect on the information base they have constructed with data from external sources as well as their own internal invention processes. In addition, they take time to articulate the steps in the process that they used to obtain, consider, refine, and test the information that was constructed around the target concept and to consider where and when they may use this process to construct information bases aligned with other concepts.[34]

Once the initial instructional activities for each of these three examples have been completed, students need to continue to process the must-learn information and abilities over an extended number of days following the completion of this first class. Teachers need to assign homework that will require students to continue working with the information in ways relevant to the outcome abilities until they have gained the proficiency expected.

This section has illustrated how the three generic classes of models of instruction may be useful in classifying three representative teaching strategies used in classrooms. In addition, specific ways in which these models operate from an IC perspective were presented.[35]

To be most effective, the actual instructional events—including the interactions between each student and the phenomena studied, each student and his/her peers and teacher, and each student and the information encountered from all sources—must be in direct alignment with the TLO, SILOA/Os, and final exam test items. Figure 2 illustrates this relationship. At the same time, the learning tasks and interactions need to help students to complete the appropriate processing tasks and to spend the time each needs to spend in order to attain and maintain the information and abilities expected.

The IC Perspective: A Viable Paradigm?

The IC perspective represents a significant new paradigm in that:

(a) This perspective represents both a synthesis and an extension of existing models and theories of cognition and learning that already serve as foundations for further practice in a number of areas in which a viable theory of cognition would be expected to be used successfully.
(b) I have no accurate data as to the extent to which scholars and practitioners are turning away from existing, competing modes of thought and activity to buy into the IC perspective. There is evidence, though, from increasing numbers of participants at my conference and workshop sessions that interest in this perspective is growing.

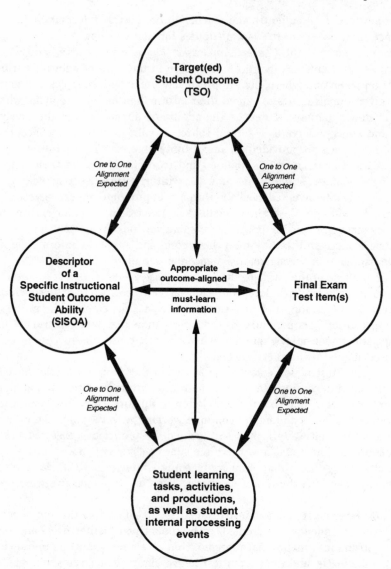

Figure 2. Four major components of curriculum decision-making and instruction in direct alignment with each other and with appropriate information that students must learn to be successful.

(c) The perspective, especially with its heavy information emphasis, is sufficiently open-ended to leave all sorts of problems for the redefining group of researchers and practitioners to resolve.

(d) This perspective, as illustrated by the contents of this chapter, both provides and leads to models from which can spring particular coherent traditions of scientific research.

Could this perspective become the dominant and guiding paradigm of the field of instructional design? The answer is, "Yes! It could." This answer is based on the fact that, as illustrated herein, the IC view can provide the foundation of assumptions, theories, concepts, and models that can guide future practice.

Without adequate infoschemata relative to how people learn and the important variables of learning, individuals engaged in the ID process are likely to make decisions based solely upon external factors such as materials, activities, and products, which may or may not be consistent with what learners need to have in order to be successful. In addition, unless they use an ID model that enables them to integrate this concern for important learning variables while they proceed through the steps in the ID process, they may complete the process, and even develop a lengthy tangible product, but implement instructional variables that are less successful than they might have been were these variables considered throughout the process.

One valuable and powerful way to help individuals to attend to learner variables, to acquire and master one or more ID decision-making models, and to accept the value of more deliberate pre-instructional planning is to facilitate their generation of tangible products that are records of their decisions. As records of their decisions, IDers can trace their decision paths, reflect upon what they have decided and why they made these decisions, consider what they thought was important and not important, and assess the quality of their own decision-making processes and decisions.

When an appropriate atmosphere is maintained while the IDer is acquiring these ID abilities, he or she tends to shift attention from just a concern for the quality of the tangible product in the form of course guides and written curriculum plans toward a conscious concern for the quality and appropriateness of the internal variables in his or her decision-making processes that generated these products. In addition, at least for the students with whom the author has been working, individuals acquire a strong sense of the interconnections among the planning, instruction, and assessment components of the ID process.

Notes

1. Formal curriculum planning and formal instructional design are not identical processes. Pre-instructional curriculum development, planning, or design, by whichever name one wants to use, includes the decision-making events from initial consideration and selection of target learner outcomes through to the task of describing specific learner outcome abilities as objectives and the writing of the final exam test items aligned directly with selected target, priority, and specific learner outcome abilities. Decisions regarding the scope and the general sequence of information and abilities that learners are to encounter and/or acquire are expected in the curriculum planning process. Decisions involving specific sequence of information and abilities for learners and the specific learning tasks and resources that may be used are additions to the curriculum planning process. However, these are essential decision points in systematic instructional design. A comprehensive instructional design model would include all of the curriculum design decisions plus the multitude of decisions regarding the actual setting up of the environment of the learner during the learning tasks and during the time allocated for instruction.

2. Besides abilities, the instructional designer may select any attainable and maintainable state or condition of being, such as "learners will be competent inquirers" or "learners will be appreciators of Impressionistic Art," as a target outcome. For the sake of brevity, this chapter will focus on outcome abilities that learners could acquire.

3. The specific courses to which the author is referring do not include segments that go into detail or depth on planning for daily instructional periods and on specific teaching models, techniques, or behaviors. At present, they emphasize the prior-to-instruction decisions, thereby stopping short of detailed planning of day-by-day instructional events and teacher behaviors.

4. Two of these models are SPINPROM (Synthesis Perceptual Information Processing and Operations Model) and TIPIOA (Taxonomy of Information Processing Indicators and Outcome Abilities), a viable alternative to Bloom's cognitive taxonomy (Stahl, 1984a, 1992a, c). Details concerning these models are available from the author. A third model, the IC Model of School Learning, is described briefly in this chapter (also, Stahl, 1989a, 1995).

5. Space does not permit an elaboration of the reasons for the avoidance of these terms and the concepts and meanings they conjure up in people's brains. A longer manuscript that deals specifically with such concepts is underway.

6. "Infobit" (plural, "infobits") is a term coined by the author in 1983 to denote any piece or bit of information or data and occurrence that will be perceived, what meaning each will have, what sense each makes to him or her, and how each will be transformed, distorted, stored and forgotten.

7. This assumes that there are no physiological problems or dysfunctional activity caused by such things as foreign substances, an internal electro-chemical imbalance, or neurological damage or deficiencies.

8. "Re-presented" is not the same as "represented." Re-presented is a Piagetian notion of retrieving something for the purpose of presenting it once again for additional consideration, assessment, and reflection, hence the use of the prefix "re-."

9. The 23 hours is a "rule of thumb" period for instructional settings because students typically return to the same class period approximately 23 hours after the class ended the previous day.

10. Besides abilities, the instructional designer could select any acquirable condition or state of being, such as "learners will be inquirers" or "learners will be appreciators of Impressionistic paintings," as a target outcome. For the sake of brevity, this chapter will focus on outcome abilities that learners could acquire.

11. The information-constructivist reconceptualization of "schemata" as "infoschemata," the characteristics, roles, and influences of infoschemata, and the rationale for the new construct are provided elsewhere (e.g., Stahl & Casteel, 1990; Stahl, 1992a).

12. Planning is any processing and decision-making tasks associated with a future action the person engages in *prior to* making final decisions before starting a particular set of actions. The final set of decisions represents the plan. One should not automatically assume that merely because some person or group is engaged in planning or has planned some action that either the decision-making processes involved or the decisions reached are quantitatively and qualitatively appropriate.

13. A large number of pre- and in-service teachers view the task of completing components of decision components of a curriculum plan outline as being something other than a set of decisions they are to make. Their perspective typically treats these steps as having little value or function relative to their own teaching and student learning and considers them as mechanical "tell me what to do and I'll do it the way you want" operations rather than as a series of important decisions that represent their personal choices and priorities aligned with actual enhancement of student learning.

14. Within the IC perspective, the label "abilities" is preferred over "skills" for several reasons, not the least of which is the notion that for the IC, learners may eventually become "skilled at" any particular ability. The term "skill" is used to denote a qualitative dimension of an ability rather than the ability itself. Consequently, one facilitates others to become skilled at an ability. It makes no sense to claim that one intends to help another become skilled at or in a skill (also see Cornbleth, 1987).

15. The label "uniprocessing ability" is used here and continues to be used since coined by the author in 1984. A new label is being sought to name the category of human-invented "thinking processes" that consists of a number of *uni*versally applicable, cross-disciplinary cognitive tasks that generate a set of information that is *uni*que to that set of processing tasks.

16. For our purposes here, this phase refers to the selection of only one outcome. Depending upon the time available and the circumstances of the learners and instructional setting, the IDer certainly may be able to select more than one outcome ability for a particular course or unit.

17. For purposes of this chapter, "unit" will be used throughout. Certainly the perspective and guidelines here are appropriate to courses, modules, programs, etc.

18. One student generated a list of over 4,500 descriptors of information in reference to one TLO without including any subject matter content not specifically mentioned in the actual statement of the TLO. This list was produced after the student had announced that the fewer than 50 descriptors originally generated were all that were possible from the target outcome selected.

19. If one or more sub-abilities has been determined and stated, then a list of descriptors is generated for each sub-ability following the same guidelines as for the TLO.

20. General suggested guidelines for courses or units of other lengths and situations are available from the author.

21. One of these words would be selected as is appropriate to the ability that each learner is to possess in relation to the piece of information that follows. Note that none of these options refers to an ex-

ternal performance or product, but rather to an internal, hence invisible, ability that learners may acquire and maintain. The descriptors of specific instructional learner outcome abilities included in step G describe the external performances and products that will be accepted as public evidence that these internal abilities exist.

22. The IDer should not begin planning by seeking out a set of General Instructional Learner Outcome Objectives. Instead the concern should be to determine the generic internal abilities that learners are to acquire and then to describe them as clearly as possible. Once these abilities are described, they may be viewed as "objectives" of instruction. This orientation helps the planner and the instructor to maintain a focus on what the learner needs to accomplish rather than what the instructor needs to "teach to," cover, or attain. Seen in this way, the objective cannot be attained unless there is sufficient evidence that the learners have attained the generic ability described.

23. The IDer should not begin planning by seeking out a set of General or Specific Instructional Learner Outcome Objectives. Instead the concern should be to determine the target and priority internal abilities learners are to acquire and then to describe these as clearly as possible. Once these abilities are described, these may be viewed as "objectives" of instruction. This orientation helps the planner and the instructor to maintain a focus on what the learner needs to acquire rather than what the instructor needs to "teach to," cover, or attain. Seen in this way, the objective cannot be said to have been attained unless there is sufficient and appropriate public evidence that the learners have attained the target and priority ability described.

24. Once again, depending upon such factors as the length of the course, the amount of instructional time actually available, etc., this number may vary from unit to unit or for the same unit with different learners.

25. The author has designed a Target Information Chart to record these descriptors. This chart enables the IDer to record other relevant decisions prior to selecting and writing descriptors of Specific Instructional Learner Outcome Abilities (SILOAs).

26. The first set of labels refer to Levels, Categories, and Subcategories of the Taxonomy of Information Processing Indicators and Outcome Abilities (TIPIOA) (Stahl, 1992c), an alternative to Bloom's cognitive model .

27. These letters indicate one of the seven categories of mastery that students could attain for a particular ability to make use of a particular infobit. "MM," for instance, represents the "Maintained Mastery" category (Stahl, 1986).

28. The taxonomic system used by the author is a highly viable alternative to Bloom's Cognitive Taxonomy, labeled the Taxonomy of Information Processing Indicators of Abilities and Outcomes (TIPIAO) (Stahl, 1992c).

29. These are referred to as "exiting performance objectives" to emphasize that these are abilities learners are to have when they are exiting the unit, rather than abilities they are to demonstrate one or more times during the unit of instruction.

30. Definitions of the specific components for each SILOO and the guidelines for constructing statements which describe them are available elsewhere (Stahl, 1992c).

31. For instance, one teacher announced to her students, who were working on group projects to present orally to their peers and who were to construct a test to measure how much their peers learned from the presentation, that a teacher never places anything on the final test that was emphasized in class, since everyone might make a good score and you couldn't separate the "good" students from the "bad" ones that way!

32. The word *pedagogy* is derived from the Greek words meaning "child" and "to lead." A *pedagogue* is a person who "leads a child"; *pedagogy* is his or her craft as a teacher/leader; and *pedagogical decisions* refer to the choices the teacher/leader makes regarding the carrying out of his/her roles of "leading" the child to become a successful learner.

33. *Permanent Storage* is a component of the IC information processing model (Stahl, 1982, 1990, 1992c). This 'storage' function is distinct from the 'scan,' 'search,' 'locate,' 'verify,' 'retrieve,' 'fabricate,' and 'assemble' functions that characterize *Long Term Memory.*

34. For those in science education, the Learning Cycle Model (e.g., Lawson, Abraham, & Renner, 1989) as it typically occurs in the classroom would be classified as a combination model of teaching.

35. Currently, a universal model of instruction, wherein all models are variations of the one, is being completed by the author.

References

Andrews, D. H., & Goodson, L. A. (1980). A comparative analysis of models of instructional design. *Journal of Instructional Development, 3*(4), 2–16.

Ausubel, D. P. (1963). *The psychology of meaningful verbal learning: An introduction to school learning.* New York: Grune and Stratton.

Ausubel, D. P. (1968). *Educational psychology.* New York: Holt, Rinehart, and Winston.

Bandura, A. (1986). *Social foundations of thought and action: A social cognitive theory.* Englewood Cliffs, NJ: Prentice-Hall.

Bartlett, F. C. (1932). *Remembering: A study in experimental and social psychology.* Cambridge: Cambridge University Press.

Beard, C. A. (1934). Written history as an act of faith. *American Historical Review, 39*(2), 219–231.

Becker, C. L. (1955). What are historical facts? *The Western Political Quarterly, 8*(3), 327–340.

Bittinger, M. L. (1968, February). A review of discovery. *The Mathematics Teacher, 61,* 140–145.

Block, J. H., Efthim, H. E., & Burns, R. B. (1989). *Building effective mastery learning schools.* New York: Longman.

Bloom, B. S. (Ed.). (1956). *Taxonomy of educational objectives: The classification of educational goals. Handbook I: Cognitive domain.* New York: Longman.

Bloom, B. S. (1976). *Human characteristics and school learning.* New York: McGraw-Hill.

Burns, R. W. (1977). *New approaches to behavioral objectives* (2nd ed.). Dubuque, IA: W. C. Brown.

Carr, E. H. (1961). *What is history?* New York: Vintage Books.

Carroll, J. B. (1963). A model of school learning. *Teachers College Record, 64*(8), 723–733.

Carroll, J. B. (1989). The Carroll Model: A 25-year retrospective and prospective view. *Educational Researcher, 18*(1), 26–31.

Casteel, J. D., & Stahl, R. J. (1973). *The Social Science Observation Record (SSOR): Theoretical construct and pilot studies.* Gainesville, FL: P. K. Yonge Laboratory School.

Cohen, S. A. (1987). Instructional alignment: Searching for the magic bullet. *Educational Researcher, 16*(8), 16–20.

Combs, A. W., Richards, A. C., & Richards, F. (1976). *Perceptual psychology: A humanistic approach to the study of persons.* New York: Harper & Row.

Combs, A. W., & Syngg, D. (1959). *Individual behavior.* New York: Harper & Row.

Cornbleth, C. (1987). The persistence of myth in teacher education and teaching. In T. S. Popkewitz (Ed.), *Critical studies in teacher education: Its folklore, theory, and practice.* Philadelphia: Falmer Press.

Croce, B. (1941). *History as the story of liberty.* London: George Allen & Unwin.

Dempster, F. N. (1988). The spacing effect: A case study in the failure to apply the results of psychological research. *American Psychologist, 43*(8), 627–634.

Dick, W., & Carey, L. (1990). *The systematic design of instruction* (3rd ed.). Glenview, IL: Scott, Foresman.

Gagné, R. M. (1985). *The conditions of learning* (4th ed.). New York: Holt, Rinehart, and Winston.

Gagné, R. M., Briggs, L. J., & Wager, W. W. (1988). *Principles of instructional design* (3rd ed.). New York: Holt, Rinehart, and Winston.

Guskey, T. R. (1985). *Implementing mastery learning.* Belmont, CA: Wadsworth.

Henson, K. T. (1980). Discovery learning. *Contemporary Education, 51*(2), 101–103.

Joyce, B., & Weil, M. (1972). *Models of teaching.* Englewood Cliffs, NJ: Prentice-Hall. [Also see three later editions.]

Kelly, G. A. (1955). *The psychology of personal constructs.* New York: Norton.

Kuhn, D., Asmel, E., & O'Loughlin, M. (1988). *The development of scientific thinking skills.* San Diego: Academic Press.

Kuhn, T. S. (1970). *The structure of scientific revolutions* (2nd ed.). Chicago: University of Chicago Press.

Lawson, A. E., Abraham, M. R., & Renner, J. W. (1989). *A theory of instruction: Using the learning cycle to teach science concepts and thinking skills.* Cincinnati, OH: National Association for Research in Science Teaching.

Mager, R. F. (1962). *Preparing instructional objectives.* Belmont, CA: Fearon.

McGhee, R. (1978). *Points of departure: Basic concepts in sociology* (alternative edition). Hinsdale, IL: Dryden Press.

Mead, G. H. (1934). *Mind, self, and society: From the standpoint of a social behaviorist.* Chicago: University of Chicago Press.

Murphey, R. (1982). *The scope of geography* (3rd ed.). New York: Methuen.

Neisser, U. (1967). *Cognitive psychology.* New York: Appleton.

Neisser, U. (1976). *Cognition and reality.* San Francisco: Freeman.

Orlich, D. C. (1989, March). Science inquiry in the common place. *Science and Children,* 22–24.

Posner, G. J., & Rudnitsky, A. N. (1994). *Course design: A guide to curriculum development for teachers* (4th ed.). New York: Longman.

Stahl, R. J. (1982). What do we know about student learning, memory, and thinking? Paper presented at the annual meeting of the National Council for the Social Studies, November, Boston.

Stahl, R. J. (1983). The domain of cognition: A viable alternative to Bloom's Taxonomy. Paper presented at the Annual Turner Seminar, July, Vail, CO.

Stahl, R. J. (1984a). Cognitive theory within the framework of an information processing model and a learning hierarchy: Viable alternatives to the Bloom-Mager systems. In R. K. Bass & C. R. Dills (Eds.), *Instructional design: The state of the art II* (pp. 149–168). Dubuque, IA: Kendall/Hunt.

Stahl, R. J. (1984b). An information-based model of information processing: Basic components and critical principles of cognitive uniprocesses. Presentation at the Annual Turner Seminar, July, Vail, CO.

Stahl, R. J. (1986). New ways of thinking about how humans think and learn: Practical synthesis models within an information processing format. Presentation at the annual conference of the Association for Supervision and Curriculum Development, March, San Francisco.

Stahl, R. J. (1987). A way of thinking about how humans think and learn: An Information-Constructivist perspective. Session presented at the biennial meeting of the Australian Association for Curriculum Studies, Macquarie University, July, North Ryde, NSW.

Stahl, R. J, (1989a). Time alone does not mastery make: Extending Carroll's Model of School Learning in light of an information processing perspective. Paper presented at the annual meeting of the American Educational Research Association, April, San Francisco.

Stahl, R. J. (1989b). Curriculum planning through instructional design: Guidelines. [Unpublished manuscript used in draft form for classes taught by the author. Manuscript is being revised.]

Stahl, R. J. (1990). What students need and do to become successful learners: An Information-Constructivist prospective of school learning. Paper presented at the annual meeting of the National Association for Research in Science Teaching, April, Atlanta.

Stahl, R. J. (1991a). The Information-Constructivist (IC) perspective: Applications to and implications for science education. Paper presented at the annual meeting of the National Association for Research in Science Teaching, April, Lake Geneva, WI.

Stahl, R. J. (1991b). Determining must-learn information directly aligned with target student outcome abilities (unpublished book chapter).

Stahl, R. J. (1992a). A context for "higher order knowledge": An Information-Constructivist (IC) perspective with implications for curriculum and instruction. *Journal of Structural Learning, 11*(3), 189–218.

Stahl, R. J. (1992b). The Information-Constructivist (IC) perspective: An introduction. Paper presented at the annual meeting of the National Association for Research in Science Teaching, March, Boston.

Stahl, R. J. (1992c). The acquisition and a range of "knowledge-based" cognitive abilities: The TIPIOA as a viable educational outcomes taxonomy. *Journal of Structural Learning, 11*(3), 219–245.

Stahl, R. J. (1992d). From 'academic strangers' to successful members of a cooperative learning group: An inside-the-learner perspective." In R. J. Stahl & R. L. VanSickle (Eds.), *Cooperative learning in the social studies classroom: An invitation to social study.* Washington, DC: National Council for the Social Studies.

Stahl, R. J. (1994). Achieving targeted student outcomes: An Information-Constructivist (IC) model to guide curriculum and instructional decisions. *Journal of Structural Learning, 12*(2), 87–111.

Stahl, R. J. (1995, January). Meeting the challenges of making a difference in the classroom: Students' academic success is the difference that counts. *Social Education, 59*(1), 47–53.

Stahl, R. J. (manuscript in preparation a). *Using models of teaching: A practical handbook.*

Stahl, R. J. (manuscript in preparation b). *Making learner-appropriate curriculum and instructional design decisions.*

Stahl, R. J., & Casteel, J. D. (1990). Roles of infoschemata and cognitive-beliefs in thinking and learning in the social studies/social sciences: An Information-Constructivist perspective. (Submitted for publication.)

Stahl, R. J., & Verdi, M. P. (1992). Using the IC perspective to guide curricular and instructional decisions toward attaining desired student outcomes of science education. Paper presented at the annual meeting of the National Association for Research in Science Teaching, Boston, March (Manuscript was revised and has been submitted for publication.).

Wedman, J. F. (1989). Overcoming resistance to formal instructional development processes. *Educational Technology Research & Development, 37*(4), 41–46.

Wittrock, M. C. (1978). The cognitive movement in instruction. *Educational Psychologist, 13,* 15–30.

Wittrock, M. C. (1986). Students' thought processes. In M. C. Wittrock (Ed.), *Handbook of research on teaching* (3rd ed.), (pp. 297–314). New York: Macmillan.

26

Rapid Collaborative Prototyping as an Instructional Development Paradigm

Laura T. Dorsey
Charter Performance Group, Inc., Indianapolis

David A. Goodrum
Thomas M. Schwen
Indiana University, Bloomington

Introduction: Models and Paradigms

Thiagarajan's (1976, p. 10) rebuke that "instructional developers spend more time building models than designing instruction" has done little to slow down the pace at which new models are churned out. Over the last three decades, the proliferation of Instructional Systems Development (ISD) models, intended to serve as a framework to guide the thinking and practices of designers in the field, has added little that is new to our understanding of the ISD process (Hannafin, 1992). The existing myriad of models can be reduced to some combination of three essential activities: analysis, synthesis, and evaluation (McCombs, 1986; Romiszowski, 1981; Thiagarajan, 1976). Unfortunately, ISD models are still "more alike than different" (Andrews & Goodson, 1980; Schiffman, 1991).

The common misuse of the term "model" in the field of instructional development (Davies, 1984) helps to explain why ISD models fail to extend our thinking and our practice. Models are representations of reality presented with a degree of organization and structure (Richey, 1986). Fidelity—an accurate and exact reflection of reality—is expected of a model whether it is intended to describe, prescribe, predict, or explain (Andrews & Goodson, 1980). ISD models, however, are widely perceived as low fidelity—not accurately reflecting what designers actually do in practice (Lange & Grovdahl, 1989; Meggary, 1983; Rowland, 1992; Thiagarajan, 1976).

445

Davies (1984) suggests that what typically is labeled an ISD model is better understood as a graphic representation of a paradigm. What appears to be a plethora of ISD models is in reality only numerous alternate characterizations of a single paradigm. Criticisms of contemporary ISD models intimate that we don't need a new ISD model. We need a new paradigm.

Criticisms of the Current ISD Model/Paradigm

Calls for a new paradigm can be deceiving. It implies that we understand and reject the paradigm underlying our current models. Research finds few articles that report quantitative or qualitative findings on the ID process itself (Molenda, 1987). Questions about the fundamental nature of ID are still unanswered. Although many intuitively recognize that the field's models do not reflect real practice, one cannot with confidence answer the questions, "what is it that ID people do, how do they do it and what is the impact of having done it?" (Dills & Romiszowski, 1987, p. 10).

Nevertheless, the general call for a new paradigm in the field, regarding both research and instructional development, continues to gain momentum (Hannafin, 1992; Streibel, 1991). Central to this call is the belief that our current paradigm is positivist in nature and results in linear, objective-driven models. Such models are perceived as inadequate or inappropriate for the complex, dynamic situations in which learning occurs. For example, Hannafin (1992), in his introduction to a special series on constructivist approaches to learning, asserts:

> While most educators concede that emerging technologies can revolutionize our historic notions of teaching and learning, some are convinced that the application of ISD methods alone will not support such a transformation. Our methods and models are primarily externally directed and content driven. They emphasize the attainment of highly prescribed objective outcomes and the organization of to-be-learned lesson content, not the largely unique and individual organization of knowledge. ISD methods, and instructional design products, are largely convergent and reductionistic in nature. They are perceived as focusing on the part rather than the whole. (p. 50)

There is also growing consensus that much of ISD is based on "empty box" procedural models (McCombs, 1986; Merrill, Li, & Jones, 1990a). Andrews and Goodson (1980, p. 3) explain that the "fidelity of a model to the actual processes it represents will diminish as the specificity of the model diminishes." It is not surprising, therefore, that when prevailing models fail to provide detailed guidelines for practice, actual practice will be seen to differ dramatically.

In addition to being criticized for a lack of detail, our predominant ID models, exemplified by the Dick and Carey model (1985), have been criticized for an overabundance. Tessmer and Wedman (1990, p. 78) emphasize its impracticality, noting standard ID models "prescribe a level of detail and complexity which is difficult, and sometimes impractical, to obtain in practice."

To the above criticisms we would add another: Instructional developers typically describe planning for the adoption and diffusion of new technologies as an activity separate from development. The common pattern is to design a technical or system change and follow it with enforced or coerced individual and organizational change. At best, potential users of the system are included as sources of data in the analysis phase of the process (Schiffman, 1991). The product of design is accepted as optimal and followed by efforts to ensure its adoption by users through the use of effective selling and transitioning strategies.

Reigeluth (1990) describes this as the "expert approach." Expert designers develop the system, which is then "marketed" to stakeholders who may "buy in" or "opt out." The weakness of this approach lies in the fact that designers are not knowledgeable about the environment in which the final product must operate. The result is implicit or explicit rejection of the system, or at best, reluctant acceptance of a solution that does not meet real needs (O'Neill, 1993).

All in all, ISD is under serious attack and reconsideration, if not awash in confusion. On the one hand it is criticized for its time and cost requirements, its impractical level of detail and complexity, its philosophical differences with emerging learning theories, and its lack of validity in reflecting actual practice. On the other hand, as Lange and Grovdahl (1989) point out, there is general agreement that ISD is desirable; even though it is suspected that it may be a term applied by many to *whatever* one is doing to produce training or instruction.

Rapid Prototyping as an Alternative ISD Model

"Rapid Prototyping," a design process used in software design, has been put forth as an alternative model that addresses many of the of conventional ISD model weaknesses. Rapid prototyping is being advanced as more congruent with authentic instructional design practices than conventional models (Tripp & Bichelmeyer, 1990), more flexible and non-linear (Dowding, 1991; de Hoog, de Jong, & de Vries, 1994; Merrill, Li, & Jones, 1990b) more cost effective (Jones, Li, & Merrill, 1992; Tessmer, 1994) and leading to higher user acceptance (O'Neill, 1993).

Whether or not rapid prototyping represents a change in paradigm, as Tripp and Bichelmeyer (1990) assert, is not possible to determine at this point. The reproach that ISD models are essentially "empty boxes," providing no more than general guidelines for practice, applies equally as well to most existing descriptions of rapid prototyping. The relatively incomplete and, at times, conflicting descriptions of how rapid prototyping applies to instructional development provide an inconsistent view of the methodology within the ISD field.

For example, Tessmer (1994) suggests rapid prototyping can serve as a method of formative evaluation as well as a design methodology, while Tripp and Bichelmeyer (1990) clearly disagree. Furthermore, the role of learners and end users of instructional products in the rapid prototyping process is also unclear. Jones, Li, and Merrill (1992) focus on gathering feedback on prototypes from subject matter experts or designers themselves; it is only implied that learners or potential users are directly involved. Tessmer (1994) indicates that either learners *or* experts are involved in the review of incremental products as part of a revision process. Tripp and Bichelmeyer (1990, p. 37) argue that "a crucial part of the prototyping process is utilization of the design with potential learners." In all these descriptions, learners seem to adopt a "reactive" role, traditional to the ISD field, whereas in other fields users serve as equal co-designers in a *participatory design* process (Greenbaum & Kyng, 1991).

What actually constitutes a "prototype" and its utilization in the development process varies. Tessmer (1994, p. 15) describes the prototype as "a working portion of the final product that is immediately implemented with a group of learners or is reviewed by experts." In this view, early design products such as videodisk storyboards are not considered prototypes. Alternately, O'Neill (1993) submits that frequently a "rough sketch" adequately furnishes users a with reliable image of how the system will look and feel. Jones, Li, and Merrill (1992) seem to agree with Tessmer that prototypes are incomplete but essentially "executable versions" of the final product.

While a rational argument and experience from other fields (e.g., Bailey 1993) support claims of improved process and product when rapid prototyping is applied to problems, it is not yet possible to judge the effectiveness and efficiency of this model. As suggested earlier, until the "empty boxes" are sufficiently filled in, its underlying paradigm cannot be characterized and potentially distinguished from other paradigms of development. Descriptions of rapid prototyping from other fields can all be relevant to the instructional designer, but it is difficult to know precisely how to apply this knowledge. It is the intent of the remainder of this chapter, therefore, to begin to explicate a model of development that incorporates a "rapid prototyping" approach. This description is intended to lay the groundwork for further research to increase fidelity and practical application of the model.

We have chosen to adopt the term *rapid collaborative prototyping*, rather than the more common label, "rapid prototyping," to emphasize an essential difference between our conception of the process and that currently found in the ISD literature—the role of the user. In our view, rapid collaborative prototyping is an iterative process of design in which *users and designers* engage as peers to simultaneously discover the problem and solution through the use of prototypes to make ideas concrete. Our understanding of rapid collaborative prototyping has evolved from our direct experience and reflection as well as a review of similar practices in other fields of design, especially the area of human factors and interface design.

Assumptions of Rapid Prototyping

In our view, three essential rudiments serve as the foundation of a model of rapid collaborative prototyping: Model building, iteration, and user collaboration are all intrinsically necessary components of a process of discovery and development.

Model Building as a Process of Discovery and Development

Analysis in the instructional development process identifies the requirements for a solution to a problem. The results of analysis (needs, learner, task) are interpolated into a design (usually on paper) that is developed into instructional materials or software and finally implemented or delivered to the users. All too often, however, the reaction of end users and clients is "That's not what I wanted at all!" And the reaction of the designer is, "But that's what you said!" Unfortunately, as well as quite naturally, most users have only a nebulous grasp of their exact needs and, therefore, cannot provide sufficient information to satisfy the requirements of traditional up-front analysis methods. A solution designed to an up-front list of functional requirements and not to the "real situated practices" of people will often be totally unsuitable (Carroll, 1994a).

Jenkins (1985, p. 2) states, "the prototyping methodology is based on one simple proposition: users can point to features they don't like about an existing system (or indicate what feature is missing) more easily than they can describe what they would like in an imaginary system." In rapid collaborative prototyping, models of a solution are built in order to detect the essential elements of a user's requirements. Tripp and Bichelmeyer (1990, p. 36) describe the rapid prototyping model of instructional development as "the building of a model of the system to design and develop the system itself." Models in this sense are consistent with Davies' (1984) definition in that they "bear a quantitative relationship to the real thing." A prototype (or model of the solution) provides the user a tangible and dynamic look at an evolving solution to—and definition of—the problem.

Rapid prototyping's emphasis on model building as a method of design echoes early design methodologies. Lawson (1980), citing Jones (1970), traces the history of design from "craft" to its current professional and technology-based status. Designing while building through trial and error characterized original design methods. The separation of design from building and, therefore, the separation of designers from builders and users, coincided with the professionalization of design. The major drawback was the time required for this approach to design. Addition of the term "rapid" to the term prototyping emphasized the major advancement that the availability of new technologies has reportedly brought to this process. Rapid prototyping returns to a "design by doing" process in which the problem and the solution are simultaneously discovered by users through the use of prototypes (Madsen & Aiken, 1993). The advantage of combining building with designing is "an astonishingly well-balanced result and a close fit to the needs of the user" (Jones, 1970, p. 19).

Iteration as a Process of Discovery and Development

Counter to the traditional linear progression model of ISD, iteration is at the heart of a rapid collaborative prototyping approach to development. In it, analytic, developmental, and evaluative activities tightly intertwine in recurring cycles (see Figure 1). Time between each successive prototype can be very short—from days to even minutes. Between each user testing, building and reconceptualizing occur. The system grows like an onion, with successive layers of refinement developing over time (Mullin, 1990). The value of "speed" in the iterative cycle is only partially its effect on the project timeline, however. Here the term *rapid* may be misleading. It is important to keep the cycle of change moving forward and keep the users and design team involved, but the real value of speed in iteration is minimal investment in effort, material, and time to operationalize each new idea. "Minimal investment" enables the design process to become a discovery process.

A 1987 study of real-world interactive system design practices among designers identifies two development models in which prototyping is utilized as part of an iterative design process (Rosson, Maas, & Kellogg, 1987, p. 139). The "phased model of development," characteristic of most prevailing ISD models, consists of a design phase followed by implementation with an evaluation phase falling somewhere between these two. In the phased model, "iteration is limited to the initial design phase, in which the prototype is a *simulation* of function that will not be implemented until later." In the "incremental model of development," implementation and design occur concurrently in an iterative manner. In this model, "the prototype *is* the system and the iteration that takes place ultimately evolves into the final system."

In our own experience with iterative prototype development, both approaches have been utilized. In the earliest design cycles, prototypes in the form of "idea sketches" and "mock-ups" that simulate the solution ideas were repeatedly developed with low-fidelity tools to enhance the discovery of the problem and alternative solutions. These initial iterative cycles of design were not necessarily intended to *evolve* into a final implementation. Later design cycles in the same project involved the use of high-fidelity "pilot prototypes" that were expected to evolve into a viable implementable solution for the intended environment of use.

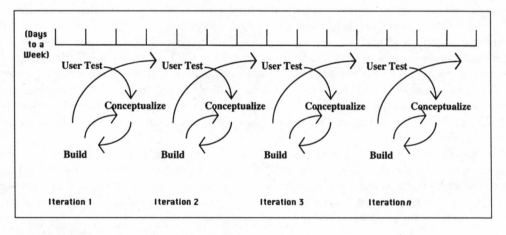

TERMINOLOGY
- **User Test**   The experience of the user operating the application in the conducting of real tasks
- **Conceptualize** The addition and refinement of problem definitions and of solution requirements
- **Build**   Realizing the additions and refinements in the application prototype

Figure 1.   Iterative design in rapid collaborative prototyping.

Collaborative User as Designer

If iteration is the heart of a rapid collaborative prototyping approach to instructional development, active participation by the user is the soul. The standard division of people into designers and users—a particularly techno-centric perspective—is beginning to blur (Trigg & Bødker, 1994). A rapid collaborative prototyping development process cannot occur without the unique knowledge users bring to the design. Users are experts in the tasks they perform, the problems they face, and the environment in which they operate, while designers are experts in project management, technology, and learning. The needs of the users drive the design process. As such, designers must be ready to reject one solution idea when a different solution better meets their needs (Good, 1992). As collaborators in the design process, users are not passive partners. Their responsibilities extend beyond their traditional role in which they might be interviewed about their needs, sign-off on a list of specifications, or test the product after it has been designed and developed. In a rapid collaborative prototyping approach to development, users are rightfully active participants, setting direction and making decisions about both the process and the product of design.

In *How Designers Think* (1980), Bryan Lawson speculates on the future role of the designer in society. Power, in Lawson's view, will either continue to reside solely in the hands of the professional designer, be consciously rejected by the designer who would now associate himself directly with user groups, or, somewhere between these two opposing roles, be cooperatively shared by designer and users. Rapid collaborative prototyping implies a clear shift in the allocation of power from the hands of the professional designer to that of the user. Precisely how much power shifts is one of the primary issues in rapid collaborative prototyping. Jenkins (1985) suggests that the user in rapid prototyping becomes the "designer" and the traditional designer becomes the "builder" of a solution. Designers in the Information Systems (IS) area operate under the belief that the efficacy of the solution is commensurate with the amount of user involvement in the development process (Carmel, Whitaker, & George, 1993). We believe, as suggested above, the equal sharing of power in a context of mutual learning and discovery is key to the model of rapid collaborative prototyping. Our own experience to date follows closely Lawson's (1980) description of the "middle path" in which the designer no longer dominates the process of design but continues to contribute specialized decision-making skills.

Historically, the designer in effect "used" the user. The user was a source of information for the designer to carry back to the design process. Following the initial needs/task assessment, the user did not hear from the designer until the pilot test, or often, not until implementation. In a collaborative prototyping model, the user "uses" the designer as an information resource and facilitator of a design process to solve his or her instructional needs. Emphasis on designer responsibility and expertise shifts more to project management, establishing realistic expectations, facilitation of structured meetings, creative brainstorming, and evaluation. Both user and designer are responsible for determining the scope and complexity of the problem, constructing and exploiting prototypes, documenting inadequacies and contributing divergent ideas.

As problematic as this transformation is for the designer, it is just as difficult, if not more so, for the user. Even when users enjoy management support for their involvement and are allocated adequate time for participation, it is a considerable leap no longer to fall back on the attitude that, "You guys are the experts." Collaboration implies not only co-control but co-responsibility for realization of the project goals.

Rapid Prototyping Principles

Admittedly, there are no clearly established methodologies for applying rapid collaborative prototyping as a design strategy. The process, as we describe it, evolved with our experience and varies from project to project. Several principles drawn from other fields, however, guided our initial activities and have been refined by our experience. We have classified the principles into four categories: Process, Interaction, Fidelity, and Feedback.

Process Principles

Process principles pertain to the fundamental character of the design process itself:

Iteratively modify the prototype several times in each design level. It is generally not sufficient to engage in a single round of build-evaluate-design activities at each level of prototyping. The design process should continue through iterative loops, making incremental changes to the prototype until the users and critical stakeholders recognize the prototype as meeting their needs as far as they are known at that point. When the user says "that's it!" the prototype can be moved to the next level of design/development.

Modify and return the prototype quickly—speed is critical. Rapid collaborative prototyping is founded on the belief that change should be positive. When a user changes his/her mind, it is a signal of progress toward the user's true needs. To ensure change is not detrimental to the process as a whole. However, response to that change must be speedy. Modifications to prototypes must be possible with minimal investment of time and effort so the user can promptly receive and confirm prototype modification.

Seek alternatives—not just modifications. Investment in any solution idea, no matter how little, leads to a reluctance to abandon that idea even when new counter information is available. Rapid collaborative prototyping seeks to minimize early investment and, therefore, early lock-in to a solution path. This requires a conscious effort to remain creative—continuously looking for creative alternatives to the problem. Multiple solutions, in the form of multiple prototypes, contribute to uncovering a wider variety of issues and lead to a more balanced solution. To adapt an old adage, "Two prototypes are better than one!"

Interaction Principles

Interaction principles pertain to the relationship among the design team members:

Regard the user as designer. As discussed earlier, direct and indirect users and other critical stakeholders, including subject matter experts and the sponsor, are experts in their environment and the work and learning tasks in which they are engaged. Design by rapid collaborative prototyping upsets the traditional boundaries of who does what in the process of design. Users are "in the driver's seat" on the design road to a *usable* and *used* solution. This does not mean, however, that "the customer is always right." It should be assumed that users are always "right" about the problem (e.g., they require being able to perform some task and can't or are confused about some point). However, users are not necessarily always right about how best to fulfill that need (Bjerknes, 1993; Rector, Horan, Fitter, Kay, Newton, Nowlan, Robinson, & Wilson, 1992). Deceptively simple suggestions may conceal a variety of needs. Solution propositions must be critically examined, no matter what the source.

Avoid the use of technical language. The value of the design team lies in its diversity of perspectives and expertise. This diversity, however, can hinder clear communication critical to the process. Technical language refers to both the language of design and of implementation. Obviously, users may not be familiar with commonly used instructional design terms. Reliance on these terms when communicating with users and clients is a communication shortcut with potentially high costs.

Maintain consistent communication with the users (Bjerknes, 1993; Good, 1992). The amount of direct user involvement in the development process will vary throughout the project. At times, designers will be building and revising prototypes away from the users. In many cases, events external to the immediate development process, such as budget or other political issues, will slow the project down. On such occasions it is important to continue to inform users of the project progress and status. Failing to do this can lead to users feeling decreased ownership and responsibility for the process as a whole.

Fidelity Principles

Fidelity principles pertain to the character of the prototype:

Employ low fidelity prototypes to gain quality feedback during early *levels of design. Employ high fidelity prototypes to gain quality feedback during* final *levels of design.* Andrews and Goodson (1980, p. 2) explain that a model is "an abstraction or simplification of a defined referent system, presumably having some fidelity to the referent system." Prototypes are models of a proposed solution and as such are assumed to have some fidelity to the solution. The amount of fidelity, or how "real life" the prototype is, depends on its purpose and when it is applied in the design process. With low fidelity prototypes, "neither the form nor the materials used in its construction have to be those of the final design, as long as the basic idea or concept can be tested" (Janson & Smith, 1985, p. 306). As Mullin (1990, p. 18) suggests, "if you can paint a believable picture, you can get a fast and accurate reading from the client on whether you understand the problem and whether or not you have a solution for it." Low fidelity prototypes paint simple abstract pictures that capture the essential elements of the solution with little realistic detail. Low fidelity prototypes are most effective in the early levels of the design process when the focusing concern is on identifying broad user needs. As the design process moves progressively toward increasing the users' hands-on interaction with the solution and the integration of the prototype into the user environment, high-fidelity prototypes, employing materials intended to be used in the final product, are appropriate (Munoz, Miller-Jocobs, Spool, & Verplank, 1992).

The prototype is effective when it allows the user to give pertinent and productive feedback (Munoz, Miller-Jocobs, Spool, & Verplank, 1992). The test of a prototype is not how well it models the final solution but rather how well it stimulates the problem discovery process. To be effective, a prototype must make the solution idea tangible so that the user can legitimately evaluate the idea in the context of their experience and environment and provide sound feedback.

Exploit the available technology (Jenkins, 1983). Rapid prototyping builds on what already works to some degree. What "works" may be derived from previous cycles of prototyping or may be drawn from sources completely outside this particular design project. In our experience we found that one man's trash (or one man's solution) might also be part of our solution. Off-the-shelf products can be effectively used as conceptual prototypes in part or full.

Feedback Principles

Feedback principles pertain to the evaluation process:

Capture what the user likes but more importantly what he/she does not like (Jenkins, 1983). Productive feedback is information that extends the design. Often, the more negative the feedback, the more useful it is as it works to clarify a previously misunderstood user need.

If the user doesn't want it fixed, don't fix it (Jenkins, 1983). "Fixing" or modifying the prototype implies the problem was previously misunderstood. Our role as designers/developers is not to change the problem but to suggest solutions to the problem. This principle is related to John Carroll's (1990) principles for minimalist design. It assumes that we depend on the learner to manage the learning situation effectively and values more what can be excluded than what can be included.

Gather data on three levels (Rector, Horan, Fitter, Kay, Newton, Nowlan, Robinson, & Wilson, 1992). Feedback on prototypes should be elicited at three levels: Micro, Midi, and Macro. Each is equally important even though one will often predominate during varying levels of the development process as a whole. For example, macro-level data is especially important during the Level 1 cycle where visions of the solution are first initiated.

Micro-level data address the "look and feel" or usability of the solution. It focuses on things such as layout and format, readability, color, content accuracy, or how a particular component of the entire product needs to be "fine-tuned" to be most serviceable.

Midi-level data address how to implement the task or learning goal in the system. It focuses on such things as sequence, navigation, organization, functionality, and content relevance.

Macro-level data address how the solution is integrated into the user environment and its potential impact on that environment.

Prerequisites to Design

Two critical activities precede a successful rapid collaborative prototyping design process: Relationship Building and Contextual Inquiry. Because of its inherent dependence on active participation by users and focus on authentic user tasks, the process must be grounded in a solid relationship with the user and an understanding of their "work-a-day world" (Moran & Anderson, 1990).

Relationship Building

The first critical requirement of a successful development process is to identify appropriate stakeholders or "co-designers" in the process. Don't underestimate the difficulty of this (Good, 1992). This activity may seem to take a disproportionate amount of time in the process as a whole. However, this investment is the foundation. Users, both direct and indirect, must not only be willing, but also available and informed about the process. Several guidelines help to identify appropriate users. Users must (1) be true representatives of the environment in which the solution will be implemented (2) be able to identify some personal benefit resulting from their participation, (3) possess the flexibility and time to devote to the design process, and (4) be experienced in the work/task of the problem focus.

Potential co-designers must be informed about how the process will occur, their role in the process, and the potential resources and constraints to the solutions. Members of the participatory design team address these aspects of the project prior to tackling the problem itself and continually throughout the entire process.

Contextual Inquiry

Focusing on the user means focusing on the workaday world in which the problem is embedded or the learning must occur. Just as the stakeholder must gain expertise in the design process, the designer must gain expertise in the problem context—the work and/or learning activities of the user. This activity, called "contextual inquiry" (Good, 1992; Wixon, Holtzblatt, & Knox, 1990) or "immersion" (Carmel, Whitaker, & George, 1993), can be performed through interviews, observations and even apprenticeships.

In a project aimed at developing an electronic case study experience for students in an advanced accounting course (Carter, Hammer, Goodrum, Saito, & Naugle, 1994), contextual inquiry involved a series of interviews with students who participated in "real life" consulting experiences. Our goal as designers was to understand the "work practices" students used to consult services with small businesses and the collaborative team environment in which this occurred. Interviews consisted primarily of facilitating students to think aloud about the actual physical and cognitive process they applied to solve the consulting problem. Our understanding of the "consulting process" provided a foundation for a simulated version of the same experience and a set of tools to support the learning/problem solving process. Similarly, the development of a course to teach technical experts to develop On-the-Job training (OJT) packages required extensive understanding of the work environment in which the OJT development would actually occur.

Cycles of the Prototyping Process

Once substantial progress is made in establishing a relationship with the stakeholder/users, and all members of the team gain at least a basic understanding of the problem context, iterative cycles of design can begin. Within each large scale development project, there are many small scale design processes which go through a full problem solving cycle to investigate options and develop a fuller understanding of the solution requirements. We have identified five levels at which these design/development cycles occur: (1) Visioning, (2) Exploring, (3) Experimenting, (4) Pilot Testing, and (5) Evolutionary Development (see Figure 2). Solution ideas, in the form of prototypes, progressively filter or funnel through these levels, becoming more concrete or tangible with each. Each level is described in detail below. These levels have been adapted in part from the work of Milton Jenkins (1983, 1985) in the field of applications systems design.

Level 1 Cycles—Creating a Vision

The design team, made up of expert designers, direct and indirect users, technical implementers and other stakeholders, joins together in the first level of design cycles to create an initial broad vision of potential solutions. The vision provides direction for the design

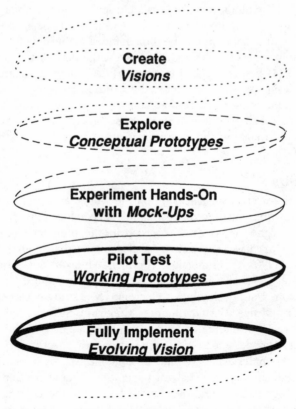

Figure 2.   Cycles of the prototyping process.

process, but it can and does change substantively as part of that same process. In fact, an essential principle of rapid collaborative prototyping—the design of multiple alternative solutions—is critically applicable at this level. Multiple visions in this first level of design cycles helps to ensure against locking-in too early and avoids early over-investment in a solution that may need to be discarded later as the problem is further understood. At this level, solutions are described with broad stroke scenarios to characterize and initiate the direction for change.

A project aimed at supporting new sales employees (Dorsey, Goodrum, & Schwen, 1993) initially conceived of a "problem" as inadequate access to product and customer information. Early visions consisted of varying distance education systems and a hypertext knowledge base. These eventually evolved into a vision of a performance support system residing on a laptop computer to be utilized in a "Virtual Office" environment. In a smaller, more traditional instructional design project, the goal was to provide all employees with basic knowledge of a new data access system within the organization. Original visions included a traditional lecture format course, a self-instructional "mystery textbook," and a simulated computer magazine, followed by discussion sessions.

Prototypes of the vision at this level are fuzzy descriptions and represent a general approach rather than specifics about the solution. They set the direction for following cycles of development. (See Figure 3 for an artist's interpretation of a vision for a professor's file cabinet transformed into an electronic resource for students.). Evaluation at this level consists of imagining the possible range of consequences to the organization and the individuals comprising it. This first level of design might occur initially in one or two design meetings, although the vision will be revisited again and again.

Specific activities that occur in this first level of the design process might include:

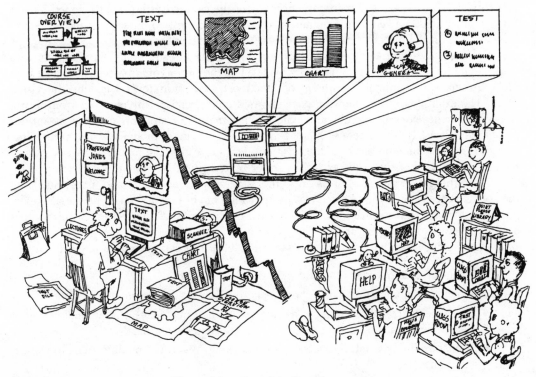

Figure 3. Level 1. Creating a vision.

- Writing a brief skeletal description of the problem as it is currently understood
- Writing a brief skeletal description of the users' requirements based on the problem understanding, e.g., basic needs in terms of the outputs or results of the solution
- Identifying resources and constraints to the project
- Estimating the scope and complexity of the project
- Brainstorming solution ideas
- For each solution idea, estimating the impact to the organization and individuals, including cost (e.g., development and implementation) and amount of change
- Prioritizing the solution visions for the next level of prototyping

Level 2 Cycles—Exploring with Conceptual Prototypes

The second level of iterative design cycles engages the collaborative design team in developing conceptual prototypes or "idea sketches" of the most promising solution options under consideration from Level 1. Graphic "cartoons" of the solution ideas developed at this stage begin to define the basic functional components and the "look and feel" of the solution options. The design team translates abstract concepts, such as "Virtual Office" "Performance Support System," or "Electronic Case Study," into simple charts, diagrams, sketches, etc., using common tools such as paper and pencil, video, drawing and word processing software, and even simple object-oriented authoring software such as HyperCard.

For example, "Virtual Office" can now be more specifically depicted as the combination of home, remote, and core office locations, tying together distributed work teams with a host of communication tools, including a fax, high speed phone lines, and laptop computers. In one of our projects, we borrowed a pre-produced video describing a "telecommuting program" to serve as our conceptual prototype of a Virtual Office. This "off the shelf" video, produced as a corporate marketing tool, incorporated many of the characteristics we envisioned for our Virtual Office and enabled us to communicate more concretely to ourselves and the rest of the design team the direction in which we were headed.

In most cases, simple drawings or examples of other already produced materials with similar qualities are most appropriate for this level of the prototyping process. The goal is to move quickly with minimal investment of time, cost, and effort toward making the vision "real." The example on the following page shows a conceptual prototype taken from a project aimed at developing a "problem solving environment" for students engaged in anthropological analysis. These "cartoons," hand drawn by the instructor in an early design meeting, begin to create a common image of the solution idea, suggesting the primary functions, early navigation issues, content issues, etc., for further investigation (see Figure 4).

With these idea sketches, users and other stakeholders can react and assess how well the solution ideas match the targeted tasks, application environment, and its potential impact on the individual and organization. Collaborative modification of the conceptual prototypes occurs as new ideas are generated.

Specific activities that occur in this second level of the design process might include:

- Using low fidelity tools to create idea sketches
- Showing/demonstrating existing products to illustrate the vision
- Using the conceptual prototypes as catalyst to elicit new ideas, test understanding of the problem and user needs, and compare alternative solutions
- Brainstorming new solution ideas and/or making "real time" modifications to the existing ones
- For each solution idea, estimating the impact on the organization and individuals
- Prioritizing the solution visions for the next level of prototyping

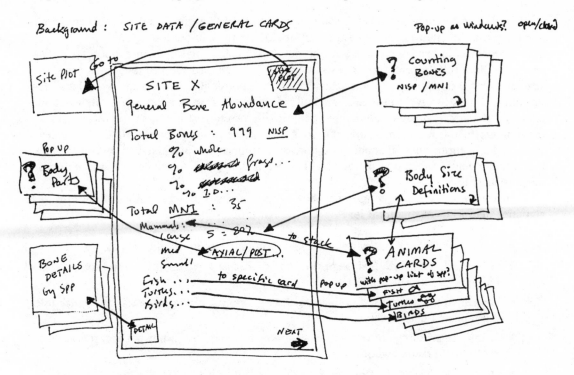

Figure 4. Level 2. Exploring with conceptual prototypes.

Level 3 Cycles—Experimenting Hands-on with "Mock-up" Prototypes

As the design process progresses, the design team moves toward enabling users to engage directly and dynamically with the solution ideas. In the third level of iterative design cycles, "mock-ups" extend the conceptual prototypes by adding a functional portrayal of the solutions. It is not necessary for prototypes at this level to actually "work," but merely to appear to work. The classic example of prototypes at this level is taken from the early development of ATM machines in which the "man behind the curtain" actually fulfilled the function of responding to user input and dispensing cash as requested. Users in this phase temporarily engage in authentic tasks typical of the context in which the solution will eventually be implemented. A Virtual Office mock-up consisted of salespersons temporarily utilizing a cubicle set up to emulate a core office space, using a laptop computer in addition to their desktop PCs to accomplish some tasks, and staging a tele-conferenced staff meeting.

In Level 2, interaction with the prototype is not very concrete, as stakeholders share in and respond to a "show and tell" demonstration of the conceptual prototype. In Level 3, stakeholders actively "use" the prototype to accomplish an authentic work or learning task. This occurs, however, outside the actual environment in which the solution will eventually be implemented—typically in a lab of some sort. Users may be allowed to take the prototype "home" but not to begin using it as part of their ongoing work or learning activities. Since the mockup only *appears* to function as intended, practical use of the prototype is impossible at this level.

Third level prototypes are incomplete. Only the *known* needs are addressed; only portions of the content are incorporated, etc. For example, if the vision of the entire solution consists of several modules with the same basic functionality and user navigation options, only mock-up one module at this level. Focusing efforts on the single module encapsulates the design issues and creates a template to efficiently develop subsequent modules in the next level of prototyping. However, if some modules contain unique functions, a single screen depicting that function might be developed for each of those modules.

Prototypes in level three need not be developed using final implementation tools. For example, the mock-up prototype of a simulated computer magazine (intended as a self-instructional text) might be a few pages constructed with basic word processing tools. Final development might involve typesetting, original art, and high gloss colored paper. The essential elements (sequence, organization, content topics, literary tone, format, etc.), however, must be apparent in the mock-up. Again, the goal is to efficiently capture the fundamental features of the solution in a dynamic prototype to further refine and detail the problem and user requirements. Evaluation of the usability, learnability, and match to task and environment is sought.

In the third level, the design team and users search to discover information. Specific activities that occur in this third level of the design process might include:

- Crafting alternative "mock-ups" of the conceptual prototypes that appear to work.
- Conducting hands-on sessions in the "lab" with users "trying out" the prototype with authentic work or learning tasks.
- Implementing "on the fly" (or minimal turn-around) modifications of the mock-ups and repeated user try-outs.
- Giving the prototype to users to take home and "play" with, but not incorporating it into their workaday world.
- Brainstorming new solution ideas and/or modifications to the existing ones.
- For each solution idea, estimating the impact to the organization and individuals.
- Prioritizing the solution visions for the next level of prototyping.

Level 4 Cycles—Pilot Testing with Working Prototypes

The fourth level of design cycles is the most critical and is the one toward which the first three levels strive to move quickly. It is not until users actually attempt to integrate solution ideas into their "work-a-day world" that true needs can confidently be identified and the solution requirements can confidently be known. Unlike a traditional design process, in which pilot testing of solutions occurs near the final stages of implementation to "debug" the solution, prototypes are "piloted" in the rapid prototyping model to discover problems and unmet needs, and to further the design (Tripp & Bichelmeyer, 1990). In level four, users employ prototype solutions to engage in actual work and learning tasks in the context of a real environment. High fidelity representations or prototypes of the solution are constructed employing, as much as possible, the materials or tools to be used in the formal product. The stretch toward high fidelity is important to test the usability and implementation issues that become more apparent now.

It is important to remember that even though high-fidelity tools are used in the development of prototypes at this level, they are still prototypes and changes should be expected and welcomed rather than feared and avoided. In a traditional development model of instructional materials, there is a tendency to professionally produce final materials for the "pilot." Until users have engaged in "design by doing" in realistic conditions, much of the need and the corresponding solution remain undiscovered. A simple, but realistic, example of the danger in this can be seen in a project involving the development of a board game as an instructional strategy to teach engineers about a new technical process. During Level 2 and 3 cycles of development, users had interactively modified with designers the game strategy, rules of the game, activity/question cards, appropriate rewards, etc., to the point at which all felt the game was "working well." It was not until the game was "piloted" in the training center that it was discovered the board game was too large to comfortably fit on any of the available tables. Since every table in the training center was a standard size, it was necessary to significantly redesign the layout of the game board to accommodate the smaller tables. Because the pilot prototype game board had been developed using informal but realistic materials and had not been professionally produced, much effort and cost to the project was saved.

The Virtual Office pilot prototype consisted of a small group of representative users officially relinquishing their private office space in the corporate building to set up a "virtual office" in their home or garage, trading their desktop PCs for laptops, and participating in all office meetings via teleconferencing– all while maintaining full responsibilities for their ongoing work activities.

The pilot prototype for the accounting case study was still several iterations away from the ideal vision. This "pilot prototype" consisted of a combination "messy text" (i.e., simulation of actual documents that might be gathered in the consulting process) and a time-stamped video of company employee interviews. This pilot prototype might be described as having medium fidelity. The video and text were to be used in the final product, but they were not yet embedded in a multimedia program to enable users to integrate and easily navigate through both. We would begin to call this a pilot prototype because the prototype was used in a "real" environment, that is, as part of a credit course for accounting majors. It did not, however, allow us to test many of the usability and implementation issues that were expected with the envisioned multimedia system.

The pilot prototype developed for the problem solving environment for anthropological analysis more closely illustrates an ideal prototype at this level. A hypertext version of the environment was developed with all the functionality known to be needed at that time. It was implemented in a credit course of fewer than 20 people, although it eventually will be used with groups of approximately 100 students at a time.

Design and development continues to occur during the pilot just as it did in the earlier levels. As much as possible, modifications are made to the prototype during the pilot as they are identified. Design changes are instigated by explicit suggestions from the users and implicit suggestions inferred from observation of the prototype in use.

Specific activities that occur in this fourth level of the design process might include:

- Constructing high fidelity prototypes, employing materials to be used in the formal implementation.
- Conducting observations and evaluative sessions with users during and after use of the prototype.
- Brainstorming new solution ideas and/or modifications to the existing ones.
- Modifying the prototype according to the feedback results.

Level 5 Cycles—Evolutionary Development

In the final level of design cycles, the design team supports users in the ongoing appropriation and customization of the solution for their evolving needs. As the organization and individuals change, so do their problems and needs. The solutions meant to support them must change as well. At this level of design, solutions are integrated into the organization in ever-widening circles of implementation with each new set of users potentially "tweaking" or customizing the solution to meet its members' unique needs or ways of working and learning. This evolutionary phase of the design process leads to a stage of implementation in which "bottom line" results can begin to be measured. Here, the solutions saturate and become integrated in the organization.

At this final level, the impetus for change is in the hands of the users as they continue to incorporate the solution into their changing work and learning environment. This does not mean that the design team abandons its proactive position in seeking feedback about user success and satisfaction. We found in our own projects that users assume that formal implementation implies a final solution. The development process, however, does not end with implementation. No solution can ever be final. The needs of any organization and set of individuals will not only evolve, but will at times require a radically different vision to meet their ever changing environment. Rapid collaborative prototyping includes the notion of continuous change.

Specific activities that occur in this fifth level of the design process might include:

- Limiting the population initially served and expanding incrementally.
- Letting the users determine when change is necessary and thus control the development time.
- Proactively seeking user feedback on a regular basis.
- Modifying the prototype according to the feedback results.

Some Rapid Collaborative Prototyping Techniques

Specific techniques employed during the rapid collaborative prototyping design process are borrowed and adapted from other models of design. Some techniques, such as "Pictive," are best suited for the early stages of the design process where vision and conceptual prototypes are being developed. Others, such as Think-Aloud Protocol, are useful tools for levels three, four, and five. A sampling of these techniques is described below.

Visual Display Brainstorming

Visual Display Brainstorming borrows heavily from traditional brainstorming and storyboarding practices developed by Disney Productions. This technique is especially beneficial when applied to early visioning efforts. Essentially, Visual Display Brainstorming combines brainstorming's fast-paced generation of ideas with the added structure and visual representation of those ideas associated with storyboarding. All members have equal opportunity to contribute ideas from their perspective, and those ideas are quickly available to the group for discussion in an organized yet flexible manner. The team facilitator guides members to select critical topics of discussion and posts these visually on a large wall or surface through the use of index cards and markers. Topic headers in a typical visioning meeting might include: Who has the Problem? What is the Problem/Need? Possible Solutions? Constraints/Obstacles? The group then responds to the highest priority topic by writing its ideas on additional index cards and posting these below the topic header on the wall. The group progressively moves through each topic header adding or deleting topics, or discussing sub-topics as it becomes appropriate.

PICTIVE (Plastic Interface for Collaborative Technology Initiatives through Video Exploration) (Muller, 1991; Muller, Wildman, & White, 1993)

PICTIVE increases user participation in the design of a computer interface. PICTIVE consists of brainstorming with low-tech objects to communicate ideas between design team members (Muller, 1991). In these video-taped sessions, users and designers physically construct and manipulate "objects" on a clean surface representing a blank computer screen. Preprepared or spontaneously created objects are made from paper, colored plastic transparencies, post-it notes, paper clips, colored markers, etc., and are used to represent the work/job tasks engaged in by the user and typical "system" objects such as dialogue boxes, etc., and menu bars. The PICTIVE technique enables users with no computer skills to actively participate in the design of the prototype.

Although "user interface" typically refers to computer-based instructional solutions, it is useful to think of it more broadly when developing prototypes. Essentially, the user interface is the tangible "look and feel" of the solution, which represents its structure, organization, functionality, etc. The "interface" for a self-study instructional magazine might include the page size and layout, font styles and sizes, chosen topics and their sequence, tone or language style, header and footer formats, graphic style, weight, grade and color of paper, etc. From this perspective, PICTIVE and other user interface design techniques can be adapted for use with a wide variety of instructional solutions.

Participatory Video Prototyping (Young & Greenlee, 1992)

Participatory Video Prototyping is an extension of the PICTIVE process developed by Michael Muller. Its primary advantage is that it captures the dynamic/interactive nature of the prototype solution. In the PICTIVE process, a videotape records the design ideas, whereas in this approach, the video recorder creates a simulation of the prototype solution and gains user feedback on the solution ideas. As in the PICTIVE technique, markers, post it-notes, colored acetate and paper, etc., create unrefined representations of the elements of the interface. Then, using a consumer camcorder on a copy stand, the interface is brought to life (Young & Greenlee, 1992). By physically manipulating the objects (e.g. a "mouse arrow" drawn on clear acetate) and starting and stopping the camera appropriately, it appears as if the prototype is dynamically responding to user input. Adding creative sound effects to the audio part of the video enhances the prototype further. The video can then be played back to a large number of users for feedback.

Think-Aloud Protocol

Think-Aloud Protocol (e.g., McAlpine, 1987) is a technique highly suited for Level 3 Prototypes. In this technique, the user or learner verbalizes every word or thought while performing an authentic work or learning task to provide information which later can be used in the revision of the prototype solution. An observer documents or chronicles the problems as well as the problem solving processes the user exhibits while completing the task, then conducts a follow-up interview to probe the user's perceived goal, major problems and causes of the problems, suggestions for revision of the prototype, etc.

Traditionally, the observer takes a passive role. However, an adaptation of the technique places the observer/designer in a more active role to probe user problems as they occur (instead of when the entire task has been completed). Revisions are made on the spot if it is at all possible.

Conclusion

When compared to the traditional phased ISD model, analysis, design, and evaluation are qualitatively different in rapid collaborative prototyping. The three components no longer exist as distinct activities in separate phases, but occur simultaneously. In fact, dissecting them for a one-to-one comparison between the two approaches runs the risk of losing sight of a critical and defining characteristic of the rapid collaborative prototyping process.

With its concomitant analysis, design, and evaluation, we consider rapid collaborative prototyping to be greater than simply a more accurate reflection of actual practice or an enhancement of the existing ISD model. It offers a fundamentally different approach to the development of instructional products. With its emphasis on stakeholders, model building, iteration, and speed, rapid collaborative prototyping offers an antidote to ISD's sad reputation for linearity, analysis-by paralysis, inefficiency, and cult of the expert.

In short, the process of making things concrete begins immediately, or after a "quick and dirty" analysis of project goals, scope, and criteria. The goal is to create dynamically, not describe statically, the results of analysis. Lengthy, up-front analysis that focuses on gathering data from and about users and ends before design begins is replaced by inquiry with users in a discovery process that continues throughout the entire project.

In essence, design is transformed into successive model building, increasing in fidelity over time. The focus is no longer on a single solution. Multiple solutions are overtly cultivated and refined for the purpose of creating viable, not 'strawman,' alternatives, and are only later abandoned or converged.

Solutions are not completed before evaluation commences. Testing of potential solutions at all occurrences of model building is meant to inform further development as well as the reconceptualization of the problem. In effect, evaluation is continuous, no longer relegated to the end of the project and thereby left open for being dropped entirely. Evaluation by the user community seeks "what works," focusing on utility as well as usability.

The most radical notion of rapid collaborative prototyping is the ownership role played by the user or learner, who is no longer a source for data and feedback, but takes on a primary ownership and decision-making role. The user or learner, in effect, becomes the designer; the traditional designer becomes more of a facilitator. There is also a clear understanding that designs are "appropriated" (Newman, 1990) or "tailored" (Trigg & Bødker, 1994) by users and learners. The design and its actual use in the real world continues to evolve. In the past, the sense within ID was that designs often failed because they were improperly implemented; more often than not, the blame was laid at the feet of the teacher or trainer. Early attraction to the use of computers for delivery of instruction was, in part, based on the sense that the 'source of error'—the teacher or trainer—could be by-passed.

The obvious point is that instructional designs are a part of a larger, real-world, social system where people use designs for their own purposes. An innovation should be defined by the consequences it has for people (Carroll, 1994b). Rapid collaborative prototyping, at the very least, capitalizes on this, including users and learners from the very beginning as stakeholders who are experts on their environments, who will live with the consequences of the design long after the designer has vanished, and who will appropriate the design, or abandon it, depending on its usefulness. Solutions no longer need to be 'marketed' or sold through yet another phase of adoption and diffusion hitched to the end of the entire development process. With the users engaged from the beginning as stakeholders, claiming expertise and decision authority, they create their own commitment and ownership. Adoption and diffusion is, in effect, another concurrent activity within the development process.

A current limitation of rapid prototyping is its close association with computer software development; it appears by association to be limited to the development of computer technology and to be dependent on computer tools themselves to be practically conducted. Our view is that model building, iteration, and user collaboration may be generally applicable to most areas of instructional development. Rapid prototyping alone does not, however, point to what should be developed or why, whether or not designs should be limited to instruction, what all and who all should be included, and so on. With its underlying principles of process, interaction, fidelity, and feedback rapid collaborative prototyping points in the direction from which a new paradigm may emerge for ISD. To elicit and explicate the entire paradigm will take a combination of research into how other fields are changing their approach to development and how these principles and practices will impact our own field.

References

Andrews, D. H., & Goodson, L. A. (1980). A comparative analysis of models of instructional design. *Journal of Instructional Development, 3*(4), 2–16.

Bailey, G. (1993). Iterative methodology and designer training in human-computer interface design. In *Proceedings of INTERCHI '93* (Amsterdam, the Netherlands), (pp. 198–205). New York: ACM.

Bjerknes, G. (1993). Some PD advice. *Communications of the ACM, 43*(4), 39.

Carmel, E., Whitaker, R. D., & George, J. F. (1993). PD and joint application design: A transatlantic comparison. *Communications of the ACM, 36*(6), 40–47.

Carroll, J. M. (1990). An overview of minimalist instruction. In *Proceedings: 23rd Hawaii International Conference on Systems Science (HICSS-23)*. New York: IEEE Computer Society.

Carroll, J. M. (1994a). Designing scenarios for human action. *Performance Improvement Quarterly, 7*(3), 64–75.

Carroll, J. M. (1994b). Making *use* of a design representation. *Communications of the ACM, 37*(12), 29–35.

Carter, M., Hammer, R., Goodrum, D. A., Saito, R., & Naugle, L. (1994). Improving the effectiveness of professional education: Learning managerial accounting via a complex case. In *Proceedings of Selected Research and Development Presentations at the Annual Convention of the Association for Educational Communications and Technology* (pp. 79–93). Washington, DC: AECT.

Davies, I. K. (1984). Instructional development: Themata, archetypes, paradigms, and models. In R. K. Bass & C. R. Dills (Eds.), *Instructional development: The state of the art, II* (pp. 8–17). Dubuque, IA: Kendall/Hunt.

de Hoog, R., de Jong, T., & de Vries, F. (1994). Constraint-driven software design: An escape from the waterfall model. *Performance Improvement Quarterly, 7*(3), 48–63.

Dick, W. (1981). Instructional design models: Future trends and issues. *Educational Technology, 21*(7), 29–32.

Dick, W., & Carey, L. (1985). *The systematic design of instruction* (2nd ed.). Glenview, IL: Scott, Foresman and Company.

Dills, C. R., & Romiszowski, A. (1987). In search of the elusive ID research study, or How do we know when (if) we are doing ID? (Instructional Design, Development, and Evaluation Working Paper, No. 25). Syracuse University, School of Education.

Dorsey, L. T., Goodrum, D. A., & Schwen, T. M. (1993). Just-in-time knowledge performance support: A test of concept. *Educational Technology, 33*(11), 21–29.

Dowding, T. (1991). Managing chaos (or how to survive the instructional development process). *Educational Technology, 31*(1), 26–31.

Glegg, G. L. (1981). *The development of design.* Cambridge, England: Cambridge University.

Good, M. (1992). Participatory design of a portable torque-feedback device. In *Proceedings of CHI '92.* New York: ACM.

Goodrum, D. A., Dorsey, L. T., & Schwen, T. M. (1993). Defining and building an enriched learning and information environment. *Educational Technology, 33*(11), 10–20.

Greenbaum, J., & Kyng, M. (1991). Design at work: Cooperative design of computer systems. Hillsdale, NJ: Lawrence Erlbaum Associates.

Hannafin, M. J. (1992). Emerging technologies, ISD, and critical learning environments: Critical perspectives. *Educational Technology Research and Development, 40*(1), 49–63.

Hannafin, M. J., & Hannafin, M. K. (1991). The status and future of research in instructional design and technology revisited. In G. J. Anglin (Ed.), *Instructional technology: Past, present, and future* (pp. 302–309). Englewood, CO: Libraries Unlimited.

Janson, M. A., & Smith, D. L. (1985). Prototyping for systems development: A critical appraisal. *MIS Quarterly, 9*(12), 305–314.

Jenkins, M. A. (1983). Prototyping: A methodology for the design and development of application systems. (Discussion Paper No. 227.) Indiana University, Graduate School of Business.

Jenkins, M. A., (1985). Prototyping: A methodology for the design and development of application systems. (Reprint Series Paper No. R603). Institute for Research on the Management of Information Systems, Indiana University. Reprinted from *Spectrum, 2*(2–3).

Jones, J. C. (1970). *Design methods: Seeds of human futures.* London: Wiley-Interscience.

Jones, M. K., Li, Z., & Merrill, M. D. (1992). Rapid prototyping in automated instructional design. *Educational Technology Research and Development, 40*(4), 95–100.

Kember, D., & Murphy, D. (1990). Alternative new directions for instructional design. *Educational Technology, 30*(8), 42–47.

Lange R. R., & Grovdahl, E. C. (1989). Does anyone really use instructional systems design? *Educational Technology, 29*(10), 34–37.

Lawson, B. (1980). *How designers think.* Westfield, NJ: Eastview Editions.

Madsen, K., & Aiken, P., (1993). Experience using cooperative storyboard prototyping. *Communications of the ACM, 36*(4), 57–63.

McAlpine, L. (1987). Think-aloud protocol: A description of its use in the formative evaluation of learning materials. *Performance & Instruction, 26*(10), 18–21.

McCombs, B. L. (1986). The instructional systems development (ISD) model: A review of those factors critical to its successful implementation. *Educational Communication and Technology Journal, 34*(2), 67–81.

Megarry, J. (1983). Educational technology: Promise and performance. *Programmed Learning and Educational Technology, 20*(2), 94–98.

Merrill, M. D., Kowallis, T., & Wilson, B.G. (1981). Instructional design in transition. In F. H. Farley & N. J. Gordon (Eds.), *Psychology and education: The state of the union.* Berkeley, CA: McCutchan.

Merrill, M. D., Li, Z., & Jones, M. K. (1990a). Limitations of first generational instructional design. *Educational Technology, 30*(1), 7–11.

Merrill, M. D., Li, Z., & Jones, M. K. (1990b) ID$_2$ and constructivist theory. *Educational Technology, 30*(1), 34–37.

Molenda, M. (1987). An agenda for research on instructional development. In *Proceedings of Selected Research and Development Presentations at the Annual Convention of the Association for Educational Communications and Technology.* Washington, DC: AECT.

Moran, T. P., & Anderson, R. J. (1990). The workaday world as a paradigm for CSCW design. In *Proceedings of the Conference on Computer-Supported Cooperative Work,* October, 1990, Los Angeles, CA (pp. 381–393). New York: ACM.

Muller, M. J. (1991). PICTIVE: An exploration in participatory design. In *Proceedings of CHI '91* (pp. 225–231). New Orleans, LA. New York: ACM.

Muller, M. J., Wildman, D. M., & White, E. A. (1993). 'Equal opportunity' PD using PICTIVE. *Communications of the ACM, 36*(6), 64–67.

Mullin, M. (1990). *Rapid prototyping for object oriented systems.* Reading, MA: Addison-Wesley.

Munoz, R., Miller-Jocobs, H. H., Spool, J. M., & Verplank, B. (1992). In search of the ideal prototype. In *Proceedings of the CHI '92 Conference* (pp. 577–579). New York: ACM.

Newman, D. (1990). Opportunities for research on the organizational impact of school computers. *Educational Researcher, 19*(3), 8–13.

Olson, G. M., & Olson, J. S. (1991). User-centered design of collaboration technology. *Journal of Organizational Computing, 1,* 61–83.

O'Neill, C. (1993). Extending the instructional systems development methodology. *Performance and Instruction, 32*(7), 5–10.

Rector, A. L., Horan, B., Fitter, M., Kay, S., Newton, P. D., Nowlan, W. A., Robinson, D., & Wilson, A. (1992). User centered development of a general practice medical workstation: The pen and pad experience. In *Proceedings of CHI '92* (pp. 447–453). New York: ACM.

Reigeluth, C. (1990). *Principles of educational systems design.* Paper presented at the 1990 Conference of the Association for Educational Communications and Technology, Anaheim, CA.

Richey, R. (1986). *The theoretical and conceptual bases of instructional design.* Letchworth, Herts., Great Britain: Garden City.

Romiszowski, A. J. (1981). *Designing instructional systems.* New York: Nichols.

Rosson, M. B., Maas, S., & Kellogg, W. A. (1987). Designing for designers: An analysis of design practice in the real world. In *Proceedings of the CHI + GI '87* (pp. 137–142). New York: ACM.

Rowland, G. (1992). What do designers actually do? An initial investigation of expert practice. *Performance Improvement Quarterly, 5*(2), 65–86.

Rowland, G. (1993). Designing and instructional design. *Educational Technology Research and Development, 41*(1), 79–91.

Schiffman, S. (1991). Instructional systems design: Five views of the field. In G. A. Anglin (Ed.), *Instructional technology: Past, present, and future.* Englewood, CO: Libraries Unlimited.

Streibel, M. J. (1991). Instructional plans and situated learning: The challenge of Suchman's theory of situated action for instructional design and instructional systems. In G. J. Anglin (Ed.), *Instructional technology: Past, present, and future* (pp. 117–132). Englewood, CO: Libraries Unlimited.

Tessmer, M. (1994) Formative evaluation alternatives. *Performance Improvement Quarterly, 7*(1), 3–18.

Tessmer, M., & Wedman, J. F. (1990). A layers-of-necessity instructional development model. *Educational Technology Research & Development, 38*(2), 77–85.

Thiagarajan, S. (1976). "Help, I'm trapped inside an ID model!" Alternatives to the systems approach. *NSPI Journal,* November, 1976, 10–11.

Trigg, R. H., & Bødker, S. (1994). From implementation to design: Tailoring and the emergence of systemization in CSCW. In *Proceedings of the Conference on Computer-Supported Cooperative Work,* October, 1994, Chapel Hill, NC. New York: ACM.

Trimby, M., & Gentry, C. (1984). State of ID systems approach models. In R. K. Bass & C. R. Dills (Eds.), *Instructional development: The state of the art, II.* Dubuque, IA: Kendall/Hunt.

Tripp, S., & Bichelmeyer, B. (1990). Rapid prototyping: An alternative instructional design strategy. *Educational Technology Research & Development, 38*(1), 31–44.

Wixon, D., Holtzblatt, K., & Knox, S. (1990). Contextual design: An emergent view of system design. In *CHI '90 Proceeding.* New York: ACM.

Young, E., & Greenlee, R. (1992). *Participatory Video Prototyping.* Paper presented at the CHI '92 Conference, Monterey, CA.

27

SALT and Accelerative Learning

Donald H. Schuster
Iowa State University, Ames

Overview

The Suggestive Accelerative Learning Techniques (SALT) method, also known as Suggestive Accelerative Learning and Teaching, utilizes aspects of suggestion similar to advertising and unusual styles of presenting material to accelerate classroom learning. The essence of this technique is using an unusual combination of physical relaxation exercises, mental concentration and suggestive principles to strengthen a person's ego and expand his/her memory capabilities plus relaxing music while material to be learned is presented dynamically. Many of the independent elements have been known here in the Western World, but Dr. George Lozanov of Sofia, Bulgaria apparently was the first to put all of these component elements together in an integrated and highly effective learning procedure called suggestopedia or SALT in the USA.

This humanistic teaching method has been evaluated in field experiments in US public school classrooms, and the component elements evaluated in analytic laboratory studies with college students. The classroom studies rather consistently show that students trained with the SALT method showed significantly higher achievement scores than the controls, sometimes with significantly better attitudes than controls. Classroom subject matter has ranged from reading, spelling, mathematics, science, art, ag education, computers, and physics to beginning German and Spanish. Grade levels have ranged from pre-school reading readiness to high school and college freshmen. Lab studies have provided significant support for the major component features of the method.

Several terms need definition. "Suggestology" is a term coined by Lozanov (1978) for the study of suggestion, theoretically and practically. "Suggestopedia" is a term also first used by Lozanov to mean the application of suggestion to education and learning, especially their improvement. "SALT" (Suggestive Accelerative Learning Techniques) started as an American synthesis from the theory of Suggestopedia but without knowing its details; we added various elements based on our own experimental investigations. SALT and Suggestopedia as terms are used interchangeably here, but there are minor differences between them. "Super-Learning" is a trade-marked term coming from Ostrander and Schroeder (1979) to refer to

467

their book on accelerative learning methods such as SALT and Suggestopedia. Finally, please note that "SALT" as used here can also refer to the SALT Society, the Society for Accelerative Learning and Teaching, now headquartered in San Diego, California, but recently renamed the International Alliance for Learning.

Introduction

The originator of Suggestopedia, Dr. George Lozanov, (1978, p. 258) lists three principles for accelerated learning:

(1) joy, absence of tension, and concentrative psychorelaxation;
(2) unity of the conscious and the paraconscious, and the integral brain activity; and
(3) the suggestive link on the level of the reserve complex.

The first means that learning should be fun and easy. The student should be in a relaxed state mentally, ready to learn and free from distractions.

The second means that the teacher integrates the teaching approach in several ways. The content of a lesson (verbal, conscious) is presented holistically with the non-verbal (beyond conscious, body language) aspects of the lesson. Words are matched appropriately with gestures and facial expressions. Integral brain activity refers to left-right brain integration as well as cortical-subcortical and emotional-rational integration.

The third means that the teacher uses waking state suggestions similar to advertising at several levels to lead the student realistically to expect that learning and memory will be improved over past performance.

Thus, SALT is based on Lozanov's three theoretical principles: joy and the absence of tension in learning; unity of the conscious and paraconscious; and suggestion is the link to the reserves of the mind. However, we need bridging concepts to go from theory to classroom implementation.

The first bridging concept is relaxation and how it affects learning, applying the principle of joy and the absence of tension in the learning process. Classroom relaxation helps students to appreciate the joy of learning. Carter (1981) researched the use of biofeedback relaxation procedures with handicapped children to help them learn. Independent variables were electromyographic biofeedback, relaxation auditory tapes, handwriting practice, and home practice. Results indicated that biofeedback relaxation was best, and listening to relaxation tapes second, in helping students learn, as measured by tests of intelligence, reading, auditory memory, and handwriting.

Relaxation/anxiety interacts with other variables to influence learning. Schuster & Martin (1980) investigated experimentally the effects of biofeedback-induced relaxation or tension of the forehead during learning and testing, chronic anxiety level, test easiness, and facilitating suggestions on learning, and retention of vocabulary words. Many significant effects occurred, but could be summarized: State-trait matching occurred for simple, low-level interactions. For example, highly anxious subjects typically did better when tensed than relaxed. The converse was true for chronically low anxiety subjects. Subjects with intermediate anxiety levels did the worst regardless of induced tension or relaxation. For higher order interactions, results significantly favored overall relaxation in keeping with suggestopedic concepts. Even the chronically anxious did better when given suggestions with an easy test and when relaxed with biofeedback prior to learning, during learning and during testing. The general conclusion seems to be that students learn better when relaxed in the classroom than when anxious and nervous.

The second bridging concept is whole brain learning, or getting more of the brain than usual involved in the learning process. We consider right brain–left brain specialization, rational–emotional integration and learning in different levels of consciousness. This includes brain theories relevant to unity of the conscious and unconscious, and tied to activities to enhance learning.

Lozanov (1978) claims students learn better when taught suggestopedically, as their minds and brains are operating in an integrated manner, emotionally-rationally, cortically-subcortically and left-right. Recent neurological findings tend to support this claim. As shown by Claycomb (1978), acquisition and retention increase dramatically when more than one area of the brain is involved. Schuster & Gritton (1986) reviewed several general theories of brain functioning, and applied the results to classroom teaching. These theories are: hemispheric specialization and their interaction (see O'Boyle, 1986), Maclean's Triune Brain, (see Holden, 1979), Taxon-Locale Memory (O'Keefe & Nadel, 1978), and Holographic Memory (Pribram & Goleman, 1979).

The third bridging concept is using suggestion to lead students to expect that their learning will be accelerated above normal. This is the suggestive link to get students to expect that learning will be easy, fun, fast and efficient. Suggestion comes in a variety of forms: verbal/non-verbal, and direct/indirect. We consider these in detail and give examples. Using suggestion in class is complex, but has always been part of good teaching.

This third basic factor on which accelerated learning depends, according to Lozanov (1978), is that students will learn according to what the teacher expects of them. The phenomenon that people perform according to what important people around them expect is well-known by the name of the *Self-fulfilling Prophecy* or the *Pygmalion Effect*, and is well-documented by Rosenthal and Jacobson (1968) among others. Suggestion by the teacher is the key to this enhanced learning expectancy. Therefore we need to discuss various types of suggestion and ways to use suggestion in the classroom.

Suggestion used in SALT is not the same as hypnosis. If the reader feels that Suggestopedia is hypnosis, then so is commercial advertising, and the word "hypnosis" loses its meaningfulness. We feel that suggestion in SALT is much closer to advertising than it is to hypnosis.

Let's analyze four different types of suggestion, following our two-way categorization by verbal/non-verbal, and direct/indirect.

1. *Direct verbal suggestion.* As an example, a teacher might tell her class, "Learning will be easy for you today." This type of suggestion is seldom used in SALT as it directly confronts students' barriers to accelerated learning, but it can be used sparingly when students are relaxed.

2. *Indirect verbal suggestion.* This type of suggestion draws on the work of Erickson (1980), who provided the following sub-types of indirect verbal suggestion, among many others:

> *Yes set.* This consists of one or more questions to which the obvious answer is "yes"; the suggestion is the last question. Example: "Isn't it a beautiful day outside today? The weekend is coming tomorrow (as the case may be)? Are you ready to learn easily today?"

> *Not doing, not knowing.* A basic aspect of Erickson's approach was to allow mental processes to proceed by themselves, to relax and to let things happen by themselves. Example: "You don't have to make any special effort in this class to learn."

> *Simple bind.* The student has free choice to choose among alternatives offered by the teacher, but all alternatives lead in the direction desired by the teacher. Example: " Do you want to learn faster this week or next?"

> *Focusing questions.* Example: "Can you imagine yourself being Darwin today as we start our biology lesson?"

3. *Direct nonverbal suggestion.* A teacher directs a behavior as reinforcement specifically to just one student in class. Example: The teacher looks directly at a girl and smiles at her when she gives the right answer to the teacher's question.

4. *Indirect nonverbal suggestion.* Nonverbal indirect suggestion for students comes from several sources: the teacher, peers, and the environment. The teacher's behavior and attitude are critical indirect nonverbal suggestions. If the teacher talks in an interesting, excited way, this suggests to the students that the material is interesting to learn.

Another example here is teacher eye contact with students. If the teacher continually keeps looking into the eyes of students around the class, this roving eye contact seems to suggest: "Are you getting this? I want you to understand."

Another nonverbal suggestion is peer pressure in the class. When students in class discover how well they have done on class tests and talk excitedly about it, other students take this suggestion that they can learn easily as well.

The classroom itself is a source of nonverbal indirect suggestion. Arrange to have the ceiling of the room a light, attractive color. Arrange the chairs if possible in a semi-circle. Turn the lights in the room down to help students relax. Use inspiring wall posters and pictures. Put potted plants and flowers around the room. These features add up to the suggestion, "This is a pleasant place to learn."

The teacher's job is to integrate classroom suggestions to lead the students to expect that learning will be fun, easy, efficient and long-lasting. Teachers can use the *SALT Teacher's Check List* (from Schuster & Gritton, 1986) to help them day-by-day to use progressively more suggestive elements in the classroom.

Philosophy

Lozanov uses six minor principles or means as a bridge between his three fundamental principles of Suggestopedia and what the trained teacher does in the classroom.

Authority is the first such means: The teacher should be an authority in two ways, knowing his/her subject matter and how to teach.

Infantilization is the second means: The teacher should induce a childlike, open attitude in students to encourage them to be receptive to the didactic material and learn it easily.

Double planeness is third: The teacher should give the same message consciously and paraconsciously. The teacher should communicate through verbal behavior and nonverbal behavior the same message in an integrated manner.

Intonation is fourth: The teacher varies speaking intonation against a background of music. When the volume and tempo of the music change, the teacher varies his/her voice to accommodate these changes artistically.

Rhythm is the fifth means: Reviewing the material with baroque music in a rhythmic manner helps memory.

Passive concert is the last means: The teacher reviews didactic material with the students in a mind set similar to expecting to go to a concert of favorite music.

These philosophical means or considerations lead to specific do's and don'ts for teachers in the classroom.

Classroom Activities

From the teacher's viewpoint there are three major phases and activities to a SALT lesson: preliminary, presentation and practice. Each in turn is sub-divided into further phases and activities.

Preliminary Phase

This is the get-ready-to-learn phase and is an important one, particularly for the first few lessons taught with SALT. After the students have learned how easy it is to learn with SALT and are enjoying learning in a relaxed manner, the teacher can reduce the time and effort spent on preliminary activities. Actually, Lozanov (1978) has eliminated any preliminary activities such as we recommend, and instead relies on a carefully trained teacher to provide the relaxation and suggestions integrated with lesson delivery. However, we feel a teacher just starting to use SALT would do well to follow our recommended preliminary activities. In fact one teacher (Prichard & Taylor, 1980) spends the first few lessons with a new class just to get the students relaxed, settled down and ready to learn easily. These preliminary activities are:

1. *Physical relaxation.* The purpose of these activities is to relax the students physically so that they can sit quietly and be ready to learn. Typically these exercises are gentle warm-up or yoga stretching exercises. Examples are stretching, bendovers, sidebends, head flops, twists, and waves of tension/relaxation up and down the body.

2. *Mental relaxation.* Mental relaxing exercises are done to get students to stop thinking about their problems, calm down, and to attend to what the teacher is saying. The teacher can use guided imagery spoken in a relaxing fashion, or request students to do their mind calming by themselves. An example of the first is for the teacher to describe slowly, with pauses, watching the sun come up in a beautiful setting. An example of the second is to have students watch their own breathing without controlling it.

These two steps can be combined, as Romen (1982) has, to produce physical and mental relaxation in one exercise.

3. *Suggestive set-up.* The purpose here is to persuade the students that learning will be fun, easy, efficient and long-lasting. We recommend suggestions for this that can be tacked on at the end of guided imagery. Examples are using the George Concept or Early Pleasant Learning Restimulation (Schuster & Gritton, 1986). The latter uses guided recall by the teacher to have students reflect holistically on some time early in their life when learning was fun and easy.

Example: "Pick some time in your life when you were learning something you liked and enjoyed. (Pause) Everybody got one? (Pause) Where were you? Imagine yourself back there enjoying it again. (Pause) Who was with you sharing the excitement? (Pause) Think about how your hands felt then. Everybody's hands feel different when excited. (Pause) Let that good feeling spread all over your body. (Pause) How did your stomach feel? Let it feel that way again. (Pause) Take a look at the eager feeling you had about learning. (Pause) Maximize that feeling of wanting to learn, and let yourself learn that same easy way today."

At the conclusion of the preliminary phase, the students should be relaxed, interested and expecting to learn today's lesson easily.

Presentation Phase

We recommend that the teacher break the lesson into three sub-phases here: Review/preview, Dramatic presentation, and Passive review with music.

1. *Review/Preview/Decode.* What is the big picture for today's lesson, and how does it fit into the course overall? A brief review of previous material can be worked into today's lesson as a point of departure. Ausubel (1960) called a special kind of lesson preview an "advance organizer", and is highly recommended from research results. The preview can be lengthy or quite brief. Example: "Today we're going to learn how to square algebraic expressions." An extensive preview is termed "decoding" the lesson.

2. *Dramatic presentation (Concert #1).* This first major presentation of the lesson is Lozanov's first concert. The teacher presents the didactic material in a dramatic, dynamic way with lively background music to stimulate students' imaginations to form sensory associations. The more mental pictures a student makes, the more associations are made with consequent better learning than without such "pictures." Schuster & Wardell (1978) provided experimental verification of this concept. Lively classical music helps image making.

3. *Passive review with music (Concert #2).* This second major presentation is Lozanov's second concert. This special review provides another set of tags or associations to help students learn. Students are asked to focus their attention on the teacher's voice and the music in a relaxed easy way. They should accept any images that come along, but not worry about generating new images this time and just enjoy the process. The students generally are more relaxed than in the previous first concert.

Lozanov claims this special mental condition is one of the suggestopedic processes that enables accelerated learning. Our research (Schuster & Mouzon, 1982) tends to bear him out. In our laboratory, students learned about 30% more vocabulary words with baroque music as a background than without music. They learned about 15% more with classical music as a background than without music as a control.

Practice Phase

In this somewhat conventional practice phase, students activate and use the material they have learned in the previous presentation phase. Sub-phases here are activation, elaboration and tests.

1. *Activation.* Here for the first time students are required to do something actively with the material previously learned. An easy example in a foreign language class is for the instructor to lead the class in a choral reading of the material previously covered. This is relatively easy, as the students merely have to read out loud along with the teacher. But note that for the first time, the students are actually doing something with the language.

Songs are very good practice exercises to help students learn to pronounce the language correctly, get the feel of the language, and learn about the culture.

Asher (1969) advocates keeping students actively involved in a language class. In his Total Physical Response (TPR), the teacher says a word or phrase, and promptly acts it out. In a Spanish class the teacher might say, "Siéntense" ("Sit down") and then sit down, requesting the students to do likewise with a gesture. Dhority (1991) makes good use of TPR in the first 10 hours of his German classes.

Another fun way to practice foreign language is an adaptation of confluent education by Galyean (1982). On a sheet of note paper pinned to the back of each student, other students with a felt pen write 3 adjectives that describe that student in a positive way. Then the student goes around the room asking questions of other students trying to guess what adjectives are written on his/her back. The purpose is to provide vocabulary drill and provide practice in saying nice things about other people.

Wenger (1974) developed several techniques appropriate here; one of his best is: What you describe in as precise and as great detail as you can will not only help you learn that material but will also expand your intellectual abilities in general. An adaptation I used in teaching a large computer programming class was: Ask the students to work in pairs; each of the students in turn describes to the other in as precise terms as possible the major points in today's material (Schuster, 1986). The emphasis is on precision and brevity, with the listening student having the right to break in to correct or add to what the first student is saying. After a few minutes these roles reverse, and the previously listening student now has responsibility for stating precisely the major points of a second topic.

2. *Elaboration.* Here students are required to use the lesson material in new and different ways. Making up short plays and skits can be used to good advantage. For example, a history teacher asked the students to make up a skit or short play on Lewis and Clark's history-making trip on the Missouri and Columbia rivers to the American west coast. The students had a lot of fun in writing the skit, which obviously had to stick fairly close to fact. The students relished the idea of using their ingenuity in devising props, and then putting on their play for the teacher and other students.

Another example is having the students go to a local restaurant or hotel where the proprietor speaks the target language; the students go there as customers and have to use the language in getting a room or ordering meals, etc. A variation on this is foreign language night at the instructor's home, where food, games and conversation are in the target language.

Two people separately have adapted SALT and speed reading techniques that are applicable to classes with a large outside-of-class reading load. Scheele (1993) reported on his "Photo Reading" and Seki (1992) on his "Speed Reading" technique at the 1992 SALT Conference in Minneapolis, MN. Both appear to be worthwhile elaborations.

3. *Tests.*　Quizzes are given at the end of every SALT lesson, usually ungraded. Grades are given on the basis of announced or scheduled tests, typically monthly or final exams.

Questions of all types are used in such quizzes. However, the teacher needs to be careful that students have had practice with the type of questions s/he uses. In following Bloom's Taxonomy (1956), for example, if you tap evaluation, be sure that your students have had practice with evaluation questions beforehand.

SALT principles and components can help on regular tests. In a controlled experiment in teaching Spanish, students did significantly better on quizzes when they relaxed briefly and reviewed their success goal imagery beforehand. SALT techniques also apply to studying outside of class. Schuster (1988) detailed how to do this in the little book *How to Learn Quickly.*

A Review of Supporting Research

Lozanov (1971, 1978) presented the results of many studies in evaluating the components of his method. Combined, these components of his method have speeded up language learning by factors of 5:1 or more.

In the following review, we include studies of teaching foreign languages with Suggestopedia or its American synthesis, SALT. We review only studies that used a laboratory-based manipulative design so as to be able to infer cause and effect.

Marina Kurkov (1977) was the first American to attempt to evaluate the suggestopedic method, adapting Suggestopedia to the teaching of beginning Russian at Cleveland State University, Ohio in 1971. The experimental class covered two quarters' worth of material in one quarter, whereas the control was taught conventionally just one quarter's worth of material. She used the same text and tests in both sections. Grades were somewhat higher in the experimental group (3.0 vs. 2.5 in the control group). With Suggestopedia, the experimental students had learned twice as much Russian in one quarter as the control students.

Bordon & Schuster (1976) performed the second American study in the context of a college Spanish class taught with an adaptation of Suggestopedia. An ANOVA design used independent variables: suggestive positive atmosphere, background music, and synchronized stimuli with breathing; all were dichotomously manipulated. All three independent variables significantly affected the acquisition and retention of learning Spanish words. The criterion was the number of words learned from a list of 50 Spanish words presented under one of the eight possible experimental conditions of the three variables. When all three of these independent variables were present, learning was 2-1/2 times better (average = 30.5) than when all were absent (average = 8.3). The intermediate interaction effects were as expected.

Schuster (1976) performed a classroom study to evaluate the suggestive accelerative Lozanov method for teaching beginning Spanish at the college level. In the fall of 1972 the author randomly selected one section of 13 sections available, while two other sections taught conventionally by other instructors but using the same text book and tests served as control. Only the instructors teaching conventionally made up the final exam, which was prepared in two parts, written and laboratory (spoken). Students taught with SALT had two contact hours per week in contrast with six for students in the control sections. On the final exam, there were no differences between averages for the experimental and control sections, plus the experimental students spent less time on homework than controls. Thus the experimental method resulted in a time saving of 3:1 in teaching beginning Spanish.

Bushman (1976a) taught Finnish with three experimental treatments to college students: one with a full Suggestopedic treatment, a second Suggestopedically, but with music and easy chairs deleted, and a third group taught conventionally. The author concluded that Suggestopedia produced better Finnish language learning. Bushman (1976b) evaluated Russian language learning with a suggestopedically taught group contrasted with a conventionally taught group. Since his major suggestopedic component consisted of finger painting with no relevance to teaching Russian, this reviewer questions the validity of his claim to having tested Suggestopedia a second time. Therefore this reviewer feels that Bushman's conclusion of the invalidity of Suggestopedia in teaching Russian is invalid in itself.

Robinett (1975) adapted some aspects of Suggestopedia to teaching Spanish with three treatments in her experimental design. Both experimental classes had higher exam scores than controls, but there were no significant differences between the two experimental classes.

Ramirez (1982) experimentally evaluated teaching English vocabulary to Chicano third-grade children. Her two experimental groups learned about twice as many words as the controls.

Wagner and Tilney (1983) claimed to have evaluated Suggestopedia in teaching German vocabulary, using three treatment conditions: one a group listening to baroque music tapes from a commercial firm, a second group without baroque music, and third a no-contact group taught in a traditional classroom. The authors monitored brain waves of the students with an electroencephalogram (EEG) while learning but reported no significant change in brain waves due to their experimental treatment. The authors claimed to have tested a commercial adaptation of Suggestopedia, but couldn't substantiate any improved, superior learning. This reviewer feels that this study and its result should be discounted and ignored for two reasons: First is that their research design was faulty, comparing a live teacher in a conventional classroom with experimental students studying language tapes in isolation (the teacher is critical in Suggestopedia). Second, their lack of brain wave reduction in students demonstrated that Suggestopedic relaxation had not been achieved, with the consequence that Suggestopedia was not being tested.

Gassner-Roberts & Brislan (1984) evaluated Suggestopedia experimentally with three sections of beginning German. This yearlong study proved the superiority of Suggestopedia over conventional teaching methods.

Garcia (1988) used a modified Suggestopedic approach in teaching English language to Hispanic elementary students. Test results supported the superiority of the experimental approach and that it facilitated the development of a good learning strategy.

Due to lack of rigorous experimental design, several additional studies support Suggestopedia in its claim of superior learning, but fail to prove it: Lahey (1974), Lemyze (1978), Philipov (1978), Prichard, Schuster, and Pullen (1980), and Zeiss (1984). In spite of this *caveat*, Palmer & Dhority (1993) analyzed extensively the results of data collected by Dhority before and after using Suggestopedic techniques in teaching college German. Compared with previous German classes taught conventionally by the same instructor, the experimental Suggestopedic class achieved posttest scores more than double those taught conventionally and with one-third the class time for instruction. The authors claimed these outstanding results merit calling this approach a model of accelerative learning.

In conclusion, the previously cited studies, using good experimental design, provide hard data to prove that Suggestopedia or its American adaptation of SALT do result in learning a foreign language some two to three times faster than controls.

Additionally, SALT or Suggestopedia have been applied successfully to the teaching of many subjects other than foreign languages. Classroom subject matter and grade levels have varied widely. Many such studies have been published in the *Journal of the Society for Accelerative Learning and Teaching*. This journal also has published articles on the theory of SALT/Suggestopedia as well as case studies and detailed analytical studies of SALT component elements. One such unusual study merits attention here: Clevenson (1994) applied accelerated learning principles to retraining his company's maintenance people in their rationale toward maintaining pumps. The criterion measure, Mean Time Between Failure (MTBF), showed that pumps ran longer between failures and down-time when maintained by personnel trained with accelerated learning than with conventional training.

In this chapter, we have covered the background of SALT (Suggestive Accelerative Learning and Teaching), the theory of SALT/Suggestopedia, how to teach with classroom applications and examples, and finally, supporting research. For further details, refer to the book by Schuster & Gritton (1986), available in Norwegian, German, Spanish, and Japanese as well as English. Extensive additional information is given in the *Journal of Accelerative Learning and Teaching*.

References

Asher, J. J. (1969). The total physical response technique of learning. *Journal of Special Education, 3*(3), 253–262.

Ausubel, D. P. (1960). The use of advance organizers in the learning of meaningful verbal material. *Journal of Educational Psychology, 51,* 267–272.

Bloom, B. *et al.* (1956). *Taxonomy of educational objectives, handbook 1: Cognitive domain.* New York: Longman.

Bordon, R. B., & Schuster, D. H. (1976). The effects of a suggestive learning climate, synchronized breathing and music on the learning and retention of Spanish words. *Journal of Suggestive-Accelerated Learning and Teaching, 1*(1), 27–40.

Bushman, R. W. (1976a). Effects of a full and a modified Suggestopedic treatment in foreign language learning. Unpublished master's thesis, Brigham Young University.

Bushman, R. W. (1976b). An intuitive vs. a rational presentation mode in foreign language instruction. Doctoral dissertation, Brigham Young University. University Microfilms 77-4818.

Carter, J. L. (1981). *Application of biofeedback relaxation: Procedures for handicapped children.* Annual report on Project No. 443CH00207, Grant No. G008001608, with the Bureau of Education for the Handicapped, US Department of Education.

Claycomb, M. (1978). *Brain research and learning.* Washington, DC: National Education Association.

Clevenson, A. B. (1994). Effectiveness of accelerated learning as a tool to facilitate a maintenance paradigm shift. *Journal of Accelerative Learning and Teaching, 19*(2), 111–130.

Dhority, L. (1984). *Acquisition through creative teaching: ACT.* Sharon, MA: Center for Continuing Development.

Dhority, L. (1991). *The ACT approach.* Philadelphia, PA: Gordon & Breach.

Erickson, M. H. (1980). *The collected papers of Milton H. Erickson on hypnosis,* Vols. I–IV. New York: Irvington Publishing.

Galyean, B. C. (1982). The use of guided imagery in elementary and secondary schools. *Imagination, Cognition and Personality, 2*(2), 145–151.

Garcia, Y. (1988). The use of Suggestopedia with limited English-speaking Hispanic elementary students. *Journal of the Society for Accelerative Learning and Teaching, 13*(3), 221–251.

Gassner-Roberts, S., & Brislan, P. (1984). A controlled, comparative and evaluative study of a suggestopedic German course for first year university students. *Journal of the Society for Accelerative Learning and Teaching, 9*(3), 211–233.

Holden, C. (1979). Paul MacLean and the triune brain. *Science, 204,* 1066–1068.

Kurkov, M. (1977). Accelerated learning: An experiment in the application of suggestopedia. *Journal of Suggestive-Accelerative Learning and Teaching, 2*(1&2), 27–35.

Lahey, L. A. (1974). An empirical test of Suggestopedia and suggestion in language acquisition. *Masters Abstracts, 12/03* Education, general.

Lemyze, J. C. (1978). Teaching French composition through Suggestopedia. *Journal of Suggestive-Accelerative Learning and Teaching, 3*(2), 129–133.

Lozanov, G. (1971). *Sugestologiya* (Suggestology). Sofia, Bulgaria: Izdatelysvo Nauka i Izkustvo.

Lozanov, G. K. (1978). *Suggestology and outlines of Suggestopedy.* New York: Gordon & Breach.

O'Boyle, M. W. (1986). Hemispheric laterality as a basis of learning: What we know and don't know. In G. D. Phye & T. Andre (Eds.), *Cognitive instructional psychology: Components of classroom learning.*

O' Keefe, J., & Nadel, L. (1978). *The hippocampus as a cognitive map.* New York: Oxford University Press.

Ostrander, S., & Schroeder, L. (1979). *SuperLearning.* New York: Delacorte.

Palmer, L. L., & Dhority, L. (1993). The 636% solution paradigm: A statistical evaluation of the extraordinary effectiveness of Lynn Dhority's US Army accelerated learning German class. *Journal of the Society for Accelerative Learning and Teaching, 18*(3&4), 237–246.

Philipov, E. R. (1978). Suggestopedia: The use of music and suggestion in learning and hypermnesia. Doctoral dissertation, U. S. International University, 1975. Condensation in *Journal of Suggestive Accelerative Learning and Teaching, 3*(2), 65–107.

Pribram, K., & Goleman, D. (1979). Holographic memory. *Psychology Today, 12,* 71–84.

Prichard, R. A., Schuster, D. H., & Pullen, C. (1980). Adopting Suggestopedia to secondary German instruction. *ADFL Bulletin, 12*(2), 31–34.

Prichard, A., & Taylor, J. (1980). *Accelerative learning: The use of suggestion in the classroom.* Novato, CA: Academic Therapy Publications.

Ramirez, S. Z. (1982). The effects of Suggestopedia in teaching English vocabulary to Spanish-dominant Chicano third graders. Master's thesis, University of Wisconsin, Madison.

Robinett, E. A. (1975). The effect of Suggestopedia in increasing foreign language. Doctoral dissertation, Texas Tech University. *Dissertation Abstracts International,* 1976, *(II-A),* 7217.

Romen, A. S. (1982). *Self-suggestion and its influence on the human organism.* New York: M. E. Sharpe.

Rosenthal, R., & Jacobson, L. (1968). *Pygmalion in the classroom.* New York: Holt, Rinehart, and Winston.

Scheele, P. (1993). *The PhotoReading whole mind system.* Wayzata, MN: Learning Strategies Corporation.

Schuster, D. H. (1976). A preliminary evaluation of the Suggestive Accelerative Lozanov method of teaching beginning Spanish. *Journal of Suggestive-Accelerative Learning and Teaching, 1*(1), 32–51.

Schuster, D. H. (1988). *How to learn quickly.* New York: Gordon & Breach.

Schuster, D. H., & Gritton, C. E. (1986). *Suggestive Accelerative Learning Techniques.* New York: Gordon & Breach.

Schuster, D. H., & Martin, D. J. (1980). The effects of biofeedback-induced tension or relaxation, chronic anxiety, vocabulary easiness, suggestion, and sex of subject on learning rare vocabulary words. *Journal of Suggestive-Accelerative Learning and Teaching, 5*(4), 275–288.

Schuster, D. H., & Mouzon, D. (1982). Music and vocabulary learning. *Journal of the Society for Accelerative Learning and Teaching, 7*(1), 82–108 .

Schuster, D. H., & Wardell, P. J. (1978). A study of Suggestopedic features that can be omitted once students learn how to learn. *Journal of Suggestive-Accelerative Learning and Teaching, 3*(1), 9–15. ED-181721.

Seki, H. (1992). Speed reading improves learning. Paper at the Annual SALT Conference, Minneapolis, MN.

Stein, B. L., Hardy, C. A., & Toten, H. (1982). The effect of Baroque music and imagery on vocabulary retention. *Journal of the Society for Accelerative Learning and Teaching, 7*(4), 341–356.

Wagner, M. J., & Tilney, G. (1983). The effect of "SuperLearning Techniques" on the vocabulary acquisition and alpha brain wave production of language learners. *TESOL Quarterly, 17*(1), 5–17.

Wenger, W. (1974). *How to increase your intelligence.* New York: Bobbs-Merrill.

Zeiss, P. A. (1984). A comparison of the effects of SuperLearning techniques on the learning of English as a second language. *Journal of the Society for Accelerative Learning and Teaching, 9*(2), 93–102.

28

Existentialistic Design and Delivery of Instruction

Terry Flynn
Organizational Design and Development Consultant
Syracuse, New York

Introduction

This chapter presents a model of instructional design and delivery which was developed for use within an industrial workplace setting. The model is an outgrowth of several assumptions about learners and instructors and their respective responsibilities to themselves and to each other. Thus, the chapter begins with some background on what those assumptions are and where they originated. The model that I propose is one that attempts to satisfy my own existential humanist theoretical orientation as well as the very practical (often bottom-line) orientation of my clients. It is in the effort to strike this tenuous balance that I have developed an existentialistic, highly interactive, client-centered approach not only to instruction, but also to instructional design.

The chapter is organized as follows: In the first section, I argue that existing ID paradigms, models, and approaches are not sufficiently generalizable to apply to workplace instruction. Thus, there is a need for a new ID paradigm which will meet the needs of workplace learners and those of the client. The second section describes the foundation of the existentialistic paradigm, its basic principles and how they apply to the topic of instructional design in general. The third section outlines the four-step instructional design process I have developed, which applies existential principles to the workplace, resulting in an existentialistic approach to instruction which best supports the needs of the learner and those of the client (that is, the learner's employer). Finally, the fourth section offers some tentative conclusions, argues for the generalizability of the existentialistic paradigm, and suggests areas requiring further research and development.

Why Existing Approaches to ID Do Not Apply

My work as an organizational development consultant has caused me to try to "train" or "educate" adults, usually within the context of a changing workplace. In doing so, I have broken most of the accepted rules of ID. I have found myself working outside any paradigm of ID that I am familiar with, and I have felt that to follow the rules would result in doing a tremendous disservice to myself as an instructor, to the potential learners entering the class, and to the client footing the bill for the instruction. I have, therefore, come to the conclusion that the field of ID, in developing its "generalizable" theories in the support of an overarching paradigm, has overlooked this population of learners, which I cannot.

Characteristics of the Learners

The following characteristics very generally describe the bulk of the workplace population: (1) They have not been in a classroom in several years; (2) for many years, they have been in an environment which has not supported or rewarded intellectual curiosity and critical thinking or has placed serious restrictions on such activity; (3) they are now in the classroom because they are *required* to be there by their employer; (4) their work lives are in a state of large-scale transition; (5) the instruction is expected to result in personal behavioral change as well as increased knowledge; (6) if they fail to master the material, they risk job loss; and (7) they view the classroom as something that takes them away from what they are really *supposed* to be doing.

These characteristics obviously do not apply to all instruction across all workplace settings. But to the extent that any of these characteristics are strongly present in the workplace setting, or in any instructional setting, most theories of ID fall short of the goal of educating. For these characteristics to be adequately and constructively addressed within the educational setting, any single ID theory would have to address all of the following (not necessarily in this order):

- the desired outcomes of the training for the sponsoring organization (the "client");
- the time frame within which the content must be mastered;
- the organizational reality outside of the classroom (or the relationship between what happens in the classroom and what happens within the workplace);
- the psychological state of the learner;
- the driving motivation of the students (the "learner");
- the price to the student of failure to master the material;
- the intellectual capabilities and learning style of the learner;
- the work-related power relationships between members of the same class;
- the nature of the content; and
- the needs of the instructor.

Brief Critique of a Sampling of ID Theories

Conditions of Learning.   The Conditions of Learning (CoL) paradigm is very appealing because of its formulaic quality. There are right and wrong answers about how to present information to learners. The progression from simpler, basic concepts to more complex ones makes ID highly predictable and standardizable; qualities which are essential to the notion of mass-production/mass delivery of instruction. Learners are typed on the basis of learning style, thereby allowing for the development of correct and incorrect approaches to instructional delivery.

But is it really the case that the CoL paradigm accurately reflects and supports the way most people learn, or are we designing a paradigm which enables standardized mass instruction to occur with as little fall-out among the student population as possible under those circumstances (i.e., when large groups of students must master the same information in a predictable, standardized manner)?

In my experience, unless learners are very highly motivated as they enter the classroom (an assumption that does not always hold within a workplace instructional setting), they will be lost if all they receive are "the basic building blocks" with little or no immediately apparent practical applications for the material. This is not a result of learners' "laziness" or inability to delay gratification. Rather, it reflects a profound understanding of the value of their time and energy, tinged with a healthy skepticism about whether "school" has anything worthwhile to offer them. The CoL paradigm does not offer a useful way to think about how and what the learners learn or what the classroom dynamics and dialogue might teach the instructor about reality as it exists for the learners.

Accelerative Learning (SALT). The Suggestive Accelerative Learning Techniques (SALT) paradigm focuses on the acceleration of learning via the use of a combination of relaxation techniques, suggestion, and activities designed to provide stimulation of multiple parts of the brain. The use of music, relaxation exercises, confidence building, and dramatic presentation of the content are all techniques which work together to improve learner engagement with and retention of the material (Schuster, 1997).

The SALT paradigm offers useful insight into ID but falls short of telling the whole story. What SALT theorists provide is a meaningful way of thinking about the classroom preconditions for learning, both in terms of the learners' psychological state(s) and in terms of the responsibility of the instructor to be aware of the classroom itself as a tool to be brought to bear on providing excellent education.

In my experience, there are certainly instances when SALT techniques would work against the instructor/learner relationship and would not enhance the learners' ability to master the material. The application of accelerated learning techniques requires up-front "buy-in" by the learners to the content and to the out-of-the-ordinary techniques often utilized by SALT practitioners. The students have to be motivated to learn the material. Otherwise, they will view the SALT techniques as being imposed by the instructor to brainwash them into accepting something (information, new behaviors, attitudes) that they would not otherwise want to accept.

These are just two examples of existing paradigms that fail to fully satisfy the requirements of workplace instruction. Since it is beyond the scope of this chapter to critique all existing paradigms, suffice it to note that existing paradigms of ID usually fail due to false constraints placed on the learners, the notion of instruction or learning, the understanding of the boundaries of the classroom, and/or the conception of the responsibilities of the instructor. In the next section, I explore how an existentialistic perspective with its broad understanding and acceptance of learners, instruction, and learning allows ID to expand its effectiveness and thus meet the needs of all parties to the instructional process.

A New Paradigm:
Existentialistic Design and Delivery of Instruction

The paradigm that best supports the reality of instructional design for a workplace classroom is founded upon the assumptions and techniques of Existential Psychology. Existentialistic Design and Delivery of Instruction (EDDI) is a modification of those tenets. Existential psychology is represented here primarily by the writings of Ludwig Binswanger (1958, especially pp. 191–213, and 1963) and Medard Boss (1977).

At the foundation of Existential Psychology are three principles or reactions and one methodology. First, Existential Psychology objects to the concept of causality as it has been carried over from the natural sciences into psychology. There are no cause and effect relationships in human existence. Second, Existential Psychology is opposed to the Cartesian notion of dualism of subject (mind) and object (body, environment, or matter). Third, Existential Psychology adamantly opposes regarding an individual as a thing that can be managed, controlled, shaped, and exploited. A person is free and is responsible for his/her existence. Finally, it is important to note that Existential Psychology relies upon the use of phenomenology, or "a method in psychology [that] seeks to disclose and elucidate the phenomena of behavior as they manifest themselves in their perceived immediacy" (Van Kaam, 1966). I have summarized their major assumptions below and will explain how they have been applied to the field of instructional design and delivery.

Principle One: Causality Is Replaced with Motivation

It is not possible to cause human behavior and therefore one can never be certain that a particular action by one party will result in a particular reaction by a second party. Rather, motivation and understanding are the operative principles in an existential analysis of behavior. Motivation always presupposes an understanding (or misunderstanding) of cause and effect. Learners will not cause (or behave in a way so as to make a desired outcome happen) an outcome without first understanding that their behavior is connected to an outcome, and that the specific outcome is desireable to them.

The implications of this assumption for instructional development are profound. The idea that motivation enables learning to occur suggests that each student's motivation to learn must be fully understood by the instructor as a necessary precondition to learning. Students must understand the connection between what is occurring in the classroom and the attainment of their personal goals. This further implies that in some cases the first task of instruction is to assist the learner in formulating an idea of what they want to achieve and why. Then and only then will the instructor and the student be able to collectively assess the value of the content of the course in helping to meet the student's goals.

Without these steps, the instructor and student run the risk that although the content may be valuable to the student, the connection between the content and an outcome desired by the learner is not clear and therefore the material is not mastered due to a lack of student motivation. The benefit of any outcome to the learner must not only be present, but it has to be understood by the learner.

It follows that all instruction must begin with the instructor learning about what reality is for the learners—not simply their intellectual development on a certain subject, but also the issues which they bring into the classroom, e.g., fear of job loss, negative learning experiences in their past, fear of inability to master the subject matter, lack of interest in or perceived need for mastery of the subject matter.

Consider a Conditions of Learning perspective with its focus on the disassembling of complex concepts into discrete blocks in order to instill the knowledge in a way that will cause higher learning to happen. Now if we replace the implied causality with a focus on learner motivation, we find a missing first step (i.e., a step enabling the instructor to understand why the student is there). What are the student's expectations? The Conditions of Learning blocks may still work but only after the instructor has helped the learner to understand the path from the Conditions of Learning blocks to the learner's desired goal. Understanding these connections forms the basis of learner motivation.

Thus, the following conclusions apply to ID: (1) instructors cannot cause learners to learn; (2) instructional materials cannot cause learners to learn; and (3) attention to fragmented components of the learner such as brain waves, relaxation levels, and isolated behavioral responses cannot cause learners to learn.

The educational experience must allow for two-way leadership and direction. Instructors must react to what they are learning about learners just as learners need to react to the instruction. Likewise, existentialistic instructors give up the illusion of control over the learning process by handing over responsibility for deciphering the "right answer" to the learners. Learners are assisted in developing new understandings through the process of coming up with answers and exploring mistakes. To best meet learners where they are, the instructor must understand the reasoning (i.e., misunderstanding) behind incorrect connections and be sensitive to the effect on learners of labeling an answer "wrong."

Principle Two: Existential Psychology Stands for the Unity of the Individual-in-the-World

Existential Psychology firmly resists the notion that human behavior can be examined or understood as resulting from environmental stimuli or bodily states. Any view that destroys the unity of the individual-in-the-world is a falsification and fragmentation of human existence. Thus, the prevalent instructional development theories which focus on learning as a function only of the mind are unacceptable. Dissection of human behavior is not countenanced, because it reduces humans to a heap of fragments that defy re-synthesis. The concept of "being-in-the-world (also called the "individual-in-the-world") is best elucidated by Martin Heidegger, the German philosopher. Heidegger's central idea is that an individual is a being-in-the-world. Humans have their existence by being-in-the-world and the world has its existence because there is a Being to disclose it. Being and world are one (Heidegger, 1962).

Within ID, this assumption can be manifested by placing emphasis on the process of learning rather than on mastery. Realignment of emphasis is beneficial because learning (the moment of "getting it") often does not occur and certainly does not need to occur in the classroom, on the day the instructor presents the material. If learners walk out of the room comfortable that they are allowed (indeed expected) to continue processing the information, they will be more likely to "get it" than if they feel humiliated because they do not already understand the material by the end of the time allotted—the "class" time. In this manner, learners are recognized as entities who continue to exist and to interact with the instructional material beyond the walls and time frame of the classroom.

Also, learners attain knowledge through assimilation of information and behaviors into themselves as individuals-in-the-world. Therefore, learning requires the participation and experience of the content. They use their classroom experiences to make connections or to better understand the connections taking place between cause and effect all around them. Thus, they learn by living the content and incorporating it into their "being-in-the-world."

SALT theorists seem to have a good start for this type of Being-in-the-World Orientation with their focus on the physical and psychological states of the learner within the classroom. But to the extent that they are attempting to cause rapid learning, as measured by retention rates, and to the extent that they maintain a narrow focus on physiological measures indicating degree of relaxation, they've missed the point. Education is not about retention. It is about motivation which results from understanding. The process of understanding cannot be restricted to or dependent upon a classroom, complete with instructor and an instructional template.

Principle Three: People Are Free and Responsible for Their Existence

Principle three is one that largely complements most humanistic ID theories, which tend to encourage respectful treatment of learners and their ability, indeed, their right, to make choices within the learning environment. Responsibility for existence, however, leads the EDDI practitioner toward a more self-directed, learner-choice focused instructional strategy, one that is less reliant on the instructor as the ever-present initiator, facilitator, and feedback provider. EDDI suggests that at the least, all responsibilities in the classroom are shared, and at the most, they belong to the learners. It is the job of the instructor to assist them in coming to that understanding and thus leading the learners toward the development of themselves as people.

Shifting from theory to reality, especially the reality of instructional development for a workplace setting, EDDI makes the following assumptions:

1. The primary function of the instructor is to assist the learner in understanding the linkage between mastery of the content and the attainment of personal goals. In order for the instructor to perform this task effectively, it will also be necessary for the instructor to be able to communicate the link between classroom occurrences, accomplishments, and behaviors and the organization's reward and discipline policies.

2. The instructor and instruction must acknowledge the world-life experiences that each individual learner brings to the classroom. At least one part of this recognition will entail the instructor recognizing organizational power relationships between individuals in the class, the fear of failure to master the material that may exist as a larger-than-life force for some learners, and the effect that widely diverse previous learning experiences might have on the population's ability to learn.

3. Learning is a function of and the responsibility of the learner. The instructor is responsible for providing the appropriate setting, materials, and activities that will allow learning to occur for the motivated learner, and to unearth motivation by linking instruction to the learner's goals. But it is also the responsibility of the instructor to hand the reigns of control over to the learners. The instructor's role then becomes that of an observer who, by reflecting to the learner or group of individuals what phenomena they observe, is able to assist the learners in deepening their understanding of causes and effects.

Putting Existentialism into Practice— A Six-Step Existentialistic Model

This section shows how the EDDI paradigm translates into a six-step model for implementing EDDI techniques. This section uses various workplace examples to demonstrate the usefulness of an existentialistic approach.

Step 1: Identify the Desired Outcomes

In an industrial setting, the task of instructing is to support the achievement of a stated organizational goal. The design of training therefore is usually driven by specific, often measurable outcomes that must be achieved. These outcomes do not usually correspond directly to a traditional field, such as math skills or communication skills, in which the outcomes are specific and often consist of narrow blocks of content relating explicitly to a particular field. Nor do they necessarily correspond directly to the desires of the individual learner. Rather, the outcome is often stated in terms of organizational performance measures for the production process or work system. The training is expected to result in the student being able to perform some task or family of tasks better, thereby achieving better operations results. Thus, in an industrial setting, the task of the training is not usually to impose desired outcomes but rather, to figure out how instruction and training might support the achievement of an already stated (and usually measurable) client objective.

When the stated goal of the training experience is tied to organizational or personal performance measures rather than to mastery of the material covered in the classroom, it is critical that the instructor and the curriculum developer do their work in conjunction with the client. Especially from an existential perspective, it is important to consider, give weight to, and balance the needs of all invested parties. Figure 1 provides a visual conceptualization of

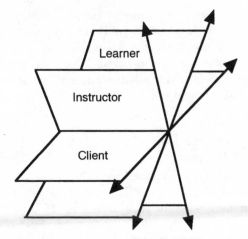

Figure 1. Interdependent planes represent the "reality" of each party. These planes intersect at the point of instruction, balancing divergent needs and experiences at a single point yet assuming constant movement and therefore, a constantly changing point of intersection.

this balancing act. Note in Figure 1 that it is at the point of intersection of the planes that instruction can happen because the instruction is designed with respect for each party's reality or "Being-in-the-world."

For example, if ACME Products hires Ivan the Instructor to come to its factory and deliver basic computer skills to the work force, it is vitally important that Ivan fully understand why ACME is interested in making this investment in its employees. It is possible that the course is being offered as a goodwill gesture by the company to its faithful and trustworthy employees. But it is more likely that ACME is willing to incur the costs of Ivan the Instructor, the cost of lost worktime, and all related costs because it expects a return on its investment. Ivan needs to know what ACME expects that return to be.

Educating people to do something that they will never have an opportunity to do can be quite frustrating and demotivating, especially for adult learners. Adults usually jealously guard their time and they tend to be very pragmatic learners. If they know they need to learn something (because it will make their lives easier, their jobs more secure, their performance better) they will exert the energy needed to learn it. Returning to the example above, Ivan is under the impression that he has been hired to deliver a basic computer skills course. But what if ACME's plant manager is willing to pay for computer skills being delivered only because she expects the employees to record their work-in-process rejects on the computer at the close of each shift. Ivan's instruction will, in all likelihood, not be adequate to make the students proficient at recording on-line rejects.

The result of such a mismatch between the client's desired outcomes and the instructor's is potentially quite costly. The students return to their job with skills and knowledge that will not result in better performance as defined by the company. The plant manager sees no return on her investment and views the training as a waste of limited company resources. The instructor is viewed as ineffective and is not asked back.

These mismatches are all too common within industrial settings for a variety of reasons. First, training/education is sometimes viewed as a panacea for all industrial woes. "If it's broke, train it." Second, many instructors are not familiar with the unique requirements of industrial clients. Third, instructors are usually hired or contracted with by the human resources or personnel department rather than directly by operations managers. Therefore, the client that the trainer interfaces with often has little awareness of the specific need or situation that drove the operations people to request instruction in a particular subject. Finally, as in most educational experiences, the instructor controls only that which goes on in the classroom. So the instructor is not in a position to change anything within the industrial setting. For example, even if Ivan the Instructor teaches the basic computer skills course perfectly and all the participants master the material, Ivan cannot change the fact that the learners will not have time in front of a computer terminal for the next six months because production volumes have shot through the roof.

Step 2: Identify the Timeframe for Achievement of Desired Outcomes

Once the desired outcomes are identified with the client and confirmed across functions within the organization, it then becomes the instructor's responsibility to work with the client to develop a realistic timeframe for achievement of the desired outcomes. This is especially important when the instruction is not a single event, but takes place over time.

For example, say the client desires instruction that will result in supervisors being better able to resolve employee grievances without having to involve higher levels of management. The instructor must provide the client with a sense of what sorts of results will be seen and when. The instructor might predict that with four hours of classroom time, the client can expect increased supervisory awareness of the costs involved in processing a labor union grievance and the benefits of relationship building with employees. With eight hours of classroom training, the supervisors will have been exposed to interpersonal communication theories and will have practiced three new communication tools. Therefore, the client should expect to see new communication tools in practice throughout the supervisory population. And so on.

This step is valuable because it allows the instructor to design the curriculum around specific (desired and perhaps rewarded) behaviors rather than by knowledge chunk or subject. It also lets the client know what behaviors it should be reinforcing and encouraging at different points. More importantly, it forces the client to identify organizational "barriers" to the practice of the new behaviors and to remove them. Without this critical action, even the best instruction/training will not result in behavioral change.

It is easy to see why the client must enable the behavioral change outside of the classroom at least as much as the instructor enables it in the classroom. Returning to the most recent example, what would happen if the supervisor-in-training decided to resolve a grievance in his department without taking it to upper management (just as instructed in training!)? He draws upon his new cadre of communication tools and conflict resolution techniques to get at the heart of the grievance. He discusses the situation with his boss and they agree, the solution is fair. He returns to the employee and they resolve the grievance. Two days later, the Personnel Manager overrules the agreement and the grievance is taken over by senior management with a very different outcome.

Whatever the cause of the supervisor being overruled, it is most likely not an instructional problem. Rather, it is highly likely that the supervisor bucked up against an organizational policy or structure that did not support his actions. The results: wasted time and money, a frustrated supervisor, and a failed initiative to decentralize grievance handling.

Step 3: Develop a Cross-Functional Client Group to Resolve Structural Issues

The instructor must be aware of what "reality" is for the learner outside of the classroom. In an industrial setting, this awareness is all the more critical because of the conscious and deliberate structure of reward and discipline mechanisms outside of the classroom which will immediately confront the learner. The classroom experience is only one part of a network of forces acting upon the learner.

Because it is not usually within the purview of the instructor to affect organizational policies and practices beyond the classroom, the instructor needs to have access to a cross-functional team from the plant which has primary responsibility for facilitating the maintenance or retention of newly learned information and behaviors by the students.

The need for an internal support team is driven by the fact that whatever is learned in the classroom is often considered somewhat suspect by the learners until they have had the chance to test it in the real world of work. If use of the new knowledge or behaviors produces positive results, it will be retained; if not, the learner will revert to tried and true behaviors or understandings. The idea that learning happens in the classroom is especially misleading in an industrial setting in which a premium is placed on being able to predict and control the behavior of employees. The organizational system itself is an educator and reinforcer. Given a disparity between the message of the instructor and that of the system, the system will win every time. It packs a greater wallop.

When the desired outcome of instruction is behavioral change, an internal support team is essential. Suppose management wanted to impress upon employees the importance of customer satisfaction. They call in an instructor from the local business school and ask him to put together a one-week course devoted to understanding the importance of customer satisfaction and solving problems identified by the customers. The instructor meets with the senior management team and they agree that the desired outcomes are: (1) employees are aware of who the customers are and what the customers' needs are; (2) employees know the key competitors and understand how our service compares to theirs; (3) employees are trained in handling customer complaints constructively; and (4) employees are trained to conduct problem-solving and trouble-shooting when a problem is identified by a customer.

Also suppose that classroom instruction is all that happens to the employees. The employees show up for their class. They spend considerable time and energy mastering the concepts and tools provided by the instructor. Each employee is somehow evaluated to ensure that he or she has completely mastered the material. The employees leave the classroom, ready to satisfy customers with a vengeance.

Upon returning to his work area, one employee notices (thanks to his increased awareness) that the parts coming off the line will not meet the customer's standards. He calls his supervisor and recommends that the line be halted until the problem is corrected. The supervisor, whose merit bonus is based on the number of parts out the door each day, tells the employee to ship the parts to the customer.

It is not easy to measure the results of the instructional experience in this example but certain outcomes should be expected. The week of instruction is totally undermined and, therefore, the expense of instruction, time off the job for learners, and materials are wasted. The employee's frustration level soars. It is not the case that the employee learns nothing from an experience like this. Quite the contrary. The knowledge gained by the employee is that learning new concepts is a waste of time because the organization will never change to allow for new behaviors, no matter how seemingly worthy the content.

Without an internal resource team in place, the story ends there. But with a team in place, the probability that follow-up will happen is greatly increased. A follow-up to the training would reveal that no one is using the skills learned. A survey is sent out to the former trainees. Barriers to implementation of the new skills are identified and responded to. Additionally, if the course were to be repeated, feedback received by the internal team could be funneled to the instructor allowing him to make adjustments in the material to further facilitate mastery of the content and application of it within that particular site.

For best results, the cross-functional team should have representatives from each major stake-holding group within the plant. The greater the number of stake holders involved, the better the chances that the instruction will get support and on-going attention both during and immediately following delivery. If it is a unionized facility, union officers are often exceptionally good at identifying ahead of time organizational barriers and constraints to the stated "desired" behaviors. They are also usually well tied into the informal communication network (i.e., the grapevine) and can give accurate feedback on the quality of the instruction, the types of additional, follow-up support needed, and the issues or problems surrounding implementation of the new skills.

Step 4: Establish the Instructional Design Team (IDT)

In most cases, it is very beneficial to involve the client not only in overseeing implementation of learning (the cross-functional client group), but also in the instructional design process. This is true even in those cases in which the client has little experience with the process of curriculum design or delivery. For this reason, I recommend the use of an Instructional Design Team or IDT. (It is often very useful for the IDT's membership to overlap with the cross-functional client group formed in Step 2.) The IDT is a cross-functional group of internal and external resource people who work with the instructional development specialist to make sure that there is near-perfect coordination between instructional content, instructional delivery, learner goals, and organizational goals. Members of the IDT (see Figure 2) are engaged in an on-going dialogue throughout the design and delivery process. This team participates in making the instructional material immediately relevant and applicable

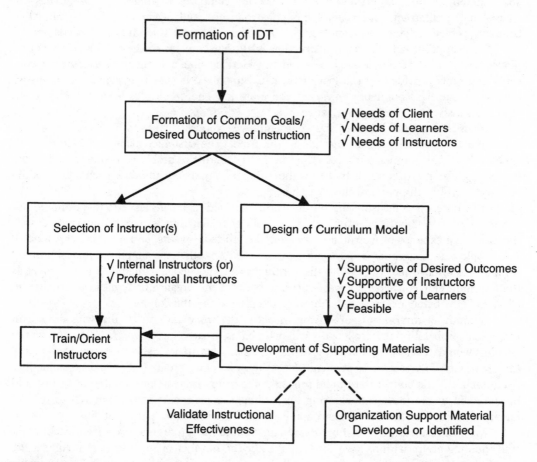

Figure 2.   Sequence of events and points of consideration for the instructional design team (IDT).

to the learners. Also, the inclusion of clients in the process of design increases the likelihood that the classroom experience will achieve the desired outcomes (established in Step 1) and that the manner of instructional delivery will match the needs of the learners.

An instructional design team might consist of 5–12 people and should be chaired by the ID professional. Some roles that can be very effective on an IDT are: professional trainer, curriculum development specialist, selected internal trainers from the plant, manager of operations, personnel manager, technical experts (either internal or external), instructional materials design specialist, and equipment vendors. The selection of people best suited for a particular project should be based on the type of training being designed (technical vs. process); the manner of delivery of the material (Will there be a manual needed? Will the instruction be delivered by internal or external instructors?); and the style of the training (use of audio-visual or other equipment; experiential vs. lecture, etc.).

The IDT accomplishes its task through a series of steps, noted in Figure 2, each leading to the development of the instruction. It is not necessary that all members of the IDT participate in all steps, but it is important for the entire team to approve the outcome of each step prior to moving onto the next step because each team member approaches the task with different concerns and different experiences. The best result will be achieved when all of the distinct points of view concur on all instructional design decisions.

The specific steps/decisions which the IDT will engage in may vary slightly from project to project, but the following list summarizes the steps of a "typical" IDT process (if indeed there is such a thing). Each step/decision will be discussed in more detail below.

A. Detail the desired outcomes.
B. Decide who will deliver the instruction and what are their needs.
C. Design a curriculum model and delivery approach.
D. Develop the supporting instructional material.

With the assistance of an IDT, the instructor is well positioned to gain an ever-deepening understanding of the client's reality. At the same time, the instructor is also in an excellent position to educate the organizational decision-makers about the potentialities and limits of classroom instruction, the vast array of instructional design options available, and the pros and cons of each selection. The entire extended conversation, which occurs over time within the IDT, makes the instructor infinitely more valuable to the client and makes the client a much more savvy and discerning consumer of instruction. If the parties work well together and respect each other's expertise, the end result is the formulation of a very strong, usually long-lasting relationship between customer/client and supplier/instructor.

A. *Detail the Desired Outcomes.* In those situations in which the scope of the content is extremely focused, as is often the case in highly job-specific subjects, this step may not be necessary. But whenever the desired outcomes span several behaviors or content areas, this step is crucial. Even under the best circumstances, an instructor working within an industrial setting is lucky to get a very general but meaningful desired behavioral outcome statement such as, "We want the production workers to function as self-directed teams." This statement, while more helpful than, say, "We want the team building course," is still insufficient for the instructor to fully formulate the ideal curricula. The curriculum development specialist needs to know what specific ideas are underlying the desired outcome. Otherwise, the instructor is caught in a guessing game that s/he cannot win. Consider the following three scenarios wherein Ivan the Instructor attempts to gain insight into what specific outcomes Frank the Client is really expecting.

Scenario One

Frank: "We want the production workers to function as self-directed teams. Can you design a course that will get them to that point by year-end?"

Ivan: "Well, let's consider what you mean by self-directed. I assume that you want the employees to be performing the duties that are currently performed by their supervisors."

Frank: "That's right. Can you do it?"

Ivan: "So the sorts of duties that the employees would have to master are production planning, budgeting, tracking attendance, and things like that?"

Frank: "Oh no . . . lets not go overboard here. I think we would be getting ahead of ourselves with all that. I was thinking more along the lines of the workers being cross trained so they could fill in for each other during breaks so we wouldn't lose so much time by shutting down and starting up the lines all the time."

Scenario Two

Frank: "We want the production workers to function as self-directed teams. Can you design a course that will get them to that point by year-end?"

Ivan: "Well, let's consider what you mean by self-directed. I assume that you want the employees to be performing the duties that are currently performed by their supervisors."

Frank: "Well, I'm not exactly sure what I mean by self-directed either. But what I do know is that as of the end of the year, we will be losing eight of our fifteen first-line supervisors and we will not be allowed to replace them. Corporate has done some bench marking and they think our overhead costs are way out of line with the competition. If we can't bring them into line, we will most likely lose our market share."

Scenario Three

Frank: "We want the production workers to function as self-directed teams. Can you design a course that will get them to that point by year-end?"

Ivan: "Well, let's consider what you mean by self-directed. I assume that you want the employees to be performing the duties that are currently performed by their supervisors."

Frank: "Yes, although you will probably have to begin with the very basics. The functional illiteracy rate for our production work force is about 35%, so we can't just jump right into most of the tasks. And I frankly don't know what the math skills are like. In general, the production work force is highly skilled but they lack formal education. That may be related to the fact that English is a second language for 50% of the work force. Who knows?"

Ivan: ". . . I see. . . . And you say you'd like the production work force functioning as self-directed teams by year end? You realize of course that this is a very ambitious goal given the need to begin with basic skills."

Frank: "Well, what I really need is to pay for this instruction in this year's budget. I just don't want to wait until next year because I'm not sure we'll have such a generous training budget. If we can get the instruction started, and paid for, by year-end, that will meet both my financial and operational goals."

In each of the above scenarios, the original statement of desired outcomes are the same. But the conversation that follows this statement in each scenerio results in a radically different understanding of what would constitute appropriate instruction. These scenarios assume, for the most part, that the client knows, if asked, what he or she needs to get out of the instruction. Often, it requires significantly more digging on the part of the instructor to assist the client in coming to an understanding of what he or she needs and, more importantly, what instruction can and cannot do to help the client move toward his or her goals. Thus, the first task to be undertaken by the IDT is to fully explore the desired outcomes for the instruction, getting as specific and tangible as possible.

It is not unusual at this point for the instructor to shift into the role of facilitator/consultant as the client tries to work through misaligned goals and conflicting organizational directions. It is also not unusual for some unresolved issues or differences of opinion to be sent back to the internal support group for resolution or clarification. Therefore, it is often expeditious to build in overlapping membership between the IDT and the cross-functional client group.

B. *Decide Who Will Deliver the Instruction and What Their Needs Are.* In many instances, there is tremendous benefit to be gained by using internal (usually non-professional) trainers rather than bringing in professional trainers from outside the organization. Insiders have decidedly more credibility with the plant population than outsiders. This is due in part to their ability to relate the content of the instruction to day-to-day life in the plant. They are also able to understand and relate better to the concerns of the learners.

On the other hand, external instructors usually have a better grasp of the big picture. They are usually better able to adapt the curriculum based on the needs of the students. They usually have years of experience teaching the material, which enables them to bring to the classroom an understanding of how learners master the content, points that are difficult to master, and techniques to facilitate learning.

It is important, when making the internal vs. external instructor decision, to keep in mind the unique characteristics of an industrial setting. Consider the potential value to the client of developing internal resources (i.e., the instructors) for future instructional needs. If the client is likely to require the course to be delivered repeatedly to the entire workforce, then it is often appropriate to create a cadre of internal instructors who are able to deliver the course without incurring the cost of an external instructor.

Related to the value of developing internal instructors to deliver an often repeated course is the potential value of having internal subject-matter experts roaming the facility as they do their regular jobs. Take, for instance, the subject of safety. Let's say the plant must conduct an annual course in meeting Occupational Safety and Health Administration (OSHA) requirements and related safety issues. Aside from the financial benefit of having internal people ready and able to instruct the course each year, there is the added benefit of having that cadre of experts acting on their knowledge for the rest of the year. They know the requirements and are thus more likely to follow them in the course of performing their daily duties. They offer a permanent role model for their co-workers and reinforce the material covered in the classroom on a regular basis.

Drawbacks of using the internal instructor approach are not inconsequential, however; the most obvious drawback is their relative lack of experience and expertise in the content area as well as in the field of instructional design and delivery. Internal instructors often require extensive training in order to function well as instructors. They usually require that instructional material be formatted specifically for them, with comprehensive instructions relating to how best to deliver the material. The end result is that they usually do not tailor the course to the unique needs of each group because they do not know what to change and are often uncomfortable changing anything.

Also, internal instructors are less likely to draw from a broad-based knowledge of the field. Especially in the case when a plant is undertaking a new way of doing something, no one in the plant is yet expert in the new procedure, technology, or structure. For example, if a plant is implementing a Just-In-Time (JIT) inventory control process, even the material planners, who are expert in inventory handling and planning, do not have abundant expertise to draw upon when it comes to JIT. The risk is that instruction becomes an exercise in the blind leading the blind due to the lack of depth of understanding on the part of the instructor.

Finally, in situations in which learners may be openly hostile to learning the material because they are opposed to the underlying change taking place, the use of internal trainers is often risky. Workers who feel, for example, that computer-regulated machines will undermine their craftsmanship may be very difficult to instruct in basic computer skills due to their lack of motivation to give up something very valuable to them. Using internal instructors is risky in such a situation because the internal instructors could be viewed by the learners as sell-outs. Therefore, they've lost their credibility before they have even begun to instruct.

While the decision to use internal or external instructors may appear to be related more to logistics than to instructional design, nothing could be farther from the truth. In the vast majority of plants, the use of internal instructors will dictate certain instructional design parameters that can be more or less restrictive depending on the skill level of the internal instructors, the amount of time and resources allotted to train the internal instructors prior to delivery of the material, and the ability and willingness of the learner population.

Instructional design for internal instructors differs from generic instructional design in that the learning environment must be made more "predictable." The "predictablity" of the learner responses is illusory and thus imposed, but the instructional design can still offer a menu for the instructors complete with an escape hatch for those situations in which the learners' response exceeded the instruction's flexibility and/or the instructor's ability.

Internal instructors falter when they are confronted with a reaction from the learner that they were not prepared for (and, for inexperienced instructors, that means they are prone to faltering). Instructors need to know how to respond to what happens. Therefore, the instructional material must be designed as a decision tree such that instructors have a map to follow for each possible response from the learner(s). These potential action paths should cover a multitude of possibilities, such as different learning styles within the classroom or across classes, literacy issues, levels of acceptance and resistance within the learner groups, and the comfort level of the instructor with different types of educational activities and exercises. It must also include a path for learner responses which are impossible for the internal instructor to adequately handle.

C. *Design a Curriculum Model and Delivery Approach.*   Given the fact that there are several differing motivations at work throughout the instructional design and delivery processes, early on it is necessary to forge a unity of purpose that is understood by and acceptable to all parties: the instructor, the learner, the client, and the instructional designer. The IDT can be helpful in identifying a lack of unity in purpose between the instructor or the instructional designer and those internal to the organization. It can also provide insight into the possible motivation of the learners, which is useful information for the instructor and the instructional designer to build upon.

At some point, it is usually necessary for all parties to put their proposed model on the table and see what happens. It is also useful to come to a more general agreement on the overall organization of the material. This decision about how to organize the content for presentation to the learners is one that should be dependent on how the information will be used within the organization and what the desired outcomes of the instruction are. If the content of the instruction was to be communication skills, for example, how should it be presented? Should week one be devoted to listening skills, week two to providing constructive feedback, week three to logical argument, and so on? Or would it make more sense, given the desired outcomes of the instruction by the client and the learners to have week one devoted to communication with co-workers, week two to communication with customers, and week three to communication with the boss?

Obviously, this example is an oversimplification, in that there are usually dozens of ways of organizing the material, and it is usually not easy to make the perfect link between in-class content and out-of-class outcomes. But the need to agree on a model is nonetheless critical in that it forces each party to consider the content of the instruction within a broad, existential context.

D. *Develop Supporting Instructional Material.*   The existentialistic approach's emphasis on learning process rather than on mastery leads to relatively unstructured support materials which allow the learner to draw conclusions and document lessons learned rather than have them imposed by the instructor. In fact, the learner is in one sense the true instructor because it is his or her choice to accept new understandings. Thus, instructional material should be substantive enough to trigger a recollection of the concepts presented and the activities experienced by the learners, but should also allow for the final conclusions or learnings to be filled in by the learners.

Also, because the existentialistic paradigm draws and builds upon the whole life experience of the learner, it is important for at least some of the instructional material (for example, workbooks) to be private. In encouraging the learners to draw from their own personal experiences and self-knowledge, the instructor must be aware of the potential risks (psychological, work-related, and personal) to the learners of too much public disclosure. Instructional materials should differentiate between thoughts that will be shared in group discussions and those that are for private reflection. There is value to be gained from allowing time for participant introspection and, therefore, this should not be abandoned. Instructors should attempt to assist the learner in forming connections between old and new understandings by allowing him or her to experience new concepts in a multitude of ways. Introspection, discussion, group exercises, simulations, role playing, and so on, should each be used to reinforce a single concept completely.

The IDT's role during this phase is to broaden the notion of "supporting instructional material" from its traditional, classroom focus. What sort of support materials should the organization be providing out of the classroom? How can other members of the organization be oriented to support those in training as the learners attempt to try out new skills or behaviors?

Finally, if the organization is committed to the use of internal trainers, it is during this stage that the skill level of the internal trainers needs to be assessed. The internal trainers need to identify the supporting materials that they will require and assist in their design and development.

Step 5: Deliver the Instruction

This step, although self-explanatory, is where the existential assumptions truly come into play. The instructor steps from the role of presenter to the role of facilitator to the role of mirror, and back again. The instructor offers suggestions as to how a piece of information could be interpreted and invites students to participate in activities. But the instructor takes the cue from the students. The students are responsible for the learning. The instructor is responsive to their needs.

The instructor recognizes and draws upon the experiences of the participants. Activities allow participants to explain and thus better understand how they got to be who they are and how they come to their current conclusions about the subjects at hand.

The instructor uses the techniques associated with Phenomenology to bring students to a better understanding of themselves and the subject matter. Phenomenology is the description of the data (literally the "givens") of immediate experience. It seeks to understand rather than to explain phenomena. Van Kaam (1966, p. 15) defines it "as a method in psychology [that] seeks to disclose and elucidate the phenomena of behavior as they manifest themselves in their perceived immediacy." By reflecting to the students what the instructor sees, the students are freed to see their behavior and underlying thoughts or assumptions more objectively. The students can then make a decision on their direction based on where they are now. For example, in a class on group dynamics, rather than lecturing on the stages of group development, the instructor might ask students to consider the different stages they had gone through as a class. The instructor might make observations about the group and the ways their interactions seemed to change over time. But the class members have equal opportunity to share and build upon their interpretation of the experience (i.e., the data).

Step 6: Evaluate and Revise

Even the best IDT cannot predict with 100% accuracy what the needs of the learners will be. It is therefore very important to allow time for the IDT to meet with the instructional designer and the instructors after initial classes to evaluate and revise the material. The focus of this meeting should be not only on what the IDT has observed, but also on what the learners have reported. That is, each class should have an evaluation form which allows for all participants in the class to reflect on what they've learned, how comfortable they are with the activities, what additional support they might need, and whether the content of the course is helping them to meet their goals. This data, combined with the feedback and reflections of the IDT and the experts, will provide all the information needed to evaluate and improve the instructional experience. This meeting will also bring to light gaps between the client's expectations and the results of the instruction. Here again, the parties may have to return to the drawing board to ensure that everyone's needs are met. By the time this spiraling process is complete, the client will feel at least as invested in the instructional material as the instructional designer does, a result that is sure to enhance his or her commitment to continued learning in the workplace.

Conclusion and Recommendations

I have argued that the Existentialistic Design and Delivery of Instruction (EDDI) paradigm dictates a certain approach to instruction which is particularly useful within a workplace setting. It attempts to go beyond existing ID theories by attending to the "whole person" of the learner across his or her life experience. This paradigm is particularly necessary in the workplace because of the important role of the client, a largely invisible role in the classroom, but one which is profoundly visible with an expanded frame of reference.

It should not be assumed, however, that the EDDI approach would only be effective in the workplace. An existentialistic approach works because it rejects the unintended, unstated, but omnipresent message of many traditional paradigms that people are to be managed, controlled, and exploited by the instructional experience. It accepts the entirety of the learners as they are, where they are. It places responsibility for learning in the hands of the learners, thereby allowing them the freedom to choose their response to the content. And it values the process of learning and of coming to understanding—the core of life's work.

References

Binswanger, L. (1958). The existential analysis school of thought. In R. May, E. Angel, & H. F. Ellenberger (Eds.), *Existence.* New York: Basic Books.

Binswanger, L. (1963). *Being-in-the-world: Selected papers of Ludwig Binswanger.* New York: Basic Books.

Boss, M. (1977). *Existential foundations of medicine and psychology.* New York: Aronson.

Brockett, R. G. (1997). Humanism as an instructional paradigm. This volume.

Heidegger, M. (1962). *Being and time.* New York: Harper and Row.

Schuster, D. H. (1997). SALT and accelerative learning. This volume.

Sisco, B. (1997). The individualizing instruction model. This volume.

Van Fossen, S., Sticht, T. G. *et al.* (1991). *Teach the mother and reach the child: Results of the intergenerational literacy action research project of wider opportunities for women.* Washington, DC: Wider Opportunities for Women.

Van Kaam, A. (1966). *Existential foundations of psychology.* Pittsburgh: Duquesne University Press.

Wilson, B. G. (1997). The postmodern paradigm. This volume.

Work in America Institute National Policy Study (1992). *Job linked literacy: Innovative strategies at work.* Scarsdale, NY: Work in America Institute.

29

Linear Instructional Design and Development

Roberts A. Braden
California State University, Chico

This chapter is about *linear* instructional design and development. That is, it is about using a systematic, *linear* procedure to design, develop, and validate instruction. The procedure is systematic in that it follows a prescribed set of steps. It is linear in that the steps are conducted in a predetermined order, one after the other. It involves design in that the procedure calls for analysis, creative planning, and decision making. It involves development as the rendering of the design. It is validated in the sense that the developed instructional materials are subjected to tryout and revision before general implementation. In short, linear instructional design and development (IDD) is what we commonly call basic instructional design, basic instructional development, basic instructional design and development, or just basic ID. It is also what people mean sometimes, but not always, when they use the term instructional systems design (ISD). For the remainder of this chapter the terms *instructional design* and *ID* will be used as synonyms for *linear instructional design and development*.

Do you get the idea that there might be a jargon problem here? Indeed there is, and it confounds the issue of identifying the elements of good practice. Those who talk about and write about ID tend to assume that they and their audience are talking about the same thing. Upon sober reflection we realize that this is often a fallacious assumption. Too frequently we are talking past each other. Too often we select our definitions and assume that our conversationalists share them. The reality is that instructional design does not mean the same thing to all people who consider themselves instructional designers. That is not surprising, since we find that the broader term instructional technology does not mean the same thing to all who identify themselves as instructional technologists. Even Seels and Richey's recent (1994) "definition" book does not provide help here. All of the following titles are in use by individuals whose role it is to "design instruction":

- Instructional designer
- Instructional developer
- Instructional technologist
- Educational technologist
- Performance technologist
- Training designer
- Curriculum designer
- Educational psychologist
- Computer educator
- Production expert/specialist
- Teacher/trainer

Does it matter? Probably. If the names are not the same, how can we expect that the intent or the approach or the results will be the same? And they are not. Certainly the *approach* is not, and that is the crux of our dilemma. Unless we can agree upon the approach—the methods—of ID, then all else is subject to disagreement. That includes disagreement over ID's function, purpose, limits, and even its legitimacy.

If, as the list of names above suggests, we cannot agree upon the role of the persons doing instructional design, how can we predict the outcome of their efforts? The answer may be that in the final analysis we do not want their efforts to be entirely predictable. We may revel in our diversity. We may cherish our differences. And we may believe that our different perspectives and our different techniques enrich the profession. Yes, most ID theorists, teachers, and practitioners probably believe those things. In a creative profession, we celebrate our differences. Usually our opposing points of view are argued in an atmosphere of tolerance. The issue to be raised here is whether we can be *too* tolerant, too accepting of every new variety of ID, too accommodating of notions that run counter to established ID as defined earlier. My answer is yes. There is no reason that we should warmly welcome every mutation of the system, or even that we should be PC (professionally correct) and pretend that we do.

The things that we have in common as designers of instruction are more important than our differences. (That is a statement of opinion for which the reader's tolerance is requested.) What do we all have in common? Well, we all have a concern for the facilitation of learning. The vast majority of us believe that *our product* is a prescription for learning. We call it instruction, and the design is accompanied by whatever it takes to support the prescribed learning event. Beyond that we begin to diverge. We share a common base of literature, full of theory and advice. Within that rich literature there are many intertwining threads, but few that are universal. Three recurring ideas are critical to the theme of this chapter. One is that we can express our ideas about how ID is to be done in a *model*. The second is that systematic design is cybernetic. That is, that it involves a feedback loop for revision or self-correction. The third is that *prescriptive* procedures and models, as contrasted with *descriptive* ones, follow a fixed (prescribed) sequence of activities.

Models

Different conceptions of the instructional technology field are nowhere more obvious than in the proliferation of ID models and in the ever growing list of alternatives to ID. There has been no shortage of models. As early as 1972, Twelker did a review of five ID models. Gropper (1977) provided an analysis of ID models used in university settings and identified ten common tasks (steps) found in those models. In 1980, Andrews and Goodson analyzed 40 models, extending Gropper's list to 14 items and concluding that instructional design models serve four purposes:

1. Improving learning and instruction by means of the problem-solving and feedback characteristics of the systematic approach.
2. Improving management of instructional design and development by monitoring and controlling the functions of the systematic approach.
3. Improving evaluation processes by means of the designated components and sequence of events, including the feedback and revision events, inherent in models of systematic instructional design.
4. Testing or building learning or instructional theory by means of theory-based design within a systematic instructional design model.

Gustafson (1981), in the first of two surveys of instructional development models, created a taxonomy of ID models with four categories: (1) classroom focus, (2) product focus, (3) systems focus, and (4) organizational focus.

The original Gustafson survey provided brief descriptions of five models which he thought belonged in the *classroom focus* category. Two of the models—those originated by Kemp (1985) and by Gerlach and Ely (1980)—have identified steps but are not linear. The Learning System Design Model created by Davis, Alexander, and Yelon (1974) is somewhat linear, but some steps can be performed simultaneously. Gustafson says of the DeCecco model that it "is not an ID model, but rather a teaching model with boxes and arrows" (De-Cecco, 1968, p. 20). That leaves only the model by Briggs (1970) as a true linear ID model in the classroom focus category. Interestingly, Gustafson found the linear nature of Briggs' model to be a potential drawback, because teachers might find the linear approach to be unacceptable.

The second Gustafson survey (1991) covers two more classroom ID models. The Heinich, Molenda, and Russell ASSURE Model (1993 and revisions) isn't even a model in a graphic sense, but merely an acronym. In contrast, the Dick and Reiser Model (1989) is primarily linear. An interesting feature of that model is its linkage of objectives to a textbook—an obvious concession to the classroom teacher who may have no control over the choice of the text. After looking at all these classroom ID models and hearing relevant comments from classroom teachers, this author would like to suggest the following axiom:

> **School teachers in K-12 do not have enough time to prepare instruction using a full systems approach model. Even truncated models and semi-linear models may be too demanding for most classroom teachers.**

Gustafson's *product development models* category yielded three examples in the second edition of his survey (1991). Linearity is implicit in the Van Patten Model (1989) and the model by Bergman and Moore (1990). The limited scope of these models is their greatest weakness. They, like so many models for the design of computer-based instruction (e.g., Criswell, 1989; Kearsley & Halley, 1987; Soulier, 1988), give short shrift to all but the strategies and production aspects of instructional design. The model by Leshin, Pollock, and Reigeluth (1992) is linear. Their seven-step procedure has been grouped with the classroom models, but could have been classified as a systems development model. Although Leshin, Pollock, and Reigeluth's model was apparently created specifically to emphasize the strategy-development aspect of ID as elaborated by their textbook, it turned out to be a comprehensive, robust model. As such it is well suited for use by either teachers-in-training or instructional design practitioners.

The third category identified by Gustafson (1991) is *system development models*. He gave five examples: (1) Instructional Development Institute (IDI); (2) Interservices Procedures for Instructional Systems Development (IPISD); (3) Dick and Carey; (4) Seels and Glasgow; and (5) Diamond. The specified characteristics for models to be included in this category include having a problem-solving orientation and *a linear development process*. Three other models in this category need to be mentioned because they are in current favor as the bases for textbooks now in use. First, there is the model by Knirk and Gustafson (1986), which is highly influenced by Gustafson's two reviews. Then there is the model by Smith and Ragan (1993), which bridges the gap between classroom models and systems development models. Third, there is the very linear model by Foshay, Silber, and Westgaard (1986). It is the model used by the International Board of Standards, and it has been incorporated in an excellent textbook by Rothwell and Kazanas (1992).

The model by Dick and Carey (1990) is being more widely taught than any other today. The steps of the D&C model are to identify instructional goals, conduct instructional analysis, identify entry behaviors and characteristics, write performance objectives, develop criterion-referenced test items, develop instructional strategy, develop and select instructional materials, design and conduct formative evaluation, revise instruction, and design and conduct summative evaluation. The steps are done in sequential order as listed, except that instructional analysis and entry behavior identification are done concurrently or perhaps iteratively. The D&C sequence parallels the steps of my own more elaborate model, which will be presented later.

The model by Seels and Glasgow (1990) is one of the examples given by Gustafson (1991) of a systems development model. However, *in its graphic form* it barely meets Gustafson's criteria for being in that category. It is not a linear model as much as it is an interactive model. The authors explain that it is iterative, but the manner in which designers may appropriately jump back and forth between steps is unclear. The ambiguity may or may not be intentional, but lack of rigor is not implied. Seels more recently has written that "ISD is generally a linear *and iterative* procedure which demands thoroughness and consistency" (Seels & Richey, 1994, p. 31, emphasis added).

Knirk and Gustafson's Synthesized Model (1986) has its components clustered into three groups. It begins with problem identification, is followed by design, and ends with development. In each grouping there are sequential steps, and there are steps that may be conducted randomly, concurrently, or iteratively. For example, the model prescribes that during design you must first develop instructional objectives, and next you do either or both of two things: indicate appropriate instructional strategies and/or choose the type of media. Similar flexibility is offered during problem determination, wherein determining entry behaviors and identifying instructional goals are steps that don't follow a forced sequence. During development, the steps of analyzing results and of revising materials are not performed in a prescribed order either, and one would assume that an analyze-revise-analyze-revise iteration cycle is intended. At all three points in the model where a choice of steps is offered, *both* must be accomplished before proceeding to the next step. Thus, the strength of this model is that it compels linearity where it matters and allows randomness or personal choice where it does not.

Smith and Ragan's model also clusters steps into three groups: analysis, strategy, and evaluation. Like Seels and Glasgow, they show that all of their steps are in a sequence which is generally followed but with great latitude for exceptions. This is reflected both in their graphic representation of the model and in the text: ". . . particular circumstances may cause a designer to modify the sequence of design steps. Many times the steps within a particular phase may occur concurrently" (Smith & Ragan, 1993, p. 7).

Another Model

To make all of the best arguments in favor of linear models requires that we examine one of them in detail. The model in Figure 1 not only is linear, it is more comprehensive than most of the models discussed so far. This model offers clarification about where ID begins and ends. It relates ID processes to the management of projects and provides an expanded evaluation component. Further, it accommodates easy graphic juxtaposition of Keller's (1983) motivational design model.

The model contains four shaded clusters of elements. Only the large cluster on the left is instructional design. The other three clusters represent project management, the design of motivation, and the implementation of instruction. Within the ID cluster are 15 distinct steps, six of which involve evaluation. All evaluation-related activities are shown in ovals. Non-evaluation procedures are presented in rectangles. ID steps will be explained in the order in which they should be performed. The importance of the output of each step as input into the next step will be clarified through the use of an input-process-output pattern of explanation.

Step 1. Determine Needs

The first ID step is to find out what the target students *need* to know about the subject under consideration. A problem or an opportunity that has come to somebody's attention serves as the trigger (input) for this step. Needs assessment has become commonplace in ID models these days and involves a basic discrepancy analysis approach. In that approach, two things are compared to each other to determine the discrepancy between them. In learning needs assessment, we generate the things to be compared. On the one hand, the status quo regarding learner skill and knowledge is evaluated. On the other hand, a consensus is reached concerning the level of skill or knowledge desired for the learners. The difference represents the "needed" learning.

Because this process may unearth many "needs" that cannot or should not be met through instruction, part of the process involves ferreting out the learning needs. Since we may discover more learning needs than we wish to meet, another part of the process is to analyze all such needs and establish priorities. In this way, we can separate the needs to be addressed by instruction from those to be left for another time and another solution.

The output of the first step, therefore, is a set of needs (one or more) which can and should be met via instruction. For a typical ID project, these results will be formalized in a needs assessment report, but very small ID teams may find that a simple list will suffice.

Step 2. Determine Goals

Those identified needed learnings are the input for the step in which we clarify and clearly state the *instructional* goals. By delaying the establishment of learning goals until needed learnings have been determined, we assure ourselves that the instruction we design will "teach" what the students need to know. Converting a set of learning needs into a set of learning goals is a straightforward procedure. Each identified need is rephrased to indicate a *performance*. The performance specified *must* demonstrate achievement of the implied skill or knowledge component. This is the behavioral part that so galls the extreme cognitivists. Individuals who are unwilling to accept the notion that we should be designing instruction intended to promote the learning of specific, predetermined competencies will not be persuaded by the conclusions of this chapter. *A basic premise of linear instructional design is that it is* [performance] *goal driven.*

Linking specific performances to abstractions, theories, and the like is problematic, of course. However, that does not mean that we can duck specifying whatever it is we want the

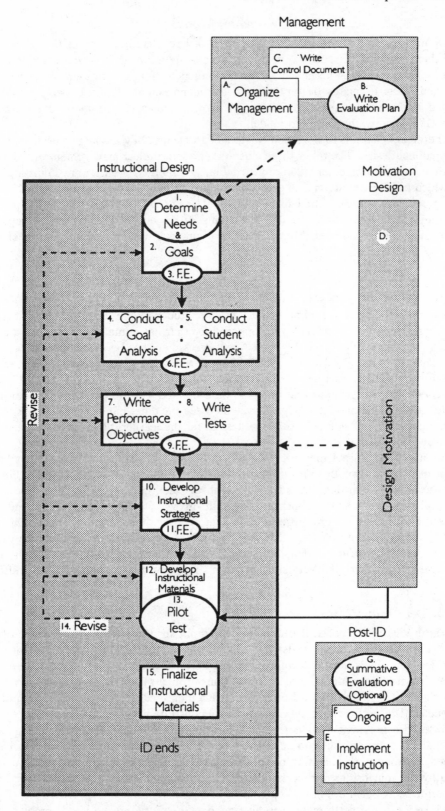

Figure 1. Top-to-bottom formative evaluation instructional design model.

learners to be able to demonstrate they have learned. Consequently, the process may require that the design team set performance goals that can be met with secondary evidence of goal achievement. In practice, we find that the more challenging the learning task, the more likely the designer will need to be creative in setting the performance goal. This prompts the second axiom:

> **Whenever instructional designers encounter a learning need that cannot be rendered into a sensical, observable, achievable student performance, they should abandon attempts to meet that need through linear instructional design techniques.**

The message is clear. ID, as defined herein, isn't the solution to every probelem—not even every teaching-learning problem. Sometimes we care not so much *what* the students learn, but *that* they learn. In those cases, we want the students to have an educational experience, but not necessarily an instructional one. In most cases of learning need, however, clear goals can be written that are instructionally achievable. To simplify the design process, it is recommended that a goal be stated for each identified need, or if needs are grouped, that a chart relating needs to goals be created. That done, a set of goal statements is the output of the second step.

Step 3. Formatively Evaluate Learning Needs and Instructional Goals

The goals statements are the grist (input) for the first of several *formative evaluation* procedures. Each place where a small "F. E." ellipse occurs in the model the symbol should be interpreted to mean that the output of the step to which it is attached will be formatively evaluated for project congruence and for quality. Further, a feedback loop is implied and revision or correction of errors is expected before the design team proceeds to the next step. Exercising quality control through formative evaluation at the points in the model marked F.E. allows us to catch errors early, before they are compounded. It also helps us to fine tune the ID process.

At the first F. E. step, we seek to verify that the goals reflect the identified needs and that indeed they are sensical, observable, and achievable. If the client has triggered the project, we determine whether the goals reflect the client's concerns, and, sequentially, we do it now rather than later. The rationale for the linear imperative at this stage is that the earlier we detect trouble, the easier the remedy. Evaluation methods at this stage range from simple checklist verification to comprehensive expert review and will vary according to the scope and idiosyncrasies of the specific project. At this and all subsequent points of formative evaluation, the evaluation begins as *product evaluation*—the evaluation of the deliverable product of the preceding step. In the event that the product is found to be flawed, the evaluation may become *process evaluation*, in which we examine our procedures to discover where we went wrong. When we conclude formative evaluation, our output is a set of unambiguous goals in which we have a high level of confidence.

Steps 4 and 5. Analyze Instructional Goals and Students

At Step 4, we analyze the goals. *Goal analysis* can be and often is performed in conjunction with step 5, *student analysis*. This is an example of two activities that need not be (and sometimes cannot be) performed in a given linear sequence. What happens in goal analysis is that we subject the goal to a questioning procedure, which results in responses that reveal the components of knowledge and skill required to master (or "do," or "perform") the goal. To facilitate discussion of goal analysis, we refer to these components—of whatever nature—simply as skills and subskills. The process enables us to arrange these skills and sub-skills in graphic form, which visualizes the knowledge structure to show the relationship of components to each other, and, in general, to clarify which subskills are prerequisite to the learning of which others.

As we identify the hierarchies and prerequisites, we use the results of student analysis to tell us which subordinate skills have already been mastered by the typical student and therefore need not be designed into the instruction. Usually we identify the subskills first and then find out whether the typical student has already learned them. However, we *can* determine everything that the typical student knows about many topics without waiting until the chart of skills and subskills has been developed. In fact, when we do the needs assessment we discover a great deal of information about student knowledge. Thus, we may already know which subskills the target students possess prior to instruction.

One output of a student analysis is a profile of the typical student. At the minimum, the profile will be limited to information about student competency levels—a statement, usually written, of what the student is expected to know and be able to do. Competencey information is generated for internal use in determining the entry level of the instruction. A wider ranging student profile might include demographic data useful for linking the specific project to generizable research findings, and it might also include social and psychometric data for use in *designing motivation.*[1]

Melding the results of goal and student analyses, we produce a composite output of the two analysis steps in the form of *a set of skills and subskills to-be-learned.* That information drives the content (subject matter) of the instruction, and as such is often the most controversial aspect of what emerges from the ID process.

Step 6. Formatively Evaluate Instructional Goals Analysis and Student Analysis

For both political and practical reasons, the next linear step is another progress check. Again, as the design team performs formative evaluation, it is looking for congruence and for quality. A subject-matter expert's review of the designer's chart of skills and subskills is highly desirable, and the informed input of a teacher or trainer who has taught similar information to similar students should be obtained if at all possible. If SMEs and experienced teachers of the topic are unavailable, the evaluator or designer should pose questions which challenge the logical continuity of the identified set of skills with the needs and goals.

Even a non-expert can often answer the question, "If the student can perform a specified skill, will that be sufficient evidence that he/she has achieved the learning goal?" It ought to be clear that if we cannot answer that question affirmatively, then we may not be creating something that will achieve our goals. In that case, unless you are a major risk taker or do not believe in instructional goals, you should not proceed with the instructional design!

Steps 7 and 8. Write Performance Objectives and Write Tests

What we are establishing here is a strong case for the linear imperative. The output of F. E. at step six is an essential ingredient (input) for writing performance objectives. Can in-

---

[1]In this chapter, the concurrent and intertwining design of motivation and instruction is acknowledged, both verbally and graphically. However, in the interest of not overwhelming readers who are having their first encounter with this model, the details of that relationship are left to another time, and readers are referred to Keller's linking of his motivation design model to Dick and Carey's model (Keller, 1987).

structional designers begin the entire process by writing objectives without benefit of a set of skills and subkills? Of course they can, but why would they? They would have no assurance that they were not including unnecessary objectives and leaving out others that are critical to what the target students need to learn about the subject.

Given a set of skills and subkills to be taught, the designer's task is to create a set of matching performance objectives and a matching set of test items. The pattern is simple. Objectives must match skills. Test items must match objectives. It doesn't matter, however, whether matching is approached on a set-by-set-by-set basis, or whether a skill is matched with both an objective and a test item before the next skill is considered. For that reason, the two steps are shown in the Figure 1 model as linked with a perforated boundary. The graphic intent is to show that Steps 7 and 8 may or may not interact with each other. When interaction does occur, the usual type of interaction is one of repetition, or as some would say, it is an iterative process. The process goes like this: Write an objective; then write a test item; then write a group of related objectives; then write matching test items; then keep moving back and forth, back and forth, until all of the skills and subskills are matched with objectives and test items.

The departure from straight line linearity described here is not a concession to those who eschew linear models. The needed skill is always identified before an objective is written. The objective is always completed before the test item. The essential order of things should not be broken. Objectives are prepared which translate things to be learned (those raw skills and knowledge components) into meaningful statements of what the student must be able to do after instruction. The objective statements are carefully crafted so that teachers and students can easily understand the circumstances under which the learners will be required to give evidence that they have learned. Furthermore, the objective statements clarify how well the student must learn the skill.

All three of these elements of the objective are important as inputs for the next step, writing a test item. A perfectly matched test item will call for the student to demonstrate the desired learning under circumstances described in the objective. The test item should require an observable and measurable response. The learning objective will be considered met only if the student's response meets the quality standards established in the objective itself.

What has been described is the simplest of Magerian theory without some of the jargon. The reason for presenting the process in this manner is to strip away the *mumbo jumbo*. Writing objectives should be easy and it should be done at a specific point in the ID process. Writing objectives that contain all of the Magerian components makes sense if those objectives are to be the basis for writing test items. When stripped to its essentials, the process can be seen as so simple and straightforward that arguments against it are blunted.

Likewise, shorn of the glitzy phrases, writing matching test items is more time consuming than mind boggling. Each test item merely needs to ask the learner to *do* whatever the objective said that he or she must learn to do. Professional expertise is required to write valid and reliable test items, but application of that expertise is easier when the function of the test items is clear and when the input is in a supportive format.

No magic is required, and herein lies one of the raps that is often laid upon systematic ID. Critics fault ID as being too lockstep. Well, if the requirement is excessive that learning objectives must match a set of identified skills and subskills, and if the requirement that test items match the objectives is also excessive, then systematic ID is too lockstep. If the critics want creativity in the ID process, they can find it in abundance, but not at Steps 7 and 8.

Step 9. Formatively Evaluate Objectives and Tests

The formative evaluation of performance objectives requires objectivity and the interjection of subjective judgment. Objectivity is required to verify that there is an objective for every identified skill or subskill that the students need to learn. Beyond that, good designers also will require a judgment that the objective is sufficient—that it covers all, not just part, of the implicit demands of the skill or subskill. Every objective should receive such scrutiny.

In a more general sense, evaluators also should look holistically at the entire set of objectives and ask, "If the students learn to do all of these things, will they have met the learning goals, and will they have overcome their lack of competency as measured in the needs assessment?" In the final analysis, everything in the ID process must meet the *litmus test* of being congruent with the learning goals.

Although many clients are indifferent to the details of the instructional design, others are curious to the point of being meddlesome. Accordingly, while the objectives are being evaluated (reviewed), they can be shared with many clients. When confronted with a "These are the specific things that your employees will learn to do" statement, the client is afforded an opportunity to voice approval or dissent. In the event that the client does not approve of the objectives, this step is the time to debate their merits. The design team may win the argument, but it may not. If not, an impasse over objectives at Step 9 affords the design team options. It may revisit the needs and revise the project accordingly. Or, it may abort the project in a timely manner. If disagreement over the desired outcomes of instruction is withheld until the end of the project and cannot be resolved at that time, the result is an unimplemented instructional program.

The formative evaluation of the test items can be extremely rigorous or quite lax, depending upon other project variables. At the least rigorous extreme, all that is required is a matching check. Just as the set of objectives should match the set of identified skills and subskills, the set of test questions should match the set of objectives. Since the testing of an objective might entail two or more test items to fully examine the behavior, the "match" is not necessarily one-to-one. Yet, the complete set of test items must completely match every behavior stated or implied, and that match should be verified prior to proceeding.

Testing for purposes of grading, as is done everywhere in schools and universities, tends to contaminate our thinking about tests. The test items created at Step 8 and evaluated at Step 9 are not written primarily for use in assessing grades. Their purpose is to provide ways to *test the instruction*, which will verify that it has facilitated the desired learning. So it is that the set of formatively evaluated test items, as the output of Step 9, becomes the most important and essential input of Step 10.

Step 10. Develop Instructional Strategies

The development of instructional strategies is the most challenging, most creative, most complex, and most misunderstood aspect of ID. Leshin, Pollock, and Reigeluth (1992) refer to this phase as specifying learning events and activities. They devote 116 pages to an explanation of how activities and events are derived for four types of learning: memorization of information, application of skills, understanding of relationships, and higher-level thinking. They make the point that "Each type of learning will require different instructional methods to produce efficient and effective instruction" (p. 136).

So far, so good. Let us add to the recipe a philosophical point of view which this author wishes were shared by every instructional designer. Let us say that whatever strategy we develop must provide the best possible guarantee that the students will be able to successfully respond to the test items. Consequently, instruction should be designed which "teaches to the test" (or at least teaches to the set of criterion-based test items created at Step 8.) This flies in the face of traditional teaching methods that use tests ritually as secret instruments for granting rights of passage. Teaching to the test is not very helpful advice for teachers who are burdened with expectations that they give grades the way that they have traditionally been given. More to the point, however, a teach-to-the-test mindset is true to the spirit of creating student-oriented instruction which has been designed to meet real student learning needs.

Once the designer buys into teaching to the test, the linear design sequence is set in place. The designer must know how the student's performance will be assessed before selecting an appropriate instructional method that will accommodate that method of assessment. Each objective with its associated test item(s) is a unique creative challenge. Fortunately, the universe of instructional delivery strategies and the ways that they can be combined is almost limitless. Linking a viable strategy to any objective is merely a matter of making good, informed choices. When objectives are sequenced into lessons, care must be taken to assure that any overall strategy "works" for every objective.

The strategy development process is informed and influenced by learning theory, technology, motivational considerations, characteristics of the target learners, and by the biases of the client or the developer. It is also influenced by pragmatic factors such as cost and convenience. Many instructional designers develop instructional strategies that reflect Gagné's (1985) events of instruction. For example, Dick & Carey (1990) collapse Gagné's nine instructional events into the following five major components of an instructional strategy: (1) preinstructional activities, (2) information presentation, (3) student participation, (4) testing, and (5) follow-through. All of these components can be addressed in a lesson plan or strategy paper which is the output of this ID step.

Step 11. Formatively Evaluate Instructional Strategies

The strategy paper must meet several tests. The presentation sequence and proposed student participation should be able to pass muster with an SME and/or an experienced teacher of the subject. The entire strategy package is subject to questions of relevance, congruence, organization, and quality. Expert opinion and peer review are quite useful at this step because with so many instructionally acceptable strategies it is easy to overlook an obviously superior approach. Additionally, even though there are numerous strategies that will work well, there may be unforeseen reasons why some or all of them are not-so-desirable. Input from other designers, evaluators, trainers, and SMEs can reveal information that mitigates against a particular strategy.

All evaluation begins with data gathering. Critical data (information) that is needed to formatively evaluate an instructional strategy package can be characterized by four "E" words—efficiency, effectiveness, economy, and elegance. The evaluator seeks to know whether the suggested strategy calls for the efficient expenditure of faculty time and whether the learning activities are efficient from the standpoint of the student. Will the suggested strategy do its primary job—promote learning effectively? Holding the strategy up to the economic light of comparative costs may doom a high technology solution but save a project, or even a designer's job. Finally, after all of the more mundane things are evaluated, the evaluator turns to assessment of the elegance factor. Some things just work together better than others. Some plans achieve the same ends as others, but in less complicated ways. When all other things are equal, some strategies are more appealing, more exciting, more interesting, just more elegant than others.

In regard to the necessity of doing formative evaluation again, and at this sequential point of the ID process, the issue is clear. The formative evaluation is desirable. It cannot be done until after the strategy materials have been developed. The only remaining question is whether or not it can be delayed until later—thrown together with all of the other formative evaluation activities. Yes, it can be delayed, but only at the peril of the instructional designer. What if the strategy is a bummer? What if the ID team develops a costly package of instructional materials to support the wrong strategy? Will the fact that you can teach with almost any medium bail you out when the end-of-project evaluation reveals that another medium or another approach would have been as good or better—and cheaper? No. The correct time to validate the strategy decisions is before committing to instructional materials.

Step 12. Develop Instructional Materials

Even though the name of this step is *Develop* Instructional Materials, the instructional designer should be in no hurry to do so. Given a strategy, the next thing to do is to determine whether or not appropriate instructional materials already exist. Only rarely will there be instructional materials that fit the strategy perfectly, but on those rare occasions it is better to adopt than to develop. Likewise, if instructional materials exist that nearly fit the strategy, then adaptation is preferable to starting over. Faculty members who teach college courses follow a similar procedure when they choose a course textbook. They routinely find the adoption of a textbook to be more practical than writing their own for every course that they teach. When the published text doesn't quite fit, the faculty members adapts—supplementing or using only parts of the book. Only as a last resort (or given some other incentive) does he or she author a new text. The faculty member's intuitive logic carries over into ID. *Instructional design does not always subsume instructional [materials] development!*

For most ID projects, the design team will be required to develop instructional materials that carry out the instructional strategy. They will first select a medium, although strategies which call for particular kinds of interactivity or particular kinds of student participation may preempt that decision. Clients and environmental constraints may also preempt the choice of a delivery medium (when the client says that she/he wants interactive CD-ROM-based instruction, a video-audio-text solution isn't going to be acceptable). Once the medium is chosen or imposed, the design team is controlled by three factors. The first is the strategy. The second is the subject matter. The third is the production methodology associated with the selected medium. Videos start with scripts, CBI begins with a flow chart or control document, overhead presentations begin with an outline and layout sketches, and so forth. In this day of specialization, it is acceptable for an instructional designer to relegate the production of media to production experts. Generalists will want to control their own productions, and that is their choice.

In the entire ID process, the production of instructional materials presents the greatest opportunity to get lost. The temptation is high to let media production values take priority over structure and purpose. In a quest for slick appearance or for generating interest (and motivation), the media producer can fall into the trap of producing *infotainment* or *edutainment* instead of instruction. To guard against this, the designer must have enough production oversight to insist that the materials being produced support the strategy.

Step 13. Pilot Test the Instruction

The pilot test is a formative evaluation of prototype instructional materials both for congruence and for instructional effectiveness when implemented. Formative evaluation methods generally are described as involving the following: expert review, one-to-one evaluation, two-to-one evaluation, small group evaluation, and field test evaluation. The evaluator may use one, several, or all of these techniques in the pilot test phase. Several experts, each with a different area of expertise, may be involved in the expert review.

All of the procedures except expert review involve exposing typical students to the designed instruction. As the names of the pilot test procedures imply, the process varies according to the number of students involved. So does the nature of the data gathered. Evaluation done with small numbers of students provides information about each segment of the instruction. Student likes and dislikes are recorded, communication problems are noted, and the effectiveness and efficiency of every small component of the instruction is brought under scrutiny.

With larger pilot test groups, the evaluator finds out how well the instruction works in settings similar to those for which it was designed. Throughout all of the formative evaluation activities, the evaluator is alert for implementation problems, weaknesses in the materials, indicators of errors in the design process, and evidence regarding student achievement of the learning goals.

The output of the pilot test is an evaluation report. If correctable flaws have been discovered, a recommendation can be made regarding the advisability of going back and making changes. The cost of revision will be weighed against the benefits to be derived from the improvements.[2] The purpose of the evaluator is not to make the revise-or-proceed decision, but rather it is to furnish the decision-maker with the best possible information upon which to base the decision.

Step 14. Revise as Necessary

The evaluation report serves as a roadmap for revision. Because design according to this linear model has included top-to-bottom formative evaluation, it is unlikely that pilot test evidence will suggest a return to one of the very early steps in the ID process. Still, the designers will go where they must if the decision to revise has been made. Revision requires reverting to the point of breakdown and working through the remainder of the model again. A nightmare project would be one that sent designers deep into the revision loop repeatedly, causing them to do it over and over until they get it right. A more realistic scenario is one in which the instructional materials are implemented several times and are fine-tuned after each tryout. For example, the instructional materials might be tweaked after a one-to-one evaluation, tweaked again after a small group evaluation, and revised a third time after a field trial. Iteration of that nature is intended in the model, and is yet another example of requiring only reasonable adherence to the linear sequence.

Step 15. Finalize Instructional Materials

Once the decision is made to forgo further revision, the design team has only to finalize the instructional package. If multiple copies are required, they must be produced. If packaging is appropriate, all of the pieces must be assembled, boxed, and whatever. Depending upon how widely the program will be disseminated, it may be advisable to send the student guide, handouts, worksheets, and the instructor's manual to the print shop. A collection of files on disk may need to be mastered onto CD-ROM. Videotape replication may be in order. It all depends upon the particular project. The logistics and clerical support for putting everything together in final form can be relegated to others by the designer, but the design team is not done until the entire instructional package is ready for marketing or implementation.

Alternatives that Challenge Linear Instructional Design

There are at least five kinds of design alternatives that challenge linear ID. The list with representative references to writings that explain or advocate each alternative follows:

1. Patrick Henry designers ("Give me liberty . . .") (Gentry, 1994; Kemp, 1985; Kemp, Morrison, & Ross, 1994).
2. Benjamin Franklin designers (". . . do not squander time . . . ," "A penny saved . . . ") (Tessmer & Wedman, 1990; Wedman & Tessmer, 1993).

---

[2]The manner in which the cybernetic feedback-for-revision loop is shown in ID models tends to be deceptive. The graphic implication is that the system is always self-correcting and that negative feedback always results in revision. In practice, errors are fed back through a costs/benefits filter, and only economically viable revisions are undertaken.

3. Pablo Picasso designers (". . . instructional development is an art, not a craft . . .") (Davies, 1981, reprinted, 1991).
4. Charles Darwin designers *(Evolution of the Species)* (Merrill, Li, & Jones, 1990a, b, c; Tennyson, 1990, 1993) .
5. Sartre-Heidegger philosopher-designers ("I am; therefore I think")—constructivists, postmodernists, critical theorists, and other postpositivists (Duffy & Jonassen, 1992; Hlynka, 1995; Jamison, 1994, and elsewhere in this book; Willis, 1995; Wilson, 1993, and elsewhere in this book; Yeaman, Koetting, & Nichols, 1994).

A serious analysis of the relative merits of linear ID vs. these contenders would require at least another five chapters. Instead, each will be acknowledged with only a brief comment.

The Patrick Henry Designers (the libertarians)

None of us wishes to be fettered by unnecessary constraints. Several of the more prominent professionals in the instructional design field truly believe that it does not make much difference where one enters the ID process (model) or what sequence one follows to design the instruction. They contend that everything in their model ought to be done, but they want the freedom and liberty to do things "as they come naturally" [read: conveniently]. Objecting to the idea of having a degree of license and a sense of freedom to exercise one's own best judgment is on par with snatching food from the mouths of babes, abusing your mother, and proposing repeal of the Bill of Rights. Why would anybody take such an unpopular stand? Therein lies the dilemma and the challenge raised by those who propose non-linear models that contain the same components we find in linear models.

What we have here is a slippery slope. Convenience comes at the cost of confidence in quality. Convenience in this instance may very well represent an element of personal style and preference more than anything else. Taken to an extreme, that slope leads to preference upon preference—and ultimately to ID as art rather than system.

Do we hear some of Patrick Henry's descendants shouting, "YES! YES! That is exactly what we wish ID to be." Maybe, and that is worrisome. This author's family tree is full of educator ancestors. They were doing artistic instructional design in the 1920s and before. If we cannot progress beyond intuition and personal preference in the way that we put instruction together, then the legitimacy and viability of the entire ID profession are open to questions none of us want to answer.

The Benjamin Franklin Designers (the pragmatists)

Benjamin Franklin didn't get on the hundred-dollar bill because he was handsome. He earned a place in history because he was a practical man. Among the many aphorisms that are his legacy are two from *Poor Richard's Almanack* (1757): "God helps them that help themselves," and "Dost thou love life? Then do not squander time, for that is the stuff life is made of." Sentiments of this sort have inspired most persons who practice instructional design to "help themselves" by cutting a corner or two along the way to "not squander time."

Actually, considering the findings of a recent study, the evidence is compelling that the majority of instructional designers cut more than a corner or two. Wedman and Tessmer (1993) found that "No [single] activity was done by all [73] respondents and only 3 of 11 activities were always done by more than 50% of respondents. Based on how many respondents always did an ID activity, there is evidence that practitioners often alter ID models, at least in terms of which activities are included, if not in terms of the sequence of activities" (p. 49).

The results of Wedman and Tessmer's inquiry were not unexpected because they were documenting something that has long been suspected. So, what does confirmation of a general laxness in ID practice mean? Is it good news or bad?

The good news is: In spite of widespread damnation for its lockstep *appearance*, evidence now exists that linear ID has never been so rigorous in practice that developers have not felt free to miss a step occasionally. Does this mean that most designers do not believe in the power of performing all ID steps? A yes answer would be bad news indeed, but the real answer is, "Probably not."

Wedman and Tessmer (1993) asked their respondents why they omitted ID activities. The two reasons most often given were (1) the decision had already been made by others [27% of all responses], and (2) there wasn't enough time [25%]. Only 22% of omissions of an activity were found to be because the designers consider the activity unnecessary. Although it is hazardous to extrapolate beyond the data given by Wedman and Tessmer, a guess based upon years of ID practice and client-developer interaction would be that the activities most likely to be judged "unnecessary" are (1) student analysis, and (2) field testing. Other project-related constraints—lack of client support and money—account for most of the remaining reasons given by respondents who even occasionally used an abbreviated model in their ID practice. Conclusion: Most designers simply yield to market pressures and opt for pragmatic short cuts. Is that bad? Probably not. Does it result in the best instructional design? Probably not (and *that* is the bad news).

Apparently, the ID practice study was done by Wedman and Tessmer to provide evidence in support of their well-known layers-of-necessity model (Tessmer & Wedman, 1990, and elsewhere). It is no surprise, therefore, that they conclude from their ID practice survey that there is a gap between ID practice and common ID models, and the existence of this gap calls for a model that mirrors practice. How does their model differ from traditional ID models? What does it leave out that other models include? What procedural changes are inherent in the layers-of-necessity approach?

Well, it includes everything—but only sometimes. When time and resources are scarce it may leave out everything except five basic components: situational assessment, goal analysis, instructional strategy development, materials development, and evaluation and revision—and each of these activities is performed at a quintessentially minimal level. Finally, the model has no graphic beginning or ending. Tessmer and Wedman (1990) say that a process with steps or stages to be completed in a prescribed sequence results in what they call overproceduralization. They believe that a prescribed ID sequence "undermines the quality of resulting instructional products" (p. 80). No evidence is given for this conclusion.

Wedman and Tessmer (1993) have said that "Most ID models are based on three assumptions that appear to be incompatible with practice" (p. 53). That statement seems to identify their assumptions more than anything else. An analysis of their writings prompts a suggestion that *The Layers-of-Necessity Model might be based upon three assumptions that appear to represent opinion and overgeneralization:* (1) an assumption that practitioners would rather do shortcut ID than do most or all ID steps; (2) an assumption that doing ID activities randomly rather than sequentially will improve the ID products; and (3) an assumption that deciding what to add to a minimalist ID model is superior to deciding what to omit from a comprehensive model. Maybe Tessmer and Wedman do not assume any of these things. Certainly, until much more evidence is available, these assumptions will not be accepted here.

As we consider taking ID shortcuts we should remember that Franklin also coined the line "A little neglect may breed mischief: For want of a nail the shoe was lost, for want of a shoe . . ." (Franklin, 1757).

The Picasso Designers (the artists)

Ivor Davies (1981, reprinted 1991) took a philosophical position at the heart of the controversies which plague ID. He staked his philosophy upon the premise that ID should be [is?] an art. Actually, he discussed ID as art, craft, and science, and he foretold that the practice of ID would be some combination of the three. So far, at least, he has been correct. His emphasis upon and preference for ID as art is what makes his position worthy of reconsideration now. The concept of ID as art challenges the underpinnings of *systematic* design.

Davies clearly stated his preference for *systemic* instructional design rather than systematic ID. The problem with arguing against his position is that he differs with proponents of linear design at the most basic point. Linear design is procedural. Yet, Davies has said that "*Instructional development itself is not a process.* . . . As an art, instructional development refers to *no particular process*" (1991, p. 102, emphasis added). He went on to describe ID as something grander than its subprocesses, something more relevant, exciting, and warm, something, well, more artistic.

That all sounds very logical and at the same time aesthetically pleasing, culturally uplifting, and idealistic. Were those bad ideas? Emphatically, no. They were, however, dangerous ideas—dangerous to linear ID, that is. Why? The answer is simple: Davies' idealism has opened a crack. Others have squeezed into and expanded the crack. The path is an easy one. Begin with art. Next comes artistic license. Soon there is just license—total license. Through this opening, the ideas of ID have mutated into (1) an unspecified activity, and (2) every kind of ID variant in an era of what can be called "Roll-Your-Own ID" (see later in this chapter).

Art in the design of instruction, when applied at the expense of craft and/or science, would be disastrous. Art alone as the basis for ID surely would be no better than mindless craft-only linear ID (if, indeed, such robotic ID exists somewhere). Ivor, be careful what you ask for. You might get it.

The Darwinian Designers (the evolutionists)

Merrill, Li, and Jones (1990a, b, c) have proposed that ID evolve. Their solution for perceived shortcomings of standard ID is to soup it up. With the aid of computers they wish to strengthen the ID process by creating what they have called second generation instructional design (ID_2). Without question, the ID process can be improved upon and profitably embellished. Without question, computers and artificial intelligence hold high promise for the practice of ID.

The Merrill-Li-Jones team began their series of articles on ID_2 by listing nine limitations of standard linear ID—which they called ID_1 (Merrill, Li, & Jones, 1990a). ID with which this author has been involved never seemed to have all of that baggage. Still, the list is useful as a perspective on how barren ID_1 might be. The Merrill team's view that ID_1 is crippled and inadequate becomes more understandable when we carefully read their ideas in a later article: "It seems to us that much of what passes for Instructional Systems Development (ISD) is based on *empty box procedural models* which indicate steps to take but not how to take these steps" (Merrill, Li, & Jones, 1990c, p. 52, emphasis added).

David Merrill is well known for making provocative statements. Well, Dave, you have done it again. Empty boxes, indeed! Those boxes are "empty" only in the *graphic* models. The explanations which accompany all of the good ID models are filled with how-to advice. A wealth of articles, chapters, and books exist which provide procedures, suggestions, and examples for every instructional design and development activity. Some of these suggestions are model-specific. Some are generic. All of this breast beating about ID failing to address this or that is disingenuous at best. Instructional design—whether it bears a one, a two, or some higher number as a subscript—is not a philosophy. It is not a knowledge base. It is not a brand of psychology. It is not some sort of villain, responsible for all of the ills of our educational system. It may be, but usually is not "empty." Instead, it is a procedure, a process, with subordinate procedures and techniques not shown in its models. Its implementation is typically laden with everything the implementor knows about educational technology, ways of knowing, ways of learning, ways of structuring information, ways of presenting information, human motivation, interactivity, relevance to the learner, deep learning, transfer, achievement of understanding at whatever level is appropriate, plus legitimate client concerns for efficiency, cost effectiveness, and return on investment. (That's the *short* list!)

Second Generation ID is evolutionary. Its authors say that "The design of instruction using ID_2 is computer based [read: evolutionary], but the delivery need not be" [read: no change] (Merrill, Li, & Jones, 1990b, p. 30). Although the authors of ID_2 clearly see their creation as something much more comprehensive than a design model, they have not abandoned ID_1 entirely. Their moderate position has been that "ID_2 is clearly cognitive in orientation but maintains the premise that a prescriptive theory of instructional design is feasible and desirable" (Merrill, Li, & Jones, 1990c, p. 54).

Second Generation ID is coming. It may or may not look exactly like the Merrill team predicts. Automating instructional design has been an ongoing effort of the United States Air Force (Spector, Polson, & Muraida, 1993). The Armstrong Laboratory at Brooks AFB, Texas, has been developing and testing an Advanced Instructional Design Advisor (AIDA). Not yet available to the public, AIDA or one of its descendants may one day be widely used to apply intelligent machine techniques to the design and development of instructional materials.

The purpose here is not to diminish the use and potential of computers in ID. Computer tools which assist in the design of instruction are already proving quite valuable. To date, however, the set of computer tools available to the vast majority of instructional designers is very limited. More powerful tools and ID-specific software, such as intelligent advisors and libraries of boilerplate strategy components, will cut design time and, if used properly, will contribute to effective instruction. At this time, however, it seems unlikely that the power tools will soon be available except in proprietary (and probably quite costly) form.

The most ambitious evolutionary ID model is that of Tennyson (1990, 1993). Like the Merrill and Armstrong Labs teams, Tennyson visualizes the computerization of ID processes. He calls his theoretical model the "4th Generation ISD Model and ISD Expert Tutor." [Imagine that. He's two generations ahead of Merrill!] Of all the computerized approaches, Tennyson's is the least supportive of procedural instructional design. Tennyson, a widely known and respected instructional technologist, seems to have lost the ID rudder on his boat. Rather than explain his model in terms of design activities, Tennyson seems to have gone adrift in a computer vortex. His descriptions are listed instead as "Authoring Activities."

The only serious threat posed by either 4th Generation ISD or ID_2 is that weak designers might rely too heavily upon them. Maybe that is what is intended. Tennyson (1993) said, "I propose a framework for the development of an ISD expert system that will assist both experienced and inexperienced instructional developers in applying advanced instructional design theory" (p. 192). Is there a real possibility that instructional design might become transformed into a computer activity rather than an instruction-focused design process? We can only wait and see.

The Sartre-Heidegger Designers (the philosophers)

The hottest term in instructional technology circles is constructivism. Trendy terms include postmodernism, alternative, situated, paradigms, cognitivism, metacognition, ontology, epistemology, and other terms from the fields of psychology and philosophy. Terms falling or fallen from grace include behaviorism, reinforcement theory, programmed instruction, performance objectives, objectivist, objectivism, positivist, systematic, competency-based, technical, and many others that have permeated the vocabulary of instructional technology for years. Instructional technology is being caught in a riptide caused by change and revision in related fields. Very few instructional technologists or instructional designers are well versed, much less expert, in areas of metaphysics. Still, the tide runs, and if we are not to be sucked under by it, we must inform ourselves.

Three philosophically driven movements deserve brief discussion: constructivism, anchored instruction and situated cognition, and postmodernism. All three movements embrace cognitivism in preference to behaviorism, and the three have so much in common that sorting them out risks distorting their essence.

Constructivism. Can constructivism and classical instructional design coexist in peace? Maybe, but some of the rhetoric verges upon the inflammatory. Even Brent Wilson (1993), the most articulate and yet most moderate advocate of constructivism, has fired this salvo: "The problem can be simply stated: ID, in its present form, is out of sync with the times" (p. 1132). Why does he think ID is out of sync? He says that its orientation, methods, and research base are behavioristic.

Wrong, Brent! Behaviorism is a strand of psychology. While ID draws upon psychological theory, it does so eclectically, and in conjunction with a covey of other theories that *collectively* determine its orientation. ID in its present form is procedural, not psychological, and although influenced by Skinner and Mager, the methods of ID procedure have been influenced even more by Gagné and increasingly by Piaget. In reality, the last vestige of behaviorism reflected in classical ID is the writing of performance objectives. In deference to the advocates of cognitivism, the field even stopped calling them *behavioral* objectives.

This is where a line in the sand must be drawn. Objectives have been under fire for years, but have outlasted all detractors (Braden, 1989). Without learning objectives, ID would be a farce. Wilson is concerned that ID is stereotyped by faculty in the field of education as "no-nonsense, results-driven behaviorism." True, there is no nonsense about objectives. They are specific and unequivocal. They specify desired results, and their application makes ID results-driven. The burning question is, why should instructional designers be embarrassed by that? It is time that we stop apologizing for what we do. It is time that we start bragging about the fact that we are able to follow an independent course. We should ignore the internecine wars of the field of psychology and proudly pick and choose from all of the available theories and research results.

But constructivism is about more than a shift in psychological theory from behaviorism to cognitivism. A debate rages over the nature of learning and instruction. Constructivists believe that individuals "construct" their own meaning. Thus, learners construct their own learning. "In this view, learning is a constructive process in which the learner is building an internal representation of knowledge, a personal interpretation of experience" (Bednar, Cunningham, Duffy, & Perry, 1992, p. 21). To hardline constructivists, that leaves no room for the idea that instruction [can be][should be] designed to teach knowledge. In the constructivist view, learning is entirely internal. In the more traditional view, learning is fostered by someone or something external (teaching or instruction).

Constructivists talk of learning in which the learner arrives at *shared negotiated meanings*—maybe with a teacher, maybe with other learners. Logically, if determining the meaning of things is delayed until the moment of learning, designers cannot determine in advance the nature of the content. Neither can they design anything specific that would fit an old fashioned definition of instruction. Do constructivism's basic tenets spell doom for instruction as we have known it? If so, widespread acceptance of radical constructivism would mean the demise of instructional design and development. Neanderthal instructional designers like this author would find that hard to accept.

Anchored Instruction and Situated Cognition. Anchored instruction is mostly a strategy. The modifier "mostly" is used because anchored instruction has enough philosophical and psychological baggage to keep it from being anything simple. Anchored instruction is a near relative to constructivistic instruction. The Cognition and Technology Group at Vanderbilt University (CTGV) were the earliest advocates of anchored instruction. Their approach

". . . represents an attempt to help students become actively engaged in learning by situating or anchoring instruction in interesting and realistic problem-solving environments" (CTGV, 1992, p. 135).

The term "anchored" implies something fixed or stable. That connotation is misleading, however, if we consider only the dynamics of anchored instruction as developed by CTGV. The "anchor" is a huge data base, a cyber-environment which provides an abundance of information resources for the learner. The dynamics for the student are absolutely *not* anchored. The student browses and moves about within the module, sucking up knowledge and understanding along the way. Students may steer a course or they may drift.

The major problem with anchored instruction may be that it has been both undersold and oversold. Any massive adoption of anchored instruction will require enormous sums of money. In that regard, it has been undersold. Without the money, the current experimental examples of anchored instruction oversell and raise unreasonable expectations. Another problem is that the unstructured experiences of learners may be extremely beneficial, but the need for structured learning activities should not be overwhelmed by a fad. Systematic ID (including linear and other forms of ID) and structured instruction are not going to go away no matter how much the constructivists and their bedfellows might yearn for that result.

Situated cognition is a term that seems to mean about the same thing as anchored instruction. Therefore, situated cognition, like anchored instruction, is primarily a strategy—just one of many strategies for fostering learning. Current proponents of situated learning include Bransford *et al.* (1990), Brown, Collins, and Duguid (1989), and Streibel (1995).

Situated cognition is neither complicated nor incompatible with traditional ID. At the crux of this approach is a golden strategy. Namely: Learning should be *situated* in a rich, real-world context. A commendable tactic of situated learning is the creation of situations that foster cognitive apprenticeship. The case studies and examples given to us by advocates of situated learning are all positive and encouraging. And why not? Good instructional designers have always attempted to tie instruction to realistic situations through the use of real-world examples. Simulations are not a new instructional method, and real-world tutoring and apprenticeships have always been arrows in the designer's quiver.

As *desirable conditions,* situated cognition's ideas fit nicely into the designer's pallet of instructional strategies. If taken to an extreme and made *mandatory conditions,* then situated cognition is doomed to be a passing fad. History tells us that Fred Keller's Personalized System of Instruction (PSI) died an ignominious death in spite of documented effectiveness. In test after test, PSI outperformed and outtaught all competing instructional strategies (see the chapter on PSI in this volume). PSI offered no strategy alternatives and in that respect was uni-dimensional. A problem with situated cognition is that it projects a uni-dimensional epistemology.

Cognitive apprenticeship may continue to be best and most frequently represented in on-the-job training, an instructional circumstance seldom structured by ID. Otherwise, situated learning should be subsumed by ID, not the other way around. Computer-based tutoring and simulation will become more powerful as computer technology unfolds, but that merely means that ID tools will be stronger. Designers will have better and more robust options, and some of those options will make learning more realistic, more worldly.

Postmodernism. The most extreme postmodern notion is that all approaches are equally valid. If we apply that idea to ID, we will open the floodgates to every sort of ID butcher one might imagine. Silly ideas do not earn serious consideration. Marginal theories may deserve respect, but they do not deserve to be given the same credance as mainstream theories.

What is the attraction of postmodernism? Like constructivism it is more heady, more abstract, more philosophical, more elusive, and more mentally challenging than positivistic, scientific, and behavioristic paradigms. For intellectually gifted individuals, it provides more to play with than mechanistic, routine, objective realities. Perhaps that is its greatest weakness as well. Subjective, or ill-defined, or metaphorical, or multidimensional, or uninterpreted, or chaotic, or highly theoretical notions are not comprehensible to the least gifted individuals. While the postmodernists continue their unending search for meaning, average citizens will search for structure. Who would support a profession forclosed to all but the brightest? Who will be the first elitist to say that only persons who have abstract reasoning skills can design instruction for the masses? Which of the social engineers who find comfort in the political potential of postmodernism will challenge egalitarian ethics by creating an intellectual glass ceiling in the instructional design workplace?

Postmodernists and constructivists are closely related—at least second cousins. For example, the learning vs. teaching dichotomy of constructivism is a factor in postmodern ideology. However, the postmodernists are more likely to reject instruction because it is *culturally contaminated* than because learning is done internally by learners (Jamison, 1994). Muffoletto (1994) and Nichols (1991) are among those who have been most outspoken in their criticism of instructional technology (and thus ID) for its lack of social conscience. Elsewhere in this volume, P. K. Jamison has posed the question: "How is instructional development a social practice?" The answer from this quarter is that it isn't, nor should it be. ID, like all of instructional technology, should be apolitical and asocial. It is a conduit and a tool which, in the wrong hands or driven by the wrong ideology, might become manipulative, doctrinaire, and oppressive. You, too, be careful what you ask for, P. K., for you, too, just might get it.

Denis Hlynka (1995) has a vision of educational technology as a platform for postmodernism. Every educational technologist will need to decide whether they share that vision. Hlynka's discourse includes ideas like empowering new voices, challenging the existing canon, shifting meanings, and other things that together seem to be anti-status quo. For this chapter on linear ID, the most chilling line from Hlynka's vision is "Educational technology operates within a nonlinear mode" (p. 118).

A non-philosopher can become befuddled perusing the literature of postmodernism. That may be what happened to this non-philosopher who came to the following conclusion: Postmodernism is a reactionary philosophy—reactionary in the sense that we use the word in politics. At heart it is a go-back-one-step philosophy. It is a philosophy that seeks a set of intellectual blinders. Yes, it seeks blinders to shield our eyes from the impact of modernism, i.e., the impact of technology. It does not seem compatible with a field that has "technology" in its name.

Roll-Your-Own ID

There is an ever-growing body of criticism of ID. Some critics have proposed new approaches. Some have not. Too many have called for nonlinear, nonsystematic ID. They are calling for intuitive, artistic ID with no structure, no rules, no constraints—instructional design of an unspecified nature. The one thing that too many of the alternatives to linear instructional design have in common is sympathy toward roll-your-own ID.

A natural resistance to regimentation fuels the desire of most of us for flexibility in what we do. We prefer guidelines to laws. However, we must never lose sight of the differences between what we *want to do*, what we *ought to do*, and what we *must do*. The research of Wedman and Tessmer (1993) tells us that the profession widely rejects a "must do" view of ID procedure. The profession has not yet been as unanimous in rejecting permissiveness by persons who wish to do whatever they want to do and still call it ID. The instructional design profession must resist accepting an attitude that each designer can *just make it up as he or she goes along.*

Far too many persons who are engaged in the sole activity of producing instructional materials are referred to as instructional designers. Roblyer (1988) called attention to common shortcomings of educational computer software: "It is . . . clear that most software is being designed based on marketing priorities, rather than to meet identified needs of specific students. . . . Software is rarely identified by objective and is most often not accompanied by other components to form a complete instructional system" (p. 9). In summarizing the research of Bialo and Erickson, Roblyer found that of 163 microcomputer courseware programs, the majority had poor or missing objectives, tests, support materials, and field testing evidence. In other words, the evidence is overwhelming that most CBI is not being developed to meet ID standards. Just because a person does CBI authoring does not mean that he or she is doing instructional design. Even instructional technologists with impeccable designer credentials occasionally fall into the trap of characterizing materials production as ID. It is only one small part of ID.

Some examples: (1) Rapid prototyping (Tripp & Bichelmeyer, 1990) is merely a technique in the production phase of an ID project that calls for CBI in its strategy. (2) Interactive television (Lochte, 1993) and interactive multimedia (Schwier & Misanchuk, 1993) are merely delivery media unless the messages they carry have gone through some sort of ID process. That would not be troublesome, if, for instance, a search through Lochte's book uncovered any reference at all to systematic design of instruction. (3) Writing CBI software (Kearsley & Halley, 1987; Tessmer, Jonassen, & Caverly, 1989) is an activity that should come quite late in the ID process. Yet, we find respected authors like Kearsley and Halley publishing an entire book on how to design interactive software which fails to even mention the relationship of authoring to total ID.

The Myths About Linear Instructional Design

Myth: Linear ID is simplistic.

The ID procedure outlined at the outset of this chapter is made up of concepts which have been explained in ways intended to be easy to understand. Understandable is not necessarily simple. The procedure of instructional design only touches the surface of what is involved in linear ID. For the procedure presented in this chapter, *the several ID steps are interwoven in a* **system** *that can only be categorized as complex.* Associated theories provide enough abstractions to satisfy the intellectually curious, but critics of ID models tend to challenge the models in isolation, ignoring the fact that the uncomplicated model is the host for a mountain of knowledge, techniques, and theories.

Myth: Linear ID is an inflexible procedure.

ID has rules made to be broken and procedures made to be altered. However, the procedure is modified when—and only when—the situation provides clear evidence that project outcomes will benefit by the deviation. *A linear ID model is a guideline, and absent reasons to the contrary, its steps should be followed.* When reasons to deviate from the guidelines of the model occur, each instance must be considered on its own merits and demerits. If the costs are few and the benefits many, the designer can easily make a considered decision to depart from the model. *Whenever ID procedure and sound professional judgment are in conflict, judgment must prevail!*

Myth: Linear ID is uncreative.

In a recent article, Dick (1995) makes a strong case that design models do not stifle creativity. Thousands have learned the principles of linear ID using Dick and Carey's textbook (1990), yet he does not believe that his model locks designers into thinking about only one step at a time. He observed that his own students tend not to be very creative at first, but

". . . the more experience they have designing instruction, the more effective, the more effi-cient and the *more creative* they will become" (emphasis added). No evidence exists to sup-port the assertion that followers of linear models are uncreative. *Creativity is not impossible nor is it forbidden in linear ID.* In whatever process a designer uses, including an unwavering linear approach, **thinking** *need not be linear.*

Myth: Linear ID is for low-level objectives only.

If we know or can find out what specific things are to be learned, linear ID is an ap-propriate design approach. A problem here is that as the content becomes more abstract, our ability to specify it becomes more limited. *Any Magerian objective at whatever "level," if cor-rectly written, can be developed into instruction using a linear ID approach.* An additional problem is that there are fewer proven strategies for teaching higher-level objectives. A de-signer must know a great deal more than which step comes next in a linear model in order to create the best instructional strategies for high-level objectives. Even so, the designer can design complicated, creative, innovative instructional strategies as a linear ID activity—de-signed at the right time and with the best possible input. While failure to prescribe an ap-propriate instructional strategy constitutes a breakdown in linear ID, it is a fault common to all other methods of preparing instruction.

Myth: Linear ID is intended to be a panacea for improving performance and instruction.

Most performance problems are not learning problems. Not all learning problems are instructional problems. Not all instructional problems warrant the expenditure of human and material resources that go into linear ID. Not all intended learning is content-specific. That is, when the purpose of instruction is to insure that students learn something, but not some-thing in particular, linear ID is no more effective than any other design approach. For knowl-edge domains that are ill-structured, extremely complex, and/or that deal with highly advanced, abstract concepts, ID will do no harm, but it may do little good. Not enough re-search has been done to adequately inform us about the best instructional strategies for af-fective objectives, ill-structured content domains, and for teaching that involves persuasion.

Myth: It really does not matter whether every step in a linear ID model is performed or whether the steps are done sequentially.

That is *the* myth that this chapter is meant to dispel. There is a reason for each step. Some steps contribute directly to the instructional product. Other steps contribute primarily to assure that we are creating the right product. Still other steps serve quality control func-tions. The steps are done in order because the output of step one is a useful input for step two, and so forth. Changing the number or sequence of the design and development steps is always an option, but it is an option with at least a minor risk that the ensuing instruction will suffer.

Conclusion

Linear instructional design and development is not the answer to every performance problem. It is not even the answer to every instructional design problem. It is, however, the best, most effective, most efficient procedure for designing instruction that is meant to teach specific things at most knowledge levels. Linear IDD is more complex than the simple boxes and arrows of any design model, but that does not diminish the utility of such models. Linear

IDD may be violated more often than it is strictly observed in daily practice, but shortcuts are more likely to be the consequence of market forces than of perceived shortcomings in the IDD process.

Linear IDD is a powerful tool. Adherence to a procedure such as the one described herein will result in the creation of instructional products that achieve their intended purpose. However, the choice of design approaches must be made with each new project, and that choice represents a professional decision. Well-trained instructional design professionals will be able to weigh situational constraints against the potential benefits of systematic design. As they do so at the inception of a new instructional design effort, the linear IDD process ought to be the first procedure considered—to be adopted if appropriate and discarded only with caution.

References

Andrews, D., & Goodson, L. (1980). A comparative analysis of models of instructional design. *Journal of Instructional Development, 3*(4), 2–16.

Bednar, A K., Cunningham, D., Duffy, T. M., & Perry, J. D. (1992). Theory into practice: How do we link? In T. M. Duffy & D. H. Jonassen (Eds.), *Constructivism and the technology of instruction.* Hillsdale, NJ: Lawrence Erlbaum Associates.

Bergman, R., & Moore, T. (1990). *Managing interactive video/multimedia projects.* Englewood Cliffs, NJ: Educational Technology Publications.

Braden, R. A. (1989). Instructional design: Objectives. *Educational Technology, 29*(10), 32–33.

Bransford, J. D., Sherwood, R. S., Hasselbring, T. S., Kinser, C. K., & Williams, S. M. (1990). Anchored instruction: Why we need it and how technology can help. In D. Nix & R. Spiro (Eds.), *Advances in computers, cognition, and multimedia: Explorations in high technology.* Hillsdale, NJ: Lawrence Erlbaum Associates.

Briggs, L. (1970). *Handbook of procedures for the design of instruction.* Pittsburgh, PA: American Institutes for Research.

Brown, J. S., Collins, A., & Duguid, P. (1989). Situated cognition and the culture of learning. *Educational Researcher, 18*(1), 32–42.

Cognition & Technology Group at Vanderbilt (CTGV). (1992). An anchored instruction approach to cognitive skills acquisition and intelligent tutoring. In J. W. Regian & V. J. Shute (Eds.), *Cognitive approaches to automated instruction.* Hillsdale, NJ: Lawrence Erlbaum Associates.

Criswell, E. L. (1989). *The design of computer-based instruction.* New York: Macmillan.

Davies, I. K. (1991) Instructional development as an art: One of the three faces of ID. In D. Hlynka & J. C. Belland (Eds.), *Paradigms regained: The uses of illuminative, semiotic, and post-modern criticism as modes of inquiry in educational technology.* Englewood Cliffs, NJ: Educational Technology Publications (reprinted from *Performance and Instruction,* July, 1981).

Davis, R., Alexander, L., & Yelon, S. (1974). *Learning systems design: An approach to the improvement of instruction.* New York: McGraw-Hill.

DeCecco, J. (1968). *The psychology of learning and instruction: Educational psychology.* Englewood Cliffs, NJ: Prentice-Hall.

Diamond, R. M. (1989). *Designing & improving courses and curricula in higher education: A systematic approach.* San Francisco, CA: Jossey-Bass.

Dick, W. (1995). Instructional design and creativity. *Educational Technology, 35*(4), 5–11.

Dick, W., & Carey, L. M. (1990). *The systematic design of instruction* (3rd ed.). New York: HarperCollins.

Dick, W., & Reiser, R. (1989). *Planning effective instruction.* Englewood Cliffs, NJ: Prentice-Hall.

Duffy, T. M., & Jonassen, D. H. (Eds.). (1992). *Constructivism and the technology of instruction.* Hillsdale, NJ: Lawrence Erlbaum Associates.

Foshay, W., Silber, K., & Westgaard, O. (1986). *Instructional design competencies: The standards.* Iowa City, IA: International Board of Standards for Training, Performance, and Instruction.

Franklin, B. (1757) *Poor Richard's almanack.* Philadelphia: Author. [available in many contemporary compilations of Franklin's writings]

Gagné, R. M. (1985). *The conditions of learning* (4th ed.). New York: Holt, Rinehart, and Winston.

Gentry, C. G. (1994). *Introduction to instructional development: Process and technique.* Belmont, CA: Wadsworth Publishing Company.

Gerlach, V. S., & Ely, D. P. (1980). *Teaching and media: A systematic approach* (2nd ed.). Englewood Cliffs, NJ: Prentice-Hall.

Gropper, G. L. (1977). On gaining acceptance for instructional design in a university setting. *Educational Technology, 17*(1), 7–12.

Gustafson, K. L. (1981) *Survey of instructional development models.* Syracuse, NY: ERIC Clearinghouse on Information Resources.

Gustafson, K. L. (1991) *Survey of instructional development models* (2nd ed.). Syracuse, NY: ERIC Clearinghouse on Information Resources.

Heinich, R., Molenda, M., & Russell, J. D. (1993). *Instructional media and the new technologies of instruction* (3rd ed.). New York: Macmillan.

Hlynka, D. (1995). Six postmodernisms in search of an author. In G. J. Anglin, *Instructional technology: Past, present, and future* (2nd ed.). Englewood, CO: Libraries Unlimited.

Jamison, P. K. (1994) The struggle for critical discourse: Reflections on the possibilities of critical theory for educational technology. *Educational Technology, 34*(2), 66–69.

Jamison, P. K. (1995, February). Recognizing the importance of critical postmodern possibilities for instructional development. Paper presented at the annual convention of the Association for Educational Communication and Technology, Anaheim.

Kearsley, G., & Halley, R. (1987). *Designing interactive software.* La Jolla, CA: Park Row Press.

Keller, J. M. (1983). Motivational design of instruction. In C. M. Reigeluth (Ed.), *Instructional design theories and models: An overview of their current status.* Hillsdalle, NJ: Lawrence Erlbaum Associates.

Keller, J. M. (1987). The systematic process of motivational design. *Performance and Instruction, 26*(10), 1–8.

Kemp, J. (1985). *The instructional design process.* New York: Harper & Row.

Kemp, J. E., Morrison, G. R., & Ross, S. M. (1994). *Designing effective instruction.* New York: Merrill.

Knirk, F. G., & Gustafson, K. L. (1986). *Instructional technology: A systematic approach to education.* New York: Holt, Rinehart, and Winston.

Leshin, C. B., Pollock, J., & Reigeluth, C. M. (1992). *Instructional design strategies and tactics.* Englewood Cliffs, NJ: Educational Technology Publications.

Lochte, R. L. (1993). *Interactive television and instruction: A guide to technology, technique, facilities design, and classroom management.* Englewood Cliffs, NJ: Educational Technology Publications.

Merrill, D. M., Li, Z., & Jones, M. K. (1990a). Limitations of first generation instructional design. *Educational Technology, 30*(1), 7–14.

Merrill, D. M., Li, Z., & Jones, M. K. (1990b). The second generation instructional design research program. *Educational Technology, 30*(3), 26–31.

Merrill, D. M., Li, Z., & Jones, M. K. (1990c). ID_2 and constructivist theory. *Educational Technology, 30* (12), 52–55.

Muffoletto, R. (1994). Schools and technology in a democratic society: Equity and social justice. *Educational Technology 34*(2), 52–54.

Nichols, R. G. (1991). Toward a conscience: Negative aspects of educational technology. In D. Hlynka & J. C. Belland (Eds.), *Paradigms regained: The uses of illuminative, semiotic, and post-modern criticism as modes of inquiry in educational technology.* Englewood Cliffs, NJ: Educational Technology Publications.

Roblyer, M. D. (1988). Fundamental problems and principles of designing effective courseware. In D. H. Jonassen (Ed.), *Instructional design for microcomputer courseware.* Hillsdale, NJ: Lawrence Erlbaum Associates.

Rothwell, W. J., & Kazanas, H. C. (1992). *Mastering the instructional design process: A systematic approach.* San Francisco: Jossey-Bass.

Schwier, R. A., & Misanchuk, E. A. (1993). *Interactive multimedia instruction.* Englewood Cliffs, NJ: Educational Technology Publications.

Seels, B., & Glasgow, Z. (1990). *Exercises in instructional design.* Columbus, OH: Merrill.

Seels, B. B., & Richey, R. C. (1994). *Instructional technology: The definition and domains of the field.* Washington, DC: Association for Educational Communications and Technology.

Smith, P. L., & Ragan, T. J. (1993). *Instructional design.* New York: Merrill.

Soulier, J. S. (1988). *The design and development of computer based instruction.* Newton, MA: Allyn and Bacon.

Spector, J. M., Polson, M. C., & Muraida, D. J. (Eds.). (1993). *Automating instructional design: Concepts and issues.* Englewood Cilffs, NJ: Educational Technology Publications.

Streibel, M. J. (1995). Instructional plans and situated learning. In G. J. Anglin (Ed.), *Instructional technology: Past, present, and future* (2nd ed.). Englewood, CO: Libraries Unlimited.

Tennyson, R. D. (1990). Integrated instructional design theory: Advancements from cognitive science and instructional technology. *Educational Technology, 26*(6), 18–28.

Tennyson, R. D. (1993). A framework for automating instructional design. In J. M. Spector, M. C. Polson, & D. J. Muraida (Eds.), *Automating instructional design: Concepts and issues.* Englewood Cilffs, NJ: Educational Technology Publications.

Tessmer, M., Jonassen, D. H., & Caverly, D. C. (1989). *A nonprogrammer's guide to designing instruction for microcomputers.* Englewood, CO: Libraries Unlimited.

Tessmer, M., & Wedman, J. F. (1990). A layers-of-necessity instructional development model. *Educational Technology Research & Develoment, 38*(2), 77–85.

Twelker, P. A. et al. (1972). *The systematic development of instruction: An overview and basic guide to the literature.* ERIC Document Reproduction Service No. ED 059 629.

Tripp, S. D., & Bichelmeyer, B. (1990). Rapid prototyping: An alternative instructional design strategy. *Educational Technology Research & Development, 38*(1), 31–44.

Van Patten, J. (1989). What is instructional design? In K. Johnson & L. Foa (Eds.), *Instructional design: New alternatives for effective education and training.* New York: Macmillan.

Venesky, R., & Osin, L. (1991). *The intelligent design of computer-assisted instruction.* New York: Longman.

Wedman. J., & Tessmer, M. (1993). Instructional designers' decisions and priorities: A survey of design practice. *Performance Improvement Quarterly, 6*(2), 43–57.

Willis, J. (1995). A recursive, reflective instructional design model based on constructivist-interpretivist theory. *Educational Technology, 35*(6), 5–23.

Wilson, B. G. (1993). Constructivism and instructional design: Some personal reflections. In M. R. Simonson & K. Abu-Omar (Eds.), *15th annual proceedings of selected research and development presentations.* Ames, IA: Association for Educational Communications and Technology.

Yeaman, A. R. J. (1994) Deconstructing modern educational technology. *Educational Technology, 34*(2), 15–24.

Yeaman, A. R. J., Koetting, J. R., & Nichols, R. G. (1994) Critical theory, cultural analysis, and the ethics of educational technology as social responsibility. *Educational Technology, 34*(2), 5–13.

PART 5

The Tactical Vantage Point: Instructional Design Micro-Strategies

30

Using Models of Instruction

Timothy P. Anderson
Nebraska Wesleyan University, Lincoln

Introduction

A model of instruction is a step-by-step process designed to achieve a particular educational outcome. No single model of instruction is designed to achieve all of the outcomes of education. This means that teachers must be able to use a variety of teaching models in order to accomplish the goals of education. When used appropriately, models of instruction are very effective in achieving educational outcomes.

It can be argued that models of instruction constitute a teaching paradigm. Paradigms include a set of assumptions, a framework describing functions, and a research design related to these functions. Instructional models include assumptions related to effective instruction and learning. There is a clearly defined framework that describes teaching models. This framework includes intended outcomes, a descriptive language, and step-by-step procedures to follow in order to achieve intended outcomes. The assumptions and framework provide a prescription for selecting models and clarifying effective instruction, which leads to a particular research design.

Bruce Joyce and Marsha Weil wrote the book *Models of Teaching* (1972). This book has become the definitive source on the models of teaching approach. Most of what is presented in this essay derives from Joyce and Weil's research on models of teaching.

The models approach to instruction will be examined in the following manner. First, key terms, such as models, strategies, and families will be defined. Next, a number of models of teaching in each family will be identified and described. Then a number of suggestions will be presented regarding the selection of models. After making suggestions on the selection of models, a process will be presented to assist teachers in acquiring new instructional models.

Definitions

Model of Instruction

A model of instruction is defined as a step by step process designed to achieve a particular outcome. There are many models of instruction. Each model has a rationale. The rationale includes the learning theory that the theory is derived from; the educational goals

521

that the model is designed to achieve; and some evidence to support the effectiveness of the model. Instructional models focus on process and product. They are sequential in their steps. It may take anywhere from a few minutes to weeks to complete the implementation of a particular model of teaching.

Joyce and Weil (1986) used a number of concepts to describe instructional models. These concepts included syntax, social system, principles of reaction, support system, and effects.

"Syntax" refers to the sequence of steps, also called phases, that are followed in implementing the model.

"Social system" refers to the classroom environment. Each model requires definite teacher-student roles and relationships. Some models require considerable teacher control and structure, while other models use little teacher control and require students to develop considerable independence.

"Principles of reaction" is defined as how teachers respond to students' responses. Each model demands a particular focus towards students and a particular response to student actions. Sometimes a teacher must be very supportive of students' responses. Other times the teacher may be very neutral toward their responses.

"Support system" refers to the particular conditions needed to successfully implement the model. For example, some models require a particular type of classroom or classroom configuration in order to function. Each model requires specific curriculum materials in order to be successful.

All models have "effects" on students. There are direct and indirect student effects. All models have intended goals or direct effects on students such as learning a specific skill. Models also have secondary or indirect effects. Some of these indirect effects are desirable, some are not.

Teaching Strategies

Teachers use models to design teaching strategies. Teaching strategies are designed to accomplish different sets of educational goals. When a teacher selects a series of teaching models based on desired outcomes and then sequences the models in a particular order so as to accomplish a series of goals, the teacher is designing a teaching strategy. Appropriately planned and delivered teaching strategies assist the teacher in attaining desired outcomes.

Families of Instruction

Joyce and Weil (1980) reviewed a large number of teaching models. They identified four groups of models, called families. The four families were the information processing family, the social family, the personal family, and the behavioral family. Teaching models were grouped into families based on desired outcomes as well as on how students learn (Joyce & Weil, 1980). These four families, together with the models from each family that are described in this chapter, are listed in Figure 1, along with the purposes of each of the models. The four-family concept has remained stable over time. However, some of the models within the families have been moved from one family to another.

Information Processing Family. The information processing family focuses on the usual academic concerns. For example, one general outcome of education in this area is to have students acquire new information. Information processing models not only assist in teaching students new information, they also teach students general thinking skills and discipline specific skills. According to Joyce and Weil (1980), information processing models de-

Family	Model	Primary Purpose of Model
Information Processing	Advance Organizer	Learn Content/Concepts Develop Habitual Thinking Skills
	Concept Attainment	Learn Content/Concepts Develop Conceptual Thinking Skills
	Concept Development	Learn Content/Concepts Develop Conceptual Thinking Skills
	Memory	Remember Large Amounts of Information
Social	Group Investigation	Develop Problem-Solving Skills Develop Group Interaction Skills
	Jurisprudential Inquiry	Develop Problem-Solving Skills Develop Interaction Skills
	Role Play	Develop Problem-Solving Skills
Personal	Non-Directive Counseling	Examine Personal Beliefs Personal Problem-Solving Skills
	Synectics	Develop Individual Creative Problem-Solving Skills
Behavioral	Direct Instruction	Develop Personal Academic and Social Skills
	Simulation	Develop Group Problem-Solving and Interaction Skills

Figure 1. Teaching models discussed in this chapter, by family.

rive from four sources. These sources include "studies on thinking, learning theorists, scholarly disciplines and developmental studies of the human intellect" (Joyce & Weil, 1986, pp. 23–24). Some of the models in this family include the concept attainment model, concept development model, memory model, and the advance organizer model (Joyce & Weil, 1980).

Social Family. The social family focuses on the social outcomes of education. One general educational outcome here is the development of solid citizenship skills. Social models are to develop citizenship through the exploration of social issues. The models are based on the belief that students best learn social values and skills through interaction with other students. These models stress the development of thinking skills, some acquisition of content, group interaction, social responsibility, and values clarification. Group investigation, role playing, jurisprudential inquiry, and cooperative learning (not treated in this chapter) models are some of the models that constitute the social family models (Joyce & Weil, 1986).

Personal Family. The personal family models include models that develop individual student abilities. These models stress the development of a positive self concept. They help students develop better emotional health. They also focus on improving individual thinking skills and developing feelings of empathy for others. These models provide opportunities for student input which, in turn, assists students in acquiring the skills needed to self-manage their learning. Many of these models are based on humanistic learning theories and help students in their own efforts to attain their maximum potentials. Models in this family include the nondirective counseling model and synectics (Joyce & Weil, 1986).

Behavioral Family. The behavioral family models also focus on maximizing student potential. However, these models are based on behavioral learning theories. These models focus on skill development, self management (such as relaxation and visualization techniques) and the changing of behavior. Two of the models in the behavioral family are the direct instruction model and simulations (Joyce & Weil, 1986).

Information Processing Family Models

As previously stated, information processing models are used to assist students in acquiring new information and developing thinking skills. Four models, the concept attainment, concept development, memory, and advance organizer models, will now be described in order to demonstrate the acquisition of new information and the development of thinking skills.

Concept Attainment Model

The concept attainment model is used to help students learn new concepts. This model also assists students in analyzing their conceptual thinking, which, in turn, assists students to improve their conceptual thinking (Joyce, 1985). This model assists conceptual development through the use of critical attributes. Critical attributes are defined as the essential characteristics that constitute a concept. This model assists students in identifying the critical attributes of a concept through the use of examples and non-examples of that concept.

Gunter, Estes, & Schwab (1990) describe the concept attainment model as an eight-step process. They state that the first step is to select and define a concept that has definite critical attributes. Clearly identifiable characteristics are necessary in order to effectively use the model. After selecting a concept, they recommend that the teacher write an appropriate definition for the lesson. However, they remind the teacher that:

> the major purpose of the lesson is to allow students the chance to author their own definition: for many reasons, student-generated definitions are often superior to the initial definition created by the teacher. In any event, the outstanding function of the concept attainment model is to provide an alternative to telling learners what to understand, allowing them, literally, to participate in their understandings. (p. 92)

The second step is to identify the critical characteristics of the concept. There are two types of attributes or characteristics. The first type is the essential or critical attribute or characteristic. Essential attributes are the defining attributes of the concept. The second type is the nonessential attribute. These attributes are associated with the concept but are not considered essential to the definition of the concept. For example, a critical attribute of a table would be table legs. Table legs are essential in defining the concept of a table. All tables have some sort of color associated with them, but color is not essential to the understanding of the concept of a table. Therefore, color in this concept is a nonessential attribute.

The third step is to develop a list of examples and non-examples of the concept. The examples must include all of the essential attributes. The non-examples must not include all of the essential characteristics of the concept. The number of examples and non-examples that need to be generated by the teacher depends on the sophistication of the concept. Sophisticated concepts contain more critical characteristics than less sophisticated concepts. Therefore sophisticated concepts need more examples and non-examples than do basic concepts. It is important to note here that exposure to multiple examples and non-examples of a concept increases the understanding and retention of the concept (McKinney, 1985). These three steps are completed before attempting to teach the concept to students.

Step four begins the actual teaching process. In this step the teacher tells the students that they will be learning a new concept. They are told the type of concept to be presented in order to focus their thinking. The students are told the teacher will present a series of examples and non-examples of the concept. They will have to analyze the examples and non-examples, identify the critical characteristics, and define the concept. The teacher then reminds the students of the type of concept to be learned and proceeds to the next step in the model.

This step, step five, consists of presenting the students with examples and non-examples of the concept. The teacher presents one example and one non-example of the concept at a time. They are usually listed on the board. The teacher asks the students to analyze the examples and non-examples in order to determine the critical characteristics. The teacher continues to present one example and one non-example at a time, as a pair, until students correctly identify all of the essential attributes.

The next step, step six, in the concept attainment model is to have students name and define the concept. Using the lists of examples and non-examples, students identify the critical characteristics of the concept and use those attributes to define the concept. They then label (name) the concept. A perfect definition is not necessary at this time. What is important is having students experience the process of naming and defining the concept.

The next step, step seven, is to test the attainment of the concept by presenting a series of unlabeled examples and non-examples of the concept. Students demonstrate understanding of the concept by correctly labeling the examples and non-examples. Students are also asked to generate their own examples and non-examples of the concept and to explain their decisions.

The last step, step eight, focuses on discussing the activity. This is a very important step. Here, students explore their thinking processes. They are asked to describe their thought processes while identifying the essential characteristics and formulating their definition. Hypothesis formation and hypothesis testing can be reviewed in this section as well as overall deductive and inductive thinking processes. The discussion ends with exploring opportunities for applying these processes in new situations (Gunter, Estes, & Schwab, 1990).

After students become familiar with what is expected of them within this model, the teacher may want to alter step five, presentation of examples and non-examples, in order to vary this activity. Instead of presenting one labeled example and one labeled non-example at a time, the teacher can list all of the examples and non-examples mixed together on the board at one time. These examples and non-examples would not be labeled. The students then look at all of the data and select individual components. They then ask the teacher if a particular piece of evidence is an example or a non-example. The teacher labels the data as the students request. In this way students have more control over the data. Students continue through the rest of the model in the same manner as previously described (Weil & Joyce, 1978a).

Concept Development Model

Another model that can be used to help students to form new concepts and learn concept formation skills is Hilda Taba's concept development model (Gunter, Estes, & Schwab, 1990). This model uses students' previously learned information to develop a concept. Since the data used to develop a concept comes from the students, the teacher has less control over the process than when using the concept attainment model already described.

Taba's concept development model is a five-step process. These steps are listing, grouping, labeling, regrouping, and relabeling (Gunter, Estes, & Schwab, 1990).

In step one, students list characteristics or examples of a concept identified by the teacher. The teacher is not required to have a definition of the concept in this model, as is the case in the concept attainment model. For example, if an instructor in a university-level education course wants to explore a concept, such as effective teaching, the instructor will probably have a list of essential characteristics and a definition in mind. The instructor in this situation can start the activity by asking students to think of past teachers and list examples of effective teaching that they have experienced.

A teacher can also use this model if he or she does not have a list or definition in mind. For example, a teacher in a new school may want to explore student's views of effective teaching practices in that school. In this situation, the teacher can ask students to think of effective teachers in the school and list positive examples of their performance. The teacher then accepts the students' list and definition for the concept. In either situation, the teacher can either ask students to write their ideas on paper first and then present them to the class or just brainstorm and verbally present examples to the teacher. However, if the teacher asks students to think about the concept first and write their answers before presenting them to the teacher, it usually improves the quality of the examples and generates wider student participation in the model. In either case, the teacher accepts all student responses and writes all responses on the board.

After a large number of student-generated examples have been presented, the teacher begins step two. Here the teacher leads the students in grouping similar types of examples. The teacher does this by asking the students to review the list. The teacher then points to the first example written on the board and asks students to identify other statements that may be similar to the first example. The teacher continues this process until each example is put into at least one group. As always, the teacher accepts all student responses and asks students to explain their decisions.

In step three, the teacher directs the students to review each group and formulate a label for it. The students then write a definition for each label using the essential characteristics of each group.

In step four, students review each group and definition. The teacher asks the students if they want to add any examples to a group, transfer an example to another group or combine groups. Here, again, the teacher accepts all student responses and asks students to justify their actions. The teacher serves as a mediator in helping students to come to agreement over differences.

Finally, after regrouping, the teacher asks students if they want to re-label or redefine any of the groups. After relabeling, the teacher reviews the thinking processes used to group and label and asks students to summarize the information and skills learned from this process (Gunter, Estes, & Schwab, 1990). At this time, the teacher may want to compare the student-generated list and definition of the concept to the teacher's list and definition. However, the teacher needs to be careful in this situation. If the student definition is compared to another definition, students may get the idea that their concept formation is not correct. This defeats the purpose of the model. If at all possible, use the student definition of the concept for the rest of the course. If the teacher sees a possible discrepancy among definitions, s/he can make suggestions in steps four and five to direct the students toward other possibilities. The teacher could also address discrepancies after the process has been completed, if it appears desirable to do so.

This model can stand alone but it is also part of Taba's more sophisticated inductive thinking teaching strategy. In this strategy, interpretation skill development and content application skill development opportunities are added to the concept formation thinking skills development steps (Joyce & Weil, 1986).

Memory Model

A third information processing model is the memory model. This model stresses data acquisition and thinking skill development. It focuses on assisting students to remember large amounts of new information and developing memorization skills through the use of mnemonics. The memory model is a four-step model (Joyce & Weil, 1986).

The first step consists of getting students to interact with the new information. This can be accomplished in a number of ways. For example, the teacher can assign the students to read the material. The teacher then has the students identify the important information. This can be accomplished by having students underline the key material. The teacher can also conduct a review session and ask students to identify and explain the material verbally. The teacher then writes the information on the board. Another way that the teacher can get students to interact with the material is to have students complete worksheets over the material. There are many ways to get students to interact with the new material; interaction with the material is the key in this stage.

The second step helps students tie the new information to be learned to information that they already know through the use of mnemonics. Students can use any one or any combination of a number of mnenomics in order to develop pictures or images of the new material. There are four types of mnemonics. They are the link method, the peg method, the method of loci, and the keyword method. The first three methods, link, peg and loci, are especially suited for remembering lists of information. The fourth method, the keyword method, is very helpful in assisting students to learn and remember new vocabulary (Glover & Bruning, 1990). Obviously, if the students are not familiar with mnemonics, the teacher needs to familiarize them with these devices and their uses.

The third step of the memory model is to have students review the images or pictures that they developed using mnemonics in the previous step and exaggerate these pictures. The more ridiculous that the pictures become, the better the opportunity for students to remember the material.

The last step in the model is to have students practice recalling the information until they have committed the new material to memory. Practice is one key to being able to recall information at the appropriate time. Teaching students to check their recall assists in the development of metacognition skills. This model, then, concentrates on assisting students to acquire new information through the use of mnenomics and developing thinking skills (Joyce & Weil, 1986).

Advance Organizer Model

The last information processing model to be presented here is the advance organizer model. This model provides a process for presenting large amounts of information to students in a meaningful manner. The advance organizer model is a three-step process (Joyce & Weil, 1980).

The first step of the process is the presentation of the advance organizer. This includes presenting and clarifying the purpose of the lesson. It also includes the presentation of the organizer itself. The organizer is a more abstract concept than the specific material that is to be learned that day. The organizer consists of definitions, connections between the different concepts to be explored, and how the concepts will be explored. Students need to understand where the material to be learned fits in with other relevant discipline-specific knowledge, as well as what needs to be learned about the concept to be studied by the class. An example of an organizer is the concept, plant. The teacher defines the concept and maps the different types of plants such as coniferous trees. The teacher describes what needs to be learned, how students will learn the material and how the material relates to other material. The organizer is usually presented in a reading or lecture format.

The second step concentrates on presenting the actual material to be learned by the students. In this step, students participate in a well-planned learning task. Using the example presented in step one, the task would concentrate on teaching about coniferous trees.

The last step reviews the learning task and organizer in order to tie the new material to existing student knowledge bases. In this step, the teacher asks the students a series of questions that allow students to review the task and explain what they learned in the activity. Students are also asked to connect the learning task to the organizer and apply what they just learned to what they already know (Joyce & Weil, 1980).

There are many other information processing models of instruction. They all, to varying degrees, stress data acquisition, thinking skills development, intelligence growth or some combination of these. When used appropriately, information processing models of teaching are effective in achieving these purposes (Joyce, Weil, & Showers, 1992).

Social Family Models

Group investigation, role playing, and jurisprudential inquiry are three models of instruction included in the social family models of teaching. The social family models stress learning in groups in order to acquire new information, develop thinking skills, develop social skills, clarify values, and explore social issues (Joyce & Weil, 1986).

Group Investigation Model

The group investigation models help students to gain new information about a topic, develop problem-solving skills, and develop group interaction skills. The group investigation model is a six-step model (Joyce & Weil, 1986).

In the first step, students are presented with a problem. This problem may be selected by the teacher or it may be initiated by students during a lesson. Through discussion, the teacher helps the students to identify or define the problem and any other relevant issue related to it.

In the second step, students examine their attitudes about the problem situation. This step is just a continuation of the discussion started in step one. Students identify their beliefs, which many times are in conflict with other students' beliefs, state their interests in the problem, and form possible hypotheses to explore later on.

In step three, students organize study plans. These can be very extensive. They include a definition of the problem, identification of the various areas to be studied and role assignments. The plan provides students with opportunities to work in research groups, and the role assignments develop student accountability.

In the fourth step, students implement the study plans. Here, students complete their roles by carrying out their assigned duties. Many times this takes them out of the classroom and into the school library or the community in order to get the necessary information required to solve the problem. The teacher continues to serve as a facilitator in this step, just as in step three. The teacher assists students in locating information and monitors group dynamics.

Students present their reports in step five. They evaluate their solution to the problem and the process used to solve it. They review and evaluate through a teacher-led discussion. This discussion is important for helping students to focus on group interaction skills and thinking processes. Students may decide that they did not solve the problem, they may not have liked the plan they developed, or they may decide to research another issue. If so, students would complete step six.

In step six, the process of defining, discussing, planning, researching and evaluating is repeated by the students. The teacher continues to serve as a facilitator for the process, which continues until the teacher and students are satisfied with their solutions (Joyce & Weil, 1986).

Role Play Model

Another social family model that teaches problem-solving skills and allows students to explore social issues and individual feelings is the role play model of instruction. This model can be described as a six-step process (Grambs & Carr, 1991) or as a nine-step process (Joyce & Weil, 1986). The six-step model will be summarized here.

Step one identifies a problem situation. The problem situation usually focuses on a historical or current social or personal issue. It can be generated by the teacher or initiated by students. If students have little experience participating in role playing activities, the teacher should probably select the issue, define the problem and develop the roles. If students are familiar with role playing, the teacher may want to act as a facilitator and let students select the issue. In this situation, students would define the problem, analyze the issue and determine the roles. In either situation, students would generate possible hypotheses to be tested in the role play in order to seek a solution to the problem.

The second step is to choose students to act out the roles identified in the previous step. Students can volunteer for roles or the teacher can appoint students to fulfill roles. The teacher should not allow one student to volunteer another student for a role. This can potentially embarrass a student and limit the effectiveness of the role play activity.

The next step, three, is to determine the line of action. After the role participants are selected, they analyze their roles and determine the line of action that will occur in the role play. They may decide to form their own hypothesis and line of action or select one presented in step one. In either case, the line of action is designed to provide a basis for resolving the problem situation. The role players must be given a few minutes alone, either in a corner of the room or outside the classroom where they can determine the line of action.

Step four occurs while the role participants are completing step three. In this step, the teacher assigns the rest of the students to observe the individual role players, some part of the line of action or the overall line of action. All students who are not participating as a role player should be assigned to observe some part or all of the role play. For example, the teacher may assign some students to observe a particular role player. The students assigned this task would be required to describe the role player's actions and would be asked to decide whether or not they believed that the role player acted as a real person would act if this was a real situation. Students assigned to observe the line of action would be asked to describe the line, determine if the line of action resolved the dilemma and if it accurately reflected a real-life situation. Assigning audience observation tasks increases student involvement in the role play and improves the quality of the final discussion in step six.

In step five, students act out the line of action. The teacher needs to focus the students on solving the problem quickly. The enactment is usually limited to three to five minutes in length. Remember, the primary goal of role playing is to test hypotheses and solve problems. Therefore, the enactment should quickly get to the point so that a number of hypotheses can be tested in one class period. This also helps the teacher to maintain an appropriate learning climate for the students. The teacher should only intervene if students get off task or if it is time to end the role play.

After the enactment is finished, the teacher leads a followup discussion. This review and analysis of the line of action is step six in the role play model. All students need to participate in the discussion critiquing the role play. This is the most important step in the process in terms of student learning. Some questions that the teacher may ask in attempting to analyze the role play include questions relating the role play to the real world. Did the students think that the role play simulated a real world situation? How could the role play be changed to better reflect the real world? What might happen if a role was changed or some of the facts, issues or actors were changed? Did the line of action solve the problem? Since the audience was previously assigned similar types of questions in step four, the discussion should flow smoothly.

The role play lesson may end here or the class may decide to change the original line of action and reenact it. If this is the case, steps one through six are repeated. Roles are discussed and assigned, the line of action is determined, observers are assigned tasks, the reenactment occurs and a followup discussion is conducted. This process continues until the teacher and students decide that the issue has been explored to everyone's satisfaction (Grambs & Carr, 1991).

Jurisprudential Inquiry Model

The jurisprudential inquiry model also provides a framework for students to explore social issues, identify conflicting values and develop thinking skills. This model is a six-step model (Joyce & Weil, 1980).

In step one, students are presented with a problem situation. The problem is one that is associated with one or more public social issues, and may be either historical in nature or a current problem. This problem may be presented in a variety of ways. It is usually presented in a case-study format either through a reading, a film or a lecture. The presentation can be made by the teacher or the students. After the problem is presented, the facts of the situation are identified and the actions of the people associated with the case are determined by the students.

In step two, students seek to identify the issues involved in the case. The teacher assists the students to identify the issues associated with the case as well as the values associated with the issues. Conflicting values are identified and one policy issue is selected for further discussion.

In step three the teacher continues the discussion initiated in step two. The discussion now focuses on helping students to identify their stance on the issue. Students state their position and identify possible consequences associated with their stance.

After students state their position on the issue, the teacher initiates step four of the model. In this step, the teacher becomes somewhat confrontational in regard to student opinions. Using the Socratic method, the teacher presents a series of questions that attack the assumptions, facts, values and conclusions of student positions. These questions usually identify conflicts in student positions and force students to develop new, more defensible positions on the issue.

If students do not change their positions in step four, they get another opportunity to change their positions in step five. In this stage, students review a number of other similar situations in order to help them test their solutions by applying them to other situations. After testing their solutions in other situations, the teacher then provides students with time to change their positions by asking them to think about their positions again and write them out. This helps students prepare for step six.

In step six, the teacher rigorously questions the students again in terms of their positions. The teacher again attacks the assumptions, facts, logic and values used to determine student conclusions. The teacher ends the process after helping students to determine if their positions will prevail under extreme conditions (Joyce & Weil, 1980).

It should also be noted that the current cooperative learning models of instruction belong to the social models family. The cooperative learning models focus on developing thinking skills, communication skills, group participation skills and social responsibility through cooperative group activities. These activities include jigsaw STAD, student teams academic division, and teams-games-tournament (Slavin, 1990). All of these models appear to be effective in achieving desired outcomes (Joyce, Weil, & Showers, 1992).

Personal Family Models

The personal family constitutes the third family of models of instruction derived by Joyce & Weil (1980). This family also focuses on a number of general educational outcomes. These outcomes include helping students to develop positive self concepts, improving the quality of student thinking, and developing empathy for others. These models are based on humanistic theories of learning, and stress self actualization. The nondirective teaching model and synectics model are two models associated with the personal models of instruction family (Joyce & Weil, 1986).

Nondirective Teaching Model

The nondirective model is a counseling model that teaches individual students how to manage and solve individual problems. This model is a five-step model (Joyce & Weil, 1986).

In step one, the teacher helps the student to focus on a particular problem. It can be an academic problem, a behavioral problem, a personal problem or a social problem. In this step, the teacher explains the ground rules for the expression of student feelings and the overall structure of the counseling process will be agreed upon by the student and teacher. The teacher serves as a facilitator and needs to be very accepting of student feelings. The student needs to identify feelings associated with the problem.

In step two, the teacher helps the student to define the problem and also attempts to help the student clarify feelings related to the problem. Again, the teacher serves as a facilitator. It is the student's exploration of self that is important.

The student continues to explore the problem in step three. Here the student talks about the problem in more detail and develops insights related to the problem. The teacher continues to be accepting and supportive of student feelings. S/he helps the student to refine the definition, clarify emotions and develop insights into the situation.

In step four the student develops a plan designed to solve the problem. The teacher supports the student by helping the student to clarify the actions to be completed and by providing a supportive atmosphere for implementation.

In step five, the student implements the plan. After a designated time, the student reports on progress made using the plan. Based on this information, the plan may then be modified or continued as is until it is completed. Designing and implementing these personalized plans not only develops problem-solving skills, but also helps students to exert control over their learning (Joyce & Weil, 1986).

Synectics

The synectics model is considered as both an information processing model (Joyce, Weil, & Showers, 1992) and a personal family model of instruction (Joyce & Weil, 1986). It is included in the information processing family since it develops a cognitive thinking skill. It is considered a personal family model since it develops creativity, which helps students to develop individual abilities; when used appropriately, it can also develop empathy (Joyce & Weil, 1986).

Gordon's synectics model is based on the use of metaphors. The model develops creativity skills by viewing familiar objects in a new and different way. The model can also be used to view unfamiliar topics and, through the use of analogies, transform the unfamiliar topics into more understandable ones. Viewing familiar objects in a new and different way is a six-step process (Gunter, Estes, & Schwab, 1990). The model for viewing unfamiliar topics is a seven-step process. The six-step process will be described first.

In step one, the teacher introduces a familiar topic or problem. The teacher and students define the problem, identify relevant data and write all important information on the board or overhead projector. The teacher accepts and writes down all student comments. This information is used in step two to form analogies.

In step two, the teacher suggests an analogy based on the information presented in the previous step. By presenting an analogy, this models the type of thinking students need to use in this model. The teacher explains the analogy and directs students to review the list from step one and then develop additional analogies. If students are familiar with the model, the teacher may eliminate the teacher-generated analogy and start step two by asking for student-generated analogies. Students are required to explain their analogies and the teacher accepts and records all student responses. After the students identify a number of direct analogies, the students select one analogy to explore further in step three.

In step three, students use the direct analogy to formulate a number of personal analogies. For example, social studies students may be reviewing the office of the president of the United States (step one). Their direct analogy (step two) may be that the office of the president is like an automobile. In step three, students develop personal analogies by answering the question "how does it feel to be an automobile?" Here students assign personal qualities to the direct analogy. All responses are explained by the students and recorded by the teacher.

In step four, students are asked to review the lists generated in the previous steps and identify words with opposite meanings. The opposite words form compressed conflicts. An example of a compressed conflict may be *hard working* and *lazy*. After developing a number of compressed conflicts, students select one conflict and explore it further in step five.

In step five, students develop new direct analogies based on the previously selected compressed conflict. As in previous steps, the students identify and explain their analogies and the teacher accepts and records all responses. After developing a number of new direct analogies, the students select the best analogy and proceed to step six of the model.

In step six, students reexamine the original problem. The original problem is compared to the new analogy, providing students with opportunities to develop new insights about a familiar topic. They also may compare the original problem with any aspect of the previous lists in order to identify additional insights (Gunter, Estes, & Schwab, 1990).

The synectics process that is used to make unfamiliar topics become familiar topics is a seven-step model (Joyce & Weil, 1986). In step one of this model, the teacher presents new information to the students on an unfamiliar topic. In step two, the teacher provides a direct analogy linking the new information to more familiar information. The students explore the analogy and in step three, students assign personal characteristics to the direct analogy by developing personal analogies. In step four, students compare the analogy to the new information and identify similarities between the analogy and new material. In step five, students explore the differences between the analogy and new material. In step six, students identify insights developed while participating in the process and in step seven, students suggest their own direct analogies. Students explain their analogies and link the analogies to the new information presented in step one (Joyce & Weil, 1986).

Non-directive teaching and synectics, then, are just two of the models included in the personal models of instruction family. Other models, such as the classroom meeting model and the awareness training model, are also effective in promoting self-actualization, empathy and helping students to develop control over the learning process (Joyce & Weil, 1986).

Behavioral Family Models

The last family to review is the behavioral family of models. As previously stated, these models are based on behaviorist learning theories and stress behavior management and skill development. Two models that are included in this family are the direct instruction model (see also the chapter in this book on Direct Instruction) and the simulation model (Joyce & Weil, 1986).

Direct Instruction Model

The direct instruction model is a six-step process (Gunter, Estes, & Schwab, 1990). The first step consists of checking previously learned material. This review helps the teacher to determine student understanding and helps students connect the past to the present.

In step two, the teacher presents the new behavioral objective. The new behavioral objective is explained, as well as the process that will be used to achieve the objective. The teacher explains how the new objective connects with previously learned material reviewed in step one. The teacher also explains how the new objective connects to future learning.

In step three, the teacher models the behavior or skill to be performed by the students. This is accomplished by presenting the information needed to complete the task, as well as by identifying, describing, and demonstrating the steps to be performed by the students. The teacher then checks for student understanding of the information and of the steps to be performed in order to accomplish the behavioral objective.

In step four, students are provided with opportunities to practice the various steps under controlled conditions. The teacher provides students with corrective feedback after they complete the steps of the task.

After the teacher determines that the students can perform the task adequately, they are assigned homework. This constitutes step five, independent practice. In this step, students complete homework assignments without assistance. The teacher provides delayed corrective feedback by reviewing the completed homework assignments. The corrected homework is always reviewed by the students. This process is continued until the students have met the objective.

After students have mastered the task, it is important to occasionally review the skill with the students. This is step six in the direct teaching model. Occasional review of student task performance with feedback from the teacher is necessary in order to retain mastery of the task (Gunter, Estes, & Schwab, 1990).

Simulation Model

The simulation model is included in the behavioral models family, since it can help students to develop physical skills (Joyce, Weil, & Showers, 1992). It can also be included in the social models family when it emphasizes group interaction and thinking skills (Joyce & Weil, 1986). This model can also be used to develop empathy, examine values and experience competition. There are four steps in this model (Joyce & Weil, 1986).

The first step is to explain the nature of simulations. Here the general goals of simulations are explained and the specific concepts to be studied are identified by the teacher.

In step two, students are introduced to the actual simulation. The teacher identifies the specific outcomes to be achieved and explains the rules of the game. The teacher also assigns the student roles and explains the line of action. The teacher can also include a short practice session in this step. The practice session provides the teacher with opportunities to check understanding and clarify any misunderstandings.

In step three, students complete the actual steps in the simulation. In this step, the teacher serves as a facilitator and referee for the game. This step may last anywhere from one class period to as many as ten or more class periods.

The final step in the simulation model is the debriefing session. In this step, the teacher leads a discussion designed to help students to evaluate the simulation. Students are asked to review the events of the game. They are asked to identify new information learned and thinking skills used during the game. They also explore the emotions that surfaced during the game. Students are then asked to list the positive and negative aspects of the game and to compare the simulation to the real world. The questions asked in this step are similar to the types of questions asked during role play follow-up discussions (Joyce & Weil, 1986).

While simulations and role play enactments share some similarities, they also differ in a number of respects. Simulations usually have more structure. The roles in simulations usually are more clearly defined and there are definite lines of action. Simulation lines of action take much longer to complete than role play enactments. Finally, simulations usually create some sort of final products that can be evaluated by the teacher and students. For example, if students were negotiating a labor contract in a business or economics course, there probably would be some sort of written document explaining the agreement between the two sides. This document can be evaluated and graded by the teacher and students. Usually, there is no time to complete a written document in a five-minute role play.

The behavioral systems model and mastery learning model are other examples of the behavioral models of teaching family. The behavioral models appear to be effective in achieving the outcomes that they were designed to accomplish (Joyce, Weil, & Showers, 1992).

Selecting Models

Models can be selected on the basis of the outcomes desired from the instruction. The model selected should match the intended instructional objective. As previously stated, models can be grouped into families based on outcomes and orientations toward learning. The outcomes range from acquiring new information and modifying behavior to increasing intelligence and self-actualization. In general, the information processing models focus on academic goals, the social family models stress group problem solving, the personal family models concentrate on personal development, and behavior models relate to behavior management.

Most models have primary outcomes and secondary outcomes (Joyce & Weil, 1986). Many times the outcomes overlap. In other words, a number of models can be used to achieve a particular outcome. Also, a model can be used to accomplish one outcome one time and can be used to achieve a somewhat different outcome the next time.

Matching models to desired outcomes is a very important factor in selecting models. However, it is not the only one. There are other very important factors that must be considered while selecting models of teaching to be used in a particular classroom.

Teachers need to consider the course goals and the content and the level of the course while selecting activities (Squires, 1988). Certain course goals eliminate certain models of teaching. Teaching is discipline specific. Some types of content do not match well with certain models. Also, the intended level of the course dictates the consideration of some models and eliminates others. For example, a course designed to develop a broad background of information in history would probably not use many simulations. This would take too much time away from lecture presentations. Simulations promote depth of understanding as opposed to the breadth of understanding that the introductory students may be required to achieve at that time.

The teacher also needs to consider individual student readiness levels and group readiness levels while selecting teaching activities (Squires, 1988). If students are not capable of understanding or completing the steps of a model, the model will not be effective in achieving the desired outcomes. Models need to be adapted to student capabilities and interests. Even though models have definite steps, the steps can be modified to meet the needs of students.

Physical, institutional and social contexts are additional factors to consider while selecting instructional activities (Squires, 1988). For example, certain simulations may require certain room arrangements and equipment in order to be effective. A school may not have the appropriate types of rooms or equipment available in order to complete the simulation. Some institutional staffs may be very traditional in their approach to teaching and not support teachers using a variety of teaching models. This can also be the case with certain traditional communities. Therefore, certain models are not appropriate for use in certain contexts.

Finally, individual teacher strengths and weaknesses need to be considered in model selection (Squires, 1988). If a teacher does not have the motivation or skill to effectively use a model of instruction, the model probably will not be effective.

Learning Models of Instruction

Teachers can learn to use new models of instruction through Joyce's four-step coaching process (Joyce & Showers, 1982). The first step in this process is to present teachers with a description of a new model of instruction. The presentation starts with the purpose of the model and the learning theory that supports it. This is followed by a description of the steps composing the model.

In step two, a demonstration of the model is presented to the teachers. This can be accomplished through an actual modeling of the steps by a professional competent in using the model or by a film of a professional using it in a classroom.

The third step provides for opportunities for practice and feedback. Here, teachers practice the steps of a model under relaxed conditions. Teachers can use the model in this situation without worrying about such concerns as classroom management. Teachers also receive feedback on their performance from a person trained in the use of that model.

According to Joyce (1982), after these three steps have been successfully completed, most teachers will have the skills needed to implement the new teaching model in their classrooms. However, his research indicates that without additional assistance, only a very few teachers, approximately 5%, will actually implement the teaching model.

In order to help more teachers to transfer new teaching models to the classroom, Joyce advocates a fourth step and calls it coaching. Joyce's coaching concept involves designating a time when a group of administrators and teachers meet as a team to discuss teaching and problems that teachers encounter while implementing new teaching strategies. These meetings are to occur on a regular basis for a couple of months after learning new models. During this time, the models are discussed, practiced and evaluated by the team. New applications for the models are developed for use in the classrooms (Joyce & Showers, 1982). According to Joyce (1982), if coaching is added to the process, over 90% of the teachers learn new models of instruction and use them in their classrooms. Other studies (Anderson, 1984) support this research.

References

Anderson, T. P. (1984). *The contextual variables in schools that promote or inhibit teachers' opportunities to use a variety of teaching models.* Unpublished doctoral dissertation, University of Nebraska, Lincoln, Nebraska.

Ausabel, D. P. (1960, October). The use of advance organizers in the learning and retention of meaningful verbal materials. *Journal of Educational Psychology, 51*(5), 267–272.

Gentile, J. R. (1988). *Instructional improvement: A summary and analysis of Madeline Hunter's essential elements of instruction and supervision.* Oxford, OH: National Staff Development Council.

Glover, J. A., & Bruning, R. H. (1990). *Educational psychology: Principles and applications* (3rd ed.). Glenview, IL: Scott Foresman.

Grambs, J. D., & Carr, J. C. (1991). *Modern methods in secondary education* (5th ed.). Orlando: Holt, Rinehart, and Winston.

Gunter, A. G., Estes, T. H., & Schwab, J. H. (1990). *Instruction: A models approach.* Boston: Allyn and Bacon.

Guskey, T. R. (1985). *Implementing mastery learning.* Belmont, CA: Wadsworth Publishing.

Joyce, B. R. (1981, Spring). Transfer of training: The contribution of coaching. *Journal of Education, 163*(2), 163–172.

Joyce, B. R. (1982, February). Speech presented to Sydney Public Schools (videotape).

Joyce, B. R. (1985, May). Models for teaching thinking. *Educational Leadership, 42*(8), 4–7.

Joyce, B. R., & Showers, B. (1980, February). Improving inservice training: The messages of research. *Educational Leadership, 37*(5), 379–385.

Joyce, B. R., & Showers, B. (1982, October). The coaching of teaching. *Educational Leadership, 40*(1), 4–10.

Joyce, B. R., Showers, B., & Rolheisen-Bennett, C. (1987, October). Staff development and student learning: A synthesis of research on models of teaching. *Educational Leadership, 45*(2), 11–23.

Joyce, B. R., & Weil, M. (1972). *Models of teaching.* Englewood Cliffs, NJ: Prentice-Hall.

Joyce, B. R., & Weil, M. (1980). *Models of teaching* (2nd ed.). Englewood Cliffs, NJ: Prentice-Hall.

Joyce, B. R., & Weil, M. (1986). *Models of teaching* (3rd ed.). Englewood Cliffs, NJ: Prentice-Hall.

Joyce, B. R., Weil, M., & Showers, B. (1992). *Models of teaching* (4th ed.). Boston: Allyn and Bacon.

Kagan, S. (1989–1990, December/January). The structural approach to cooperative learning. *Educational Leadership, 47*(4), 12–15.

Larson, G. (1984). *Lesson design.* Unpublished manuscript.

Mayer, R. E. (1979, Spring). Can advance organizers influence meaningful learning? *Review of Educational Research, 49*(2), 371–383.

McKibbin, M., Weil, M., & Joyce, B. R. (1977). *Teaching and learning: Demonstration of alternatives.* Washington, DC: AACTE.

McKinney, C. W. (1985, January). A comparison of the effects of a definition, examples and nonexamples on student acquisition on the concept of "transfer propaganda." *Social Education, 49*(1), 66–70.

Mosston, M., & Ashworth, S. (1985, May). Toward a unified theory of teaching. *Educational Leadership, 42*(8), 31–34.

Orlich, D. C., Harder, R. J., Callahan, R. C., Kauchak, D. P., Pendergrass, R. A., & Keogh, A. J. (1990). *Teaching strategies: A guide to better instruction* (3rd ed.). Lexington, MA: D. C. Heath.

Platten, M. (1991, March). Teaching concepts and skills of thinking simultaneously. Paper presented at the National Art Education Conference, Atlanta, GA.

Rischling, D. L. (1986). *Instructional decision making.* Unpublished manuscript.

Slavin, R. E. (1987). *Cooperative learning: Student teams.* Washington, DC: National Education Association.

Slavin, R. E. (1990). *Cooperative learning: Theory, research, and practice.* Englewood Cliffs, NJ: Prentice-Hall.

Squires, G. (1988). Teaching and training: A contingent approach. *Newland Papers No. 15,* Hull University, England.

Strong, R. W., Silver, H. F., & Hanson, R. (1985, May). Integrating teaching strategies and thinking styles with the element of effective instruction. *Educational Leadership, 42*(8), 9–15.

Taba, H. (1967). *Teacher's handbook for elementary social studies.* Palo Alto: Addison-Wesley.

Weil, M., & Joyce, B. R. (1976). *Academic models of teaching.* Omaha, NE: Center for Urban Education.

Weil, M., & Joyce, B. R. (1978a). *Information processing models of teaching. Expanding your teaching repertoire.* Englewood Cliffs, NJ: Prentice-Hall.

Weil, M., & Joyce, B. R. (1978b). *Social models of teaching: Expanding your teaching repertoire.* Englewood Cliffs, NJ: Prentice-Hall.

Weil, M., Joyce, B. R., & Kluwin, B. (1978). *Personal models of teaching: Expanding your teaching repertoire.* Englewood Cliffs, NJ: Prentice-Hall.

Zeleny, L. D. (1973). *How to use simulations* (How to Do It Series No. 26). Washington, DC: National Council for the Social Studies.

31

Precise Instructional Design: Guidelines from Precision Teaching

Ogden R. Lindsley
Behavior Research Company
and
University of Kansas, Lawrence

Overview

This chapter presents the guidelines for instructional designers that would follow from the discoveries and methods of Precision Teaching. First described are the what, where, and why of Precision Teaching. Next shown is how Precision Teaching fits Kuhn's definition of a scientific field or paradigm. Six major Precision Teaching principles are then described, followed by evidence of its superior effectiveness. Precision Teaching do's and don'ts for instructional design are listed, followed by myths that block fluent learning. Some special problems encountered in designing computer assisted instruction are mentioned. Next, two competing viewpoints are specified followed by models supporting daily charting, and teaching to fluency. Concluding weak points and concluding strong points are spelled out.

What Is Precision Teaching?

Precision Teaching is a system of tactics and strategies for the self-monitoring of learning. I have recently described Precision Teaching in more detail elsewhere (Lindsley, 1992a). The most visible sign of Precision Teaching is the Standard Celeration Chart (see Figure 1 on page 541) on which students monitor, project, and analyze their own learning easily and daily. This is called "the chart" by students. At Precision Teaching's core are daily timed practice sessions. Students develop both fluency and accuracy in frequent, short (usually one minute), daily practice sessions. These are called "timings" by students. Students practice by themselves on carefully designed practice sheets. Both questions and answers must have no more than one or two letters or syllables for rapid performance at frequencies above 60 per minute. These "practice sheets" must have more questions than could ever be answered in the allotted time. This gives the frequency scores real meaning since no one can ever finish; there is just too much on each sheet.

In addition to the charts, timings, and practice sheets, Precision Teaching strategies have developed inductively from hundreds of thousands of students, teachers, and supervisors. Here are a few slogans expressing these strategies:

"The child knows best."	Try each student's own improvement suggestions before other's.
"A dot a day makes an A."	Charted daily practice is essential and guarantees top grades.
"Different strokes for different folks."	Expect different practice sheets, error drill, explanations, rewards, and penalties for each student.
"Jaws gobbles up math."	The learning picture with steep acceleration of corrects and steep deceleration of errors looks like a wide open shark's mouth, and is the best learning picture to most rapidly climb every learning curriculum.
"Celerate, then celebrate."	Socially celebrate steep learning slopes as they happen.

Mostly a monitoring, practice, and decision-making system, Precision Teaching combines powerfully with any curriculum approach. The combination always refines the curriculum by pinpointing spots in the ladder that need more or different steps. The combination always produces much more learning than the curriculum produced alone. Our very first combination was with the Canadian Montessori curriculum in a class for exceptional children (Fink, 1968). Combinations of Precision Teaching with Direct Instruction (Engelmann & Carnine, 1982) have been used successfully at the Quinte Learning Centre (Maloney & Humphrey, 1982), the Haughton Learning Center (Freeman & Haughton, 1993a), and the Cache Valley Learning Center (Desjardins & Slocum, 1993). The latest (a triple combination) is with Direct Instruction and Tiemann-Markle instructional design (Markle, 1983; Tiemann & Markle, 1990) in the Morningside Phonics Fluency (Johnson, 1992a), and the Morningside Mathematics Fluency (Johnson 1992b; Johnson & Streck, 1992).

What Are the Origins of Precision Teaching?

Precision Teaching came from laboratory free-operant conditioning. This history has also been described recently (Lindsley, 1971a; 1990). A broader, more scholarly history covers its roots in nineteenth century physiology and medicine (Potts, Eshelman, & Cooper, 1993). Briefly put, we applied the principles that had guided our laboratory research with chronic psychotic patients from 1953 through 1964 (Lindsley, 1960) in inexpensive classroom research.

The reason for doing this was that almost all early appliers of operant methods to classroom teaching used operant reinforcers, schedules, and descriptive terms, but they did not use rate of response (Bijou & Baer, 1961). I considered rate or frequency of response to be Skinner's greatest contribution, since it had proven to be 30 to 600 times more sensitive than percent correct, percent of time observed on task, or response duration in our human laboratory research.[1] So, to me, this was overlooking Skinner's most powerful contribution. I could not get the early applied behavior analysts to change their recording methods—and still haven't been able to. Neither was I able to convince students of mine to enter education and try to install response frequency in classroom teaching. So, in desperation, I closed my Harvard Medical School laboratory and entered teacher training in Special Education at the University of Kansas Medical Center to try to get frequency used by teachers and students to monitor classroom performance.

Precision Teaching was developed in special education, where it was absolutely necessary to individualize instruction fully (Lindsley, 1971a). Later it became clear that frequency monitoring methods were even more powerful when used in regular classrooms with regular (Beck, 1981) and gifted (Duncan, 1972) classes.

Reacting to teachers' complaints that they were unable to practice Precision Teaching because of lack of support from their building principals, I moved in 1972 into the administrator training program to produce doctorates in educational administration who were well versed in Precision Teaching. I had hopes that these school administrators would not only support precision teachers, but would set up building-wide Precision Teaching programs. As it turned out, these precision principals did support a teacher or two, but were too controlled by the entrenched myths of the school district, other teachers, and parents to be able to install anything as drastic as self-charting by students. Here and there a principal tried it and was promptly removed, usually with trumped up charges like "insubordination," or "overly demanding of teachers," or "installs 18th century educational practices." No one looked at improvements in the academic performance of students.

Why Precision?

We chose the word "precision" to describe the daily performance monitoring feature taken from free-operant conditioning. This would clearly distinguish it from Behavior Modification and Applied Behavior Analysis, also taken from free-operant conditioning, that used single subject research design, operant descriptive terms, and emphasis on consequences, but used traditional percent correct and percent of time observed on task. At that time it seemed important to make the word for our methods an adjective rather than a noun, so that practitioners could see that their methods were mainly left intact and were merely improved by more precise daily monitoring feedback (Lindsley, 1972, p. 9). We envisioned Precision Counseling, Precision Social Work, Precision Administration, and Precision Law—all united by a common research and monitoring system. Precise Self-management actually got going as a field for a while (Duncan, 1969, 1971; Johnson, T. S., 1972), but its practitioners left for the more lucrative fields of law and clinical psychology, where the high pay is for contact hours and there is no motive to improve effectiveness by performance monitoring.

Why Self Counting and Charting?

One of our first classroom discoveries was that student's performance often improved when they merely counted and recorded it. Charting their own performance, so they could see their daily progress, often produced further improvement. Student self-counting and charting made maintaining daily charts of three to four academic and one or two social behaviors possible in a classroom of 30 students without need for external observers or teacher

---

[1]In one of our many laboratory examples, one puff on a cigarette produced an interruption and brief acceleration in a patient's response frequency with no effect on percent correct in a free-operant discrimination task. It took smoking at least one cigarette (30 puffs), and sometimes a whole pack of cigarettes (600 puffs) to show effects on percent correct discrimination. This meant that frequency was a 30 times to 600 times more sensitive response measure than percent correct.

assistants (Starlin, 1971). The students conducted their own timings, monitored by a friend, and charted and filed their own charts on the classroom walls.

Why the Standard Celeration Chart (SCC)?

During the first year of teacher training, I noticed that in a three-hour weekly class of 18 teacher trainees, we could not share more than three or four student charts per night. The trainees usually procrastinated, waiting to update their charts the night before the class in which they were scheduled to present. This meant they monitored their student's learning charts only once or twice a semester! Daily recording has little value if it is only analyzed once a month.

One night, when 40 minutes were taken by a trainee to present her student's chart, I noticed that the majority of the time had been spent describing the counting and charting details. And even then, others in the class had misunderstood what was happening to the student's learning. I then realized that we must have a standard chart to eliminate this endless, error producing world of highly different personal charts made by each student and teacher. Often teachers made up a different chart scale for each student in their class.

Later that night I designed our first standard chart. It was called a "Standard Behavior Chart" because it covered the full range of human behavior frequencies—from one a day, to 1,000 per minute. This chart had a multiply (logarithmic) scale up the left for frequencies, and an add (arithmetic) scale across the bottom for days of the week. It was designed to cover a school semester of daily practice on one 8.5 by 11-inch sheet.[2] We experimented with different paper and ink colors to find the light blue that produced the fewest errors with school children charting in black pencil. Charts were made commercially available and a handbook describing standard chart features and uses was published (Pennypacker, Koenig, & Lindsley, 1972). Later we discovered inductively that all human behavior frequencies grew by multiplying and decayed by dividing—as straight lines on the chart (Koenig, 1972). This meant that students could project their learning courses from two weeks of daily charted performance to see when they might reach their aim. This made baselines and reversal research designs unnecessary, since deviation from the projected course could be used to determine the effect of instructional procedure changes.

Figure 1 displays a sample Standard Celeration Chart together with its standard charting conventions taken from an article by Owen White (White, 1986). Even later, when we started recording group and organizational performances, we made charts for weekly, monthly, and yearly frequencies.[3] These charts were designed to synchronize with the daily chart so that a growth line showing doubling every growth (celeration[4]) period was at the same angle (34°) on each chart. Lower left to upper right corner represented doubling every week, every month, every six months, or every five years, depending on the chart. What this set of four charts had in common was the angle of that celeration line so that users could directly perceive learning magnitude without resorting to protractors or formulas. Organizational and national performance also grew and decayed as straight lines on these charts as did personal

---

[2]At first we tried to get one full calendar year on a sheet, but the lines were too close for easy student charting.

[3]Daily, weekly, monthly, and yearly Standard Celeration Charts are available by mail order from Behavior Research Company, P.O. Box 3351, Kansas City, KS 66103.

[4]The term "celeration" was coined for the general class of both acceleration (gradual increase in frequency) or deceleration (gradual decrease in frequency). "Celeration" was not in Webster's unabridged dictionary (Gove, 1961), but it should have been. "Celeration" follows so naturally that even first graders learn the concept and use the term correctly almost immediately.

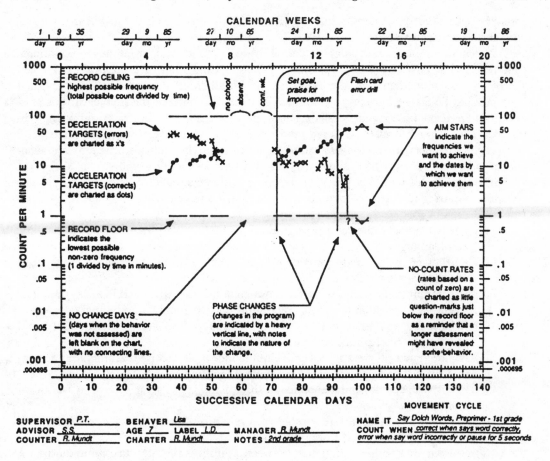

Figure 1. Standard Celeration Chart and charting conventions.

behavior on the daily charts. Organizational performance was more accurately projected on these charts by free-hand than by using least squares and geometric projection formulas from the data (Oliva, 1981).

The major advantages of the Standard Celeration Chart are that the *magnitude* of learning (celeration) can be directly seen and compared within and between student charts. Learning is easily projected by simple straight-line extrapolation. Changes in learning are not seen as simple increases or decreases; but are seen in more detail as either immediate jumps or gradual turns or combinations such as jump up and turn down.

A practical advantage of the Standard Celeration Chart is that valuable teacher, student, or researcher time is not wasted trying to figure out the coordinates of a unique learning chart. Using the Standard Celeration Chart in our in-service teacher training classes reduced case presentation time from a median of 20 minutes to a limit of two minutes per case! A teacher can survey the wall-posted personal charts of his/her 30 different students in less than 10 minutes to determine which students need help today.

Precision Teaching Fits Kuhn's Definition of a Scientific Paradigm

Thomas Kuhn defined a scientific field or paradigm by the two characteristics of: (1) attracting an enduring group of students, and (2) being sufficiently open-ended to leave all sorts of problems for practitioners to solve (Kuhn, 1970). Precision Teaching clearly satisfies both these requirements.

An enduring group of students is demonstrated by a journal, an annual international conference, and university based doctoral and master's programs. The *Journal of Precision Teaching* is now more than a decade old, edited by Claudia McDade, and currently published from Jacksonville State University, Jacksonville, Alabama. A conference is held each year. Doctorates in Precision Teaching are available from the Universities of Florida, Washington, Central Washington, and Texas at Denton, and Ohio State, Tennessee State, and Utah State Universities,[5] to mention the longest established. Strong undergraduate programs are available at Jacksonville State and Youngstown State Universities,[6] among others.

The open-ended nature of Precision Teaching is demonstrated by at least twenty major questions requiring further classroom and/or laboratory research. These include:

(1) Further proof of the multiplying nature of human performance, daily variability, and learning.

(2) Further proof that daily practice produces more learning than twice the amount of practice every other day.

(3) Further proof that daily practice in two channels (see-write and hear-say) produce steeper learning than the same amount of practice in only one channel (see-write).

(4) How many and what practice channels produce the most efficient and rapid progress up curriculum ladders?

(5) Is more rapid progress up a curriculum ladder produced by teaching accuracy before fluency or by teaching fluency before teaching accuracy?

(6) Further support for independence of three parts of behavior change or learning—jumps, turns, and bounce.

(7) Are there any other differences between reinforcers that produce jump-ups (in addition to turn-ups) and those that do not?

(8) Are there any other differences between punishers that produce jump-downs (in addition to turn-downs) and those that do not?

(9) Are there any differences between behaviors that are jumped-up by reinforcers and those that are not?

(10) At exactly what frequencies for what performances does fluency occur?

(11) How does fluency relate to laboratory "behavioral momentum" (Nevin, 1992)?

(12) How does fluency relate to generalization (stimulus equivalence) (Epstein, 1985)?

(13) How does fluency relate to generative instruction (Johnson & Layng, 1992)?

(14) Is it necessary to establish accuracy prior to building fluency?

(15) What are the best tactics for establishing endurance?

(16) What are the rules for shortening facts to permit fluent performance (>60 per min.)?

(17) What variables produce abrupt changes in daily variance (increases or decreases)?

(18) What variables produce gradual changes in daily variance (converges or diverges)?

(19) Is the learning of learning (celeration of celeration) linear on a multiply scale (equal distances are the same multiple) as is learning, or does the learning of

---

[5]At Florida, contact William Wolking or Henry Pennypacker. At Washington, contact Thomas Lovitt or Owen White. At Central Washington, contact Libby Nesselroad Street. At Texas at Denton, contact Guy Bedient or Sigrid Glenn. At Ohio State, contact John Cooper. At Tennessee State, contact Robert Spangler. At Utah State, contact Timothy Slocum, Richard West, or Richard Young.

[6]At Jacksonville State in Jacksonville, Alabama, contact John Brown or Claudia McDade. At Youngstown State in Youngstown, Ohio, contact Stephen Graf.

learning require a power scale (equal distances are same powers or number of times it multiplies by itself)?

(20) What changes in the way Precision Teaching is presented and taught will produce more acceptance by the public school, educational research, and behavior analysis establishments?

Precision Teaching has produced many more research questions, but this list of twenty clearly proves it is open-ended.

Precision Teaching's Six Major Principles

Precision Teaching's six major principles are:

(1) self-chart performance frequency daily,
(2) use Standard Celeration Charts,
(3) separately chart desired and undesired pairs,
(4) aim at fluency,
(5) monitor learning (celeration), and
(6) teach in more than one channel at once.

(1) *Self-chart performance frequency daily.* Our early research demonstrated that self-charting was preferred by learners over teacher charting, and it was more efficient since each second grader could easily maintain as many as 19 different academic charts (Starlin, 1971). Also, the only way we could guarantee that the learners could read charts and knew how steeply they were learning was when each learner kept and maintained his or her own charts. We also discovered that one-minute timings each day produced steeper learning than two one-minute timings every other day. Such data convinced us that, as with athletics and the performing arts, academic practice must be daily.

(2) *Use Standard Celeration Charts.* Precision teaching requires Standard Celeration Charts for four reasons. First, chart reading time is reduced by a factor of ten when charts are standard. With over 10 charts for each learner in a classroom of 25 students, it would be impossible to read all 250 charts in a few minutes if they were all different. There is a tremendous saving of teacher time when the students maintain and read their own charts. Students only ask for their teacher's advice when they and their charting partner are stumped and need help in suggesting a curricular improvement to increase the slope on one of their learning charts.

The second reason Standard Celeration Charts are required is that they represent learning to do and learning not to do as straight lines on the chart. Straight line projections are easy to make by eye or by ruler. Differences in the slope of these straight learning lines are easy to estimate in comparing steepness of learning within and between charts.

The third reason Standard Celeration Charts are required is that they both normalize and equalize the variance (daily bounce) period. Normalizing makes the daily up-bounce the same size as the down-bounce. Equalizing makes the total daily bounce the same distance on the chart when it is bouncing from three to nine per minute as when it is bouncing from 30 to 90 per minute. The normalized and equalized bounce makes it much easier to project the learning lines.

The fourth reason Standard Celeration Charts are required is that with normalized daily bounce, it is possible to recognize statistically significant outliers on the chart which could not have happened by chance alone. These exceptional outlier days permit inductive discovery of unique variables to improve the learning. Exceptionally good days (peaches) reveal things to do to improve the learning. Exceptionally poor days (lemons) reveal blocks and problems to avoid in improving the learning. It is interesting that this normalizing and equalizing of the variance on the Standard Celeration Chart is very similar to the normalized and additive variance required by traditional parametric statistics.

(3) *Separately chart desired and undesired pairs.* In the early days we called these "fair pairs," thinking it was only fair to accelerate a performance if we were trying to decelerate a performance (Duncan, 1969). Later, when it became clear that corrects and errors independently accelerated and decelerated, we called these academic pairs "learning pictures" (All, 1977). There were 13 different patterns of learning pictures in a single class of junior high school students.

(4) *Aim at fluency.* At the core of Precision Teaching practice is fluency building. This comes mainly from classroom practices and discoveries, led by Eric and Elizabeth Haughton (Haughton, 1974).[7] When elementary school students performed basic tool skills (e.g., add facts) at frequencies from 100 to 200 per minute, they had more retention, more endurance, and more application (generalization) than when they were taught to full accuracy but at lower frequencies, around 20 per minute (Haughton, 1981). These advantages of teaching to fluency have been found at all grade levels, including graduate school courses. Fluency has been shown to increase confidence (Binder, 1990). Fluency has also been the aim in teaching industrial sales persons new product knowledge (Binder & Bloom, 1989). Recently fluency has been related to the laboratory derived concept of "behavioral momentum" (Nevin, 1992), to generalization and stimulus equivalency (Epstein, 1985), and to generative instruction (Johnson & Layng, 1992).

(5) *Monitor learning (celeration).* Since performance frequency is a dot on the Standard Celeration Chart (SCC), and learning is a line of dots connected across days, both performance and learning can be easily seen on the SCC at once. That is the true power of the SCC. Many who use the SCC in their teaching actually do not monitor the learning or slope. They merely monitor the performance frequency by seeing how high up the chart their dots are. They ignore the slopes of the lines. Hence, they ignore the learning (celeration). It is easy to tell by looking at the charts in a classroom whether learning is being monitored. If most of the charted lines are flat, or only very slightly sloped at 10 degrees (celeration of x1.1 per week), it is a dead give-away that the class is not focused on learning. The whole class could regularly produce learning slopes of 34 degrees (celerations of x2.0 per week) when learning is monitored and the celeration aim is at least doubling every week! Celerations of x2.0 per week are routine and expected at Morningside School and Malcolm X Community College (Johnson & Layng, 1992).

(6) *Teach in more than one channel at once.* Performance channels are Precision Teaching's way of describing precisely and in plain English the input-output relationship of a particular practice method. The rules are: active verbs, present tense, with a verb and object for the input stimulus and the related verb and object for the output response. For example: "see the capital letter "A,"—write the lower case letter "a." That is one throughput "see-write" channel. Another might be "see the picture of the dog—say its sound." That is a "see-say" channel. And again, "see the picture of the dog—write its sound (e.g., bow, wow)." That is a see-write channel. Ever since we discovered that learning to read in three different graded readers each day produced independent learning pictures (Johnson, N. J. A., 1971), it also became clear that learning the same material in different channels produced different learning pictures.

---

[7]Maximizing frequency existed as a seed in the parent free-operant laboratory research. It was essential to design rat levers and pigeon keys that did not put ceilings on the response frequency. Back as far as 1938, Skinner was unhappy that the levers used in his classic research published in *The Behavior of Organisms* took one second to reset. This placed a 60 per minute ceiling on the rats' response frequency. Skinner immediately designed new levers that could be operated up to 300 times per minute and placed no ceiling on the animals' performance.

The more different channels skills or concepts are taught in, the more generalization to other environments occurs. Eric Haughton was working on large matrixes of learning channels when he died in 1985. He had reported some of this work at annual Precision Teaching conferences, but none was in print. No one has systematically followed up on this work. Teaching to several learning channels at once appears to produce stronger performance, steeper learning, and more generalization, and is more fun for both learner and teacher. Ideal mixes of learning channels for particular skills need to be discovered. Learning channels research is one of the most promising yet most neglected in the field of Precision Teaching.

How Effective Is Precision Teaching?

Wherever Precision Teaching has been used, it has almost always doubled student learning at a median additional cost per teacher per year no higher than $90 (Albrecht, 1984). That figures out to be only $3 per student per year over current costs.

Precision Teaching has been selected as a nationally accredited educational model— Great Falls (Beck, 1976; Beck & Clement, 1991). Precision Teaching has had some success in public schools in special education. However, the strong bias against structure, monitoring, and frequent timed practice has kept it out of most public school regular classrooms. This is tragic because it could be used to develop a strong base of fluent tool skills in the pre-primary grades which would prevent many of the so-called learning and attention disorders which appear in the later grades.

Precision Teaching's most effective demonstrations are in learning centers and private schools which are not limited by anti-practice bias and lock-step curriculum controls. The Quinte Learning Centers in Belleville, Ontario (Maloney & Humphrey, 1982), the Haughton Learning Center in Napa, California (Freeman & Haughton, 1993a), and the Cache Valley Learning Center in Logan, Utah (Desjardins, 1993) are only three of the successful learning centers using Precision Teaching methods. The high effectiveness of one of the private schools using Precision Teaching is described below.

Morningside Academy in Seattle was established in 1980 and combines Precision Teaching to fluency with Direct Instruction and Tiemann-Markle instructional design. Teaching children with learning and attention problems, Morningside guarantees two grade levels gain per year in all subjects or tuition money back. In the seven years since offering the guarantee, Morningside has never had to return tuition for failing to produce two grade level gains per year (Johnson, 1989).

In 1987, Morningside added an adult literacy program in reading, mathematics, and writing for the Job Training and Partnership Act. Morningside agreed to be paid only for those students who progressed at least two grade levels in two skills in 21 months. Of the 32 African-American males in the first group, 29 exited with skills above the national eighth-grade literacy standard. They gained an average of 1.7 grade levels in two skills per month (20 hours of instruction). The U.S. government standard requires only one grade level gain per 100 hours of instruction. Therefore, Morningside Academy produces over 10 times the gain required by the government standard. Morningside's director attributed part of this success to the contingency that the faster the students advance, the sooner Morningside is paid (Johnson & Layng, 1992; Snyder, 1992).

In 1991, the Morningside Model was disseminated to the Academic Support Center at Malcolm X College in Chicago. During five weeks in January, April, May, June, and July, Malcolm X tutors were trained to teach a sequence of over 250 objectives in mathematics, from simple addition through solving ratios and equations with one unkown, a span of about six grade levels. The tutors practiced their new teaching skills with each other between training visits. The learners had high school diplomas but could not read at the the sixth grade level. Beginning in July, for three hours per day, four days per week (Monday through Thursday) for six weeks, the learners were tutored and practiced to fluency. Every Friday the tutors met with Johnson, Layng, and their in-training supervisors to share charts, discuss successes, brainstorm problems, and have their questions answered. Learners with entry math skills at the fifth grade level gained over six years in math computation, and over two years in math concepts and problem solving. After only 20 hours in timed reading practice, learners gained an average of 1.1 years in reading level (Johnson & Layng, 1992).

All of these gains at Seattle and Chicago occurred without any homework! None to turn in. None to grade.

Precision Teaching Do's and Don'ts for Instructional Design

There are more than a dozen guidelines for designing instruction that follow from discoveries made by precision teachers and their supervisors (Lindsley, 1992a). These are counter-intuitive and go against the common and cherished beliefs of most educators now in power. Traditional instruction is designed to be too slowly paced, and involves too little practice, too few practice channels (only see-write), and too little learning progress feedback.

Here I briefly list ten Do's and three Don'ts drawn from Precision Teaching discoveries.

Do count the number of all learner practice actions.
Do time each practice session.
Do shorten learner responses to two syllables to permit frequencies up to 200 per minute.
Do have more practice sheet questions than any student can answer in the allotted time.
Do have more negative instances than positive instances in practice materials.
Do teach and require practice of the same material in several channels each day.
Do build fluency first and accuracy later.
Do separately chart both correct and error frequencies each day (learning pictures).
Do use standard celeration charts so straight-line projections can be made by eye.
Do use standard celeration charts so amounts of learning can be compared by eye.
Don't monitor percent correct.
Don't use finishing an assignment as a reward.
Don't assign homework. (If you do it *must* be both timed and charted.)

This list could be extended by going further into detail. However, readers should get the flavor of Precision Teaching from these thirteen Do's and Don'ts.

Myths that Block Fluent Learning

At least twelve myths entrenched in our culture block fluent learning. These are deep seated and very difficult to overcome by argument alone. In combination they are deadly! No wonder public school instruction is so ineffective! The only way to overcome these myths is to produce learning two to ten times greater than public school learning without using the tactics suggested by the myths. This must be done in private learning centers. Several of these centers were described earlier. The twelve blocking myths follow:

(1) Performance improves by adding. WRONG!
    It improves by multiplying.

(2) There is an ideal curriculum and system for all children. WRONG!
    Ideal learning needs are more unique than students' clothing needs.

(3) See-Saw Theory—as corrects go up, errors must go down. WRONG!
    Correct and error learning are independent.

(4) Things learned generalize automatically to other situations. WRONG!
Performing is specific to the situation it was practiced in. Generalization must be carefully taught, using fluency and different channels.

(5) Feedback is effective even if it comes a week after the performance. WRONG!
Corrective feedback (did, didn't) should come immediately after performing.
Instructive feedback (do, don't) should come just before the next performance.

(6) Understanding must come before skills are learned. WRONG!
Understanding is not necessary. It is a luxury!
Understanding is most effective AFTER the skill is fluent.
In academics, the mind still rules and is thought to learn more by understanding than practice.
We know daily practice is essential in performing arts and sports.
But we still believe understanding is more important than practice in academics.

(7) A strong positive self-concept is required before skills can be learned. WRONG!
A strong positive self-concept results from (comes AFTER) fluent, accurate skills.
Telling learners they are good before they are fluent doesn't fool them; they know better—you merely invalidate your approval.

(8) Accuracy must come first before speed. WRONG!
Our most effective learning picture starts with high error frequencies (60 per min) and low correct frequencies (10 per min)— called "Jaws cross-over."

(9) A high frequency of errors will break the learner's spirit. WRONG!
High error frequencies decelerating rapidly each week build curricular spirit.

(10) A high frequency of errors will teach the learner bad habits. WRONG!
Learners actually need more practice on what not to do than on what to do.

(11) Thirty minutes are needed for a topic, so one minute sessions are useless. WRONG!
Charted practice sessions as small as 10 second "sprints" are more effective than long 20 to 30 minute sessions.

(12) Speed tests produce anxiety which blocks what the learner really knows. WRONG!
This only appears when the learner is only tested a few times each semester.
With daily timed practice, the timing anxiety disappears within two weeks.

This list of entrenched myths that block teaching to fluency and rapid learning could be enlarged. There are several other entrenched myths about learning and performance that are just plain wrong. However, this list is long enough to give a notion of the kind of cultural blocks that effective teaching practices face in public school application.

Special Problems with Computer Assisted Instruction

From 1985 to 1992, I advised a corporation which produced authoring systems for computer assisted instruction and custom courses for Fortune 500 clients. This company tried to combine the very best principles and procedures from Applied Behavior Analysis and Precision Teaching in its authoring system and courses (Silverman, Lindsley, & Porter, 1991a). Four major problems were encountered. First, the company executive officers and programmers believed more in the incorrect popular myths of how best to learn than they did in Precision Teaching's proven results. This produced almost constant stumbling, misinterpretation, and time-wasting in instructional design. They wanted the instruction to be comfortable for the student throughout. Second, there was a very real problem in getting the computer programs to refresh the screens fast enough to permit fluent students to respond at the exciting speeds of 60 a minute and above. Computer arcade games do this, but it was like pulling teeth to get the programmers to make courseware that fast. Third, almost all clients wanted to use the courses in single sessions of two or three hours duration, treating this new technology very much like their familiar training lectures and workshops. They were told that they would get much better learning and learner satisfaction from brief daily practice sessions, but almost none used the courses that way. Fourth, almost all of the clients said they purchased the company's courses because of guaranteed results. But few looked at the results, and only one customer compared the results of the training with the employees' on-the-job performance (Silverman, Lindsley, & Porter, 1991b).

It is possible, if the developers *and users* of computer programs believe in fluency enough to override their cultural myths, to develop and use computer programs that get up to low fluency of 30 answers per minute. Both "Think Fast," developed for the IBM PC by Joseph Parsons[8] and "FluentLearn," developed for the Macintosh by Claudia McDade[9] accomplish 30 per minute. But these frequencies are far below the fluencies of 60 to 100 per minute reached with properly designed and used fluency cards. Fluency cards are called "SAFMEDS" to remind users that they must "**S**ay **A**ll **F**ast a **M**inute **E**very **D**ay **S**huffled." And SAFMEDS' frequencies are far below the high fluencies of 200 to 300 per minute reached in see-say channels using properly designed practice sheets (Freeman & Haughton, 1993a). And practice sheet frequencies are below the high fluencies of 400 to 500 per minute reached in the think-say (sometimes called free-say) channel in which learners freely respond to directions with no immediate limiting stimuli (Freeman & Haughton, 1993b).

Competing Viewpoints

There are two almost insurmountable competing view points that Precision Teaching must defeat. The first is the general cultural entrenchment of measurement habits of percent and base ten scaling. The second is the dominant small group research design with its associated intermittent measurement, independent observer, and analysis of variance probability statements.

Closely related to the small group research design is the extreme resistance to self-recorded data and a total dependence upon data observed by more than one "external observer." This brings up their stress on reliability to the exclusion of validity. How many times the teacher smiled at Tommy is *only* validly recorded by Tommy. (How many times that two observers saw the teacher smile at Tommy may produce a comforting notion of reliability, but if Tommy didn't see the smiles, then the "reliable" records are not valid). Statistical dogma assumes that you can't have validity without reliability. But you certainly can.

Variability is a datum—what we call daily bounce—not an error! This principle is further described in detail elsewhere (Johnston & Pennypacker, 1980).

Models Supporting Precision Teaching's Daily Charting

Formative evaluation (Bloom, Hastings, & Madaus, 1971) and curriculum-based measurement (Deno, 1985) are both measurement models related to the daily counting and charting of Precision Teaching. Precision Teaching developed independently at approximately the same time as formative evaluation, and 15 years before curriculum-based measurement.

---

[8]*Think Fast* for the IBM PC is commercially available from Joseph A. Parsons, University of Victoria, P. O. Box 1700, Victoria, B.C., Canada V8W 2Y2.

[9]*FluentLearn* for the Macintosh is commercially available from McLAB, Inc., P. O. Box 571, Jacksonville, AL 36265.

Precision teaching is the ultimate in formative evaluation. Not only is the performance monitored while it is changing rather than after, but the performance on each and every day is recorded, charted, and projected in real time. Having learners count and chart their own performance in Precision Teaching ties the evaluation even more closely to the performance than when psychologists or teachers test occasionally during formative evaluation.

Models Supporting Precision Teaching's Fluency Aims

Englemann's "firming" procedure (Englemann & Bruner, 1968) and Bloom's "automaticity" goal (Bloom, 1986) are both related to the fluency aims of Precision Teaching. Precision Teaching fluency aims developed independently at about the same time as Englemann's firming and 15 years before Bloom published his goal of automaticity.

In the Direct Instruction model, "firming" of mathematics and reading skills is related to fluency (Engelmann & Bruner, 1968; Engelmann & Carnine, 1970). Reading and arithmetic skills are considered firm when the student can perform them quickly and accurately. This firm performance is only loosely and not precisely defined. Questions such as "How does one know when a student is fluent" or "What is the frequency criterion for fluency" are as yet unresolved for Direct Instruction users (Williams & Albin, 1984).

Bloom's "automaticity" of performance, which he now claims should be one of the goals of instruction (Bloom, 1986) is related to fluency. However, "automaticity" is not precisely described. From reading Bloom, one cannot tell how you determine precisely when a performance is "automatic." Programming and practice frequencies are not given for producing automatic performance. Bloom does not even mention whether practice must be daily or not in order to produce automaticity. Also, the notion of automaticity was in the literature (Denekla & Rudell, 1974; Haughton, 1972, 1974) years before Bloom wrote about it.

Concluding Weak Points of Precision Teaching

The weakest points of Precision Teaching are its confrontations with entrenched but faulty cultural myths and practices. I have recently described the paradox of how the work ethic, discipline, and competition are avoided in our public school academics, but welcomed in athletics (Lindsley, 1992b). Precision Teaching is seen as comprising all three of these and so is also avoided. "Drill and practice" is currently bad news in education, while "learning styles," "whole language," and "facilitated communication" are *in.*

The weakest point of Precision Teaching is its confrontation with massive cultural entrenchment of percent correct. Ron Holzschuh spent two years of post-doctoral research comparing the sensitivity and productivity of percent correct with frequency correct and incorrect as classroom performance measures. He found that frequencies correct and incorrect picked up 40 times more effects of routine changes in teaching procedures than did percent correct (Holzschuh & Dobbs, 1966). Also, teaching decisions based on percent correct monitoring were less productive and more difficult to make because the teachers could not tell what was happening to the correct or error learning. For example, if percent correct was staying the same, teachers could not tell whether the correct and error frequencies were both accelerating, both maintaining or both decelerating—they simply knew that the proportion was the same. For another example, if percent correct was increasing, the teacher did not know whether this was because both corrects and errors were accelerating with the corrects accelerating more steeply, whether the corrects were maintaining and the errors decelerating, or whether both corrects and errors were decelerating with the errors decelerating more steeply. These three different learning pictures require different remedial teaching procedures, which cannot be prescribed based on percent correct. This was true for different subject matters, and different grade levels. Ron concluded with the statement, "Percent is the worst thing that ever happened to education."

Base-five scaling (five fingers = one hand) is another entrenched procedure in education that Precision Teaching confronts. It has proven extremely difficult to get administrators and researchers to count the frequency of complaints or feelings of satisfaction with a school or its methods. The entrenched habit is to have parents, students, teachers, or administrators rate their satisfaction on a scale of five. The majority of research studies over the last two decades in educational administration have used questionnaires, Likert scales, small group design, and the analysis of variance, and as far as I know has discovered nothing of import.

Possibly the next weakest point is the educational establishment's entrenched use of tests and educational and school psychologists to do the testing. There is just no need for regular testing once each student's actual timed practice and learning is charted daily. In anticipation of resistance from school psychologists, I joined the Association for School Psychology and applied for and obtained American Board of Professional Psychology certification as a School Psychologist. I spent several years trying to recruit school psychologists to become learning specialists and advise teachers in solving the learning problems revealed on their student's charts. It seemed to me a natural (Lindsley, 1971b). They were in the schools. They were better trained in research and statistics than teachers. Presumably they liked numbers and general concepts and different learning and teaching techniques. However, I overlooked one thing. School Psychologists were imprinted with and dedicated to testing. Testing was their life, their blood. I advised them to estimate Binet and WRAT scores to get out from behind their long list of students who had already been placed in special classrooms by teacher request and now must be tested to justify the placement. This would be so that they could get into the classrooms and help teachers. We found out that the school psychologists preferred to have a huge pile of untested students in their in-basket—it was their security blanket. They were *testers*. In no way would they become *teacher helpers!*

Probably the next weakest point is its confrontation with the educational research establishment. Educational researchers should welcome Precision Teaching's power, find some cooperating public school classrooms, and start collecting what would be to them massive amounts of valid learning data already processed and charted. All they would have to do is collect and analyze the results. But they are now so caught up in their tactical procedures that they cannot even think, much less research, outside of the frame of their Latin Square, small group, reversal, crosstabs, analysis of variance and covariance research designs. These are so cumbersome that the researchers hardly ever get a study done on over two hundred students learning in real time under different curricular conditions.

One of the most powerful research potentials that Precision Teaching fell upon is the opportunity to determine rapidly the most effective of several curricula by trying three or more on the same student at the same time.

It looks like we may have to wait for a new generation of educators to adopt Precision Teaching methods. Max Planck once said, "A new scientific truth does not triumph by convincing its opponents . . . but rather because its opponents eventually die" (Barber, 1961, p. 597). In the same vein, Skinner sadly said, "I am convinced now that science never progresses by converting . . . It really takes a new generation" (Hall, 1967).

Concluding Strong Points of Precision Teaching

The strongest point of Precision Teaching is that it works! It is one of the few measurement systems that *always* greatly enhances rather than interferes with the performance being monitored.

It is universal—all-inclusive. Every performance, from the most minute keyboard action or phonic utterance (Johnston, T. S., 1972) through previously considered unmeasureable events like thoughts, feelings, and urges (Calkin, 1981; Duncan, 1971) to global performances like books written and major creative ideas had, can be counted and divided by the time over which they were counted, and charted. Everything we have seen charted, from felt fetal kicks (Edwards & Edwards, 1970) to world armed attacks (Taylor & Hudson, 1975), accelerates as straight lines on Standard Celeration Charts.

It is sensitive. Precision Teaching learning pictures have proven to be two to forty times more sensitive to changes in learning conditions than other monitoring and evaluating methods (Holzschuh & Dobbs, 1966). It reveals aspects of learning never before seen clearly.

It reveals two very different kinds of learning processes—jumps and turns. Jump-ups or jump-downs in frequency (performance) occur and are independent of turns in celeration (learning). At this time we know very little about what causes jumps and turns, the relationships between them, or why they are independent. We do know this independence poses serious problems for education and applied behavior analysis. We do know that a large proportion of the published data charts in the literature contain counter-turns (Lindsley & Rosales-Ruiz, 1984). A counter-turn is a jump-up followed by a turn down, or a jump-down followed by a turn-up. Counter-turns are counter-productive because over time you lose the effect you are trying to produce. In jump-ups followed by turn-downs, the abrupt, immediate effect of the reinforcer is gradually lost by the later deceleration (satiation) in the performance frequency. In jump-downs followed by turn-ups the abrupt, immediate effect of the punisher is gradually lost by the later acceleration (adaptation) in performance frequency.

Precision Teaching does not provide a comprehensive theoretical framework for understanding instructional design. This is because it is primarily an inductive system. If there is an underlying theory, it is that frequency monitoring on standard celeration charts is powers of ten more sensitive than percent or duration monitoring. However, even this has been proven by classroom research—so it is more correctly thought of as a proven method than a theory.

However, Precision Teaching does provide a comprehensive framework in which instructional development procedures and models can be evaluated while being developed, compared after development, and enhanced during their use later in the classroom.

Precision Teaching methods are the most powerful tools yet discovered to aid instructional design. Designers stubbornly resisting using these promising new tools seriously handicap the poor student required to learn from their imprecisely designed materials. Designers using the powerful tools of precision teaching, monitoring trial learner's Standard Celeration Charts continuously throughout instructional development, will earn my blessing, and the endearing gratitude of generations of student learners. They also will have earned the proud title *Precise Instructional Designer,* or *Precision Designer* for short.

References

Albrecht, P. L. (1984). *Summary of ten major school precision teaching programs.* Unpublished doctoral dissertation, University of Kansas, Lawrence.

All, P. (1977). *From get truckin' to jaws, students improve their learning picture.* Unpublished master's thesis, University of Kansas, Lawrence.

Barber, B. (1961). Resistance by scientists to scientific discovery. *Science, 134,* 596–602.

Beck, R. J. (1976). *Report for the Office of Education Dissemination Review Panel, 1976, Special Education.* Great Falls Public Schools, Precision Teaching Project: Great Falls, MT.

Beck, R. J. (1981). *High School Basic Skills Improvement Project: Validation Report for ESEA Title IV-C.* Great Falls Public Schools, Precision Teaching Project: Great Falls, MT.

Beck, R., & Clement R. (1991). The Great Falls Precision Teaching Project: An historical examination. *Journal of Precision Teaching, 8*(2), 8–12.

Bijou, S. W., & Baer, D. M. (1961). *Child development: Vol 1. A systematic and empirical theory.* New York: Appleton-Century-Crofts.

Binder, C. V. (1990, Sept.). Closing the confidence gap. *Training,* 49–56.

Binder, C. V., & Bloom, C. (1989, Feb.). Fluent product knowledge: Application in the financial services industry. *Performance and Instruction,* 17–21.

Bloom, B. S. (1986). Automaticity: The hands and feet of genius. *Educational Leadership, 43*(5), 70–77.

Bloom, B. S., Hastings, J. T., & Madaus, G. F. (1971). *Handbook on formative and summative evaluation of student learning.* New York: McGraw-Hill Book Company.

Calkin, A. B. (1981). One minute timing improves inners. *Journal of Precision Teaching, 2*(3), 9–21.

Denekla, M. B., & Rudell, R. (1974) Rapid "automatized" naming of pictured objects, colors, letters, and numbers by normal children. *Cortex,* 186–202.

Deno, S. L., (1985). Curriculum-based measurement: The emerging alternative. *Exceptional Children, 52*(3), 219–232.

Desjardins, A. (1993). Teaching addition and subtraction word problems. *Journal of Precision Teaching, 10*(2), 25–28.

Desjardins, A., & Slocum, T. (1993). Integrating Precision Teaching with Direct Instruction. *Journal of Precision Teaching, 10*(2), 20–24.

Duncan, A. D. (1969). Self application of behavior modification techniques by teen-agers. *Adolescence, 6*(4), 541–556.

Duncan, A. D. (1971). The view from the inner eye: Personal management of inner and outer behaviors. *Teaching Exceptional Children, 3*(3), 152–156.

Duncan, A. D. (1972). The gifted count and chart. In J. B. Jordan & L. S. Robbins (Eds.), *Let's try doing something else kind of thing: Behavioral principles and the exceptional child* (pp. 51–55). Arlington, VA: Council for Exceptional Children.

Edwards, D. D., & Edwards, J. S. (1970). Fetal movement: Development and time course. *Science, 169,* 95–97.

Engelmann, S., & Bruner, E. (1968). *DISTAR reading level I.* Chicago: Science Research Associates.

Engelmann, S., & Carnine, D. W. (1970). *DISTAR arithmetic I.* Chicago: Science Research Associates.

Engelmann, S., & Carnine, D. (1982). *Theory of instruction: Principles and applications.* New York: Irvington.

Epstein, R. (1985). The spontaneous interconnection of three repertoires. *Psychological Record, 35,* 131–143.

Fink, E. R. (1968). *Performance and selection rates of emotionally disturbed and mentally retarded preschoolers on Montessori materials.* Unpublished master's thesis, University of Kansas, Lawrence, KS.

Freeman, G., & Haughton, E. (1993a) Building reading fluency across the curriculum. *Journal of Precision Teaching, 10*(2), 29–30.

Freeman, G., & Haughton, E. (1993b) Handwriting fluency. *Journal of Precision Teaching, 10*(2), 31–32.

Fuchs, L., & Deno, S. L. (1981). *A comparison of reading placements based on teacher judgement, standardized testing and curriculum-based measurement* (Research Report No. 53). Minneapolis: University of Minnesota, Institute for Research on Learning Disabilities.

Gove, P. B. (Ed.). (1961). *Webster's third new international dictionary of the English language (unabridged).* Springfield, MA: G. & C. Merriam Co.

Hall, M. H. (1967). An interview with "Mr. Behaviorist": B. F. Skinner. *Psychology Today, 1*(5), 20–23, 68–71.

Haughton, E. C. (1972). Aims—growing and sharing. In J. B. Jordan & L. S. Robbins (Eds.), *Let's try doing something else kind of thing: Behavioral principles and the exceptional child* (pp. 20–39). Arlington, VA: Council for Exceptional Children.

Haughton, E. C. (1974, March). Define your act and set your fluency goals in personal, social, and academic areas. *Special Education in Canada, 48*(2), 10–11.

Haughton, E. C. (1981). REAPS. *Data Sharing Newsletter.* Waltham, MA: Behavior Prosthesis Laboratory.

Holzschuh, R. D., & Dobbs, D. (1966). *Superiority of rate correct over percent correct.* Unpublished manuscript, Educational Research, University of Kansas Medical Center.

Johnson, K. R. (1989). *Executive summary.* Morningside Corporation (810 18th Ave., Seattle, WA 98122).

Johnson, K. R. (1992a). *Morningside phonics fluency: A Precision Teaching approach.* Seattle: Morningside Academy.

Johnson, K. R. (1992b). *Morningside mathematics fluency: A Precision Teaching approach.* Seattle: Morningside Academy.

Johnson, K. R., & Layng, T. V. J. (1992). Breaking the structuralist barrier: Literacy and numeracy with fluency. *American Psychologist, 47*(11), 1475–1490.

Johnson, K. R., & Layng, T. V. J. (In Press). The Morningside Model of generative instruction. In R. Gardiner, D. Sainato, J. O. Cooper, T. E. Heron, W. L. Heward, & J. Eshleman (Eds.), *Behavior analysis in education: Focus on measurably superior instruction:* Pacific Grove, CA: Brooks/Cole Publishing Company.

Johnson, K. R., & Streck, J. (1992). *Scope and sequence: Morningside mathematics: Revised edition.* Seattle: Morningside Academy.

Johnson, N. J. A. (1971). *Acceleration of inner-city elementary school pupils' reading performance.* Unpublished doctoral dissertation, University of Kansas, Lawrence.

Johnson, T. S. (1972). Precision therapy is the way to go. In J. B. Jordan & L. S. Robbins (Eds.), *Let's try doing something else kind of thing: Behavioral principles and the exceptional child* (pp. 40–50). Arlington, VA: Council for Exceptional Children.

Johnston, J. M., & Pennypacker, H. S. (1980). *Strategies and tactics of human behavioral research.* Hillsdale, NJ: Lawrence Erlbaum Associates.

Koenig, C. H. (1972). *Charting the future course of behavior.* Unpublished doctoral dissertation, University of Kansas, Lawrence.

Kuhn, T. S. (1970). *The structure of scientific revolutions* (2nd ed.). Chicago: The University of Chicago Press.

Lindsley, O. R. (1960). Characteristics of the behavior of chronic psychotics as revealed by free-operant conditioning methods. *Diseases of the Nervous System, 21* (monograph supplement), 66–78.

Lindsley, O. R. (1971a). Precision Teaching in perspective: An interview with Ogden R. Lindsley; Ann Duncan, interviewer. *Teaching Exceptional Children, 3*(3), 114–119.

Lindsley, O. R. (1971b). The beautiful future of school psychology: Advising teachers. In M. C. Reynolds (Ed.), *Proceedings of the Conference on Psychology and the Process of Schooling in the Next Decade: Alternative Conceptions* (pp. xxiii, 116–120). Minneapolis: Univ. of Minnesota, Dept. of AudioVisual Extension.

Lindsley, O. R. (1972). From Skinner to Precision Teaching: The child knows best. In J. B. Jordan & L. S. Robbins (Eds.), *Let's try doing something else kind of thing: Behavioral principles and the exceptional child* (pp. 1–11). Arlington, VA: Council for Exceptional Children.

Lindsley, O. R. (1990). Precision teaching: By teachers for children. *Teaching Exceptional Children, 22*(3), 10–15.

Lindsley, O. R. (1992a). Precision Teaching: Discoveries and effects. *Journal of Applied Behavior Analysis, 25,* 51–57.

Lindsley, O. R. (1992b). Why aren't effective teaching tools widely adopted? *Journal of Applied Behavior Analysis, 25,* 21–26.

Lindsley, O. R., & Rosales-Ruiz, J. (1984 May). Standard celeration meta-charting of overcorrection literature. In W. L. Heward (chair), *Exploring and assessing response deceleration procedures.* Symposium conducted at the 10th Annual Convention of the Association for Behavior Analysis, Nashville, TN.

Maloney, M., & Humphrey, J. E. (Interviewer). (1982). The Quinte Learning Center: A successful venture in behavioral education—an interview with Michael Maloney. *The Behavioral Educator, 4*(1), 1–3.

Markle, S. M. (1978, 1983). *Designs for instructional designers.* Champaign, IL: Stipes Publishing Company.

Nevin, J. A. (1992). An integrative model for the study of behavioral momentum. *Journal of the Experimental Analysis of Behavior, 57,* 301–316.

Oliva, C. M. (1981). *A comparison of the accuracies of five future projection methods.* Unpublished doctoral dissertation, University of Kansas, Lawrence. *Dissertation Abstracts International,* 1982, *42,* 2956A (University Microfilms No. 81–28, 733).

Pennypacker, H. S., Koenig, C. H., & Lindsley, O. R. (1972). *Handbook of the standard behavior chart.* Kansas City, KS: Precision Media.

Potts, L., Eshelman, J. W., & Cooper, J. O., (1993). Ogden R. Lindsley and the historical development of Precision Teaching. *The Behavior Analyst, 16,* 177–189.

Starlin, A. (1971). Charting group and individual instruction. *Teaching Exceptional Children, 3,* 135–136.

Silverman, K., Lindsley, O. R., & Porter, K. L. (1991a). Overt responding in computer-based training. *Current Psychology: Research and Reviews, 9*(4), 373–384.

Silverman, K., Lindsley, O. R., & Porter, K. L. (1991b). A computer intelligent tutoring system versus on-the-job tutoring. *Journal of Organizational Behavior Management.*

Snyder, G. (1992). Morningside Academy: A learning guarantee. *Performance Management Magazine, 10,* 29–35.

Taylor, C., & Hudson, M. (1975). *World handbook of political and social indicators.* New Haven: Yale University Press.

Tiemann, P. W., & Markle, S. M. (1990). *Analyzing instructional content: A guide to instruction and evaluation* (4th ed.). Champaign, IL: Stipes Publishing Company.

White, O. R. (1986). Precision Teaching—Precision Learning. *Exceptional Children, 52,* 522–534.

Williams, J. A., & Albin, R. (1984, Spring). Fluency and skill maintenance by the handicapped. *Direct Instruction News,* p. 20.

32

Applying the Individualizing Instruction Model with Adult Learners

Roger Hiemstra
Syracuse University
Syracuse, New York

Introduction

As Brockett describes in his chapter in this book, the humanism paradigm provides another framework for approaching the design and delivery of instruction. In keeping with the basic tenets of humanism, a better way of describing such instructional design (ID) or delivery efforts is to say that they involve facilitating learners to take increasing responsibility for their own learning. Maslow (1976) and Rogers (1977) have alluded to this as involving the total person in learning.

Humanism generally refers to beliefs about freedom and autonomy, and holds that "human beings are capable of making significant personal choices within the constraints imposed by heredity, personal history, and environment" (Elias & Merriam, 1980, p. 118). Humanist principles stress the value of specific and individual human needs. Some primary humanist assumptions include the following: (a) human nature is inherently good; (b) individuals are free, autonomous, and capable of making major personal choices; (c) human potential for growth and development is virtually unlimited; (d) self-concept plays an important role in growth and development; (e) individuals have an urge toward self-actualization; (f) reality is defined by each person; and (g) individuals have responsibility to both themselves and others (Elias & Merriam, 1980).

The humanism paradigm is receiving increasing attention from some instructional designers who are attempting to make their instructional systems more "responsive to the needs of the individual student" (Miller & Hotes, 1982, p. 22). Humanism, what Hollis (1991) describes as a "theory of learning," supports some approaches to help improve instructional effectiveness. Many mediated approaches to learning, for example, are based on assumptions that learners can and will assume responsibility for making learning decisions.

Kramlinger and Huberty (1990) also pay attention to the wisdom and experience participants can contribute to instructional activities, and suggest that this involves learners becoming more reflective on personal experiences and more self-directed in their acquisition of new knowledge or skill. Brockett and Hiemstra (1991) created what they call the PRO (Personal Responsibility Orientation) model to provide a definitional framework for self-directed involvement and to describe corresponding interactions between learners, instructors, and the societal conditions within which learning occurs.

The purpose of this chapter is to describe how a teaching and learning process based on humanism, what Sisco in his chapter refers to as "Individualizing the Instructional Process" (II), can be implemented at the tactical or lesson level with adult learners. The II model is a teaching and learning process premised not only on humanism, but also on ideas about the empowerment of learners. Much of the model's development was supported by various research efforts to define and describe self-directed learning (SDL). Most SDL research in the past three decades has demonstrated that adult learners generally prefer to take considerable responsibility for their own learning. Thus, there is considerable value in considering the humanism paradigm as a foundation for instructional design.

Opportunities for Learner Control

Many traditional teaching, training, or ID situations limit opportunities for personal learner involvement and decision-making because control over content or process remains in the hands of experts, designers, or teachers who depend primarily on didactic, behaviorist, or cognitivist approaches (Kramlinger & Huberty, 1990). In essence, some teachers have difficulty accepting the humanistic philosophical underpinnings crucial to adults accepting increased responsibility for learning. They may even accept certain humanistic beliefs but feel compelled to employ a more directed instructional approach because of organizational or traditional expectations about teaching and the design of instruction.

As Hollis (1991) notes:

> . . . traditionally, instructional technologists have largely ignored the humanists' ideas among all the available theories from which to draw upon and incorporate into their schemes. Theoretically, instructional technology has been based on research in human learning and communications theories. In reality, more borrowing of ideas is needed, especially from the ranks of the humanists. (p. 51)

The II process assumes that there are various aspects of teaching, learning, or ID over which learners can assume some control (Hiemstra & Sisco, 1990; Patterson, 1973; Valett, 1977). For example, many learners can determine some of their personal learning needs by using a variety of assessment or diagnostic instruments. Often a learner is capable of controlling or making decisions through a learning contract or some other planning tool about the sequence of certain learning materials (Knowles, 1986). Many learners are very capable of deciding the pace or approach in acquiring new knowledge (Hiemstra, 1995).

Other aspects of the learning process over which learners can assume some responsibility include such functions as setting goals, specifying the learning content, choosing instructional methods, controlling elements of the learning environment, promoting the nature of any introspection or critical thinking, and selecting evaluation techniques. Many of these aspects will be detailed in the next section.

Individualizing Instruction: The Process in Action

As an adult basic education instructor, Sarah Roberts was familiar with the need to build self-confidence in her learners. She recalled how many came to the learning center with low self-esteem, but a sincere desire to improve themselves. The learners were not always realistic about their personal goals nor the time needed to accomplish them, so Sarah strived to set a tone of encouragement tempered with realistic expectations. She believed that small, incremental gains, coupled with lots of positive feedback, lead to later success.

Sarah's views about the educational process were consistent with most other teachers at the learning center where she worked. She and her colleagues believed that the best way to instruct adults was through an individualizing process. This meant that each and every learner was helped to assume increasing responsibility for their learning. Although many of the learners initially required a good deal of structure, the idea of individual control and accountability was constantly reinforced. As a result, most flowered under such conditions and Sarah felt the reason for this was related to the instructional process practiced at the center. (Hiemstra & Sisco, 1990, pp. 77–78)

Although Sarah Roberts is a fictitious person, her story is not unrealistic. The individualizing process described in this vignette consists of six steps: (a) Carrying out various activities prior to the first session, such as developing a learning rationale, preplanning certain learning experiences, and securing a variety of potential learning resources; (b) facilitating or creating a positive learning environment, including attention to physical, psychological, and social aspects; (c) developing the instructional plan, including active involvement of participants in assessing personal and relevant group needs, ascertaining the relevance of past experience, and prioritizing knowledge areas to be covered; (d) helping learners identify appropriate learning activities and techniques; (e) facilitating various learning experiences and monitoring learner progress; and (f) evaluating individual learning outcomes in various ways. Building on aspects of the humanism paradigm, in the II process the instructor's role is to manage and facilitate a learning process: "Optimum learning is the result of careful interactive planning between the instructor and the individual learners" (Hiemstra & Sisco, 1990, pp. 47–48).

There are several specific roles an instructor or facilitator undertakes in the II process:

1. Serving as a content resource or specialist on some topics.
2. Managing an interactive process involving learners in determining their own learning needs, rather than pre-supposing a generic set of needs.
3. Arranging and employing the resources necessary for a group of learners to accomplish their personal goals, including such actions as finding or creating new resources, obtaining knowledge or expertise on new areas, and arranging for the availability of outside experts.
4. Making available a wide variety of instructional experiences to maintain learner interest.
5. Using various instructional techniques for stimulating and motivating learners (Wlodkowski, 1985, presents several strategies for motivating adult learners).
6. Helping learners develop positive attitudes and feelings about their self-directed learning abilities.
7. Maintaining some understanding of how well each learner is doing at reflecting on personal learnings.
8. Facilitating learners in evaluating their personal achievements in various ways, such as traditional testing, instructor or collegial critiques of written materials, personal interviews between the facilitator and a learner, and self-evaluation.

Most of these roles are based on the humanist assumptions described earlier in the chapter and the notion that learners can and will assume increasing responsibility for their own learning. The following sections describe how various steps in the II process make use of these roles.

Activities Prior to Meeting
Learners the First Time

As with most educational endeavors, in the II process an instructor's activities do not begin at the time of any initial contact with learners. An organizational structure for participatory planning is required, various learning materials must be prepared, and considerable thinking about how to involve learners must take place. In other words, an instructor should carry out considerable planning and preparation.

However, there are some differences an instructor must consider in comparison to what normally takes place in many of the more traditional teaching and learning approaches or those based on other than the humanist paradigm. In many respects, more advanced planning is required in an individualized setting than in more structured ones, because needs are specified during initial interactions between instructor and learners and often they are refined throughout the process. Thus, advance preparation for potential learning activities in a variety of possible areas may be required. The following describes some of the many actions typically taking place prior to that first contact with learners.

Pre-Planning Efforts. II is differentiated from many other instructional processes in that no course, training session, or workshop can be completely developed prior to meeting with the learners. Each group of learners will be different, new or unexpected needs frequently emerge during the needs assessment efforts, and new learning resources and experiences will constantly be required.

Early in any pre-planning efforts, there is a need to determine or understand necessary competencies or requirements. For example, most instructors or trainers must wear an institutional hat of some sort and be responsible for ensuring that subsequent learning experiences are within normal individual or organizational expectations. There may be governmental or other regulations which mandate certain learning requirements. In addition, most participants will anticipate acquiring certain types of knowledge or skill.

Thus, if a training program or course has already been presented at least one time, then defining competencies may mean simply refining those identified in earlier planning work. However, when a new learning experience is being developed, then the process of determining competencies may involve considerable background research, conferring with colleagues, anticipating learners' expected proficiencies, estimating the amount or type of learning activities needed, and thinking about how various learning experiences can be blended together. Whatever efforts are utilized, clearly understanding the necessary learning requirements provides a background for acquiring various learning resources and estimating needed learning experiences.

Securing Learning Resources. As noted earlier, in the II process an instructor assumes a variety of roles, including such functions as facilitating the learning process, supporting self-directed learning, and providing a variety of resources, as well as the more traditional presentation of information on several topics. Thus, providing learners access to various learning materials or resources is required.

This involves finding, building, designing, and developing a variety of resource possibilities, such as a large collection of films, video tapes, and even learning experiences out in the community or within the larger organization sponsoring the training activity. In other words, a facilitator needs to provide information and resource possibilities related to many aspects of any learning endeavor. Therefore, advance planning helps to ensure that certain materials and specialized resource people are available to learners.

Workbook of Supplemental Materials. It is important, too, to create a workbook or study guide of supplemental materials that describe, support, and enrich the learning experience. This includes such features as syllabus information, explanation of any learning requirements, learning activity descriptions, bibliographic references, learning contract materials including examples (described later in this chapter), and any special materials not easily obtainable.

The advantage of developing a supplemental study guide is that it typically emerges from any advance planning and collection of resource material. It is never possible to plan everything because of unexpected directions determined through needs assessment activities. However, a well designed workbook is appreciated by learners and it provides a foundation on which subsequent and evolving learning can be based.

Creating a Positive Learning Environment

In the II process there are several activities that are important to establishing an effective learning climate. As noted before, they grow out of the humanist paradigm that stresses the value of individual decision-making. The purpose of this section is to describe these activities and what usually happens during the first few hours of student/teacher contact.

Initial Contact with Learners. Actual content delivery begins literally within the first session's initial minutes in many teaching and learning approaches (Pratt, 1984; Sisco, 1991). This assumes that each learner there is ready to receive information from the trainer or teacher. Subsequently, what often happens is that information about a topic is delivered in a lecture format. Learners may even be discouraged from seeking clarification of learning goals, content being covered, or future expectations of the instructor.

The II process, however, assumes that typical adult students have considerable life and work experiences that can become the basis for future learning. Most adults are capable and usually desirous of assuming some personal control over the learning process. It is in the first few hours together that attitudes about what is possible are formed.

Thus, it is important that the first time learners are together and the instructor helps them to become acquainted with each other. This serves to elaborate on the varied nature of experiences among participants and serves as a means for building potential collegial relationships. When possible to do so, place the learners in a circle or "U"-shape so good eye contact with each other is possible. This is known as a sociopetal setting (chairs in rows is known as a sociofugal arrangement and it normally discourages interactions or makes them more difficult—Hiemstra, 1991a; Vosko, 1991).

Various techniques can be used to help people become acquainted, such as the use of name tags or large index cards folded to look like a tent with the learner's name (using a first name or nickname is recommended) printed on the outside in large enough letters so that they can be easily seen from across the room or table. Other techniques include having people introduce themselves one by one around the circle or dividing the class into groups of two so that members of pairs can become acquainted with each other; subsequently, each member of the pair introduces his or her new friend to the rest of the group. Sisco (1991) describes several other techniques that can be used.

Some instructors not accustomed to the II process may have reservations about using this initial time for helping learners become acquainted rather than for informational presentations. However, a small investment of time at the beginning of a course or training session can reap extra rewards later on in terms of learner enthusiasm, respect for each other, and ideas regarding whom to work with on any learning projects. In essence, a humanistic respect for others underlies this feature.

Arranging for and Monitoring the Physical Space. An appropriate physical space is important to successful teaching and learning. This may entail insisting on certain rooms or spaces for your course or training session prior to when it starts or finding another setting if the original space becomes inadequate or inappropriate (Hiemstra, 1991a). Occasionally it may even be necessary to request additional breakout rooms to accommodate small group discussion or work sessions.

Many adults also thrive in settings that are informal in nature and where collegial networking is encouraged. In those learning situations where small group discussion is utilized, move the chairs into the sociopetal or circular pattern noted earlier. If the chairs are not comfortable, encourage learners to take charge of their own comfort by bringing in their own chairs or cushions. Obviously, there are many other aspects of the physical environment that need managing or assessing, including such things as table size, accessibility for the disabled, and appropriate voice amplification.

Ensuring that the learning space is comfortable, accessible, or usable will take time and energy both before a learning experience begins and throughout the time it is underway. It frequently necessitates a facilitator arriving at a room early to monitor the conditions, bringing in extra chairs or tables, and spending countless hours rearranging the furniture or making coffee. It may mean monitoring the temperature, worrying about the level of lighting in a space, and ensuring that adequate time for refreshments or other breaks is available. However, such attention to the physical side of a learning environment usually helps build positive learning attitudes among learners.

Dealing with Psychological/Emotional Conditions. An effective learning environment involves more than just attention to various physical features:

> A learning environment is all of the physical surroundings, psychological or emotional conditions, and social or cultural influences affecting the growth and development of an adult engaged in an educational enterprise. (Hiemstra, 1991a, p. 8)

Figure 1 provides a checklist that can be used to determine if various concerns about a learning environment are met.

For example, there are various psychological or emotional conditions that may impact on learners in a multitude of ways. Pratt (1984) and Sisco (1991) talk about this as the need to deal with those feelings, thoughts, and questions learners may have about a new learning experience. Mahoney (1991) suggests that many adults carry "baggage" or outside influences into the learning setting that can adversely affect their ability for successful participation. Brown, Hastings, and Palmer (1970) describe how bio or circadian rhythms may affect a person's ability to perform at certain times of the day. Thus, it is important in the II process that an instructor deal with such conditions as humanistically as possible in creating a positive learning environment.

Understanding the Social/Cultural Influences. A third aspect of any learning environment concerns the various social and cultural complexities that instructors and learners face as they engage in any educational endeavor. Many social and cultural aspects will influence learner performance or participation in both visible and subtle ways. Unfortunately, for many instructors it is often difficult or it feels uncomfortable to deal with some of the social or cultural dilemmas that exist any time you bring a group of learners together.

For example, Collard and Stalker (1991) assert that the various social or cultural understandings related to gender differences often result in oppression and exploitation even in the classroom. The predominance of males as members of teaching, training, or design faculties often is a visible sign, but there frequently are situations in which oppression may exist in less visible ways. By way of illustration, Kolodny (1991) describes how in a biomedical engineering program, females dropped out at higher rates than men in later stages of their training because of approaches the faculty used in the classroom:

> When presented with the detailed medical history of a specific patient, the women generally excelled in the problem solving needed to develop a biomedical solution. Though they didn't name it as such, these young women were using empathy as a learning strategy. What frustrated them was that instructors rarely introduced specific case histories; raw data abstracted from case studies made up the bulk of the material presented in the classroom. In that learning context, the men performed better than the women. And the women switched majors. (p. A44)

SENSORY CONCERNS	SEATING CONCERNS	SOCIAL/CULTURAL CONCERNS
___ Adequate lighting ___ Absence of glare ___ Lighting adequate for A/V devices ___ Attractive/appropriate colors and decorations ___ Adequate acoustics ___ Adequate sound amplification ___ Any noise to be reduced or eliminated ___ Temperature adequate for season of the year ___ Adequate ventilation or adequate air conditioning ___ "Warm" or "caring" setting	___ Adjustable seats or alternative choices ___ Adequate cushioning if used for long periods ___ Can person's legs be crossed comfortably? ___ Straight back and flat pan for people with back problems ___ Adequate sturdiness/size ___ Easily moved around ___ Seat height from floor incorporated into plans ___ Left handed learner provided for	___ Overt or subtle gender discrimination existing ___ Overt or subtle age discrimination existing ___ Overt or subtle racial discrimination existing ___ Facilitators trained for age, race, and gender sensitivity ___ Sociopetal discussion/seating relationships facilitated ___ Knowledge of various for cultures and associated histories ___ Women learners disempowered or devalued in any way

FURNISHINGS CONCERNS	GENERAL CONCERNS	PSYCHOLOGICAL/EMOTIONAL CONCERNS
___ Adequate table or writing space ___ Can furnishings be rearranged for small group work or sociopetal needs? ___ Table space available for refreshments/resources ___ If sitting at tables, can the learners cross their legs? ___ If learners sit at tables, can tables be arranged in a square, circle, or U-shape? ___ Absence of ragged or sharp edges on all furnishings ___ Adequate sturdiness for all furnishings ___ Can learners see each other adequately when seated? ___ Can learners see facilitator adequately when seated?	___ Adequate access/egress to site for learners ___ Adequate signage to direct learners to appropriate sites ___ Lavatory/cafeteria/refreshment machines nearby ___ Adequate parking nearby ___ Adequate lighting in parking area and building hallways ___ Adequate space shape and size in learning site ___ Breakout rooms/areas available if needed ___ Does the learning site have flexibility and provide for learner movement if needed? ___ Learners facilitated in using computer technology	___ Learners helped to become acquainted with each other ___ Learners helped to feel at ease and relaxed ___ Special attention given to the very first encounter with learners ___ Barriers learners may face addressed by facilitators ___ Barriers learners may face addressed by administrators ___ Learners helped to take more control of own learning ___ Facilitators trained in adult learning literature and theory ___ Facilitators trained in adult teaching techniques and theory

Figure 1. A checklist for analyzing the learning environment.
[Adapted from Hiemstra (1991b) and Hiemstra & Sisco (1990)]

Belenky, Clinchy, Goldberger, and Tarule (1986), Gilligan (1982), Hayes (1989), Moir and Jesseo (1992), Tannen (1990), and The Group for Collaborative Inquiry (1993) are some of the voices urging instructors to better understand women's ways of knowing, study, and discourse.

Colin and Preciphs (1991) talk about stereotypic perceptual patterns regarding people and even racism that exist in some learning situations. They suggest that many educators do not overtly confront existing inaccurate perceptions or racism but instead focus on safer or more non-threatening issues. Tisdell (1993) describes how power relationships based on race, class, age, and gender can affect adult learning. This means that instructors in the II process, as well as those using any other process, must constantly dig deep inside themselves to confront racism, gender bias, or other social or cultural issue that may inhibit the learning environment.

Creating an Informal Learning Environment. In many traditional teaching and learning situations, a teacher or trainer typically works at the front of the room presenting information, tightly directing the learning experiences, and creating a fairly formal situation in which the instructor is perceived as the expert and learners are expected to receive information or knowledge from that expert. Obviously, this is not the situation with all teachers operating from something other than the humanist paradigm. However, when it is the case, learners in such settings often become dependent on what the instructor says or does. In many instances this "dependent" learner may spend considerable energy worrying about future evaluations or tests or trying to "figure out" what an instructor wants or expects.

Thus, another important function within the II process is the establishment of an informal learning environment. This means that the facilitator comes to be seen as something other than the sole or primary expert and instead becomes more of a colleague who helps learners think about multiple ways for obtaining knowledge. Involved, too, is promoting in learners a reliance on self and an assumption of personal responsibility for learning. This usually facilitates learners taking early ownership for personal involvement in any subsequent learning activities.

Developing the Instructional Plan

In more traditional teaching and learning approaches, instructors plan most of the content, activities, and experiences. However, step three in the II process involves spending some initial time describing to learners several expected focal points for subsequent learning, but not specifying all the topics, activities, or experiences that may be encountered in the course. Thus, rather than prejudging what is best for a particular group of learners, time is allotted for determining exactly what should be studied.

Assessing Individual and Group Needs. Developing a learning plan together is important in promoting feelings of personal ownership by learners. For example, the first few hours of a II learning experience include some efforts to determine both individual and group needs. This involves such activities as completing a needs diagnosis form, discussing such needs and ways to prioritize them with fellow students, and facilitating ways individual needs can be compared with group needs to indicate areas for concentrated study by each person outside of what is covered during group sessions. Figures 2a and 2b detail a typical needs assessment tool that could be used during this step in the II process.

After assessing the needs of this group of learners, the instructor's role at this point is to design a logical flow of events for meeting group needs. This normally involves developing a session-by-session schedule that now resembles more traditional instructional schedules or plans. It includes information on learning topics, events, activities, assignments, and resources. An instructor often can utilize many of the resources and learning activities developed or compiled during the pre-planning efforts of Step One. However, the needs diagnosis process will have identified some needs that are unique to that particular group, so new or redesigned learning experiences and resources are often required.

Such a design or learning plan is shared with learners at the next possible opportunity for their review and feedback. After such feedback, any necessary modifications are made, although, if possible, some flexible time should be included to meet some of the needs that will emerge or evolve during the remainder of the learning process. The next procedure is to provide the final plan to learners as the framework they are to use to understand what is happening in subsequent group sessions and as a basis for the design of their individual learning contracts. In essence, a percentage of time has been devoted at the beginning of the group sessions to tailoring a learning plan aimed at meeting unique needs of a specific group of learners.

DIAGNOSTIC FORM

Name   Date

The diagnostic form is designed to assist you in assessing your level of competence and need related to possible content areas for the course, for personal study, and for assisting in the construction of a learning contract. The information will help you identify and develop many of the professional competencies required to understand adult learners and adult learning. The information will also help your instructor in planning to meet the needs of this group.

For each potential content area, please check the most relevant column indicating a "self-rating." Any specific needs that are not met by course experiences should guide your personal emphasis on learning activities and the development of a relevant learning contract.

To assist in the decision regarding which column to check for each area, use the information below. Make your best estimation of current strengths and weaknesses. In addition, please feel free to add other content areas you believe are related to the course content or for which you have special needs.

DK If you are uncertain regarding the relation between the listed area and your current level of need or competence and you would like or need to explore this relation further through discussion, reading, independent study, etc.

LO If your current competence related to the listed area is especially low, but could be raised toward a desired level through specific learning experiences.

MD If your past experiences have provided part of the desired competence and some learning experiences would develop the remainder.

HI If your past experiences have substantially developed the listed area.

Figure 2a. A typical needs assessment tool.

Developing a Learning Contract. A learning contract is a tool utilized by learners to plan for and specify many of the activities, experiences, and resources of relevance to their involvement in a course or training event. Knowles (1986) provides a variety of examples and approaches to using learning contracts. Figure 3 portrays a typical learning contract.

In the II process, the contract enables learners to match their individual needs with those group activities and experiences described in the learning plan. Some learners' needs will match fairly closely the overall group needs, so they will spend individual time studying some of the group topics in considerable detail. Others will have identified needs as important for intensive personal study that are not scheduled for inclusion in group sessions.

Detailing goals, learning resources, timelines, evaluation criteria, and learning verification strategies serve to facilitate good planning and build personal ownership for subsequent

Potential Content Areas	Self-Rate Your Competence			
	DK	LO	MD	HI
1. Adult learning theory and research				
2. Barriers to learning/participation				
3. Developmental differences among and between men and women				
4. The adult as learner				
5. The theory of margin (load/power concepts)				
6. Motivation for adult learning				
7. Stages of development/life transitions				
8. General learning theory				
9. Learning/cognitive styles				
10. Learning how to learn				
11. Self-directed learning				
12. Facilitator roles and responsibilities				
13. Perspective transformation/paradigm shifts				
14. Application of theory to various settings				
15. A personal philosophy of working with adults as learners				
16. Other (or use back side for other needs)				

Now that you have completed your self-ratings, please go back and numerically rank each "LO" you checked according to perceived importance. Think of this in terms of the amount of time you should allot outside of the time spent on in-class discussions. This might help you think about areas of concentration for your individual projects and in the design of your learning contract.

Figure 2b.   A typical needs assessment tool *(continued).*

study efforts. Frequently, the instructor can provide various kinds of support in terms of suggesting possible learning activities, materials, and resources (the next section provides some information on learning activity possibilities). Feedback from the instructor or trainer in terms of any needed clarification or change or to provide additional information usually is an added feature.

Learning Activity Identification

The fourth step in the II process is the identification of various learning efforts or activities that build knowledge and develop those competencies appropriate to the needs the learners have identified. Some of this work will have started at the preplanning stage (Step One), but some of it will involve new efforts in response to the various needs identified for that particular group of learners.

Learner: __John Doe__   Course: __# IDE 502 Adult Learning__

What are you going to learn (objectives)?	How are you going to learn it (resources/strategies)?	Target date for completion	How are you going to know that you learned it (evidence)?	How are you going to prove you learned (verification)?
Improve my ability to participate in a class	Actively participate in the face-to face sessions	End of course	Self-perceptions about contributions	Seek feedback from instructor and colleagues
Improve my general understanding of adult learning theory, literature, and research	1. Actively participate in the course 2. Complete a learning contract	1. End of the course 2. First draft by fifth week	1. Keep a log of my learnings 2. Approved first draft and second draft if needed	1. Ask instructor for feedback 2. All contract tasks completed
Acquire much more information about adult learning literature	1. Read the two texts 2. Read at least 10 journal articles and/or other items related to adult learning	End of course	1. Reading log (see term project) 2. A book review	Ask instructor for feedback on both
Improve my understanding of myself as a learner	1. Complete at least three self-assessment instruments 2. Talk to colleagues at work about my learning strengths and weaknesses	1. End of the course 2. Throughout the course	Write a paper that summarizes my personal findings and describes some of the implications for improving my work as a learner and with learners	Ask both instructor and several colleagues at work for some feedback
Develop new understanding of my own philosophy for working with adults as learners	1. Participate in the class mini workshop on philosophy 2. Complete the philosophy instrument in the workbook. 3. Talk with colleagues about "work" philosophy	1. When it is presented 2. End of course 3. Throughout the course	Write a statement of personal philosophy that represents both my own and my work situation	Ask both instructor and my supervisor for some feedback
Improve my understanding of basic adult learning theory	1. Participate in class discussion about theories 2. Read several books and articles on theories	1. Throughout the the course 2. By end of course	The written report and my subsequent discussion of the implications with my colleagues	Ask instructor and my work colleagues for feedback on my understanding and proposed implications
Enhance my understanding of the implications for work from the knowledge on adults as learners	1. Read at least four books listed in the bibliography 2. Annotate ideas, reflections, and new learnings in a reading log	End of course	Extensive reading log where I will both summarize and interact with my readings	Ask instructor for feedback

Figure 3.   A simulated learning contract for a course on adult learning.

This typically involves describing in a workbook (or in subsequent information presented to learners) information about such learning activities, how learners can access necessary learning resources, and how they can think about recording or organizing some of the new knowledge they acquire. The next major section describes some learning activity possibilities.

There are two remaining steps in the II process. The fifth step, carrying out and monitoring the progress of initial planning efforts, begins to parallel the more traditional instructional processes. It involves implementing a variety of learning activities, resources, and experiences in keeping with the learning plan mutually negotiated between the instructor and learners. This might entail lecturing about certain topics; however, to maintain interest, other techniques that can be used include group discussion, case study analysis, role playing, debates, teaching teams, outside experts, computerized programs, and even electronic discussions.

The sixth step, evaluation and feedback, involves helping learners to assess the value of their own learning efforts as well as critiquing the instructor and the instructional process.

This typically is tied to learning contract plans and frequently requires considerable and on-going feedback from the instructor. Such evaluative information also can provide benchmark data for subsequent times that the course or training session is conducted.

Learning Activity Ideas

There are many possible learning activities, strategies, and approaches. The II process involves helping learners become aware of such possibilities and planning for their use as part of the learning contract development effort. This section's purpose is to describe a few of these as examples.

Information Collection and Critical Reflection Approaches

There are a number of ways that learners can gather information and think critically about it in terms of meeting learning needs, acquiring new information, or promoting aware-ness of what is possible. One is called an interactive reading log. This involves a procedure whereby learners record and reflect on information they acquire pertaining to one or more of their individual needs. Such information can come from books, periodicals, audio-visual materials, and electronic communications.

The idea is to interact with the material by simulating a dialogue with the author(s), recording areas of agreement and disagreement, or reading in a manner that Knowles (1975) calls a proactive approach so as to determine some of the motivations or questions the orig-inal author might have set. Elbow (1973, 1981) describes another technique he calls "cooking," in which the reader attempts to determine an interaction of contrasting and conflicting ma-terials in a document and ascertain the heart of any content.

Following is a summary of some tips or strategies pertaining to interactive reading activities:

1. An interactive reading log involves a series of reactions to those aspects of any lit-erature piece the reader finds particularly meaningful or provocative.
2. Items selected for inclusion or reactive responses can include a variety of written in-formation or material disseminated in other forms and can contain part or all of such items.
3. Readers can skip some sections which don't appear interesting or relevant, skim others, and read others more carefully for intensive interactions.
4. No particular guidelines are mandated for any learner in terms of the type, quan-tity, or nature of the reading or even subsequent recording and interacting. Instead, in keeping with the humanistic paradigm and as a means for helping learners as-sume considerable personal responsibility, each learner can be encouraged to find a personal interactive reading and recording style.
5. Readers can be encouraged to raise various questions about the nature of written materials, such as do they appear to be supported by research or experience, can they be verified, and do they appear to have practical utility.

There are other approaches that can be used, too. Christensen (1981), Gross (1977), and Progoff (1975) describe some excellent uses of a journal or diary for recording personal feel-ings and reflections about topics being studied. Jones (1995) describes how portfolios can be used to collect, record, and display information. Brookfield (1989) describes a variety of ways that critical reflection can be enhanced through helping adults explore alternative ways of thinking and acting. Creating theory logs and media logs are other examples.

Small Group Activities

Inherent to success in the II process is a belief in synergism, which not only makes energy, excitement, and new learnings possible, but often multiplies them when two or more people study and discuss information or knowledge together. For example, several learners joining together in a study group on some topic related to the course typically review and critique some written material on a topic of mutual interest in order to obtain various opinions on meanings and implications for practice or research. Such opinions or discoveries usually are shared, critiqued, and recorded in some fashion.

For instance, a typical small group experience involves a few people discussing material they have read. There might be stimulator or discussion questions prepared by the instructor. They might engage in some type of debate in which certain group members deliberately take one side of an issue and other group members another side. On other occasions, learners themselves will generate questions.

After discussion over some period of time, perhaps from only a few minutes to several hours and ranging over multiple times talking together, it is not unusual to ask or expect that group members will develop some written materials as a response or summary. The facilitator or instructor usually provides some sort of feedback in the form of written or oral comments as a mechanism to help students obtain outside opinions on how well they did in understanding the information. Figure 4 provides an example of a study group description sheet that is shared with learners.

STUDY GROUP ACTIVITY

I. Preparation
   A. In forming a group from among your classmates, determine how you will meet and communicate.
   B. Determine workable meeting times or communication procedures and select a group coordinator.
   C. Select some aspect of teaching or training adults you would like to study.
   D. Select two or more journals and/or two or more books related to the study group's focus so that each person is reading at least two articles or two chapters.
   E. Divide up the reading responsibilities based on such criteria as availability, variety, controversies, etc.
   F. Prepare article abstracts or chapter summaries for use in the study group. Submit the summaries to each other.
   G. Meet in person one or more times and discuss the materials thoroughly.

II. Presentation
   A. Produce a group report summarizing the materials discussed and the general focus of the direction. In other words, devise some method to record the primary points made during the preparation and discussion.
   B. The length typically varies from 10–25 pages.
   C. Submit the group report prior to the end of the course. Keep at least one copy among the group members.

III. Educational Goals for the Activity
   A. To help you increase personal knowledge regarding the central theme of the study area.
   B. To assist you in becoming acquainted with differing points of view.

IV. Miscellaneous
   A. Grading on this activity will include self-evaluation ratings and the instructors' subjectivity on a pass or incomplete basis and in relation to your learning contract.
   B. Written feedback will be provided.

Figure 4. Example of a study group description sheet.

Agency Visits

There usually are a number of learning resources or relevant educational experiences existing within any community (Hiemstra, 1992). One way to obtain exposure to such resources or experiences is to have learners visit agencies, organizations, or programs related to the content area under study. Various schema are available for understanding the nature of such agencies (Hiemstra, 1992; Schroeder, 1980). This is a practical way for learners to obtain information or knowledge through observations, interviews, and various evaluative techniques.

Another useful technique for obtaining new knowledge or experience is to facilitate for learners a mini-internship of some sort within an agency. This might involve shadowing a leader within the organization for several hours. It might include participating in several meetings held within the agency. It might even involve assuming certain ad hoc responsibilities, such as helping to plan or implement some event.

Specialized Study Effort

Another technique is for a student to carry out some type of special study away from the classroom or training session. This might involve studying some aspect of the community or an organization that is related to the subject matter under review. It could include an analysis of how some actions are carried out by various decision-makers. It might involve the development of a special product or resource that could be used by an organization to enhance some aspect of their outreach effort.

Conclusions

These are only a few of the learning activities that are possible. Most skilled instructors or trainers will develop a variety of such activities as they gain experience both with the II process and with any course or training program.

The II process is a proven way of organizing and carrying out instruction with adult learners. However, it is predicated on the humanist paradigm and a belief that such learners are both capable and desirous of assuming increasing responsibility for their own learning, growth, and development. It is hoped that this chapter and the Brockett and Sisco chapters will stimulate readers to consider the paradigm's potential in effective design and delivery of instruction.

References

Belenky, M. F., Clinchy, N. Goldberger, L., & Tarule, J. M. (1986). *Women's ways of knowing: The development of self, voice, and mind.* New York: Basic Books.

Brockett, R. G., & Hiemstra, R. (1991). *Self-direction in learning: Perspectives on theory, research, and practice.* New York: Routledge.

Brookfield, S. D. (1989). *Developing critical thinkers: Challenging adults to explore alternative ways of thinking and acting.* San Francisco: Jossey-Bass.

Brown, F. A., Hastings, J. W., & Palmer, J. D. (1970). *The biological clock: Two views.* Orlando, FL: Academic Press.

Christensen, R. S. (1981, Oct.). Dear diary—a learning tool for adults. *Lifelong Learning: The Adult Years*, 4–5.

Colin, S. A. J., & Preciphs, T. K. (1991). Perceptual patterns and the learning environment: Confronting white racism. In R. Hiemstra (Ed.), *Creating environments for effective adult learning* (New Directions for Adult and Continuing Education, Number 50). San Francisco: Jossey-Bass.

Collard, S., & Stalker, J. (1991). Women's trouble: Women, gender, and the learning environment. In R. Hiemstra (Ed.), *Creating environments for effective adult learning* (New Directions for Adult and Continuing Education, Number 50). San Francisco: Jossey-Bass.

Elbow, P. (1973). *Writing without teachers.* London: Oxford University Press.

Elbow, P. (1981). *Writing with power: Techniques for mastering the writing process.* New York: Oxford University Press.

Elias, J. L., & Merriam, S. (1980). *Philosophical foundations of adult education.* Malabar, FL: Krieger.

Gilligan, C. (1982). *In a different voice: Psychological theory and women's development.* Cambridge, MA: Harvard University Press.

Gross, R. (1977). *The lifelong learner.* New York: Simon and Schuster.

Group for Collaborative Inquiry. (1993). The democratization of knowledge. *Adult Education Quarterly, 43,* 43–51.

Hayes, E. R. (1989). Insights from women's experiences for teaching and learning. In E. R. Hayes (Ed.), *Effective teaching styles* (New Directions for Adult and Continuing Education, Number 43). San Francisco: Jossey-Bass.

Hiemstra, R. (1991a). Aspects of effective learning environments. In R. Hiemstra (Ed.), *Creating environments for effective adult learning* (New Directions for Adult and Continuing Education, Number 50). San Francisco: Jossey-Bass.

Hiemstra, R. (Ed.). (1991b). *Creating environments for effective adult learning* (New Directions for Adult and Continuing Education, Number 50). San Francisco: Jossey-Bass.

Hiemstra, R. (1992). *The educative community.* Syracuse, NY: Syracuse University Publications in Continuing Education.

Hiemstra, R. (1995). Helping learners take responsibility for self-directed activities. In R. Hiemstra & R. Brockett (Eds.), *Overcoming resistance to self-direction in learning* (New Directions for Adult and Continuing Education). San Francisco: Jossey-Bass.

Hiemstra, R., & Sisco, B. (1990). *Individualizing instruction for adult learners: Making learning personal, empowering, and successful.* San Francisco: Jossey-Bass.

Hollis, W. F. (1991). Humanistic learning theory and instructional technology: Is reconciliation possible? *Educational Technology, 31*(11), 49–53.

Jones, J. E. (1995). Portfolio assessment as a strategy for self-direction in learning. In R. Hiemstra & R. Brockett (Eds.), *Overcoming resistance to self-direction in learning* (New Directions for Adult and Continuing Education). San Francisco: Jossey-Bass.

Knowles, M. S. (1975). *Self-directed learning.* New York: Association Press.

Knowles, M. S. (1986). *Using learning contracts.* San Francisco: Jossey-Bass.

Kolodny, A. (1991, February 6). Colleges must recognize students' cognitive styles and cultural backgrounds. *Chronicle of Higher Education,* A44.

Kramlinger, T., & Huberty, T. (1990). Behaviorism versus humanism. *Training and Development Journal, 44*(12), 41–45.

Mahoney, V. L. (1991). Adverse baggage in the learning environment. In R. Hiemstra (Ed.), *Creating environments for effective adult learning* (New Directions for Adult and Continuing Education, Number 50). San Francisco: Jossey-Bass.

Maslow, A. (1976). Education and peak experience. In C. D. Schlosser (Ed.), *The person in education: A humanistic approach.* New York: Macmillan.

Miller, B. W., & Hotes, R. W. (1982). Almost everything you always wanted to know about individualized instruction. *Lifelong Learning: The Adult Years, 5*(9), 20–23.

Moir, A., & Jesseo, D. (1992). *Brain sex.* New York: Dell Publishing.

Patterson, C. H. (1973). *Humanistic education.* Englewood Cliffs, NJ: Prentice-Hall.

Pratt, D. D. (1984). Teaching adults: A conceptual framework for the first session. *Lifelong Learning: An Omnibus of Practice and Research, 7*(6), 7–9, 28, 31.

Progoff, I. (1975). *At a journal workshop.* New York: Dialogue House Library.

Rogers, C. R. (1977). *Carl Rogers on personal power.* New York: Delacorte Press.

Schroeder, W. L. (1980). Typology of adult learning systems. In J. M. Peters & Associates. *Building an effective adult education enterprise.* San Francisco: Jossey-Bass.

Sisco, B. R. (1991). Setting the climate for effective teaching and learning. In R. Hiemstra (Ed.), *Creating environments for effective adult learning* (New Directions for Adult and Continuing Education, Number 50). San Francisco: Jossey-Bass.

Tannen, D. (1990). _You just don't understand: Women and men in conversation._ New York: William Morrow.

Tisdell, E. J. (1993). Interlocking systems of power, privilege, and oppression in adult higher education classes. _Adult Education Quarterly, 43,_ 203–226.

Valett, R. E. (1977). _Humanistic education: Developing the total person._ St. Louis: C. V. Mosby.

Vosko, R. S. (1991). Where we learn shapes our learning. In R. Hiemstra (Ed.), _Creating environments for effective adult learning_ (New Directions for Adult and Continuing Education, Number 50). San Francisco: Jossey-Bass.

Wlodkowski, R. J. (1985). _Enhancing adult motivation to learn._ San Francisco: Jossey-Bass.

33

Strategic Teaching Framework: An Instructional Model for Learning Complex, Interactive Skills[1]

Thomas M. Duffy
Indiana University, Bloomington

In this chapter, I describe the Strategic Teaching Framework (STF) instructional model for supporting the development of complex, interactive skills. The model grew out of our[2] efforts to support teachers in adopting new approaches to teaching. The result of that work was the design of a hypermedia-based information system, the Strategic Teaching Framework Information System (STFIS)[3] (Fishman & Duffy, 1992), and the Reflective Problem Solving Instructional System.

While the current STF model is related to teacher education, we see STF as a more general model applying to any complex practice, e.g., counseling, sales, consulting, troubleshooting a complex system, etc. As the examples indicate, while our focus has been on the interaction between people, the STF model could readily be applied to an individual's use of complex technology (see, e.g., Rowland, 1991). Perhaps the limitation in the generality of the model is to situations in which performance:

- is dynamic, demanding the ability to continuously adapt responses to situational cues (see, e.g., Suchman, 1987), and/or
- involves an ongoing complex interaction.

I begin this chapter by considering the teacher education need that STF addresses and how that need was translated into an instructional goal. Our development of the instructional model to meet this need was guided by certain assumptions about how people learn and what it means to "understand." After discussing the key assumptions we have made about learning, I describe the two components of the STF model: the Information System and the Reflective Problem Solving Instructional System. In each case, I first describe the principles (instructional and design) that guided the development process and then describe the actual implementation. I conclude by summarizing the general characteristics of the model.

The Problem: A Need for New Approaches to Teaching

Teaching practices have come under tremendous scrutiny of late, in large measure because of the widespread dissatisfaction with the results of those practices. The typical teaching practice has been most often characterized as didactic instruction in which information is presented to children to learn with little consideration for the use of that information. The textbook dominates, in large measure dictating both the content and the process of learning. Children, of course, learn in this environment—they pass the test. But, unfortunately, much of what is learned remains inert and disconnected from the demands and issues of everyday life (Bransford, Franks, Vye, & Sherwood, 1989). In essence, the emphasis tends to be on the acquisition of a domain of knowledge with little instruction focusing on the use of that knowledge in larger contexts.

Professional teaching associations in all the content areas are now calling for a new, more student-centered approach to teaching[4] (AAAS, 1993; Brooks & Brooks, 1993; Mathematics Association of America, 1991; NCTM, 1991; Rutherford & Ahlgren, 1990). The National Council of Teachers of Mathematics, one of the first to define the new goals for teachers and teaching, notes that in this new instructional environment, teachers must be proficient in—among other things—"selecting mathematical tasks to engage students' interests and intellect; providing opportunities to deepen students' understanding of the mathematics being studied and its applications; orchestrating classroom discourse in ways that promote the investigation and growth of mathematical ideas; using, and helping students use, technology and other tools to pursue mathematical investigations; seeking, and helping students seek, connections to previous and developing knowledge; [and] guiding individual, small-group, and whole-class work" (NCTM, 1991, p. 1).

The emphasis in mathematics, as well as in the other disciplines, is on engaging the learner in authentic uses of information and on increasing the student's responsibility and ownership for the learning activity. The goal is to engage the learner in authentic activity (cognitive and behavioral) as part of a learning community. There are a wide variety of instructional strategies that can be used to achieve these constructivist goals, but several instructional strategies in particular have been emphasized. First, instruction should be centered around problems or the big issues in a domain; these problems and issues are used to provide a larger context or anchor for specific learning activities (see, e.g., CTGV, 1992). Second, collaborative groups are used to create a discourse community for sharing and testing ideas against alternative perspectives. Third, instructional strategies that link abstract and concrete representations of a concept, e.g., using manipulatives in mathematical problem solving or developing a local history in the social sciences, serve to support the interplay of concrete and abstract thinking.

Underlying all of these strategies is an important change in the relationship between teacher and learner. We all agree that in the learning process the teacher and the learner are working together in the child's zone of proximal development. However, as Scardamalia and Bereiter (1991) put it, the key question is, who has ownership of the work in that zone? In traditional instruction, the teacher is in control, identifying in detail what is to be learned, how it is to be learned, and the criteria for learning. The learner's job is to follow the teacher's directions. In the new learning environments, the student more fully shares ownership of the learning environment and hence the teacher must be responsive to the child.

The role of the teacher changes from a presenter of information to that of coach, guide, collaborator and a multiplicity of other roles related to supporting and challenging the child's thinking. This shift in the teacher's role can be characterized in terms of a shift from teaching actions that are dictated by a pre-specified plan to teaching that is dictated to a greater degree by the current situation (Suchman, 1987). By the "current situation," I mean the instructional goals of the teacher, the response of the child or children to the particular question or task, and all other factors in the immediate context that might influence the moment-to-moment actions of the teacher. Under the traditional approach to instruction, the materials could be designed so that the teacher simply "executed" the instructional plan, following the script. Clearly this will be impossible in this new instructional environment. To be effective in this dynamic environment, the teacher must be guided by a stable pedagogical framework (simple procedures or a script will not do) and be able to reflect on and apply that framework in an automatic fashion while responding to the classroom dynamics. In essence, the plan is under constant revision in response to the current context and guided by the pedagogical framework. In Schön's (1987) terms, the teacher is a reflective practitioner who reflects-*in*-action.

The Instructional Goal

Our goal was to design an instructional system that would help teachers to develop this new approach to teaching. It seemed clear to us that there was a need not just for learning new teaching strategies or procedures but also a new pedagogical framework for thinking about or interpreting those strategies. The pedagogical framework is critical to the details of how a strategy is implemented and integrated with the rest of instruction and hence it is critical to overall effectiveness of the strategies.

The teaching strategies addressed included having the children work collaboratively and the use of problem solving activities in which the students use information rather than simply "mastering" the domain.[5] Using the language of NCTM, quoted above, the use of problem solving, collaboration, and other strategies are meant to engage student's interests and intellect, promote discourse that leads to investigation and the growth of ideas, and deepen their understanding. In sum, we saw the central goal as shifting the teacher's focus from instruction, and hence on what he or she is doing in the classroom, to one of learning, in which the focus is on the child's thinking and how to support the child in developing more effective thinking skills in the domain.

Our task, then, was to promote both conceptual change and the development of new teaching strategies. However, as the research literature has amply demonstrated, conceptual change is not so easily achieved. It cannot be taught through didactic presentation and it is not going to be obtained through a weekend workshop. Rather, the change must arise from the learners' (our teachers') own construction of a model of learner-centered teaching and from a collaborative environment in which they can test their constructions, evaluate alternative perspectives, and reflect on their own teaching.

In summary, the general call for restructuring the teaching and learning environment was the impetus for this project. The learning or instructional goals arose from our analysis of the national call for the restructuring of teaching as well as from our analysis of the research and theory on teaching and learning. Achieving those goals will require a system that will support long-term professional development.

Assumptions About Learning

The design of our learning environment was guided not only by our analysis of the instructional needs of the teachers, but also by our assumptions about learning and understanding. Three key assumptions were made about learning.

Knowledge is *in* our interactions with the environment. This is perhaps the most fundamental assumption about learning: learning is in our experiences. The content, the context, the learners' goals and the activity of the learner are all inextricably linked in determining what is learned. A fundamental implication of this is that we cannot distinguish between "learning about" and "learning"; it is all learning! To understand what is learned, we must understand this complex learning environment.

Traditional information processing views of learning also emphasize the active processing of the learner. The active learning in those traditional models determines how strongly the information was stamped into memory (rehearsal) or how well it is embedded into the cognitive networks in our heads (elaborative encoding). However, there is little question as to what is learned—it is still an information transmission model and simply a matter of effective storage of the message.

The constructivist view of learning is illustrated by considering the task of designing instruction to aid learners in becoming experts in some domain: expert chess players, expert auto mechanics, expert instructional designers, etc. In conducting an analysis of the instructional requirements we might, for example, use the program SemNet to capture the semantic network of the expert's knowledge (Allen & Hoffman, 1993) and then ask the expert to elaborate on each of the nodes so that we would have a concept map with an expert elaboration on each node in the map. Now, how do we use that information to develop new experts? Surely no one would propose that we teach the map to the learners with the assumption that when they can produce the same map and elaborate it in the same way, they will have expert knowledge. At least we certainly hope no one would propose this! Yet, when we look at the system of schooling and when we look at much of teacher training, we see exactly this model of instruction—learners master the content of textbooks written by experts.

In contrast to this knowledge transmission view, we would argue that we must look at the experiences of the expert—not what is stored in the expert's head—and provide those experiences for the learner. The understanding of the expert is indexed by the experiences of the expert—and thus those experiences—not the knowledge base or current understanding—must be the focus of instruction. Of course we cannot replicate the actual experiences of the expert and as instructional designers we do not want to do that—it simply would not be efficient. However, the point I wish to make is that when we are designing instruction, we should be focusing on the activities of the learner as much if not more than on the information base used in those activities. These activities must engage the learner in authentic, cognitive challenges (Honebein, Duffy, & Fishman, 1993).

We assume that the expert understanding is developed through reflection on what it means to learn; through observation and analysis of teacher and learner activities in relationship to their understanding of learning; and through testing their views in the classroom. Thus, these are the expert's interactions with the environment that are the authentic activities we must provide our learners. The design of our instructional system must promote this analysis and reflection. We must support the learners in developing their own visions of learning and their own approaches to teaching that is consistent with those visions. We must also support them in testing their understanding.

The goal is truly to automatize—not to automatize procedures, but rather to automatize the interpretative application of the pedagogical model in the process of teaching. That is, the goal is the development of the ability to reflect-in-action. The teaching strategies offered must not be "how to" in a detailed prescriptive fashion, but rather must provide the opportunity for the teacher to learn.

Understanding develops as learners test their representations (constructions) against alternative representations. The constructivist view outlined in the previous paragraphs is often interpreted as meaning that "anything goes," i.e., any individual's construction is as good as that of anyone else. Nothing could be further from the truth. Constructivists emphasize the social nature of learning in general and collaborative learning in particular. Indeed, a key strategy for testing understanding is through discussion in a social/collaborative environment. The goal is to see how one's own view compares to other views, to see what evidence or focus others brought to bear in working on the same problem, and to evaluate the perspectives of others. A second strategy for testing understanding is to see how well it works. At base, this means addressing the question of how well it accounts for what we "know" about the world or how well it "solves" the problem. The goal, as Rorty (1991) notes, is to develop viable understandings and to continually seek to increase viability.

The implication of this assumption about learning is that the design of our instructional system must provide mechanisms for teachers to test their understanding against alternative views and to test their understanding in actual teaching practices.

What is learned is determined in large part by the goals of the learner. Too often in instructional design, we focus on the instructional goal and ignore the goals of the individual learners. Task analysis and instructional sequencing are organized around the instructional goals. From our constructivist point of view, the goal of the learner is central to determining what is learned. This is really a corollary to the assertion that understanding is a constructive process. An individual's goal in learning, i.e., the individual's purpose for learning, determines what is attended to and, perhaps more importantly, how we understand what we attend to. We have different understandings and different memories of a content domain depending on the puzzlement or goals that guided the learning. Underlying this statement is the assumption that the learning process is guided by and organized around each individual's own learning goals. Dewey (1938) talked about a "perturbation" being the stimulus for learning, while Piaget (1977) talked in terms of learning occurring through accommodation of information which cannot be readily assimilated into existing schema. Here we use the term "puzzlement" to reflect the learner's goal, i.e., to describe the inadequate understanding that directs the constructive process.

In school, the goal of the learner is typically to pass the test. What is attended to when studying a text, and how it is attended to, will depend on whether the student expects an essay test, a multiple choice test, or a short answer test. It will also depend on the student's understanding of the teacher's item construction practices, e.g., the tendency to ask trick questions or to focus on definitions. The importance of the goals of the learners in determining understanding is perhaps most obvious to anyone who has taught a course to adults who have diverse, real world experience. In contrast to the "academic" understanding we so often demand and that the younger students all too willingly provide, the understanding of these mature students is typically contextualized in their previous work experiences. They want to apply the learning to their lives and their jobs and so how they understand the concepts is contextualized in these concrete uses of knowledge.

This understanding of learner goals impacts the design of our learning environment at two levels. At the most basic level, we clearly have a learning goal of aiding teachers in adopting a new conceptual framework and new teaching strategies. If the teacher does not adopt this basic goal, then the system can be of little help. Hence, if the principal simply dictates the learning requirement, we have little expectation that the necessary conceptual change will occur. At another level, however, given that the teachers have a goal of change, the learning environment must be designed to support and challenge the learner's focus. Rather than an instructional system that has predetermined instructional paths that the learner must follow, we designed an information system and then provided guidance and support in using this system to construct and test understanding of this new view of learning and its realization in the classroom.

The Instructional Model

The constructivist learning principles described in the previous section led us to the development of an instructional model that has two basic components: (1) an information system, to aid teachers in developing and testing their understanding of learner-centered approaches to teaching; and, (2) an instructional strategy that would provide support for the process of working with the information base and for applying that understanding to their classroom practices.

In developing this model, we have not addressed strategies for motivating the learners to adopt any particular learning goal. We make the presumption that the learner comes to the system with these goals already established. We are providing tools to aid the learners in achieving their goals—the model is designed to aid the learners in resolving *their* problems. In the specific instance of aiding teachers in adopting a learner-centered approach to teaching, there are two likely sources from which this goal might have developed: the teacher's own dissatisfaction with his or her classroom and the desire to restructure; or, the discussion through the professional organizations where goals are being set that are consistent with this framework for teaching (AAAS, 1993; NCTM, 1989, 1991; Rutherford & Ahlgren, 1990).

Strategic Teaching Framework Information System
Design Principles

The metaphor guiding the design of STFIS is that of visiting a classroom in which expert teaching is observed, information about the teaching is obtained, and questions are posed. The expert teachers in some sense are models, but the goal is not to support the student-teachers in imitating the expert's teaching process, but rather to provide experts as a vehicle for analyzing and reflecting upon the teaching strategies.

These teachers and their classrooms are the core of our learning support materials, and thus the process of identifying the master teachers is critical. The master teachers are ones who have been identified as exemplary by the North Central Regional Education Laboratory in their national survey of experts who were involved in teacher training and were major contributors to the educational research on teaching in their subject matter area (Jones, Knuth, & Duffy, 1993). Three criteria guided the process for selecting the elementary mathematics teachers used in our first module. First, they were identified as teachers who worked with collaborative groups, used problem solving as the primary approach to teaching, and used questioning techniques that were learner centered to help the student become an effective decision maker and problem solver.

The second criterion in selecting teachers was that they were judged as exemplary by experts in the field. We must emphasize that the goal was not to find "perfect" teachers; such a goal is obviously impossible to achieve. Rather, it was to find someone who was simply an extremely effective teacher recommended by leaders in the field.

The third criterion was that the teacher could articulate what he or she was trying to accomplish. As I will describe in a moment, reflection on the teaching is a critical component of the design of our information system, and hence it was critical that the teachers could articulate a coherent pedagogical perspective that guided their teaching.

These master teachers provided the core of the information system—they were the key resources for building the STFIS. Four design principles guided our use of these master teachers as an information resource.

1. Focus on teaching process within content domains. Our focus is on general strategies for teaching, regardless of content, and on the pedagogical model underlying those strategies. However, we recognize that an understanding of the strategies and the pedagogy must be contextualized in the content. Hence, we focused on developing separate modules for each major content domain (mathematics, social studies, language/English, and science) and range of grade levels (elementary, middle, and high school). The idea is that the learner can study the pedagogy and strategies within the context of the content domain and age level that they work with. We have completed, and are currently field testing, the Elementary Mathematics module.

While we feel it is necessary to contextualize the instruction in the specific content/age level domains, we did not engage in further decomposition of the content areas. That is, methods courses in teacher education focus on how to decompose and present specific content in the domain, e.g., how to decompose and sequence the teaching of whole numbers, fractions, multiplication of decimals, etc. We could not include this level of content linkage in our system. Rather we focus on a class period of instruction and the particular content that was taught during that period. The reflective problem solving instructional strategy that guides the use of the information system is used to support the teachers in transferring the understanding of that context to the specific content they are teaching at the time.

This concern about the linkage of content and classroom teaching strategies is both a practical and a theoretical issue. At the practical level, one simply cannot link the classroom strategies to all content topics. This is not only true of teaching but of virtually any complex environment, e.g., sales training or troubleshooting complex equipment. Rather, we must train for transfer. Nonetheless, at a theoretical level, there is considerable research indicating how strategies are embedded in the deep understanding of specific content and hence transfer in general is difficult to obtain (see, e.g., Chi, Glaser, & Farr, 1988). We have addressed the issue by embedding our instruction in an exemplar of the content area (i.e., a particular topic) and then supporting the transfer process by promoting the learner's (teacher's) reflection and transfer to new topics. The issue of transfer is a concern for us, as it should be to all instructional developers, and is the focus of our research related to the use of STF.

2. Bring the richness of the classroom to the learner. This goal has several design implications. Most importantly, the richness of the classroom interaction is best captured in video and hence the STFIS is centered around classroom video. However, the impact of this design goal extends beyond simply providing video, to the determination of the nature of that video.

- *Situated action.* If we are going to capture the richness of the classroom then we must capture the situated action of the teacher in that classroom. That is, the "richness" of teaching—the expertise—is not in the teacher's execution of a pre-specified procedure but in the teacher's adaptation of approaches to the particular situation. It is in how the teacher integrates instructional goals with the interaction with the children. The implication of this is that STFIS must provide video of "real" classroom interaction. Scripted or otherwise idealized interactions will not do, for they fail to capture the richness of authentic instruction. Thus, STFIS centers around video of unrehearsed and unscripted classroom instruction. We attempted to capture the "normal" interactions of the expert teachers.

- *Integrated instruction.* If we are going to capture the richness of the classroom, then we cannot focus on isolated teaching strategies. Rather we must capture the richness reflected in the orchestration of instruction over the class period. Particular teaching strategies must be understood in the larger, complex teaching environment. The videos in the information system are of whole class periods of instruction. The user can visit a class, much as one might physically do, and watch how the class period is orchestrated.

In realizing this goal, we videotaped several class periods of each of our master teachers using three cameras. Because the focus was on capturing the natural flow of instruction, the camera crew had to be flexible in tracking the action. One camera focused on the students talking, another on the teacher, and a third provided wide angle shots of the class as well as shots of other interesting events that might occur out of the focus of the other cameras. The richest class period, with the best video, was selected for use in STFIS. This video was edited to capture the complete flow of the instructional period. A 50-minute class period might be edited to 45 minutes (we edited out deadtime and time when there was inadequate video/ audio). Note how this approach contrasts with the traditional approach of focusing on particular strategies—here we are focusing on the master teacher working with the children.

3. The understanding of effective teaching must arise out of the learner's own analysis of the master teachers. In designing STF, we did not want to "teach" the learners the "correct" strategies, but rather our goal was to support them in constructing and testing their own understanding of the instruction. As I discussed in the previous section, we viewed it to be essential that the teachers engage in an analysis of the instruction, constructing and, most importantly, testing their own analyses of the teaching (see, for example, the discussion by Spiro *et al.*, 1992, of cognitive flexibility theory). The reality is that a whole array of management, teaching, and content issues are "important" in a rich and dynamic classroom. These design principles led to a design in which the content was presented in an information system rather than taught to the learner. There were several critical design considerations in developing the information system from this perspective:

- *Provide Multiple Models.* Within the Elementary Mathematics module, we provide three master teachers, all within the constructivist framework but each realizing the constructivist goals using different strategies. For example, one teacher has a very formalized approach to collaborative groups. The students work in teams of four and while all are responsible for all aspects of problem solving, they have particular responsibilities to the group as well. Another teacher has a very loose structure in which students work in pairs and are supported in establishing their own working strategies and investigatory goals. The third teacher has groups of five to six students focused on a specific real-world problem for which they must develop and justify a solution. While the particular methods differ considerably, all three teachers reflect the same basic student-centered goals. They listen to the student and question the student based on that student's representation of the problem; they encourage multiple-solution strategies; and they encourage reflection on the process. Offering these alternative classrooms serves two goals. First, it de-emphasizes method and increases the emphasis on the conceptual framework. For example, there are many strategies for organizing collaborative groups, but the important learning issues in any group are in promoting a discourse community in the content domain (using the language of mathematics) and testing one's understanding. Second, providing multiple classrooms offers the potential for the learner to identify a teaching style that is most compatible with his or her personality. In our instructional strategy, which we discuss later, we encourage the learner to focus on one teacher—a teacher who has a compatible style—focusing on understanding the multiple occurrences of the strategy during the class period as well as the integration of the various strategies that result within the instructional "orchestration." It is only after some level of understanding and implementation of these strategies is achieved that we propose that the learners engage in an in-depth analysis of the other teachers' uses of the strategy. This approach differs somewhat from the cognitive flexibility approach (Spiro *et al.*, 1992). We agree that crisscrossing cases and concepts is essential to building a rich understanding of the concepts. However, we think that the integration of the application of the various strategies (pedagogical concepts) by a single teacher is critical. Understanding the strategies in the context of orchestrating the teaching/learning is central. Therefore, we emphasize beginning with a more integrated analysis of a single case, which can then serve as a reference point for the learners when they begin crisscrossing cases and concepts. Also, rather than moving from simple to complex, our emphasis is on understanding the teaching context that best reflects the approach the learner would like to achieve. (If one teacher's approach is more simplistic, it does little good to study that approach if it is not the style consistent with that of the learner.)[6] Thus we see the need to support the learners as they work in the complex environment.

- *Provide Multiple Perspectives.* Rather than defining what is important in each of the classrooms, we chose to offer multiple perspectives on what was important. Again, our goal was to support the teachers in their analysis, rather than to preach to them as to what is important. We collected perspectives from three sources: the teacher in the video, a mathematics educator, and we offered our own perspective. The basic procedure for collecting these perspectives was as follows: We asked the teachers or the mathematics educators to watch the video with us, treating us as a learner trying to adopt this approach to teaching. Their task was to help us understand what was important about the teaching, what might be done differently, and what could be improved. There were no instructions to comment on any specific aspects of the instruction—simply to comment on what they felt was important for a teacher wanting to adopt this approach. Our analysis indicated that the content of the comments could be classified into four categories: management, teaching strategies, the problem and content used, and assessment. Therefore, we organized the comments into these categories and attached them to the video at the points to which they applied. In this way, the learner can watch the classroom, pause at any point, and get three perspectives as to what is important in that particular classroom event. Thus, rather than telling the learner what is important, we provide support—points of view—for their own analysis of what is important.

4. Support the teachers in becoming a part of a community of learners. We think it is essential that the learners/teachers collaborate with other teachers within their school as well as in other schools as they attempt to develop, evaluate, and refine their thinking and practice about learner-centered instruction. In essence, the core features of the learning activity in the STF model—analyzing and reflecting on teaching and considering alternative perspectives—must become part of an actual community of practice. Encouraging and supporting this process is central to the reflective problem-solving instructional strategy. The STFIS was also designed with features that encourage and support collaboration, such as:

- *Notetaking.* We provided a notetaking capability in STFIS that operates much like the expert perspectives. Users can write notes and append them to the video so that they and others can look at their notes on specific events in the video. An index organized by authors also allows the user to review the notes by particular individuals. This strategy for notetaking serves two purposes. First, it encourages the user to become a part of the STFIS rather than simply viewing it as a source of expert information. The user adds his or her perspective along with that of the experts that are built into the system. Second, the notetaking provides the mechanism for collaboration among fellow teachers.

- *Network access.* We think it is important that the collaboration extend beyond the school to form a more diverse community of learners. This not only provides richer perspectives on strategies, but it helps assure that the effort to restructure teaching transcends the day-to-day demands of the school. To support this collaboration, we have provided access to the Internet or other networks relevant to the teacher. This is the least developed component of the STFIS since it only becomes usable once a base of user sites is established.

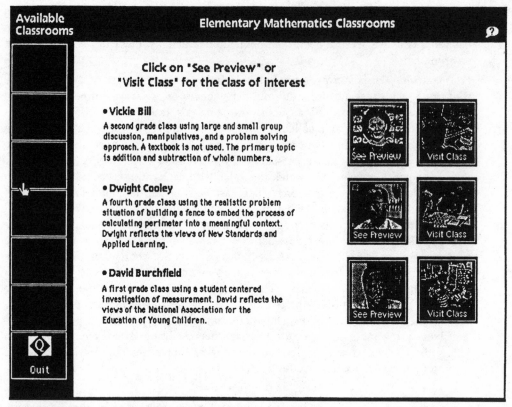

Figure 1. Table of contents screen from Strategic Teaching Frameworks.

Implementing the Design Principles

The previous section outlined the primary design principles for the STFIS. In this section, I describe the system resulting from those principles using the Elementary Mathematics module as the particular implementation.

A learner first encounters a table of contents screen in STFIS (Figure 1). The three classrooms available in the module are briefly described in a text format, and previews are available that provide an overview of the class along with some classroom video. When a classroom is selected for study, the individual can click on "visit classroom." Once in the classroom, all information addresses the teaching in that classroom.

The classroom screen for one teacher, Vicki Bill, is shown in Figure 2. The general controls for navigation and access of special tools are in a column on the left. It is here that the user obtains a summary of the flow of the class and the primary activities.

The top portion of the screen is the video control area. The classroom is divided into sixteen events. These events were imposed to create natural stopping points for listening to perspectives or for discussing the teaching. They represent points in the classroom instruction at which the teacher changes tasks or changes her focus from one group to another—they are natural interruption points. The user can watch the class all the way through or can go to specific events. The activity in each event is shown at the top of the screen when the event is selected. The events are also listed in the documentation and in the information base.

The perspectives on the teaching are available in the lower left portion of the screen. For this classroom we have the perspectives of: Vicki Bill, the classroom teacher; Pete Kloost-

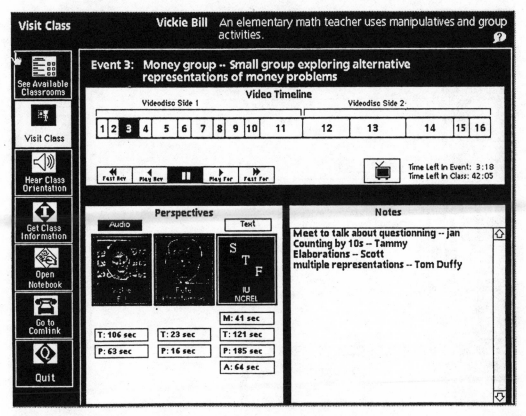

Figure 2. The "visit classroom" screen for examining the teaching of the teacher, Vicki Bill. The screen is divided into four areas: general control, video control, perspectives on the particular events in the classroom, and notes taken by the users on the particular events.

erman, a mathematics education professor; and the STFIS development team. These perspectives change as the user goes from one event to another. The symbols for the perspectives on this event indicate that there is commentary on management (M), teaching strategies (S), and the structure of the problem solving content (P). There are no comments on assessment (A) in this event. The user can either listen to or read the perspective by first selecting "audio" or "text" and then clicking on the perspective.

The notes on the event entered by the learners working with the program are shown in the lower right portion of the screen. Here we see that there are four notes on this event. The notes are attached to the events, so the notes that are shown change as the learner changes events. The learner can add a note at any time by clicking on the notebook icon in the left column of the screen, which opens a word processing window (Figure 3). In saving the note, a title and the author's name are entered. The note title and author name are then listed in the note window as well as in author and event indexes. The note can be accessed from any of these locations by clicking on the title.

This "visit classroom" screen is a temporally organized database that follows the flow of the class. We also provide a conceptually organized database related to the class. After users study the class and identify issues or strategies to study in more detail, they can select the "get information" icon in the left column to go to the conceptual database shown in Figure 4. The conceptual database consists of:

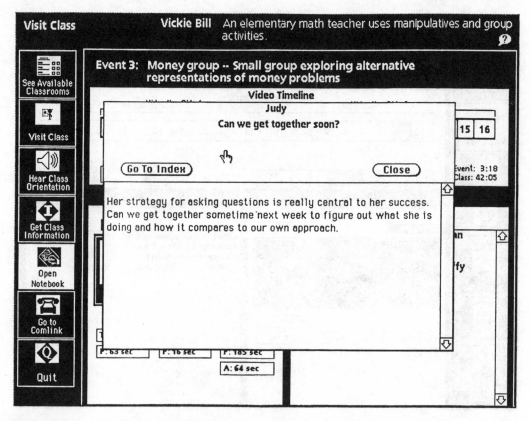

Figure 3. The notetaking facility available to the user when visiting a classroom. Notes appear with the particular teaching event they reference and are also available in indexes organized by events and by authors of the notes.

- perspectives and clips of video from the classroom;
- interviews with the teacher and other experts; and
- references to articles that are in a physical library that accompanies the computer system.

This information is organized into eight major categories shown at the top of the screen (see Figure 4). We use the same four categories used in the "visit classroom" environment but we also have included information on how to plan for these classes (e.g., lesson plans) and issues in the overall process of adopting this approach to teaching. Finally, we provide articles that the classroom teacher has identified as critical to her thinking and we provide access to all of the classroom events.

When a major topic is selected, subtopics under that topic appear in the lower left window. These subtopics are grounded in the expert analyses of the video and the classroom events. That is, the topics are there because they were identified in the perspectives or in the expert interviews or they are clearly a part of the teaching in the class. While there is considerable overlap across the three classrooms, there are differences in the subcategories that reflect the differences in particular teaching strategies.

When a subtopic is selected, the information available is shown in the lower right window. When users click on a perspective, they view the particular segment of video and the particular part of the commentary relating to that subtopic. Selecting an article yields the

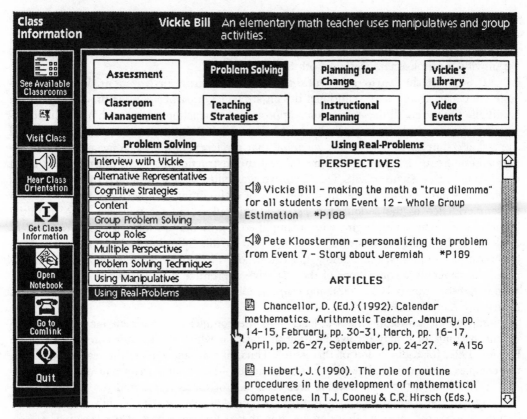

Figure 4. The information base screen provides a conceptually organized access to the events in the classroom and to other, elaborative material.

reference for that article in the library and an index of the other database topics. Interview data is simply the auditory presentation of the interviewee's comments.

The STF Reflective Problem-Solving Instructional System

The Strategic Teaching Framework Information System is a database that teachers can access as they strive to develop a new conceptual framework and strategies to be used in that framework. In this section, I focus on the instructional strategy guiding and supporting learners in the use of STFIS. The reflective problem-solving instructional strategy does not provide instruction in how to teach, nor does it provide definitions of teaching strategies. As I have discussed throughout this chapter, how to teach is a constructive activity of the learner and not something to be presented in a didactic format. Rather, the instructional strategy focuses on guiding, supporting, and challenging the learner in the process of using STF to develop a learner-centered approach to teaching in his or her classroom. It is process instruction or coaching rather than content instruction.

Instructional Principles

The reflective problem-solving instructional strategy emphasizes change as a process in which learners move iteratively through the steps of: analyzing the use of an instructional strategy and the conceptual basis for its use; adapting and implementing the strategy in their classrooms; and reflecting on that implementation in terms of the pedagogical success. There are three instructional principles underlying this instructional strategy. I first discuss these principles and then outline the implementation of the instructional strategy in the guidance we provide to the learners working with STFIS.

1. Support the learners in working in the authentic environment. With this principle we depart from many traditional design strategies in which the learning environment is initially simplified. In these traditional approaches, instruction begins with a simplified environment and complexity is gradually added. Thus, both the context or the environment and the task are simplified. In contrast, we argue that the learners must be engaged in the complex and authentic learning environment,[7] and the instructional system must support them in working in that environment. The Cognitive Flexibility theory presented by Spiro and his colleagues is most explicit about the importance of maintaining complexity. Spiro *et al.* (1992) present evidence of the serious and *persistent* misunderstandings that can arise in initial learning when instruction begins with a simplified representation (also, see Osborne & Wittrock, 1983, for examples of these persistent errors.) While Spiro has been most articulate on this issue of complexity, maintaining the complexity of the environment is also either implicitly or explicitly a component of the cognitive apprentice model (Lave & Wenger, 1991), anchored instruction (CTGV, 1992), and virtually all instructional models in the constructivist framework (Perkins, 1992).

Support or scaffolding for the learner in the complex environment may involve providing coaching, or it may involve limiting the task for which the learner is responsible (see Perkins, 1992, for a discussion of this issue). Thus, like an apprentice, the learner works in the complex environment, but the tasks are initially limited and performance is supported. As expertise grows, the tasks become more complex or more varied and the support structures are gradually withdrawn. Because the learner is always working within the full or authentic context, the meaning that derives from that context is a part of the learning.

2. A problem-based learning instructional strategy will most effectively support the learners. The learner comes to the instruction with a problem. The teacher then asks: "How do I adopt a learner-centered approach to my teaching?"; "How do I get my children more actively involved in the learning activity?"; "How do I give the students more responsibility and still assure that I really met the objectives for the course to be met?" There is no "right" answer to these questions. There is no set of procedures that can be handed to the teacher. This problem of effective teaching is a complex, ill-structured problem, in which there are many options and no clear-cut correct answer.

We have found that the problem-based learning approach developed by Barrows and his colleagues (Barrows, 1992) provides a theoretically sound and useful instructional framework for this type of a learning goal. The instructional approach can be summarized as follows:

- The problem is the stimulus for learning, and all learning arises from working on the problem. In our case, the problem is to adopt a learner-centered approach to teaching.

- The learners are responsible for all learning and all decisions related to the problem. The learners own the problem.

- Learning is collaborative. Learners work together to generate and evaluate ideas and help one another in understanding particular issues.

- The instructor is a facilitator of the problem-solving process. The facilitator does not engage in Socratic dialogue or in any other way teach the content. Rather, he or she simply asks questions to stimulate the students to reflect on where they are going, where they are coming from, if they understand the concepts or principles they are talking about, if they have considered all the options, etc.

3. The instructional tasks move from simple to complex. Rather than simplifying the learning materials, we ask the learners to begin with a restricted learning task in the complex, authentic teaching environment. This is consistent with the apprenticeship model in which the learner gradually takes on larger and more central tasks in the learning environment.

We have found that when teachers seek to change, they want to make the entire change at once and they simply get lost in the complexity of what they are trying to accomplish. Hence, our instruction guides them to first watch the entire STFIS class (visit the classroom) and compare their teaching to what is happening in the class. After watching the class, we suggest that they identify one or two aspects of the teaching that they would like to incorporate within their teaching and then return to the video and begin an in-depth analysis of those approaches.

While we think it is important that the teachers define their own issues, we offer suggestions for those who do not have a sense of where to start. We suggest that they might most profitably focus on the questioning strategies and the way the teacher responds to the child's answers. We also suggest that they might: examine the strategy for using collaborative groups and what it means to collaborate; examine the design of problems in relation to learner ownership and the variety of teaching objectives embedded in the problem; or the methods for assessing the children during the course of the class period. Mastering and adapting specific aspects of the teaching approaches to their classroom and understanding them from the conceptual framework is the beginning of the change process. Task complexity increases in two ways. First, the task moves from analysis to implementation and reflection. Second, this is an iterative process in which more teaching strategies are integrated into the the analysis and implementation, and the implementation involves an increasing part of the teacher's class.

4. Promote conceptually based reflection on the new teaching practices. The goal is for the learners to become reflective practitioners who reflect-in-action while teaching (Schön, 1987). The concept of the reflective practitioner emphasizes the importance of the practitioner maintaining a reflective awareness of his or her practice. But more importantly, it emphasizes the ability to reflect-in-action. Rather than the execution of pre-specified plans, the concept of the reflective practitioner focuses on situated actions (Suchman, 1987). In effect, the environment is seen as dynamic and the successful practitioner is one who can recognize and respond to that dynamic environment in a conceptually consistent manner.

In the reflective problem-solving instructional strategy, the learner begins by examining the teaching of the expert teachers, interpreting it from the learner-centered teaching perspective. As the skill at reflecting on the actions of the teaching of others develops, the learner tries out these new strategies and reflects on his or her own teaching practices. The goal is not to simply execute a plan, but to constantly reflect upon what was done from the new conceptual framework. Learning begins with reflection (analysis) on the action of the STF teachers and reflection on one's own teaching. As reflection becomes more automatic and interpretation of the conceptual grounding of the teaching practices becomes more facile, the learner will begin to reflect-in-action, i.e., the learners will be reflective of their practices in the process of teaching.

Implementing the Instructional Principles

The STF Information System is designed to be placed in schools to support long-term professional development. This significantly impacts the alternatives available for implementing the reflective problem-solving instructional strategy. We have begun with an experimental implementation in which we have tried to maintain the facilitator role described in the earlier discussion of problem-based learning. In that study (Chaney, 1994), over the course of a semester, fourteen teachers at a rural school used STFIS as the primary resource for beginning the process of adapting learner-centered teaching strategies in mathematics. The teachers worked in groups of three or four, meeting weekly for an hour and a half to work with STFIS. The facilitator participated with each of the groups as they worked with STFIS, but avoided prescribing or teaching content or strategies. Rather, she encouraged their analysis of the STFIS teachers following the principles outlined in the previous section, and, in particular, she emphasized the need to move iteratively and in small steps through analysis, implementation, and reflection.

For the wider distribution of the STFIS, we attempt to implement components of the reflective problem-solving instructional strategy in written instructions that accompany STFIS. These instructions provide the structure but not the coaching or situated facilitation that the facilitator provided in Chaney (1994). The emphasis is on guiding the learner's constructive process. The instructions do not present content on teaching (definitions, etc.). Indeed, the written orientation provided gives only the briefest description of learner-centered instruction, even though it is the focus of the teachers' goals. The open description states in part:

> All of the classrooms in STF Information System reflect a learner-centered approach which focuses on the thinking process of the student as he or she works in a content area. That is, the teachers attend to and respond to the thinking of the children as they work on content area problems. While we think the teachers in STF Information System exhibit many excellent attributes in their teaching and management of the classroom, we primarily focused on three attributes in selecting the teachers:
>
> - the use of problem solving tasks as a central component of their instruction;
> - the use of collaborative groups as a strategy for helping the children to manage the problem-solving process and to test their ideas and evaluate other ideas;
> - a focus on the thinking processes of the children and how the children represent problems and solution strategies.

The remainder of the guidance focuses on the process of change, rather than the nature of the teaching strategies. The written instructions provide an orientation to the process that states in part:

> We do not believe that effective teaching is simply a matter of following a procedure or a recipe. Rather, a teacher's beliefs about learning determines how teaching strategies are implemented. [Therefore] we want you to get to know the STF teacher and how that teacher thinks about what he or she is doing. The goal is to develop an overall perspective on teaching and observe how it is realized in the classroom by the teacher. However, we also want to present other points of view on that teaching—we believe that there is value in understanding how others interpret what is happening in that classroom. We want you to critically examine the flow of the class period and the interplay of strategies—teaching, management, assessment, and problem solving strategies. The goal is to understand the overall make-up of the classroom—to develop your own perspective on the classroom. Once you have done that, you can compare it to your own teaching and begin to identify the changes you would like to make. We certainly think that a group of colleagues working as a team is most valuable. The team will help to sustain motivation and provides a mechanism through which you can test and refine your ideas.

We then outline the multiple-step process for using STFIS in adopting a learner-centered approach in their classroom. The steps are entirely process oriented with one exception: the learners are directed to pay particular attention to the way in which the teachers interact with and question the students. The key steps that we outline are as follows:

1. **Select a classroom.** Begin by identifying a classroom in your module that you are most comfortable with. We think it is a good idea to study one classroom intensely and then later use the other classrooms to enrich your repertoire.

2. **Watch the class all the way through.** Study the overall flow of the class. Compare the teacher's approach with what you are doing. In this first viewing, just get an overall sense of what the strategies are and how the teacher orchestrates a class. Begin to identify what you find to be particularly interesting. We expect that you will disagree with some of the things the teacher does—or will see them as not fitting your class. That is okay, as long as you are in agreement with the overall student-centered, problem-solving based approach. Use disagreements in a constructive manner to refine your own approach.

3. **Begin an analytic examination of the class.** Look at the teaching with a critical eye. What is important about what is going on? What makes the class work? Listen to the perspectives available for each event and compare the views to your own. *Compare the teaching to your own approach and identify similarities and differences.*

4. **Analyze the teacher's approach to interacting with the children.** We think the pattern of interaction requires special attention. The manner in which teachers interact with the children is central in all STF classrooms. In our mind, this is the key to the success of the approaches. We are convinced that no matter what change you make in the classroom, the success of that change will depend on how you interact with the children. The attributes we think are common across the STF classrooms are:

   — There is a lot of questioning and very little telling. The teacher is focused on listening to the student rather than telling the student what he or she should be doing.

   — The questions focus on how the child is thinking. Rather than emphasizing a solution, the questioning emphasizes how the child represents the problem; how he or she thinks about the problem.

   — The learner's point of view is important. There is no template against which answers are measured, but rather the teachers are trying to understand the child's ideas.

   — The questions are designed to aid the learner in correcting misunderstandings or expanding on a point. That is, rather than correcting the student, the teacher asks questions to help the student notice errors and new possibilities.

   Spend as much time as you can looking at the questioning strategies and at the teacher's attention to the learner. A real understanding will only arise out of your study of the class.

5. **Target a change you would like to make and a topic that you will be teaching sometime in the next month that will be the starting point for your change.** It is now time to go to the information base. You have been visiting the classroom to get a perspective on the overall integration of activities. Now you need to develop a detailed understanding of the strategy you will be implementing. There might be several subtopics in the database relevant to your goal, so do explore. You can read articles that provide conceptual as well as how-to frameworks. You can look at specific parts of the classroom that are relevant to your focus, and you may find some interview data that will address the particular issue. You certainly will want to look under "Implementing Change" and the "Change Process." Approach the database with the goals of designing a lesson on the topic you selected using a particular strategy. You need to understand the strategy both conceptually and in its practical application. You will need to work through how to integrate the rest of your teaching strategies and your management strategy—and how you will assess the students.

6. **Try out the lesson in the classroom.** This is not a one shot deal, so just go for it. The goal here is to get feedback on the approach you are developing so that you can refine it. Therefore:

- Try to reflect on what you are doing and what the children are doing as you carry out your plan.

- Invite another teacher from the group into your classroom for peer coaching. Share your plan and your goals and ask him or her to take notes during the class to give you feedback. The goal is to obtain supportive feedback that focuses on the particular strategy (critiquing must be focused if it is to work)

- Consider asking someone to videotape your class. You can use the videotape to support your own reflection.

7. **Reflect on your tryout and begin to develop a new, "revised" plan to further improve your approach.** It is important to do this as soon as possible after your tryout. Use whatever feedback resources you have. Additionally, view the relevant portions of the class again and reflect on details of the activities in comparison to what you did. The idea is to use the STF class to key you into issues that may be relevant to understanding what the strengths and weakness were in the execution of your own plan. Return to the database and review the information that you felt was most helpful. Seek additional items of information to further refine your approach. We expect that as you develop the new approach, you will turn to the conceptual items more frequently to refine your view of the learning environment.

8. **Repeat steps 5–7 until you begin to feel comfortable with the new approach.** We cannot emphasize enough that this is a gradual process. It is not a one shot attempt with either success or failure, but rather, you are engaging in a process of learning and reflecting.

9. **Identify another new approach you want to implement and repeat steps 6 to 9.**

While the use of written instructions provides the overall structure for the change process, it, of course, cannot provide the critical, situated facilitation of analysis and reflection. Because ongoing support for the teachers thinking is critical in the reflective problem-solving instructional strategy, we are exploring the use of technology to provide linkages to and among the schools and teachers using STFIS. We have explored the use of audio conferencing to link small groups of schools and a facilitator[8], but coordinating times for synchronous, multi-site discussion is difficult, to say the least. We see the use of the Internet as holding great potential for supporting asynchronous collaboration among the community of teachers. There are a number of projects that are beginning to use the network environment to support problem solving in ways compatible with our goals, and they are achieving considerable success (Duffy, 1994; Edelson & O'Neil, 1994; Harasim, 1993; Scardamalia, Bereiter, Brett, Calhoun, & Lea, 1992). While we have provided the foundation for the Internet access in STFIS, the interface for collaboration still needs to be refined. Thus, as implementation progresses, we see the written instructions as providing the basic implementation of the reflective problem solving strategy. It provides guidance on the overall structure for the change process. The Internet collaborative environment will provide the situated facilitation of analysis and reflection as the teachers seek to understand and implement a learner-centered approach to teaching.

Summary and Conclusions

In this chapter, I have described an instructional model that is designed to support individuals in learning to function effectively in complex, ill-structured environments. By "ill-structured," I mean that the environment does not repeat itself, but rather is dynamic and calls for dynamic responses. Furthermore, there is no clear certainty that one's response is the "best" or most effective to use. This is characteristic of a wide variety of real world contexts, especially those involving the interaction between people, e.g., sales, teaching, negotiating, medical treatment, etc., or working with a complex system, e.g., the economy, complex equipment, social service systems, etc.

Because the environment is dynamic, there are no fixed procedures to be executed. Rather a wide range of strategies must be adapted or even created in response to the situation. The individual must interpret the situation, moment to moment, constructing responses. If the individual's performance is to be coherent, then these interpretations and the selection and adaptation of strategies must be guided by a conceptual framework or theory. That conceptual framework is the lens through which we view the situation—it guides us in identifying what is important in the situation and guides us in responding. The expert is guided almost automatically by this conceptual framework and thus the expert is reflecting-in-action, in the terminology of Schön (1987). The goal in learning—and the goal that guides the instructional design process—is for the teachers to develop both a repertoire of strategies and an interpretive framework that will support them in assembling and adapting the strategies to the particular situation.

The model assumes that the learner arrives motivated to learn. Thus, the learning scenario is one of a learner faced with an ill-structured problem: "How can I learn to function successfully in this environment?" It is assumed that the learning occurs in the process of solving this problem. That is, we cannot tell the learner how to adopt a new approach, in part because there is no one correct approach. Rather, the learner, by engaging in active analysis and testing of the strategies will develop the rich understanding of an expert.

Three types of *content based* instructional materials are made available to the learner. The central resource is a video of each of several experts performing in the environment. These examples serve as models that the learner can analyze. Thus, the examples are designed to capture the dynamic nature of actual teaching. They capture the complexity of the context and the performance, rather than being simplified representations. We have found CD-ROM or videodisk to provide the most effective resource for both capturing the dynamic nature of the teaching and permitting analysis of that teaching. The availability of multiple examples or models provides two advantages. It offers more opportunity for the learner to find a particular style that is most compatible with his or her own style, e.g., formal vs. informal. Additionally, the contrast of approaches avoids focusing on the specific procedures and helps to develop the more general framework that guides the use of the particular strategies (Merrill & Tennyson, 1977).

The second set of resources is access to alternative perspectives on the expert performance and on the adaptation of that expert performance to other contexts. The learner is engaged in constructing an understanding not only of the particular strategies, but of the conceptual framework or set of principles that guide the use of the strategies. The multiple perspectives from individuals who have the same goal help the individual to see alternative interpretations of the dynamic environment and alternative ways of adapting the strategies. It allows the learners to test and refine their understanding.

The third set of content based resources are less context bound—that is, books and other materials on the concepts and strategies the expert used, e.g., collaborative groups. These resources aid in enlarging and enriching the interpretations of the conceptual framework and the strategies. The expert performance and the learners' own context serve as the anchors for interpreting these materials. These articles provide a rich web of information to aid the learner in building links between the expert's and the learner's teaching practices. Thus, these are not materials to be mastered, but rather to be used.

What I have described thus far are resource materials. The *instructional process* is one of supporting the learner in using these materials. We have identified the learner's task as one of solving an ill-structured problem. The instructional role is to provide support and guidance in that activity. The support is at two levels: the micro level of analysis and discussion and the overall sequencing of the learning process. The micro-level support is designed to aid the learner in reflecting on and testing his or her own understanding and in promoting collaboration. In the overall guidance, the learner is supported in moving through the following steps:

- **Observation.** The learner stands on the periphery and watches the expert performance. In terms of teacher education, the learner "visits the classroom."

- **Analysis.** The learner begins an analysis of the expert performance, contrasting it to his or her approach, e.g., how the teacher works with collaborative groups, assesses the students, asks questions, etc.

- **Focusing.** The learner identifies one or two strategies that are seen as most interesting and most usefully incorporated into his or her own performance, e.g., the use of problems or questioning strategies. The learner engages in an in-depth analysis of the strategies, studying their use in that particular class as well as the more general principles related to the use of the strategy.

- **Adaptation.** As understanding develops, the learner plans for the incorporation of the strategies in his or her own environment. That is, the context for thinking of the strategy now shifts to a particular context in which the user will use the strategy, e.g, the teacher will decide with which topic he or she will try a problem solving approach and the new approach to interacting with the children.

- **Testing.** The learner tries out the new strategies.

- **Reflection.** The learner engages in reflection on the success of the strategies. The performance is contrasted to the expert performance not in terms of matching that procedure, but in terms of the success of the dynamic interaction in the environment, e.g., the learning of the students and the interactions with the students.

- **Revise and test again.** There is no expectation that the learner will feel comfortable with the new approaches initially. Indeed, the reflective process is central to learning, and thus we would expect many iterations.

- **Extend.** As the learner begins to feel comfortable, he or she will incorporate new strategies into the repertoire. In essence, the learner begins to take over more and more of the expert performance.

In essence, the learner begins with reflection on the action of experts and then moves into his or her own activity. The reflection on the expert performance shifts to reflection on his or her own actions. Additionally, the learners are encouraged to begin focusing on specific strategies that they see as most relevant and useful and, as they understand the underpinnings for the strategies and can adapt it to their own contexts, they begin to integrate the new strategies and build a richer understanding of the process.

Central to this model is the constructive activity of the learner. This is an ill-structured environment, and these are no clearly correct responses to be "discovered." Rather, learners must build linkages between theory and practice, and they must develop the ability to interpret the practice such that that interpretation comes to guide their own practice.

Notes

1. Work on this chapter was supported in part by funding from the North Central Regional Education Laboratory. My thanks to Beau Jones, Scott Grabinger, Don Cunningham, John Savery, and Curt Bonk for their useful comments on an earlier draft of the chapter.
2. A large and very talented group of designers and developers have worked on this project over the last couple of years. They all made valuable contributions. Those members who have been part of

the process since inception are: Randy Knuth and Beau Jones at the North Central Regional Educational Laboratory and Buck Brown, Tammy Chaney, and Tom Duffy at Indiana University.

3. Strategic Teaching Framework Information System is a product of Indiana University and the North Central Regional Educational Laboratory.

4. Everyone recognizes that the approaches being called for have a long history in education. They are not new historically. However, they are new in the current educational and societal context. The label "new" should not detract the reader from the real issues of the implications of the current focus for the practice of instructional design.

5. In our terms, mastery involves a combined effect of domain relevant knowledge and domain relevant problem solving skills—the ability to engage in authentic problem solving in the domain.

6. This difference in approaches may reflect the fact that we are focusing on more dynamic learning, calling for a sequence of situated actions.

7. Authenticity, and hence the limits of complexity, is defined in terms of the complexity that we expect the learner to be able to manage at the end of instruction (Honebein *et al.,* 1993)

8. This effort has been directed by Carol Fine at the North Central Regional Educational Laboratory.

References

Allen, B., & Hoffman, R. P. (1993). Varied levels of support for constructivist activity in hypermedia-based learning environments. In T. M. Duffy, J. Lowyck, & D. Jonassen (Eds.), *Designing environments for constructive learning.* Heidelberg: Springer-Verlag.

American Association for the Advancement of Science (1993). *Benchmarks for science literacy: Project 2061.* Washington, DC: American Association for the Advancement of Science.

Barrows, H. S. (1985). *How to design a problem-based curriculum for the preclinical years.* New York: Springer Publishing Co.

Barrows, H. S. (1992). *The tutorial process.* Springfield, IL: Southern Illinois University Medical School.

Bransford, J. D., Franks, J. J., Vye, N. J. & Sherwood, R. D. (1989). New approaches to instruction: Because wisdom cannot be told. In S. Vosniadou & A. Ortony (Eds.), *Similarity and anological reasoning* (pp. 470–497). New York: Cambridge University Press.

Brooks, J. G., & Brooks, M. G. (1993). *The case for the constructivist classroom.* Alexandria, VA: The Association for Supervision and Curriculum Development.

Chaney, T. (1994). *Design and evaluation of a constructivist instructional model to support conceptual change: A case study of elementary mathematics teachers.* Bloomington, IN: Indiana University.

Chi, M., Glaser, R., & Farr, M. (Eds.). (1988). *The nature of expertise.* Hillsdale, NJ: Lawrence Erlbaum Associates.

Cognition & Technology Group at Vanderbilt (1992). Technology and the design of generative learning environments. In T. Duffy & D. Jonassen (Eds.) *Constructivism and the technology of instruction: A conversation.* Hillsdale, NJ: Lawrence Erlbaum Associates.

Dewey, J. (1938). *Logic: The theory of inquiry.* New York: Henry Holt.

Duffy, T. M. (1994). *Corporate and community education: Achieving success in the information society.* Unpublished paper. Bloomington, IN: Indiana University.

Edelson, D., & O'Neil, K. (1994). *The CoVis collaboratory notebook: Computer support for scientific inquiry.* Paper presented at the Annual Meeting of the American Educational Research Association, New Orleans, LA.

Fishman, B., & Duffy, T. M. (1992). Classroom restructuring: What do teachers really need? *Educational Technology Research and Development, 40,* 221–239.

Harasim, L. (1993). Collaborating in cyberspace: Using computer conferences as a group learning environment. *Interactive Learning Environments.* 3, 119–130.

Honebein, P., Duffy, T. M., & Fishman, B. (1993). Constructivism and the design of learning environments: Context and authentic activities for learning. In T. M. Duffy, J. Lowyck, & D. Jonassen (Eds.), *Designing environments for constructive learning.* Heidelberg: Springer-Verlag.

Jones, B. F., Knuth, R., & Duffy, T. M. (1993). Components of constructivist learning environments for professional training. In T. M. Duffy, J. Lowyck, & D. Jonassen (Eds.), *Designing environments for constructive learning.* Heidelberg: Springer-Verlag.

Lave, J., & Wenger, E. (1991). *Situated learning: Legitimate peripheral participation.* New York: Cambridge University Press.

Mathematics Association of America (1991). *A call for change: Recommendations for the mathematical preparation of teachers of mathematics.* Washington, DC: Author.

McMahon, T. A, Carr, A. A., & Fishman, B. J. (1992). *Hypermedia and constructivism: Three approaches to enhanced learning.* Paper presented at the meeting of the Association for Educational Communications and Technology, Washington, DC.

Merrill, M. D., & Tennyson, R. (1977). *Teaching concepts: An instructional design guide.* Englewood Cliffs, NJ: Educational Technology Publications.

Milter, R. G., & Stinson, J. E. (in press). Educating leaders for the new competitive environment. In G. Gijselaers, S. Tempelaar, & S. Keizer (Eds.), *Educational innovation in economics and business administration: The case of problem-based learning.* London: Kluwer Academic Publishers.

National Council of Teachers of Mathematics (1989). *Curriculum and evaluation standards for school mathematics.* Reston, VA: Author.

National Council of Teachers of Mathematics (1991). *Professional standards for teaching mathematics.* Reston, VA: Author.

Osborne, R. J., & Wittrock, M. (1983). Learning science: A generative process. *Science Education, 67,* 489–508.

Perkins, D. N. (1992). What constructivism demands of the learner. In T. Duffy & D. Jonassen (Eds.), *Constructivism and the technology of instruction: A conversation.* Hillsdale, NJ: Lawrence Erlbaum Associates.

Piaget, J. (1977). *The development of thought: Equilibration of cognitive structures.* New York: Viking Press.

Rorty, R. (1991). *Objectivity, relativism, and truth: Philosophical papers, vol. 1.* Cambridge: Cambridge University Press.

Rowland, G. (1991). *Problem solving in instructional design.* Unpublished doctoral dissertation. Bloomington IN: Instructional Systems Technology, Indiana University.

Rutherford, F. J., & Ahlgren, A. (1990). *Science for all Americans.* New York: Oxford University Press.

Scardamalia, M., & Bereiter, C. (1991). Higher levels of agency for children in knowledge building: A challenge for the design of new knowledge media. *The Journal of the Learning Sciences, 1,* 37–68.

Scardamalia, M., Bereiter, C., Brett, C., Calhoun, C., & Lea, N. S. (1992). Educational applications of a networked communal database. *Interactive Learning Environments, 2,* 45–71.

Schön, D. (1987). *Educating the reflective practitioner.* San Francisco: Jossey Bass.

Spiro, R. J., Feltovich, P. L., Jacobson, M. J., & Coulson, R. L. (1992). Cognitive flexibility, constructivism, and hypertext: Random access instruction for advanced knowledge acquisition in ill-structured domains. In T. Duffy & D. Jonassen (Eds.), *Constructivism and the technology of instruction: A conversation.* Hillsdale, NJ: Lawrence Erlbaum Associates.

Suchman, L. A. (1987). *Plans and situated actions.* New York: Cambridge University Press.

34

Instructional Transaction Theory

Richard W. Cline
Jean A. Pratt
M. David Merrill
Utah State University, Logan

Introduction to Instructional Transaction Theory[1]

Instructional transactions[2] are the essence of Instructional Transaction Theory (Merrill, 1985). The purpose of this theory is to invent procedures for teaching knowledge and skills in a more organized and efficient way than has been possible with previous instructional design theories. Instructional transactions shells[3] are the methods being developed for teaching knowledge and skills, and ID Expert is the software tool being developed as the vehicle to develop and deliver the instruction. This chapter describes the history of instructional transaction theory, what it is, and how it is currently being implemented.

Much of the computer-based instruction (CBI) occurring in public school classrooms and private industry lacks sound instructional design. This is due to the significant amount of time and the expertise it takes to apply instructional design principles to CBI. Current instructional design and development practices have an estimated development/delivery ratio for computer-based instruction that exceeds 200 hours of labor for one hour of instruction (Lippert, 1989). Other estimates suggest ratios exceeding 500:1 just for programming. There is a critical need for significantly improved methodology and tools to guide the design and development of high-quality computer-based instruction.

In almost all areas other than education, the impact of computerization has been to increase productivity by reducing labor costs, or allowing greater production from the same labor. Tasks that at one time might require days or weeks could now be accomplished in minutes or hours. One reason for this achievement is that computers provide a tool that enables an algorithm to be rapidly performed over and over. An algorithm is a sequence of computations that can be repeated over and over with different data. We treat subject-matter content as data and use the automated instructional algorithms to vary the representation of that content.

Instructional transactions are instructional algorithms: patterns of learner interactions (usually far more complex than a single display and a single response) which have been designed to enable the learner to acquire a certain kind of knowledge or skill. We have identified 13 different instructional transactions which each know how to teach a specific type of knowledge. These instructional algorithms require only the input of the content or subject matter in order to automatically develop the interactions that the learner will see.

ID Expert is a tool that automates the development of computer-based instruction via transaction shells. It is an Instructional Design Expert System. ID Expert is targeted toward users with minimal instructional design experience, but is powerful enough to enable the experienced instructional designer to manipulate the instructional design strategies. ID Expert has built-in instructional design and flexible instructional strategies to assist an author using this tool to concentrate more on the content and display than on how to design instruction. A novice instructional designer needs only provide the subject-matter content and representational resources. ID Expert does the rest. This tool also allows an author to manipulate how instruction is presented through changeable parameters of the instructional strategies. An experienced instructional designer can assess the learners' characteristics and then, with a few simple mouse clicks, change the learner interaction to best meet the needs of the learners.

History of Instructional Transaction Theory

To fully understand Instructional Transaction Theory (ITT), one must understand the foundational theoretical premises upon which it was designed. The evolution of ITT into an accepted instructional design theory and software (ID Expert) parallels Merrill's progressive approaches to automating instructional design.

Merrill developed component display theory (CDT) in the late 1960s as an extension to Gagné's nine conditions of learning theory. Merrill agreed with Gagné (1965) that performance-based learning outcomes could be categorized in several ways and that different learning outcomes required different specific operations of events of instruction. Merrill suggested, though, that *performance* (Gagné's only dimension) was too limiting and should be combined with *type of content* to form a two-dimensional classification system which could represent a variety of different presentation types, using only a few types of discrete displays.

TICCIT (Time-shared Interactive, Computer-Controlled Information Television) was the application of CDT to instructional situations. TICCIT (still in use at Brigham Young University) was developed and tested in the 1970s. TICCIT (Merrill, 1980) is an interactive system which gives the student control over instructional displays which contain only one kind of information each. The student selects the type of instructional display which best meets his/her instructional need at that time based upon the student's aptitude and prior learning. Each instructional idea—concept, procedure, or principle—is presented in each of three modes: rule, example, and practice.

Reigeluth and Merrill later developed elaboration theory (Reigeluth, Merrill, Wilson, & Spiller, 1994) to extend component display theory. Elaboration theory suggests that students learn most effectively if they are allowed to interact with a simple representation of the terminal task and then are guided through increasingly complex representations. Elaboration theory is based upon the macro strategies of sequencing instruction according to cognitive learning structures, synthesizing the relationships among ideas to provide a holistic view of the instruction, and summarizing the instructional concepts via preview and review. System-generated instructional control and guidance gradually fades out, forcing an increase in learner control and cognitive processing.

In the mid-1980s, Merrill extended his original component display theory to take advantage of the increased presentation and intervention capability of existing computers and the current research on cognitive learning structures for the purpose of more effective instruction (Merrill, 1994). The new CDT proposed to present *experiential content* by having the computer simulate real-life experiences for the student, interact with the student, and coach the student through complex tasks. Merrill planned to accomplish this real-time interaction via transactions: the mutual, dynamic, real-time give and take which is possible through a computer. Transactions, the vehicle for instructional transaction theory, were conceived with the new component *design* theory.

The new CDT incorporated portions of Gagné's theory as well as elaboration theory. The new CDT was based on the assumption that there are different kinds of learning outcomes. There are different instructional conditions to promote those learning outcomes. And these are different types of cognitive structures and processing necessary to achieve the different types of learning outcomes.

The new CDT also included four principles designed to guide the acquisition of learning. The *cognitive structure principle* stated that instruction should promote the development of that cognitive structure most consistent with the desired learning performance. The *elaboration principle* stated that instruction should promote the incremental elaboration of the most appropriate cognitive structure to enable the student to achieve increased generality and complexity in the desired learning performance. The *learner guidance principle* stated that instruction should promote that active cognitive processing which best enables the student to use the most appropriate cognitive structure in a way consistent with the desired learned performance via such techniques as "fading." The *practice principle* stated that instruction should provide the dynamic, ongoing opportunity for monitored practice that requires the student to demonstrate the desired learned performance, or a close approximation of it, while the system monitors the activity and intervenes with feedback both as to result and as to process.

The new CDT also introduced the concept of *course organization*: a representation of the ideas to be taught in the course and the relationship between those ideas, including control mechanisms (based on the elaboration principle rather than Gagné's prerequisite objectives hierarchies) which guide the student's progress through the course organization.

The application of the new CDT was through the development of the Instructional Systems Design Expert system (ISD Expert) in 1987. ISD Expert automated the presentation, inquisitory, and practice displays via instructional algorithms. The instructional algorithms used different transactions to achieve different learning outcomes. The content and resources used to represent the content were stored in a separate knowledge database and resource library (in contrast to frame-based CAI in which content and resources are contained within each display frame). The separation of instructional strategies from the content and resources provided a major feature for ISD Expert.

ISD Expert began as an implementation and testing of the new Component Design Theory. The design and development process resulted in a refinement of the product (now referred to as ID Expert to distinguish it from the traditional ISD model). With the development of ID Expert came the formalization of a new theory based upon a new generation of instructional design. Merrill recognized the inadequacy of the traditional instructional design system to meet learner's needs based on findings from the cognitive sciences and the development of high technology. Merrill made a paradigmatic shift from the traditional ISD-based CDT to a second generation instructional design theory (ID$_2$): instructional transaction theory (ITT).

A Shift in Paradigms

Kuhn (1970) suggests that paradigm shifts are gradual because those who have bought into a particular paradigm attempt to patch its anomalies and don't recognize them as counter-instances of the paradigm. This is what we see with the first generation of instructional design (ID$_1$). ID$_1$ was developed before the increased accessibility and capability of computers for the use of instruction. Although a good system, it lacked the robustness and functionality necessary to accommodate the potential power of the computer. ID$_2$ manipulates the computer, not as an electronic page-turner, but as an expert system which guides and monitors the instructional process. ID Expert is one application of instructional transaction theory which represents the second generation of instructional design.

A major shift in thinking with instructional transaction theory is in the way the instructional content is organized. ITT still follows the fundamental assumption that different instructional conditions are required to promote different learning outcomes in accordance with Gagné and Merrill's earlier theories. ITT extends this notion to prescribe specific instructional strategies based upon links between specific components of knowledge content.

Knowledge content in ITT is organized into "frames" or categories of learning outcomes, which each require a corresponding instructional strategy. The different frames are individually detailed and corporately linked together via elaborations, which are characteristic, descriptive, and associative values of the knowledge content. Elaborations break down the knowledge into its descriptive components, classify groups of knowledge content according to shared characteristics, and link knowledge content to other, related content. The resulting instructional knowledge structure is represented as an Elaborated Frame Network (Merrill, Li, & Jones, 1990b) in which data in one part of the EFN is affected by and affects data in another part of the EFN through the elaboration links. The result to the student is a more logical mapping of the instructional content to match what we now know about the cognitive mental structures in order to facilitate learning.

Use of the computer facilitates the ID_2 process, although ID_2 is certainly not limited to the use of the computer. ID Expert is the instructional software tool (based on the instructional transaction theory) that was used to test the ID_2 model. ID Expert prompts the user to think beyond the breakdown of knowledge into discrete sets typical of traditional content analysis by having the user categorize the detailed content by learning outcome. ID Expert then takes advantage of built-in, reusable instructional algorithms (i.e., instructional transactions) which know how to teach the different types of learning outcomes represented by the Elaborated Frame Network. Within each instructional transaction, ID Expert has four built-in interaction modes which provide the different learning conditions necessary to promote the acquisition of the different learning outcomes. ID Expert also knows what knowledge content is linked to other knowledge content in the Elaborated Frame Network as well as the value of the elaboration links, so it can intelligently build the instruction in a manner most consistent with the way learners learn. A more illustrative method of describing the paradigmatic shift from ID_1 to ID_2 may be to compare the two models.

Comparison of ID_1 and ID_2

Merrill, Li, and Jones (1990a) define the first generation instructional design (ID_1) as "the most widely applied instructional design theory [which] is based largely on the work of Robert M. Gagné and his associates at Florida State University . . . and is often equated with the term *Instructional Systems Development* (ISD)" (p. 7). Merrill *et al.* identified several limitations of the first generation instructional design (ID_1), which make it inadequate as a foundation upon which to build effective instructional theory. The more effective approach of the second generation instructional design (ID_2) much better serves as the foundation for instructional transaction theory. Table 1 is a breakdown of the comparison.

Discussion of ID_1 and ID_2 Concepts

First generation instructional design methods break the knowledge down into components such as facts, concepts, principles or procedures, but fail to provide the complex interrelationships among the components. ID_2 teaches integrated sets of knowledge and skills based upon the findings in cognitive psychology, which suggest that learning occurs within the construction and elaboration of mental models built from schema or frame networks.

Table 1. Comparison of ID$_1$ and ID$_2$ concepts.

ID$_1$ (Inadequate concepts)	ID$_2$ (More adequate concepts)
Individual content components: Facts concepts, principles, procedures	Integrated knowledge/skill sets: Frame, schema, mental model
Content oulines: Hierarchy diagrams	Knowledge structures: Elaborated Frame Network
Course organization: Segments, Lessons, Units	Course organization: Components, abstractions, associations
Passive presentations	Interactive transactions
Basic display elements: Rules, examples, practice	Integrated interactions: Interaction modes, transactions, transaction families
Labor-intensive/not cost-effective	Flexible and reusable

ID$_1$ is based upon a bottom-up, prerequisite hierarchy in which the learner masters one piece of knowledge content before moving to the next piece. ID$_2$ uses the cognitive learning-based concept of the Elaborated Frame Network (EFN). The EFN represents knowledge as frames which are comprised of specific values and which link to other frames, which teach a different, yet related knowledge. This is different from the traditional programming definition of "frame."

ID$_1$ breaks the course organization into the traditional categories of segments, lessons and units. ID$_2$ also breaks the course into lessons and then segments, but goes a step further and categorizes knowledge into transactions based upon the purpose of instruction. ID$_2$ is comprised of *component transactions* which teach the component parts, steps, or events of a knowledge object, *abstraction transactions* which teach a learner to use a skill acquired from one set of instances or classes with a previously unencountered instance or class, and *association transactions* which teach the learner to integrate information from two or more knowledge frames into a coordinated set of knowledge and skill.

Much of the current computer-based ID$_1$ is passive. The computer is little more than an electronic page-turner. ID$_2$ requires active mental engagement from the student to process the information via the interaction modes within each transaction. The student cannot simply "click to proceed," but must select or enter the correct information as prompted by the system.

ID$_1$ instructional strategies are comprised of basic display elements (e.g., definitions, examples, and practice), which must be created for each lesson. ID$_2$ is composed of four interaction modes (present, explore, practice and test), which each know how to interact with the student and can be used repeatedly with any type of subject-matter content. Subject-matter content is represented by transaction families, which can teach any combination of parts, steps, or events. The system treats subject-matter content as data, which it processes through its automated instructional algorithms. The system determines which combination of instructional interaction modes are necessary to teach the specified learning outcome.

Instructional transactions enable the design and development of flexible and reusable instructional software. This is achieved by the separation of subject matter content from the instructional strategies used to teach the content and the resources used to illustrate the instruction.

The transaction shell is content-flexible because it allows a teacher to enter and modify instructional content easily and to specify the amount of information that a student needs to learn.

The transaction shell is instructional strategy-flexible because it allows a teacher to customize instructional strategies. The teacher has a variety of instructional strategies to choose from by changing the default values of related instructional parameters.

The transaction shell is content-reusable because the same knowledge base may be used to accomplish a set of instructional functions, such as presentation, remediation, and practice, by customizing the instructional strategies. The content is separate from the resources used to illustrate it, so can be used in a variety of instructional contexts.

The transaction shell is instructional-strategy reusable because it separates the subject matter content and the instructional strategies. The knowledge structure of the shell may be used to represent a variety of subject matters, making the shell reusable. Once a subject matter or a portion of subject matters has been represented using the knowledge structure of a particular transaction shell, the instructional strategies are available and can be customized for teaching the materials.

Frames vs. Transactions

Most authoring systems are frame-based. Their architecture is that of a file cabinet or data base of frames or displays, which are pre-composed and pre-stored. These displays consist of one or more screens to be presented to the student. These displays can contain graphic images, video, audio, and/or text. The usual strategy is to present information to the student and ask one or more questions concerning the material. Based on the student's response, the next display is chosen from the data base. This is a very limited branching programmed-instruction model of tutorial instruction.

ID Expert is based on the computing metaphor, that of an algorithm plus data comprising a program. In ID Expert, the algorithm is an instructional strategy and the data is the knowledge to be taught. Rather than the single branching instructional algorithm that characterizes most authoring systems, ID Expert contains a library of different instructional algorithms. These algorithms have been preprogrammed, and each one knows how to teach a particular kind of knowledge. Designing an instructional strategy in ID Expert is a matter of selecting the appropriate instructional algorithms for a given knowledge element or elements (i.e., categorizing the content according to the desired learning outcome). This instructional algorithm is then customized for a particular student population or specific subject-matter topics.

In contrast to programmed-instruction's algorithm of branching, ID Expert has many different instructional algorithms, which can be configured in many different ways. The instructional designer can tailor the instruction to a specific learner audience by either changing the audience characteristics and accepting ID Expert's default instructional strategy, or by manipulating the instructional design strategy parameters directly. Either option requires only a few simple mouse clicks.

Separating the Knowledge Base, Instructional Strategies, and Subject Matter

The instructional transaction theory is unique because (a) it separates specific subject matter content from its underlying structures, and (b) it separates subject matter content from the instructional strategies necessary to teach the content. They are achieved through the knowledge base and instructional parameters.

A knowledge base is a representation of the entities, activities, and processes of the knowledge and skills to be taught. It contains all the information, the knowledge and mediated resources necessary to carry on instructional interactions with students to teach the content. For each entity, the knowledge base contains the information about its components as well as its relationships with other subject-matter entities. The knowledge base itself is independent of the subject-matter domain. This gives a transaction the capability of being reused to teach a variety of content by filling in its knowledge structures with information specific to the knowledge or skill being taught (Li & Merrill, 1990).

The instructional parameters allow a transaction to be customized to meet the needs of an individual student or to serve a specific instructional function (e.g., basic instruction or remediation). We have identified a number of important categories of parameters, including presentation mode, instructional control, display, practice, and feedback. Each transaction has a set of carefully researched instructional parameters that affect the instructional interactions and strategies. Each parameter has a default value determined by research or derived from the designers' experience. A default value set contains the default values for all parameters. It represents the typical situation in which the transaction operates. Once the knowledge acquisition is completed, the transaction is ready to use.

Instructional Transaction Shells

An instructional transaction is a mutual, dynamic, real-time give-and-take between an instructional system and a student in which there is an exchange of information. It is the complete sequence of presentations and reactions necessary for the student to acquire a specific type of instructional goal. It requires active mental effort by the student. Its effectiveness is determined by the match between the nature of the student's interaction and resulting mental processing with the type of task and subject-matter content to be learned (Merrill, Li, & Jones, 1991).

Different kinds of knowledge and skills require different kinds of transactions. The necessary set of these instructional transactions are designed and programmed once, like other applications, such as spread sheets and word processors. These instructional programs are called instructional transaction shells. These transaction shells can then be used with different content topics as long as these topics are of a similar kind of knowledge or skill. For instance, the Identify transaction teaches the component parts of an entity, while the Execute transaction takes a learner through each sequential step of an activity.

A transaction shell consists of four primary components (see Figure 1): interactions and an *interaction manager*, which cause the transaction to occur; *instructional parameters*, which enable the instruction to be customized for a given learner population, learning task, and environmental situation; a *knowledge base* containing a structural representation of all the knowledge to be taught; and a *resource data base* containing mediated representations of the knowledge to be taught. A transaction shell has three authoring systems: a *transaction configuration system, a knowledge acquisition system*, and *resource editors*.

Transaction shells incorporate intelligence about instructional design in several ways. First, the functions and methods of each transaction shell enable the type of interactions most appropriate for acquiring a given type of knowledge. The designer does not need to reinvent appropriate instructional designs for every application. Second, the knowledge base includes a syntax for knowledge representation that not only enables transactions to use this knowledge, but assures that the knowledge included is complete and consistent. Third, intelligence in the knowledge acquisition system enables subject-matter experts to supply the necessary knowledge without knowing the formal syntax of the knowledge representation system. Fourth, the parameters of each transaction shell identify those ways that these interactions can vary for different learner populations and different tasks. Fifth, intelligence in the transaction configuration system contains instructional design rules relating learner and task attributes to various values on the instructional parameters. Thus, the instructional designer needs to supply only descriptive information about the learners and the task. The configuration system can select a pattern of instructional parameter values consistent with this

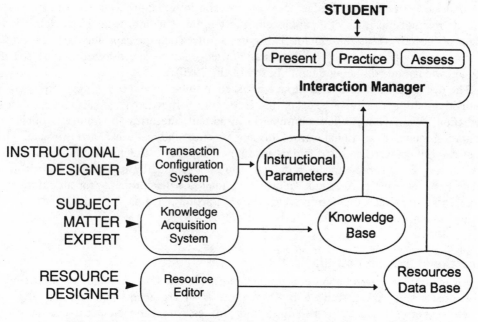

Figure 1.   Components of an instructional transaction shell.

information. However, the configuration system is merely a guide; a designer has access to all of the parameters and can adjust the value of groups of parameters or individual parameters to more adequately fine-tune a particular transaction instance.

Structure of the Elaborated Frame Network

We propose to represent knowledge in terms of objects which we call frames. The frames we define here are different from those in traditional frame-based authoring systems referred to earlier. Each frame in ID Expert has an internal structure (slots, which contain values for the structure), and links to other frames. These (both internal and external) are termed elaborations of the frame. The set of all elaborated frames together, which contains all the knowledge to be instructed by a course, is called an elaborated frame network (Merrill *et al.* 1990b). In other words, an elaborated frame network is an external representation of the same knowledge and skill which comprise a mental model.[4] An elaborated frame network is comprised of knowledge frames, including their internal structures and the connections (organization and elaboration) among these frames.

Frames

It is hypothesized that there are three kinds of frames:

- *Entity Frames.* Entities are things in the real or imagined world, including objects (natural objects and manufactured devices), creatures (animals and persons), places (natural and constructed), and symbols. Examples of entities include the Washington Monument, a computer, Abraham Lincoln, and pi. We assume that there can be no instruction without at least one entity involved.

- *Activity Frames.* An activity is some group of actions performed, or which could be performed, by the learner. Examples of activities include operating a device, using a formula to perform a calculation, and participating in a social interaction, such as group decision-making.

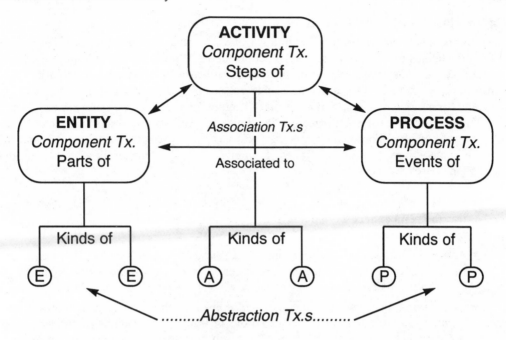

Figure 2.   Elaborated frame network.

- *Process Frames.* A process is some group of actions outside the learner, including physical and social events in the real or imagined world. The distinction between an activity and a process has to do with the role of the learner. If the learner is or could be the actor in the activity, then the actions are analyzed as an activity, with the learner's potential role central to the analysis and instruction. If, on the other hand, the learner could not be an actor and the actions could occur entirely external to the learner, then the actions are analyzed as a process. For example, the procedure to service a machine, which will be performed by the learner, is an activity; replicating a cell in biology is a process.

Transaction Families

A transaction family is an Elaborated Frame Network represented by a linked Process, Entity, and Activity frames—a PEA-net. A PEA-net is an association that frequently occurs in most subject matters. The entity is that object, or those objects, which are acted on; the activity is that which is done by the learner either with or to the entity; and the process is the consequence of this activity in terms of some event or set of events that change the properties of the object. Learning about the entity helps the learner to understand what the object is in terms of its parts, their locations, and their functions. Learning the activity helps the learner to acquire the skills for manipulating the object. Learning the process enables the learner to know the consequences of his or her actions and to make predictions about future consequences.

Certain associations are necessary to build adequate knowledge representations. An entity can stand alone as the object of instruction, but an activity or process always requires the presence of an entity. In other words, whenever there is an activity or process in a knowledge base, there is always a potential link to its PEA-net partners. There is always an associated entity affected by an activity and often an associated process that is the consequence of the activity. Whenever there is a process in a knowledge base, there is always an associated entity whose properties are changed by the transformation of the process and often an associated activity on which the occurrence of the process is conditional (Merrill, 1993).

Elaborations/Classes of Transactions

Instructional transactions can be grouped into a limited number of classes. The nature of the interactions for a given class of transactions depends on the types of knowledge structure(s) that the transactions seek to promote and the learner performance enabled by these transactions. We assume that different knowledge structures require different types of instructional transactions. We also assume that different transactions promote the acquisition of different types of learner performance. We have identified three primary classes of transactions or types of elaborations: component transactions, abstraction transactions, and association transactions (Merrill, Li, Jones, & Hancock, 1997). Further descriptions of the transaction classes are as follows:

- Component transactions correspond to the internal structure of a frame. For an entity, the components are parts of the entity; for an activity, steps; and for a process, events and causes.

- Abstraction transactions correspond to a "kinds-of" class/subclass hierarchy into which the frame may be classified. Abstraction transactions represent the generality of entities, activities, and processes.

- Association transactions provide meaningful links to other frames in the network. Associations are non-hierarchical aggregations of frames. An example of an association is a process linked with another process, each of which may be used as an analogy for the other.

ID Expert currently utilizes only the component transactions, although the abstraction and association transactions are detailed in the design specifications. There are three classes of component transactions: identify, execute, and interpret.

An *identify* transaction teaches entities and their parts, by presenting the names, locations, and descriptions of the parts. The identify transaction also allows students to explore information about the parts and to practice their knowledge about names, locations, and descriptions of the parts. Finally, the students are tested on their knowledge about the entity.

An *execute* transaction teaches activities and their steps. The steps of the activity are presented, one by one, including the name, description, and demonstration of each step. The execute transaction allows the students to explore information about the steps of the activities and to practice their knowledge about names, descriptions, and demonstrations of the steps. Students are also tested on their knowledge about the activity and its steps.

An *interpret* transaction teaches processes and their events. The events of a process are presented, one by one, including the name, description, and a demonstration of each event. The interpret transaction allows students to explore information about the events of the process and to practice their knowledge about names, descriptions, and demonstrations of the events. Students are again tested on their knowledge about the process and its events.

There are five classes of abstraction transactions: judge, classify, generalize, decide, and transfer (Merrill, Jones, & Li, 1992).

The *judge* transaction enables the learner to acquire the ability to order the instances of a given class on the basis of one or more of the dimensional properties.

The *classify* transaction enables the learner to acquire the ability to sort or classify instances as to class membership. It answers the question, "What is it?"

The *generalize* transaction is the inverse of the classify transaction. Generalize transactions enable the learner to acquire the ability to identify as members of a more general class what appear to be distinct instances or classes.

A *decide* transaction enables the learner to acquire the ability to select one alternative from another. It answers the question, "Which do I select?"

A *transfer* transaction enables the learner to acquire an abstraction model, that is, a generalized set of steps for an activity, or a generalized set of events for a process, and to apply this abstraction model to a previously unencountered class or instance of the activity or process.

We have also identified at least five classes of association transactions: propagate, analogize, substitute, design, and discover.

A *propagate* transaction enables the learner to acquire one set of skills in the context of another set of skills.

An *analogize* transaction enables the learner to acquire a process or activity or entity by likening it to a different process or activity.

A *substitute* transaction enables the learner to acquire an alternative activity or process by comparison to a previously learned similar activity or process.

A *design* transaction enables a learner to invent a new activity or entity or process, or to improve an existing one.

A *discover* transaction enables a learner to find a new entity, activity, or process.

Instructional Transaction Interactions

Adequate interactions are not passive; they require relevant mental effort on the part of the learner. An interaction can vary in terms of the level of mental effort required. Relevant mental processing causes the learner to actively construct the appropriate mental model of the target knowledge structure(s). Asking an appropriate rhetorical question, which requires no overt response, may require far more active mental processing than having the learner respond overtly by pushing the return key to turn the page. A transaction in which the interactions all require the learner to engage mental processes directly related to the knowledge structure being promoted will be more effective than one in which many of the interactions are passive or are less related to the mental processes represented by the knowledge structure. The degree of mental effort required should not be an alternative, rather, a given transaction should be defined such that its interactions require all the mental processing that is necessary for the learners to acquire the target knowledge structure(s).

The type of transaction and the components of its knowledge base limit the interactions that are possible within a given transaction shell. Different classes of transactions will have different types of interactions. Nevertheless, all transactions should include interactions that are characterized by certain interaction modes. Four interaction modes have been identified: presentation, exploration, practice, and test (Merrill, Li, & Jones, 1991).

The interactions modes are defined as follows:

- *Presentation.* This mode is the primary way that knowledge is conveyed to the learner. Present does not imply passive interaction; an adequate presentation may involve a great deal of interaction. The learner is presented information (i.e., location, name, and description of parts, steps, or events, and any attached, illustrative demonstrations).

- *Exploration.* This mode enables the learner to have a quick look at the knowledge without extensive interaction. The learner explores the information given in the presentation mode by clicking on one piece of the information linked to the part, step, or event (e.g., name or location). The system then displays the rest of the component information (e.g., description and demonstration).

- *Practice.* This mode enables the learner to consolidate his or her knowledge. Practice provides an opportunity for the learner to demonstrate, generalize, elaborate, integrate, and extend new skills. The system provides the *Correct Answer* as feedback to incorrect learner responses so that learners can learn from their mistakes.

- *Test.* This mode enables ID Expert to determine the extent to which the learner has internalized the knowledge. To what extent is the learner able to remember the knowledge, use the knowledge, and apply the knowledge? Assessment is similar to practice, but with most of the learning supports removed so as to enable the learner to demonstrate knowledge acquisition in situations which resemble real-world settings. The learner must recall the correct information from memory and apply that knowledge. The only feedback the learner receives is a score at the end of the testing exercise.

Instructional Transaction Shells: Responsibilities, Methods, and Parameters

Responsibilities

The instructional design prescriptions of first generation instructional design are characterized as "best case" prescriptions. We have identified different prescriptions for each of several performance-content outcomes in our earlier work on component display theory. These prescriptions identify values for a number of variables which characterize the best instructional strategy for each of the possible outcomes. These prescriptions, however, do not identify the range of values for the many parameters which characterize each prescription, nor do they indicate conditions for which these parameters should assume different values. In other words, each outcome classification has a "best case" prescription, and deviations from this prescription are left to the individual instructional designer. Transaction shells do not merely represent a best case. By changing its parameter values, a shell can be configured in many ways to represent a complete range of instructional interactions (Merrill, Li, & Jones, 1992).

Several instructional responsibilities are necessary in order for an instructional transaction to successfully interact with a learner. All instructional transactions, regardless of the type of knowledge or skill they teach, must be capable of performing these responsibilities. The specific methods and parameters that are necessary for a given type of transaction to accomplish these responsibilities will differ from one class of transactions to another. In fact, the difference in the way these responsibilities are accomplished by different classes of transactions is one of the characteristics that distinguishes one class of transactions from another.

Each responsibility is accomplished via several *methods*. These methods are specific activities that enable the responsibility to be accomplished. They require values on a number of instructional *parameters*. These parameter values determine exactly how a given method is applied in a given transaction instance. The interactions enabled by a given transaction can exhibit a considerable variance, depending on the values assigned to the parameters which constrain its methods. Instructional design via instructional transaction shells consists of selecting parameter values appropriate for a given learner population and particular learning task. These parameter values then enable the methods of each responsibility to carry out this responsibility in a way consistent with the requirements of a given learning situation.

All instructional transactions must include the following responsibilities: *knowledge selection, knowledge sequence, interaction management,* and *interaction enactment.*

Select Knowledge. From all the knowledge associated with a given transaction instance, the knowledge selection responsibility determines that part of the knowledge which will be taught during a particular enactment of the transaction. Each of the frames in the knowledge base may include a large number of components: parts, steps, or events. Each of these knowledge frames may be implemented by several different mediations in the instructional resource data base. The amount of available knowledge often exceeds that which needs to be presented during a given enactment of the transaction. When a transaction is sent a message to do its job, the first parameters it needs are those which tell it about all the knowledge that is available and which specific knowledge elements are to be included during this enactment of the transaction.

Sequence Knowledge. The knowledge sequence responsibility determines which of the selected knowledge elements is presented next. Whenever the amount of knowledge to be included in a given enactment of a transaction exceeds that which should be presented simultaneously, then an instructional transaction requires sequence parameters to indicate how this knowledge should be partitioned and sequenced. Knowledge acquisition is facilitated if the knowledge is partitioned into mind-size pieces; on the other hand, knowledge assessment often requires the learner to interact with the knowledge as a whole. A given instructional transaction, regardless of the type of knowledge taught, should be able to invoke a variety of instructional sequences.

Manage Interactions. The instructional management responsibility determines how the student will interact with the selected and sequenced knowledge. Instructional management is accomplished by the selection of an *instructional strategy.* An instructional strategy is a sequence of *interaction modes,* each of which knows how to either present information, explore information, facilitate the student's practice of the skills promoted, or assess the student's knowledge and skills. The management responsibility also determines when a learner should move to the next interaction mode in the strategy. Instructional strategies can vary from providing information to promoting mastery of the knowledge and skills involved in the transaction. The type and sequence of interaction modes vary from one strategy to another. A given instructional transaction, regardless of the type of knowledge taught, should be able to invoke a variety of instructional strategies.

Enact Interactions. The instructional enactment responsibility determines how each interaction mode in a given strategy carries out its responsibility. The enactment responsibility determines the role that a given interaction will play, whether presenting information, enabling practice, or assessing a student. The enactment responsibility specifies how the interaction presents information, constrains learner responses, and/or reacts to the learner's responses. The enactment responsibility also determines how each interaction is adjusted to provide the type of interaction most appropriate to a given student and subject matter. A given interaction mode, regardless of the type of knowledge taught, should be able to modify the nature of its interaction with the student in a variety of ways.

Methods

A transaction accomplishes each of its responsibilities via a set of methods. A method is a set of activities carried out by the responsibility in the process of enacting the transaction. The way that a particular method accomplishes its role is determined by a set of specific parameters.

All transactions include knowledge selection methods for *partitioning* knowledge, *portraying* knowledge, and *amplifying* knowledge; knowledge sequencing methods for routing the learning through the selected knowledge and *guiding* the learner's advancement; interaction management methods for *prioritizing* interactions and *expediting* the learner's acquirement of the knowledge involved in the interaction; and interaction enactment methods for *presenting, exploring, enabling practice,* and *assessing knowledge.*

Select Knowledge. The knowledge selection responsibility is accomplished via three methods: knowledge partitioning, knowledge portrayal, and knowledge amplification.

Partition Knowledge. Learners can process only a limited amount of information at any one time. Working memory can effectively consider less than 7 plus or minus 2 chunks of information simultaneously. When more information is presented, previous information is lost from working memory. Effective instruction therefore requires that when the amount of information to be presented exceeds that which can be effectively handled by short-term memory, this information needs to be divided into mind-sized pieces. The *knowledge partitioning* method accomplishes this task by first selecting from the knowledge available to the transaction that knowledge which will be taught, and second, while making this selection, dividing the knowledge into mind-sized pieces or segments.

Portray Knowledge. A primary advantage of learning from an instructional situation is that the learner can be brought into contact with a much wider scope of knowledge via the mediation of this knowledge than would be possible if the learner was required to learn only from the real world or on-the-job. Not only can a wider scope of knowledge be presented, but this knowledge can be mediated in ways that enable it to be more effectively learned than learning it from its naturally occurring state. The *knowledge portrayal* method selects from the various mediations available in the resource data base those knowledge mediations that will be used by the current enactment of the transaction.

Amplify Knowledge. The knowledge to be taught can be divided into primary knowledge and ancillary knowledge. Primary knowledge is the information that is the focus of a particular instructional intervention. Ancillary knowledge is additional information that is prerequisite to the primary knowledge, that provides nice-to-know information related to the primary knowledge, that provides a context or setting for the primary knowledge, or which makes the primary knowledge easier to learn. The *amplify* knowledge method selects from the available ancillary knowledge that which will be included in a particular enactment of the transaction.

Sequence Knowledge. The knowledge sequencing responsibility is accomplished via two methods: *routing* the learner though the selected knowledge and *guiding* the learners advancement through the selected knowledge.

Route Learner. A path sequences the knowledge segments for a given student. The route learner method determines an appropriate path through the selected knowledge—that is, at any point in the instruction, it determines which knowledge segment a given learner should study next.

Guide Advancement. The guide advancement method determines when a learner has received maximum benefit from study of a given knowledge segment, and when the student should move to the next knowledge segment. Under learner control, this method also provides appropriate information to enable the leaner to choose from alternative paths.

Manage Interactions. The interaction management responsibility is accomplished via two methods: *interaction prioritization* and *acquirement expediation.*

Prioritize Interactions. Each transaction consists of a number of possible *interaction modes.* An instructional strategy is an ordering of these interaction modes for a given student. This method determines which interaction mode should be engaged next for a given student.

Expedite Acquirement. Acquirement refers to the learner's internalization of the knowledge and skill being taught by a given transaction. Interaction modes are the means by which this acquirement is accomplished. The expedite acquirement method determines when the student has received maximum benefit from one interaction mode and should move to the next in order to optimize this acquirement. Under learner control, this method also provides appropriate information to enable the learner to choose from alternative interaction modes.

Enact Interactions. The interaction enactment responsibility is accomplished via four methods, each one corresponding to one of the four primary interaction modes described earlier in this chapter: *present knowledge, explore knowledge, enable practice,* and *assess knowledge.*

Present Knowledge. The present method is the primary way that knowledge is conveyed to the learner.

Explore Knowledge. This mode enables the learner to have a quick look at the knowledge without extensive interaction.

Enable Practice. Practice provides an opportunity for the learner to demonstrate, generalize, elaborate, integrate, and extend new skills.

Assess Knowledge. Assessment is similar to practice but with most of the learning supports removed to enable the learner to demonstrate knowledge acquisition in situations which resemble real-world settings.

Parameters

A transaction shell is a piece of computer code that, when delivered to a student via an appropriate delivery system, causes a transaction to occur. A transaction configuration system enables the instructor or designer to provide values for a wide range of instructional parameters. We define parameters as the different instructional design strategy settings that are changeable. These parameters control the nature of the interactions with the learner. A transaction shell has three authoring subsystems, as described earlier.

For example, in ID Expert, the instructional development tool designed to test the ITT theory, the designer can change the instructional design strategy at any level of the course organization hierarchy. At the segment level, the designer can specify transaction sequence, interaction sequence, and display of transaction properties. The transaction sequences are comprised of *Learner Control*, *Prerequisite* (the learner must attain mastery of specified transactions prior to moving on to the next transactions, *Linear* (the learner must proceed sequentially through the transactions), and *Integrated* (the system moves the learner directly from one transaction to the next as specified by the interaction sequence and without a display of each transaction's properties). At the transaction level, the designer can specify the selection, timing, and sequencing of component display, mastery criterion, feedback type and source, and mode of learner response. This ability to change instructional design parameters enables the designer to customize the instruction to a specific target audience.

Learner and System Control. Learner control has attained widespread popularity in recent years, but indications are that not every learner can make good decisions about his or her own learning. An adequate transaction should allow both learner and system controlled interactions. A transaction needs to have the capability to direct learner activity as well as having the learner control the interaction; it needs to include both learner controlled and system controlled interactions. The degree of learner control provided in any given situation is a function of the familiarity, motivation, aptitude, and attitude of the individual learners involved. These learner characteristics are all manipulatable parameters within ID Expert's Audience Configuration dialog box.

There are four different interaction modes through which the learner interacts with the system: Present, Explore, Practice, and Test. These interaction modes are under either system or learner control. Under system control (SC), the system sequences the displays and responses in the interaction mode. Under learner control (LC), the learner sequences the displays and responses. LC overview enables the learner to explore the knowledge structure(s); SC overview systematically overviews the knowledge structure(s) as prescribed by the instructional designer. LC presentation enables the learner to explore the knowledge in any order; SC presentation systematically sequences the knowledge for the learner. SC sequencing of knowledge is especially important if sequencing is an important factor in the knowledge content. LC practice allows the learner to engage in practice opportunities in any order; SC practice presents practice opportunities one-by-one in a predetermined systematic order (Merrill *et al.*, 1991).

Use as a Rapid Prototyping Tool

ID Expert's flexible instructional strategies and built-in interaction modes make it an ideal rapid prototyping tool (Jones, Li, & Merrill, 1992). In contrast to traditional ISD models which require the designer to wait until the end of the front-end, data-gathering process before a prototype can be developed, ID Expert offers users the capability of walking into a client's office with a lap-top computer, visiting with the client about the subject-matter content, and developing a prototype on the spot, using placeholders or existing resources in place of the appropriate resources. The instructional designer can offer a number of different prototypes based upon the client's needs, using a whole series of different design approaches, until both the client and the instructional designer are satisfied with the prototype. Prototyping with ID Expert is faster than with traditional ISD models. It also provides the client and the instructional designer with a mutually clear idea of the final product. This makes it much more cost-effective than traditional ISD models, which lack a high correspondence between the user's view and design at the *beginning* of the instructional design process.

Another reason ID Expert makes an excellent rapid prototyping tool is that it allows the instructional designer to focus on the design and not on the tool. As Jones *et al.* (1992) state: "Designers of instructional products should think more about expository sequences, assessment, and learner control, and less about buttons, fields, placement of graphics on the screen, and program code" (p. 97). ID Expert's built-in instructional strategy and interaction modes enable the user to concentrate on creativity, without having to worry about screen display or programming languages. Everything but the subject-matter content is built in to the system.

Automatic Configuration of Transactions

One goal of Instructional Transactions is to make instructional development more efficient—an order of magnitude more efficient. But if even a simple instructional transaction (e.g., learning the names of the parts of some entity) requires the large number of parameters identified in this paper, then doesn't concern with all of these parameters make the instructional design more time consuming rather than less? The answer is "yes" and "no." "Yes" if a designer had to individually set all of these parameter values in order to design a piece of instruction, or worse, had to concern him- or herself with each of these variables in designing unique instruction; then the time would increase. Paradoxically, "hand-wired" instructional design must be concerned with all of these parameters anyway, but we do so implicitly rather than explicitly. "No" if a piece of computer code captures how to teach identification and if all of these parameters are part of the code but not made explicitly available to the designer; then the instructional design can be significantly more efficient.

A given designer would, via the transaction configuration system, provide information about students and the task. A set of rules (intelligence) in the transaction configuration expert system converts this information into a set of default values for the parameters of the transaction shell. The designer can then immediately inspect an enactment of the instruction and modify it by either changing the original input information about students and the task or, if necessary, by explicitly changing a given parameter value affecting the part of the instruction he or she wants to modify. The process is analogous to using many of the modern computer interfaces. Programming in Windows or on the Macintosh is far more complex than earlier systems, but the resulting user interface, for the non-programmer, is much easier to use. In a similar way, the level of detail suggested by this chapter is necessary in order to program an instructional transaction shell, but, once in place, the subject matter expert user will be able to design and develop technology based instruction much more easily (Merrill *et al.*, 1991).

Audience Rules

In any classroom or workplace, there are people that have different needs, background experience, motivation levels, and learning levels. The purpose of audience configurations is to create instruction for the target audience. The instructional designer can create a new audience and define the values for that audience, which will then determine the instructional strategy. The values that can be set for an audience include the motivation level, experience level, and learning level of the student within ID Expert's Audience Configurations dialog box. The *Motivation* and *Experience* levels both include a "High" and "Low" parameter setting. The *Learning Levels* include *Mastery, Familiarity, Basic,* and *Overview. Mastery* means the learner must carry out a procedure or thoroughly understand a process. *Familiarity* means the learner needs enough information to supervise or manage. *Basic* means the learner needs enough information to make a decision or selection (e.g., deciding upon the best business management plan or selecting the correct answer from a test). *Overview* means the learner needs information only (e.g., with a new employee orientation or a product demo-kiosk).

ID Expert changes the instructional parameters within the built-in instructional design strategies, as the author changes the audience values. The result is effective, quality instruction that is produced automatically without additional input from the subject-matter expert or inexperienced instructional designer. The author is also optimizing the use of time by using ID Expert's default parameter settings, thereby reducing development costs.

Effects of Different Audience Settings

When the author sets the values for an audience within the Audience Configuration dialog box, ID Expert automatically sets the parameters throughout all of the instructional parameter dialog boxes.

There are two main categories of control that are directly affected by changes in the audience configuration parameters: the interaction sequence and the practice/test component sequence. The system provides *Learner Control* over the interaction sequence to learners who are assessed as being highly motivated to learn. The system can also prescribe a *Remedial* interaction sequence, which first assesses the learners' mastery of the content and then, based on the learners' performance, either moves them forward to the next transaction or back to the present and/or Explore interaction modes for remedial help. The system places learners with *Low* experience and motivation levels into a *Standard* interaction sequence and takes them sequentially through each of the four interaction modes.

ID Expert also changes the Practice/Test interaction modes and response modes based on the defined learner characteristics. The system selects a *Simultaneous* practice sequence for learners requiring a *Basic* or *Mastery* level of learning and a *Sequential* practice sequence for learners requiring a *Familiarity* level of learning. In the *Simultaneous* mode, the learner must complete all the selected responses for one component prior to advancing to the next. In the *Sequential* mode, the learner must go through all the components with one response mode before proceeding to the next response mode, and so on, until all the components have been completed using all the response modes.

ID Expert provides two response modes for the learner: recognize and recall. In the *Recognize* response mode, the learner need only click on the correct response to select it from a display of all available responses. In the *Recall* response mode, the learner must recall from memory the correct response and enter (by typing) that response into the response prompt box. ID Expert provides the instructional designer with a *Keywords* function so that learners can answer in their own words as long as they include the key words of the content as specified by the instructional designer.

As an example of changed instructional design strategies based on defined learner characteristics, a user could create an audience called "Novice" and assign the following parameters to that audience:

> Motivation = Low
> Experience = Low
> Learning Level = Mastery

ID Expert automatically takes the student through the Presentation interaction, then through Practice and Test sequentially. In the Practice interaction, the student is required to type in the name and description of the parts instead of just recognizing them from a list. The Test interaction is identical to Practice, except that the student does not receive immediate feedback. The student must get 90% or better to pass the test.

The instructional designer could use the same knowledge base and change the audience configuration as follows in order to meet the learning needs of a different audience:

Motivation = High
Experience = High
Learning Level = Overview

These values would typically be for a person in a supervisor's role or one who does not need to know the material well but needs an overview of the content. ID Expert provides the Explore interaction mode with learner control according to the values above. Learner control gives the student the ability to select what to do next. The student can decide not only what transaction to study next, but also what interaction mode to engage in within the selected transaction.

The instructor can select the desired audience from the list of previously created audience configurations in the Audience drop-down menu in the Course Organization window. The Audience menu gives the instructor the ability to customize the same course for a variety of audiences.

Custom Parameter Setting for Multiple Transaction Versions

In addition to creating audience configurations by setting the values for Motivation, Experience, and Learning Level, the user can open the Design Transaction Strategy dialog box to manually set parameters according to the identified instructional needs of the learners. Hence, an audience configuration can be completely controlled by the built-in instructional strategies, which follow the values set for Motivation, Experience, or Learning Level. Or, an audience configuration can use these value settings in conjunction with preferences for instructional strategies set by the instructional designer. Finally, the instructional designer can customize every instructional strategy parameter according to his or her own instructional design preferences.

Benefits of Automatic Configuration

One of the benefits of automatically configuring the instructional design strategies is the inherent ability to create different versions of the course for different audiences. The amount of time and money saved is tremendous because the same course can be used for a variety of audiences. For example, supervisors requiring an overview of the training content can receive one version of the training while their subordinates receive a different version of the same training. The instructional designer can define a "Supervisor" audience in the Audience Configuration's dialog box, which automatically modifies the instructional transactions according to the Supervisor's needs. An additional audience called "Novice" could then be defined, which automatically changes the instructional transactions for the needs of the beginners.

Current Testing and Development

Research and development of ID Expert and other tools to test instructional transaction theory continues at Utah State University. Some of these tools include the *Learning Environment Builder* (a tool for developing multimedia exploration-simulation environments), *Language Listening Tutor* (a tool for developing situated multimedia language learning experiences), *Electronic Textbook Builder* (a tool for developing multimedia books), and the *Electronic Workshop* (a tool used by technical writers to create multimedia instruction with automated practice).

Future Design for Online Adaptation of Instruction

If we can adjust instructional transaction parameters while creating instruction, then we can also adjust these same parameters during run-time, thereby providing automatic reconfiguration of the transaction and real-time adaptation of instruction. This capability is especially important due to the changing instructional needs of students. An instructor can currently select a previously created audience, which automatically changes the parameters accordingly, or create a unique audience, which changes the instructional strategy. In the future, ID Expert's *Facilitator* will act as a guide or coach to the learner. The Facilitator will assist the learner in developing an instructional strategy. A meta-issue here is not just the acquisition of knowledge, but the transformation of students into efficient learners. If the learner does not respond to an instructional strategy defined by the designer, then the Facilitator can choose a different instructional strategy which better fits the learner's learning style as identified through interaction with the system.

Notes

1. Portions of this chapter were previously published in *Educational Technology.*
2. M. David Merrill first introduced the idea of an instructional transaction in 1985. Subsequently Li & Merrill (1990) described instructional transactions in more detail.
3. To avoid the frequent repetition of the entire phrase "instructional transaction" or "instructional transaction shell" we will often adopt the shorter "transaction" or "transaction shell." The reader should understand that the modifier "instructional" is understood in this shorthand usage.
4. We make no claims about how cognitive structure is organized and elaborated, as this is not well understood. We stand on the weaker and more defensible assumption that we can analyze the organization and elaborations of knowledge outside the mind, and presume that there is some correspondence between these and the representations in the mind.

References

Gagné, R. M. (1965). *The conditions of learning* (1st ed.). New York: Holt, Rinehart, and Winston.

Jones, M. K., Li, Z., & Merrill, M. D. (1992). Rapid prototyping in automated instructional design. *Educational Technology Research & Development, 40*(4), 95–100.

Kuhn, T. S. (1970). *The structure of scientific revolutions* (2nd ed.). Chicago: University of Chicago Press.

Li, Z., & Merrill, M. D. (1990). Transaction shells: A new approach to courseware authoring. *Journal of Research on Computing in Education, 23*(1), 72–86.

Lippert, R. C. (1989). Expert systems: Tutors, tools, and tutees. *Journal of Computer-Based Instruction, 16*(1), 11–19.

Merrill, M. D. (1980). Learner control in computer based learning. *Computers & Education, 4,* 77-95.

Merrill, M. D. (1985). Where is the authoring in authoring systems? *Journal of Computer-Based Instruction, 12*(4), 90–96.

Merrill, M. D. (1993). Instructional transaction theory: Knowledge relationships among processes, entities, and activities. *Educational Technology, 33*(4), 5–16.

Merrill, M. D. (1994). The new component design theory: Instructional design for courseware authoring. In D. G. Twitchell (Ed.), *Instructional design theory* (pp. 353–366). Englewood Cliffs, NJ: Educational Technology Publications.

Merrill, M. D., Jones, M. K., & Li, Z. (1992). Instructional transaction theory: Classes of transactions. *Educational Technology, 32*(6), 12–26.

Merrill, M. D., Li, Z., & Jones, M. K. (1990a). Limitations of first generation instructional design. *Educational Technology, 30*(1), 7–11.

Merrill, M. D., Li, Z., & Jones, M. K. (1990b). Second generation instructional design (ID$_2$). *Educational Technology, 30*(2), 7–14.

Merrill, M. D., Li, Z., & Jones, M. K. (1991). Instructional transaction theory: An introduction. *Educational Technology, 31*(6), 7–12.

Merrill, M. D., Li, Z., & Jones, M. K. (1992). Instructional transaction shells: Responsibilities, methods, and parameters. *Educational Technology, 32*(2), 5–27.

Merrill, M. D., Li, Z., Jones, M. K., & Hancock, S. W. (1997). *Instructional transaction theory: Transaction shells.* Manuscript in preparation.

Reigeluth, C. M., Merrill, M. D., Wilson, B. G., & Spiller, R. T. (1994). The elaboration theory of instruction: A model for sequencing and synthesizing instruction. In D. G. Twitchell (Ed.), *Instructional design theory* (pp. 79–102). Englewood Cliffs, NJ: Educational Technology Publications.

35

Automating the Design of Adaptive and Self-Improving Instruction

Jianping Zhang
Andrew S. Gibbons
M. David Merrill
Utah State University, Logan

Computer-based instruction (CBI) technology has demonstrated its ability to carry out several education and training functions effectively, and the use of interactive instructional technologies has experienced a dramatic increase in recent years. However, this technology will be a viable solution to education and training problems only if the cost of developing new instructional products can be made much more competitive with the cost of developing traditional instruction. This focuses attention directly on the tool software that is used for the creation of interactive instructional systems: the authoring system.

Authoring systems allow an author, normally an instructional designer or a subject-matter expert, to create computer-based instruction in a timely and cost-effective way. This is achieved by eliminating the complex and costly programming step and by allowing the designer to build structures of instructional logic out of tailored program code or logical primitives. The earliest authoring systems were programming languages, but ones in which the code necessary to carry out instructional functions was bundled within designer-friendly macros such as "ask (a question)" and "display (a graphic)." Later authoring systems incorporate menus to allow authors to build logic and display plans. Most recently, graphical authoring interfaces have reduced some of the author's choices to simple drag-and-drop mouse actions.

Solving the programming problem for authors with authoring systems has greatly influenced the productivity of development of computerized instruction, and the number of computer-based products has increased geometrically. However, the current conception of authoring systems has not solved the problem to a sufficient degree. A cost barrier still exists to the use of computer-based instruction, and the quality of current instructional products still appears to be far below the potential promised by the computer. Existing authoring systems have not supplied the answer to the problem for two reasons: (1) the increasing popularity of computerized instruction and rapid developments in computer technology have resulted in the expectation of steadily increasing sophistication in the product, and pressure is always on authoring systems to "un-program" increasingly complex display and logic functions; (2) even though the expensive programming burden has been lifted from the author's shoulders, there remains an equally costly and unnecessarily repetitive design process burden which still rests squarely on the designer. Authoring systems, which are mainly logic-builders and offer little instructional design assistance, have done almost nothing to alleviate this problem (Merrill, 1985). Moreover, there has developed an unexpected and still existing shortage of qualified instructional designers trained to carry out the rigorous design process.

Authoring Systems and Design Systems

In order to develop computer based instruction using existing authoring systems, both a subject matter and instructional design expertise must be involved. The subject matter expert possesses content expertise, and the instructional designer is trained in the construction of systems that instruct well. Designing effective computer based instruction using an authoring system requires considerable interaction between the subject matter expert and the instructional designer. This instructional design process is most labor intensive. Only the best-funded training programs can afford to be computer-based, and many organizations that are attracted to the concept of computer-basing recoil when they discover the size and technical expertise of the infrastructure they must build in order to implement CBI by themselves—even assuming the use of an authoring system.

One response to this problem has been the oversimplification of the concept of computer-based instruction and a departure from the original conception of the computer as an *active* instructional agent. Contemporary computer-based instruction has fallen into a pattern dictated mainly by the economics of the available authoring tools. Linear and simple branching tutorials are the most convenient and least expensive form of computerized instruction created by authoring systems, and therefore they are by far the most numerous products produced. It is not a matter of effectiveness, because several alternative forms of the computer-based instructional product (such as the simulation) surpass the tutorial in effectiveness. These alternatives are also more costly to build, however, so they are much less frequently built. The mass of computer instruction products today are sub-optimal in terms of both cost and quality.

The early concept of computer-based instruction placed a high value on the ability of the computer to adapt the interaction to the momentary needs and condition of the student (Stolurow, 1969). Different students have different backgrounds, capabilities, motivations, and habits of learning. The early vision of computer-based instruction was motivated by the notion that the computer, capable of lightning-fast decisions, could deliver instruction appropriate to the dynamic momentary needs of the individual student. Today, instructional designers find it difficult to make instruction adaptive to the individual, even when they have clear plans as to how that can be achieved. This is because the authoring tools which they use make it very difficult to do so. This is a little-discussed failure of existing authoring systems.

To create adaptive instruction, an authoring system must provide the author with tools with which to build and then control the administration of instructional primitives to the student. Whereas existing authoring systems allow the author to create sequences of logic and displays, an authoring system for adaptive instruction will ask the designer to supply the raw materials from which logic and displays can be created at the time of instruction. Furthermore, it will allow the instructional event driver to select the best instructional strategy based on student performance data at the time of instruction but not before. Such an authoring system must allow the designer to specify or select rules to control the administration of these elements to the student. There is no capability of this type in existing authoring systems.

Self-improving Instruction

Some time after the original dream of the adaptive instructional system, there arose the idea that a computer-based instructional system could further improve its performance by learning from its own experience. One of the most valuable qualities of a human instructor is the ability to improve instruction through experience, which includes practice and feedback. In time, this learning capacity can turn a young, inexperienced instructor to a seasoned and powerful teacher. Our common perception is that an instructor who would never improve his or her skills is hardly a good instructor. This comparison might be applied as well to a computerized instructional system. A system with no capability to modify or update instructional strategies and curriculum and the rules for administering them must be looked upon as only a mechanical device.

Toward a Solution

If computer-based instructional technology is to have a role in the solution of America's educational and training problems, then the tools for creating computer-based instructional products must change radically so that the products themselves can change in form and power. The new tools must at the same time reduce the costs of development by an order of magnitude and place in the hands of the designer the primitives from which truly adaptive, non-tutorial, and experience-sensitive instructional systems can be built.

To address this problem, the ID_2 Research Team at Utah State University has embarked on a program of technological research to develop an authoring tool capable of automated and high-rate authoring for instruction which is both adaptive and capable of self-improvement. The ID Expert system has been under design for over five years (Merrill & Li, 1989) and is intended for use by both novice subject-matter experts and experienced instructional designers. This chapter describes the planned growth of the ID Expert system, with emphasis on the future adaptive and self-improving qualities it must possess.

Historical Trends

Many systems have demonstrated the ability to create instruction adapted to individual students. Adaptations have been demonstrated in subject-matter sequencing (Westcourt, Beard, & Gould, 1977), subject-matter treatment (Lesgold, 1987), selection of instructional strategies and tactics (Woolf & McDonald, 1984), tutorial dialogue construction (Carbonell, 1970; Clancey, 1983), system-generated explanations of student-generated constructions (White & Frederiksen, 1986), system-generated explanations in response to student interrogation (Clancey, 1983), construction of student-prescribed demonstrations (Forbus, 1984; Stevens, Roberts, & Stead, 1983), coaching (Burton & Brown, 1979; Shute & Glaser, 1986), selection of problem type (White & Frederiksen, 1986), selection of problems (Burton, 1982; Kimball, 1982), selection of progressive problem sequences (Barr, Beard, & Atkinson, 1976; White & Frederiksen, 1986), and provision of feedback and advice (Brown, Burton, & Bell, 1975).

As well as adaptive instructional systems, there have been laboratory examples of "learning" systems: systems capable of improving their own instructional practice based on experience with instructing students. A system described by Kimball (Kimball, 1982) is capable of identifying student solutions to symbolic integration problems which are better than its own and adjusting its knowledge base when it finds a superior student solution path. O'Shea (O'Shea, 1979) describes a system which is capable of adjusting instructional strategy based on instructional experience.

The benefits of both adaptive and self-improving systems have so far been confined primarily to the laboratory as research results. Very few adaptive or self-improving systems have seen extended use in day-to-day instructional settings. Moreover, commercially-available authoring tools do not provide the average designer or subject-matter expert with the capability to create adaptive or self-improving instruction at low cost. This results in a continuing isolation of the designer from applied experimentation with innovative products and forms a gap between what has been demonstrated as possible and what the available tools empower. The ID Expert system hopes to eventually bridge that gap.

Instructional Transaction Theory

The design of the Instructional Design Expert (IDX) system is based on Instructional Transaction Theory (ITT) (Merrill, Li, & Jones, 1991). Transaction theory maintains that the basic building block of instruction should be the instructional transaction. This principle applies particularly to the highly interactive medium of computer-based instruction, in which the most powerful vehicle for learning is the pattern of interactions between student and computer.

A transaction is a sequence of related interactions between an instructional driver program and a student, in which there is a mutually-responsive interchange of information. From the computer, the student receives instructional messages, demonstrations, directions, requests for responses, feedback and correction. From the student, the computer receives requests for information, requests for instructional treatments of various kinds, and responses which can be analyzed in order to reach conclusions regarding the progress of the student's learning.

A "transaction" differs from the notion of "frame," upon which the majority existing authoring tools are built. A frame is a pre-programmed and stored quantity of message and logic that is linked either closely or loosely with other frames into a sequence. A mostly linear arrangement of frames is the hallmark of the great bulk of computer-based instruction today, particularly that which has been created using available authoring tools. A transaction, in contrast, is a non-sequenced set of possible interaction primitives which is given definition and sequence only at the time of instruction by the means of control data which is passed to it by a transaction manager function.

Twelve classes of generic instructional transactions have been identified (Merrill, 1987; Merrill, Li, & Jones, 1992a,b) as well as numerous specialized transaction patterns. A transaction class is distinguished by the types of instructional primitive it includes, the types of content and message primitives it is equipped to handle, and the set of parameters that is required to cause it to function during instruction. The Execute Transaction, which teaches students to execute a procedure, must be aware of "steps" in a procedure and uses parameters which specify demonstration types and levels of prompting during practice. The Interpret Transaction, in contrast, teaches students to understand observable processes and the principles that drive them. It is aware of the "stages" of a process, which are much different from the steps of a procedure, and requires parameters which specify types of experimental interactions with the student.

Instructional transactions are designed and programmed once within programs called transaction "shells." Once created, transaction shells have parameterized message slots which can be used with different bodies of specific content, as long as they are of a similar kind of knowledge or skill. Authoring using transaction shells consists of creating knowledge bases which are keyed to the structures of multiple transaction shells and configuring the control

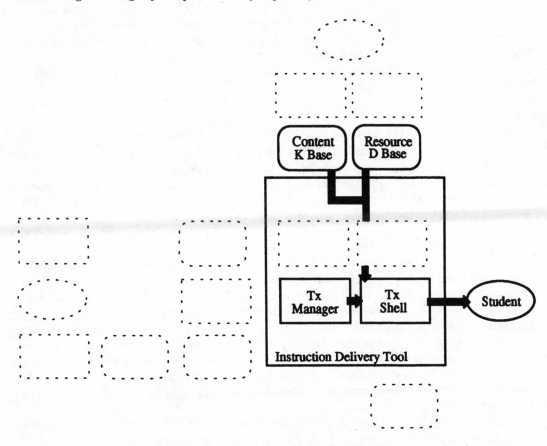

Figure 1.   ID Expert during instruction.

parameters. This may be done by supplying set values to the shell in advance of instruction or, as is explained later in this chapter, by allowing an expert system to supply the values during instruction.

Separability of Content and Interaction Patterns

An important assumption of Transaction Theory is that instructional content and resources, the raw materials from which instructional messages are constructed, can be separated from the interactions between computer and student which constitute instructional strategy. This assumption allows transactions to be generic and to be applied to any content during instruction (Jones, Li, & Merrill, 1990; Merrill, 1992) so long as it is structured properly.

Transaction Theory makes the second assumption that all subject matters possess regularities of structure that allow them to be represented within a common-form knowledge base. This assumption ensures that the organization of knowledge to be instructed will be regular, so that it can be acted upon by the complementary organization of the strategies incorporated in transactions. These two assumptions foreshadow the basic mechanism of the ID Expert system, which is illustrated in Figure 1.

At the time of instruction, the structure of subject-matter content and display resources from the content knowledge base and resource data base respectively are combined for delivery to the student. Rather than being pre-composed, instruction is free to take any of a number of forms at any moment, depending on the prescriptive data sent to the transaction shell from the transaction manager.

Control and Adaptability of Instruction

The source of control data within ID Expert is of the greatest importance, because the mechanism for supplying this control data determines the degree of adaptability of the instruction. If control data supplied to a transaction shell is predetermined by the instructional designer and pre-stored in the computer until the time of instruction, then there is little difference between the instruction it produces and instruction created by a frame-based authoring system. Only certain paths are possible for the student, and all of them are pre-determined by the designer.

If, on the other hand: (1) the control data passed from the Transaction Manager to the Transaction Shell is derived at the time of instruction, (2) the transaction shell is made up of an appropriate set of instructional primitives, and (3) a robust and varied set of raw materials has been stored in the knowledge and resource bases, then the instruction can be made highly adaptive to the individual student. The only limits to adaptability will be: (1) the quality of content and display resources, (2) the conclusions that can be reached by rule-based inference from the student's response patterns, and (3) the set of primitive instructional interaction forms which have been included within the transaction shell. It is, in part, the set of expert instructional rules in the transaction manager function that gives the system the name of ID "Expert."

Earlier designs of ID Expert specify that the source of the data used by the transaction manager be the Monitor and Advisor, aided by data from both student and course data bases. These are included into a feedback loop in Figure 2.

The function of observing student responses to instruction is assigned to the Monitor, which records the responses and screens them to identify patterns of interest to the Advisor. Patterns of interest depend on the momentary context of instruction, and the Monitor must be aware of the function being carried out by the transaction shell at each moment in order to know which patterns to anticipate.

The Advisor is assigned the function of interpreting the pattern data forwarded to it by the Monitor and selecting the transaction manager's next strategy goal. It does this using data from the Student Record Data Base, which contains the student's characteristics, instructional history, and learning preferences and styles, and from the Course Delivery Knowledge Base, which contains knowledge about task characteristics, instructional parameters, and course definitions.

When the Advisor arrives at a decision, it sends the result to the Transaction Manager, which in turn composes an array of parametric data to condition the transaction shell for the next interaction with the student. This array includes data on the classes of content to be requested from the knowledge base, the resources to be drawn from the resource data base for display construction, the type of interaction to be used, logical values for the control of repetition and feedback, tolerance values for response comparison, and screening patterns of interest to the Monitor. The Advisor is capable of acting in this prescription mode for those portions of instruction that are under system control. It is also capable of acting in an advisory mode for students working under their own direction but toward an explicit instructional goal.

Figure 2 shows that the transaction shell in use at a given moment is selected by the Transaction Manager from a library of shells. Within the space of a few minutes of instruc-

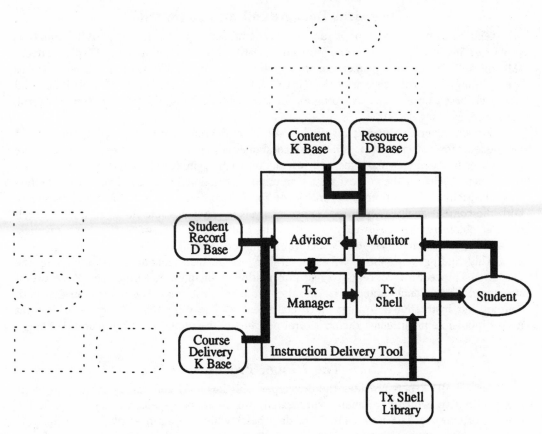

Figure 2. Monitor, Advisor, and data bases provide adaptation.

tion, a student working under student control might request or be prescribed definitions, procedural information, and demonstrations of principle-related phenomena. Supplying this would involve the use of multiple transaction shells, of which the student would know nothing, since the instructional surface would be seamless.

ID Expert and Design

In addition to delivering adaptive instruction, ID Expert is a design system. It was conceived by a team, the ID_2 Research Team, whose title, "ID_2," stands for "Second Generation Instructional Design." ID_2 symbolizes the team's belief that current instructional design principles and practices must be questioned and improved if the field of instructional design is to continue to progress (Merrill, Li, & Jones, 1990a, b).

The incorporation of automated design into ID Expert has several desirable outcomes: (1) It makes the creation of reliably effective computer-based instruction accessible to developers who may lack training in instructional design, (2) it creates leverage for the productivity of the developer, and (3) it opens the door to re-use and multiple uses of knowledge bases and transaction shell structures. Automated design is made possible by the assumptions of content-strategy separability and consistent knowledge structure already described.

Historical Background and Rationale

The assumption that content and instructional strategy can be regarded separately is supported by both theoretical and applied research. Merrill's Component Display Theory (Merrill, 1983) was an early precursor to the current Instructional Transaction Theory. It was used as the basis for the design of the TICCIT CAI system (Bunderson & Merrill, 1974), and was itself based on an extensive program of research on the teaching of concepts (Merrill, Tennyson, & Posey, 1992).

Merrill's concept research resulted in the identification of a family of logically-related components for concept instruction. These components were used during research as the core of a set of instructional messages and interactions which produced predictable learning results when applied in the context of a structured instructional strategy. This learning effect was consistent across concepts, regardless of specific content, and the structural nature of both the content analysis and the strategy analysis made it possible for even novice developers to obtain results consistently. A substantial body of research supports the effectiveness of instruction designed using this structural technique (Merrill, 1994).

This finding generalizes across several types of instructional goals, including the teaching of procedures, concepts, verbal information, principles, and processes. Wide use of structured instructional strategies has resulted from this discovery. The realization that both content and instructional strategy have consistent and learning-related structures is what makes it possible to automate the structural portions of instructional design using ID Expert.

The Design Process

Because ID Expert provides the developer with low-level content, message, and interaction primitives which have been incorporated into transaction shells, the process of design consists of entering data into a family of data bases which are used at the time of instruction to condition the selection and operation of transaction shells and the selection of content. Figure 3 illustrates these knowledge bases in relation to the rest of the system, along with the interfaces which serve them.

The designer, who may be either a non-design-trained subject-matter expert or an instructional technologist, can enter design decisions into any of the data bases. Of these, only two, the Content Knowledge Base and the Resource Data Base, absolutely require entries. The designer's window to the data bases is an interface which appears seamless to the designer but which is shown in Figure 3 as separate input channels.

Each data base contains data relevant to particular instructional decisions. The Course Configuration Tool accepts data related to the structure of the course intended by the designer. The data describing course decisions are stored in the Course Delivery Knowledge Base. The Knowledge Acquisition Tool accepts data for the Content Knowledge Base, one of the two central elements of the system. The Resource Editor allows the designer to associate the names of resources (any form of multimedia resource, such as video, audio, text, or animation) with entity attributes and states; this resource data is placed into the Resource Data Base. The Student Record data base, not shown with its own interface entity, holds data related to individual students. It contains both student characteristic and student historical data which is used to tailor instructional decisions to the individual. A fifth data base, the Course Authoring Knowledge Base, functions to assist with the entry of course delivery data and also participates in the self-improvement function of the system which is described later.

A large body of data may be entered into these four data bases, depending on the designer's wishes and the level of detail that he or she has decided to work at. ID Expert is designed to allow both professional designers and designers-by-designation (normally subject-matter experts pressed into training service) to express designs at any level of detail and to influence instruction at any level through the setting of instructional parameters.

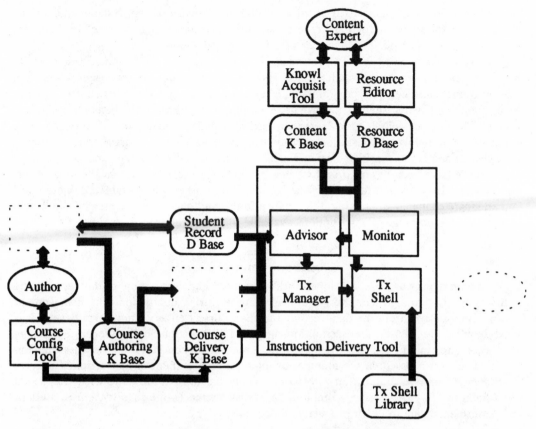

Figure 3. Interfaces for entry of data bases.

Designers and Non-Designers

The complete list of variables placed at the designer's discretion is enormous. Because there are so many potential decisions, and because not all designers wish to or are qualified to make decisions respecting each possible choice, the system has been designed to allow design to be accomplished at several levels. To suggest the possibilities, four levels are described here.

Level 1—Design by Default. The most convenient level of design possible consists of deferring the design to the system and relying on the set of default values built into the system for each content and strategy decision point. Transaction shells are constructed with automatic defaults which are only used if the designer or if the instructional rules of the system fail to override them. The low-effort designer need only enter content into the knowledge base with a set of matching resources. The defaulted system will be capable of providing complete instruction from that beginning, including the construction of courses from the knowledge base.

Level 2—Minimal Design. A second level of design involves making a moderate number of design decisions by entering parametric data for them after making the requisite entries into the *content* knowledge and resource data bases, and then relying on the defaults of the system to make the remainder of the design decisions. This level of design is actually a whole spectrum of levels, because the designer may choose to enter a little parametric data, much data, or somewhere in between. The largest number of designers will fall into this category.

Level 3—Maximal Design. The third level of design envisions the designer making deliberate plans for every instructional choice and entering parametric data for all of them into the appropriate data base. This designer uses few or no defaults.

Level 4—Design Extension. The fourth level of design involves the modification, extension, or creation of a new transaction shell. Though ID Expert automates design, it does not prevent trained designers and programmers from creating new transaction shell varieties, nor from modifying existing shells. The primitives employed in transaction shells are very fine-grained. They can be combined to create a transaction shell for new types of student-system interaction. The family of transaction shells which has been named in ID_2 literature so far is still evolving and is not considered by any means to be a closed set. In fact, specialized transaction shells have been designed and created by the ID_2 Research Team in the area of foreign language training, and future projects are planned in other areas. Trained designers will find adequate challenge in creating new shell varieties, and once they are created, shells will be sharable, so the range of shell options available to users will grow with time.

Management

ID Expert provides the developer with messaging and interaction primitives and the ability to specify, through data, how they will be used during instruction. The management of instruction derives from the data recorded in the Course Delivery Knowledge Base as it is acted upon by the Advisor, Transaction Manager, and Transaction Shell. A separate management system for instruction in ID Expert is not a reasonable consideration, because the concept of ID Expert is based on the moment-by-moment management of instruction. The term "management" used in conjunction with ID Expert has meaning in the same sense that it had when Stolurow (1969) described computer-based instruction as the involvement of student and performance data in every instructional decision.

Self-improvement of Instruction

The ability of ID Expert to adapt instruction to individual students through management has been described. The ID Expert design also includes a self-improving capability through which the system will be able to learn from its own instructional experience and improve the quality of its decisions. Figure 4 adds this final element to the ID Expert design.

The ID Expert instructional rules are the final arbiter of the course of events to be followed during instruction. As ID Expert instructs students, data accumulates which can be used for learning by the system concerning the effects of variations in treatment, both within individual students, and between students. Using this data in conjunction with special analysis programs, the system will be self-improving.

Current Status of ID Expert

To this point, this chapter has described the design of the ID Expert system in its mature state. Over five years of design and development work have brought the ID Expert design to its current state. Of the functions described above, some have been implemented and some are awaiting implementation.

ID Expert has gone through several generations to this point. Early versions of ID Expert were constructed on VAX and Macintosh platforms using standard programming languages and expert system design tools. These early versions were a valuable proving ground for the selection of programming tools. Later programming efforts were centered on the personal computer using C++ as the programming vehicle and Microsoft Windows as the interface vehicle, which we hoped would ensure maximum portability of the finished product.

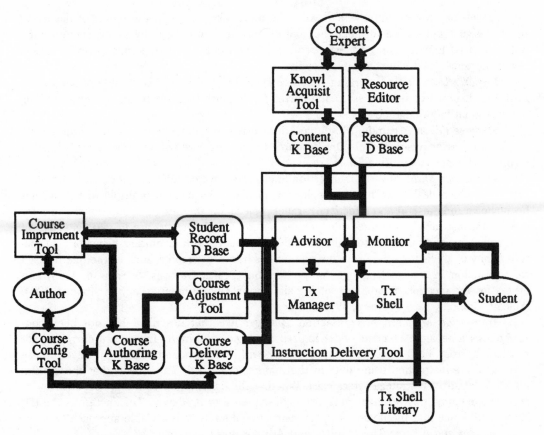

Figure 4. Complete ID Expert system with self-improvement.

Most recent efforts have centered on the use of object-oriented programming tools and are exploring the use of knowledge objects and live simulations as the source of knowledge (see, for instance, Gibbons & Anderson, 1994). Experience with early tools and approaches has convinced the ID_2 Research Team that an object-oriented approach to system development will offer the greatest future flexibility and the most efficient path for programming, and a variety of tools are being tested currently.

ID Expert has been developed under contracts with multiple sponsors. Moreover, multiple lines of development have been pursued in the past, with more than one of them attempting to attain productized status. Several ongoing projects related to ID Expert currently serve as proving grounds for conceptual and programming technique experiments but are intended in time to merge with the main thrust of ID Expert development, which is the completion and productization of a fully-functional ID Expert system. The current functionality of the ID Expert system is described below. Figure 4 may be used as a reference for the functional components named.

Content Knowledge Base. A working Content Knowledge Base exists and is capable of supporting the new developments described. Extensions are currently being made that improve the object-orientation of the knowledge base. This is necessary in order to include the capability for designing and authoring simulations within future ID Expert versions.

Knowledge Acquisition Tool. Multiple versions of the Knowledge Acquisition Tool exist. However, a knowledge acquisition tool is extremely dependent upon its interface, and these existing versions can be improved. It will take much experience in the hands of users and much design modification to meet the goal of an interface for use by non-designers unfamiliar with ID Expert knowledge base structure. The interface of ID Expert is under design review currently, and will continue to evolve.

Resource Data Base. A working Resource Data Base exists and is capable of supporting future ID Expert expansion. Resourcing currently supports multiple forms of representation for individual knowledge objects.

Resource Editor. A working Resource Editor exists in conjunction with the interface for the Knowledge Acquisition Tool. The Resource Editor interface will improve along with that of the Knowledge Acquisition Tool.

Transaction Shells. Several Transaction Shells exist or are under development. The Identify shell, which deals with memory behavior, has been incarnated multiple times and has been shown to be useful and effective. Parallel projects for the design of additional shells for procedural instruction (Execute) and process instruction (Interpret) are in various stages of completion. In additon to these skills related to the instruction of unitary behaviors, a separate family of shells for specialized instruction has begun to emerge, such as the one focused for instruction in foreign language comprehension (Drake, Gibbons, & Schwab, 1995) and others for the creation of problem-solving simulation environments (Lacy & Gibbons, 1994; Wolcott, Gibbons, Lacy & Sharp, 1994).

Transaction Manager. A Transaction Manager like that described has not been constructed as a separate element of ID Expert. Strategies within ID Expert are currently administered from hard-wired strategy patterns within transaction shells. However, these patterns drive instruction using data in the manner described. This means that the mechanism for data-driven strategies does exist. Whether the data comes from a pre-set strategy or an adaptive computing mechanism is of no consequence to ID Expert. This fact gives the ID_2 Team confidence that the data-driving of instructional strategy is a viable approach.

Monitor and Advisor. The Monitor and Advisor do not yet exist.

Transaction Shell Library. The Library does not exist as an independent functioning entity. Instead, there exists now a conceptual bin which contains all of the shells which have been developed, which are called into use in individual lessons.

The remainder of the functions described in Figure 4 do not exist at present. This includes: the Student Record Data Base, the Course Delivery Knowledge Base, the Course Configuration Tool, the Course Authoring Knowledge Base, the Course Adjustment Tool, and the Course Improvement Tool.

The Prospect

The ID Expert system as described has evolved through multiple versions, and at each incarnation certain design goals have been targeted to improve the functionality and efficiency of the system. Testing of the product has taken place for each stable product, and findings have been used to improve the next round of design. The test results obtained so far lead to the following conclusions.

(1) The basic design concept of ID Expert, which includes generation of instruction from a structured knowledge base using transaction shells, is sound. The goal of a completed and functional system is attainable.

(2) The goals for increased efficiency of authoring are attainable. Assuming the development of well-designed user interfaces, efficiency goals should pose no problem. The four levels of authoring (default, minimal, maximal, extender) are expected to influence productivity, with more deeply involved designers requiring greater amounts of time to complete their work. However, the speed with which each level of author will be able to work is expected to compare favorably with authors working at similar levels with other authoring tools. The possibility of batch entry of knowledge and resource data bases and extensions of

the user interface for power users is expected to promote additional efficiency for authors.

(3) The goal of creating multiple transaction shells for the creation of varied forms and textures of instruction is attainable and practical. Several varieties of transaction shell have already been developed or are under development. The method for combining them with seamless transitions is under design, and work toward that capability will be started in the near future.

(4) The goal of making the system accessible and usable by non-designers is attainable. Numerous users at universities and in industry have conducted beta testing of the current version of ID Expert. Though the current interface is not considered optimal, it has been found to be adequate in the hands of an understanding user. Improved interfaces will empower increasing numbers of less experienced and trained users.

(5) The goal of placing instruction under control of a runtime adaptive function is practical and well within the realm of the possible. There are practical limits to the amount of computing possible during instruction without causing delays, and the number of controllable variables that research has shown to influence instructional effectiveness is yet modest. However, several structural strategic variables suggest themselves immediately for manipulation, and the ID Expert system is structured in a way that makes it easily modifiable to incorporate manipulation of new variables. Many dimensions of adaptability are represented in the ID Expert system as it is currently configured, and many new dimensions will be added over time.

(6) The goal of achieving a self-improving system is difficult, but achievable. The ability to obtain useful and reliable changes to instructional rules depends upon the quality of the data which can be obtained from instructional protocols. This is a factor within the control of the system designers, since it is they who will define for the system the sampling guidelines which will control the selection of cases and examples for use in system self-modification.

Future Growth

The ID_2 Research Team will continue to develop toward the adaptive and self-improving version of ID Expert described in this design. The ideals which have guided the design of ID Expert development to this point will continue to influence it. They are:

1. Increased authoring efficiency.
2. Authoring by non-designers.
3. Knowledge-basing of instruction.
4. Application of sound instructional principles through content-independent strategy structures.

If ID Expert reaches these goals, it will be a powerful and productive tool. It will be capable of producing a wide variety of computer-based instructional forms possessing a high degree of variability and controllability, yet it will do so with high efficiency compared to existing authoring tools. Most importantly, it will bring the technology of adaptive and self-improving instructional systems within the reach of the average developer and will empower the non-designer to create effective computer-based instruction.

In order to continue toward this overall goal, several sub-goals will be used as way points. The order in which these goals are presented below does not indicate the order in which they will be addressed.

Goal: Creation of the Student Record Data Base

The Student Record Data Base will be constructed to accumulate student record data. This will represent the model of the student's knowledge as well as a great deal of knowledge about the student that can be used in selecting and tailoring an instructional approach. Data will be stored for individual students and for student population composites.

Each individual student record will store information about the student under several categories, representing an expansion in the amount and types of data normally kept on students by a management-related data base. Categories contemplated include at present:

Student Entering Characteristics
> *Educational background, psychometric data, personal factors affecting instruction, skill level measures on entry, competencies certified, and level*

Student Instructional History
> *History of courses taken within the system, achievement levels attained, results of course studies (completed or not completed)*

Student Preferences
> *Favored display styles, favored strategy styles, favored content sequence styles, favored control styles, favored interaction patterns*

Student Instructional Setting Adjustments
> *Student-specific defaults to the standard instructional plan to be used as seed values at the beginning of instruction*

Student Instructional Goals
> *Names of courses to be completed, personal criterion levels, timing criteria*

Goal: Improvements in the Knowledge Acquisition System

We have described plans and projects underway for improvements to the author interface and the knowledge base. The author interface of ID Expert must support knowledge acquisition, resource acquisition, and instructional plan acquisition. It must be flexible enough and generic enough to do this not only for existing transaction shells, but also for an expanding family of shells, both generic and specialized. Maintaining the efficiency of the interface will be a key goal.

During knowledge capture, the future plans for the interface call for addition of an automatic mode to the manual mode of knowledge acquisition which now exists. In the current version of ID Expert, the subject-matter expert takes the initiative in entering knowledge base data, and the system provides no guidance to the user beyond an extensive context-sensitive help system. The author must currently be somewhat familiar with the organization and operation of the ID Expert knowledge base. The addition of an automatic mode will provide guidance to the author during knowledge acquisition. The interface acting in this mode will be capable of extracting knowledge base structures and their interrelations from the answers an author supplies to interface-generated questions.

Future developments will also more clearly define the relationship between the contents of the knowledge base and the resource base. Maintaining a clear distinction between the two will be a key to the generalizability of the system across more complex transaction types and the future accommodation of object-oriented and intelligent resources which will manage their own display to the student.

Goal: Development of the Transaction Manager

The Transaction Manager function will be separated from the transaction shells where it now resides. As it separates, it will assume control of several functions required for the execution of more complex varieties of shell-driven instruction. For instance, the design for the Execute (procedure-using) and Interpret (process understanding) shells require that simulations be provided for student manipulation and demonstrations. To carry out their instructional function, these simulations must be controlled by the strategy plan embedded within the transaction. Since several shells will share this function, the transaction manager will provide a centralized control mechanism for simulations.

Other generalizable functions will gravitate to the transaction manager as it evolves, including management of the display (all media channels), dispatch of data to the various data bases that make use of the instructional record, communication with the Advisor-Monitor system for the control of instruction, and integration and sequencing of transaction shells during instruction.

Goal: Development of the Advisor and Monitor

The Advisor and Monitor functions will be built together and in progressive stages of functionality. The earliest Monitor will consist of a data siphon which simply captures data from instruction uncritically. A second element of this early Monitor will examine the data off-line and make overnight adjustments to instruction parameters. A later Monitor version will include pattern recognition capabilities for the sorting of instructional data in real time. This will allow the companion version of the Advisor to make its recommendations and parameter adjustments during instruction.

The Advisor will become the centerpiece of curriculum control and instructional management. Its decisions—which will be implemented either as recommendations to the student or enforced through execution of options—will range from the highest levels (selection of lessons, segments, and transactions) to the lowest levels (selection of resources and messaging options for one display). The Advisor will be responsible for selecting instructional goals as well as the strategic means supporting their attainment. It will become the manager of transaction shells, specifying their ordering and featuring (through parameterized settings) for a particular student and instructional task. Because of its range of interest, the rule sets of the Advisor will eventually become somewhat compartmentalized and will provide a valuable design exercise in instructional management.

The ability of the Monitor to recognize useful patterns of student performance will improve over time as the resolution of its view increases. The Monitor will also tend to become compartmental because its interests will vary from high-order patterns and trends in between-lesson performance to display-to-display communication and interaction patterns and their influence on performance. Both Advisor and Monitor will be designed in a way that permits the addition of new rules—new expertise—to be added rapidly.

Goal: Development of Additional Transaction Shells

A quality transaction shell depends upon a sound conception of effective instructional strategy. The twelve shells currently outlined are generic instructional strategy shells corresponding with basic learning types proposed by Gagné (1985), Merrill (1994), and Bloom (1956). In addition to these generic shells—from which curricula can be constructed—additional specialized shells will be designed and created for the instruction of specific skill complexes, such as the comprehension of spoken or written foreign languages. Work on this type of shell is currently underway, as well as work on generic shells for instructing procedures and processes. Transaction shells will eventually be capable of duplicating virtually any form of instruction, any strategic approach, or any surface appearance, including discovery, exploration-based, and simulation-based learning, as well as hypermedia forms and performance support systems. The creation of multiple shells will accomplish at the same time the formation of the Transaction Shell Library.

Goal: Development of the Course Configuration Tool

Two levels of instructional plan data are now entered through the author interface: (1) strategy configurations to guide the execution of individual transaction shells, and (2) course configurations that govern the ordering of transaction shells and content.

The current elements of course structure are: course, lesson, segment, and transaction. Course, lesson, and segment are traditional designations which acquire meaning only as the designer creates them, and which frequently correspond to topic divisions rather than performance plateaus. ID Expert as an automated design tool will evolve its own set of goal-defined course structures and incorporate them into future versions.

Design rules within ID Expert will assist the author in designating course components with respect to these performance targets. It will do so through a Course Configuration Tool with three modes of operation: manual, consulting, and authoring.

The manual mode currently exists. Authors now designate course elements at the course, lesson, segment, and transaction levels. At the segment level, the author configures the transaction shell with instructional settings or accepts defaults.

In consultation mode a built-in "consultant" will be on call for advice on course configuration. In certain circumstances it will be capable of intervening with cautionary messages and recommendations. Explanations for the consultant's recommendations will be provided at the author's request. Through these explanations, an author will be able to learn from the consultation tool and improve his/her instructional design skills. As a course is created, the consultant will also perform consistency checks and report to the author on the state of completion of the authoring task.

In the authoring mode, the Course Configuration Tool will perform the course configuration process automatically. It will examine the contents of the content knowledge base before assigning a course structure and making transaction shell assignments. These decisions will be made according to a set of design rules contained in the Course Authoring Knowledge Base. As segments, lessons, units, and ultimately the course are formed or a transaction is configured, the configuring tool will show it to the author for approval or modification. Default values will be used for the configuration of transaction shells.

Goal: Development of the Course Delivery Knowledge Base

As the Advisor and Monitor are developed, the Course Delivery Knowledge Base will be developed as well. This knowledge base will store decision rules and parameters that are the distillate of data from instruction that has been acted upon by the Advisor. The Course Delivery Knowledge Base will be the place where the Advisor stores its instructional rules.

Goal: Development of the Course Authoring Knowledge Base

Operation of the Course Configuration Tool will depend heavily on the content's Course Authoring Knowledge Base. This data base will contain course authoring knowledge in the form of rules and cases.

The rules in the Course Authoring Knowledge Base will consist of course organization rules, appropriate for structuring instruction in any subject matter. The initial set of rules will be based on the best available research. As the Course Improvement Tool is created, these rules will be improved through the experience of the system. As well as course structuring rules, the Course Authoring Knowledge Base will contain rules for configuring transactions.

The cases in the Course Authoring Knowledge Base will consist of student records created from instructional interactions which list relevant student characteristics, the learning goal of the interaction, the course structure, the instructional strategy used, the performance evaluation result, and the feedback given. Cases will be dynamically created during the process of instruction. Initially, the Course Authoring Knowledge Base will contain no cases, but only rules. These initial rules will be used to guide the construction of the initial curricula and instructional strategies.

After these curricula and instructional strategies have been used to deliver courses to a number of students, student records will have been created. From these records, the ones that are representative will be selected as cases and stored in the Course Authoring Knowledge Base. These new cases will be used to update the existing curricula and instructional strategies and create new curricula and strategies.

In the completed Course Configuration Tool, the consultation and authoring modes will share an inference engine, which is the key component of the Tool. This inference engine will be capable of simple rule-based and case-based reasoning. When a decision is being made, the inference engine will attempt to retrieve a case that was used to assign a decision to a similar problem. Case data will be stored in the Course Authoring Knowledge Base. If the best case available in the Authoring Knowledge Base is not adequate to make the new decision, then the inference engine will either extract a solution from the retrieved case or modify the solution to the retrieved case until an adequate fit is found.

Goal: Development of the Course Improvement Tool

The function of the Course Improvement Tool will be to maintain and improve the rules and cases in the Course Authoring Knowledge Base. This tool will have two main components: a case-based learning component, and an inductive learning component.

The case-based learning component will maintain the cases in the Course Authoring Knowledge Base by adding, removing and generalizing on them. This will improve the system's available knowledge for guiding the author.

The inductive learning component will maintain the rules in the Course Authoring Knowledge Base. After a large number of student records are accumulated in the Student Records Data Base, existing rules in the Course Authoring Knowledge Base may be modified or discarded if they are not consistent with the records, and new rules will be generated if necessary from records that are not covered by any rules.

An inductive machine learning algorithm will be used to generate new rules and modify (specialize or generalize) existing rules from a set of given examples.

Goal: Development of the Course Adjusting Tool

The Course Adjusting Tool will dynamically adjust instruction for a given student at the time of instruction; it is the immediate mechanism for making instruction adaptive. Adjustments are triggered by bad student performances and negative feedback from the student.

After the completion of a transaction, the student will be evaluated and feedback will be provided by the immediate transaction shell. The result of the evaluation, along with the student's feedback, will be passed to the Course Adjusting Tool and analyzed. If no adjustment is needed, instruction will continue, using the same controlling data. If adjustments are proposed by the Course Adjustment Tool, the adjustment, together with an explanation, will be reported to the student in student control mode. Spontaneous reactions, comments, or requests from the student may also initiate an adjustment.

Course adjustment is accomplished in the same manner as course construction. The Course Improvement Tool performs both rule-based and case-based reasoning using the course authoring knowledge (rules and cases) and the instructional content meta-knowledge. The task of course adjustment is simpler and smaller than the task of course construction, because most adjustments made by the Course Improvement Tool are minor and local to transactions.

Goal: Networking

Networking is a practical concern. It is necessary to permit data gathering from individual instructional sessions to a central store for storage, analysis, and expert rule-updating. It is indicative of the state of the art in computer-based instructional management that little is said or written about this function, which is a *sine qua non* for efficient, fault-free, and loss-free management of the data for multiple students within a common courseware base. A network is essential at instruction time for an adaptive system due to the mass of data, rules, and parameters that must be consulted in order to make the requisite decisions for one student. Though running of courseware can and probably should be the designated role of the individual work station, a constant communication with a central management server will be increasingly necessary as the sophistication of adaptive functions and the amount of data involved in moment-by-moment decision-making increases.

Goal: Links to the ID process

The name of the ID_2 Research Team indicates that the development of the ID Expert system entails more conceptual groundwork than the creation of an author tool and has more goals than the reduction of authoring costs. Authoring is only one step of a larger process for designing and then developing a comprehensive instructional product with all of its supporting features, certification systems, and documentation.

Because it is only one step of a larger process, authoring must fit harmoniously into its place. It must accept data and decisions from prior stages of the process as well as passing its own data and decisions on to other stages in a useful form. ID Expert must make use of the task analysis (instructional goal data), the target population analysis (student characteristic data), and media selections. It must coordinate with the syllabus or curriculum process and the overall course or product design process. It will feel the influences of management, implementation, and evaluation planning decisions and may in many cases have to carry out tasks in service of those plans.

As well as filling its function within the design process, ID Expert has impact on the process itself and suggests ways in which it might change. The objectives analysis process, for instance, has been automated within ID Expert to the point at which ID Expert can automatically generate standard-form instructional objectives from knowledge-base data supplied by the subject-matter expert. By designating which objectives will be instructed, the subject-matter expert can outline a curriculum (syllabus) for computer-based instruction automatically. Future versions of ID Expert will include advisory systems to assist subject-matter experts in making these decisions and will have default instructional rules which will decide automatically if that is desired.

Conclusion

Computer-based instructional technology will become a greater force in the future of education and training. Systems like ID Expert will be necessary, however, in order to bring economies to the production of the large bodies of courseware that are needed. Just as other mass-audience technologies have matured beyond the day of the small-workshop artisan, computer-based instruction must be producible in quantity without reducing the quality of the experience. Indeed, the quality of computer-based instruction must greatly improve over what is now offered if it is to remain a viable instructional option. ID Expert represents the first of many such quantity- and quality-producing systems for computer-based instruction that will be required.

References

Barr, A., Beard, M., & Atkinson, R. C. (1976). Information networks for CAI curriculums. In O. Lecareme & R. Lewis (Eds.), *Computers in education.* Amsterdam: North-Holland.

Bloom, B. S. (Ed.). (1956). *Taxonomy of educational objectives: The classification of educational goals. Handbook I: Cognitive domain.* New York: Longman.

Brown, J. S., Burton, R. R., & Bell, A. G. (1975). SOPHIE: A step towards a reactive learning environment. *International Journal of Man-Machine Studies, 7,* 675–696.

Bunderson, C. V., & Merrill, M. D. (1974). The design and production of learner-controlled courseware for the TICCIT system: A progress report. *International Journal of Man-Machine Studies, 6,* 479–492.

Burton, R. R. (1982). Diagnosing bugs in a simple procedural skill. In D. H. Sleeman & J. S. Brown (Eds.), *Intelligent tutoring systems.* London: Academic Press.

Burton, R. R., & Brown, J. S. (1979). An investigation of computer coaching for informal learning activities. *International Journal of Man-Machine Studies, 11,* 5–24.

Carbonell, J. R. (1970). AI in CAI: An artificial intelligence approach to computer-assisted instruction. *IEEE Transactions on Man-Machine Systems, 11*(4), 190–202.

Clancey, W. J. (1983). GUIDON. *Journal of Computer-based Instruction, 10*(1), 8–14.

Drake, L., Gibbons, A. S., & Schwab, S. (1995). Computerized language listening; A tool for authoring video-based lessons. A paper presented at the Annual Meeting of the Association for Educational Communications and Technology, February, 1995, Anaheim, CA.

Forbus, K. (1984). An interactive laboratory for teaching control system concepts. *BBN Report # 5511.* Cambridge, MA: Bolt, Beranek, & Newman.

Gagné, R. M. (1985). *The conditions of learning* (4th ed.). New York: Holt, Rinehart, and Winston.

Gibbons, A. S., & Anderson, T. A. (1994). Model-centered instruction. A paper presented at the Annual Conference on Automated Authoring, Department of Instructional Tecnology, Utah State University, August, 1994.

Jones, M. K., Li, Z., & Merrill, M. D. (1990). Domain knowledge representation for instructional analysis. *Educational Technology, 30*(10), 7–32.

Kimball, R. (1982). A self-improving tutor for symbolic integration. In D. Sleeman & J. S. Brown (Eds.) *Intelligent tutoring systems.* London: Academic Press.

Lacy, M., & Gibbons, A. S. (1994). The library location simulation at USU. A paper presented at the Region 8 Conference of the Association for Educational Communications and Technology, May, 1994, Park City, UT.

Lesgold, A. M. (1987). Toward a theory of curriculum for use in designing intelligent instructional systems. In H. Mandl & A. M. Lesgold (Eds.), *Learning issues for intelligent tutoring systems.* New York: Springer-Verlag.

Merrill, M. D. (1983). Component display theory. In C. M. Reigeluth (Ed.), *Instructional design theories and models: An overview of their current status.* Hillsdale, NJ: Lawrence Erlbaum Associates.

Merrill, M. D. (1985). Peter Dean lecture: Where is the authoring in authoring systems? *Journal of Computer-based Instruction, 12*(4), 90–96.

Merrill, M. D. (1987). Prescriptions for an authoring system. *Journal of Computer-based Instruction, 14*(1), 1–8.

Merrill, M. D. (1992). Instructional transaction theory: Knowledge relationships among processes, entities, and activities. ID_2 Research Team Technical Report, Department of Instructional Technology, Utah State University.

Merrill, M. D. (1994). *Instructional design theory* (D. G. Twitchill, Ed.). Englewood Cliffs, NJ: Educational Technology Publications.

Merrill, M. D., & Li, Z. (1989). An instructional design expert system. *Journal of Computer-based Instruction, 16*(3), 95–101.

Merrill, M. D., Li, Z., & Jones, M. K. (1990a). Limitations of first generation instructional design. *Educational Technology, 30*(1), 7–11.

Merrill, M. D., Li, Z., & Jones, M. K. (1990b). Second generation instructional design (ID_2). *Educational Technology, 30*(2), 7–14.

Merrill, M. D., Li, Z., & Jones, M. K. (1991). Instructional transaction theory: An introduction. *Educational Technology, 31*(6), 7–12.

Merrill, M. D., Li, Z., & Jones, M. K. (1992a). Instructional transaction theory: Classes of transactions. *Educational Technology, 32*(6), 12–26.

Merrill, M. D., Li, Z., & Jones, M. K. (1992b). Instructional transaction shells: Responsibilities, methods, and parameters. *Educational Technology, 32*(2), 5–27.

Merrill, M. D., Schneider, E. W., & Fletcher, K. A. (1980). *TICCIT.* Englewood Cliffs, NJ: Educational Technology Publications.

Merrill, M. D., Tennyson, R. D., & Posey, L. O. (1992). *Teaching concepts: An instructional design guide* (2nd ed.). Englewood Cliffs, NJ: Educational Technology Publications.

O'Shea, T. (1979). A self-improving quadratic tutor. *International Journal of Man-Machine Studies, 11,* 97–124.

Shute, V., & Glaser, R. (1986). An intelligent tutoring system for exploring principles of economics. *Technical Report.* Learning Research and Development Center, University of Pittsburgh, Pittsburgh, Pennsylvania.

Stevens, A. L., Roberts, B., & Stead, L. (1983). The use of a sophisticated interface in computer-assisted instruction. *IEEE Computer graphics and applications, 3,* 25–31.

Stolurow, L. (1969). Some factors in the design of systems for computer-assisted instruction. In R. C. Atkinson & H. A. Wilson (Eds.), *Computer-assisted instruction: A book of readings.* New York: Academic Press.

Westcourt, K., Beard, M., & Gould, L. (1977). Knowledge-based adaptive curriculum sequencing for CAI: Application of a network representation. *Proceedings of the National ACM Conference,* Seattle, Washington (pp. 234–240). New York: Association for Computing Machinery.

White, B. Y., & Frederiksen, J. R. (1986). Progressions of qualitative models as foundations for intelligent learning environments. *BBN Report #6277.* Cambridge, MA: Bolt, Beranek, & Newman.

Wolcott, L., Gibbons, A. S., Lacy, M., & Sharp, J. (1994). Navigating the information environment: An instructional simulation of information retrieval processes for university students. A paper presented at the Annual Meeting of the Association for Educational Communications and Technology, Nashville, TN.

Woolf, B. P., & McDonald, D. D. (1984). Building a computer tutor: Design issues. *IEEE Computer, 17*(9), 61–73.

36

Structural Communication: A Tactical Paradigm for Implementing Principles from Constructivism and Cognitive Theory

Elisa J. Slee
Portland State University
Portland, Oregon

Rob S. Pusch
Syracuse University
Syracuse, New York

Recently, several authors have advocated that cognitive considerations be incorporated into instructional design based on instructional systems development (ISD) (Hannafin, 1992; Rieber, 1992; Ryder & Redding, 1993). Ryder & Redding (1993) point out that the procedures for implementing ISD steps have "not been updated to incorporate findings from research on cognition and information processing" (p. 76). In addition, a review of existing computer-based programs indicates that many of them follow a behaviorist, "cookbook" approach to instruction (Tobin & Dawson, 1992).

Designs have been criticized as being "externally centered" (Hannafin, 1992) and failing to include advances in cognitive psychology and information processing. Lebow (1993) has suggested that part of the criticism may be due to the tendency of theorists to treat "constructivism" as a method when it is actually a philosophy, and ISD as a philosophy when it is actually a method. He suggests five principles that may represent an answer to the question, "for what problems is constructivist philosophy the solution?" These are:

1. Maintain a buffer between the learner and the potentially damaging effects of instructional practices.

2. Provide a context for learning that supports both autonomy and relatedness.
3. Embed the reasons for learning into the learning activity itself.
4. Support self-regulation through the promotion of skills and attitudes that enable the learner to assume increasing responsibility for the developmental restructuring process.
5. Strengthen the learner's tendency to engage in intentional learning processes, especially by encouraging the strategic exploration of errors. (p. 5)

One purpose of instruction should be to help the learner gain a better understanding of his or her world. To do this the learner must be an active participant in learning. This active participation allows the learner to integrate new material into existing knowledge, leading to deeper processing (Craik & Lockhart, 1972), and so resulting in greater retention of new information. Therefore, instruction should be designed to encourage learners to actively participate in learning.

What existing instructional "methods" or "techniques" do we have that incorporate some of these principles? We feel that Structural Communication is one such technique. While it was originally developed in the late sixties, it embodies many of the principles of a constructivist *philosophy* toward learning as well as principles based upon developments in *cognitive* theory.

In this chapter, we will review the cognitive approach to instruction, describe Structural Communication, and then review research findings and how they fit into the philosophy of constructivism in ISD and cognitive theory. Finally, we will discuss the strengths and limitations of Structural Communication as a paradigm.

The Cognitive Approach to Learning

Over the past two decades there has been a shift from "behaviorism" to "cognitivism" in examining learning. The primary focus of the "cognitive" approach to learning is on how processing affects the understanding and retention of information. This approach is said to be learner centered and is concerned with cognitive processing, with an emphasis on the mental models of the content constructed by the individual learner. Whereas some cognitive psychologists have examined processing in terms of long- and short-term memory, others, such as Craik and Lockhart (1972), have focused upon levels of processing. This approach considers what factors influence depth of processing, such as prior knowledge and overt or covert activities.

Levels of processing theory looks at retention of information as related to the depth, or spread, of encoding. The theory suggests that the more deeply information is processed, the longer a memory trace will persist. But what does this have to do with the construction of mental models and understanding of material? The depth of processing is also related to the degree to which information is organized in memory and related to prior knowledge. The level to which information is processed is related to the degree that the information is analyzed and organized by the learner.

How does this "levels of processing" model translate into the development of classroom activities that will aid processing? Let's consider an example. When a teacher is introducing a science unit on the principle that hot air rises, he or she might ask students to think of examples of this phenomenon in their daily lives. A "good" teacher does this because he or she knows that if the students have some living example, then they will be better able to create a link from prior knowledge or experience to the content presented in class, and consequently better organize and remember the information.

Methods of instruction contain a vast number of activities that purport to promote various levels of processing. An activity that promotes processing is rehearsal or repetition. This technique is often used when learners are trying to memorize information. While this does lead to the formation of a memory trace, it is not one that is very permanent.

Activities that promote more permanent memory traces, hence deeper processing, are activities that require learners to analyze and organize information. These activities also promote the relation of new material to prior knowledge. The use of these activities to promote deeper understanding of material are discussed more specifically in Wittrock's (1974) generative model of learning. The basic premise of the generative model is that the learner is not a passive receptacle of information, but that the learner actively constructs his or her own meaning of material. This active process results in the understanding of the material. Wittrock proposed that learners use a variety of generative strategies in the construction of this meaning. Examples of generative learning strategies include the generation of images, illustrations, summaries, headings, inferences, outlining, critical comments, analogies, and concept mapping (Linden & Wittrock, 1981).

The generative model of learning is based on studies of memory and retention (Wittrock, 1985). Generative strategies increase the processing load of learners, thereby affecting depth of processing. One way to help learners is to develop instructional units that will encourage them to see the connections between ideas in a passage.

A method that could encourage this would structure learning in a manner designed to promote "higher level, synthesis learning," with the goal being understanding. Such a method was developed in the late sixties. This method is called Structural Communication (Egan, 1972). Understanding is "inferred if a student shows the ability to use knowledge appropriately in different contexts, and to organize knowledge elements in accordance with specified organizing principles" (Egan, 1972, p. 66). We will now describe Structural Communication.

Structural Communication

Bennett and Hodgson (Hodgson, 1972) developed an instructional technique called Structural Communication. The original developmental work was performed in the late sixties and early seventies at the Institute for the Comparative Study of History, Philosophy, and the Sciences, in London, U.K. The primary purpose of the institute was to conduct "research into methods of analyzing and organizing knowledge, aiming to develop practical techniques which can lead to more effective thinking and more insightful understanding" (Egan, 1976, p. ix). The technique was designed to encourage creative thinking in learners, allowing them to create an understanding of a topic, not simply memorize facts.

While the development of Structural Communication may have been a reaction to linear and branched programmed instruction, we must keep in mind that it is still a form of programmed instruction. The inventors did not throw out all of the ideas of programmed instruction. Egan (1976) discusses the similarities of all programmed instruction and contrasts Structural Communication to linear and branched programmed instruction in three areas: individualizing, efficiency, and control. Table 1 summarizes this comparison.

Structural Communication takes the best of programmed instruction, the ability to individualize instruction—the increased efficiency and increased control—and adds to this the ability to account for different learning styles and increased learner control. Furthermore, it breaks away from the behaviorist paradigm of the mind or a "black box" and "knowledge as behavior" and incorporates at least some elements that can be considered in line with constructivist philosophy and cognitive paradigms.

Model of Thinking Behind Structural Communication

Structural Communication is based on a model of thinking constructed by Bennett and Hodgson. This model contains four levels of thinking: creative, conscious, sensitive, and automatic. Bennett and Hodgson viewed traditional programmed instruction as relevant to teaching at the two lowest levels of thinking, automatic and sensitive, which are useful for the learning of involuntary habits and reproductive thinking.

Table 1. Structural Communication and Programmed Instruction.

	In Common	**Contrast**
Individualizing	Programmed instruction makes it possible to include strategies, pacing, and feedback that is tailored to the needs of individual learners.	Linear programming allows for self-paced instruction, but does not account for differences in learning style. Branched programs do increase the possibility of accounting for learning styles, but this is still limited. Structural Communication was designed to make it possible that no two learners take the same path through the instruction.
Efficiency	Programmed instruction allows for increase in efficiency when compared to teacher led instruction.	While both linear and branched programs increase the efficiency in certain types of subject matter, they tend to be limited to reproductive or low levels of thinking. Structural Communication was designed to encourage creative thinking so can be adapted to a greater variety of subject matter.
Control	Programmed instruction allows for greater control over the learning process.	Traditional linear and branched programs allows the program's author to maintain control over what the student learns. Structural Communication, since it encourages creative thinking, increases the control the learner has on what is learned.

The intent of Bennett and Hodgson was to devise a technique that would actively engage learners in higher, more creative levels of thinking, and provide a great deal of freedom in the learning process. Bennett notes its "basic requirement. . .is to be able to reproduce conditions of challenge and response that elicit judgment, creativity, decision making and hypothesis formation" (Egan, 1976, p. 15). Learners need to be allowed to construct connections between concepts presented in instruction and to get feedback that indicates where their thinking is inconsistent or they have misperceptions, but they should not be presented with one correct answer. This learning situation is best described as a guided discussion. The goals of such a situation are:

- learners must create an answer;
- learners must integrate the concepts and facts of the instructional material;
- they must be provided with feedback that points out inconsistencies in their thinking;
- the instruction must be individualized;
- there can be more than one answer; and
- learners need to be able to infer from the material.

The object was to construct a form of programmed instruction that could simulate guided discussions or essay writing. Instruction had been all too passive. Bennett and Hodgson wished to create a program which would encourage active learning. The inventors designed the Structural Communication technique to be of value for social learning of different kinds (Egan, 1976). Hodgson made the following distinctions between the learning of knowledge and learning for social action: The learning of knowledge assumes there is a single truth, concentrates on finding the solutions to problems, reduces the variety of options, and removes feeling from learning. On the other hand, learning for social actions assumes that there are multiple truths, sees feeling as important to learning, assumes that learning occurs in social settings, and concentrates on raising issues and problems (Hodgson, 1972).

Structural Communication (SC) was designed to promote learning for social action. The inventors of SC felt that the learning that occurs in school is inseparable from the social situations in which it is learned. This is consistent with both the cognitive approach to learning and the constructivist philosophy, both of which view social context as critical to the content and form of learning. They felt that learning for social action was critical for the transfer of learning from the classroom to practical situations (Egan, 1976). The distinctions between the learning of knowledge and the learning for social action are evident in the actual components Bennett and Hodgson designed into the Structural Communication technique. The components of the technique are presented below and will be followed by a review of the research conducted using the Structural Communication technique.

The Structural Communication Technique

The typical components of a Structural Communication unit are *intention, presentation, investigation, response matrix, discussion section,* and *viewpoints.* Figure 1 provides an overview of the components which are described below. A description and an example of each of the components is presented.

Intention: An overview of the case study presented by the author. The intention is used to provide a context for the content of the study unit.

Example of Intention: This study unit will examine the implementation of a management information system at TYCON Construction products. We will follow the introduction of a new order and entry system.

Presentation: This is the subject matter of the study unit. The presentation could be anything from a text-based passage to a novel or a play. This could also be any sort of computer mediated instruction, including simulations.

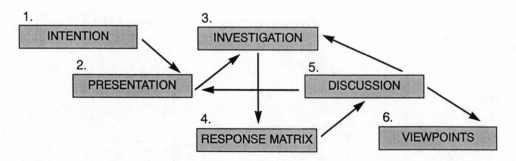

Figure 1. Overview of the components of Structural Communication, from Egan, 1976.

Example of text from the Presentation: In this particular example, the Presentation consisted of a 2,000 word business case study. What follows is an excerpt from this text.

> Chuck was 32 years old and the staff assistant to the director of marketing for TYCON Construction Products. His problems had begun nearly two years earlier. TYCON had been experiencing difficulties in processing orders. A boom in construction had caused manufacturers' deliveries to TYCON to be irregular, late, and sometimes even canceled. Thus, TYCON's inventory was erratic; customers and sales personnel couldn't depend on prompt deliveries. Furthermore, because some customers' payments were three, four, and five months overdue, the marketing department wanted to check customer credit before authorizing orders. Unfortunately, since TYCON had over 8000 customers, authorizations were extremely time consuming.

Investigation and Response Matrix: The purpose of the investigation section is for the learner to interact with the subject matter. There are typically between three to five questions or "problems" concerning the content of the presentation. A learner formulates a response to the investigative questions by selecting items from a response matrix. A *response matrix* is comprised of a set of some ten to thirty facts, theories, or principles about the subject of the presentation. A learner selects items from the matrix that he or she feels are relevant to composing an answer to the problem or question presented. The same matrix is used for all of the questions presented, and any given item can be selected for one or more questions. Questions typically require a higher level of analysis of the material. A learner must organize and interrelate various aspects of the *presentation* in order to answer the questions posed. This is meant to be a very open-ended form of responding, similar to outlining an essay.

Example of question for Investigation: What major factors would support Tom's termination? *Example of an excerpt from a Response Matrix:*

No documentation existed for systems development	No backup system was available and TYCON could not return to the original system	Users were not involved in the project
1	2	3
Lack of understanding of system integration	Lack of communication involving management, users, and committee members	Programmers quit and their programs had to be rewritten
4	5	6

Manufacturer deliveries to TYCON irregular **7**	TYCON's inventory erratic **8**	Customers could not depend on prompt deliveries **9**
4-Man committee met five times during a 3 month period to create proposal for management **10**	Chuck technically in-experienced and unsure of himself **11**	TYCON needed to buy or lease equipment to implement this new system **12**
Customers do not pay bills promptly **13**	Slow processing of credit authorizations **14**	Small but effective data processing department **15**
Implementation done by plunge method **16**	Lack of internal DP analysts capable of systems analysis **17**	Initial project schedule compressed by 33% **18**

Outside consultants hired only after system failed **19**	Data processing did not know about new product line **20**	Lack of periodic review **21**
System requirements and specifications kept changing **22**	Data processing staff were highly motivated **23**	4-Man committee stopped meeting for ten months **24**
Major portions of the system were incompatible **25**	No pre-testing was done before final implementation **26**	Only minor bugs appeared after implementation **27**
Tom Jackson fired **28**	Poor project review made at 10 months **29**	DP said project delays were external and out of their control **30**

Discussion: The discussion section includes both a response analysis and *comments*. The learner is directed to read specific discussion comments by means of the response analysis. The *response analysis* may be a set of "if-then" rules such as: "If you included three or more of items 2, 4, 7, 8, or 30 from the response matrix you should read comment A." This process of analysis and advice giving may be automated by a computer. The discussion *comments* are used by the author to provide feedback to the learners regarding errors or misperceptions and to suggest alternative but valid viewpoints. The author of the study unit uses the discussion comments to argue for the inclusion of necessary items which the student omitted or for the exclusion of irrelevant items. The comments can also be employed to highlight secondary factors which are important in the investigation of the question and to highlight relationships between various aspects of the subject matter contained in the presentation as it relates to a given question. For example, if a learner failed to include an essential item from the *response matrix*, s/he would be directed to read a specific comment, in which the author would describe why this element was essential. Likewise, if a certain response pattern indicates that a reader has only selected matrix items of secondary importance to the question posed, the discussion comment would highlight how these were related to the subject and also point out other factors that should be considered.

The discussion comments distinguish this method from other variations of "programmed instruction." The author of a Structural Communication study unit writes the discussion comments in advance. Given that there is no one right answer, the author attempts to anticipate particular responses that a reader might construct when using the matrix and writes the discussion comments in such a way that they serve to assist the learner in further analyzing the information. The discussion comments also identify further relationships between component elements of information and serve to reconstruct the learner's schema of the domain of knowledge under study.

Example of a Response Analysis: If you included three or less of 2, 4, 5, 16, 20, 25, 26, read comment D.

Example of a Comment: You have missed some of the major factors contributing to Tom's termination. Remember to focus specifically on Tom's area of responsibility, and to evaluate how well he carried them out. Tom clearly should not have implemented a system without pretesting, and he should have protected the company by avoiding the plunge method - the riskiest of all options. Just as importantly, Tom should have understood the entire system integration, and held frequent meetings to ensure meeting everyone's requirements. Tom clearly did not perform his job well, as evidenced by his lack of knowledge of the new product line and the system incompatibilities.

Viewpoints: This section is used to provide summarizing comments on the subject matter, alternative viewpoints, and links to future lessons. The author may present his or her viewpoint or biases on the content of the study unit. This section can also be used to direct students to further reading or activities.

Example of excerpt from a Viewpoints: In this case, the Viewpoint was presented to the class during a lecture following the case. What follows is an excerpt. . . . As you can see, TYCON's problems with the order entry and billing system resulted from a number of factors. . . .

An additional optional component of a Structural Communication study unit is called the *coherence index.*

Coherence Index: The *coherence index* is a method developed by Bennett and Hodgson to obtain a numerical assessment of the learner's understanding of the questions presented. Their primary assumption is that "the response the student records to each problem reflects his attempt to organize elements from the matrix into a satisfactory whole" (Egan, 1974, p. 54). For each question, every item in the response matrix is given a weighting between −2 and +2, depending on its significance and relevance to the question. For example, an item considered to be clearly irrelevant is given a weighting of −2 and an item of importance would be weighted +2. The set of weightings which represents a student's response to the question is then called his/her *coherence index.* If there were four questions in the study unit, one would have four coherence indices, one for each question of the unit. These separate indices could be summed for a 'total score' for the study unit. Hodgson and Bennett (Egan, 1974) considered the *coherence index* to be an objective measure of how well a student organizes knowledge about the specific topic in the study unit.

Using a Structural Communication Study Unit

A learner using a study unit designed according to the Structural Communication technique first studies the material in the *intention* and *presentation* sections, and then proceeds to the *investigation.* In the *investigation,* questions and problems are posed to challenge the learner to identify and make connections between the various aspects of the subject matter being investigated (Egan, 1974). He or she constructs a response by selecting items from the *response matrix.* This activity requires that the learner carefully analyze and interrelate information in the *presentation* material when generating a response. The authors of Structural Communication (Egan, 1974) conceived of this as the learner "constructing" a response, because he/she selects items which when combined represent a coherent, complex, and personally generated answer to a question. Unlike typical "programmed instruction," the items from the response matrix may be used in answering more than one question. Thus, the goal is not to find the 'right' item from the *response matrix* for each question, but to consider carefully which items from the matrix are relevant when combined with other items, in a particular context.

After the learner chooses the items from the *response matrix,* s/he proceeds to the *discussion* section. The *discussion* section of a Structural Communication study unit is comprised of two parts. First, the reader must analyze his/her response (*response analysis*). In most Structural Communication study units, this is performed by the learner. The learner would work through a series of if-then rules such as, "If you included matrix items 2, 16, 18, and 21, read comment A." This procedure can be automated if the lesson is presented via a computer. The computer executes the if-then rules and automatically branches the learner to the appropriate comment. Upon completion of the study unit, the learner may be directed to a section called *viewpoints,* in which summary comments about the unit are made. The instructor may also choose to present the *viewpoint* as a discussion in class, rather than as the text of the study unit. Finally, the *coherence index* may or may not be employed as a measure of the learner's understanding of the unit.

Research on Structural Communication

This section describes research on Structural Communication. Research on Structural Communication is best organized historically. The early writings primarily described the technique and its uses. Following this period, there were a number of years during which the technique went unexplored. Recently, however, a group of researchers, primarily at Syracuse University and Concordia University, have 'revived' the technique, and conducted research using it as an instructional method.

While there are several articles which describe the uses and examples of Structural Communication study units (see, for example, Egan, 1972, 1976; Hodgson & Dill, 1970a, 1970b, 1971), limited research on this instructional technique has been reported. Hodgson and Dill (1970a, 1970b, 1971), in three articles in the *Harvard Business Review,* describe a Structural Communication business case study exercise. Readers were invited to mail in their responses to the questions posed at the end of the case. A coherence index was calculated for each question. One notable result was that the reader response was higher than for any other case study presented up to that time in the *Harvard Business Review.* In addition, the coherence index improved over problems one through four, suggesting that a certain skill was involved in using this instructional technique.

Since Hodgson first described Structural Communication in the late sixties, a number of study units have been produced in both the United Kingdom and the United States (Whittington, 1974). These units were produced for schools and businesses and covered a variety of subject areas such as: management, health, social studies, mathematics, and the environment. Whittington (1974) interviewed teachers, students and trainers at schools and businesses that had used the technique. His interviews focused on the effectiveness of Structural Communication, as well as areas for possible improvements. On the whole, the students enjoyed the Structural Communication study units. Likewise, the teachers enjoyed the technique, and found the response matrix to be effective in generating responses. Teachers often used the study units as a group exercise and suggested some notable areas for improvement. First, the teachers felt that additional materials such as films could be used to supplement the presentation. Also, the teachers felt that it would be helpful to leave some blank items on the matrix so that students could fill in ideas or comments of their own. Finally, the trainers and teachers felt that Structural Communication had a "dual nature" (Whittington, 1974, p.60). That is, they considered Structural Communication to be both a teaching and a learning strategy.

This conclusion was echoed by Hodgson (1974) in a paper summarizing the progress and future directions for the technique. He indicated that field work in the United Kingdom suggested that Structural Communication was essentially a process technique and that the preparation of the material must vary for the specific application. He also suggested that much more room must be left for the user to insert his own content of experience" (p. 6).

Romiszowski (1976) performed a feasibility study that compared a Structural Communication study unit on set theory developed by Fyfe and Woodrow (1969) to existing materials for teaching set theory. The Structural Communication study unit was successful in teaching concepts and principles of set theory at a greater depth of understanding than the existing materials. However, the subjects of the study had difficulty with the reading level of the unit. Romiszowski felt this was a limitation of the specific materials used, not of the Structural Communication technique.

The next mention of Structural Communication in the literature was an article by Baath (1979), suggesting that it could possibly be a model for correspondence education. During the next several years, there were no reports on Structural Communication. However, with the widespread use of microcomputers, a number of researchers began to reexamine the Structural Communication technique. Mitchell and Meilleur-Baccanale (1982) compared Structural Communication to regular textual presentation. Eighty-one undergraduate subjects studying systems analysis were tested on immediate recall and understanding as well as delayed understanding. The experimental group using Structural Communication outscored the prose group by 58% on the test of immediate recall. Similarly, the Structural Communication group scored 51% higher on the delayed post-test. The authors concluded that the Structural Communication technique was superior to regular textual material for this particular subject matter.

The authors also investigated whether there were any differences in recall and understanding between learners classified as "holists" and as "serialists" (Mitchell & Meilleur-

Baccanale, 1982). While the authors did not find any significant differences in this study, they attributed this to unequal sample sizes in the cells; in particular, few serialists actually completed the Structural Communication units. One might expect that the structure of a Structural Communication study unit forces learners to engage more in the processing of material. The discussion comments can serve to aid in the analysis of information, thus improving the post-test scores. The control group was allowed to review the text for as long as it wished, however, there was no "structure" to this unlimited review time; and so the information might not have been processed.

Another study, conducted by Romiszowski, Grabowski, and Damadaran (1988), examined the use of Structural Communication to increase the processing of information in a simulation. The authors noted that on successive trials of an interactive video (IV) business case simulation, *Decision Point*, learners did not improve their scores. The authors designed a Structural Communication unit for the purpose of "debriefing" students in order to increase their processing of information. Students who participated in the Structural Communication debriefing exercise did, in fact, improve their scores as they worked through the *Decision Point* simulation during a second trial. This suggests that the Structural Communication debriefing helped learners to analyze the case study information more effectively than the IV presentation alone and thereby acted as an aid to deeper processing.

A computer-based version of the debriefing exercise for *Decision Point* has been developed (Romiszowski, Grabowski, & Pusch, 1988). This includes two versions, one with "short" question stems and one with "long" question stems. The "long" question stems are hypothesized to provide some orienting information related to questions. A future study hopes to determine whether orienting information aids in processing by providing a link to the learners' prior experience with the simulation.

In a more recent study, Mitchell and Emmott (1990) investigated a print-based version of the case study published earlier by Hodgson and Dill in the *Harvard Business Review*. They compared the print-based study to one automated on a computer and hypothesized that individuals classified as "serialists" or "surface processors" would perform less well than "holists" or "deep processors" as measured by the coherence index. They also hypothesized that the coherence index for all subjects using the computer version would be greater than for those using the print version. Their results generally supported these hypotheses. However, the holists only outperformed the serialists on the paper version of the case study exercise. Mitchell and Emmott (1990) suggest that the paper version calls for more processing on the part of learners, since they have to analyze for themselves which feedback comments would be relevant. The computer-based version supplies this prescription automatically.

Hodgson (1974) suggested that the technique be expanded to include more of the individual user's experience. Concept mapping is one strategy which might do this. Taylor (1990) investigated how the use of concept maps affected performance on a computer based Structural Communication study unit on nutrition. Thirty undergraduates were randomly assigned to three versions of the units: study units with instructor generated concept map, learner generated concept map, and no concept map. Students in the control group (no map) completed the protein module. All students in the experimental groups first completed a module introducing them to concept mapping. Following this module, students in the first experimental group completed the protein module using the designer's concept map. Students in the second experimental group practiced concept mapping using a module on fats and then made their own concept map while completing the protein module. It was found that learners who used either instructor generated or learner generated concept maps outperformed the group that did not use this strategy at all. While the mean score of the group that generated its own map was higher than the group with the instructor generated map, the difference was not statistically significant. The authors noted that while time to complete the protein module was not recorded, it was probable that the group which generated its own concept maps spent more time on the module and this could have contributed to the better performance.

In another study using mainframe technology to present a case study in management information systems, Slee (Pusch & Slee, 1990) examined "interactivity" and increasing learner interaction. Field independent and field dependent learners were presented two different versions of a Structural Communication study unit. In the first version, students selected items from the response matrix and were immediately branched to the appropriate discussion comments. In the second version, students performed the if-then response analysis themselves, and then selected which comments they wished to read. All learners were given the opportunity to make a comment after each question investigated. Finally, upon completion of the case study, all learners commented to the instructor regarding the computer based training experience via electronic mail. One interesting result of the study was the nature of the comments learners made upon receiving the discussion comments. A significant number of students continued an "academic dialogue" when they were given the opportunity to make a comment, arguing in response to the discussion comments received. Other individuals used the opportunity to comment to reinforce themselves in a social way, saying such things as, "This is really fun; I'm good at this." Finally, other learners used the comment space to write evaluations of the software. In addition, many of the students who performed the if-then response analysis themselves chose to examine more comments than they would have been branched to, had the system been fully automated. This was an exploratory study; however, it suggests that some students may actually seek additional information when given the opportunity. The overall email comments about the computer-based training experience were extremely positive. Students cited the ability to "make comments" and continue the discussion with the instructor via email as "fun," "interesting," and "informative."

Romiszowski and Abrahamson (1992) have continued to explore the effects of enabling learners to make comments in response to the discussion comments provided in the unit. They tested a paper based Structural Communication study unit on the novel *Animal Farm* with eighth grade students and are currently preparing a HyperCard version for experimental testing. In the initial field testing of the unit, the authors found that the students reacted to the Structural Communication unit as if it were a formal test. Despite being told that there were no 'right' or 'wrong' answers, the students were concerned with finding the correct answer. In addition, students were discouraged by the length of the unit (8 pages) and the numerous corresponding response comments. Romiszowski and Abrahamson are undertaking further research to determine to what extent these effects are the product of the sociocultural traditions of the K–12 classroom, the Structural Communication methodology, or the medium used to present it.

For this purpose, a Structural Communication shell has been developed in HyperCard which enables the selection of a variety of study units that may be presented automatically to the student. The shell also tracks exactly how the learner utilized the unit. A characteristic of this shell is that it allows for student generated comments and insights to be added to the already prepared materials and to be shared between students and tutors as a form of an in-depth, student generated seminar. This fusion of pre-design study exercises with collaboration group discussion by email has been applied to the computer delivery of case study methodology (Romiszowski & Chang, 1992).

Strengths and Limitations of Structural Communication as a Paradigm for Tactical Planning

Kuhn (1970) has written that for a model to be considered a paradigm, it must show achievements that were (1) "sufficiently unprecedented to attract an enduring group of adherents away from competing modes of scientific activity," and (2) be "sufficiently open-ended to leave all sorts of problems for the redefined group of practitioners to solve." How does Structural Communication fit Kuhn's two requirements?

We feel that, in many ways, SC was a technique "designed before its time." That is, in the 1960s, microcomputers were a thing of the future. Consequently, the technique was somewhat cumbersome to implement, especially in terms of the response analysis. However, it still had a number of adherents, and several adaptations were made to the technique when it was actually implemented. One such adaptation was using the technique in group discussions with a facilitator, rather than as programmed instruction for individuals. Another adaptation was abandoning the "coherence index" as a summative measure. Many of the research studies used different types of measures of comprehension (such as concept level posttest scores) due to the difficulty in calculating the coherence index. In the thirty years since it was invented, it has attracted a steady stream of adherents. Now, with the widespread availability of microcomputers and multimedia applications, it can be expected to attract even more. These technologies eliminate the difficulties associated with analyzing the various responses. In addition, multimedia capabilities can serve to enhance the presentation of the case study elements, and networking abilities allow for expanding the opportunity for student input into discussion comments. Thus, it seems that while perhaps SC may be criticized for only attracting only a limited number of adherents, it certainly has had an enduring attraction, with several citations appearing in the literature over the years.

As far as being sufficiently open-ended for research and practical application, we feel that these two areas are exactly the strengths of the SC technique, particularly in light of recent developments in cognitive psychology and paradigm shifts in the field of educational technology. Such shifts advocate paying more attention to the individual learner and how he/she processes information. Hannafin and Gall (1990) have defined "learning environments" as "comprehensive, integrated systems that promote engagement through student-centered activities, including guided presentations, manipulations, and explorations among interrelated learning themes." These systems serve to deepen comprehension by integrating tools, resources, and pedagogical features. We feel that Structural Communication is an emerging tactical paradigm to do just that because it engages the learner in a dialogue that encourages deeper analysis of the information. There are no "right" or "wrong" answers according to SC; rather, incorrect perceptions are viewed as opportunities for further exploration and discussion. This view is consistent with a constructivist philosophy. An area of further research, using the SC technique, would be to explore what design features of the technique lend themselves best to further exploration of errors and deepening of comprehension. For example, it could be that using a student-generated electronic forum (Romiszowski & Abrahamson, 1992), based upon students' comments to the author-generated discussion comments, increases comprehension. In addition, with the advancement in technologies, it would be possible to track students' comprehension levels, and as a summative test, present them with a new case study to analyze, rather than computing the coherence index.

The SC technique is certainly open to practical applications. One particular area that comes to mind is in the design of automated case study exercises to be used at business schools. Business schools have used the case study methodology in traditional lecture format to present coursework for decades. Now, many more individuals and colleges are exploring the possibility of offering degrees via correspondence. Structural Communication is the perfect technique for such applications. The case study could be presented using multimedia and the students' responses sent to the instructor via electronic mail. Then, the response analysis would be performed automatically and the discussion comments sent to the student. At this point, the instructor could decide that the student should make comments on the discussion comments and have them entered into a class forum or sent privately back to the instructor. In turn, the instructor could analyze the students' comments and make global comments to the class.

In conclusion, it seems that Structural Communication can be considered an emerging tactical paradigm, according to Kuhn's definition. Also, it fits well as a technique for designing "learning environments" which are consistent with the constructivist philosophy and developments in research in cognitive psychology.

References

Baath, J. A. (1979). Correspondence education in the light of a number of contemporary teaching models. Malmo: University of Lund, Department of Education.

Craik, F. I. M., & Lockhart, R. S. (1972). Levels of processing: A framework for memory research. *Journal of Verbal Learning and Verbal Behavior, 11*, 671–684.

Egan, K. (1972). Structural Communication: A new contribution to pedagogy. *Programmed Learning and Educational Technology, 9*(2), 63–78.

Egan, K. (1974). Beyond linear and branching programmed instruction. *British Journal of Educational Technology,* 5 (2), 36–58.

Egan, K. (1976). *Structural Communication.* Belmont CA: Fearon Publishers.

Fyfe, R. M., & Woodrow, D. (1969). *Basic ideas of abstract mathematics.* Centre for Structural Communication: University of London Press, London.

Hannafin, M. (1992). Emerging technologies, ISD, and learning environments: Critical perspectives. *Educational Technology Research and Development, 40*(1), 49–63.

Hannafin, M., & Gall, J. (1990, October). Emerging instructional technologies and learning environments: From instruction- to learner-centered models. Paper presented at the annual meeting of the Association for the Development of Computer-Based Instructional Systems.

Hodgson, A. M. (1972). Structural learning in social settings: Some notes on work in progress. *Programmed Learning and Educational Technology, 9*(2), 79–86.

Hodgson, A. M. (1974). Structural Communication in practice. In *APLET Yearbook of educational and instructional technology 1974/75.* London: Kogan Page.

Hodgson, A. M., & Dill, W. R. (Sept./Oct. 1970a). Programmed case: The misfired missive. *Harvard Business Review,* 140–46.

Hodgson, A. M., & Dill, W. R. (Nov./Dec. 1970b). Programmed case: Sequel to the misfired missive. *Harvard Business Review,* 105–110.

Hodgson, A. M., & Dill, W. R. (Jan./Feb. 1971). Programmed case: Reprise of the misfired missive. *Harvard Business Review,* 140–45.

Kroenke, D., & Dolan, K. (1987). *Business computer systems: An introduction* (3rd ed.). New York: Mitchell Publishing.

Kuhn, T. S. (1970). *The structure of scientific revolutions* (2nd ed.). Chicago: University of Chicago Press.

Lebow, D. (1993). Constructivist values for instructional systems design: Five principles toward a new mindset. *Educational Technology Research and Development, 41*(3), 4–16.

Linden, M., & Wittrock, M.C. (1981). The teaching of reading comprehension according to the model of generative learning. *Reading Research Quarterly, 17*(1), 44–57.

Mitchell, P. D., & Emmott, L. (1990). Eliminating differences in comprehension due to cognitive style through computer-based instructional systems. Paper presented at the meeting of the Association for the Development of Computer-Based Instructional Systems, San Diego, CA.

Mitchell, P. D., & Meilleur-Baccanale, D. (1982). Differential effects of wholist and serialist learning style on learning with Structural Communication. In *Progress in cybernetics and systems research.* New York: John Wiley & Sons.

Pusch, W., & Slee, E. J. (1990). Structural Communication: A forgotten application of cognitive theory. *Instructional Development, 1*(2), 11–16.

Rieber, L. P. (1992). Computer-based microworlds: A bridge between constructivism and direct instruction. *Educational Technology Research and Development, 40*(1), 93–106.

Romiszowski, A. J. (1976). *A study of individualized systems for mathematics instruction at the secondary level.* Unpublished doctoral dissertation, The University of Technology, Loughborough, United Kingdom.

Romiszowski, A. J. (1986). *Developing auto-instructional materials: From programmed texts to CAL and interactive video.* London: Kogan Page.

Romiszowski, A. J., & Abrahamson, A. (1992). *The Structural Communication methodology as a means of teaching George Orwell's Animal Farm: Paper and computer-based instruction.* Paper presented at the meeting of the Association for Educational Communications and Technology, Washington, DC.

Romiszowski, A. J., & Chang, E. (1992). Hypertext contributions to computer mediated communication: In search of instructional models. In M. Giardina (Ed.), *Interactive multimedia environments: Human factors and technical considerations in design issues.* New York: Springer-Verlag.

Romiszowski, A. J., Grabowski, B. L., & Damadaran, B. (1988). *Structural Communication, expert systems, and interactive video: A powerful combination for a nontraditional CAI approach.* Paper presented at the meeting of the Association for Educational Communications and Technology, New Orleans, LA.

Romiszowski, A. J., Grabowski, B. L., & Pusch, W. S. (1988). *Structural Communication: A neglected CAI methodology and its potential for interactive video simulations.* Paper presented at the meeting of the Association for the Development of Computer-Based Instructional Systems, Washington, DC.

Ryder, J. M., & Redding, R. E. (1993). Integrating cognitive task analysis into instructional systems development. *Educational Technology Research and Development, 41*(2), 75–96.

Taylor, S. G. (1990). *Concept mapping in Structural Communication.* Unpublished master's thesis, Concordia University, Montreal, Canada.

Tobin, K., & Dawson, G. (1992). Constraints to curriculum reform: Teachers and the myths of schooling. *Educational Technology Research and Development, 40*(1), 81–92.

Weinstein, C. E., & Mayer, R. E. (1986). The teaching of learning strategies. In M. C. Wittrock (Ed.), *Handbook of research on teaching* (pp. 315–327). New York: Macmillan.

Whittington, R. B. (1974). *A report on the effectiveness of Structural Communication.* Unpublished report, Simon Fraser University, B. C., Canada.

Wittrock, M. C. (1974). Learning as a generative process. *Educational Psychologist, 11,* 87–95.

Wittrock, M. C. (1985). Teaching learners generative strategies for enhancing reading comprehension. *Theory into Practice, 24*(2), 123–126.

37

Subliminal Perception Studies and Their Implications for Incorporating Embedded Communications into Instructional Design Products

James M. King
University of Georgia, Athens

Introduction

Experimental psychologists have been studying subliminal perception for over one hundred and thirty years and a great number of those who have studied the subject appear to believe that subliminal perception does occur. At the same time there has been continual controversy in the research community as to the viability and validity of many of the past and present studies. Subliminal perception or persuasion seems to be one of those subjects in which there is very little middle ground. Most researchers appear to either accept the existence of subliminal effects or strongly discount the entire area as a valid research pursuit. The early studies dealt primarily with subliminal imagery, while recent studies have concentrated on both subliminal audio and visual imagey.

As instructional message designers, we attempt to consider all aspects of an instructional design project along with the impact of the visual and audio content of that production. Is there a paradigm or model for message designers to follow in the process of turning out instructional and training materials? Obviously, there are many instructional design models which provide the basic framework for proceeding with the "construction" of a finished product. The current design models might be considered the guidelines for putting together the "blueprints" of a project. Message design, the actual "hammer and nail process" of designing materials, does not enjoy the luxury of existing paradigms to ease or speed the process.

Message designers do depend upon principles of design based on the behavioral and cognitive sciences. Books such as Fleming and Levie's (1993) *Instructional Message Design:*

Principles from the Behavioral and Cognitive Sciences provide research-based principles that guide designers in the decision making process related to the look and feel of a finished product. We always wonder what more can be done to make the message or communication more effective. One area that has not been addressed by Fleming and Levie (1993), Soulier (1988), Kemp (1985), Pettersson (1989), or any other authors writing in the instructional or message design area is the function of subliminal imagery and subliminal audio in learning. The area of subliminal perception (SP) has attracted a great deal of interest in the popular press, and surprisingly, there is a fairly large body of research concerning various aspects of SP. Subliminal perception has been and will continue to be a controversial topic both among the general populace and within the scientific community. The fact that *Time* Magazine devoted space in the Grapevine Section of the March 1, 1993 issue to the Russian efforts on mind control research demonstrates that subliminal perception is still worthy of news coverage. The *Time* (1993) report follows:

Mind Control Is a Terrible Thing to Waste

AS THE COLD WAR DEFROSTS, AMERICANS AND RUSSIANS ARE DISCOVERING common interests: rock music, fast food and . . . **MIND CONTROL TECHNOLOGY.** Former KGB General George Kotov has told American visitors about Russian research into "acoustic psycho-correction." The process involves transmitting commands into the subconscious through static or white-noise bands. The U.S. Army says it's 'looking into' these reports. (p. 9)

This type of news coverage, alluding to mind control, has been popular with the press, but is ranked by many in the mainstream of psychology, advertising and instructional design as being as newsworthy as UFO sightings.

The current popular fascination with subliminal perception began in the summer of 1957 in a Fort Lee, New Jersey movie theater. There, James Vicary conducted an experiment in message design that reverberated around the world. Vicary, head of a New York marketing and opinion-research firm, exposed over 45,000 people to two subliminal advertising messages, "Eat Popcorn" and "Drink Coca-Cola." His reported results were that theater popcorn sales increased 57.5% and that Coca-Cola sales increased on the average of 18.1%.

The news media quickly picked up on the story and wire services around the globe reported the effects of Vicary's study. The immediate reaction from the general public was an outcry against the use of embedded or subliminal ads in motion picture or television advertising. Patterson (1958), in *The Commonweal*, gave this description,

. . . All over the country newspapers announced the debut of a new kind of invisible advertising, one whose special claim was that it could stir people to buy corn flakes and toothpaste without letting them know they were being prodded. Throughout their accounts of the process, reporters scattered terms like 'brainwashing,' 'manipulating,' and 'something out of George Orwell' freely. Clearly, there was a wide-spread fear that a sinister new force had been added to the dark arts of mass persuasion. (p. 72)

However, it was not until 1962 that Vicary admitted that the data had been fabricated to boost his failing advertising agency. In the meantime, the Vicary study spurred a high level of public interest and is still referred to as a landmark study in the area of subliminal perception.

As Whitaker (1975, p. 17) states, "the mere mention of subliminal perception seems to produce Orwellian visions of 'mind control.'" Public outcry against the alleged powers of subliminal perception reached its height in the 1960s, epitomized by cartoons depicting people rushing out and buying things they didn't need or want as a result of secretly implanted subliminal cues from films or TV. The immediate appeal of subliminal communication to the message designer, teacher, college professor or industrial trainer is that such methods could be the answer to the persistent problem of student motivation and attention. The idea of presenting almost any message and embedding the true lesson material subliminally appears to have great promise. So, just what are subliminals and what do we know about their real ability to impart knowledge or effect behavior?

A Review of Popular Studies

Anthony Pratkanis in his article entitled *The Cargo-Cult Science of Subliminal Persuasion* (1992) states that there have been several waves of popular interest in subliminal persuasion. The first wave occurred at the turn of the twentieth century when interest in "spiritual self-help" groups such as "New Thought" became popular. "New Thought" ". . . stated that the mind has unlimited but hidden power that could be tapped-if one knew how-to bring about a wonderful, happy life and to exact physical cures" (p. 264).

The next wave occurred in the early 1970s when Wilson Bryan Key published a series of books purporting to uncover subliminal seduction techniques that not only were effective in film and video media, but were prevalent in print advertising. Key (1973) argued in what Pratkanis (1992) declares a "pseudo-scientific method" that messages aimed at inducing sexual arousal were embedded in print advertising. Key supposedly discovered embedded messages in product ads contained in publications ranging from *Newsweek* to *Playboy* magazines, as if you needed to embed subliminal sexual messages in *Playboy*.

Pratkanis (1992) states that the current wave of interest in subliminal perception began in the late 80s and continues into the 90s, with entrepreneurs creating a $50-million dollar-plus industry in subliminal self-help audio and video tapes. These tapes are supposedly designed to improve everything from self esteem to sexual responsiveness.

Purpose

Just what is the basis for subliminal persuasion or subliminal perception? Is there a research base upon which to build a set of guidelines or model for incorporating subliminal messages into instructional design? If subliminal perception techniques are effective, what are the ethics of using subliminal messages? These are a few of the issues this chapter will attempt to explore.

Definitions

Before tackling the hows and whys of subliminal research, a few operational definitions will help set the stage.

Subliminal Perception–perception of a stimulus which is below the threshold of conscious awareness. The threshold of conscious awareness is not fixed and varies from subject to subject and under changing environmental conditions.

Supraliminal Perception–conscious perception of a stimulus. While supraliminal stimuli may be perceived, they may not be internalized because of competing stimuli.

Subliminal Imagery Studies– studies dealing with the effects of subliminal imagery, including motion pictures, video and print imagery. Images are inserted into existing material by slide insertion, candlepower ratio levels or tachistoscopic projection.

Subliminal Audio Studies– studies dealing with the effects of subliminal audio, including psycho-acoustical concealment, back-masking, white-sound masking or electronic synchronization.

Threshold of Awareness– the point at which a subliminal image or sound approaches perception. The threshold varies with subjects and situational conditions.

Research

Research into subliminal perception has been carried out for over 150 years. Many of the studies are based upon sound research practices. But many are open to question, both for their inadequate or missing controls and the scientific or pseudo-scientific motivations of the researchers involved in the studies. Presented here are the summaries of some of the major studies conducted since the 1900s. They vary in type and procedures, with most dealing with subliminal visual perception and a few focusing on subliminal auditory perception. One study even deals with subliminal perception of weights.

Baker (1937) reports experiments by Suslowa as early as 1867 that were the precursors to later subliminal imagery studies. Suslowa was concerned with the effects of electrical stimulation on his subjects' abilies to make two-point threshold discriminations. It was found that their ability to discriminate one- from two-point stimulation was not reduced even when the intensity of the electrical stimulation was so low that the subjects were not aware of its presence.

Dunlap (1900) used the popular Müeller-Lyer illusion in which a line is made to appear shorter or longer than a second line of equal length by the direction of arrows at the end of the lines. (Figure 1) The Müeller-Lyer illusion still appears in many basic psychology texts today. In Dunlap's experiment the arrows which created the illusion were subliminally presented and then measured by getting the subjects' judgments on the relative length of the two presented segments. Dunlap found that ". . . for each subject the large majority of the sets compare as they would if the illusion were operative." He further states that "the imperceptible illusion-figure is active in producing psychical results," but further study is required to substantiate these conclusions.

Pratkanis (1992) reports that neither Tichener and Pyle (1907) nor Mabro and Washburn (1908) were able to replicate Dunlap's results, but Dunlap's study became the basis for many following studies. Pratkanis notes that 30 years later, Joseph Bressler:

> . . . was able to reconcile the empirical differences between Dunlap and his opponents. Bressler (1931) found that as the subliminal angles increased in intensity—that is, as they approached the threshold of awareness—the illusion was more likely to be seen. This finding, along with many others, served as the basis for concluding that there is no absolute threshold of awareness—it can vary as a function of individual and situational factors—and led to the hypothesis that, on some trials, subjects could see enough of the stimulus to improve their guessing at what might be there. (p. 265)

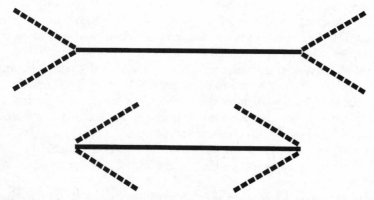

Figure 1.   Müeller-Lyer illusion used in numerous subliminal studies.

Bressler (1931) conducted a controlled study to demonstrate that unaware cues produce perceptual illusions by his use of an adaptation of Dunlap's Müeller-Lyer figure. He used different sets of figures with the subliminal arrows of different predetermined stimulating power. His results indicated that the subliminal arrows definitely affected the subjects' judgments of the lengths of the supraliminal segments and that the magnitude of the effect varied directly with the strength of the stimulus.

Dixon (1981) reports that Pierce and Jasthrow conducted experiments in 1884 to determine if subjects could discriminate between objects with imperceptible weight variation. Subjects were able to discriminate much better than chance would allow; however, the differences the subjects perceived were so small that they had no confidence in their judgments. This was among the first studies to measure a subject's awareness concerning whether they perceived a stimulus or whether they felt they were merely guessing.

Baker (1937) concluded that subjects were able to discriminate diagonal from vertical crossed lines and a dot-dash from a dash-dot auditory pattern in subliminal presentations. Miller (1940), who presented his subjects with five geometric figures at four different levels of intensity below the threshold concluded that as the intensity of the stimulation was reduced so was the subjects' ability to discriminate.

Adams (1957) summarized the significant findings of 76 studies of subliminal perception or "behavior without awareness," concluding that subjects in most of the studies were able to discriminate both aural and visual stimuli at a greater-than-chance levels.

Lloyd Silverman (1976) developed the "subliminal psychoanalytic dynamic activation" (SPA) line of research which has led to additional controversy. Silverman's research is based on the premise that many psychiatric disorders result from specific underlying conflicts. Silverman's procedure involves subliminally exposing subjects to emotionally charged words. Some of the sample phrases used in Silverman's and other researchers' studies have included: "MOMMY AND I ARE ONE," (MIO) paired with neutral phrases such as "PEOPLE ARE WALKING" (PAW). It is claimed that both disturbed and normal subjects exhibit beneficial effects after exposure to the symbiotic frame "MOMMY AND I ARE ONE," while the neutral "PEOPLE ARE WALKING" elicits no response. In many of these studies it appears that subliminal stimulation had an adaptive, enhancing effect on behavior.

The SPA technique involves, basically, the following design, as described by Weinberger (1992):

> Most have a within-subject design. Typically, subjects are seen twice, once for an experimental and once for a control session, with the order counterbalanced across subjects. Many recent studies have used a between-subject design, one usually used when looking at the effects of subliminal messages on various interventions. The experimental session involves presentation of what is presumed to be a psycho-dynamically active stimulus; the control session is presumably a neutral or inert message. Unmasked stimuli are presented via a tachistoscope for 4 ms; there are usually four exposures in each session 10 s apart. Subjects are unable to report seeing anything more than flickers of light. Sometimes discrimination trials follow the experiment . . . (p. 172)

Weinberger further describes the SPA procedures as follows:

> Double-blind procedures are in force throughout the experiments. That is, neither the subject nor the experimenter knows the content of the stimulus. The subject is ignorant by virtue of stimulus subliminality, and the experimenter is unaware of stimulus content because the stimuli are prepared and coded in advance of sessions by another experimenter. (p. 172)

Not all studies have been as conclusive. While subjects in laboratory controlled studies do appear to perform at better-than-chance levels in tests of perception of subliminal images and audio messages, commercial applications have not proved as conclusive.

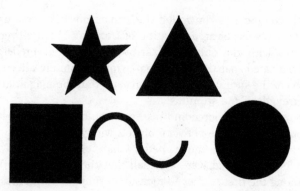

Figure 2. Five abstract symbols used by J.G. Miller and by DeFluer and Petranoff in several subliminal studies.

One of the first commercial tests of subliminals occurred in Great Britain in 1956 preceding Vicary's experiment in the New Jersey movie theater. Whitaker (1975) reports that the British Broadcasting Corporation ". . . as a part of its regular broadcasts, transmitted the words 'Pirie Breaks World Record' at a speed described as subliminal." (p. 19). Viewers were asked if they detected the message and many said that they did, but that raised the question of whether, in fact, the message was at a subliminal level.

In 1957, WTCO TV in Bangor, Maine conducted a subliminal experiment by broadcasting a "public service" announcement embedded in regular programming. The experiment yielded "negative results." DeFluer and Petranoff (1959) conducted a two-part experiment to determine the effectiveness of subliminals in television. In the first part of the experiment they used a set of five abstract symbols that were first used by J. G. Miller (Figure 2). Miller's experiment with the five symbols had successfully demonstrated subliminal perception under traditional projection methods. Defluer and Petranoff embedded the five symbols in 15-minute blocks of a feature-length motion picture presented to 25 subjects over a closed circuit television system. They used a process of "supering" the symbols over the television picture at a level of 1% of the video level. The remaining 99% of the video level masked the "super" and subjects were not consciously aware of the embedded figures.

The movie was stopped at 15 minute intervals and subjects were asked to identify the symbol that had been embedded. The results showed a 34% accuracy, which DeFluer and Petranoff reported as 14% above pure chance.

In the second part of the experiment, DeFluer and Petranoff broadcast subliminal "supered" messages at the 1% level during a nightly broadcast of feature length movies. One message, "Watch Frank Edwards," referred to the program immediately following the feature movie. The second message, "Buy___," referred to three products available at local food markets. The experiment was conducted over a five week period and the messages were alternated nightly.

The broadcast occurred over WTTV in Indianapolis, Indiana and the viewing audience was not made aware of the subliminals. At the end of the five-week period it was concluded that the subliminal images had "no measurable effects" on the television audiences' viewing or buying habits. This real-world experiment, in which variables could not be easily controlled, demonstrated that subliminals may not have the impact that many would impart to them.

Wilson Bryan Key has contributed to what Pratkanis (1992) calls "Cargo-cult Science." Pratkanis states that "Key argued that subliminal techniques were not just limited to television and movies. Cleverly hidden messages aimed at inducing sexual arousal are claimed to be embedded in the photographs of print advertisements. Key found the word *sex* printed on everything from Ritz Crackers to the ice cubes in a Gilbey Gin ad" (p. 265).

Pratkanis further states that "Key was successful in linking the concept of subliminal persuasion to the issues of his day. The 1970s were a period of distrust by Americans of their government, businesses, and institutions. Key claimed that big advertisers and big government are in a conspiracy to control our minds using subliminal implants" (p. 265).

Controversy

Controversy has surrounded subliminal perception from the very beginning. The original studies in the late 1800s and early 1900s came at a time when people were interested in spiritualism and mesmerism. The idea that the mind could process undetectable images and sounds reinforced the sense of the mystic, of man's innate ability to be more than the sum of his parts. The controversy over the "power" of subliminal persuasion exploded in the summer of 1957 when word of Vicary's experiments in a New Jersey movie theater both stunned and frightened the general population. Outcries were heard around the world about the threat of this powerful tool that the advertising media now possessed, which could mold the consumer's mind to buy whatever industry wanted to market. Newspaper columnists, magazine editors, radio and TV newscasters all reported the power of this new "subliminal" tool to provoke buying frenzies in the consumer.

Validity, as to the effectiveness of subliminal persuasion, was added to these journalistic protestations about subliminal persuasion when the Federal Communications Commission called for an investigation of the Vicary study and the National Association of Broadcasters banned the use of subliminal advertising. No one made an attempt to replicate the Vicary study, but many accepted the results as valid. Years later in an interview with *Advertising Age*, Vicary admitted that he had fabricated the study to bolster his failing advertising company. Pratkanis (1992) states that in the 1962 interview with *Advertising Age*, "circumstantial evidence suggests that this time Vicary was telling the truth" (p. 261). So it appears that one of the greatest outcries over subliminal persuasion and the "knee jerk" reaction to contain it were all promulgated by a fabricated study.

But the subliminal controversy does not end with Vicary's acknowledgment that his study was false. Other players, or more correctly, "evangelists," entered the subliminal picture. The most prominent or "visible" player in the 1970s was Wilson Bryan Key. Key (1973, 1976, 1980, 1990) has made a very good living authoring a set of books with titles including *Subliminal Seduction, Media Sexploitation, The Clam-plate Orgy,* and *The Age of Manipulation: The Con in Confidence and the Sin in Sincere.* Each of these books purports to review in a scientific manner the "insidious", sexually laden messages that are embedded in the print media, ranging from ads for Gilbey's Gin to cover art on *Glamour* magazine. In fact, Key uses what could be described as pseudo science to "prove" his thesis. Key's latest book was reviewed by John O'Toole (1989), President of the American Association of Advertising Agencies. O'Toole wonders: "Why is there a market for yet another re-run of this troubled man's paranoid nightmares?" (p. 26).

In the process of compiling this chapter, the author checked out over 20 books from the university library related to subliminal perception. Many of these books are well written and the authors have attempted to pursue the study of subliminals in a scholarly manner. Several books of note included Norman Dixon's (1981) *Preconscious Processing,* and *Perception Without Awareness* by Bornstein and Pittman (1992). Ironically, if a book is judged by its cover, at least in terms of how used it appears, then Wilson Bryan Key's book, *Subliminal Seduction,* wins the prize. Not only was the outside worn, but the margins were thoroughly marked and many key passages underlined. It can easily be imagined how many college students at this university have used Key's books as a primary source for information related to subliminals, while avoiding or discounting the more in-depth and scientifically based books on the subject. The author suspects this pattern is not restricted to this university, but is a common happening nationwide.

In an article by Michael Lev (1991), John O'Toole, president of the American Association of Advertising Agencies, is quoted as saying, "There is no such thing" (as subliminal advertising). "The issue persisted partly because college professors frequently used the Key books in media courses" (Section D, p. 7, Column 1). Lev also reports that in a recent survey conducted by Ogilvy and Mather, 61 percent of 800 people surveyed believed that subliminal advertising existed, and 56 percent believed that it is effective. The survey, with a 3 percent margin of error, gives us a pretty good clue as to what Americans think about subliminals. Pratkanis (1992) reports that "just nine months after the Vicary story first broke, 41 percent of survey respondents had heard of subliminal advertising. This figure climbed to 81 percent in the early 1980s, with more than 68 percent of those aware of the term believing that it was effective in selling products" (p. 261). Pratkanis reports that most people learned about subliminals through the mass media or courses in high school and college. Books like Key's have been a major contributor to the perpetuation of the myth of subliminal advertising. Advertisers have begun spoofing subliminal advertising by taking advantage of its appeal to the American consumer. Seagram's has run a series of ads asking you to find the "hidden" image. One can only wonder what Wilson Bryan Key thinks of Seagram's "subliminal" ad campaign.

Key is not the only "subliminal evangelist" working the market. Eldon Taylor (1988) has also written a pseudó scientific book, *Subliminal Learning: An Eclectic Approach,* which introduces one to the wonders of subliminal audio and videotapes. Taylor has written a book to support the use of subliminal self-help audio and videotapes and to dispel some of the controversy that surrounds this currently popular mind-expansion technique. The writing style used and the references to "scientific" studies conducted would lead the reader to believe that the designs of subliminal self-help tapes and videos are based upon sound scientific research. In fact, most of the studies cited either were not conducted under controlled conditions or more often were conducted by the very companies that market the tapes. Taylor cites both Bryan Wilson Key and Vance Packard as authorities on the evidence for the existence of subliminal persuasion techniques. Vance Packard (1957), author of *Hidden Persuaders,* is possibly the "father" of pop paranoia, finding government and industrial intervention into every corner of the psyche of America. Taylor wraps his book in pseudó science and appeals to the masses through the premise that our minds can be easily molded by subliminal messages. In fact, Taylor is trying to build a case for the use of subliminal audio and videotapes because he has a vested interest in Progressive Awareness Research, Inc., one of the many companies marketing subliminal materials.

Another book which deserves close scrutiny is one by John David Oates (1991), entitled *Reverse Speech: Hidden Messages in Human Communication.* Oates "investigates" the use of reverse speech or the process of "back masking," first used by the Beatles in some of their music. Great controversy surrounds the embedding of sexual or satanic phrases within the tracks of popular music. Again, the basic belief is that these hidden or subliminal messages psychodynamically affect our actions, usually in detrimental ways. The most recent media-grabbing case involved the rock group *Judas Priest.* Two teenagers in Reno, Nevada committed suicide, and their parents brought suit against *Judas Priest* and CBS Records, Inc., claiming that a back-masked phrase, "Just Do It," was the contributing factor in the deaths of the two boys. Ironically, Bryan Wilson Key served as an expert witness for the plaintiffs. The court ruled in favor of *Judas Priest* with the judge stating that "The scientific research presented does not establish that subliminal stimuli, even if perceived, may precipitate conduct of this magnitude. There exist other factors which explain the conduct of the deceased independent of subliminal stimuli." (*Vance & Belknap v. Judas Priest & CBS Records,* 1990) Although Judas Priest was exonerated, the controversy surrounding subliminal perception, and particularly back masking, still continues. Each month at least one popular press magazine or newspaper prints an article or references material about subliminal perception.

Are subliminals, particularly audio and video subliminals, effective? The general consensus from well controlled research studies dealing with graphically or textually embedded images is that subliminal perception is a "real" phenomenon, meaning that subjects exposed to subliminal images under well controlled conditions do respond in posttests at better than chance levels when asked to identify or associate the subliminals. Masling (1992) states that "Not only does learning occur when stimuli are presented below the level of conscious awareness, but some types of performance are actually enhanced by subliminal exposure" (p. 262).

Dixon (1981), in his book on preconscious processing, concludes that:

1. . . . the brain may respond to external stimuli which, for one reason or another, are not consciously perceived. The effects of such stimuli may be almost as varied as those of sensory inflow which *does* enter consciousness.

2. . . . the characteristics of preconscious processing are indeed consistent with certain general principles of biological adaptation.

3. If these data (cognitive theories and clinical practice) are valid then they compel a view of the body/mind relationship quite different from that traditionally held. And if *this* is so then we must perforce rethink all those theories which took it as axiomatic that awareness must mediate between stimulus and response, and that the 'lowly' operations of preconscious processing are remarkable only for their simplicity. (p. 262)

Moore (1992) reports that reviews of research findings in subliminal perception have provided very little evidence that stimuli below observers' subjective thresholds influence motives, attitudes, beliefs, or choices. "Studies that do purport to find such effects are either unreplicated or methodologically flawed in one or more ways . . ." (p. 274).

While studies with subliminal imagery have shown positive results, subliminal audio research has not satisfactorily demonstrated the effectiveness of embedded communications. Again, Moore (1992) states that "Subliminal tapes represent a change in modality from visual to auditory, and now subliminal stimulation is supposedly being harnessed for a more noble purpose—psychotherapy, clearly a less crass objective than that of covert advertising" (p. 276). Apparently, the many more variables and intervening factors at work in audio research do not produce the consistent results that have been obtained with graphic or textual studies. Again, under well-controlled laboratory conditions, some audio research studies have shown significant effects. However, according to Pratkanis, Eskenazi, and Greenwald (1990), in two studies conducted with commercial self-esteem and memory subliminal tapes, they could find no effect (improvement or decrement) on either self-esteem or memory. Other researchers have found the same results. Treimer and Simonson (1986) and Merikle and Skanes (1992) all found no effect in multiple studies they have carried out over the past 8 years using various commercially available products. Merikle (1988) even demonstrated, by using audio spectroscopic analysis, that some subliminal audio tapes have no perceptible (as measured electronically) subliminal signal.

So what is the bottom line as far as instructional developers and message designers might be concerned? Yes, the phenomenon of subliminal perception, at least at the visual level, does exist, and might have practicality under certain learning conditions. Is it a technique that should be incorporated into training or instructional materials? Can the environment and the presentation be maintained in a controlled enough manner to assure the effectiveness of the subliminals? Is it worth the effort?

Ethics

What are the ethics of incorporating subliminals into training or instructional materials? Just because we can do it, should we? When designing materials for learning, at first it may be felt that anything that is necessary to assure mastery is appropriate. But is it fair to embed a hidden message or meaning into your materials? Should students know they are receiving subliminal messages? The current litigious society we live in says you better label anything you produce; not just with the fact that it contains subliminal images, but also that whatever the content, we can't guarantee that it will be effective nor can we guarantee that it won't harm you. Heaven help us if the lawyers would ever let us claim that materials are effective and will accomplish what they are designed to do. So, if you want to use subliminal audio or graphics within a product, let the students know about it. A better tack would be to give each student the option of using the subliminal materials at his or her own discretion. Students may use subliminals if they feel that it will assist them in mastering the materials more quickly. Using graphic or textual subliminals within a computer program may be viewed by a student as an effective option. While audio subliminals have shown little effectiveness, many researchers have found that students "felt" they had learned the material "better" because the subliminals were present. In fact, students did not learn better or remember more when subliminals were used, but if students think they are doing better, is there anything wrong with students feeling positive about their learning experience?

Conclusion

There is no doubt that subliminal perception research is a controversial area. Moore (1992) says that, "Subliminal advertising and psychotherapeutic effects from subliminal tapes are ideas whose scientific status appears to be on par with wearing copper bracelets to cure arthritis" (p. 279). While there is a body of subliminal research and a group of serious and dedicated scientists pursuing the answers to questions in this area, the serious scientific research efforts take a back seat to the mass media reports and subliminal "evangelists" stumping the country selling their books and tapes. Masling (1992) indicates that three groups have been involved in serious subliminal research: clinical psychologists interested in unconscious motivation, and social and cognitive psychologists concerned with perceptual and cognitive processes at or below the level of awareness. Even within the serious scientific community, the research of those who venture into the study of subliminals is sometimes ridiculed by their colleagues. Dixon (1981) writes that "Even today, when the reality of unconscious perception has been confirmed beyond reasonable doubt, there remains in some quarters a legacy of almost unshakable resistance. Manifestations of this resistance, however, do seem to have changed—from active refutation to ignoring of the irrefutable!" (p. 181). Dixon was not talking about the general population, but about many of his peers in the field of psychology.

How do we as instructional developers and message designers deal with subliminal perception? On a base level, subliminals should be viewed as just another tool or technique that is available for us to use in creating the "best" instructional materials. But, in reality, subliminal perception as a design technique probably can play only a small part in the overall design of any project. We have so many better tools or techniques available to us, based on design principles formulated over years of research. Just in the area of perception, Winn (1993), in Fleming and Levie's (1993) *Instructional Message Design*, lists over 70 design principles that, if applied properly, will have more effect than subliminal perception. If subliminal perception techniques can be harnessed and incorporated as a tool for creating better message designs, then we should use them as we would any other option we have open to us. Our current knowledge and skill with incorporating subliminals into designs is embryonic at best. If you want an adventure you might try incorporating subliminals into your next project. But, be prepared to expect questions, criticism and possibly controversy.

References

Adams, J. K. (1957). Laboratory studies of behavior without awareness. *Psychological Bulletin, 54,* 388–405.

Baker, L. E. (1937, January). The influence of subliminal stimuli upon verbal behavior. *Journal of Experimental Psychology, 20,* 84–100.

Bornstein, R. F., & Pittman, T. S. (1992). *Perception without awareness: Cognitive, clinical, and social perspectives.* New York: The Guilford Press.

Bressler, J. (1931). Illusion in the case of subliminal visual stimulation. *Journal of General Psychology, 5,* 244–251.

DeFluer, M. L., & Petranoff, R. M. (1959). A televised test of subliminal persuasion. *Public Opinion Quarterly, 23,* 168–180.

Dixon, N. F. (1981). *Preconscious processing.* New York: John Wiley & Sons.

Dunlap, K. (1900, September). Effect of imperceptible shadows on judgments of distance. *Psychological Review, 7,* 435–453.

Fleming M., & Levie, W. H. (Eds.). (1993). *Instructional message design: Principles from the behavioral and cognitive sciences* (2nd ed.). Englewood Cliffs, NJ: Educational Technology Publications.

Kemp, J. E. (1985). *The instructional design process.* New York: Harper & Row Publishers.

Key, W. B. (1973). *Subliminal seduction: Ad media's manipulation of a not so innocent America.* Englewood Cliffs: Prentice-Hall.

Key, W. B. (1976). *Media sexploitation.* Englewood Cliffs, NJ: Prentice-Hall.

Key, W. B. (1980). *The clam-plate orgy.* Englewood Cliffs, NJ: Prentice-Hall.

Key, W. B. (1990). *The age of manipulation: The con in confidence, the sin in sincere.* Englewood Cliffs, NJ: Prentice-Hall.

Lev, M. (1991, May 3). No hidden meaning here: Seagram goes 'subliminal.' *The New York Times,* Section D, p. 7.

Mabro, H. M., & Washburn, M. F. (1908). The effect of imperceptible line on the judgment of distance. *American Journal of Psychology, 19,* p. 242.

Masling, J. M. (1992). What does it all mean? In R. F. Bornstein & T. S. Pittman (Eds.), *Perception without awareness: Cognitive, clinical, and social perspectives* (pp. 259– 276). New York: The Guilford Press.

Merikle, P. M. (1988). Subliminal auditory tapes: An evaluation. *Psychology & Marketing, 46,* 355–372.

Merikle, P. M., & Skanes, H. E. (1992, October). Subliminal self-help audiotapes: A search for placebo-effects. *Journal of Applied Psychology, 77,* 772–776.

Miller, J. G. (1940). The role of motivation in learning without awareness. *American Journal of Psychology, 53,* 229–239.

Mind control is a terrible thing to waste. (1993, March). *Time,* p. 9.

Moore, T. E. (1992). Subliminal perception: Facts and fallacies. *The Skeptical Inquirer, 16*(2), 273–281.

Oates, D. J. (1991). *Reverse speech: Hidden messages in human communication.* Indianapolis: Knowledge Systems, Inc.

O'Toole, J. (1989). [Review of *The age of manipulation*]. *Advertising Age, 60,* p. 26.

Packard, V. (1957). *Hidden persuaders.* New York: Affiliated Publishers.

Patterson, J. (1958, April). Invisible salesman. *The Commonweal,* p. 71.

Pettersson, R. (1989). *Visuals for information: Research and practice.* Englewood Cliffs, NJ: Educational Technology Publications.

Peirce, C. S., & Jastrow, J. (1884). On small differences of sensation. *Memoirs of the National Academy of Sciences, 3,* 73–83.

Pratkanis, A. R. (1992). The cargo-cult science of subliminal persuasion. *Skeptical Inquirer, 16*(2), 260–272.

Pratkanis, A. R., Eskenazi, J., & Greenwald, A. G. (1990, April). What you expect is what you believe (But not necessarily what you get): On the effectiveness of subliminal self-help audiotapes. Paper presented at the meeting of the Western Psychological Association, Los Angeles, CA.

Silverman, L. H. (1976). Psychoanalytic theory: The reports of my death are greatly exaggerated. *American Psychologist, 31,* 621–637.

Soulier, J. S. (1988). *The design and development of computer based instruction.* Boston: Allyn and Bacon, Inc.

Suslowa, M. (1863). Veranderungen der hautgefule unter dem einflusse electrischer reizung. *Zeitschrift fur Rationelle Medicin, 18,* 155–160.

Taylor, E. (1988). *Subliminal learning: An eclectic approach.* Salt Lake: Just Another Reality Publishing, Inc.

Tichener, E. B., & Pyle, W. H. (1907). Effect of imperceptible shadows on the judgment of distance. *Proceedings of American Philosophical Society, 46,* 94–109.

Treimer, M., & Simonson, M. R. (1986, January). Old wine in new bottles: Subliminal messages in instructional media. Paper presented at the Annual Convention of the Association for Educational Communications and Technology, Las Vegas, NV.

Vance and Belknap v. Judas Priest and CBS Records. 86-5844/86-3939. Second District Court of Nevada (1990).

Weinberger, J. (1992). Validating and demystifying subliminal psychodynamic activation. In R. F. Bornstein & T.S. Pittman (Eds.) *Perception without awareness: Cognitive, clinical, and social perspectives* (pp. 170–190). New York: The Guilford Press.

Whitaker, R. (1975, Nov./Dec.). Subliminal perception: Myth or magic? *Educational Broadcasting,* 17–20.

Winn, W. (1993). Perception principles. In M. F. Fleming & W. H. Levie (Eds.), *Instructional message design: Principles from the behavioral and cognitive sciences* (2nd. ed.). Englewood Cliffs, NJ: Educational Technology Publications.

38

The Algo-Heuristic Theory and Methodology of Learning, Performance, and Instruction as a Paradigm

Landamatics International, New York

Introduction

The AHT as a Paradigm

Most theories and methods are created to resolve certain practical and/or theoretical problems. The Algorithmico-Heuristic Theory (AHT) of Learning, Performance, and Instruction (labeled *Landamatics* by some American scholars, i.e., in the *Encyclopedia of Psychology*) is no exception to this rule. It was devised to offer an effective solution to a number of theoretical and practical issues for which there has been no satisfactory solution in educational theory and practice for a long period of time.

The AHT can be viewed as a paradigm because:

- It clearly *formulates the psychological and educational problems* that it addresses.

- It identifies the *root causes* of those problems.

- It contains specific *conceptualizations and explanations* of the problems addressed.

- It offers a *conceptual apparatus* for a systematic description of these problems and their causes.

- It offers a *system of distinctive methods* for resolving those problems in a systematic and reliable way.

- The offered methods are *objective* and *replicable*.

661

- The offered methods are sufficiently *general (generic)* and *comprehensive* to be applied to different kinds and levels of education and training, as well as to different kinds and levels of learning and performance.

- The results of applying the methods are measurable and can be compared with the results of applying other methods.

The AHT meets another criterion of a paradigm, as pointed out by Kuhn (1970): It has created a following. Thousands of teachers in the former USSR, where the AHT was developed in the early 1950s, applied the AHT in their educational practices and achieved a dramatic improvement in learning and performance of students at all levels of education. Also, a number of books and numerous articles describing various applications of the AHT or its further development have been published in many countries (e.g., Bung, 1973; Bussman, 1970; Carpay, 1976; Coscarelli, 1978; Gentilhomme, 1964; Gerlach, Reiser, & Brecke, 1977; Horabin & Lewis, 1977; Kopstein, 1977; Lánsky, 1969; Lewis, 1967; Lewis & Horabin, 1977; Merrill, 1977, 1980; Scandura, Durnin, Ehrenpreis, & Luger, 1971; Schmid, Portnoy, & Burns, 1976; Sholomij, 1969, 1973; Tulodziecki, 1972; Vermersch, 1971; Zemke & Kramlinger, 1982; and Zierer, 1972).

AHT's Content Area and Overall Objectives

Reading current publications on critical thinking, an impression often arises that the task of teaching students how to effectively learn and critically think is a new task that arose relatively recently. In fact, it is a very old task which has concerned philosophers and educators from ancient times. This false impression arises in large part because at different times the task has been formulated in different words and within different contexts. The real issue is that for centuries there didn't exist *effective, explicitly formulated, systematic, reliable and replicable* methods of teaching thinking and problem solving. This does not mean that there didn't exist teachers who knew how to teach thinking. But these teachers discovered their methods by themselves through their own experience; they never developed their methods to the level of explicit and precise conceptualization and methodology, i.e., to the level of theory, which would have made those methods systematic, reliable, and replicable. As a rule, good instructional methods developed by these teachers died with the death of the teachers who found or discovered them. Attempts by psychologists and educational scientists to theoretically describe the methods used by these teachers often led to theories and practical recommendations which were either vague or incomplete or one-sided.

Instructional theories and methods have always existed which absolutized certain components of complex thinking and learning processes (for example, associations). Their authors believed that by teaching these particular components in a certain way, it would be possible to form *all* the mental skills and abilities that were desirable in students, and thus all the goals (tasks, objectives) that were viewed as important would be achieved.

A list is presented here of some of the tasks in teaching thinking and in developing the ability to effectively learn, which have been formulated as instructional objectives by numerous authors at different times and in different words:

1. It is important to give students not only knowledge but to teach them how to apply it.
2. It is important to give students not only knowledge but to teach them how to think, solve problems, and make decisions.
3. It is important to teach students not only knowledge but to form thinking skills and abilities.
4. It is important to teach students not only how to think but also to develop their intelligence.

5. It is important not only to transfer knowledge (information) to students but also to teach them how to obtain knowledge (information) by themselves, i.e., how to learn.
6. It is important to make learning and problem solving as active as possible and overcome the passivity that is characteristic of many students.
7. It is important to teach students not only rules, laws, theorems, and other theoretical propositions, but also how to discover these propositions on their own.
8. It is important to teach students how to solve not only standard problems but nonstandard (creative) problems as well. (In other words, to teach both non-creative and creative thinking.)
9. It is important to teach students not only knowledge about objective phenomena and processes but also about knowledge itself, i.e. *meta*-knowledge.
10. It is important to teach students not only the ability to solve problems and make decisions but the ability to manage and control their own mental processes as well.

Different authors give different—often incompatible and even contradictory—recommendations as to how to achieve these objectives. In addition, those recommendations are frequently not specific enough or are simply vague. All this leads to the fact that in practice, educational practitioners (teachers, instructors, trainers) often fail to achieve the objectives of which they are well aware and which they, as a rule, want to achieve.

Studies conducted within the AHT framework identified a number of factors which cause problems in achieving the outlined objectives. Among them, in particular:

(a) teachers don't often have a *clear* and sufficiently *detailed* understanding of the *internal mechanisms* of "objects" (cognitive phenomena) involved in learning and cognitive activity;
(b) teachers don't often know what *precisely* to do in order to achieve each and all of the instructional objectives they want to achieve, i.e., they don't know the precise *"how to"* of the instructional process as related to each of the instructional objectives;
(c) teachers not infrequently use methods which are either inappropriate for the mental processes they want to form in students, or are inadequate, or incomplete, or unsystematic, or unreliable.

AHT is an attempt to build a comprehensive and unifying *theory* of, and a detailed *methodology* for, the systematic and reliable teaching of knowledge and thinking in a way that leads to the development of general cognitive abilities and intelligence.

From its inception, the creators of this theory intended to overcome the vagueness and confusion that is characteristic of many notions used in instructional science. They also intended to clearly formulate the methods (the "how to") of practical instruction which follows from such a unifying theory.

Obviously, in the limited space of one chapter, it is impossible to describe the theory and the methodology in sufficient detail to guarantee the effacy of its use by the practitioner. Therefore, this chapter will only outline the foundation and the basic principles of the AHT which are essential for its description as a paradigm.

Conceptual Apparatus of the AHT:
Basic Definitions and Differentiations

Each well-designed theory is based on a limited number of basic notions (concepts) and propositions which reflect (a) the essential *characteristics* of the objects (phenomena) described by the theory and (b) the *relationships* between these objects (phenomena), as well as the relationships between their characteristics. All other concepts and propositions in the theory are *derived* from these basic ones.

Since individual phenomena described by the theory have both common and distinctive features, it is very important to show the commonalities and differences among phenomena. Only this will provide a *cohesive* and *logically organized* picture of the content domain studied by the theory and prevent confusions that normally arise when the theory is not well organized logically.

The next section provides the description of the basic notions (concepts) used in the AHT and of their relationships.

Knowledge and Thinking

Knowledge

Knowledge is a reflection in our minds of objects or phenomena in the form of images, concepts, or propositions. To know something means to have an image of that object, and/or a notion of it, and/or be able to state a proposition about it.

When one closes one's eyes, one can see in his/her mind a *picture* of certain objects, for example, of a pencil. This picture is a mental *image*.

The ability to *explain* what a pencil is by *verbally stating* (listing) the characteristic *features* of a pencil is an indication that a person has a *notion (concept)* of it. (Whether the concept is correct or incorrect is a different matter.)

The ability to *give a definition* of a pencil or *make a statement* about its attributes is an indication that a person has knowledge of a pencil in the form of a *proposition*.

Thus, knowledge exists in three major forms: images, concepts, and propositions:

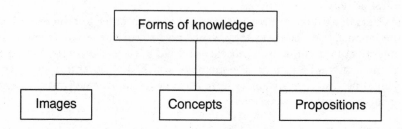

It is well known that people may have knowledge of certain objects in the form of images but not in the form of concepts (one may *depict* an object, make a *drawing* of it, but have difficulties in isolating and verbally listing its characteristics).

It is also possible that a person may have knowledge in the form of a concept (i.e., be able to list an objects' characteristics) but not be able to give their logically correct definitions or formulate their related rules.

A person, of course, may have the knowledge of objects in all three forms. Knowledge may reflect *external* objects of phenomena or *internal* processes or states of the person himself or herself.

Knowledge may also reflect another knowledge and thus be a *meta*-knowledge. There may be knowledge that reflects meta-knowledge, thus representing meta-knowledge of the *second order*.

Knowledge may be divided into types depending on whether it reflects *objects (sub-stantive* knowledge) or *actions* with objects *(procedural* knowledge).

Knowledge can be classified on some other logical grounds as well.

Thinking

It is common knowledge that a person may be very knowledgeable but not very smart. And vice versa: he may be smart but not very knowledgeable. This makes it obvious that knowledge and thinking are different things.

The difference, simply stated, is this: While knowledge is a *reflection* in our mind of objects and phenomena, thinking is *operation* on (or with) reflections (i.e., on knowledge) which allows one to produce from the given knowledge some other knowledge (for example, to create a new image, to draw a conclusion from some proposition, etc.).

Physical and Mental Actions (operations)

Physical Actions

What does it mean to operate on knowledge? More generally, what does *operating* precisely mean? The notion of operating implies some *actions*. To operate a factory, for example, means to do certain things to the factory's objects to achieve a certain product or achieve other goals. Operating consists of certain *actions*; for example, *to turn on* a machine, to *set* a certain regimen of its work, and so on.

The actions (or "operations") we just mentioned are *physical (practical)* actions. (We will be using the terms "action" and "operation" interchangeably.) The notion of physical actions is simple and everyone has it: physical (practical) actions deal with *material, tangible* objects and bring about their physical, material changes, or *transformations*. Sharpening a pencil or turning it around are different *transformations* of a pencil caused by different *actions* performed on it.

However, the notion of an action is not limited to physical (practical) actions. For example, when talking about someone's thinking processes, we may ask a person the question: "What did you *do* in your *mind* that led you to that decision?" The natural question is what "*doing something in the mind*" means.

Mental Actions

Doing something in the mind definitely implies some *actions*. But the mind cannot perform physical actions that transform material, tangible objects. What it can do, however, is to transform *reflections* of objects in our mind, i.e., images, concepts or propositions. The actions by which the transformation of images, concepts and propositions is carried out are *mental* actions.

Many mental actions are congruous to physical actions. For example, by physically sharpening a pencil we change *(transform)* its objective mass and shape; by physically turning it around we *transform* its objective spatial orientation. Mental actions we perform on a pencil's image are similar to the physical actions we performed on the real pencil: we can *transform* the image of a blunt pencil into an image of a sharpened pencil; we can *turn around* the original image and thus change its spatial orientation in our mind.

The transformations we perform in our mind via mental actions are *real* transformations performed by *real* actions. The difference between physical and mental actions is only that the former are performed on tangible *objects* while the latter are performed on their intangible *images*.

Mental actions—and the transformations they bring about—can be performed not only on images but on *concepts* and *propositions* as well. We are able to *eliminate* in our mind one or another characteristic of an object reflected in a concept, *add* characteristics, *replace* them, and so on. We are also able to carry out different mental actions on propositions, *changing* them in a variety of ways and thus *transforming* them.

Knowledge, Mental Actions, and Mental Processes

In a wide sense of the word, a *process* is the *creation* and *transformation (change)* of objects or phenomena, their attributes, states, or relationships. Mental processes are actuations in the mind and transformations of *knowledge* (images, concepts and propositions) and/or of *mental operations*.

It is very rare, if ever, that solving a problem or making a decision can be done by using some *single* knowledge unit or a single mental operation. Usually, cognitive processes involve *sets* of knowledge units and mental operations. Depending on the previous instruction, learning and experience, knowledge units and mental operations are *organized* in certain *systems*. Since the principles of organization may be different in different people and for different situations, these systems may have different *structures*.

In the framework of the AHT, special interest is placed on the process of *actuation* of knowledge units and mental operations in the course of thinking. As a rule, people have in their minds thousands of knowledge units and mental operations. However, when they solve problems and make decisions they use (apply) only some of them. To be able to apply them, they must first be *actuated*. Failure to actuate the needed knowledge unit(s) and/or operation(s) makes it impossible to use (apply) them in the course of solving a problem, and thus leads to a failure to find a solution.

Ways of Actuating Knowledge and Actions

Passive and Active Processes

Knowledge units and mental operations can be actuated in three basic ways:

(a) externally by outward stimuli (tangible objects and/or instructions);
(b) internally by other knowledge units or mental operations; and
(c) internally by verbal self-instructions as to what to do in order to perform some task or achieve some goal.

Actuation in cases (a) and (b) is based on associations formed in previous learning and experience. Actuation in these cases occurs *by association, involuntarily,* i.e., *automatically, by itself.*

An example is provided by the occasion of seeing the house where a friend used to live, which might bring about a mental image of the friend. Or, when a request to "give me a pen" actuates the appropriate action of giving. Another example is when a mental image of a singer or his name actuates a song that he sang (or vice versa). Or, performing one action in the process of starting a car—provided that this process has been automatized sufficiently—actuates another action to be performed.

Processes actuated by association are **passive** *processes since they occur without any special effort, i.e., by themselves.* But actuation in case (c) is different. A situation or a problem may automatically actuate certain knowledge units and mental operations which may not be adequate for finding a solution. However, if a person *knows what to do* in order to find a solution and *gives himself a corresponding self-instruction*, this self-instruction may actuate necessary physical and/or mental actions *which were not actuated automatically by association.*

For example, consider a student who is trying to solve a geometric problem. Perception of a diagram of an isosceles triangle automatically—by association—actuates in the student's mind the knowledge of three of the attributes of isosceles triangles (out of five that exist and in principle are known to him). These attributes, however, don't lead to the finding of a solution. Then he asks himself a question (self-question): "What are the other attributes of isosceles triangles?" (This self-question performs the function of a self-instruction: "Find other attributes.") The self-question (self-instruction) actuates mental actions of *voluntary search in the memory for those attributes of an isosceles triangle* which *did not come to mind by involuntary association, by themselves.*

Thus, self-instructions actuate certain physical or mental actions that in turn actuate certain knowledge (images, concepts and/or propositions) which were not actuated by association but whose use (application) was necessary in order to solve the problem.

Self-instructions and their corresponding mental or physical actions are thus able to *overcome associations*. Overcoming associations is a prerequisite—and, as a rule, a necessary condition—for solving any kind of non-standard, creative problem; this kind of problem is creative exactly because associations actuated by the problem conditions don't lead to the solution.

Processes that involve the actuation of knowledge and actions through the use of self-instructions, thereby leading to the overcoming of association-activated knowledge and actions, are **active** *processes.*

The ability of self-instructions to actuate knowledge units and actions not actuated by association lies at the foundation of *self-guidance, self-regulation and self-control*. This ability makes humans capable of breaking out of the fatal dominance of associations formed by past experience and thus makes it possible for them to avoid becoming slaves to their associations.

The Anatomy and Makeup of Verbal Instructions and Operations

Consider a simple instruction: "Give me a pen, please." The instruction contains two basic components:

(a) an indication of an *action* to be performed ("give");
(b) an indication of an *object* with which the action is to be performed ("a pen") and of an *object* towards which it is to be directed ("me").

In the AHT, the first component of an instruction is called the "action component;" the second component—the "object component."

The object component of an instruction reflects the fact that most human actions are *object-directed* and are performed with objects—physical or mental (images, concepts and/or propositions). Instructions which don't contain object components often don't make sense. Such is, for example, a request (instruction): "Please, give." Give what? Give to whom?

Instructions may indicate not only actions but their attributes (characteristics) as well (e.g., "give *immediately*"). They also may indicate not only objects but their attributes and/or relationships (e.g., "give a *red* pen," "give a *better* pen," etc.). Thus, the components of instructions can be crudely divided into two groups: those related to actions and their characteristics, and those related to objects and their characteristics and relationships.

Processes, Instructions and Prescriptions

We have just seen that verbal instructions and self-instructions are a powerful tool for actuating physical and mental actions. Further, these mental actions are capable of further actuating knowledge units (images, concepts, and propositions) and of transforming (changing) them. Since mental processes involved in solving problems are, as a rule, made up of *sets* or *systems* of mental *actions (operations)*, *sets or systems of instructions or self-instructions* are needed for guiding those processes.

A set or system of verbal instructions or self-instructions which actuate physical and/or mental operations needed for solving a problem or a class of problems constitutes a *prescription*.[1]

Instructions making up prescriptions can exist in a *categorical* form (like "give me a pen") or in a *conditional* form (like "if it's raining, take an umbrella"). Conditional instructions are actually *rules* which prescribe a mode of action in specified conditions.

Processes Guided and Not Guided by Prescriptions

In the AHT, processes actuated by verbal prescriptions (or self-prescriptions) or transformed following prescriptions (or self-prescriptions) are called *prescription-guided*. If the prescription is an algorithm or a rule, then the process is *algorithm-guided* or *rule-guided*; if it is an heuristic or a set of heuristics, then it is *heuristic-guided*. A characteristic feature of all prescription-guided processes is that before performing an action(s), a person turns to an outward instruction(s) or gives herself a self-instruction(s): "Do this," "do that," and so on.

In those instances in which mental processes are not prescription-guided (i.e., they are actuated and/or transformed by external or internal actuators other than instructions or self-instructions), it is very often possible to *state certain instructions in rule form in accordance* with actual operations performed by a person, even though that person isn't even aware of such a rule. For example, when confronting certain situations or solving certain problems, suppose that a person always automatically reacts to condition m by operation M and to condition n by operation N. Her actions can be described by the following rule: "If m, do M, but if n, do N." Since, however, the person does not reproduce this rule in her mind before performing these operations, her actions are *not* rule-guided. Moreover, a person may not be consciously aware of the conditions that actuate his actions and therefore may not be able to formulate the rule according to which he acts. (For example, if asked why in one situation he did M and in another situation he did N, he may say, "I don't know. I just *felt* what should be done in each of the situations, but I can't explain what specific factors in each of the situations caused me to perform those actions.") But because there is a certain *regularity* in the person's actions, this regularity can be discovered and a rule such as those indicated above can be *used to describe* his actions. This has been called *according-to-rule* actions.

Thus, in the context of the AHT it is important to distinguish actions (processes) performed *by* rules (rule-guided actions) and actions (processes) performed *according to* rules which are not rule-guided. This distinction is important for a better understanding of the AHT methodology of learning and instruction, as well as the AHT-based instructional design, which takes special care to convert prescription-guided mental processes into according-to-prescription (or according-to-rule) processes.

Algorithmic and Non-Algorithmic Prescriptions and Processes

It was discovered within the AHT that all prescriptions and processes can be broken down into two large classes: algorithmic and non-algorithmic, with the latter in turn broken down into semi-algorithmic, semi-heuristic, and heuristic. Here is a graphic representation of the classification:

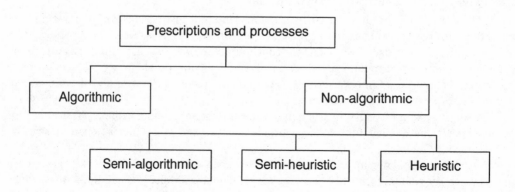

Algorithmic Prescriptions and Processes

An *algorithmic prescription*, or an *algorithm*, is a system of instructions[2] (in a particular case, rules) that:

(a) are addressed to relatively elementary physical and/or mental operations which the addressee knows how to perform;
(b) are unambiguous;
(c) determine uniform performance of the appropriate operations;
(d) are applied to all problems of a given class; and
(e) guarantee a solution—and an identical solution—to any problem of a given class.

Algorithmic prescriptions define *regular* processes whereby identical conditions bring about identical operations. Here is an example of an algorithmic prescription (~ means "not" or negation):

If there is a circumstance a, do A.
If not-a (~a) but b, do B.
If not-a (~a) and not-b (~b), but c, do C.
If not-a (~a) not-b (~b) and not-c (~c), do D.

In a symbolic representation, where the arrows mean "if . . . , then":

a → A.
~a & b → B.
~a & ~b & c → C
~a & ~b & ~c → D.

In a flowchart representation where a plus means yes and a minus means no, the algorithm would look like this:

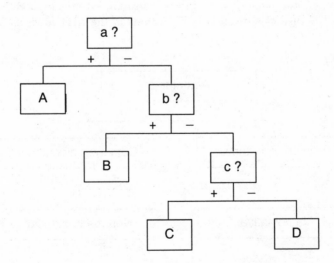

An *algorithmic process* is a regular system of operations (processes) that are either performed by following an algorithmic prescription (an algorithm) or are not performed by following an algorithm but can be described by an algorithm. In the first instance, the algorithmic process is an *algorithm-guided* process, in the second instance it is an *according-to-algorithm* process.

An *algorithmic problem* is a problem for which an algorithm is known or that is performed by an algorithmic process which can be algorithmically described, the latter meaning that an algorithm can be constructed in accordance with the process.

It is important to note that with regard to many problems for which an algorithm is not known or that are not currently solved by an algorithmic process, it is often not known in advance whether the problem is algorithmic or not. The only way to obtain an answer is to *try* to find an algorithm. If an algorithm has been found, then the problem is algorithmic. If it hasn't been found, then it is still not known whether the problem is algorithmic (algorithmizable). Potentially, there are two possible situations here:

(a) the problem may be algorithmic (algorithmizable) in nature but people might have failed to find the algorithm, or
(b) the problem is not algorithmic (algorithmizable) in nature and an algorithm will never be found.

The issue is that it is often not known which of the two situations exists.

Until the middle of the 1950s, the notion of an algorithm was considered purely mathematical. In studies conducted by this author, however, it was discovered that processes similar to the mathematical algorithmic processes existed in solving all kinds of problems, not just mathematical. It was also discovered that it was possible to devise prescriptions similar to mathematical algorithms which were capable of guiding the processes of solving non-mathematical problems in the same way in which mathematical algorithms guided the processes of solving mathematical problems. The discovery of non-mathematical algorithmic processes and non-mathematical algorithms made it possible to *generalize* the notion of an algorithm, making it *broader* than the notion of a mathematical algorithm.

The broader notion of an algorithm, encompassing both mathematical and non-mathematical algorithms, was termed in the AHT a *human algorithm*. The notion of a mathematical algorithm became a particular case of human algorithms. Later, with the advent of computers, the notion of a *computer algorithm* was introduced in computer science and artificial intelligence. The final classification of algorithms in the AHT looks as follows:

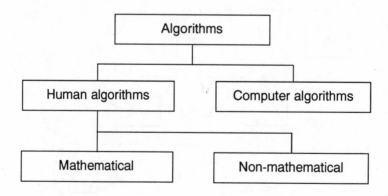

Here is an example of a human non-mathematical algorithm. In a lesson on lenses there is the following description of the kinds of lenses:

Kinds of Lenses. There are two basic kinds of simple lenses. Light bends when it passes through either kind. Lenses that are thicker in the middle than at the edges are called *convex, converging,* or *positive.* Parallel light rays passing through a convex lens bend inward so that they meet at a point on the other side. Lenses that are thicker at the edges are called *concave, diverging,* or *negative.* Parallel rays passing through a concave lens bend outward so that they spread apart.

A Plano-Convex Lens has one plane surface and one convex surface. It is used in certain types of slide projectors.

A Plano-Concave Lens has one plane surface and one concave surface. It is combined with other lenses for cameras.

A Double-Convex Lens has two convex surfaces. It is used in various magnifying glasses.

A Double-Concave Lens has two concave surfaces. It is used in reducing glasses.

A Concavo-Convex Lens has one convex surface of greater curvature than the concave surface. It is used to help correct farsightedness.

A Convexo-Concave Lens has one concave surface of greater curvature than the convex surface. It is used to help correct nearsightedness.

These descriptions give characteristics of different kinds of lenses but do not say what one should *mentally do* in order *to identify* the kind (category) to which some given lens belongs. *Mental operations* to be performed in the process of identification are to be *inferred* by students from the descriptions. This may be not an easy task, as is confirmed by the fact that many students who can state the characteristics of lenses (which means that they have knowledge of the attributes of lenses) make errors in identifying actual lenses. The *cause* of their difficulties is this: Knowing the characteristics of lenses given in the descriptions, they don't know how to *turn the descriptions into a prescription,* i.e., into an *algorithm of actions* (in this instance, the algorithm for the identification of the proper category for a given lens).

Here is a *non-mathematical human algorithm,* designed by the author, that precisely indicates what one should mentally do in order to easily identify a kind (category) of any lens:[3]

ALGORITHM

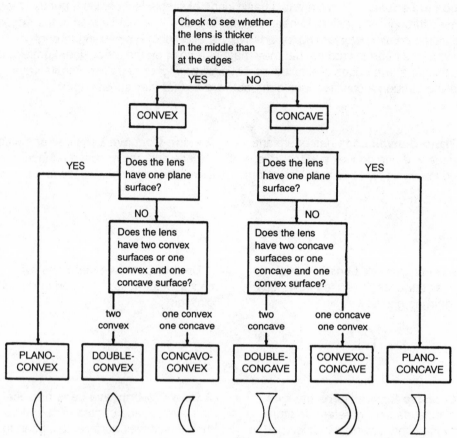

Semi-algorithmic Prescriptions and Processes

It is easier to explain the difference between *algorithmic* and *non-algorithmic* prescriptions and processes by example than by definitions. In the examples that follow, two specific situations and their appropriate instructions will be contrasted and analyzed.

Example 1. Suppose there is a bookshelf with books, and that there is only one book in a red binder. One person says (gives an instruction) to another: "Give me the red book, please." Here the request (instruction) is unambiguous, contains no uncertainty, and would definitely lead to achieving the desired result, if performed. Moreover, if this instruction is given to different people, they would select the same book. In other words, the *results* of carrying out this instruction by different people would be the *same*.

The performance of this instruction leads to the desired results because:

(a) it precisely specifies the action to be performed and this action is *relatively elementary* for the person to whom it is addressed ("give");

(b) it precisely specifies the *field of objects* from which the sought-for object is to be chosen or selected (this fields is "the books on the bookshelf");

(c) it precisely specifies the *criterion* that is to be used to identify the sought-for object ("red binder");

(d) the criterion is *sufficient* to allow the performer to select one specific object from the specified field.

The listed characteristics of the instruction *completely determine* the action, its objects, and its results, and don't require any independent mental processes to be performed by the one to whom the instruction is addressed.

This is why this *instruction* is *algorithmic* and the *action* performed to realize this instruction is an *algorithmic* action.[4]

Example 2. The same bookshelf now contains two books with red binders. The request (an instruction) made to a person is, "Give me a red book, please." This request (instruction as to what to do) is similar—but not identical—to the request in Example 1. However, in contrast to the previous instruction, this one contains a degree of *uncertainty* because it did not specify which of the two red books to give. Different people performing this instruction may select different books.

The characteristics of this instruction are these:

(a) it precisely specifies the action to be performed, which is *relatively elementary* for the person ("give");
(b) it precisely specifies the *field* of objects from which the sought-for object is to be chosen or selected (this field is "the books on the bookshelf");
(c) it precisely specifies the *criterion* that is to be used to identify the sought-for object ("red binder");
(d) the criterion, however, is *not sufficient* to ensure that the person selecting the book will select one specific object (the desired book) out of the two books meeting the criterion.

Thus, the listed characteristics of the instruction *do not completely* determine the action's object and thus the action's results. The instruction contains a *certain* (although very small) *degree of uncertainty*. This degree of uncertainty requires a certain *independent mental process* (a conscious or unconscious decision, simple as it is) to determine which object to select in order to carry out the instruction.[5]

In the AHT, instructions with such characteristics are termed *semi-algorithmic*. A *system* of such instructions geared to solving problems of a particular class is a *semi-algorithmic **prescription***. A set of operations performed in the realization of a semi-algorithmic prescription—or which can be described by a semi-algorithmic prescription stated in accordance with the operations actually required and performed—is a *semi-algorithmic **process***.

A *semi-algorithmic **problem*** (task) is one that can be solved (performed) by following a semi-algorithmic prescription or by carrying out an according-to-semi-algorithmic prescription process which can be described by a semi-algorithmic prescription.

The mental processes that a semi-algorithmic problem (task) requires the performer to execute are slightly different from those that an algorithmic problem (task) requires.[6] Specifically, in Example 2, the semi-algorithmic problem requires an *independent* solution as to which particular object to select among all those which meet the insufficient criterion (or the criteria) contained in the instruction. This in turn requires the creation and use of some *independent* additional criterion or criteria which are not contained in the instruction.

Semi-heuristic Prescriptions and Processes

Example 3. The same bookshelf, but the request (instruction for what to do) in this case is different: "Give me an *interesting* book." In the request to give me an interesting book, the criterion for selection is not well specified and contains an uncertainty: What does "interesting" precisely mean? What is interesting for one person may not be interesting for another person. What is interesting for *this* person? Which book to choose? Obviously, should this instruction be given to different people, they may chose not only different books within the *same category*, but different books within *different categories* (for example, one may chose a book interesting from the science point of view, another one a book interesting from the entertainment point of view).

The characteristics of this instruction are these:

(a) it precisely specifies the action to be performed which is *relatively elementary* for the person ("give");

(b) it precisely specifies the *field* of objects from which the sought-for object is to be chosen or selected (this field is "the books on the bookshelf"); but

(c) it *does not* precisely specify the *criterion* that is to be used to identify the sought-for object ("interesting").

As with the instruction in Example 2, this one also *does not* completely determine the action's object and its result. But the degree of uncertainty in this instruction is considerably greater because it concerns the uncertainty in the criterion for selection. This in turn requires a *much more complex independent mental process* to carry out the instruction.

In the AHT, instructions with such characteristics are termed *semi-heuristic*. A set (system) of such instructions is a *semi-heuristic* **prescription**. A set (system) of operations performed in the realization of a semi-heuristic prescription—or which can be described by a semi-heuristic **prescription** formulated in accordance with such operations—is a *semi-heuristic process*.

A *semi-heuristic problem* (task) is one that can be solved (performed) by following a semi-heuristic prescription or by carrying out an according-to-semi-heuristic prescription process that can be described by a semi-algorithmic prescription.

Mental processes which a semi-heuristic problem (task) requires that the performer execute are different from those that algorithmic and semi-algorithmic problems (tasks) require.[7] Specifically, semi-heuristic problems require an *independent* specification of the criterion (or criteria) that would allow a person to select some specific object (or objects) as a solution to the problem.

Heuristic Prescriptions and Processes

Example 4. Children, in a single-subject multiple-trials experiment, were shown two nails on the wall which were at a particular distance from one another. The task (problem) was formulated as follows: "Find *some way* to mark the same distance on the other wall."

It was not permitted to use the hand as a measuring instrument (the distance between fingers). There were a number of objects in the room: a bookshelf with books, a radio set, two plates with apples, a few bottles of perfume, a sheet, pencils, a few dishes, several utensils and some other things. But there was no ruler, or a measuring tape, or a cord, or string, or rope.

Most children found themselves in a difficult position and could not find a solution. One child, however, went to the bookshelf, pulled out a book and used it as a measuring instrument (the distance was "nine books"). Another child used a pencil for the same function.

When a child could not find a solution (i.e. find some *object* and some *actions* with that object that would solve the problem), a suggestion (a suggestive instruction) was given to him: "Find some *object* in the room by which you can measure the distance." If this did not help, another suggestion was given: "Can you use a book as a measuring instrument?." In cases when even this didn't help, the instruction was, "Take the book, put one of its ends against the left one of the nails and then start turning the book around on the wall until you reach the other nail. Count the number of book lengths between the nails. Afterwards, use this procedure on the other wall to mark the distance." The experiment showed that those children who the previous instructions didn't help could solve the problem with the last instruction.

Let us consider the instruction contained in the formulation of the problem: "Find *some way* to mark the same distance on the other wall."

The characteristics of the instruction are these:

(a) it indicated the action to be performed ("find") which, however, might *not* have been *relatively elementary* for all the children ("How to find?," "Which specific actions to perform?").

(b) it *did not* specify the *field* of objects within which some object that could be used as a measuring device could be found (Where to look for such an object: Among plates with apples? Among bottles of perfume? Among dishes? Utensils? Office supplies? Books?)

(c) it *did not* specify the *criterion* that is to be used to identify the sought-for object (i.e., it did not specify the object's *attribute(s)* that could be used in finding the object by which the problem could be solved).

In all previous examples (Examples 1–3), the tasks—and the corresponding algorithmic, semi-algorithmic and semi-heuristic instructions—*specified the field* of objects in which the requested object was to be found or selected: it was the set of books.[8]

In addition to the specification of the field, a *criterion for selection was indicated:* "the *red* book," "a *red* book," "an *interesting* book," although, as was noted, the criteria differed among these examples in the degree of specificity.

In all of the previous examples, 1 through 3, the process of performing the task involved some *search*—however simple and elementary it was. But this search was in the *specified, predefined field.* In Example 4, however, the field of search was *not* specified or predefined ("find some *way* to mark . . ."). Was the object to be used for solving the problem an apple (i.e., did it belong to the *class* of apples?), or a bottle of perfume (i.e., did it belong to the *class* of bottles?), or a book? The problem as formulated in the instruction contained in the problem formulation required a *search* in an *unspecified, undefined field.*

In the AHT, *problems* that require a search in an unspecified or undefined field are termed *heuristic,* or truly *creative.* From this, it follows that heuristic (creative) *processes* are only those which involve a search in undefined fields.

Heuristics, according to the AHT definition, are nothing other than *instructions* (heuristic instructions) which guide the processes of searching in unspecified or undefined fields.[9] Heuristic instructions can contain different degrees of specificity (or, what is the same, contain different degrees of uncertainty) and thus have different *guiding power.*

Utilization of High Uncertainty Heuristics—
One of the Drawbacks of Conventional Instruction and Training

Many heuristics conventionally used for helping students, trainees, workers, and others to solve problems and to perform tasks are often so general and contain such a high degree of uncertainty that they become practically useless.[10] One of the objectives of the AHT is to find or create heuristics which contain less uncertainty and thus acquire higher guiding power. The greater the guiding power, the more useful the heuristic.

It is important to emphasize that finding heuristics with "reduced uncertainty" is not only the task of teachers, trainers, managers, manuals writers, and others whose function (or at least one of their functions) is to guide students, trainees, employees and other people. It is one of the important tasks of students and other problem solvers as well. Any means used for guiding people from the outside should become a means for *self-guidance.*

Relativity of the Notions of Algorithmic and Heuristic Problems,
Processes, and Instructions

In analyzing Example 4 above, we qualified the instruction "Find *some way* to mark the same distance on the other wall" as a heuristic, for it required that a search be performed in an undefined field. Suppose, however, that this instruction is given to someone who knows a solution to this problem. Would that person need to conduct a search in an undefined field? Obviously, no. This means that *for him*, this problem and the instruction *would not be heuristic*, and the process by which he would perform the task *would not be creative*. The instruction (problem formulation) will actuate in his mind a known sequence of associatively connected known actions which he would then simply carry out. He would carry out an *algorithmic process*.

From this example it is clear that a problem which is heuristic (creative) for one person may be non-heuristic (non-creative) for another person. Moreover, a problem which had been creative for a *given person* before she found a solution would become non-creative once he has found (or learned) the solution. This is also true with regard to algorithmic and other types of problems, processes, and instructions.

For example, an instruction to "Find the adverb in the sentence" will be an algorithmic instruction for those who know what an adverb is and how to find it. But it will *not* be an algorithmic instruction for those who don't know what an adverb is and/or how to find it.

A request (instruction) to "Give me an interesting book" will be *semi-heuristic* for those who don't know what is interesting to the person asking for a book, but this request (instruction) will be *semi-algorithmic or algorithmic* for those who know the interests of the person asking for an interesting book.

Thus, the notions of heuristics and algorithms (and semi-algorithms or semi-heuristics) are not absolute. They are *relative*. Characteristics of problems, processes, and instructions such as, for example, heuristic or algorithmic are *not inherent* characteristics. They *acquire* certain characteristics—i.e., *become* either heuristic or algorithmic—only in relation to the current state of mental processes of those to whom they are addressed or who would perform or use them. That is why it is that to say that one problem is creative but another one is not does not make sense without indicating *to whom* the statement is directed.[11]

Interlacing of Algorithmic and Heuristic Processes, Tasks, and Problems

A great many tasks, problems, and job functions are purely algorithmic or algorithmizable. (The overwhelming majority of tasks in the popular professions are algorithmic or semi-algorithmic in nature.) But there are few, if any, tasks, problems, and job functions that are purely heuristic (creative).

As a rule, creative tasks are tightly interwoven with algorithmic tasks and contain a lot of algorithmic elements. All *technical aspects* of performing creative tasks are usually algorithmic.

Hence the importance of identifying the algorithmic components of creative tasks, of developing algorithms for their learning and performance, and imparting these algorithms to students, trainees, and non-experts. Mastering the algorithmic components of creative processes would free the performers' minds to concentrate on the truly creative components of tasks and problems and thereby raise the overall effectiveness of creative processes.

Algorithmic Tasks and Activities Which Just Look Creative

When experts perform complex tasks by way of algorithmic processes of which they are unaware, these tasks often appear creative not only to the outsiders, but also to the experts themselves. Just the assumption that such tasks may not need creativity sometimes is enough to arouse experts' sincere indignation—so deep is their conviction that they use creativity.

The AHT methods allow one to determine the true nature of the processes involved in performing complex tasks—whether they are algorithmic, or truly creative, or just look creative. If the last is the case, then the AHT enables one to uncover deeply hidden complex algorithms which lie at the foundation of the seemingly creative activity.

Classification of Algorithms

Human algorithms can be classified on the basis of different logical grounds, depending on the objectives for which algorithms are designed, the subjects to whom they are geared, the nature of processes they guide, the characteristics which are to be achieved by using algorithms, and so on (see also Landa, 1982). Following are examples of some of the classifications offered by the AHT:

Classification 1. Binary and multiple-choice algorithms.

Classification 2. Deterministic and probabilistic algorithms.

Classification 3. Algorithms of practical activity and of (pure) cognitive activity, the latter in turn divided into algorithms of perception, of memorization, of thinking, etc.

Classification 4. Algorithms of identification and of transformation.

Classification 5. Algorithms of performance, of learning, and of teaching.

Classification 6. Effective and ineffective algorithms, the former in turn divided into efficient and inefficient algorithms.

Classification 7. Mathematical, linguistic, engineering, medical, etc., algorithms.

Classification of Non-Algorithmic Prescriptions

Some of the grounds for classification of the non-algorithmic prescriptions are the same as those underlying the classification of the algorithmic prescriptions (for examples the grounds underlying classifications 3, 4, 5, 6, and 7 above). However, there are some grounds which are specific to the classification of non-algorithmic prescriptions.

For example, heuristic prescriptions may differ by the following characteristics (among others):

1. The *degree of uncertainty* contained in heuristic instructions (heuristics). Some heuristics, as was mentioned above, may be more *specific* than others and therefore would have a greater guiding power.

2. The *content of the field of search* to which the heuristics are addressed. They may be addressed to the *fields of objects* among whom the search is to be carried out, or to the *fields of actions* when the creative task consists of finding an action which would solve a problem, or to both kinds of fields.

3. The *nature of objects within a field* to which heuristics are addressed. They may be addressed to searches among *tangible* objects or to searches among *mental* objects (images, concepts or propositions).

4. The *kind of search* the heuristics are guiding. Some heuristics may guide a *directed* search, some others a *random* search.

There exist some other characteristics by which non-algorithmic prescriptions differ from each other and on whose ground they may be classified (see Landa, 1976, chapters 5–8).

General Methods of Thinking

The term "method" (as well as "procedure") has several meanings in science. One meaning is "a set of structured *operations*." Another meaning is "a set of structured *instructions* as to what operations to perform." When one says that "the method by which a person *solved* a problem was *effective*," he has in mind a person's system of *operations* (a problem cannot be solved by instructions, only by actions). When, however, one says that a person "*formulated* an effective method of solving problems," then clearly *instructions* are meant.

We will be using the term "method" in both senses, with its specific meaning being clear from the context.

It was indicated above that an algorithm is a system of instructions that allows one to solve *any problem* of a given class. In this respect, an algorithm can be viewed as *a general method of thinking* for solving problems of the respective class. The same is true with respect to non-algorithmic, and specifically heuristic, prescriptions.

Consider, for example, the following three heuristics: "When starting to solve a problem, separate what is given from what is to be found (obtained, determined, proven, etc.)," "refer to what is given and isolate all the attributes of the given object(s)"; "refer to what is to be found (obtained, determined, proven, etc.) and isolate all the sufficient conditions of the objects or relationships to be found" (Landa, 1976, Chapter 8).

Although the above three heuristics were initially identified and formulated for solving geometric problems of proof, it is obvious that they are more general and can be applied to solving all kinds of problems, not just geometric ones. Thus, the sets (systems) of both algorithmic instructions and non-algorithmic instructions represent general methods of thinking.

It is obvious that the degree of generality of methods of thinking—both algorithmic and non-algorithmic—may be different, and the more general the method of thinking, the more powerful it is. It was shown in AHT research that there even exist general (universal) methods of thinking which are applicable to all subjects regardless of any specific content.

An example of how such a general method of thinking can serve a system of instructions and their corresponding operations is furnished by the problem of identifying objects whose defined attributes are connected *conjunctively* (by the logical conjunction AND). Similarly, a second example is provided by the same problem applied to the identification of objects whose attributes are connected *disjunctively* (by the logical conjunction OR). It turned out to be possible to build general *content-free* methods of thinking whose operations and their systems are determined exclusively by the *logical structure of attributes* rather than by the content (Landa, 1974, Chapter 8). Moreover, it turned out to be possible to teach even relatively small children such general methods of thinking (Landa, 1974, the Section entitled "Logic Lesson," pp. 352–387)[12].

The Notions of Intelligence and General Cognitive Skills in the AHT

Careful analysis of the characteristics of intelligence as a cognitive phenomenon[13] from the point of view of the concept of general methods of thinking has led to the conclusion *that general intelligence is nothing other than a mastery of a system of generalized methods of thinking* which enable a person to find effective solutions to most problems and classes of problems in different subject areas.

This notion of intelligence is based on the AHT's assumption that there exist a finite number of general cognitive operations, and these become components of different specific systems of operations (methods) geared to solving most kinds of problems.

If we designate each of the general mental operations by a specific letter, then one can think of a pool of general mental operations as an alphabet: $a, b, c, d, e, \ldots, n$. Using such a representation, each general method of thinking can be thought of as a *word* in this alphabet. Thus, for example, the general method of finding a proof may be represented as a combination of operations (a word), *abdeghpt*, or the general method of building a hypothesis as a combination (a word), *agptsu*, and so on.

If it is true that general intelligence is nothing other than a set (system) of generalizable methods of thinking, then it is obvious that:

(a) the basic operational components of intelligence can be identified;
(b) the basic systems of operational components (i.e., general methods of thinking for solving specified classes of problems) can be defined; and
(c) intelligence can—and should be—taught via teaching these generalizable mental operations and their systems—general methods of thinking for solving general classes of problems.

As far as the relationships between the notion of *general intelligence* as a set of general methods of thinking and the notion of *general cognitive abilities* is concerned, this relationship can be easily explained by using the following simple analogy. Let us assume that in order for a person to perform a certain task, a connection between some factor a and some action A should be formed in his or her mind. Because this connection (association) is a necessary condition for performing the task, it is obvious that prior to the formation of the connection, the person could not properly react to factor a and thus properly perform the task—he or she didn't have the required *ability*.

Assume that the training was then conducted and the connection was formed. After the connection has been formed, it can exist in two states: *actuated* (active) and *not actuated* (passive, latent). The *ability* to react to factor a by performing action A is nothing other than the *formed* connection in the latent, *non-actuated (or pre-actuated)* state which has the *potential* to be actuated. Once actuation occurs, the ability as a *potential* for actuation turns into an *actively functioning process* which makes up the mechanism of actual *performance*.

By analogy, *general cognitive abilities* are nothing other than the *formed generalized methods of thinking in the latent pre-actuated state* ready to be actuated by the appropriate external or internal actuators which turn the latent (passive) knowledge and operations into an actively functioning process of thinking.

Similar to the notion of *general cognitive abilities* is the notion of *general cognitive skills*. When we say that a person has a skill to do something, we don't mean that he is doing this now. We mean that he *can*, or *is able*, to do this when necessary. Thus, the notion of a skill as a *potential* to do certain things is the same as the notion of an ability. The difference between them may, on a connotation level of everyday language, lie only in the degree of generalization: ability is a more generalized skill. But if we add the word "general" (or "generic") to the words "cognitive skills," then the meanings of the terms "general cognitive abilities" and "general cognitive skills" become the same.

The AHT's Specific Problem Domain and Objectives

Discovery of The Root-Cause of the Inability of Conventional Instruction to Teach Students Methods of Thinking and to Develop Their General Intelligence

In the Introduction, some general causes of the failure of conventional instruction to teach thinking in a systematic and reliable way were indicated. Now it is possible to specify those causes and to reveal their common root-cause.

1. The studies conducted in the framework of the AHT showed that expert thinkers and performers, including teachers, are unequally aware of the different components of the processes involved in performing practical and cognitive tasks and solving problems. Specifically, it was found that expert thinkers and performers are aware mostly of the following components:

(a) physical actions involved, and
(b) knowledge used.

However, they are largely unaware of the mental actions (operations) they carry out in their minds when performing tasks and solving problems.

2. The assessment of the degree of experts' awareness of the mental operations component of mental processes showed that it does not exceed 30%. And this 30% is what is being taught to students in academia and to the trainees and novices in any profession. The extensive unawareness of the mental operations involved in thinking and performance manifests itself in the fact that teachers and trainers usually transfer to students the *results* of their mental processes (final and intermediate) rather than the *processes themselves*. They commu-

nicate to students the solutions (final and intermediate) rather than how they *arrive* at these solutions. They fail to tell the students what they *mentally do* and in what order, for example, to see a relation between data, determine a rule or a theorem to be used, figure out the physics law to be applied when solving a certain physics problem, and so on.

3. Teachers and trainers are especially unaware of the unconscious *algorithms and non-algorithmic processes (general methods of thinking)* they use when performing tasks and solving problems. As a result, they, as a rule, don't teach them.

4. The considerable unawareness on the part of teachers of their own mental processes could have been compensated for by the knowledge of those processes—and their corresponding methods of thinking—received from psychology and instructional science in the course of teacher training. However, these sciences so far have not been involved, to any appreciable extent, with discovering algorithms and other general methods of thinking important for effective learning and problem solving. This leads to the result that teachers very often simply don't know them. Neither do they know how to discover them on their own, should they realize the critical importance of teaching general methods of thinking to students.

Typical Ways in Which Students Learn and Solve Problems When Not Taught General Methods of Cognitive Activity

Transferring to students and trainees in professional training only about 30% of the mental operations and methods they need to know and master in order to successfully learn, perform tasks and solve problems leads to the following consequences:

1. Students don't know how to effectively acquire knowledge in the process of learning and how to apply knowledge in the process of thinking and solving problems. They experience difficulties in learning and performance and, as a result, become low achievers.
2. Many students become able to *memorize* and *mechanically reproduce* what teachers teach them (including the *external* flow of reasoning with regard to the specific problems selected by a teacher for demonstration), but are unable to generate their own reasoning with regard to new problems, i.e., unable to think for themselves.
3. Not knowing how to think and solve problems, many students use the only method available to them—blind trial and error, which expresses itself in guessing. For many students, guessing becomes an habitual approach to solving all kinds of problems, a style of mental activity.
4. Only a small percentage of students are able to discover, through trial and error, those 70% of the mental operations and their systems (algorithmic and non-algorithmic processes and methods) which underlie the ability to successfully learn and solve problems. As a result, this small percentage of students, and only they, develop in themselves general intelligence.

The AHT's Specific Objectives

At the inception of the AHT, the specific objectives had been formulated as follows:

1. Develop a *set of techniques for getting inside the minds of expert* learners, performers, and problem solvers in order to uncover their largely unconscious mental processes (algorithmic and non-algorithmic), which underlie the experts' ability to effectively learn, perform and solve problems.

2. Actually *discover the experts' algorithmic and non-algorithmic processes* for various types (classes) of tasks and problems, including those involved in effective learning.

3. *Break down* the discovered processes into *relatively elementary knowledge units and mental operations*, and *identify their connections* (systems).

4. Explicitly *describe* the uncovered mental operations and their systems (processes) as algorithmic and non-algorithmic methods.

5. *Improve* and *generalize* to an even greater degree (if and when possible) the methods of learning and thinking learned from the experts in order to create more powerful *super-expert* algorithms and heuristics.

6. Use the discovered or improved algorithmic and non-algorithmic methods as *models (blueprints)* of what should be formed in the minds of students and novices in professional training in order to create out of them expert learners, performers and problem solvers.

7. *Convert descriptions* of the algorithmic and heuristic methods into *prescriptions* as to what students and novices *should do* in their minds in order to be able to learn and perform as effectively as experts.

8. Create a *methodology of instruction* which would enable teachers and trainers to:
   - effectively *teach students and novices the mental processes used by experts* (especially, their general algorithmic and heuristic methods of cognitive activity);
   - *replicate*, via specific algo-heuristically based instruction, the *mental processes of experts* within students and novices, and do it in a *systematic, reliable* and relatively *fast* way—without the need for students and novices to go through years of conventional experience in order to become expert learners, performers and problem solvers;
   - *develop* in students, as a result of teaching them expert-level general methods of thinking, *general cognitive abilities (general intelligence)*.

9. Create a new type of *algo-heuristically based* textbooks and learning materials, as well as computer-based interactive multimedia courseware, for use in various disciplines. These materials would be able to effectively teach not only content-specific knowledge and skills but also general content-free methods of thinking.[14]

10. Create a methodology for courseware design and programming that would enable instructional designers to make media-based instruction that is *diagnostic, adaptive, and individualized*.[15]

The Generic Nature of the AHT

The AHT methods of penetrating the minds of experts and uncovering their unconscious algorithmic and heuristic processes are most general. They apply to expert learners and performers in any field. General also are the methods for describing algorithmic and heuristic processes, of breaking them down into more elementary component knowledge units and mental operations, and of replicating the mental processes of experts in the minds of students, novices, and non-expert performers via algo-heuristically based instruction. The AHT methodology allows one to uncover, analyze and replicate the mental processes underlying the performance of the most varied kinds of tasks and the solution of the most varied kinds of problems. In particular:

- simple or complex
- well-structured or poorly structured
- routine or non-routine
- deterministic or probabilistic
- having just one solution or more than one solution
- involving uncertainties and risk or not involving such.

The generic nature of the AHT makes it possible to effectively apply it to the improvement of learning and instruction not only in education but in industry, business, and government as well. (For some results of the latter area of application see Landa, 1993.)

AHT's Instructional Principles and the Prerequisites for Their Realization

Most principles described in this section are formulated for use in mass instruction in a group (classroom) setting. Some of the principles can be modified if the instruction is individualized. Modifications are discussed below in Principle 9 which deals with individualization in the teaching and learning of general methods of thinking.

Principle 1.   **Students and novices should be taught expert-level mental processes and general methods of learning and thinking (intelligence) explicitly, and in a systematic and reliable way.**

Prerequisite 1.1.   To realize this principle, it is necessary to *uncover* (or discover) the largely unconscious algorithmic and non-algorithmic mental processes and general methods of thinking as practiced by experts, and then to perform their *componential microanalysis* in order to identify their sufficiently elementary components (psychological "atoms" and "molecules"), as well as the connections between them (their structure).

Prerequisite 1.2.   To realize this principle, it is also necessary to give an explicit *structural description* of the discovered expert-level mental processes and general methods of thinking as *human algorithms* or *heuristics*. The description should be as detailed as is necessary to serve as a precise *model (blueprint)* of what is to be formed in the minds of students and novices to achieve the objectives of teaching students thinking and of developing their general intelligence.

Principle 2.   **Students and novices should be taught general methods of thinking in the context of each of the disciplines, with the demonstration of the generic nature of general methods of thinking by using examples from various disciplines. Students must be made aware of the interdisciplinary nature of the general methods of thinking and their applicability to varied contents.**

Prerequisite. 2.1. Teachers of each of the disciplines (say, mathematics) should select examples from other disciplines (say, grammar, biology, social sciences, etc.) which require the same methods of analysis and reasoning to solve problems as in their original discipline, and to make students see the commonality in the methods.[16]

Principle 3.   **Formation in students of the expert-level mental processes and general methods of thinking should proceed as a constructive, engineered process whereby complex mental entities (e.g., a certain method of reasoning) are built from their components (knowledge units and mental operations), and each of the components is built from its sub-components (more-elementary knowledge units and mental operations).**

Prerequisite 3.1.   To realize this principle, a *successive componential* and *structural analysis of each* knowledge unit and mental operation is to be conducted, and appropriate graphs (trees) of knowledge and operations are to be built. The successive componential analysis should continue until reaching the *level of fragmentation* at which the elements being added to the tree can be considered *elementary for the students being taught.*

Here is an *example of a successive componential analysis.*In order to be able to solve problems of class A, it is necessary to perform operations *m, n, o, p.* In order to be able to perform operation *m,* it is necessary to be able to perform operations *e, f, g.* In order to be able to perform operation *e,* it is necessary to be able to perform operations *a* and *b.* But we know (or have established through a test) that the students already know how to perform a and *b,* they have a mastery of these operations. Thus, operations *a* and *b* are elementary for them; they don't need to be taught these operations, from which it follows that these operations don't need to be further fragmented. Thus the instructor or the media-based instructional system designer can draw on these operations as already formed and use them as a basis for forming operations of a *higher level or higher order.* As can be seen, the successive componential and structural analysis of cognitive processes and methods of thinking is a *top-down* process, whereas their actual formation in the course of instruction is a *down-top* process.

Principle 4. **The level of detail of the algorithms and heuristics to be taught should be adapted to the current level of students' knowledge and operations, so that the algorithms or heuristics would contain instructions that students know how to perform, and are able to perform.**

Prerequisite 4.1. To realize this principle, a preliminary analysis of the level of students' cognitive development (i.e., what they know and are able to do) should be conducted. The results of such an analysis will determine the level of detail to which the algorithms and heuristics to be taught are to be broken down (fragmented).

Principle 5. **Since the level of cognitive development of different students within a group or class may be different, certain instructions in algorithms and heuristics may be sufficiently elementary (i.e., performable) for some students and not elementary (not performable) for some other students. If this is the case, it is important to teach each student those sub-algorithms for performing those instructions (operations) which are not elementary for him or her.**

Prerequisite 5.1. To realize this principle, instructional designers and teachers should discover and have available sub-algorithms and sub-heuristics for each instruction and operation which is to be taught in the context of teaching algorithms or heuristics.

Here is an example of the above principles. Let us suppose that for determining the punctuation in a sentence according to a certain punctuation rule, it is necessary to identify the type of a sentence (whether it is simple or compound), which in turn requires the ability to find a subject(s) and a predicate(s). If students have already been taught how to find a subject and a predicate in a sentence, then, when teaching an algorithm for determining the type of a sentence, a teacher may proceed from the assumption that instructions like "find a subject(s) in the sentence" and "find a predicate(s) in the sentence" are elementary for the students (i.e., they know how to perform these operations errorlessly). Let us further suppose that in the course of teaching the algorithm it turned out that for some students these operations were not elementary and they either didn't know how to perform them or made errors in their performance. In this case, it is necessary for the teacher to have handy the sub-algorithms for identifying subjects and/or predicates in a sentence and, before proceeding with the teaching of the algorithm, take a step back and teach those sub-algorithms to students who don't already know them (this can be done, for example, in the course of remedial instruction). Sometimes, it is necessary to move down to an even lower level(s) and start teaching sub-sub-algorithms. It is clear, however, that before all operations on the sub-algorithmic levels have been formed, it is impossible to effectively teach and learn higher level operations of the algorithm. What was said with regard to algorithms and sub-algorithms is true with regard to heuristics and sub-heuristics as well.[17]

Principle 6.   **The teaching and learning of algorithms (algorithmic prescriptions) and heuristics (heuristic instructions) is not a goal in itself; it is rather a means to effectively teach their respective mental processes (knowledge units and mental operations).[18]**

Principle 7.   **The teaching and learning of *algorithms* (algorithmic prescriptions) and *heuristics* (heuristic instructions) is not a goal in itself. It is also a means to teach students the abilities of *self-guidance, self-regulation, and self-control.* This becomes possible because algorithms and heuristics are important *tools* for self-guidance, self-regulation, and self-control. The learning and mastery of these tools develops in students the ability to manage not only their physical behavior but their mental processes as well.**

Principle 8.   **It is important to teach students not only—and not even so much—the ready-made algorithmic and heuristic methods, but also *how to discover algorithms and heuristics* on their own. The teaching of methods for the independent discovery of methods has a higher educational value than simply imparting to students the ready-made algorithms and heuristics.[19]**

Principle 9.   **Teaching students and novices ready-made algorithms and heuristics and their corresponding algorithmic and heuristic processes can be done in different ways. The method of preference at a particular time and for particular students is determined by the conditions specified in the following rules:**

Rule 9.1. If an algorithmic prescription or a set of heuristics is relatively small (up to five instructions), it can be introduced to students as a whole at the very beginning of their instruction.

Rule 9.2. If an algorithmic prescription or a set of heuristics is long enough (more than five instructions), don't introduce it to students as a whole at the very beginning. Introduce it instruction by instruction or by small blocks of instructions.

Rule 9.3. Don't request students to memorize instructions. Instructions and their corresponding mental operations will be memorized involuntarily in the course of practicing or through application.

Rule 9.4. Having introduced an instruction, provide exercises which will provide practice for students in performing the instructions' corresponding operation. It is important to vary the content of these exercises as much as possible in order to provide for faster generalization of the practiced operation. Continue practicing the operation until it becomes internalized and automatized (i.e., until it is performed smoothly and swiftly without referring to the instruction or giving himself/herself a self-instruction).

Rule 9.5. Move on to the teaching of the next instruction (operation) only after the previous one was internalized and automatized, and practice it alone in the same way in which the previous operation was practiced.

Rule 9.6. After a related pair of operations have been internalized and automatized, provide exercises which require application and utilization of *both* operations. Continue practicing the performance of both operations until they merge into a *single block* of operations.

Rule 9.7. Practice each subsequent operation separately, and then join it to the already developed block of operations, thus gradually enlarging the block. Continue the process of adding new operations to the already formed block of operations until all the operations making up the algorithmic or non-algorithmic process are combined (merged) in the final large block.[20]

Rule 9.8. Gradually build the graphic representation (for example, a flowchart on the blackboard) of the gradually formed algorithmic or heuristic process. Once an operation has been formed, formulate the corresponding instruction and include it in the flowchart. Once the next operation has been formed and added to the previous one, formulate the next instruction and add it to the already formulated instruction, and so on.[21,22]

The snowball principle of forming complex systems of mental operations makes the acquisition and assimilation of methods of thinking not only an *easy* process; it provides for a *systematic* and *reliable* learning of methods of thinking with *guaranteed* results. The snowball methodology eliminates the need for memorizing prescriptions and effectively leads to the learning of mental *processes* rather than of *prescriptions* as to what to do mentally in order to solve a specific problem or make a specific decision. Instructions here are just a temporary *means* to actuate the operations which are to be learned. Once an operation has been internalized and automatized through practicing, the *need for instructions and self-instructions vanishes* and the learned operation starts to be actuated by problem conditions and other operations rather than by instructions. Because instructions and self-instructions are no longer needed and used, they often begin to be forgotten. Learning and thinking begin to function in a "natural way" when people don't normally tell themselves at each step of the thought process what they have to do. If we liken instructions to crutches, we can say that crutches were very useful for learning how to "mentally walk," but once learning has occurred, no crutches are needed any longer. They can be thrown away or kept for the occasion when for some reason a person might forget how to do a certain step in the process of walking.

The snowball methodology fulfills another important function. It transforms a *successive* performance of mental operations, following an algorithm or a set of heuristics, into a *simultaneous, or parallel*, performance. According to the AHT, the simultaneous performance of mental operations lies at the foundation of both *intuition* and *pattern recognition*. (For more detail, see Landa, 1982.) The snowball methodology is thus not only an effective way of teaching students general methods of thinking, but also a way of forming both intuition and pattern-recognition abilities.

Principle 10. **If proper technical means of instruction are available, it is important to individualize the teaching of general algorithmic and non-algorithmic methods of learning and thinking, and adapt the method of instruction to the individual characteristics of students, including their individual cognitive style.**

No true individualization of instruction is possible if the teacher has to teach a sufficiently large group of students all at the same time. Only personal computers provide the real possibility to individualize instruction and make it truly adaptive. Students' individual characteristics affect all aspects of learning, including the learning of general methods of thinking. Therefore, adaptation to these individual characteristics is highly desirable, as it makes learning easier and more productive.

With regard to learning general methods of learning and thinking, students differ, as was found in the AHT studies, in the following respects:

(a) Some students prefer to discover methods on their own, while some others prefer to receive them in the ready-made form.

(b) Some students prefer to first learn and master a mental operation and then have this operation formulated as an instruction of what to do, while some others prefer to first clearly understand, in the form of an instruction, what they have to do and then practice the appropriate operation.

(c) Some students prefer to know the entire method (say an algorithm) in advance of practicing individual operations, while some others don't care about knowing the whole method in advance, as it is difficult for them to grasp its complexity without having learned its component operations. Therefore they prefer to learn the method in an instruction-by-instruction (or operation-by-operation) manner.

(d) Some students don't need a lot of practice in performing each operation in order to internalize and automatize it, while some others need a substantial amount of practice. (There is obviously a continuum in the number of exercises needed by different students.)

(e) Some students generalize operations on the basis of just one to two similar examples or exercises (there exist students who don't need any examples at all), while some others need varied examples for the generalization to occur.

There exist some other individual differences in learning general methods of thinking as well. The AHT's approach to individualization should not be understood as a passive adaptation to students' individual characteristics. (For example, from the fact that a student doesn't like to discover algorithms but prefers to receive them in the ready-made form, it does not follow that the instructor should not teach him/her the methods of algorithm discovery, and that all algorithms should be given to him/her in the ready-made form.)

The AHT promotes an *active* adaptation, which means the following: The instruction must not to be under the thumb of the *weak* characteristics of a student's cognitive activity when the strong characteristics are valuable and desirable. Instruction should *strengthen* the weak characteristics as much as possible. On the other hand, it should draw on the already available *strong* characteristics of the student to the greatest possible degree in teaching both content and in developing the weak characteristics.

A simple example will illustrate this principle. A low level of activity of a student's mental processes is its *weak* characteristic, while the desirable characteristic is a high (or higher) level of activity; this is the *strong* characteristic of a student's mental processes. To develop a strong (active) characteristic (a high degree of mental activity), the instruction should strengthen this characteristic (activity level) as much as possible. If on the other hand, a student is able to generalize operations from just one or two examples or exercises (this is a strong characteristic), then the instruction should draw on this characteristic and the student should not be given more examples or exercises than he minimally needs.

In this section, only some basic principles of the algo-heuristically based instruction have been described. In order to realize each of the principles in practice, the instructional designer and teacher have to know the 'how to' of realization. In other words, they have to know the algorithms (or at least the semi-algorithmic methods) of the instructional actions. In the AHT, a number of such instructional (teaching) algorithms and semi-algorithms have been developed. They are so unambiguous and detailed that they can be taught to instructional designers and teachers in a systematic and reliable way, similar to how teachers teach students algorithms of certain mathematical operations. Development of instructional (teaching) algorithms opens up prospects for radical and dramatic improvement of instructional design methodology, as well as of the processes of teacher performance and teacher training.

How the AHT Methodology of Teaching General Methods Affects Students' Knowledge, Cognitive Abilities, Learning, and Thinking

Here are some of the effects produced in students as a result of teaching them general methods of thinking, as established by the AHT studies:

- Students learn that all chunks of *knowledge have a structure* and that *different contents* (within the same discipline or across different disciplines) *may have the same logical structures.*

- Students learn basic common (general) structures of knowledge and acquire the ability to *identify the knowledge structure of any knowledge* within any discipline.

- Students begin to understand that *methods of acquiring and handling knowledge* (methods of learning and problem solving) are *determined* not only, and not even so much, by the specific *content* of the knowledge as by its *logical structures.*

- Students begin to understand that there exist *common (general) methods* of acquiring and handling any knowledge that are determined by *common (general) structures of knowledge* rather than by its specific content.

- Students come to know how each general type of knowledge structure determines the method for its own handling.

- Students become able to *see (identify) common structures* in different knowledge contents, and then to *derive methods of handling this knowledge from its type of structure.* This develops an important *interdisciplinary* approach to learning and thinking and important interdisciplinary skills.

- Acquisition, generalization, and sufficient mastery of general methods of learning and thinking *create the ability to successfully handle all kinds of content and solve all kinds of subject-specific problems* which, according to the AHT, is the substance and manifestation of *general intelligence.*

- Learning not only general methods of thinking but methods for discovering these methods (i.e., methods of higher order) *develops within* students *different levels of meta-knowledge*, as well as the *ability to move*, when needed, *from the knowledge and methods of one level (order) to the knowledge and methods of another level (order).*

- Knowledge of the components of general methods of thinking, the components' logical structures and their designs, *enables students to analyze* not only how other people think but *their own thinking* as well, and to *improve these methods of thinking* when needed.

- Awareness of one's own mental processes and knowledge of algorithmic and non-algorithmic instructions (in particular, heuristics) *enables students to exercise self-regulation and self-control* of their cognitive processes (for verbal instructions are the essential psychological *tool* of self-regulation and self-control).

- Independent or guided discovery of methods of thinking (especially algorithms) develops such qualities of mind *as attention to detail,* a habit of *identifying* and *considering multiple conditions* which may affect actions and their results, a habit of *carefully analyzing connections between conditions* and *actions* and/or *decisions,* as well as a habit of *testing and verifying assumptions and hypotheses.*

- Independent or guided discovery of methods of thinking (especially algorithms) develops a habit of searching for *general approaches* to solving *specific problems* rather than just looking for specific *solutions.*

- The testing of algorithms in the course of their discovery or creation develops a *sensitivity to ambiguities* in students and a habit of *expressing* ideas and thoughts *accurately, precisely and concisely.*

- Using algorithms as guides for solving problems develops a habit to *think thoroughly* and *in a well organized* and *systematic manner.*

Thus, it would be justified to say that the AHT methodology of teaching general methods of learning and thinking develops not only certain qualities of learning and thinking in students, but also certain qualities of mind that grow into personality traits, as mental habits become more generalized and steady.

The AHT theory and methodology was applied to teaching various disciplines in grade school and colleges, as well as to improving training and performance in industry, business and government. Table 1 summarizes the comparative effectiveness of the conventional and the AHT-based methods of instruction in teaching selected academic disciplines.

Notes

1. Verbal instructions may sometimes be replaced by symbols (like a stop sign on the road or an arrow on a map) which then perform the function of verbal instructions.

2. In an extreme case, a prescription can consist of just one instruction,

3. The logic of designing this algorithm and the ways of leading students to figuring it out on their own is described in Chapter 6 in Reigeluth (1983). As will be shown below, one of the AHT's major objectives is not to simply give students ready-made algorithms, but to teach them general methods of turning descriptions into prescriptions and thus devising algorithms on their own. (For more detail on how to turn descriptions into prescriptions and teach students to devise algorithms of identification on their own, see Landa, 1974, Chapters 8, 10, and 15.)

4. As was said above, a system of *instructions* of this type geared to solving problems of a particular class is an *algorithmic **prescription*** or simply an **algorithm**. A system of algorithmic *actions* like the one just cited is an *algorithmic **process**.* A problem (task) which can be solved (performed) by using an algorithm (given from the outside or known by a person, i.e., stored in the memory) is an *algorithmic **problem*** (task).

5. The larger the field of choice, the greater the degree of uncertainty which requires, in turn, a greater degree of independence of the mental process—unless, of course, the selection of the book is performed randomly.

6. In a system of instructions, some instructions may be algorithmic and some others semi-algorithmic. If a system of instructions contains at least one semi-algorithmic instruction, we would call the entire prescription semi-algorithmic. This also will be true of semi-heuristic and heuristic prescriptions discussed below.

Table 1. Effectiveness of AHT-based methods.

Subject matter	Abilities tested	Conventional method	Landamatics method	Times better
Mathematics (geometry)	Ability of junior high school students to solve problems of proof	25% of test problems were solved after 1-1/2 years of conventional instruction	87% of test problems were solved after 7 hours of algo-heuristic instruction	3.5 times[1]
Physics	Ability of junior high school students to solve more than 40% of problems of average and high level of difficulty	None of students	88% of students	88.0 times[2]
Grammar of native tongue	Ability of junior high school students to classify a sentence	Error rate = 29.5%	Error rate = 6%	4.9 times[3]
Foreign language (English)	Ability of college students to comprehend 80 to 99% of sentences in a complex written scientific text	3.2% of students	88.5% of students	27.6 times[4]
Medicine	Ability of 6th year medical students to solve diagnostic problems in radiology	Error rate = 64%	Error rate = 4%	16 times[5]
Theory of music	Ability of college students to perform assignments requiring application of complex music-related concepts	Failure rate = 34%	Failure rate = 7%	4.8 times[6]

1. L. Landa, 1974, p. 255.
2. G. Weiser, 1969.
3. L. Landa, 1974, pp. 551–52.
4. A. Pesochin, 1974.
5. L. Naumov, 1973.
6. Z. Volynskaya, 1974.

7. In a case in which a semi-heuristic problem includes algorithmic and/or semi-algorithmic sub-problems, the processes which a semi-heuristic problem requires to be performed are executed in *addition* to the algorithmic and semi-algorithmic processes.

8. In the algorithmic instruction (Example 1), not only the *field* of objects was specified, but also the *object* within the field as well ("the red book," which was the single one on the shelf).

9. In the literature on psychology and artificial intelligence, the word "heuristic" is given a large variety of meanings. For example, some view heuristics as *rules*, specifically "rules of thumb" (e.g., Feigenbaum & Feldman, 1963; McGraw & Harbison-Briggs, 1989; Scott, Clayton, & Gibson, 1991; and many others), while some others view them as *processes* (e.g., Newell, Shaw, & Simon in Feigen-

baum & Feldman, 1963). Some authors utilize the term in both senses (e.g., Miller, Galanter, & Pribram, 1960). Some understand by heuristics the methods of solving problems, as well as the science which studies such methods (Polya, 1972). Sometimes the term "heuristic" is used to mean "a non-hierarchical direct association between concepts" (Clancey, 1985); sometimes it is used to mean a descriptive representation (or "perspective") of knowledge (Harmon & King, 1985). There exist also a number of other understandings and definitions which frequently are vague and non-operational. A good overview of some earlier notions of heuristics was given in Boden (1977).

10. An example of a heuristics with a high degree of uncertainty: If you can't find a solution to a problem, examine the problem from different angles (Polya, 1972).

11. For more details about the notion of relativity in classifying problems as algorithmic or non-algorithmic, see Landa (1974), Chapter 2.

12. The importance of structural analysis and of the structural approach to instructional design is also strongly emphasized by J. Scandura in his theory of structural learning (Scandura, 1973, 1983).

13. We emphasize the *cognitive* ability, since according to the theory of multiple intelligences, there exist other varieties of intelligence (Gardner, 1983). The question arises, of course, of why different kinds of important ability should be called "intelligences."

14. It must be emphasized that the formation of *content-free* methods of thinking can be done only through working within *specific contents* (mathematical, grammatical, biological, etc.) by the *gradual abstracting* from that content its general structural characteristics. From the discussion in the previous section, it follows that "content-free" does not mean "no-content." It simply means that in the course of formation of general methods of thinking, the content of thinking shifts from *specific objects and their characteristics to the general structures* of those objects and characteristics, with general structures becoming the content of general methods of thinking. But those structures (as do any structures) exist only within specific contents; they are general structures *of* specific contents.

15. Special emphasis is made in the AHT on the importance of diagnostics (and assessment) of not just the *character* and *level* of students' knowledge, skills and abilities (this is more or less satisfactorily done currently via conventional tests), but on the diagnostics of the cognitive *mechanisms* underlying the character and cognitive levels. Specifically, these mechanisms include the diagnostic determination, for example, of which of the required mental operations either exist or don't exist in the student's mind, which mental operations are performed or not performed in the course of solving certain problems, which connections exist between knowledge and operations, and which knowledge units and/or operations are actuated or not actuated in the course of performing certain tasks and solving certain problems.

In the AHT, such diagnostics were called *psychological trouble-shooting diagnostics* (for more detail, see Landa, 1976, Chapter 11). This kind of diagnostics identifies not only *what* a student knows and is able to do, and *how well* the student knows what s/he knows and does what s/he is supposed to do, but also why s/he can or cannot do certain things—which *specific mental operations* "work" or don't "work" in his or her mind. And, if they work, what *functional characteristics* the working operations have (e.g., what are their actuators, what is the degree of their generalization, what is the speed of their actuation, and so on).

Only the psychological trouble-shooting diagnostics of the *internal mechanisms* of students' mental processes makes it possible to "repair" those mechanisms when they don't function or don't function properly, and repair them effectively and fast. In this respect, the psychological trouble-shooting diagnostics open up radically new ways of treating students in the course of instruction. A good medical treatment acts not only, and even not so much, on the external *symptoms* of diseases (like a headache), but on the internal pathological *mechanisms—causes—*which bring about those symptoms. Likewise, the instruction based on the trouble-shooting diagnostics deals not only with the externally displayed *states* of students' knowledge and skills (what and how they know and what and how they can do), but also with the *causes* of those states: what works or doesn't work in the student's mind, which leads to a given state. Once a malfunction in a psychological mechanism has been identified (diagnosed) it becomes clear how to treat it. It is common knowledge in medicine that one and the same symptom (for example, a headache) should be treated differently depending on its cause. The same approach is applied in algo-heuristic adaptive instruction based on the psychological trouble-shooting diagnostics: One and the same error, for example, is handled differently depending on its psychological cause.

That is why the notion of diagnostic, adaptive, and individualized instruction in the AHT implies not only the conventional type of diagnostics and adaptation (which is the diagnostics of the *states* of students' knowledge and skills, and adaptation to them), but also the diagnostics of the psychological *causes* of those states, identification of the internal mental operations which lie behind the states and determine them.

It should be noted that as early as the middle of the 1960s, the author's associates were able to create a new type of adaptive textbook which was capable of psychological trouble-shooting and of effecting an individualized instruction which adapted not only to the states of students' knowledge and skills but to the psychological mechanisms of those states and, in particular, to their causes (see, for example, Yudina & Granik, 1970; Yudina, 1973). Computers provide an incomparably mightier tool for carrying out this kind of "higher order" adaptation and individualization and make instruction based on the psychological trouble-shooting diagnostics much easier and more efficient.

16. For an example of how it can be done—and was done—see Landa (1974), pp. 355–377.

17. Teachers often teach "current" knowledge and skills without making sure that the *foundation prerequisite sub-algorithmic and sub-heuristic operations* have been formed in all students. This leads to low achievements and inability to learn on the part of those students whose foundation prerequisite sub-algorithmic and sub-heuristic processes have not been formed or were defective. The situation may be easily remedied if a teacher knows how to troubleshoot the causes of a learning or performance problem and what prerequisite sub-algorithmic and sub-heuristic processes have to be taught. Unfortunately, teachers, as a rule, are not trained in how to do all of this and therefore cannot cope with the students' learning and performance problems.

18. Knowledge of algorithmic and non-algorithmic prescriptions (methods) represents an important type of procedural *meta*-knowledge which has direct bearing on the ability to consciously and purposefully guide and regulate one's own mental processes.

19. There exist not only general algorithmic and non-algorithmic methods for learning and solving problems but also *methods for discovering such methods, i.e., methods of higher order* which are based on a higher order *meta*-knowledge. Since, however, the discovery of methods is often a very time-consuming process, it is as a practical matter impossible to base all the instruction on the discovery method. Therefore, in practical terms, the discovery method of teaching methods of learning and thinking should be combined with the method of directly teaching students ready-made algorithms and heuristics.

20. This process of building up a complex system of mental operations by adding new operations to the already-formed blocks reminds the author of making a big snowball by adding more snow to the already existing ball. In the AHT, it has been dubbed "a snowball principle" for forming complex algorithmic and non-algorithmic processes.

21. Thus, students will be exposed to the whole algorithmic or heuristic prescription only at the end of forming the actual algorithmic or heuristic process; i.e., after the process has already been formed. The function of such a graphic representation of the whole—and often complex—process is to serve as a *summary* of what has already been learned and as a *reference* in case, at some point in the future, an operation(s) to be performed may slip the mind or be forgotten.

22. The formulation of instructions and their graphic representation should grow together with the growing body of learned operations. However, some students prefer the formulation of instructions before the operations have been practiced. These variations, however, don't substantially affect the effectiveness of the technique ("the snowball principle of forming mental processes") described in this rule.

References

Boden, M. (1977). *Artificial intelligence and natural man.* Hassocks, UK: The Harvester Press.

Bung, K. (1973). *Towards a theory of programmed learning instruction.* The Hague/Paris, Mouton.

Bussman, H. (1970). *Die Anwendung der Algorithmentheorie Landa's auf eine anschauliche Problemlösungsaufgabe aus der pädagogische Psychologie.* Dissertation. Die Philosophische Fakultät der

Rheinisch-Westfälischen Technischen Hochschule Aachen.

Carpay, J. A. M. (1976). Foreign language teaching and meaningful learning. A Soviet Russian Point of View. *ITL Review of Applied Linguistics*, University of Leuven.

Clancey, W. J. (1985, Dec.). Heuristic classification. *Artificial Intelligence, 27*(3).

Coscarelli, W. (1978). Algorithmization in instruction. *Educational Technology, 18*(2).

Corsini, R. J. (Ed.). (1984). *Encyclopedia of psychology.* New York: John Wiley & Sons.

Feigenbaum, E. A., & Feldman, J. (Eds.). (1963). *Computers and thought.* New York: McGraw-Hill.

Gardner H. (1983). *Frames of mind: The theory of multiple intelligences.* New York: Basic Books.

Gentilhomme, I. (1964). Optimisation des Algorithmes d'Enseignement. *La Pedagogie Cybernetique, 4.*

Gerlach, V., Reiser, R., & Brecke, F. (1977). Algorithms in education. *Educational Technology, 17*(10).

Harmon, P., & King, D. (1985). *Expert systems.* New York: John Wiley & Sons.

Horabin, I., & Lewis, B. (1977, Summer). Fifteen years of ordinary-language algorithms. *Improving Human Performance.*

Kopstein, F. (1977). What is algorithmization of instruction? *Educational Technology, 17*(10).

Kuhn, T. S. (1970). *The structure of scientific revolutions.* Chicago: University of Chicago Press.

Landa, L. N. (1974). *Algorithmization in learning and instruction.* Englewood Cliffs, NJ: Educational Technology Publications.

Landa, L. N. (1976). *Instructional regulation and control: Cybernetics, algorithmization, and heuristics in education.* Englewood Cliffs, NJ: Educational Technology Publications.

Landa, L. N. (1982). The improvement of instruction, learning, and performance: Potential of "Landamatic Theory" for teachers, instructional designers, and material producers. An interview. *Educational Technology, 22*(10&11).

Landa, L. N. (1983). The Algo-Heuristic Theory of Instruction. In C. M. Reigeluth, (Ed.), *Instructional design theories and models: An overview of their current status.* Hillsdale, NJ: Lawrence Erlbaum Associates.

Landa, L. N. (1987). A fragment of a lesson based on the Algo-Heuristic Theory of Instruction. In C. M. Reigeluth, (Ed.), *Instructional theories in action: Lessons illustrating selected theories and models.* Hillsdale, NJ: Lawrence Erlbaum Associates.

Landa, L. N. (1993). Landamatics ten years later. An interview. *Educational Technology, 33*(6).

Lánsky, M. (1969). Learning algorithms as a teaching aid. In *RECALL: Review of Educational Cybernetics and Applied Linguistics.* London: Longman.

Lewis, B. (1967). *Three essays in ordinary language algorithms.* London: London University Institute Monograph.

Lewis, B., & Horabin, I. (1977). Algorithmics 1967. *Improving Human Performance Quarterly, 6,* 2–3.

McGraw, K. L., & Harbison-Briggs, K. (1989). *Knowledge acquisition: Principles and guidelines.* Englewood Cliffs, NJ: Prentice-Hall.

Merrill, P. F. (1977). Algorithmic organization in teaching and learning: Literature and research in the USA. *Improving Human Performance Quarterly, 6,* 2–3.

Merrill, P. F. (1980). Representations for algorithms. *NSPI Journal, 19*(8).

Miller, G. A., Galanter, E., & Pribram, K. (1960). *Plans and the structure of behavior.* New York: Holt.

Naumov, L. B. (1973). *Report on testing algorithms for x-ray diagnostics* (in Russian). Novosibirsk.

Polya, G. (1972). *How to solve it.* Princeton, NJ: Doubleday.

Pesochin, A. (1974). *Teaching via algorithms.* Moscow: Kharkov, Medical College Publishing House.

Reigeluth, C. M. (Ed.). (1983). *Instructional design theories and models: An overview of their current status.* Hillsdale, NJ: Lawrence Erlbaum Associates.

Reigeluth, C. M. (Ed.). (1987). *Instructional theories in action: Lessons illustrating selected theories and models.* Hillsdale, NJ: Lawrence Erlbaum Associates.

Scandura, J. M., Durnin, J. H., Ehrenpreis, W., & Luger, G. (1971). *An algorithmic approach to mathematics: Concrete behavioral foundations.* New York, Harper & Row.

Scandura, J. M. (1973). *Structural learning I: Theory and research.* London: Gordon and Breach Science Publishers.

Scandura, J. M. (1983). Instructional strategies based on the structural learning theory. In C. M. Reigeluth (Ed.), *Instructional design theories and models: An overview of their current status.* Hillsdale, NJ: Lawrence Erlbaum Associates.

Schmid, R., Portnoy, R., & Burns, K. (1976). Using algorithms to assess comprehension of classroom text material. *Journal of Educational Research, 69.*

Scott, A. C., Clayton, J. E., & Gibson, E. L. (1991). *A practical guide to knowledge acquisition.* Reading, MA: Addison-Wesley.

Sholomij, K. M. (1969). On the difference between heuristic and non-heuristic programs (in Russian). *Voprosy Psikhologii, 2.*

Sholomij, K. M. (1973). On one of the formal methods of designing optimal identification algorithms (in Russian). In L. Landa (Ed.), *Issues in algorithmization and programming of instruction, Vol. 2.* Moscow: Prosveshchenie Publishing House.

Tulodziecki, G. (1972). *Beiträge der Algorithmenforschung zu einer Unter-richtswissenshaft.* Athenäum Pädagogischer Verlag Schwann.

Vermersch, P. (1971). Les algorithmes en psychologie et en pedagogie. Definition et intérêts. *Le Travail Humain, 1.*

Volynskaya, Z. A. (1974). *On the possibility and expediency of using programmed instruction methods for teaching theory of music.* Ph.D. dissertation abstract (in Russian), Moscow.

Weiser, G. A. (1969). *Teaching students general methods of thinking for solving physics problems.* Ph.D. dissertation abstract (in Russian), Moscow.

Weiser, G. A. (1973). On methods of students' thinking in solving physics problems (in Russian). In L. Landa (Ed.), *Issues in algorithmization and programming of instruction, Vol. 2.* Moscow: Pedagogica Publishing House.

Yudina, O. N. (1973). Diagnostics of psychological causes of students' errors in algorithm-based vs. conventional instruction (in Russian). In L. Landa (Ed.), *Issues in algorithmization and programming of instruction, Vol. 2.* Moscow: Pedagogica Publishing House.

Yudina, O. N., & Granik, G. G. (1969). On some methods of dynamic adaptation of instruction to students on the basis of trouble-shooting of the psychological causes of errors. In L. Landa (Ed.), *Issues in algorithmization and programming of instruction, Vol. 1.* Moscow: Prosveshchenie Publishing House.

Yudina, O. N., & Granik, G. G. (1970). *Russian: A programmed textbook and exercises, Part 2* (in Russian). Moscow: Pedagogica Publishing House.

Zemke, R., & Kramlinger, T. (1982). *Figuring things out: A trainer's guide to needs and task analysis.* Reading, MA: Addison-Wesley.

Zierer, E. (1972). Using algorithmic procedures in foreign language learning. In *RECALL: Review of Educational Cybernetics and Applied Linguistics.* London: Longman.

PART 6

The Logistics Vantage Point: Technology-Based Paradigms

39

Structured Writing as a Paradigm

Robert E. Horn
The Lexington Institute
Lexington, Massachusetts

Introduction

Thomas Kuhn (1962, 1970) suggests that "normal science" consists of "research based upon one or more past scientific achievements that some particular community acknowledges for a time as supplying the foundation for its further practice." These achievements were (1) "sufficiently unprecedented to attract an enduring group of adherents away from competing modes of scientific activity," and (2) "sufficiently open-ended to leave all sorts of problems for the redefined group of practitioners to solve." He then states that this is his definition of a paradigm: "Achievements that share these two characteristics I shall henceforward refer to as paradigms." Although Kuhn goes on to use the word "paradigm" in at least twenty-one distinct meanings (as catalogued by Masterman, 1970), this is the only place where he explicitly defines the term. Others have broadened the meaning of "paradigm" and still others have used the term as a metaphor for any theory or method or approach, large or small.

If any writing or instructional design approach can be called a paradigm within Kuhn's definition, I will claim that structured writing most certainly qualifies. And if Kuhn's concept of paradigm can be metaphorically extended beyond the sciences to the realm of practical methodology of communication, then structured writing surely qualifies there as well. My approach in this chapter will be to describe what I believe to be the salient characteristics of structured writing and to describe the "past achievements" that supply "the foundation for further practice." Then I will demonstrate briefly how these achievements have been "sufficiently unprecedented to attract an enduring group of adherents away from competing modes of scientific activity" and finally, I will describe some of the sorts of issues in research and evaluation that structured writing focuses on today.

What Are Some of the Problems that
Structured Writing Addresses?

Structured writing has been developed to address many of the perennial problems most people have when working on a complex written communication task. Instructional design certainly qualifies as such a complex task. Some of these perennial problems are:

- How should I organize the mass of subject-matter material?
- How can I keep track of the structure? How can the reader keep track?
- How can I make the structure of the document and the subject matter more obvious?
- How do I analyze the subject so that I am sure that I have covered all of the bases?
- How do I know the coverage is complete? How will the reader understand this scope?
- In large analytic and communication tasks, how do I track multiple inputs, different levels of reader competence and rapidly multiplying and increasingly demanding maintenance requirements?
- If I am working in an organization with a large number of writers, how do I provide the plan for a group of writers and how do I manage the group—efficiently—so that it will appear to the reader that there is a unity or organization, structure, analysis, style, graphic display and format?
- How do I sequence the final document so that it will present the information to different levels of readers in the most useful manner?
- How do I organize the linkages so that different readers with different backgrounds can get what they want from it easily and quickly?
- What formats are optimum to enable users to make sense of the document as a whole and through the window of the current display?
- How do we make instructional writing optimally effective and efficient?

These problems are not unique to instructional design. They are addressed one way or another by every person who writes a document. But they are the major issues faced by the paradigm of structured writing. The remainder of this chapter will examine how structured writing helps writers tackle these questions.

What Are Some of the Presuppositions of
Structured Writing?

In this section I will present several of the major presuppositions of structured writing to provide the background that I used to formulate the paradigm of structured writing.

I have used these presuppositions without entering current cognitive science debates as to whether or not we really use some kinds of representations within our minds and brains. Rather, I simply observe that when we communicate, we do use representations.

Presuppositions about Subject Matter. I begin with what seems obvious, namely that, since we communicate with each other using physical mediums, we have to represent what we do in sentences and images. Thus, any subject matter consists of all the sentences and images used by human beings to communicate about that subject matter. So, with sentences and images, we have all we need to fully analyze a subject matter. I acknowledge that subject matters exist that can only be learned by intense observation, practice and nonverbal feedback (such as an exotic martial art). I acknowledge the issues raised by Polanyi in his concept of tacit knowledge, i.e., that certain knowledge is learned by observation of fine motor movements and unvoiced values which go beyond the sentences that represent a subject matter. But I sidestep them. Structured writing only deals with that which can be written. Practical communication in commerce, science, and technology teaches, documents or communicates something. Therefore, I assume that what is important enough to learn is capable of being rendered in sentences (or diagrams).

I also assume that the most important regularities to understand in a subject matter are those that exist between sentences. Many of the studies of language begin and end with the study of words and sentences in isolation. Subject matters are tight relationships between many clusters of sentences and images. So, if we are to analyze subject matters properly (i.e., efficiently and effectively) for communication and training, we must understand the relationships between sentences. Why is it that certain sentences should be "close" to each other in an instructional document in order to convey the subject matter easily to a new learner?

Presuppositions about readers. There were a number of assumptions about the users (or readers). I took it as axiomatic that different readers and learners may want to use a given document in a variety of ways. Readers may use any of the following approaches to a given document: scanning to decide whether to read the communication at all, browsing to find interesting or relevant material, analyzing critically the contents, studying to be able to remember the subject matter, etc. And, in general, it is difficult to predict what learners and readers will do with a given piece of instruction or communication.

Documents often have hundreds or even thousands of users. Each document has a different interest and relevance to each user. Each must therefore serve many people having many purposes. If possible, it is important to optimize among several functions in the same document.

Presuppositions about Writing. When I developed structured writing, I also introduced what turned out to be a fairly radical assumption: *A new paradigm in communication and learning requires a new basic unit of communication.* Revolutions in paradigms in physical theory have in part come about from the different concepts of the most basic particle (from the atom as a singular unit, to the Bohr model of the atom as a subvisible solar system, to electrons as rings of probability, to the discovery of subatomic particles, etc.). Revolutions in linguistic theory came about with the invention of grammar as a unit of analysis. The behavioral paradigm in instructional design came after Skinner's invention of the stimulus–response unit. Similarly, the invention of the information block (discussed below) qualifies as a major turning point in the history of the conception of basic units.

Most training is not formal training. It does not take place in the classroom with documents called training manuals. It takes place on the job with whatever documentation is at hand. I have heard that only one-tenth of training is formal classroom training. Nine-tenths never gets accounted for in the financial or other reports of a company as training. Thus, in my list of major assumptions is this one: Anything that is written is potentially instructional. Therefore, in so far as possible: A writer should design each communication to potentially be "instructional" even if its ostensible job may be as a memo or a report or as documentation.

Another focus of the structured writing presuppositions gives importance to the scientific research on how much people forget. We forget most of what we learn within three weeks of learning it. I have noted that we must build "learning-reference systems" in order to deal with these problems (Horn *et al.,* 1969). Since then we have used the term "reference based training" (Horn, 1989a) to cover this area. Others have invented the delightful term "just in time training" to cover an essential aspect of this training need. And later I specified the domains of memos and reports as another arena in which writing with instructional properties takes place (Horn, 1977).

With this survey of the assumptions underlying the paradigm, let us take a look at the actual components of the structured writing approach.

Analogy	Description	Notation	Specified Action
Block Diagram	Diagram	Objectives	Table
Checklist	Example	Outlines	Stage Table
Classification List	Expanded Procedure	Parts-Function Table	Synonym
Classification Table	Table	Parts Table	Theorem
	Fact		When to Use
Classification Tree		Prerequisites to	
Comment	Flow Chart	Course	WHIF Chart
Cycle Chart	Flow Diagram	Principle	Who Does What
Decision Table	Formula	Procedure Table	Worksheet
Definition	Input-Procedure-Output	Purpose	
	Non-example	Rule	

Figure 1. Most frequently used block types (in domain of relatively stable subject matter). This chart is reproduced by permission of The Lexington Institute, publishers of *Mapping Hypertext* by R. E. Horn.

What Are the Components of the Structured Writing Paradigm?

My early analyses began with the detailed examination of actual sentences, illustrations, and diagrams that appeared in textbooks and training manuals. My investigation involved trying to establish a relatively small set of chunks of information that (1) are similar in that they cluster sentences (and diagrams) that have strong relationships with each other and (2) frequently occur in various kinds of subject matter. This analysis focused, thus, on the relationship between the sentences in subject matter. The result of this analysis was the invention of the information block as a substitute for the paragraph. The taxonomy that resulted is now known as the information blocks taxonomy for relatively stable subject matter (shown in Figure 1).

Definition: Information Blocks

Information blocks are the basic units of subject matter in structured writing analysis. They replace the paragraph as the fundamental unit of analysis and the form of presentation of that analysis. They are composed of one or more sentences and/or diagrams about a limited topic. They usually have no more than nine sentences. They are always identified clearly by a label. Three examples of information blocks are shown in Figure 2. Information blocks are normally part of a larger structure of organization called an information map (see below for explanation of maps). In short, they are a reader-focused unit of basic or core parts of a subject matter.

Example of an Information Block

What do information blocks look like? It is important to notice that different types of blocks vary widely in appearance and construction. For example, below is one of the most simple-looking types of blocks (but one that has standards for construction more stringent than most), a definition block:

Definition: The Master Payroll File is a group of records containing all of the payroll and employee information used by the weekly payroll program.

How Is a Block Different from a Paragraph?

Let us examine some of the characteristics of this example of an information block and see how it differs from paragraphs. First, we must note that there is no topic sentence in the information block. Topic sentences are absent or irrelevant in much of structured writing, so much so that they are not taught in a structured writing course.

Second, it is worth observing that there is no "nice to know" but irrelevant information in the information block. Note that the only information it contains is information that is relevant to defining the term Master Payroll File. Paragraphs typically have a lot of nice to know information.

Third, note that the block has a label. One of the mandatory requirements for blocks is that they always have a distinguishing label, chosen according to systematic criteria (Horn, 1989a). Paragraphs have no such requirement, although they may be randomly labeled, depending upon the taste of the writer.

Fourth, all definitions in a given structured document would be consistent with these characteristics. Paragraphs have no requirement for consistency within or between documents. These are some of the main characteristics that distinguish the block from a paragraph.

This first example is a very simple block. While this block is one sentence long, many types of blocks contain several sentences, diagrams, tables, or illustrations, depending upon their information type. (See Figure 2.) Typical blocks are several sentences in length, and might contain different kinds of tables. Diagrams comprise other kinds of information blocks.

How Does Structured Writing Handle Cohesion and Transition?

There is no "transitional" information in the information block, but principles for writing prose encourage or require it. The need for coherence, cohesion, and transition is handled in a completely different manner in structured writing. While this is a huge topic (Halliday and Hasan, 1976), suffice it to say that much of the burden of coherence is placed on the labeling structure and much of the transition requirement is placed on one type of block, the introduction block, that frequently appears at the beginning of information maps.

The Four Principles

All information blocks are constrained by four principles used to guide structured writing:

The first of these is the *chunking principle.* It derives from George Miller's basic research (Miller, 1956), which suggests that we can hold only seven plus or minus two chunks of information in human short-term memory. Our formulation of the principle states: Group all information into small, manageable units, called information blocks and information maps. Small (in information blocks) is defined as usually not more than seven plus or minus two sentences. While others lately (e.g., Walker, 1988) have recommended modularity (i.e. dividing information into labeled chunks) as a principle of structured writing, I have insisted that information blocks turn out to be "precision modularity" (Horn 1989a, 1993) because of the operation of three other principles with the chunking principle and because I believe we have shown that blocks sorted using our taxonomy (see below) offer much greater efficiency and effectiveness of composition and retrieval.

The second principle we use in helping to define the information block is the *labeling principle.* It says: Label every chunk and group of chunks according to specific criteria. It is beyond the scope of this paper to get into all of these criteria. They consist of guidelines and standards, some of which cover all blocks, some of which cover only specific types of blocks

Information Block Containing a Table

Decision

IF the book is . . .	THEN send the patron . . .	AND send . . .
available	the book	an invoice to the Billing Unit.
not available • never owned • lost	Form 25	--
checked out with no waiting list	Form 66	a copy of Form 66 to Circulation Desk.
checked out with a waiting list	Form 66 and Waiting List Notice	a copy of Form 66 to Circulation Desk.

Information Block Containing One Sentence and One Diagram

Diagram

The terminal is held in place in the connector cavity by a locking tang, and the attached cable allows you to move and position the terminal.

Information Block with Several Sentences and Several Diagrams

Procedure

Step 1	Step 2	Step 3
Push the cable forward until it will no longer slide.	Insert the K8889 tool through the hole on the opposite side and gently pull the cable out.	Inspect the terminal. Replace if necessary and then replace the cable by inserting it into the locking tang.
Example:	**Example:**	**Example:**

Push   K8889
                    Pull
                    Cable   Push

This Chart is reproduced by permission of The Lexington Institute, publishers of *Mapping Hypertext* by R. E. Horn

Figure 2.   Some different kinds of Information Blocks.

or even parts of blocks. I have claimed elsewhere (Horn, 1992a) that it is the precise specification of different kinds of blocks that permits the identification of context and limits for these criteria, thus saving them from being bland and overly abstract and thus largely useless guidelines.

The third principle used in developing the information block is the *relevance principle*. It says: Include in one chunk only the information that relates to one main point, based upon that information's purpose or function for the reader. In effect it says, if you have information that is nice to know, or contains examples or commentary, the relevance principle demands that you put it some place else and label it appropriately: but do not put it in the definition block.

The fourth principle is the *consistency principle*. It says: For similar subject matters, use similar words, labels, formats, organizations, and sequences.

Answering Some Objections to Blocks

Some have commented that information blocks are not particularly unique or novel. They say, for example, that information blocks are only what paragraphs, when written properly, should be. I have answered many of these claims elsewhere (Horn, 1992a). If extraneous information is excluded from an information block (as it should be, following the relevance principle), the discourse is changed radically. If the materials for cohesiveness and transition in paragraph-oriented writing are put into the labels, and if the labeling system is relevant and consistent, the appearance and usefulness of the whole piece of writing is changed tremendously. If the subject matter is divided into appropriate-size chunks (using the chunking principle and the taxonomy of information blocks), the form of discourse is changed decisively. If all of these changes are made together in the same document, the text usually has much less intertwined prose with multiple threads and allusions. It is a far more usable text to scan, to read and to memorize.

Blocks by Themselves Qualify Structured Writing as a Paradigm

By itself, the invention of the information block might qualify structured writing as a separate and new paradigm for analysis and writing. But we used these new distinctions to build a powerful analytic tool for gathering information about and specifying the subject matter in instructional or documentation writing. Simply revising the basic unit has radically shifted the rhetoric of exposition in the documents in which structured writing is used.

Topic—Block Matrix of a Subject Matter

To aid analysis of subject matter for instructional and documentation purposes, I conceptualized the subject matter as a topic-block matrix, shown schematically in Figure 3.

The reader will note that the topics from the subject matter are arranged along the top of the matrix. This is done according to a group of guidelines provided as a part of the structured writing system. The block types (see Figure 1 for list) are arranged along the vertical axis. The resulting cells in the matrix represent information blocks into which the sentences and diagrams from the subject matter are placed. Examination of the blank spaces show the analyst what information may still be not written down and hence perhaps not known. Specific templates have been developed which permit the analysts to know with a high degree of certainty which block should be filled in for a specific topic. An example of this would be a template which would specify these three block types for a concept: definition, example, and (optionally) non-example.

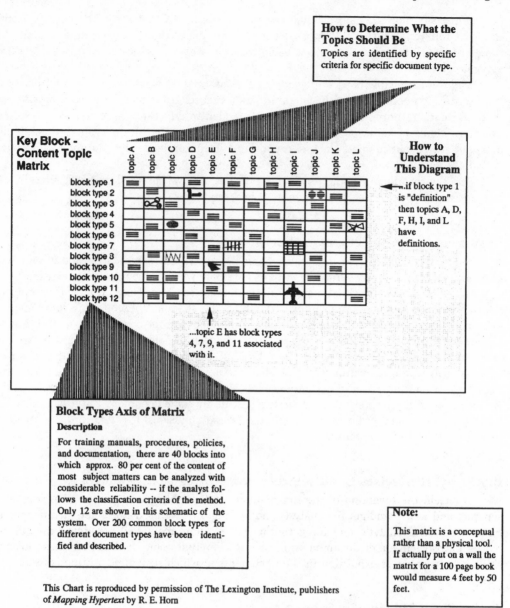

Figure 3.   Block Type-Content Topic Matrix.

Systematic Labeling

Another key component of structured writing was the development of a system of consistent labeling of parts of a document. Obviously labeling is not unique to structured writing. Many books follow a more or less systematic labeling guideline. But when combined with the new units of communication, the information block and the information map, the systematic labeling becomes a powerful communication device. In a recent article (Horn, 1993), I summarized the benefits of such a systematic approach to labeling. Systematic labeling:

- enables readers to scan content to see what they want to read
- enables readers/learners to find what they are looking for in a consistent, relevant, complete manner;

- enables the analyst/writer to manage the intermediate stages of information gathering and analysis in a more efficient way;

- enables learners to anticipate learning problems by showing the structure of the subject matter to them.

Definition: Information Maps

Information Maps are a collection of more than one but usually not more than nine information blocks about a limited topic. In general, one can think of an information map as approximately one to two pages in length, but some maps (of certain well-specified types) run several pages in length and some maps are composed of only one information block. Maps both (1) aid the writer in organizing large amounts of information during the analysis phase and (2) help the reader to understand the structure of the subject matter and the document. Maps may be sequenced hierarchically or in other clearly defined ways such as task or prerequisite order. Maps are assembled during the sequencing phase of the writing process, into parts, sections, chapters and documents depending upon communication purpose and reader needs. (For an example, see Figure 4.)

Discourse Domains

Communication in business takes place in some fairly routinized forms. This fact enables us to identify some major domains of discourse. We begin such an analysis by asking questions about specific domains such as: How does a report of a scientific experiment differ from a sales presentation or a policy manual? They differ in many ways. They differ as to who the authors are, how the authors have come to know the subject matter, what can be assumed about the audience of the communication, what level of detail is used, what content is communicated.

In addition to the "what are the differences" questions, we can ask the "what are the similarities" questions. How are all reports of scientific experiments alike? How are all sales presentations alike? The analysis of these similarities and differences is what is called domain analysis in structured writing. It involves examining the relationships between author and reader of different kinds of documents and the "stances" and points of view that can be seen as a result. This analysis yields specific block types that can be expected in specific kinds of documents. The domain of relatively stable subject matter has already been introduced in this chapter as the one that comprises the subject matter used in training and documentation writing (see also below).

So, in the Information Mapping method, a domain of discourse is defined as the specification of information blocks of a particular class of documents, all of which share the same type of author-reader assumptions and the same stance or point of view towards subject matter.

Some examples of domains of discourse (Horn, 1989a) have been studied extensively. They are:

- the domain of relatively stable subject matter, which is that domain of subject matter which we think we know well enough to teach it in a course or write introductory training material about it.

- the domain of disputed discourse, which is that subject matter about which we know enough to chart its disagreements.

Other domains such as those of business report and memo writing have been studied (Horn, 1977). Still others remain to be carefully identified and mapped.

Comparing 17.1.0	Regular Data Values, and . . .	Non-Regular Data Values
Introduction	Some data have patterns. They progress by fixed increments.	Some data do not show any pattern of intervals between the values.
Definition	Data are called regular when the values of a data vector progress from some initial value with some fixed interval to another value, and then optionally from that to still other values by even increments.	Data are called "non-regular" data when they have no systematic pattern of intervals between them.
Example One	Time data show frequent regularities. Samples of blood collected from a laboratory animal every hour on the hour might be called SAMPLEHRS and might look this way: SAMPLEHRS = 6, 7, 8, 9, 10	Most measurement data do not exhibit systematic regularities that are fixed intervals between values, so they are usually non-regular data. Here is an example: LABMEAS = .01, .09, .04, .3
Use This Input Statement	Input with Computed Clause Statement	Standard Input Statement
Comment	This statement permits you to input regular data in a very compact form and is much quicker to type than a normal input statement.	This statement should be used for normal data entry.
Related Pages	Input with Computed Input Statements, 22 Standard Input Statement, 21 Variables, 19	

This Chart is reproduced by permission of The Lexington Institute, publishers of *Mapping Hypertext* by R. E. Horn

Figure 4.   Example of an Information Map.

Information Types

Blocks in the domain of relatively stable subject matter can be sorted into seven basic classifications, which we call the "information types."

The seven information types are:

- Procedure
- Process
- Concept
- Structure
- Classification
- Principle
- Fact

This is a key set of categories for specifying and describing how human beings think, especially about what we have called relatively stable discourse domains. Structured writing guidelines have been developed that permit the information blocks to be assigned to one or more of these information types. An example would be the assignment of definitions and examples to the information type "concept" or the assignment of a flowchart to the information type "procedure." This permits the identification of what has come to be called "key block" information, the information which you must have to fully analyze an individual topic of a subject matter. Key blocks enable writers to anchor their writing firmly and reliably to the centrally important structure of a subject matter. (For further information, see Horn, 1989a, Chapter 3.)

The information types theory is used to help the analyst/writer identify specific information that is needed for each topic. These information-type templates specify the key information blocks needed to ensure completeness and accuracy of the analysis.

Systematic Integration of Graphics

From its conception, the structured writing paradigm recognized the importance of graphics (illustrations, diagrams, photographs) as an integral part of any writing with a practical purpose. This meant that we had to specify exactly where such graphics would communicate better than words by themselves. And this led to the identification of specific blocks within the overall scheme which are required to have some kind of graphic, because the communication was likely to be better than if the same message were conveyed only by words. This is also paradigmatic change. Certainly in the past, words and images had been used together. But graphics were regarded either as a "tacked on" afterthought or as decorations, not as a mandatory and integral part of the message (see Horn, 1993, for a fuller treatment of this point).

Systematic Formatting

Much reading in the Age of Information Overload is actually scanning. We must continually identify that which we don't have to read. We are always looking for the salient parts. This makes the requirement for aiding scanning paramount in the specification of formatting. There have been a variety of formats identified that meet this criteria. Structured writing is most often associated with a single format: that of having the map title at the top and the block labels on the left-hand side of the page. But this is only one of the many possible formats of structured writing that aid scanning (see Horn, 1989a, for others). The topic of formatting is also the one that has produced the most confusion about structured writing. Many people have observed only the strongly formatted versions of documents written according to the analytic methods of structured writing and have concluded that "it is only a format." Since the analysis and structuring of the document is part of the process of producing the document, much of the highly disciplined thinking that goes into producing the documents is not immediately visible. But the number of trained writers of structured writing has grown to over 150,000 world-wide, and the discernment that something more than format goes into structured writing has gradually become the norm rather than the exception.

Systematic Life-Cycle Approach to Document Development

Documentation and training materials often last a long time. The amount of time from drafting to final discard of a document can be years and sometimes decades. Many business documents are frequently revised and updated. This means that a methodology for writing must have in place a facility for rapid revision and updating as well as cost-effective initial development. The structured writing paradigm has made paradigmatic changes in how documents can be updated and revised. Because the basic units of organization, the information blocks, are easily isolatable from each other (unlike other paradigms of writing and formatting), they can be much more easily removed, changed or replaced. Previous and more literary rhetorics provide a great deal of difficulty to the writer managing the life cycle of the document, because such literary rhetorics have an intricate and highly interwoven approach to organization. Managers involved in preparing foreign language translations also report major efficiencies of translation because of the simplification of rhetorical structure. Needless to say that the structured writing approach propagates rapidly in a business environment in which costs of publication are closely watched.

What Structured Writing Shares with Other Paradigms

Not all of the components of structured writing are novel. Such total novelty is not a requirement for a paradigm. Structured writing shares the use of words and sentences with other forms of writing. Many of the conventions and rhetorical guidelines for good, clear writing of sentences are incorporated without change. Moreover, when serving a purely instructional function, most of the guidelines regarding the design of practice exercises, tests, criteria-based instruction, etc. are used wholesale.

Behavioral research from instructional design, such as Merrill and Tennyson's (1977; Merrill, Tennyson, & Posey, 1992) work on teaching concepts, has also been incorporated into the structured writing paradigm. This research serves to strengthen the instructional properties of documents whose initial or primary use is not instructional, but which at some time in the life cycle of the document must provide formal or informal training. Moreover, as another example, much of the collection of research-based design imperatives in Fleming's and Levie's (1978, 1993) work on message design supported and strengthened the research foundations of the structured writing paradigm, as have many individual pieces of research since then.

What Makes Structured Writing "Structured"?

One of the claims of structured writing is that there exist particular dimensions along which technical or functional writing can be described (if observing it from the point of view of an outside observer) or composed (if attempting to develop some document using it). It seems to me that we can describe several scales of structure or dimensions along which a piece of prose would be placed. Some of these scales are:

The Chunking Scale.   This scale might be described by the question "to what degree can the between-sentence units be clearly chunked into separate chunks, each of which serves only one purpose?"

Most ordinary prose paragraphs would be placed on the low end of this scale simply because they mix functions. For example, many paragraphs mix introductory and definitional functions, while highly structured writing keeps them separate. I have itemized and described forty such functions for chunks (which I call information blocks) appearing in the domain of relatively stable subject matter (the domain of text books, procedure and policy manuals, etc.). Dividing subject matter strictly according to this taxonomy of chunks produces highly structured chunking.

Making the structure visible with labels. Does such a highly chunked writing style produce highly structured writing? To some degree it does. But there are other dimensions to consider. One of these has to do with whether or not the reader can actually see the structure by glancing at the page. Three factors contribute significantly to making the structure visible.

One factor is whether or not the chunks are labeled. If the chunks are clearly and functionally labeled, the reader will be able to scan the labels and get a gist of the document as a whole. The second factor is actually a group of design elements that include format (where the labels are placed) and type style (such as size and boldness of the labels). A third factor is whether there is a systematic application of labeling—the application of the consistency principle.

So we have three more possible scales or dimensions of "structuredness" to consider. Clearly most prose falls down badly on these scales, while methods that have a labeling system will be rated as more "structured." And to determine "structuredness" we must use a multi-dimensional approach.

The Between-Chunk Sequencing Structure. All of the dimensions of structure discussed so far could be done and we might rate the writing as poorly structured, because the way in which the chunks are put together does not present a clear structure to the reader.

There are many ways to arrange the sequence of chunks in a piece of writing. For example, arranging them hierarchically is one frequently used way. Here again there are at least two distinguishable factors: (1) Is the document organized according to some larger organizing scheme, such as the concept of nine different kinds of hypertrails as a basis for the structuring of sequencing (Horn, 1989a) and (2) Can the reader see this at a glance? So again we have both the "inner organization" principle and the formatting principle at work.

These and other "dimensions" and their attendant scales might be devised to make a precise determination of structuredness in individual pieces of writing.

Is Structured Writing "Sufficiently Unprecedented" and Has It Attracted an "Enduring Group of Adherents"?

Kuhn suggests that the paradigm must show achievements that were "sufficiently unprecedented to attract an enduring group of adherents away from competing modes of scientific activity."

Structured writing also qualifies as a paradigm in that it was presented all at once as a complete methodology, rather than incremental additions. This is not to say that no improvements or additions have been made. The major structures and components of structured writing have endured over 25 years (Horn, 1993). To review, the components that appeared together all at once are:

- The invention and description of the information block as a new kind of basic unit of communication that permits the use of truly structured writing;

- The precise specification of different kinds of information blocks for specific purposes, and in particular the specification of approximately 40 information blocks that comprehend over 80 percent of the domain of relatively stable subject matter and the specification of other clusters of block types for memos, reports, proposals and other document types;

- The invention of a content analysis approach of question and information types that clusters different information blocks to guide question asking and ensure completeness in the initial analysis of the subject matter;

- The invention and description of an intermediate unit of structured writing, the information map, that permits easy and natural topic clustering;

- The development of a comprehensive and systematic set of criteria for labeling blocks and maps;

- The systematic specification of where graphics should be used and where text would be better;

- The development of easy-to-scan formats that exactly fit with the analysis methodology and categories to aid learning and reference.

We have already described how these different characteristics and components represented dramatic departures from the customary practice at the time structured writing was introduced. Even today, the conventional literary approach is still taught in most writing and instructional design courses, although many technical writing courses are adopting some kind of structured approach.

In recent years, the group of adherents to the structured writing paradigm has been growing by approximately 20,000 persons annually. The total number of users stands somewhere around 150,000 as this chapter is written. These are primarily people in industry: instructional designers, people who write documentation and reports, managers who write memos and proposals, developers who build online and hypertext applications. Many of these people are taught in the largest companies in the world by a licensing arrangement which qualifies instructors to teach within a company that has made a commitment to training all of the relevant staff in the methodology. A considerable group of researchers has focused attention on the structured writing methodology as well (see next section). Altogether, one can confidently note that structured writing has attracted an "enduring group of adherents."

Is Structured Writing Sufficiently "Open-Ended" for Research and Practical Application?

Kuhn's definition of paradigm requires that the theory be "sufficiently open-ended to leave all sorts of problems for the redefined group of practitioners to solve." Structured writing qualifies by this criteria in that it has produced a robust, ongoing stream of research and evaluation both in universities and in industry.

One test of this requirement is to ask if there have been major problems solved within the methodology after the initial paradigm was presented. There have been several. In 1977, a major extension of the methodology was made to the crafting of memos and reports. (Horn, 1977) Here the concept of the information block was kept intact, but a new domain was surveyed which resulted in the identification of fifteen basic types of reports and memoranda in industry and the identification of blocks that acted analogously to the key blocks in the domain of relatively stable structured subject matter. The formatting was modified and extended to incorporate requirements of the report and memo contexts. The idea of the map was modified in several ways while keeping its major purpose and the systematic criteria for the labeling of blocks was extended slightly.

A similar major extension was made in 1988 (Belerive & Horn, 1988) by extending the approach to the preparation of proposals. Most of the major extensions used for reports were reexamined and found appropriate for proposals. A few modifications were made in the basic methodology to adapt it to the proposal context in industry. Similarly, in 1989, the approach was applied to writing for computer-user documentation (Horn, 1989b).

The structured writing approach has been shown to be analogous to other types of structured methodologies and can incorporate them into its larger dominion. One such area is argumentation analysis (Horn, 1989a, Chapter 7), which enables analysts to examine the form of argumentation presented by an author or speaker at various levels of detail in a diagrammatic way.

Another dimension of open-endedness should also be noted. From the beginning, I made no effort to complete the methodology. I have always said that the taxonomy of 40 information blocks for relatively stable discourse covers 80 percent of the subject matter. Why only try to achieve 80 percent? Why not attempt to identify 99 percent of the information-block types? First, 80 percent coves a lot of territory. Since key blocks that identify the core information in a subject matter fall among this 80 percent, the most fundamental information is guaranteed to be there. Secondly, it would not be cost effective to try to specify all of the rest of the blocks. They tend to be idiosyncratic to particular subject matters and instructional contexts. Rather, I decided to go up a level of abstraction at that point and develop criteria for making new information blocks. What the writer does about the other 20 percent is to devise new block types. I used this open-endedness in my proposals to improve the writing of scientific reports and abstracts (Horn, 1989a, Chapter 8). Others have taken this approach in literally thousands of situations in writing industrial applications. This approach provides a continuous open-endedness to the methodology. I might also mention that, in a similar area, writers are encouraged to combine different kinds of maps to suit the documents they are creating.

A recent survey (Horn, 1992b) notes fifteen doctoral dissertations that focused on structured writing. One reviewer (Clark, 1993) was "surprised to see that most of the research done on the method has evaluated its effectiveness on learning outcomes, not retrieval speed or accuracy." (That was not surprising to me since the structured writing paradigm grew out of the instructional design context, not the conventional writing context.) Clark continued "Of the ten studies summarized [in detail in Horn, 1992b], seven focused on learning and only two on retrieval time. In the learning studies, most compared the effectiveness of [structured writing] with 'conventional' materials on test scores. In two of the studies time was controlled; in the others learners studied as long as they wished." Figure 5 shows the results of the studies summarized in Horn, 1992b. Clark concluded "It seems that there is fertile research soil to till with future studies that focus on speed and accuracy of retrieval from large reference documents prepared using various layouts. More cognitively-oriented research that includes protocol analysis while learners read would not only help to document effectiveness, but also would gain insight into the reasons for the effectiveness. Certainly reduction of cognitive loading would be one reasonable hypothesis to explore in comparing structured to conventional reference materials."

Many companies have now trained thousands of people in the structured writing methodology. More studies are needed to examine the impact of implementing the method throughout an entire organization. One such study (Holding, 1985) studied the impact of training 180 managers in structured writing seminars at Pacific Telephone. She looked at the results on both the writers and the readers (by interviewing their supervisors). On the writer side, there were decreases in writing time and increases in clarity, as well as improvement in analytical and organizing skills; which is not surprising, given the extreme focus on analysis and organization in structured writing courses. All of the supervisors surveyed stated that the amount of time it takes to read a document, using the method taught in the structured writing course, decreased. The mean decrease in the amount of time was 32 percent. Other advantages the supervisors reported included faster approval (of reports and memos) due to the methods used in the course (83%). The supervisors and writers agreed that writers wrote their required letters and memos before deadlines. Further research along these lines would prove useful to other implementers.

		Measured by Number Right or Errors	Time to Do Task	Supervisor Appraisal
Initial Learning	**Immediate Recall**	Stelnicki: 32% higher scores on facts; 41% higher on concepts Soyster: 13% higher scores Romiszowski: 10% higher scores Burrell: 53–59% better on tests Webber: 38% higher scores on the criterion tests	Romiszowski: 10% faster Webber: IM version was 50% faster	
	Long Term Recall	Soyster: No difference (attributed to motivation factors by the researcher) Webber: IM version provided 85% or better accuracy when starting on the job.		
Retrieval	**Had Previously Used the Materials**	Jonassen & Falk: 33% higher scores with IM	Baker: IM had 12–21% better reading speed	
	Had Never Seen the Materials Before	Schaffer: 54.5% fewer errors with IM		
On-the-Job Application			Holding: Supervisors reported 32% decrease in reading time for persons receiving reports written in IM. 84% of IM users report increase in writing speed after taking course.	Holding: Supervisors reported 100% of those who received training had productivity increase. Course was rated: • very effective 63% • effective 30% • somewhat effective 7%

> **Key:**
> IM = Information Mapping's method. Names are names of principal investigators on specific research studies.

This Figure is reproduced with permission from the Lexington Institute, publishers of *How High Can It Fly? Examining the Evidence on Information Mapping's Method of High-Performance Communication* by Robert E. Horn.

Figure 5.   Results of major research studies on structured writing.

The structured writing field has generally had to rely on research from cognitive psychology, educational research, and other fields for the close examination of its components and writing guidelines. There is a rich vein of potential research in this area as well. I have noted elsewhere (Horn, 1992a) that, while research in naturalistic settings such as jobs, classrooms and laboratories are important, those settings may be the "wrong place to attempt to measure certain effects." I urged the field to devote more research time in the next phase of research to isolating variables. It would, for example, be helpful to know how much of the dimensions of "structure" contribute to the overall effects.

There is virtually unanimous agreement that much of what we read will be stored on computers in the next ten years. That conversion to online access and reading is proceeding steadily and is expected to accelerate. The availability of hypertext functions provides many opportunities for just-in-time instruction, but also provides managers with a panoply of problems (see Horn, 1989a, Chapter 2 for a survey of these problems). I have claimed that structured writing will help solve a good many of these problems (Horn, 1989a, Chapter 5).

It would seem that structured writing easily meets Kuhn's criterion of being "sufficiently open-ended to leave all sorts of problems for the redefined group of practitioners to solve" while at the same time providing practical solutions to today's busy instructional design practitioners.

References

Belerive, P., & Horn, R. E. (1988). *Unbeatable proposals for the strategic advantage.* Waltham, MA: Information Mapping, Inc.

Clark, R. (1993, Feb.). Review of *How high can it fly* by R. E. Horn. *Performance and Instruction,* 43–44.

Fleming, M., & Levie, W. H. (1978). *Instructional message design: Principles from the behavioral sciences.* Englewood Cliffs, NJ: Educational Technology Publications.

Fleming, M., & Levie, W. H. (Eds.). (1993). *Instructional message design principles from the behavioral and cognitive sciences* (2nd ed.). Englewood Cliffs, NJ: Educational Technology Publications.

Halliday, M. A. K., & Hasan, R. (1976). *Cohesion in English.* London: Longman

Holding, E. (1985). *An evaluation of the effectiveness of the Information Mapping Methodology and "Effective Reports, Proposals and Memos."* San Francisco, CA: Pacific Bell.

Horn, R.E. (1966). A terminal behavior locator system. *Programmed Learning, 1.*

Horn, R. E. (1977). *Writing management reports.* Waltham, MA: Information Mapping, Inc.

Horn, R. E. (1986). *Engineering of documentation–The Information Mapping approach* (available from Information Mapping, Inc.)

Horn, R. E. (1989a). *Mapping hypertext: Analysis, linkage, and display of knowledge for the next generation of on-line text and graphics.* Lexington MA: The Lexington Institute.

Horn, R. E. (1989b). *Strategies for developing high-performance documentation.* Waltham, MA: Information Mapping, Inc.

Horn, R. E. (1992a). Clarifying two controversies about Information Mapping's method. *Educational and Training Technology International, 2*(29), 109–117

Horn, R. E. (1992b). *How high can it fly? Examining the evidence on Information Mapping's method of high performance communication.* Lexington, MA: The Lexington Institute.

Horn, R. E. (1992c, Jan.). How to get little or no effect and make no significant difference. *Performance and Instruction,* 29–32.

Horn, R. E. (1992d). Commentary on *The Nurnberg Funnel. Journal of Computer Documentation, 16*(1), 3–10.

Horn, R. E. (1993, Feb.). Structured writing at twenty five. *Performance and Instruction,* 11–17

Horn, R. E., Nicol, E., Kleinman, J., & Grace, M. (1969). *Information Mapping for learning and reference.* Cambridge: I.R.I. (A.F. Systems Command Report ESD-TR-69-296).

Horn, R. E., Nicol, E., & Roman, R. *et al.* (1971). *Information Mapping for computer-learning and reference.* Cambridge: I.R.I. (A.F. Systems Command Report ESD-TR-71-165).

Kuhn, T. S. (1962, 1970). *The structure of scientific revolutions.* Chicago: University of Chicago Press.

Masterman, M. (1970). The nature of a paradigm. In I. Lakatos & A. Musgrave (Eds.), *Criticism and the growth of knowledge.* Cambridge: Cambridge University Press.

Merrill, M. D., & Tennyson, R. D. (1977). *Teaching concepts: An instructional design guide.* Englewood Cliffs, NJ: Educational Technology Publications.

Merrill, M. D., Tennyson, R. D., & Posey, L. (1992). *Teaching concepts: An instructional design guide* (2nd ed.). Englewood Cliffs, NJ: Educational Technology Publications.

Miller, G. A. (1956, March). The magic number seven, plus or minus two: Some limits on our capacity for processing information. *Psych. Rev., 63*(1), 81–96.

Walker, J. H. (1988). The role of modularity in document authoring systems. In *ACM Conference on Document Processing Systems,* Santa Fe, NM, December 5–9.

40

Analysis Versus Intuition in the Classroom: A Model of Expertise and the Role of Computers in Achieving It

Hubert L. Dreyfus and Stuart E. Dreyfus
University of California, Berkeley

Introduction

To determine the proper place of computers in the classroom, a theory of learning is required. If learning consists in abstracting more and more sophisticated rules from examples, as thinkers from Socrates to Kant to Piaget have held, then the computer could serve both as tutor and tutee. As tutor, the computer would be programmed with the rules describing a particular domain, such as physics, and the rules for coaching that the teacher has acquired from experience. If these rules were complete enough, the computer could do the job of the teacher with the advantage that each student could progress at whatever speed was commensurate with his or her interest and ability. As tutee, the computer could be programmed by the student to produce geometrical figures or to simulate the movement of a pendulum, etc. In thus programming the computer, the student would learn the rules governing the phenomena in some particular domain while also acquiring the capacity to think procedurally like a computer.

The above attractive proposals assume that the mind is a computer with a program, a view now widely accepted in philosophy and psychology. This same information-processing model of the mind has led to high hopes but serious disappointments in the field of artificial intelligence (Dreyfus, 1992). No one yet has produced generally accepted evidence as to how the brain or mind works when it learns and thinks; therefore, before accepting this assumption uncritically, we had best begin by looking at the phenomenon itself.

The phenomenon of learning a new skill has been neglected by the philosophical tradition because philosophical reflection only takes place when everyday successful, skillful coping has broken down, and the agent is presented with some obstacle or problem. Then thinking strategically or procedurally is in order. The traditional mode of reflection has passed over the way we acquire and activate our everyday skills. If we describe the stages adults go through in acquiring a new skill, whether it be a bodily skill such as driving or an intellectual skill such as chess playing, we find five distinguishable stages.

Stage 1: Novice

Normally, the instruction process begins with the instructor decomposing the task environment into context-free features which the beginner can recognize without benefit of experience. The beginner is then given rules for determining actions on the basis of these features, like a computer following a program.

For purposes of illustration, let us consider two variations: a bodily or motor skill and an intellectual skill. The student automobile driver learns to recognize such interpretation-free features as speed (indicated by his speedometer) and distance (as estimated by a previously acquired skill). Safe following distances are defined in terms of speed; conditions that allow safe entry into traffic are defined in terms of speed and distance of oncoming traffic; timing of gear shifts is specified in terms of speed, etc. These rules ignore context. They do not refer to traffic density or anticipated stops.

The novice chess player learns a numerical value for each type of piece regardless of its position, and the rule: "Always exchange if the total value of pieces captured exceeds the value of pieces lost." He also learns that when no advantageous exchanges can be found, center control should be sought, and he is given a rule defining center squares and one for calculating extent of control. Most beginners are notoriously slow players, as they attempt to remember all these rules and their priorities.

Stage 2: Advanced Beginner

As the novice gains experience actually coping with real situations, he begins to note, or an instructor points out, perspicuous examples of meaningful additional components of the situation. After seeing a sufficient number of examples, the student learns to recognize them. Instructional maxims now can refer to these new situational aspects recognized on the basis of experience, as well as to the objectively defined non-situational features recognizable by the novice.

The advanced beginner driver uses (situational) engine sounds as well as (nonsituational) speed in his gear-shifting rules. He shifts when the motor sounds like it is straining. He learns to observe the demeanor as well as position and velocity of pedestrians or other drivers. He can, for example, distinguish the behavior of the distracted or drunken driver from that of the impatient but alert one. No number of words can take the place of a few choice examples in learning these distinctions. Engine sounds cannot be adequately captured by words, and no list of objective facts enables one to predict the behavior of a pedestrian in a crosswalk as well as can the driver who has observed many pedestrians crossing streets under a variety of conditions.

With experience, the chess beginner learns to recognize over-extended positions and how to avoid them. Similarly, he begins to recognize such situational aspects of positions as a weakened king's side or a strong pawn structure despite the lack of precise and universally valid definitional rules.

Stage 3: Competence

With increasing experience, the number of features and aspects to be taken into account becomes overwhelming. To cope with this information explosion, the performer learns, or is taught, to adopt a hierarchical view of decision-making. By first choosing a plan, goal or perspective which organizes the situation, and by then examining only the small set of features and aspects that he has learned are relevant to that plan, the performer can simplify and improve his performance.

A competent driver leaving the freeway on a curved off-ramp may, after taking into account speed, surface condition, criticality of time, etc., decide he is going too fast. He then has to decide whether to let up on the accelerator, remove his foot altogether, or step on the brake. He is relieved when he gets through the curve without mishap, and is shaken if he begins to go into a skid.

The class A chess player, here classed as competent, may decide, after studying a position, that his opponent has weakened his king's defenses so that an attack against the enemy king is a viable goal. If the attack is chosen, features involving weaknesses in his own position created by the attack are ignored as are losses of pieces inessential to the attack. Removal of pieces defending the enemy king becomes salient. Successful plans induce euphoria and mistakes are felt in the pit of the stomach.

In both of these cases, we find a common pattern: detached planning, conscious assessment of elements that are salient with respect to the plan, and analytical rule-guided choice of action, followed by an emotionally involved experience of the outcome.

The experience is emotional because choosing a plan, a goal or a perspective is no simple matter for the competent performer. Nobody gives him any rules for how to choose a perspective, so he has to make up various rules which he then adopts or discards in various situations depending on how they work out. This procedure is frustrating, however, since each rule works on some occasions and fails on others, and no set of objective features and aspects correlates strongly with these successes and failures. Nonetheless, the choice is unavoidable. While the advanced beginner can hold off using a particular situational aspect until a sufficient number of examples makes identification reliable, to perform competently requires choosing an organizing goal or perspective. Furthermore, the choice of perspective crucially affects behavior in a way that one particular aspect rarely does.

This combination of necessity and uncertainty introduces an important new type of relationship between the performer and his environment. The novice and the advanced beginner, applying rules and maxims, feel little or no responsibility for the outcome of their acts. If they have made no mistakes, an unfortunate outcome is viewed as the result of inadequately specified elements or rules. The competent performer, on the other hand, after wrestling with the question of a choice of perspective or goal, feels responsible for, and thus emotionally involved in, the result of his choice. An outcome that is clearly successful is deeply satisfying and leaves a vivid memory of the situation encountered as seen from the goal or perspective finally chosen. Disasters, likewise, are not easily forgotten.

Remembered whole situations differ in one important respect from remembered aspects. The mental image of an aspect is flat; no parts stand out as salient. A whole situation, on the other hand, since it is the result of a chosen plan or perspective, has a "three dimensional" quality. Certain elements stand out as more or less important with respect to the plan, while other irrelevant elements are forgotten. Moreover, the competent performer, gripped by the situation that his decision has produced, experiences the situation not only in terms of foreground and background elements but also in terms of opportunity, risk, expectation, threat, etc. As we shall soon see, if he stops reflecting on problematic situations as a detached observer, and stops thinking of himself as a computer following better and better rules, these gripping, holistic experiences become the basis of the competent performer's next advance in skill.

Stage 4: Proficiency

Considerable experience at the level of competency sets the stage for yet further skill enhancement. Having experienced many situations, having chosen plans in each, and having obtained vivid, involved demonstrations of the adequacy or inadequacy of the plans, the performer involved in the world of the skill "notices," or "is struck by," a certain plan, goal or perspective. No longer is the spell of involvement broken by detached conscious planning.

Since there are generally far fewer "ways of seeing" than "ways of acting," after understanding without conscious effort what is going on, the proficient performer will still have to think about what to do. During this thinking, elements that present themselves as salient are assessed and combined by rule to produce decisions about how best to manipulate the environment.

On the basis of prior experience, a proficient driver approaching a curve on a rainy day may sense that he is traveling too fast. Then, on the basis of such salient elements as visibility, angle of road bank, criticalness of time, etc. (the factors used by the competent driver to decide that he is speeding), he decides whether to take his foot off the gas or to step on the brake.

The proficient chess player, who is classed as a master, can recognize a large repertoire of types of positions. Recognizing almost immediately and without conscious effort the sense of a position, he sets about calculating the move that best achieves his goal. He may, for example, know that he should attack, but he must deliberate about how best to do so.

Stage 5: Expertise

The proficient performer, immersed in the world of his skillful activity, sees what needs to be done, but decides how to do it. With enough experience with a variety of situations, all seen from the same perspective but requiring different tactical decisions, the proficient performer gradually decomposes this class of situations into subclasses, each of which share the same decision, single action, or tactic. This allows the immediate intuitive response to each situation, which is characteristic of expertise.

The expert chess player, classed as an international master or grandmaster, in most situations experiences a compelling sense of the issue and the best move. Excellent chess players can play at the rate of 5–10 seconds a move and even faster without any serious degradation in performance. At this speed they must depend almost entirely upon intuition and hardly at all upon analysis and comparison of alternatives. We performed an experiment in which an international master, Julio Kaplan, was required rapidly to add numbers presented to him audibly at the rate of about one number per second, while at the same time playing five-seconds-a-move chess against a slightly weaker, but master level, player. Even with his analytical mind completely occupied by adding numbers, Kaplan more than held his own against the master in a series of games. Deprived of the time necessary to see problems or construct plans, Kaplan still produced fluid and coordinated play.

Kaplan's performance seems somewhat less amazing when one realizes that a chess position is as meaningful, interesting, and important to a professional chess player as a face in a receiving line is to a professional politician. Almost anyone can add numbers and simultaneously recognize and respond to faces, even though each face will never exactly match the same face seen previously; and politicians can recognize thousands of faces, just as Julio Kaplan can recognize thousands of chess positions similar to ones previously encountered. The number of classes of discriminable situations, built up on the basis of experience, must be immense. It has been estimated that a master chess player can distinguish roughly 50,000 types of positions.

It seems that a beginner makes inferences using rules and facts just like a heuristically programmed computer, but that with talent and a great deal of involved experience, the beginner develops into an expert who intuitively sees what to do without applying rules. The philosophical tradition has given an accurate description of the beginner and of the expert facing an unfamiliar situation, but normally an expert does not reason. He does not solve problems. He does what normally works and, of course, it normally works.

Note that this description of skill acquisition reverses the traditional view, since we see the learner moving, not from the concrete to the abstract, but from abstract rules to a repertoire of concrete cases.

This model of skill acquisition has important implications for the use of the computer in education. To begin with, the best, indeed the only, proper use of the computer is not as a coach or as a tutee, but as a drill sergeant for beginners. Beginners need drill and practice to improve in any domain. Whereas computers can acquire a rule in one fell swoop, human beginners need repetition for three reasons. They need to fix the rule in their memory. They need to learn to apply it to a variety of different cases. They need to learn that context effects are irrelevant. Such practice, in which the beginner is confronted by a variety of simplified cases, is easily and attractively provided by the computer.

If one tries to use the computer as tutor beyond the beginning level to produce improved performance by teaching more complex rules, the computer will have the counterproductive effect of keeping the learner on the early level of analysis and preventing the natural development of a repertoire of typical aspects and typical whole situations which are required to produce intuitive expertise.

Likewise, the computer can serve successfully as tutee for a beginning student who can thus be led to discover the rules of geometry or grammar. However, the plan of educators like Seymour Papert (1980), who wish to use the computer to get students to think procedurally like a computer in everyday domains of knowledge, even sports, will either fail, as the natural development of intuition takes place, or, if the teacher succeeds in forcing the student to think procedurally, the result will be an inferior level of skill in which every new situation is confronted as a problem. In neither case will the student achieve the sort of intuitive expertise we acquire in any domain in which we have sufficient talent and experience.

One might hope that one could get around these problems by programming a computer coach who, like an experienced teacher, would know how to give hints, point out typical aspects, answer questions, and motivate the sort of practice which will produce expertise. This hope is based upon the idea that one can use artificial intelligence (AI) techniques to give the computer the rules that underlie the skill of being a good teacher. But if the above five-stage model of skill acquisition is correct it applies to the teacher's knowledge and skills too, so therefore one would expect the AI approach to computer-aided instruction (CAI) to fail. Indeed, after early optimism thirty years ago, when Patrick Suppes (1966), one of the leading American theorists, predicted that, thanks to the computer, by the turn of the century each student would have "the personal services of a tutor as well informed and responsive as Aristotle," CAI has run into unexpected and serious trouble. Almost everyone, including Suppes, now agrees that before computers can be successful tutors they need to be able to understand continuous speech, carry on a conversation with the learner, represent the common-sense knowledge that is used by the learner in mastering any domain, and abstract and use rules for coaching. Research in each of these areas has reached an impasse—the very impasse that one would expect if all these abilities depend upon an expert in each of these skills who has accumulated a large repertoire of prototypical situations, rather than a set of rules operating upon objective features abstracted from the environment.

Even if the mind at some deep level does operate by applying rules to features, a view supported by the philosophical tradition but for which there is not a shred of neurological or psychological evidence, this should not be of any comfort to the workers in CAI. For if the expert teacher is unaware of such rules he cannot give them to the programmer who would like to capture the teacher's expertise in a computer program. Moreover, if the learner, to progress, must abandon analysis and act intuitively, as experiments on concept acquisition suggest, then teaching the child to approach all problems procedurally will stand in the way of skill acquisition even if skill acquisition consists in acquiring unconscious rules.

On the positive side, computers can give children the opportunity to take an active and imaginative part in the study of domains which are otherwise difficult or impossible to bring into the classroom: evolution is too slow, nuclear reactions too fast, probability too counter-intuitive, factories too big, much of chemistry too dangerous.

If a teacher is explaining how money grows at a given interest rate, for example, the computer can simulate the growth, compressing each year into a second, and graphically exhibit the outcome. By changing a number the student can vary the interest rate and immediately observe the effect. Simulations of biological and environmental systems have also been developed. In the future such simulations will surely become more common, helping students of all ages in all disciplines develop their intuition.

Along with simulation, another promising use of computers is in the creation of learning environments. Here, rather than the computer teaching some particular goal or skill, it serves as a toolkit for coping with events in a micro-world. In the course of using the tools, the user figures out how to solve problems in the micro-world and so learns the conceptual structure of the domain.

There is no doubt that a child playfully interacting with such software learns the conceptual structure of the game domain. It seems clear too that the child acquires problem-solving skills such as the ability to break down a problem and solve it step-by-step and to formulate strategies that can be used to organize and chose among the available step-by-step procedures. Such a game would presumably take a beginner as far as competence.

Unfortunately, game designers seem to think that mastery consists in grasping more and more complex conceptual domains by means of more and more sophisticated problem-solving skills. This leads to games in which the learner solves progressively more difficult problems, where "more difficult" means problems which require going beyond the previous solution. This sort of game may well lead to ever-increasing competence, but it inhibits crossing the line to intuitive expertise, since as soon as one begins to perfect a skill one finds oneself back in the role of a beginner.

A more intuitive learning game would begin like a problem-solving game, requiring that the learner discover a procedure for arriving at the solution to a problem. This would enable the student to arrive at competence while fostering the sort of involvement required for going further. But then, once the learner had the procedure well in hand, the program would encourage the student to forget the procedure and leap directly to the solution. Finally, the program would lead the learner to jump intuitively to the solution in situations that were similar to the one with which he or she was already familiar.

If we want our educational system to produce experts and our society to have the benefit of human expertise in all areas of life, we must resist the computer model of the mind, and the concomitant tendency to try to use computers in education beyond the beginning level. Computers can and should be used only to provide the drill and practice, by means of which human beings take the first step in their progress from analytic problem solving to intuitive action, and as interactive models of domains in order to help students develop their intuitions.

References

Dreyfus, H. L. (1992). *What computers [still] can't do* (3rd ed.). Cambridge, MA: MIT Press.
Papert, S. (1980). *Mindstorms: Children, computers, and powerful ideas.* New York: Basic Books.
Suppes, P. (1966). The uses of computers in education. *Scientific American, 215*(3).

41

Hypermedia: Harbinger of a New Instructional Paradigm?

Terry K. Borsook
All About Health, Inc.
Toronto, Ontario

Imagine a huge pile of red bricks on the ground. Not very impressive. But return in a few months when those bricks have been summoned together to form a house. The "meaning" of those bricks, literally, the building blocks of the house, depends entirely on how they are connected. They can just as easily be assembled into a warehouse, a retail store or a house of worship. The bricks remain identical in each case. Only the arrangement changes. But that, as we will see, makes all the difference.

Why should we think any differently of knowledge? Why should we confine ourselves to a structure that some architect has planned? Why not avail ourselves of the opportunity to rearrange the bricks of knowledge in a way that suits our own purpose, needs, background, existing knowledge, and desired perspective? If meaning comes from how elements are connected and if traditional media discourage the rearrangement of those connections, then we have been handicapped all along. If you can appreciate the advantage of being able to form your own structures, then you have a glimpse at the remarkable potential of *hypermedia*.

Shifting Paradigms

Imagine a new accessibility and excitement that can unseat the video narcosis that now sits on our land like a fog. Imagine a new libertarian literature with alternative explanations so anyone can choose the pathway or approach that best suits him or her; with ideas accessible and interesting to everyone, so that a new richness and freedom can come to the human experience; imagine a rebirth of literacy. (Nelson, 1987; p. 1/4)

Despite its proclamation as a revolutionary information and learning tool, as a weapon believed to be a bastion of democracy and freedom, hypermedia has always seemed like a solution in search of a problem—or perhaps a solution whose problems might outweigh its benefits. Yet it has an intuitive appeal that persists. It seems to be one of those things that we *know* is right because it just *feels* right. It is this intuitive appeal, recently proposed cognitive learning theories, and dizzying progress in technology that have synergistically fueled the surge in hypermedia research and development.

When the CD-ROM first became available, people were not quite sure what to do with the immense storage capacity it offered. The CD-ROM's acceptance was agonizingly slow, especially when held up against the breakneck advancements in other areas of computers and electronics. The problem was that there were no enticing titles for consumers. Developers were thinking in terms of *more*. The white pages for the entire country, the full text of encyclopedias, research indexes and abstracts, to name a few of the early entrants, were not enough to interest consumers. A completely new way of looking at how to use the capacity of the CD-ROM was needed. It was only once people realized that the vast storage capacity of a CD-ROM offered entirely *new* possibilities did it flourish. A paradigm shift occurred almost overnight.

What Exactly Is Hypermedia?

Hypertext (and its multimedia cousin, hypermedia) is not a thing you can hold in your hand or a particular software product. It is a technique for accessing information with a computer. To best appreciate what makes hypermedia so special, it is important to understand it in relation to other media and methods. Some media are more interactive than others—that is, they permit more control over sequencing. Consider how you are reading this chapter. Chances are, you started at the beginning and, more or less, read straight through. You may have skipped some parts, re-read others, jumped directly to the last paragraph to read the conclusion, or skimmed it, reading only a few words here or there. Books are not, regardless of widely held claims to the contrary, completely linear. They *do* permit a degree of interactivity. Now, consider a videotape. About the only thing you can do with a videotape is play it. True, you could start playing it from any point and watch a segment for however long you wish, but the awkwardness of moving around and finding a specific place on a tape precludes much in the way of interactivity.

Now, let us look at hypermedia. A hypermedia system permits a great deal more flexibility than does videotape. It allows one to access any information in whatever manner and in whatever sequence one wishes. That is, with hypermedia, information access is completely interactive (nonsequential) and is dictated by the needs of the individual, not by a sequence predetermined by an author. Of course, this large degree of learner control is not an advantage in all situations. For example, lower ability learners have a difficult time in such a free-form environment, are often confused, and score less well on performance tests than do similar lower ability students in more structured instructional environments. So hypermedia is not ideal for everyone all the time.

But all of this is rather abstract. We turn now to an analogy that will, it is hoped, explicate the nature and potential of hypermedia so that you will be able to make informed training and performance enhancement decisions. Books, videotapes, and other essentially linear media can be considered analogous to a subway train. You can travel forward and backward (flip the pages ahead and back; fast forward and rewind); you can get on and off at any point (using the table of contents and index; fast forward to a particular point on the tape), and you can travel for however many stops you wish (stop reading after the first chapter; stop tape after part II). No one would dispute the value of a train—it can be very effective and efficient in taking us where we need to go. But if you wish to explore and learn about a city, the subway train is absolutely inadequate. What you need is a car.

Traveling in a car along Main Street, if you see something interesting over to the right, you turn down a side road to explore. While on that side road, you may encounter some interesting shops that you also would like to explore. After leaving the shops, you continue down the road and encounter a cobblestone street with interesting old buildings that you think would be fun to investigate, so you turn onto that street. After a while, you decide that you would like to return to Main Street so that you can travel to a different part of town. The flexibility you have in a car—to go where you want to go, stay for as long as you want to stay, and visit places in whatever order you want to visit them—is what hypermedia is all about.

It is this level of exploratory freedom that is at the heart of hypermedia. The truth is that we are only beginning to understand the opportunities of hypermedia. But that does not mean that we need to wait until all the research has been done and we know everything there is to know about it before we can start using it. Following is a closer examination of the unique advantages of hypermedia, along with a consideration of its limitations.

Terminology

What exactly is hypermedia anyway? There is often some confusion regarding exactly what hypermedia is and what it is not. Five terms—interactive video, interactive multimedia, multimedia, hypertext, and hypermedia—are often used interchangeably, yet represent distinct ideas.

Interactive video (IV) combines the "interactive capability of the computer with the unique properties of video presentations" (Chen, 1990, p. 6). The typical interactive video arrangement includes a videodisc player connected to a personal computer, with the computer controlling the presentation of the video in response to interaction with the user. IV refers specifically to the *computer-videodisc player* combination. IV is a subset of interactive multimedia.

Interactive multimedia refers to any computer-based configuration in which some combination of video, computer-generated graphics, sound, animation, and voice is used (see Ambron & Hooper, 1988, 1990; Stefanac & Weiman, 1990). These multimedia elements can either come from external sources, such as videodisc players, VCRs, or audio equipment, or they can be generated internally, such as when video, sound, or graphics are stored digitally on a hard disk or optical disk. What gives interactive multimedia its interactivity is the computer. Without the computer, the result is simply multimedia.

Of all the five terms, *multimedia* is the most difficult to define. The term has been used to refer to everything from slide shows to extravaganzas complete with multiple monitors, animation, video, sound, and text. It would be easy to remember that multimedia stands for multiple media except that the term media can mean many things. "Media" can include slides, audiotapes, videotapes, videoconferencing, animation, films, music, voice, paper, or even someone shouting through a megaphone. Media can be instructional or not; it can be interactive or not; and it can be computer-based or not. While the focus of interactive video, interactive multimedia, and multimedia is on the technology, the focus of *hypermedia* is on method—a method that so happens to be most suited to the computer.

An understanding of hypermedia depends on an understanding of its related term, *hypertext*. Quite different from the continuous flow of text inherent in traditional presentations of information, hypertext breaks up the flow into modules. "By modularizing information, users have the option of selecting the next module, which may include an elaboration or example of the present idea or an entirely new idea to be compared with the previous one" (Jonassen, 1989, p. 7).

Hypertext is often described as a computer-based method of nonsequential reading and writing—a technique with which chunks, or *nodes*, of information can be arranged and rearranged according to an individual's needs, previous knowledge, curiosities, etc. (Begoray, 1990; Conklin, 1987; van Dam, 1988; Hall *et al.*, 1990; Jonassen, 1989). Hypertext not only *presents* information as a book does, it also *represents* information. As discussed earlier in this paper, meaning is derived from the arrangement of information. The implication here is two-fold:

1. Meaning is not static, but rather, dynamic—changing as the arrangement of nodes changes.
2. Meaning resides in the relationships between the nodes, not in the nodes themselves. This insight is intriguing and has exciting implications for learning.

According to Kearsley (1988), hypertext should improve learning by focusing attention on the relationships between ideas rather than on isolated facts. Associations provided by the links in hypertext should facilitate retrieval, concept formation, and comprehension.

Hypermedia, a term often used interchangeably with hypertext, is simply multimedia hypertext (Nielsen, 1990). That is, hyper*media* extends hyper*text* to include the full range of information forms: sound, graphics, animation, video, music, as well as text. As hypermedia is the more inclusive of the two terms, this chapter will use the term hypermedia as a catch-all term referring to both text-based and multiple media-based systems.

Why Use Hypermedia?

Information Can Be Layered

Depending on their level of knowledge, learners can obtain information in however much detail they desire. They could simply read through a description of a surgical procedure or they could ask for definitions of terms, diagrams of various anatomical regions, and a full-motion video of the procedure being performed by a master surgeon. Linear media, such as books and videotapes, force the author to decide on a single presentation of the information for an assumed audience with an assumed level of knowledge and experience (see Carr, 1988; Raybould, 1990).

It is as if users could fly above the landscape of information contained in a hypermedia system and could swoop down to obtain a closer, more detailed view of the detail and intricacies, or fly higher to see the bigger picture—how everything fits and functions together. Hypermedia allows users to assume whatever level (altitude) is needed or desired as they traverse the information space.

The potential of this unique characteristic of hypermedia becomes evident when we consider the dilemma faced by a designer of an exhibit on nutrition. She is forced to make some very difficult decisions regarding the level and type of information that she will provide visitors. If she keeps the information very simple and fundamental, visitors who have a basic knowledge of nutrition will find the information offered at the exhibit uninteresting. If, on the other hand, she makes it too technical and detailed, she risks losing a good deal of the population who know very little about the subject. So she is forced to compromise. She must walk a precarious balance that mixes enough detail to keep her more knowledgeable patrons interested, while not overwhelming others who have little or no previous knowledge in the area.

Such a system is designed to fit the masses, all the individuals who possess some "average" level of knowledge, are of "average" age, and who have "average" needs and interests.

Hypermedia offers a way out of this conundrum of the average. Each presentation is tailored to the uniqueness of each individual who walks up to the system. This individualizing or layering of information communication is ideally suited to the talents of hypermedia. The whole issue of "beating the average" will be discussed further later in the chapter.

Information Can Be Re-used

The advantage just described suggests that nodes may be re-used, freeing authors from having to constantly re-invent the wheel. Common libraries of glossaries, diagrams, animations, videos and sounds could be made available on which any hypermedia document may draw. Authors merely need to draw links between their own material and these common library items. Such a system would save authors a significant amount of work and would thus decrease authoring time (see Bevilacqua, 1989). Authors benefit since they are free to focus on the original contributions of their writing. Readers benefit since they have quick and easy access to a wide assortment of high quality support material which they may choose to view as they wish.

Learners See Only Relevant Information

It has been argued that the key to efficient and effective learning may be the ability to pick out only the relevant information from books and other sources, without getting swamped by extraneous information. Hypertext is the ideal technology for zeroing in on just the information one needs (Raybould, 1990).

Hypermedia can ameliorate *information anxiety*, a term coined by Richard Saul Wurman (Wurman, 1989), that refers to the feeling of being surrounded and overwhelmed by information. People often suffer from information anxiety when faced with the daunting task of wading through multiple thick books, watching entire videos, listening to audiotapes and attending lectures, all just to obtain that part of the information one needs.

Hypermedia Provides a Useful Interface for Accessing Information in Many Different Forms

Hypermedia is one of the best methods available for giving learners a way to access different types of information in different ways. One hypermedia-based anatomy system allows learners to explore the anatomy of the foot by presenting information in a wide variety of ways (A.D.A.M.). For example, learners can click on any part of the foot to obtain a pop-up label of what that structure is; they can slide a control bar to "peel" back successive layers of the foot; they can click on the name of a surgical procedure and a diagram of the relevant area of the foot will pop up and the appropriate parts will be highlighted; clicking somewhere else can call up a full-motion video showing a surgeon performing the procedure.

A picture of a human heart can be accompanied by a motion video segment depicting blood flow through the ventricles, detailed drawings, textual explanations of anatomy and processes, and heartbeat sounds. All of this information can be immediately available at the click of an on-screen button. The quick and easy retrieval of related information in its different forms helps to build stronger relationships between these pieces of information than would result if one had to stop reading a textbook, retrieve a videotape, then an audiotape, then a carousel of slides, etc. Hypermedia offers an ideal environment in which to exploit the benefits of quick and easy access to information in all its myriad forms.

Hypermedia Offers a Way to See Issues, Ideas, and Concepts from Several Perspectives

Whether one is studying classical literature or cardiology, complex concepts are best learned when students can approach the material from different perspectives. Indeed, recent research (Spiro & Jehng, 1990; Spiro *et al.*, 1991) shows that in order to learn complex material, learners must see that same material at different times, in different situations, for different purposes and from different conceptual perspectives. Hypertext is ideally suited for such a purpose.

When I was a young boy, I was fascinated by the globe I got as a birthday present. I enjoyed looking at where my own country was in relation to the rest of the world and I marveled at all the mysterious foreign lands that existed on the other side of the globe from my own. But I was puzzled. North America, where I was located, was on the *side* of the planet, or so it seemed. If it was on the side, then standing perpendicular to the ground, I should be able to look down and see the sky!

I came to realize that the reason for my puzzlement derived from my assumption that there was an up and down in space and that the proper way to view Earth was the way all table-top globes are oriented, with North America above South America (relative to the table-top, that is). As soon as I changed my perspective, I was freed to view North America as being just as easily "on top" as on the "side" of the planet, and a whole new understanding emerged. It appears, then, that we can change the universe (at least what we think we know about the universe) by changing our perspective.

We need not think on a wordly scale in order to appreciate the power of perspective. Say that you have never seen an orange before and you slice it in half. You see something like the illustration below:

If you were to stop there, you would not realize that had you sliced it cross-wise, you would see something quite different:

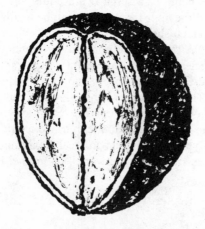

Most would agree that having the opportunity to view the orange from two perspectives lends a better understanding of oranges. If it takes multiple slices to understand an orange, imagine how many "slices" it would take to understand the human cardiovascular system, or the economy, or the ecology? And yet when we read books or watch videos to learn about something, we get an impoverished view of the world. Linear media that require individuals to read/view information in more or less one sequence simply cannot support the exploration of phenomena from multiple perspectives.

What's a Dalmatian? A canine? A pet? A spotted animal? A mammal? A fireman's companion? A Dalmatian can be associated with a myriad of things. Now try to imagine the best way to classify a mouse. As a member of a group of animals called rodents? As a strange pet to have? As an undesirable house companion? Mice, like Dalmatians and everything else in the world, can fall under any number of classification schemes.

The meaning we ascribe to a concept depends entirely on which classification scheme or set of associations is accessed. This access depends on the situation (i.e., context). Indeed, to the age-old question, "What is the meaning of life?," the answer is probably, "It depends." It depends on how we look at things, when we look at them, and even to what things we choose to attend. In other words, it depends upon how we construct our personal reality—how we perceive the world and even what we choose to include in our view of it. How we perceive the world and what we choose to include are not themselves static. They change with the context.

So what does a childhood misunderstanding have to do with knowledge and learning? What does an astronomical curiosity have to do with more day-to-day concerns of earthbound individuals and organizations? A lot! To understand why, we must first explore the differences and similarities between information, knowledge, and understanding. Of the three, information is the only one that does not need the human mind to exist. Information is "out there" in the world. Information is the building block for knowledge and, in turn, for understanding. Knowledge is what happens to information as it is transformed by the human brain into a vast interconnected network of information, contexts, sensory experiences, and emotions.

As soon as we add an experience, emotion, or other cognitive elements to some information, it becomes knowledge. In a sense, knowledge is personalized information. A surgeon who reads about a new surgical technique in a journal has acquired information, but when the surgeon thinks about how he or she could use the same technique for different patients, the information has been transformed into knowledge. To say that we understand something means that we have available multiple views and perspectives. To make the important distinctions among information, knowledge and understanding clearer, let us consider the journey from simply having information about somebody, to knowing her, to understanding her. Joan has brown eyes and short hair. She majors in both biology and chemistry. These are bits of information—facts. When I connect this information with what I know about biology and chemistry, the possible career aspirations of people who major in these subjects and the quality of the university, I can infer that she may wish to go to medical school. This mixture of interconnected bits of new and old information, personal experience, and inference all combine to yield knowledge. Understanding Joan is to know a wide variety of things about her and to have seen her in a wide variety of situations. My understanding of Joan increases to the extent that my repertoire of knowledge expands.

Hypermedia Mirrors the Way the Brain Works

It is true that, as Morariu (1988) says, no one is quite certain just how information is organized in the mind, but it is also true that, curiously, several different psychology and learning theories triangulate on hypertext as an effective learning technology. Cognitive flexibility theory (Spiro & Jehng, 1990; Spiro *et al.*, 1991), generative learning theory (Wittrock, 1974a, 1974b, 1979), schema/semantic network theory (Brown, Collins, & Duguid, 1989; Jonassen, 1985; Suchman, 1987), and dual coding theory (Clark & Paivio, 1991; Paivio, 1986) all point in the direction of hypermedia as an ideal instructional technology (see Fiderio, 1988).

Information Can Be Personalized

Obviously, different people have different purposes (e.g., browsing to satisfy curiosity vs. being tested on the material this Friday), different backgrounds (e.g., never worked with computers before vs. computer expert), different levels of knowledge (e.g., novice vs. expert), work in different contexts (school library vs. museum) and have different expectations/motivations (e.g., "This is going to be fun" vs. "I hate this!"). Since in a hypermedium, information is divided into modules, one idea per module, it is relatively easy for the modules to be rearranged according to individual needs (Carr, 1988). Both authors and users can personalize trails through the information space (collection of modules). Authors can lay down predetermined trails through the material, different trails being appropriate for users possessing different needs or knowledge. For example, a "beginner's trail" would guide users through nodes that offer introductory comments, explain terms, go into more detail and even provide quiz nodes with which users could test their understanding of the material. An "expert's trail" might breeze through all the support material and provide access to material that is more specialized and complex. Users could select from a selection of trails, the ones most appropriate for them. They could also record their own trails as they course through the material, which they then could choose to traverse again at a later time. Such personalized subsets of an entire hypermedia corpus are called *webs* (Meyrowitz, 1986; Yankelovich *et al.,* 1988).

Hypermedia Can Be Enhanced with Other Technologies

In what Martin (1990) refers to as intelligent documents, hypermedia systems can contain expert knowledge in the subject area. Such a built-in expert system could query users and then provide guidance on traveling through the information space based on the user's needs as they unfold. It's like having an expert advisor sitting beside you. Electronic performance support systems (EPSSs), essentially sophisticated, computer-based job-aids, are based on the marriage of hypermedia and expert systems (Geber, 1991). As Richard Horn says (quoted in Geber, 1991, p. 25), "Instead of giving people a finished course, you give them Legos and let them snap them together any way they want."

Hypermedia Conveys Complexity

Decades of research in fields as diverse as organizational theory, ecology, medicine, and family studies has increasingly chiseled away at our hopes for simple cause and effect relationships to explain the world. What could be simpler than using the handle on a water faucet to fill a glass with water? Peter Senge (1990) reminds us that even this seemingly mundane task actually requires a feedback system that is anything but linear. We think that we are controlling (i.e., causing) water to fill the glass, but in fact, this is only half true. It may be just as validly stated that the water is controlling (i.e., causing) our hand.

As we fill the glass, we watch the water level to see if the desired level has been reached. In other words, we monitor the "gap" between where we are and where we want to be. As the gap narrows—as the water level approaches the desired level—we adjust the faucet to slow the flow of water. So the water controls our hand every bit as much as the converse. This entire process is a system involving five variables that interact in such a way that each is both a cause and an effect of the others.

Thinking systemically messes up our comfortable notion of linear cause and effect. What makes this process a system is the feedback loop. The flow of water causes the water level to rise. The rising level causes the perceived gap to narrow, which causes the faucet position to either remain the same, slow the flow or stop the flow which, in turn, influences the water flow, which influences the current water level, and on and on. So does the faucet position cause the water flow or does the water flow cause the faucet position? Thinking systemically involves the initially uncomfortable realization that every variable is both a cause and an effect. The view "I am controlling the rate of flow of water into the glass" reflects only half the system. It would be equally true to say that the level of water in the glass is controlling my hand!

Most important for our discussion here is that our current educational strategies and technologies are inadequate to convey the richness of systems. Print and video are essentially linear. It is extremely difficult to convey the dynamics of a changing system of interacting variables that both influence and are influenced by each other.

Of course, some subjects are inherently more complex and systemic in nature than others. For example, medicine and English literature are by nature highly complex.

The problem is that despite the inherent complexity of the material, it must be simplified. Complex systems must be reduced to simplified models in order to make them understandable.

The computer is the only device that allows a learner to peer into the parts while preserving a sense of how the parts comprise the whole. To understand why this capability is so powerful and so important, consider how we might attempt to understand human behavior. Imagine trying to understand a person's behavior by merely observing a single action extracted from a context or set of circumstances. If we see a man complaining, we cannot simply assume that humans in general or this man in particular, would complain all the time (although it seems that some do). We need to look at the situation, the person's history, the content of the complaint and the manner in which the complaint is expressed in order to understand why the man is complaining. That is, in order to understand a complex phenomenon, it is entirely inadequate to simplify by extracting parts of the whole, because the meaning of the parts (e.g., someone complaining, or smiling, or walking, or helping) depends on the way these parts are arranged into a whole (e.g., the situation, a person's background, events that transpired earlier, etc.). Hypermedia is a unique instructional strategy that permits one to zero in on smaller concepts, processes, and procedures while concomitantly retaining the essence of a complex phenomenon. It is this feature that makes computer-based learning so exciting.

Planned Serendipity

One of the main criticisms leveled against hypermedia is that because it does not impose a sequential reading of information, it is impossible to ensure that learners will acquire all the necessary information. This argument is predicated on a largely questionable assumption—that viewing information equals learning the information. Unfortunately, presenting information is no guarantee that any of it will be learned. And unless the material is of a simple nature and all that is desired is rote memorization, mere exposure to it is not enough to make it meaningful. I maintain that while a learner may not actually see everything when using hypermedia, the quality of the learning may be better—that is, the extent to which the material has been related to or integrated with one's store of knowledge is likely to be greater with hypermedia.

Planned serendipity can be a useful way to learn and to make learning more exciting. Planned serendipity refers to an environment that has been designed to facilitate the discovery of related gems of information. For example, Trumbull, Gay, and Mazur (1992) describe a hypermedia system on cultural entomology called *Bughouse*. To help orient users to the system, an interface metaphor of a Victorian country house and its grounds is employed. Users move through the house and the grounds by clicking buttons on the screen. The familiar context of a house and its surroundings encouraged users to browse around, feeling relatively secure that they would not get lost in "hyperspace." Greater exploration means greater likelihood of a serendipitous encounter with an unexpected, yet useful piece of information. Trumbull *et al.* found that subjects who mostly used the browsing feature of the system were more likely to appreciate the extent, richness, and complexity of the information available than were individuals who used either a sequential (index) or a guided navigation/location strategy.

Challenges

Cognitive Overhead

Cognitive overhead is the "additional mental overhead required to create, name and keep track of links" (Conklin, 1987, p. 40). In a hypermedia system, there is the actual information itself and the mechanisms for accessing that information. Cognitive overhead increases to the extent that the access and organization mechanisms demand more mental effort. The goal, then, is to keep these mechanisms as transparent as possible. This essentially comes down to the issue of user interface design, a whole art and science in itself! Although research has been conducted in this area and some suggestions made (Nielsen, 1990), cognitive overhead persists as a limitation of hypermedia.

Lost in Hyperspace

This problem is due to the inherent nature of hypermedia. When users are allowed to wander freely from node to node, there is always an imminent danger of getting lost. Conklin (1987) calls this the *disorientation problem.* Different strategies have been attempted to circumvent the possibility of getting lost. HyperTies, developed by Ben Shneiderman (Shneiderman, 1987, 1989), is based on the encyclopedia metaphor, with information being divided up into *articles.* Articles may be accessed in any of three ways: Through a table of contents, an index, or by clicking on highlighted words embedded throughout the text. Presumably, the familiar structure of an encyclopedia ameliorates the problem of feeling lost. In addition, at all points in the system, the name of the current article is shown at the top of the screen and the screen last visited is printed at the bottom. Selecting this latter item allows users to back up through the system, revisiting all the screens previously visited but in reverse order. The familiar encyclopedia structure and tools (table of contents, index), the article titles and the ability to back up all help keep users oriented.

Another orientation method, perhaps compatible with the HyperTies design, is the use of *maps* (Nielsen, 1990; Yankelovich *et al.*, 1988). Maps typically consist of two dimensional diagrams composed of icons representing documents with lines drawn between icons to represent conceptual links between those nodes. Although such a device is intuitively appealing and does work for small collections of hypermedia documents, but as the collection gets larger and larger the maps become increasingly impractical. Nielsen (1990) in an attempt to overcome this limitation, divides the maps up into global and local views, the former providing an overview of the entire corpus and the latter showing what nodes are immediately connected to the one currently being viewed. This approach helps, but it is not entirely the answer.

Martin (1990) offers yet another approach to the problem of disorientation. Like Shneiderman, Martin's approach models the hypermedia system on something with which most people are already familiar, the outline processor. To start, the user is presented with an outline that is completely collapsed with only the main headings showing. Users can expand headings as they wish. Martin feels that the only way to ensure that users will not get lost is to structure the material in the form of a hierarchy. In addition, he recommends several intelligent hypermedia navigation features, including the following:

- The system could mark places of interest to each user.
- The user could leave bookmarks.
- The user could leave notes at any point.
- The system could adapt its navigation paths to the user's needs.
- An expert system could recommend paths. (p. 83)

The issue of navigation in hyperspace remains a hurdle to surmount for designers of hypermedia systems. However, an ever expanding array of creative approaches to learner navigation (Beasley & Lister, 1992; MacKenzie, 1992; Nelson & Palumbo, 1992; Smeaton, 1991; Trumbull, Gay, & Mazur, 1992) promises to enable learners to exploit the advantages of hypermedia without succumbing to its number one weakness.

Ushering in a New Paradigm

Perhaps the most exciting thing about hypermedia is not in the technique itself, but in the type of thinking it promotes. Hypermedia is not just another instructional strategy or information retrieval technology. It's promise is its impact on the way we, as educators, think about design. This recognition holds implications for both designers and learners.

Let us first consider the designer's perspective. Instructional design has traditionally been (and still is, by and large) a highly linear affair—linear in the *process* of development and in the *end product* of that development (e.g., seminar, workbook, videotape, even traditional CAI). For example, a chapter on planning and authoring CAI lessons in a book edited by the highly respected, established instructional designers Leslie Briggs, Kent Gustafson, and Murray Tillman (Briggs, Gustafson, & Tillman, 1991) advocates that nine events of instruction unfold as the learner proceeds:

1. Gaining attention
2. Informing the learner of the lesson objective
3. Stimulating recall of prior learning
4. Presenting stimuli with distinctive features
5. Guided learning
6. Eliciting performance
7. Providing informative feedback
8. Assessing performance
9. Enhancing retention and learning transfer

To be sure, these are useful techniques and their inclusion in any instructional endeavor, computer-based or not, will ensure enhanced learning when compared to the outcomes from a design of a learning experience that does not include them. But in the world of hypermedia, where exploration is king, the designer has considerably less control over exactly what the learner will experience.

Better Than Average

The designer must jettison some hard-won precepts regarding how instruction happens. First, as designers, we have become accustomed to conceiving our creations for some mythical "average" learner. We have had to assume that all learners using our product are similar in all the ways that matter (e.g., reading skills, background, education level, etc.). Thus, designers have handicapped themselves. The real tragedy is that we approach design for computer-based programs in much the same way. Of course, this is very understandable, but it is a terrible waste. The computer has the power to personalize instruction in ways that would make the designer of the past very envious. Everything is up for grabs now. The computer can adjust its presentation based on a host of variables such as student demographics, interests, gender, educational background, reading ability, and cultural heritage. Perhaps even more exciting is the computer's potential to make adjustments "on the fly." For instance, the computer can offer more complex material to learners who seem ready for it, and suggest material for review to those who require further explanation.

Interactivity Is Where It's At

Interactivity is one those concepts that everyone talks about but that no one can easily define. We hear that books are *not* interactive and that computer software *is* interactive. This myth must be disposed of. The truth be known, every method of instruction ever devised is interactive to some degree, falling somewhere on a continuum between two theoretical (impossible) extremes (i.e., completely non-interactive vs. completely interactive). Even that phenomenon that everyone loves to hate, the lecture, is at least minimally interactive to the extent that the lecturer can alter his or her talk depending on feedback from the audience (i.e., facial expressions, body posture, number of raised hands, rate at which people are leaving, etc.). It all depends on how the medium is used.

All of the preceding may sound academic, but it is important for the following reason: It points up the idea that instructional vehicles are neither, in and of themselves, interactive nor non-interactive. Just because it is on a computer does not automatically make it interactive. And just because it is delivered via an ostensibly linear medium, such as a lecture or videotape, does not make it non-interactive. The crucial factor that makes the difference is how that medium is used. A computer does not guarantee greater interactivity. It only provides the *opportunity* for greater interactivity. How we choose to exploit the opportunity is the challenge before us as designers and teachers.

But the question remains, what exactly is interactivity? Interactivity is, quite simply, the opportunity to affect the course of a communication. The extent to which a medium offers this opportunity is the extent to which it can be considered interactive. Thus, interactivity can be quantified and measured. Such a measurement scheme should prove useful to designers, educators, and learners themselves, and is being pursued by the author.

The crux of the issue is that if the opportunity for interactivity is one of the unique features of the computer, and interactivity is so helpful, then it behooves us to think in terms of learner input when designing instructional programs.

When designing highly interactive programs, keep the following in mind:

- Avoid telling the learner. Instead try to set up an environment that urges learners to ask questions, explore, form hypotheses, analyze, synthesize, predict, evaluate and construct. In short, get learners to do something, anything.

- One of the most powerful ways to learn is through problem-based learning. With this method, a scenario is given that includes some problem (or problems) that must be identified and solved. Learners are thus provided a context within which to apply their knowledge. Of course, problems can be constructed that elicit the application of specific material that is particularly important. Understanding is made richer the more connections one has made between bits of knowledge. Since drawing connections is what hypermedia is all about, it is easy to see how it can be an ideal tool for problem-based learning.

- Provide as much informative feedback as possible. People learn a great deal from feedback, and it is, indeed, what we depend on to derive learning through experience. Every time a learner does something on the computer, valuable information becomes available that the computer can use to both offer detailed feedback to the learner and to adapt itself to the learner. The outcome of this evaluation should be made available to learners as soon as possible.

Students who are experiencing difficulty with a subject are often referred to tutors. What makes the tutor helpful is that he or she can diagnose the cause of the student's difficulties, explain the material accordingly and adjust the presentation depending on feedback from the student (i.e., blank stare, misunderstanding, wrong answers, etc.).

Although the superiority of one-on-one tutoring is widely recognized, it is reserved for special cases because of the scarcity of the funds and the personnel to provide such an opportunity for all.

But this restriction of tutoring to special cases is becoming obsolete because the computer can come remarkably close to matching the interactive and individualizing abilities of a human tutor. True, technology is a long way from being able to detect subtle facial changes, and computers are hard pressed to "understand" all but the most straightforward of sentences. However, the capabilities they *do* possess remain largely untapped.

Breaking Up Is Hard to Do

Another key concern for the instructional designer developing a hypermedia system is the concept of interdependent modules. Traditional instruction lines everything up in a neat column. It remains for the learner merely to proceed up the column. New bits of knowledge are built upon a foundation of previous bits. The designer can be more or less confident that the material will be traversed in the correct order so that he or she can write progressively more advanced material.

But the situation is quite different for the hypermedia designer. Hypermedia information must be modularized and stored as "nodes." These nodes are linked by both designer and learner.

With *non*computer-based instruction, you build the street (i.e., an outline) and then place the buildings along the street. With hypermedia, you begin by creating the buildings and then erect them all over the city.

Live Versus Dead Space

We have become so accustomed to working with what I call "dead space"—media such as paper, videos, audiotapes and other vehicles of essentially one-way communication. But the computer is "live space." It can be made to offer a clickable, askable, hearable, and explorable learning environment. One can read about a saxophone in a book. But in a CD-ROM product from Microsoft, one can click on a speaker icon to hear how it sounds, click on its parts to see close-ups with more detailed information, click on a Sound Box icon to "play" the instrument, hear how it sounds in jazz, orchestral or big band ensembles, listen to the various ways it can be played (e.g., "harsh tone," "soft tone"), click on another button to view it from various perspectives, and click on yet another button to see what other instruments are related to it and go off exploring these. For some instruments, such as the timpani or tambourine, clicking on the image of the instrument produces its sound! With this program and others like it, there is a sense that one has been invited into a world where things are alive and waiting for us to discover them.

Some Issues

Reading Versus Authoring Hypermedia

If learning is a constructive process, then authoring one's own hypermedia project may be even more effective than simply traversing the paths laid down by someone else. If the brain forges understanding by linking knowledge together in different ways, where context and purpose are the setting within which understanding is constructed, then it is reasonable to predict that authoring one's own hypermedia project may be even more powerful than experiencing another's creation. The *process* of creating the project may be the key to this power. Whether, how, and to what extent this is true needs to be assessed empirically. This research may yield valuable information on how people learn.

Social Psychological Issues

The advantages of teams are becoming increasingly clear. There are some interesting questions to consider here. How can collaborative work be facilitated in hypermedia documents? How can collaborative hypermedia tools affect how people work and accomplish goals together? How should these tools operate?

Personality Issues

Certain personalities may be more suited than others to the network structure of hypermedia. Perhaps those who desire to exercise more control over various aspects of their lives would work better with hypermedia than those who desire to exercise less control. The latter group may be quite happy with material that leads them through sequentially.

Context/Environment

Some contexts may be better suited for hypermedia than others. A museum setting in which users intend to simply browse may be ideal for hypermedia, whereas a setting in which users have specific questions in mind and intend to seek out specific information may or may not be as well suited for hypermedia.

Learner Intentions

This is different from purpose. The purpose of a hypermedia system may be to teach lower gastrointestinal anatomy. The intention of one learner, though, may be to compare and contrast various related color drawings in the database. Another user may intend to explore the myriad connected concepts, images and animations as they come up. So, it is important to catalog what intentions users may have, and to ensure that the system you are either creating or purchasing can accommodate as many of these as possible.

Subject Matter

It is very possible that some subject matters are more amenable to presentation through hypermedia than are others. For instance, it may be that a course on basic reading skills may be best learned linearly, since advancing through the material depends on mastery of previous material. Further research is needed to ascertain the characteristics of subjects that either lend themselves or do not lend themselves to hypermedia.

Combinations

What type of system is best for a novice who only wants an introduction to a field, or alternatively, for a novice who needs to learn a great deal about a field, or for a novice using a system in a museum and who does not know what he wants?

At the Intersection of Hypermedia and Learning Theory

Humans are perceived by cognitive theorists as being processors of information, acquiring knowledge and skills by way of interactive internal processes. These internal processes are orchestrated by a set of control processes which are personal and are reflective of both innate abilities and individual experience.

The various theories proposed by cognitive psychologists as well as strategies employed by cognitively-oriented educators and instructional designers exhibit a basic cohesion in that humans are viewed as processing information by actively attending to stimuli, accessing existing knowledge to relate to new information, realigning the structure of that existing knowledge to accommodate the new information, and encoding the restructured knowledge into memory (Jonassen, 1985). The meaning that the individual ascribes to information is viewed as idiosyncratic and as actively constructed from a base of existing knowledge (Winn, 1988). Our active participation in the construction of this new knowledge is viewed as a critical component for accessing and retrieving prior knowledge in the interpretation of new information (Weinstein, 1978). As we explore some of these ideas of how we learn and apply knowledge, it will become obvious that activity as well as *inter*activity are integral components of both theory and its application in the technology of hypermedia.

Cognitive Flexibility Theory

Many instructional systems fail, claim Rand Spiro and his colleagues, because they do not take into consideration the *ill-structuredness* of many complex domains (Spiro & Jehng, 1990; Spiro *et al.*, 1991). *Cognitive flexibility theory* is an attempt to explain how the brain makes sense of ill-structured domains (i.e. domains that are complex and in which there is little regularity from one case to another).

Essentially, the theory states that cognitive flexibility is needed in order to construct an ensemble of conceptual and case representations necessary to understand a particular problem-solving situation. The idea is that we cannot be said to have a full understanding of a domain unless we have the opportunity to see different case representations from that domain.

According to Spiro *et al.* (1991), the learning of advanced knowledge requires an approach to learning that is quite different from that required for the learning of introductory material. The fundamental problem running throughout many learning efforts is "oversimplification." Oversimplification occurs in different forms. For example, *additivity bias* occurs when parts of complex entities are studied and it is assumed that these parts can then be reintegrated as a whole while retaining their original complex characteristics. Another example is *discreteness bias*, in which continuous processes are divided up into discrete steps. Yet another form of oversimplification includes *compartmentalization bias*, in which highly interrelated, interdependent concepts are considered in isolation from one another without consideration of how they interact.

Cognitive flexibility theory is an answer to the necessity of mastering complex subjects without falling prey to oversimplification in any or all of its forms. Basically, the theory posits that in order to learn complex material, the learner has to see that same material at different times, in different situations, for different purposes and from different conceptual perspectives (Spiro *et al.*, 1991). Complete schemata are constructed to the extent that learners are exposed to multiple knowledge representations and multiple interconnectedness of the complex material to be learned.

Given the tenets of cognitive flexibility theory and what we know about the unique characteristics of hypermedia, it is easy to see the promising fit between the technology of hypermedia and the manner in which we best learn complex subject material. To make the potential fit of hypermedia to cognitive flexibility theory even stronger, recall that hypermedia is nothing more than a tool to link nodes (chunks of information, or "conceptual elements") together in meaningful ways. This capability matches precisely the requirements of cognitive flexibility theory—the ability to see different aspects of a complex subject area from different perspectives in different contexts.

Hypermedia, therefore, has properties that are consistent with the needs of cognitive flexibility theory. For example, conceptual elements in the hypermedia environment can be rearranged so that several elements can be viewed together. For another purpose, or in a different situation, these same conceptual elements could be arranged differently. Recall that it is the arrangement and relationships among nodes that give meaning to information. By freely rearranging nodes according to specified features/properties depending on different needs, different contexts, and different problems, learners have a powerful tool with which to learn and understand complex material in all its forms, in different situations, and in its entirety.

Information Processing

Information processing is proposed as an interactive system. An individual uses the physical senses to make sense out of the stimuli of the environment. This sensory recognition involves the individual's long-term memory, experiences, abilities, and expectations. Information is first received and recognized and is then either encoded and stored for later retrieval or is lost. The stages of information processing—recognition, short-term (working) memory storage, and long-term memory storage—are dependent on internal processes. What we remember, therefore, is a result of interactions within this system of active internal processes.

The system processes information by first recognizing patterns. If information is first recognized, it can then take on meaning. To extend our discussion of the concept of the Dalmatian dog, for example, we would first process the information presented by recognizing the pattern of the letters *DOG*. The combined alphabet letters *D, O,* and *G,* however, are not just recognized as individual letters in terms of how they are shaped; they represent a host of associations which have already been mentioned. Whether we are able to recognize this word and give it meaning each time we see the letters *DOG* depends on whether the information about *DOG* is stored in long-term memory and can be retrieved into short-term memory (working memory) when called upon.

According to information processing theory, retention of information is attributed to basic processes—attention, selective perception, rehearsal, encoding, and retrieval—all of which occur throughout the three information processing stages. Current theorists put more emphasis on these processes and how they are effected than on the stages in which they occur. To increase the probability that information is acquired, stored, and retrieved, we must somehow effect attention, selective perception, rehearsal, encoding, and retrieval. As processing occurs, information and skills are recorded to form stronger links to nodes and more pathways to stored information. According to theorists, information must be adequately encoded, stored, and retrieved to be remembered. Thus, *any* retention aid should encourage extra processing of information to increase links to stored skills. According to Tulving and Thomson (1973), the degree of accessibility of information stored in long-term memory is dependent on the strength of the cues encoded during acquisition. Strong cues, such as those cues which may be generated through hypermedia, are more likely to result in recall.

Case-Based Reasoning

Case-based reasoning is an educational paradigm in which learning depends on a memory of specific experiences, or "cases" (Riesbeck & Schank, 1989). Medical and law schools have long utilized case-based instructional techniques in their curricula. Cases provide the means with which students can learn why, when, and how knowledge is applicable. In order to avoid the "inert knowledge problem" (see Whitehead, 1929), learners must have the opportunity to organize new knowledge appropriately and know how and in what situations to apply this knowledge. The important point here is that instruction is more effective when anchored in meaningful problem-solving environments similar to those in which students will find themselves when solving real-world problems.

If the usefulness of information depends on an ability to recall it when appropriate, then it is important that cases be presented in such a way as to provide contextual cues to properly index information in memory. Hypermedia may facilitate this indexing by presenting information along with appropriate contextual cues. Ferguson *et al.* (1991) have created a hypermedia case-based learning environment that helps organize information in the same way in which the information will have to be organized when applied to some task.

Generative Learning

Cognitive principles suggest that learning is an active, constructive process in which learners generate meaning for information by accessing and applying existing knowledge. Generative learning theory incorporates this principle of cognitive psychology (Wittrock, 1974a, 1974b, 1979). The theory maintains that meaning for material is generated by activating and altering existing knowledge structures so as to interpret new information and encode it effectively for future retrieval and use. In Wittrock's (1974b) model, meaningful learning (learning with understanding) is a rational and transferable process:

> . . . the generative model predicts that learning is a function of the abstract and distinctive, concrete associations which the learner generates between his prior experience, as it is stored in long-term memory, and the stimuli. Learning with understanding, which is defined by long term memory plus transfer to conceptually related problems, is a process of generating semantic and distinctive idiosyncratic associations between stimuli and stored information. (p. 89)

Comprehension, according to the generative model, requires the proactive transfer of existing knowledge to new material. Wittrock (1990) maintains, for example, that generative reading focuses on constructive or generative processes usually considered characteristic of good written composition. In other words, reading, like good writing, involves generative cognitive processes that create meaning by building relations among the parts of the text to be learned as well as between the text and what the learner already knows, believes, and has experienced. Learning activities which require the learner to relate new information to an existing knowledge structure depend on complex cognitive transformations and elaborations that are individual, personal, and contextual in nature. Generative learning activities, then, can be thought of as strategies which foster not only learning but learning-to-learn (Brown, Campione, & Day, 1981). The student is not only transforming the content being learned, but is also practicing these transformation activities. In these learning activities, information is transformed and elaborated into a more individual form for the learner, thereby making the information more memorable as well as more comprehensible.

Semantic Networks

The nature of traditional media such as paper and video forces a linearity onto its content. Authors must arrange their work hierarchically so that one idea flows into the next, with ideas subsumed under other ideas. As we have discussed earlier, however, the mind is anything but a linear thinking machine. Ideas are *not* arranged as on a scroll with one neatly leading to the next. In fact, it appears that the mind consists of endlessly intertwined webs of interrelated ideas, emotions and skills.

Quillian (1968) developed the idea of active structural networks (ASN) in an effort to capture and depict the ostensibly network-like nature of the brain. These networks consist of nodes (chunks of information) and labeled links (relationships) between nodes. Everything someone knows is encoded into the active structural networks of the brain. Furthermore, networks serve as structures within which new information is integrated with knowledge already possessed by the learner. Learning, then, involves the acquisition of new chunks of information and their connection to related chunks of information both new and old.

It is easy to see how active structural networks function by speaking in terms of schema theory. Schemata consist of interconnected sets of ideas which are further linked to other schemata. Meaningful learning takes place when new ideas are linked to other new ideas and when all are somehow assimilated into existing networks of schemata. While it might seem that the connections between nodes and between schemata are fixed except when new learning is taking place, the fact is quite the opposite. Relationships within and between schemata are defined in terms of context. We remember and process ideas and reprocess old ideas differently, depending on the context.

From these perspectives, it does not make sense to speak of an Absolute Truth about anything in our world, since the meaning of anything depends on how we perceive it in relation to other things. This position is at the foundation of the increasingly popular educational movement, *constructivism.* Suchman (1987) argues that there is no ultimate reality. Instead, reality is relative and is the outcome of a constructive process. It is one's experience with an idea and the context of which the idea is a part that are used together to construct a meaning of that idea (Brown, Collins, & Duguid, 1989).

All of this brings us back to the limitations of paper, video, and other linear systems. If learning involves the manipulation of networks of information, and if the relationships binding these networks change depending on the context, the inadequacies of linear systems become clear. Within hypermedia, information can be rearranged, analyzed, shifted, and molded to suit the needs of each individual and the context in which the material is learned and/or applied. Hypermedia is a technology which can assist its users in constructing their schemata according to context and to individual needs and characteristics. The exact ways in which hypermedia can be made to facilitate schemata processing, however, requires a good deal more empirical research.

Dual Coding Theory

The central theme underlying semantic network theory is that information is not simply filed away under a single heading, but rather is integrated in some way into a highly interconnected network of data and the relationships between those data. Dual coding theory (DCT) goes further in that it postulates that mental representations of ideas and events are stored in distinct verbal and nonverbal symbolic modes and that these representations retain the pattern of sensorimotor activation present during encoding (Clark & Paivio, 1991; Paivio, 1986).

One of the structural assumptions underlying DCT is that connections are formed both within verbal and nonverbal representations (associative connections) as well as between the two forms of representation (referential connections). For example, an associative connection would be one in which thinking about computers might remind you of related terms such as monitor, printer, and perhaps even frustration. A referential connection would be present if the word "mouse" conjured up memories of images of mice, the squeaking sounds they make and a sensation of anxiety. Thus, both *inter* and *intra*-associative structures exist between and within the two symbolic systems.

Mental representations are activated by related nodes in the network of associated nodes. Thoughts can activate associated nodes and then spread, resulting in a complex pattern of spreading activation among nodes and links in the network.

This last example points out an important assumption of DCT specifically, as well as of active structural networks generally. As the activation of nodes and associations spread out, it tends to weaken. It is easy to see how a thought of a Dalmatian could activate the thought of the dog's owner. But it becomes increasingly ridiculous to speak of strong associations between verbal and nonverbal mental representations because, ultimately, everything is related! DCT, then, provides a plausible explanation of how the brain deals with units of information, in both verbal and nonverbal forms, which are more or less related to one another.

Another interesting aspect of DCT relevant to our discussion of hypermedia is that it emphasizes the role of past experience in the development of mental representations. Although two individuals may have the same experiences, their mental representations of these experiences will be different in significant ways as a function of their past experiences.

DCT makes it easy to see how beneficial hypermedia can be. First, one of the implications of DCT is that the more sensory modes in which mental representations are stored, the more likely it is that they will be remembered. Hypermedia makes it easy to access related information in a wide variety of forms.

Another implication of DCT is that the particular mental representations constructed by individual learners depend on context. If different people construct different representations of reality in order to conform to their individual contexts and experiences, then it follows that any tool that helps people to personalize the information structure would be beneficial.

The idea of a spreading wave of activation suggests that it might be useful to assign values to links emanating from each node. The values assigned would represent the strength of the conceptual relationships between nodes. These values would indicate to users which of several links are the strongest, and would thus help users to decide which links to traverse. Of course, there is no reason why users themselves could not be provided with the means of assigning values to links. Much research remains to be done in this area.

Dual coding theory has much in it that recommends hypermedia. It is a comprehensive theory of learning and suggests many implications for education. Its main idea is that all knowledge is constructed in the brain in many different forms and is different from person to person. All of this points up the need for learning and information acquisition tools that facilitate associative processing of information in a variety of forms. Hypermedia is such a tool.

Conclusion

The idea of a machine based on associative indexing is not new (Bush, 1945), but the technology to materialize that vision is only now becoming available, with exciting new capabilities just over the horizon. While we explore these possibilities, however, we must not forget that the technology must *work for humans,* not the converse.

An attempt should be made to bridge the gap between what we know about how we learn and apply knowledge and a new technology that promises to augment the brain's functioning in a way never before possible. Hypermedia has been trumpeted as a revolutionary device to help us deal with the geometrically increasing pool of information in the world.

All of these benefits are kudos to the technology of hypermedia itself. The real intrigue of hypermedia, however, derives from its unique ensemble of characteristics which tantalizingly corroborate evidence regarding the way we learn and apply that learning.

Hypertext/hypermedia may not be appropriate for everybody in all situations and for all purposes, but then, it is an empirical question what these situations and purposes are. Exploiting the full potential of hypermedia will require nothing less than a dramatic change in the way instructional systems are designed.

References

Ackerman, M. J. (1989). New media in medical education. *Methods of information in medicine, 28,* 327–331.

A.D.A.M. Software (1994). *A.D.A.M. The inside story.*

Akscyn, R. M., McCracken, D. L., & Yoder, E. A. (1988). KMS: A distributed hypermedia system for managing knowledge in organizations. *Communications of the ACM, 31*(7), 820–835.

Ambron, S., & Hooper, K. (Eds.). (1988). *Interactive multimedia.* Redmond, WA: Microsoft Press.

Ambron, S., & Hooper, K. (Eds.). (1990). *Learning with interactive multimedia.* Redmond, WA: Microsoft Press.

Ambrose, D. W. (1991, Dec.). The effects of hypermedia on learning. *Educational Technology,* 51–55.

Bannister, G. (1988, Oct.). Not too hyper for the classroom. *Computers in Education,* 6–7.

Beasley, R. E., & Lister, D. B. (1992). Application report: User orientation in a hypertext glossary. *Journal of Computer-Based Instruction, 19*(4), 115–118.

Begeman, M. L., & Conklin, J. (1988, Oct.). The right tool for the right job. *Byte,* 255–268.

Begoray, J. A. (1990). An introduction to hypermedia issues, systems and applications areas. *International Journal of Man-Machine Studies, 33,* 121–147.

Bevilacqua, A. (1989, Feb.). Hypertext: Behind the hype. *American Libraries,* 158–162.

Bigelow, J. (1988, March). Hypertext and case. *IEEE Software,* 23–27.

Borgman, C. L. (1986). The user's mental model of an information retrieval system: An experiment on a prototype on-line catalog. *International J. of Man-Machine Studies, 24,* 47–64.

Bourne, L. E., Dominowski, R. L., Loftus, E. F., & Healy, A. F. (1986). *Cognitive processes* (2nd ed.). Englewood Cliffs, NJ: Prentice-Hall.

Briggs, L. J., Gustafson, K. L., & Tillman, M. H. (Eds.). (1991). *Instructional design: Principles and applications* (2nd ed.). Englewood Cliffs, NJ: Educational Technology Publications.

Brown, A. L., Campione, J. C., & Day, J. D. (1981). Learning to learn: On training students to learn from texts. *Educational Researcher, 10,* 14–21.

Brown, J. S., Collins, A., & Duguid, P. (1989). Situated cognition and the culture of learning. *Educational Researcher, 18*(1), 32–42.

Bush, V. (1945, July). As we may think. *Atlantic Monthly,* 101–108.

Byers, T. J. (1987, April). Built by association. *PC World,* 244–251.

Campbell, B., & Goodman, J. M. (1988). HAM: A general purpose hypertext abstract machine. *Communications of the ACM, 31*(7), 856–861.

Campbell, R. (1989, March). (I learned it) through the grapevine: Hypermedia at work in the classroom. *American Libraries,* 200–205.

Carlson, D. A., & Sudha, R. (1990). Hyperintelligence: The next frontier. *Communications of the ACM, 33*(3), 311–321.

Carr, C. (1988, Aug.). Hypertext: A new training tool? *Educational Technology, 28*(8), 47–50.

Casabianca, L. (1988, Summer). Ted Nelson: Hypermedia magician. *HyperMedia,* 23–25.

Chen, L. C. (1990). Interactive video technology in education: Past, present, and future. *Journal of Educational Technology Systems, 19*(1), 5–19.

Clark, R. C. (1989). *Developing technical training: A structured approach for the development of classroom and computer-based instruction materials.* Reading, MA: Addison-Wesley.

Clark, J. M., & Paivio, A. (1991). Dual coding theory and education. *Educational Psychology Review, 3*(3), 149–210.

Conklin, J. (1987, Sept.). Hypertext: An introduction and survey. *IEEE Computer,* 17–41.

Crane, G., & Mylonas, E. (1988, Nov.). The Perseus project: An interactive curriculum on classical Greek civilization. *Educational Technology, 28*(11), 25–32.

van Dam, A. (1988). Hypertext '87: Keynote address. *Communications of the ACM, 31*(7), 887–895.

Dede, C. (1988). The role of hypertext in transforming information into knowledge. At *NECC.* Dallas, TX.

Dixon, B. N. (1986). The Grolier electronic encyclopedia (a review). *CD-ROM Review, 1*(1), 1–15.

Dixon, B. N. (1986). Making miracles. *CD-ROM Review, 1*(1), 20–24.

Duffy, T. M., & Jonassen, D. H. (1991, May). Constructivism: New implications for instructional technology? *Educational Technology, 31*(5), 7–12.

Ertel, M., & Oros, J. (1989, Jan.). A tour of the stacks: Hypercard for libraries. *Online,* 45–52.

Ferguson, W., Bareiss, R., Birnbaum, L., & Osgood, R. (1991). *ASK Systems: An approach to the realization of story-based teachers.* Manuscript.

Fiderio, J. (1988, Oct.). A grand vision. *Byte,* 237–244.

Franklin, C. (1988a, March). An annotated hypertext bibliography. *Online,* 42–46.

Franklin, C. (1988b). The hypermedia library. *Database, 11*(3), 43–48.

Frisse, M. (1988a, Oct.). From text to hypertext. *Byte,* 247–253.

Frisse, M. (1988b). Searching for information in a hypertext medical handbook. *Communications of the ACM, 31*(7), 880–886.

Frisse, M. E. (1990, Jan.). The case for hypermedia. *Academic Medicine,* 17–20.

Garg, P. K. (1988). Abstraction mechanisms in hypertext. *Communications of the ACM, 31*(7), 862–870.

Garrett, N., Smith, K., & Meyrowitz, N. (1986). Intermedia: Issues, strategies, and tactics in the design of a hypermedia document system. In *Conference on Computer-Supported Cooperative Work* (pp. 163–174). Austin, TX, Dec. 3–5.

Geber, B. (1991, Dec.). Help! The rise of performance support systems. *Training*, 23–29.

Gentner, G., & Stevens, A. (1983). *Mental models.* Hillsdale, NJ: Lawrence Erlbaum Associates.

Goodman, D. (1987, Oct.). The two faces of HyperCard. *Macworld*, 122–129.

Haan, B. J., Kahn, P., Riley, V. A., Coombs, J. H., & Meyrowitz, N. (1992). Iris hypermedia services. *Communications of the ACM, 35*(1), 36–51.

Haavind, R. (1990). Hypertext: The smart tool for information overload. *Technology Review, 93*(8), 42–50.

Halasz, F. G. (1988). Reflections on notecards: Seven issues for the next generation of hypermedia systems. *Communications of the ACM, 31*(7), 836–852.

Hall, P. A. V. *et al.* (1990). Hypertext systems and applications. *Information and Software Technology, 32*(7), 477–490.

Harris, M., & Cody, M. (1988, Nov.). The dynamic process of creating hypertext literature. *Educational Technology, 28*(11), 33–40.

Hicken, S. (1991). Learning in tasks that incorporate natural versus unnatural mappings: An example using aircraft instrument comprehension. *Educational Technology Research & Development, 39*(1), 63–71.

Hodges, M. E., & Sasnett, R. M. (1993). *Multimedia computing: Case studies from MIT Project Athena.* Reading, MA: Addison-Wesley.

Humphreys, D. (1988, Oct.). Cutting the hyper from hypercard. *Computers in Education*, 13–15.

Hutchings, G. A., Hall, W., Briggs, J., Hammond, N. V., Kibby, M. R., McKnight, C., & Riley, D. (1992). Authoring and evaluation of hypermedia for education. *Computers and Education, 18*(1–3), 171–177.

Jackson, M. S. (1990). Beyond relational databases. *Information and Software Technology, 32*(4), 258–265.

Jackson, M. S. (1991). Tutorial on object-oriented databases. *Information and Software Technology, 33*(1), 4–12.

Jaffe, C. C., Lynch, P. J., & Smeulders, A. W. M. (1989). Hypermedia techniques for diagnostic imaging instruction: Videodisk echocardiography encyclopedia. *Radiology, 171*, 475–480.

Jonassen, D. H. (1985). Generative learning vs. mathemagenic control of text processing. In D. H. Jonassen (Ed.), *The technology of text, Vol II.* Englewood Cliffs, NJ: Educational Technology Publications.

Jonassen, D. H. (1986). Hypertext principles for text and courseware design. *Educational Psychologist, 21*(4), 269–292.

Jonassen, D. H. (1987). Assessing cognitive structure: Verifying a method using pattern notes. *Journal of Research and Development in Education, 20*(3), 1–14.

Jonassen, D. H. (1988, Nov.). Designing structured hypertext and structuring access to hypertext. *Educational Technology, 28*(11), 13–16.

Jonassen, D. H. (1989). *Hypertext/hypermedia.* Englewood Cliffs, NJ: Educational Technology Publications.

Jonassen, D. H. (1991a, June). Thinking technology. *Educational Technology, 31*(6), 35–37.

Jonassen, D. H. (1991b). Hypertext as instructional design. *Educational Technology Research & Development, 39*(1), 83–92.

Kay, A. (1988, Summer). Alan Kay on hypermusic: The art of people amplification. *Multimedia*, 42–44.

Kearsley, G. (1988, Nov.). Authoring considerations for hypertext. *Educational Technology, 28*(11), 21–24.

Keough, L. (1988, July). The persistence of hypertext. *Computer Decisions*, 60–63.

Kinnel, S. (1988, June). Comparing HyperCard and Guide. *Database*, 49–54.

Kinzie, M. B. (1990). Requirements and benefits of effective interactive instruction: Learner control, self regulation, and continuing motivation. *Educational Technology Research & Development, 38*(1), 1–21.

Kinzie, M. B., & Berdel, R. L. (1990). Design and use of hypermedia systems. *Educational Technology Research and Development, 38*(3), 61–68.

Knussen, C., Tanner, G. R., & Kibby, M. R. (1991). An approach to the evaluation of hypermedia. *Computers and Education, 17*(1), 13–24.

Kreitzberg, C. B. (1990). Supporing peak performance through multimedia. *Multimedia Review, 1*(4), 31–42.

Kreitzberg, C. B., & Shneiderman, B. (1988). Restructuring knowledge for an electronic encyclopedia. In *Proceedings of the International Ergonomics Association's 10th Congress*, Sydney, Australia, Aug. 1–5.

Lippincott, R. (1990, Feb.). Beyond hype. *Byte*, 215–218.

Locatis, C., Charuhas, J., & Banvard, R. (1990). Hypervideo. *Educational Technology Research & Development*, 38(2), 41–49.

Locatis, C., Letourneau, G., & Banvard, R. (1989). Hypermedia and instruction. *Educational Technology Research & Development*, 37(4), 65–77.

MacKenzie, I. S. (1992). Beating the book: Megachallenges for CD-ROM and hypertext. *Journal of Research on Computing in Education*, 24(4), 486–498

Mahler, S., Hoz, R., Fischl, D., Tovly, E., & Lernau, O. Z. (1991). Didactic use of concept mapping in higher education: Applications in medical education. *Instructional Science*, 20, 25–47.

Maida, A. S. (1985). Selecting a humanly understandable knowledge representation for reasoning about knowledge. *International Journal of Man-Machine Studies*, 22, 151–161.

Marchionini, G. (1988a, Nov.). Introduction to special issue on hypermedia. *Educational Technology*, 28(11), p. 7.

Marchionini, G. (1988b, Nov.). Hypermedia and learning: Freedom and chaos. *Educational Technology*, 28(11), 8–12.

Marchionini, G., & Shneiderman, G. (1988, Jan.). Finding facts versus browsing knowledge in hypertext systems. *IEEE Computer*, 70–80.

Martin, J. (1990). *Hyperdocuments & how to create them.* Englewood Cliffs, NJ: Prentice-Hall.

McArthur, J. R., Bolles, J. R., Fine, J., Kidd, P., & Bessis, M. (1989). Interactive computer-video modules for health sciences education. *Methods of Information in Medicine*, 28, 360–363.

McClelland, B. (1989, Jan.). Hypertext and online: A lot that's familiar. *Online*, 20–25.

McKnight, C., Richardson, J., & Dillon, A. (1989). The construction of hypertext documents and databases. *Infomediary*, 3, 33–42.

McLeod, D. (1991). Perspective on object databases. *Information and Software Technology*, 33(1), 13–21.

Megarry, J. (1987). Hypertext and compact discs: The challenge of multimedia learning. In N. Rushby (Eds.), *Technology-based learning: Selected readings.* New York: Nichols Publishing.

Meyrowitz, N. (1986). Intermedia: The architecture and construction of an object-oriented hypermedia system and applications framework. In *OOPSLA '86 Proceedings* (pp. 186–201). Portland, OR, Sept. 29–Oct. 2.

Misanchuk, E. R., & Schwier, R. A. (1992). Representing interactive multimedia and hypermedia audit trails. *Journal of Educational Multimedia and Hypermedia*, 1, 355–372.

Morariu, J. (1988, Nov.). Hypermedia in instruction and training: The power and the promise. *Educational Technology*, 28(11), 17–20.

Nelson, T. H. (1987). *Literary machines.* South Bend, IN: The Distributors.

Nelson, W. A., & Palumbo, D. B. (1992). Learning, instruction, and hypermedia. *Journal of Educational Multimedia and Hypermedia*, 1, 287–299.

Nielsen, J. (1990). The art of navigating through hypertext. *Communications of the ACM*, 33(3), 296–310.

Norman, D. A. (1983). Some observations on mental models. In D. Gentner & A. Stevens (Eds.), *Mental models* (pp. 7–14). Hillsdale, NJ: Lawrence Erlbaum Associates.

Ores, P., & Dommer, A. (1991). Hypertext in the '90s: Hype or reality? *Desktop* p. 57–61.

Paivio, A. (1986). *Mental representations: A dual-coding approach.* New York: Oxford University Press.

Puterbaugh, G., Rosenberg, M., & Sofman, R. (1989, Nov./Dec.). Performance support tools: A step beyond training. *Performance & Instruction*, 1–5.

Quentin-Baxter, M., & Dewhurst, D. (1992). A method for evaluating the efficiency of presenting information in a hypermedia environment. *Computers and Education*, 18(1–3), 179–182.

Quillian, M. R. (1968). Semantic memory. In M. Minsky (Ed.), *Semantic information processing* (216–270). Cambridge, MA: MIT Press.

Raybould, B. (1990, July). Choosing the right hypertext product for performance support. *CBT Directions*, 13–20.

Reid, J. C., & Mitchell, J. A. (1991). The improvement of learning in computer-assisted instruction. *Journal of Educational Technology Systems*, 19(4), 281–289.

Riesbeck, C., & Schank, R. (Eds.). (1989). *Inside case-based reasoning.* Hillsdale, NJ: Lawrence Erlbaum Associates.

Ritchie, I. (1989). Hypertext: Moving towards large volumes. *The Computer Journal, 32*(6), 516–523.

Saffo, P. (1987). What you need to know about hypertext. *Personal Computing,* 166–173.

Schwartz, M., & Delisle, N. (1987). Contexts—A partitioning concept for hypertext. *ACM Trans. on Office Information Systems, 5*(2), 168–186.

Senge, P. (1990). *The fifth discipline. The art & practice of the learning organization.* New York: Doubleday/Currency.

Shetler, T. (1990, Feb.). Birth of the blob. *Byte,* 221–226.

Shneiderman, B. (1987). User interface design for the hyperties electronic encyclopedia. In *Proceedings of Hypertext '87* (pp. 199–204). UNC Raleigh, NC.

Shneiderman, B. (1989). Reflections on authoring, editing, and managing hypertext. In E. Barrett (Ed.), *The society of text.* Cambridge, MA: MIT Press.

Shneiderman, B., & Kearsley, G. (1989). *Hypertext hands-on!* Reading, MA: Addison-Wesley Publishing.

Shultz, E. K., Brown, R. W., & Beck, J. R. (1989). Hypermedia in pathology: The Dartmouth interactive medical record project. *AJCP,* 91 (supplement)(4), S34–S38.

Smeaton, A. F. (1991). Using hypertext for computer-based learning. *Computers and Education, 17*(3), 173–179.

Smith, J. B., & Weiss, S. F. (1988). Hypertext: Introduction to special issue on hypertext. *Communications of the ACM, 31*(7), 816–819.

Smith, K. E. (1988, March). Hypertext—linking to the future. *Online,* 32–40.

Smith, W. R., & Hahn, J. S. (1989). Hypermedia or hyperchaos: Using HyperCard to teach medical decision making. In *Proceedings of the thirteenth annual symposium on computer applications in medical care* (pp. 858–863). Washington, DC, November 5–8: The Computer Society of the IEEE.

Spiro, R. J., Coulson, R. L., Feltovich, P. J., & Anderson, D. K. (1988). Cognitive flexibility theory: Advanced knowledge acquisition in ill-structured domains. In V. Patel (Ed.), *Tenth annual conference of the Cognitive Science Society* (pp. 375–383). Hillsdale, NJ: Lawrene Erlbaum Associates.

Spiro, R. J., Feltovich, P. J., Jacobson, M. J., & Coulson, R. L. (1991, May). Cognitive flexibility, constructivism, and hypertext: Random access instruction for advanced knowledge acquisition in ill-structured domains. *Educational Technology, 31*(5), 24–33.

Spiro, R. J., & Jehng, J. (1990). Cognitive flexibility and hypertext: Theory and technology for the nonlinear and multidimensional traversal of complex subject matter. In D. Nix & R. Spiro (Eds.), *Cognition, education, & multimedia: Exploring ideas in high technology.* Hillsdale, NJ: Lawrence Erlbaum Associates.

Spiro, R. J., Vispoel, W., Schmitz, J., Samarapungavan, A., & Boerger, A. (1987). Knowledge acquisition for application: Cognitive flexibility and transfer in complex content domains. In B. C. Britton & S. Glynn (Eds.), *Executive control processes in reading* (pp. 177–199). Hillsdale, NJ: Lawrence Erlbaum Associates.

Stefanac, S., & Weiman, L. (1990, April). Multimedia: Is it real? *Byte,* 116–123.

Stevens, G. H. (1992). Hypertext and hypermedia definitions and design issues. At Annual Convention of the Association for Educational Communications and Technology, Washington, DC.

Suchman, L. (1987). *Plans and situated actions: The problem of human-machine communication.* Cambridge, UK: Cambridge University Press.

Swift, M. K. (1991, June). Hypertext: A tool for knowledge transfer. *Journal of Systems Management,* 3–37.

Timpka, T. (1989). Introducing hypertext in primary health care: A study on the feasibility of decision support for practitioners. *Computer Methods and Programs in Biomedicine, 29,* 1–13.

Tognazzini, B. (1990, Winter). Principles of multimedia visible interface design. *Multimedia Review,* 18–22.

Trumbull, D., Gay, G., & Mazur, J. (1992). Students' actual and perceived use of navigational guidance tools in a hypermedia program. *Journal of Research on Computing in Education, 24*(3), 315–328.

Tulving, E., & Thomson, D. M. (1973). Encoding specificity and retrieval processes in episodic memory. *Psychological Review, 80,* 352–373

Wasylenski, L. (1988, Oct.). Using HyperCard in the classroom. *Computers in Education,* 8–9.

Weaver, P. A., & McCleary, K. W. (1990, Aug.). Hypertext: Publishing method of the future. *Cornell H.R.A. Quarterly,* 108–110.

Weinstein, C. E. (1978). *Elaboration skills as a learning strategy.* In H. F. O'Neil (Ed.), *Learning strategies.* New York: Academic Press.

Weldon, L. J., Mills, C. B., Koved, L., & Shneiderman, B. (1985). The structure of information in online and paper technical manuals. In *Proceedings of the Human Factors Society—29th annual conference* (pp. 1110–1112). Santa Monica, CA.

Werkman, R. F., Abell, T. L., & Hahn, J. S. (1990). Hypermedia to oracle: A gastrointestinal endoscopy database. In *Proceedings of the fourteenth annual symposium on computer applications in medical care*. Washington, DC, Nov. 4–7.

Whitehead, A. N. (1929). *The aims of education*. New York: Macmillan.

Williams, G. (1987, Dec.). HyperCard: HyperCard extends the Macintosh user-interface and makes everybody a programmer. *Byte*, 109–117.

Winn, W. (1988). *Rethinking instructional design procedures in light of cognitive theory*. Unpublished manuscript, University of Washington, Seattle.

Winn, W. (1991). Diagrams as aids to problem solving: Their role in facilitating search and computation. *Educational Technology Research & Development, 39*(1), 17–29.

Winn, W., & Li, T.-Z. (1991). Diagrams as aids to problem-solving: Their role in facilitating search and computation. *Educational Technology Research and Development, 39*(1), 17–29.

Wittrock, M. C. (1974a). A generative model of mathematics learning. *Journal of Research in Mathematics Education, 5*, 181–197.

Wittrock, M. C. (1974b). Learning as a generative process. *Educational Psychologist, 11*, 87–95.

Wittrock, M. C. (1979). The cognitive movement in instruction. *Educational Researcher, 8*(2), 5–11.

Wittrock, M. C. (1990). Generative processes of comprehension. *Educational Psychologist, 24*(4), 345–376

Wurman, R. S. (1989). *Information anxiety*. New York: Doubleday.

Yankelovich, N., Haan, B., Meyrowitz, N., & Drucker, S. M. (1988, Jan.). Intermedia: The concept and the construction of a seamless environment. *IEEE Computer*, 81–96.

Yankelovich, N., Meyrowitz, N., & van Dam, A. (1985, Oct.). Reading and writing the electronic book. *IEEE Computer*, 15–30.

Yoder, E., Akscyn, R., & McCracken, D. (1989, May). Collaboration in KMS: A shared hypermedia system. In *Proceedings of the CHI'89*, Austin, TX.

42

Computer Mediated Communication

Alexander J. Romiszowski
Jason Ravitz
Syracuse University
Syracuse, New York

Introduction: Why Is CMC a New Paradigm?

A working definition of computer mediated communication is "communication between different parties separated in space and/or time, mediated by interconnected computers." Computer mediated communication (CMC) is a generic term now commonly used for a variety of systems that enable people to communicate with other people by means of computers and networks. Well-known examples of such systems include computer conferencing, electronic mail, discussion lists, and bulletin boards. However, there are yet other possible applications of CMC both in the work environment and in education and training.

In the work environment, a common and growing phenomenon is collaborative work by individuals or groups who are separated from each other by either time or distance. This has come to be called Computer Supported Cooperative Work (CSCW) (Grief, 1988). In the education and training context, in addition to computer "conferencing," we can set up computer-mediated discussions of a more focused nature as exemplified by the so-called "Virtual Classroom" (Hiltz, 1986, 1990), computer-mediated seminars and case study discussions (Romiszowski & DeHaas, 1989; Romiszowski, Jost, & Chang, 1990), and computer-mediated job "performance support systems" (Gery, 1991). The variety of alternative modalities is large and growing.

As we move into the age of synergy between the cognitive sciences, computer sciences, and telecommunications, we are continually being faced with new possibilities for communication over distances. As an example, the recent movement towards multimedia computing has already found an application in computer-based audiographic conferencing systems with multimedia support for visual communications and in desktop-video conferencing systems that provide two-way digitized video communication between remote sites. Voicemail systems are also being applied in education and training contexts to enable asynchronous audio conferencing or multi-way communication between people at remote sites (Bernard & Naidu, 1990; Iskandar, 1994; Romiszowski & Iskandar, 1992).

We have recently seen hybrid applications that involve a combination of computer-based instruction and computer-mediated discussions between students at a distance (e.g., Romiszowski & Chang, 1992, 1994). Indeed, computer-based collaborative work almost invariably involves such a combination. Some authors see such hybrid "fourth generation distance education systems" as playing a central role in future technology-based education (Lauzon & Moore, 1989).

It is increasingly common to encounter systems that combine the use of information accessed from remote databases with CMC interchanges between users. The computer network combines the permanent nature of written communication with the speed and to some extent the dynamicism of spoken telephone communication. Moreover, unlike the telephone, the real-time communication of CMC can provide a shared context, and a rich structure that supports continued evolving use (Curtis, 1995). The existence of distributed databases represents not only an explosion of access to information, but also represents the accumulation and development of new knowledge from a distributed group of users as they become information providers as well as consumers. How is this information processed, synthesized, criticized, and turned into knowledge? This is one of the many questions CMC researchers seek to address (e.g., Koschmann *et al.*, 1993). These advances will largely be excluded from this chapter, though occasionally they may be mentioned as future developments with implications for future research questions. Additionally, the computer science research involved in CMC (e.g., object-oriented, multimedia environments, virtual reality markup language, tool development, and so on) will not be addressed here as we are concentrating on CMC as a new communication paradigm.

So, is CMC a new communication paradigm? In order to be counted as a new paradigm, CMC must meet the criteria set forth by Kuhn (1962) and summarized by the editors of this volume in Chapter 1:

(1) it represents a significant departure from past practices;
(2) it has attracted a large number of followers;
(3) it raises unprecedented research issues that promise to be of concern for some time.

Additionally, we should add a fourth criterion as follows:

(4) it has given rise to a new group of practitioners and leaders who have embraced the technology and who are not afraid of change.

Although CMC can be (and is) used to support traditional activities that represent non-paradigmatic change, this chapter deals with the ways in which it does represent a paradigmatic shift in communication, business, and education. Although CMC is not always used in groundbreaking ways, it would seem that we are in the process of a major transformation of the communication habits and patterns of our society. It is not necessary to detail all the recent CMC research here to illustrate that it does have the attributes of a new paradigm. CMC represents a significant departure from past practices; it has attracted large numbers of researchers; it raises unprecedented research issues that promise to be of concern for some time; and it is being embraced as part of their practice by significant numbers of educational leaders. In the following sections we shall analyze the current state of CMC from these four perspectives, and also the impact it is having on business and educational settings.

CMC as a Departure from Previous Practice

A computer network can act as a communication medium just as if it were a printed book containing text and graphics, a video broadcasting system, or a telephone. However, the computer brings certain characteristics to the communication process that the majority of previously available communication media did not offer.

Highly Interactive Communication

The first of these characteristics is the capability of supporting complex processes of interaction between the participants. Unlike the limited interactivity available in other forms of computer-based learning, such as CAI, the possibilities for interaction and feedback in CMC environments are almost limitless, being a function of the creativity and personal involvement of the participants in the on-line discussion. The feedback messages do not have to be pre-prepared and stored as is the case with computer-assisted instruction (CAI). Also, the participants are able to some extent to express within their messages not only the bare content but also their personal viewpoints and, to a limited extent, the emotional overtones that may be present. Thus, the potential for interaction in a CMC system is both more flexible and potentially richer than in other forms of computer-based education.

Multi-Way Communication

Another aspect of the communication process is that it is essentially multi-way communication. At the very least, the communication is two-way, as in the case of two people exchanging messages in an electronic mail environment. More often, however, the communication is multi-way, between all the participants of a group who may receive and respond to messages from all the other participants.

One point which should be considered is whether unlimited multi-way communication is in fact always desirable within an educational situation. Many participants in computer conferencing have expressed frustration and disappointment with the difficulty they have had in sorting out relevant from irrelevant information, due to the fact that there are so many participants contributing messages on a variety of different topics. One approach to creating some order in this chaos is through the development of special-purpose educational CMC software environments that may break down a complex conference into sub-themes and issues held in separate "areas" as if it were in separate rooms in a convention center (for example, CoSy and PARTIcipate are software packages that support this). Conferencing software can automatically link the incoming messages into discussion threads so that the users of the CMC system can get a clear idea of the structure of previous discussions. Hypertext environments have also been applied to breaking down a large group of participants into small groups for intensive discussion, replicating in the on-line environment the classroom-based techniques of seminars or case studies (Chang, 1994; Romiszowski & Chang, 1992).

Synchronous or Asynchronous Communication

Finally, the communication process may have both synchronous and asynchronous characteristics. We understand synchronous communication to be communication between two or more people in real time, such as a classroom-based face-to-face discussion, or a telephone conversation. In asynchronous communication, the participants are not both on-line at the same time, (e.g., correspondence by letter or fax). There are advantages and disadvantages to each of these forms of communication. For example, in an asynchronous communication process, one loses a certain degree of spontaneity and dynamism, but on the other hand gains time to analyze the message received, reflect on the appropriate response, if necessary, make reference to other information sources, and compose and edit the final response with all due care. Different educational situations may depend for their success on different mixes of these factors. The interesting aspect of using the computer as a communication medium is that it is possible to use it both as a synchronous communication medium like a telephone or an asynchronous communication medium like a fax system at will, depending upon what is ideally required by the particular situation (Rawson, 1990; Sheffield & McQueen, 1990).

Pervasiveness of CMC

Origins of CMC Networks

Computer mediated communication is in fact one of the earlier modes in which computers have been used within the education process. Before CAI was more than an idea in the minds of certain researchers, computer networking and conferencing systems were already implemented, initially to facilitate communication among researchers. Indeed, it was in response to the fear of a possible war damaging the potential of researchers to continue to work that many of the major universities and government research institutions of the US were linked by a network named ARPANET, which was so designed as to offer multiple communication paths between the various nodes or sites in the network (Elmer-Dewitt, 1994). The idea was that if certain sites are knocked out, the remaining sites could still communicate with each other independently of the particular geographic location of the disabled sites. This characteristic of the ARPANET system has been maintained in its successors such as Bitnet and the Internet. Indeed, the Internet is in effect a worldwide network of ARPANET-like local regional networks (Jacobson & Zimpfer, 1992).

Proliferation of the Networks

The linking of all regional networks to all the others creates multiple pathways of access from any one node in any one network to any other node in any of the other networks. This powerful web of electronic communication has become an indispensable tool for research and collaborative work in the scientific community. During the last few years, the academic exclusivity of Internet has broken down as an ever-increasing number of commercial providers have opened access to anybody willing to subscribe.

Corporate Uses of CMC

In the area of business communications, CMC has already become firmly established. Today, most of the major companies in the US and Europe either rent or maintain their own data and personal communication networks. This enables all departments to communicate effectively and efficiently by electronic means, both within their corporate network and increasingly over the Internet. One aspect of increasing importance in these systems is the use of electronic mail, computer conferencing, and increasingly, computer supported cooperative work between individuals or groups who may be scattered in different regions of a country or even on different continents. The "globalization" of business communication has become a necessary contribution for staying competitive.

The tendency to this "whole world" view of telecommunications coupled with the possibility of digitizing and storing messages for transmission at more convenient or more economical times is transforming the whole socio-political structure of business communications and is now also beginning to impact on personal communications.

Educational Uses of CMC

In education, a particular growth area is the use of computer mediated communication systems, not only for distance education when the participants are separated physically, but also for more convenient communication on the same campus. Applications include institutions that utilize CMC as a principal mode of instruction and communication between tutors and students for whole courses, programs that run a few course units by means of CMC, and the use of CMC as a support medium for enrichment in otherwise conventional courses. Kuehn (1988) suggests that electronic mail can extend classroom discussions, increase the ease of evaluating student assignments, increase the connectedness of students and faculty, and increase both the social as well as the intellectual impact from this means of communication. However, such developments are not free of problems.

One of the problems identified in the educational uses of computer conferencing is that of teacher workload. Experiences from the NKI Electronic College in Norway show that teachers' main reservation about educational CMC is the open-ended demand on their time (Paulsen, 1992). As early as 1988, Hiltz noted that teaching an on-line course, at least the first time, was a bit like parenthood. "You are 'on duty' all the time, and there seems to be no end to the demands on your time and energy" (Hiltz, 1988, p. 31). Nevertheless, many educators who are enthusiastic about the use of this new teaching medium have adapted strategies from small-group and interactive face-to-face techniques to the on-line world. Examples include: seminars, learning partnerships, group projects, team presentations, simulations and role plays, peer counseling and self-help groups. These and other strategies are described in Miller (1991). Thus, one area of research concerns the development of tools, skills, and procedures to improve and facilitate this process. Further research questions are discussed in the following section.

Research Issues in CMC

An Emerging Research Agenda

Research surrounding CMC parallels the expansion of this technology. Journal articles begin appearing with frequency around 1984, although the roots of research in the field go back to the 1960s and earlier (Hiltz & Turoff, 1978). Regular academic conferences were convened and several edited books devoted to CMC began to appear around the early 1980s (Harasim, 1990b; Kaye, 1992a; Kerr & Hiltz, 1982; Mason, 1993; Mason & Kaye, 1989). Since 1990, scholars have developed several comprehensive bibliographies. Among these, Romiszowski (1992) and Burge (1992) each list approximately 400 references—from conference proceedings, edited book chapters, professional papers, and journal articles.

Now there is a constant stream of conference proceedings and edited books appearing at the rate of several per year, some devoted to specific and others to general aspects of research and development in CMC. Notable among recent publications are the anthology on *Collaborative Learning through Computer Conferencing,* edited by Kaye (1992a, 1992b), the volume edited by Waggoner (1992), the *Proceedings of the Third Teleteaching Conference* held in Trondheim, Norway, edited by Davies and Samways (1993), and regular Conference Proceedings emanating from such universities as Wisconsin at Madison, USA; Guelph in Ontario, Canada; and the Open University in the United Kingdom. We also see Computer Supported Collaborative Learning (CSCL) as a subset of Computer Supported Cooperative Work (CSCW). We consider CSCW to be a new educational paradigm (Koschmann, in press).

Examination of the earlier materials finds many of them to be anecdotal in nature, written by pioneers in implementing CMC technology for educational purposes, promoting the exciting educational possibilities of this new medium, and reporting case descriptions of their own experiences with these innovations. However, some basic research was performed; a 1992 survey found over 35 CMC studies completed or in progress (Cole, Beam, Karn, & Hoad-Reddick, 1992). These authors report that the majority of studies came out of a quantitative/positivist paradigm. However, they argue, as does Mason (1992), that interpretist and critical theory paradigms may be more appropriate for studying the CMC environment. So far, few studies have been performed from these "neo-qualitative" perspectives.

As mentioned above, a large proportion of the earlier writings and indeed some of the current writings on CMC are exploring the potential of CMC rather than reporting hard research. As an example, among the 400 publications listed in the bibliography prepared by Romiszowski (1992), only some 10% to 15% were research studies. This compares to 25% on overviews, reviews, applications, trends, and policy; another 15% on design, development, and implementation strategies; 15% on the hardware, software, systems, and logistics; another 20% on aspects of networking, and hardware and system related issues; finally, some 15% on descriptions of database access and CSCW projects or applications.

The research papers can be further classified into several areas of interest. First, there are issues of general concern, such as: the access to CMC and whether it has a democratizing or elitist impact on society; the quality of on-line information and its equivalence to printed material (particularly relevant in the case of on-line journals); the social impact of CMC on the users; methods of implementation and use in both distance education and in conventional courses; and research aspects of software capability, design, and utilization.

A second group of research interests can be generally referred to as "teaching and learning concerns." These include: the content and objectives that may be treated by CMC; the process of interactivity and interaction as it occurs in CMC; appropriate learning strategies and tactics that may be employed in CMC; aspects of learner control or system control of CMC systems; and the effectiveness or other outcomes of CMC used for educational purposes.

A third group of research interests may be best referred to as implementation concerns. These include: aspects of student participation or non-participation and their attitudes; attitudes and participation styles of instructors and teachers using CMC; aspects to do with the implementation and administration of CMC systems; and logistic and planning aspects to do with staff and support systems.

Because of the difficulty of reaching CMC users, often separated by space or time, most research efforts to date involved survey research, either through electronic or conventionally distributed questionnaires (see, for example, Grabowski *et al.*, 1990; Phillips & Pease, 1987; Ryan, 1992). Another relatively popular method is the evaluative case study (e.g., Mason, 1990; Phillips, 1990; Phillips, Santoro, & Kuehn, 1988). However, many researchers recognize the value of automatic computer-based recording of communications transactions, and have sought to capitalize on usage, interaction, and transcript information directly available from the conferences (Henri, 1992; Levin, Kim, & Riel, 1990; Mason, 1992; Tucker, 1991). Harasim (1987) first used mainframe computer records to analyze student access times and dispersion of participation in a graduate computer conference.

There is little use to date, in the study of CMC, of qualitative approaches based on observation and interviewing (either in-person or over the telephone). This is so for several reasons: (a) the labor intensity of qualitative research study; (b) the expense and difficulty of contacting ex-CMC users; and (c) the relatively recent acceptance of qualitative research in education. Some more recent studies, for example, Eastmond (1993) and Burge (1993), have, however, adopted such a methodology. Emerging technologies may soon help to overcome or eliminate some of the difficulties of this form of research. For example, the British Open University in 1996 embarked on a project that uses new software developments available on the Internet to conduct and manage the data collection and analysis of interactive interviews and discussions. By the end of 1996 this project will have integrated data collected from some one hundred thousand participants who will have been interviewed via the World Wide Web.

Nevertheless, the most glaring omission in CMC research continues to be the lack of analytical techniques applied to the content of the conference transcript. Given that the educational value of computer conferencing is much touted by enthusiasts, it is remarkable that so few evaluators are willing to tackle this research area. One of the pioneers in this field is Henri (1992), who presents an analytical framework for categorizing five dimensions of the learning process exteriorized in messages: participation, interactions, social, cognitive and metacognitive. Another is Mason (1992), who has attempted to draw up a typology of conference messages related to the educational values they display. We hope to see more research like this in the future.

Changing Technologies

One important trend already mentioned is the explosive rate at which new technologies for communication are being disseminated. The current multimedia and hypermedia developments have already been absorbed into CMC educational environments, producing systems that, at least in principle, have the potential for vastly improving the rather unstructured and text-based modes of communication that were the characteristic of earlier CMC systems. The incorporation of graphics, audio, video and in the future perhaps even simulations of a virtual reality nature, which may all be transmitted across the digital information superhighways (e.g., via technologies based on the World Wide Web) presents the potential for much richer CMC environments and promises to attract new types of users.

Most of the research completed so far is related to the earlier forms of text-based CMC. Some of these results may be equally valid within the future multimedia distance education systems. However, we may expect many new issues and research questions to emerge as these broad-band multimedia, multi-modal communication systems link both people and remote databases into one seamless information and communication environment.

Replicate or Innovate?

Another issue which is increasingly facing CMC researchers and practitioners is whether this medium should be considered as an alternative way of implementing previously well tried teaching/learning strategies or whether the medium itself may lead to the implementation of novel strategies that previously were not used. Among the research and development work that has followed the line of replication of the past, a notable trend is illustrated by the "Virtual Classroom" methodologies that have been implemented and researched by Roxanne Hiltz and her collaborators (Hiltz, 1986, 1990). This work has focused on the replication of well tried classroom-based teaching/learning strategies in a networked environment. Variations on the virtual classroom might include the virtual conference room (that is, computer conferencing), the virtual seminar room, and the virtual case study discussion room, each implying a specific set of teaching/learning strategies (Romiszowski, 1993).

A non-conventional example of a popular use of CMC is to supplement conventional classroom-based instruction with group exercises or projects that participants "take home," where they continue to interact with both teacher and colleagues through the medium of CMC. This approach, although not new with respect to its project work details, is novel in that it extends the possibilities for group interaction (Grabowski *et al.*, 1990). An example of a somewhat more novel approach is the trend towards the implementation of learner controlled environments that may combine the use of information resources stored remotely as a hypermedia network of information, together with computer supported collaborative project work between groups of individuals utilizing the CMC capabilities of the network (Chang, 1994; Romiszowski & Chang, 1992, 1994).

Technological Synergy

Yet another important trend is the technological synergy between the computer sciences, the cognitive sciences, and the telecommunications sciences, which is offering a host of possibilities, such as artificial intelligence software that may act as an intelligent interface between remote library databases and students or may in other ways facilitate the learning process. One possibility that is not yet a full reality is the capability of a computer mediated communication system to handle instant translation so that group discussions may take place between participants from different countries, the groups using their own native languages in the process.

Another area of current technological development which is yet to show its promise in practice is virtual reality or, in other words, the physical simulation of personal closeness and involvement in a particular environment. It is possible to imagine CMC systems of the future that will not be open to the criticism of the loss of non-verbal communication elements such as expression, gesture, or even touch. The applications of these new technological possibilities are yet unresearched. However, progress in the field is so rapid that it is not too early to consider some of the research issues that such new technological possibilities might pose. How would such integration work, what would it depend on, what will be its capabilities and what are the expected timelines and costs for making this available? Additionally, what are the trade-offs for learning? For example, does moving from a text to a visual medium entail less use of imagination? Does it present problems for the visually impaired who currently use text readers?

Changing Theories and Philosophies

CMC provides a rich arena for the work of educational theorists. Theoretical and philosophical "camps" are locked in fervent debate on CMC-related issues. One notable current debate which impacts on the role of CMC in education is the "constructivism vs. objectivism" debate. The constructivist viewpoint is often aligned with CMC and opposed to CAI, which is seen as an objectivist approach to teaching and learning (Cunningham, Duffy, & Knuth, 1993; Kaye, 1992b). Some constructivists who align themselves with CMC argue that the Internet itself represents the active ongoing creation by the participants of something that did not exist before, and therefore it is an exemplar of constructivism in action.

Another not-so-recent debate which has been revived in relation to the use of CMC is the "humanism vs. mechanism" issue. The humanists see the personal interaction between people that CMC allows as an important element in the appropriate use of computers in education. A similar debate on the "cognitive vs. behaviorist psychology" platform may lead to positions being taken either for or against the use of CMC (Morrison, 1989).

Other groups of theorists argue for CMC from the standpoint of learning as "conversation." In this viewpoint, the teaching/learning process is seen as a form of conversation (whether real or in the mind of the learner) which leads to an "agreement" on the meaning of specific content. It is argued that CMC, through the provision of real opportunities for conversation, might be a more appropriate medium for the development of those types of learning objectives for which a conversational approach is of particular importance, i.e., higher order learning objectives associated with problem solving and critical thinking skills (Romiszowski & Corso, 1990).

Yet other philosophical/theoretical viewpoints that have been brought to bear on the relevance and appropriateness of CMC are Habermas' theory of un-dominated communicative action (Boyd, 1990) and Postmodernism (Soby, 1990). All of these different theoretical and philosophical viewpoints are interesting but are largely unresearched. Some current research is beginning to address certain issues in this field. For example, Chang (1994) compared several different methods of organizing a CMC discussion of a Harvard Business Case. These methods differed in the extent to which they reflected a constructivist or an objectivist philosophy. He found no significant difference between the treatments with respect to their effectiveness, but the more objectivist treatments were more efficient in terms of the use of student time. However, much more work is necessary in order to validate the claims and counterclaims and to develop a robust set of principles for the selection, design and use of CMC environments in education and training.

Extent of Theory/Knowledge Base

CMC scholarship tends to proudly acclaim the educational merits of this technology for a variety of reasons—access, collaboration, interactivity, self-direction, and experiential learning to name a few—yet few of these are grounded in systematic, rigorous inquiry. As more and more research accumulates, the ability to use CMC to manage the resulting information would appear to be important as a microcosm and testing ground for this approach to information management and knowledge construction. This research and the resulting discussion among practitioners at all levels of the educational system contributes to a knowledge base about developing CMC. It is the explicit goal of some projects to use electronic networks to build knowledge resources and to support processes of collective learning (Ravitz, 1995).

The CMC knowledge base, albeit small at present, is growing at a very fast rate, due to the number of researchers who are devoting their attention to the issues. At the present time, the sheer volume of research activity on CMC exceeds most other areas of educational technology research and development. Furthermore, not only are there many interested researchers, but the opportunities for research are multiplying as the number of real-world CMC applications grows.

CMC Leadership and Practice in the Real World

Electronic Networks and Future Education and Training

The development of telecommunications and digital data transmission is revolutionizing the way that business is performed. People are working and communicating ever more by means of computer-based work stations that support databases, electronic mail and a host of other information tools. As electronic communication networks become more ubiquitous, easier to use and more powerful, the trend towards electronic, networked, business communications will grow rapidly. As a result, people will spend an increasing proportion of their time at workstations and proportionately less in live meetings (Vallee, 1982; Zuboff, 1988).

As economic realities shift towards ever decreasing costs of electronic communication and ever increasing costs of transport, space, lighting, heating, and teaching salaries, the tendency towards distance education methods, particularly electronically delivered distance education, is likely to increase yet further. In the light of this situation, it is important to verify to what extent the use of CMC can be an effective alternative to conventional methods of teaching and learning.

The U.S. telephone company, AT&T, for example, has already moved towards the massive use of "teletraining" in place of conventional classroom-based courses for most of its sales and management training needs. The major part of sales and management training in AT&T is now delivered by this method (in 1989, over 69,000 employees participated at least once in some form of teletraining) and results overall are considered to be quite satisfactory (Chute, 1990). The rapid expansion in use of electronic teletraining is being driven, as always, not so much by considerations of effectiveness, but rather by economic factors. AT&T has reported an overall reduction of over 50% in the costs per student hour of training. This cost saving comes almost entirely from savings in travel and subsistence costs (incurred when employees participate in centrally organized "place-based" courses) as well as from reduced loss of productivity due to a reduction in the time employees are away from their jobs (Chute, 1990; Chute *et al.*, 1988).

There is a similar growth in the practical grassroots acceptance of CMC in the formal education sector. If one of the functions of a new paradigm is to create opportunities for new real-world practices, with new leadership and new relationships developing, clearly CMC performs this function. Leadership is frequently seen to come from the more remote areas that have the most to gain from access to CMC resources via networks, e.g., at University of Minnesota's Crookston campus where, with support from IBM, every student receives a laptop computer from their student fee, and every building is being networked (Peterson, 1995). Athabasca University in Alberta is a premier distance learning center which has committed strongly to the use of CMC as a principal course delivery medium (Holt & Gismondi, 1995), and George Washington University offers a Master's degree program in Educational Technology Leadership that relies on CMC as an essential element (Kearseley, Lynch, & Wizer, 1995).

New Forms of Education and Training

In this section, we examine the CMC paradigm in relation to some others presented in this book. Because the impact of CMC is felt across society, it converges with paradigm shifts described throughout this volume, both in business and education. CMC supports the business shifts described by Davies (in this volume) to global markets; it supports boundaryless training and operation, and a process orientation. Communications between businesses represent authentic learning opportunities and can help provide just-in-time training. Davies states that "In most of American business today, over 60% of work is carried out by high performance work groups." This almost always involves the use of CMC, at least internally within an organization. CMC accompanies a changed role for the manager, the trainer, and the subject matter expert as their availability and access to employees in the field is transformed. Re-engineering of companies requires new levels of communication across an increasingly flat organization. Additionally, he states that for instructional technologists, "design and development, under the new paradigm, has become a multi-functional, multi-level, high performance team activity." These are only a few of the ways we see the impact of CMC in this domain of new business practice.

CMC is also related to the shifts in education that include, for example, reflective conversation and cooperative learning as outlined by Wilson (in this volume). Increasingly, learning dialogues and group processes are directly supported by CMC, as also are role playing exercises, simulation-games and case studies. In many cases situated learning, as described by Orey and Nelson (in this volume), is supported by CMC as on-line mentorships are made available to learners and interaction within a "community of practice" is fostered via computerized networks. The ability of CMC to support social interactions can maximize learning by making a connection between learning and authentic settings as the classroom increasingly interacts with the local community, its people and resources (Klingenstein, 1995). In these cases, learners develop skills for communicating within the community, making a contribution to and benefiting from their participation in discussions. Reciprocal teaching and the development of communal knowledge and memory all can be supported by computer networks (see Orey & Nelson, in this volume).

In another chapter in this volume, Dreyfus and Dreyfus present the case that the real role of computers in the instructional process is much more limited than many authors would lead us to believe. In all the cases quoted above, however, the computer network plays the role of a communication medium that links people to people, rather than a "teaching machine" that takes over some of the functions of an instructor or facilitator. Therefore we do not see the above comments to be in conflict with the position taken by Dreyfus and Dreyfus. This observation is yet one more reason for considering CMC as a new paradigm for technology-based teaching. It represents a move away from the previously prevalent view of the computer's role in education, so well summarized by Taylor (1980) as "Tutor, Tool and Tutee," to a new perception of the computer (network) as "Medium" using the term in McLuhan's (1964) sense of "Extensions of Man." (See also the discussion of extensions in Chapter 1 of this volume.)

There are also other pressures, both organizational and philosophical, that are increasing the amount of autonomy, self-directedness, and responsibility that learners have with respect to their own education and development. From the philosophical side, there is the viewpoint that people should have more control over what they learn and how they learn it. This viewpoint is embodied in the principles of modern adult education, or andragogy. It also reflects earlier humanist traditions (see the three chapters by Brockett, Hiemstra and Sisco in this volume). They are further strengthened by the modern concepts of continuing or "permanent education," which spring from the realization that change in society, and particularly in the workplace, is now so fast that everyone is of necessity involved in a process of lifelong learning. This need for updating may in some respects be very specific and personal for each individual. Hence the growing popularity of the "Open Learning" concept as a modular approach to education that can take anyone from wherever they are at present to wherever they need/want to be in a given domain, relatively independently of the needs/ wants of other people (Paine, 1988).

Given the increasingly competitive nature of business in the international marketplace and the critical importance that access to and use of up-to-date information and methods plays in a company's competitiveness, it is not surprising that the concept of human resources development as "self-development" is taking root. This concept sees keeping up-to-date and employable as the responsibility of every employee. The employer's responsibility is to make this possible, by helping to identify the needs of the individual and by facilitating access to the resources necessary to satisfy those needs. This will call less frequently for lengthy courses organized either within the company or by outside providers, but will instead make much more use of networking, access to external databases and electronic libraries, small specialist group teletraining, and self-instruction in all its forms (Eurich, 1990).

As the trends outlined above expand through the business community, similar trends will be seen in relation to adult education, especially in the growing use of distance education in formal educational institutions. To some extent, similar economic factors may lead to a greater use of distance education and electronic networking as the prime delivery media for certain courses. More ubiquitous, however, will be the use of electronic communication media to support conventional courses. One reason for this is the organizational and pedagogic benefits that such systems can offer conventional courses; another is that it will be seen to be the duty of education to use such systems in order to prepare its graduates for the realities of a workplace where they will be obliged to use them.

This last point really brings home the importance of conducting research now on how these technologies afford new types of high quality educational experiences, i.e., before networks become used widely for the replication of existing processes. Analysis of more innovative uses today can advance effective learning models to be used in future networked communication systems. This focus is particularly important, as we know much less about how to converse effectively on electronic networks than we do about electronic self-instruction. There is a long history of and fairly developed technology for the design, development and delivery-at-a-distance of self-study materials. There is much less known about the running of effective group-discussion sessions at a distance.

Such teaching methods as seminars or case studies are traditionally implemented in small or medium sized face-to-face groups, led by skilled and experienced "facilitators." Much of the success of these teaching methods is ascribed to the facilitators and the skill with which they focus discussion; guide the approaches adopted by the participants; use the natural group dynamics to stimulate interest, participation and deep involvement; pull together what has been learned in the final debriefing discussion; and so on. Can such participatory discussion methods be effectively orchestrated at a distance, electronically? How might this be done? Before considering the strategic levels that must be addressed to answer the above questions, let us review a little theory and also some of the research that is already available on this topic.

Two Paradigms Compared

It may help to compare and contrast two alternative paradigms, or maybe philosophies, which can be seen in the real-world practice of education—we shall refer to them as the "instructional" and the "conversational" paradigms. These are summarized in tabular form in Table 1.

The "instructional" paradigm is the one that has driven much (though by no means all) of the research and development of the past 30 years that has been performed under the

Table 1.   Two teaching paradigms supported by CMC.

Process Components	Paradigm Processes	
	"INSTRUCTION"	"CONVERSATION"
OBJECTIVES: (output) (why?)	specific pre-defined products standard	general negotiable processes variable
MESSAGES: (input) (what?) (when?) (who?) (whom?)	designed pre-prepared instructor one-to-many	created on-line participants many-to-many
INTERACTION: (process—focus) (analysis) (feedback) (complexity)	behaviors criterion-ref. corrective one-layer-thick	ideas content/structure constructive interwoven layers
DISTANCE EDUCATION: (examples)	Correspondence Courses	Teleconferencing Videoconferencing
	Computer- Mediated Communication	Computer- Mediated Communication

label of educational (or instructional) technology. The "conversational" paradigm may be seen as the basis of much of the work done on small group study, group dynamics, experiential learning and so on. In relation to distance teaching specifically, one may notice at the bottom of Table 1 that the self-instructional "study module" or typical correspondence course may serve as a good example of the instructional paradigm. Synchronous teleconferencing, both audio and video based, is, on the other hand, a good example of the conversational paradigm in action. CMC, however, is seen as being able to support both conversational and instructional paradigms.

For example, joint cooperation on the analysis and development of a hypertext document satisfies all the basic requirements of a conversation between the participants. The study of an on-line version of a maintenance manual for an aircraft in order to learn a particular set of troubleshooting procedures satisfies the requirements of instruction. This versatility of CMC systems and their potential integration with on-line information sources such as hypertext makes them particularly interesting systems to study with a view to their rational adoption in education and training (Horn, 1989; Romiszowski, 1990).

A Plan for the Future:
Research and Development Agenda

It is clear that future technological synergy will be offering ever more powerful communication alternatives. Researchers are trying to be proactive and anticipative of technological change and its potential impact, both for good and bad, on education and training systems. This chapter illustrates the variety of ways that CMC is impacting business training and education. Agendas are being set at the national level, e.g., a National Information Infrastructure is being constructed in Singapore (Lewis & Romiszowski, 1995) and the United States (National Information Infrastructure Advisory Council, 1995) with an expected impact on businesses, universities, schools, and communities.

Previous sections of this chapter illustrated an abundance of research concerns at various levels. Researchers are concerned with issues involved in the making of sensible policy decisions regarding CMC: strategic planning decisions, tactical decisions within specific CMC projects, and logistic decisions concerning the tools of CMC. In this section we propose an outline of a research and development agenda that hopefully can help to make more sense of the role of CMC within the future "networked society." We have organized our observations on a multi-level model that parallels Gilbert's (1978) model of vantage points and is indeed the organizational model used for the major sections of the present volume. In this way, the reader may relate the content of this section, which is specific to CMC, to the overall paradigmatic picture of instructional development that is presented in the book as a whole.

Level of Policy/Culture/Philosophy: Acceptability of CMC

CMC is expected to have a direct impact on societal changes and therefore on education, specifically on the goals, the content, the delivery methods in the macro sense (for example, to what extent will the demand for distance education grow and in what sectors of the market) and so on. Additionally, it will shape the way new technological developments can offer solutions to some of education's current or anticipated problems. This particular area of research is especially prone to what we have called the "moving target problem"; technological change is happening at such a rate that the prediction of futures may be considered to be a continuing task rather than a project that can be done once and for all during a particular decade. Indeterminate technologies prevent one from knowing the outcome of implementation until after the fact (Berman, 1981; Itzkan, 1994/1995). The implications of not evaluating the alternatives in advance, or of evaluating them incorrectly are potentially very great, both in terms of misapplied project funding and in terms of possible disappointment with end results of an innovation.

Technology and the citizens of society exist within a complex system which has economic, political and other types of pressures and constraints. A very clear example of possible misjudgments can be seen in plans over the past several years based on the assumptions that certain technological improvements would be available within certain time spans. In the mid and late 1980s, many millions of dollars were invested in the United States into the "Education Utility." This concept was based on the assumption that within a year or two, all schools would be networked with sufficient bandwidth to enable a provider of educational information located at a distance to offer better service than the established system of book sellers, printers, and videotape producers (Gooler, 1986). Nearly ten years have gone by and the Education Utility concept has not become a reality on a grand scale (although there are numerous "mini-education utilities" that have been implemented by corporations or by state or local institutions). The technology is here but the political will and the economic pressures to make it available are not. It is important to note that setbacks are more often a result of human limitations than technological ones.

The above is especially troublesome given that one policy issue confronting CMC is that computer technology often significantly increases the gap between the "haves" and the "have-nots." Most CMC use is institutional, but as Eastmond (1993) reports, whether or not adults value this sort of experience often depends on their occupational status and socialization. Therefore, research must be carried out through a broad systemic approach involving the analysis of as many as possible of the factors that may play a part in the actual shaping of the future.

Some researchers also express concern that CMC builds global networks while reducing proximate neighborhood and family ties, that it may alter peoples' work and communication patterns significantly and may de-humanize interpersonal interaction (Eastmond, 1992; Zuboff, 1988). Levinson (1990) counters (without a research basis) that the technologies are more effective than we imagine in conveying human communication. Many anecdotal reports have noted that friendly relationships developed in spite of reduced cues, that participants became more casual and humorous over time, and that this medium invites more equitable participation. Additionally, the advent of community-wide networks supports their local as well as distant uses (Klingenstein, 1995) and may add a sense of connectedness as opposed to fragmentation.

The Strategic Level: Organizational Research/Development

The next level of research concerns strategic decisions in the context of overall planning of CMC systems and their integration into broader-based education and training systems. One important issue concerns strategies for effective dissemination of CMC in actual educational systems. The British Open University (OU) is currently engaged in finding answers to the research questions concerned with "scalability" of CMC. How can the undoubted successes of small group educational computer conferencing scale to distance education efforts? While some students valued electronic contact with their tutor and found that the medium reduced the isolation often reported by distance learners, the pedagogical benefits of this were shown to be highly dependent on the quality and quantity of the tutor input.

The larger the CMC network, the richer the resource for information exchange. However, depersonalization also occurs and so individuals are less likely to know the position, background, and expertise of those with whom they communicate. The problem of tutor workload is another critical issue (Mason & Kaye, 1989). It is the conclusion of those involved in many of these trials that no ideal model has yet been identified for applying these successes to large courses of 1000 to 5000 students (Mason, 1994). Some of the suggestions under consideration include: the extension and enhancement of peer learning groups; the use of 'master classes' in which a few students interact with an expert while the remainder can only read; increased input from central academic staff who normally write courses rather than interact with students; the use of World Wide Web facilities integrated with conferencing facilities; and the development of a few specialist conferencing tutors rather than the expectation that all tutors will be trained and paid for conferencing duties.

A variety of uses of conferencing are jumbled together amongst these suggestions and it is important to distinguish them: conferencing used for teaching (transmission of the content of the course) and conferencing used for tutoring (supporting the student); conferencing used for course delivery (of articles, updated material, directives from the course team) and conferencing used for interaction (between students and teachers). Over the next few years as the OU expands into continental Europe, it intends to make extensive use of computer conferencing. During this period, the OU expects to experiment widely with a variety of large-scale conferencing models.

The Tactical Level: Instructional Research

Perhaps one of the most important areas for tactical research at the moment is to investigate the potential applications and specific methodologies for collaborative learning. This research is examining the available tools and describing the additional tools that would be desirable. These may include shared workspaces, the sharing of documents, and even the possibility, through virtual reality, of being in almost physical contact with collaborators who are in reality at a distance.

A second important research area for the future is the design and evaluation of specific CMC environments for the implementation of particular types of instructional activities. These may include simulation games, small group discussions, group assignments or case study discussions. These techniques, which are typically practiced in small groups facilitated by a skilled expert, are among the techniques that are most valued for the development of critical thinking, problem solving and other higher-order cognitive skills. As society progresses into the age of technology, ever more of the routine tasks performed by human beings will be taken over by computers (whether they be physical tasks performed by robots or intellectual tasks performed by expert systems). The area for human employability will be more and more restricted to those types of tasks that computer systems cannot perform effectively. Some of these will be tasks that are very reliant on interpersonal skills, empathy and human contact. Others will be the tasks of the "knowledge worker," that is, the person who can perform intellectual tasks beyond the capability of computer software. As an ever greater proportion of the jobs performed by humans have these characteristics, there will be an ever greater need for critical thinking and creativity skills, and therefore an increasing need for educational methodologies and techniques that are effective at developing them.

Here we have a somewhat paradoxical situation. Small group face-to-face meetings which most effectively teach these skills will become more expensive as compared with the falling costs of various telecommunications-based methodologies. Therefore, we may be able to afford ever less (in terms of teaching methodologies) of what we require ever more—unless we can implement on CMC networks techniques for small group discussion on a wide scale. As an example, the work performed by Romiszowski and Chang (1992) and Chang (1994) is focused exactly on this particular problem, concentrating on the replication in a CMC environment of effective business case analysis and discussion methodologies.

Level of Logistics or Tools: Software and Networks Research

As new tools become available, will they be used to support traditional teaching, or will they offer the potential for the use of teaching strategies that were not possible with the previous technologies at our disposal? There is an obvious need for keeping utilization research abreast of tool development so that we have rational plans for the use of the new tools and technologies as they become available. Otherwise, we run the risk of being swept away by the appearance of the tools without a chance for their prior evaluation.

Opinions vary as to the significance of the software and its impact on the learning environment. For example, Eastmond (1992) contends that the "user-friendliness" and transparency of the system for enabling participants in CMC to use software features heavily impacts the CMC experience and the learning approaches taken with the media. An example of the way the software capabilities may influence a student's success and the overall success of a CMC experience was identified by Romiszowski and DeHaas (1989) and Romiszowski and Jost (1989) in analyzing the dynamics of educational computer conferences of a seminar-like nature held within a typical electronic mail environment. These studies identified two major problems experienced by both the participants and the CMC exercise organizers. The participants experienced a loss of the "sense of structure" of the discussion. The messages as received in their mailboxes in a linear stream did not reflect the sequence of the various arguments within the parallel discussions that were going on in the seminar. The result was that participants typically only recalled the most recent messages and did not relate them clearly to earlier messages. At the end of the conference, it was found that participants varied considerably in terms of their overall general view of what had been discussed and decided upon. A second problem, which may be considered more a problem for the organizers than for the participants, was the problem of "loss of control" over what exactly would be discussed. Maybe partly as a consequence of the loss of a sense of structure on the part of the students, the students would tend to pick up on a recently circulated message and respond to it out of context, often leading the discussion into a completely new area. It was found that the task of bringing discussants back onto the original topic was much more difficult in the CMC environment than would normally be the case in face-to-face discussion.

It was shown that these two problems were largely caused by the software environment within which the conferences were taking place. Modifying this environment greatly diminished both of the problems. A structured discussion environment within a hypertext software package was developed that would automatically create separate discussion areas in memory for each topic and automatically created links between relevant messages that could later be followed with ease (Romiszowski & Chang, 1992).

Some Concerns for the Future

Educational CMC takes place within an institutional context with learning as the desired outcome of this activity. This section focuses first on various learning concerns which have surfaced with the use of this medium. Next, it shifts to address institutional concerns such as the characteristics and participation of students, administration and implementation, and staff and support issues. The purpose is not to provide a comprehensive overview of the literature, but to indicate the variety of research issues being addressed concerning CMC and education. Our discussion of these issues is generally in agreement with the learning theory paradigm shift described by Wilson, and the business paradigm shift described by Davies (both elsewhere in this volume).

Teaching/Learning Concerns

The characteristics of CMC, although changing rapidly, still shape the instructional and communication activities they support. Perhaps the most obvious question to arise is whether CMC, which is still primarily text-based, is equally suited for various subject matters (Florini, 1990). As the capabilities of CMC change to include more powerful tools coupled with audio, visual and kinesthetic information, the range of subject matters supported by CMC will broaden. Wells (1992) surveyed courses being taught at both the undergraduate and graduate levels in the following subject areas: computer science, foreign languages, group performance skills, history, humanities, physics, statistics, education, engineering, management, and media studies. Wells suggests that subjects best suited to CMC are those that involve discussion, brainstorming, problem-solving, collaboration, and reflection. Interactivity, which in this context may best be defined as the capability for participants to receive specific feedback to their contributions of any length from any other member of a CMC discussion group, is touted as a primary advantage of this medium (Feenberg, 1989; Harasim, 1989; Moore, 1991). Studies of message exchange patterns support the perspective that communication patterns are more democratic and group discussion oriented than typically would be found in classrooms or other telecommunications settings (Harasim, 1989; Levin, Kim, & Riel, 1990; Siegel, Dubrovsky, Kiesler, & McGuire, 1986). Eastmond (1993) suggested that CMC isn't inherently interactive, but instead depends largely on participation frequency, timely contributions by members, and the nature of the messages that are posted.

CMC has also been proclaimed as uniquely suited for collaborative study (Harasim, 1989; Harasim, 1990a; Kaye, 1992a, 1992b). However, Eastmond (1993) found that a competitive model of computer conferencing was equally adaptable to CMC, and that the collaborative model did not work equally well for all students. Siegel *et al.* (1986) investigated the effects of CMC on communication efficiency, participation, interpersonal behavior and group choice. They found that CMC groups interacted less and took longer in the decision-making process than similar groups in face-to-face discussion. On the other hand, the CMC group members tended to behave as equals, whereas there was evidence of social inequality and of unequal participation in the face-to-face group.

Romiszowski and Chang (1992) have performed several studies investigating techniques by which the CMC environment could promote the same level of cognitive processing and interactivity that may occur in a one-on-one tutorial between a student and an expert teacher. The strategy employed involved the use of an initial, partially pre-prepared exercise that invites a student to create a structural "picture" of all related elements relevant to the solution of a particular complex, multi-faceted problem. This complex student response is then the basis of a CMC discussion which may take place either between student and tutor or between a group of students commenting on each others' alternative solutions. This adaptation of a methodology called "Structured Communication" has shown itself to be effective for implementing such interactive teaching methods as the Harvard Business Case methodology. Furthermore, it reduces the amount of human facilitator or monitor interaction necessary in order to lead the exercise to a satisfactory conclusion (Chang, 1994; Romiszowski, 1990; Romiszowski & Chang, 1992).

Several researchers have examined the learning strategies students employ when engaged in on-line study. Burge (1993) used structured, open-ended interviews to study how students think they learn through CMC. Learning strategies she found students using fell into the following major categories: making choices, expressing their viewpoints, group interaction, and the organization of information. Eastmond (1993) found that distance students who took courses through computer conferencing transfered learning-to-learn approaches from other instructional contexts. These transferred elements included study patterns, time scheduling, working with others, establishing attitudes, setting goals, seeking task and structure information, and demonstrating competence. However, the nature of this novel instructional context also required them to develop idiosyncratic ways of dealing with the on-line learning environment. Some CMC-specific strategies they employed included: dealing with multiple discussions, information overload, asynchronicity, and textual ambiguity, as well as processing the on-line information and determining what contributions to make.

Some proponents of CMC see the principal use and value of the medium as an emancipatory communication medium, totally under control of the users, for whatever purpose they wish to use it. There is no doubt that such a medium of communication was a missing aspect in most conventional distance education systems of the past.

There are also problems that need to be addressed when using CMC as an integral part of a course. Some of these spring from the asynchronous qualities of CMC. Not only is the discourse "multi-level" in that several different topics may be in simultaneous discussion, but it is also "multi-speed" (Romiszowski & DeHaas, 1989). Unlike face-to-face, or real-time teleconferencing, in which the participants communicate during one fixed period of time, CMC allows one to choose when to respond to another participant's comment. This offers the benefit of allowing one to think out a more structured, more complex response, and the benefit of being able to participate at times that are personally convenient. This same factor can also generate communication difficulties, including procrastination and even failure to respond altogether. Riel and Levin (1990) have identified characteristics of successful networking projects, which include establishing the expectation of a response (in addition to easy and equal access to the technology, common interests or shared experiences, group goals, structured tasks, and physical separation to encourage use).

Assessment of student achievement in CMC courses versus that obtained through correspondence or classroom formats is reported in only a few studies. For example, Cheng, Lehman, and Armstrong (1991) compared achievement, attitudes, time-on-task, and interaction between groups involved in each of the three types of instructional formats in a graduate course about microcomputers. In another study, Phelps *et al.* (1991) compared both the effectiveness and the costs of a computer mediated communication course in the U. S. Army.

In this study, the CMC students tended to score somewhat higher than those taking the conventional courses. However, the CMC courses had higher dropout rates. As regards costs, once the initial conversion and start-up costs are recovered, the CMC courses were found to cost 48% less than the equivalent conventional courses. In general, evaluation of CMC, like other research issues, is and will continue to be an ongoing concern.

Implementation Concerns

Most small-scale uses of computer conferencing begin at the grassroots level with a few enthusiastic teachers, but its eventual acceptance within a large institution usually requires backing at the highest level. Implementing a program of on-line teaching can raise major policy issues. For example, there is the question of incentives and remuneration of faculty who teach via telecommunications. Very few institutions currently acknowledge the extra effort and time involved in teaching via CMC with additional payment. Furthermore, the academic promotion process does not adequately reward faculty for taking on teleconferencing duties. Lack of recognition continues to be a significant deterrent to growth and acceptance amongst faculty. This issue is bound up with the much more complex and long-term issue of whether the use of CMC saves organizations money. There is growing acceptance of the notion that turning to CMC is not a route to major cost-cutting, but rather it is a means of extending access to courses, improving the quality of courses being offered, and meeting the need for flexible learning which cannot be otherwise met.

Teaching via computer conferencing requires a high degree of familiarity with the system's features and architecture, and the training and support of teachers and students are critical aspects of any educational program using this medium. While it is relatively easy to train teachers and students to use a CMC system, it is much more difficult to teach the skill of moderating such a course: how to promote discussion, devise activities and encourage interaction. Experienced on-line teachers have written guidelines (Brochet, 1989; Kerr, 1986), but in the end, teachers have to find their own style through practice. A recent research-based analysis of this issue is provided by Spitzer *et al.* (1994). Based on the experience of their LabNet project for teachers, they offer suggestions, e.g., for when to use different communication styles (including timing and tone), inviting others to join discussions, bridging private and public discussions, forming groups and getting acquainted with each other, keeping quality high, asking and answering questions, and maintaining continuity and ongoing group involvment.

Institutions with large CMC programs often operate a help desk for queries about equipment and communications systems; smaller programs also usually provide some staff resource to give advice to students with technical difficulties. However, given the technical complications of the current telecommunications scene, some organizations adopt the policy of expecting students to turn elsewhere, e.g., to local service dealers, for this support.

Managing and supporting equipment through its lifetime is another issue which some institutions face for the first time with telecommunications. For some organizations, a whole new unit and type of staff are necessary. Many underestimate the extent of the commitment required by telecommunications. According to Maloy and Perry (1991), to understate the budget required to operate, maintain, and upgrade the system, and to train students and staff to operate it, is to undercut its assimilation into the instructional process. When this happens, technology remains supplemental, making it even more vulnerable to cost reductions.

The Learner's Concerns

Just a few studies touch upon the life situation, goals, and personal factors which affect the pursuit of a formal education by the distance student. Robinson (1992) looked at demographic characteristics of distance students at a Canadian university and found that the majority of them were working women, pursuing an education part-time. Most of them had prior university experience.

Likewise, little research addresses distance students' perceptions of education and of their distance learning, although it does appear from anecdotal reports that class differences affect participation in courses taught using computer conferencing. Middle class students find it easier to access the computer network and they discuss actively on the system. In contrast, working class students contribute less in reactive responses, but their participation increase over time. Roberts (1990) compared distance students with traditional students and found that distance university students held learning and career oriented goals—not social and cultural ones. These students were self confident, independent, achieving, and persistent. However, differences in goals and academic self-concept were found across gender, class, experience, and income level. Grint (1989) found that students thought it difficult to carry out conversations in asynchronous time and felt they were overloaded with trivial information before being able to contribute. They were inhibited by their impression of a large, "lurking," anonymous audience that would read their contributions. Students perceived that unless they contributed facts, which was difficult in the new subject matter area they were studying, their additions to the conference were unimportant. Therefore, they disliked reading the opinions of other students on-line. Status and gender affected participation among those studied by Grint, also.

Harasim's (1987) research using two graduate courses taught through computer conferencing is probably the most telling about how students perceive this medium. Using both quantitative and qualitative approaches, she found that students spent longer on-line than they were required to do by the course, and they felt that this medium was effective. Students listed the advantages of computer conferencing as: increased interaction, access to a group, the democratic environment it fostered, the convenience of access, their control over the instructional process, the motivation they had to participate, and the textual nature of the computer conferencing medium. The disadvantages they mentioned about this medium were the information overload they felt, the medium's asynchronicity (which caused delayed responses), difficulty they felt following on-line discussions, the loss of visual cues with this communication, increased access inconvenience, and health concerns about computer radiation.

The literature abounds with comments from teachers recording their personal learning experiences in adopting and adapting this medium (Gunawardena, 1992). One of the rewards to be gained through computer conferencing is the flexibility it gives them to work at their convenience, instead of at set times. The role of the computer conferencing teacher is quite different from that of the traditional classroom instructor or lecturer. Course design becomes more important. Preparation entails the structuring of conferences and topics, and the design of activities and small group work. During a computer conferencing course, the teacher must adopt the role of facilitator, not content provider. The facilitator needs to pay careful attention to welcoming each student to the electronic course, and reinforcing early attempts to communicate. "In the first few weeks, I make sure that my notes in the conference specifically reference prior student notes. I send many individual messages to students suggesting resources, and generally reaching out to students. The coaching function is key to easing the students' transition to computer mediated communication" (Davies, 1989, p. 82).

While the teacher's role is particularly time consuming in the initial phase of a computer conferencing course, that role usually shrinks as students take over the discussions. Nevertheless, some reports indicate that teachers spend up to twice as long, overall, to deliver a course via computer conferencing as they do to give a course using traditional means. Given that CMC is so time consuming, why are so many teachers willing to teach electronically? The reason lies in the reported reward: tremendous satisfaction in working towards the goal of developing independent, questioning learners.

Conclusion: So How Is CMC a New Paradigm?

In sum, we have shown that there is a growing body of research across society at different levels within the business and educational systems involving the development and use of CMC for learning. The criteria set forth earlier have clearly been met.

The future of computer conferencing is undoubtedly one of great mergers as CMC becomes integrated with the capabilities of synchronous media, multimedia, and the whole panoply of desktop facilities. This merger is already happening at the leading edge with integrated text, sound and graphics being exchanged on higher speed networks. The growth area for CMC lies with individuals and organizations creating and using resources available over networks like the Internet, from both public and commercial network providers.

The role of the on-line instructor will increasingly be that of guide to these resources, and facilitator of learners and teams as they produce new resources. It will be interesting to see what types of needs computer conferencing will fulfill with the advent of cheap audio and visual connections. How will the advent of synchronous messages enhance interactions, e.g., to what degree will the added stimulation of voice and visual communication overcome learners' inertia and be more compelling to respond to than text?

Another trend predicted to continue is international on-line connections—for example, collaborations amongst students studying similar courses at different institutions. School children carrying out multi-cultural investigations are a powerful and inexpensive resource for extending the classroom walls. It would be naive to think that communication will automatically lead to greater knowledge, increased respect for individual and cultural differences, and a new appreciation of similarities. But a more peaceful world will not evolve without communication. The technology of CMC does not lead directly to the answers, but the dialogue it supports is a significant way for people to begin to embrace the common questions (Wells, 1993, p. 85).

As new forms of computer conferencing arise, the current text-based forms of CMC will fall increasingly toward the trailing edge of technology. However, they will continue to find specialized uses in education and training. Old computer equipment will be perfectly adequate for textual communication, and could be used with those who currently cannot afford access. By comparison with multimedia conferencing, text-based computer conferencing will remain an inexpensive technology that will continue to grow at the grassroots level. In the short term, conferencing systems with improved interfaces will find increasing markets, and learners will increasingly have to adapt to the interactive and collaborative paradigm they represent. However, this technology-led growth will eventually meet a new generation of users reared with the computer and schooled in international communication, and then tele-learning will become the norm rather than the exception.

References

Berman, P. (1981). Toward an implementation paradigm. In R. Lehming & M. Kane (Eds.), *Improving schools.* Beverly Hills, CA: Sage Publications.

Bernard, R. M., & Naidu, S. (1990). Enhancing interpersonal communication in distance education: Can voice-mail help? *Educational and Training Technology International, 27*(3), 293–299.

Boyd, G. (1990). Appropriate uses of computer mediated communication systems for education: Conferencing "R-PLACES." *Educational and Training Technology International, 27*(3), 271–275.

Brochet, M. (1989). Effective moderation of computer conferences: Notes and suggestions. In M. Brochet (Ed.), *Moderating conferences.* Guelph, Ontario: Computing Support Services, University of Guelph.

Burge, E. J. (1992). *Computer mediated communication and education: A selected bibliography.* Toronto, Canada: Distance Learning Office, Ontario Institute for Studies in Education.

Burge, E. J. (1993). *Students' perceptions of learning in computer conferencing: A qualitative analysis.* Unpublished doctoral dissertation. University of Toronto, Toronto, Canada.

Chang, E. (1994). *Investigation of constructivist principles applied to collaborative study of business cases in computer mediated communication.* Unpublished doctoral dissertation. Syracuse University, Syracuse, NY.

Cheng, H., Lehman, J., & Armstrong, P. (1991). Comparison of performance and attitude in traditional and computer conferencing classes. *The American Journal of Distance Education, 5*(3), 51–64.

Chute, A. G. (1990). Strategies for implementing teletraining systems. *Educational and Training Technology International, 27*(3), 264–270.

Chute, A. G. *et al.* (1988). Learning from teletraining. *American Journal of Distance Education, 2*(3), 55–63.

Cole, S. L., Beam, M., Karn, L., & Hoad-Reddick, A. (1992). *Educational computer mediated communication: A field study of recent research.* Toronto, Canada: Ontario Institute for Studies in Education.

Cunningham, D. J., Duffy, T. M., & Knuth, R. A. (1993). The textbook of the future. In C. McKnight (Ed.), *Hypertext: A psychological perspective.* London: Ellis Horwood.

Curtis, P. (1995). Lecture, Northeastern University, Boston, MA, 3/13/95.

Davies, L. (1989). Facilitation techniques for the on-line tutor. In R. Mason & A. R. Kaye (Eds.), *Mindweave: Communication, computers, and distance education.* New York: Pergamon Press.

Davies, G., & Samways, B. (Eds.). (1993). *Teleteaching: Proceedings of the IFIP-TC3.* Amsterdam: North Holland Publishers.

Eastmond, D. V. (1992). Effective facilitation of computer conferencing. *Continuing Higher Education Review, 56*(1&2), 23–34.

Eastmond, D. V. (1993). *Adult learning of distance students through computer conferencing.* Unpublished doctoral dissertation. Syracuse University, Syracuse, NY.

Elmer-Dewitt, P. (1994). Battle for the soul of the Internet. *Time, 144*(4), 50–56.

Eurich, N. P. (1990). *The learning industry: Education for adult workers.* Princeton, NJ: The Carnegie Foundation for the Advancement of Teaching.

Feenberg, A. (1989). The written world: On the theory and practice of computer conferencing. In R. Mason & A. R. Kaye (Eds.), *Mindweave: Communication, computers, and distance education* (pp. 22–39). New York: Pergamon Press.

Florini, B. M. (1990). Delivery systems for distance education: Focus on computer conferencing. In M. G. Moore (Ed.), *Contemporary issues in American distance education* (pp. 277–289). New York: Pergamon Press.

Gery, G. (1991). *Electronic performance support systems.* Boston: Weingarten Publications.

Gilbert, T. F. (1978). *Human competence.* New York: McGraw-Hill.

Gooler, D. D. (1986). *The education utility: The power to revitalize education and society.* Englewood Cliffs, NJ: Educational Technology Publications.

Grabowski, B. *et al.* (1990). Social and intellectual value of computer mediated communications in a graduate community. *Educational and Training Technology International, 27*(3), 276–83.

Grief, I. (1988). *Computer-supported cooperative work: A book of readings.* San Mateo, CA: Morgan Kaufmann.

Grint, K. (1989). Accounting for failure: Participation and non-participation in CMC. In R. Mason & A. R. Kaye (Eds.), *Mindweave: Communication, computers, and distance education* (pp. 189–191). New York: Pergamon Press.

Gunawardena, C. (1992). Changing faculty roles for audiographics and online teaching. *The American Journal of Distance Education, 6*(3), 58–71.

Harasim, L. M. (1987). Teaching and learning on-line: Issues in computer mediated graduate courses. *Canadian Journal of Educational Communication, 16*(2), 117–135.

Harasim, L. M. (1989). Online education: A new domain. In R. Mason & A. R. Kaye (Eds.), *Mindweave: Communication, computers, and distance education* (pp. 50–62). New York: Pergamon Press.

Harasim, L. M. (1990a). Online education: An environment for collaboration and intellectual amplification. In L. M. Harasim (Ed.), *Online education: Perspectives on a new environment* (pp. 229–264). New York: Praeger.

Harasim, L. M. (Ed.). (1990b). *Online education: Perspectives on a new environment.* New York: Praeger.

Henri, F. (1992). Computer conferencing and content analysis. In A. R. Kaye (Ed.) *Collaborative learning through computer conferencing: The Najaden papers* (pp. 115–136). New York: Springer-Verlag.

Hiltz, S. R. (1986). The "virtual classroom": Using computer mediated communication for university teaching. *Journal of Communication, 36*(2), 95–104.

Hiltz, S. R. (1988). *Teaching in a virtual classroom. Volume 2 of a virtual classroom on electronic information exchange system (EIES): Final evaluation report.* Newark, NJ: New Jersey Institute of Technology.

Hiltz, S. R. (1990). Evaluating the virtual classroom. In L. M. Harasim (Ed.), *Online education: Perspectives on a new environment* (pp. 133–183). New York: Praeger.

Hiltz, S. R., & Turoff, M. (1978). *The network nation: Human communication via computer.* New York: Addison-Wesley.

Holt, P., & Gismondi, J. (1995). *Integrating virtual spaces into open learning systems* (pp. 102–129). Proceedings of the Mid-continent Institute's Fourth Annual Innovations in Education Conference, Minot State University, Minot, ND.

Horn, R. E. (1989). *Mapping hypertext.* Lexington, MA: The Lexington Institute.

Iskandar, H. (1994). *The efficiency of different methods of providing feedback to distance learners in a developing country.* Unpublished doctoral dissertation. Syracuse University, Syracuse, NY.

Itzkan, S. (1994/1995). Assessing the future of telecomputing environments: Implications for instruction and administration. *The Computing Teacher, 22*(4), 60–64.

Jacobson, T., & Zimpfer, S. (1992). *The global distribution of selected computer network resources.* Paper presented at the August 1992 Conference of the International Association for Mass Communication Research, Guaruja, Brazil.

Kaye, A. R. (Ed.). (1992a). *Collaborative learning through computer conferencing: The Najaden papers.* New York: Springer-Verlag.

Kaye, A. R. (1992b). Learning together apart. In A. R. Kaye (Ed.), *Collaborative learning through computer conferencing: The Najaden papers.* New York: Springer-Verlag.

Kearseley, G., Lynch, W., & Wizer, D. (1995). The effectiveness and impact of online learning in graduate education. *Educational Technology, 35*(6), 37–42.

Kerr, E. (1986). Electronic leadership: A guide to moderating online conferences. *IEEE Transactions on Professional Communications, 29*(1), 12–18.

Kerr, E. B., & Hiltz, S. R. (1982). *Computer mediated communication.* New York: Academic Press.

Klingenstein, K. (1995). *Common ground: Community networks as catalysts.* Proceedings of the Annual Meeting of the Internet Society. Honolulu, HI, June 27–30.

Koschmann, T. (in press). Paradigm shifts and instructional technology. In T. D. Koschmann (Ed.), *CSCL: Theory and practice of an emerging paradigm.* Mahwah, NJ: Lawrence Erlbaum Associates

Koschmann, T., Newman, D., Woodruff, E., Pea, R. D., & Rowley, P. (1993). *Technology and pedagogy for collaborative problem solving as a context for learning.* Report on a CSCW '92 Workshop. ACM SIGCHI Bulletin, 25(4), 57–60.

Kuehn, S. (1988). *Discovering all the available means for computer assisted instruction: Adapting available university facilities for the small to medium-sized course.* (ERIC Document Reproduction Service No. ED 294 284.)

Kuhn, T. S. (1962, 1970). *The structure of scientific revolutions.* Chicago: University of Chicago Press.

Lauzon, A. C., & Moore, G. A. B. (1989). A fourth generation distance education system: Integrating computer-assisted learning and computer conferencing. *The American Journal of Distance Education, 3*(1), 38–49.

Levin, J. A., Kim, H., & Riel, M. M. (1990). Analyzing instructional interactions on electronic message networks. In L. M. Harasim (Ed.), *Online education: Perspectives on a new environment* (pp. 185–214). New York: Praeger.

Levinson, P. (1990). Computer conferencing in the context of the evolution of media. In L. M. Harasim (Ed.), *Online education: Perspectives on a new environment* (pp. 3–14). New York: Praeger.

Lewis, J. H., & Romiszowski, A. J. (1995). *Networking and the learning organization.* Paper presented at the IDLA Conference on "Networking into the 21st Century." Indonesia, October, 1995.

Maloy, W., & Perry, N. (1991). A Navy video teletraining project: Lessons learned. *The American Journal of Distance Education, 5*(3), 40–50.

Mason, R. (1990). *Home computing evaluation: Use of CoSy on DT200, 1989.* (Center for Information Technology in Education. CITE Report No. 99). (ERIC Document Reproduction Service No. ED 320 541.)

Mason, R. (1992). Methodologies for evaluating applications of computer conferencing. In A. R. Kaye (Ed.), *Collaborative learning through computer conferencing: The Najaden papers* (pp. 105–116). New York: Springer-Verlag.

Mason, R. (Ed.). (1993). *Computer conferencing: The last word.* Victoria, BC: Beach Holmes Publications.

Mason, R. (1994). Computer conferencing and the Open University. *Computers in Teaching Initiative Support Service, CTISS File, 17,* 5–7.

Mason, R., & Kaye, A. R. (Eds.). (1989). *Mindweave: Communication, computers, and distance education.* New York: Pergamon Press.

McLuhan, M. (1964). *Understanding media: The extensions of man.* New York: McGraw-Hill.

Miller, A. J. (Ed.). (1991). *Applications of computer conferencing to teacher education and human resource development.* Proceedings from an International Symposium on Computer Conferencing at the Ohio State University, June 13–15.

Moore, M. G. (1991). *Computer conferencing in the context of theory and practice of distance education.* Proceedings of the International Symposium on Computer Conferencing (pp. 1–9). Columbus, OH: Ohio State University.

Morrison, J. L. (1989). *Impact of computer conferencing upon refining problem-solving skills.* Proceedings of the 31st International ADCIS Conference.

National Information Infrastucture Advisory Council. (1995, March). *Common ground: Fundamental principles for the national information infrastructure. First report.* U.S. Department of Commerce, Washington, DC.

Paine, N. (1988). *Open learning in transition: An agenda for action.* London: Kogan Page.

Paulsen, M. F. (1992). The NKI electronic college: Five years of computer conferencing in distance education. In M. F. Paulsen (Ed.), *From bulletin boards to electronic universities: Distance education, computer mediated communication, and online education* (pp. 2–17). The American Center for the Study of Distance Education, University Park, Pennsylvania.

Peterson, W. (1995). *Moving to a notebook computer environment.* Mid-continent Institute's Fourth Annual Innovations in Education Conference, Minot State University, Minot, ND, November 9–12.

Phelps, R. H., Wells, R. A., Ashworth, R. L., & Hahn, H. A. (1991). Effectiveness and costs of distance education using computer mediated communication. *The American Journal of Distance Education, 5*(3), 7–19.

Phillips, A. F., & Pease, P. S. (1987). Computer conferencing and education: Complementary or contradictory concepts? *The American Journal of Distance Education, 1*(2), 44–52.

Phillips, C. (1990). Making friends in the electronic student lounge. *Distance Education, 11*(2), 320–333.

Phillips, G. M., Santoro, G. M., & Kuehn, S. A. (1988). The use of computer mediated communication in training students in group problem-solving and decision-making techniques. *The American Journal of Distance Education, 2*(1), 38–51.

Ravitz, J. (1995). *Building collaborative on-line communities for K–12: Observations concerning networking theory and practice* (pp. 71–83). Proceedings of the Mid-continent Institute's Fourth Annual Innovations in Education Conference, Minot State University, Minot, ND, November 9–12.

Rawson, J. H. (1990). Simulation at a distance using computer conferencing. *Educational and Training Technology International, 27*(3), 284–292.

Riel, M., & Levin, J.A. (1990). Building electronic communities: Success and failure in computer networking. *Instructional Science, 19,* 145–169.

Roberts, L. H. (1990). *Educational goals and self-concepts of distance learners at Empire State College.* Unpublished doctoral dissertation. Nova University, Ft. Lauderdale, FL.

Robinson, R. (1992). Andragogy applied to the open college learner. *Research in Distance Education, 4*(1), 10–13.

Romiszowski, A. J. (1990). Computer mediated communication and hypertext: The instructional use of two converging technologies. *Interactive Learning International, 6,* 5–29.

Romiszowski, A. J. (1992). *Computer mediated communication: A selected bibliography. Educational Technology Selected Bibliography Series, Vol. 5.* Englewood Cliffs, NJ: Educational Technology Publications.

Romiszowski, A. J. (1993). Telecommunications in training. In *ASTD Handbook of Training Technology.* Alexandria, VA: American Society for Training and Development (ASTD).

Romiszowski, A. J., & Chang, E. (1992). Hypertext's contribution to computer mediated communication: In search of an instructional model. In M. Giardina (Ed.), *Interactive multimedia learning environments*. Berlin: Springer-Verlag.

Romiszowski, A. J., & Chang, E. (1994). Alternative strategies for collaborative study of business cases by computer mediated communication. *Instructional Developments, 4*(1). Syracuse, NY: Syracuse University.

Romiszowski, A. J., & Corso, M. (1990). *Computer mediated seminars and case studies.* Paper presented at the 15th World Conference on Distance Education, Caracas, Venezuela. International Council for Distance Education (ICDE).

Romiszowski, A. J., & DeHaas, J. (1989). Computer mediated communication for instruction: Using e-mail as a seminar. *Educational Technology, 29*(10).

Romiszowski, A. J., & Iskandar, H. (1992). *New telecommunications and voicemail technologies in distance education.* Proceedings of the 16th World Conference on Distance Education, Bangkok, Thailand. International Council for Distance Education.

Romiszowski, A. J., & Jost, K. (1989). *Computer conferencing and the distance learner: Problems of structure and control.* Proceedings of the Fifth Annual Conference on Teaching at a Distance, Madison, Wisconsin, August 8–10, 1989.

Romiszowski, A. J., Jost, K., & Chang, E. (1990). *Computer mediated communication: A hypertext approach to structuring distance seminars.* In Proceedings of the 32nd Annual International Conference of the Association for the Development of Computer-based Instructional Systems (ADCIS).

Ryan, R. (1992). International connectivity: A survey of attitudes about cultural and national differences encountered in computer mediated communication. *The Online Chronicle of Distance Education and Communication, 6*(1).

Sheffield, J., & McQueen, R. J. (1990). *Groupware and management education: Matching communication medium to task requirements* (pp. 181–182). Proceedings of the Third Guelph Symposium on Computer Mediated Communication.

Siegel, J., Dubrovsky, V., Kiesler, S., & McGuire, T. W. (1986). Group processes in computer mediated communication. *Organizational behavior and human decision processes, 37*, 157–187.

Soby, M. (1990). *The postmodern condition and distance education computer conferencing and communicative competence* (pp. 112–120). Proceedings of the Third Guelph Symposium on Computer Mediated Communication.

Spitzer, W., Wedding, K., & DiMauro, V. (1994). *Fostering reflective dialogues for teacher professional development.* Cambridge, MA: TERC.

Taylor, R. P. (Ed.). (1980). *The computer in the school: Tutor, tool, and tutee.* New York: Teachers College Press.

Tucker, R. W. (1991). Editor's desk: Virtual assessment. *Adult Assessment Forum, 1*(3), 3–4.

Vallee, J. (1982). *The network revolution: Confessions of a computer scientist.* Berkeley, CA: And/Or Press, Inc.

Waggoner, M. D. (Ed.). (1992). *Empowering networks: Computer conferencing in education.* Englewood Cliffs, NJ: Educational Technology Publications.

Wells, R. (1992). *Computer mediated communication for distance education: An international review of design, teaching, and institutional issues* (ACSDE Monograph No. 6). University Park, PA: The American Center for the Study of Distance Education.

Wells, R. (1993). The use of computer mediated communication in distance education: Progress, problems, and trends. In G. Davies & B. Samways (Eds.), *Teleteaching: Proceedings of the IFIP TC3 Third Teleteaching Conference, Trondheim, Norway.* Amsterdam: North-Holland.

Zuboff, S. (1988). *In the age of the smart machine.* New York: Basic Books.

Early versions of this chapter received considerable input from Dan Eastmond and Robin Mason, to whom the authors are most grateful.

43

Simulation and Computer-Based Instruction: A Future View

Andrew S. Gibbons
Utah State University, Logan

Peter G. Fairweather
T. J. Watson Research Center, IBM
Yorktown Heights, New York

Thor A. Anderson
M. David Merrill
Utah State University, Logan

Introduction

This chapter reviews several factors pointing to a future in which the use of computer-based instructional simulations will increase dramatically. Simulation is one of the most powerful forms of instruction a computer can deliver, yet its level of use is surprisingly low in proportion to its power. The purpose of this chapter is to discuss the trends and forces which will probably change the way we think about simulations and bring closer to reality the concept of a simulation-based curriculum.

There are several conditions which favor re-examination of simulation as an instructional tool:

1. *The market for CBI is broadening; funds for CBI are easier to obtain.* Only a decade ago, in order to sell a CBI product, one had to begin by selling the concept of computerized instruction itself. This is no longer true.
2. *The concept of CBI itself is maturing in the minds of consumers; expectations are escalating.* The tutorial sequence with inserted questions, which seemed like such a grand achievement two decades ago, is aging, along with monochrome displays and key-

board-centered interactions. Interactivity and interface are important issues today, and increasingly software sales are being made by interaction styles and support systems, since most products offer the same basic set of capabilities. This increase in the user's desire to interact with products in more sophisticated ways is true of instructional computing as well.

3. *The tools of the programmer are becoming much more powerful, capable, and efficient.* Features of instructional products which used to require extensive programming are now relatively simple, thanks to highly efficient construction tools. With minimal effort, most programmers can create scrolling windows, pull-down menus, and sophisticated control structures. Manipulation of screen content is also becoming more sophisticated and at the same time more simple. Instructional interactions which used to be "don't ask" are now "I'll have it for you in a couple of hours."

4. *Educators are revising their conception of curriculum and asking for products which teach performance.* Recently, all curricular areas from mathematics and science to language arts, languages, and social studies are changing the expected outcomes of instruction. Curriculum emphasis is shifting toward the ability to apply, to solve, to design, to plan, and to manipulate representations, and away from the ability to remember and manipulate abstract verbal structures. In training as well, the shift is toward performing rather than informing. These shifts are forcing CBI designers for both educational and training products to consider environment-based rather than topic-based products.

5. *Models of learning distinguish declarative and procedural knowledge types.* Both basic research and experimental instructional development have illustrated the utility of separating knowing "what" from knowing "how" and, more importantly, for devising specific techniques for the teaching of each.

These trends, along with falling computer costs and increasing computer speed and power, are favorable to the increased use of simulation. However, before simulation can attain use levels comparable with other instructional means, several things must happen:

New developer mindset. Instructional designers must change the way they think about computerized curriculum products. Instead of thinking of the instructional computer as an amplifier or a duplicator—both metaphors which suggest distributing an identical message to the members of a large audience—developers must envision the computer as a creator of working environments within which students solve problems that will instruct them. Instead of thinking of better ways for telling a message on the computer screen, developers must think of better ways for structuring environments that teach with a minimum of telling and a maximum of application.

New instructional technology. In order to use simulations to a greater extent within education and training curricula, instructional designers must broaden their mindset relative to instruction itself. Current conceptions of computer-based curriculum depend heavily on a compartmentalized tutorial instructional form, and modern computer-managed instruction (CMI) systems trivialize the computer's actual participation in the management of instruction by catering to this conception. A new instructional technology must offer new conceptions of curriculum in which the primary building block is carefully-selected and structured performance challenges—in the form of a progressive sequence of increasingly complex microworlds. To do so, the field must come to grips with complex instructional issues highly pertinent to instructional simulation: issues such as coaching, prompting, feedback for extended performances, assessment, unobtrusive measurement, instruction during problem-solving, data abstraction, selection of optimal problem sequences, and forms of management which take into account a much broader range of student performance data and task characteristics.

Simulation authoring tools. Authoring tools which favor the creation of simulations must become as available and as usable as tools which favor tutorials. Such tools will make the modeling of physical and conceptual systems easy. They will allow the developer to create environments for exploration and effectuation within which the student can move about as if in the real world. These new tools, since they will deal with the design of environments and events rather than with set sequences of message and interaction, will confront difficult interface challenges.

Low-cost products. Most importantly, both tools and techniques must be developed that make the creation of simulated environments and sequences of problems within those environments much less expensive than they are now. In the same way that developers have invented tools for mass-producing tutorials, they must turn their attention to ways for the mass-production and management of families of simulation problems through which students can move in an order calculated to meet their individual needs.

This chapter describes advances toward these goals:

- It defines *instructional* simulation and relates it to other instructional forms.
- It relates the use of instructional simulation to instructional strategy.
- It describes three forms of instructional simulation: the location simulation, the model simulation, and the hybrid simulation.
- It relates the design of simulations to the issue of instructional scope and instructional goals.
- It proposes a technology for integrating instructional goals with simulations, at the same time weaving simulation into the instructional plans of the larger instructional product.
- It describes six classes of instructional feature which can accompany a simulation: coaching, feedback, representation, control structure, scope dynamism, and embedded didactics.
- It describes a trend in authoring tools which will make instructional simulations and their instructional features easier and less costly to construct.

What Is Simulation?

The practice of building simulations for a variety of purposes—systems analysis, product and process design, and scientific research—has been general for well over two decades. Briefly, a simulator *simulates* something. That something may be a physical system or a conceptual system: a set of things that really exists, or things that we only think exist but have never experienced directly, like atomic nuclei and black holes. A simulation can simulate the operation of a mechanical device, the running of trains according to a schedule, a day's worth of telephone calls across a telephone network, or the explosion of a star. To do this, the simulation temporarily creates a set of *things* through the means of a program and then relates them together through cause-effect *relationships*, which may be expressed to the computer in the form of "if-then" rules or mathematical expressions. As a simulation runs, changes in the state or value of one thing propagate to influence the states and values of other things.

This is the basic mechanism of simulation, and it is an extremely useful tool. Without simulations, the design of large buildings, cars, bridges, and telephone switches would become impossible; much scientific research would come to a halt, and our knowledge of how things work would be greatly impeded. The growth of our technology-rich society would be stalled without simulations.

What Is *Instructional* Simulation?

Most general-purpose simulations are constructed to explore how a specific system (a bridge, a star, or the earth's atmosphere) will react to a given set of inputs. In an instructional simulation, the system being modeled is already understood by the one constructing it, and the purpose for simulating it is not to explore system behavior but to provide a model which can serve as a base for instruction. In a sense, this assigns to the simulation the role historically filled by the physical model. Because of the unique capabilities of the computer, its models can be incredibly diverse, realistic, and potentially more complex and detailed than the physical model. Moreover, the computer's models are dynamic in their response to the desires and informational needs of the student, and the computer can simulate models which are abstract, which physical models find difficult.

Discussions of instructional simulation frequently begin with provocative descriptions of simulation examples rather than with a definition. This is probably due to the great variety of forms taken by instructional simulations. Instructional simulations vary so widely in appearance, in the quality of the experience they produce, in their operation, and in their instructional purpose that they resist being placed under a single definition. Moreover, definition is difficult because there are many simulation look-alikes and feel-alikes which are not instructional simulations.

A definition of instructional simulation is important, however, not because *simulation* needs defining, but because *instructional* does. A definition will differentiate instructional simulations from simulations in general and allow us to concentrate attention on the principles for the design of their *instructional* features. Instructional simulations share several characteristics:

1. *They are simulations.* They model either a physical system from the real world, a conceptual system, or an environment. They focus on a specific portion of the real—or imagined—world and only model that.
2. *They engage the learner in interactions.* Instructional simulations accept input from the student and then respond in two ways: (1) they give the normal response computed by their model rules, and (2) they perform additional instructional functions that have been planned by an instructional designer.
3. *They are reactive and execute non-linear logic.* They respond to learner actions as well as changes in their own internal states. Actions can be performed in an unconstrained order, and the results of actions are not always easy to predict because they are computed.
4. *Their design reflects an intended instructional function.* Instructional simulations are designed to promote the attainment of specified instructional goals. They possess instructional features which support the attainment of those goals.

One can learn from general purpose simulations quite successfully. However, an *instructional* simulation possesses additional instructional features that support the attainment of specified learning goals. When a general purpose simulation is used for instruction, it normally falls to a teacher or instructor to supply both the instructional goal and the auxiliary messages and interactions, in effect turning the general purpose simulation into an instructional one. The notion of an *instructional* simulation is simply a recognition of the *full instructional context* in which simulations are normally used. This presents the opportunity to formalize the principles for designing and automating that instructional context.

The emphasis on instructional goals may be a concern to those who favor exploratory and less-structured approaches to learning. Some feel that explicit instructional goals restrict what a student may learn from an experience, and this has created a tension among instructional designers, which obscures the real instructional questions. Students will, in fact, learn what they choose to learn because they are humans. By creating a product for use in instruction, a designer is expressing a learning goal and hoping that a student will choose to learn in harmony with that goal—that the student will temporarily choose that goal as his or her own. A designer cannot prevent a student from learning unless information and necessary interactions are deliberately denied. Therefore, instructional simulations constitute a more flexible form of instructional tool which can be used by the student for learning that is unintended by the designer yet not denied by the design. In this sense, they constitute, as Rieber (1994) describes, a point for merging the extreme views on both sides of the instructional goal question, laying ". . . the foundation of interactive learning environments where structure and motivation are optimized without subverting personal discovery, exploration, and ownership of knowledge."

Even exploratory/experimental environments such as LOGO (Abelson & diSessa, 1981; Papert, 1980) have implicit goals in the broadest sense, and their particular use is most often accompanied by a challenge or an assignment to the student to discover one or more principles or processes by experimenting within the environment. This constitutes an instructional goal within the definition of this chapter, and such uses are considered to label the tool, under those conditions, as an "instructional simulation." Therefore, the designation "instructional" does not describe the product itself but the manner and context in which it is used.

Relation to Other Instructional Forms

For some instructional purposes, a simulation is embedded within a tutorial framework. In these cases, the simulation mechanism is placed under the control of the tutorial's instructional strategy through a "bridle" that allows the strategy to control the simulation. The tutorial strategy can send instructions through the bridle, causing it to initialize its values, start, stop, reset, or run for a set number of cycles. The tutorial context in this case supplies part of the instructional message, and the simulation also supplies some appropriate display elements correlated to the states of its model variables. In some cases, the order of control is reversed: The simulation is the main instructional vehicle and possesses within itself resources and strategies for didactics in addition to the usual capability for supporting demonstrations and practice.

Asking which of these two arrangements is superior (tutorial with embedded simulation, or simulation embedding tutorial) is inappropriate. If instructional simulation is to become integrated in use with other forms of instruction, there must emerge a new mindset which amalgamates traditional forms of instruction with new arrangements which are neither exclusively tutorials nor exclusively simulations. This will introduce a new curriculum metaphor into computer-based instruction, because the basic measure of instruction will have changed.

An instructional simulation has a scope which is defined in terms of: (1) the manner in which it is used (i.e., embedded vs. embedding), (2) that portion of the world that it models, and (3) the instructional goals it is designed to promote. An earlier section of this chapter hinted at the relationship between the simulation scope and the instructional scope. The two may coincide or differ. The *instructional scope* of a simulation refers to the performance or set of performances it is designed to instruct and support during one instructional event. The *simulation scope* refers to the portion of the world simulated and the full range of task-actions which can be supported and recorded by the environment. A simulation environment with a particular *simulation scope* may support several individual instructional events, each with its own *instructional scope*. This is a critical distinction, and failure to make it will cause simulation designers to confuse the simulation environment with the instructional event carried out within it. Designers who are used to the "one objective, one lesson" point of view are especially prone to this confusion. But simulations create a new measure of instruction: the instructional event. The simulation scope is the background upon which the event takes place.

An instructional simulation is also defined in terms of the levels of fidelity and resolution with which it represents the world to the user. *Fidelity* refers to the *precision* and *accuracy* with which the simulation mimics the cause-effect linkages of the real world. *Resolution* refers to the level of *detail* or *granularity* at which it represents the real world to the user. The resolution of a simulation is analogous to the resolution of a computer screen: the higher the level of resolution, the more detail can be discriminated. Resolution also includes the dimension of time and defines the granularity of all sensory experiences provided by the simulation.

The most important elements of an instructional simulation are its *instructional features*. They are independent of the formulas and rules housed within the simulation's model. They are also independent of the specific content or subject matter being simulated. On the other hand, they are directly related to the goals of instruction. In the same way that we now discuss the strategy of a tutorial independently of its subject matter, we must come to discuss the instructional features of a simulation. The instructional features carry out the strategic intentions of a simulation and are what makes the simulation instructional.

A simulation's instructional features carry out a major portion of its instructional messaging. They perform instructional functions like those of the instructional features of other forms of instruction, but because of the unique logical structure of simulations, the experience to the student can feel very different. Instructional features of simulations, just as those of other forms of instruction, are used to draw or guide attention, to relate displayed elements, to direct action, to augment memory, to catalyze analysis and use of the instructional message, to emphasize, to create proportion, to create confidence and interest, to compliment, and to correct. There is no strand of continuous message in a simulation like the one normally found in more traditional forms of instruction, so designers must conceive new patterns of instructional interaction which implement messaging functions. The messages of a simulation are generated by models and by instructional features which monitor the models, instructional goals, and the student performance. A later section of this chapter discusses the instructional features of simulations in more detail.

Simulation and Macro-Strategy

Instructional simulations must be viewed as taking part in a larger instructional plan and overall strategy. Some refer to this as the macro-strategy (Reigeluth, 1983) level of instruction: the level *above* the individual "instructional event" or "lesson." The use of a simulation's instructional features depends on this overall strategic plan and on the student's performance across several instructional events, as well as on the momentary instructional goal and student performance within the immediate instructional event. For instance, the withdrawal of coaching support during practice must be based on a larger pattern of maturing learning capability within the student beyond the horizon of one event, as well as on student performance in the current event.

The instructional plan of a simulation must be seen as part of the larger strategic plan of an instructional product: a product which may include many instructional forms. Only if instructional designers begin to see instructional means such as tutorials, simulations and job aids working together in this larger perspective of meta-strategic planning will it be possible to integrate them harmoniously for the attainment of higher-level learning goals.

Organization of Simulations for Instruction

Certain instructional functions are typically carried out in service of instructional goals. A generic model has evolved through common practice which many instructional designers use for arranging the conditions of learning for an instructional objective. It includes the instructional stages of:

1. *Presenting* information to the learner which is directly relevant to the skill or knowledge being learned.
2. *Demonstrating* how the information is applied in the creation of a performance, or demonstrating cause-effect relationships within the content.

Presentation and demonstration are normally accompanied by specialized sub-functions which intend to assist the student to digest the content, relate the digested elements to previous knowledge, and accommodate it within the structures of previous learning through assimilation and reorganization.

3. *Providing* opportunity to *practice* the target performance under a variety of conditions and standards.

Testing, which is normally added to this list of stages, may be viewed as a form of practice in which all instructional features have been turned off until the performance is completed and assessed.[1]

These instructional stages correspond generally to ones proposed by Alessi and Trollip (1991) and Reigeluth and Schwartz (1989). Both, in turn, are based on general models of instructional stages proposed by Gagné (1985) and Merrill (1983, 1987, 1994).

Simulation is particularly adept at carrying out practice and demonstration stages of instruction. In fact, its use in the past has been isolated almost entirely to those two functions. However, the authors consider simulations to be suitable vehicles for presentation as well, though this requires the average designer to modify traditional views about how that function is accomplished. We believe that simulations are capable of all stages of instruction.

General Elements of Instructional Simulation

The experience which an instructional simulation can provide derives from two aspects: its *model* and its *environment*. A model, as its name implies, models some system. An environment can be a model itself or an access route to a computed model. Environments are made up of *locations*. On the basis of these definitions, we divide the world of instructional simulations into three broad classes which define different types of experience for the user, at the same time influencing the tools required for building them. The classes are: (1) location simulations, (2) model simulations, and (3) hybrid location-model simulations.

---

[1]Many designers take this list of instructional functionalities literally. They use it to supply an inflexible physical structure for their instructional products. Others realize that the ordering and isolation of the funtions is not critical but simply use the fact that the functions must somehow and somewhere be performed within the instruction. They see that it is the mixing of these functions in various ways which creates the rich texture of instructional experiences found in the interesting and useful variety of instructional forms.

The Location Simulation

A pure location simulation is one in which the environment is the extent of the simulation. The simulation model consists of a set of "locations" which students move into and out of in any order they choose. Each location is a "place" where the student can obtain information from the simulation and/or perform actions. Locations may or may not have a visible manifestation, but each has controls with which the student can move between locations within the environment.

The Aspen videodisc (Brand, 1987; see also Fletcher & Rockaway, 1986) provides an example of navigation between locations, even though the Aspen product itself does not fit the definition of an instructional simulation. The Aspen videodisc was the first surrogate travel videodisc. Within the town of Aspen, Colorado it allowed a user to control the direction of travel through streets and buildings, turning at intersections to enter new streets or to observe the interior spaces of buildings. Each main control (or decision) point can be considered the anchor point of a "location" within the Aspen environment.

A location simulation requires only that there be one or more locations, each of which provides some sensory input or information to the student, relative to a problem which is being solved or a task which is being accomplished. Paths between locations and movement controls allow navigation to take place. Locations may take many forms, and many types of action may be performed at a location, depending on the designer's purpose. Conceptually, a location may be a room, a geographic location, or a thing, like a book page. It may also be an event, such as an interruption by the voice of an environment character with a message or a call through the telephone on the wall. It may also be a speech from a conversation with a person, or simply a sound which is heard.

The Aspen videodisc is only a set of locations within a video environment. It has no instructional goal and no instructional features. Therefore, by itself it is not an instructional simulation, though it expresses connected locations within an environment. Aspen was intended as a demonstration of the videodisc's ability to support the surrogate exploration of an environment—a tour of the city. It is not an instructional simulation.

The Model Simulation

A pure model simulation is one in which a computed model is the central feature of the simulation, rather than a set of locations. A model is made up of model components, each of which has one or more properties, which in turn have one or more possible discrete values or a range of continuous values. Rules or formulas within the model cause the change of the value of one property to propagate to other properties:

If
> *the temperature (property) of the ocean surface (model element) increases (value)*
then
> *the rate of evaporation (property) of the ocean surface (model element) increases (value)*
and
> *the temperature (property) of the ocean surface (model element) decreases (value).*

This is accomplished according to the model's mathematical formulas and rules. A model simulation is the one most frequently used within current instruction and is probably the type most often associated with the concept of simulation in the minds of instructional designers.

Models are so versatile that they can be made to mimic the behavior of almost any physical or conceptual system. Giving students direct experience observing or manipulating a model can produce powerful learning. Building around this model an instructional goal and a set of instructional features creates an instructional simulation, which extends the power of the model to instruct, improves the instructor's knowledge of the knowledge state of the student, and increases the efficiency of the instruction. A properly sequenced plan of observations and manipulations of the model can increase its instructional value even more, and careful attention to the manner in which the model represents data about its various states to the student raises the effectiveness to an even higher plateau.

The Hybrid Location-Model Simulation

A hybrid location-model simulation is one in which both a set of locations and a model are essential to the function of the simulation. In this type of simulation, a student moves throughout a set of locations, obtaining information and performing actions. Certain actions within locations produce changes to the values of a model which is connected behind the scenes to the activated control. This touches off a flurry of computation within the model which results in changed states, which in turn makes new information available at one or more locations. For instance, in a hybrid simulation of a computer network, there might be several locations—multiple work stations, a host computer, and a cable connection box—at which the states and condition of the network can be observed. A message typed into the network at one work station location might result in changes to the display of another work station, or the connection of a cable at one location might result in the change of a work station's display at another. Since the student cannot be in all locations at once, these various manifestations of the common network model are only seen as the student moves from location to location.

All model simulations are in fact hybrids, because at least one location (information-obtaining and control-activating point) is created for a model to act as an interface between the model and the student. This interface supplies information to the student from the model and carries control inputs to the model from the student. A model may also have connections to multiple locations.

The function of a location is two-fold, however, and if both functions are not remembered, the location becomes merely an interface element. Locations can be given *interpretability* if they are designed so that each new location discloses to the student one or more specific items of information relative to performance or to the solution of a problem. Defined in this way, a location is a structural element of the environment related to the structure of the problem itself, and movements between locations can be used in the judgment of performance.

Hybrid simulations can create very realistic environments for interaction with students. The instructional use of hybrid simulations is reported in descriptions of a cross-country flight planning simulation (Gibbons, Trollip, & Karim, 1990; Gibbons, Waki, & Fairweather, 1990), maintenance simulations (Gibbons, 1996; Gibbons, Rogers, & King, 1991), and pilot emergency training simulations.

Instructional Simulation Look-Alikes

Certain forms of non-simulation (non-model or non-environment) instruction mimic the look-and-feel of simulations under a narrow range of conditions, but have substantial differences from them outside of that range. These include the path simulation and the visual simulation. Though each is highly effective within its own domain of use, neither can be considered a true simulation, and neither can support the same instructional goals as a true simulation.

Path simulation. The path simulation is a tutorial logical form which appears and feels like an instructional simulation. A path simulation is a very effective instructional form during the early stages of procedure learning. The logic of a path simulation is almost identical to a quiz made up of chained multiple-choice questions. In place of textual questions, however, the student is presented with a graphic action environment, and instead of textual or numeric answers, the student responds by clicking or touching the area of the display which represents the performance of an action.

If the response of the student is the anticipated one, then positive feedback may be presented verbally, but the most important effect for the student is the graphic presentation of the natural system response that would normally follow the action: a light goes on, a sound is heard, or some other evidence of success is sensed. Because the correct response to each question—each "response opportunity"—chains the student directly into the next one, it is difficult for a correctly responding student to tell that he or she is not in a fully-responsive simulated environment. However, when the student makes an unexpected or incorrect response, the effect is very different. A true simulation would model the result of the incorrect response as faithfully as the correct one, but a path simulation stops to correct the student, directs the student to make the correct response, and returns the student to the response point where the error occurred.

The path simulation, which looks so much on the surface like a model simulation, differs in many ways from a real model simulation. The only thing that it "simulates" is the correct response path that the student is expected to follow. Deviations from the path are quickly corrected, and the student is placed back on the "simulated" path. This degree of immediate correction and support is valuable to students in early stages of instruction on procedures which follow a prescribed order of steps. But for instruction for which the goal is more complex and involves integrated forms of decision making or problem solving, and in which the order of actions is uncertain or changeable, the path simulation is inadequate. Other dissimilarities between path and model simulations include their very underlying logical structure. Path simulations are easily constructed by authoring systems, using concatenated multiple-choice questions and realistic, non-verbal display material. Model simulations can be created using authoring systems, but only with much difficulty, programming, and expense. The current tool of choice for building model simulations is a programming language of some type, though that will soon change due to emerging tools discussed in a later section.

Visual simulation. The visual simulation is a form of representation and not a simulation at all. A visual simulation allows a student to view some process or procedure as an observer but prevents the student from interacting with a model that underlies the visualization. This is because the model in a visual simulation has been simplified to the point at which it cannot react to learner actions. It is a representation which cannot be interactive in any way unanticipated and unplanned by the designer.

Visual simulations are extremely useful for conveying to the student a mental image of the cause-effect or sequential characteristics of a process or procedure. The learning possible, however, is limited to the visual designer's foresight in anticipating the student's informational needs.

Simulation as Instruction

We need stronger technological and theoretical guidelines for the integration of simulation as instruction. New principles must be found to describe not only how simulations themselves can be employed as instructional tools, but to provide guidelines for the integration of simulations with other instructional varieties to form larger, focused instructional products. Up to the present, much of the writing on simulation has been done from the perspective of the simulation builder. It tends to dwell on the problems of creating simulations, the interesting features of simulations, and the use of simulations in various isolated education and training applications. Use of simulations within a larger instructional context is frequently described as desirable, but few guidelines are offered for doing so. This has the practical effect of isolating rather than integrating simulation with other instructional means.

In order to relate simulation to instructional strategy, Alessi and Trollip (1991) describe simulations with reference to a four-phase model of instruction consisting of presenting information, guiding the student, allowing practice by the student, and assessing student learning. Reigeluth and Schwartz (1989) similarly place simulations within the context of three basic acts: acquisition, application, and assessment. However, these are prescriptive positions. What rationale is there for the use of simulations from the point of view of learning theory?

Shuell (1990) and others (Glaser & Bassok, 1989) propose that learning of the types undertaken in educational and training settings is a phased process consisting of plateaus of integration. Shuell suggests the existence of three phases of learning: (1) an initial phase of fact learning and structure-borrowing, (2) an intermediate phase of new structure formation, and (3) a terminal phase of behavior automatization. Anderson (Anderson, 1983, 1993) also proposes a model of human learning which progresses through phases of declarative learning, proceduralization, composition, and strengthening through use.

The principles of instructional design link specific classes of learning with specific strategic manipulations (Gagné, 1985; see also Gibbons, 1977 for a description of taxonomic systems which were given birth by this principle prior to Gagné). This strategy-linking improves the focus and precision of instructional designs.

However, instructional strategy is dynamic within learning types as well as across them. The type of instructional support required in the early stages of memory or concept or principle learning is different from that which is needed in the final stages. Shuell's and Anderson's conceptions of *phases* or *stages* of learning help us to recognize that instructional strategy is a dynamic process rather than a static formula. This suggests additional uses of simulation for instructional purposes.

The phases of instruction give simulations their instructional context and suggest ways in which they should be integrated with other instructional forms, including tutorials and job-aids. As important as this is, however, it has not been matched by a corresponding technology of analysis and synthesis during instructional design that allows simulations to be incorporated systematically within curricula, so the bridge which has been thrown across the gulf between simulation and other forms of instruction does not quite reach the opposite bank.

At least one of the missing planks for this bridge is a revised approach to the designer's use of tasks and objectives, and this raises the issue of *instructional scope*. One of the main impediments to increased use of simulation is confusion over the setting and control of instructional scope for individual instructional events. Simulation confuses this issue because one simulation scope can be used as the stage for the enactment of several instructional scopes.

Instructional scope defines the focus of intention of the instructional designer at any given instructional moment by identifying the behavior or performance which is the target of instruction. Instructional objectives are traditionally used to designate instructional scope. They tend to work well when the instructional target is a single behavior or a small number of behaviors. However, the system of objectives as it is now practiced begins to break down above that level.

In current practice, the early stages of instruction for a comprehensive body of skills, knowledge, and attitudes target individual elements of skill and knowledge. Designers frequently apply methods of task and objectives analysis in order to identify and isolate lower-level instructional goals. The analysis methods in general use are equal to the task of fragmenting knowledge and skill into small units for individual attention, but they are inadequate for reversing the analytic process and creating, through synthesis, conglomerate goals that integrate these isolated capabilities, once learned, into the complexes of flexible and expert behavior called for in everyday situations. Advanced stages of instruction should focus on the integration of isolated capabilities into complexes of ability which approach the real-world performance threshold. Glaser and Bassok (1989) name as an important research task ". . . to design programs that test approaches to the integration of competent performance" (p. 659). Justified criticism (Collins, Brown, & Newman, 1987; Gagné & Merrill, 1990) has been leveled at current instructional design practice because it frequently ignores this need and produces "basics-only" courses in which students learn fragments which are never combined into wholes.

Work Model Synthesis

To fill the need for defining and designing integrative paths, we suggest a technique called "work model synthesis," which in the instructional design process fits into the hiatus between Analysis (following objectives analysis) and Design (prior to media selection and syllabus construction), the point at which the designer switches from analytic to synthetic activities.

The work model is an important construct for instructional designers because it is a unit of synthesis rather than analysis. Whereas the purpose of task and objective analysis is to separate out and to de-structure a performance, the purpose of the work model is to combine and to re-structure it. Work model synthesis is the complement to task and objective analysis. The work model was first described by Bunderson, Gibbons, Olsen, and Kearsley (1981). A work model methodology is described by Gibbons (1988), and the technology of work models has been successfully applied in the design of high-performance, high-criticality training systems (Gibbons, Bunderson, Olsen, & Robertson, in press; Gibbons & Robertson, 1994).

By definition, a work model is an agglomerate instructional goal, complete with behavior(s), condition(s), and standard(s) of performance. It may consist of a single task, a single objective, or any combination of tasks and objectives which are to be instructed, practiced, or tested in combination. Each work model comprises the occasion for one instructional event—independently-schedulable and delivered via a single instructional medium or media combination. The work model is a mapping entity. The instructional event that it represents does not correspond exactly with what designers traditionally call a "lesson." In fact, it gives a new and more precise meaning to the term "lesson" by defining not only its target behavior but the performance environment in clear and unambiguous terms, regardless of whether that target behavior is of the scope of one objective or of a large cluster of objectives and tasks.

In the sense that a work model constitutes one instructional event—a single instructional occasion using a single media combination—it resembles a lesson, but a work model may also be many things different from what is normally called a "lesson." This is because the work model is an expression of instructional goal, performance, or intent and not just a unit of time or a topic. For instance, a work model may split the instruction normally related to one instructional objective into two parts when the intention (the instructional strategic goal) of the parts is sufficiently disparate to require handling of the presentation in a different medium from the practice and at a different time. The first work model may consist of only the presentation portion of the instruction, and the second of only the practice portion. Later work models may focus on individual tasks performed at an intermediate level of standard under a specified set of (relatively uncomplicated) conditions. From there, additional work models may follow, which make task execution more difficult by either raising the standard or by introducing new or more challenging conditions or both. Finally, tasks can be combined in any variety to form an intermediate level work model which represents partial real-world performance.

New tasks are introduced into work models incrementally, resulting in a potentially large number of work models. These new tasks need not be introduced in any particular order, and the selection and succession of work models is a major design issue. This point should be emphasized: the order in which new tasks appear within work models is *not* fixed by hierarchical position in a task analysis. Within a simulated context, one or more lower-level tasks not included within a work model may be supplied by the performance environment. This removes the student's responsibility to perform them entire and allows the student to practice simplified versions of the more integrated task without being required to perform the whole task.

The work model is a very flexible container which expands to fit the momentary capacity and performance goals of the student, and when it is used properly, it can define a path of learning challenges which moves the student from novice to proficient behavior. It can also be used by the designer to define a complete family of problem settings and versions which may be used by students to progress toward integrated performance, each student taking a path particularly suited to his or her learning speed and trajectory.

Implications

The work model has both practical and theoretical implications.

Theoretically, it is used to define a path for the integration of behavior through successive stages. Each work model is in effect a meta-instructional objective that combines performances together for practice purposes (or splits them, according to the need). Therefore, it is the tool by which the designer provides the best path of instructional challenges during the intermediate stage of instruction.

Practically, the work model is the individual element of instruction. When a syllabus or curriculum is created that specifies the permissible order or orders of instruction, it is the work model (also named the "instructional event") which is placed into sequence. Moreover, when instructional media are assigned during a process called media selection, it is the individual work model to which a medium is assigned. Finally, when an instructional product is produced, it is the work model, or instructional event, which normally represents one independently authorable and producible element of the course product. The work model (instructional event) is the element assignable by computer-managed instruction (CMI) systems to students for study, and data resulting from instruction can be referenced to the individual work model and the tasks within it. Thus, the work model is the central focus of many important design and instruction functions in a way that neither objectives alone nor the undefined notion of "lesson" can possibly be.

The mapping of the work model is from tasks and instructional objectives to work models. The mapping may be one-to-one, one-to-many, or many-to-one, as shown in Figure 1.

We must assume that even after the tools for capturing the expertise of an expert performer are perfected, as described in Lesgold, Chipman, Brown, and Soloway (1990), the notion of work models will still be necessary. Capturing expertise is the nominal purpose of the task and objectives analysis processes which are currently used by instructional designers. Work model synthesis is necessary in order to group the elements of expertise, once identified, into suites of expert performance for the student to use as stepping stones or performance plateaus during learning and practice. This incremental introduction of increasingly complex tasks is described as an essential feature of the apprenticeship model of learning described by Collins, Brown, and Newman (1987). (See also Burton, Brown, & Fischer, 1984, for an excellent discussion of how work models can be linked into "increasingly complex microworlds.")

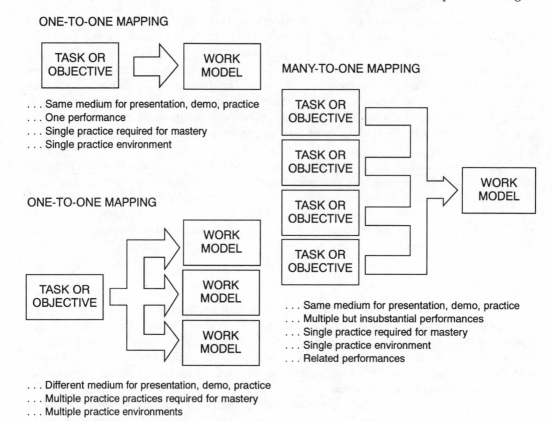

Figure 1. Task/objective-to-work-model mappings.

Work Models and Simulation

Using work models does introduce a new step into the instructional design process, but it is not certain whether this is an entirely new step or simply the formalization of steps which designers have been taking for years without recognizing the formal process, principles, and constructs which should guide them. The main benefit of work model synthesis is that it brings system, order, and the capability for more precise control to the otherwise confusing and imprecise process of defining syllabus events. It allows syllabus and media decisions to be made in a rational and data-based manner. It encourages more careful consideration of the need to include simulation in the curriculum and increases the chance that what is designed will incorporate appropriate levels of integrative practice for the target population for each instructional task. Moreover, once syllabus decisions are made and tested in use, they are revisable on the basis of the data which accumulates from use, enabling adjustments to be made with more precision than would otherwise be possible.

The use of work models has been shown to be useful in industrial training as well as in virtually all non-industrial complexes of performance. It has been applied by students to content as diverse as Pinyin (Romanized Chinese) language reading skills, tennis serving skills and strategy, library research skills for elementary children, scientific process skills for the same population, and spoken foreign language comprehension for all languages. The more complexly integrated the performance, the more useful the work model technique has been, whether the subject of instruction is motor-biased or not.

The use of work models facilitates the appropriate incorporation of simulation within curricula in several ways. First, work models align instructional media concerns with instructional strategy concerns, then allow portions of the instructional strategy for a single instructional objective to be split off for separate designer treatments using separate media assignments. The presentation phase of instruction for an objective can be carried out in a medium that is appropriate for its strategic requirements, frequently a presentation-oriented medium, while the practice phase can be carried out in another that suits its practice requirements, frequently a simulation.

Second, using work models encourages definition of intermediate-level task and objective combinations which require practice as a group and allows the selection of an appropriate instructional medium for them. Most often, the appropriate medium for intermediate-level instruction is some form of simulation.

Third, using work models encourages the notion of incrementality in designing paths toward real-world performance. Instead of thinking of simulation as one level of practice on the path toward real-world performance, it suggests that a progressive family of simulated environments may be used, each distinguished by its level of fidelity (conditions), scope of task and objective inclusion (behavior), and level of expected performance (standard). The variation of these dimensions should suggest to the designer a multi-dimensional field of possible work model "stepping stones." The designer's task becomes one of selecting the best path for the student to move across the field—not stopping at each point on the path, but only those which optimize progress for the student.

The notion of progressive models in the building of complex behavior capabilities has been shown to be important, not only for the facilitation of learning, but for the prevention of model flaws in the student's learning which might impede further independent use of the knowledge. (See, for instance, White & Frederiksen, 1990.) Our conclusion is that the more complex the performance being trained, the greater the need for work models and the more likely the need for simulation. If work models are used, the more likely the simulation will be well-integrated with other instructional forms and with a larger curriculum.

Instructional Features of Simulations

Instructional features distinguish instructional simulations from general purpose simulations. A student may learn from experiencing a general purpose simulation, but instructional features guide, catalyze, inform, and support learning processes and so amplify the effectiveness and efficiency of the simulation. The instructional goal is relevant because goals—and measurements of student performance relative to goals—determine *when* instructional features will be activated and *what* and *how much* they will communicate to the student. The notion of an instructional feature is meaningless without a goal, because without one there is no reference point from which the actions of an instructional feature can be planned.

Some instructional features are programs which can be added to or subtracted from simulations as independent modules,[2] but some of them also represent qualities of the message communicated to the student, which make it easier or harder to learn from a simulation. The sections which follow describe instructional features in more detail, following a brief review of learning processes which appear to have implications for these features.

Learning and Instructional Features

There appear to be at least two major varieties of learning goal: *verbal-semantic goals* and *performance goals*. Anderson (1993) describes a learning process that encodes knowledge

---

[2]See, for instance, Wenger's (1987) description of modularity as a dimension of flexibility in the design of intelligent tutoring systems (p. 265).

in both declarative and performance form. A key element in the Anderson theory of learning is the relationship between knowledge in its declarative form and in its action-ready form. Anderson maintains that the action-ready form is derived through transformation of the declarative form into a compiled and proceduralized form, and that the two forms of knowledge are therefore closely related.

Snow and Lohman (1989) divide their discussion of educational testing along the lines of verbal and performance tests. Verbal-semantic instructional goals promote the ability to reproduce from memory or to manipulate verbal and semantic structures. Gagné (1985) characterizes this type of learning as "verbal information." He separates it from the classes of beyond-verbal learning called "intellectual skills" and "cognitive strategies" whose nature is manifested directly in the execution of acts (either visible or covert) and not simply in the reproduction or manipulation of verbal or semantic structures.

When Bunderson and his co-workers (Bunderson, Gibbons, Olsen, & Kearsley, 1981) describe the concept of the work model, they refer to a phenomenon called the "lexical loop" as the alternative to performance-centered instruction. The lexical loop is the tendency for instruction to slip into a verbal metaphor and teach "about" rather than "how to." Bunderson and his colleagues suggest that the great mass of modern instruction—in both schools and in industry—is delivered from the metaphor of *verbal* goals, despite the fact that the instruction is intended to bring about a change in the student's *performance* capability. It creates the lexical loop defined by Bunderson and his associates (Bunderson, Gibbons, Olsen, & Kearsley, 1981). In their words:

> The students are expected to translate the verbal abstractions back into the skills/knowledge of the expert. They are expected to create a model of the performance of the expert from verbal abstractions. This is the lexical loop. (p. 207)

Collins, Brown, and Newman (1987) and Lesgold and Lajoie (1989) refer to this as the problem of "inert knowledge." It is only possible for this mismatch between performance expectations and verbal instructional means to exist because of separate learning paths for verbal and performance goals which are illustrated in Figure 2, which is based on Anderson's theory. As the diagram shows, knowledge of both declarative and performance types may be obtained by either instructional or self-instructional paths. A student may be instructed directly in order to bring about declarative learning. This instruction may include presentations of information, helps for the encoding and storage process, and practice to provide the occasion for storage and to proceduralize recall. Then, according to Anderson's theory, further direct instruction, with an additional supply of information, helps, and different forms of practice, can assist the student to convert that declarative knowledge into procedural knowledge.

However, in many cases we learn from direct experience rather than from an instructor. Means of self-instruction include exploration, inquiry, experimentation, self-examination, and retrospection on raw experience. The absence of a prepared informational presentation on the self-directed learning path forces us to construct our own declarative knowledge using observation, assumptions, inference, and deduction. Likewise, we can support our own conversion of knowledge from the declarative to the procedural form by copying what we observe of competent performance and by using the same deductive and inferential techniques to fill in the missing parts. The self-instructional case describes learning without an instructor as well as learning in which the instructor's techniques are deficient or faulty. If the instructor fails to supply the necessary information, we can activate self-instructional techniques and supply the missing portion. And if the instructor fails to supply the necessary practice environment and supports with which to convert declarative into procedural knowledge, then we can supply that too. The assumption on the part of instructors and training organizations that students will make this transformation from verbalism to performance capability on their own lies at the core of the prevailing body of teaching methods in our society today for both training and education.

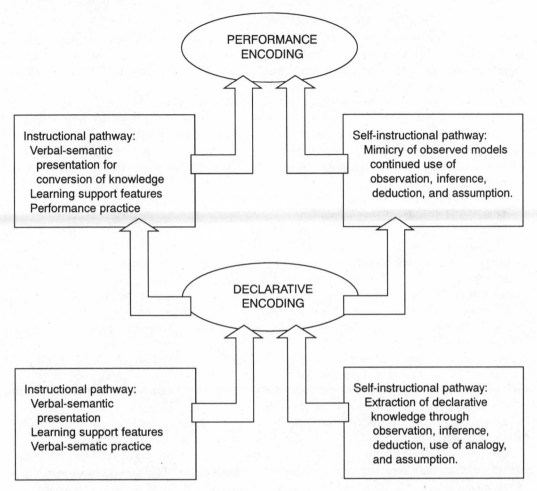

Figure 2. Different paths to learning for verbal and performance encoding goals.

Students learn early in their careers, and mostly on their own, the techniques for converting declarative knowledge into performance capability through the self-instructional pathway shown in Figure 2. Much, if not most, of what we learn as humans is learned through our interpretation of direct experience and through the cause-and-effect linkages which we detect or infer as a result of that experience. This is probably why students can learn from simulations and why they are so adept at learning from them. Simulations communicate efficiently with the learning processes because they approximate more closely the experiential language through which we are most apt to learn anyway.

The strictly experiential model of learning, however, has serious drawbacks. Students learning unaided from experiential sources are prone to faulty observation, misinterpretation, and incorrect inference (Champagne, Gunstone, & Klopfer, 1985). The instructional features found in all forms of instruction—and which are especially important in instructional simulations—represent a designer's plan to provide the necessary supports for instruction while at the same time ruling out as far as possible error and misconception due to misinterpretation of experience. This is the point of the "cardinal principles of instruction" identified by Merrill (1987). The function of instruction is not to replace experience with verbalization, but to provide support during directed experience to ensure that what is learned is accurate and complete.

Instructional Features and Instructional Goals

Instructional features are predicated upon and draw their definition from instructional goals. Without goals, instructional features can only act as tour guides and commentators to facilitate exploration, inquiry, and self-directed learning through experience (Wenger, 1987). As Collins, Brown, and Newman (1987) state it: ". . . the content of the coaching interaction is immediately related to specific events or problems that arise as the student attempts to carry out the target task." (p. 17.) Instructional goals are statements of learning intent. When an instructional goal is present, it influences the operation of the instructional feature and helps the feature determine how to respond to the student, which includes influencing the content of messages and interaction. This is true of the classes of instructional features described in this chapter.

Though it is common among instructional designers to think mainly of instructional goals as singular, isolated, static points at high levels toward which students move (such as the "lesson objective"), some intelligent tutoring systems employ systems of instructional goals that change moment by moment during instruction. The tutoring system GUIDON (Clancey, 1979), for instance, passes the goal structure used by an expert system to solve a diagnostic problem in MYCIN to an expert tutor which uses it to select and carry out its own tutorial functions. An improved version of the same system, named NEOMYCIN (Clancey, 1988), reorganizes the knowledge base to include a more complete representation of the expert's diagnostic rules so that they also can be included in the formation of instruction. (See also Lesgold, 1988.)

We believe that there are at least two sets of instruction-related goals in operation during instruction. One set is *performance* goals: performance targets that the student is hoped to achieve. The second is the *strategic* goals. Strategic goals represent the intention of the designer to support the learning process through specific strategic moves which may include sending messages to the student, interacting with the student, or receiving a non-judgable (data) message from the student. Strategic goals govern the instructional acts which are performed: messages and interactions. Strategic goals remain in effect until performance goals are satisfied or until either system or student disengages from instruction. In order to accomplish a learning goal, several strategic goals may need to be selected, used, and discarded.

Control of instruction, whether live or computer-based, consists of the moment by moment selection of, first, performance and then strategic goals. Under instructor-led or system-led instruction, selection is by the teacher or the system. A live teacher monitors the learner constantly, selecting a succession of performance goals with corresponding strategic goals that will support their attainment. At a particular moment during instruction, the performance goal may be, "The student will demonstrate verbal encoding of the principle [being taught]." One appropriate strategic goal in response to this would be the compound goal, "Present the principle and then check for successful verbal encoding."

Goals decompose hierarchically. The strategic goal, "Present the principle" may decompose into the subgoals, "Verbalize the principle to the student" and "Present a mnemonic to aid memory for the principle." This would adhere to one philosophy of memory instruction—one which stresses the use of memory aids. A different philosophy could lead to the selection of different subgoals, such as, "Verbalize the principle to the student" and "present a cause-effect summary of the principle which can be used to re-generate the rule from memory." Moreover, depending on still further philosophical differences in teaching strategy, two designers might reorder the verbalization goal and the cause-effect summary goal with respect to each other, and the presentation may take the form of a guided discovery in which the student participates quite actively, using cause-effect observations as the means of generalizing to the principle.

Strategic goal patterns are fixed in a logical sequence in some forms of instruction but have tended to be more free to vary in others. Part of the excellence of a great instructor lies in the ability to pick a more excellent sequence of performance goals, along with excellent sequences of matching strategic goals. Another skill of teaching excellence is knowing when to abandon or modify an ineffective goal for a new goal. An instructional simulation accepts interactions from the student in any order. It might therefore have a dynamic goal engine, able to recognize moment by moment the one or more momentarily appropriate performance goals, making it able then to form corresponding strategic goals that would enable its instructional features to support learning in an intelligent way. This design was tried in the LISP Tutor (Anderson, Farrell, & Sauers, 1984; Anderson, Conrad, & Corbett, 1993), which determines, moment by moment, the legitimacy of the student path compared to an expert's solution in order to detect errors and provide feedback.

If this view of goals is not complicated enough, there is yet another set of goals in operation during learning which have relevance to the design of instructional features of a simulation: the student's own intentions or learning goals. These are of importance in simulated environments which provide tools to the student for solving problems along with a specific problem requiring use of the tools. In order for instructional features to assist the student in this type of environment, it must have the ability to know or discover what the student was intending—the student's strategic goal—at a given moment during interaction. Discovering this goal may be as simple as asking the student for clarification during feedback or as complex as trying to infer intentions from a performance trace.

Six Classes of Instructional Feature

We describe six classes of instructional feature for simulations: (1) coaching systems, (2) feedback systems, (3) representation systems, (4) control systems, (5) scope dynamism, and (6) embedded didactics. **Coaching** is *prospective*; it assists the student to prepare to act in advance of the act itself. **Feedback** follows an act or the lack of an act where one should be performed. Its use by the student is *retrospective*, and it causes the student to suspend action-directed processing in favor of recalling and reconstructing past events in order to repair knowledge. **Representations** are the means by which information is conveyed to the student. They include visual, audible, and otherwise sense-able communications from an instructional source. The proper organization and use of representations is perhaps more important in simulations than in any other form of instructional experience, because to a greater extent than in any other, the student is responsible for interpreting the representations received rather than having them interpreted for him or her by the context of the sequential message. The **controlled change** of scope is a powerful simulation instructional technique. **Scope dynamism** refers to the selection and ordering of instructional scopes, which in simulation terms translates to problem progressions. **Embedded didactics** are instructional resources and messages which are encapsulated within or blended within simulation environments. They are an important feature that helps turn a simulation into an instructional simulation. The sections which follow describe these six classes of instructional feature.

Coaching Systems

Coaching is a complex of several instructional acts. Coaching messages vary in content, depending on the momentary strategic *goal*, the particular *aspect* of the student's performance which is being supported, and the *degree* to which it is being supported. Coaching in general seems to have three functions: support for the student memory processes which are under development, proportioning of the instructional message, and the mapping of learning opportunities for the student.

Support for student memory processes. One form of coaching consists mainly of support for the timing and content of the student's memory retrieval process during performance. It is a reminder system for what to retrieve and why to retrieve it. Coaching's purpose is not only to ensure a satisfactory performance at the present moment but to assist the student in strengthening patterns of performance and their sequences for future performances. Therefore, they are an important part of the conversion of declarative knowledge into procedural form. As the student's own retrieval patterns strengthen, prolonged coaching is unnecessary and probably detrimental.

Coaching supports action and decision making by the learner for the learning of both verbal-semantic behavior and performance. This includes assisting the student with observation, analysis, goal-selection, performance selection, and performance execution. A list of the specific acts supported might include the ones in Table 1 below.

This set of questions leads to matched coaching messages, also shown in Table 1, which vary, depending on the momentary performance and strategic goals, and which can also vary relative to the status of the student and the phase of instruction. A coaching system can be a temporary "scaffold" (Collins, Brown, & Newman, 1987) to support the student's integration of memory activity with performance activity.

The content of memory coaching messages is generally of two types: *occasion* and *substance*. Occasion refers to *when* to remember; substance refers to *what* to remember. The ultimate capability of a coaching system is to be what is commonly called a "job aid" or "learning coach." If the parameters of a dynamic coaching system were set to provide full support, the result would be a step-by-step, moment-by-moment performance support system capable of leading the student through the performance of a complex task. If the coaching system was intelligent and had within itself the ability to model performance, it would not only be capable of performing demonstration acts, but also of providing a running commentary on its own performance prior to and during each one. Thus coaching, in a sense, blends at the edges with the function we would normally call "demonstration." As we will see, it blends at another edge with some of the functions of feedback as well. However, the overlap in neither case is complete. There are functions reserved strictly to coaching and others reserved strictly to feedback and demonstration. In actuality, every coaching system is a subset of that complete coach, and the threshold for messaging to the student is based on a setting by the designer.

Proportioning. As well as learning what to remember and when, students must also learn which elements of knowledge and performance are of greater importance to competent performance. Learning of proportional import is accomplished through coaching and through feedback, through the frequency of recurring messages and the urgency or emphasis which they are given.

Opportunity mapping. Coaching can also act, as Wenger (1987) describes, to help those who:

> . . . overlook learning opportunities and get stuck on "plateaus" of proficiency. Making them aware of further possibilities is the task of a coach: his purpose is not to lecture, but to foster the learning inherent in an activity itself by pointing out existing learning opportunities and by transforming failures into learning experiences. (p. 124)

Feedback Systems

As an instructional technique, feedback is required for more than theoretical reasons; it is required because students demand it. When it is not given, there is a sense of incompleteness: the feeling of having been ignored or snubbed. Tutorial designers seldom fail to provide feedback following a student response. However, in general practice simulation, designers frequently fail to provide any feedback at all beyond a statement of the overall result of the simulation exercise—what tutorial designers call "knowledge of results" feedback.

Table 1. Memory activities supported by coaching and related messaging implications.

Activity supported	Question	Message implications
Choice of information processing action	What should I do next?	"It is time to select a course of action that will satisfy your goal."
Observing	What should I be alert for?	"Since you saw the first wisp of color in the acid solution, watch the response to the next drop of base carefully."
	Where should I be attending?	"The coda symbol is placed here, above the staff."
	Is what I saw a cause for action?	"The bubbles popping on top of the pancake may mean that it is done on the bottom."
Goal selection	What should I try to do now?	"Have you completed your isolation of the fault to one circuit board?"
Action/performance selection	What is the best way to accomplish my goal?	"Have you considered using the split-half method to eliminate parts of the circuit board which are good?"
Action/performance execution	What should I do next? (Step)	"As a next step in making this measurement, you ought to consider placing your measurement probes."
	What should I do next? (Decision)	"To decide which point to measure from: (1) trace the signal path on the schematic toward the first known fault and (2) pick a point half way between."
Self-monitoring and evaluation	Am I doing this correctly?	"Ask yourself: Is this the next logical step in setting up the meter to take a measurement?"
	Was this the right thing to do?	"Think through your decision process for picking this point: Does it meet the criteria for 'most accessible measurement point'?"
	Was it the right time?	"Ask yourself: Has the meter been set up to protect it from high voltages?"
	How could I have done better?	"Take a moment to consider at least one other possible way to make this test and ask if that way has any advantages."

Every simulation supplies some degree of "natural" feedback (Reigeluth & Schwartz, 1989). This consists of the visible or otherwise-sensed responses of the simulation's model to the manipulations of the student. It is a common but mistaken opinion, especially among trainers, that little or no additional "artificial" feedback is required for use with simulations. Natural feedback is expected to bear the full weight of instructional effect. This belief is not supported by research (Anderson & Skwarecki, 1986). We believe that the need for artificial feedback is as strong in simulations as in any form of instruction. We also believe that this is an important question for research. Feedback may be even *more* valuable in conjunction with simulation-based learning than in other forms, since the act of learning from direct experience is more likely to produce errors and misconceptions than learning from carefully controlled text and graphic sequences. The type of integrated performance which is learned in an instructional simulation is also assumed to have at least as much, if not more, requirement for self-monitoring by the student, an important capability which is established mainly with the assistance of artificial feedback.

The role of feedback in instruction has not been formally defined since the decline in popularity of behaviorist theory. The centrality of the feedback concept to behaviorist learning theory has made it difficult to bring a new, cognitive, meaning to the old behaviorist term. Current research in feedback struggles hard to throw off this legacy of inherited meaning, and it is not certain how successfully that effort is proceeding (Gibbons, 1993).

For the purposes of this chapter, feedback is defined as any message to the student that is contingent upon the outcome of a judgment of one or more actions by the student, normally actions taken in response to a performance opportunity provided by the instruction. Providing feedback may require: (1) some mechanism for recording the student's performance, (2) an analysis and judgment of the performance to find both excellent and erroneous patterns of action, and (3) a diagnosis of error causes so that appropriate correctives can be implemented.

At least five functions of feedback can be identified within the framework of cognitive theory:

Give student knowledge of right/wrong. Right/wrong feedback should be provided as a courtesy to the student, if for no other reason. The feedback system must use the current goal of instruction as well as knowledge of the phase of learning to determine the timing and placement of this message. If the scope of the instructional goal is wide, and if the phase of learning is a later one, then knowledge of results might be given at the end of a prolonged sequence of performance. If the conditions are opposite—narrow scope and early learning phase—then feedback messages might come after any incorrect response. An interesting feature of many simulations is the absence of a single right answer and a merging of the right/wrong dimension into a continuum of judgment assessments. Using this judgment rating continuum effectively in the instruction of "soft" skills is at the same time a challenge and an opportunity for the simulation designer. At any rate, it represents a radical departure from the standard view of feedback and its functions.

Supply content for corrective knowledge remedy. Cognitive theory, in contrast to behaviorism, assumes a student responsible for the self-management of his or her own learning. If that ideal is not always true, then it should be one of the goals of instructional theory based on cognitive principles to help it to be so for individual students. In the absence of research results to the contrary, designers should give students access to any feedback information that might encourage and support self-management of learning.

Content can be supplied as part of the feedback message which enables the student to revise knowledge structures, since part of the self-management of learning includes maintenance of one's own knowledge. This content can be supplied in a number of forms:

Description, demonstration, or modeling of expert performance
Comparisons with expert performance
Simple replay of student activity with commentary
Enumeration of error points only
Comparison with peers or norms
Restatement of content

Support for recovery and move-ahead. Once an error has been published and pinpointed, the feedback process can continue by attempting to administer messages and interactions that support the student in self-remediation. These may come in the form of suggestions, prescriptions, menu choices, or mandatory interactions. Students can be asked to re-try the performance that was faulted one or more times, or new examples can be presented for solution. A short didactic message can be given, or a later tutorial may be scheduled. A system with dynamic scope selection may even designate a future problem for the student which involves the faulted performance as one of its elements. This is the mechanism used in a training system for the Patriot guided missile system which is described later.

Establish self-monitoring. This neglected function of feedback may well turn out to be one of the most important. Glaser and Bassok (1989) stress the role of feedback in establishing self-regulatory capability as an important outcome of learning. (See also Burton, Brown, and Fischer, 1984.) Collins, Brown, and Newman, (1987) discuss the self-monitoring of performance as one of the major outcomes of the use of cognitive apprenticeship principles.

Deal with attitude and motivation of the student. The student at the time of feedback has slightly different feelings than at a time of instruction. A performance has been offered, and it is to be judged. The student may be either certain or anxious, and when the judgment is adverse in some aspect, it can create feelings of frustration, impatience, anger, and lowered confidence. In many cases the effects of such feelings are relatively minor, but in some cases students begin to question their willingness to proceed with instruction. A feedback message must help the student place bad news in perspective and can do so in many ways.

One of the ways is to provide good news. The notion of feedback has become associated with correction in general, and yet a live instructor will carefully consider every opportunity to compliment good aspects of performance because doing so at the right time can bolster student morale and release new energies to the learning task. The principle of noticing the positive was recommended by Burton and Brown (1979) but has been largely ignored. This may be due to the underlying conception, expressed within the same paper, that learning is largely a process of "debugging" knowledge structures. This is a non-constructive, reactive view of the learning process. It tends to lead to activities which are corrective. Descriptions of learning theory which specify the use of positive feedback will perhaps change this negative bias in feedback.

A way to help a student keep negative feelings in proportion during feedback is to make feedback indirect. Instead of presenting its message directly and bluntly, a feedback system can ask the student questions which will lead to a success experience. This places the initiative directly back on the student and changes the feedback experience from a correction to a self-correction. Most students' errors are relatively minor and result from inattention, hastiness, memory faults, or timing errors, so the student in many cases knows the right thing to do to correct a fault and can be brought to a correct answer by skillful questioning. An example of this indirection is found in dialogues provided by Lepper and Chabay (1987). In many respects, the instructional computer still has a great deal to learn from the human instructor.

Representation Systems

The representation of information to the student is an integral function of an instructional simulation. The phrase "representation of information" often connotes some form of graphic, but as it is used here, it refers to the total set of sensory channels used to transfer information to the student, including graphic, textual, tabular, auditory, tactile, kinesthetic, and olfactory. We name representation as an instructional feature of simulations because representations vary widely in their capability to transmit information to the student efficiently and understandably, and yet they are a highly controllable element of instruction. The representational principles used by a designer either enhance or limit the instructional ability of a simulation.

Bayman and Mayer (1984) related the mental models formed by students to graphic and verbal representations provided during instruction. They demonstrated that the completeness of the representations provided influenced the resulting mental models, and hypothesized that incorrect mental models would lead to inappropriate or faulty extensions of procedure when more complex computations were required. White (White, in press-a, in press-b; White & Frederiksen, 1990) has based a major program of research leading to the development of the QUEST system on the design and sequencing of model sequences through which a student is expected to pass during instruction. White describes how her microworlds for sixth-grade instruction in physics ". . . incorporate a variety of linked alternative representations for force and motion . . ." in order to facilitate the learning of them through a ". . . series of increasingly sophisticated models for reasoning about how forces affect the motion of objects" (White, in press-a). This broader definition of representation is an important expansion which shifts our attention from just illustrations and causes us to think of representations more as threads or progressions of many-channeled representation over time. It also shifts our attention away from merely static representations.

Representations for instructional simulations make special demands on the student because many of the contextual cues present in traditional instructional forms are not present in a simulation experience. Many of the habits for the decoding of tutorial displays do not transfer readily to simulations. As students use a simulation, they are frequently learning to interpret new representations—new images of the simulated world—at the same time they are expected to be learning from the simulation. Learning from simulation often imposes large but possible information processing burdens on the student. Poor representations add to this burden, sometimes to the point of restricting rather than enhancing learning. Simulation displays are frequently non-verbal and are organized spatially rather than sequentially. Motion is often involved, and change may occur at several places or in multiple channels (e.g., sound *and* graphic) within one representation simultaneously, making focus and the sequence of scanning a display into critical factors. Sometimes a variety of constantly-changing elements within a representation must be tracked and correlated by the student, and in most cases, the conclusions the student reaches due to this correlation is part of the information intended to lead to learning. In some cases, such as pilot training, the appropriate pattern of scanning itself is one goal of instruction. Time and space are therefore elements of representation.

Four aspects of representation which have special relevance to instructional simulations include: the representation trace, the timing and channeling of message elements, the focus of representations for message bearing, and the structuring of representation and information-conveying frameworks to reduce processing loads.

Representation trace. The representation trace is the simulation's ability to maintain a historical residue of past representation states within student view. In a simulation, the trace is important because it contains the very contrasting information that allows the student to learn from successive repetitions—sometimes called "experiments"—of the simulated experience. An example will illustrate the dimensions of this notion of trace.

A camera simulation provided by a major authoring software vendor has many excellent features. It is attractive and realistic and encourages learning about camera exposure through the exploration of a camera's controls. When controls have been set and the film has been advanced, clicking the shutter "takes" a picture and shows the result on the screen. Resetting the controls, advancing the film, and clicking again replaces the first picture with the picture taken at the new settings. The representation's trace in this simulation consists of (1) the visible settings of the camera and (2) the single picture which has been taken most recently at those settings. By manipulating the settings systematically in an experiment, a student can self-instruct on the relationships between the settings and picture qualities of contrast, light quality, depth, and image brightness.

One of the authors asked a graduate-level class in simulation design what they would do if they could modify the trace of this simulation to improve the amount of useful information it provided to the student. Two general schools of thought formed after some discussion. The first school of thought said that the camera should be reduced in size to make room on the screen for the display of the "history" of all of the slides taken, as if the screen were a large light table. Each slide taken would be added to the light table in the order of being taken and labeled with its exposure settings. The theory was that this historical trace would allow greater comparison between setting combinations and encourage more ambitious and systematic experiments by the student. In fact, the light table might be laid out with labels in such a way as to suggest (but not constrain) certain experiments.

A second school of thought recommended the abandonment of the camera itself altogether, replacing it with a "cube" of pictorial history. The dimensions of the cube would represent the camera's three independent variable settings. The purpose of the cube would be to allow the student to look along any dimension of the cube, noting the effect of incremental changes in the setting represented by that dimension. A key element of this plan was that the student should be able to see from three to five pictures along any dimension selected at any time from the student's current position. (Could we call this the span or the horizon of the trace?) This would allow the student to see the not only the absolute differences from picture to picture but the rate of change as well: the "envelope" of acceptable picture qualities. In effect, this would be like placing the student within a cubic space full of pictures with the ability to walk along any dimension, studying the dimensional change. Of course, angular dimensions would be traversable as well, showing the student the effects of changes on two or more dimensions at once. One provision of the "cubic" point of view was that the instructional goal was not to learn operation of the camera's controls but to learn the effects of the controls on picture quality. This position also supported the addition of (1) other picture subjects or content to the set, and (2) pictures taken in different light conditions ranging from bright and direct to dim and indirect.

This example illustrates that the amount of information available to the student in a simulation's representation can vary greatly and that the representation can influence the amount of information a student must hold in memory at one time. The multiple pictures provided by the "light table" design improved the amount of information available to the student over the original single-picture display, and the burden on student memory was reduced by it. The information available increased even more with the "picture cube" form of representation. Does it also reduce memory? Does it increase the "sense" of the picture-space defined by the settings? These are interesting and researchable questions.

This example also illustrates that both the content and the structure of a representation are related to the instructional goal. The "picture cube" design group recommended the elimination of the camera from the representation altogether: not a wise decision if the instructional goal pertained to the physical act of setting the camera's controls, but perfectly reasonable if the goal centers upon the relationship between camera settings and picture qualities.

The use of the representation is more than a matter of displaying information to the student. The representation also interacts with the student's sense of self-directed exploration and learning. If the picture cube is filled with pictures before the student arrives to inspect it, what will be the effect on the student's inspecting and attending process? Will the immediate overload of information represented by the picture-filled cube reduce the amount of attention the student will pay to each picture and each set of contrasts offered? There are reasons to suspect that it would be better to let the student fill the cube by taking pictures one at a time, noting each set of differences and contrasts provided by each new picture.

Timing and channeling of message elements. Another dimension of representation is timing. Mayer and Anderson (1991) studied the encoding of instructional message information relative to a process (the operation of a bicycle pump). They determined that the timing of the arrival of the audio and graphical content of demonstrations influenced the ability of students to reason using the process knowledge that was conveyed. If visual and auditory channels of information did not arrive simultaneously, performance on a test of reasoning about pump operation suffered.

Even in tutorials, the element of time is just beginning to be mastered. The addition of new message channels by multimedia has increased the importance of authoring tool features which allow designers to coordinate the timing of animations, audio messages, text and graphic messages, and video sequences. Some difficulties yet exist in the coordination of some multimedia channels, and designers still must in some cases "design around" tool shortcomings. Instructional simulations will continue to make the timing of messages of all kinds more complex and yet more important.

Focus of representations. The purpose of a simulation representation is to make salient certain trends or patterns in information or data generated by the simulation and to make it easy for students to compare trends with each other across a range of varying conditions. Larkin and Simon (1987) emphasize the subtle but powerful influence of representations on human information processing by pointing out the relative differences in (mental) computations necessary to obtain information which is usable for problem solving from different forms of representation: verbal and diagrammatic. They ask us to:

> . . . consider a set of points represented in either a table of x and y coordinates or as geometric points on a graph. Visual entities such as smooth curves, maxima, and discontinuities are readily recognized in the latter representation but not in the former. (p. 70)

Larkin and Simon conclude that memory encoding is influenced by representation and that a representation that fails to make particular items of information salient in effect hides that information from the person, both at the time of recognition during instruction and at the time of search during problem solving. They show how this secondary encoding influences the process of problem solving directly. They demonstrate, for instance, how changes in the representation add to or diminish the perceptual and memory load for the person, depending on the form of representation chosen and the prior, compiled knowledge possessed by the student. This principle and the manner in which the authors illustrate it suggest that designers must discover principles for matching representations with problem structures and instructional intention in systematic ways. Most significantly, Larkin and Simon's principles:

> . . . not only provide an explanation of why diagrams can be so useful, but also provide a framework for further study of the knowledge required for effective diagram [representation] use. (p. 99)

Research by Powers, Lashley, Sanchez, and Shneiderman (1984) performed prior to the writing of Larkin and Simon supports the Larkin-Simon theory in detail, predicting that a combination of tabular and diagrammatic representations, each providing its information in a problem-relevant form and thus making it more salient and usable, was more effective than either of the representations in isolation. Slusarenko and Worner (1989) demonstrate how a single powerful representation of the complex relationships between a source and one or more observers in the doppler effect can not only facilitate a student's understanding of observations but also lead to accurate predictions in complicated variations of the effect, while at the same time eliminating the need to memorize formulas and rules—at least for the purposes of comprehension and prediction.

Structuring information-conveying frameworks. The structure of a display and its population with graphic objects can convey volumes of information immediately to a user if a particular metaphor is chosen (see Cates, 1994). This is the whole point of the desktop, windows, and notebook metaphors selected for use in the interfaces of major computer operating systems. Not only does a user know readily what each object on the screen represents, but actions which can be performed are also suggested to the user without the need for training. Analogies, metaphors, and familiar patterns can be used in the structure of simulations as well to reduce the processing required in order to obtain information from the display.

Not only does the representation figure into the size of the memory burden, but it influences the manner in which information is encoded as well (see Larkin & Simon, 1987). Ward and Sweller (1990) point out that not only the provision of worked examples but also particular methods of formatting them influence their effectiveness of the instruction of mathematics. Citing earlier research in which worked examples had a greater effect on performance than even practice opportunities, they report current research that concludes the format of worked examples to be a major influence on the acquisition of rules and their automation in a way that less-well formatted examples does not match.

Fitter and Green (1979) describe several dimensions of representations that influence rapid assimilation and understanding of the cause-effect relationships they contain. They propose five main principles for structuring representations for improved communication of the patterns within their data:

1. Relevance: The placement of the data to be observed in the most observable and usable form. The example of syntax diagrams of Pascal are offered as an example of information that is ready to use in tracing errors within Pascal statements. An informal experiment is described showing time differences in the use of the syntax diagrams and the more linear Backus-Naur form. However, differences in understanding of Pascal statements is not found, indicating the rather specific focusing property of representations on not only the student's attention but on the processing and use of the information as well.

2. Restriction: The restriction of elements of a representation so that they are more unambiguously interpretable. The authors provide an example that shows that this may result in a slightly larger representation but that the representation itself will be given more meaning and interpretability. The point the authors emphasize is that reducing the representation may in some cases confound the information conveyed to the student, reducing the completeness of the representation and actually hiding needed information from the student.

3. Redundant recoding: The coding of information in a readily-visible spatial form when the information already contains the same data in a logical form. The authors use the example of an indented versus unindented representation of computer code heavily loaded with nested loops. The authors also recount an interesting experiment in which they found the solving of a simple problem highly reactive to the order in which the elements of data were presented.

4. Revelation and responsiveness: The design of representations which allow the user to see the forces, structures, or processes underlying surface forms. The authors describe how a representation can function as a "conceptual window" into underlying processes.

5. Revisability: The economy of revising a representation. The authors point out that in the case of redundantly recoded representations, the revision may be made more complex because each change requires attention to two dimensions of representation rather than one.

Control Systems

The controls provided to a student determine to a great extent the information which she or he can obtain from the simulation. Visual simulation provides limited information to the student because its behavior cannot be controlled along certain dimensions. Therefore, the only information available to the student in a visual simulation is that which is placed there deliberately by the designer. Model or location simulations provide the potential for a great deal more information to be accessed by the student because additional variations of modeled system behavior and environmental exploration are made available for student observation. When, in addition, a suitable set of controls is made available to the student, with which the simulation and its representation can be influenced and explored, the amount of information which can be obtained expands even further.

Simulation controls fall into three main categories: (1) controls which influence simulation behavior, (2) controls which influence the representation of the model or environment to the student, and (3) controls which control the simulation session itself. A designer faces several tough trade-offs during the selection, configuration, and surfacing of controls. By selecting too many or too few controls, or by configuring them with too many or too few optional modes, the designer presents the student with either overchoice or information deficit. By creating surface representations of the controls which are hard to operate or hard to decipher, the designer places the control in front of the simulation in the student's attention.

Scope Dynamism

Scope dynamism is a change in the intended scope of learning. The manipulation of scope for instructional effect has been a tool of both teachers and designers for at least as long as there have been training wheels on bicycles. When teachers and designers define the instructional goal, they define the scope of instruction. When they change or select instructional scope specifically for the purpose of improving learning, they engage in scope dynamism.

A scenario is comprised of a learning problem or task—one work model—and the simulation itself supplies an environment within which the problem can be solved or the task accomplished. As described in an earlier section, it is the scope or work model that represents one instructional event. One simulation environment may support several instructional events. This is why scope dynamism is an instructional feature of simulations: designers may arrange sequences of scopes within a single environment in an order that enhances instructional impact.

Burton, Brown, and Fischer (1984) define the concept of "increasingly complex microworlds" which is the essential mechanism of scope dynamism. However, there are *two* types of scope dynamism, and within the type of educational measurement environments described as third- and fourth-generation measurement systems by Bunderson, Inouye, and Olsen (1989), both types will be required. The two types of scope dynamism are *within*-problem dynamism and *between*-problem dynamism.

Within-problem scope dynamism means that the designer has made provision for increasing the instructional challenge of a problem by adding tasks, changing conditions, or raising criteria during the execution of one simulation problem. Between-problem dynamism means that the designer has made provision for selecting problems in a particularly beneficial order. The dimensions which change between problems are the same ones that change within problems: task, conditions, and criterion.

The concept of scope dynamism responds to Vygotsky's (1978) principle of "zone of proximal development." A designer plans the succession of scopes in such a way that students advancing through a sequence of problems are not challenged beneath or beyond this zone, which varies for students individually. Within this zone, competent performance is possible, but growth is demanded by challenge. Research by White (White, in press-a, in press-b; White & Frederiksen, 1990) has established the importance of carefully selecting and ordering scopes—in her case, expressed in terms of mental model progressions—to achieve a gradually increasing range of performance capability in the student while at the same time avoiding the introduction of misleading models or models which compete with the learning of later extensions.

Work models, discussed earlier as a means of organizing and sequencing instructional events, are a tool for achieving scoping dynamics. A single work model consists of a specified group of tasks and objectives practiced under a given set of conditions to a given standard of acceptable performance. Any of these can vary. In some cases, designers find it useful to introduce one set of tasks and then hold that set constant throughout several instructional events while variations of conditions make the task more difficult to perform or while increasingly high levels of performance are required. In other cases, designers find it useful to introduce several tasks independently at a consistent level of condition and criterion difficulty, then to bring tasks together, at the same time gradually increasing the difficulty through condition adding and the criterion adjustment as well. This conception of scope manipulation provides a difficult challenge to the designer of instructional simulations. The choice of possible scopes is enormous, even for relatively simple task suites. For complex performances, the choice of scopes is overwhelming. Brown, Burton, and Fischer (1984) provide an excellent and extensive set of principles for the achievement of between-problem scoping dynamics, all of which are testable hypotheses.

Embedded Didactics

"Didactic" as it is used in this chapter refers to messages or presentations of performance-related content as well as demonstrations of the relationships within that content, which are provided with direct instructional intent, and without the assumption that the student has been previously exposed to the content. Collins, Brown, and Newman (1987) emphasize the role of demonstrations and directed content messages provided by a master as an important ingredient in a system of cognitive apprenticeship. This recognition of the need for these didactic elements in a complete system of instruction, especially one aimed primarily in the development of skilled performance, is important.

A basic model of instruction which includes "telling," "showing," and "doing" was referred to earlier. Simulations are so much associated with "doing" that their capacity for "telling" and "showing" (important avenues toward "doing") has been neglected.[3] Perhaps this is because our collective image of simulations has tended to include its use to teach technical subjects, mainly using models as a vehicle, and with instructor-supplied didactics.

Some of the concepts described in this chapter, particularly the notion of scoping dynamics, increases the desirability for didactic features to be incorporated within instructional simulations. Other ideas from this chapter, particularly the idea of location simulations and the dramatic scenarios they make possible, suggest ways in which the didactic function can be included without appearing to change what the simulation's interactive and participative experience into a receptive one.

Bringing the instructional message closer to where the performance is taking place is a concept with great face validity. We feel that the concept of cognitive apprenticeship (Collins, Brown, & Newman, 1987) will become a great influence on the design and construction of instructional simulations in the future. As it does, there will be a change in the types and

---

[3]Interestingly, a corresponding atrophy has occurred in the world of tutorials, where "telling" and "showing" have been emphasized at the expense of "doing."

content of the didactic messages and the manner in which demonstrations are staged and comments are made. There will be an increased emphasis on the modeling of expert-like thinking in the messages, and the representations used in demonstrations will be structured and emphasized in ways which complement that thinking. Students will be given control over the content, level, and order of the didactic message. What now exist as hinting systems will become student-controlled reference systems in realistic simulations, and newsy or suggestion-bearing personalities within the problem's population in dramatic ones. Didactics will supply only that level of assistance that will allow the student to move ahead as a self-directed learner.

Instructional Features and Traditional Thinking

If we are to apply the instructional features described above effectively during simulations, we must change some of our traditional images of instruction, many of which are not sound instructional principles but rather artifacts of common design practice and folklore:

Separation of presentation and practice. The traditional view of instruction tends to look upon presentation and practice as isolated functions: We present information and then engage the student in practice intended to anchor that information in memory before proceeding ahead to the next body of information. Simulation-based learning challenges the student to gain information within the context of practice or exploration, often in bits and pieces, as clues or from casual observation. Frequently the moment of gaining knowledge and applying it occur close together and at a much more fine-grained level than traditional practice supports.

Ordering of presentation and practice. Telling is normally expected to precede using in traditional instructional forms. How can you ask a student about information which has not been provided? In simulation-based instruction, the technique of presenting a problem for which the student does not have the information is sometimes used. The student is placed in the position of determining information needs and then satisfying them. This upsets the normal order of "telling-then-using." In some cases, it is failure at performance that alerts a student to the need for declarative knowledge.

Visibility of presentation forms. During traditional instruction, it is easy to recognize when you are being taught, but in simulation learning, the presentations come less frequently in forms that are recognizable as presentations. Information which is relevant to a problem solution, and that normally would be given in presentation form, can be embedded within a simulated environment in many subtle ways; straightforward presentations which look like traditional presentations can become less common.

Instructor control. Classroom habits which we all have learned tell us when it is time to become passive receivers of information. Each of us has a set of skills that we were taught specifically for use while in this mode: note-taking, occasional questioning, polite discussion, and others. Simulation-based instruction denies the student a passive role. It requires that a student take action in order to be instructed. The sequence of action within a simulation is controlled by the student. The instructor can only guide, comment, correct, and suggest through the use of instructional features. Also, an instructor can select the order of challenges given to the student.

Head-on approach to instruction. Traditional tutorial forms have all the subtlety of a jackhammer. They tell you what you are going to learn, then make you learn, then test you on your learning. This "fill-then-spill" formula is so familiar to students that the "cram-then-scram" behavior has been invented to cope with it; in high school and undergraduate college studies, this has been elevated to a lifestyle. Simulation-based instruction takes an indirect route to learning which has a less obvious structure. Instruction is not necessarily directed nor controlled by the instructor. Features in this type of instruction are less centralized and sometimes harder to identify: they tend to become engines rather than specific messages and contingencies rather than certainties. Designers are forced to deal with principles and to create functions which may be invoked at any time during a problem. Instruction becomes much less the traditional and comfortable (for the designer) sequence of messages at pre-scheduled points in the instruction.

Compartmentalized view of instruction. We are used to having our instruction tied up in discrete tutorial packages. Once we finish a package, we need not deal with it again. Simulation-based instruction is contained in a different type of package: the environment. A family of related problems may share the same environment, and a student may return many times to the same simulated office, workshop, laboratory, or setting—each time for a slightly more challenging task, for the same task under more challenging conditions, or for the same task at a higher standard of performance.

Simulation and Cognitive Apprenticeship

The concept of cognitive apprenticeship described by Collins, Brown, and Newman (1987) provides a powerful context for the schooling of integrated performance. It incorporates all of the ideas discussed in this chapter and provides an organizing framework for implementing them. Cognitive apprenticeship recognizes that learning is a phased process; it recognizes the need for the basic instructional acts of presentation, demonstration, and practice, and places them into a larger instructional context aimed at establishing competent performance; it provides for early support of student performance through coaching and feedback in its notion of scaffolding; it anticipated the dynamism of instructional features by prescribing withdrawal of scaffolding as the student's performance strength increases; it recognizes the power of example in learning a new performance.

The key elements of cognitive apprenticeship are not major modifications of current instructional theory but an organization of them within the centuries-old apprenticeship metaphor and an expansion to include methods for making visible the key elements of mostly-invisible cognitive performances. Simulations fitted with instructional features supply an excellent vehicle for the implementation of cognitive apprenticeships, as Collins, Brown and Newman themselves suggest.

Simulation Tools

One impediment to the increased use of instructional simulation is the problem of tools. The inferior tools instructional designers have today for simulation building yield fewer but more expensive simulations. Moreover, they usually exhibit only a few of the features discussed here. Current frame-based authoring tools and the courseware they help to build have formed a kind of "feature symbiosis" that retards innovation in CBI. In their quest for productivity, courseware tool designers capture those features that authors use most frequently or which mark the most rapid and easy path to results for tool users. By the same token, authors tend to shape their development strategies in terms of the tools they have available. For example, computer-based instruction dealing with automotive engine repair might well use surrogate travel through the engine via visual "menus" to learn part names, locations, and functions. However, if the designer's chosen authoring tool facilitates the construction of verbal menus, then verbal menus will more likely be used as the navigation tool.

Although tools to create general purpose simulations are common, tools to create *instructional* simulations are rare, but they are emerging, and preliminary experience affirms their potential to control the costs of developing this form of instruction. What characteristics do these tools have that recommend them for these development tasks over frame-based authoring tools?

They contain objects that, abstractly at least, belong to the same domain as that to be
simulated

Their objects communicate in some way to permit them to be linked together into functioning complexes in a variety of ways

They permit authors to create new types of objects within the domain to be simulated

They contain objects specially tailored for the simulation of processes that accompany
instruction.

Frame-based or consolidated authoring tools are used for direct development of courseware message components. Their approach might be called-message-centered. In contrast, effective simulation tools permit authors to first span the semantic gap by creating new objects
in the domain to be simulated (e.g., switches, dials, vats, schedules) and then to assemble
them into a working system or model. This approach, which gives the student some degree
of access to the model created, may be called model-centered (Anderson & Gibbons, 1995;
Gibbons & Anderson, 1994; Gibbons & Fairweather, in press). This approach separates authoring process into two parts: (1) the creation or definition of the objects in terms of primitives functions of the system and, once these domain objects have been synthesized (2) their
connection and articulation into a working simulation. We also suggest that there is a third
step to authoring: (3) the creation or configuring of instructional features with respect to the
simulations.

The creation of domain-specific objects might seem to be an unnecessary extra step.
After all, why not simply create the simulation out of the base primitives the authoring tool
offers? While that might seem more direct, it doesn't address the principal problem facing
simulation development: the semantic gap between the domain of the tool and that of the
problem to be solved. By creating a set of domain-specific objects, the author unifies these
domains and solves the simulation problem in terms of the problem instead of in terms of
the tool. For example, a simulation involving a flight navigation system can be expressed in
terms of navigation system switches, displays, headings, and way-points, instead of authoring
system integers, floats, pointers, or bytes.

Furthermore, by creating a set of domain-specific objects, the author can draw upon
them again and again to solve additional problems in the same domain. Object reuse can
powerfully affect the economics of multi-simulation development projects by permitting the
first tier effort to be carried out once and the results of that activity used to create a series
of simulations. (An early software game, Bill Budge's *Pinball Construction Kit* (Budge, un-
dated), illustrates this point. Players are given the objects (e.g., balls, flippers, spinners, and
bumpers) out of which they can assemble an infinite number of different pinball games.
(Here we see that once the semantic gap is crossed, the work becomes enjoyable enough to
become the game itself.)

There are many implications of this model-centered view of instruction and product design. Among them is the concept of the instructional "player," which is illustrated in Figure
3. The model in this view supplies fresh, simulation-derived knowledge for the function of
message construction carried out by the instructional "players," each designed to use the
knowledge from the simulation in several instructional or supporting ways (Gibbons & Anderson, 1995). Tutorial-form instruction is created by a tutorial player which embeds the
knowledge within sequences of message and practice interactions. Problem-based forms of instruction are created from the same model by a problem player which is capable of using the
same model, in conjunction with special problem description data, to create a simulated performance situation. Forms of knowledge reference (an encyclopedia article) and performance
support (task-aiding) would be created by players devised to interpret, arrange, and communicate model-derived knowledge for those purposes. Thus, the same simulated model of a
telephone could be used with different "players" for tutorials on the internal processes and

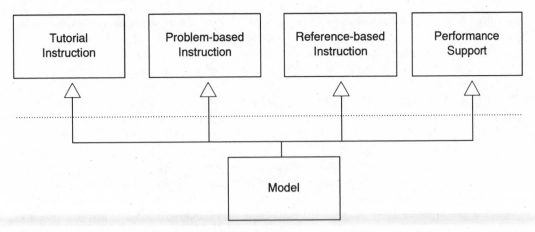

Figure 3. The "player" concept in which a single simulation model supplies content for numerous uses.

operating procedures of the telephone, maintenance problems in which faults were detected and repaired, interactive encyclopedic articles on telephones, and a task-support for telephone operation.

Tools for *Instructional* Simulation

As suggested earlier, although virtually any simulation can stimulate learning, most are not instructional. What, then, would be the characteristics of tools that can build not only general, event-based simulations, but add the unique features that make them instructional simulations as well?

We can look to currently-available consolidated (frame-based) development tools for at least part of the answer. Those tools, it will be recalled, have isolated logic and display features that are commonly used in instruction, and package them into units such as menus, timed displays, constructed-response capture and judging, or animations. These features must likewise be present in a simulation authoring tool to support the goal and purpose setting, information highlighting, and feedback mechanisms that make up the directed instruction that can accompany the simulation.

However, instructional simulations not only simulate; they supply instructional features as well. These teaching functions are dynamically applied, based on what can be observed or inferred from the student's performance. This has several implications. A simulation model of some *(simulation)* scope must be running, while at the same time one or more additional functions must be active to provide the more direct instructional functions (within some *instructional* scope) as well as monitoring student response patterns to determine the need for and content of interruptive instructional functions such as coaching or feedback.

This kind of computing lies beyond the scope of the typical frame-based or message-centered authoring tool; there is little provision for economical creation of the simulations themselves, let alone their instructional features. To achieve the power sought, experimental systems have been almost exclusively programmed in computer languages associated with artificial intelligence such as Lisp, Prolog, and OPS5. Frame-based authoring systems trade power for ease of use and productivity and have no means for representing the goal structures out of which intelligent tutoring strategies are woven. *Ad hoc* welding of frame-based authoring tools to knowledge representation languages, while accomplishing the task, remains too difficult to be practical (Fairweather, Gibbons, Rogers, Waki, & O'Neal, 1992). For authoring systems to meet the demands of instructional simulations, they must have capabilities which allow separate instruction, modeling, and monitoring functions to be operating in parallel and with some independence. Systems with these capabilities are becoming commercially available.

New and emerging authoring tools use object-oriented programming methods and, in many cases, user-friendly interfaces to empower designers to accomplish complex simulations which have the ability to instruct. Though these tools are not the same effortless tools that designers have dreamed of for decades, and though there is for each one some burden of programming, these tools still attack the problems of cost and ease of use. It is by far less difficult and less costly to build a model simulation using these tools than with traditional frame-based tools. We feel that they will eventually allow the creation of instructional simulations at productivity rates and costs comparable to or below those for tutorial creation. Easy-to-use design tools that encourage the creation of simulations will place an upward pressure on design conceptions, and the end of the lexical loop will be possible as a new conception of curriculum itself—more evenly biased toward the use of simulations with instructional features—asserts itself and encourages the formation of a new vision of computer-based instruction systems.

Conclusion

Several factors have been reviewed in this chapter that point the way to increased and more effective use of simulation. Simulation appears to be one of the more powerful forms of computerized instruction. However, the future of the computer itself as a main tool for instructional delivery depends in large part on changes in our thinking, our design habits, our design principles, and our tools in order to make simulations the main dish at the instructional feast.

References

Abelson, H. A., & diSessa, A. (1981). *Turtle geometry: The computer as a medium for exploring mathematics.* Cambridge: MIT Press.

Alessi, S. M., & Trollip, S. R. (1991). *Computer-based instruction: Methods and development* (2nd ed.). Englewood Cliffs, NJ: Prentice-Hall.

Anderson, J. R. (1983). *The architecture of cognition.* Cambridge, MA: Harvard University Press.

Anderson, J. R. (1993). *Rules of the mind.* Hillsdale, NJ: Lawrence Erlbaum Associates.

Anderson, J. R., Conrad, F. G., & Corbett, A. T. (1993). The LISP tutor and skill acquisition. In J. R. Anderson (Ed.), *Rules of the mind.* Hillsdale, NJ: Lawrence Erlbaum Associates.

Anderson, J. R., Farrell, R., & Sauers, R. (1984). Learning to program in LISP. *Cognitive Science, 8,* 87–129.

Anderson, J. R., & Skwarecki, E. (1986). The automated tutoring of introductory programming. *Communications of the Association for Computing Machinery, 29*(9), 843–849.

Anderson, T. A., & Gibbons, A. S. (1995). Architecture for a tool to create model-centered instruction. *Apple's East/West Authoring Tools Group CD-ROM.* Apple Computer, Inc., Advanced Technology Group, Authoring Tools Program, Cupertino, CA.

Bayman, P., & Mayer, R. E. (1984). Instructional manipulation of users' mental models for electronic calculators. *International Journal of Man-Machine Studies, 20,* 189–199.

Brand, S. (1987). *The media lab: Inventing the future at MIT.* New York: Viking.

Bunderson, C. V., Gibbons, A. S., Olsen, J. B., & Kearsley, G. P. (1981). Work models: Beyond instructional objectives. *Instructional Science, 10,* 205–215.

Bunderson, C. V., Inouye, D. K., & Olsen, J. B. (1989). The four generations of computerized educational measurement. In R. E. Linn (Ed.), *Educational measurement* (3rd ed.). New York: American Council on Education and Macmillan Publishing Company.

Burton, R. R., & Brown, J. S. (1979). An investigation of computer coaching for informal learning activities. *International Journal of Man-Machine Studies. 11,* 5–24. Also published in D. Sleeman & J. S. Brown (Eds.) (1982), *Intelligent tutoring systems.* New York: Academic Press.

Burton, R. R., Brown, J. S., & Fischer, G. (1984). Skiing as a model of instruction. In B. Rogoff & J. Lave (Eds.), *Everyday cognition: Its development in social context.* Cambridge, MA: Harvard University Press.

Cates, W. M. (1994). Designing hypermedia is hell: Metaphor's role in instructional design. A paper presented at the annual meeting of the Association for Educational Communications and Technology, Nashville, TN.

Champagne, A. B., Gunstone, R. F., & Klopfer, L. E. (1985). Instructional consequences of students' knowledge about physical phenomena. In L. H. T. West & A. L. Pines (Eds.), *Cognitive structure and conceptual change.* Orlando, FL: Academic Press.

Clancey, W. J. (1979). Tutoring rules for guiding a case method dialogue. *International Journal of Man-Machine Studies, 11,* 25–49.

Clancey, W. J. (1988). Acquiring, representing, and evaluating a competence model of diagnostic strategy. In M. T. H. Chi, R. Glaser, & M. J. Farr (Eds.), *The nature of expertise.* Hillsdale, NJ: Lawrence Erlbaum Associates.

Collins, A., Brown, J. S., & Newman, S. E. (1987). Cognitive apprenticeship: teaching the craft of reading, writing, and mathematics. Technical Report No. 403, Center for the Study of Reading, University of Illinois, Champaign, Illinois.

Fairweather, P. G., Gibbons, A. S., Rogers, D. H., Waki, R., & O'Neal, A. F. (1992). A model for computer-based training. *AI Expert, 7*(12), 30–35.

Fitter, M., & Green, T. R. G. (1979). When do diagrams make good computer languages? *International Journal of Man-Machine Studies, 11,* 235–261.

Fletcher, J. D., & Rockaway, M. R. (1986). Computer-based training in the military. In J. A. Ellis (Ed.), *Military contributions to instructional technology.* New York: Praeger Publishers.

Gagné, R. M. (1985). *The conditions of learning and theory of instruction* (4th ed.). New York: Holt, Rinehart, and Winston.

Gagné, R. M., & Merrill, M. D. (1990). Integrative goals for instructional design. *Educational Technology Research and Development, 38*(1), 23–30.

Gibbons, A. S. (1977). *A review of content and task analysis methodology.* Technology Report #2. San Diego, CA: Courseware Incorporated.

Gibbons, A. S. (1988). Instructional event (work model) analysis. Unnumbered technical report, Wicat Systems, Incorporated.

Gibbons, A. S. (1993). *Interactive instruction and feedback* (book review). *Educational Technology Research and Development, 41*(4), 104–108.

Gibbons, A. S. (1996). Evaluators and extended feedback models in aviation CBT. In G. Hunt (Ed.), *Designing instruction for human factors training in aviation.* Aldershot, UK: Avebury.

Gibbons, A. S., & Anderson, T. A. (1994). Model-centered instruction. Paper presented at the Sixth Summer Institute on Automated Authoring of Computer-based Instruction, Utah State University, Department of Instructional Technology, Logan, UT.

Gibbons, A. S., & Anderson, T. A. (1995). Automated authoring for tutorial-based simulations. *Apple's East/West Authoring Tools Group CD-ROM.* Apple Computer, Inc., Advanced Technology Group, Authoring Tools Program, Cupertino, CA.

Gibbons, A. S., Bunderson, C. V., Olsen, J. B., & Robertson, J. (in press). Work models: Still beyond instructional objectives. *Machine-Mediated Learning.*

Gibbons, A. S., & Fairweather, P. G. (in press). *Designing computer-based instruction.* Englewood Cliffs, NJ: Educational Technology Publications.

Gibbons, A. S., & Robertson, J. (1994). The challenge system: Performance-based testing merged with instruction. Paper presented at the Association for the Development of Computer-based Instructional Systems, Nashville, TN.

Gibbons, A. S., Rogers, D. H., & King R. V. (1991). The maintenance evaluator: Feedback for extended simulation problems. Paper presented at the Ninth Conference on Interactive Instruction Delivery, Society for Applied Learning Technology, Kissimmee, FL.

Gibbons, A. S., Trollip, S. R., & Karim, M. (1990). The expert flight plan critic: A merger of technologies. *Educational Technology, 30*(4), 32–35.

Gibbons, A. S., Waki, R., & Fairweather, P. G. (1990). Adding an expert to the team: The expert flight plan critic. *Interactive Learning International, 6*, 63–72.

Glaser, R., & Bassok, M. (1989). Learning theory and the study of instruction. *Annual Review of Psychology, 40*, 631–66.

Larkin, J. H., & Simon, H. A. (1987). Why a diagram is (sometimes) worth ten thousand words. *Cognitive Science, 11*, 65–99.

Lepper, M. R., & Chabay, R. W. (1987). Socializing the intelligent tutor: Bringing empathy to computer tutors. In H. Mandl & A. Lesgold (Eds.), *Learning issues for intelligent tutoring systems*. New York: Springer-Verlag.

Lesgold, A. (1988). Toward a theory of curriculum for use in designing intelligent instructional systems. In H. Mandl & A. Lesgold, (Eds.), *Learning issues for intelligent tutoring systems*. New York: Springer-Verlag.

Lesgold, A., Chipman, S., Brown, J. S., & Soloway, E. (1990). Intelligent training systems. *Annual Review of Computer Science, 4*, 383–94.

Lesgold, A., & Lajoie, S. P. (1989). Apprenticeship training in the workplace: Computer-coached practice as a new form of apprenticeship. *Machine-Mediated Learning, 3*, 7–28.

Mayer, R. E., & Anderson, R. B. (1991). Animations need narrations: An experimental test of a dual-coding hypothesis. *Journal of Eduactional Psychology, 83*(4), 484–490.

Merrill, M. D. (1983). Component display theory. In C. M. Reigeluth (Ed.), *Instructional design theories and models: An overview of their current status*. Hillsdale, NJ: Lawrence Erlbaum Associates.

Merrill, M. D. (1987). A lesson based on the component display theory. In C. M. Reigeluth (Ed.), *Instructional design theories in action: Lessons illustrating selected theories and models*. Hillsdale, NJ: Lawrence Erlbaum Associates.

Merrill, M. D. (1994). The new component design theory: Instructional design for courseware authoring. *Instructional Science, 16*, 19–34. Also published in M. D. Merrill (1994), *Instructional design theory*. Englewood Cliffs, NJ: Educational Technology Publications.

Papert, S. (1980). *Mindstorms: Children, computers, and powerful ideas*. New York: Basic Books.

Powers, M., Lashley, C., Sanchez, P., & Shneiderman, B. (1984). An experimental comparison of tabular and graphic data presentation. *International Journal of Man-Machine Studies, 20*, 545–566.

Reigeluth, C. M. (1983) Instructional design: What is it and why is it? In C. M. Reigeluth (Ed.), *Instructional design theories and models: An overview of their current status*. Hillsdale, NJ: Lawrence Erlbaum Associates.

Reigeluth, C. M., & Schwartz, E. (1989). An instructional theory for the design of computer-based simulations. *Journal of Computer-Based Instruction, 16*(1), 1–10.

Rieber, L. P. (1994). An instructional design philosophy of interaction based on a blending of microworlds, simulations, and games. A paper presented at the annual meeting of the Association for Educational Communications and Technology, Nashville, TN.

Shuell, T. J. (1990). Phases of meaningful learning. *Review of Educational Research, 60*(4), 531–547.

Slusarenko, V., & Worner, C. H. (1989). Graphical representation of the classical Doppler effect. *The Physics Teacher, 27*(3), 171–172.

Snow, R. E., & Lohman, D. F. (1989). Implications of cognitive psychology for educational measurement. In R. E. Linn (Ed.), *Educational measurement* (3rd ed.). New York: American Council on Education and Macmillan Publishing Company.

Vygotsky, L. S. (1978). *Mind in society: The development of higher psychological processes*. Cambridge, MA: Harvard University Press.

Ward, M., & Sweller, J. (1990). Structuring effective worked examples. *Cognition and Instruction, 7*(1), 1–39.

Wenger, E. (1987). *Artificial intelligence and tutoring systems*. Los Altos, CA: Morgan Kaufmann Publishers.

White, B. Y. (in press-a). ThinkerTools: Causal models, conceptual change, and science education. To appear in *Cognition and Instruction*.

White, B. Y. (in press-b). Intermediate causal models: A missing link for successful science education? To appear in R. Glaser (Ed.), *Advances in instructional psychology, Volume 4*. Hillsdale, NJ: Lawrence Erlbaum Associates.

White, B. Y., & Frederiksen, J. (1990). Causal model progressions as a foundation for intelligent learning environments. *Artificial Intelligence, 24*, 99–157.

44

Intelligent Tutoring Systems: Toward Knowledge Representation

John D. Farquhar
Penn State University, Harrisburg

Michael A. Orey
University of Georgia, Athens

Introduction

Instructional design is primarily concerned with prescribing methods for the optimization of learned outcomes (Reigeluth, 1983). The Intelligent Tutoring System (ITS) paradigm is a relatively new method of instruction with convincing capability to effect modern theories, assumptions, and practices within the design of instruction (Jones & Winne, 1992; Lawler & Yazdani, 1987; Sleeman & Brown, 1982).

The practice of ITS is based in the field of cognitive science, which Gardner (1987) describes as an interdisciplinary endeavor encompassing artificial intelligence, cognitive psychology, philosophy, anthropology, neuroscience, and linguistics. With the strongest ties to artificial intelligence and cognitive psychology, ITS challenges traditional methods of instructional design from an external perspective. This chapter discusses the value of the ITS perspective, providing important considerations for the maturation of instructional design principles and processes.

A clear description of the ITS paradigm is attempted with a discussion of the following assertions made by ITS researchers:

- Instruction which is adaptive to the needs of each individual student is most effective.
- Instruction is most adaptive to student needs when the selection and sequencing of instructional events is performed *dynamically*.
- Knowledge representations can effectively direct the dynamic selection and sequencing of instructional events.
- Useful knowledge can be computationally represented.

805

Adapting Instruction to Individual Needs

The need to consider individual differences within systems of instruction has been the subject of discussion for many years (Glaser, 1977; Thorndike, 1911; Weisgerber, 1971). *Adaptive instruction* is a method which considers individual differences in ability, knowledge, interests, goals, self-efficacy, and learning styles with respect to desired educational outcomes (Glaser, 1977). Adaptation is achieved through the manipulation of instructional variables.

Instructional adaptations can be classified at two levels: macroadaptation and microadaptation. *Macroadaptation* refers to global, long-term variations within a curriculum such as the selection of appropriate content. *Microadaptation* describes the immediate, moment-to-moment accommodations such as individualized feedback, reinforcement, and pacing.

In the classroom, macroadaptation takes the form of curriculum recommendations based upon individual assessments of abilities and styles. The research into Aptitude-Treatment Interaction (ATI) is concerned with finding optimal instructional treatments or methods of instruction that are best suited to individual differences. Microadaptation is the term applied to common and frequent variations that occur throughout a lesson which serve to adjust the instruction to the unique needs of the learner. The systematic design of instruction often employs microadaptations through the provision of feedback (Gagné, Briggs, & Wager, 1977).

Optimizing adaptation in instruction is the subject of considerable research. A much cited study by Bloom (1984) compared a wide variety of instructional methods from individual tutoring to large-group instruction. According to Bloom, students who learn from individualized tutoring will on average score two standard deviations higher than students who learn from large-group instruction. This difference can be attributed to the increased level of adaptability available with individualized tutoring. Creating computer-based systems that maximize instructional adaptations through individualized tutoring is the *Holy Grail* of ITS research.

Achieving Adaptation

Whenever an informed decision is made to select one instructional approach over another, an adaptation has occurred. Many mediums of instruction, both instructor-based and instructor-independent, are capable of instructional adaptation. Two methods of empowering instructional mediums with adaptive capabilities include planned adaptation and dynamic adaptation.

Planned Adaptation

Mediums of instruction making use of planned adaptation include programmed-instruction texts and "teaching machines" (Lumsdaine & Glaser, 1960; Saettler, 1990). These mediums possess the capability to make the much desired adaptations in the delivery of instruction by *branching* individual learners to alternative units, or frames, of information. If the unique needs of the individual learner can be appropriately evaluated and planned for, these mediums are capable of delivering successful, although limited, adaptation of instruction.

The well-established medium of Computer-Assisted Instruction (CAI) also uses branching as a primary means of providing adaptation. One of the major tasks of a CAI designer is to determine in advance the most appropriate *sequence* of frames. The sequencing task is accomplished through an extensive analysis of the content and the intended audience. Once a sequence has been determined, the program is developed as planned.

A major drawback of CAI is that designers must *anticipate* responses by the learner and determine feedback or alternative instructional sequences from such responses. All responses to interactions must be explicitly planned and "encoded" into the material, including "unexpected" responses made by the student. In the end, the adaptive character of the program reflects the sum of decisions made by the designer. While offering a number of advantages over classroom activities, such as individualized pacing and feedback, these systems are rigid and unresponsive to many possible learning interactions due to their static organization.

In addition, the process of developing highly adaptive materials through branching routines is a task of diminishing returns, requiring exponentially more design and development effort for each level of complexity. Attempts to make CAI systems more responsive to diverse individual needs dramatically increases planning and development efforts. The formidable task of producing highly adaptive systems of instruction solely through the use of static branching routines has led researchers to consider alternative approaches.

Dynamic Adaptation

An alternative to the static branching approach is to *dynamically* employ the selection of instructional strategies within the program itself. Dynamic adaptation analyzes learning performance as instruction is delivered, providing data for the ongoing selection of strategies. Recognition of student needs is accomplished on a "moment-by-moment" basis, supplying a "finer grain" of adaptability than possible with planned instructional frameworks (Ohlsson, 1986).

The ideal dynamic instructional decision-maker is the human tutor (Bloom, 1984). Studies of human tutoring indicate that tutors monitor the progress of students very closely, frequently assisting them as they encounter problems (Merrill, Reiser, Ranney, & Trafton, 1992). The assistance given by a tutor is modulated to the specific behavior of the students. Strategic decision-making is the essence of providing tutoring assistance. Merrill *et al.* (1992) describe the human-tutoring experience as one of *collaborative problem-solving*, in which both the tutor and the tutee contribute to problem resolution.

The execution of dynamic adaptation requires constant evaluation of the problem situation. Each time a student reaches an impasse, tutors perform a number of analyses. They evaluate the student's current understanding of the problem, determine an appropriate solution path, and select an intervention strategy with the highest learning gain (Littman, Pinto, & Soloway, 1990; Merrill *et al.*, 1992). The central goal of ITS development has been to model the analysis processes, or decision-making behaviors, of human tutors. To perform such activities, the ITS must have a certain "understanding" of the *learner*, the *domain*, and appropriate *pedagogical principles*. This understanding, or intelligence, takes on the form of knowledge representations.

Knowledge Representations

The representation of knowledge is the key component of intelligent systems, allowing them to actively perform analyses and model cognitive processes of the learner, the domain, and pedagogical principles. The ability to model cognitive processes and form knowledge representations is the central methodological shift away from static branching toward the development of highly adaptable, dynamic instructional systems.

An intelligent system, much like an instructional designer, evaluates information concerning the learner, the domain, and strategies of instruction in order to select, sequence, and appropriately deliver instruction. Dede (1986) describes Intelligent Tutoring Systems as having an understanding of *what, whom,* and *how* they are teaching. In addition, the system must employ a method of *communicating* with the student.

While the literature is inconsistent regarding nomenclature, intelligent systems are composed of four types of knowledge representations: (1) the expert model, (2) the student model, (3) the instructional expert, and (4) the user interface. These components exist in differing degrees in all true intelligent systems.

The Expert Model

The *expert model* is a representation of the expert's knowledge of a content domain. The design and development of this representation is achieved through the process of *knowledge engineering* in which relationships within the domain are analyzed and encoded into a model. This process is somewhat analogous to an instructional designer's *task analysis;* however, the end product of knowledge engineering is often an "executable" model. Expert models which are executable can provide an answer or a solution to a set of problem "inputs" which are not specifically planned for by the designer.

One of the first intelligent systems, SCHOLAR (Carbonell, 1970), was able to respond to carefully worded questions about the domain topic (South American geography). For example, students could receive answers to questions such as "What is the area of Brazil?" In addition, the system would pose similar questions to the student. Supporting these interactive sessions, SCHOLAR contained a knowledge base of information represented in the form of a *semantic network.* A semantic network is a structure of information consisting of nodes and links in which the nodes are individual units of information and links are the relationships or interconnections between nodes.

Knowledge represented by the expert model serves two major purposes. The expert model is the *source* of the knowledge to be communicated as well as the *standard* for evaluating the student (Wenger, 1987). The standard that the model uses in the evaluation can be the processes involved in the solution of a problem, or simply the end result. Expert models, therefore, may model the decision-making processes in human-like fashion or they may provide the correct solution by other means. An example of the latter is the arithmetic coach, WEST (Burton & Brown, 1982).

In WEST, students manipulate a set of arithmetic symbols in order to make the "best move" on a game board. For each problem, the expert model determines the best move by a computational "brute force" method which evaluates all possible outcomes, then selects the best. This method is appropriate for a computer asked to solve given problems in mathematics; however, the human performance of such problems is often achieved by other means. In this case, the standard of performance for the learner is the set of "best moves" as determined by the expert model.

The extent to which the expert model's decision-making processes are visible to the student describes the model's *transparency.* Completely opaque or "black box" expert models do not make available to the student those processes by which the problem is solved. In addition to WEST, the expert model within SOPHIE (Brown, Burton, & deKleer, 1982) solved domain problems (in this case, electronic troubleshooting) through a computational process which was not expected of or even provided to the student. While black box models are capable of initiating helpful interactions by recognizing patterns of student behavior, they are limited to providing only surface-level tutoring. On the other hand, "glass box" models are capable of presenting the internal structure and decision-making processes of the expert model, thus allowing for deep-level tutoring (Anderson, 1988).

The Student Model

To be adaptive to student needs, the intelligent system must have some knowledge of individual abilities and cognitive states. The representation of the current cognitive state of the student is the *student model.* The process of developing the student model is a problem of *diagnosis.* Diagnostic processes evaluate student behavior to infer a student model. The model is used in conjunction with other components of the system (such as the instructional expert) to determine when and how tutorial interventions should occur.

Interventions employed in adaptive systems include a variety of computer-generated responses such as recommending different approaches or providing new, slightly more difficult problems. In these examples, knowledge of the student's current understanding of the domain problem is essential. Methods for modeling student knowledge involve locating either missing conceptions or misconceptions (VanLehn, 1988). Models with missing conceptions describe student knowledge as a subset of expert knowledge, whereas models with misconceptions include extraneous knowledge outside the expert model.

One common method of modeling missing conceptions is the use of an *overlay student model*. In this method, "the student model can be visualized as a piece of paper with holes punched in it that is laid over the expert model" (VanLehn, 1988, p. 62). The overlay student model identifies knowledge that is known as well as unknown by the student. The program SCHOLAR would "flag" nodes of information within the semantic network, identifying pieces of information that the student should know (O'Shea & Self, 1983). Intelligent systems developed by Anderson (1989, 1992) follow a process of *knowledge-tracing* whereby the acquisition of knowledge is identified as the student becomes engaged in problem sets.

Another common method of developing a student model is the assembly of both missing conceptions and misconceptions from the expert model and the use of a *bug library*. Compiled from a variety of sources such as analyses of student behaviors, or predictions from learning theories, bug libraries are collections of misconceptions that are common to a particular domain.

The Instructional Expert

Adaptive instruction implies the use of strategies of instruction appropriate for the individual. A system capable of performing intelligent adaptive instruction would have at hand a number of principles and processes involved in selecting, sequencing and enacting appropriate strategies. The *instructional expert* (sometimes referred to as the teaching module, tutor, pedagogical, or instructional module) mimics the actions of a model educator in effectively adapting instruction for the student.

The instructional expert relies upon information provided from both the expert model and the student model. An analysis of this information determines instructional actions, such as selection and sequencing of material, as well as when and how to intervene. Essentially, the goal of the instructional expert (and ultimately the system as well) is to provide instructional interactions that bring about a match between the student's cognitive processes (as interpreted by the student model) and domain cognition (as described by the expert model).

The User Interface

The process of communication between the student and the system is performed through a *user interface*. Often, the student is engaged in an activity or a simulated environment while the system makes meaningful responses. In some intelligent systems, the interactive environment is such a dominant feature that the *simulation component* is described as an additional ITS feature (Burns & Parlett, 1991). This may be indicative of the importance of interface design as seen by many developers of ITS (Bonar, 1991).

The main task of the user interface is to provide clear communication between student and system. This communication can be abstract in nature, as in SCHOLAR (Carbonell, 1970), within which interactions were performed through a dialogue of text, or more concrete, such as the manipulation of graphical dials to simulate steam plant operations, as in STEAMER (Burton, 1988). Ideal interfaces are those that are able to communicate knowledge in the form that best represents the knowledge being communicated (Bonar, 1991).

Criticisms and Limitations

Since its fairly recent inception, the ITS community has made many claims of imminent success in the development of new instructional systems. Early developers exhibited perhaps the loftiest of expectations, exclaiming that true mimicry of a human tutor could be achieved in a few short years (Carbonell, 1970). Advocates have even asserted that intelligent systems, by nature of their high adaptability, may be particularly suited to American culture, providing an answer to America's low international standing in mathematics education (Anderson, 1992). Many claims made by the ITS community have been met with criticism. This section presents the most prominent criticisms and limitations of ITS, each followed by our comments.

Evidence of Effectiveness

Perhaps the most common criticism of ITS development has been the lack of demonstrable success (Rosenberg, 1987). The collective cry from the critics has been: "Show us!" While the results of comprehensive evaluations are limited, there is now strong support for the success of ITS (Anderson, Boyle, & Reiser, 1985; Legree & Gillis, 1991; Shute & Glaser, 1990).

Legree and Gillis (1991) present a review of several studies in ITS. They argue that if you consider research that has been conducted over a substantial period of time covering substantial amounts of material, the effect size of ITS is about 1.0. Bloom (1984) argued that the most effective instructional strategy is human tutoring, which he calculated to have an effect size of 2.0. Traditional CAI seems to have an effect size of about 0.4 (Kulik & Kulik, 1987). This would imply that ITS developers have substantiated some of their claims relative to their goal of developing a medium as effective as one-on-one human tutoring.

Additional studies have turned to qualitative methods to examine the impact of ITS. One such study (Schofield, Evans-Rhodes, & Huber, 1989) examined the effects of a geometry tutor on seven classes in one high school. The results indicated that the teachers' roles changed from provider of instruction to personal tutor for the children having difficulties in the class and that the students became more involved in the learning effort. In sum, while there are only a few large scale evaluations of ITS, they do seem to support the ITS approach.

Based Upon a Theory of Learning

There seems to be some misplaced criticism toward ITS, reproaching the field for its lack of a theory of learning (Rosenberg, 1987). However, John Anderson, a leading ITS researcher, is the author of one of today's most detailed and influential learning theories (Anderson, 1989). Anderson's model, the ACT* Theory, describes human thought as a construct of production systems operating much like an algorithmic computer. This theory has led to the use of *model-tracing* as one of the most common and effective ITS techniques (Anderson, Boyle, & Reiser, 1985). Merrill *et al.* (1992) also found that model-tracing was very similar to the techniques employed by human tutors. Thus, the learning theories supporting a substantial amount of ITS development are robust and useful enough to support effective learning.

Similarly, Brown and VanLehn (1980) developed a plausible theory (Repair Theory) for explaining the nature of children's errors in performance as it relates to learning. VanLehn (1993) has continued his work on computational theories to the point where he has now created a program called Cascade. This program simulates the way humans learn and has been developed by considering a wide range of data that is available about the way people learn.

The Computational Representation of Knowledge

The field of ITS, due to its use of artificial intelligence techniques, is also a player in a large debate concerning the computational representation of knowledge (Casti, 1989; Dennett, 1991; Dreyfus, 1992; Penrose, 1989). Essentially, the argument against ITS would be phrased: "Accurate computational representations of human knowledge are impossible since the character of human thought relies upon non-algorithmic features such as *intentionality* and *intuitiveness*." Advocates of the opposite position claim that the mind operates much like a computer.

Dreyfus and Dreyfus (this volume) stake the position that human knowledge at the expert level does not involve the application of learned rules. Rather, they claim that expert performance is the act of exhibiting "intuition." The progression from novice to expert, in the opinion of Dreyfus and Dreyfus, is the abandonment of critical analyses to a state of intuitiveness, where one "sees" the answer without effort.

We reject this characterization of skilled performance. Developing expertise is not a magical process through which one leaps from the acquisition of rules to the application of intuition (unless intuition is defined as the unconscious application of complex rules). Instead, the development of expertise is primarily a process of gradual automatization of learned rules (Anderson, 1990). While cognitive psychologists such as Anderson have developed theories based upon a body of evidence, Dreyfus and Dreyfus seem to have developed their theory of intuitive expertise based upon their own intuitions (see their reference list).

However, this debate is perhaps moot as models of expertise *can be* effectively represented. Regardless of their accuracy in representing human understanding, intelligent computer systems *are* capable of performing expertise in many complex tasks such as playing chess. Thus, they are capable of demonstrating this knowledge within learning environments.

Limited Applicability

Another common criticism of ITS is directed at its limited applicability. Most successful examples in the field seem to be limited to certain domains of knowledge (e.g. mathematics, computer programming, electronic trouble-shooting). Additionally, Dreyfus and Dreyfus (this volume) claim that computers cannot aid in skill acquisition at the expert level.

While initial efforts in the ITS field were limited to a few domains, the ITS methodology is growing and will continue to grow to new domains. Self (1988) suggests that since early ITS programs were developed by researchers themselves, the domains were limited to areas immediately accessible to the researchers (e.g. computer programming). As ITS development techniques become refined, we expect to find the applicability of ITS in all areas of instruction.

The additional allegation concerning ITS (that ITS' methods cannot be used for the development of expert knowledge) is again misplaced. This allegation rests upon the argument that expert knowledge cannot be computationally represented, thus making it impossible to provide computer tutoring at that level. While we agree with Dreyfus and Dreyfus (this volume) that the development of human expertise requires thousands of hours of practice in a variety of situations and circumstances, it seems that the computer is an *ideal* tool for providing such varied environments. As long as the expert performance of a domain can be executed by a computer, that performance can be tutored by the computer.

We will concede to one limitation of the applicability of ITS. Developing an expert model seems to require a domain that is "well-defined." The development of expert models in areas of knowledge that represent "ill-defined" problems may be virtually impossible to build. In these areas, we expect future instructional systems to integrate ITS elements within the delivery of complex simulated situations.

Why Teach Algorithmic Knowledge?

Related to the issue of teaching "well-defined" knowledge, there is a criticism of ITS that asks: "If a computer system can be built to solve a particular problem, why is it important to teach this knowledge?" There are three responses to this question as discussed by Anderson (1988).

The first response is the argument of robustness. While machines are quite capable of fully providing many functions, it seems pertinent to have people with the same or similar capabilities as backup. Knowledge of "critical" functions is important for humans to possess in case of machine failure or unavailability. Just as we rely upon spell-checkers for much of our daily communication, we hope to have the ability to communicate at times when without a spell-checker.

A second response is the establishment of prerequisite knowledge. Just as a calculator can perform all of our calculation needs, a basic proficiency in mathematics is necessary to carry out more complicated tasks in statistics or budgeting.

Finally, as a third response, there is the response that a programmed tutor can teach *part* of an extremely complex skill, even if the complete skill is ill-defined. Most ill-defined problems have well-defined components.

Lack of Instructional Approaches

While it seems obvious that the effective delivery of instruction is central to the development of intelligent systems that teach, the instructional expert component has received the least attention from researchers and developers of all the ITS components (McFarland & Parker, 1990). McFarland and Parker claim that Intelligent Computer-Assisted Instruction (ICAI) programs "have failed to use instructional design approaches or systematic teaching. Rather than assuming that this knowledge base of pedagogy does not exist, ICAI researchers should examine research findings and best practices of education and training to determine how the events of effective instruction can be clarified and codified" (McFarland and Parker, 1990, p. 211).

In defense of such issues, it should be noted that most ICAI programs deal with very specific domain topics and have often incorporated strategies of instruction specific to the domain. However, the incorporation of more design principles and practical learning theories is an obvious need that is beginning to be addressed (Anderson, 1989). Others such as Park, Perez, and Seidel (1987) have been quite specific about how this can be done. Much of their work focuses on how more traditional instructional strategies found in the field of ISD can be applied to ITS systems.

Development Time

Perhaps a more devastating criticism of ITS is that most systems that have been developed have taken enormous amounts of time and run on only very expensive machines that are not readily available to learners. This same criticism has been leveled against CAI in general (Merrill, Li, & Jones, 1990) with estimates reaching 500:1 (500 hours of development for every 1 hour of instruction). ITS estimates can be even more severe. However, just as tools are being built to streamline this development time for CAI, efforts are also underway to reduce development time for ITS. Much of this effort has focused on development tools. Some are using hypermedia tools (Orey, Trent, & Young, 1993), while others are building tools from the ground up (Munro, Johnson, Surmon, & Wogulis, 1993). In addition, many of the systems that are being developed run on microcomputers.

Summary

ITS is a paradigm that is distinct from any predecessor. It has emerged from the interdisciplinary work performed in the areas of artificial intelligence and cognitive psychology. This perspective is ideal for the design of computer-based learning systems, since it couples research from advanced computational techniques with research on human learning. Because

ITS has emerged from these fields, not out of an instructional systems design perspective, its view is unique and powerful.

At the center, ITS *represents* knowledge. The methodology employs useful representations of the content, of the learner, and of teaching to adapt to individual learning needs. While many criticisms have been leveled against ITS throughout its 20-year history, these criticisms are either outdated or misrepresent the practice. Since the inception of the field (Carbonell, 1970), research experiments and practical products have demonstrated that Intelligent Tutoring Systems possess great value. We recommend the continued use and investigation of the method as an alternative to traditional instructional design principles and processes.

References

Anderson, J. R. (1988). The expert module. In M. C. Polson & J. J. Richardson (Eds.). *Foundations of intelligent tutoring systems* (pp. 21–53). Hillsdale, NJ: Lawrence Erlbaum Associates.

Anderson, J. R. (1989). The analogical origins of errors in problem solving. In D. Klahr & K. Kotovsky (Eds.), *Complex information processing: The impact of Herbert A. Simon* (pp. 343–372). Hillsdale, NJ: Lawrence Erlbaum Associates.

Anderson, J. R. (1990). *The adaptive character of thought.* Hillsdale, NJ: Lawrence Erlbaum Associates.

Anderson, J. R. (1992). Intelligent tutoring and high school mathematics. In *Proceedings of Second International Conference,* ITS 1992, Montreal, Canada

Anderson, J. R., Boyle, C. F., & Reiser, B. J. (1985). Intelligent tutoring systems, *Science, 228,* 456–462.

Bloom, B. (1984). The 2 sigma problem: The search for methods of group instruction as effective as one-to-one tutoring. *Educational Researcher, 20*(4) 231–241

Bonar, J. G. (1991). Interface architectures for intelligent tutoring systems. In H. Burns, J. Parlett, & C. Redfield (Eds.), *Intelligent tutoring systems: Evolutions in design* (pp. 35–68). Hillsdale, NJ: Lawrence Erlbaum Associates.

Brown, J. S., Burton, R. R., & deKleer, J. D. (1982). Pedagogical, natural language and knowledge engineering techniques in SOPHIE I, II, and III. In D. Sleeman & J. Brown (Eds.), *Intelligent tutoring systems.* New York: Academic Press.

Brown, J. S., & VanLehn, K. (1980). Repair theory: A generative theory of bugs in procedural skills. *Cognitive Science, 4,* 379–426.

Burns, H., & Parlett, J. W. (1991). The evolution of intelligent tutoring systems: Dimensions in design. In H. Burns, J. Parlett, & C. Redfield (Eds.), *Intelligent tutoring systems: Evolutions in design* (pp. 1–12). Hillsdale, NJ: Lawrence Erlbaum Associates.

Burton, R. R. (1988). The environment module of intelligent tutoring systems. In M. C. Polson & J. J. Richardson (Eds.), *Foundations of intelligent tutoring systems* (pp. 21–53). Hillsdale, NJ: Lawrence Erlbaum Associates.

Burton, R. R., & Brown, J. S. (1982). An investigation of computer coaching for informal learning activities. In D. Sleeman & J. S. Brown (Eds.), *Intelligent tutoring systems* (pp. 79–98). New York: Academic Press.

Carbonell, J. R. (1970). AI in CAI: An artificial intelligence approach to computer-assisted instruction. *IEEE Transactions on Man-Machine Studies, 11*(4), 190–202.

Casti, J. L. (1989). *Paradigms lost: Images of man in the mirror of science.* New York: William Morrow.

Dede, C. D. (1986). A review and synthesis of recent research in intelligent computer-assisted instruction. *International Journal of Man-Machine Studies, 24,* 329–353

Dennett, D. C. (1991). *Consciousness explained.* Boston: Little, Brown, and Co.

Dreyfus, H. L. (1992). *What computers (still) can't do.* Cambridge: MIT Press.

Gagné, R. M., Briggs, L. J., & Wager, W. W. (1977). *Principles of instructional design.* New York: Holt, Rinehart, and Winston.

Gardner, H. (1987). *The mind's new science: A history of the cognitive revolution.* New York: Basic Books.

Glaser, R. (1977). *Adaptive education: Individual diversity and learning.* New York: Holt, Rinehart, and Winston.

Jones, M., & Winne, P. H. (1992). *Adaptive learning environments: Foundations and frontiers.* New York: Springer-Verlag.

Kulik, J. A., & Kulik, C. C. (1987). Review of recent research literature on computer-based instruction. *Contemporary Educational Psychology, 12,* 222–230.

Lawler, R. W., & Yazdani, M. (1987). *Artificial intelligence and education: Learning environments and intelligent tutoring systems.* Norwood, NJ: Ablex.

Legree, P. J., & Gillis, P. D. (1991). Product effectiveness evaluation criteria for intelligent tutoring systems. *Journal of Computer-Based Instruction, 18*(2), 57–62.

Littman, D., Pinto, J., & Soloway, E. (1990). The knowledge required for tutorial planning: An empirical analysis. *Interactive Learning Environments, 1,* 124–151.

Lumsdaine, A. A., & Glaser, R. (1960). *Teaching machines and programmed learning.* Washington, DC: DAVI.

McFarland, T. D., & Parker, O. P. (1990). *Expert systems in education and training.* Englewood Cliffs, NJ: Educational Technology Publications.

Merrill, M. D., Li, Z., & Jones, M. K. (1990). Limitations of first generation instructional design. *Educational Technology, 30*(1), 7–11.

Merrill, D. C., Reiser, B. J., Ranney, M., & Trafton, J. G. (1992). Effective tutoring techniques: A comparison of human tutors and intelligent tutoring systems. *The Journal of the Learning Sciences, 2*(3), 277–305.

Munro, A., Johnson, M. C., Surmon, D. S., & Wogulis, J. L. (1993). Attribute-centered simulation authoring for instruction. In P. Brna, S. Ohlsson, & H. Pain (Eds.), *Proceedings of Artificial Intelligence in Education* (pp. 42–49). Edinburgh, Scotland: AACE.

Ohlsson, S. (1986). Some principles of intelligent tutoring. *Instructional Science, 14,* 293–326.

Orey, M., Trent, A., & Young, J. (1993). Development efficiency and effectiveness of alternative platforms for intelligent tutoring. In P. Brna, S. Ohlsson, & H. Pain (Eds.), *Proceedings of Artificial Intelligence in Education* (pp. 42–49). Edinburgh, Scotland: AACE.

O'Shea, T., & Self, J. (1983). *Learning and teaching with computers.* Englewood Cliffs, NJ: Prentice-Hall.

Park, O., Perez, R. S., & Seidel, R. J. (1987). Intelligent CAI: Old wine in new bottles, or a new vintage? In G. Kearsley (Ed.), *Artificial intelligence & instruction: Applications and methods.* Reading, MA: Addison-Wesley.

Penrose, R. (1989). *The emperor's new mind: Concerning computers, minds, and the laws of physics.* New York: Oxford University Press.

Reigeluth, C. (1983). Instructional design: What is it and why is it? In C. Reigeluth (Ed.), *Instructional design theories and models: an overview of their current status.* Hillsdale, NJ: Lawrence Erlbaum Associates.

Rosenberg, R. (1987). A critical analysis of research on intelligent tutoring systems. *Educational Technology, 27*(11), 7–13.

Saettler, P. (1990). *The evolution of American educational technology.* Englewood, CO: Libraries Unlimited.

Schofeld, J. W., Evans-Rhodes, D., & Huber, B. R. (1989). *Artificial intelligence in the classroom: The impact of a computer-based tutor on teachers and students* (Contract No. N00014-85-K-0664). Office of Naval Research, Cognitive Science Program: Cognitive and Neural Sciences Division.

Self, J. (1988). *Artificial intelligence and human learning.* New York: Chapman and Hall.

Shute, V. J., & Glaser, R. (1990). A large-scale evaluation of an intelligent discovery world: Smithtown. *Interactive Learning Environments, 1,* 51–77.

Sleeman, D., & Brown, J. S. (1982). *Intelligent tutoring systems.* New York: Academic Press.

Thorndike, E. L. (1911). *Individuality.* Boston, MA: Houghton Mifflin.

VanLehn, K. (1988). Student modeling. In M. C. Polson & J. J. Richardson (Eds.), *Foundations of intelligent tutoring systems* (pp. 55–78). Hillsdale, NJ: Lawrence Erlbaum Associates.

VanLehn, K. (1993). CASCADE: A simulation of human learning and its application. In P. Brna, S. Ohlsson, & H. Pain (Eds.), *Proceedings of Artificial Intelligence in Education* (pp. 42–49). Edinburgh, Scotland: AACE.

Weisgerber, R. A. (1971). *Perspectives in individualized learning.* Palo Alto, CA: Peacock.

Wenger, E. (1987). *Artificial intelligence and tutoring systems.* Los Altos, CA: Morgan Kaufmann Publishers.

45

The Learning Systems Repository: A Conceptual Framework

Charles Atkinson
MacroLearning Systems, Ltd.
Cambridge, Massachusetts

Overview

This chapter introduces and describes the Learning Systems Repository (LSR), a comprehensive data-based model for instructional systems design, development, storage, and delivery. The LSR is a multi-level, multi-dimensional integration of paradigms and bodies of theory from psychology, information science, instructional technology, brain science, and computer science. It utilizes and combines these paradigms and theories into a standardized system of software and courseware that can accommodate and provide access to knowledge in any domain, learning mode, organizational format, delivery medium, learning level, and language. It reflects current and projected trends in business, training, and society in general. The LSR incorporates many of the paradigms discussed in this book. It provides a practical, real-world proving ground for these paradigms in that, to achieve widespread acceptance and use, they must be able to effectively interface with each other within and between projects and products like the LSR.

Background and History

New paradigms are very rapidly reshaping information science. A continuing revolution in the design and manufacture of computer hardware is producing standardized, interchangeable, and reusable components that can be assembled ever faster, cheaper, and with higher quality. Object-oriented technology is producing software in which processing methods and data are combined in self-contained units that permit easier identification, access, and combination for use.

Object-oriented technology provides an engineering model that can be extended to any complex system in which processes and information can be combined into objects. It offers an especially valuable approach for education, in which knowledge and instruction can be combined into discrete learning units, which can then be selected and assembled as needed to create effective learning systems. The LSR is a model for the creation, storage, and delivery of such object-oriented learning systems.

The conceptual basis for the LSR was initially conceived in a collaborative project with Schering AG, a leading international pharmaceutical company headquartered in Berlin, Germany.

In 1987, I entered into a contract with Schering AG to design and develop a large-scale database learning system for their various product and sales training programs. Schering recognized that the pharmaceutical industry (and industry in general) had entered the information age and, to be competitive, it needed to change into a *knowledge* company. It believed that that the capability to make the most up-to-date and relevant instruction and information available to audiences worldwide would be a critical factor in business success.

Superior products would still be a key requirement, but equally important would be the ability to support those products with the right information and instruction, at the right time, to the right audiences, for the right applications. No longer would it be sufficient to use information technology only for documentation and tracking of sales and marketing facts and figures. Technology could provide the means to acquire, organize, and disseminate the *concepts and competencies* needed to manage, market, sell, distribute, diagnose, prescribe, purchase, apply, and utilize the company's pharmaceutical products. This would produce a significant competitive advantage in the pharmaceutical marketplace.

The Schering project has continued and is ongoing. It represents a significant economic and intellectual investment in the development of a practical, multi-dimensional, multi-lingual, and multi-representational database learning system which now incorporates:

- Capability to accommodate and access multiple learning modes and media.
- Capability to address audiences with differing learning levels and learning styles.
- Capability for differing languages.
- Structured learning evaluation tools.
- Courseware development standards and tools.
- Courseware authoring software.
- Metastructures for organizing knowledge into curricula, courses, course modules, lessons, and knowledge elements that can be selected, sorted, and combined according to user needs and interests.
- Metastructures for defining courseware attributes and capability for profiling courseware attributes to create specific user versions.

The Schering project was a touchstone for initiation of the LSR—a new education paradigm. The LSR expands on the principles and capabilities of the Schering work in a model that centers around the application of object-oriented technology to the acquisition, development, database storage, and distribution of courseware. Like the Schering project, it combines courseware, database learning system software, applications software, operating systems software, computer hardware, and communication and telecommunication components.

Problems and Opportunities

The creation of new knowledge takes place continuously and at an ever-accelerating rate. New technologies emerge. New production processes are invented. New products are developed. New sales and marketing techniques are used. New data is produced and disseminated. And this knowledge explosion is accompanied by increasing difficulty in organizing and gaining access to information by users.

The enormous quantities of new information and the pace of information change create a crucial need to produce new learning products much more rapidly and frequently than in the past. We are facing an urgent requirement to acquire, develop, store, distribute, and deliver information and instruction worldwide.

Current methodologies for building new learning systems are no longer appropriate to meet the challenge. Courseware development is an extremely expensive effort, sometimes taking months and years, too often with unpredictable results. It costs too much, takes too much time, and requires too much expertise and experience. Too often, success depends more on the talent and creativity of the individual developer than on the efficiency of the work process or the technology employed.

In development of new learning systems, it has generally been necessary to build each learning application as a completely new effort, often reinventing similar materials that already exist. This is true for many reasons:

- It may be difficult to find relevant learning materials that were previously developed. The existence of such materials may be undocumented or their location may be unknown.

- Relevant materials may target an inappropriate audience, or exist in an inappropriate format, or have an inappropriate learning level.

- Needed content knowledge or expertise may reside in the repertoire of an instructor or designer who is not available.

- Even when relevant materials are found and useful documentation exists, content is generally so embedded in a specific instructional mode, media application, or language that it is difficult and costly to extract the useful content or convert the format.

For all of these reasons, it is often easier to start from scratch than to reuse existing educational materials for a new project. In fact, even when relevant materials can be found, when documentation exists, and when format and structure are appropriate, the difficulty of modifying existing materials and the scope of changes required to create a new version often make it preferable to start fresh and essentially reinvent the wheel.

Vision

The LSR vision is to make knowledge available to everyone, tailored to individual learning needs, enhancing productivity, promoting innovation, and creating substantial improvements in the quality of life. The educational paradigm for achieving this vision is an object-oriented repository of learning systems for all areas of human knowledge, available globally for the acquisition, development, storage, distribution, and delivery of information and instruction through telecommunications, hardware, and software networks.

Goals

The goals for development and implementation of the LSR can be defined in three general categories. Specific goals in each category are presented below:

❑ **Goals for LSR capability**
- Utilizing specific standards for system design, tools, applications, materials distribution and access, system implementation, and system support.

- Using a layered, modular architecture for organization, search, and delivery of learning materials.
- Delivering knowledge from a comprehensive learning materials database.
- Increasing the quality, value, and effectiveness of learning experiences to exceed current standards for excellence.
- Utilizing telecommunications, hardware, and software technologies to provide rapid distribution and access to learning materials, with reduced costs.
- Assembling learning materials to meet the specific needs, repertoire, language, learning skills, and preferences of the individual user.

❑ **Goals for LSR utilization**

- Providing access to learning systems that address global requirements for information and instruction.
- Encouraging worldwide learning systems development for LSR application.
- Providing access to learning systems for specific local applications and requirements.

❑ **Goals for learning systems design and development**

- Utilizing specific standards for courseware design and development.
- Knowledge engineering to make optimal use of reusable parts in learning systems development (finding, refining, and repurposing previously developed learning systems and parts of learning systems).
- Reducing the cost of building learning systems (by up to 70% of current costs).
- Reducing the time required for learning systems development (by up to 75% of current time requirements).
- Using relevant learning, brain dominance and behavior theories in learning systems development.
- Designing new learning systems for potential combination and reusability.
- Optimizing strategies for chunking and packaging learning materials.
- Designing new learning systems for easy updating and adaptability; designing large learning systems for easy scalability.

Technology Roadmap

To understand the current and future impact of technology and how it affects the LSR, it is useful to look at the processes of technological evolution. Evolutionary change related to the LSR can be conveniently viewed in five tiers, each representing one domain of technological capability. The five domains are independent, but related to each other as shown in Figure 1.

The first, second, and third tiers show the evolution of technological capability in telecommunications, computer hardware, and computer operating systems. Evolutionary development moves from left to right, with inexorable progress to the fifth generation in every tier. The fourth tier shows the evolution of applications software; its fifth generation is where LSR database software is being implemented. The fifth tier shows the evolution of knowledge; its fifth generation is where LSR learning systems are being implemented. It is expected that a fully operable LSR knowledge utility will be in place and operable worldwide by the year 2,000.

	1st Generation	2nd Generation	3rd Generation	4th Generation	5th Generation
5th Tier: Knowledge	Hierarchical	Networked	Relational	Object-Oriented	Knowledge Utility
4th Tier: Software	Style Manual	Word Processing	Authoring System	Application Suites	Groupware
3rd Tier: Oper. System	Manual Typing	Word Processing	Single Hardware	Multiple Hardware	Interoperable
2nd Tier: Computer	Typewriter	Word Processor	Personal Computer	Client/Server	Client/Server
1st Tier: Telecom.	Mail	Telephone	Fax/LAN	Internet/WAN	World Wide Web

Figure 1. Tiers and generations in a technology roadmap.

Paradigms and Theories

Although the so-called educational revolution started in the 1950s, instructional technology is still an immature science. It provides only the beginnings of an accepted body of theory and standards of practice to which a majority of educators subscribe. The paradigms presented in this book are evidence that educational technology is still a developing arena, with many new theoretical constructs that hold promise for educational developers and practitioners.

Among the various educationally-related theories that are available, I believe that theories of learning, behavior, brain dominance, chaos, and database architecture offer models and principles which are central to learning systems development. These theories provide key ingredients for the conceptual framework of the LSR.

Learning Theory

Learning theory provides a primary foundation for conceptualizing the courseware to be developed and stored in the LSR. It offers rules, guidelines, and models for:

- Analyzing competencies to be taught.
- Setting learning goals.
- Selecting modes and media of instruction.
- Determining learning methodologies.
- Developing learning materials.
- Specifying the dimensions and methods for evaluating learning progress.

Behavior Theory

Behavior theory provides a second foundational leg for the design and development of LSR courseware. Based on the applied analysis of behavior, it focuses on what the learner knows, says, and does. Using schedules and contingencies of reinforcement to develop desired behaviors, it is characterized by:

- The organization and coding of competencies to be acquired:
  - —knowledge, primarily in the form of concepts and facts;
  - —skills, primarily in the form of procedures, practice processes, and problem-solving approaches; and
  - —performance, the merging of knowledge and skills in task accomplishment.
- Specification of learning objectives with respect to targeted competencies.
- Rules, guidelines, and models for teaching/learning of generalizations, discriminations, concepts, and other behavioral elements.

Brain Dominance Theory

Brain dominance theory offers a four-quadrant *whole brain model*, illustrated in Figure 2, for understanding differing modes of thinking and learning.

This thinking and learning preference model provides an organizing principle for LSR courseware design and development. In accordance with the model, LSR courseware will be designed so that knowledge, skill, and performance elements are delivered in a whole brain fashion. Courses will be rational, well organized, interpersonal, visual and conceptual.

Chaos Theory

Chaos theory provides constructs and guidelines for recognizing, defining, and codifying repetitive patterns in apparent chaos. The concept of repetitive patterns is an important key to LSR courseware design and LSR effectiveness.

Repetitive knowledge and learning structures can bring order to the (chaotic) complexities of learning. Repetitive knowledge patterns, problem-solving patterns, learning organization patterns, and learning process patterns become a familiar part of the learner's repertoire. They all help to make the learning task easier.

Database Theory

The most important LSR feature is its capability to organize learning materials in a modular way so that they can be selected from an object-oriented database. The modular-

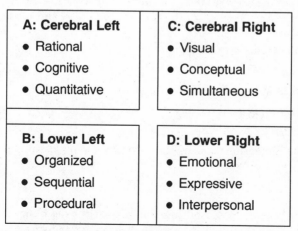

Figure 2. A four-quadrant whole brain model.

ization of learning materials is an old instructional idea that is expanded and improved through object orientation. What is new is that each learning module becomes a completely self-contained object which can be defined at any level in a hierarchical (layered) courseware structure. Each module is a reusable object that can stand on its own or be combined with others, but is not dependent on or "hardwired" to any other module. This means that:

- Modular objects can be curricula, courses, chapters, lessons, or lesson elements.
- Modular objects can be mixed, matched, and/or assembled into composites that provide larger and more powerful modules.
- The format and/or content of any module can be inherited (copied) separately or together.
- Modules can be defined in classes according to common patterns of content, structure, and behavior.

Object technology and object-oriented development standards will allow LSR courseware to be developed at a fraction of the time and cost of conventional courseware.

System Organization and Access

Object oriented technology provides a paradigm for organizing and gaining access to the LSR. LSR organization must permit easy identification, finding, and manipulation of any modular knowledge object from a collection that potentially includes millions of such objects—in multiple knowledge domains, multiple instructional modes, multiple media, multiple languages, at differing learning levels, designed for differing target audiences, and in multiple hierarchical layers.

Metaphorically, the organization and access task is like finding a particular needle among a vast number of different needles in a field of many different types of haystacks. Accomplishing this task imposes three requirements:

1. Need for a structured organizational schema that effectively classifies types of haystacks and types of needles into a manageable number of discrete categories.
2. Need for a prescriptive methodology that effectively describes and identifies each separate needle according to unique characteristics.
3. Need for a simple procedure to select any one or more particular needles from their particular haystacks and to manipulate them according to user need.

The LSR meets these needs in a layered approach which incorporates the following functional capabilities. Each capability is described following the list.

- Layers
- Object attributes
- Database navigation
- Object views
- Knowledge document templates
- User interactivity
- Competency testing and learner tracking
- Assembly agents

Layers

The LSR will organize modular knowledge objects in a layered hierarchical structure of directories, curricula, courses, modules, chapters, lessons, and lesson elements. Each layer will serve as a database of knowledge objects that can be selected, sorted, combined, viewed and otherwise manipulated in various ways.

Layering eliminates monolithic databases and provides enormous search economy. The rule of "nested nines" provides that only four layers of discrimination, with nine objects in each layer, provides the capability to search and select from more than 6,000 different objects. Five layers bumps the number of objects to almost 60,000; six layers to more than 500,000. And as the number of objects in each layer is increased, the number of total objects that can be searched increases geometrically.

An illustrative analogy of the power of layering can be drawn from layering of the view from Apollo 13. In *five layers of search*, Apollo 13's overall view can be focused on a specific room in a single house:

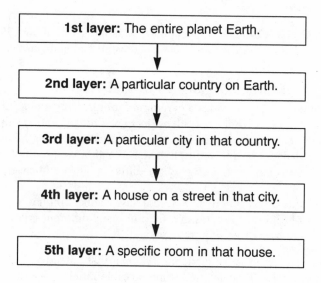

Object Attributes

The LSR will provide a detailed profile which defines the attributes of each knowledge object so that the process of identification, search, and selection can be directed to any specific object that is desired. Attribute specifications will include (but not be limited to) such descriptors as:

- Title
- Topic and content abstract
- Author
- Date of publication or most recent update
- Language
- Instructional mode
- Medium
- Length in pages and/or user time
- Intended target audience
- Learning level

Database Navigation

The LSR will provide multiple ways of searching for any knowledge object that has been identified by layer and/or attributes. Navigation techniques will include (but not be limited to) such search methods as:

- Finding and selecting by specific words or phrases.
- Finding and selecting by attribute profile.
- Sorting by size, date, topic, alphabetic order, or any other defined criteria.

Object Views

A significant LSR advantage will be the capability for object views—the ability to look at the overall knowledge repository and the knowledge objects in it from any desired perspective. Object views will permit the user to merge, mix, match, and sort knowledge objects in multiple ways. The user will be able to customize courseware to specific learning levels, media, personal learning style, and/or individual thinking preferences.

Knowledge Document Templates

Digital document templates will be provided for all major learning formats and media to support and standardize LSR courseware development. Each template will incorporate learning structure and process, so that the need is minimized for developers to be instructional technologists. Each template will enable the developer to put subject matter content in the right place for effective learning.

User Interactivity

The LSR will enable interactive participation by users. Interactivity will be provided in four principal ways:

- Learning interactions which are specifically designed into courseware as an integral part of the learning experience.
- On-line interactions with the system through input of notes and comments on courseware and learning experiences.
- On-line interactions with other users in group learning settings.
- On-line authoring of courseware when such authoring is authorized.

Competency Testing and Learner Tracking

LSR courseware will incorporate criterion-referenced (goal-based) assessments for evaluation of learning performance and competency achievement. Assessments may be at the lesson or any larger courseware level. Internal quizzes, case problems, and other learning progress checks will allow self-assessment during the learning experience. Final assessments will measure mastery. Objective final assessments will be provided for organizational use in formal learning settings.

Learning performance will be tracked against curriculum, course, and lesson learning objectives. Performance feedback will guide remedial study and/or or future learning assignments.

Assembly Agents

The LSR will incorporate software mini-programs which serve as agents for run-time assembly of knowledge objects into composite courseware products. This assembly capability will enable the creation of learning experiences that meet the specific needs of the user on an on-line, real-time basis.

Courseware Development Process

Conventional courseware development is a "waterfall" process in which each development stage provides a foundation for the next stage. Typical *conventional development* incorporates a waterfall cascade of stages as illustrated below:

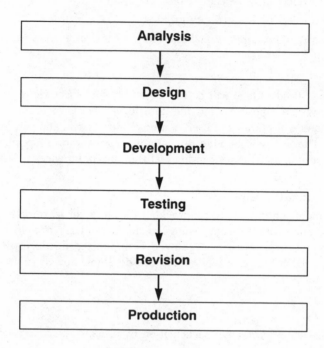

Object technology permits a radical change from the conventional courseware development process. The rapid object assembly approach offers a much simpler and faster process.

Since object technology permits courseware to be assembled from existing, reusable knowledge objects, there can be an enormous gain in developmental effort and time. There is no need for the consecutive stages of the waterfall process. Content available in relevant knowledge objects from existing courseware can account for a large proportion of the content needed. Finished courseware can be produced largely from such knowledge objects. In some cases, existing course materials can provide 80–90% of the materials needed for creation of new courseware.

Standards and Implementation Requirements

The LSR will consist of educational materials stored in an object-oriented database. This will represent a radically new learning/teaching application. Learning materials exist independently of a database. And databases exist independently of learning materials. The challenge is to design learning materials for the LSR so that they can be stored in and accessed from the LSR object database, and to design the database so that it will accept LSR learning materials. A significant obstacle in meeting this challenge is that the fields in a standard relational database are not designed for the variable nature of educational materials, especially the very wide spectrum of multimedia educational materials anticipated for incorporation in the LSR.

	Platform	Tools	Applications	Distribution	Support
Courseware	Modular knowledge objects	Development guidelines; document	Specific courseware	Documentation and training	Documentation and training
Software	Object technology programs	Authoring guidelines and software	Specific software	Documentation and training	Documentation and training
Repository	Object-oriented knowledge	Catalogues and user guidelines	User-selected information	Documentation and training	Documentation and training

Figure 3. The LSR product and service model.

Not only are educational materials not optimally designed for a standard database, but also, there is essentially no standardization in the construction of educational materials. For the LSR, this imposes a mandate to construct a conceptual framework of courseware and software standards that will permit an effective marriage between LSR software and courseware. In addition, development tools which incorporate database software and authoring software will be needed to create or convert learning materials and create applications for use.

The codification of standards, supported by appropriate software tools, will provide a platform for development, conversion, and storage of learning materials as objects in the LSR database.

When development, conversion, and storage of learning materials has been accomplished, the system can be implemented, courseware can be distributed from the database, and the overall system supported with appropriate methodology and training.

Taken together, LSR courseware plus software provide the knowledge repository. The platform, tools, application, distribution, and support functions for courseware, software and the repository are summarized in the model shown in Figure 3.

Current Issues and Efforts

Implementation Stages

LSR implementation can be described in a series of stages:

- *Seeding Stage.* The seeds that have served as the stimuli for the conception of the LSR include the various theories, technologies, organizational schema and development methodologies that are introduced in this chapter. Together, these foreshadow the paradigm shift reflected in the LSR. The seeding stage is effectively over, but additional seeds may emerge as work progresses on LSR development and implementation.

- *Concept Stage.* The LSR concept stage is currently ongoing. The most important concepts are presented in this chapter. In summary, the big idea is to create an object-oriented database for the acquisition, development, storage, and global distribution of courseware in all modes and media, and for all audiences.

- *Prototype Stage.* A working LSR prototype is in development. It incorporates platform products such as *Lotus Notes* and storage and transmission products such as CD-ROMs and the World Wide Web.

- **Market Development Stage.** A commercial LSR product will emerge when prototype development and testing is completed, and when the availability of appropriate software and courseware standards and tools permit wide-scale development of LSR object-oriented courseware that provide for reusability and rapid assembly. The development and codification of required standards will be the most difficult implementation task.

- **Steady State Stage.** It is projected that the LSR will be mature and stabilized by the year 2000. A critical mass will be reached in object technology and other relevant technologies. Necessary infrastructure will be available in advanced generations of such systems and products as the World Wide Web; *Windows 95*; *Lotus Notes*, and *Notes* for the World Wide Web.

Criteria for Evaluation

LSR success will be defined by achievement of the following system capabilities:

- A robust platform of standards will permit the effective marriage of LSR software and courseware.
- LSR software will accept the widest spectrum of courseware in all modes and media.
- LSR tools will be available to support object-oriented courseware development.
- The process of creating software will be largely automated, and will be based on assembly of reusable knowledge objects.
- All LSR courseware will be profiled by applicable attributes.
- Specific LSR courseware versions will be created by profiling user applications against courseware attributes.
- LSR courseware will be accessible worldwide, and will be widely used.

The Long-Range Future

There will soon be a critical mass in the tidal wave of technology, making it possible to realize the vision of a global LSR that is implemented on the information superhighway for all areas of knowledge, all audiences, and all learning modes and media. Looking into the future, this LSR can provide an interconnected global *knowledge utility* that potentially connects everyone on the planet.

Each node on the LSR network can be an individual learner or a community of learners. All learners will be simultaneously using, generating, and sharing knowledge. Learning experiences, assembled at run time, will be specifically designed to meet the needs and interests of individual users.

46

Instructional Development for a Networked Society

Alexander J. Romiszowski
Syracuse University
Syracuse, New York

The Future Technology-Based Society: A Scenario

The Future of Work

As the world moves into the 21st century, it is predicted that the next decade or two will bring more change in the way we live, work, and learn than occurred during the whole of the previous century. Computer technology is replacing the human being in a multitude of functions, both physical and intellectual. The life-cycle for new products, processes, and services is ever shorter. As a result, a typical person working in an organizational context will be required to participate in a process of continual learning and updating in order to keep abreast of the changes in technologies, techniques, and tools that are used in order to perform productive work.

This prognosis of continuing and accelerating change may present some paradoxical future scenarios. For example, on the one hand, information is coming to be regarded as an organization's most important resource, and knowledge of relevant information is characterized as being synonymous with power. On the other hand, knowledge is to be ever more freely available to ever wider sections of the population, as a result of massive investments in telecommunication and computer network infrastructures, of which the current Internet is only the proverbial tip of the iceberg. If it is really true that the possession of unique knowledge places a person or an organization in a position of economic, political, or social advantage, then one effect of the democratization of access to knowledge should be the leveling out of some of the previous advantages that one organization or individual may have possessed over another. History suggests, however, that no society can survive and prosper without some embodiment of the principle of the survival of the fittest; without some process by which leaders may emerge. The resultant 21st century construct which has emerged is the knowledge-based organization and its principal employee, the "knowledge worker."

The knowledge worker is somebody who earns a living by using knowledge in order to create new knowledge. The knowledge worker must have well developed capabilities of critical analysis in order to be able to select from the vast array of available information that which is of relevance and value to "keeping ahead" of the competition, and a high measure of creativity in order to invent or develop the new knowledge that may offer a competitive advantage. In the future fast moving and open information society, this advantage will not last very long before the new knowledge becomes public knowledge and many people or organizations may act on it. Therefore, the task of knowledge workers will be to continually renew the process of knowledge creation, thus keeping themselves, or their employers, ahead of the competition.

Such high levels of critical insight and creativity are what traditionally single out the exceptionally intelligent human beings from the rank and file. When computer software becomes more capable and intelligent and replaces many of the routine tasks formerly performed by human beings, then maybe the only area of future occupation in which human beings will excel will be in this form of creative knowledge work. The goal of the aspiring educated human being may therefore be focused ever more on the acquisition of the necessary skills needed to be a successful knowledge worker. The purpose of this concluding chapter of this volume is to investigate in what way such a societal trend, if indeed it comes about, would affect education and training needs, processes, and delivery systems as we move into the next century.

A Systems Analysis of Knowledge Work

In order to try to make sense of the future into which we may be moving, we could do worse than to adopt the well-tried and tested "systems approach" to the design of a scenario of the educational and training systems of the future. As a first step in this process, we must perform a systems analysis of the "end-product" of the proposed new educational system, that is, the new type of "knowledge work" that, it is postulated, will become prevalent in the networked society of the 21st century.

The basic conceptual model of a "system" is some "process," acting within some "context," from which it acquires resources or "inputs," and to which it delivers results or "outputs" (see the chapter by William Hug in the present volume for a more complete account of systems thinking). The process component is often depicted as a "black box" to indicate its often incompletely understood complexity. In our scenario, the process component is our knowledge worker or, if we wish to take a broader view, an organization which is keeping abreast of its competition by engaging in knowledge work.

The principal input to this process is the existing knowledge or information that has already been discovered, organized, and made available in meaningful and useful ways. However, the amount of information in the world in general is estimated to be doubling every few years. The more information there is, the more it tends to become difficult to find the specific information that may be of particular relevance to a particular activity or problem situation that we may be facing at a specific point in time. We are faced with the paradoxical situation of having to act more quickly in order to keep abreast of change, but, as the total amount of information available to us increases, finding the task of new knowledge generation more difficult and possibly slower than in the past.

If we now turn to the output side of our system, we see a similar dilemma. The expected output from knowledge work is some form of creative and unique solution or suggestion for "keeping ahead of the competition." We are faced with the paradoxical situation that all of us, as individuals or organizations, will be forced to adapt faster and more creatively to an ever-changing environment in order to be able to survive and prosper. On the other hand, this very activity of rapid, inventive knowledge generation and its implementation in order to keep abreast of change will contribute to the acceleration of the process of change within the environment, thus forcing us to adapt and invent still more.

We therefore see, both on the input and the output sides of our system, that new technologies on the one hand offer us tools with which to deal with the new challenges that a changing society or workplace presents and, on the other hand, those same technologies actually are responsible for the changes that are generating these new and ever-changing challenges. Is there a danger that these forces for ever faster and greater change may lead society to a point at which the whole system disintegrates? Such catastrophes happen in electrical, electronic, and other types of engineering systems when there is an absence of an effective control system. Where would we expect to look for the control system in our scenario?

The general systems theory principles of homeostasis and regulation suggest that a control system, to be effective, must be similar in complexity and variety to the system being controlled (Ashby, 1956). This implies that whatever regulatory systems exist in society as a whole, every process component must possess its own self-regulating mechanisms. In our scenario, this implies that, for example, government legislation and controls cannot hope to control the directions of change in future society without the cooperation of the economically active organizations that compose that society. And these organizations are not fully "under control" if their key workers do not collaborate toward the same set of global objectives. In short, the responsibility of the knowledge worker goes beyond the creation of new knowledge in order to deal successfully with environmental change but encompasses also the judgment of which changes should be promoted and which should be controlled in order that the overall system does not get into a state of disequilibrium. How may the knowledge workers of the future develop the abilities to control change so that this change may be beneficial to the majority of citizens as well as to the organizations that employ them?

The often suggested answer to this sort of question is "through appropriate education and training." But what are the skills and competencies that the next generation of the world's citizens should master in order to become effective and responsible knowledge workers? And what are the key methodologies of the educational systems required by society in the 21st century in order to implement this new curriculum? In order to form a model of the curriculum, we once more start by conceptualizing the outcomes of this future educational process, that is, the key competencies of an effective knowledge worker.

Competencies of the Knowledge Worker, and How to Promote Them

One increasingly important competency in the future society will be "self-directed-learning." Much emphasis is being placed in modern school curricula on "learning to learn," as a response to the realization that, in the future, learning will be a lifelong occupation, largely occurring outside of the formal educational institution (Benson, 1994). One area for lifelong learning, already evident in modern highly computerized organizations, is the need to continually learn to use new tools for the accessing, processing, and transformation of information into new knowledge. These tools today typically take the form of software application packages. The very rapid rate of substitution of these tools and their increasing sophistication has led to a significant conceptual reorganization of the training function in such environments. The talk today is of "just-in-time training" (Carr, 1992; Goodyear & Steeples, 1992; Plewes, 1992). Just as the concept of just-in-time inventory control in business management signifies an attempt to keep inventory levels very close to the levels of utilization so that purchases are made just when required, so in the area of knowledge and skills acquisition through training, the just-in-time concept argues that the person who requires a new skill should learn it at the time when it is required and never before.

Just-in-time training, in its implementation, implies a high level of individualization and self-direction in the training and education processes, so that each individual may learn just what he or she needs at the time he or she needs it. Almost by definition, this implies a radical change in the training delivery systems from place-based and time-fixed group instruction (characteristic of our conventional education in the past) to on-the-job distributed training that may be utilized, under learner-control, at any appropriate time or place. This, in turn, implies the use of technology-based training delivery systems (Benson, 1994).

The just-in-time training concept is congruent with the general principles of "performance technology." The identifying characteristic of the performance technology approach is to relate all training and education activity to its effect on relevant job-related performance that may be measured, tracked and evaluated on a regular basis (Clark, 1994; Gilbert, 1978; Langdon, 1991). In the performance technology approach, training and education are but a part of the total armory of techniques for enhancing and maintaining human performance in the organization. Other techniques are: just-in-time information provision in the form of reference material or job aids; improved incentives; improved feedback on the results of performance; appropriate consequences (both rewards and punishments); and so on (Davies, 1994; Gilbert, 1978; Harless, 1992; Rossett, 1992). The performance technology movement is well positioned to solve at least part of the growing needs for change in how education and training equips the future knowledge worker (see also the chapters by Gilbert, Davies, and Doughty & Romiszowski in the present volume).

Self-Directed Knowledge Acquisition and Hypermedia

That, however, is not the whole picture. On the input side, in order to perform as a creative knowledge worker, the person must first access the information that is available and relevant, in order to put it to use. In order to facilitate this process, the information should be available in a well organized form. The organizing of vast amounts of information into meaningful structures is no easy task. The difficulty lies partly in the complexity of analysis required to come to conclusions about how best to organize and present subject matter to a variety of different user groups with different motives for using the information. It comes also from the sheer enormity of the task given the vast amount of information that is generated every year. Finally, it comes from the difficulty of arranging access to the resulting vast libraries of information for the potential end-users.

A technology-based solution to these issues has been proposed in the form of hypertext or hypermedia systems. The concept of a "universe of information" composed of electronically interlinked documents was suggested by computer scientists as early as Bush (1945). The concept was realized in practice by Englebart (1963) and Nelson (1965). It was only in the last decade or so, however, that the large-scale implementation of the concept has resulted in practical hypertext systems available to the public at large (Conklin, 1987; McAleese, 1989). (See also the chapter by Borsook in the present volume.)

The first practical action that popularized the hypertext concept outside of the computer science and research areas (and introduced it particularly in education) was the "bundling" of HyperCard with the Macintosh personal computer in the mid-1980s. This resulted in the development of many small hypertext systems by teachers who often shared their products with other teachers. It also resulted in the development of other, similar tools, such as ToolBook, that allowed the users of other hardware platforms to develop hypertext products. This, incidentally, helped to extend the versatility of the original HyperCard products by combining the "linking" capabilities of hypertext tools with the emerging "multimedia" capabilities of the new generation of personal computers, to create the basis for the "hypermedia" products that are now flooding the educational marketplace.

The Metacognitive Skills of Information Analysis

Another important aspect to consider is that of the skills and capabilities required by the knowledge worker in order, first, to locate and, second, to assess the value of specific items that are "out there" in the expanding universe of information. The skills of locating information in a complex and vast library are not easy to master. The user can be helped, however, by a combination of systems for the organization of information and for on-line help. A second set of skills, also not that easy to master, are necessary for the analysis and evaluation of information once it is located, to judge whether it is useful for the particular task which one is trying to accomplish. These are the "critical thinking skills" that most educational curricula attempt to develop, but at present only seem to succeed in doing so with a small proportion of the population. As we move, though, into the age of the knowledge worker and the knowledge organization, the importance of these skills will increase. We may even reach the situation wherein only those human beings who can demonstrate a high level of skill in critical analysis will be likely to hold down a challenging and well-rewarded job. Therefore, improvement in the effectiveness of education in this area of skill building is a critical issue.

Critical analysis skills development is the area of research that has concerned many cognitive scientists in recent years. One aspect of the problem is concerned with making sense of the information available. However well organized and well communicated some of the information sources may become, it is unrealistic to expect that all information generated in the world of the future will be written by expert communicators, or be subjected to analysis and reorganization by instructional designers. It will often fall on the end-user to make sense of imperfectly structured and communicated information sources. Research on techniques of information analysis, such as Concept Mapping (not to be confused with Information Mapping, which will be discussed later) has demonstrated the potential for improving students' information analysis and comprehension skills (Novak, 1991). (See also the chapter by Novak in the present volume.) These techniques are now being applied both to the improvement of electronic on-line communications by the incorporation of concept maps as advance organizers, content guides or browsing tools in on-line information resources (Reader & Hammond, 1994; Schroeder, 1994), and to the development of improved skill in dealing with on-line study materials by special preparatory concept-map drawing exercises (Naidu & Bernard, 1992; Russell & Meikamp, 1994).

The Skills of Creative Problem Solving

Let us now move from the input-output (information and performance) considerations that we have been addressing so far to the "process"; that is, the activity of the knowledge worker when utilizing relevant available knowledge to create useful new knowledge. The role of the knowledge worker will be to add value to existing knowledge by transforming it into more application-specific knowledge that, for a time, will be the unique property of that individual or organization. This highlights yet one more critical set of thinking skills. In addition to the skills of analysis, used to identify relevant knowledge, and the skills of evaluation to judge the usefulness of this knowledge for the task at hand, the knowledge worker must possess skills of synthesis, or the putting together of ideas in novel ways in order to create new ideas.

We are here using the terms of analysis, synthesis, and evaluation as used in Bloom's taxonomy of objectives in the cognitive learning domain (Bloom *et al.*, 1956) to describe the higher-order outcomes of learning associated with creative or productive thinking. The fact that Bloom's taxonomy has been around for a long time as a theoretical construct for instructional designers does not imply that education and training systems necessarily always do a good job of developing these creative thinking skills. As we progress into the 21st century, however, the importance of appropriate strategies and methodologies for the development of these three categories of creative thinking skills will become increasingly important. It may be argued that this is where the core curriculum of any basic schooling system should focus its attention in the future. At least a part of the current interest in constructivism (see the chapter on this topic by Wilson in this volume) and its practical implementation in the school (see the chapter by Duffy) stems from this change of focus in the curriculum.

The above mentioned observation that educational systems may not always do a good job in the area of higher order thinking skills should not be taken to imply that there is no known methodology or technology appropriate for their development. Many successful programs for the development of critical thinking skills have been developed and implemented. Analysis of such programs reveals that they tend to have certain characteristics in common. They tend to use "experiential learning" techniques. They tend to set up learning situations which present a problem or a complex task for the learners to deal with and then encourage and assist the learners to draw general conclusions and establish general principles that may explain or predict across a range of similar situations (Romiszowski, 1981; Steinaker & Bell, 1979). One teaching methodology that is particularly successful in the development of critical thinking is the case study method. This typically puts the student in the situation of having to deal with a real or simulated problem. Study of the specific case then leads to a discussion in which general principles and concepts which underlie the case are identified and then tested out on other case examples for verification of their general validity. Other techniques used for the development of critical thinking include small group discussions, simulation games, project-based work, and collaborative problem solving activities. It may be noted that most of the techniques known to work in this type of learning situation involve small group interaction, in-depth discussion, a lot of interchange of ideas between the participants, and an approach to the conduct of the teaching/learning activity that is flexible, collaborative, and "conversational." Another term that is often associated with this group of instructional techniques is "experiential" learning (Romiszowski, 1984). We shall address the specific characteristics and importance of this group of techniques later in this chapter.

The Areas of Competency, and Related Technologies

To summarize so far, we note that the mix of key competencies that are required by tomorrow's knowledge workers involve, on the "output" side, a range of performance-related competencies, not only in terms of successful and creative solutions to novel problems but also in terms of efficient and rapid learning of the use of new tools and techniques that are constantly appearing in the job environment. In this area, the relatively older traditions of instructional design continue to be relevant and useful. It is possible to identify specific knowledge and skills required in order to master the tools of the job. The one difference is that as the tools are replaced at ever greater frequency, the emphasis in the teaching/learning process is on quick, just-in-time learning. The emphasis is also on not learning the details of utilization of a tool if some sort of on-the-job reference or performance support system proves to be adequate.

On the "input" side, the skills of information access, location, analysis, and evaluation are of importance. Here we may see the need for better information provision through better structuring and on-line support of tomorrow's electronic libraries, through better authoring of the materials to be included in these libraries, and also through improving the skills of our citizens in dealing with complex and vast libraries of information accessible over networks from a distance.

In the middle, between input and output, is the "process" that transforms existing knowledge into new knowledge. This is seen as the major point of importance in future educational provision for the citizens of a highly technological and networked society. In this area, the methodologies of experiential learning and reflective learning are seen as the best available models at this time.

In short, we see that the development of the range of competencies required by tomorrow's knowledge workers will require a range of approaches that will involve a mix of educational approaches based on a mix of technologies. The design of information to make it more accessible, more understandable, and more useful draws heavily on information science and becomes a specialized form of *information technology*. The techniques that address the need to master new job skills, maybe without formal instruction, through a process of just-in-time training, or by means of on-the-job performance support, draw heavily on what we now know as *performance technology*. Finally, in the process part of the system, where the creative knowledge work occurs, we see the need for some of the more humanist, constructivist, and cognitivist approaches that have been in the forefront of educational research and development in the last few years. We may possibly refer to this cluster of new techniques as "thinking technology."

We will address these productive-thinking-process-related aspects of our model later in this chapter. What this analysis suggests, however, is that all areas of competency noted here are of importance, so all of the traditions or technologies of education just mentioned must play their part in an appropriately designed educational system and curriculum.

Delivery and Design Technologies for the Future Curriculum

Electronic Performance Support Systems

Let us now consider some of the technologies and some of the methodologies that may be of particular relevance in each of the three areas of critical competence that we have identified. To start with the output side of our picture, the performance technology approach to design typically uses a mix of instructional materials and reference or job aid materials to support the performer in the job situation. In future networked societies, it will be ever more common to find that both the training materials and reference materials are in fact electronically stored and distributed. This performance-support software may be either stand-alone, for example, a CD-ROM disc accessed on an individual personal computer, or it may be networked from some central server to many users. This trend to on-line performance support is a natural tendency, not only because of the potential benefits that electronic delivery and control of learning and reference materials may have, but also because in the networked society or job environment, the computers, and networks are already there for other reasons, and it is both economical and convenient to use the same tools and distribution systems for learning and reference materials. As this tendency developed, we have recently witnessed the birth and rapid growth of "electronic performance support systems" (Gery, 1991; Milheim, 1992; Stevens & Stevens, 1995).

An electronic performance support system, or EPSS, is an integrated system of training and reference materials, possibly some software tools such as special purposes spreadsheets, or simulation "shells" for testing out hypotheses, and whatever else may help to both develop and maintain the performance of persons carrying out a particular set of tasks. This integrated system of job-related information is delivered to those persons, on-line, as part of the software that supports their job, by means of a general purpose computer/workstation that typically performs other job related functions as well.

In the United States, such electronic performance support systems are now being implemented by a rapidly increasing number of organizations for a variety of job-related training and support purposes. They are being used in technical and engineering contexts (Gery, 1995), in service industry contexts (Dorsey *et al.*, 1993), and indeed to support teachers in some of their planning tasks (Gayeski, 1995). Some of the large organizations that have invested heavily in EPSS and thus have reduced or even replaced more conventional approaches to education and training in the organization are American Express, AETNA Insurance, IBM, and Chrysler Corporation. An area of application in which EPSSs are beginning to impact the average citizen is in the use of computer software application packages. Several instructional design and development organizations are now specializing in the marketing of more or less sophisticated EPSSs for commercially available business and home consumer software. One such company, National Education Training Group, now offers some hundreds of titles of training/performance support software for most of the popular end-user packages from software houses such as Microsoft, Lotus, and Novell. Some of the software houses, notably Lotus, are now beginning to market their actual software packages (such as Lotus 1-2-3) on a CD-ROM disc together with a full suite of electronic performance support tools, such as reference manuals, detailed CAI tutorials, and sets of "typical application examples" to serve as models. It may not be so long before the idea of going to a course in a classroom in order to learn to use a new computer software package will appear as archaic and unnecessary as the ancient school curricula that insisted on teaching a classical (dead) language to all students, whatever their area of specialization. As powerful computer networks become economically available, it may become possible to download "on demand" and "just-in-time" a performance support package for just about any commercially available software package.

Multimedia, Hypermedia, Internet, and Information Superhighways

On the "input" side of our picture, growth in the provision of hypertext and hypermedia systems and the implementation of powerful networks (such as the Internet and the promised future information superhighways) points the way in which technology is leading us in relation to the organization, storing, and distribution of information to end users. Although we are not yet there, the promise is that in a short time, most citizens of the world will be in a position to economically access just about any information in the world. Although the technology enthusiasts may be a little over-optimistic in terms of timelines, the signs are that we are heading towards much cheaper and more democratic access to the world's stores of information.

Whether this trend will mean an improvement in how society actually *uses* information is yet to be seen. The evidence from countries in which multiple channels of television are normally available is that most citizens use only a few of these channels on a regular basis. If today the typical USA resident regularly uses only four or five out of the forty or fifty channels that are piped to the household, what may be the position some years down the line when 500 channels are available in every house? Will the citizens still be using only five out of the 500 on any regular basis? And if a proportion of the channels are made available either for education or public access information distribution as opposed to entertainment, what is the likelihood that if people choose to access these channels they will benefit as much as they hoped to in terms of identifying useful information, understanding it, and learning how to use it in practice? Not only will the average citizen require an above-average level of skill in navigating through information networks and identifying points which are worth paying attention to among the so many that are not, but also the networks of information must be so organized that an average citizen without a superhuman capability of information analysis will indeed have the capabilities of identifying what is out there and which parts of it are of relevance and value.

Most hypertext and hypermedia products have, to date, been "stand-alone" systems, in that although they offer the end-user the possibility of "browsing," or "navigating" a particular knowledge domain in a flexible, learner-directed manner, that browsing is limited to the information documented in a particular CD-ROM or other media package. The vision of Nelson (1973, 1980, 1987) and other hypermedia enthusiasts, of a global system of interlinked information sources that ultimately would provide access to all the world's information resources for all the world's citizens, remained a theoretical construct until very recently. Indeed, attempts in the USA to implement the beginnings of such a system in the mid 1980s, under the name of the "Educational Utility" (Gooler, 1986) failed miserably. Now, a decade later, spurred by the explosive growth of the Internet, the concept is entering the realms of practical implementation and use. The World Wide Web, now the preferred manner of accessing the information resources of the Internet, is a hypertext system that allows the contributors of information to create links between their contributions and any of the other documents, or "sites," existing in the system, and allows the Internet users to navigate freely from one site to another by simply clicking on the highlighted indicators of existing links.

How close are we today to realizing Nelson's dream of universal democratic access to the world's information resources? Perhaps not as close as some people would have us believe. There are several reasons for this. One that immediately springs to mind, especially in the context of nations such as Indonesia, Brazil, Russia, or Angola, where the telecommunication infrastructure is not as developed or as freely accessible as in, say, Europe, Australia, Singapore, or the USA, is the time and resources that will have to be spent in order to make today's emerging technologies truly available and affordable on a worldwide basis.

A second, more easily overlooked, reason is that even in the technologically "developed" nations, the currently existing infrastructure is not up to coping with the traffic that will result from exponentially expanding use of the Internet, both in terms of information providers and end-users. Already there are signs of the system being over-extended, particularly at certain times of the day. Continuing growth in the size of information resources and the volume of end-user traffic must be accompanied by proportional growth in the capacity of the networks to carry the traffic. This is a not an insignificant investment, even for the richer, developed nations.

A third, yet more easily overlooked, reason for caution is the limited capacity of the end-users to find their way through an "exploding universe" of information in an effective and efficient manner. Finding relevant information in conventional libraries has always been problematic and difficult. The advent of hypertext has introduced an additional set of "micro" problems to the previously existing "macro" issues of information search and retrieval. In addition to previous difficulties of finding relevant documents (books, papers, articles), the reader is faced with difficulties in finding relevant information within the document. One major user problem in many currently available hypertext systems is described as the "lost in hyperspace" effect (Edwards & Hardman, 1989; Yankelovich *et al.*, 1988). The readers navigate in a non-linear pattern from one "node" of information to another following potentially interesting or relevant "links" and soon lose their bearings, as if in a maze, unclear as to where they have arrived in the domain of study and why they are there. The undisputed technical advantages of making information more easily and more democratically available are to some extent undermined by human skill limitations on effectively using such an information network.

Whereas the responses to the two earlier-cited reasons lie in the domains of the technology itself (coupled to economic and political decisions as regards necessary financial resources), the solutions to this third reason lie within the domain of the social and cognitive sciences and the related technologies of communication and education. One future area of work for the instructional systems design and development professional will be in the area of on-line information systems, to help solve both the "macro" issues of information systems design from the human engineering viewpoint and the "micro" issues of the design of non-linear, browsable, hypermedia documents that are understandable and really useful to the end-user.

The "macro" level of design will draw strongly on existing techniques for the organization of information libraries, coupled to innovative techniques for providing "librarian support" to the end-user by automated means. This is one of the few areas in which artificial intelligence research has so far produced tangible products, in the form of "expert systems" that effectively and efficiently replicate the user-help capabilities of the skilled librarian (Bailey, 1992; Denning & Smith, 1994; McCrank, 1993; Morris, 1991). These new developments are now beginning to be applied to the design of "search engines" for use in global networks such as the Internet (Price-Wilkin, 1994; Valauskas, 1995).

The "micro" level of design will focus on the principles and procedures for the development of "hyperdocuments" of various types, especially as relates to the organization of information so that it is of the maximum value to the maximum range of possible end-users and, at the same time, so organized that readers may freely navigate from one detailed item of information to another while always maintaining a clear vision of the "big picture" and their position within it. Among the many attempts to develop authoring techniques for this purpose, the structured writing methodology named "Information Mapping" is an early development (Horn, 1969, 1973) that has proven its power in many contexts (Romiszowski, 1976), and has continued to mature and grow in versatility (Horn, 1989; Romiszowski, 1986). (See the chapter by Horn, in the present volume, for a full account of Information Mapping and its advantages.)

The future roles of instructional designers and developers in this sector of our scenario will concentrate on applying effective techniques for the organizing of information in networks and also applying techniques for the development of information organization and analysis skills in the population. In relation to the former, the methodologies of structured writing, such as the Information Mapping system, may serve at least as the beginning of the development of powerful technologies for the creation of information networks that are really of use to human beings. In relation to the latter point, the techniques of subject matter organization, such as Concept Mapping, may be used in order to develop the information analysis and evaluation skills that the knowledge workers of the future will require.

Computer Mediated Communication (CMC)

Let us now consider the knowledge workers themselves and their process of critical and creative thinking. A technology that holds much promise is Computer-Mediated-Communication (CMC). (This is described more completely in a separate chapter in this volume by Romiszowski and Ravitz.) CMC is a much broader concept than "computer conferencing." It includes any form of organized interaction between people, utilizing computers or computer networks as the medium of communication. The attractions of CMC for future educational systems are many. First of all, it is yet one more, and particularly versatile, approach to the delivery of "distance education." There are powerful political, economic, and social arguments that support the extended use of distance education methods in the future.

There are other characteristics of CMC, however, that are of value even if the educational process is not or should not be carried out at a distance. For example, the "asynchronous" nature of interpersonal communication in a computer network, where individuals read messages and then respond in their own time, taking as long as they need to think out their responses, holds promise in certain contexts as compared to more conventional methods of group discussion (Romiszowski & Corso, 1990; Romiszowski & DeHaas, 1989). Although face-to-face meetings may have advantages in terms of interpersonal and social contact, nonverbal communication and so on, they also have disadvantages. They are held in "real time" which, apart from possibly making it difficult or impossible for some people to participate due to other commitments or geographical distance, may limit in some cases the amount of planning and analysis or the amount of participation that individuals who do attend may have time for. Face-to-face meetings may also limit participation due to various forms of personal inhibition.

CMC is probably the fastest growing area of educational technology research and development at the moment (Romiszowski & Mason, in press). However, we still are not in a position to be able to design CMC systems that will effectively implement particular group-learning strategies with the same amount of confidence that we have when designing a computer-based instruction package or a set of on-line reference materials as job-performance-aids for a project geared towards the mastery of certain job skills. Nor are we yet as knowledgeable or skillful in the use of CMC as we are beginning to be in the organization of meaningful networks of information within the electronic communication networks that are beginning to link all parts of the world. Of the three areas that we have identified, the CMC area is the most promising for the development of the reflective thinking and creative planning skills that are required to close the gap between information and performance in knowledge work. For the time being, however, we know little about how to implement CMC for the effective development of creative thinking skills.

It is in the area of CMC, therefore, that the greatest need exists for research and development on the design and development of creative thinking training programs. Once more, here we meet an interesting and paradoxical problem. On the one hand, we have identified the critical thinking (or creative problem solving) area as being of paramount importance for the knowledge worker of the future and therefore, ultimately, for the employability of the human race. We have also identified the types of teaching-learning techniques that seem to be most effective in this area. These tend to be experiential exercises followed by interpersonal interaction in small groups, and with facilitators to guide the group towards useful conclusions. The small-group-discussion teaching-learning methodologies have always been relatively expensive, as they involve small groups of students at one place and time with highly skilled and experienced group facilitators. In the future, with falling technology costs and all manner of distance education hardware/software systems appearing on the market at economical prices, the small group learning methodology will appear as a luxury that we can afford to use but sparingly. Yet it is exactly this methodology that we currently know how to use effectively for the development of critical thinking skills. The paradoxical situation, therefore, is that in the changing technological and economical climates that will develop as we move into the 21st century, we may get less and less of what we need more and more.

As the impact of technology on society is at least partly to blame for this paradoxical problem, it would be appropriate if we could find a solution to the problem within that same technology. Over the last few years, a number of research studies have been performed to investigate the utilization of the case study methodology within computer networks as opposed to small group meetings (Romiszowski, 1990; Romiszowski & Chang 1992, 1995; Romiszowski, Grabowski, & Damadaran, 1988; Romiszowski, Grabowski, & Pusch, 1988). The results of these studies will not be repeated in detail here. It is important, however, to highlight two emerging conclusions. First, if properly planned and implemented, computer-mediated conversations may be just as effective as small group discussions for the development of a wide range of higher order decision-making and planning skills. Second, the key to the design of effective instructional CMC environments may be found in the application of a scientific theory of conversation. In addition to instructional technology, performance technology, and information technology, the field should develop and apply a conversation technology.

Conversation Theory and Design Technology

Teaching and Learning as Conversation

One way of looking at the three areas of key competencies, the associated training needs and the emerging methodologies for satisfying those needs is to use the four terms—information, instruction, performance, and conversation—and to associate each of these terms with the word technology. We already speak of information technology and associated information system design skills, instructional technology with its associated instructional system design skills, and performance technology with its associated performance support system design skills. The suggestion made here is to introduce one further (possibly new) construct of a "technology of conversation" with its associated "conversational system design skills."

This terminology is not commonly used, but it is probably fair to say that good teachers, particularly of open-ended subject matter such as philosophy, history, and the social sciences in general, are by definition good conversationalists. They deal with the analysis, synthesis, and evaluation of complex, abstract ideas, as opposed to the mastery of precise, observable performances or behaviors. These complex ideas may be modeled as some form of network or structure that exists in the mind of the teacher or the subject expert.

A major objective of teaching in such subject areas is in some way or other to confront the student (and the student's current state of organization of ideas) with the teacher's, other subject experts' (and perhaps other students') alternative (maybe richer and certainly different) structures of ideas on the same subject. This interchange, which is a part of all of the group discussion methodologies we mentioned earlier, occurs through the process of conversation.

In this context, a conversation is an opportunity for one partner to externalize, through language, the interrelationships between ideas that exist in the mind, and another partner to capture with reasonable accuracy the structure of relationships, and so be able to infer, from what was said, what has in fact been thought. The process of analysis of the pattern of relationships (and the absence of other expected relationships) demonstrated through the conversation is the major way by which a teacher or a colleague may help another person to re-think his or her position in relation to some topic or other. The process of conversation has been in use in society and in education for as long as language has existed. Why should we not therefore focus on developing a science of effective conversation and then utilize that science in order to develop a set of principles for action, that is, a technology of educational conversation? This idea is not new. Indeed, it is the basis for a rather sophisticated approach to considering higher level educational interactions as being examples of conversations and the development from that concept of a learning-teaching model named Conversation Theory (Pask, 1976, 1984).

The Reflective Conversation: Theory and Practice

Conversation, in Pask's theory, is presented as both a very simple and a very complex phenomenon. We will here concentrate on the simple connotation, limiting ourselves to just considering that many teaching-learning interactions can be analyzed and thought of in terms of a conversational interchange between two or more entities. The word "entity" is used to emphasize that a "conversation" may be held between two or more people, but also between two or several groups of people, and indeed it is possible to have a conversation with oneself in which one plays out two or more "entities."

It is appropriate in this context to refer to the work of Donald Schön on the analysis of the common characteristics of world-class professionals in fields such as management, architecture, or medicine (Schön, 1983). Schön, in his book entitled *The Reflective Practitioner*, demonstrated that the one common trait of most outstanding professionals in areas in which critical thinking is of utmost importance, is the ability to "converse reflectively" with themselves. The common factor that Schön identified as underlying excellence in higher order cognitive professional practice was the routine of reflecting, on a daily basis, on what happened during the professional activities of the day, why what happened happened, what may have happened had certain factors been somewhat modified, and so on. In short, the key to excellence is being able to hold a "debriefing session" with oneself on the higher order principles, concepts, and theories that may explain the actual practical events of the day.

If the world's outstanding professional practitioners seem to be outstanding because they have an outstanding level of skill in carrying on an "educational conversation" with themselves, surely the development of such skills may be one important goal in a curriculum for the 21st century. How may such skills be developed? In his later book *Educating the Reflective Practitioner*, Schön (1987) makes several suggestions for approaches to the development of reflective thinking, or self-analytical skills. By and large, the route to learning to "talk to yourself" effectively is to be put into a position where you have to talk to others. To talk means to exchange through words (maybe with the occasional help of visual communication) a verbal picture of the mental picture of a complex phenomenon that we have in our mind. The art of this form of conversation is what seems to be developed by small group discussion techniques such as brainstorming, case study and so forth. If, as was indicated earlier, we may not get enough opportunity to use these techniques in their conventional form in the high-tech world of the future, then maybe we should devote effort to designing technology-based conversational techniques that might substitute for the small group classroom-based ones we already have.

Structural Communication and the Conversational Use of Networking

This area of research is not absolutely new. One technique aimed at developing a conversational interchange between a learner and printed study materials was developed in the United Kingdom in the late 1960s and was named Structural Communication (Egan, 1972, 1976; Hodgson, 1974). This technique bears some similarity to the programmed instruction techniques of its time, and in its current computer-based application bears some similarity to computer-assisted instruction. However, it differs in the way in which it asks for responses and interactions from students and the nature and manner of supply of feedback.

The essential characteristics of a Structural Communication exercise are, first, to set a series of interconnected, open-ended and complex problems in a particular domain of study, then to furnish a device called a response matrix, which is a very complex multiple-choice question mechanism that allows students to respond by selecting a combination or pattern of responses from an extensive menu of twenty or more items; the pattern of response may then be analyzed in the light of expert knowledge to identify whether certain critical relationships between important concepts and ideas have been included or omitted from the student's response. This analysis allows the material to diagnose certain apparent differences in cognitive structure between the expert responsible for the writing of the exercise and the student using the exercise (and indeed between different students who are using the exercise). The final stage is the selection, on the basis of the registered response patterns, of appropriate combinations of feedback messages that may alert students to how their thinking process on the topic is organized and how it might be organized in different ways. In short, the exercise gets students to think again about the subject in question, without necessarily implying that they were right or wrong in their original thinking. (In another chapter included in the present volume, Slee and Pusch present a full description of the Structural Communication method and related research.)

The methodology of Structural Communication has been extended in recent years to allow for deeper and more extensive but highly focused conversation on specific aspects of the domain under study (Romiszowski, 1990; Romiszowski & Chang, 1992, 1995). After an initial software-driven round of interaction that follows the model described above, any further doubts, queries, disagreements, or misunderstandings may be further dealt with by inviting original student free-form text input and then routing these student comments/queries to other participants or to tutor-facilitators (who may be at a distance) by means of a conventional electronic mail network connection. In this way, the conversation may continue beyond the initial exercise, to replicate in all significant respects a small-group discussion or one-on-one tutorial.

This use of computer-mediated-communication (CMC) as a supplement to a rather special form of computer-assisted instruction (CAI) appears to hold much promise for the educational systems of the networked society of the future. Current experience with educational applications of the more conventional forms of computer conferencing and networking is not all positive (Romiszowski & Jost, 1989). One of the problems with conventional computer conferences is that many people contribute ideas into a common pool which has to be sorted through by reading in a sequential manner, whereas the actual ideas are interrelated to each other in anything but a linear and sequential manner. Many people desist from computer conferencing because the load of reading a lot of possibly irrelevant and marginal contributions in order to discover the few "gold nuggets" of important information is not a cost-effective use of their time. Others complain that the computer conference, like many live conferences, can suffer from being dominated by a small group of exceptionally industrious and productive participants who, in effect, browbeat the others into keeping silent.

In a computer conference based on an initial Structural Communication exercise along the lines described above, the ensuing discussions take place in a large number of separate sub-discussions already focused on specific aspects of the overall problem area being studied. In this way, automatic order is injected into the computer conference, a particular person possibly taking part in six or more separate mini-conferences on half a dozen issues of personal interest, within a total of maybe twenty mini-conferences running at the same time, all generated by one initial exercise. This approach also minimizes the need for human moderating to keep order among the messages (essential in many conventional types of computer conferences) and therefore makes it a more attractive and cost effective way of utilizing networks for education on a regular basis. The decomposure of a complex discussion into an organized set of mini-discussions automatically classifies the messages, so that a person who is joining the discussion may easily pick up not only the last few messages but the overall structure of what has been discussed.

Conclusion

Towards a Technology of Conversation for a Networked Society

The research-based advantages mentioned above are examples of some of the principles of a new emerging technology of conversation design. The Structural Communication methodology is probably only one among many approaches that may help designers to get effectiveness, efficiency, and real "added value" from the use of computer networks in the educational environments of the future. The computer network is seen by many as a key component in systems designed to achieve the priority educational objectives for the knowledge worker of the 21st century.

The COMPUTER NETWORK, however, is merely a technological device to link together human beings into collaborative CONVERSATIONAL NETWORKS, in which they can exchange ideas and share materials, often stored and presented as hypertext or hypermedia INFORMATION NETWORKS. But the object of the whole exercise is ultimately to help individuals to build their own (and to enable them to help others build their own) CONCEPTUAL NETWORKS of interrelated ideas, strategies, and theories that are essential for the processes of critical analysis and evaluation of existing knowledge and the creative synthesis of new knowledge: the essential components of knowledge work and the key to employability and professional satisfaction in the future.

The four quite separate, but interrelated, concepts of NETWORK presented in this paragraph illustrate the real meaning that we should ascribe to the popular term "Networked Society." We should look beyond the *delivery-system* aspects of the physical hardware and software of future networks to the full systemic meaning of the term: the *"input"* aspects related to the structuring of information in "user-friendly" networks; the *"output"* aspects related to the development of 23 critical thinking skills and powerful networks of concepts and principles in the mind of the learner; and the *"process"* aspects of the REFLECTIVE CONVERSATION as a prime methodology for the development of these skills and conceptual networks.

Towards a Conversation on the Future of Instructional Development

This is the last chapter in the section devoted to delivery-system-related paradigms of Instructional Development. It has been written, therefore, with a view to future developments, both in technology and in society, as it is impacted by technology. The impact of technology on society is the emergence of the "knowledge worker" as the model, or exemplar, of the future citizen. Analysis of this model of the future output of educational and training systems led us to identify key areas of competence that should form the basis of future curricula. Evaluation of past practices and current developments led us to identify key areas of future instructional development activity.

This is also the last chapter of the book. As such, it offers an opportunity to synthesize the ideas presented earlier, in separate chapters, into a more integrated, or systemic, view of the future of instructional development. For example, the key areas of ID, mentioned above, illustrate that some of the new ideas and trends, such as constructivism, should integrate with, but not replace, earlier approaches based on behaviorist, cognitivist, or humanist theories of learning. The current trend towards just-in-time training and performance support systems will continue to rely heavily on the older technologies and techniques of computer-assisted instruction and job-aids in combination with recent ideas on learner-control and andragogy. The current need for electronic hypermedia reference materials will be largely satisfied by ID techniques derived from earlier materials development technologies, such as structured writing, in combination with more recent ideas on visual communication, multimedia, user-friendly interface design, and intelligent on-line help systems. And the future emphasis on the development of critical-thinking skills will combine earlier research and practice in the use of small-group instruction techniques with more recent ideas and development in such diverse areas as reflective learning, constructivist learning, and situated cognition, on the one hand, and computer-based simulations, interactive distance education systems, and intelligent tutoring systems on the other.

The future scenario presented in this chapter may act, therefore, as a context within which to compare, contrast, and (above all) integrate ideas from diverse sources into a more powerful and more diversified approach to ID. Theoretical, philosophical, and cultural foundations of the field are of value and relevance to the extent that they lead to strategic and tactical decisions that "make sense" in the light of prior research and are then found to "make a difference" in the real-world contexts of learning and transfer of learning to work, play, and life in general.

The lesson we may draw from the analysis of our future scenario is that the new ideas and techniques add to but seldom completely replace the old. In the opening chapter of this book, the editors make the case for considering the field of instructional development to be multi-paradigmatic. The exact "mix" of predominant paradigms may change over time, but the field has never been fully dominated by one exclusive paradigm. In the sections and chapters that followed, many of the well established and accepted paradigms, as well as a few newly-emerging candidates, have been presented. This final chapter presents the reader with the opportunity to consider the probable future "paradigm mix" that will underpin ID in the 21st century. One future scenario is presented and one set of conclusions is drawn from it. But this is only the first step in what (hopefully) may develop into an ongoing conversation on the future of instructional development in the future Networked Society.

References

Ashby, W. R. (1956). *An introduction to cybernetics.* London, UK: Chapman and Hall.

Bailey, C. W. Jr. (1992). The intelligent reference information system project. A merger of CD-ROM, LAN, and expert system technologies. *Information Technology and Libraries, 11*(3).

Benson, G. M. Jr. (1994). *The lifelong learning society: Investing in the new learning technology market sector.* Stephentown, NY: Learning Systems Engineering.

Bloom, B. *et al.* (1956). *Taxonomy of educational objectives, handbook 1: The cognitive domain.* New York: Longman.

Bush, V. (1945). As we may think. *Atlantic Monthly, 176*(1), 101–8.

Carr, C. (1992). *Smart training: The manager's guide to training for improved performance.* New York: McGraw-Hill.

Clark, R. C. (1994). Hang up your training hat. *Training and Development, 48*(9), 61–63.

Conklin, J. (1987). Hypertext: An introduction and survey. *IEEE Computer, 20*(9), 17–41.

Davies, I. K. (1994). Process re-design for enhanced human performance. *Performance Improvement Quarterly, 7*(3).

Denning, R., & Smith, P. J. (1994). Interface design concepts in the development of ELSA, an intelligent electronic library search assistant. *Information Technology and Libraries, 13*(2), 133–47.

Dorsey, L. T. *et al.* (1993). Just-in-time knowledge performance support: A test of concept. *Educational Technology, 33*(11).

Edwards, D. M., & Hardman, L. (1989). Lost in hyperspace: Cognitive mapping and navigation in hypertext environments. In R. McAleese (Ed.), *Hypertext: Theory into practice.* Norwood, NJ: Ablex Publishing Corp.

Egan, K. (1972). Structural Communication: A new contribution to pedagogy. *Programmed Learning and Educational Technology, 9*(2), 63–78.

Egan, K. (1976). *Structural Communication.* Belmont, CA: Fearon.

Englebart, D. (1963). A conceptual framework for the augmentation of man's intellect. In P. W. Howerton & D. C. Weeks, *Vistas in information handling, vol. 1: The augmentation of man's intellect by machine* (pp. 1–29). Washington, DC: Spartan Books.

Gayeski, D. M. (1995). DesignStation 2000: Imagining future realities in learning systems design. *Educational Technology, 35*(3), 43–47.

Gilbert, T. F. (1978). *Human competence: Engineering worthy performance.* New York: McGraw-Hill.

Gery, G. (1991). *Electronic performance support systems.* Boston, MA: Weingarten Publications.

Gery, G. (1995). Attributes and behaviors of performance centered systems. *Performance Improvement Quarterly, 8*(1).

Goodyear, P., & Steeples, C. (1992). IT-based open learning: Tasks and tools. *Journal of Computer Assisted Learning, 8*(3), 163–86.

Gooler, D. D. (1986). *The education utility: The power to revitalize education and society.* Englewood Cliffs, NJ: Educational Technology Publications.

Harless, J. (1992). Wither performance technology? *Performance and Instruction, 31*(2), 4–8.

Hodgson, A. M. (1974). Structural communication in practice. In A. J. Romiszowski (Ed.), *APLET Yearbook of Educational and Instructional Technology—1974/75.* London, UK: Kogan Page.

Horn, R. E. (1969). *Information Mapping for learning and reference.* Lexington, MA: Information Resources, Inc.

Horn, R. E. (1973). *Introduction to Information Mapping.* Lexington, MA: Information Resources, Inc.

Horn, R. E. (1989). *Mapping hypertext.* Lexington, MA: The Lexington Institute.

Langdon, D. (1991). Performance technology in three paradigms. *Performance and Instruction, 30*(7), 1–7.

McAleese, R. (1989). *Hypertext: Theory into practice.* Norwood, NJ: Ablex Publishing Corp.

McCrank, L. J. (1993). Reference expertise: Paradigms, strategies and systems. *Reference Librarian, 40.*

Milheim, W. D. (1992). Performance support systems: Guidelines for system design and integration. *Canadian Journal of Educational Communication, 21*(3), 243–52.

Morris, A. (1991). Expert systems for library and information services: A review. *Information Processing and Management, 27*(6), 713–24.

Naidu, S., & Bernard, R. M. (1992). Enhanced academic performance in distance education with concept mapping and inserted questions. *Distance Education, 13*(2), 218–33.

Nelson, T. H. (1965). The hypertext. Paper presented at the 1965 Congress of the International Federation for Documentation. Washington, DC: International Federation for Documentation.

Nelson, T. H. (1973). A conceptual framework for man-machine everything. In AFIPS *Proceedings*. Montvale, NJ: AFIPS.

Nelson, T. H. (1980). Replacing the printed word: A complete literary system. In S. H. Livingston (Ed.), *Information Processing 80*. New York: North Holland.

Nelson T. H. (1987). *Literary machines*. San Antonio, TX: Nelson.

Novak, J. (1991). Clarify with concept maps. *Science Teacher, 58*(7), 44–49.

Pask, G. (1976). Conversational techniques in the study and practice of education. *British Journal of Educational Psychology, 46*.

Pask, G. (1984). Review of conversation theory and a protologic (or protolanguage). *Educational Communication and Technology, 32*(1), 3–40.

Plewes, T. J. (1992). Workforce trends, workplace trends: How they dictate a changing education and training strategy. Paper presented at the "Work Now and in the Future" Conference, Portland, Oregon, November.

Price-Wilkin, J. (1994). A gateway between the World Wide Web and PAT: Exploiting SGML through the Web. *Public Access Computer Systems Review, 5*(7), 5–27.

Reader, W., & Hammond, N. (1994). Computer based tools to support learning from hypertext: Concept mapping tools and beyond. *Computers and Education, 22*(1–2), 99–106.

Romiszowski, A. J. (1976). *A study of individualized systems for mathematics instruction at post-secondary levels*. Ph.D. Thesis, University of Loughborough, UK.

Romiszowski, A. J. (1981). *Designing instructional systems*. London, UK: Kogan Page.

Romiszowski, A. J. (1984). *Producing instructional systems*. London, UK: Kogan Page.

Romiszowski, A. J. (1986). *Developing auto-instructional materials*. London, UK: Kogan Page.

Romiszowski, A. J. (1990). The case method, interactive media and instructional design. Proceedings of the 7th International WACRA Conference. Needham, MA: World Association for Case Method Research and Application.

Romiszowski, A. J., & Chang, E. (1992). Hypertext's contribution to computer-mediated-communication: In search of an instructional model. In M. Giardina (Ed.), *Interactive multimedia environments* (pp. 111–30). Heidelberg: Springer-Verlag.

Romiszowski, A. J., & Chang, E. (1995). Hypermedia networks for case-study discussions in distance education. Paper presented at the World Conference on Distance Education, Birmingham, UK.

Romiszowski, A. J., & Corso, M. (1990). Computer-mediated seminars and case studies: Possible future trends for in-service training and development by means of interactive distance education. Paper presented at 15th World Conference on Distance Education, Caracas, Venezuela.

Romiszowski, A. J., & DeHaas, J. (1989). Computer-mediated-communication for instruction: Using E-mail as a seminar. *Educational Technology, 29*(1).

Romiszowski, A. J., Grabowski, B. L., & Damadaran, B. (1988). Structural Communication, expert systems, and interactive video: A powerful combination for a non-traditional CAI approach. *Proceedings* of AECT National Conference.

Romiszowski, A. J., Grabowski, B. L., & Pusch, W. S. (1988). *Structural Communication: A neglected CAI methodology and its potential for interactive video simulations*. Paper presented at the ADCIS Annual Conference.

Romiszowski, A. J., & Jost, K. (1989). *Computer conferencing and the distance learner: Problems of structure and control*. Paper presented at the 1989 University of Wisconsin Conference on Distance Education.

Romiszowski, A. J., & Mason, R. (in press). Research on computer mediated communication. Chapter in D. Jonassen (Ed.), *Handbook of research on educational technology*.

Rossett, A. (1992). Performance technology for instructional technologists: Comparisons and possibilities. *Performance and Instruction, 31*(10), 6–10.

Russell, R., & Meikamp, J. (1994). Creativity training—A practical teaching strategy. Proceedings of annual conference of the American Council on Rural Special Education, Austin, TX.

Schön, D. A. (1983). *The reflective practitioner: How professionals think in action*. London, UK: Temple Smith.

Schön, D. A. (1987). *Educating the reflective practitioner*. San Francisco, CA: Jossey-Bass.

Schroeder, E. E. (1994). Navigating through hypertext: Navigational technique, individual differences, and learning. *Proceedings* of R & D Section, 1994 AECT Conference, Nashville, TN.

Steinaker, N. W., & Bell, M. R. (1979). *The experiential taxonomy: A new approach to teaching and learning.* New York: Academic Press.

Stevens, G. H., & Stevens, E. F. (1995). *Designing electronic performance support tools.* Englewood Cliffs, NJ: Educational Technology Publications.

Valauskas, E. J. (1995). *Britannica Online:* Redefining encyclopedias for the next century. *Database, 18*(1), 14–18.

Yankelovich, N. G. *et al.* (1988). Issues in designing a hypermedia document system: The intermedia case study. In S. Ambron & K. Hooper (Eds.), *Interactive multimedia* (pp. 33–85). Redmond, VA: Microsoft Press.

Author Index

Subject Index